September 1–4, 2015
Guzelyurt, Northern Cyprus

**Association for
Computing Machinery**

Advancing Computing as a Science & Profession

HT'15
Proceedings of the 26th ACM Conference on
Hypertext & Social Media

Sponsored by:
ACM SIGWEB

In cooperation:
ACM SIGCHI

Supported by:
Middle East Technical University Northern Cyprus Campus

Association for Computing Machinery

Advancing Computing as a Science & Profession

The Association for Computing Machinery
2 Penn Plaza, Suite 701
New York, New York 10121-0701

Notice to Past Authors of ACM-Published Articles

ISBN: 978-1-4503-3628-4 (Digital)

ISBN: 978-1-4503-4026-7 (Print)

Additional copies may be ordered prepaid from:

ACM Order Department
PO Box 30777
New York, NY 10087-0777, USA

Phone: 1-800-342-6626 (USA and Canada)
+1-212-626-0500 (Global)
Fax: +1-212-944-1318
E-mail: acmhelp@acm.org
Hours of Operation: 8:30 am – 4:30 pm ET

Printed in the USA

Foreword

It is our great pleasure to welcome you to the *26th ACM Conference on Hypertext and Social Media*. The ACM Conference on Hypertext and Social Media (HT) has a long-standing tradition of being the premium venue for high quality peer-reviewed research on theory, systems and applications for hypertext and social media. This year, in its 26th edition, HT2015 focuses on the role of hypertext and hyperlink theory on the web and beyond, as a foundation for approaches and practices in the wider community, through contributions related to *Digital Connectivity*, *Data Connectivity*, and *Digital Humanities*. As a result, the conference is concerned with all aspects of modern hypertext research, including social media, adaptation and personalisation, user modeling, linked data and semantic web, dynamic and computed hypertext, and its application in digital humanities. Thus, HT2015 gives researchers and practitioners a unique opportunity to share their perspectives with others interested in the various aspects of modern day hypertext and social media.

The call for papers attracted submissions from Asia, North America, Australia, Europe, and Africa. We have received 60 Full Technical Papers, 17 Short Papers, 14 Poster and Demo Papers. Our program committee reviewed and accepted the following: 24 Full Technical Papers (40%), 10 Short Papers and 6 Poster and Demo Papers. This year's conference also includes two distinguished keynote speakers. Their valuable and insightful talks can and will inspire researchers for the future of hypertext and social media research:

- *The Near Future is Hybrid,* Yiannis Laouris

- *From Small Sensors to Big Data: How the Sensor Web is Changing Our World,* Barry Smyth

Putting together HT2015 was a team effort. We first thank the authors for providing the content of the program. We are grateful to the program committee and the Track Chairs for the three tracks, Shlomo Berkovsky and Markel Vigo for Digital Connectivity, Oscar Corcho and Erjia Yan for Data Connectivity, and Jacco van Ossenbruggen and Markus Strohmaier for Digital Humanities, who together with all program committee members and reviewers worked very hard in reviewing papers and providing feedback for authors. We also thank our Workshop and Tutorial Chairs Alvin Chin and Ethan Munson, our Posters and Demos Chair Jessica Rubart, our Doctoral Consortium Chairs Denis Parra and Christopher Trattner, our Proceedings Chair Claus Atzenbeck, our Treasurer and Local Chair Ilknur Celik, Our Student Support Chair Ethan Munson, our Publicity Chairs Federica Cena and Michael Yudelson, and our Web Chair Sukru Eraslan for all their contributions to the conference and these proceedings. Finally, we thank Middle East Technical University Northern Cyprus Campus (NCC) and ACM for their support.

We hope that you will find this program interesting and thought provoking and that the conference will provide you with a valuable opportunity to share ideas with other researchers and practitioners from institutions around the world.

Yeliz Yesilada
HT2015 General Chair
METU NCC, Cyprus

Rosta Farzan
Program Co-Chair
University of Pittsburgh, USA

Geert-Jan Houben
Program Co-Chair
TU Delft, the Netherlands

Table of Contents

Keynote 1

Session 1

Session 2

Session 3

Keynote 2

Session 4

Session 5

Session 6

Session 7

Demonstrations

Poster Abstracts

Late-Breaking Abstracts

2015 ACM Conference on Hypertext and Social Media Organization

General Chair:	Yeliz Yesilada *(Middle East Technical University Northern Cyprus Campus)*
Program Chairs:	Rosta Farzan *(University of Pittsburgh, USA)* Geert-Jan Houben *(Delft University of Technology, The Netherlands)*
Track Chairs **Digital Connectivity:**	Shlomo Berkovsky *(CSIRO, Australia)* Markel Vigo *(University of Manchester, UK)*
Track Chairs **Data Connectivity:**	Oscar Corcho *(Universidad Politécnica de Madrid and LocaliData, Spain)* Erjia Yan *(Drexel University, USA)*
Track Chairs **Digital Humanities:**	Jacco van Ossenbruggen *(Centrum Wiskunde & Informatica CWI* *and VU University, The Netherlands)* Markus Strohmaier *(GESIS/University of Koblenz-Landau, Germany)*
Workshop and Tutorial Chairs:	Alvin Chin *(BMW Group, USA)* Ethan Munson *(University of Wisconsin-Milwaukee, USA)*
Posters and Demos Chair:	Jessica Rubart *(University of Applied Sciences Ostwestfalen-Lippe, Germany)*
Doctoral Consortium Chairs:	Denis Parra *(Catholic University of Chile, Chile)* Christopher Trattner *(Norwegian University of Science and Technology, Norway)*
Proceedings Chair:	Claus Atzenbeck *(Hof University, Germany)*
Student Support Chair:	Ethan Munson *(University of Wisconsin-Milwaukee, USA)*
Caring, Child Care and **Disability Support Chairs:**	Andy Brown *(BBC, UK)* Caroline Jay *(University of Manchester, UK)*
Treasurer and Local Chair:	Ilknur Celik *(Middle East Technical University Northern Cyprus Campus)*
Publicity Chairs:	Federica Cena *(University of Torino, Italy)* Michael Yudelson *(Carnegie Learning, Inc., USA)*

Local Publicity Chair:	Elgin Akpinar *(Middle East Technical University, Turkey)*
Web Chair:	Sukru Eraslan *(Middle East Technical University Northern Cyprus Campus)*
SIGWEB Representative and Liason:	Simon Harper *(University of Manchester, UK)*
Program Committee Digital Connectivity Track:	Maristella Agosti *(University of Padua)*
	Liliana Ardissono *(University of Torino)*
	Maria Bielikova *(Slovak University of Technology in Bratislava)*
	Peter Brusilovsky *(University of Pittsburgh)*
	Iván Cantador *(Universidad Autónoma de Madrid)*
	Federica Cena *(Department of Computer Science, University of Torino)*
	David Chin *(University of Hawaii)*
	Owen Conlan *(Trinity College Dublin)*
	Paul De Bra *(TU/e)*
	Ernesto Diaz-Aviles *(IBM Reseach)*
	Vania Dimitrova *(School of Computing, University of Leeds)*
	Peter Dolog *(Department of Computer Science, Aalborg University)*
	Erik Duval *(Departement Computerwetenschappen, K. U. Leuven)*
	David Garcia *(ETH Zurich)*
	Cristina Gena *(Department of Computer Science, University of Torino)*
	Simon Harper *(University of Manchester)*
	Eelco Herder *(L3S Research Center)*
	Sharon Hsiao *(Arizona State University)*
	Michael Kurtz *(Harvard-Smithsonian Center for Astrophysics)*
	Séamus Lawless *(Trinity College Dublin)*
	Pasquale Lops *(University of Bari)*
	Alexander O'Connor *(Trinity College, Dublin)*
	Daniel Romero *(University of Michigan)*
	Xiaolin Shi *(Microsoft Corporation)*
	Carsten Ullrich *(DFKI GmbH)*
	Julita Vassileva *(University of Saskatchewan)*
	Ruben Verborgh *(Ghent University – iMinds)*
Program Committee Data Connectivity Track:	Jean-Paul Calbimonte *(EPFL)*
	Irene Celino *(CEFRIEL)*
	Fabien Gandon *(Inria)*
	Raúl García-Castro *(Universidad Politecnica de Madrid)*
	Tudor Groza *(The Garvan Institute of Medical Research)*
	Raf Guns *(University of Antwerp)*
	Christophe Guéret *(Data Archiving and Networked Services DANS)*

**Program Committee
Data Connectivity Track
(continued):**

Aidan Hogan *(DCC, Universidad de Chile)*
Kim Holmberg *(Åbo Akademi University, Finland)*
Pavan Kapanipathi *(Wright State University)*
Xiangnan Kong *(Worcester Polytechnic Institute)*
Vincent Larivière *(EBSI-Université de Montréal)*
Vanessa Lopez *(IBM Research)*
Pablo Mendes *(IBM Research Almaden)*
Heiko Paulheim *(University of Mannheim)*
Isabella Peters *(ZBW-German National Library of Economics)*
Milan Stankovic
(Sépage & STIH, Université Paris-Sorbonne, France)
Raphaël Troncy *(EURECOM)*
Dietmar Wolfram *(University of Wisconsin-Milwaukee)*

**Program Committee
Digital Humanities Track:**

Harith Alani *(KMi, The Open University)*
Jisun An *(Qatar Computing Research Institute)*
Martin Atzmueller *(University of Kassel)*
Giovanni Luca Ciampaglia *(Indiana University)*
Puschmann Cornelius
(Alexander von Humboldt Institute for Internet and Society)
Mathieu D'Aquin
(Knowledge Media Institute, the Open University)
Fabian Flöck *(GESIS Cologne)*
David Garcia *(ETH Zurich)*
Daniel Gayo-Avello *(University of Oviedo)*
Denis Helic *(KTI, TU-Graz)*
Laura Hollink *(VU University Amsterdam)*
Andreas Hotho *(University of Würzburg)*
Antoine Isaac *(Europeana & VU University Amsterdam)*
Robert Jäschke *(L3S Research Center)*
Jaap Kamps *(University of Amsterdam)*
Nicolas Kourtellis *(Yahoo Labs)*
Q. Vera Liao *(University of Illinois at Urbana Champaign)*
Suzy Moat *(University of Warwick)*
Claudia Müller-Birn *(Freie Universität Berlin)*
Daan Odijk *(University of Amsterdam)*
Jürgen Pfeffer *(Carnegie Mellon University)*
Daniele Quercia *(Yahoo Labs)*
Rossano Schifanella *(University of Turin)*
Mützel Sophie *(University of Lucerne)*
Wouter Van Atteveldt
(Vrije Universiteit, afdeling Communicatiewetenschap)
Taha Yasseri *(Oxford Internet Institute, University of Oxford)*

Program Committee
Doctoral Consortium: Alejandro Bellogin *(Universidad Autónoma de Madrid, Spain)*
Alessandro Bozzon *(TU-Delft, Netherlands)*
Robin Burke *(De Paul, USA)*
Vania Dimitrova *(Leeds University, UK)*
Alexander Felfernig *(Graz University of Technology, Austria)*
Jill Freyne *(CSIRO, Australia)*
Eduardo Graells *(Telefonica, Chile)*
Eelco Herder *(L3S, Germany)*
Sharon Hsiao *(Arizona State University, USA)*
Bart Knijnenburg *(University of California Irvine, USA)*
Ralf Krestel *(HPI, Germany)*
Yu-ru Lin *(University of Pittsburgh, USA)*
Alan Said *(Recorded Future, Sweden)*
Markus Schedl *(JKU, Austria)*
Claudia Wagner *(GESIS, Germany)*
Arkaitz Zubiaga *(University of Warwick, UK)*

Hypertext 2015 Sponsor & Supporter

Sponsor: sig web

In cooperation: SIGCHI

Supporter:

MIDDLE EAST TECHNICAL UNIVERSITY
NORTHERN CYPRUS CAMPUS

The Near Future is Hybrid

Yiannis Laouris
laouris@cnti.org.cy
Future Worlds Center
Nicosia, Cyprus

The exponential growth of the web, in connection with all its derivatives and all scientific, social, economic and other consequences, created the widely accepted notion that the future(s) is (are) digital. This could not be more wrong and more misleading. Indeed, at least for the next couple of decades, the futures are hybrid in all aspects and in practically all domains. For example, we are still far away from an educational system that operates only in virtual worlds. Friends' circles in social networking sites turn out to serve primarily the sustainability of existing real world friendships. While simulations and software (virtual instrument) solutions were trendy during the last few decades, we now witness a rapid development in robotics. Flying (i.e., drones), ground robots (i.e., robot dogs), and microcontrollers, fully equipped with sensors and actuators are about to massively populate every natural or man-made environment.

This talk will discuss how underlying principles of hybrid futures evade and dictate developments in every aspect of IT, ranging from education and HCI, to visualizations and digital humanities, all grounded in the intelligent linking between software algorithms and physical infrastructures.

The implications for the Anthropocene will be highlighted and discussed.

HT '15, September 1–4, 2015, Guzelyurt, Northern Cyprus.
ISBN 978-1-4503-3395-5/15/09.
DOI: http://dx.doi.org/10.1145/2700171.2790379

Small-Scale Incident Detection based on Microposts

Axel Schulz[*+] Benedikt Schmidt[*] Thorsten Strufe[†]

[+]Business Intelligence Marketing	[*]Telecooperation Lab	[†]Faculty of Computer Science
DB Fernverkehr AG	Technische Universität Darmstadt	Technische Universität Dresden
Germany	Germany	Germany

ABSTRACT

Detecting large-scale incidents based on microposts has successfully been proposed and shown. However, the detection of small-scale incidents was not satisfyingly possible so far, though the information that is shared during such local events could improve the situational awareness of both citizens and decision makers alike.

In this paper, we propose an approach for small-scale incident detection based on spatial-temporal-type clustering. In contrast to existing work, (1) we employ three distinct properties that define an incident, (2) we use a hybrid approach to reduce the computational overhead, and (3) we extract generalized features to increase robustness towards previously unseen data. Our evaluation in the domain of emergency first response shows that our approach identifies 32.14% of all real world incidents recorded for the city of Seattle just using on tweets. This result greatly outperforms the state of the art, which only detects about 6% of the real-world incidents. Also, a precision of 77% shows that we efficiently discard irrelevant information.

Categories and Subject Descriptors

H.3.3 [**Information Storage and Retrieval**]: Information Search and Retrieval—*Information filtering*; I.2.7 [**Artificial Intelligence**]: Natural Language Processing—*Text analysis*

General Terms

Algorithms; Experimentation

Keywords

Microblogs; Event Detection

1. INTRODUCTION

Improving situational awareness—"the perception of the elements in the environment within a volume of time and space, the comprehension of their meaning, and the projection of their status in the near future" [7]—is one of the main goals for efficient decision making in emergency management. With the changing information

HT '15, September 1–4, 2015, Guzelyurt, Northern Cyprus.
Copyright is held by the owner/author(s). Publication rights licensed to ACM.
ACM. ISBN 978-1-4503-3395-5/15/09 ...$15.00.
DOI: http://dx.doi.org/10.1145/2578726.2578744.

landscape in the World Wide Web, citizens express their observations and inferences about real-world crisis events more frequently using social media [18, 11]. However, detecting valuable information during small-scale incidents such as fires and car crashes imposes new challenges that have rarely been tackled so far.

The few approaches that address small-scale incident detection primarily rely on one basic property, i.e., the textual content of tweets. However, relying on textual content may be insufficient. Consider a car crash. Many crashes happen every day and last for few couple of hours on different roads. Small-scale incident detection that analyzes tweets for incidents needs to distinguish the different crashes to achieve good precision and recall. Therefore, additional knowledge of the time and location is needed to distinguish and aggregate information that relates to the same or to different incidents.

This also applies to the type of the incident, if, for instance, a tweet relates to a car accident or a fire. We follow the specification of the Federal Emergency Management Agency [4] and consider an incident as "an unexpected event in the real-world typically resulting in a damage or injury, which happens at a certain place, at a certain time, and which can be described by a type.". In other words, an incident is specified by three properties: (1) incident type, (2) location, and (3) time period. Consider the following example of a complete incident specification: an incident of type *car crash* with location *Interstate I-90* and time *February 7, 2015, 11:43:00*.

Having this said, there are different problems that complicate the extraction of the three properties that define an event from tweets:

- Problem 1 - Location: Only about 1-2% of all tweets contain exact geographic information.

- Problem 2 - Time: Tweets have a creation time and their content may contain statements about the time of an incident, yet neither, either or both may reflect the actual time and duration of the incident.

- Problem 3 - Type: Due to the large amount of information shared everyday, incident-related information needs to be differentiated from irrelevant information with high precision.

In this paper, we present a holistic small-scale incident detection approach that addresses all aforementioned problems of small-scale incident detection. We focus on the clustering of incident-related microposts using information about the spatial and temporal dimension as well as the incident type of an incident mentioned in a tweet. The following techniques are applied to increase the quality of our approach. Spatial information is enriched by geotagging tweets that are not explicitly geotagged based on an extension of our earlier work on the geolocalization of tweets [19]. Also, incident types are identified based on tweet classification [22]. A crucial challenge is the development of a classification approach that does not overfit on the training data but which works well on previously unseen microposts. We address this challenge by feature generalization based on *Semantic Abstraction* [20].

Our approach is evaluated in a study that examines small-scale incident detection using tweets. In discussions with emergency managers we came up with the requirement that the error of detections should not exceed 500 meters in distance and 10 minutes in time. This threshold is used to asses the quality of the approaches. Our evaluation is the first one on high quality ground truth data, i.e., based on the Seattle Real Time Fire Calls[1] data set, which provides information about real-world incidents registered by the Seattle administration.

Using 802k unfiltered tweets as provided by the Search API and the real-world data, we show that our small-scale incident detection approach detects more than 50% of the real-world incidents just using tweets. Furthermore, 32.14% of these are detected to be within a range of 500m and 10min to the real incident. This recall is a clear advantage over the best competitors within the state of the art [3, 5, 24], which detect less than 6% of the incidents – an insight we gain by the first study on incident detection with real data for these approaches. Also, more than 77% of the incident clusters created with our approach are indeed related to incidents, which indicates a high precision and a significant reduction of irrelevant information.

In summary, our contributions are the following:

- We propose an end-to-end pipeline for small-scale incident detection. The pipeline is based on clustering of event-related microposts using information about the spatial and temporal dimension as well as the event type of an event mentioned in a tweet.

- We propose a hybrid approach, employing supervised classification of tweets *before* detecting event clusters. Thus, our approach reduces the computational overhead of the event clustering and improves precision.

- By extracting generalized features using Semantic Abstraction, our approach is more robust to previously unseen data. This is especially important, as only a limited amount of data can be used for training a supervised classification model.

- We provide the first comparison of state of the art approaches in the domain of incident detection based on microposts and a high-quality ground truth. Furthermore, we show that our approach outperforms existing works significantly.

The remainder of this paper is structured as follows. We present and discuss related work. Next, our approach is described. In an evaluation, we compare our approach to the existing state of the art on small-scale incident detection. We conclude with a summary and discussion of future work.

2. RELATED WORK

In the last years, research coped with event detection on short and unstructured texts such as tweets [2]. Approaches in this area focus on either unspecified events (e.g., when no prior information about an event is known) such as [3], while others are specialized towards detecting pre-defined types of events. In the following, we omit presentation of general approaches for large-scale event detection for which an overview can be found in [2].

Related approaches can be differentiated according to four dimensions. (1) the classification of the event type, i.e., the detection

[1] http://seattle.data.gov

of specific or unspecific events. (2) the clustering approach used for aggregating related information to event clusters. (3) the use of spatial and temporal information to provide more accurate clustering results.

Classification of the event type.

Small-scale event detection without specifying the event type was conducted by [5, 27, 25]. In contrast to the approaches designed for detecting unspecific events, other approaches focus on detecting specific events such as incidents. [6, 12, 18] focus on specific large-scale events, whereas the works of [1, 10, 14, 15] are related to specific small-scale events such as incidents.

Clustering of related information.

The existing approaches vary depending on the clustering approach. Commonly, unsupervised clustering techniques are used such as k-means and hierarchical approaches [1], single-pass clustering [3], graph-based clustering [10], or density-based clustering [5]. Also, topic modeling based on the tweet's text was used for aggregating related information [6]. Furthermore, the text is used to create statistical models [15], e.g., for burst detection.

Other approaches were developed to use metadata during the clustering process. [25] make use of geotags and apply simple spatial clustering. [12] and [24] follow a spatio-temporal clustering approach. For this, a spatial and temporal bounding box is defined to which extent newly incoming information is aggregated.

A common problem of unsupervised approaches is that the clusters mostly remain unlabeled, thus, the combination of unsupervised clustering with supervised classification was conducted in rare cases. This is due to the fact that supervised approaches are only necessary if specific event types such as incidents need to be detected and the types are known beforehand. In this case, different classifiers such as SVMs were used [3, 18].

Spatial and temporal information.

The majority of the presented related work relies on the message text, i.e., tweets are clustered based on text similarity. Temporal metadata is mostly used for detecting changes in the frequency tweets are created or words are used. Some approaches also include temporal metadata in the clustering process [14, 18]. However, none of the presented approaches makes use of temporal expression recognition as we do. Some approaches which focus on detecting small-scale events, use spatial information [6, 15, 12, 24, 14] while others propose approaches for geotagging [25, 5, 10, 18]. The former approaches allow higher precision, while in the latter ones more information is available.

In contrast to the presented state of the art, we propose a straightforward clustering of unknown event-related data using information about the location, the time period as well as the event type of an event mentioned in a single tweet. Furthermore, our proposed approach is a hybrid approach, employing supervised classification of each tweet before clustering. This way, we are able to reduce the computational overhead as the number of tweets can be significantly reduced, thus, clustering as well as preprocessing steps are much faster. Furthermore, our approach makes use of geotagging as well as temporal extraction, which are only applied in rare cases in related work.

3. SYSTEM DESIGN

In the following section, we present our approach for small-scale incident detection with a focus on the incident properties type, location and time (see Figure 1):

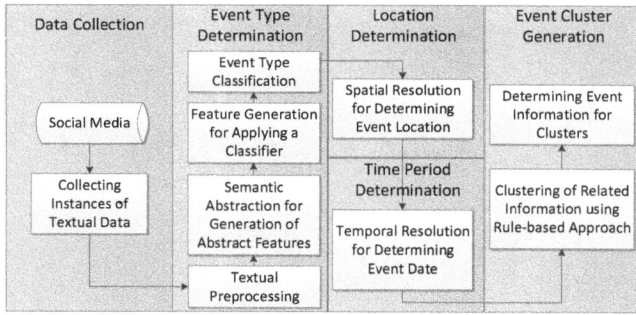

Figure 1: Approach for detecting events and clustering event reports.

I. Collection: A prerequisite is the collection of tweets and the corresponding user profiles.

II. Incident Type Determination: The first processing step classifies the tweets. Beginning with classification helps to differentiate whether a tweet is related to an event or not at a very early stage of the processing pipeline. This is highly important, as we deal with a low proportion of relevant, small-scale incident-related tweets in the large input stream. Thus, the early classification dramatically reduces the number of tweets to be processed in all following steps because all further steps will process only incident-related tweets. We decided to use a supervised classification model to allow fast labeling of incident-related tweets. The process step to train this model includes preprocessing and feature generation. For training the classification model, we complement commonly used features with abstract feature groups derived using Semantic Abstraction [20]. For creating these abstracted features, we use automatic named entity and temporal expression recognition to introduce abstract features based on the occurrence of location and temporal mentions. Also, background information provided by Linked Open Data (LOD) is used to obtain new features that are universally applicable.

III. Location Determination: To determine the spatial location of an incident, we make use of all information present in the user profile as well as the message text to infer a likely location of an incident. The process is based on our work on geolocalization [19].

IV. Time Period Determination: We derive the time of the incident addressed in a tweet from the tweet's text and its creation date. Identification of the time when the incident actually happened is often neglected in related approaches; however, it is useful information to distinguish incidents, which is necessary in the clustering process.

V. Incident Cluster Generation: Tweets that refer to same incident are clustered. For this, we do not only rely on the message text as done in related approaches, but we also use the three properties that define an incident, i.e., type, location and time period, enabling a much faster and more precise clustering. Based on the resulting clusters, a decision maker can consume all tweets that refer to the same incident.

4. SEMANTIC ABSTRACTION

The described system design combines supervised classification to identify incident-related tweets and unsupervised clustering to extract actual incidents. Before we report the interplay between both in detail, we focus on the classification approach. Obviously, a classification approach is required capable of dealing with the user-generated content and its inherent heterogeneity. Users tend to use abbreviations or non-standard vocabulary in their posted content. Also, named entities such as street names used in tweets are likely to be related to the location where a text was created or they are biased towards certain topics. To address this by a robust classifier we have focused on feature generalization by a technique called Semantic Abstraction (SA).

With SA we generalize text features to improve classification performance by (1) replacing already present tokens with a more general token and (2) introducing a set of additional features derived from background knowledge about the text at hand. For creating these abstracted features, we use automatic named entity and temporal expression recognition to introduce abstract features based on the occurrence of location and temporal mentions as well as background information provided by LOD.

Semantic Abstraction using Location Mentions.

For every incoming tweet, location mentions (e.g., "I-90") are extracted and replaced with a common token "LOC" (see Listing 1), before preprocessing is applied. We identify location mentions using named entity extraction with the Stanford Named Entity Recognizer[2]. The NER model was retrained based on a labeled dataset of 800 tweets containing location mentions. The resulting classifier provides more than 90% accuracy for detecting location mentions on this dataset. As a result, location mentions are later on represented as TF-IDF features as well as n-grams. Furthermore, we count the number of location mentions in a tweet and add this as an additional feature.

Listing 1: Example tweet with location mention and the same tweet with the replaced location mention.

```
car crash on  I-90 , right lane closed
                ↓
car crash on  @LOC , right lane closed
```

Semantic Abstraction using Temporal Expressions.

As another abstraction approach, we extract temporal expressions from tweets, which are tokens or phrases in a text that serve to identify time intervals such as "yesterday". For identifying temporal expressions, we adapted the HeidelTime [23] framework. The framework relies on regular expressions to detect temporal expressions. As the system was developed for large text documents with formal language, it needed to be adapted to work on short and unstructured microposts. We also extended the HeidelTime tagging functionality to detect temporal expressions such as dates and times. The detected expressions are then replaced with two annotations: "DATE" and "TIME".

Listing 2: Replaced temporal expression example.

```
 friday afternoon  in heavy traffic
        ↓
 @DATE  in heavy traffic
```

---

[2]http://nlp.stanford.edu/software/CRF-NER.shtml

As a result, the temporal expression in the example tweet shown in Listing 2 is replaced with our annotation. Also for this approach, abstracted temporal mentions result in additional TF-IDF features, n-grams, as well as the number of temporal mentions in a tweet.

Semantic Abstraction using Linked Open Data.

We use LOD as a source of background information about entities as an additional feature generation step. For instance, different named entity mentions in tweets are used synonymously to refer to the same entity. "NYC" or "The Big Apple" all refer to the same city *New York City*. With simple text similarity measures, this relationship is undetectable. However, as all mentions relate to the same URI in DBpedia, this background knowledge about an entity can be used as additional features.

We use the RapidMiner LOD extension [17] to extract additional features from LOD. The extension recognizes entities based on DB-Pedia Spotlight[3] to get likely URIs of the detected named entities. Then, these URIs are used to extract the direct types and categories of an entity. Each extracted type and category is then added as an additional feature, with each feature encoding the number of words that are present in the tweet that have the same URI. In Listing 3, two newly added features for two example tweets are shown.

Listing 3: Extracted DBpedia properties for two tweets.

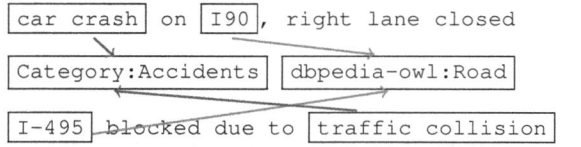

```
car crash  on  I90 , right lane closed

Category:Accidents   dbpedia-owl:Road

I-495  blocked due to  traffic collision
```

The SA-generated features play an important role in the system design presented in the following.

5. SYSTEM FOR SMALL-SCALE INCIDENT DETECTION

In the following, we provide detailed information about the actual property extraction steps of the process specified in the system design section.[4]

5.1 Incident Type Determination

In this step, we decide on the incident-relatedness of a tweet. For this, an incident type is assigned to a tweet or it is classified as not incident related. The type is assigned using automatic classification techniques. As a result of this, information related to incidents is identified in large amounts of potentially available information items. As already mentioned, assigning the incident type before conducting further processing steps such as spatial or temporal resolution allows filtering out irrelevant information, significantly reducing the amount of data that needs to be processed in the following steps.

In the following we give an overview of all steps conducted for training a model for incident type classification (see Figure 2 for an overview).

Preprocessing

Preprocessing converts the text of a micropost into a structured representation so it can be used for feature generation, which is

Figure 2: Semantic abstraction and feature generation steps for training a classification model for automatic incident type classification.

foundation for the subsequent processing steps. First, we identify abbreviations in tweets and replace them with the corresponding word using a slang dictionary[5]. Second, we apply Semantic Abstraction to identify and replace location mentions and temporal expressions with their respective common token.[6] Third, based on the resulting text, we conduct tokenization. Thus, the text is divided into tokens. Every token is then analyzed and non-alphanumeric characters are removed or replaced. Finally, all tokens are normalized using lemmatization.

Feature Generation

Once the preprocessing was applied, the modified texts are used to generate several features. To identify the most valuable features, we conducted a comprehensive feature selection, analyzing the value of each feature for the overall classification performance. In section 6, the evaluation results of the best feature combinations are shown.

Depending on the classifier, we found that word-n-grams or char-n-grams perform best. In addition, we add TF-IDF scores as well as syntactic features such as the number of explanation marks, question marks, and upper case characters as features.

Additionally, we use Semantic Abstraction to generate features that help training a more generalizable model. Generalization refers to (1) replacing already present tokens with a more general token and of (2) introducing a set of additional features derived from background knowledge about the text at hand. We add the number of location and temporal mentions present in the text and we use Linked Open Data (LOD) as a source of interlinked information about entities to generate additional and more general features for text classification.

As a result of the feature generation step, a machine learning model is trained that can be applied on all incoming data. This way, noisy information is filtered out prior clustering, keeping only the incident-related tweets. In the following, we call those incident-related tweets *incident reports*.

5.2 Location Determination

The second property to specify an incident is its location. To determine the spatial dimension of a tweet, we extended our geolocalization approach presented in [19] to allow street-level geolocalization of tweets. Geolocalization of tweets without attached geoposition is highly important because only a limited number of about 1-2% of all tweets are explicitly geotagged. The applied geolocalization approach uses an estimation of the city and country

---

[3]http://spotlight.dbpedia.org
[4]The source code is available upon request.

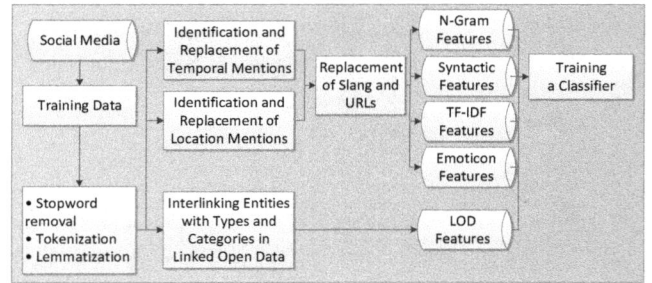

[5]http://www.noslang.com/
[6]Semantic Abstraction using LOD is applied on the unprocessed text for feature generation.

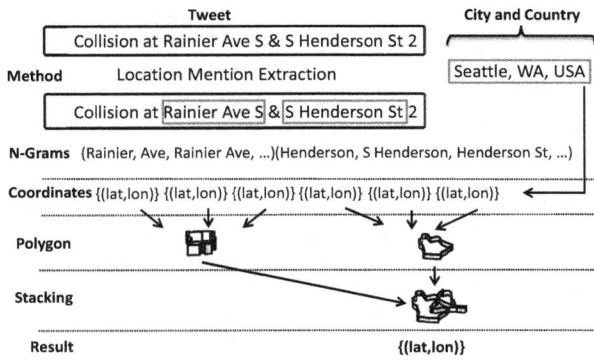

Figure 3: Extended geolocalization approach based on the approach presented in [19].

where a tweet was send from and additionally considers location mentions extracted from the tweet message (see Figure 3).

The process works as follows. As a first step, we use the location mention extraction approach as presented before to detect possible location mentions in the tweet message. Based on this information, we create triples of combinations of consecutive words (word-n-grams) to determine likely location names. We then use geocoding APIs such as the MapQuest Nominatim API[7] to map each n-gram to a location in the corresponding city. This results in several sets of coordinate pairs for each n-gram. Based on these pairs, we create a polygon. As a last step, we remove redundant polygons as some n-grams refer to the same location. Once all polygons are determined, they are stacked one over the other. The highest area in that height profile is then found, and its polygon outline is determined as the intersection of the contributing polygons. In this case, the polygon is used as estimation of the location where an incident mentioned in a tweet has happened.

This approach allows the street-level geolocalization of the message focus of tweets. In a preliminary evaluation we found that the approach is able to estimate the location of an incident described in a tweet with a median distance of 250m. For this, we manually geocoded 100 event-related tweets and compared our estimation with the ground truth.

Metrics:

To evaluate our approaches, we compared the coordinate pair estimation of each approach with a ground truth. For evaluating the performance of each spatial indicator and the combined approach for the geolocalization of a tweet, we use the device location as ground truth. For determining the user's residence and geolocalizing event-related tweets, we used the manually provided geotags as ground truth.

5.3 Time Period Determination

The third property to identify is the time period of an incident reported in a tweet. The obvious usage of the tweet creation date is unreliable because people also report on past incidents. To address this, we use the creation date of a tweet as base for our estimations. Subsequently, the data is adjusted by using the temporal expression annotations generated in the preprocessing. All temporal expressions are extracted and combined with the creation date to calculate the date when the incident most probably occurred.

---

[7] http://developer.mapquest.com/web/products/open/nominatim

Listing 4: Example tweet for determining likely point in time of an incident.

```
Yesterday, people died in a car accident.
```

For instance, given the tweet in Listing 4 created on Friday 15, 2015, we can use our mechanism to estimate Thursday 14, 2015, as a likely point in time when the accident occurred as the tweet is referring to "yesterday".

As a result of the spatial and the temporal resolution, each incident report is assigned a GPS coordinate pair as well as a point in time the message refers to.

5.4 Incident Cluster Generation

As a third step, a rule-based approach is used for creating clusters of related information and finally detecting incidents. We rely on type, location and time period determined before to conduct clustering. This is an important difference to related work that applies clustering based on tweet content.

Our rule-based clustering works as follows. An incident described by a newly incoming incident report is compared to the previously reported incidents. For the outcome of this comparison, we differentiate two cases for matching of *incident reports* and previously reported incidents:

- No match to existing incident: If no existing incident could be detected, a new *incident cluster* is created comprising the spatio-temporal and incident type information of the incident report.

- Match to existing incident: If the newly reported incident lies within the spatial and temporal extent and shares the same incident type as an existing incident, then the incident report is added to the existing incident cluster.

To conduct this matching, we follow a rule-based approach. A rule specifies the spatial and temporal extent as well as the incident type that is used to assert the equivalence of a new incident report and an existing incident cluster. A new incident report is aggregated with an existing incident cluster if its spatial and temporal extent falls within the extent that the rule asserts to the existing incident and if it shares the same incident type. These rules are described as a triple of the form:

$$\langle incident\_type, radius, time \rangle \quad (1)$$

The spatial extent is a radius in meters drawn around the spatial location of the incident. The temporal extent is a timespan in minutes calculated from the creation time of the initial incident. The incident types are the types of small-scale incidents that are differentiated using the supervised classification approach. In Algorithm 1, the final algorithm for our approach is shown.

The example rule $\langle Car\_Crash, 50m, 30min \rangle$ asserts that each reported incident of the type "Car Crash" is identical to a previously reported incident if it is of the same type, within a range of 50 meters, and within a time interval of 30min. Thus, the corresponding tweet is assigned to the incident cluster.

In the case of a successful match between an incident report and an incident cluster, the spatial information of the incident report and the incident cluster are merged. The spatial locations of the incidents are merged to a weighted mean location. The weights take the ratio of $1 : N$ between the newly reported incident and the existing incident, where N is the number of reports that are already associated with the existing incident. This ensures that all incident reports have the same impact on the mean incident location. In contrast, the temporal dimension is not merged, but the time of the

Algorithm 1: Algorithm for rule-based clustering.

Data: Incident reports IR
Result: Incident clusters C

```
1  forall the Incident reports ir in IR do
2  |   Get all rules R applicable for incident types of ir
3  |   forall the rules r in R do
4  |   |   Get all existing incident clusters C within time
   |   |   interval of r
5  |   |   forall the clusters c in C do
6  |   |   |   if Distance(c,ir) < radius of r then
7  |   |   |   |   if incident type is (sub)type of rule types then
8  |   |   |   |   |   Aggregate tweet to incident cluster
9  |   |   |   |   |   Reevaluate rules for new incident
10 |   |   |   else
11 |   |   |   |   Create new incident cluster c
```

(temporally) first report is used as the time of the incident. This allows finding a more likely date of an incident.

As the spatial and temporal resolutions are prone to errors, the clustering was designed to cope with incomplete information: Missing spatial information is replaced with a common spatial center, e.g., the center of the city for which the tweets are used; Missing temporal information is replaced with the creation date of the tweet. Thus, even with one or two missing characteristics, we are still able to build clusters, preserving *potentially* important information.

With the help of these three steps, a rule engine can compute whether incident reports are clustered if they describe the same incident or not. Initially, the specification of these rules requires domain knowledge in emergency management, though, it would be possible to automatically derive rules based on real-world data. Therefore, we argue that these rules should at least initially be specified by domain experts (e.g., emergency managers) to match incident types according to their needs.

6. EVALUATION

In the following we report on two evaluations to asses the quality of our small-scale incident detection process. In a pre-study, we present the quality of our approach for classifying the type of the incident mentioned in a tweet. In the main study, we show the comparison of our approach for detecting small-scale incidents with related approaches.[8]

6.1 Pre-Study: Incident Type Determination

The determination of the incident type is a crucial step in our small-scale incident detection approach because the classification of the tweet serves as a filter to limit the workload for all later processing steps. Thus, high accuracy of the classifier is required. To realize this, special attention was given to this step and we introduced features based on Semantic Abstraction. In the following, we evaluate the performance of our classifier. Please note that our goal was not to compete with existing classification approaches, but to provide a suitable model for the incident detection pipeline.

Dataset

We focus on three specific small-scale incident types which were identified to be the most common incident types in the city of Seat-

tle, WA based on our analysis of the Seattle Fire Calls dataset. The dataset is a source of official and frequently updated incident information and provides high-quality data about incidents. The tree classes of very common and distinct incident types and the neutral class used for the evaluation are: *car crash*, *fire*, *shooting*, and *not incident related*.

We collected public tweets in English language using the Twitter Search API in a 15km radius around the city centers of Seattle, WA and Memphis, TN. We focused on data from these two cities to avoid overfitting to regional terms of one city. This gave us an initial set of 7.5M tweets collected from November 19, 2012, to February 7, 2013, for Memphis, TN and Seattle, WA.

To build a classification model a dataset of tweets annotated with incidents was used as ground truth and training set. For training we focused on a small, high quality set. We created the dataset using the following steps. First, we applied incident keyword filtering as presented in [22]. From the resulting set, we randomly selected 2,000 tweets containing at least one incident-related keyword. These tweets were manually labeled by three researchers of our research department that have experience in emergency management and data labeling. Every tweet was labeled by each researcher. To assign the final coding, the majority of all coders had to agree on a label. In the case of disagreement, issues were resolved in a group discussion. The final dataset used in the pre-study is **4-CLASSES**: 2,000 tweets (328 fire, 309 car crash, 334 shooting, 1,029 not incident related).

Our evaluation shows that the dataset contains sufficient training data to construct a classifier of high accuracy. Thus, we assume that neither the fact that the dataset does not represent the typical distribution of incident-related tweets nor the even low number of 2,000 tweets affected the evaluation of the classifier.

Metrics

To measure classification performance we report the accuracy (ACC) and the micro-averaged F1-Measure (F).

Algorithms

We focused on a multinomial Naive Bayes (NB) and a Support Vector Machine (SVM) classifier, due to their excellent performance in text classification tasks [16]. We relied on the LibLinear implementation of an SVM with linear kernel as it has been shown that for a large number of features and a low number of instances, a linear kernel is comparable to a non-linear one [9]. Our goal is to optimize the performance of the overall classifier. Therefore, we evaluated the best parameter settings for the slack variable c whenever an SVM was used. All results were determined applying a stratified 10-fold cross validation.

We compared the following feature groups: Word-n-grams and char-n-grams with $n = \{1..5\}$, syntactic features, TF-IDF scores, and Semantic Abstraction using LOD, location mentions and temporal mentions.[9]

Though we conducted an intensive evaluation of multiple feature combinations, it is important to note that we did not evaluate all possible combinations, but only those combinations that seem to provide better classification results. Furthermore, we were interested in finding the best feature combination that allows classifying our dataset. However, for future evaluations one might also try to reduce misclassification of certain classes.

---

[8]The datasets will be published at http://www.doc.gold.ac.uk/~cguck001/IncidentTweets/

[9]A more detailed evaluation of Semantic Abstraction can be found in [20].

Table 1: Classification results using our feature set on the 4-CLASSES dataset. Binary weighting using an SVM and term-frequency weighting using NB are shown in comparison with a majority class approach.

Features	c	Accuracy	Micro-avg. F1
Majority Class		51.45%	34.96%
Best (SVM/binary)	0.125	90.10%	90.05%
Best (NB/tf)		88.15%	88.08%

Results

In Table 1, the classification results for a simple baseline approach using the majority class compared to classifiers with the best feature combinations are shown.[10]

The evaluation of several n-gram combinations showed that for an SVM word-3-grams with binary weighting and for a NB classifier char-5-grams and term-frequency weighting give the highest performance. Also, conducting Slang and URL replacement prior generating the n-grams was valuable. Furthermore, adding the syntactic feature group and TF-IDF scores was beneficial. Finally, Semantic Abstraction prior generating n-grams gave the best performance.

In summary, the classifier trained on this dataset is able to classify incident-related tweets with an accuracy of more than 90%. With this level of accuracy, we are able to precisely differentiate noise from incident-related tweets. Further justifications of these results are provided in the next study.

6.2 Main Study: Incident Detection

The second study compares the small-scale incident detection performance of our approach with the state of the art. The state of the art was re-implemented following the respective papers. We assessed on small-scale incident detection performance of our approach and the state of the art. Therefore we compare the result for a stream of tweets with an official incident database as a gold standard.

Dataset

Our main goal is to evaluate how well real-world incidents are detected. Therefore we decided to use information from an existing emergency management system as gold standard. For this, we used the Seattle Fire Calls dataset that contains official incident information shortly after an incident was reported to the Seattle Fire Department. Though the Seattle Fire Calls dataset provides a huge amount of incident information per day, we do not expect it to contain all incidents that actually occurred. Still, the official source provides a high-quality ground truth for small-scale incidents.

To compare the real-world incidents with incidents determined from tweets, we collected a two-day sample of tweets using the Twitter Search API in a 15km radius around Seattle, WA. For this study, we used the ***complete and unfiltered*** dataset that could be retrieved to show the applicability of our approach on a large amount of data. The used sample is not a complete sample of tweets for Seattle. However, the number of tweets should be sufficient to cover different small-scale incidents. Therefore it enables us to compare the performance of existing approaches for small-incident detection. Most importantly, we did *not* apply any further pre-filtering, resulting in the dataset **INC-TW**: 802K tweets for Seattle from March 11, 2014, to March 13, 2014.

---

[10]Please note that we did not want to compare classification approaches as we did for instance in [22].

Furthermore, we collected real-world incident data in the same period to allow correlation of tweets and real-world incidents. As the incident types provided by the Seattle Fire Department are more fine-grained than our three types, we aggregated the incident types present in this dataset to match our types (see Table 2). The final ground truth dataset used for our evaluation consists of 84 real-world incidents from Seattle, **INC-S**: 21 car incidents, 61 fire incidents, and 2 shooting incidents.

Metrics

Our goal is to extract as much real-world incidents as possible, therefore we report recall. With recall as the percentage of real-world incidents detected of all real-world incidents in the same time period. Furthermore, we want to understand how much of the captured data actually is about incidents. Therefore we report precision. Both definitions rely on the assumption that an incident is detected if at least one tweet is contained in an incident cluster matching the real-world incident. For precision and recall we follow the definitions of [13] and [26].

Algorithms

In the evaluation, we compared different state of the art clustering approaches. As we aimed to detect small-scale incidents, we wanted to detect real-world incidents within a 500m radius and within a 20min time interval. These parameters were provided by emergency managers we interviewed in the course of our work. All approaches were restricted accordingly. Though our geolocalization approach is able to estimate the location of an incident with a median distance of 250m, we decided to follow the parameters of the emergency managers, thus, allowing our approach to be more imprecise. Nevertheless, we also present the results that could be achieved with a different spatial radius.

Related Approaches: For comparing with the state of the art, we re-implemented three approaches that do not need a specific number of clusters to be created as input. We omit comparisons of partitioning algorithms such as k-means and hierarchical approaches because these showed as too slow to be applied on our large datasets.

The selected systems represent the state of the art in the field of small-scale incident detection. Noteworthy, the event-related information extracted by the state of the art extracts less incident information (location, type, time) than the approach we report in this paper. Most importantly, for most approaches cluster centers are created around explicitly geotagged tweets as no automatic geolocalization is used. We decided to re-implement all approaches 'as-reported', thus, we added no additional enhancements that were specifically designed for our approach. This way we ensure a fair comparison between systems as these were initially designed.

We considered the following approaches:

- As a first approach, we re-implemented the density-based clustering presented by Boettcher and Lee [5] that uses DB-Scan [8]. This approach was chosen because it provides high precision for detecting small-scale incidents. The approach depends on two parameters "Epsilon" and "Min points" that define the closeness and density of instances. As the optimal values are not known in advance, we evaluated several combinations of both parameters using a greedy grid search approach.

- As a second clustering approach, we re-implemented the geospatial clustering presented by Walther and Kaisser [24] as the most recent approach for small-scale incident detection. Also, this approach relies on a spatio-temporal clustering thus being highly related to our approach.

Table 2: Recall of our approach differentiated by incident type.

Incident Type	Real-world Incident Type	# Real-world Incidents	Recall (overall)	Recall (<500m,±10min)
Car Incident	Motor Vehicle Accident Motor Vehicle Accident Freeway Medic Response Freeway Car Fire Car Fire Freeway	21	71.42%	38.09%
Fire Incident	Fire In Building Fire In Single Family Resd. Automatic Fire Alarm Resd. Auto Fire Alarm	61	52.46%	29.50%
Shooting Incident	Assault w/Weap. 7 per Rule Assault w/Weapons Aid	2	50%	50%
All		84	57.14%	32.14%

- As a third approach, we re-implemented an online single-pass clustering as used by Becker [3], which is commonly used for detecting incidents of unspecific type. We decided to use Leader-follower clustering as a fast algorithm, for which the threshold parameter was optimized in the evaluation.

For all approaches, we used the euclidean distance similarity metric based on a tweets' tokens weighted using the TF-IDF scores.

The selected approaches were applied on all 802K tweets, which contain more than 20k explicitly geotagged tweets. However, as we were interested in a 20min temporal extent and due to clustering performance, we separated INC-TW into 20min time intervals and applied the respective algorithms on the resulting windows. This does not affect overall performance, as temporal information is present for all tweets.

After applying the algorithms, we conducted a spatio-temporal filtering to finally allow correlation with real-world incidents. We selected only clusters that are within a 500m radius and a ±10min time interval of a real-world incident. For applying this filtering, we followed the same spatial and temporal merging strategy as used with our approach. Thus, spatial locations of the individual tweets in a cluster that have GPS coordinates are merged to a weighted mean location. If all tweets in a cluster did not have GPS coordinates present, the cluster was discarded as this could not be related to an incident. As a temporal dimension for a cluster, the creation date of the oldest tweet in the cluster was used.

Our goal was to compare the recall of all approaches. Therefore we omit any post-processing (i.e., posterior supervised classification of the resulting clusters) presented in related works which solely improves precision. We assumed that the resulting clusters are perfect incident-related clusters, thus, boosting the performance of related approaches. Therefore, we manually evaluated every resulting cluster to check whether it corresponds to the real-world incident. Additional merging of clusters would not provide any benefit with respect to recall.

Rule-based Clustering: For our approach, we applied the spatio-temporal-type clustering as described in Section 5.

1. **Classification:** For detecting the type of incident, our supervised classification approach was applied. A model was trained on the 4-CLASSES dataset introduced in the pre-study which comprises 2,000 tweets. The classifier was then applied to all tweets in the newly collected dataset for Seattle, INC-TW. All tweets with probability >70% were chosen for further processing. Choosing a lower probability would result in too many misclassified tweets as a manual evaluation of the classified tweets showed. As a result, the classifier identified 1,271 incident-related tweets with the respective incident types. These tweets were sent by 685 distinct users. However, the actual number of incident-related tweets might be higher due to the limitations of a supervised approach.

2. **Spatio/Temporal Resolution**: Next, our approaches for detecting the point in time of an incident and the approach for geolocalization of tweets were applied on each tweet. This gave us spatio-temporal information for each incident report, which is needed for our matching approach. Most importantly, of the 1,271 tweets only 25 tweets contain an exact GPS coordinate, thus, more than 98% of the tweets would not be used by our approach if no geolocalization would be applied.

3. **Rule-based Clustering**: Finally, the rule-based clustering was applied on the prefiltered tweet dataset containing the spatial, temporal, and type information. We created a single rule *{Incident_Type, 500m, 10min}* for each incident type {Crash, Fire, Shooting}. Using our clustering algorithm, the 1,271 tweets were aggregated to 366 distinct incident clusters.

Results

The results of evaluating the correlation to real-world incidents are shown in Table 2. For our evaluation, i.e., the correlation of incidents derived from the tweets with real-world incidents, we calculated the recall using the detected incidents and the real-world incident information. To decide whether an incident detected with our approach matches the real-world incident, all tweets in each incident cluster were manually compared with respect to the incident type and the spatial location mentioned in each tweet. If at least one incident-related tweet was contained, a match of the incident cluster to the real-world incident was confirmed.

Recall for Incident Detection: In the case the rule *{Incident_Type, 500m, 10min}* is applied, 32.14% of the real-world incidents could be detected. This is a very precise result given the strict temporal and spatial boxing. Furthermore, if no spatial boxing was applied, we were able to detect 57.14% of the incidents reported in the official emergency management system using just information present in tweets. Also, the individual recalls for each incident type are high with more than 50% without spatial boxing and more than 29% with spatial boxing for each incident type. However, the results for the shooting incidents may not be representative as only two shooting incidents occurred in this time period.

In Table 3, a comparison of our approach with related approaches is shown. For these approaches it is the first comparison with a real-world ground truth. The table shows the best results achieved with the respective parameter settings.

Table 3: Comparison of approaches for small-scale incident detection.

Our Approach	Recall
	32.14%
Boettcher and Lee [5] (MinPoints=1, Epsilon=0.4)	3.53%
Walther and Kaisser [24]	4.76%
Single-pass clustering (Threshold=0.8)	5.88%

The results indicate that we are able to detect five times more real-world incidents compared to the best related approach, which has a recall of 5.88%. One reason for the low recall of related approaches is that no geolocalization of tweets is applied. Thus, the overall number of clusters with GPS information that matches the actual real-world incident is of course lower. Furthermore, the temporal resolution helps to identify the date of the incident more accurately compared to other approaches.

Another advantage of our approach is that it provides clusters labeled with the type of incident while related approaches create unlabeled clusters and do also create clusters with information not related to incidents at all. As said before, for our evaluation we assumed that all clusters created with related approaches are incident related. However, detecting actually incident-related clusters is a necessity for real-world applicability.

Average Cluster Size: The results in Figure 4 show that applying clustering techniques as used in related work results in a set of clusters containing many tweets. With the best parameter settings for DBScan as used by Boettcher and Lee [5], eight clusters were detected with an average number of 478 tweets. In these large clusters many irrelevant tweets are contained, which would need to be excluded with high computational costs. With the single-pass clustering, 132 clusters were created with an average number of five tweets. The spatio-temporal clustering by Walther and Kaisser [24] applies clustering based on spatial proximity. The 274 resulting clusters contain two tweets per cluster on average. A simple reason for large cluster sizes is that clustering is applied on all 802K tweets and, in general, no pre-selection or post-processing is applied. However, cluster sizes might change whenever further processing is involved.

In contrast, our approach excludes potentially irrelevant information *before* clustering, which results in clusters that are very likely incident-related. Furthermore, the 366 clusters created with our approach are small in size with an average of four tweets; thus, detecting relevant information is much easier done manually.

Precision for Incident Detection: As we wanted to understand how many of the clusters actually are about incidents, we manually analyzed the clusters created with our approach. We found that we get a precision of 77% for detecting incidents with our approach. This high precision shows that we do not sacrifice precision for recall. This result is quite surprising, as this incident information was not contained in the official emergency management system. A reason for this could be that some incidents are not covered by the official system, for instance, if no police was called. However, the results allow detecting potentially valuable information for emergency management.

Influence of Spatial Extent: We also evaluated the effect of changing the spatial extent (see Figure 5). With a decreasing spatial extent, the recall drops significantly. However, even with a spatial extent of $100m$ still a recall of 7.14% is achieved.

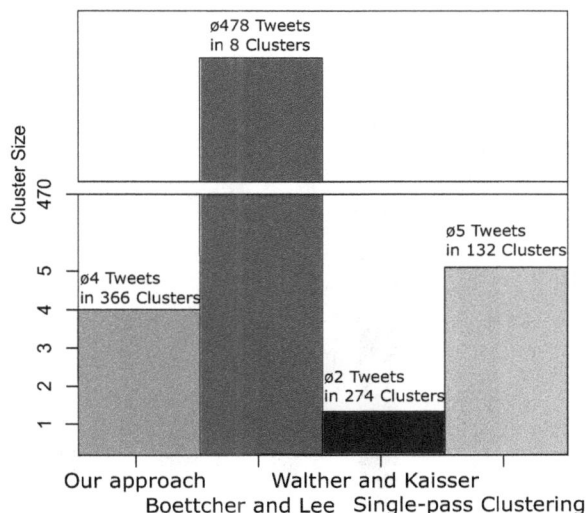

Figure 4: Average number of tweets for each cluster.

Summary: Summarized, we outperform related approaches for detecting real-world incidents. The average number of four tweets is contained in each incident cluster. This containment underlines that detecting small-scale incidents with a low amount of data is possible with our approach. Furthermore, the average time the tweets in an incident cluster were generated is three minutes and 52 seconds after the real-world incident was reported to the emergency management organization. This shows that indeed timely information can be retrieved.

We showed that our rule-based incident clustering is capable of detecting more than 50% of real-world incidents published in an emergency management system. Furthermore, we detected 32.14% of the incidents within a 500m radius and within ±10min. These results are more than five times better compared to related approaches. Also, a precision of 77% indicates that the created clusters could be valuable for decision making.

7. CONCLUSION

In this paper, we presented a spatio-temporal-type clustering algorithm, which is able to detect incidents based on microposts. For this purpose, we solved the problems of inferring the time, location, and type of incidents information is shared about. This allows for precise spatio-temporal localizations and improves clustering quality.

Evaluating our approach, we demonstrated its capability to detect more than 50% of real-world incidents published in an emergency management system[11]. Our approach detects 32.14% of the incidents within a 500m radius and within a time interval of ±10min around the actual event. These results are more than five times better than prior art. The main reason for this improvement can be attributed to the hybrid nature of our approach; the increase of geotagged information as well as the more accurate temporal information, which allow our approach to cluster based on type, time and location. Furthermore, our approach has a precision of 77%, thus, most information we provide is highly relevant for decision makers. This is a result of conducting supervised classification before clustering. Also, incorporating Semantic Abstraction as introduced in this paper, assures that the approach is robust against the het-

---

[11]http://seattle.data.gov

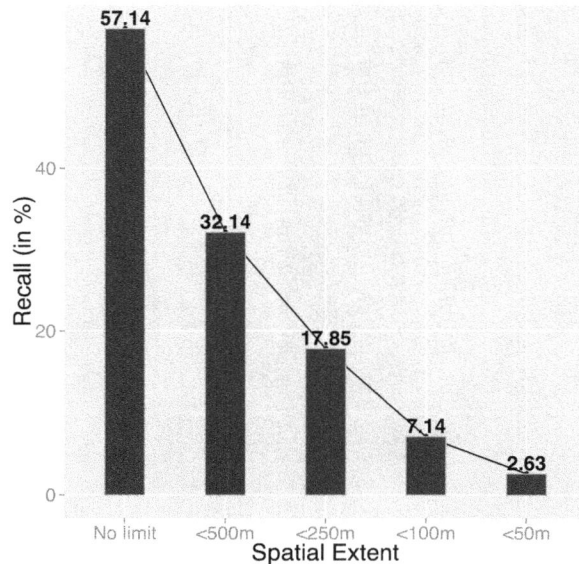

Figure 5: Influence of spatial extent on recall.

erogeneity of user-generated content. We are optimistic that our approach will actually be able to help decision makers to make use of new information sources for an improved, quicker, and better situational awareness during incidents.

Though, this paper focuses on the domain of small-scale incident detection, the approach is not limited to this domain. The presented approach is applicable to small-scale event detection in general, as only labeled data for training the supervised model would need to be provided to identify relevant event-related information for other domains. All other steps remain as presented. However, for more generic types or small-scale events, training an accurate classification model may not be an easy task due to too generic event types. In these cases, approaches such as active learning might help training these model (see for example [21]).

We will investigate several points of improvement in the future. As shown in the evaluation, different sources of user-generated content might be integrated into the clustering process to allow detecting an even higher fraction of incidents. We additionally want to detect additional information such as the number of injured people, or affected buildings, which are comprised in the aggregated event clusters, using multi-label classification. We also want to apply our approach to other types of events.

8. REFERENCES

[1] AGARWAL, P., VAITHIYANATHAN, R., SHARMA, S., AND SHROFF, G. Catching the long-tail: Extracting local news events from twitter. In *Proc. ICWSM 2012* (2012), AAAI Press.

[2] ATEFEH, F., AND KHREICH, W. A survey of techniques for event detection in twitter. *Computational Intelligence* (2013).

[3] BECKER, H. *Identification and Characterization of Events in Social Media*. PhD thesis, Columbia University, 2011.

[4] BLANCHARD, W. Select emergency management-related terms and definitions. Online, 2006. Accessed: 01.04.2014.

[5] BOETTCHER, A., AND LEE, D. Eventradar: A real-time local event detection scheme using twitter stream. In *Proc. GREENCOM '12* (2012), GREENCOM '12, IEEE, pp. 358–367.

[6] CHAE, J., MACIEJEWSKI, R., BOSCH, H., THOM, D., JANG, Y., EBERT, D. S., AND ERTL, T. Spatiotemporal social media analytics for abnormal event detection and examination using seasonal-trend decomposition. In *Proc. VAST '12* (2012), IEEE, pp. 143–152.

[7] ENDSLEY, M. R. Design and evaluation for situation awareness enhancement. In *HFES* (1988), pp. 97–101.

[8] ESTER, M., PETER KRIEGEL, H., SANDER, J., AND XU, X. A density-based algorithm for discovering clusters in large spatial databases with noise. In *Proc. KDD'96* (1996), AAAI Press, pp. 226–231.

[9] HSU, C.-W., CHANG, C.-C., AND LIN, C.-J. A practical guide to support vector classification. Technical report, Department of Computer Science, National Taiwan University, 2003.

[10] HUA, T., CHEN, F., ZHAO, L., LU, C.-T., AND RAMAKRISHNAN, N. Sted: Semi-supervised targeted-interest event detection in twitter. In *Proc. KDD '13* (2013), ACM, pp. 1466–1469.

[11] IMRAN, M., CASTILLO, C., LUCAS, J., MEIER, P., AND VIEWEG, S. Aidr: Artificial intelligence for disaster response. In *WWW'14* (2014), pp. 159–162.

[12] JADHAV, A., WANG, W., MUTHARAJU, R., AND ANANTHARAM, P. Twitris: Socially influenced browsing. In *Semantic Web Challenge 2009, ISWC'09* (2009), ACM.

[13] LI, C., SUN, A., AND DATTA, A. Twevent: Segment-based event detection from tweets. In *Proc. CIKM '12* (2012), ACM, pp. 155–164.

[14] LI, R., LEI, K. H., KHADIWALA, R., AND CHANG, K. C.-C. Tedas: A twitter-based event detection and analysis system. In *Proc. ICDE'12* (2012), IEEE, pp. 1273–1276.

[15] MARCUS, A., BERNSTEIN, M. S., BADAR, O., KARGER, D. R., MADDEN, S., AND MILLER, R. C. Twitinfo: aggregating and visualizing microblogs for event exploration. In *Proc. CHI'11* (2011), ACM, pp. 227–236.

[16] MCCALLUM, A., AND NIGAM, K. A comparison of event models for naive bayes text classification. Technical report ws-98-05, AAAI Press, 1998.

[17] PAULHEIM, H. Exploiting linked open data as background knowledge in data mining. In *Proc. DMoLD'13* (2013), CEUR-WS.org.

[18] SAKAKI, T., AND OKAZAKI, M. Earthquake shakes twitter users: real-time event detection by social sensors. In *Proc. WWW '10* (2010), ACM, pp. 851–860.

[19] SCHULZ, A., ET AL. A multi-indicator approach for geolocalization of tweets. In *Proceedings of ICWSM'13* (2013), AAAI Press.

[20] SCHULZ, A., GUCKELSBERGER, C., AND JANSSEN, F. Semantic abstraction for generalization of tweet classification: An evaluation on incident-related tweets. In *Semantic Web Journal: Special Issue on Smart Cities* (2015).

[21] SCHULZ, A., JANSSEN, F., RISTOSKI, P., AND FÜRNKRANZ, J. Event-based clustering for reducing labeling costs of event-related microposts. In *Proceedings of ICWSM'15* (2015), AAAI Press.

[22] SCHULZ, A., RISTOSKI, P., AND PAULHEIM, H. I see a car crash: Real-time detection of small scale incidents in microblogs. In *ESWC'13* (2013), Springer-Verlag, pp. 22–33.

[23] STRÖTGEN, J., AND GERTZ, M. Multilingual and cross-domain temporal tagging. *Language Resources and Evaluation 47*, 2 (2012), 269–298.

[24] WALTHER, M., AND KAISSER, M. Geo-spatial event detection in the twitter stream. In *Proc. ECIR'13* (2013), Springer-Verlag, pp. 356–367.

[25] WATANABE, K., OCHI, M., OKABE, M., AND ONAI, R. Jasmine: A real-time local-event detection system based on geolocation information propagated to microblogs. In *Proc. CIKM '11* (2011), ACM, pp. 2541–2544.

[26] WENG, J., AND LEE, B.-S. Event detection in twitter. In *Proc. ICWSM'11* (2011), AAAI Press.

[27] XIE, K., XIA, C., GRINBERG, N., SCHWARTZ, R., AND NAAMAN, M. Robust detection of hyper-local events from geotagged social media data. In *Proc. MDMKDD '13* (2013), ACM, pp. 2:1–2:9.

Did You Expect Your Users to Say This? Distilling Unexpected Micro-reviews for Venue Owners

Wen-Haw Chong, Bing Tian Dai, and Ee-Peng Lim
Singapore Management University
80 Stamford Road, Singapore 178902
whchong.2013@phdis.smu.edu.sg, btdai@smu.edu.sg, eplim@smu.edu.sg

ABSTRACT

With social media platforms such as Foursquare, users can now generate concise reviews, i.e. *micro-reviews*, about entities such as venues (or products). From the venue owner's perspective, analysing these micro-reviews will offer interesting insights, useful for event detection and customer relationship management. However not all micro-reviews are equally important, especially since a venue owner should already be familiar with his venue's primary aspects. Instead we envisage that a venue owner will be interested in micro-reviews that are *unexpected* to him. These can arise in many ways, such as users focusing on easily overlooked aspects (by the venue owner), making comparisons with competitors, using unusual language or mentioning rare venue-related events, e.g. a dish being contaminated with bugs. Hence in this study, we propose to discover unexpected information in micro-reviews, primarily to serve the needs of venue owners.

Our proposed solution is to score and rank micro-reviews, for which we design a novel topic model, Sparse Additive Micro-Review (SAMR). Our model surfaces micro-review topics related to the venues. By properly offsetting these topics, we then derive unexpected micro-reviews. Qualitatively, we observed reasonable results for many venues. We then evaluate ranking accuracy using both human annotation and an automated approach with synthesized data. Both sets of evaluation indicate that our novel topic model, Sparse Additive Micro-Review (SAMR) has the best ranking accuracy, outperforming baselines using chi-square statistics and the vector space model.

Categories and Subject Descriptors

H.4 [**Information Systems Applications**]: Miscellaneous; H.2.8 [**Database Applications**]: Data Mining

Keywords

Micro-review, tip, ranking, Foursquare, unexpected

HT '15, September 1–4, 2015, Guzelyurt, Northern Cyprus.
ⓒ2015 ACM. ISBN 978-1-4503-3395-5/15/09 ...$15.00.
DOI: http://dx.doi.org/10.1145/2700171.2791024.

1. INTRODUCTION

In recent years, the prevalence and increased popularity of micro-blogging services have resulted in huge volumes of related data being collected. Various platforms such as Foursquare and Twitter provide rich context and fine-grained data. These have led to new possibilities for data mining applications and knowledge discovery tasks.

In particular, Foursquare[1] allows users to provide short reviews about specific venues. Unlike other platforms where review mining has been extensively explored [15, 18, 25, 17], Foursquare reviews are shorter and more succinct[2]. We call such short reviews as *micro-reviews* [27, 20] to differentiate them from traditional reviews. Foursquare micro-reviews are also known as tips and we use both terms interchangeably. While Foursquare is popular, this is not the only source of micro-reviews. Micro-reviews can also be found in micro-blogging platforms such as Twitter due to users writing about their experiences with products or businesses. Micro-reviews thus represent a wealth of information that can be exploited for applications in recommender systems and customer relationship management systems.

In this work, we approach micro-review mining with the aim of providing value to *venue owners*. We differentiate venue owners from venue visitors or customers which we shall simply refer to as users. With the growing popularity of social media, there is value for owners of physical venues, e.g. restaurants, to exploit social media for outreach, publicity and business improvement. In particular, micro-reviews serve as a form of feedback for venue owners, one that is gathered at little effort and cost. However, deriving useful information from the mass of data requires some effort. In fact, a popular venue can easily garner hundreds/thousands of tips over time. This justifies the need for content distillation techniques.

To the best of our knowledge, the needs of venue owners have been neglected in prior work [15, 18, 12, 19, 21] which largely focused on serving users. Intuitively, we expect venue owners and users to have very different needs in terms of useful information. While users may be deciding on venue visitations or trying to understand venue characteristics, venue owners should be more or less familiar with their own venue characteristics and what they are offering. However, given that users can write about almost anything, it is likely that *some micro-reviews will be relatively less expected to the venue owner*. This forms the primary motivation for our work. We envisage that from the venue owner's per-

---

[1] www.foursquare.com
[2] There is a character limit of 200 for Foursquare

spective, unexpected micro-reviews should be more useful in providing new nuggets of information.

Unexpected micro-reviews can be due to various reasons. Through analyzing the Foursquare data used in our experiments, we envisage some possibilities as follows:

1. **Problem-related**: Describing aspects that may have been overlooked or given little emphasis by venue owners, e.g. parking problems mentioned in relation to food venues

2. **Competition**: Making comparisons with competitors, e.g. mentioning that the same item at some competing restaurant tastes better.

3. **Event**: Describing new unexpected information or an event , e.g. finding bugs in a dish

4. **Linguistic**: Containing language or words that are less frequently used. Such language features are often found in micro-reviews with highly negative or highly positive sentiment.

Note that the above are not necessarily mutually exclusive. For example, a micro-review can be describing an event in a highly negative manner. As an illustration, Table 1 displays four selected tips for a cafe in Singapore. From the perspective of an average venue owner (one who wishes to attract customers), the first tip is least expected. The second tip describes construction noise that affects business, but is external to the venue and which may be easily overlooked, especially if the venue owner is not always physically present. Hence this tip should be relatively unexpected as well, compared to the bottom two tips. For more examples, refer to case studies in Section 4.

| Really lazy staff here. Lotsa tables not cleared, litters all over the floor, and even cockroaches running around! Staff just hide in their cozy aircon counter and slack about. Is this Starbucks?! |
| It's a good place to watch the world go by but the double construction at the Royal Plaza Hotel and Shaw Centre makes it too noisy to enjoy the scene. Wait a few months for construction to stop. |
| Best part is that it's open 24 hrs. |
| great taste coffee... |

Table 1: Sample tips for a cafe in Singapore.

Henceforth, we propose to compute scores for each micro-review for ranking. Formally our research task is: *For a venue of interest, assign scores to its micro-reviews such that micro-reviews that are unexpected have higher scores.* After this, we rank and extract the top ranking micro-reviews. Venue owners may then decide on further actions after examining high ranking micro-reviews. Also note that in the current work, we do not differentiate unexpected micro-reviews by the underlying reasons, deferring this to future research. In our setting, we also assume most micro-reviews to be relevant to their associated venues, i.e. containing related information. Should there be irrelevant micro-reviews, these can first be filtered out using existing techniques [8, 1].

We propose a topic modeling approach for computing micro-review scores. Our exploration is driven by how we expect a micro-review to be generated. Intuitively users talk about various topics in micro-reviews, related to the venues they

visit. One can imagine that if a micro-review can be explained well in terms of a topic or attributed to some notion of a background, then it is not that unexpected after all. Hence with a model for the expected, we can offset the expected to derive the unexpected. With this intuition, we design a novel topic model based on a sparse generative framework [10]. The proposed topic model, **Sparse Additive Micro-Reviews (SAMR)** regards the generation of micro-reviews as a process jointly driven by the background, user-generated topics and the venue. We then score and rank each micro-review by combining appropriate model parameters.

Finally we recognise that ideally, venue owners should be included in the model. However this is currently not possible since micro-reviews are primarily written by users, not venue owners. Instead we have used topics and implicitly venue types to circumvent this. For example, the average owner of a dining venue should expect food and service-related topics to explain well the many micro-reviews he received. If not, then there may be cause for attention.

Contributions. In summary, our contributions are:

- We propose to mine unexpected micro-reviews to serve the needs of venue owners. This problem has been largely unexplored.

- We have designed a novel topic model, SAMR for the proposed problem. Coupled with an appropriate scoring scheme, SAMR outperforms compared baselines in both manual and automated evaluation.

- To assess ranking accuracy, we have conducted experiments with human annotators. Given a pair of micro-reviews ranked differently by competing approaches, annotators are tasked to vote for the micro-review that they deemed to be more unexpected. The SAMR model is superior, attracting 70% of the votes. (Refer to Section 5).

- For automated large scale evaluation, we construct *pseudo-venues* by mixing micro-reviews from different venues. In this manner, for each pseudo-venue, we obtain the ground truth set of unexpected micro-reviews for ranking. On measuring the ranking accuracy, the SAMR model is superior in precision. (Refer to Section 6).

2. RELATED WORK

Review Summarization. Instead of micro-reviews, much prior work [15, 18, 25, 17] had focused on mining longer reviews from e-commerce platforms, e.g. Amazon.com.

In review summarization, a well studied review mining problem, multiple reviews of an item are processed to select a set of sentences/phrases covering different representative aspects of an item, e.g. service quality for a restaurant. For example, Hu and Liu [15] selected sentences that express opinions on item aspects and compiled them into a summary, along with opinion statistics. Lappas and Gunopulos [18] exploited opinions differently and defined a review to be more confident if its expressed opinion agrees with the majority. Their objective is then to find a compact set of high-confidence reviews covering aspects selected by the user. Tsaparas et al. [25] reformulated summarization as a maximum coverage problem such that one selects a limited number of reviews that cover attributes from both positive/negative viewpoints. Lappas et al. [17] proposed a more constrained coverage problem in that reviews are selected to also preserve the distribution of different opinions.

The above summarization techniques have been successfully applied on non-micro reviews and should be easily extendible to micro-reviews. On the other hand, summarization results may be of less value to the average venue owner, since they should already be familiar with one's own venue. Instead, we provide a different value proposition by extracting unexpected micro-reviews. Our work is hence distinct in this aspect.

Supervised Review Mining. Previous works have also attempted to [12, 19, 16, 32] assign review scores based on a general notion of usefulness. These mainly rely on supervised techniques that fit a model using labeled data. The work by Ghose and Ipeirotis [12] used annotated data to fit regression models with review usefulness and sales impact as the dependent variables. Liu et al. [19] utilized rated reviews, i.e. reviews accompanied by online usefulness votes, to build a regression model. They determined that the reviewer expertise, writing style and timeliness are crucial factors affecting review usefulness. Kim et al. [16] applied SVM regression on rated reviews to model review usefulness, with the findings that review length, unigrams etc are relevant model input features. Similarly, Zhang and Varadarajan [32] applied regression on rated reviews for review usefulness scoring.

As can be seen, the targeted audience is again the users or customers, rather than the venue owners. The two roles will have different notions of usefulness. For example, while users may find a micro-review useful if it describes the signature dish of a restaurant, the restaurant owner already knows his signature dish and may derive less value. To date, there is also no collection of labels in terms of whether a micro-review is expected or not. Hence our problem is rather less straightforward and the absence of labeled data makes it difficult to apply supervised techniques.

Micro-blog/micro-review mining. Micro-reviews have some resemblance to micro-blogs, e.g. tweets, as both are short length in nature. There are also parallels if we regard the events or topics in micro-blogs to be analogous to items in micro-reviews. For micro-blog mining, a popular track [26, 14, 2, 30] is to model the interestingness/popularity of micro-blogs, where it is assumed that more popular/interesting micro-blogs will lead to more retweets. For example, Uysal and Croft [26] used a decision tree and a learned ranking function, to rank micro-blogs for each user based on his propensity to retweet each micro-blog. Both Hong et al. [14] and Alhadi et al. [2] employed classifiers to model and predict micro-blog interestingness/popularity. Lastly, Yang et al. [30] predicted retweeting behaviors as well, but in a semi-supervised framework using the factor graph.

Popularity has also been studied in the context of micro-reviews. Vasconcelos et al. [27] have utilized micro-review features and online user voting data to fit classification models for popularity. Other than popularity, other researchers [20, 7] focused on identifying sentiment polarity in micro-reviews. It is quite obvious that popular nor sentiment bearing micro-reviews cannot be equated to unexpected micro-reviews which are the subject of this work.

3. APPROACHES

We denote the number of users, venues and topics as U, V and K respectively. Also let the word vocabulary size be W. A topic is indicated by z, a venue by v and a word by w. A micro-review is represented by $\mathfrak{m}$ and has $|\mathfrak{m}|$ words. We also denote the micro-review count for user u as $n(u)$. We introduce other notations in an inline manner for easier reading.

We first discuss our proposed topic model, followed briefly by the baseline approaches.

3.1 Sparse Additive Micro-Reviews

To design a model for unexpectedness, it may be easier to start with *what is expected*. Hence our topic model's generative process is based on how we expect a micro-review to be formed. We then devise the micro-review unexpectedness scores for ranking. Readers seeking a quick understanding of the model can review the generative process below and the scoring schemes in Section 3.1.4.

Our proposed topic model: **Sparse Additive Micro-Reviews (SAMR)** utilizes the Sparse Additive Generative framework (SAGE) [10] introduced by Eisenstein et al. for topic modeling. Unlike traditional Latent Dirichlet Allocation (LDA)-based models [6], the SAGE framework is based on inferring *facet* deviations in log-space from a background distribution. In a Bayesian network, facets are parent nodes representing some factors which directly influence a probability distribution on a child node. For example, the word distribution in a document can be affected by facets such as topics and the authorship.

Eisenstein et al. [10] asserts several advantages of the SAGE framework which motivate our choice. In this framework, a child node, e.g. a word node, can be generated by multiple facets simultaneously without a latent switch to indicate which facets are active at any one time. It is also easy to enforce sparsity to avoid overfitting and generative facets can be combined additively in log-space. The latter facilitates the design of scoring schemes by facet addition or subtraction.

3.1.1 Generative process

We begin with a high level description of our model, which encapsulates how we expect a micro-review to be formed. Figure 1 presents the plate diagram while Table 2 summarizes model parameters which consist of all the facets.

We first assume a global background distribution over topics. Based on personal interest and the types of venues one visit, a user's topic set will differ to some extent from the global distribution, i.e. he 'deviates' from the background. For example, a user who frequents night spots may focus more on clubbing related topics. Thus in the model, the user generates topic deviations η^{USER} which are combined with the background topic facet η^0 to obtain the conditional topic distribution.

At the next level, the topics generate deviations affecting the background distribution over venues and words. For words, we specify that the distribution is concurrently conditional on three facets: the background ϕ^0, topic ϕ^{TOPIC} and venue ϕ^{VENUE}. Note that unlike LDA-based models, no latent switch is required per word to indicate the active facet. With the SAGE framework, we assume that all facets are jointly responsible for every word in an additive manner.

Due to the short lengths of micro-reviews, we also assume that each micro-review covers only one topic.

Intuitively the background word facet ϕ^0 implies that every word has some baseline occurrence frequency (in log space) at any venue while venue facets ϕ^{VENUE} mean that venues elevate or depress word frequencies through positive/negative deviations. Similar interpretation can be applied for user topics ϕ^{TOPIC}. For venue frequencies, the topic facet θ^{TOPIC} results in deviation from the background θ^0, e.g. a dining venue is more likely for food-related topics.

Note that deviations are computed in log space and additional facets can be included in an additive manner. The different facets are also readily combined to compute conditional distributions. For example, denote the background word facet as η^0 with the k-th element η^0_k corresponding to the k-th topic. Similarly let $\eta^{USER}_{u,k}$ be the (u,k)-th element of the user facet for topics η^{USER}. Then the probability of topic k conditional on the background and user u is:

$$p(z = k|\eta^0_k, \eta^{USER}_{u,k}) = \frac{exp(\eta^0_k + \eta^{USER}_{u,k})}{\sum_{i=1}^{K} exp(\eta^0_i + \eta^{USER}_{u,i})} \quad (1)$$

which is an element from a multinomial vector. Other component distributions can be similarly written out.

Model Parameters	Dimension	Symbol
Background topic facet	$1 \times K$	η^0
User-dependent topic facet	$U \times K$	η^{USER}
Background venue facet	$1 \times V$	θ^0
Topic-dependent venue facet	$K \times V$	θ^{TOPIC}
Background word facet	$1 \times W$	ϕ^0
Topic-dependent word facet	$K \times W$	ϕ^{TOPIC}
Venue-dependent word facet	$V \times W$	ϕ^{VENUE}

Table 2: Model Parameters

Formally for each micro-review $\mathfrak{m}$, the model's generative process is as follow:

1. The user first samples a topic: $p(k|\eta^0_k, \eta^{USER}_{u,k})$

2. The background venue facet and sampled topic jointly generate the venue v: $p(v|\theta^0_v, \theta^{TOPIC}_{k,v})$

3. The background word facet, sampled topic and observed venue jointly generate the bag of words in the micro-review: $\prod_{w \in \mathfrak{m}} p(w|\phi^0_w, \phi^{TOPIC}_{k,w}, \phi^{VENUE}_{v,w})$

We next discuss model regularization and inference. Readers less keen on technical details can skip directly to Section 3.1.4 describing the scoring scheme.

3.1.2 Regularization

Thus far, we have described an additive model for generating micro-reviews. However the model is not yet a sparse one. Sparsity is important to speed up parameter learning as well as assist model interpretation by retaining only those deviations that are more significant. To achieve sparsity, we utilize the 0-mean Laplace distribution as the prior, implying that the model likelihood function is L_1 regularized. Thus we penalize large parameter values and drive most of them towards 0. For example, the topic facet results in non-zero deviations from the background for only a small set of words instead of for all words.

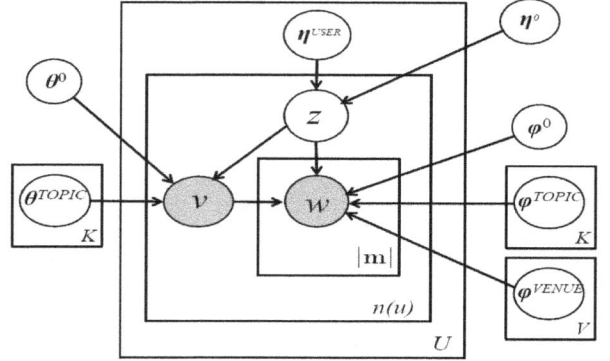

Figure 1: The SAMR topic model in plate notation

3.1.3 Inference

Since the model likelihood and parameter gradients are readily computable, we apply EM learning for parameter inference. The EM-steps are iterated until the log likelihood converges. In the E-step, we hold the model parameters constant and sample topics for every micro-reviews conditional on the old topics. To sample a topic $z_{\mathfrak{m}}$ for micro-review $\mathfrak{m}$ with user $u_{\mathfrak{m}}$, venue $v_{\mathfrak{m}}$ and word vector $\boldsymbol{w}_{\mathfrak{m}}$, we use the following sampling equation:

$$z_{\mathfrak{m}} \sim p(z_{\mathfrak{m}} = k|\eta^{USER}_{u_{\mathfrak{m}}}, \eta^0)p(v_{\mathfrak{m}}|\theta^{TOPIC}_{z_{\mathfrak{m}}=k}, \theta^0)$$
$$p(\boldsymbol{w}_{\mathfrak{m}}|\phi^{TOPIC}_{z_{\mathfrak{m}}=k}, \phi^0, \phi^{VENUE}_{v_{\mathfrak{m}}}) \quad (2)$$

which is readily expanded in the same manner as eq(1). In the M-step, we fix the sampled topic assignments and maximize the model parameters via a proximal gradient based optimization technique.

First we present gradients which are required for optimization. All gradients take on an intuitive form of actual/observed frequencies minus the expected frequencies imposed by the model. The gradients for the topic facets are as follows:

$$\partial\eta^0_k = \sum_{u=1}^{U} n(u,k) - \sum_{u=1}^{U} n(u)p(z = k|\eta^0_k, \eta^{USER}_{u,k}) \quad (3)$$

$$\partial\eta^{USER}_{u,k} = n(u,k) - n(u)p(z = k|\eta^0_k, \eta^{USER}_{u,k}) \quad (4)$$

where $n(u,k)$ is the number of micro-reviews from user u assigned to topic k and $n(u)$ is user u's total micro-review count. The gradients for the venue facets can be derived as:

$$\partial\theta^0_v = \sum_{k=1}^{K} m(k,v) - \sum_{k=1}^{K} m(k)p(v|\theta^0_v, \theta^{TOPIC}_{k,v}) \quad (5)$$

$$\partial\theta^{TOPIC}_{k,v} = m(k,v) - m(k)p(v|\theta^0_v, \theta^{TOPIC}_{k,v}) \quad (6)$$

where $m(k,v)$ is the number of times venue v is assigned topic k and $m(k)$ is the total occurrences of topic k over all venues. Finally, there are 3 sets of gradients for the word facets. For brevity, denote $p(w|\phi^0_w, \phi^{TOPIC}_{k,w}, \phi^{VENUE}_{v,w})$ as $\alpha_{w|(k,v)}$. The gradients can be written as:

$$\partial\phi^0_w = \sum_{v=1}^{V} \sum_{k=1}^{K} d(k,v,w) - \sum_{v=1}^{V} \sum_{k=1}^{K} d(k,v,w)\alpha_{w|(k,v)} \quad (7)$$

$$\partial\phi_{k,w}^{TOPIC} = d(k,.,w) - \sum_{v=1}^{V} d(k,v,w)\alpha_{w|(k,v)} \quad (8)$$

$$\partial\phi_{v,w}^{VENUE} = d(.,v,w) - \sum_{k=1}^{K} d(k,v,w)\alpha_{w|(k,v)} \quad (9)$$

where $d(k,v,w)$ is the number of times word w at venue v is assigned to topic k.

With the computed gradients, we then derive an updating rule using the Iterative Shrinkage Thresholding Algorithm (ISTA)[5]. It has been shown [5] that the L_1 regularized problem can be solved iteratively by the following:

$$\mathbf{x}_t = \arg\max_{\mathbf{x}} \left\{ \frac{1}{2\tau}\|\mathbf{x} - (\mathbf{x}_{t-1} + \tau\nabla f(\mathbf{x}_{t-1}))\|^2 - \lambda\|\mathbf{x}\|_1 \right\} \quad (10)$$

where $f()$ is a function to be maximized (i.e. likelihood in our case), $\mathbf{x}$ is the parameter vector, τ is the learning rate and λ is the regularization term. For our model inference, the parameters are the various facets described earlier.

By differentiating and solving eq(10), we obtain the following update rule for each element:

$$x_t = \begin{cases} \rho + \lambda\tau, & \rho > -\lambda\tau. \\ \rho - \lambda\tau, & \rho < \lambda\tau. \\ 0, & \text{otherwise.} \end{cases} \quad (11)$$

where $\rho = x_{t-1} + \tau\partial f/\partial x_{t-1}$.

3.1.4 Scoring schemes

With the inferred model, we now devise scoring schemes for ranking micro-reviews. Recap that we seek to extract micro-reviews that are unexpected. Now we consider how to offset the expected in order to derive unexpectedness score for each micro-review. Intuitively, if a micro-review can be explained well by a topic sampled from the venue, then we regard it as not that unexpected after all. For example, an Asian food venue will have many micro-reviews that are described well by, say an Asian food topic. Thus such micro-reviews will not be that unexpected. This implies that our scoring scheme should offset the effects of topics.

Recall from the generative process, that both the venue and micro-review topic lead to deviations of each micro-review word from the background. Deviations are computed in log-space, which facilitates addition and subtraction. Hence to offset the effect of the topic for each word, we can simply subtract the topic-dependent deviations from the venue-dependent deviation. Given a micro-review, we repeat this computation over all its words. By then averaging over all the words, we derive the micro-review score. Also note that the background is already implicitly accounted for in the deviations, hence we do not subtract the background again. We term this scoring scheme as SAMR(vt). Formally a micro-review score is computed as follows:

$$\text{SAMR(vt)} : score(\mathfrak{m}) = \frac{1}{|\mathfrak{m}|} \sum_{w \in \mathfrak{m}} (\phi_{v_{\mathfrak{m}},w}^{VENUE} - \phi_{z_{\mathfrak{m}},w}^{TOPIC}) \quad (12)$$

To ascertain the effect of topic subtraction, we compare the above scoring scheme with an alternate scheme, SAMR(v), where we use solely the venue-dependent word deviations:

$$\text{SAMR(v)} : score(\mathfrak{m}) = \frac{1}{|\mathfrak{m}|} \sum_{w \in \mathfrak{m}} \phi_{v_{\mathfrak{m}},w}^{VENUE} \quad (13)$$

	Venue A (Corpus A)	Not venue A (Corpus B)	Total
Freq. of word w	a	b	$a+b$
Freq. of other words	c	d	$c+d$
Total	$a+c$	$b+d$	$a+b+c+d$

Table 3: Contingency table for venue analysis. The bracketed column headers illustrate traditional usage in corpora analysis.

The micro-review score can also be generated using other functions. One possibility is to use the maximum word score of constituent words such that micro-reviews that mix expected and unexpected words are not penalized by the former. For brevity in the current paper, we only present results with the averaging function.

3.2 Baselines

Our hypothesis is that by modeling and offsetting topics, we can better extract unexpected micro-reviews. Hence for comparison, we consider baseline approaches that do not consider topics at all.

3.2.1 Chi-squared Statistics

We start with the chi-squared statistic, which has a simpler expected model for word usage in micro-reviews. This has been used in corpora analysis to analyze linguistic differences between different text corpora, e.g. between British and American English [13]. For this task, works such as [28, 22] applied the chi-squared test to identify words with significant differences in usage frequency across different corpora. There is an expected usage frequency for each word based on proportions and without any notion of topics. Specifically the following test statistic is used:

$$\chi^2 = \sum_i \frac{(O_i - E_i)^2}{E_i}, \quad E_i = \frac{M_i \sum_j O_j}{\sum_j M_j} \quad (14)$$

where O_i and E_i are respectively the observed and expected frequencies of the targeted word in corpus i, which in turn has M_i number of words. χ^2 follows the chi-squared distribution under the null hypothesis, i.e. targeted word has no difference in usage frequency across different corpora.

Hypothesis testing leads to rejecting/not rejecting the null hypothesis. This is not required in our problem and omitted. Instead we aim to compute a venue-specific score for each word and subsequently for each micro-review. We treat venues as analogous to corpora and utilize the test statistic χ^2 directly as word scores. The basic idea is that words deviating more from their expected frequencies for a given venue are more unexpected, thus giving larger χ^2 values. The score for each micro-review is then obtained by averaging its word scores. We refer to this scheme as χ^2 scheme.

For comparing a word usage across two corpora, it is convenient to represent information in a 2×2 contingency table. In our case, we treat the venue of interest as one corpus and all other venues as the second corpus. This results in a slightly modified contingency table as shown in Table 3. From the table, the test statistic is computed as:

$$\chi^2 = \frac{(a+b+c+d)(ad-bc)^2}{(a+b)(c+d)(a+c)(b+d)} \quad (15)$$

3.2.2 Corrected Chi-squared Statistics

In computing the chi-square statistic, one in fact approximates the *discrete* binomial distribution of observed frequencies with the *continuous* chi-squared distribution. It has been argued [31],[11, p.14] that the approximation error is overly large for small sample sizes, i.e. when at least one cell in the contingency table has expected frequency < 5. To mitigate this, the Yates' continuity correction [31, 11, 4] was proposed to reduce the error. The corrected statistic for the 2×2 contingency table is computed as:

$$Y^2 = \sum_i \frac{(|O_i - E_i| - 0.5)^2}{E_i} = \frac{\zeta(|ad - bc| - 0.5\zeta)^2}{(a+b)(c+d)(a+c)(b+d)} \quad (16)$$

where $\zeta = a + b + c + d$.

For large sample sizes, the correction effect is negligible. We refer to this scheme as the Y^2 scheme.

3.2.3 Frequency based Weighting

Lastly, we consider the case where each word is assigned its TF-IDF score [23, 29]. TF-IDF scores are computed by regarding each venue as a document made up of all its micro-reviews. To avoid introducing new terminology, we term this scoring and ranking approach as the *TF-IDF* scheme.

4. QUALITATIVE ANALYSIS

In this section, we cover qualitative analysis, giving examples of unexpected micro-reviews that are uncovered for sample venues. We apply the SAMR(vt) scoring scheme on Foursquare venues in Singapore. We include venues with at least 15 micro-reviews, thereby obtaining 3,150 venues with 56,997 micro-reviews generated by 25,189 users. We also remove stop words and rare words (< 5 occurrences). Unexpected micro-reviews due only to rare words is a trivial problem, which we are not focusing on.

We set the number of topics at 10 and initialize them randomly. Following inference, our eventual model has a sparsity of 81.9% for the topic-word facet and 99.4% for venue-word facet, i.e. 99.4% of the word deviations due to venues are 0.

We then manually examined the results for dozens of venues. Since it is required to put oneself in the shoes of the venue owner, some subjectiveness may be involved in assessing whether a micro-review is unexpected or not. We also do not assert the fact that all venues have unexpected micro-reviews. This depends very much on how users write their micro-reviews. Through subsequent experiments with annotators and pseudo-venues, we seek a fair evaluation given the presence of any subjectiveness.

Table 4 illustrates the top 3 micro-reviews for 3 sample Foursquare venues, as ranked by the SAMR(vt) scheme. For the venue 'Fish & Co.', the first and third micro-reviews are rather unexpected for a food venue. The second tip on the swordfish collar is not mentioned by most customers and may be an unexpected positive comment. For 'Meng Kitchen Traditional Taste', users had focused on restaurant name and certain easily overlooked aspects of food and service. Lastly, one can see much comparison with competitors for 'Texas Chicken'. As described in the introduction, this is one reason where micro-reviews can be unexpected. Importantly, such micro-reviews can help the venue owner in improving his products/services to beat or at least match the competition.

Fish & Co. (Seafood/American Restaurant)
There's a cute girl here ;) hahaha!
Still the best in cooking the Swordfish Collar!
eat pray love
Meng Kitchen Traditional Taste (Asian/Chinese Restaurant)
True fact. Did u know that the correct name of meng's kitchen is actually Ming Fa.
Omg the uncle got some problem listening I said I don wan chili twice and end up with chili again
All the noodle is tasty! But the portion and ingredient always get lesser and lesser):
Texas Chicken (Fried Chicken Joint, Fast Food Restaurant)
Will never eat here again.. Popeye n KFC is better..
Get out of here. Their chicken's terrible. Cross over to Novena Square for KFC instead. If you have money, Kenny Rogers. If you have time, head to Popeye's at Toa Payoh
Chicken like rubber

Table 4: 3 sample Foursquare venues (names in bold) and their top 3 unexpected micro-reviews listed below respective venues. Venue categories are in brackets.

Topics. Next, we show that the SAMR model is able to surface topics discussed by users. The topics indicate user interest and are represented by positive deviations in certain words. Table 5 presents the top 10 positive deviating words for each topic. The topics are easily interpreted, hence indicating that the SAMR model is appropriate.

We also recap the notion of deviations. For example if the micro-review topic is on 'Service' in Table 5, the word 'rude' will deviate positively from the background such that it has higher occurrence probability.

Venue Types. Lastly our model provides a topic for each micro-review. Since each venue is described by multiple micro-reviews, it is easy for one to obtain a representation per venue in terms of distribution over topics. Such a representation is indicative of the types of venues. For example, one will expect a dining venue to have a mixture of food and service-related topics. In addition, the representation granularity is adjustable. If a more fine-grained representation is desired, one should define a larger number of topics, i.e. parameter K.

For example, Figure 2 illustrates the topic distribution for the venue 'Meng Kitchen Traditional Taste', where the topic labels are from Table 5. This venue has a Foursquare category of Asian/Chinese restaurant. As can be seen, topics on local cuisine are dominant, followed by service and dining style, thus providing a good indication of the venue type.

To conclude this section, qualitative analysis assures us that the topic model provides reasonable results that can be interpreted properly. We next cover quantitative evaluation.

5. EVALUATION WITH ANNOTATORS

5.1 Experiment Setup

In this section, we present quantitative evaluation results using human annotators. Our dataset is the set of micro-reviews from Singapore Foursquare venues, which we have

Service: rude slow waited attitude customer orders mins poor waitress customers	
Relaxation: chill hang relax band live ambience quiet music atmosphere beers	
Western Cuisine: garlic bacon mushroom cheese onion potato olio aglio ink fries	
Desserts: cream chocolate ice vanilla strawberry caramel blended mocha choc milo	
Local Cuisine 1: tom yong foo tau chop rice cutlet curry yam chicken	
Local Cuisine 2: kway mee teow goreng hokkien nasi lemak hoon bee chor	
Dining Style: xiao reasonable bao prices quality price western affordable sashimi buffet	
Bubble Tea: bubble jelly pearl milk juice sugar gong tea koi pearls	
Promotions: card discount call appreciated treasure license daily forget check save	
Transport/Amenities: bus station mrt park marina exit interchange car wifi mall	

Table 5: Top 10 positive deviating words for each topic. The topic labels are manually assigned.

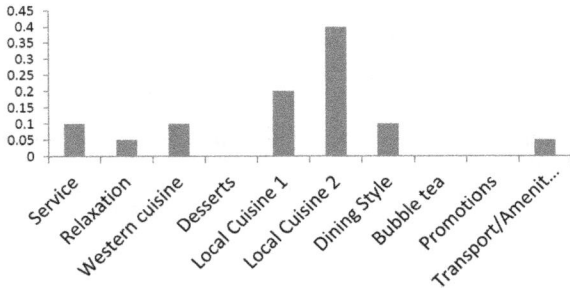

Figure 2: Topic distribution of 'Meng Kitchen Traditional Taste', as aggregated from micro-reviews. The venue is an Asian/Chinese restaurant.

covered in the previous section. We invite 6 participants not involved in this work to compare ranked pairs of micro-reviews. All participants have resided in Singapore for many years and are generally familiar with the characteristics of local venues.

For ease of voting, we limit voting options to two: χ^2 and SAMR(vt) scoring schemes, which we determine to be best performing from a separate experiment (see Section 6). First we rank micro-reviews using χ^2 and SAMR(vt) schemes, such that we obtain a ranked list for each venue per scheme. Then we select 30 venues whose results are least correlated in terms of the Spearman rank coefficient, i.e. venues where the schemes disagree the most. For each of this venue, we select 3 pairs of micro-reviews where the competing schemes disagree the most in terms of ranks. For each pair, the annotator is asked to put himself in the venue owner's perspective and decide which micro-review is relatively more unexpected. To assist the annotator, we also provide the venue category as indicated in Foursquare. The annotator can skip pairs for which he is undecided.

For example, Table 6 illustrates a sample pair for voting. The first micro-review is one that is ranked high by

one scheme, say A and low by the other scheme, say B. The opposite is true for the second micro-review. Hence if the annotator regards the first micro-review as more unexpected, then it is equivalent to a vote for scheme A. Also note that annotators are not aware of the underlying scoring schemes.

cheese baked potato is a must-have!
It's the only second Halal Outlet!!

Table 6: Sample micro-review pair from a venue with category 'Diner and American Restaurant' for voting.

We also quantify agreement between annotator pairs with Bangdiwala's B-statistic [24]. Let x_{ij} be the number of pairs where the first annotator had voted for scheme i and the second annotator had voted for scheme j. The B-statistic ranges from 0 to 1 and is defined as:

$$B = \frac{\sum_{j=1}^{2} x_{jj}^2}{x_1 \cdot x_{\cdot 1} + x_2 \cdot x_{\cdot 2}} \quad (17)$$

where $x_1 \cdot = \sum_{j=1}^{2} x_{1j}$ and all summations are over decided pairs. We use the B-statistic instead of Cohen's Kappa [9] due to the following paradox [3]: when marginals are imbalanced, Kappa is low even when observed agreement is high. In our case, SAMR(vt) attracting the majority of the votes will push down the Kappa value.

5.2 Results

For the least correlated 30 venues between χ^2 and SAMR(vt) schemes, the average Spearman coefficient is -0.45. From these venues, we then derive 90 micro-review pairs for voting. Table 7 displays the voting results. Separately Table 8 displays the agreement between annotators.

Annotator	SAMR(vt)	χ^2	Undecided
1	66 (75.0)	22 (25.0)	2
2	68 (75.56)	22 (24.44)	0
3	61 (67.78)	29 (32.22)	0
4	33 (78.57)	9 (21.43)	48
5	58 (64.44)	32 (35.56)	0
6	54 (60.0)	36 (40.0)	0

Table 7: Voting results by annotators. Numbers are vote counts and bracketed numbers are percentage in favor of each scheme, considering each annotator's decided pairs.

Annotator	1	2	3	4	5	6
1	-	0.630	0.622	0.870	0.557	0.549
2	-	-	0.498	0.775	0.527	0.373
3	-	-	-	0.684	0.433	0.501
4	-	-	-	-	0.527	0.559
5	-	-	-	-	-	0.423

Table 8: B-statistic agreement between annotators, considering only decided pairs. We show only the upper half of the symmetric table for less cluttering.

Table 7 shows that all annotators favor SAMR(vt) in surfacing unexpected micro-reviews. For example, annotator 1 casted 66 votes for SAMR(vt) and 22 votes for χ^2, leaving 2 pairs where he's undecided. The vote proportion ranges from 60% to 70+% across all annotators. On average,

SAMR(vt) is favoured with 70.2%, compared with 29.8% for χ^2, suggesting that SAMR(vt) is clearly superior. In tandem, Table 8 shows that the annotators' agreement with one another is substantially higher than what is expected by chance, i.e. value 0. On average, the B-statistic value is 0.568.

We also note that annotator 4 is highly conservative. Compared to the others, he had many more undecided pairs. Nonetheless considering only his decided pairs, the agreement rate with others is still high. This implies that he is voting only for pairs where his confidence is high and fast decisions can be made. For other annotators, votes were casted for most pairs, leading to more disagreements. However overall agreement is still high and in favor of SAMR(vt).

The annotators did comment that it is easier to decide for some micro-review pairs while certain pairs require more subjectivity to judge. This is also evident from examining the voting results since 'easier' pairs should experience more agreement. For example, for Table 6, 4 out of 6 annotators select the second micro-review as being relatively more unexpected (also ranked high by SAMR(vt)), supporting the notion that micro-reviews about an American restaurant being halal may be less expected than one describing a staple dish of cheese baked potato. In other comments, an annotator mentioned that if he is the venue owner, micro-reviews with negative sentiments will be more unexpected, since his goal would have been to provide good products and services.

Next, we move on to a second set of quantitative evaluation, one that is totally devoid of any annotator subjectivity.

6. EVALUATION WITH PSEUDO-VENUES

6.1 Pseudo-venues

Although we have conducted experiments with human annotators, we desire evaluation on an even larger scale, e.g. involving hundreds of venues and thousands of micro-reviews. Such an experiment is extremely expensive using annotators. To mitigate any human subjectivity, it is also desired to have as many annotators as possible. In view of these difficulties, we propose a more scalable experimental approach that can be easily applied on large corpora to assess ranking accuracies.

The idea is to mix micro-reviews from a pair of venues to construct *pseudo-venues*. Basically each pseudo-venue contains dominantly the micro-reviews of one venue and a small fraction of micro-reviews that are injected from another venue of a different function. The injected micro-reviews can then be treated as unexpected micro-reviews.

For example, consider a Chinese restaurant pseudo-venue. First sample a Chinese restaurant, and some of its micro-reviews. We then inject a small fraction of micro-reviews from another venue that is *not* a Chinese restaurant, e.g, an Ethiopian restaurant. The injected micro-reviews should then be relatively more unexpected (and thus ranked higher) since the focus should be on Ethiopian food or other aspects more specific to Ethiopian restaurants. We stressed that this applies in the probabilistic and not absolute sense, as injected micro-reviews can mention generic, widely applicable characteristics, e.g. slow service or opening hours. Some non-injected micro-reviews can be unexpected as well, e.g. bugs in the Chinese restaurant.

Pseudo-venue construction is easy since Foursquare venues are already categorized by functions. There are 9 coarse categories[3], e.g. shopping, food etc., which are broken down into more fine categories, e.g. shoe store, Turkish restaurant. At each level of the hierarchy tree, there are large and small categories with different number of member venues. In our experiments, we have constructed each pseudo-venue by mixing micro-reviews from a large and a small category.

In summary, we construct a pseudo-venue as follows:

1. Designate a set of small and a set of large categories. From each of the 2 sets, sample a category.

2. Sample a venue from the sampled small category$\rightarrow venue_s$ and a venue from the sampled large category$\rightarrow venue_l$.

3. Let $n_s \leq n_l$. Sample n_s micro-reviews from $venue_s$'s micro-reviews $\rightarrow \{\mathsf{m}_s\}$ and n_l micro-reviews from $venue_l$'s micro-reviews$\rightarrow \{\mathsf{m}_l\}$

4. Construct $\{\mathsf{m}_s\} \cup \{\mathsf{m}_l\}$ as the pseudo-venue's micro-reviews. Regard $\{\mathsf{m}_s\}$ as ground truth micro-reviews that are unexpected for the pseudo-venue.

Table 9 illustrates a pseudo-venue used in our experiments. The pseudo-venue was constructed using 5 micro-reviews from a theme park as $venue_s$ and 15 micro-reviews from a food venue as $venue_l$.

Universal Studios Singapore ($venue_s$), n_s=5
Ride the Mummy's revenge.
definitely have to try the mummy's revenge roller coaster ride!!!
Revenge of the Mummy, highly recommended! Shrek 4-D Adventure is pretty good as well!
Shrek 4D Adventure is a must-go for all families. A 3D adventure with 4D effects! Absolute fun but do return your Ogre-Vision glasses after the show!
The crews are all friendly!!! Nice management :) too bad cyclone-human hasn't opened yet :(
Beach Road Prawn Mee Eating House ($venue_l$), n_l=15
Great prawn & pork rib noodle (soup)
Nice but expensive. Can't eat it every week...
Have the Ngo Hiang as side dish with the prawn noodles... Great combination!
They should really start to serve soft drinks as well!
Prawn Noodles here is a Die Die Must Try!! Must have it with the tasty soup

Table 9: An example pseudo-venue constructed from 2 actual venues (in bold). For brevity, only a small sample of micro-reviews from the food venue ($venue_l$) are shown. Food items mentioned in its micro-reviews are local cuisine, e.g. Ngo Hiang is a form of minced pork roll.

6.2 Experiment Setup

We use Singapore and Malaysian Foursquare venues separately to generate datasets of 2 different settings: S5+15 and M5+15. For each setting, we generate 10 datasets which are different due to sampling conducted for their pseudo-venues. Each dataset consists of 100 pseudo-venues and remaining venues that have not been sampled for constructing pseudo-venues. Note that ranking accuracies can only be computed from pseudo-venues. We also filter off venues with less than 15 micro-reviews. In actual applications, ranking is unnecessary if a venue has too few micro-reviews.

---

[3]https://developer.foursquare.com/categorytree

S5+15: This uses Singapore venues. Each pseudo-venue consists of 20 micro-reviews with 5 as the ground truth unexpected micro-reviews, i.e. $n_s = 5, n_l = 15$. We designate the 3 largest and 3 smallest categories as large and small categories respectively. The large categories are 'Food', 'Shop & Service' and 'Residence'. The small categories used are 'Arts & Entertainment', 'College & University' and 'Nightlife Spot'. The unprocessed data consists of 2,827 and 20,769 venues in both category sets. Filtering out venues with too few micro-reviews and including the pseudo-venues, each dataset consists of 3,100+ venues with 56,000+ micro-reviews.

M5+15: We use Malaysian restaurant venues with $n_s = 5, n_l = 15$. The categories are now more fine-grained and in terms of restaurant types. We use the largest 3 restaurant categories ('Asian', 'Malay', 'Chinese') as large categories. This encompasses 3,178 venues. We regard other restaurant categories as small categories (1,974 venues), excluding 483 venues with unclear restaurant categories. On average, each processed dataset consists of around 1,900 restaurant venues with 35,500 micro-reviews.

For both settings, we apply all previously described approaches: TF-IDF, χ^2, Y and SAMR topic model with SAMR(v) and SAMR(vt) scoring schemes. For the SAMR settings, we use 20 topics. We omitted tuning the number of topics although this may potentially achieve even better ranking accuracies. For model inference, we use 25 EM iterations, with 50 gradient descent iterations in the M-step. The learning rate τ was set at 2.0E-4.

6.3 Accuracy Metrics

Mean Precision. We use the mean precision at position k, $\mathbf{MP}(k)$ to measure ranking accuracy. First we compute the precision at k for each pseudo-venue. Given a pseudo-venue's k highest ranked micro-reviews $\{\mathfrak{m}\}_k$, this is the proportion of micro-reviews that are unexpected, i.e. $Prec(k) = \{\mathfrak{m}\}_k \cap \{\mathfrak{m}_s\}/k$.

As described in the previous section, we generate multiple datasets for testing, each with 100 pseudo-venues. Hence, we average $Prec(k)$ over multiple pseudo-venues and datasets to obtain the mean precision.

Mean Average Precision. We denote the mean average precision over multiple pseudo-venues and datasets as **MAP**. This is based on Average Precision (AP), which has been widely used in document retrieval tasks. For a pseudo-venue, AP attains a perfect accuracy of 1 if all micro-reviews from $\{\mathfrak{m}_s\}$ are ranked higher than all micro-reviews from $\{\mathfrak{m}_l\}$. AP can be computed as:

$$AP = \sum_i Prec(i)\Delta r(i) \qquad (18)$$

where $\Delta r(i)$ is the change in recall from position $i - 1$ to i. For each pseudo-venue, we also evaluate the summation over all its ranked micro-reviews (instead of just the top k).

6.4 Results

Tables 10 and 11 present the mean precision (MP) and mean average precision (MAP) figures for the settings: S5+15 and M5+15 respectively. Standard deviations are bracketed. For each setting, we applied the 5 discussed scoring schemes. Also recall that SAMR(v) and SAMR(vt) are different scoring schemes based on the same topic model SAMR.

Firstly we note the low accuracy figures obtained across the board. This can be explained by our observations that many injected micro-reviews cover common food items or

	MP(1)	MP(5)	MAP
SAMR(vt)	**0.289 (0.037)**	**0.330 (0.024)**	**0.420 (0.016)**
SAMR(v)	0.095 (0.018)	0.108 (0.012)	0.272 (0.006)
TF-IDF	0.167 (0.027)	0.169 (0.018)	0.308 (0.013)
χ^2	0.277 (0.041)	0.253 (0.019)	0.369 (0.012)
Y^2	0.226 (0.032)	0.211 (0.016)	0.338 (0.012)

Table 10: Results on Singapore venues (S5+15). Standard deviations are bracketed. Best results are bolded.

	MP(1)	MP(5)	MAP
SAMR(vt)	**0.252 (0.056)**	**0.269 (0.029)**	**0.370 (0.025)**
SAMR(v)	0.098 (0.023)	0.122 (0.018)	0.276 (0.012)
TF-IDF	0.143 (0.031)	0.142 (0.014)	0.287 (0.013)
χ^2	0.226 (0.032)	0.193 (0.015)	0.323 (0.013)
Y^2	0.185 (0.033)	0.165 (0.016)	0.303 (0.015)

Table 11: Results on Malaysian restaurant venues (M5+15).

generic issues, e.g. service, while some non-injected micro-reviews can be unexpected as well. These have the effect of lowering ranking precision in pseudo-venues. However we are primarily interested in *how the competing approaches perform relative to each other*. The experiment setup and results are already adequate for such an analysis.

For all experiment settings, SAMR(vt) consistently outperforms other approaches across all metrics. The second best performer is the χ^2 scheme. Comparing these 2 approaches with the Wilcoxon signed rank test, the difference is *statistically significant* (beyond p-value of 0.05) for most settings and metrics: MP(5), MAP for S5+15 and M5+15.

χ^2 is based on differences against a simple model for expected word usage while SAMR(vt) offsets information from topics and the fact that topics and expected word usage are dependent on venues. Hence the latter is a richer model that is able to explain more of the expected, in deriving the unexpected. Both approaches also outperform the simple TF-IDF baseline.

We also note that Y^2, which is the continuity corrected version of χ^2, underperforms the latter in all settings. Thus approximation error in computing the χ^2 statistic for small data (i.e. rare words with limited usage) is not crucial for ranking accuracy here.

Interestingly SAMR(v) is consistently the worst performing approach in all settings. The single difference between SAMR(v) and SAMR(vt) is that in the former, we do not consider micro-review topics and use only the venue-dependent word deviations for scoring words. In contrast, SAMR(vt) offsets the effect of micro-review topics and achieves better accuracies. Simply put, if a micro-review contains words that are easily explained by just knowing its topic indicator, then the words are less likely to be unexpected. It is thus necessary to subtract off the topic-dependent word deviation as what SAMR(vt) has done.

In summary, supported by consistent results from 2 different settings, we now conclude that SAMR(vt) outperforms other approaches.

7. CONCLUSION

We have proposed the problem of identifying unexpected micro-reviews to serve the needs of venue owners. We envisage that the results can be used for various purposes, such as event detection, service improvement or identifying competitors. We then explore various approaches to solve the problem. Our best performing approach is scores derived from a novel topic model, SAMR, with which we use to account for the 'expected' and derive the unexpected.

Our work is extendible in several aspects. For example, it will be useful to explain why a micro-review is unexpected. This requires much deeper modeling and analysis of the context. Micro-reviews can then be clustered by their underlying reasons.

Related to the above, one can apply sentiment analysis on top of the current work. Obviously, a micro-review can be unexpected in either a positive, negative or neutral manner. A highly negative unexpected micro-review may be cause for concern. On the other hand, a highly positive unexpected micro-review may be useful in publicity or branding strategies.

Lastly, our proposed topic model can be adapted to other domains such as traditional reviews from ecommerce platforms. A key point is that traditional reviews are usually much longer than micro-reviews and hence the assumption of one topic per review will no longer hold. With some modifications, we can model multiple topics in a single review. The scoring schemes will need to be adjusted as well.

8. ACKNOWLEDGEMENTS

This research is partially supported by DSO National Laboratories, Singapore; and the Singapore National Research Foundation under its International Research Centre@Singapore Funding Initiative and administered by the IDM Programme Office, Media Development Authority (MDA).

9. REFERENCES

[1] A. Aggarwal, J. M. Almeida, and P. Kumaraguru. Detection of spam tipping behaviour on Foursquare. *WWW*, 2013.

[2] A. C. Alhadi, T. Gottron, J. Kunegis, and N. Naveed. Livetweet: Monitoring and predicting interesting microblog posts. *ECIR*, 2012.

[3] F. AR and C. DV. High agreement but low kappa: I. The problems of two paradoxes. *J Clin Epidemiol*, 1990.

[4] M. Baroni and S. Evert. Statistical methods for corpus exploitation. *Corpus linguistics: An international handbook*, 2:777–802, 2009.

[5] A. Beck and M. Teboulle. A fast iterative shrinkage-thresholding algorithm for linear inverse problems. *SIAM Journal on Imaging Sciences*, 2:183–202, March 2009.

[6] D. M. Blei, A. Y. Ng, and M. I. Jordan. Latent dirichlet allocation. *JMLR*, 3(993):1022, 2003.

[7] D. Carlone and D. Ortiz-Arroyo. Semantically oriented sentiment mining in location-based social network spaces. *FQAS*, 2011.

[8] N. Chen, J. Lin, S. C. H. Hoi, X. Xiao, and B. Zhang. AR-miner: mining informative reviews for developers from mobile app marketplace. *ICSE*, 2014.

[9] J. Cohen. A coefficient of agreement for nominal scales. *Educ Psychol Meas*, 1960.

[10] J. Eisenstein, A. Ahmed, and E. Xing. Sparse additive generative models of text. *ICML*, pages 1041–1048, 2011.

[11] B. S. Everitt. *The analysis of contingency tables.* Chapman and Hall, 1992.

[12] A. Ghose and P. G. Ipeirotis. Designing novel review ranking systems: predicting the usefulness and impact of reviews. *ICEC*, 2007.

[13] K. Hofland and S. Johansson. *Word frequencies in British and American English.* The Norwegian Computing Centre for the Humanities, 1982.

[14] L. Hong, O. Dan, and B. D. Davison. Predicting popular messages in twitter. *WWW*, 2011.

[15] M. Hu and B. Liu. Mining and summarizing customer reviews. *KDD*, 2004.

[16] S.-M. Kim, P. Pantel, T. Chklovski, and M. Pennacchiotti. Automatically assessing review helpfulness. *EMNLP*, 2006.

[17] T. Lappas, M. Crovella, and E. Terzi. Selecting a characteristic set of reviews. *KDD*, 2012.

[18] T. Lappas and D. Gunopulos. Efficient confident search in large review corpora. *ECML/PKDD*, 2010.

[19] Y. Liu, X. Huang, A. An, and X. Yu. Modeling and predicting the helpfulness of online reviews. *ICDM*, 2008.

[20] F. Moraes, M. Vasconcelos, P. Prado, D. Dalip, J. Almeida, and M. Gonçalves. Polarity detection of Foursquare tips. *SocInfo*, 2013.

[21] T.-S. Nguyen, H. W. Lauw, and P. Tsaparas. Using micro-reviews to select an efficient set of reviews. *CIKM*, 2013.

[22] D. Roland, D. Jurafsky, L. Menn, S. Gahl, E. Elder, and C. Riddoch. Verb subcategorization frequency differences between business-news and balanced corpora: the role of verb sense. *WCC*, 9, 2000.

[23] G. Salton and C. Buckley. Term-weighting approaches in automatic text retrieval. *Information Processing & Management*, 24(5), 1988.

[24] V. Shankar and S. I. Bangdiwala. Observer agreement paradoxes in 2x2 tables: comparison of agreement measures. *BMC Medical Research Methodology*, 2014.

[25] P. Tsaparas, A. Ntoulas, and E. Terz. Selecting a comprehensive set of reviews. *KDD*, 2011.

[26] I. Uysal and W. B. Croft. User oriented tweet ranking: A filtering approach to microblogs. *CIKM*, 2011.

[27] M. Vasconcelos, J. Almeida, and M. Gonçalves. What Makes your Opinion Popular? Predicting the Popularity of Micro-Reviews in Foursquare. *SAC*, 2014.

[28] T. Virtanen. The progressive in NS and NNS student compositions: evidence from the International Corpus of Learner English. *ICAME*, 17, 1996.

[29] H. Wu, R. Luk, K. Wong, and K. Kwok. Interpreting tf-idf term weights as making relevance decisions. *ACM Transactions on Information Systems*, 26(3), 2008.

[30] Z. Yang, J. Guo, K. Cai, J. Tang, J. Li, L. Zhang, and Z. Su. Understanding retweeting behaviors in social networks. *CIKM*, 2010.

[31] F. Yates. Contingency tables involving small numbers and the chi-squared test. *Journal of the Royal Statistical Society Supplement*, 1, 1934.

[32] Z. Zhang and B. Varadarajan. Utility scoring of product reviews. *CIKM*, 2006.

Sentiment-based User Profiles in Microblogging Platforms

Francisco J. Gutierrez
Computer Science Department
University of Chile
Beauchef 851, 3rd floor
Santiago, Chile
frgutier@dcc.uchile.cl

Barbara Poblete
Computer Science Department
University of Chile
Beauchef 851, 3rd floor
Santiago, Chile
bpoblete@dcc.uchile.cl

ABSTRACT

Twitter has become one of the major platforms for self-expression in the Social Web, mostly due to its adoption by mobile users and its short message format. This presents endless possibilities for social behavior researchers that, for the first time, have access to massive amounts of data generated by humans. Nevertheless, most of the current research on emotions in social platforms focuses on reactions to particular events, or crowd behavior. In this article we present our research in the identification and characterization of user sentiment profiles in online social media. By analyzing a dataset of more than 36,000 users, we identify several distinctive groups, according to similarities in their sentiment behavior. We study differences and similarities between these profile clusters and present detailed statistics. We found that a large number of Twitter users can be grouped in nine distinct profiles according to the strength and polarity of their sentiment. Researchers and practitioners can benefit from our approach to characterize Twitter users in several scenarios, such as social recommendation, and mood estimation.

Categories and Subject Descriptors

H.3.3 [**Information Storage and Retrieval**]: Information Search and Retrieval—*Clustering*; H.3.1 [**Information Storage and Retrieval**]: Content Analysis and Indexing

General Terms

Measurement, Human Factors

Keywords

Sentiment polarity; Twitter; user modeling; social media; data analysis

1. INTRODUCTION

Today we largely communicate using text-based mechanisms, such as online social media. While these services allow for a connection that overcomes geographical barriers, these tools lack non-verbal cues [29] that facilitate the understanding of another's emotions. Therefore, a particular interest in the research community has been devoted to understanding the relation between social expression in verbal communication with that in text-based communication media, such as social networking services, instant messaging, microblogging, and email [15].

One of the most basic affective states that can be analyzed is sentiment, which corresponds to the positive or negative orientation that a person adopts given a certain stimulus. However, detecting the sentiment attached to every message from a large dataset is "a challenging task, prone to errors, subject to ambiguity, and proposes several technological and research challenges" [20]. Furthermore, what is often done in sentiment analysis is to assess the opinion of many users on a specific topic, product or event. Since people typically express a huge variety of topics, mixing positive, neutral and negative feelings, it is hard to actually classify users in terms of how outspoken their opinions are, in positive, negative or both senses.

If we were able to recognize the affective state of a person when using microblogging services for self-expression and social interaction, we could improve not only the quality of their communication and broad user experience with computing systems, but also positively impact their health and quality of life. Indeed, by taking into account detailed information about the common characteristics of groups of users in these platforms, it is possible to envisage several applications, such as: directed marketing campaigns, link recommendation following sentiment homophily, and mood detection and intervention in individuals suffering emotional derailment due to personal issues, unexpected local or global events, or mental disorders.

The identification and characterization of sentiment-based user profiles would also broaden research questions in computational sociology. For instance, it would be possible to measure and monitor the individual behavior of members in a physical community by monitoring their digital traces in online social networks and social media. This eventually leads to identifying characteristic patterns of larger social groups.

In this research, our main goal is to identify and characterize emerging sentiment-based user profiles from their text contributions in microblogging platforms. In this context, Twitter currently emerges as one of the most used applications for social interaction and self-expression, where its users can freely express themselves [18]. Therefore, this social media platform is ideal for accessing a large dataset, which is representative enough for retrieving meaningful and valuable knowledge.

The main contributions of our study are two: (1) propose a methodology to cluster users based on their sentiment polarity trace over a particular time period, and (2) present an analysis and characterization of those profile clusters over a large dataset of Twitter users. The particularity of our approach is the possibility of identifying distinct user profiles according to sentiment measures, which in turn is more appropriate when analyzing user behavior on a large scale. In addition, it would be possible to envisage how to weigh users' opinions aiming to mitigate the influence of the most outspoken users when analyzing overall sentiment about a given topic.

We identified a set of nine user profiles, which are statistically different among each other according to the strength of sentiment expression along both positive and negative polarities. The study results show that Twitter users consistently stay in one profile cluster, which makes related work in sentiment analysis more meaningful. Indeed, if the analysis showed that the average expression of each user's sentiment were systematically different from time to time, then studies of user sentiment analysis would be less grounded.

Aiming to identify context-specific characteristics in Twitter, we measured how the users in the identified profiles share information. While there are differences in the retweeting behavior (i.e., sharing with other users a message that he or she considers relevant), other tweet-level indicators such as the use of hashtags or mentioning other users are not clearly different between most groups. Finally, we did not find a clear or significant correlation between the amount of published tweets by a user, and the expression of their sentiment behavior.

The rest of the article is structured as follows. The next section reviews and discusses related work. Then we present the followed approach for inferring user sentiment profiles. We next characterize the identified profiles according to their sentiment patterns, and tweet-level measures. The following section is devoted to the study findings, as well as drafting practical applications that rely on the characterization of sentiment at a user level. Finally, we present the conclusion and offer perspectives on future work.

2. RELATED WORK

The problem of detecting affective states in Twitter is not new. In fact, several studies have been published on understanding the temporal patterns in people's mood changes [8, 15], the relation between weather and emotions [16, 21], the influence of geographical location with mood [19, 22, 23, 26], and the influence of Twitter mood as a stock market predictor [3]. While these research works are interesting from a sociological point of view, they analyze specific behavior patterns, and then aggregate them in some way for large-scale analysis. On the contrary, our goal is to study sentiment patterns by aggregating tweets at a user level.

De Choudhury, Counts and Horvitz [7] extensively used social media data, particularly tweets, to detect emotion and behavior states in order to build a model for predicting postpartum changes. Similar studies have explored how to measure post-traumatic stress disorder in Twitter [6], as well as bipolar and seasonal affective disorder [5]. In addition, Golbeck et al. [13] studied how to predict user personality with Twitter data. In this case, the authors limited the data collection process to a maximum of 2,000 tweets per user, and a sample of 50 participants. From a methodological point of view, the relevance of these works is that they show it is indeed possible to aggregate user Twitter data to generate valuable and reusable knowledge.

One of the applications that can be derived from the analysis of user profiles with similar sentiment is the generation of personalized communication strategies. For instance, Twitter can be actively used in personalized campaigns in politics [9], and in market analysis [17]. In this latter case, the authors propose a hybrid text-based and community-based method targeted to market analysis, where demographic data of Twitter users can be inferred through their tweets and by clustering followers and followees.

Another application is the possibility of improving health and quality of life. Indeed, there is scientific evidence that the mood of a person can change the mood of others, even in the case where the interaction is conducted through text-based mechanisms [14], and in large social networks [11]. For instance, Salathé et al. [25] found that the diffusion of behavioral traits in Twitter is strongly content-dependent, where the exposure to negative sentiment is contagious, but the exposure to positive sentiment is generally not. Similarly, Fan et al. [10] found a significant strong correlation in the expression of sentiment between a pair of users if they interact frequently, where the correlation of negative sentiment is significantly higher than that of positive sentiment. These findings show practical considerations when envisioning facilitating the recommendation of social links between two or more people.

Following this line of reasoning, text-based indicators in Twitter can also aid in the understanding of behavioral cues in terms of social relationships. For instance, Romero et al. [24] found that the usage of hashtags can predict the emergence of social relationships, and that the interaction between the initial adopters of a hashtag can predict its future popularity. Furthermore, sentiment homophily in Twitter (i.e., similar sentiment of two people towards mutual interest) can actually be used for improving the likelihood of two users to follow each other [30], given that happiness is indeed assortative in online social networks [2], particularly in the reciprocal reply network structure of Twitter [1].

The particularity of the approach we follow in our research is that it is based on the identification of user profiles by an aggregated analysis of their individual digital traces (i.e., Twitter timelines). Instead, most prior work relies on aggregating sentiment indicators at crowd level (i.e., using tweets directly retrieved from the Twitter stream), and the overall analysis has the risk to be biased by the opinions of the most outspoken users. While this latter approach allows the characterization of large-scale behavior, it does not necessarily characterize individual differences among users in a microblogging platform.

3. MODELING SENTIMENT PROFILES

The objective of this work is to identify emerging sentiment-based user profiles directly from their published contributions in Twitter. Therefore, to achieve this goal, we follow the pipeline presented in Figure 1.

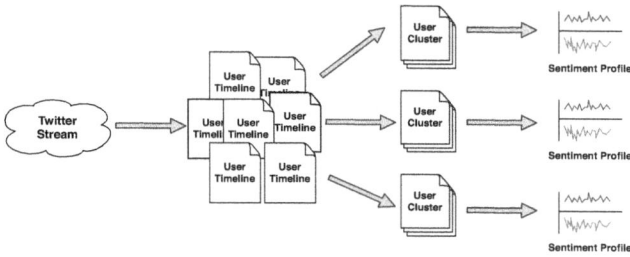

Figure 1: Pipeline for identifying sentiment-based emerging profiles.

The stages covered in the pipeline are:

1. Building a dataset, containing public tweets retrieved from user timelines.

2. Processing for each user his/her tweets and extracting the sentiment polarity (positive and negative) for each one.

3. Clustering users according to common properties in their sentiment polarity distributions, following both positive and negative dimensions.

4. Identifying independent profiles according to the values of sentiment strength along each polarity axis: positive and negative.

Each user is modeled using a joint feature vector comprising the expression of sentiment across two dimensions: positive and negative. Each dimension comprises N components, corresponding to the mean values of sentiment strength computed along N time periods. Therefore, the vector modeling each user is of dimension $2N$. Formally:

$$ U_k = \left\langle \frac{\sum_{j=1}^{t_1} p_{1,j}}{t_1}, \ldots, \frac{\sum_{j=1}^{t_N} p_{N,j}}{t_N}, \frac{\sum_{j=1}^{t_1} n_{1,j}}{t_1}, \ldots, \frac{\sum_{j=1}^{t_N} n_{N,j}}{t_N} \right\rangle, $$

where N is the number of observation points considered in the model; $p_{i,j}$ is the positive strength score of the tweet j during the observation point i; $n_{i,j}$ is the negative strength score of the tweet j during the observation point i; and t_i is the total number of tweets posted by the user U_k during the observation point i.

Following the representation above, a profile will be a finite collection of users. Formally, the profile P_i is represented as:

$$ P_i = \{U_1, U_2, \ldots, U_M\}, $$

where M is the total number of users U_k, $1 \leq k \leq M$, considered in the profile P_i.

4. DATA PROCESSING

In this section we describe in detail how we follow the stages in the pipeline for constructing sentiment-based user profiles in Twitter.

4.1 Dataset Construction

In order to be able to construct distinguishable sentiment profiles, we need to count with both, a list of currently active usernames, and their publicly available timelines. As a

further restriction, these users must belong to the English-speaking Twittersphere, due to the available tools for performing accurate sentiment analysis. Indeed, most of currently available state-of-the-art sentiment classifiers are optimized to accurately work with text written in English.

While it is possible to use the Twitter Developer API to retrieve at most 3,200 tweets of a given user, we still need to sample a set of usernames. To achieve this task, we analyzed the TREC-2011 Microblog Dataset [28], a dataset designed to be "a representative sample of the Twittersphere, where important and spam tweets are included".

Given that in this research we intend to sample users who tweet in English, we filter the messages in TREC-2011 that are written in English, according to the given metadata for each tweet. We also filter those tweets linked to accounts that today respond with a 404 error status (not found), meaning that the accounts are no longer available. Finally, to select the accounts that will be used in the study, we take the list of distinct authors of the filtered tweets. Due to the Twitter Developer API restrictions to download public user timelines (i.e., limit calls in time frames of 15 minutes and Twitter terms and conditions), we opt to take a random sample of 65,000 users from the available authors in the filtered TREC-2011 dataset.

For each user, we then download his/her public timeline. For each tweet, we retrieve its full content in text format, as well as its timestamp indicating the user local date and time in which it was published. In other words, since timestamps are retrieved considering the particular time zone in which the user has set his/her account, tweets are mutually comparable following a temporal dimension. For instance, one tweet published at 12:00 GMT will be marked as if it were published at 14:00 if it was originated from an account set in Central Europe (GMT +2:00), or at 8:00 if it was set somewhere along the East Coast (GMT -4:00).

An initial observation of the retrieved user timelines shows that users have different activity patterns. In other words, there are quite active users (who post a high number of tweets each day), while there are other users who post just one or two tweets per day. In order to limit a possible influence of unbalanced activity levels in the expression of sentiment among Twitter users, we initially stratify users according to this parameter.

From the sample of randomly selected users, we set a threshold of 200 tweets as a minimum for a user to be considered into the analysis. This leads to an observation group of 62,538 users. For each one of these users, we compute the time s/he spent on publishing 200 tweets (i.e., the time difference between the timestamps of the first and the tweet in position 200 in their timelines). Then, the activity level of a user corresponds to the number of tweets published in that time frame; i.e.,

$$ Activity\ level = \frac{200}{t_{200} - t_1}, $$

where t_i corresponds to the timestamp (in seconds) of the tweet in the position i in the timeline.

Having computed the activity level for all users, we then proceed to stratify them. The distribution of these values is presented in Table 1.

Given the highly skewed distribution of these values, we split the users with higher activity levels into two groups: those who are outliers with regard to this measure, and those

	Activity level [tweets / sec]
Minimum	0.0000007
1st quartile	0.0000058
Median	0.0000199
3rd quartile	0.0000724
Maximum	2.3260000

Table 1: Activity levels for users in the sampled group.

who remain in the fourth quartile after reordering the distribution without the observed outliers. Therefore, Table 2 shows how we set thresholds values to stratify users.

Group	Activity level [tweets / sec]	Activity level [tweets / day]
Group #1 (G1) *Outliers*	$[0.00008, \infty[$	$[7, \infty[$
Group #2 (G2) *4th quartile*	$[0.00004, 0.00008[$	$[3.5, 7[$
Group #3 (G3) *3rd quartile*	$[0.00002, 0.00004[$	$[1.8, 3.5[$
Group #4 (G4) *2nd quartile*	$[0.000006, 0.00002[$	$[0.5, 1.8[$
Group #5 (G5) *1st quartile*	$[0, 0.000006[$	$[0, 0.5[$

Table 2: Thresholds for stratifying users according to their activity levels.

In other words, from now on we consider that users in Group 1 post an average number of at least 7 tweets per day, while users in Group 5 tweet occasionally, with an average production of 1 tweet every 2 days.

4.2 Measuring User Sentiment Polarity

The next step in our pipeline consists in measuring the sentiment for each user's tweets. To achieve this, we follow the benchmark conducted by Bravo et al. [4], which states that there are two major state-of-the-art classifiers for dealing with microblogging messages. These solutions are: SentiStrength (*SentStr*), which focuses on short social messages written in English and claims to have "human-level accuracy" [27]; and Sentiment140 (*Sent140*), optimized for dealing with Twitter messages [12].

Following the results of Bravo et al. [4], SentiStrength outperforms Sentiment140 when we compare their F_1 measures. F_1 corresponds to the harmonic mean of precision (i.e., the probability that a randomly selected instance is relevant) and recall (i.e., the probability that a randomly selected relevant instance is retrieved), which is often used in machine learning for comparing the relative performance of two or more classifiers. Therefore, we choose SentiStrength for computing the sentiment of the study sample tweets. SentiStrength assigns two polarity values: one positive and one negative, in a scale ranging from -5 to +5. The global sentiment polarity and strength of a tweet will be the sum of the assigned values in each dimension. For instance, given the following tweet:

```
"Hey @ladygaga, I really loved your concert tonight.
It was epic!!"
```

SentiStrength assigns it a value of +5 along the positive axis and -1 along the negative axis, accounting then for a global sentiment of +4, which corresponds to a strongly positive tweet. Instead, in the following case:

```
"I hate working on Mondays :-( #bummer"
```

SentiStrength assigns the values +1 and -4, resulting then in a global sentiment of -3, which corresponds to a negative tweet.

Using the timeline of each user in the study sample, and we compute the sentiment strength and polarity for each one of his/her tweets. In order to make these values comparable among users, and limiting the influence of external factors that would add noise to the sentiment signal (e.g., unexpected local or global events), we aggregate their sentiment scores on a daily basis and we restrict the observation period to a time-span of 30 consecutive days. In other words, we take for all users a subset comprising all their tweets published between August 16, 2014 and September 14, 2014. Therefore, the obtained sentiment traces will be computed for all users under a same time frame. In particular, if a user does not have a tweet in a given time point, s/he will be assigned a value of 0 for both dimensions (i.e., positive and negative) in that point, as s/he will not have positive nor negative tweets. This is to ensure consistency in the definition of the joint vector model for each user presented in section 3.

4.3 Clustering Users

Given that we sample a period of $N = 30$ consecutive days, we use the user model representation as a space of vectors of dimension 60, where the first 30 components represent the daily mean sentiment strength score along the positive axis for each observation point, and the last 30 components represent the daily mean sentiment strength score along the negative axis for each observation point. The number M of profiles to be generated will be empirically determined.

As aforementioned, users are initially stratified in five groups according to their activity levels. After independently computing the vector space model for each group, we conduct clustering analysis to explore if it is possible to identify emerging patterns of users sharing similar sentiment distributions across both positive and negative polarities. This analysis is also conducted independently in each one of the five groups.

We use the K-means algorithm with Euclidean distance. First, we choose empirically a "good" value for K, the number of clusters. In fact, a good value for K should ensure that the within-sum-of-squares (SSE) is minimal, whereas the between-cluster-sum-of-squares (BSS) is maximal. In other words, a good clustering solution is obtained when the values are grouped in a cluster are as close as possible, but clusters are simultaneously as separated as possible.

To obtain the value of K, we use the L-curve method (also known as the *elbow* method), in which we look at the variance of SSE values as a function of the number of clusters. This method consists in choosing a number of clusters so that adding another cluster does not give a much better modeling of data.

After obtaining a good value for the number of clusters in each group, we apply the K-means algorithm and deduce a clustering solution, grouping users according to similar sentiment strength across each sentiment polarity axis. Each cluster leads then to a representative curve modeling positive and negative sentiment, where the centroid in each component corresponds to the representative sentiment strength score for each observed day.

Of the obtained clustering solutions for each group, we note that the size of a certain amount of clusters is highly underrepresented with regard to the number of users covered in each group. At an initial stage, we keep in the analysis just those clusters that cover at least 5 % of the users in each group. This leads to an observation subsample of 36,102 users, which corresponds to 57.73% of the original observation group. Given that the underrepresented obtained clusters may be possibly attributed to an excess of noise in the sentiment signal, we will study more in depth the characteristics of these users in future work.

For understandability, we label each obtained cluster with a sequential code, mapping the user group according to activity level, and the cluster the user belongs to. In particular, for group #1 we identify clusters G1A through G1H; for group #2, G2A through G2F; for group #3, G3A through G3C; for group #4, G4A through G4D; and for group #5, G5A and G5B.

4.4 Identifying Sentiment Profiles

In order to observe a possible correspondence between the observed sentiment strength across different clusters (given that we initially stratified users according to their activity levels), we compute the pairwise distance matrix among each pair of clusters. Furthermore, in order to observe detailed similarities and differences among each pair of clusters, we compute the distance matrices independently along each sentiment polarity. We then apply hierarchical clustering to identify similar groups along each sentiment polarity. Figure 2 depicts a heat map of the distance matrix values for positive sentiment. Color intensity maps the value of pairwise distance between each pair of groups: darker cells represent groups that are distant, while lighter cells represent vectors that are close to each other.

We identify that the hierarchical clustering leads to the following groupings along the positive polarity axis:

- Clusters G1I, G1G, G2B, G3C, G4C, and G5B

- Clusters G1D, G2E, G5A, G1B, G4D, and G3A

- Clusters G2F, and G1F

- Clusters G4B, G4A, G1E, G1A, G1H, G1J, G2D, G2A, G3B, G1C, and G2C

Similarly, we perform hierarchical clustering to the distance matrix computed along the negative polarity axis. Figure 3 depicts the corresponding heat map.

In this case, we identify the following groupings derived from hierarchical clustering along the negative polarity axis:

- Clusters G1J, G1F, and G1H

- Clusters G2A, G1C, G2F, G4B, G1E, G3B, G2D, G1A, and G1G

- Clusters G1D, G5A, G2E, G4D, and G3A

- Clusters G2C, G4A, G4C, G1I, G3C, G2B, G1B, and G5B

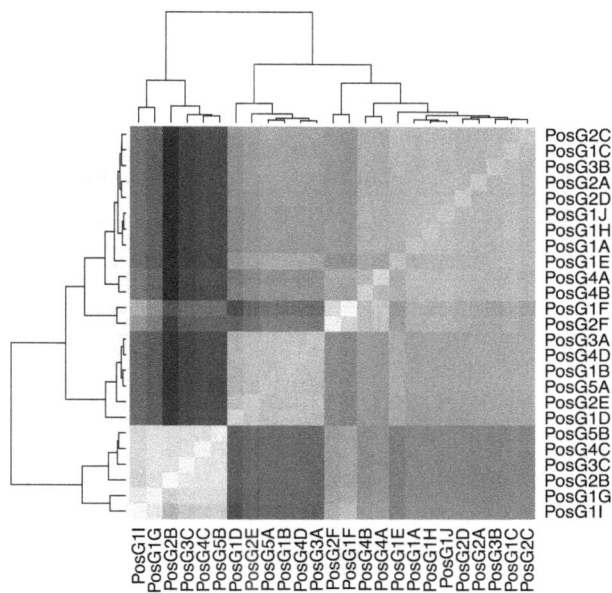

Figure 2: Heat map displaying pairwise distance between each pair of positive clusters, grouped by hierarchical clusters.

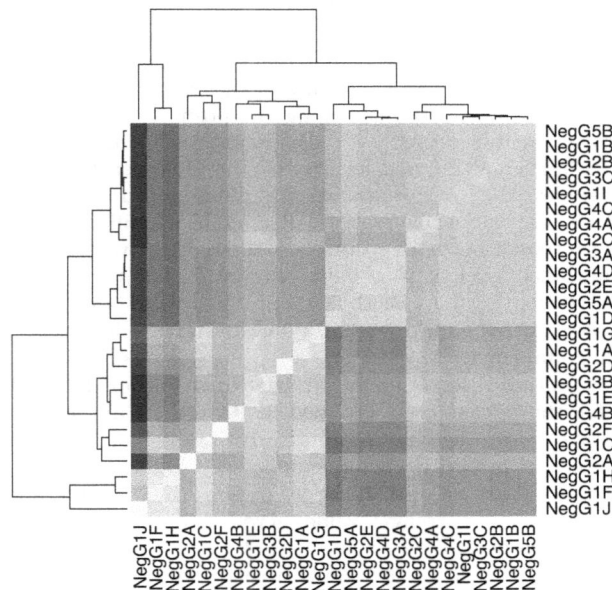

Figure 3: Heat map displaying pairwise distance between each pair of negative clusters, grouped by hierarchical clusters.

Since both positive and negative sentiment strength were independently computed for each obtained cluster, we can match the groups across each hierarchical clustering. In other words, we now proceed to intersect the clusters that simultaneously belong to the same hierarchical clusters along the positive and negative axes. For instance, given that G1H and G1J both belong to the same hierarchical clusters along each sentiment polarity, we group them together. This leads to the emergence of nine distinct sentiment profiles. Table 3 shows how these profiles are formed, and the relative size of these profiles with regard to the size of the subsampled observation group.

Profile	Clusters	Relative size
P1	G1B	6.0%
P2	G1F	1.9%
P3	G1G	3.1%
P4	G2F	1.2%
P5	G1H, G1J	7.1%
P6	G2C, G4A	6.3%
P7	G1D, G2E, G3A, G4D, G5A	33.9%
P8	G1I, G2B, G3C, G4C, G5B	15.1%
P9	G1A, G1C, G1E, G2A, G2D, G3B, G4B	25.5%

Table 3: Composition of identified profiles and relative size.

5. RESULTS

In this section we present the main characteristics of the identified sentiment profiles that coexist in the studied subsample of the English-speaking Twittersphere.

5.1 Characterizing Sentiment Profiles

The identified profiles (P1 - P9) are statistically different with regard to sentiment strength expression. Indeed, pairwise differences in the values of sentiment strength between each pair of profiles along the positive axis are statistically significant at $p < 0.05$, except for P1 and P7, P5 and P6, P5 and P9, and for P6 and P9. However, the pairs of profiles who are not statistically different along positive polarity actually show statistically significant differences in the sentiment strength values across the negative axis at a significance level of $p < 0.05$. Figure 4 shows the sentiment strength values for the nine profiles, along both polarity axes. Error bars represent a 95% confidence interval for each component.

An initial observation of strength distribution for each profile shows that users grouped in P1 and P7 are less expressive than other users. Contrarily, Twitter participants grouped in profile P8 show significantly higher sentiment strength. Users grouped in larger profiles (i.e., P7, P8, and P9) show similar strength values across different days in the observation period.

There is no clear correlation between positive and negative sentiment expression for all profiles. For instance, users with the lowest score in the positive axis (i.e., P1 and P7) do not show the lowest scores in the negative axis; while users with the highest score in the positive axis (i.e., P8 and P9) show different sentiment strength scores in the negative axis. Correlation between positive and negative sentiment in each profile only shows significant values for profiles P3 (ρ=−0.13, p<0.01), and P7 (ρ=−0.28, p<0.01).

5.2 Tweet-level Metrics

In a first attempt to characterize the identified sentiment profiles, we use tweet-level metrics. This responds to the analysis of whether or not domain-specific measures, such as the usage of retweets, hashtags, mentions, and URLs, lead

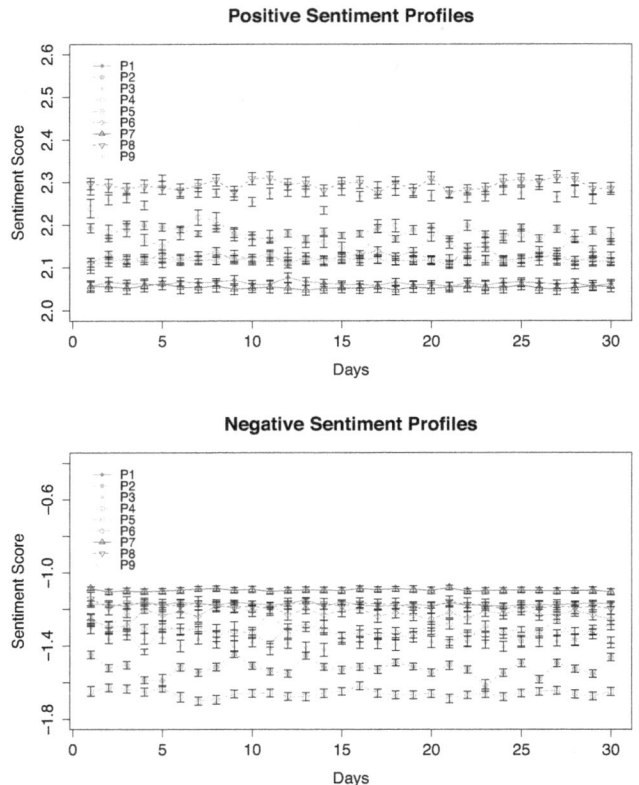

Figure 4: Sentiment strength profiles. Error bars represent the 95% confidence interval for each component.

to differences in the information sharing behavior of Twitter users with different sentiment strength expressions.

For each user in the observation subsample, we count the number of: posted retweets (`RT @username: ...`), tweets containing one or more hashtags (`#`), tweets with a mention to another user (`@username`), and tweets containing one or more hyperlinks (`http://...`). We then aggregate these results according to the identified sentiment profiles, and obtain ratio values for making these measures comparable. Figure 5 shows bar plots comparing the measured values among all studied profiles. Error bars represent the 95% confidence interval for each value.

Data does not follow a normal distribution, verified through independent Kolmogorov-Smirnov tests for each computed measure ($p < 0.001$ in each case). Therefore, given that parametric tests are not applicable in this situation, we perform pairwise Mann-Whitney U tests to study differences among the obtained values for each sentiment profile. Table 4 summarizes the results of these tests.

There are no clear differences in how Twitter users share information, when they are grouped according to their sentiment expression. For instance, the most noticeable differences are in the low usage of retweets by members of profile P8 with regard to all others. Similarly, users grouped in P6 show the highest usage of hashtags in their tweets, which is significantly higher than most of other groups. Regarding the propagation of information through hyperlinks (i.e.,

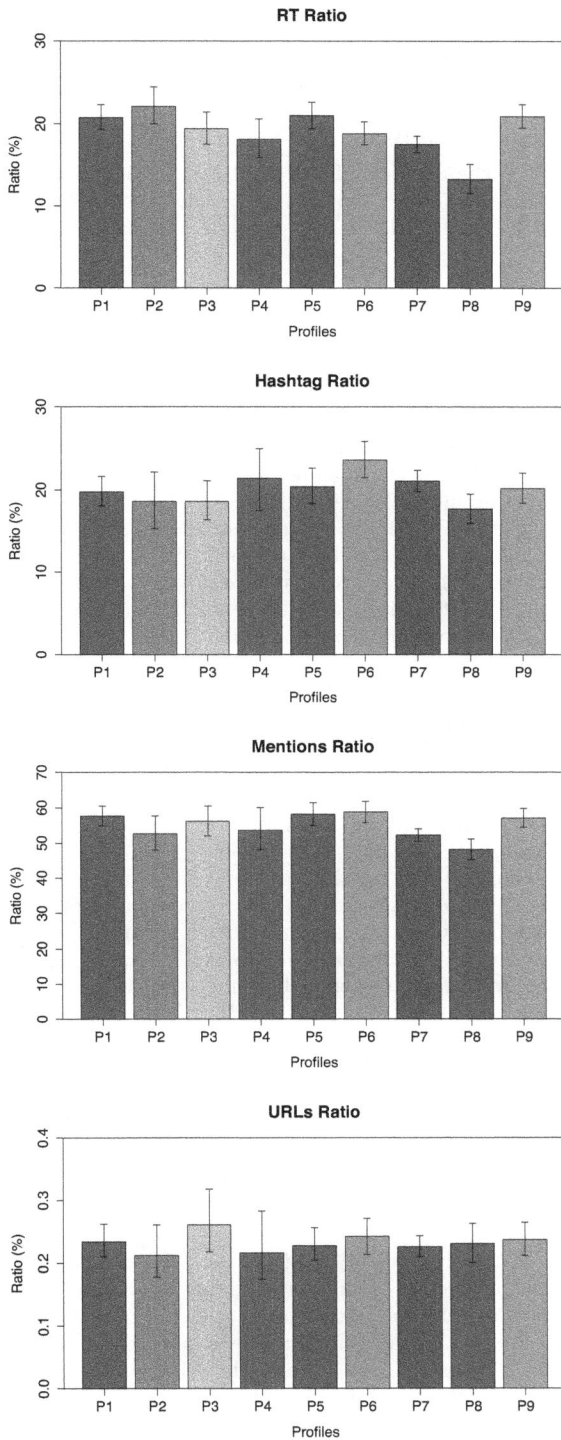

RT Ratio

Hashtag Ratio

Mentions Ratio

URLs Ratio

Figure 5: Tweet-level metrics. Error bars represent the 95% confidence interval for each value.

URLs), members in profile P3 show the highest ratio, even though it is quite small (less than a 0.3% of the analyzed tweets included an explicit URL).

RT	P1	P2	P3	P4	P5	P6	P7	P8	P9
P1	X								
P2	−	X							
P3	−	*	X						
P4	−	−	−	X					
P5	−	−	*	−	X				
P6	−	−	−	−	−	X			
P7	*	*	−	−	*	*	X		
P8	**	**	**	**	**	**	**	X	
P9	−	−	−	−	−	−	−	**	X

#	P1	P2	P3	P4	P5	P6	P7	P8	P9
P1	X								
P2	−	X							
P3	−	−	X						
P4	−	−	−	X					
P5	−	−	−	−	X				
P6	**	**	**	−	**	X			
P7	−	*	**	−	−	*	X		
P8	−	−	−	*	*	**	**	X	
P9	−	−	−	−	−	**	**	−	X

@	P1	P2	P3	P4	P5	P6	P7	P8	P9
P1	X								
P2	*	X							
P3	−	−	X						
P4	−	−	−	X					
P5	−	*	−	−	X				
P6	−	**	*	−	−	X			
P7	*	−	−	−	*	**	X		
P8	**	−	*	−	**	**	**	X	
P9	−	−	−	−	−	*	−	**	X

URLs	P1	P2	P3	P4	P5	P6	P7	P8	P9
P1	X								
P2	−	X							
P3	−	−	X						
P4	−	−	−	X					
P5	−	−	−	−	X				
P6	−	−	−	−	−	X			
P7	−	−	**	−	−	−	X		
P8	−	−	**	−	−	−	−	X	
P9	−	−	−	−	−	−	−	*	X

Table 4: Mann-Whitney U tests. The symbol − indicates that difference is not statistically significant, * means that difference is significant at p < 0.05, while ** at p < 0.01.

6. DISCUSSION

In this research we identified and characterized sentiment patterns in a large dataset of tweets, when they are retrieved and processed at a user level. In order to accomplish this task, we used data and clustering analysis techniques.

6.1 Study Findings

Using the K-means algorithm and hierarchical clustering, we identified nine different user profiles with regard to sentiment expression. The differences in the identified sentiment profiles are due to the strength in the expression of both positive and negative sentiment by Twitter users. However, we did not find a statistically significant strong correlation between level of activity and sentiment strength in either scale.

The identified clusters group a total of 36,102 users, which represents a 57.73% of the initial sampled group for conducting the analysis. Being able to detect these groups implies that it is possible to identify clusters of users who show similar behavior in terms of sentiment strength expression. However, to build a scalable sentiment-based user model, it is necessary to count with a large amount of user timelines, which is highly time-consuming, due to the restrictions imposed by the terms and conditions of the Twitter Developer API.

When comparing at a lexical level the most extreme profiles with regard to sentiment strength (i.e., P8 –the most positive one–, with P5 –the most negative–), we note that there are subtle differences in the frequency and extension of the used vocabulary. Table 5 lists the ten most frequent words in profiles P5 and P8.

Profile P5 (sentiment scores: −1.7, +2.1)

1	fatal
2	traffic
3	injury
4	accident
5	love
6	watch
7	high
8	free
9	hazard
10	area

Profile P8 (sentiment scores: −1.1, +2.3)

1	free
2	contest
3	artpop
4	happy
5	love
6	live
7	birthday
8	summer
9	watch
10	music

Table 5: Representative words of profiles P5 (most negative) and P8 (most positive).

In both lists, we have removed stopwords (i.e., commonly used words that have very little meaning, such as pronouns, conjunctions, prepositions, and common verbs). We also computed the term-document matrix for all clusters using tf-idf weighting, and we filtered the words that appear frequently in most of the obtained profiles.

While the differences related to the kind of words used in each profile can be attributed to the sentiment strength expression across both axes, the extension and term frequency of the vocabulary is dependent on the relative size of both profiles (7.1% for P5, and 15.1% for P8).

Finally, we studied if domain-specific features of Twitter (i.e., the ratio of retweets, hashtags, mentions, and hyperlinks in the posted tweets of a user) are dependent on the expression of sentiment in each profile. We did not find any statistically significant strong correlation that holds for all profiles. However, particular features, such as the retweeting and replying behaviors show differences among certain profiles.

6.2 Applications

Based on the analysis of the identified sentiment profiles for Twitter users, in this section we present two applications that can be envisaged using the proposed methodology.

6.2.1 Link Recommendation Following Sentiment

Yuan et al. [30] explored how to use sentiment homophily to build a model that helps predict if two Twitter users could become "friends" (i.e., build a follower-followee relationship). Therefore, it is plausible to envisage the design of recommender systems based on the sentiment expression of Twitter users, particularly when exploiting homophily. Moreover, Bollen et al. [2] show that happiness is indeed assortative in online social networks such as Twitter, and particularly, Bliss et al. [1] provide evidence supporting that the reciprocal reply network structure of Twitter also exhibits assortativity with regard to positive sentiment expression.

One question that then arises when envisioning the characterization of sentiment-based profiles is to study at what extent the closer nodes in the target's social network share similar sentiment strength traits with the target user. This leads to the formation of a hypothesis relating the sentiment strength traits of a given user to those of his/her closer nodes. In particular, the validity of this hypothesis can be explored by extending the proposed methodology to retrieving and analyzing Twitter timelines of the followers and followees of a particular user.

Consequently, it is possible to study whether there is a formal relation between sentiment homophily and preferential attachment in an individual's social network. If valid, this hypothesis has the potential to derive implications to design recommender systems that not only deal with link recommendation, but also with products and services relying on user-generated ratings and opinions, such as Amazon purchases or Netflix movie recommendations.

6.2.2 Mood Detection and Intervention

The role of social media analysis in the detection and monitoring of mental disorders, such as post-partum depression [7] and post-traumatic disorder [6] has recently brought the attention of the research community.

One particular application of the analysis of sentiment-based user profiles is monitoring the digital trace of an individual. This has the potential to ease the process of determining possible anomalies in the expression of his/her sentiment that could lead to provide evidence of negative mood variations. For instance, this can be evidenced if an individual consistently shows the characteristic behavior of a certain profile, and after a certain period he or she displays the characteristic behavior of a different (negative) sentiment profile.

From a technical point of view, this suggests additional research initiatives such as exploring and understanding the dynamics of sentiment-based user profiles. In particular, examples of possible areas to explore are: the influence of user personality in the dynamics of sentiment expression, and how members react to traumatic situations, high-impact global events, or unexpected situations in general.

6.3 Ethical Considerations

Even if publicly available tweets were the main data source for this research, it is clear that this approach may give rise to ethical and privacy issues. Although we worked with publicly available data, we did our best to maintain user privacy during the study. In particular, we ensured that the collected information would not be identifiable and explicitly preserved the anonymity of timeline owners. We declare that we did not perform any attempt to cross reference information with any other source, including other social media platforms. In particular, once we downloaded the tweets for a particular user, we assigned a random identifier to the timeline file, and did not keep track of the mapping between such identifier and the actual timeline owner's username.

6.4 Study Limitations

Given that we rely on an external sentiment classifier, the identification of user profiles are highly biased toward the lexicon used by this tool. In addition, we recognize limitations in our methodology, provided that some profiles would have been overlooked due to noise, instead of a true sentiment signal in data. In any case, we still consider our findings to be meaningful, as we managed to accomplish the objective of identifying distinct sentiment patterns using Twitter data retrieved and aggregated at user level.

7. CONCLUSIONS AND FUTURE WORK

With this research we identified and characterized a set of nine statistically different sentiment-based user profiles in Twitter. We show a pipeline to generate individual profiles and cluster them according to similar characteristics linked to the expression of positive and negative sentiment. The particularity of the followed approach is that we retrieve and analyze tweets directly from user timelines, instead of aggregating crowd-level sentiment indicators retrieved from the Twitter stream.

The identified profiles group 36,102 users. Being able to detect these groups implies that it is indeed possible to identify clusters of users who show similar behavior in terms of sentiment strength expression.

Aiming to characterize the obtained profiles, we analyzed the information sharing behavior of the profiled users, but we did not find clear differences in this behavior among all profiles. Instead, the most characteristic feature of the identified groups is the expression of sentiment strength. Therefore, an important contribution of this paper is to show that Twitter users consistently stay in one profile cluster, at least over a 30-day period, which makes other works in sentiment analysis more meaningful.

Finally, we illustrate as well how the proposed methodology can be extended to exploit the identified user profiles in concrete applications. As future work we envisage to analyze individual users to investigate the stability of the identified sentiment clusters, and we plan to study the applicability of the proposed approach in sentiment-based personalization, such as personalized movie recommendations in Netflix or Amazon persuasive mechanisms to drive purchase behavior.

8. ACKNOWLEDGMENTS

The authors were partially supported by FONDECYT Grant 11121511 and the Millenium Nucleus Center for Semantic Web Research under Grant NC120004. The work of Francisco J. Gutierrez has been supported by the Ph.D. Scholarship Program of CONICYT Chile (CONICYT-PCHA / Doctorado Nacional / 2013-21130075).

9. REFERENCES

[1] C. A. Bliss, I. M. Kloumann, K. D. Harris, C. M. Danforth, and P. S. Dodds. Twitter reciprocal reply networks exhibit assortativity with respect to happiness. *Journal of Computational Science*, 3(5):388 – 397, 2012. Advanced Computing Solutions for Health Care and Medicine.

[2] J. Bollen, B. Gonçalves, G. Ruan, and H. Mao. Happiness is assortative in online social networks. *Artificial Life*, 17(3):237 – 251, 2011.

[3] J. Bollen, H. Mao, and X. Zeng. Twitter mood predicts the stock market. *Journal of Computational Science*, 2(1):1 – 8, 2011.

[4] F. Bravo-Marquez, M. Mendoza, and B. Poblete. Combining strengths, emotions and polarities for boosting Twitter sentiment analysis. *Proceedings of the Second International Workshop on Issues of Sentiment Discovery and Opinion Mining, WISDOM 2013, Chicago, Illinois, USA, August 11-14, 2013.*, 2013.

[5] G. Coppersmith, M. Dredze, and C. Harman. *Proceedings of the Workshop on Computational Linguistics and Clinical Psychology: From Linguistic Signal to Clinical Reality*, chapter Quantifying Mental Health Signals in Twitter, pages 51–60. Association for Computational Linguistics, 2014.

[6] G. Coppersmith, C. Harman, and M. Dredze. Measuring post traumatic stress disorder in twitter. In *Proceedings of the Eighth International Conference on Weblogs and Social Media, ICWSM 2014, Ann Arbor, Michigan, USA, June 1-4, 2014.*, 2014.

[7] M. De Choudhury, S. Counts, and E. Horvitz. Predicting postpartum changes in emotion and behavior via social media. In *Proceedings of the SIGCHI Conference on Human Factors in Computing Systems*, CHI '13, pages 3267–3276, New York, NY, USA, 2013. ACM.

[8] P. S. Dodds, K. D. Harris, I. M. Kloumann, C. A. Bliss, and C. M. Danforth. Temporal patterns of happiness and information in a global social network: Hedonometrics and twitter. *PLoS ONE*, 6(12):e26752, 12 2011.

[9] G. S. Enli and E. Skogerbø. Personalized campaigns in party-centred politics. *Information, Communication & Society*, 16(5):757–774, 2013.

[10] R. Fan, J. Zhao, Y. Chen, and K. Xu. Anger is more influential than joy: Sentiment correlation in weibo. *PLoS ONE*, 9(10):e110184, 10 2014.

[11] J. H. Fowler and N. A. Christakis. Dynamic spread of happiness in a large social network: longitudinal analysis over 20 years in the framingham heart study. *BMJ (Clinical research ed.)*, 337, 2008.

[12] A. Go, R. Bhayani, and L. Huang. Twitter sentiment classification using distant supervision. *Processing*, pages 1–6, 2009.

[13] J. Golbeck, C. Robles, M. Edmondson, and K. Turner. Predicting personality from twitter. In *Privacy, Security, Risk and Trust (PASSAT) and 2011 IEEE Third Inernational Conference on Social Computing*

(SocialCom), 2011 IEEE Third International Conference on, pages 149–156, Oct 2011.

[14] J. T. Hancock, K. Gee, K. Ciaccio, and J. M.-H. Lin. I'm sad you're sad: Emotional contagion in cmc. In *Proceedings of the 2008 ACM Conference on Computer Supported Cooperative Work*, CSCW '08, pages 295–298, New York, NY, USA, 2008. ACM.

[15] J. T. Hancock, C. Landrigan, and C. Silver. Expressing emotion in text–based communication. In *Proceedings of the SIGCHI Conference on Human Factors in Computing Systems*, CHI '07, pages 929–932, New York, NY, USA, 2007. ACM.

[16] A. Hannak, E. Anderson, L. F. Barrett, S. Lehmann, A. Mislove, and M. Riedewald. Tweetin' in the rain: Exploring societal-scale effects of weather on mood. In *Proceedings of the Sixth International Conference on Weblogs and Social Media, Dublin, Ireland, June 4-7, 2012*, 2012.

[17] K. Ikeda, G. Hattori, C. Ono, H. Asoh, and T. Higashino. Twitter user profiling based on text and community mining for market analysis. *Knowledge-Based Systems*, 51(0):35 – 47, 2013.

[18] I. L. B. Liu, C. M. K. Cheung, and M. K. O. Lee. Understanding twitter usage: What drive people continue to tweet. In *PACIS*, page 92. AISeL, 2010.

[19] L. Mitchell, M. R. Frank, K. D. Harris, P. S. Dodds, and C. M. Danforth. The geography of happiness: Connecting twitter sentiment and expression, demographics, and objective characteristics of place. *PLoS ONE*, 8(5):e64417, 05 2013.

[20] B. Pang and L. Lee. Opinion mining and sentiment analysis. *Found. Trends Inf. Retr.*, 2(1-2):1–135, Jan. 2008.

[21] K. Park, S. Lee, E. Kim, M. Park, J. Park, and M. Cha. Mood and weather: Feeling the heat? In *Proceedings of the Seventh International Conference on Weblogs and Social Media, ICWSM 2013, Cambridge, MA, USA, July 8-11, 2013.*, 2013.

[22] D. Quercia, L. Capra, and J. Crowcroft. The social world of twitter: Topics, geography, and emotions.

In *Proceedings of the Sixth International Conference on Weblogs and Social Media, Dublin, Ireland, June 4-7, 2012*, 2012.

[23] D. Quercia, D. Ó. Séaghdha, and J. Crowcroft. Talk of the city: Our tweets, our community happiness. In *Proceedings of the Sixth International Conference on Weblogs and Social Media, Dublin, Ireland, June 4-7, 2012*, 2012.

[24] D. M. Romero, C. Tan, and J. Ugander. On the interplay between social and topical structure. In *Proceedings of the Seventh International Conference on Weblogs and Social Media, ICWSM 2013, Cambridge, MA, USA, July 8-11, 2013.*, 2013.

[25] M. Salathé, D. Vu, S. Khandelwal, and D. Hunter. The dynamics of health behavior sentiments on a large online social network. *EPJ Data Science*, 2(1), 2013.

[26] H. A. Schwartz, J. C. Eichstaedt, M. L. Kern, L. Dziurzynski, R. E. Lucas, M. Agrawal, G. J. Park, S. K. Lakshmikanth, S. Jha, M. E. P. Seligman, and L. H. Ungar. Characterizing geographic variation in well-being using tweets. In *Proceedings of the Seventh International Conference on Weblogs and Social Media, ICWSM 2013, Cambridge, MA, USA, July 8-11, 2013.*, 2013.

[27] M. Thelwall, K. Buckley, G. Paltoglou, D. Cai, and A. Kappas. Sentiment in short strength detection informal text. *J. Am. Soc. Inf. Sci. Technol.*, 61(12):2544–2558, Dec. 2010.

[28] TREC. TREC 2011 Microblog Dataset, 2011. http://trec.nist.gov/data/tweets/. Last visited: June 11, 2015.

[29] J. B. Walther. Impression development in computer–mediated interaction. *Western Journal of Communication*, 57(4):381–398, 1993.

[30] G. Yuan, P. K. Murukannaiah, Z. Zhang, and M. P. Singh. Exploiting sentiment homophily for link prediction. In *Proceedings of the 8th ACM Conference on Recommender Systems*, RecSys '14, pages 17–24, New York, NY, USA, 2014. ACM.

Breaking Bad - Understanding Behavior of Crowd Workers in Categorization Microtasks

Ujwal Gadiraju, Patrick Siehndel, and Besnik Fetahu
L3S Research Center
Appelstr. 9a
30167 Hanover, Germany
{gadiraju, siehndel, fetahu}@L3S.de

Ricardo Kawase
mobile.de
Marktplatz 1
14532 Europarc Dreilinden, Germany
rkawase@team.mobile.de

ABSTRACT

Crowdsourcing systems are being widely used to overcome several challenges that require human intervention. While there is an increase in the adoption of the crowdsourcing paradigm as a solution, there are no established guidelines or tangible recommendations for task design with respect to key parameters such as *task length*, *monetary incentive* and *time required for task completion*. In this paper, we propose the tuning of these parameters based on our findings from extensive experiments and analysis of '*categorization*' tasks. We delve into the behavior of workers that consume categorization tasks to determine measures that can make task design more effective.

Categories and Subject Descriptors

H.4 [**Information Systems Applications**]: Miscellaneous

Keywords

Crowdsourcing; Workers; Behavior; Categorization; Microtasks; Incentives; Task Length

1. INTRODUCTION

With the advent of the Internet age and its ubiquity, more and more people are turning towards standardized crowdsourcing platforms in order to service needs requiring large-scale human input. Amazon's Mechanical Turk[1] was the first such crowdsourcing platform to gain widespread popularity, followed by CrowdFlower[2]. Over the last decade there has been a considerable amount of research that has investigated means to improve the quality of results produced via crowdsourcing, and methods to measure performance metrics such as reliability or accuracy of workers in the crowd [5, 10]. However, not all task administrators are well-versed with using the existing platforms to their full potential. This

[1]https://www.mturk.com/mturk/
[2]http://www.crowdflower.com/

HT '15, September 1–4, 2015, Guzelyurt, Northern Cyprus.
© 2015 ACM. ISBN 978-1-4503-3395-5/15/09 ...$15.00.
DOI: http://dx.doi.org/10.1145/2700171.2791053.

is largely due to two major reasons; (i) there are either few or no concrete guidelines that are task specific and aid an administrator during the important phase of task design, and (ii) there are no existing principles based on which a task administrator can adjust important parameters such as length of a task, or incentive to be offered in order to obtain optimal results in the presence of any limiting constraints.

In this paper, we aim to take the first steps towards tackling the aforementioned challenges by studying the behavior of workers in a crowdsourcing paradigm with varying parameters (task length and incentive), through extensive experiments. We discuss our observations that can aid a task administrator with adjusting key parameters during the task design phase. Based on our study of their behavior, we model workers in the particular task type of '*categorization*'. We choose this task type since it is one of the most popularly crowdsourced task within the taxonomy of microtasks introduced in our previous work [3]. By relying on behavioral metrics for crowd workers, and investigating the behavior flow of workers within tasks, we establish the following guidelines to obtain optimal results from crowdsourced *categorization tasks*. A task administrator is recommended to design tasks with; (i) low to moderate monetary incentives (of the order of a few USD cents), (ii) shorter task lengths (of the order of a few minutes), and (iii) provide ample time to the workers for task completion (we recommend defining the minimum limit, but not the maximum).

2. RELATED LITERATURE

Earlier works have shown that task specific features of microtasks affect different types of microtasks differently [1, 3]. Here we study categorization tasks, discuss findings from earlier works that hold for this type of tasks, and present advances through our work.

2.1 Task Design and Quality of Results

Marshall et al. analyzed workers who took surveys on Amazon's Mechanical Turk and examined how the characteristics of the surveys influenced the reliability of the data produced [8]. We build on a similar premise and gather data from categorization tasks with varying settings, in order to conduct a meaningful analysis of worker behavior and arrive at sound insights for task design.

Mason et al. studied the effect of varying financial incentives on the performance of workers [9]. Authors conclude that increasing monetary incentives of microtasks attracts more workers to the tasks but does not improve the quality of the results produced. We study this effect in categorization microtasks, while additionally analyzing optimal incentives as per the length of a task. In contrast to our work in this paper, previous works have investigated methods to improve the quality of the results produced and the reliability of workers in crowdsourcing tasks in general. Oleson et al. present a method to achieve quality control for crowdsourcing, by providing training feedback to workers while relying on programmatic creation of gold data [10].

2.2 Worker Behavior - Influential Factors

Eickhoff et al. acknowledged the importance of understanding worker behavior in order to develop reliability metrics and design fraud-proof tasks [2]. Kazai et al. used behavioral observations to define the types of workers in the crowd [7]. By type-casting workers as either sloppy, spammer, incompetent, competent, or diligent, the authors expect their insights to help in designing tasks and attracting the best workers to a task. While the authors correlate these types to the personality traits of workers, we aim to unravel how the behavioral patterns of workers vary with changes in the task design in categorization microtasks. Eickhoff et al. additionally evaluated factors such as the size of microtask, interface used and composition of the crowd [1]. Based on this the authors suggest to design microtasks in a manner that discourages malicious workers. The authors acknowledge that there can be varying effects based on the type of crowdsourced tasks. We thereby, take this further by evaluating the impact of task length and incentives on workers behavior of categorization tasks, while utilising behavioral metrics and task-related characteristics.

3. TASKS DESIGN

We aim to analyse the behavior of workers during the consumption of 'categorization' tasks, under varying task conditions (with respect to length of the task and incentive offered). In order to do so, we deployed 9 different image categorization tasks on CrowdFlower catering to varying task settings. From each task that was deployed we collected responses from 100 distinct workers in the crowd.

We varied the parameters of length and monetary incentives, according to which the categorization tasks were deployed. We experimented with three different variations in the length of the task (20, 30, and 40 units[3]). At the same time, we considered 3 different monetary offers of 1, 2, and 3 USD cents.

3.1 Categorization Tasks

Each categorization task was formulated with very clear instructions and help-snippets, in order to avoid introducing bias or bad responses due to poor task design. Figure 1 shows an example of the categorization task that workers had to perform for each unit in the task. An image was presented and workers had to select the most suitable category in each Set (1-5) consisting of 10 different categories. Since the aim of the task was to assess performance related behavior of workers under varying task related circumstances, it was important to ensure that there was no ambiguity within the categories provided as options. Hence, we manually tailored each unit by choosing images that are

---

[3]On CrowdFlower a *unit* is the basic building block of a task. So, n units in a task implies that a worker has to complete n workflows of the same type.

comprehensible, explicit and unambiguous. In addition, we hand-picked unmistakeable categories for each set, such that the correct category is easy to match for any diligent worker. In order to reflect realistic categorization tasks, we added 9 additional categories apart from the correct one for each of the five sets of options. By doing so, we also minimize the chance of workers selecting the accurate options at random.

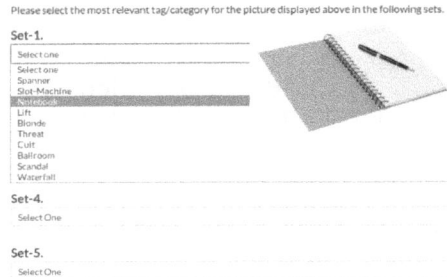

Figure 1: Workers were asked to select the most suitable category corresponding to each image displayed in the unit within the task (image is overlayed here).

For each unit, workers were required to select a category from the first set (Set-1), and the selection from the next 4 sets was made optional. By doing so we can measure the extra effort that a worker puts into the task to help the task administrator, as discussed in later sections. This design choice was motivated by the findings of Rogstadius et al., where the authors found that framing a task as helping others increases the intrinsic motivation of workers, and improves the quality of the responses produced [11].

Tasks were deployed non-concurrently such that at any point in time, there was no more than one task available to the workers for consumption. By doing so, we curtail the bias which may otherwise have crept in owing either to the consumption of the categorization tasks with higher incentive, or through workers getting too used to this particular task design. In addition, it is important to note that we randomized the order in which different workers received the units within a task.

3.2 Dataset

In total we collected 27,000 unit judgments with at least one tag provided (from mandatory Set-1). In 88% of the cases (23,767) workers provided answers for all sets (Set-1 through to Set-5). The average time to complete the task was 11.3 minutes for tasks with 20 units, 16.4 minutes for tasks with 30 units, and 18.6 minutes for tasks with 40 units. In total, 900 workers participated in our study. We present no further information regarding gender, age, etc. due to the anonymous identity of workers.

4. DATA ANALYSIS

First, we present some definitions which will be used hereafter in this paper. These definitions relate to the behavior of microtask workers in a crowd.

Ineligible Workers. Crowdsourcing microtasks present the workers in the crowd with a task description and a set of instructions that the workers must follow, for successful

Table 1: Consistency in the difficulty of units within a task across all configurations.

Task Configuration (Units X USD cents)	20x1	20x2	20x3	30x1	30x2	30x3	40x1	40x2	40x3	Average Accuracy in %
Accuracy in %	92.90 ±1.25	90.95 ±2.42	91.40 ±1.67	90.90 ±2.19	88.97 ±1.94	87.14 ±2.28	90.00 ±2.33	85.95 ±2.47	88.03 ±3.72	89.58 ±2.25

task completion. Those workers who do not conform to the priorly stated pre-requisites, belong to this category.

Tipping Point. The first point (i.e., the unit index) at which a worker begins to provide unacceptable responses after having provided at least one acceptable response, is called the *tipping point* [4].

Beaver Workers. Some workers put in additional effort in order to help out the task administrator by answering optional questions. Such hard-workers are called *beavers*, and the additional effort is referred to as *extra effort*.

We find 9 *ineligible workers* who used browser-embedded translators in order to attempt these tasks[4]. Such workers may or may not provide valid responses, but their responses cannot be used by the task administrator since they do not satisfy the pre-requisites. We discard these workers from further analysis. Despite requiring to provide only one mandatory response from the 5 sets of categories, we observe that several workers (over 88%) go the extra mile by providing responses and identifying categories from additional sets.

4.1 Consistency of Units within a Task

In this paper, since we aim to study the behavior of workers as they proceed through a task, it is important to ensure that the difficulty in answering each unit accurately is consistent throughout the task. We ensure that each unit within a task can be easily categorized, and each set has only one category that directly relates to the corresponding image.

Table 1 presents the average accuracy that workers attain within each task configuration. In each task, workers received the units for completion in a randomized order. We observe that every configuration begets an accuracy around 90% with little standard deviation. This confirms that the task design does not introduce bias through the potential variance in the consistency of units comprising the task.

Due to the nature of the task design and setup, we expect workers to achieve an accuracy of 100% without any hindrance. However, owing to possible drifts in attention spans of workers or boredom induced by the repetitive nature of the categorization task, workers could commit mistakes inadvertently. We therefore decide to tolerate 10% incorrect responses from each worker with respect to each task. Based on the simplicity of these particular categorization tasks, we reason that any further incorrect responses should not be merely alluded to the inattentiveness of workers. Hence, we consider the following definitions.

Bad Workers. We define *bad workers* as those workers who answer 10% or more of the units within a categorization task incorrectly.

Poor Starters. We define *poor starters* as those bad workers whose first 2 responses within a categorization task are incorrect.

4.2 Tipping Point

As observed in our previous work [4], we find that several workers provide acceptable responses to begin with, before derailing towards poor accuracy. We thereby investigate this tendency of workers to trail off into providing inaccurate responses, and present our findings here.

Figure 2 presents a comparison between the number of poor starters and bad workers across the different tasks that we deployed. We observe that as the length of the task increases, the number of *bad workers* also increases. In addition, we find that an increase in monetary incentive also increases the number of *bad workers*. This reinforces the findings of [2], where the authors discuss that higher monetary incentives correlate positively with the number of malicious workers attracted to the task. As a consequence we also observe that for a fixed length of a task, the average tipping point of workers decreases with an increase in monetary incentive. This is due to the increase in the number of bad workers to a task with increasing incentive, since *bad workers* tend to 'tip' relatively early in a task. We do not observe a discernible trend in the case of *poor starters*.

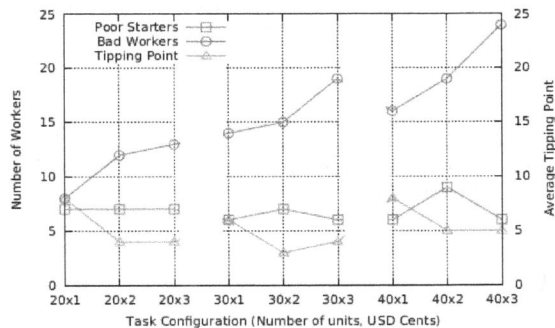

Figure 2: Number of *Poor Starters* and *Bad Workers*, and the average *Tipping Point* of workers across different tasks.

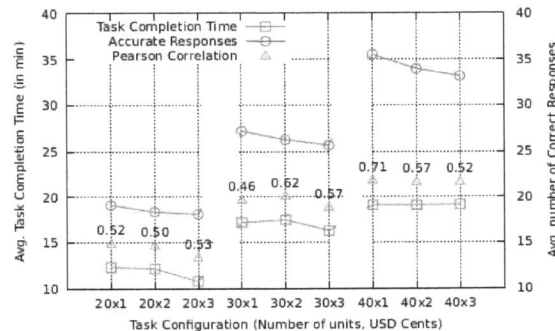

Figure 3: Correlation between the average task completion time (scaled on the y-axis) and average accuracy of workers for all tasks (scaled on the y2-axis).

---

[4]This information can be extracted based on the results from CrowdFlower.

4.3 Completion Time vs Worker Accuracy

We computed the average time that workers take to complete the tasks and their corresponding average accuracy, for all task configurations (different task lengths and varying incentives). Figure 3 presents our findings. We see that for a fixed length of the task, the average accuracy of workers increases with an increase in the task completion time, with high Pearson Correlation (see Figure 3).

We notice that this observation holds across the tasks with varying task lengths (20, 30, and 40 units). Our findings align with previous works where authors have shown that with an increase in monetary incentive, there are more workers who are attracted to a task, but the accuracy of the workers is not effected [9]. At the same time, an increase in the monetary incentive increases the number of malicious workers that are attracted to the task, since their priority is to attain immediate financial gains through quick task completion [6, 12].

4.4 Worker Behavior within a Task

We also studied the worker behavior specifically within each task, across all the task configurations, i.e., how a worker's accuracy evolves as one proceeds through the index of units; from the first till the last unit within the given task. Table 2 presents our findings of the correlations between the *unit index* (UI) and *accuracy* of a worker, the accuracy of a worker and the amount of *extra effort*, and finally the *unit index* and the amount of *extra effort*. The correlation is measured using Pearson's **r**. Note that the unit index represents how far along a worker is within a task during the task consumption.

Table 2: Evolution of the *accuracy* and *extra effort* of workers through the course of a task, across different task configurations.

Task Configuration (Units X USD cents)	Pearson's r (UI,Accuracy)	Pearson's r (Extra,Accuracy)	Pearson's r (UI,Extra)
20x1	0.25	0.22	-0.58
20x2	-0.42	0.14	-0.57
20x3	-0.49	0.68	-0.69
30x1	-0.64	0.71	-0.71
30x2	-0.27	0.46	-0.64
30x3	-0.61	0.80	-0.66
40x1	-0.68	0.80	-0.74
40x2	-0.48	0.70	-0.80
40x3	-0.75	0.71	-0.75

The general trend we observe, is that as a worker proceeds from the first unit to the last unit of a task, the worker's accuracy decreases. Here the accuracy is computed only on the compulsory responses from Set-1 for each unit, and the optional sets are not considered. From the Table 2, in column 2 we can see that the negative correlation grows stronger with increasing length of the task.

Next we study the relationship between the *extra effort* that workers exert and their accuracy within the task (once again we consider only the first set which is compulsory for each unit, while computing a worker's accuracy). We find that workers that exert more extra effort tend to project higher accuracies within the tasks (see column 3). We can see that this positive correlation grows stronger as the length of the task increases. We reason that this is due to the fact that it is more taxing to exert *extra effort* in longer tasks. If

workers, still go the extra mile and do so, it indicates their genuine attempt to provide the most suitable responses.

Finally, we investigate the longevity of workers exerting extra effort within a task, i.e., we study whether workers continue to exert the same effort as they progress through the units within a task. We find that as workers proceed through towards task completion they exert lesser extra effort (see column 4). As the length of the tasks increases, this negative correlation between the unit index and the extra effort from workers grows stronger.

4.5 Scrutiny of Extra Responses

We take a closer look at the extra responses obtained from the workers through the optional categorization sets (Set-2 through to Set-5) for all the units within tasks, across varying configurations. Table 3 presents the aggregated responses from the 9 task configurations, with respect to each of the 5 sets of options for category selection.

Table 3: Responses of workers with respect to each set of categories, aggregated across varying task configurations (% Wrong and % Correct are w.r.t. non-skipped responses.)

Response Type	Set-1	Set-2	Set-3	Set-4	Set-5
% Skipped	-	10.30	10.86	11.19	11.47
% Wrong Responses	9.23	9.52	10.92	11.58	13.31
% Correct Responses	90.77	90.48	89.08	88.42	86.69

Since the first set was made compulsory, no workers were allowed to skip Set-1. We find that the percentage of correct responses with respect to the extra responses received, gradually decreases from Set-1 to Set-5. We observe that workers tend to skip more optional sets as they proceed from Set-2 to Set-5. This is understandable, considering that workers may find it tedious to exhibit altruistic extra effort throughout the course of a task. Interestingly, of those responses which are provided by workers from Set-2 to Set-5, the percentage of wrong answers gradually increases.

4.6 Workers Breaking Bad

In addition to the method presented in previous work [4] to measure the tipping point of workers, we adopt another approach to assess the tipping point of *bad workers* by adjusting it for honest mistakes from workers. We define this relatively less aggressive measure as the *adjusted tipping point* (ATP). Since workers may lose attentiveness or get bored in repetitive tasks, honest workers may stumble at certain units. However, due to the ease of the task as mentioned earlier we do not expect workers to trail towards providing poor responses consecutively.

Adjusted Tipping Point. Workers that consecutively respond to at least 10% of the units within the task incorrectly, are said to have an *adjusted tipping point*. The index of the first unit at which the worker provided the first string of 10% or more incorrect answers is the ATP of the worker.

Breaking Worker/Breaker. A bad worker who exhibits an Adjusted Tipping Point is said to be a breaker.

For example, consider a task with 30 units, and a worker who responds to units 7,8, and 9 incorrectly. The given worker thus consecutively provided incorrect responses to 10% of the questions. The worker is hence said to be a *breaker* and the worker's ATP is 7. In case workers depict multiple strings of inaccurate responses, the ATP is consid-

Table 4: Types of workers and average ATP of *breakers*, with respect to varying task configurations.

Task Configuration (Units X USD cents)	Perfect Workers	Poor Starters	Bad Workers	Breakers	Avg. ATP
20x1	85	7	8	1	1
20x2	72	7	12	5	1
20x3	76	7	13	6	3
30x1	68	6	14	8	4
30x2	63	7	15	8	2
30x3	62	6	19	13	4
40x1	67	6	16	10	4
40x2	57	9	19	10	4
40x3	51	6	24	18	9

Table 5: Correlation between acceptable answers and workers' trust score.

Task Configuration	20x1	20x2	20x3	30x1	30x2	30x3	40x1	40x2	40x3
Correlation	0.85	0.82	0.66	0.76	0.74	0.71	0.67	0.78	0.55

ered to be the index of the first unit of the first occurrence of such a string of responses.

Table 4 presents our findings with respect to the distribution of the different kinds of workers and the ATP of *breakers*. We note that as the length of the task increases, the number of *perfect workers* decreases while the number of *bad workers* and *breakers* increases. We find no significant fluctuation in the number of *poor starters* across varying task configurations. An interesting observation is that with an increase in monetary incentive for a fixed length of the task, we see that the ATP of *breakers* increases to a higher unit index. This tells us that although malicious workers may be prone to getting attracted to tasks with higher rewards (as can be observed from the number of *bad workers* in each task), higher incentives can delay the adjusted tipping point. With an increase in monetary incentive for a fixed length of the task, we do not observe a significant trend with respect to the ATP of *breakers*. However, across different task lengths we observe that with an increase in task length the ATP of workers increases as well.

4.7 Can we trust the 'trust-score'?

CrowdFlower additionally provides a trust-score for the workers. This trust score, a value between 0 and 1, represents the accuracy of a worker in a job. Here, we draw a comparison between our findings and the trust-score provided by the platform.

Ideally, all workers could achieve a perfect score, given the simplicity of the tailored units. However, in total we identified 299 workers who did not manage to complete the task perfectly. Under our relaxed definition of *bad workers* which tolerates 10% of inaccuracy, we identified 56 bad workers. Table 5 shows the correlation between the trust-score and the number of correct answers given by the workers. In all cases we see a strong correlation, meaning that workers with a higher trust-score provided by the platform, indeed tend to perform better.

The average trust-score of all workers in the dataset is 0.64. Considering only the trust-scores of bad workers, the average is significantly lower, 0.39. However, we found out that 22 workers (out of the 56 bad workers) have trust-scores above 0.64. This indicates that although the platform associates them with high trust scores, these workers end up providing unacceptable responses, which based on our setup can only be attributed to malicious intent.

4.8 Caveats and Limitations

We ensured that each worker participated in only one of the deployed tasks by leveraging worker IDs. In this way, we eliminated the influence of some users who could perform all the tasks, additionally excluding the influence of learning and familiarity with the job, that a worker might bring from one task to another. With more experiments that stretch the limits of length of the task as well as monetary incentives offered, we can propose boundaries for these parameters. This will form a part of our imminent future work.

5. DISCUSSION AND CONCLUSIONS

We find that *bad workers* are attracted to tasks with relatively high monetary incentives when compared to those with relatively low incentives, despite being of the same length and requiring the same amount of effort for task completion. This shows that it is of prime importance for a requester to fine-tune the incentive offered, in order to obtain optimal results. From our study we find that it is safer to err on the lower side of the monetary incentive offered for a task, to attain more accurate responses from the crowd. Since we establish that the *task completion time* of a worker is strongly and positively correlated to the worker's accuracy, adequate time must be provided to the crowd for task completion. For optimal results, it is therefore safer to err on the higher side of the time required.

We establish that the accuracy of workers decreases as they proceed in a task, more so towards the end of longer tasks. This shows that a task administrator can profit by splitting a relatively long task into shorter ones before deploying it to the crowd. Our findings suggest that for extracting ideal output from a crowd, it is safer to err on the shorter side with respect to the length of a task.

By giving workers an option to provide additional work through their *extra effort*, we can gather more information regarding the worker and deduce the nature of the worker. We find that workers that exert more extra effort tend to perform with higher accuracies within the tasks. Thus, by identifying and treating these different types of workers accordingly, one can improve the effectiveness of categorization tasks. Finally, this paper sets important ground work for future work. Through further experiments we plan to quantify the limits and guidelines presented in this work.

Acknowledgements. This work has been partially funded by the European Commission within the 7th Framework Programme (Grant Agreement no: 600908).

6. REFERENCES

[1] C. Eickhoff and A. de Vries. How crowdsourcable is your task. In *Proceedings of the workshop on crowdsourcing for search and data mining (CSDM) at the fourth ACM international conference on web search and data mining (WSDM)*, pages 11–14, 2011.

[2] C. Eickhoff and A. P. de Vries. Increasing cheat robustness of crowdsourcing tasks. *Information retrieval*, 16(2):121–137, 2013.

[3] U. Gadiraju, R. Kawase, and S. Dietze. A taxonomy of microtasks on the web. In *Proceedings of the 25th ACM conference on Hypertext and social media*, pages 218–223. ACM, 2014.

[4] U. Gadiraju, R. Kawase, S. Dietze, and G. Demartini. Understanding malicious behavior in crowdsourcing platforms: The case of online surveys. In *Proceedings of CHI'15, CHI Conference on Human Factors in Computing Systems*, 2015.

[5] P. G. Ipeirotis, F. Provost, and J. Wang. Quality management on amazon mechanical turk. In *Proceedings of the ACM SIGKDD workshop on human computation*, pages 64–67. ACM, 2010.

[6] N. Kaufmann, T. Schulze, and D. Veit. More than fun and money. worker motivation in crowdsourcing - a study on mechanical turk. In *AMCIS*, 2011.

[7] G. Kazai, J. Kamps, and N. Milic-Frayling. Worker types and personality traits in crowdsourcing relevance labels. In *Proceedings of the 20th ACM international conference on Information and knowledge management*, pages 1941–1944. ACM, 2011.

[8] C. C. Marshall and F. M. Shipman. Experiences surveying the crowd: Reflections on methods, participation, and reliability. In *Proceedings of the 5th Annual ACM Web Science Conference*, WebSci '13, pages 234–243, New York, NY, USA, 2013. ACM.

[9] W. Mason and D. J. Watts. Financial incentives and the performance of crowds. *ACM SigKDD Explorations Newsletter*, 11(2):100–108, 2010.

[10] D. Oleson, A. Sorokin, G. P. Laughlin, V. Hester, J. Le, and L. Biewald. Programmatic gold: Targeted and scalable quality assurance in crowdsourcing. *Human computation*, 11:11, 2011.

[11] J. Rogstadius, V. Kostakos, A. Kittur, B. Smus, J. Laredo, and M. Vukovic. An assessment of intrinsic and extrinsic motivation on task performance in crowdsourcing markets. In *ICWSM*, 2011.

[12] J. Ross, L. Irani, M. Silberman, A. Zaldivar, and B. Tomlinson. Who are the crowdworkers?: shifting demographics in mechanical turk. In *CHI'10 Extended Abstracts on Human Factors in Computing Systems*, pages 2863–2872. ACM, 2010.

Content Virality on Online Social Networks: Empirical Evidence from Twitter, Facebook, and Google+ on German News Websites

Irina Heimbach
TU Darmstadt
Dept. of Economics and Law
heimbach@emarkets.tu-darmstadt.de

Benjamin Schiller
TU Dresden
Faculty of Computer Science
benjamin.schiller1@tu-dresden.de

Thorsten Strufe
TU Dresden
Faculty of Computer Science
thorsten.strufe@tu-dresden.de

Oliver Hinz
TU Darmstadt
Dept. of Economics and Law
hinz@emarkets.tu-darmstadt.de

ABSTRACT

The virality of content describes its likelihood to be shared with peers. In this work, we investigate how content characteristics impact the sharing likelihood of news articles on Twitter, Facebook, and Google+. We examine a random sample of 4,278 articles from the most popular news websites in Germany categorized by human classifiers and text mining tools. Our analysis reveals commonalities and subtle differences between the three networks indicating different sharing patterns of their users.

Categories and Subject Descriptors

J.4 [**Social and Behavioral Sciences**]: Economics; G.3 [**Probability and Statistics**]: Correlation and regression analysis

General Terms

Measurement; Economics; Human Factors

Keywords

Online social networks; Content virality; News articles

1. INTRODUCTION

The digitization and emergence of Internet-based services altered human communication in many respects. While we had to cut out or copy a newspaper article in the past to share it with others, we can easily send a link to an interesting article or a funny video to our friends, colleagues, and relatives via email or share them on *online social networks* (OSNs)

HT '15, September 1–4, 2015, Guzelyurt, Northern Cyprus.
© 2015 ACM. ISBN 978-1-4503-3395-5/15/09 ...$15.00.
DOI: http://dx.doi.org/10.1145/2700171.2791032.

like *Facebook*, *Twitter*, and *Google+* nowadays. Some content attracts high attention and becomes *viral*, exhibiting an almost contagious behavior [16, 5]. We define *content virality* as some feature of the content that enhances its likelihood to be shared in different communication channels, distinct from *content popularity* which is commonly measured by the total number of accesses to the content. For a discussion of alternative measures of virality, we refer to [16]. As argued by [16], virality is strongly related „to the content being spread, rather than to the influencers who spread it".

The phenomenon of online content sharing belongs to the general domain of diffusion processes, where the characteristics of the diffusing object - be it a product, an idea, a piece of information, or behavior - play an important role. While the impact of characteristics of physical products are well studied in this context, e.g., relative advantage and complexity as key factors of adoption [38], the characteristics of digital products are insufficiently investigated. The studies by Berger and Milkman [7] and Guerini et al. [16] constitute laudable exceptions and investigate the content characteristics in a structured manner. The study by Berger and Milkman [7] finds that positive and emotionally written New York Times articles are shared more frequently. Furthermore, in their sample, articles which evoke strong emotions like anger and awe are shared more often. Although they controlled for several factors and their findings are robust and confirmed in experiments and a field study, the research on drivers of content virality warrants further examinations. The study by Guerini et al. [16] proposes prediction models for different alternative measures of virality using support vector machines.

Studies by Szabo and Huberman [45], Berger and Iyengar [6], Aral and Walker [3], and Schulze et al. [42] investigate diffusion outcomes in context of different communication channels and design sharing mechanisms. Their findings suggest an interrelation between content characteristics and the characteristics of the channel, a relation that has not been studied so far.

Therefore, we intend to study the interplay between the shared content and the use of different channels. In this work, we investigate how content characteristics impact the sharing likelihood of news articles on the OSNs Twitter, Facebook, and Google+. We examine a random sample of 4,278 articles from the most popular news websites in Germany categorized by human classifiers and text mining tools.

Understanding the reasons why some content becomes popular is of high relevance for theory and business practice, as the media industry is challenged by the development of Internet-based services and has to face the transition of social life into the digital environment. First, more and more readers substitute printed magazines and newspapers with online content which is currently often still free of charge. But as more and more media companies like the New York Times [1] shift to freemium business models, knowledge about the drivers of content virality could be useful for sophisticated pricing strategies for online content [31]. Second, the authors might craft purposefully content that goes viral. Third, if the authors are not willing to adapt or even purposefully write content with the aim that it becomes popular and viral in different social media, the results of our research can provide then at least useful suggestions in selecting the appropriate channel for the message. For example if the content provider knows that Facebook users are more interested in funny and entertaining stories than in well-investigated profound polarizing articles, then it might focus its social media strategy on other, more suitable, OSNs than Facebook. The problem of selecting appropriate communication channels is becoming more relevant, as more instant messengers, OSNs and content aggregators emerge offering their own sharing plugins, e.g., like the messenger WhatsApp in 2014. Due to limited space on the website and especially for mobile ones, the content providers will be not able to place all social plugins around a content and will be forced - sooner or later - to deal with the problem of selecting the most appropriate communication channels for spreading their content online. Finally, understanding and knowing on which OSN a content will be shared more can allow content providers to match ads to the audience of that OSN [31].

The remainder of this paper is structured as follows: First, we review the existing research on information diffusion and content characteristics as a driver of such diffusion in Section 2. Then, we present our data set, our estimation model, variables, and the estimation approach in Section 3. In Section 4, we present and discuss the results of our analysis. Finally, in Section 5, we summarize our work and conclude with implications for research and business practice.

2. RELATED WORK

Previous research on content sharing and on the related fields of word of mouth (WOM) and information diffusion has a long research history. Previous research has shown the importance of WOM for increased sales [15, 9], for the adoption and discovery of new products and ideas [40, 11, 14, 13, 32, 5], and for other economic processes like on bidding behavior in online auctions [22]. Further, previous research tries to identify influential people in social networks [1, 20, 26], investigates how network structures impact social contagion [4, 30], and tries to determine how this information can be used to improve viral marketing strategies [27, 37, 47, 21]. Other research investigates temporal and topological patterns of information diffusion [33, 45, 50].

---

[1] available on `http://bit.ly/15xv06J`

Individuals decide every time they receive a viral message, a piece of content, or some other information whether and to whom they forward it [36, 43]. Newer studies address the motives to transmit content [36, 19, 25, 43, 23, 6] and the characteristics of product or content [16, 7, 10, 8, 42]. Previous studies show that motives to share content are related to altruism [36, 23, 35] as many people want to help others. This becomes also evident as content with high practical utility is shared rather often [7].

Content characteristics for their part are the least studied component of the social communication. Phelps et al. [36] find that the most forwarded emails contain jokes and chain letters but they do not further differentiate between content characteristics. In contrast, the study by Berger and Milkman [7] classifies New York Times articles on several dimensions and provides deep insights into the main drivers of content virality. An important content factor is its sentiment. The findings on its impact however are ambiguous [17, 7, 2]. Mazzarol et al. [35] report that the received word of mouth is both positive and negative but always with rather extreme values. Rosen and Tesser [39] state that people are reluctant to send negative WOM preventing building negative attitude towards their personalities. Berger and Milkman [7] find that positive content is shared more often. Contradictory to Berger and Milkman [7], Hansen et al. [17] analyze three samples from Twitter and find that negative news-Tweets are more likely to be re-tweeted but the popularity of non-news-Tweets relates to a positive sentiment of the content. Angelis et al. [2] find in a series of laboratory experiments that people tend to generate positive WOM about their own experiences but to transmit negative news about the experiences of others.

Content sentiment is tightly related to the content's emotionality. Dobele et al. [12] analyze real viral marketing campaigns and show that the success of a campaign is highly related to the emotionality of its messages. According to Berger and Milkman [7] content evoking high-arousal emotions like awe and anger activate people to share it with their peers. Content related to deactivating emotions like sadness is shared less frequently [7].

In his seminal work, Rogers [38] has already highlighted the importance of the communication channel in disseminating a product or a new idea. Studies by Szabo and Huberman [45], Berger and Iyengar [6], Aral and Walker [3] and Schulze et al. [42] find differences in diffusion processes between different communication channels or the different design of sharing mechanisms within a communication channel. An unpublished study by Berger and Iyengar [6] finds that discontinuous communication channels (email or text posts) give the conversational partners an opportunity to select the most interesting topic or brand in contrast to continuous channels (phone and face-to-face) over which people discuss the topic which just crosses their mind. As digital content is often shared via OSNs using social plugins, the characteristics of each OSN might have an effect on the sharing probability. Aral and Walker [3] investigate how the sharing mechanism (broadcast vs. personalized referrals) impacts the reach of a Facebook application. The very recent study by Schulze et al. [42] evidences the existence of a mismatch between the product characteristics to be promoted over an OSN and the users' perceptions of the network. Szabo and Huberman [45] find that while content shared on Digg.com saturates very quickly, YouTube videos keep receiving attention for a long time. The findings of these three studies let suppose that content characteristics and the characteristics of an OSN could interact, a question that has not been studied yet. Further, the differences in use of OSNs might reflect their different user groups. Therefore, it is important to know who the users of the different OSNs are and how they can be characterized by content they share over the respective OSN.

Our study is distinct from the stream of research on predicting content popularity from the early users' reactions to content such as, e.g., the number of early votes on Digg.com and number of comments on discussion forums and sites [29, 31, 45]. [29] propose a model for prediction of content popularity on discussion forums dpreview.com and myspace.com using a Cox proportional hazard regression using the number of comments and the number of links in the first hours after publishing. Other studies in this field apply similar research designs. In contrast, we concentrate on inherent content characteristics like content's sentiment and emotionality, topic and which particular emotions it evokes. We also control for author characteristics like writing complexity and author's fame as well as for publishing timing like day-of-the-week and time-of-the-day.

Therefore, we perform a deeper analysis of the drivers of content virality in three different OSNs.

3. DATA, CODING, AND ESTIMATION

Our data set comes from a large-scaled, still ongoing project which collects data of all articles appearing in the most popular German online newspapers and magazines[2] since January 2012 [41]. Using web crawlers, we record an article's title, a link to the full text, the name of the magazine, and the category where it is published. For two weeks after an article's publication, web crawlers visit the web sites every 3 hours and capture the number of Tweets (Twitter), One-ups (Google+), and Shares (Facebook). Here, Tweets refers to the number of Tweets that contain an article's URL. For Facebook, Shares is the sum of Likes, Comments, and Shares that is commonly displayed. In addition, we record whether an article is published on the main page or on subpages only. Given the immense number of articles in our database (454,888 articles published between March 1st and September 30th, 2012), we drew a random sample of 4,278 (about 1%) for this study. Then, we coded articles with respect to several dimensions. Table 1 gives a brief description of the dimensions and the data sources.

Using SentiStrength [46][3], a German dictionary for automated sentiment analysis, we quantified the positivity and emotionality of articles. Positivity is defined as the difference between the shares of positive and negative words in an article [7]. Emotionality is quantified as the total share of positive and negative words [7].

Next, we engaged four human coders to classify articles on further dimensions. The coders were not informed about the research question and were asked to rate articles on the four emotional dimensions (anger, anxiety, awe, and sadness), on the dimensions surprise, practical utility, and interest, and to note the authorship of the articles. We used the coding instructions provided by Berger and Milkman [7][4]. Each ar-

ticle was encoded by one of the coders on a five-point Likert scale [34] according to the extent to which an article evokes certain emotions or might be, e.g., of practical relevance. We trained the coders on a test set of articles to ensure good inter-coder reliabilities of up 0.7 and higher (pairwise Holsti-Index [24]).

Further, we control for the number of pictures and videos included in the article as it may affect content virality. Articles featured with pictures and videos may benefit from increased attractiveness and thus might be shared more on OSNs as shown for user profiles in a business-related OSN [44].

Table 3 gives examples of articles which score highly on different content dimensions. As expected, an article about the new love of German television hostess Michelle Hunziger, is written positively. The disqualification of the German cycling team during the world cup has a high value for anger while a report about child mortality is classified as sad. These examples show that the characteristics we determined for the articles fits well with their respective content.

Author characteristics may also affect content virality. We distinguish the first author's gender since male and female authors might have different writing styles which can impact an article's popularity [7]. Well written articles are more likely to be read, and thus are more likely to be shared. Thus, we control for writing complexity measured by applying the Flesch-Reading-Ease metric, a scale that is so ubiquitous that it is bundled with popular word processing programs and services such as Microsoft Office Word, WordPerfect, and WordPro[5]. We additionally introduce a dummy variable that measures whether the article is based on the reports of news agencies. These articles tend to be very early common knowledge, so that readers believe that everybody is already aware of this information and they therefore refrain from sharing them. We also control for the author's reputation that may also influence an article's virality. We approximated the author's reputation by counting the search hits at the search engine *Bing*[6] for the author's name plus the keyword "author".

Furthermore, we control for position, time [50], and attention competition factors [49]. Most readers start reading online magazines from the home page. So articles which are published there, are more likely to be read and thus to be shared on OSNs. Therefore, we include a variable to describe whether an article appeared on the home page or not. We extracted sections an article was published from the URLs and compress them into 13 distinct categories. These sections are cars, career, society, culture, lifestyle, politics, local, travel, humor, sports, technology, business, and science. Furthermore, there might be time effects on the number of recommendations in OSNs. We control for the time when an article is published. From that, we create 8 dummy variables for 3-hours-periods and seven dummies for the day of the week. Articles which appear at 10:00 p.m. may draw less attention than articles which appear at 10:00 a.m. Similarly, articles which appear on a weekend might have less recommendations as users spend their spare time otherwise than on the Internet. Therefore, we represent the day of the week of an article's publication in 7 dummy variables. We further use a linear time trend that captures the steady growth of each OSN over time. Finally, we account for

---

[2]available on `http://www.alexa.com/`
[3]available on `http://bit.ly/1xs2V1r`
[4]available on `http://bit.ly/1xs35WF`

[5]available on `http://bit.ly/1IMRW9s`
[6]available on `http://www.bing.com`

(a) Number of articles per time slot

(b) Number of articles per day of the week

(c) Number of articles per category

(d) Distribution of Share, Tweet and One-up count (for $x \leq 20$)

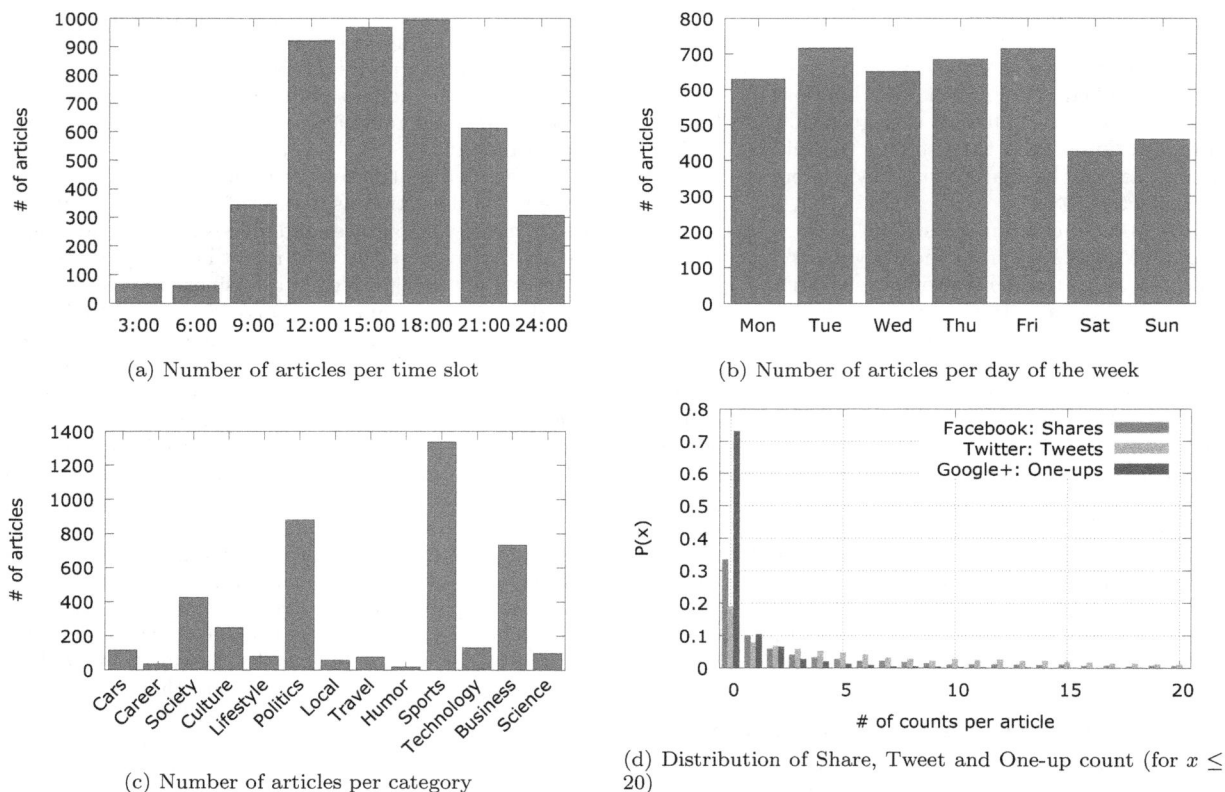

Figure 1: Statistics for the 4,278 randomly selected articles from German news websites

a magazine's reach and for the number of articles published on the same day. Magazines with higher reach are expected to have more readers who might share articles on OSNs. We completed our data by the moving average monthly reach of newspapers and magazines from the media agency AGOF[7]. As argued by [49], the number of articles is expected to negatively affect the number of recommendations on OSNs due to limited attention of people.

Summary statistics of our dependent variables and other dimensions are given in Table 2. Figure 1d shows the distributions of # of Facebook Shares, Twitter Tweets, and Google+ One-ups, which follow Zipf's law: A huge part of articles gained few recommendations and only few articles were highly shared with peers in the respective OSN. 59.49% of articles are based on reports of news agencies. 11.97% of articles are written by female first authors. 21.30% of articles are published on the start page of the respective news medium. Figures 1c, 1a, and 1b show the distributions of the selected articles along the dimensions article section, time of the day, and day of the week. Our random sample contains a disproportionately high share of sports-related articles, which is caused by the European Championship in Summer 2012. The distributions over the day-of-the-week and time-of-the-day dimensions are plausible.

As our dependent variables take on discrete, non-negative values (i.e. represent count data), we choose a negative binomial regression to analyze our research question. Methods developed for modeling count data (Poisson regression, ne-

gative binomial regression, zero inflation, hurdle models etc.) explicitly account for the particular aspects of such data like the preponderance of zeros, small values and the discrete nature of the dependent variables and therefore are better suited than the linear multiple regression approach [28]. We do not apply the Poisson regression model, as it assumes equality of the conditional mean and variance functions (equidispersion). The most common method is then negative binomial model that accounts for overdispersion (variances exceed means) of the data [28].

The estimation equation looks as follows:

$$Prob(Y = y_i | x_i) = \frac{e^{-\lambda_i} \cdot \lambda_i^{y_i}}{y_i!} \quad (1)$$

with

$$\lambda_i = e^{x_i' \cdot \beta + \epsilon} \quad (2)$$

where y_i measures the number of Shares, Tweets, and One-ups in the respective OSN for article i and x_i is the vector describing article i on the different dimensions. ϵ is a gamma distributed error with unity mean and variance α [28]. We used robust standard errors to account for heteroscedasticity in our data set.

4. RESULTS

The results (estimated coefficients, standard errors, and the respective significance levels (p-values) are listed in Table 4. As a reference category in our estimation, we selected an article written by a male first author and published in a

[7]available on http://www.agof.de/

Table 3: Exemplary articles which score highly on different dimensions

Variable	Original German Title (and English translation)
Positivity	Neues Glück für Michelle Hunziker: Mit Tomaso auf Wolke sieben
	New felicity for Michelle Hunziker: with Tomaso on cloud nine
Emotionality	Macaulay Culkin: Sein Vater fürchtet um sein Leben!
	Macaulay Culkin: His father father fears for his life
Anger	Radsport WM: Deutsche Teamsprinter disqualifiziert
	Cycling worldcup: German team is disqualified
Anxiety	Nach Fukushima: Japans Regierung erwägt ersten AKW-Neustart
	Japan plans to re-start nuclear power plants
Awe	Wie Guerilla-Gärtner illegal Städte begrünen
	How Guerrilla gardeners plant greenery on cities
Sadness	Bericht von Unicef: Kindersterblichkeit seit 1990 weltweit halbiert
	Unicef report: Child mortality halved since 1990
Surprise	Forderung nach Abschaffung des Paragrafen 173: Grünen-Politiker Ströbele will Inzest erlauben
	German politician Ströbele wants to change law to legalize incest
Practical Utility	Die zehn schönsten Wanderrouten
	10 most beautiful hiking routes
Interest	Chinesischer Jugendlicher: Eine Niere im Tausch für ein iPad
	Chinese teenager exchanges kidney for an iPad
First Author Fame	Ein Witz von Guido Knopp
	A joke by Guido Knopp
Writing complexity	EZB-Mitarbeiter fordern Inflationsschutz für Rente
	European central bank employees demand protection of retirement pays from inflation
Number of Pictures	18 deutsche Filme sind in Cannes am Start
	18 German movies are part of Cannes
Number of Videos	So drücken Sie Ihre Energie-Rechnung
	A guide how to lower your energy bill

culture section on Wednesday between 9:00 p.m. and midnight (Constant term in Table 4).

First, we observe a steady growth of sharing for Google+ ($p < .01$) and a slight decrease for Twitter ($p < .1$) which is captured by our linear time variable representing the publication time. The sharing activities on Facebook seem to stagnate. We also find some periodical patterns: On Google+ and Facebook, articles receive most recommendations on Fridays. For Twitter, there is no difference between Wednesdays (the reference day) and any other day of the week. Facebook users refrain from sharing online content on Sundays. With respect to the time-of-the-day effects there are no significant differences for Google+. Articles have a higher chance to be shared by Facebook users between 6:00 a.m. and 2:00 p.m. ($p < .01$) compared to the reference category published between 9:00 p.m. and midnight. Twitter users tweet less between 12:00 p.m. and 9:00 p.m. ($p < .01$).

With respect to the section where the article is listed, we observe some commonalities and some strong differences between the three OSNs. Articles related to career are likely to be shared on all three OSNs. In contrast, sports-related articles are less likely to be shared. Facebook and Twitter users are less likely to share articles about cars, for Google+ this effect is not significant. Whereas Twitter and Google+ users seem to be interested in business-related articles, Facebook users are less likely to share them with their peers ($p < .1$). Generally, Twitter and Google+ users seem to resemble each other with respect to their recommendation of articles related to politics, technology, and science compared to the reference category (culture). Google+ users also prefer to share lifestyle- and travel-related articles with their peers. Twitter users do not share funny articles with their peers (section humor). With exception of some aforementioned sections, for Facebook, there seem to be no differences in the sharing likelihood of articles in remaining sections. This finding might indicate the high heterogeneity and more equally distributed preferences of Facebook users.

With respect to different emotional and other content dimensions, we found no significant effect for positively written articles and negative effect for emotionality ($p < .01$) in all three OSNs. It seems that German readers do not value very emotional articles highly. This finding can be caused by cultural differences or the fact that good journalism pursues goals and practices, such as objectivity, neutrality, and fact verification [48]. As the effect of the message's sentiment is controversially discussed in the previous research [2, 39, 7, 17], future research should try to identify the reasons for this dissenting result.

In line with previous research [7], we do find that sadness has a negative impact on sharing in Google+ and Twitter ($p < .05$). We further find that anger ($p < .01$) is a good predictor for the virality of the content in all three OSNs. If anger increases by 1 unit, the log expected number of Tweets, One-ups, and Shares increases by 0.119, 0.26, and 0.283 respectively. Awe has an impact on sharing via Facebook, and surprise on Google+. The users of all three OSNs value interesting articles ($p < .01$ for Twitter and Facebook, $p < .05$ for Google+). Contradictory to our expectations and in line with [42], Facebook users share less articles with practical utility ($p < .1$) while the effects for Twitter and Google+ are insignificant.

Table 4: Estimation results of negative binomial regression, standard errors in parentheses (*: $p < .10$, **: $p < .05$, ***: $p < .01$)

Dimension	Tweets			One-ups			Shares		
Positivity	0.031	(0.030)		0.047	(0.088)		0.012	(0.055)	
Emotionality	-0.106	(0.018)	***	-0.191	(0.050)	***	-0.114	(0.024)	***
Anger	0.119	(0.021)	***	0.260	(0.046)	***	0.283	(0.047)	***
Anxiety	-0.004	(0.025)		0.040	(0.050)		-0.033	(0.055)	
Awe	0.013	(0.022)		0.029	(0.049)		0.158	(0.055)	***
Sadness	-0.048	(0.022)	**	-0.124	(0.051)	**	-0.052	(0.049)	
Surprise	0.028	(0.023)		0.088	(0.048)	*	0.076	(0.050)	
Practical utility	0.015	(0.022)		-0.008	(0.044)		-0.106	(0.054)	*
Interest	0.070	(0.023)	***	0.106	(0.047)	**	0.185	(0.051)	***
# of pictures	0.007	(0.002)	***	0.006	(0.005)		0.020	(0.007)	***
# of videos	-0.038	(0.033)		-0.190	(0.088)	**	-0.066	(0.095)	
Female first author	-0.297	(0.066)	***	-0.172	(0.120)		0.027	(0.179)	
Writing complexity	-0.007	(0.001)	***	-0.013	(0.003)	***	-0.014	(0.003)	***
News agency	-0.653	(0.048)	***	-0.828	(0.102)	***	-0.972	(0.117)	***
First author fame	1.81e-5	(8.91e-6)	**	4.03e-5	(2.40e-5)	*	6.6e-5	(2.27e-5)	***
Position	-0.120	(0.044)	***	0.357	(0.107)	***	0.440	(0.120)	***
Section: cars	-0.622	(0.138)	***	-0.244	(0.312)		-0.934	(0.414)	**
Section: career	0.627	(0.165)	***	0.742	(0.292)	**	0.652	(0.357)	*
Section: society	-0.072	(0.099)		0.242	(0.196)		-0.256	(0.302)	
Section: lifestyle	0.113	(0.168)		0.876	(0.284)	***	0.142	(0.406)	
Section: politics	0.302	(0.095)	***	0.495	(0.175)	***	-0.072	(0.276)	
Section: local	-0.031	(0.300)		0.725	(0.662)		1.020	(0.673)	
Section: travel	0.066	(0.130)		0.576	(0.348)	*	0.027	(0.379)	
Section: humor	-0.689	(0.260)	***	-0.338	(0.408)		-0.727	(0.541)	
Section: sports	-0.876	(0.0928)	***	-1.067	(0.196)	***	-1.801	(0.273)	***
Section: technology	0.865	(0.122)	***	1.915	(0.225)	***	0.229	(0.377)	
Section: business	0.360	(0.090)	***	0.409	(0.175)	**	-0.467	(0.270)	*
Section: science	0.281	(0.144)	*	1.302	(0.252)	***	0.372	(0.421)	
Publication time	-5.48e-4	(3.30e-4)	*	0.002	(7.07e-4)	***	1.71e-4	(7.68e-4)	
Time of day: 03:00	-0.151	(0.137)		-0.427	(0.333)		-0.186	(0.420)	
Time of day: 06:00	-0.208	(0.169)		-0.261	(0.353)		-0.362	(0.440)	
Time of day: 09:00	0.107	(0.103)		0.170	(0.218)		0.781	(0.221)	***
Time of day: 12:00	-0.235	(0.0912)	**	0.139	(0.186)		0.515	(0.189)	***
Time of day: 15:00	-0.304	(0.090)	***	-0.068	(0.190)		0.371	(0.197)	*
Time of day: 18:00	-0.340	(0.089)	***	-0.181	(0.183)		0.017	(0.187)	
Time of day: 21:00	-0.318	(0.096)	***	-0.002	(0.203)		0.343	(0.212)	
Day of week: Mon	-0.071	(0.067)		0.095	(0.152)		-0.0991	(0.176)	
Day of week: Tue	0.101	(0.072)		0.398	(0.144)	***	0.263	(0.169)	
Day of week: Thu	-0.051	(0.064)		0.073	(0.142)		0.215	(0.155)	
Day of week: Fri	0.003	(0.067)		0.310	(0.147)	**	0.435	(0.161)	***
Day of week: Sat	-0.116	(0.126)		0.181	(0.290)		-0.292	(0.314)	
Day of week: Sun	-0.161	(0.119)		-0.090	(0.276)		-0.718	(0.301)	**
Constant	3.078	(0.303)	***	-0.564	(0.692)		3.892	(0.808)	***
# of articles	-3.8e-4	(1.25e-4)	***	-4.39e-4	(3.01e-4)		-0.001	(3.39e-4)	***
Monthly reach	1.2e-4	(7.49e-6)	***	1.1e-4	(1.64e-5)	***	2.0e-4	(1.88e-5)	***
$Ln\ \alpha$	0.090	(0.031)	***	1.203	(0.058)	***	1.293	(0.029)	***
N		4278			4278			4278	
Pseudo R^2		0.071			0.102			0.055	

Table 1: Dimensions, sources, and values for data coding

OSN Statistics		
# of Tweets	Web crawler	$\mathbb{N}_0^+$
# of One-ups	Web crawler	$\mathbb{N}_0^+$
# of Shares	Web crawler	$\mathbb{N}_0^+$
Content characteristics		
Positivity	SentiStrength	$\mathbb{R}$
Emotionality	SentiStrength	$\mathbb{R}^+$
Anger	Human classifier	$\{1\ldots5\}$
Anxiety	Human classifier	$\{1\ldots5\}$
Awe	Human classifier	$\{1\ldots5\}$
Sadness	Human classifier	$\{1\ldots5\}$
Surprise	Human classifier	$\{1\ldots5\}$
Practical utility	Human classifier	$\{1\ldots5\}$
Interest	Human classifier	$\{1\ldots5\}$
Article features		
# of pictures	Human classifier	$\mathbb{N}_0^+$
# of videos	Human classifier	$\mathbb{N}_0^+$
Author characteristics		
Female first author	Human classifier	$\{0,1\}$
Writing complexity	Flesch Reading Test	$\{0\ldots100\}$
News agency	Human classifier	$\{0,1\}$
First author fame	Bing search	$\mathbb{N}_0^+$
Attention competition		
Position	Web crawler	$\{0,1\}$
Section (13)	Web crawler	$\{0,1\}$
Publication time	Web crawler	Datetime
Time of day (8)	Web crawler	$\{0,1\}$
Day of week (7)	Web crawler	$\{0,1\}$
Monthly reach	Media agency	$\mathbb{N}_0^+$
# of articles	Web crawler	$\mathbb{N}_0^+$

Table 2: Dataset statistics for selected dimensions

Dimension	Mean	Std. dev.
# of Tweets	11.88	19.90
# of One-ups	0.99	3.86
# of Shares	36.19	175.42
Positivity	-0.15	0.89
Emotionality	1.40	2.16
Anger	2.28	1.16
Anxiety	1.98	1.07
Awe	1.72	0.90
Sadness	2.04	1.12
Surprise	2.47	1.02
Practical utility	1.77	0.96
Interest	3.02	0.92
# of pictures	3.37	9.14
# of videos	0.12	0.45
Writing complexity	67.64	15.37
First author fame	571.34	1967.92
# of articles	1859.38	336.09
Monthly reach	6205.76	2915.20

We find support that article complexity has a positive impact on virality, which is in line with the study by Milkman and Berger [7]. We also find support for the notion that the first author's fame and the article location on the website is a strong, positive predictor for virality in all three OSNs. In line with the study by [44], we find that the number of pictures used in the article has a positive impact on the sharing likelihood in Facebook and in Twitter ($p < .01$). We also controlled for the source of the article's content and used a dummy variable for news agencies as source. If news agencies are the source of the information, the article is less frequently shared in all three OSNs ($p < .01$) as we already hypothesized.

Our results highlight that the predictors for virality are more complex than previous research suggests and that there are subtle differences between different communication channels. Hence, more research is needed in this area to better understand the phenomenon of virality.

5. SUMMARY AND CONCLUSION

Although there is a huge bulk of literature on word of mouth, social contagion, and viral marketing, research on the impact of content characteristics on sharing behavior is scarce. We therefore investigate how content characteristics

impact the sharing likelihood of news articles in three different OSNs: Twitter, Facebook, and Google+. We examined a random sample of 4,278 articles from the most popular news and magazine websites in Germany published in 2012. We used human classifiers as well as text mining tools to categorize the content and enriched the data with control variables.

Our analysis reveals commonalities and subtle differences between the three OSNs examined which highlights that different sharing patterns should be expected from different audiences. We find that emotionality has a negative effect on virality which means that articles without strong emotions are more frequently shared in OSNs. Articles with interesting and anger evoking content go viral in all three OSNs. In line with previous research, we find that sadness is negatively related to content virality in Twitter and Google+ while awe positively influences the likelihood of articles to be shared on Facebook. Articles with high practical utility are less shared on Facebook. Twitter and Google+ users are more likely to share articles related to politics, business, technology, and science. Google+ users are more likely to share articles related to lifestyle and career. In contrast, articles about sports are less likely to be shared in all three OSNs. Finally, we find that articles based on the reports of news agencies are less likely to go viral in all three OSNs, indicating that users prefer original articles.

Our results are valuable for journalists as they can use the results to write more viral articles. If the journalists do not know how to write viral articles purposefully, publishers could at least adapt their social media strategies. As we mention in the introduction, content providers face the problem of selection of appropriate communication channels due to emergence of new sharing, communication and networking services. As our results indicate, Google+ and Twitter users are more interested in technology, science, business and politics related news and content. Content providers might then adapt their website design and prominently feature such content with social plugins from Google+ and Twitter. Otherwise, the spreading of the content that is less appealing to Google+ and Twitter users might be fostered in other, more suitable, OSNs. Most content providers start now to apply systems which track users' journeys (from where a user comes and where she goes) allowing to automate their marketing decisions [18]. Based on the insights provided by our study, publishers could also develop prediction tools that automatically optimize the placement of advertisements which ultimately could increase profits [31, 18].

Our study does not come without limitations. First and most importantly, sharing behavior does not necessarily relate to reading behavior. For example, some readers may shy away from sharing articles that evoke sad feelings although it might be interesting to read them. Therefore future research could study the interrelation between reading and sharing content. Secondly, we can only give advice from a macro perspective. There might be segments within the user population that show completely different patterns of sharing. The high variances and standard errors in our results suggest a more sophisticated analysis. Researchers and practitioners might especially be interested in understanding the role of opinion leaders as they ignite diffusion processes. Thirdly it seems fruitful to understand the relation between individual characteristics and content sharing behavior. It is likely that for example narcissistic people share other content than introverted people. To examine this research question, it would however be necessary to have information on sharing behavior and on the psychographics of the sharing individuals.

In conclusion, there are a number of potentially interesting avenues for future research. The intersection between psychology, sociology, and computer science provides promising new questions that also have value for business practice.

6. REFERENCES

[1] N. Agarwal, H. Liu, L. Tang, and P. S. Yu. Identifying the influential bloggers in a community. In *Proceedings of the 2008 international conference on web search and data mining*, pages 207–218. ACM, 2008.

[2] M. D. Angelis, A. Bonezzi, A. M. Peluso, D. D. Rucker, and M. Costabile. On braggarts and gossips: a self-enhancement account of word-of-mouth generation and transmission. *Journal of Marketing Research*, 49(4):551–563, 2012.

[3] S. Aral and D. Walker. Creating social contagion through viral product design: A randomized trial of peer influence in networks. *Management Science*, 57(9):1623–1639, 2011.

[4] M. Bampo, M. T. Ewing, D. R. Mather, D. Stewart, and M. Wallace. The effects of the social structure of digital networks on viral marketing performance. *Information Systems Research*, 19(3):273–290, 2008.

[5] J. Berger. *Contagious: Why things catch on*. Simon and Schuster, 2013.

[6] J. Berger and R. Iyengar. How interest shapes word-of-mouth over different channels. *Available at SSRN 2013141*, 2012.

[7] J. Berger and K. L. Milkman. What makes online content viral? *Journal of Marketing Research*, 49(2):192–205, 2012.

[8] J. Berger and E. M. Schwartz. What drives immediate and ongoing word of mouth? *Journal of Marketing Research*, 48(5):869–880, 2011.

[9] J. A. Chevalier and D. Mayzlin. The effect of word of mouth on sales: Online book reviews. *Journal of marketing research*, 43(3):345–354, 2006.

[10] C. M. Chung and P. R. Darke. The consumer as advocate: self-relevance, culture, and word-of-mouth. *Marketing Letters*, 17(4):269–279, 2006.

[11] J. Coleman, E. Katz, and H. Menzel. The diffusion of an innovation among physicians. *Sociometry*, pages 253–270, 1957.

[12] A. Dobele, A. Lindgreen, M. Beverland, J. Vanhamme, and R. Van Wijk. Why pass on viral messages? because they connect emotionally. *Business Horizons*, 50(4):291–304, 2007.

[13] R. Garg, M. D. Smith, and R. Telang. Measuring information diffusion in an online community. *Journal of Management Information Systems*, 28(2):11–38, 2011.

[14] M. Gladwell. *The tipping point: How little things can make a big difference*. Hachette Digital, Inc., 2006.

[15] D. Godes and D. Mayzlin. Using online conversations to study word-of-mouth communication. *Marketing Science*, 23(4):545–560, 2004.

[16] M. Guerini, C. Strapparava, and G. Özbal. Exploring text virality in social networks. In *ICWSM*, 2011.

[17] L. K. Hansen, A. Arvidsson, F. Å. Nielsen, E. Colleoni, and M. Etter. Good friends, bad news-affect and virality in twitter. In *Future information technology*, pages 34–43. Springer, 2011.

[18] I. Heimbach, D. S. Kostyra, and O. Hinz. Marketing automation. *Business & Information Systems Engineering*, 57(2):129–133, 2015.

[19] T. Hennig-Thurau, K. P. Gwinner, G. Walsh, and D. D. Gremler. Electronic word-of-mouth via consumer-opinion platforms: What motivates consumers to articulate themselves on the internet? *Journal of interactive marketing*, 18(1):38–52, 2004.

[20] S. Hill, F. Provost, and C. Volinsky. Network-based marketing: Identifying likely adopters via consumer networks. *Statistical Science*, pages 256–276, 2006.

[21] O. Hinz, B. Skiera, C. Barrot, and J. U. Becker. Seeding strategies for viral marketing: an empirical comparison. *Journal of Marketing*, 75(6):55–71, 2011.

[22] O. Hinz and M. Spann. The impact of information diffusion on bidding behavior in secret reserve price auctions. *Information Systems Research*, 19(3):351–368, 2008.

[23] J. Y. Ho and M. Dempsey. Viral marketing: Motivations to forward online content. *Journal of Business Research*, 63(9):1000–1006, 2010.

[24] O. R. Holsti. *Content analysis for the social sciences and humanities.* Addison-Wesley Reading, MA, 1969.

[25] A. Java, X. Song, T. Finin, and B. Tseng. Why we twitter: understanding microblogging usage and communities. In *Proceedings of the 9th WebKDD and 1st SNA-KDD 2007 workshop on Web mining and social network analysis*, pages 56–65. ACM, 2007.

[26] Z. Katona, P. P. Zubcsek, and M. Sarvary. Network effects and personal influences: The diffusion of an online social network. *Journal of Marketing Research*, 48(3):425–443, 2011.

[27] D. Kempe, J. Kleinberg, and É. Tardos. Maximizing the spread of influence through a social network. In *Proceedings of the ninth ACM SIGKDD international conference on Knowledge discovery and data mining*, pages 137–146. ACM, 2003.

[28] P. Kennedy. *A guide to econometrics.* MIT press, 2003.

[29] J. G. Lee, S. Moon, and K. Salamatian. An approach to model and predict the popularity of online contents with explanatory factors. In *Web Intelligence and Intelligent Agent Technology (WI-IAT), 2010 IEEE/WIC/ACM International Conference on*, volume 1, pages 623–630. IEEE, 2010.

[30] K. Lerman and R. Ghosh. Information contagion: An empirical study of the spread of news on digg and twitter social networks. *ICWSM*, 10:90–97, 2010.

[31] K. Lerman and T. Hogg. Using a model of social dynamics to predict popularity of news. In *Proceedings of the 19th international conference on World wide web*, pages 621–630. ACM, 2010.

[32] J. Leskovec, L. Backstrom, and J. Kleinberg. Meme-tracking and the dynamics of the news cycle. In *Proceedings of the 15th ACM SIGKDD international conference on Knowledge discovery and data mining*, pages 497–506. ACM, 2009.

[33] J. Leskovec, M. McGlohon, C. Faloutsos, N. S. Glance, and M. Hurst. Patterns of cascading behavior in large blog graphs. In *SDM*, volume 7, pages 551–556. SIAM, 2007.

[34] R. Likert. A technique for the measurement of attitudes. *Archives of psychology*, 1932.

[35] T. Mazzarol, J. C. Sweeney, and G. N. Soutar. Conceptualizing word-of-mouth activity, triggers and conditions: an exploratory study. *European Journal of Marketing*, 41(11/12):1475–1494, 2007.

[36] J. E. Phelps, R. Lewis, L. Mobilio, D. Perry, and N. Raman. Viral marketing or electronic word-of-mouth advertising: Examining consumer responses and motivations to pass along email. *Journal of advertising research*, 44(4):333–348, 2004.

[37] M. Richardson and P. Domingos. Mining knowledge-sharing sites for viral marketing. In *Proceedings of the eighth ACM SIGKDD international conference on Knowledge discovery and data mining*, pages 61–70. ACM, 2002.

[38] E. M. Rogers. *Diffusion of innovations.* Simon and Schuster, 2010.

[39] S. Rosen and A. Tesser. Fear of negative evaluation and the reluctance to transmit bad news. *Journal of Communication*, 22(2):124–141, 1972.

[40] B. Ryan and N. C. Gross. The diffusion of hybrid seed corn in two iowa communities. *Rural sociology*, 8(1):15–24, 1943.

[41] B. Schiller, I. Heimbach, T. Strufe, and O. Hinz. Development of social network usage in germany since 2012. Technical report, Technische UniversitÄd't Darmstadt, 2014.

[42] C. Schulze, L. Schöler, and B. Skiera. Not all fun and games: Viral marketing for utilitarian products. *Journal of Marketing*, 78(1):1–19, 2014.

[43] A. T. Stephen and D. R. Lehmann. Why do people transmit word-of-mouth? the effects of recipient and relationship characteristics on transmission behaviors. Technical report, working paper, Columbia University, 2009.

[44] T. Strufe. Profile popularity in a business-oriented online social network. In *Proceedings of the 3rd Workshop on Social Network Systems*, page 2. ACM, 2010.

[45] G. Szabo and B. A. Huberman. Predicting the popularity of online content. *Communications of the ACM*, 53(8):80–88, 2010.

[46] M. Thelwall, K. Buckley, G. Paltoglou, D. Cai, and A. Kappas. Sentiment strength detection in short informal text. *Journal of the American Society for Information Science and Technology*, 61(12):2544–2558, 2010.

[47] M. Trusov, A. V. Bodapati, and R. E. Bucklin. Determining influential users in internet social networks. *Journal of Marketing Research*, 47(4):643–658, 2010.

[48] Y. Tsfati, O. Meyers, and Y. Peri. What is good journalism? comparing israeli public and journalists' perspectives. *Journalism*, 7(2):152–173, 2006.

[49] F. Wu and B. A. Huberman. Novelty and collective attention. *Proceedings of the National Academy of Sciences*, 104(45):17599–17601, 2007.

[50] J. Yang and J. Leskovec. Patterns of temporal variation in online media. In *Proceedings of the fourth ACM international conference on Web search and data mining*, pages 177–186. ACM, 2011.

A Dynamical Model of Twitter Activity Profiles

Hoai Nguyen Huynh[*]
1. Institute of High
Performance Computing
Agency for Science
Technology and Research,
Singapore
2. Complexity Institute
Nanyang Technological
University, Singapore
huynhhn@ihpc.a-
star.edu.sg

Erika Fille Legara[†]
Institute of High Performance
Computing
Agency for Science
Technology and Research,
Singapore
legaraeft@ihpc.a-
star.edu.sg

Christopher Monterola[‡]
Institute of High Performance
Computing
Agency for Science
Technology and Research,
Singapore
monterolac@ihpc.a-
star.edu.sg

ABSTRACT

The advent of the era of Big Data has allowed many researchers to dig into various socio-technical systems, including social media platforms. In particular, these systems have provided them with certain verifiable means to look into certain aspects of human behavior. In this work, we are specifically interested in the behavior of individuals on social media platforms—how they handle the information they get, and how they share it. We look into Twitter to understand the dynamics behind the users' posting activities—tweets and retweets—zooming in on topics that peaked in popularity. Three mechanisms are considered: endogenous stimuli, exogenous stimuli, and a mechanism that dictates the decay of interest of the population in a topic. We propose a model involving two parameters $\eta^\star$ and λ describing the tweeting behaviour of users, which allow us to reconstruct the findings of Lehmann *et al.* (2012) on the temporal profiles of popular Twitter hashtags. With this model, we are able to accurately reproduce the temporal profile of user engagements on Twitter. Furthermore, we introduce an alternative in classifying the collective activities on the socio-technical system based on the model.

Categories and Subject Descriptors

J.2 [**Computer Applications**]: Physical Sciences and Engineering; J.4 [**Computer Applications**]: Social and Behavioral Sciences; I.6 [**Computing Methodologies**]: Simulation and Modeling

---

[*]https://sites.google.com/site/nelive/

[†]http://www.erikalegara.net/

[‡]http://www.chrismonterola.net/

HT '15, September 1–4, 2015, Guzelyurt, Northern Cyprus.
© 2015 ACM. ISBN 978-1-4503-3395-5/15/09 ...$15.00.
DOI: http://dx.doi.org/10.1145/2700171.2791029.

Keywords

Social networks; information diffusion; modelling

1. INTRODUCTION

The study of information diffusion from gossip spreading [15, 16], to the propagation of viral memes [20, 23, 10], fads, and trends [24, 2, 22], and even word-of-mouth marketing [8, 13] has become increasingly interesting especially in this era of "Big Data." Current technologies and methods have allowed researchers to look more closely into the social network fabric—the medium at which the proliferation of various entities takes place. Questions relating to how fast information travels or what kind of information captures the most audience have piqued the interest of many researchers [3, 25, 17, 11, 5]. Various approaches have been implemented to shed light into these. Researchers have looked into the role of a network's degree of connectivity, modularity, and various centrality measures, among other things [25, 17, 11, 5]. Efforts have also been put in understanding the degree of social "influence" of entities on each other [19, 9, 6]. Many have also investigated the nature of topics that are being diffused in a social system.

In this work, we propose a model that aims to capture the various aspects of these approaches—we do not only look at the network structure in isolation, but also augment it with particulars on the nature of the information being spread, and the individuals' tendencies to spread such information or "inject" new ones. Particularly, we investigate the observations described in [14] on the dynamical classes of collective attention in Twitter where they defined four groups depending on the temporal features of their popularity dynamics. We initially introduce two free parameters intrinsic to the users' behaviours, λ and $\eta^\star$, where λ quantifies the rate of decay at which a user would spread a given information and $\eta^\star$ is the threshold an agent has that determines whether or not he/she propagates information from the users he/she follows. The rules defined are then implemented in an empirical Twitter network obtained from the Stanford Large Network Dataset Collection [18].

This paper is structured as follows: we first describe the data and model in Sec. 2, then present the results and discussions in Sec. 3, and finally summarise and establish our conclusions in Sec. 4.

2. DATA AND THE MODEL

2.1 Data

The dataset utilised here is a set of 115 hashtags used by Lehmann *et al.* in [14]. It contains the time series of number of tweets and distinct users for each of the hashtags. Each time series centers around a day on which the number of relevant tweets attain their maximum "popularity," and spans from seven days before to seven days after the day of the peak. The full data collected in [14] contain 130 million Twitter messages appearing in the period of approximately 6 months from November 20, 2008 to May 27, 2009. We point the readers to reference [14] for further details on the dataset utilised here for model fitting and verification.[1]

2.2 The model

2.2.1 Definitions and rules

The model is defined on a general network $\mathcal{N}$ with N nodes, each node representing a *user*. Each user i has F_i "*followers*" and L_i "*leaders*" whom he/she follows. This leader-follower relationship results to a directed network. It is also worth noting that although the Twitter network structure is dynamically changing in the real-world, here we only consider a static structure given the relatively short time frame we are considering, which is two weeks. Note that when a user i follows another user j, the follower sees all the tweets that j posts; if, on the other hand, user i visits the profile page of j, i will not only see the tweets, but also the retweets and replies that user j posts.

Three mechanisms are incorporated in our model. Two of which, exogenous and endogenous, define the manner at which information is propagated in the system [14, 7]. The endogenous process involves a re-posting of someone else's tweet ("*retweet*"), thereby propagating/diffusing the same tweet across the social network. On the other hand, when new information is "injected" in the social network system, an exogenous process is said to have taken place. In addition to these two mechanisms, a third one is regarded as well that accounts for the decay of the level of the activities involving a specific topic on Twitter. To encapsulate, our model incorporates these three processes: (1) injection of new information into the network, (2) spreading of information in the network, and (3) decay of information after a peak.

The key features of the model proposed are quantified in two parameters $\eta^\star$ and λ—characterising the spreading of information and the decay of activities in the network, respectively. The parameter $\eta^\star$ quantifies the *threshold of influence* of leaders on their followers, determining whether or not a follower would take action such as retweeting and/or replying to a tweet, consequently exposing his/her own followers to the information. In other words, $\eta^\star$ encapsulate the level of contagion of a piece of information in the network. On the other hand, the parameter λ quantifies the *rate of decay of interest* of a user in the information after a certain point in time. It could be seen that, in our model, the build-up in activities before a topic's peak in popularity is solely reflected by the parameter $\eta^\star$, while the decay in activities after the peak is the interplay between the two parameters $\eta^\star$ and λ.

To make the model results comparable with the data we have at hand, we use the scale of one day as one time unit. The rules and flowchart of implementation of the model are described in Fig. 1. The model is updated sequentially, *i.e.* the state of a user i at time t only depends on the state of the network *before* time t but not at time t.

2.2.2 Assumptions

The model constructed makes the following assumptions on the tendency of a user to tweet and retweet. A user posts an original[2] tweet if he/she is exposed to some new information outside of his/her Twitter network, *i.e.* from external sources (or has some original ideas to share). A user who follows a lot of other users tends to rely solely on his/her social network for information and, hence, retweets more often than "injects" new information from external sources. On the contrary, a user who has a huge following tends to be more active in posting original ideas or new tweets rather than just reposting others'. These assumptions on tendencies are illustrated in Fig. 2.

Let us consider a user i ($i = 1, 2, \ldots, N$) who follows L_i leaders $l(i, j)$ ($j = 1, 2 \ldots, L_i$) and who has F_i followers. The probability that user i is exposed to external sources is

$$\rho_i(t) = A_i \chi(t - t_0),\qquad(1)$$

in which A_i represents the activeness of i in following news and propagating to other people, and $\chi(t - t_0)$ the coverage by the media. In general, the temporal profile of external media coverage satisfies the limiting conditions

$$\begin{cases} 1 \geq \chi(x) \geq 0 \ \forall x \\ \chi(0) = 1 \\ \lim_{|x| \to \infty} \chi(x) = 0 \end{cases}\qquad(2)$$

We, however, assume that within a narrow window of time around the event, the media coverage is consistent and stays approximately constant so that $\chi(x \sim 0) \approx 1$. By the assumption described above, the activeness A_i takes the form

$$A_i = \frac{F_i}{F_{max}} \times \left(1 - \frac{L_i}{L_{max} + F_i}\right)\qquad(3)$$

to reflect the assumption that a user having more followers tends to be active in following news and can introduce interesting stuff, but that is offset by having many leaders—as in such case, the user tends to rely on the leaders for information rather than tweeting so himself/herself as illustrated in Fig. 2(a) (see, for example, [12]).

Upon external exposure, the probability of a user i to tweet T_i depends on: (1) the interest of user σ_i in the nature of the information or the particular topic under consideration, (2) the level of interest $\tau_i(t - t_0)$ as a function of time, and (3) his *hesitancy* to tweet H_i.

$$T_i = \sigma_i \tau_i(t - t_0) - H_i.\qquad(4)$$

The level of interest $\tau_i(t - t_0)$ is high during and before the event, and decays with rate λ after the event

$$\tau(x) = \begin{cases} 1 & \text{if } x \leq 0 \\ \exp(-\lambda x) & \text{if } x > 0 \end{cases}.\qquad(5)$$

---

[1]This is an aggregated dataset containing the daily number of tweets for each hastag and was generously provided by Bruno Gonçalves, see Acknowledgement.

[2]"Original" in this sense is used in a loose fashion. It only means that the post is not a *retweet*.

for every time step:

    for each user of the network:

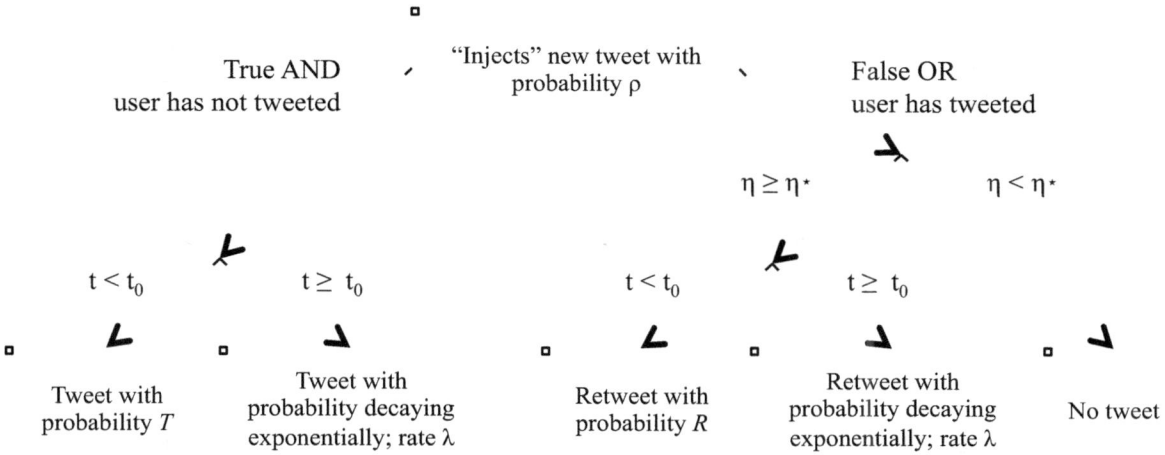

True AND
user has not tweeted

"Injects" new tweet with probability ρ

False OR
user has tweeted

$\eta \geq \eta^\star$ $\eta < \eta^\star$

$t < t_0$ $t \geq t_0$ $t < t_0$ $t \geq t_0$

Tweet with probability T

Tweet with probability decaying exponentially; rate λ

Retweet with probability R

Retweet with probability decaying exponentially; rate λ

No tweet

Figure 1: **Rules of the model proposed in this work.** t_0 is the day of the peak and η is the amount of activities by the user's leaders accumulated after his last tweet.

The hesitancy to tweet (also retweet) depends on the number of leaders and followers a user has as illustrated in Fig. 2(b). The less leaders or followers a user has, the more hesitant he is to retweet because of the lack of engagement and/or motivation to do so. Hence,

$$H_i = \frac{1}{L_i + F_i + 1}. \qquad (6)$$

Here, we also assume that $\sigma = 1$ indicating that we only focus on the topics that are of interest to the users.

Next, we define the average influence of all leaders of a user i as

$$I_i = \frac{1}{L_i} \sum_{j=1}^{L_i} F_{l(i,j)}, \qquad (7)$$

in which $F_{l(i,j)}$ is the number of followers that the leader $l(i,j)$ has.

In addition, we quantify the amount of exposure user i has to the influence of his/her leaders in the following equation:

$$Y_i(t) = \sum_{\substack{\text{all leaders} \\ l(i,j) \text{ having} \\ \text{tweeted} \\ \text{recently} \\ \text{before } t}} F_{l(i,j)}. \qquad (8)$$

And the necessary condition for retweeting is

$$Y_i \geq \eta^\star I_i. \qquad (9)$$

Upon this condition is met, the user i retweets with probability

$$R_i(t - t_0) = \sigma_i \tau_i(t - t_0) - H_i, \qquad (10)$$

which takes the same form as Eq. (4) in which H_i represents the hesitancy as described in Eq. (6).

The number of leaders who tweeted recently, *i.e.* after the user's last tweet and before current time t, is denoted as $\eta_i(t)$. The total number of possible retweets by user i at time t is given by

$$\nu_i(t) = \sqrt{\frac{\eta_i(t)}{\eta^\star} \times \frac{Y_i}{\eta^\star I_i}}, \qquad (11)$$

in which we only take the integer part and take 0 as 1 because the number of retweets is at least 1 if the user retweets.

If the user retweets, it does not necessarily mean that he would retweet all n tweets. The probability to retweet R means that he tweets at least one tweet. Therefore, it could be calculated that each of his n possible retweets carries probability $r = 1 - \sqrt[n]{1 - R}$.

By identifying the two key parameters λ and $\eta^\star$, we can expect to observe four different types of users' behaviour in response to an event, as illustrated in Fig. 3. The four types correspond to four quadrants in the $(\lambda, \eta^\star)$ parameter space, namely lowly contagious-slow decaying, lowly contagious-fast decaying, highly contagious-slow decaying and highly contagious-fast decaying.

3. RESULTS AND DISCUSSIONS

The empirical network we use for simulation was obtained from Stanford Large Network Dataset Collection [18]. The entire network is a combination of $1,000$ ego networks with $81,306$ nodes and $1,768,149$ links, a diameter of 7, and a clustering coefficient of 0.5653. We run the simulation starting from δt days before a topic peaks in popularity t_0 (we also refer to this one as "event") until 7 days after t_0. δt can vary from 0 to 7, mimicking the fact that the amount of activities related to an event becomes significant up to δt days before the event. $\delta t = 0$ corresponds to sudden events while a large value of δt indicates an anticipated one. It is noteworthy that by varying δt, we effectively include a third parameter in our model, which characterises the injection of information into the network.

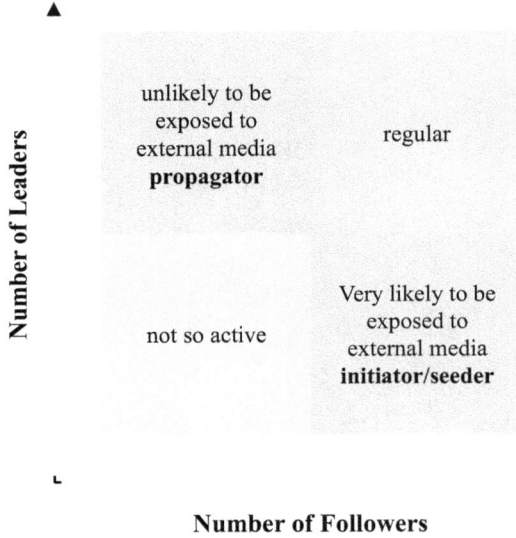

(a) Tweeting behaviour of different types of Twitter users based on their number of leaders and followers. Each type corresponds to the likelihood of being exposed to external media.

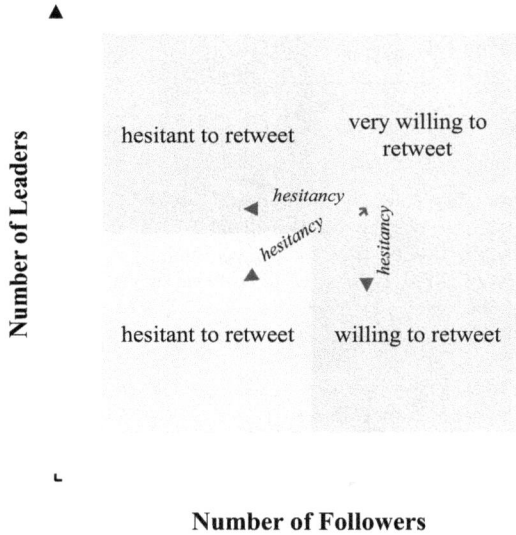

(b) Retweeting hesitancy of different types of Twitter users based on their number of leaders and followers. The arrows indicate the directions of increasing hesitancy, *i.e.* when the number of leaders or followers decreases.

Figure 2: Behaviour patterns of different types of users according to their number followers and leaders.

We then scan the $(\lambda, \eta^\star)$ parameter space in the steps of $\Delta\lambda = 0.1$ ($\lambda \in [0; 4]$) and $\Delta\eta^\star = 1$ ($\eta^\star \in [1; 60]$) to produce different time series for the number of tweets as well as the number of (distinct) users everyday and identify the ones that reproduce the empirical observations by using the distance metric introduced below. Since this is a Monte-Carlo simulation that involve generation of random numbers, we perform 50 runs with distinct seeds for the random number

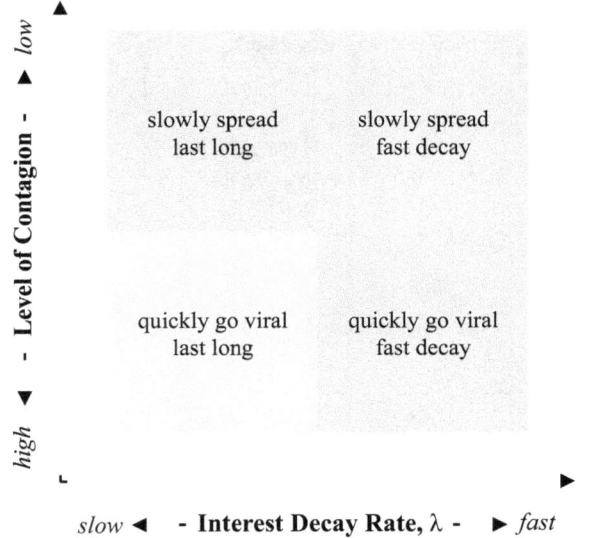

Figure 3: Distribution of different types of event in the $(\lambda, \eta^\star)$ parameter space.

generator for each set-up, *i.e.* the triplet $(\delta t, \eta^\star, \lambda)$, and take the average results.

3.1 Validation of the model

We compare the data generated by our model to the empirical data by calculating the matching score of the two profiles which are quantified by the fraction of users or tweets on a single day. In details, let $\boldsymbol{P} = (P_1, P_2, \ldots, P_N)$ be the profile of the tweets produced by our model, *i.e.* P_i is the fraction of tweets on day t_i within the entire period from t_1 to t_N. By definition, we have

$$\sum_{i=1}^{i=N} P_i = 1. \tag{12}$$

Similarly, $\boldsymbol{Q} = (Q_1, Q_2, \ldots, Q_N)$ is the corresponding profile of the tweets in the data collected by [14].

We compare $\boldsymbol{P}$ and $\boldsymbol{Q}$ by introducing the metric

$$\delta(\boldsymbol{P}, \boldsymbol{Q}) = \frac{1}{N}\sqrt{\sum_{i=1}^{i=N}\left(\frac{P_i - Q_i}{\max{(P_i, Q_i)}}\right)^2}, \tag{13}$$

which quantifies the (normalised) "distance" between the two profiles. It is obvious that when the two profiles are identical $\boldsymbol{P} \equiv \boldsymbol{Q}$, *i.e.* $P_i = Q_i \ \forall i = 1, 2, \ldots, N$, the distance is $\delta(\boldsymbol{P}, \boldsymbol{Q}) = 0$. This is a normalised measure so that the maximum possible value of δ is 1.

In Eq. (13), when $P_i = Q_i = 0$, the term $\left(\frac{P_i - Q_i}{\max{(P_i, Q_i)}}\right)^2$ does not have any contribution to δ. Finally, we set a tolerance threshold $\theta = 0.04$ such that all the terms with $P_i + Q_i \leq \theta$ do not have any contribution to δ.

Using the metric introduced above and after visually verifying the plots (Fig. 4), we consider measures with $\delta(\boldsymbol{P}, \boldsymbol{Q}) \leq 0.08$ good and discard the rest. Of the 115 hashtags, about 80% (88/115) result to good fits—both for the number of users and number of retweets. The remaining 20% fall into

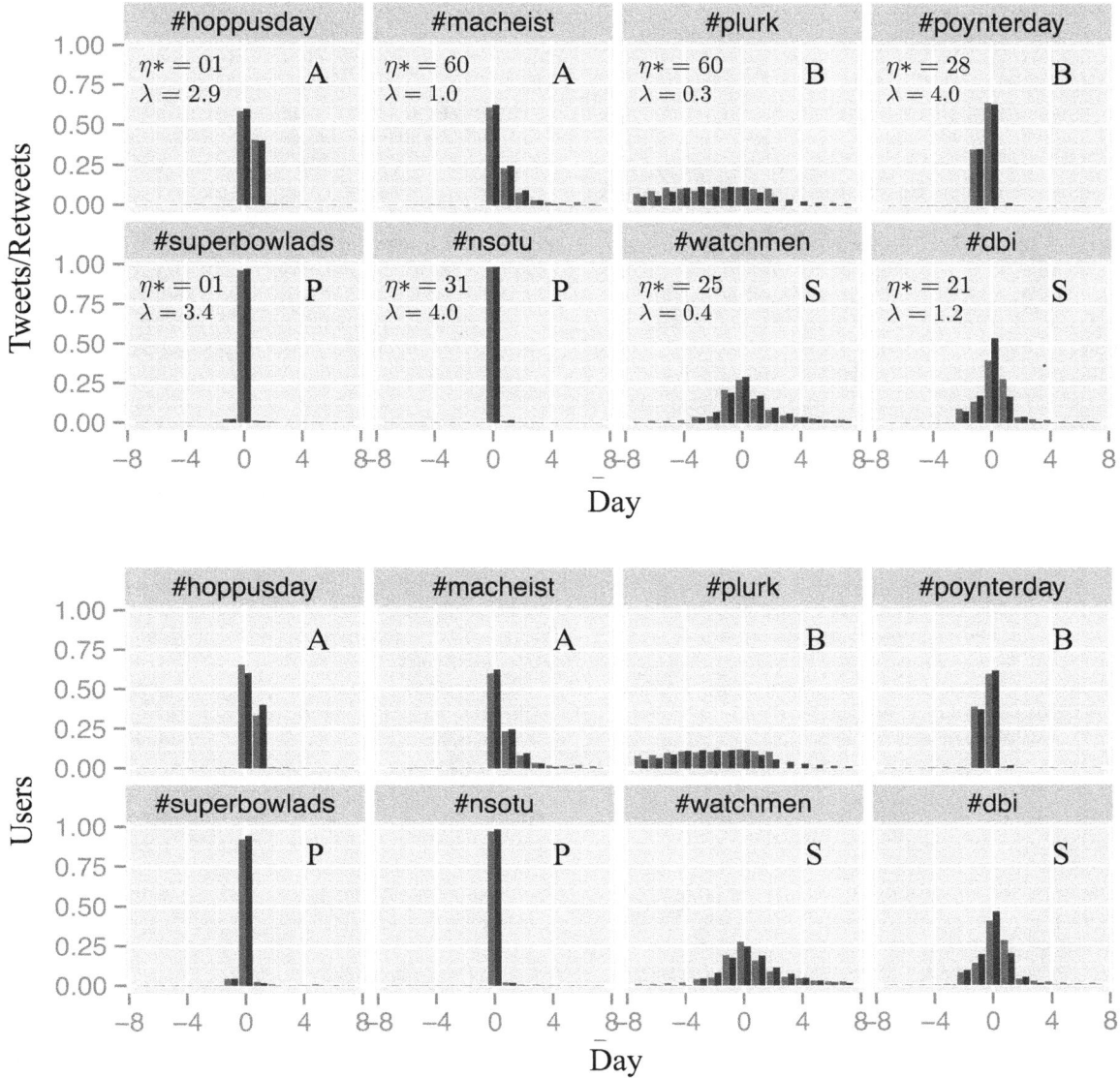

Figure 4: Time series of activities (top) and users (bottom). Results from the model (blue) shown together with the data (red) presented in [14] for classes A, B, P, and S, respectively.

the groups of activities distributed before and symmetric around the peak day [14], which have significant amounts of activities distributed prior to the events. This demonstrates that the proposed model, in spite of it being capable of capturing the main features in the collective attention build-up and decay of users before and after the event day, requires additional framework that would quantify the "sense of time" of the users—whether or not an event is approaching [1]. This aspect will be investigated and reported elsewhere.

It is worth noting that while it is not straightforward to know how many times a user would tweet or retweet in a day, we have shown that our assumptions in Sec. 2.2.2 for the users' activities work well in estimating both the number of users and retweets in most cases. Moreover, the fact that we could reproduce the temporal profiles of activities (see

Fig. 4) using our model with only two user-intrinsic parameters and an effective third parameter for external factors, justifies and validates our assumptions and hypotheses in identifying the key mechanisms of information spreading in social networks.

3.2 Classification of hashtag types

With the estimated parameter values, we generate the plot for the distribution of the hashtags on the two-dimensional parameter space of η^* and λ, as shown in Fig. 5. From the plot, we can observe the clustering pattern corresponding to different types of event shown in Fig. 3, with only a few outliers. It is quite evident that there is a clustering of large points at the bottom left corner of the plot, which correspond to the events that quickly go viral and last long.

Those events appear many days before the peak and generate significant amount of activities afterward. The other three clusters contain small points signifying the events start not so long before their peak of activities.

As illustrated by the colors of the data points in Fig. 5, we can also observe that the distribution of the points correspond very well to the classification of dynamical classes reported in [14], *i.e.* the points for each of the four classes can be segregated into distinct clusters (with exception of a few points in class of activities concentrating before the peak, see below). The four classes are called A, B, P and S, respectively, in this work for convenience of the discussion. Class A describes events where the associated activities are concentrated after a topic peaks in popularity. Class B, on the other hand, refers to the events where the activities occur before the peaks. Class P consists of events where the activities are concentrated on a single day. Finally, Class S contains events that have significant activites before, on and after the peak day. Our results show that the clusters described above also reveal the existence of subclasses within each of the classes. In Fig. 5, we can generally identify 7 clusters of data points (or hashtags) which show very good correspondence to the classification in [14].

From the fittings, we can observe two subgroups in the class with activities concentrating after the peak, *i.e.* class A (after). One group shows long range behaviours in which the activities span over a long period of time reflected by slow decay of interest (small λ) but high spreading threshold (large $\eta^\star$). The other group shows short range behaviours in which the activities span over a very short period of time reflected by low spreading threshold (small $\eta^\star$) but very fast decay of interest (large λ).

For the class with activities concentrating before the peak, *i.e.* class B (before), we also observe two subgroups. One group shows long range behaviours in which the activities span over a long period of time reflected by long appearance before the peak but high spreading threshold (large $\eta^\star$). The other group shows short range behaviours in which the activities span over a very short period of time reflected by very short appearance before the peak but very low spreading threshold (small $\eta^\star$).

For the class with activities concentrating at the peak, *i.e.* class P (peak), the values of the parameters suggest two subgroups, both of which have very fast decay of interest (large λ). One group shows contagious behaviours in which the events appear very shortly before the peak but generate a lot of activities due to low spreading threshold (small $\eta^\star$). The other group shows inert behaviours due to very high spreading threshold (large $\eta^\star$).

The class with activities distributed symmetrically around the peak, *i.e.* class S (symmetric), generally has low spreading threshold (small $\eta^\star$) and slow decay of interest (small λ).

In Fig. 4, we show the different profiles for each of the classes described above.

3.3 Content analysis

After revealing the existence of the classes and subclasses of the hashtags, we turn to looking at content of each hashtag and learn how it is related to the apparent classification. In Appendix A, we have a table showing the hashtags together with their corresponding type and class (and subclass, according to our results above). The table is organised in such a way that the top rows contain the "simple" hashtag types, in the sense that the hashtags of those types generally belong to one class identified by our model. The rows further down at the bottom of the table contain more complicated hashtag types whose tweets fall into different classes.

From the table, it could be seen that hashtags in the categories of activism (#ie6, #pman) or technology (#safari, #safari4, #skype) indicate events that capture attention in a long period of time and make impact that keep people discussing. These events are called for attention on a particular matter, *e.g.* campaign or of great interest and impact to many people, *e.g.* technology products. The peak in these events are usually associated with a symbolised or iconic activities on that day, *e.g.* rally of people in a place or release of a product. The hashtags in the category of charity (#twestival, #protest) indicate events that generate activities before a peak but soon decay after that. This is because these events usually call for people's support to achieve a certain goal (*e.g.* fund raising, signature collection). And once the goal has been achieved, people are no longer interested in the follow-up. The hashtags in the category of marketing generally exhibit sudden appearance. That could be explained by the strategies of marketers releasing incentives to advertise their products. But our results show that it also depends on the type of product and how it is advertised to determine the dynamical behaviours of people's attention to it.

The hashtags in other categories generally spread across different classes with no easy way of relating the content to the class. Nevertheless, content type like the Twitter (word) games spontaneously started by some user(s), which appear in all of the classes and subclasses identified in the work, could provide a very useful set-up to study what type of content would become popular in a social setting [4, 21]. Further analysis of the meaning of the hashtags and the content of the tweet messages containing the hashtags will be explored and reported elsewhere.

3.4 Discussions

The classification of hashtags allows us to identify their general features in terms of how people react to the information they receive and also possibly infer their content. Overall, class S (symmetric) occupies the bottom left quadrant of the parameter space $(\lambda, \eta^\star)$. In this quadrant, the threshold $\eta^\star$ is low and the rate of decay λ is also low. They correspond to events that can easily spread (due to low threshold) and can last after a topic peaks in popularity (low rate of decay), *e.g.* movie (#watchmen), technology release (#safari, #skype) or activism (#pman). Our model in this study can reconstruct the data very well up to $\delta = 4$ days before the peak but generally falls through beyond that. This suggests a different pattern in people's behaviour when spreading the information when the "sense of time" is relevant, *i.e.* before and near the event associated with the information.

On the other hand, class P (peak) occupies the right half of the parameter space, which corresponds to events that decay very quickly after the peak. They can further be categorised into two groups: the upper one (high threshold $\eta^\star$) corresponds to events that capture immediate attention but decay immediately, *e.g.* unexpected and unpopular political events (#spectrial, #nsotu) or occasional media events (#grammys, #oscars); and the lower one (low threshold $\eta^\star$) corresponds to the events that spread very quickly (it ap-

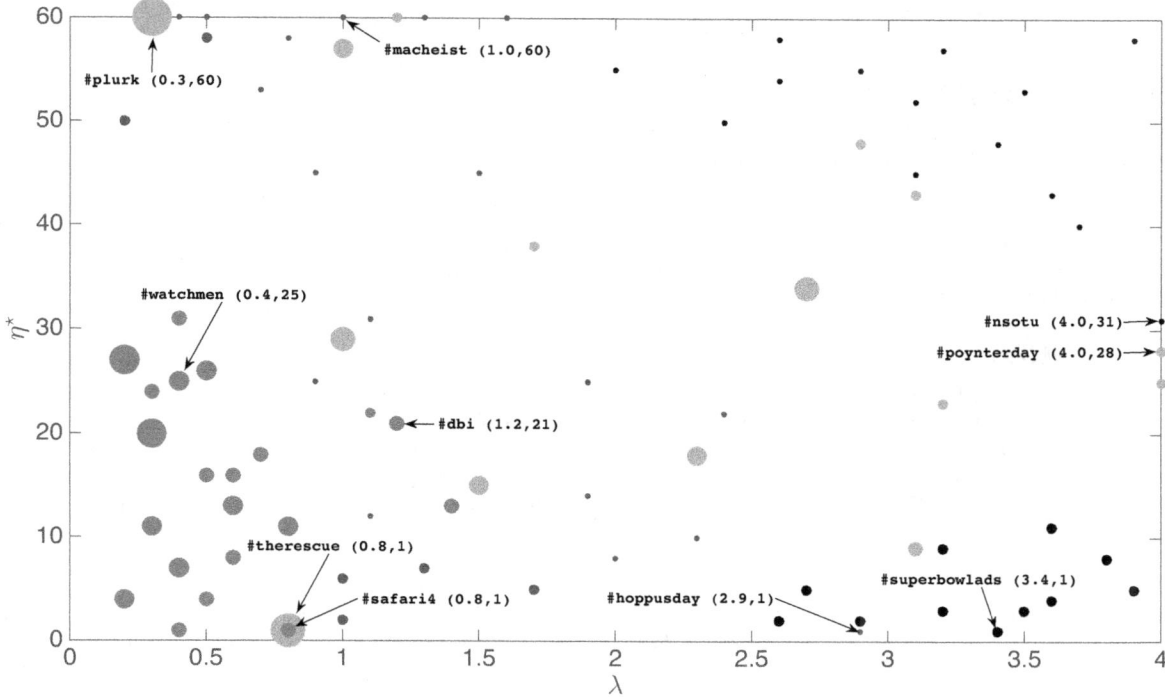

Figure 5: Fitted parameters η^* and λ showing clustering patterns. The circles of larger size correspond to large value of δt. The colours (online) of the data points are determined by the classed identified in [14], red for S, black for P, blue for A and green for B.

pears one or two days before the peak) and also decay very quickly, *e.g.* sport events (#nfl, #superbowl). The remaining two classes A (after) and B (before) can both be divided into two groups: (1) low threshold, high decay rate; (2) high threshold, low decay rate. The difference between them is the time the users become aware of the events. Events in class A are sudden and people continue to discuss them due to either low decay rate (long last), *e.g.* lobbying marketing campaign (#macheist), or low threshold (easy to spread), *e.g.* honouring popular stars (#hoppusday). Events in class B depict anticipation where people already discuss the topics even before their popularities peak—this contributes to large amounts of activities before the peak, *e.g.* new feature of Twitter (#plurk) or anticipated show (#poynterday). The events in this class, however, display scattered pattern and in some rare cases make overlap with class S (#therescue).

It needs to be emphasised that the model proposed is straightforward and concise—carrying the heuristic and intuitive assumptions on the online behaviours of users, given the knowledge of their social network's structure. Yet, the model produces the dynamical behaviours observed in real data and allows us to gain insights on the clustering of topics—telling us about the different natures of the contents being circulated in the social media, and how these clusters relate to the classes presented in [14]. This signifies that the three mechanisms included in the model are essential and sufficient in accurately describing the dynamics behind the collection attention of users on a Twitter network.

Knowing the relevant factors that influence the dynamics behind information spreading and trend setting is crucial for various aspects of society which can range from governance to politics, and marketing. Everyday, we are overwhelmed with terabytes of information originating from various social media sources as people share news, comments, opinions, and updates in their blogs, microblogs, and homepages; and on Facebook, Twitter, and Instagram, among others. The key for the stakeholders is to know how to manipulate and strategize, if possible, their messages and campaigns such that theirs will stand out to attract attention and not get lost in the vast sea of online information.

What we have presented herewith so far is a model that recaptures the previous trends for certain issues and topics by describing certain attributes of the agents involved in the social network. The next important question is whether or not we can use this knowledge to reshape the trend profiles of the different information types. Our work hints on the importance of knowing the kind of audience on which a product, an idea, or a campaign has possible influence. That aspect to some extent is quantified in our model as the parameters λ and $\eta*$.

4. CONCLUSIONS

In this work, we proposed a model using three mechanisms that underlie the tweeting and retweeting behaviours of users on Twitter. These behaviours correspond to perceiving and propagating information in a social network. Despite the simplicity of the model, we are able to capture the general patterns of behaviours observed in real data. In particular, we have not only illustrated the four dynamical classes reported by Lehman *et al.* [14] but also demonstrated the existence of further subclasses in three of the classes.

5. ACKNOWLEDGMENTS

We would like to acknowledge Bruno Gonçalves and Yang Bo for meaningful and useful discussions. We thank Bruno for sharing with us the aggregated dataset for use in this study. HNH thanks Chew Lock Yue at the NTU Complexity Institute for his support. This research supported by Singapore A*STAR SERC "Complex Systems" Research Programme grant 1224504056.

6. REFERENCES

[1] V. Alfi, G. Parisi, and L. Pietronero. Conference registration: how people react to a deadline. *NATURE PHYSICS*, 3(11):746, NOV 2007.

[2] Y. Altshuler, W. Pan, and A. Pentland. Trends Prediction Using Social Diffusion Models. In *Social Computing Behavioral - Cultural Modeling and Prediction*, pages 97–104. Springer Science+Business Media, 2012.

[3] S. Asur, B. A. Huberman, G. Szabo, and C. Wang. Trends in social media: Persistence and decay. In *5th International Conference on Weblogs and Social Media*, page 434, 2011.

[4] C. Castillo, M. El-Haddad, J. Pfeffer, and M. Stempeck. Characterizing the life cycle of online news stories using social media reactions. In *Proceedings of the 17th ACM Conference on Computer Supported Cooperative Work & Social Computing*, CSCW '14, pages 211–223, New York, NY, USA, 2014. ACM.

[5] K. Chung, Y. Baek, D. Kim, M. Ha, and H. Jeong. Generalized epidemic process on modular networks. *Physical Review E*, 89(5), may 2014.

[6] D. Cosley, D. P. Huttenlocher, J. M. Kleinberg, X. Lan, and S. Suri. Sequential influence models in social networks. In W. W. Cohen and S. Gosling, editors, *ICWSM*. The AAAI Press, 2010.

[7] R. Crane and D. Sornette. Robust dynamic classes revealed by measuring the response function of a social system. *PNAS*, 105(41):15649–15653, October 2008.

[8] J. Goldenberg, B. Libai, and E. Muller. Talk of the network: A complex systems look at the underlying process of word-of-mouth. *Marketing Letters*, 12(3):211–223, 2001.

[9] M. Granovetter. Threshold Models of Collective Behavior. *American Journal of Sociology*, 83(6):1420, may 1978.

[10] N. O. Hodas and K. Lerman. The simple rules of social contagion. *Scientific Reports*, 4:4343, 2014.

[11] Y. Ikeda, T. Hasegawa, and K. Nemoto. Cascade dynamics on clustered network. *J. Phys.: Conf. Ser.*, 221:012005, apr 2010.

[12] H. Kwak, C. Lee, H. Park, and S. Moon. What is twitter, a social network or a news media? In *Proceedings of the 19th International Conference on World Wide Web*, WWW '10, pages 591–600, New York, NY, USA, 2010. ACM.

[13] E. F. Legara, C. Monterola, D. E. Juanico, M. Litong-Palima, and C. Saloma. Earning potential in multilevel marketing enterprises. *Physica A: Statistical Mechanics and its Applications*, 387(19-20):4889–4895, aug 2008.

[14] J. Lehmann, B. Gonçalves, J. J. Ramasco, and C. Cattuto. Dynamical classes of collective attention in twitter. In *Proceedings of the 21st International Conference on World Wide Web*, WWW '12, pages 251–260, 2012.

[15] P. Lind, L. da Silva, J. Andrade, and H. Herrmann. Spreading gossip in social networks. *Physical Review E*, 76(3), sep 2007.

[16] P. G. Lind, L. R. da Silva, J. S. Andrade, and H. J. Herrmann. The spread of gossip in American schools. *Europhys. Lett.*, 78(6):68005, jun 2007.

[17] A. Louni and K. P. Subbalakshmi. Diffusion of Information in Social Networks. In *Intelligent Systems Reference Library*, pages 1–22. Springer Science+Business Media, 2014.

[18] J. McAuley and J. Leskovec. Learning to Discover Social Circles in Ego Networks. In *Proceedings of the 2012 Neural Information Processing Systems Conference*, 2012.

[19] S. Myers, C. Zhu, and J. Leskovec. Information diffusion and external influence on networks. In *Proceedings of the 18th ACM SIGKDD International Conference on Knowledge Discovery and Data Mining*, KDD '12, pages 33–41, New York, NY, USA, 2012. ACM.

[20] J. Ratkiewicz, M. Conover, M. Meiss, B. Gonçalves, S. Patil, A. Flammini, and F. Menczer. Truthy. In *Proceedings of the 20th international conference companion on World wide web*, WWW '11. ACM Press, 2011.

[21] A. Rudat and J. Buder. Making retweeting social: The influence of content and context information on sharing news in twitter. *Computers in Human Behavior*, 46(0):75–84, 2015.

[22] Y. Sano, K. Yamada, H. Watanabe, H. Takayasu, and M. Takayasu. Empirical analysis of collective human behavior for extraordinary events in the blogosphere. *Phys. Rev. E*, 87:012805, Jan 2013.

[23] L. Shifman and M. Thelwall. Assessing global diffusion with web memetics: The spread and evolution of a popular joke. *Journal of the American Society for Information Science and Technology*, 60(12):2567–2576, dec 2009.

[24] T. Tassier. A model of fads fashions, and group formation. *Complexity*, 9(5):51–61, 2004.

[25] L. Weng, J. Ratkiewicz, N. Perra, B. Gonçalves, C. Castillo, F. Bonchi, R. Schifanella, F. Menczer, and A. Flammini. The role of information diffusion in the evolution of social networks. In *Proceedings of the 19th ACM SIGKDD international conference on Knowledge discovery and data mining - KDD '13*. ACM Press, 2013.

APPENDIX

A. HASHTAG TYPE *vs.* ITS CLASS

The 88 hashtags used in this study. They belong to 13 types of event. Full description of the meaning of the hashtags could be found in [14].

Class →	A		B		P		S
Hashtag type ↓	High $\eta^\star$	Low $\eta^\star$	High $\eta^\star$	Low $\eta^\star$	High $\eta^\star$	Low $\eta^\star$	Low $\eta^\star$
Activism (2)							#ie6 #pman
Technology (3)							#safari #safari4 #skype
Charity (2)			#twestival #protest				
Sport (6)			#masters			#superbowlads #nfl #superads09 #nfldraft #superbowl	
Honour (3)		#hoppusday		#poynterday #asot400			
Holiday (3)		#aprilfools	#easter				#happy09
Convention (10)		#rp09 #mix09 #leweb	#macworld				#w2e #ces #ces09 #drupalcon #cebit #25c3
Awareness (3)		#earthday		#earthhour #therescue		#horadoplaneta	
Marketing (5)	#glmagic #free #macheist	#skittles			#evernote		
Media (9)	#bsg #bachelor	#americanidol #starwarsday #phish			#grammys #oscars #oscar		#watchmen
Political (10)		#g20		#rncchair #teaparty	#spectrial #nsotu	#budget	#inaug09 #davos #coalition #hadopi
Disruption (14)	#amazonfail #peace #swineflu #bushfires	#googmayharm #winneden			#gfail #gmail #schiphol #blackout	#snowmageddon #mikeyy	#h1n1 #influenza
Twitter (17)	#yourtag #blogger #socialmedia	#unfollowfriday	#tweepme #firstfollow #plurk	#iloveyou #myfirstjob	#nerdpickup #oscarwildeday #3hotwords #oneword	#crapnames #followme	#dbi #politics

The Role of Structural Information for Designing Navigational User Interfaces

Dimitar Dimitrov
GESIS
Cologne, Germany
dimitar.dimitrov@gesis.org

Philipp Singer
GESIS
Cologne, Germany
philipp.singer@gesis.org

Denis Helic
Graz University of Technology
Graz, Austria
dhelic@tugraz.at

Markus Strohmaier
GESIS and University of
Koblenz-Landau
Cologne, Germany
strohmaier@uni-
koblenz.de

ABSTRACT

Today, a variety of user interfaces exists for navigating information spaces, including, for example, tag clouds, breadcrumbs, subcategories and others. However, such navigational user interfaces are only useful to the extent that they expose the underlying topology—or network structure—of the information space. Yet, little is known about which topological clues should be integrated in navigational user interfaces. In detail, the aim of this paper is to identify what kind of and how much topological information needs to be included in user interfaces to facilitate efficient navigation. We model navigation as a variation of a decentralized search process with partial information and study its sensitivity to the quality and amount of the structural information used for navigation. We experiment with two strategies for node selection (quality of structural information provided to the user) and different amount of information (amount of structural information provided to the user). Our experiments on four datasets from different domains show that efficient navigation depends on the kind of structural information utilized. Additionally, node properties differ in their quality for augmenting navigation and intelligent pre-selection of which nodes to present in the interface to the user can improve navigational efficiency. This suggests that only a limited amount of high quality structural information needs to be exposed through the navigational user interface.

Categories and Subject Descriptors: H.5.3 [**Information Interfaces and Presentation**]: Group and Organization Interfaces—*Web-based interaction* H.5.4 [**Information Interfaces and Presentation**]: Hypertext/ Hypermedia—*Navigation*

Keywords: Navigation; Decentralized Search; Structure; Networks; User Interfaces

HT '15, September 1–4, 2015, Guzelyurt, Northern Cyprus.
© 2015 ACM. ISBN 978-1-4503-3395-5/15/09 ...$15.00.
DOI: http://dx.doi.org/10.1145/2700171.2791025.

1. INTRODUCTION

With the increasing amount of information made available to people on the Web every day, it has become increasingly difficult to build information systems that can be navigated in an efficient way. Information systems that deliver strong intuition about the choices made available to their users through the interfaces are efficient at guiding the user to the needed piece of information. Thus, they are considered good at supporting activities such as *navigation* or *browsing*. In order to improve navigability, new interfaces—e.g., tag clouds, breadcrumbs, subcategories—have been introduced. In Figure 1, we see an example of a tag cloud. Besides other aspects of tag cloud design [27], tag clouds—as well as all other kinds of user interfaces—are only useful for augmenting navigation to the extent to which they are able to expose the underlying structure of the information space [10]. Yet, little is known about what kind of and how many topological clues should be integrated in navigational user interfaces.

Problem. Consequently, in this paper, we want to study the problem of properly exposing the topological structure of the information space through an interface. This problem has two dimensions: (i) Which are the important structural properties that contribute to properly exposing the hidden structure of the information space and (ii) how much should we know about them in order to navigate efficiently? Knowing which nodes in a network are important and how to identify them is crucial for navigation. Such knowledge could reduce the amount and nature of information needed for improving the users' understanding about the information space resulting in better navigational efficiency. Subsequently, we next derive and discuss the two main research questions that we want to tackle in this article.

Research questions. (i) What kind of and (ii) how much structural information is needed for efficient navigation? Regarding the first research question, we are specifically interested in deriving important structural properties of the information space that should be exposed through an interface in order to properly guide users' navigation. Related work [2] has suggested that the degree—as a proxy of a node's popularity—is a very good navigational feature in networks with a power law degree distribution. Yet, little is known about the effect of the clustering coefficient as a navigational feature on the efficiency of navigation. The clustering coefficient may be feasible as navigational feature due to its importance for the emergence of the small world property of a network. Small world networks are

Figure 1: **A tag cloud enabling navigation from The Rolling Stones page on last.fm.** Exemplary user interface used for navigation in many online information systems. The tag clouds among other web interfaces are useful to the extent that they expose the underlying structure of the information space. Identifying the most important tags *from a navigational perspective* is crucial for providing efficient support.

known to be particularly navigable[18, 31]. In this paper, we investigate whether nodes with a specific clustering coefficient have an impact on navigation and we study how the clustering coefficient can be used to identify them. Furthermore, regarding the second research question, we are interested in determining the amount of structural information needed for navigation and if this depends on the quality of the structural information.

Approach and methods. We approach the research questions by analyzing the structural properties of four different networks. Initially, we take a look at their shortest path distance, degree and clustering coefficient distributions, and classify them by their expected navigability according to [4]. To model navigation, we use the message-passing algorithm *decentralized search* which is inspired by the small world experiment by Stanley Milgram [22]. Several versions of the algorithm can be found in literature [21, 18, 19, 30, 2, 1]. Decentralized search has already been demonstrated to be useful for modeling navigation in information networks [13]. For studying which and how much information is needed for efficiently navigating a network, we utilize an adaption of the algorithm which we call *partially informed* decentralized search. The partially informed decentralized search models a user who is limited in her exposure to the structure of the information space and thus, has just a weak or limited understanding of the topology of the information space. We study two strategies for selecting important nodes with regard to their popularity and clustering coefficient. With both strategies, the algorithm navigates by popularity. With simulations, we compare the partially informed decentralized search with the random search and the fully informed decentralized search. In our setting, random search corresponds to a user who is clicking at random and has no intuition. We also make a comparison between the two strategies for node selection to test the importance of the exposure of the user to the underlying structure of the information.

Findings and contributions. The most prominent finding is the surprisingly small amount of structural information needed for efficient navigation and the supportive properties of the clustering coefficient for identifying nodes important for navigation. By and large, our findings suggest that only a limited amount of high quality structural information needs to be exposed through the navigational user interface. Additionally, we empirically demonstrate the sensitivity of decentralized search as a navigational model on the kind of structural information utilized. The navigational performance of decentralized search appears to depend on the amount of high quality structural information provided.

Structure. The rest of this paper is organized as follows. After discussing related work in Section 2, we present an adaptation of

decentralized search and two strategies for selecting nodes with high structural importance used in the experimental setup in Section 3. In Section 4, we give detailed overview of the used datasets. In Section 5, we present our results and formulate our findings. Next, Section 6 discusses the findings and their implications for the design of navigational user interfaces. Finally, we conclude the paper and provide some directions for future work in Section 7.

2. RELATED WORK

The decentralized search algorithm is inspired by research conducted in the 1970s by Stanley Milgram who studied the structure of the American society and conducted the famous *small world experiment* [22]. For this experiment, Milgram asked randomly selected people from Nebraska to forward a packet to a stock broker in Boston. If participants did not know the target personally, they were asked to forward the packet to personal contact that they thought might know the target better. These persons then should repeat this process. Even though there were quite some restrictions, the experiment showed that the average chain length of letter trails that reached the target was around six.

Motivated by this small world experiment, researchers [21, 18, 19, 30, 2, 1] have developed the so-called *decentralized search algorithm* that tries to find a path between a *start node* and a *target node* in a network by passing a message from a node to one of its immediate neighbors also called *candidate nodes*. What information is available and how it is used for selecting one of the candidate nodes is decisive for the success of the search. For a detailed description of the decentralized search algorithm, please refer to Section 3.1. Next, we delve into related work and discuss navigation using homophily (Section 2.1), navigation using popularity (Section 2.2), models for user navigation (Section 2.3) and the role of clustering for navigation (Section 2.4).

2.1 Navigation Using Homophily

There are different models based on node similarity or homophily for generating small world networks in which decentralized search is very effective. The two main models are *grid-based* and *hierarchy-based*. The first *grid-based model* was proposed by Watts and Strogatz in [31]. This model places nodes on a two-dimensional grid in a way that nodes with high similarity have small grid distance. In order to assure the emergence of the small world property, the model puts long links between the nodes that are similar, but still locally far away on the grid. This model was improved by Kleinberg in [19, 18] where he concentrated on the length of the long links. He showed that efficient search is only possible for certain values of the clustering exponent of the model which is responsible for placing the long link connections between the nodes.

The *hierarchical model* was proposed independently by Kleinberg [20] and by Watts et al. [30]; these models are also generative. In hierarchical models, similar nodes are placed near to each other in a hierarchy. The probability of two nodes being connected in the hierarchical model not only decreases with their hierarchical distance but also it decreases exponentially. Another generative model was proposed by Boguñá et al. in [4] where they assumed that nodes form a *hidden metric space*. The topology of the metric space determines the distance between the nodes in the metric space and models the probability of a link between them in the generated network. The model also possesses a parameter that is responsible for the clustering in the network. This clustering parameter, like the clustering exponent in Kleinberg's grid model, is also responsible for expressing the homophily of the nodes in the network. The main limitation of these models is the global information about the node's position on the grid or in the hierarchy.

2.2 Navigation Using Popularity

Since estimating similarity between nodes is not easy, Adamic et al. [2] concentrated on the degree of nodes. They proposed an algorithm for efficient search in power law networks which makes use of the power law degree distribution to support the node selection. The algorithm keeps track of a node's identity and uses information about the node's degree and the node's neighbors' degree. The biggest difference to the models elaborated in Section 2.1 is the absence of global information about the target node and its position in the network. Adamic et al. showed that degree-based navigation works fairly well in power law degree distributed networks in comparison to Poisson degree distributed networks. Additionally, in power law degree distributed networks, random walks tend to select high degree nodes and achieve good results in those kinds of networks.

2.3 Model for User Navigation

Decentralized search has a long tradition as a model for user navigation in different types of networks. In [13], Helic et al. showed that decentralized search can be used to model user navigation in information networks. The differences and the similarities between the click traces produced by decentralized search with hierarchical background knowledge and actual user navigation were studied by Trattner et al. [29]. Research on the navigational efficiency of different types (broad and narrow) of hierarchical background knowledge conducted by the authors showed that both types are useful. However, broader hierarchies performed better under the limitations introduced by the user interface [11].

2.4 The Role of Clustering

In [31], Watts and Strogatz used the characteristic path length and the clustering coefficient to define the class of navigable networks. The characteristic path length is the averaged shortest path length over all nodes in the network. The clustering coefficient can be interpreted as the probability of a link to exist between two randomly picked neighbors of a node [23]. In a network $G = (V, E)$, where V is a set of nodes and E is a set of edges, $E \subseteq V \times V$. Let $N(u)$ be the neighborhood of the node u and d_u the degree of the node u. The local clustering coefficient $C(u)$ is then defined as the fraction of pairs of neighbors of the node u that are themselves neighbors:

$$C(u) = \frac{|e_{vw} \in E : v, w \in N(u)|}{d_u(d_u - 1)/2}. \tag{1}$$

An alternative definition of the class of navigable networks was given by Boguñá et al. [4] who showed how the navigability of a network depends on its degree distribution and its clustering coefficient. In the models described in Section 2.1 and Section 2.2, the clustering exponent plays an important role for the emergence of the small world networks and it is crucial for navigation.

In [16, 17], the authors studied the impact of the clustering exponent on the navigability of a network, i.e., they showed for different network sizes how the change of the clustering exponent affects the effectivity and the efficiency of four different decentralized search versions. In the next Section 3, we will present an adaptation of decentralized search—partially informed decentralized search—and we will use the degree distribution and clustering coefficient of the networks to identify the nodes for which the partially informed decentralized search will be able to make an informed decision.

3. METHODOLOGY

Decentralized search is an established model for navigation. Our goal is to estimate the amount and type of structural information that allows efficient navigation. To this end, we extend the decentralized search algorithm in a way that allows us to simulate navigation with limited amount and different kinds of structural information. By doing so, we can tackle the research questions posed in Section 1. Next, we describe (partially informed) decentralized search in Section 3.1 before we discuss strategies for node selection in Section 3.2 and conduct our experiments in Section 3.3.

3.1 Decentralized Search

In Figure 2, we see an example of both a *fully informed* as well as a *partially informed decentralized search* in a network. The goal is to find the path between node 1 (purple) and node 33 (yellow). The fully informed version of decentralized search uses the degree information as shown in the first row of the table presented in Figure 2 and navigates greedy by degree. Let I be an *informed set* of nodes for which the algorithm can take an informed decision regarding the degree of the candidate nodes. In the case of fully informed search $I = V$, this means that the algorithm possesses the degree information about all nodes in the network. This allows it to rank all candidate nodes by their degree and to select the node with the highest degree. The green arrows show how navigation proceeds for this version of the algorithm. The red arrows show a path produced by the partially informed version of decentralized search. In this version, we only have a fraction of the popularity information as shown in the second row of the table in Figure 2 and the informed set I is a proper subset of V. The partially informed decentralized search ranks the nodes by their degree and selects the node with the highest one only if the set of candidate nodes C contains nodes whose popularity value is available in $I \cap C \neq \emptyset$; otherwise, it picks one node at random. In both versions of the algorithm, we avoid already visited nodes and we terminate the search if the target node is in the set of candidate nodes. For completeness, Figure 2 also highlights an example path of an *uninformed random walker* (blue arrows) that simply picks adjacent nodes at random for navigating.

With the partially informed version of decentralized search, we can estimate the amount of information really needed for navigation in a network. By varying the fraction of the nodes where the popularity is available, we can derive the sensitivity of the algorithm to the amount of popularity information. Thus, this allows us to study our research questions at interest regarding what kind of and how much structural information is necessary for efficient navigation.

Using the methodological concepts explained, we conduct our experiments in Section 3.3. We focus on using the degree of the candidate nodes to model the popularity of nodes. Degree corre-

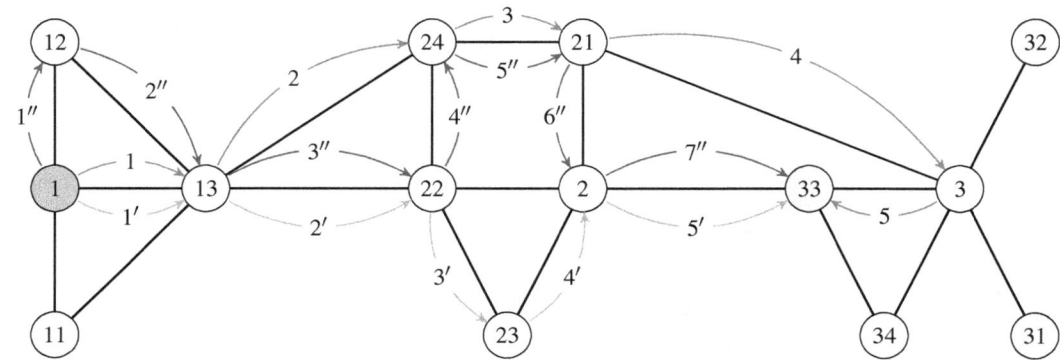

Popularity/Node	1	11	12	13	2	21	22	23	24	3	31	32	33	34
Degree (fully informed, $I = V$)	3	2	2	5	4	3	4	2	3	5	1	1	3	2
Degree (partially informed, $I \subset V$)	-	-	-	5	-	-	-	-	3	5	-	-	-	-

Figure 2: **Different versions of decentralized search.** *Green:* The arrows show the path produced by a *fully informed decentralized search.* *Red:* The arrows show the path produced by a *partially informed decentralized search.* *Blue:* The arrows represent the path produced by a *uninformed random walker.* The table shows the information provided to the algorithm for selecting the next step. The first row of the bottom table contains the popularity scores of all nodes $I = V$ provided to the fully informed decentralized search and the second row contains only a small portion of all popularity scores $I \subset V$. Fully informed and partially informed decentralized search apply greedy neighbor selection. The partially informed search selects a random node when no information is available. Although finding the shortest path between the nodes 1 (purple node) and 33 (yellow node) is possible with both versions of decentralized search, in general this is not the case because the algorithm can take an informed decision only on the local level.

sponds to the number of links attached to the node [23] and it is a local metric:

$$d_u = \sum_{v \in V} a_{uv} \qquad (2)$$

Thus, when we speak about fully and partially informed decentralized search, we speak about fully and partially informed on a local level. If the algorithm was informed on the global level—in other words, if we possessed the adjacency matrix A of the network G—we would be able to calculate the shortest path, which is highly unlikely for real user navigation in large information networks on the web.

3.2 Strategies for Node Selection

In the following, we define two strategies for selecting structurally important nodes: the popularity strategy and the clustering strategy. The nodes selected by these two strategies are elements of the informed set of nodes for which the partially informed decentralized search is going to possess the information about their popularity (i.e., degree) in the network. With these strategies, we can study how the kind of structural information affects navigation.

Popularity Strategy. We sort the nodes by popularity in descending order and take just the top k% of the sorted list. For these nodes, the algorithm will make an informed decision regarding the popularity of the nodes. The idea behind the popularity strategy for node selection is the same as the idea to navigate by popularity, namely highly popular nodes are very well connected. Selecting a highly popular node increases the probability of finding the target node under the nodes' neighbors.

Clustering Strategy. We sort the nodes by clustering coefficient in ascending order and take just the top k% of the sorted list. For these nodes, we again provide the popularity value of the nodes to the algorithm. Consider that with this strategy the algorithm also navigates greedy by degree.

The rationale behind the clustering strategy for node selection is that nodes with low clustering reduce the probability of a link to exist between two random neighbors of a node. This means that selecting a node with low clustering will provide nodes where the neighbors are not connected. The absence of a link between two neighbors of a node can be interpreted in the way that the neighbors are just too different. This would imply that selecting nodes with low clustering would provide nodes whose similarity between the neighbors is very small and this would allow navigation between clusters in the network. On the other hand, low clustering means that in this network region there is a *structural hole* as defined by Burt in [5]. The absence of connections between the nodes in these regions of the network will give even a higher importance to the existing connections resulting in a higher importance of the nodes in these regions.

3.3 Evaluating Navigational Efficiency

As emphasized, we conduct experiments with two distinct strategies for selecting the node members of the informed set having also different informed set sizes. With the popularity and clustering strategy (see Section 3.2), we examine how the exposure of the structure of the information space through the interface affects the efficiency of navigation. Furthermore, with the size of the informed set, we investigate how much structural information is needed for efficient navigation.

We conduct experiments on four different networks (see Section 4): (i) Wikipedia for schools (topological link network), (ii) Facebook (ego network), Twitter (ego network) and (iv) DBLP (co-authorship network). The four datasets can be seen as representatives of popular networks in information system on the web. For each network, we generate thousand navigational missions containing of one *start node* and one *target node* chosen randomly with at least one path between them. The goal for the algorithm is to reach the target nodes. We break up the search after 20 iterations on the small networks (Wikipedia for schools and Facebook) and

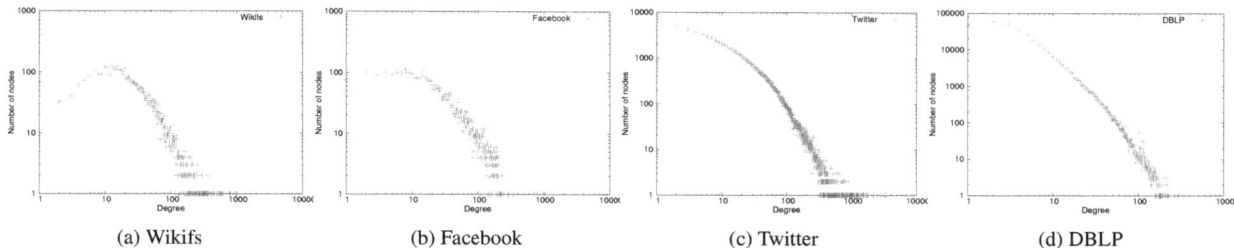

| (a) Wikifs | (b) Facebook | (c) Twitter | (d) DBLP |

Figure 3: **Degree distributions on log scaled axes.** We see that all networks have a power law like degree distributions. This implies that degree greedy navigation will be very successful. For α-values cf. Table 2.

50 iterations on the big networks (Twitter and DBLP). We conduct experiments with degree as local popularity metric.

Note that for a set of size 0% of all nodes in the network, we navigate without any structural information. With this setting, the partially informed decentralized search reduces to a uninformed random walker (cf. Figure 2) which can serve as a baseline for our experiments as it corresponds to a third (random) strategy for selecting important nodes. For a set size of 100%, we navigate with all available information. This means that the partially informed search upgrades to a fully informed decentralized search.

As we are interested in examining the impact of the amount and kind of structural information provided to the partially informed decentralized search algorithm, we also need to evaluate the efficiency of the algorithm. To that end, we focus on two metrics: the *success rate* and the *stretch*. Success rate and stretch respectively measure the effectivity and efficiency of the search. We calculate the success rate as:

$$s = \frac{|W|}{|P|} \qquad (3)$$

It is the fraction of the set of successful missions W and the set of all missions in the simulation P. The success rate measures the percentage of cases in which the algorithm was able to find the target node. Thus, the success rate measures the effectivity of the algorithm. To measure the efficiency of the algorithm, we consider the stretch defined as:

$$\tau = \frac{1}{|W|} \sum_{s,t \in W} \frac{h(s,t)}{l(s,t)}. \qquad (4)$$

Technically, the stretch is calculated by dividing the length of the path produced by the algorithms $h(s,t)$ with the length of the shortest path $l(s,t)$ between the start and the target nodes and then averaging over all nodes.

4. DATASET DESCRIPTION

In this section, we give a thorough description of the studied datasets and their structural properties. We analyze four different networks (cf. Table 1) taken from the Stanford Large Network

Dataset Collection[1]. The *Wikipedia for schools* network represents the topological hyperlink network derived from Wikipedia articles for teaching purposes referred to as Wikipedia for schools (Wikifs). The *Facebook* and *Twitter* datasets are ego-networks. Finally, the *DBLP* dataset represents a co-authorship network.

Navigability of networks. In Figure 3, we see the degree distributions of the different datasets. All networks exhibit power law like degree distributions at least for the tail. To get an initial idea of the navigability of these networks, we apply the method presented by Boguña et al. [4] who studied navigability of networks by looking at their clustering coefficients and power law exponents. In Table 2, we see that the values of the clustering coefficient of all networks are in the range defined in [4]. Additionally, we determine the power law exponent of the degree distributions with the methods presented in [6, 3]. We see that if we try to fit the power law distribution for the whole range of data points ($x_{min} = 1$), all networks are navigable according to Boguña et al. [4]. This is not the case, if we try to find the best power law fit and let the method estimate the best x_{min}. In this case, only the Facebook network is efficiently navigable.

Inequality of degree distributions. The Gini index is a metric that reviews the inequality in the degree distributions. A Gini index of zero means that the degree is equally distributed over the network, whereas a Gini index of one means that one node of the network possesses all links. In Table 3, we highlight the Gini index and the corresponding functions generating distributions with such inequality for the four datasets at hand. The corresponding generating functions support the results of the estimated first data point. We see that Wikipedia for schools, Facebook and DBLP possess Gini indices of 0.54. The inequality in the degree distribution is more explicit in the Twitter network. Inequality in the degree distribution is important for achieving good results with greedy navigation since it assures easy decision making.

---

[1]http://snap.stanford.edu/data/index.html

Table 1: **Datasets collection.** The table shows the network type and the number of nodes and edges. Two networks are directed and two undirected. For each network type there is a small and a big network regarding the nodes and the edges.

Name	Type	Nodes	Edges
Wikifs	directed	4,604	119,882
Facebook	undirected	4,039	88,234
Twitter	directed	81,306	1,768,149
DBLP	undirected	317,080	1,049,866

Table 2: **Small world classification of the datasets.** Depending on the point from where we try to fit the power law in the distribution (from the first data point or x_{min} estimated automatically), we see that either all of the networks are efficiently navigable (the clustering coefficient C and the power law exponent α are in the range defined by Boguña et al. [4]) or just the Facebook network. Table 3 suggests that we have higher trust in the results of the second row where the x_{min} is placed automatically.

Network	C	α, x_{min}	SW?	α, x_{min}	SW?
Wikifs	0.27	1.25, 1	✓	3.05, 142	✗
Facebook	0.61	1.26, 1	✓	2.51, 47	✓
Twitter	0.57	1.30, 1	✓	3.27, 188	✗
DBLP	0.63	1.48, 1	✓	3.26, 29	✗

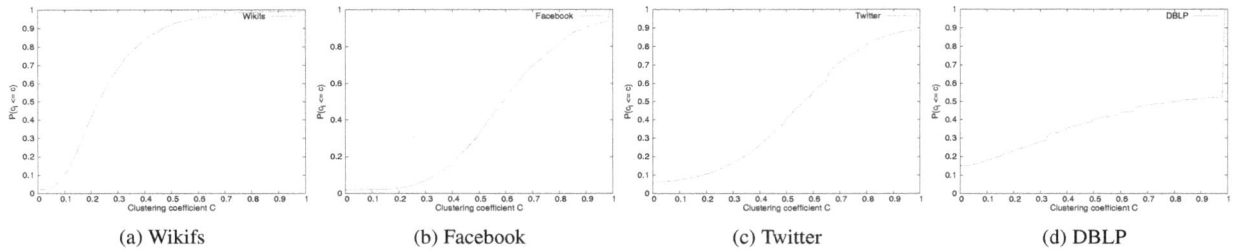

(a) Wikifs	(b) Facebook	(c) Twitter	(d) DBLP

Figure 4: **Clustering coefficient distribution.** Most nodes in Wikipedia for school have clustering around 0.2 meaning that the network has no clearly defined clusters. Facebook and Twitter exhibit similar distributions despite the different network size; there is a fraction of nodes with clustering near zero and a bigger fraction of nodes with very high clustering near one. All other nodes have clustering coefficient nearly uniformly distributed between zero and one. Very characteristic for the DBLP network is the high clustering coefficient; around half of the nodes have a clustering coefficient of around one.

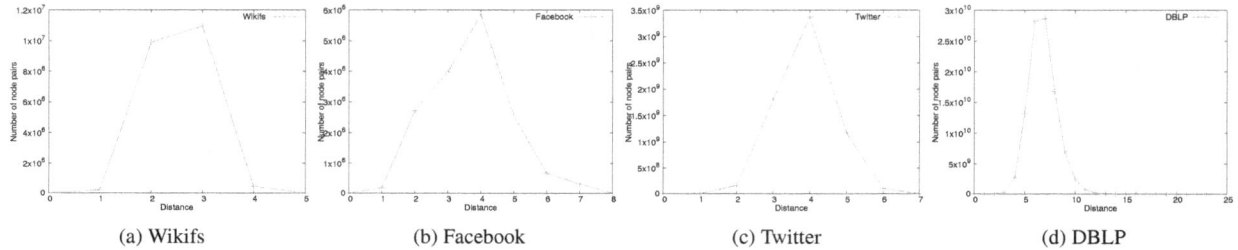

(a) Wikifs	(b) Facebook	(c) Twitter	(d) DBLP

Figure 5: **Shortest distance distributions.** Most of the node pairs in Wikipedia for schools have very short shortest paths; this makes this network very efficiently navigable. We see that the Facebook and Twitter networks have very similar distributions despite the different network size. Also, in these networks most of the node pairs have very short shortest paths. DBLP is the most difficult to navigate considering the fraction of node pairs with relatively long shortest paths.

Pareto principle. Since all networks possess power law like degree distributions, the Pareto principle suggests that we will need at least 20% of the nodes to achieve similar success rates and stretches for the networks with the popularity strategy and partially informed decentralized search as with a fully informed decentralized search. Additionally, we see that only one network is navigable according to the classification of Boguña et al.[4] (if we use higher x_{min} values), thus, we cannot necessarily expect the popularity strategy with smaller amounts of nodes to perform well in these networks. The results presented in Section 5 contradict this intuition. We believe that this is tightly related to the clustering coefficient distributions for the four networks.

Differences in clustering coefficient distributions. In Figure 4, we see that the networks possess very different profiles regarding the clustering coefficient distributions. We see that the Facebook and Twitter networks exhibit similar clustering coefficient distributions, despite the different network size. In these networks, most of the nodes have a clustering coefficient between 0.3 and 0.7. Nodes in DBLP exhibit very high clustering coefficients and most of the nodes in Wikipedia for schools have a clustering coefficient between 0.1 and 0.5. Thus, we also expect to see differences in the results produced by the clustering strategy for node selection.

Shortest path distributions. Beside the clustering coefficient and the degree distribution of a network, the shortest distance distribution is also important for the emergence of the small world property

Table 3: **Gini Index.** The table shows the Gini index of the used networks and the corresponding distribution functions.

Network	Wikifs	Facebook	Twitter	DBLP
Gini Index	0.54	0.54	0.64	0.54
$f(x)$	x^2	x^2	x^3	x^2

of a network [31] which significantly increases its navigability. The shortest distance distribution also provides insight into how difficult it generally is to navigate a network. In Figure 5, we can see the shortest distance distributions of studied networks. For the Wikipedia for schools network, we see that most of the node pairs have a shortest distance of three. The Facebook and Twitter network exhibit a bit longer shortest distance, whereas DBLP has the longest shortest distance distribution.

5. RESULTS

In the following, we provide the results of our empirical evaluation. For both node selection strategies presented in Section 3.2, the decentralized search algorithm navigates greedy by degree. The amount of information needed for efficient navigation depends on the type of the structural information used and differs in the distinct networks.

Popularity strategy results. First, the popularity strategy tries to identify important nodes based on their popularity. Figure 6 shows the success rate and stretch for this strategy in all networks. In this case, the algorithm achieves with just 1% of the nodes similar efficiency results as with 100%. For Facebook, the partially informed decentralized search achieves slightly worse results than the fully informed search already with 2% for navigation by degree and the same or even a bit better results with 25% of the nodes. For this setting, the algorithm achieves similar performance as the fully informed decentralized search for Wikipedia for schools and Twitter also already with 1% of the nodes. We see that navigation in DBLP is very difficult in general. The best results in this network are realized with 2-3%.

Clustering strategy results. The clustering strategy tries to identify structurally important nodes based on their clustering coefficient. Figure 7 shows the success rate and stretch for greedy navigation

(a) Success rate

(b) Stretch

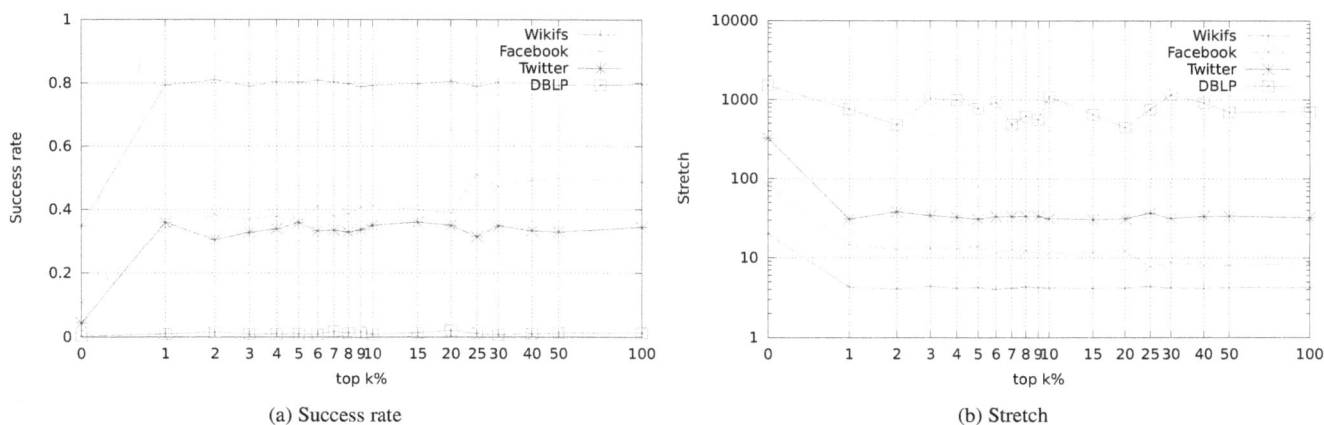

Figure 6: Success rate (s) and stretch (τ) for popularity strategy for different amount of information. *Left (a):* The success rate achieved for the popularity strategy and degree as popularity metric—the higher the better. To improve readability, we added one to all values and logarithmically scaled the x axis which shows the amount of information used. *Right (b):* The stretch achieved for the popularity strategy and degree as popularity metric—the lower the better. To improve readability, we added one to all values and scaled the axes logarithmically. We can see that we can achieve the success rate and stretch levels of fully informed search already with very small amount of information—about 1-2%. Strongly outperforming the fully informed search is not possible with this strategy.

by degree. We see that for Wikipedia for schools and Twitter the success rate initially falls with increasing amount of information, and then it jumps to the level of the fully informed search at 2% and 6% for Wikipedia for schools and Twitter, respectively. For Facebook, we observe very interesting success rate values since we are able to achieve considerably better results with less structural information. The success rate grows from 1% to 6% of the nodes to a value higher than the value achieved by the fully informed search (100%). After a drawback between 6% and 9% of the nodes, the success rate achieves even better results than for 6% with 15% of the nodes. Using more than the top 15% of the nodes worsens the success rate to the level of fully informed search. As before, we can see that navigation in DBLP is also very difficult with this strategy. The best results in this network are realized with 30% of the structural information.

Findings. Next, we summarize the results in the following two main findings answering the research questions tackled throughout this work as proposed in Section 1.

(i) What kind of structural information is needed for efficient navigation? Strongly outperforming the fully informed search with the popularity strategy is not possible. With increasing amount of information about the popularity, the success rate and the stretch improves continuously. With the clustering strategy, it is partly possible to substantially outperform the fully informed search. There is an initial drawback in success rate and stretch in all networks with the clustering strategy. After this initial drawback the success rate and the stretch increase until the levels of the fully informed search or even outperform the fully informed search.

Finding 1: Our results suggest that nodes with high popularity and low clustering are very important and can guide navigation very well and thus, should be exposed to the user through the interface.

(ii) How much structural information is needed for efficient navigation? With the popularity strategy, the levels of success rate and stretch produced by the fully informed decentralized search are achieved already with 1% of the popularity information. With the

clustering strategy, the levels of success rate and stretch produced by the fully informed search are achieved with a bit more information than with the popularity strategy, depending on the network.

Finding 2: Our results suggest that with intelligent selection of nodes based on their structural properties, we can significantly reduce the amount of information that is needed to be presented to the user in navigational interfaces without reducing the efficiency of navigation.

---

6. DISCUSSION

In Section 6.1, we start with a discussion and interpretation of our results (cf. Section 5) tailored around the research questions posed in Section 1. In Section 6.2, we discuss the implications followed by an elaboration of the advantages and limitations of our approach in Section 6.3.

6.1 Discussion and Interpretation of Results

Quality of Structural Information—Popularity vs. Clustering. Ranking the nodes by popularity and clustering is a good way to identify structurally important nodes. Furthermore, if the popularity information is combined with small amounts of clustering information which is a local metric, we can navigate even more efficiently. Nodes with high popularity and low clustering are very important and can guide navigation very well and should be exposed to the user through the interface. Knowing the important nodes on the local level regarding popularity and clustering can result in reducing the amount of nodes that need to be exposed to the user. This way we would be able to relax constraints of the screen size [12]. The initial drawback in the performance of the algorithm for this strategy can be explained by the degree distributions of the informed set of nodes. If the set is too small, there are not enough nodes with high popularity. Once the informed set has a sufficient amount of nodes for which the user has an intuition not only about the popularity but also about the clustering coefficient of the nodes, the user can navigate more confidently towards the target.

(a) Success rate

(b) Stretch

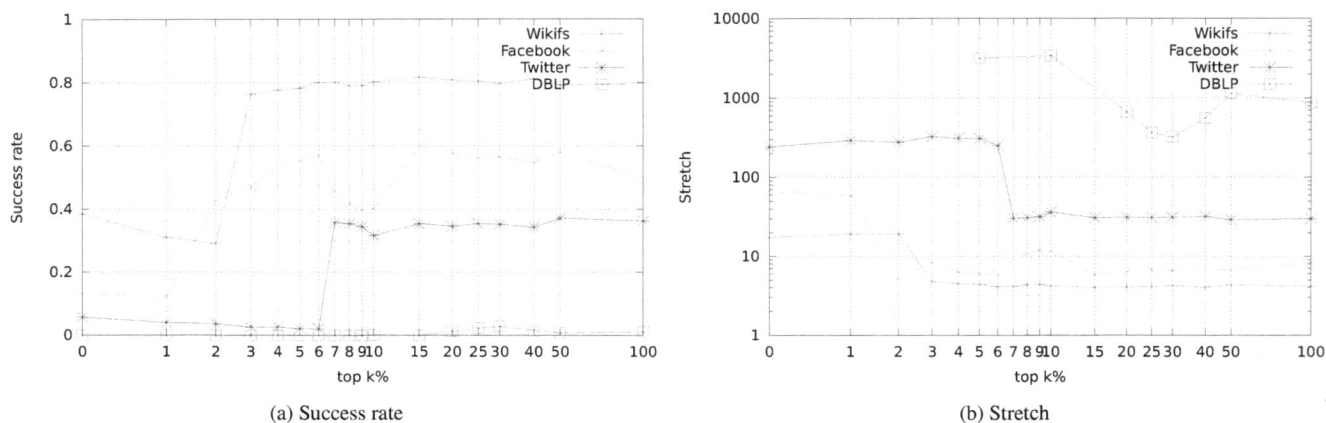

Figure 7: **Success rate** (s) **and stretch** (τ) **for clustering strategy for different amount of information.** *Left (a):* The success rate achieved for the clustering strategy and degree as popularity metric—the higher the better. To improve readability, we added one to all values and logarithmically scaled the x axis which shows the amount of information used. *Right (b):* The stretch achieved for the clustering strategy and degree as popularity metric—the lower the better. To improve readability, we added one to all values and scaled the axes logarithmically. We can see that for achieving the success rate and stretch levels of fully informed search (100%) we need slightly more information with the clustering strategy compared to the popularity strategy presented in Figure 6. Nonetheless, with this strategy, we are also able to outperform the fully informed search in some networks by only utilizing a low amount of clustering information.

Amount of Structural Information—Partially vs. Fully Informed Search. Surprisingly low amount of structural information is needed to achieve the same or even better results than with all information. This finding is really surprising if we consider the level of inequality in the degree distributions suggested by the Gini index and the exponent of the power law degree distribution (cf. Table 2 and Table 3). For the popularity strategy, outperforming the fully informed search is not possible, whereas for the clustering strategy we are able to top the results produced by the fully informed decentralized search.

6.2 Implications

Navigation in online networks is supported by smart user interfaces like tag clouds, breadcrumbs, subcategories and related categories. Normally, these navigational user interfaces make use of algorithmically preprocessed information about the content of the network. Our results have direct implications for these algorithms and for the ways data is presented to the user through the navigational interfaces.

Rethinking algorithms. Our findings suggest to reorganize the way we build hierarchies and to rethink algorithms creating hierarchies like [15, 12, 26, 7, 32]. In [12], the authors showed that the ability of hierarchies to guide navigation is significantly reduced through the restrictions introduced by the user interfaces. The main problem identified by the authors was that the top level of the hierarchies produced by the algorithms have too many subcategories—i.e., a too high *branching factor*. To tackle this problem, they adapted one of the best known algorithms for hierarchy induction proposed by Heymann and Garcia-Molina [15]. This algorithm creates a hierarchy by producing a similarity network. The hierarchy is then developed by ranking the nodes in the similarity network by popularity. Nodes are then placed in the hierarchy in a descending order of their popularity and their similarity to nodes that are already in the hierarchy. This way, nodes with high popularity are placed in the top of the hierarchy and nodes with low popularity at the bottom. Our results suggest an alternative ranking for the nodes of the similarity network. The results of the popularity strategy suggest that we should concentrate on the top 1% of the nodes in the network and try to produce a

hierarchy with a well structured top. In contrast, the order of the bottom levels of the hierarchy is not really important, since we are able to achieve the same efficiency in navigation with only 1% of the nodes. This result also suggests that even if we break the semantics in the low levels of the hierarchy, we still will be able to navigate efficiently. Hints of how we should reorganize the top levels of the hierarchy are given by the clustering strategy we presented. We can re-rank the nodes of the similarity network considering not only their popularity, but also their clustering coefficient.

Our result could also be applied to the adapted version of the algorithm by Heymann and Garcia-Molina [15] proposed by Helic and Strohmaier [12] which generates a hierarchy in two stages. First, it produces hierarchies with a given branching factor. The largest hierarchy is called the main tree and all other hierarchies are then added to the main tree. After sorting the hierarchies by size, they are attached to the main tree in a way that preserves the branching factor of the hierarchy. Here, we could again try to re-rank the most popular nodes also by their clustering and put them in the main tree as suggested by the clustering strategy.

Presentation and information scent. Our results suggest that for efficient navigation, only a very small amount of local popularity and clustering information is necessary. Thus, we can derive that for efficient navigation, the user needs to have a good intuition only about the most important nodes in the network. Exposing the nodes with high structural importance through the user interface does not ensure that the user is going to select them. If the user has no sufficient knowledge and understanding of the most important nodes, the system has to deliver the explanation and in this way strengthen the *information scent* of the user for these specific nodes [24, 25]. By providing additional information about the important nodes regarding popularity and clustering, the information system would help the user to create an intuition about the presented choices. Assuring that a user has a high understanding about the topology of the information space—high exposure to the structurally most important nodes—would allow us to reduce the actual amount of nodes that are presented to the user though the interfaces. Without such information, random navigation performs well, which is con-

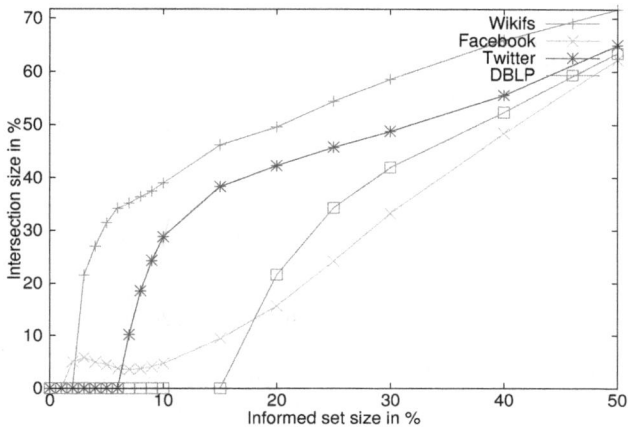

Figure 8: **Informed sets overlap.** The intersection size in percentage for the popularity and clustering strategy for the different informed sets sizes (except for 100%, $I = V$) of nodes used in the experiments in Section 3.3. For the datasets at hand, there is no big overlap in the informed sets selected by the two strategies. Additionally, with increasing set size the overlap does not necessarily increase as so the efficiency of navigation (cf. Figure 6 and Figure 7).

sistent with previous results for navigation by popularity in power law networks [2].

Helic et al. [14] studied the navigability of social tagging systems and showed that the tagging networks are power law networks. They showed that limiting the tag cloud size to practically feasible sizes (e.g., 5%,10%) does not affect the navigability. Our results suggest that we can reduce the tag cloud size even further to 1% of the nodes, according to the popularity strategy. In the same work, the authors also provided theoretical and empirical arguments against existing approaches of tag cloud construction. Possible improvements of these approaches can be achieved for instance with alternative rankings considering the clustering of the tagging network as the results of the clustering strategy presented.

6.3 Advantages and Limitations

In the following, we would like to address some limitations and advantages of our work.

Correlation between strategies. It has been shown that networks might exhibit a negative correlation between the degree and the clustering coefficient of nodes based on the formal definition of the clustering coefficient [28]. Due to this negative correlation, it is possible that there is big overlap in the informed sets created by the popularity and clustering strategy in this work. That is why it is important to quantify up to which extent the two strategies for important node selection differ in the experiments conducted in Section 3.3. In Figure 8, we illustrate the size of the intersection of the popularity and clustering strategies for all datasets for different sizes of the informed sets of nodes. Overall, we can see that the overlap of nodes between the two strategies is considerably low for smaller set sizes. Not surprisingly, with increasing set size, the overlap is generally rising as the chance of overlapping node selection increases. However, as it can be seen in Figure 6 and Figure 7, an increasing overlap does not reflect an increase in the performance of the partially informed decentralized search. By and large, these observations support the importance of the findings from Section 5 and give a confirmation that both strategies select mostly

different nodes and structurally important nodes that could support navigation.

However, there might exist some few nodes that are highly beneficial to be included in an informed set for efficient navigation. Both strategies might select them early on and as soon as they include these nodes, efficiency increases drastically. Thus, in future work, we plan on further investigating the overlaps between both strategies which might also help us to find even better (potentially smaller) informed sets that can guide navigation well.

Alternative strategies for node selection. With our experiments, we have concentrated on the degree and clustering coefficient as metrics for measuring the structural importance of nodes. Above, we have discussed the potential correlation between both strategies but have also shown that the overlap is low for small informed sets. Nonetheless, other strategies might be amendable. For example, previous work [28] has suggested an alternative way to calculate the clustering coefficient by removing the degree bias (cf. Equation 1). By utilizing this method, we might be able to further investigate the differences of both strategies for finding important nodes for navigation. Also, we could simply try to implement strategies for node selection that produce mostly distinct sets of nodes. By doing so, we might be able to further improve our approach potentially leading to even better results in terms of success rate and stretch. Nodes of the distinct sets selected by the strategies can then be exposed to the user through the navigational interfaces. Also, there exist other thinkable metrics (e.g., k-core and link irregularity) describing the structure of a network that can be applied in straightforward fashion [8, 9]. We leave these investigations open for future work.

Alternative user models. In our experiments we utilized a greedy neighbor selection if at least one of the candidate nodes is in the informed set of nodes otherwise we selected one at random. This models a user who always follows her intuition if it has one. Although this is a valid user model it is a very simple one. In future work we plan to experiment with alternative neighbor selection mechanisms that model a user who is greedy or stochastic to different extents in following her intuition [13]. Additionally, it is also thinkable to use different informed sets at different stages of the search e.g., the informed set created with the popularity strategy can be used in the beginning of the search where the user is interested in exploring the information space, whereas the informed set created with the clustering strategy can be applied in stages of the search where bridging a gap between two clusters is needed.

Global information. One limitation of the decentralized search is the amount of global information used for navigation. The models presented by Watts et al. [30], Kleinberg [18, 19] and Boguña et al. [4] make use of the global position of the target node. One could argue that partially informed decentralized search is using to much global information in the sense that it uses the information about the distribution of the degree and clustering coefficient. A way to tackle the problem would be to make a random sample of n% (i.e., 30%) of the nodes and apply the popularity and the clustering strategies only at these n% of the nodes in the network.

7. CONCLUSION

Navigational interfaces are only useful for augmenting navigation to the extent to which they are able to expose the underlying structure of the information space. In this paper, we have been interested in studying (i) which and (ii) how much structural information is necessary for properly exposing the hidden structure of the information space. To that end, we have utilized an adapted version—i.e., partially informed—of the message passing decentralized search algorithm. This adaption allows to model a user that is limited in her exposure to the structure of the information space having only limited knowledge about the topology of the information space. In detail, we have focused on two strategies for selecting important nodes based on their (i) popularity and (ii) clustering coefficient.

With simulations on four distinct datasets, we have observed that a surprisingly low amount of structural information is needed by the partially informed version of decentralized search in order to achieve the same or even better performance than the fully informed decentralized search. Besides the popularity, for choosing structurally important nodes, also the clustering coefficient has turned out to be a good indicator for this task. The clustering strategy would expose nodes of high structural importance to the user which can be used to reduce the amount of information offered to the user and relax constraints posed by the limited size of the screen. Our results have implications on the algorithms used for the structuring of the information space. These algorithms should take into account the supportive properties of the clustering coefficient for navigation.

In future work, we would like to propose and evaluate another version of decentralized search that models exploitation on the local level. In this version, we plan on combining centrality metrics as proxies for popularity and clustering information as a proxy of homophily. With this extended version, we would like to study how the clustering coefficient can be used to jump from one network region to another or to stay in the same cluster and explore it.

Acknowledgments. This work was partially funded by the DFG in the research projects "PoSTs II" and "dalraSearchNet" (SU 647/13-2) and by the FWF Austrian Science Fund research project "Navigability of Decentralized Information Networks" (P24866).

8. REFERENCES

[1] L. Adamic and E. Adar. How to search a social network. *Social Networks*, 27, 2005.

[2] L. Adamic, R. Lukose, A. Puniyani, and B. Huberman. Search in power-law networks. *Physical Review E*, 64, 2001.

[3] J. Alstott, E. Bullmore, and D. Plenz. powerlaw: A python package for analysis of heavy-tailed distributions. *PLoS ONE*, 9, 2014.

[4] M. Boguna, D. Krioukov, and K. C. Claffy. Navigability of complex networks. *Nat Phys*, 5, 2009.

[5] R. S. Burt. *Structural holes: The social structure of competition*. Harvard University Press, 2009.

[6] A. Clauset, C. R. Shalizi, and M. E. Newman. Power-law distributions in empirical data. *SIAM Review*, 51, 2009.

[7] I. Dhillon, J. Fan, and Y. Guan. *Efficient Clustering of Very Large Document Collections*. Kluwer Academic Publishers, 2001.

[8] S. N. Dorogovtsev, A. V. Goltsev, and J. F. F. Mendes. K-core organization of complex networks. *Physical Review Letters*, 96, 2006.

[9] E. Estrada. Quantifying network heterogeneity. *Physical Review E*, 82, 2010.

[10] M. A. Hearst. *Search User Interfaces*. Cambridge University Press, 2009.

[11] D. Helic, C. Körner, M. Granitzer, M. Strohmaier, and C. Trattner. Navigational efficiency of broad vs. narrow folksonomies. In *Proceedings of the Conference on Hypertext and Social Media*. ACM, 2012.

[12] D. Helic and M. Strohmaier. Building directories for social tagging systems. In *Proceedings of the International Conference on Information and Knowledge Management*. ACM, 2011.

[13] D. Helic, M. Strohmaier, M. Granitzer, and R. Scherer. Models of human navigation in information networks based on decentralized search. In *Proceedings of the Conference on Hypertext and Social Media*. ACM, 2013.

[14] D. Helic, C. Trattner, M. Strohmaier, and K. Andrews. On the navigability of social tagging systems. In *Proceedings of the International Conference on Social Computing*. IEEE, 2010.

[15] P. Heymann and H. Garcia-Molina. Collaborative creation of communal hierarchical taxonomies in social tagging systems. Technical report, 2006.

[16] W. Ke and J. Mostafa. Strong ties vs. weak ties: Studying the clustering paradox for decentralized search, 2009.

[17] W. Ke and J. Mostafa. Scalability of findability: Effective and efficient ir operations in large information networks. In *Proceedings of the International Conference on Research and Development in Information Retrieval*. ACM, 2010.

[18] J. Kleinberg. Navigation in a small world. *Nature*, 406, 2000.

[19] J. Kleinberg. The small-world phenomenon: An algorithmic perspective. In *Proceedings of the Symposium on Theory of Computing*. ACM, 2000.

[20] J. Kleinberg. Small-world phenomena and the dynamics of information. *Advances in neural information processing systems*, 1, 2002.

[21] J. Kleinberg. Complex networks and decentralized search algorithms. In *Proceedings of the International Congress of Mathematicians: invited lectures*, 2006.

[22] S. Milgram. The small world problem. *Psychology Today*, 61, 1967.

[23] M. Newman. *Networks: An Introduction*. Oxford University Press, 2010.

[24] P. Pirolli. Computational models of information scent-following in a very large browsable text collection. In *Proceedings of the Conference on Human Factors in Computing Systems*. ACM, 1997.

[25] P. Pirolli and S. Card. Information foraging. *Psychological Review*, 106, 1999.

[26] A. Plangprasopchok, K. Lerman, and L. Getoor. Growing a tree in the forest: Constructing folksonomies by integrating structured metadata. In *Proceedings of the International Conference on Knowledge Discovery and Data Mining*. ACM, 2010.

[27] C. Seifert, B. Kump, W. Kienreich, G. Granitzer, and M. Granitzer. On the beauty and usability of tag clouds. In *Proceedings of International Conference on Information Visualisation*. IEEE, 2008.

[28] S. N. Soffer and A. Vazquez. Network clustering coefficient without degree-correlation biases. *Physical Review E*, 71, 2005.

[29] C. Trattner, P. Singer, D. Helic, and M. Strohmaier. Exploring the differences and similarities between hierarchical decentralized search and human navigation in information networks. In *Proceedings of the International Conference on Knowledge Management and Knowledge Technologies*. ACM, 2012.

[30] D. Watts, P. Dodds, and M. Newman. Identity and search in social networks. *Science*, 296, 2002.

[31] D. Watts and S. Strogatz. Collective dynamics of 'small-world' networks. *Nature*, 393, 1998.

[32] S. Zhong. Efficient online spherical k-means clustering. In *Proceedings of the International Joint Conference on Neural Networks*. IEEE, 2005.

Wisdom of the Crowd or Wisdom of a Few?
An Analysis of Users' Content Generation

Ricardo Baeza-Yates
Yahoo! Labs
Barcelona, Spain
rbaeza@acm.org

Diego Saez-Trumper
Universitat Pompeu Fabra
Barcelona, Spain
dsaez-trumper@acm.org

ABSTRACT

In this paper we analyze how user generated content (UGC) is created, challenging the well known *wisdom of crowds* concept. Although it is known that user activity in most settings follow a power law, that is, few people do a lot, while most do nothing, there are few studies that characterize well this activity. In our analysis of datasets from two different social networks, Facebook and Twitter, we find that a small percentage of active users and much less of all users represent 50% of the UGC. We also analyze the dynamic behavior of the generation of this content to find that the set of most active users is quite stable in time. Moreover, we study the social graph, finding that those active users are highly connected among them. This implies that most of the wisdom comes from a few users, challenging the independence assumption needed to have a wisdom of crowds. We also address the content that is never seen by any people, which we call digital desert, that challenges the assumption that the content of every person should be taken in account in a collective decision. We also compare our results with Wikipedia data and we address the quality of UGC content using an Amazon dataset. At the end our results are not surprising, as the Web is a reflection of our own society, where economical or political power also is in the hands of minorities.

Categories and Subject Descriptors

H.2.8 [**Database Management**]: Database applications-Data mining;; J.4 [**Computer Applications**]: Social and Behavioral Sciences

General Terms

Human factors, measurement.

Keywords

Social networks; user generated content; wisdom of crowds.

HT '15, September 1–4, 2015, Guzelyurt, Northern Cyprus.
Copyright is held by the owner/author(s). Publication rights licensed to ACM.
ACM 978-1-4503-3395-5/15/09 ...$15.00.
http://dx.doi.org/10.1145/2700171.2791056.

1. INTRODUCTION

The wisdom of crowds is a well known concept of how "large groups of people are smarter than an elite few, no matter how brilliant, they are better at solving problems, fostering innovation, coming to wise decisions, and even predicting the future" [20]. On the other hand, although all people that use Internet can contribute to web content (or any type of activity), most people do not. In fact, in any social network, the set of people that just looks at the activity of others (passive users or *digital voyeurs*) is much larger than the people that is active. Similarly, among the active users most of them do little, while a few do a lot (*digital exhibitionists*). We are interested in the characterization and interplay of these groups of people regarding the generation of content.

Let us take a specific case, say the world of blogs in the Web. Most people do not have a blog and few people have good blogs. Conversely, most blogs are not read and few blogs are well read. Indeed, people contribute to content in a social network or in the Web because they have the (possibly wrong) perception that someone will look at and read their contribution. This perception that they are speaking to the whole world, when the truth is that most of the time they are speaking alone, creates a very long tail of content that nobody sees, a huge *digital desert* where people write to an empty audience, metaphorically speaking.

Although we believe that there is a high correlation between the quality of content and the activity of users interacting with that content, in this paper we explore this process: how people contributes to content and what is the impact of the content generation process in the so called wisdom of crowds. As we cannot study this in the context of the whole Web, as most usage data is private, we use two different datasets: a small sample of New Orleans Facebook users and a large one coming from a micro-blogging platform, Twitter. Both are good case studies for the problem being tackled. In fact, today Facebook and Twitter are the two largest social networks in term of users. In one of these cases we estimate a weak lower bound of how much of the UGC produced is never seen. We also compare the content generation process in these social networks to the content generation of Wikipedia as well as the estimations of unique users per month that visit that website.

Moreover, using another UGC dataset from Amazon's movies reviews, where the quality of content it is explicitly rated, we study the relation between quantity and quality of content produced by people, finding also that the majority of high-quality content is generated by a small set of users.

Our main results are:

- The percentage of users that generate more than 50% of the content is small, less than 7% in our two examples;

- These top users are quite stable in time, more than 70% of the initial people in our two examples stay on that group during all the time observed;

- The quality of content it is not strongly correlated with amount of users' activity, but;

- Given that quality of content it is (almost) equality distributed among users, more active users produces - in absolute numbers - more high quality content than less active users.

- The number of users that do not contribute to the generation of content is the majority of them, some because of inaction while others because their content is not taken in account;

- There is a significant volume of content that nobody sees, and hence is not taken in consideration; and

- The bias seems to be even worse in non social contexts such as content creation in Wikipedia, where there are also is higher amount of content that is never visited.

The reminder of this paper is organized as follows. Sections 2 and 3 give the background. Sections 4 to 6 present the experimental results and discuss them.

2. RELATED WORK

The concept of the wisdom of crowds was introduced by Francis Galton in 1907 [6], and used by James Surowiecki in his seminal book "The Wisdom of Crowds" [20], where he posits –among other things– that the aggregated knowledge of a group would be bigger than the knowledge of any of its single components. Although wisdom is difficult to measure, on the Web this concept has been translated –and widely applied– as using the data provided directly (*e.g.*, content) or indirectly (*e.g.*, clicks) by users to discover knowledge in a *crowd sourcing* approach [14, 9, 5, 8]. A good example of how this wisdom can be used, is exploiting the clicks that users do after issuing a query in a web search engine. This allows to extract semantic relations between queries in an automatic manner [1, 2, 3]. Therefore, in this example and others, more user generated content implies more knowledge that can be potentially discovered.

In Online Social Networks, wisdom can be related to the amount of content produced by users. Previous studies suggests that the amount of user's activity (*e.g.*, number of *tweets*) it is related with her/his number of followers [19], and also with the monetary value that they produce [18]. Similarly, in social graphs –where node in-degree has a power-law distribution [10, 13, 11, 7]– most of the content produced (*i.e.*, activity) is generated by a small subset of users, while the majority of users act as passive information consumers [16]. Moreover, previous studies have shown that the around 50% of URLs consumed in Twitter are produced by a tiny portion of users (less than 1%) [22]. However, while previous work shows that to have a lot of followers cannot be considered as synonym of influence [4], nowadays we do not know enough about most active users. In this paper we try to understand the importance and characteristics of most active users regarding the generation of content.

3. EXPERIMENTAL FRAMEWORK

3.1 Assumptions and Definitions

We consider that each unit of activity (tweets or posts) is *one unit of content* and that the overall activity is proportional to the wisdom of the crowd. A possible variation is to consider the length of the text of the tweet or the post. Nevertheless, as these texts are small (e.g. tweet length is capped by 140 characters), the results should be similar. Later on this paper, we discuss about the content's quality, and how it relates with the concept of wisdom.

To distinguish top contributors (*wise users* or digital exhibitionists) from the rest of the active users, we use the following arbitrary definition for a given time period: wise users are the set of most-active users such that they contribute with 50% of the content (or half of the wisdom). Other definitions are possible, for example based in a larger percentage, but we consider that 50% is already a majority of the content. Nevertheless, the results would be similar as all the distributions involved resemble power laws. We call the rest of the users, in fact, the majority of them, *others*.

3.2 Datasets

We use two different datasets from two different kind of social networks: Twitter, a micro-blogging social network; and Facebook, a pure social network. For all the experiments we consider only the active users, meaning users that have shown some posting activity in the time period considered.

Facebook: This dataset corresponds to the New Orleans Facebook's Regional Network[1] [21]. We have two lists: the first one contains the social graph (friendships) and a second list with user-to-user *wall posts* (where u,v means user v posting in u's wall), and the timestamp. All these data has been anonymized.

The social graph has 1,545,686 edges between 63,731 users. The information about *wall posts* has 876,993 actions, with 39,986 users doing at least one post (active users). Hence, we can estimate that at least 37% of users are passive or inactive. Notice that these are users that have a public profile, so although the set is partial, is what can be compared to other datasets based on public data as the next one.

This dataset has *wall posts* from 14th of September 2004 to 22th January of 2009 according to Table 1. We use the last three years as the two first are too small. The Pearson correlation of the number of posts with respect to the number of friends, using a logarithmic transformation to linearize the distributions, is 0.64. That is, the distributions are partially correlated. The distribution of posts versus users follows a power law of parameter -1.58.

Twitter: Our dataset contains almost all the tweets done in Twitter between March 1st until May 31st of 2009. We also have the complete social graph of Twitter for that period. This information is a subset of the dataset obtained in [4]. Specifically, tweets are represented as a list of pairs (user id, timestamp), and the social graph is an adjacency list.

The social graph has 1,963 millions of edges between 42 million of users (688 million edges between 12 millions of

---

[1]Regional Networks were deprecated by Facebook in August of 2009.

Time Period	#Active Users	#Posts
1 Year (2006)	73K	8K
2 Years (2006-2007)	304K	18K
3 Years (2006-2008)	448K	18K
All (2004-2009)	876K	39K

Table 1: Details of the Facebook dataset.

Time period	# Users	# Active Users	# Tweets
Month 1	28M	4.7M (16.7%)	109M
Month 2	37M	7.3M (19.7%)	164M
Month 3	42M	6.9M (16.4%)	167M
All	42M	12.1M (28.8%)	440M

Table 2: Details of the Twitter data set.

Time period	# Users	# Active Users	# Tweets
1 Week	39M	3.9M (10.0%)	48M
2 Weeks	40M	5.4M (13.5%)	95M
3 Weeks	41M	6.4M (15.6%)	141M

Table 3: First three weeks of May, cumulative, for the small Twitter dataset.

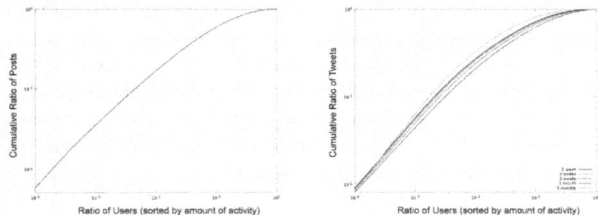

Figure 1: Cumulative distribution of user activity in Facebook (left) and Twitter for the 3 weeks dataset (right).

active users). The activity considers 440 million of tweets produced by the active users. In fact, the number of non-active users (71%) is more than 2.4 times larger than the number of active users (29%). Hence, our analysis would be more striking if we take percentages over the whole user population.

Our Twitter data has two limitations: (i) we have "only" the last 3,200 tweets from each user, but we have found only 167 of users with more tweets than this threshold in around 50 millions users;[2] and (ii) from the social graph, we cannot establish when each edge was created, therefore we are working with the final snapshot of that graph.

In order to study the UCG with different time granularity, in our experiments we use this dataset in two different ways: first, the full dataset split in months and next, a smaller sample where we split in weeks the first three weeks of May. Tables 2 and 3 gives the details of them. The distribution of tweets versus users can be approximated by a power law of parameter -2.1. On the other hand, the Pearson correlation of the number of tweets with respect to the number of followers, using again the logarithmic transformation, is 0.68. That is, the distributions are again partially correlated.

---

[2]In any case, this implies that our results are a good lower bound because we are trimming the most active users.

Group	Average in-degree		Gamma index	
	Facebook	Twitter	Facebook	Twitter
Wise	100.5	1723.5	9.7×10^{-3}	7.0×10^{-5}
Others	29.1	81.5	6.2×10^{-8}	2.4×10^{-6}
Active	34.1	112.6	3.8×10^{-4}	4.6×10^{-6}

Table 4: Average in-degree and Gamma index by group.

4. EXPERIMENTAL RESULTS

4.1 Wise and Others

We start by finding the proportional sizes of the user groups defined in the previous section. Figure 1 shows that the distribution of user activity is very skewed. For Twitter - Figure 1 (right) - where we have more data points, we show that the distribution also depends on the time window considered, as a longer time window implies that a smaller group of users produced most of the content. For three years, we found that in the Facebook dataset, the wise users were just 7.0% of the total. On the other hand, in a period of three months, we found that in the Twitter dataset the wise users accounted for just 2.4% of them.

In the case of the Twitter dataset, looking at the social graph we found that even though wise users are less than 3%, they concentrate more than the 35% of the incoming edges, therefore they have also a higher in-degree (see Table 4). On the other hand, in the Facebook dataset, 7% of the users concentrate 21% of the links. This is not surprising as the Facebook social graph is more sparse as friendship is bidirectional and both users have to accept the relation.

To measure the connectivity of each group, we use the Gamma index, that is the ratio between the links observed over all possible links in the complete graph of active users [15]. A larger Gamma Index means higher connectivity into the graph. In Twitter we see that wise are the most cohesive group. In Facebook the differences are even bigger, as wise users are five orders of magnitude more cohesive than the rest. Differences between Twitter and Facebook might be due to the different nature of the link creation process in each platform (in Facebook both parts needs to agree to create a link, while in Twitter each user can decide alone) and the type of graph. However, in both cases wise users are more cohesive than the rest, suggesting that they are a highly connected elite.

We can partially compare these results to the content generation process of Wikipedia. Indeed, according to data published by Wikipedia itself, the top 10,000 editors produce 33% of the content editions. Considering that there are almost 20.8 million registered editors, the top editors represent just 0.04% of them. As the number of passive users, that is, people that use Wikipedia but do not contribute with content, is more than one billion, the percentage of active editors with respect to the total number of users is negligible. Something similar happens with the creation of the almost 4.5 million Wikipedia articles in English, where the 2,005 most prolific authors account for the creation of 50% of the articles [17]. This is less than 0.01% of registered editors, and this number would be even smaller if non-registered users could be taken into account.

Class	Wise (%)	Total Active Users
1 year	906 (11,8%)	7663
2 years	1528 (8,7%)	17572
3 years	2591(6,8%)	38144

Table 5: Wise users per year (Facebook dataset).

Time period	Wise (%)	Active Users
1 week	231,620 (5,8%)	3,979,668
2 weeks	247,435 (4,7%)	5,362,828
3 weeks	254,616 (4,0%)	6,415,867
1 month	256,663 (3,7%)	6,943,311
3 months	294,230 (2,4%)	12,183,943

Table 6: Wise users in different time periods for the Twitter dataset.

Class	Wise from the beginning	(%)
1 year	906	100
2 years	671	74
3 years	653	72

Table 7: Users that were in the wise group in the first year and stay there (Facebook).

Time period	Wise from the beginning	(%)
1 week	231,620	100
2 weeks	203,098	87
3 weeks	192,870	83

Table 8: Users that were in the wise group in the first week and stay there (Twitter).

4.2 Evolution Along Time

Now we find the percentage of wise users for different periods of time for both datasets. Results are detailed in Tables 5 and 6. This shows that even though the percentage of wise users decreases with larger time windows, the absolute number is pretty stable. However, are those wise users always the same? Table 7 shows the percentage of users that were in the wise group in the first year and stay there in the next two years for the Facebook dataset. Table 8 shows the percentage of users that were in the wise group in the first week and stay there during the next two weeks for the small Twitter dataset. As can be seen the wise users are very stable, as more than 70% or 80% remains after three years or weeks, respectively.

In Figure 2 we show the dynamics of the wise and others groups, during three years or months for both datasets, showing the percentage of people that come from the groups in the previous month as well as the percentage of new users. The numbers displayed in the edges, represents the percentage of users going to a given group in previous/next time slot. Outgoing edges pointing to previous time slot (*e.g.* from month 2 to month 1) shows where the users come from, while edges pointing to the next time slot shows the destiny of those users. For example, in Figure 2 (b), in month 2, 66% of wise users come from the wise group in month 1, 27% from others and, 7% from *new* users (users that were not active in month 1). Next, 92% of those wise users, stay in the wise group in month 3, and 8% went to *others*. Another way to understand this, would be look at symmetric

edges. For example, in month 3, 1% of the *new* users went to wise group, while 4% percent of the total of wise users come from *new* users.

Overall, we can see that groups are quite stable if we do not consider new users. In fact, at the end of three periods, most of the *wise* users have always been in this group, for example in Figure 2 (a), 74% of *wise* users stay in that group from year 1 to year 2, and then 98% stay in that group from year 2 to year 3, confirming the stability of this group.

4.3 The Digital Desert

In this section we analyze the phenomena of the content that is uploaded for some users, but is never seen by anyone else. We refer to this content as the *digital desert*. We can estimate a lower bound for the content that is never seen for the case of the Twitter dataset.[3] In fact, a lower bound for the digital desert can be computed as the percentage of content generated by people that has no followers.[4] This percentage of people is only 0.06% for the wise group but 20.58% for the *others* group. This accounts for 0.03% and 1.08% of the whole content, respectively. Hence, the digital dessert in this dataset is at least 1.11%. Although small, this implies that the opinion of some people is not really considered and hence is not part of the collective wisdom.

The size of the digital desert increases if we look at another kind of UGC platform such as Wikipedia. Comparing the logs of requested pages in the English Wikipedia during a month (June 2014)[5] with the new content added in the previous month (May 2014) we see that from the 1,350,554 articles edited/added during that month, 31% of them were not visited[6] in June. This is an upper bound for the digital desert in this dataset and time period.

5. QUALITY OF THE WISDOM

In previous sections we have used an arbitrary definition of wisdom that is directly related with the amount of content produced by users. However, one can argue that quantity of content produced (*i.e.,* activity) does not imply equal contribution to the global wisdom. To address this problem we need to measure the quality of content. Unfortunately, it is not simply to measure content quality in a social network, because it would be difficult to define what is a "good tweet" or a "good post" in Facebook. One option is to relate quality with popularity (*e.g.*, retweets or likes), but such metric would be clearly biased towards popular users. Therefore, it is preferable to use a dataset where the quality of users' contributions it is clearly ranked by the readers. A good example of such kind of content are Amazon's products reviews, where readers can evaluate the helpfulness of a review by answering yes or no to the following question: "Was this review helpful to you?"

Specifically, we use a public Amazon's movie reviews dataset released by [12] in 2013. This dataset contains

---

[3]For the Facebook Dataset we cannot estimate the size of the digital desert because was obtained through a snowball sampling.

[4]Potentially, content uploaded by users without followers can be reached through the search page of Twitter or a generic search engine. However, tweets posted by users without followers are unlikely to be top-ranked in any search results.

[5]https://dumps.wikimedia.org/other/pagecounts-raw/

[6]These visits include humans and bots.

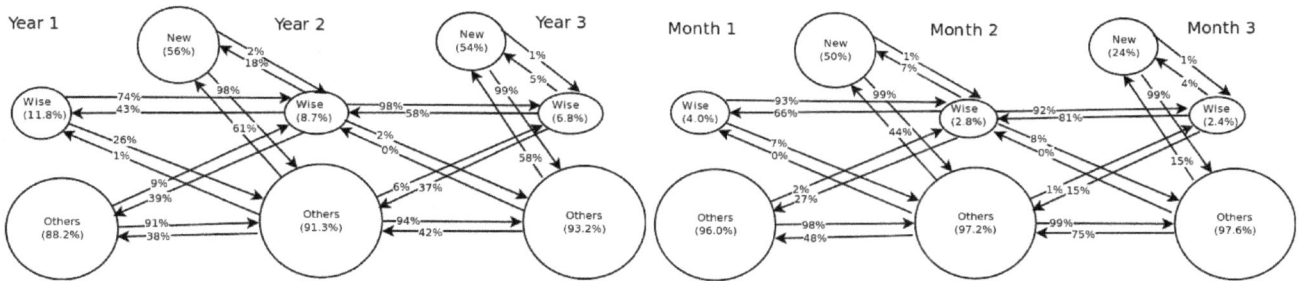

Figure 2: Dynamic behavior of users' groups for Facebook (left) and Twitter (right). Labels on edges represent the percentage of users coming/going from/to a given group to another.

almost 8 million reviews, from 889,176 users, of around 250K different movies, in a period of 15 years (from 1997 to 2012). From each review we have –among other things– the (anonymized) author, the content, and also a field called "helpfulness", that contains the number of readers that have rated the review as helpful or not.

In order to make this data comparable with the previous experiments, first we divided users in wise and others, following the definition given in Section 3.1 that based in the amount of activity (previously number of post or tweets, now number of reviews). In this case we found that 4% of users produced 50% of all reviews. This is similar to Facebook (7%) and Twitter (2%), suggesting that the process of content generation is comparable with the previous cases. For future comparison we denote this group of users as activity-based-wise.

Next, we want to redefine wisdom by adding the dimension of content's quality. To do that, we say that users are contributing to the wisdom only if each review has been rated as helpful by at least one reader. The intuition behind this definition is that if a review helped at least one user, the review is a contribution to the total wisdom. Obviously, stronger requirements can be imposed (e.g., that at least 50% of the users rating a review found it useful). However, our definition will establish a lower bound for the content's value. Hence, now the total wisdom will be the sum of all helpful reviews. Surprisingly, we found that 64% of the reviews were helpful for at least one reader, and 66% of users have produced at least one helpful review, showing that a wide group of users contribute to the total good content and that almost two thirds of the whole wisdom generated is valuable. However, breaking down the results we found that –again– just 2.5% of the users produced 50% of the total helpful reviews. We denote these users as quality-based-wise. Moreover, we found that quality-based-wise users is a *proper* subset of the activity-based-wise users in this dataset.

We also compute the (review) entropy for each user. To that aim, we grouped the reviews of each single user, and then computed the Shannon entropy in that text. Interestingly, we found that the Spearman correlation between activity and entropy is low (0.32), while the correlation between entropy and helpfulness is slightly higher (0.43). Figure 3 shows that from a certain level of users' entropy the reviews tend to be more useful, but that also there is a saturation point where more entropy does not imply more helpfulness. This relation between entropy and value (helpfulness) is useful to generalize these results because we expect that users that introduce more information per word

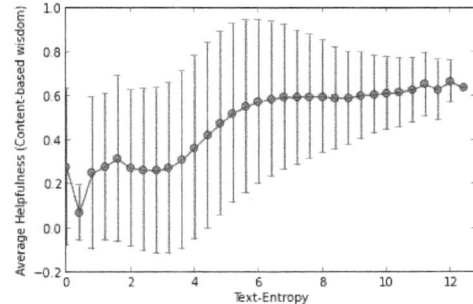

Figure 3: Average Helpfulness of users according to text entropy in their reviews.

(i.e., higher text entropy) are –at the same time– adding more wisdom.

6. CONCLUSIONS AND FUTURE WORK

Our results, added to social influences, undermines the independence principle that is needed to have a real wisdom of crowds [20], as the percentage of people that produces most of the content is really small. Moreover, if we consider that very active people is highly connected among them, compared with the rest of users, creating a cohesive elite. The diversity principle is also challenged, as many users do not contribute to the wisdom, either because they do not exercise this option or because their opinion is not taken in account (the digital desert).

The distribution of how people contribute to wisdom becomes more skewed when a filter of quality is introduced. Although many people show the capability of producing helpful content, the majority of such content is produced by just a subset of the elite.

The datasets used are already a bit old, but on the other hand one of them is complete and less noisy than a more current dataset, as at that time Twitter had less spam than nowadays. For sure the results in other datasets would be different, but we believe the issues addressed in this paper will remain valid for the majority of UCG.

Finally, although we would like to believe that the Web is a more democratic environment as all the people has the same opportunities, at the end the Web mimics our society. Indeed, the economic or political power in most countries belongs to a minority of the people. Even when explicit decisions must be taken through elections or referendums, many people choose not to exercise their right to vote.

7. REFERENCES

[1] R. Baeza-Yates and A. Tiberi. Extracting semantic relations from query logs. In *Proceedings of the 13th ACM SIGKDD international conference on Knowledge discovery and data mining*, pages 76–85. ACM, 2007.

[2] P. Boldi, F. Bonchi, C. Castillo, D. Donato, A. Gionis, and S. Vigna. The query-flow graph: Model and applications. In *Proceedings of the 17th ACM Conference on Information and Knowledge Management*, CIKM '08, pages 609–618, New York, NY, USA, 2008. ACM.

[3] H. Cao, D. Jiang, J. Pei, Q. He, Z. Liao, E. Chen, and H. Li. Context-aware query suggestion by mining click-through and session data. In *Proceedings of the 14th ACM SIGKDD international conference on Knowledge discovery and data mining*, pages 875–883. ACM, 2008.

[4] M. Cha, H. Haddadi, F. Benevenuto, and K. Gummadi. Measuring User Influence in Twitter: The Million Follower Fallacy. In *Proc.of the 4th Int'l AAAI conf. on Weblogs and Social Media (ICWSM)*, Washington DC, USA, 2010.

[5] A. Fuxman, P. Tsaparas, K. Achan, and R. Agrawal. Using the wisdom of the crowds for keyword generation. In *Proceedings of the 17th international conference on World Wide Web*, pages 61–70. ACM, 2008.

[6] F. Galton. Vox populi (the wisdom of crowds). *Nature*, 75, 1907.

[7] R. Gonzalez, R. Cuevas, R. Motamedi, R. Rejaie, and A. Cuevas. Google+ or google-?: dissecting the evolution of the new osn in its first year. In *Proceedings of the 22nd international conference on World Wide Web*, pages 483–494. International World Wide Web Conferences Steering Committee, 2013.

[8] C. Hsieh, C. Moghbel, J. Fang, and J. Cho. Experts vs the crowd: Examining popular news prediction perfomance on twitter. In *Proceedings of ACM KDD conference, Chicago, USA*, 2013.

[9] A. Kittur and R. E. Kraut. Harnessing the wisdom of crowds in wikipedia: quality through coordination. In *Proceedings of the 2008 ACM conference on Computer supported cooperative work*, pages 37–46. ACM, 2008.

[10] H. Kwak, C. Lee, H. Park, and S. Moon. What is twitter, a social network or a news media? In *Proc.of Int'l conf. on World wide web*, WWW'10, pages 591–600, NY, USA, 2010. ACM.

[11] G. Magno, G. Comarela, D. Saez-Trumper, M. Cha, and V. Almeida. New kid on the block: Exploring the google+ social graph. In *Proceedings of the 2012 ACM conference on Internet measurement conference*, pages 159–170. ACM, 2012.

[12] J. J. McAuley and J. Leskovec. From amateurs to connoisseurs: modeling the evolution of user expertise through online reviews. In *Proceedings of the 22nd international conference on World Wide Web*, pages 897–908. International World Wide Web Conferences Steering Committee, 2013.

[13] A. Mislove, M. Marcon, K. P. Gummadi, P. Druschel, and B. Bhattacharjee. Measurement and Analysis of Online Social Networks. In *Proceedings of ACM SIGCOMM Internet Measurement Conference*, 2007.

[14] M. Paşca. Organizing and searching the world wide web of facts–step two: harnessing the wisdom of the crowds. In *Proceedings of the 16th international conference on World Wide Web*, pages 101–110. ACM, 2007.

[15] C. Ricotta, A. Stanisci, G. Avena, and C. Blasi. Quantifying the network connectivity of landscape mosaics: a graph-theoretical approach. *Community Ecology*, 1(1):89–94, 2000.

[16] D. M. Romero, W. Galuba, S. Asur, and B. A. Huberman. Influence and passivity in social media. In *Machine learning and knowledge discovery in databases*, pages 18–33. Springer, 2011.

[17] K. Rutherford. The few who write Wikipedia. https://en.wikipedia.org/wiki/Wikipedia: Wikipedia_Signpost/2014-01-22/Special_report, 2014. [Online; accessed 19-Jun-2014].

[18] D. Saez-Trumper, Y. Liu, R. Baeza-Yates, B. Krishnamurthy, and A. Mislove. Beyond cpm and cpc: determining the value of users on osns. In *Proceedings of the second edition of the ACM conference on Online social networks*, pages 161–168. ACM, 2014.

[19] D. Saez-Trumper, D. Nettleton, and R. Baeza-Yates. High correlation between incoming and outgoing activity: a distinctive property of OSNs? In *Fifth International AAAI Conference on Weblogs and Social Media,*, Barcelona, Spain, 2011.

[20] J. Surowiecki. *The Wisdom of Crowds: Why the Many Are Smarter Than the Few and How Collective Wisdom Shapes Business, Economies, Societies and Nations*. Random House, 2004.

[21] B. Viswanath, A. Mislove, M. Cha, and K. P. Gummadi. On the Evolution of User Interaction in Facebook. In *Proceedings of the 2nd ACM SIGCOMM Workshop on Social Networks (WOSN'09)*, Barcelona, Spain, August 2009.

[22] S. Wu, J. M. Hofman, W. A. Mason, and D. J. Watts. Who says what to whom on twitter. In *Proceedings of the 20th international conference on World wide web*, pages 705–714. ACM, 2011.

Machine Classification and Analysis of Suicide-Related Communication on Twitter

Pete Burnap
School of Computer Science
and Informatics
Cardiff University
burnapp@cardiff.ac.uk

Gualtiero Colombo
School of Computer Science
and Informatics
Cardiff University
colombog@cardiff.ac.uk

Jonathan Scourfield
School of Social Sciences
Cardiff University
scourfield@cardiff.ac.uk

ABSTRACT

The World Wide Web, and online social networks in particular, have increased connectivity between people such that information can spread to millions of people in a matter of minutes. This form of online collective contagion has provided many benefits to society, such as providing reassurance and emergency management in the immediate aftermath of natural disasters. However, it also poses a potential risk to vulnerable Web users who receive this information and could subsequently come to harm. One example of this would be the spread of suicidal ideation in online social networks, about which concerns have been raised. In this paper we report the results of a number of machine classifiers built with the aim of classifying text relating to suicide on Twitter. The classifier distinguishes between the more worrying content, such as suicidal ideation, and other suicide-related topics such as reporting of a suicide, memorial, campaigning and support. It also aims to identify flippant references to suicide. We built a set of baseline classifiers using lexical, structural, emotive and psychological features extracted from Twitter posts. We then improved on the baseline classifiers by building an ensemble classifier using the Rotation Forest algorithm and a Maximum Probability voting classification decision method, based on the outcome of base classifiers. This achieved an F-measure of 0.728 overall (for 7 classes, including suicidal ideation) and 0.69 for the suicidal ideation class. We summarise the results by reflecting on the most significant predictive principle components of the suicidal ideation class to provide insight into the language used on Twitter to express suicidal ideation.

Categories and Subject Descriptors

[Computer Science]: artificial intelligence, text analysis, Web-based interaction, human safety

1. INTRODUCTION

It is recognised that media reporting about suicide cases has been associated with suicidal behaviour [29] and con-

HT '15, September 1–4, 2015, Guzelyurt, Northern Cyprus.
© 2015 ACM. ISBN 978-1-4503-3395-5/15/09...$15.00.
DOI: http://dx.doi.org/10.1145/2700171.2791023.

cerns have been raised about how media communication may have an influence on suicidal ideation and cause a contagion effect between vulnerable subjects [14]. With the advent of open and massively popular social networking and microblogging Web sites, such as Facebook, Tumblr and Twitter (frequently referred to as social media), attention has focussed on how these new modes of communication may become a new, highly interconnected forum for collective communication and, like news media reporting, lead to contagion of suicidal ideation.

Social science and medical research have investigated the impact that communication on the topic of suicide via the World Wide Web may have on vulnerable subjects, with particular attention to the younger generation [9]. [2] conducted a qualitative study by interviewing young adults who engage in suicidal behaviours and use websites dedicated to these themes. [31, 5] also conducted online searches for Web resources containing suicide-related terms and describing suicide methods. They presented a qualitative analysis of the resources they discovered and concluded that, although neutral and anti-suicide Web sites occurred most frequently, pro-suicide forums and Web sites encouraging suicidal behaviour were also present and available, suggesting that more prevention plans specifically focused on Web resources are required. Building on this, [19] have reviewed online suicide intervention and prevention literature, concluding that there is a lack of published evidence about online prevention strategies and more attention is required to develop and evaluate online preventative approaches. [33] also studied the impact of Facebook suicide notes on suicidal behaviour, reporting that it was not yet clear to what extent suicide notes on online social media actually induce copycat suicides. They note that suicide and social media effects deserve further evaluation and research.

Other studies have focused on the written communication of suicide on the Web via bulletin boards [18], newsgroups [24], chat rooms [4], and web forums [22]. These are mostly qualitative analyses and where quantitative data are used in web-related suicide studies, they tend to rely solely on human classification, which is difficult to implement at scale. Computational methods have only been used in a small number of suicide communication studies.

Some studies report a positive correlation between suicide rates and the volume of social media posts that may be related to suicidal ideation and intent [37, 20]. There is also a developing body of literature on the topic of identifying suicidal language on Twitter [15, 35], but very few attempts to use machine classification to automatically identify suicidal language and differentiate between this and other forms of suicide-related communication, such as awareness raising and reporting of suicides. The differentiation is a requirement for the purposes of analysing the characteristics of suicidal ideation on social media. [10, 8] study depression and other emotional states expressed via social media. Suicidal language is likely to include emotive content and possible signs of depression but we do not suggest depression and suicidal ideation are synonymous in this paper. Two very recent papers presented the results of Twitter studies aiming to classify 'risky' language [1] and levels of 'distress' [16] - both reporting classification performance that has potential for improvement (around 60-64%). An important step in providing support to suicidal social media users is to understand how suicidal ideation is communicated. Recent studies have shown that people are more likely to seek support from non-professional resources such as social media, rather than risk social stigmatisation by seeking formal treatment [16].

Thus, our study aims to contribute to the literature on understanding communications on the topic of suicide in social media by (i) creating a new human-annotated dataset to help identify features of suicidal ideation, (ii) creating a set of benchmark experimental results for machine learning approaches to the classification of suicidal ideation, and (iii) developing a machine classifier capable of distinguishing between worrying language such as suicidal ideation, and flippant references to suicide, awareness raising about suicide and reports of suicide. This last contribution is especially relevant to quantify actual volumes of worrying language on social media for the purposes of understanding risk to human safety, as opposed to all references to suicide. The research presented in this paper comprises an analysis of data collected from the microblogging website Twitter, the text of which has been classified into one of seven suicide-related categories by a crowdsourced team of human annotators. We then use a range of machine learning classification methods to identify suicidal ideation in tweets and analyse the predictive features of suicidal ideation to help explain the language used by perceived suicidal social media users.

2. RELATED WORK

The Durkheim project is aiming to mine social media data to identify markers of harmful behaviour[1]. The project will study a group of US war veterans who will opt-in to share their Twitter, Facebook and LinkedIn posts over time. There are so far no publicly available results from this study but the group has recently published the results of a suicide prediction task, using text from the clinical notes of US war veterans to identify text-based statistically significant *signals* of suicidality, with around 60% accuracy [30]. They found clinical notes of people who had died through suicide frequently recorded behaviours indicative of fear, agitiation and delusion.

Written text has also been analysed in a number of recent studies that have analysed suicide notes and developed machine classifiers to identify topics and emotions expressed by people who have taken their lives [17, 34, 27, 39, 23, 12]). Many of these papers attempt to classify text at a sentence level, which would suggest short strings much like those that would be posted to social media. However, suicide notes are

written by people who have accepted suicide and then go on to harm themselves, whereas the current research is particularly interested in identifying suicidal thinking or ideation prior to self-harm, which may differ from the language used in suicide notes. Additionally, handwritten notes, even at sentence level, are not constrained by string length. Twitter posts are limited to 140 characters, which forces authors to use short, informal language that may differ from the way they would normally express feelings on paper. Finally, social media data are noisy, contain a broad range of topics, and language use varies over time. These features arguably make the task of classifying suicidal ideation more complex than it would be in a discrete recording of pre-suicide thoughts and feelings in a suicide note.

A small number of studies have investigated the communication of suicidal ideation on social media. However, they are mainly focused on a comparison with national death rates. For example, in Korea [37] and the US [20] research has attempted to identify a positive correlation between the frequency of suicide-related posts on social media and the number of recorded suicide cases. Suicide related posts were identified using a set of keywords relating to general concepts such as suicide and depression [37] or relating to suicide methods [20].

[15] analysed the Twitter posts of a person who had recently died through suicide. They studied the posts sent in the twenty-four hours prior to death, finding an increase in positive emotions (though not statistically significant) and a change in focus from the self to others as the time of death approached. As this was only a single person study, and given the fact the person had attempted to make the posts rhyme (thereby perhaps using different language to achieve this), the authors propose larger studies of a wider range of Twitter posts. They used the Linguistic Inquiry and Word Count (LIWC) software to identify parts of speech, emotional words and cognitive processes among other concepts [26]. LIWC was also used in [16] as a sampling technique to identify 'sad' Twitter posts that were subsequently classified using a machine learning into levels of distress on an ordinal scale, with around 64% accuracy in the best-case.

Also studying linguistic features of suicidal ideation, [35] used an online panel of young (early 20s) Twitter users to examine the association between suicide-related tweets and suicidal behaviour. They identified that particular phrases such as "want to commit suicide" were strongly associated with lifetime suicide attempts, the most powerful predictor of future suicide. They also noted that other phrases that suggest suicidal intent, such as "want to die", were less strongly associated. The variation here could suggest the flippant use of such phrases on social media when having a bad day - hence the additional challenges posed to classification of suicidal ideation on social media. Finally, [1] used machine learning to classify 'risky' and 'non risky' Tweets, as defined by human annotators, with an accuracy of around 60%. They created word lists to represent a number of topics and emotions related to suicide, finding references to insults, hurt and bullying in the 'risky' category.

3. DATA

3.1 Data Collection and Annotation

Rather than manually developing a word list to represent suicidal language, we generated a lexicon of terms by collect-

---

[1]http://www.durkheimproject.org/news/durkheim-project-will-analyze-opt-in-data/

ing anonymised data from known suicide Web forums, blogs and microblogs, and asking human annotators to identify whether it contained references to suicidal ideation. First we collected user posts from four known Web sites identified by experts in the field [31, 5] as being used to discuss suicidal themes for support and prevention. The selected Web sites either had dedicated sections[2],[3] or are specifically designed for suicidal discussions[4],[5]. Then we collected data from microblogging site Tumblr [6] - specifically, content containing self-classified suicidal ideation (i.e. text posts 'tagged' with the word 'suicide').

For each of the resulting Web sites we then collected an equal number of 200 posts, retrieved in chronological order, with a total of 800 text posts. These posts, and 1000 posts randomly selected from the Tubmlr sample, were subsequently human annotated using the crowd-sourcing online service Crowdflower[7]. To avoid difficulties in the annotation of long pieces of text we discarded posts having a length greater than the five percent longer than the average post length for each of the websites considered. Human annotators were asked to identify content containing suicidal ideation using a binary criteria by answering the question 'Is this person suicidal?'.

We then applied the Term Frequency/Inverse Document frequency (TF.IDF) method to the corpus of annotated documents in order to identify terms that appear frequently in the suicidal ideation class but appear with less frequency in the non-ideation class. This process identifies terms that can be used to distinguish between the two classes. In the TF.IDF process we considered n-grams of 1 to 5 words in length, and ranked the top 500 terms. These terms were further analysed by two experienced suicide researchers to remove terms not specifically related to suicide, as well as duplicate keywords. This resulted in a final list of 62 keywords and phrases that suggested possible suicide intent. Illustrative examples are *asleep and never wake*, *don't want to exist* and *kill myself*. These search terms were then used to collect data from Twitter via the Twitter Streaming Application Programming Interface (API).

Twitter data were collected for a continuous period of six weeks from 1st February 2014 using the suicide-related search terms, resulting in a dataset of over four million posts. In parallel we monitored traditional media over the same period to identify the names of reported suicide cases in England. We then retrieved a second data set from Twitter using the name and surname of the deceased as search keywords. Here, the underlying idea was to collect different types of posts with a connection to suicide other than those more directly expressing suicidal ideation (which was the aim of the first dataset collection). All names were removed from the text before analysis.

Following the data collection we produced a random sample of 1000 tweets from both datasets, with 80% of posts from the collection of suicide related search terms, and the remaining from the 'names' dataset. The human annotation task was repeated using the same crowdsourcing service.

---

[2]http://www.experienceproject.com

[3]http://www.enotalone.com

[4]http://www.takethislife.com

[5]http://www.recoveryourlife.com

[6]https://www.tumblr.com

[7]http://www.crowdflower.com

This time human annotators were asked to classify data into either one or more of the six suicide related categories listed below, or into the seventh category representing tweets that cannot be classified into any of them. This coding frame was developed with expert researchers in suicide studies to capture the best representation of how people generally communicate on the topic of suicide.

Table 1: Types of Suicidal communication with relative % proportion in dataset

class	description	% of dataset
c1	Evidence of possible suicidal intent	13
c2	Campaigning (i.e. petitions etc.)	5
c3	Flippant reference to suicide	30
c4	Information or support	6
c5	Memorial or condolence	5
c6	Reporting of suicide (not bombing)	15
c7	None of the above	26

Text annotation can be a subjective task, so to limit the amount of subjectivity we required at least 4 human annotations per tweet as per the convention in related research [36]. CrowdFlower provides an agreement score for each annotated unit, which is based on the majority vote of the trusted workers [21]. Because the crowdsourcing service continues to recruit workers until the task is complete, there is no guarantee that all workers will annotate the same set of units. Therefore we cannot calculate traditional interrater reliability (IRR) scores, such as Krippendorf's Alpha or Cohen's Kappa to determine agreement between all annotators. However, CrowdFlower has been shown to produce an agreement score that compares well to these classic measures [21]. Based on the output from our annotator task we can determine agreement on each unit. The purpose of the experiments performed in this paper are to establish the accuracy of a machine classifier when assigning tweets to a particular class of suicidal communication, and thus it is the agreement score for the unit of analysis (each tweet), and not the overall human agreement for all units that is important for validation. We removed all tweets with less than 75% agreement - again, following established methods from related research [36], and discarded any where less than three out of four annotators (75%) agreed on the dominant class for each tweet. Annotators were allowed to select multiple class labels and the majority choice was taken. The distribution of tweets to classes from c1-c7 is shown in Table 1. Note that the dominant class was flippant and improper use of suicide-related phrases and expressions, with actual suicidal intent or thinking being in the minority (about 13% of the total). The fact that four people unknown to each other and without being influenced by each other's annotations could agree to this level would suggest that it is possible for human annotators to agree on what constitutes the language of suicidal ideation, and what is simply a flippant reference to suicide. The resulting dataset of 816 Tweets was subsequently used to train a machine learning classifier (details are provided in the next section), which is only slightly below the dataset sizes of other similar analyses of emotive content on social media (e.g. [25, 36, 3, 7]).

3.2 Feature Preparation

We used the text of the tweets in order to train and test

a number of machine classifiers to identify suicidal ideation and differentiate between this and other types of suicide-related communication, including flippant references to suicide. Three features sets were derived from the text as follows:

- Features representing *lexical characteristics* of the sentences used, such as the Parts of Speech (POS), and other *language structural features*, such as the most frequently used *words* and *phrases*. These are standard features used in most text mining tasks. References to self and others are also captured with POS – these terms have been identified in previous research as being evident within suicidal communication;

- Features representing *sentiment, affective and emotional features and levels* of the terms used within the text. These were incorporated because of the particularly emotive nature of the task. Emotions such as fear, anger and general aggressiveness are particularly prominent in suicidal communication [1]

- Features representing ideosyncratic language expressed in short, informal text such as social media posts within a limited number of characters. These were extracted from the annotated Tumblr posts we collected to try and incorporate the language used on social media that may not be identified using standard text mining features.

3.2.1 Feature Set 1

For the first set of features, and part of the second set, we derived features used in [34], published within the special issue on *sentiment analysis of suicide notes* [28]. We will refer to this set of features as *Set*1. More specifically, the *Set*1 feature set included the following:

- *Parts of Speech.* We used to the Stanford Part-Of-Speech (POS) Tagger[8] to assign each word in a Tweet a POS label. Examples are nouns (broken down into singular, plural, proper), verbs (specifying tenses such as present, past and present participle), 1st vs 3rd person references, adjective and adverbs (comparative, superlative), pronouns (personal, possessive), as well as other tags representing conjunctions, determiners, cardinal numbers, symbols, and interjections. For each of POS we considered the frequency of each in a Tweet as a feature.

- *Other Structural Features.* For this we considered the inclusion of negations in the sentence (total number), the specific use of a first person pronoun (either singular or plural), and external communication features such as the inclusion of a URL in a tweet or a mention symbol (indicating a retweet or reply).

- *General Lexical Domains.* These features represent general lexical categories such as home, religion, psychology, sociology, etc. These were extracted using WordNet Domains labels,[9]

- *Affective Lexical Domains.* These are a set of categories specifically related to domains representing 'affective' concepts. These include concepts representing moods, situations eliciting emotions, or emotional responses such as joy, anger, grief, sadness, enthusiasm, surprise, love, hate, and happiness; but even more specific sub-categories such as amicability, belligerence, bad-temper, unrest, and trepidation; and opposites such as positive-negative concern, negative fear, positive-negative suspense, self-esteem, self consciousness, self-pity, and self-deprecation. These are very appropriate for the specific language we are investigating in this study.

- *Sentiment Score.* Using SentiWordNet[10] each words is assigned a score between zero and one for both positivity and negativity. The sum all words in a Tweet were used as features.

- *Words.* The most frequently used *words* and *n-grams* in terms of (first 100) unigrams, bigrams and trigrams contained in the training set.

- *Keyword list.* We also included each of the 62 keywords derived from the Web form text that were used for the pre-filtering search (e.g. 'asleep and never wake', 'don't want to try anymore', 'end it all', 'isn't worth living', 'my life is pointless', 'kill myself', 'to live any more", 'want to end it', 'want to disappear', 'want to die', etc..). Each of the search terms were included as individual features together with one global binary feature representing the inclusion of any of them in a Tweet.

3.2.2 Feature Set 2

Given the psychological and emotional expressiveness of suicidal ideation, we then explored a second set of features by using the Linguistic Inquiry and Word Count *LIWC* text analysis software [26] to extract more specific labels representing affective emotions and feelings within the text. We refer to these features as *Set*2. These include a more extensive breakdown of categories that may be more suitable for the particular language of emotional distress that we would expect to be present in suicidal ideation. Examples are related to death, health, money, religion, occupation, and achievement, senses (e.g. feeling, hearing, seeing), and three other groups of terms related to 'cognitive mechanisms', 'affect', and 'social words'. These can be further broken down into labels representing family, friends, humans; anxiety, anger, sadness and positive and negative emotions; and terms related to certainty, inhibition, insight, causal, inclusivity and exclusivity. A subset of these features (sadness) were used in [16], but we have incorporated a wider range of the feature set to enable us to distinguish between distress and other forms of suicide-related communication (e.g. grief, support and reporting).

3.2.3 Feature Set 3

Next, due to the noisy nature of social media, where short, informal spelling and grammar are often used, we developed a set of regular expression (RegEx) and pattern matching rules from our collection of suicide-related posts collected

---

[8]http://nlp.stanford.edu/software/tagger.shtml
[9]http://wndomains.fbk.eu

[10]http://sentiwordnet.isti.cnr.it

from social networking website Tumblr. We refer to these features as *Set3*. These were annotated as part of the human annotation process conducted earlier and introduce language from short informal text related to the six suicide related categories to assist the classifier. Examples of these expressions for each class (numbered 1-6 here) include:

1: '.+((\cutting |\depres|\sui)|\these|\bad|\sad).+ (\thoughts| \feel).+' to represent phrases such as 'suicidal / cutting / bad / these . . . thoughts / feelings'; '.+\wan\w.+d[ie].+' for expressions as 'want/wanted/wanting to die'; '.+\end.+ (\all|\it|\life).+' for sentences with 'end/ending it all' and 'end my life'; and '.+ (can.+|don.+|\take).+(\go|\live|\anymo| \cop|\alive).+' covering a wide range of phases including 'can't take anymore', 'can't/don't want to live/cope anymore', 'don't want to be alive', 'can't take it anymore', and 'can't go on'. In addition, we added a list of individual words and n-grams including 'trigger warning', 'tw', 'eating disorder', 'death', 'selfharm' and 'self harm', 'anxiety', and 'pain'.

2: '.+(\need|\ask|\call|\offer).+\help.+' related to phrases as 'call/offer for/of help' and individual terms as 'shut' (e.g. website shut down) and 'stop' (e.g. bullying).

3: '.+(\kill|\hat\throw)' for phrases including 'kill/killing /hate myself', '.+(\f**k.+' for swearwords such as 'f**k/ f**king', '.+ (\boy\girl).+(\friend)' for expressions with 'boyfriend' and 'girlfriend', and '.+(\ just)\.+(\like).+' covering expression including 'just' . . . like'. In addition, some words related to general topics such as 'work' and 'school' have also been included since they are representing contexts more favourable to flippant language rather than genuine expression of distress and suicidal intent.

4: '.+(\talk|\speak).+to.+(\one|\some|\any).+' related to phr-ases as 'talk / speak to someone/somebody' and words such as 'web', 'blog', 'health' , and 'advice'.

5: '.+miss.+(\you|\her|\him).+' related to phrases such as 'miss/missing you/her/him' and '.+(\kill|\die|\comm).+(day| month|year).+' to represent specific time references.

6: '.+(\took|\take).+\own.+\life.+' covering expressions including 'took/taken his/her own life' and words related to suicide methods such as 'hanged', 'hanging' and 'overdose'.

Note that the regular expressions included in the third class representing flippancy were also identified within those related to the first suicidal class (and vice versa). However, we decided to associate RegExs to only one of the two classes according to the nature of the annotated tweets, for example phrases as 'hate myself' or 'kill myself' were frequently associated with flippant posts whereas terms such as 'wanted to die' and 'want to end it' were more likely to be included in tweets containing evidence of suicidal thinking.

3.2.4 *Data-driven Features*

We built a fourth feature set that we will refer to as the *combined* set, incorporating the union of all of the features in the three previous groups. Given the large number of features associated with each tweet, and potential for co-linearity between features in the *combined* set, we applied *Principal Component Analysis (PCA)* as a dimension reduction procedure to convert the set of all possibly correlated variables within the *combined* set into a new set of linearly uncorrelated features (called principal components).

The text of the tweets was also incorporated as a feature set for all experiments. We transformed each Tweet into a word vector using ngrams of size 1 to 5, and retained between 100 and 2000 words (in increments of 100, 300, 500, 1000, 1500 and 2000). The optimum performance was 1-3grams with 500 words retained, and we only present these results in this paper.

4. MACHINE CLASSIFICATION METHOD

4.1 Baseline Experiments

We first conducted baseline experiments using the Weka machine learning libraries[11]. We used the four derived features sets with the most popular classifiers from the special issue on classification of suicidal topics in [27]. These were *Support Vector Machine (SVM)*, *Rule Based (we used Decision Trees (DT))*, and *Naive Bayes (NB)*.

Support Vector Machines (SVM) have been shown to work very well with short informal text [25, 38], including promising results when classifying other mental health issues [11]. Feature vectors are plotted in high-dimensional space and hyperplanes (lines that separate the data points) are used to try and find the optimum way to divide the space such that the data points belonging to the different human assigned classes are separated. Multiple hyperplanes can be used and the optimal hyperplane will be the line that maximizes the separation between classes. Rule-based approaches are able to iteratively identify the feature from a set of training data that maximises information gain in a classification exercise - or put another way, it quantifies the significance of how using one feature as a rule to classify a tweet as suicidal ideation, reduces the uncertainty as to which class it belongs to. Performing this step multiple times creates a hierarchical and incremental set of rules that can be used to make classification decisions. We used a J48 decision tree (C4.5) to perform rule-based experiments. Finally, given the prevalence of individual words or short combinations of words that would be associated with suicidal ideation, it is logical to incorporate probabilistic classifiers into the experiments as they make classification decisions based on the likelihood of feature occurrence. Specific terms and phrases prevalent in each class can be identified and learned by the classifier. We implemented a Naive Bayes algorithm as a probabilistic approach.

4.2 Ensemble Experiments

The individual baseline experiments produced a set of results that achieved a reasonable performance but clearly required refining (see Table 2). This could suggest that the sample was not large enough to allow the classifier to learn a suitable set of predictive features. It could also suggest the features themselves were either not adequate to represent the latent meaning that human annotators identified when assigning each tweet to a class, or the features were not being suitably utilised during the learning phase. Both sample size and feature set limitations led us to incorporate an *ensemble* classification approach, which enabled us to combine the base classifiers and different methods of feature sampling during the learning phase. There are two very popular ensemble approaches. One is Boosting [13] (e.g. AdaBoost), which aims to 'boost' the performance of a classifier by iteratively adding a new classifier to the ensemble where each new classifier is trained on data for which the previous iteration performed poorly. An advantage of this is that, for

---

[11]http://www.cs.waikato.ac.nz/ml/weka/

smaller samples, the more difficult to classify instances can be focussed on to improve classifier performance. However, this approach has also been reported to reduce classifier accuracy by forcing new classifiers to focus on difficult data points at the sacrifice of other data. The second popular method is Bagging [6], which takes a bootstrap sample of data points and trains a classifier on each sample, averaging out the probabilities for each class across all classifiers in the ensemble.

In [32] the authors propose an ensemble approach known as Rotation Forest (RF), which splits the feature set into a number of smaller sets before sampling from each set and running Principal Component Analysis (PCA) on each subset, creating a number of different principal components for each subset of features, and subsequently building a number of classifiers using these. This approach showed a performance improvement over Bagging and Boosting and provided a logical choice of method to refine our baseline classifiers, given the 1444 features all measuring properties of the text, possible colinearity between features, and variance of features in the training data. We hypothesised that splitting the features into a number of subsets and deriving a range of principal components from these, rather than deriving principal components from all features at once, would reduce the number of false negative results by using a wider range of principal components. We therefore repeated the experiments from the baseline phase with a RF ensemble classifier.

Ensemble meta classifiers can incorporate a number of combined baseline classifiers. We experimented with incorporating all the classifiers used in the baseline experiments to determine how the principles of RF could improve these. As the initial results showed varying performance between classifiers - for example, the NB produced the lowest numbers of false positives using Set1 and Set3, but SVM produced the lowest false negatives in both cases - we chose to incorporate a second metaclassifier within the RF that used a voting principle as a mechanism to assign the label with maximum probability across all base classifiers to new instances. SVM, J48 Decision Tree and Naive Bayes classifiers were integrated within the RF classifier as an ensemble, with the classifier producing the maximum probability for new instances being selected for each classification decision. We ran two experiments with the RF approach - one with all three baseline classifiers and another with just NB and SVM classifiers. Table 3 shows the notable difference in performance when using DT to classify suicidal ideation, thus it was dropped and the ensemble approach performed much better. We have only reported the results of the NB and SVM combination.

5. RESULTS AND EVALUATION

We used a 10-fold cross validation approach in the evaluation of our classification experiments. This approach iteratively trains the classifier on 90% of the training data and tests on the remaining 10%. After 10 iterations, the results are calculated by taking the mean accuracy across all models. The results are provided in this section at two levels. Tables 2 and 3 present the results for each of the baseline classifiers - Naive Bayes (NB), J48 Decision Tree (DT), and Support Vector Machine (SVM). Each row represents the results using a different set of features. The final column in the table provides the results of the Rotation Forest (RF)

ensemble classifier. Table 2 provides the weighted average results across all classes, while Table 3 provides the results of the key class of interest - suicidal ideation. Evaluation followed standard classification measures of *Precision* measuring false positives, *Recall* measuring false negatives, and *F-measure* a harmonized mean. In the Tables we represent the best scores in bold, and the best precision and recall for each feature set in italic.

Table 2: Machine Classification Results: All classes

Feature \ Classifier		NB	DT	SVM	RF
Set1	P	*0.694*	0.635	0.692	0.672
	R	0.681	0.641	*0.689*	0.667
	F	0.681	0.637	*0.682*	0.664
Set2	P	0.683	0.620	0.698	*0.703*
	R	0.667	0.622	0.696	*0.702*
	F	0.667	0.620	0.689	*0.696*
Set3	P	0.694	0.638	0.690	*0.708*
	R	0.679	0.642	0.686	*0.707*
	F	0.680	0.636	0.680	*0.702*
Combined	P	0.674	0.622	0.695	**0.732**
	R	0.659	0.617	0.689	**0.729**
	F	0.658	0.617	0.690	**0.728**
PCA (combined)	P	0.607	0.552	0.594	*0.647*
	R	0.561	0.547	0.586	*0.591*
	F	0.563	0.549	0.581	*0.591*

Table 3: Machine Classification Results: Suicidal Ideation

Feature \ Classifier		NB	DT	SVM	RF
Set1	P	0.514	0.464	**0.657**	0.587
	R	*0.731*	0.410	0.564	0.474
	F	0.603	0.435	*0.607*	0.525
Set2	P	0.491	0.397	*0.652*	0.589
	R	*0.705*	0.372	0.577	0.423
	F	0.579	0.384	*0.612*	0.493
Set3	P	0.505	0.530	*0.647*	0.614
	R	*0.705*	0.449	0.564	0.449
	F	0.588	0.486	*0.603*	0.519
Combined	P	0.496	0.447	0.551	*0.644*
	R	0.718	0.487	0.692	**0.744**
	F	0.586	0.466	0.614	**0.690**
PCA (combined)	P	0.400	*0.446*	0.441	0.438
	R	0.590	0.526	0.385	*0.628*
	F	0.477	0.482	0.411	*0.516*

The three baseline models perform similarly across all classes for feature set 1,2 and 3, with SVM slightly outperforming NB in most cases, and DT performing least well (see Table 2). In two out of 3 cases NB achieved the best precision score and SVM the best recall in all three - leading us to test an ensemble approach. It is interesting to note that combining all feature sets led to only a 0.001 improvement in precision and actually reduced recall by 0.07 when compared to *Set 2*. Furthermore, applying a dimension reduction method - principle component analysis - led to a further reduction in performance when applied to all features (see bottom three rows of Tables 2 and 3). However, when the training data was split into smaller samples, with principle components derived for each sample - thus broadening the diversity of components while retaining complexity - we saw a performance increase, going from a maximum performance of P=0.695 and R=0.689 to P=0.732 and R=0.729 across all classes when applying the RF approach combined with a Maximum Likelihood voting metaclassifier.

When digging deeper into the key class of interest - the suicidal ideation class - we see a reduced performance for all base classifiers (see Table 3). The confusion matrix for the best performing classification model (see Table 4) shows that this is largely due to confusion between c1 (suicidal ideation) and c3 (flippant reference to suicide). This was always going to be a challenge given the subjective nature of the task and the difficulty human annotators found in agreeing on this. Sarcasm and irony are notable text classification challenges that are yet to be resolved. This is primarily due to the same language often being used in serious and flippant cases. However, the SVM baseline classifier still achieved a Precision performance of 0.657, which was in fact the best performance - even better than the RF classifier. Indeed, the baseline SVM generally outperformed the other base classifiers, and the RF ensemble, for the individual sets of features. This is in line with other existing research in this area, though we have achieved a higher performance. Yet when combining all features, and applying principle component analysis to smaller subsets of training data, the RF model performed significantly better than any other classification model for the suicidal ideation class. The maximum Recall was 0.744, which is only a slight improvement of 0.013 over the NB baseline using *Set 1*, but the maximum F-measure was 0.69 as compared to 0.61. These results suggest that the ensemble of multiple base classifiers with a maximum probability meta classifier offers a promising way forward for the multi-class classification of suicidal communication and ideation in 'noisy' short informal text, such as social media posts. The 'none of the above' confusion also suggests there may be other latent topics not present in our set of class labels. Identifying these may be a useful task for future research. Table 5 provides P, R and F results for the best performing classifier across all classes for comparison.

Table 4: Confusion matrix for the best performing classification model

class	c1	c2	c3	c4	c5	c6	c7
c1	*58*	0	15	0	0	0	5
c2	0	*18*	1	4	0	4	1
c3	11	0	*143*	0	1	5	17
c4	0	4	5	*18*	0	2	6
c5	1	1	1	0	*31*	1	1
c6	0	6	9	7	2	*76*	4
c7	20	0	23	0	2	4	*94*

6. DISCUSSION

In this section we analyse the components produced by running the Principle Component Analysis (PCA) method on the *combined* set that resulted in the best set of results, as shown in Tables 2 to 5. The application of PCA reduced the features set from 1444 to 255 attributes in terms of main

Table 5: Precision, Recall, and F-measure for the best performing classification model

class	P	R	F
c1	0.644	0.744	0.690
c2	0.621	0.643	0.631
c3	0.726	0.808	0.765
c4	0.621	0.514	0.563
c5	0.861	0.861	0.861
c6	0.826	0.731	0.776
c7	0.734	0.657	0.694

components. For the seven suicide related classes we show in Tables 6 and 7 the most representative principal components and briefly discuss what each class represents in terms of the features in the component and the particular language used in it.

Note that while the distribution of the components per class mirrors the total number of annotation per class (therefore penalising the classes less represented in our data set such as 'memorials') in Tables 6, 7 and in the related discussion we are giving priority to the most representative class of posts containing evidence of possible suicidal intent. We can observe the following characteristics of the features included for each class component:

c1: Many of the features that appear dominant in the suicidal ideation class are those related to phrases and expressions identified in the suicide literature as being significantly associated within the language of suicide. In particular, beside a limited number of uni/bi/tri-grams generated directly from the training set, the terms derived from a number of suicide related Web sites were fundamental in classifying suicidal ideation in Twitter data. As were the regular expression features derived from Tumblr posts. Examples like 'end it all now' and 'want to be dead' and regex including expression of 'depressive/suicidal/self harming' ...'thoughts /feelings' appear strongly related to suicidal ideation and are clearly discriminating for this specific class. Other terms (such as 'killing myself' and the regex containing 'die' ... 'my sleep') become effective for classification when used besides other attributes such as lexical features that express surprise, exaggeration and emphasis (e.g. adverbs ('really'), predeterminers (e.g. 'such' 'rather')), and words mapped to specific 'affective' domains such as 'alarm' and 'misery'. Note that some other concepts and terms appear with a negative correlation as expressions of opposite affective states, such as 'security' and 'admiration'.

c2: For the class representing campaigning and petitions we can observe more general concepts, again expressed by regular expressions and language clues (word-lists in our terminology), such as 'support/help', 'blog' as well as more specific terms (e.g 'safety plea') and expressions ('put an end to this'). Some of the Wordnet domain features require further examination as they appear confusing at first - for example 'racing' is picking up on the words 'run' and 'running' that are related to campaigns.

c3: As the confusion matrix in Table 4 shows, the class concerning a 'flippant' use of suicidal language is the one presenting the major difficulties in classification, since it includes many of the same linguistic features of suicidal ideation. However, the principal components derived for this class identify certain attributes that are the opposite type of sentiment from emotional distress. These include affective states such as 'levity', 'gaiety', 'jollity', and 'cheerfulness', as well as popular conversational topics, such as casual remarks about the weather. The confusion occurs where phrases such as 'kill myself' are used frivolously.

c4: The class representing posts related to information and support (and prevention) appear mostly represented by specific words (often unigrams and 'tags') directly linked to the support services (e.g. #police, #officers, internet and suicide) and/or topicality (such as sexual references ('#lgtb'), and the domains of self-harm and #suicide).

c5: For the class concerning memorial messages, as may be expected, direct mentions of the name of the deceased appear highly influential as well as 'time' references (e.g. 'a month ago', 'a year since') in association with terms such as 'killed' and 'died' (well captured by one of our regular expressions). In addition labels and tags as 'rip' and terms expressing 'love' 'and 'affection' are also part of the components associated with this class. Again, we see some Wordnet domains appearing - 'mathematics' and 'agriculture' are related to specific words such as 'add' and 'grow'.

c6: The class concerning news reports related to suicide presents features such as words representing sources of information (e.g. #bbc news), types of news (research study or statistical report), and direct mentions of the name of the deceased (as well as general concepts related to the particular case, such as in the one here reported of the 'TV' domain). Note that the last three classes of memorial, information/support, and news reporting all share the common characteristics of including URL links within the tweets which, consequently, does not result in an effective feature for discrimination between these different classes.

c7: Finally, the class of posts annotated as not related to any of the previous classes exhibits attributes such as general phrases related to self doubt (such as 'what's wrong with me and 'hate myself') and emotional states (such as 'jitteriness' and 'admiration'). These are phrases that could appear in tweets relating to emotional distress but are also clearly evident in general everyday 'chatter'.

7. CONCLUSION

In this paper we developed a number of machine classification models built with the aim of classifying text relating to communications around suicide on Twitter. The classifier distinguishes between the more worrying content, such as suicidal ideation, and other suicide-related topics such as reporting of a suicide, memorial, campaigning and support. We built a set of baseline classifiers using lexical, structural, emotive and psychological features extracted from Twitter posts. We then improved on the baseline classifiers by building an ensemble classifier using the Rotation Forest algorithm, achieving an F-measure of 0.728 overall (for 7 classes, including suicidal ideation) and 0.69 for the suicidal ideation class.

We summarised and attempted to explain the results by reflecting on the most significant predictive principle components of each class to provide insight into the language used on Twitter around suicide-related communication. From this analysis we observed that *word-lists and regular expressions (regex)* extracted from online suicide-related discussion fora and other microblogging Web sites appear capable of capturing relevant language 'clues', both in terms of single words, n-grams (word-lists) and more complex patterns.

Table 6: Principal components per class

c1 - Evidence of possible suicidal intent
0.185word_list1_end it all_521+0.185end it all+0.179it all now +0.179all now+0.175it all
0.149word_list1_want to be dead_554-0.133_-0.129i think +0.125word_list1_to commit suicide_547+0.114really
0.149word_list1_want to be dead_554+0.145wn_affect11_alarm _496-0.123number of adverb superlative_211-0.121word_list7 _relationship_780+0.118regEx_class6_+.+\report.+_701
0.153thinking about killing+0.153about killing myself +0.153about killing+0.147so im+0.147wn_affect11_misery_314
0.119number of predeterminers_206+0.117regEx_class1_+.+ ((\cutting|\depres|\sui)|\these|\bad|\sad).+(\thoughts|\feel) .+_667+0.115wn_domain_astrology_160-0.106bombing
0.231regEx_class1_+.+(\bdie).+(\bmy).+\bsleep.+0.177word _list_want to be dead_554-0.155wn_domain_dentistry_113 -0.146wn_affect11_security_277-0.129wn_affect11_admiration

c2 - Campaigning (i.e. petitions etc.)
0.25 word_list2_support_746-0.134wn_domain_racing_84 +0.119regEx_class2_+.+blog.+_683+0.113wn_domain_jewellery
0.189safety+0.188plea+0.188safety plea+0.188plea over
0.187end to+0.187word_list_ put an end to this_540 +0.187an end to+0.187an end+0.152r i

c3 - Flippant reference to suicide
0.112wn_domain_meteorology_166+0.11 to live+0.107 wn_affect1_jollity_333+0.107wn_affect11_levity_327 +0.107wn_affect11_levity-gaiety_378
0.14 word_list_ want to be here anymore_575-0.13number of existentials (there)_196+0.126wn_affect11_cheerfulness_459 -0.111so-0.111really
0.162wn_affect11_jollity_333+0.162wn_affect11_levity_327 +0.162wn_affect11_levity-gaiety_378+0.128or +0.113wn_domain_meteorology_166
-0.159myself-0.144regEx_class3_total_662-0.136regEx_class3_+. +(\to).+(\kill|\disapp).+_672-0.125to kill myself-0.125to kill

c4 - Information or support
0.152and anxiety self-harm+0.152challenge+0.152 challengesexps to#lgbt+0.152young people#mylgbthealth
0.175#police #officers in+0.175#suicide preventiontoday +0.175#suicide prevention+0.175officers trained+0.175#police
0.21 internet & suicide+0.21 between internet & +0.21 & suicide http+0.21 & suicide+0.21 internet

c5 - Memorial or condolence
0.155regEx_class5_+.+(\kill|\die|\comm).+(day|month| year.+_692+0.138wn_domain_mathematics_117 +0.13 wn_domain_agriculture_104-0.12wn_domain_tax_126 -0.116number of interjections_215
0.125wn_affect11_love_324+0.125love+0.112rip *name_ replaced*+0.11 rip *name_replaced*+0.107rip

c6- Reporting news of someone's suicide (not bombing)
0.178bbc news+0.15 number+0.15 deaths by+0.15 deaths by suicide+0.15 number of+0.15 by suicide from
0.158research-0.123off-0.107self+0.106to study link+0.1 see_626
0.129regEx_class6+.+friend.+_690+0.12 friend_608-0.114regEx _class2_+.+blog.+_683-0.101adverb_599+0.101killed
+0.144self+0.121wn_domain_tv_184+ 0.101*name_replaced*13+0.101*name_replaced*+0.093dead

These appear particularly effective for the suicidal ideation class, expressing emotional distress. *Lexical and grammar features* such as POSs appear mostly ineffective and scarcely present in the principal components (only some mentions as predeterminers, existential clauses and superlatives that, however, also relate to more specific 'affective' language features than only pure lexical ones). *Affective lexical domains*, appear instead very relevant (such as those represented by the WordNet library of 'cognitive synonyms') and able to well represent the affective and emotional states associated to this particular type of language.

Concepts and labels representing broader semantic domains (also derived form the WordNet library) are, on the contrary, not effective. In fact, although they appear rather numerous as attributes within the principle components they reveal to be, on close inspection, for the majority of cases irrelevant and mostly generated by a 'confusion' and 'misrepresentation' of words (such as sentences like 'my reason crashed' associated to the 'motor-racing' domain, and 'suicide watch' associated to 'numismatic').

Sentiment Scores generated by software tools for sentiment analysis appear also ineffective and either scarcely or not at all included within the principal features of each class. Note that this is true for both basic tools that only provide a binary representation of positive and negative score values (SentiWordNet) as well as more sophisticated text analysis software that generate sentiment scores over a larger range of labels representing emotional states (LIWC).

Table 7: Principal components per class

c7-None of the above
0.15 dont want +0.149word_list_ dont want to be here_518 +0.149regEx_class7_+.+(\don.+).+(\wan.+).+here.+_707
0.136to live+0.133live+0.124hate myself +0.113hate myself for+0.113myself for
0.213regEx_class1_+.+(\die).+(\my).+\sleep.+_677 +0.2 wn_affect11_jitteriness_335+0.147wn_affect11_admiration _501+0.132wn_domain_mythology_135+ 0.207regEx_class1_+.+(\die).+(\my).+\sleep.+_677
+0.133wn_domain_town_planning_79-0.12wn_domain_painting _121+0.12bombing

A classifier for suicide-related language could potentially make an important contribution to suicide prevention. Monitoring individual social media accounts via keywords that suggest possible suicidal ideation is controversial territory, as shown by the recent withdrawal of the Samaritans Radar app in the UK [12] but there is nonetheless potential for such a lexicon to contribute to prevention in some way, as long as acceptability to social media users is thoroughly investigated. The 'real-time' identification of aggregate levels of suicide-related communication at scale in online social networks, which could be facilitated by the ensemble classifier produced in this research, is one possible approach. This could potentially aid the identification of emerging suicide clusters and the concentration of suicidal communication following particular events such as a celebrity suicide. Our classifier goes beyond the recognition of suicidal language insofar as it also aids identification of other kinds of communication, in recognition that social media platforms can be used for

multiple purposes, including the reporting of news and marshalling of campaigns. Monitoring of suicide news reporting in social media is another potential avenue where text mining and machine classification techniques could be applied. The identification of flippant use of suicidal language could be especially useful. The methods needs further development, ideally with a larger sample of social media postings, and application to platforms other than Twitter. Finally, we note that it is important to retain collaboration with domain experts in suicidology throughout the experimental and interpretation phases of future research to improve classification accuracy by incorporating prior knowledge of the characteristics of suicidal language - especially given the significance of the affective features in this paper.

8. ACKNOWLEDGMENTS

This is independent research commissioned and funded by the Department of Health Policy Research Programme (Understanding the Role of Social Media in the Aftermath of Youth Suicides, Project Number 023/0165). The views expressed in this publication are those of the author(s) and not necessarily those of the Department of Health.

9. REFERENCES

[1] A. Abboute, Y. Boudjeriou, G. Entringer, J. Aze, S. Bringay, and P. Poncelet. Mining twitter for suicide prevention. In *Natural Language Processing and Information Systems*, volume 8455 of *Lecture Notes in Computer Science*, pages 250–253. Springer, 2014.

[2] D. Baker and S. Fortune. Understanding self-harm and suicide websites. *Crisis: The Journal of Crisis Intervention and Suicide Prevention*, 29(3):118–122, 2008.

[3] L. Barbosa and J. Feng. Robust sentiment detection on twitter from biased and noisy data. In *Proceedings of the 23rd International Conference on Computational Linguistics: Posters*, pages 36–44. Association for Computational Linguistics, 2010.

[4] K. Becker and M. H. Schmidt. When kids seek help on-line: Internet chat rooms and suicide. *reclaiming children and youth*, 13(4):229–230, 2005.

[5] L. Biddle, J. Donovan, K. Hawton, N. Kapur, and D. Gunnell. Suicide and the internet. *Bmj*, 336(7648):800–802, 2008.

[6] L. Breiman. Bagging predictors. *Machine learning*, 24(2):123–140, 1996.

[7] P. Burnap, O. F. Rana, N. Avis, M. Williams, W. Housley, A. Edwards, J. Morgan, and L. Sloan. Detecting tension in online communities with computational twitter analysis. *Technological Forecasting and Social Change*, 2013.

[8] M. D. C. S. Counts and M. Gamon. Not all moods re created equal! a exploring human emotional states in social media. 2012.

[9] K. Daine, K. Hawton, V. Singaravelu, A. Stewart, S. Simkin, and P. Montgomery. The power of the web: a systematic review of studies of the influence of the internet on self-harm and suicide in young people. *PloS one*, 8(10):e77555, 2013.

[10] M. De Choudhury, S. Counts, E. J. Horvitz, and A. Hoff. Characterizing and predicting postpartum

depression from shared facebook data. In *Proceedings of the 17th ACM Conference on Computer Supported Cooperative Work & Social Computing*, CSCW '14, pages 626–638, New York, NY, USA, 2014. ACM.

[11] M. De Choudhury, M. Gamon, S. Counts, and E. Horvitz. Predicting depression via social media. In *ICWSM*, 2013.

[12] B. Desmet and V. Hoste. Emotion detection in suicide notes. *Expert Systems with Applications*, 40(16):6351–6358, 2013.

[13] Y. Freund and R. E. Schapire. A desicion-theoretic generalization of on-line learning and an application to boosting. In *Computational learning theory*, pages 23–37. Springer, 1995.

[14] M. Gould, P. Jamieson, and D. Romer. Media contagion and suicide among the young. *American Behavioral Scientist*, 46(9):1269–1284, 2003.

[15] J. F. Gunn and D. Lester. Twitter postings and suicide: An analysis of the postings of a fatal suicide in the 24 hours prior to death. *Present tense*, 27(16):42, 2012.

[16] C. Homan, R. Johar, T. Liu, M. Lytle, V. Silenzio, and C. Ovesdotter Alm. Toward macro-insights for suicide prevention: Analyzing fine-grained distress at scale. In *Proceedings of the Workshop on Computational Linguistics and Clinical Psychology*, pages 107–117, Baltimore, Maryland, USA, June 2014. Association for Computational Linguistics.

[17] Y.-P. Huang, T. Goh, and C. L. Liew. Hunting suicide notes in web 2.0-preliminary findings. In *Multimedia Workshops, 2007. ISMW'07. Ninth IEEE International Symposium on*, pages 517–521. IEEE, 2007.

[18] A. Ikunaga, S. R. Nath, and K. A. Skinner. Internet suicide in japan: A qualitative content analysis of a suicide bulletin board. *Transcultural psychiatry*, page 1363461513487308, 2013.

[19] N. Jacob, J. Scourfield, and R. Evans. Suicide prevention via the internet: A descriptive review. *Crisis: The Journal of Crisis Intervention and Suicide Prevention*, 35(4):261, 2014.

[20] J. Jashinsky, S. H. Burton, C. L. Hanson, J. West, C. Giraud-Carrier, M. D. Barnes, and T. Argyle. Tracking suicide risk factors through twitter in the us. 2013.

[21] V. Kolhatkar, H. Zinsmeister, and G. Hirst. Interpreting anaphoric shell nouns using antecedents of cataphoric shell nouns as training data. In *EMNLP*, pages 300–310, 2013.

[22] M. T. Lehrman, C. O. Alm, and R. A. Proaño. Detecting distressed and non-distressed affect states in short forum texts. In *Proceedings of the Second Workshop on Language in Social Media*, pages 9–18. Association for Computational Linguistics, 2012.

[23] M. Liakata, J.-H. Kim, S. Saha, J. Hastings, and D. Rebholz-Schuhmann. Three hybrid classifiers for the detection of emotions in suicide notes. *Biomedical informatics insights*, 5(Suppl 1):175, 2012.

[24] P. Matykiewicz, W. Duch, and J. Pestian. Clustering semantic spaces of suicide notes and newsgroups articles. In *Proceedings of the Workshop on Current Trends in Biomedical Natural Language Processing*, pages 179–184. Association for Computational Linguistics, 2009.

[25] A. Pak and P. Paroubek. Twitter as a corpus for sentiment analysis and opinion mining. In *LREC*, 2010.

[26] J. Pennebaker, M. Francis, and R. Booth. *Linguistic Inquiry and Word Count: A computerized text analysis program*. 2001.

[27] J. Pestian, H. Nasrallah, P. Matykiewicz, A. Bennett, and A. Leenaars. Suicide note classification using natural language processing: A content analysis. *Biomedical informatics insights*, 2010(3):19, 2010.

[28] J. P. Pestian, P. Matykiewicz, M. Linn-Gust, B. South, O. Uzuner, J. Wiebe, K. B. Cohen, J. Hurdle, and C. Brew. Sentiment analysis of suicide notes: A shared task. *Biomedical informatics insights*, 5(Suppl 1):3, 2012.

[29] J. Pirkis and R. W. Blood. Suicide and the media. *Crisis: The Journal of Crisis Intervention and Suicide Prevention*, 22(4):155–162, 2001.

[30] C. Poulin, B. Shiner, P. Thompson, L. Vepstas, Y. Young-Xu, B. Goertzel, B. Watts, L. Flashman, and T. McAllister. Predicting the risk of suicide by analyzing the text of clinical notes. *PloS one*, 9(1):e85733, 2014.

[31] P. R. Recupero, S. E. Harms, and J. M. Noble. Googling suicide: surfing for suicide information on the internet. *Journal of Clinical Psychiatry*, 2008.

[32] J. J. Rodriguez, L. I. Kuncheva, and C. J. Alonso. Rotation forest: A new classifier ensemble method. *Pattern Analysis and Machine Intelligence, IEEE Transactions on*, 28(10):1619–1630, 2006.

[33] T. D. Ruder, G. M. Hatch, G. Ampanozi, M. J. Thali, and N. Fischer. Suicide announcement on facebook. *Crisis: The Journal of Crisis Intervention and Suicide Prevention*, 32(5):280–282, 2011.

[34] I. Spasić, P. Burnap, M. Greenwood, and M. Arribas-Ayllon. A naïve bayes approach to classifying topics in suicide notes. *Biomedical informatics insights*, 5(Suppl 1):87, 2012.

[35] H. Sueki. The association of suicide-related twitter use with suicidal behaviour: A cross-sectional study of young internet users in japan. *Journal of affective disorders*, 2014.

[36] M. Thelwall, K. Buckley, G. Paltoglou, D. Cai, and A. Kappas. Sentiment strength detection in short informal text. *Journal of the American Society for Information Science and Technology*, 61(12):2544–2558, 2010.

[37] H.-H. Won, W. Myung, G.-Y. Song, W.-H. Lee, J.-W. Kim, B. J. Carroll, and D. K. Kim. Predicting national suicide numbers with social media data. *PloS one*, 8(4):e61809, 2013.

[38] C. Yang, K. H. Lin, and H.-H. Chen. Emotion classification using web blog corpora. In *Web Intelligence, IEEE/WIC/ACM International Conference on*, pages 275–278. IEEE, 2007.

[39] H. Yang, A. Willis, A. De Roeck, and B. Nuseibeh. A hybrid model for automatic emotion recognition in suicide notes. *Biomedical informatics insights*, 5(Suppl 1):17, 2012.

Detecting Changes in Suicide Content Manifested in Social Media Following Celebrity Suicides

Mrinal Kumar[†], Mark Dredze[‡], Glen Coppersmith[‡], Munmun De Choudhury[†]
[†]College of Computing, Georgia Institute of Technology
[‡]Human Language Technology Center of Excellence, Johns Hopkins University
{mkumar73, munmund}@gatech.edu, mdredze@cs.jhu.edu, coppersmith@jhu.edu

ABSTRACT

The Werther effect describes the increased rate of completed or attempted suicides following the depiction of an individual's suicide in the media, typically a celebrity. We present findings on the prevalence of this effect in an online platform: r/SuicideWatch on Reddit. We examine both the posting activity and post content after the death of ten high-profile suicides. Posting activity increases following reports of celebrity suicides, and post content exhibits considerable changes that indicate increased suicidal ideation. Specifically, we observe that post-celebrity suicide content is more likely to be inward focused, manifest decreased social concerns, and laden with greater anxiety, anger, and negative emotion. Topic model analysis further reveals content in this period to switch to a more derogatory tone that bears evidence of self-harm and suicidal tendencies. We discuss the implications of our findings in enabling better community support to psychologically vulnerable populations, and the potential of building suicide prevention interventions following high-profile suicides.

Categories and Subject Descriptors

H.4 [**Information Systems Applications**]: Miscellaneous

Keywords

social media; suicide; Werther effect; mental health; Reddit

1. INTRODUCTION

The "Werther effect" describes the increased rate of completed or attempted suicide following media reported incidents or depiction of celebrity suicides [19]. Naturally, the Werther effect is a highly regarded phenomenon in media effect research — prior literature has examined ways of exploiting findings on the effect to inform journalistic practices, as well as to guide suicide prevention programs [32].

However, key to the success of these interventions is the ability to measure the prevalence of the phenomenon as well as quantifying its manifestation in psychologically vulnerable populations. Unfortunately, scientific evidence in support of the Werther effect

HT '15, September 1–4, 2015, Guzelyurt, Northern Cyprus.
© 2015 ACM. ISBN 978-1-4503-3395-5/15/09 ...$15.00.
DOI: http://dx.doi.org/10.1145/2700171.2791026.

has been either qualitative, specific to particular populations, self-report based, or based on government or agency reported suicide rates [5, 16]. Due to the sensitive nature of suicide, gathering data on suicidal ideation or attempts to corroborate existence of the Werther effect, especially the epidemiological extent of the phenomenon, has been challenging [32].

Online social media platforms, such as Twitter, Facebook, Reddit, and Tumblr, are popular outlets for people seeking information and social support, including issues around a variety of psychological and health challenges [37, 38, 13]. An attractive feature of these platforms is that they allow for anonymous or pseudonymous participation. Thus, they provide individuals with a candid platform of expression, especially around conditions that are considered socially stigmatized, such as suicide and mental illness [6].

In this paper, we leverage data derived from a widely adopted suicide support forum called "SuicideWatch"[1]. This community is hosted on the popular social media Reddit. Through analysis of historical posts and associated metadata, we examine attributes of suicidal ideation and suicide interest, specifically relating to the Werther effect. Our underlying assumption is that such a forum can provide us information about individuals who are likely prone to suicidal thoughts or tendencies. Moreover, this comes at a scale previously unavailable, spanning thousands of individuals, thus enabling rigorous statistical analysis. The ability to analyze the content of the messages shared on this forum further allows us derive language and behavior related attributes associated with the Werther effect. The main contributions of this paper are:

- We show notable increases in the posting frequency on the forum following reports of celebrity suicides. This change is persistent after accounting for baseline expected variability in posting activity, and in contrast to other mental health forums on Reddit.

- We include linguistic measures of behavior, obtained from content shared on the forum. We find that posts following celebrity suicides express greater negativity, raised cognitive bias, increased self-attentional focus, and lowered social integration in the aftermath of celebrity suicides.

- We utilize n-gram and topic model analyses to show that expressions of self-derogatory behavior, depictions of suicidal tendencies, and detachments from the social realm are more frequently discussed after celebrity suicides.

Broadly, we aim to aid suicide prevention, one of the leading causes of death in the United States. While suicide is the 10th leading cause of death[2], it rises to the third position for people aged

---

[1]http://www.reddit.com/r/suicidewatch
[2]Per data from 2013: http://www.cdc.gov/nchs/fastats/leading-causes-of-death.htm

15-24,[3] a demographic known to extensively use social media.[4] An ability to measure existence and prevalence of the Werther effect from large-scale online data may help moderation efforts on these platforms, especially in periods that succeed high-profile celebrity suicide. Online interventions may also be built to extend careful advice and help to individuals identifying with a particular suicide event and therefore at an increased risk of future suicide.

Privacy Note: All social media data used in this paper are publicly available. At no time did we contact or interact with a user. Given the sensitive nature of this research, we took care to anonymize the data in analysis and presentation, so as to minimize any inadvertent disclosure of personal information, or information that may reveal cues about an individual's online identity. Approval was obtained from the relevant institutional review boards.

2. BACKGROUND

2.1 Werther Effect and Copycat Suicides

A number of studies have found evidence, both anecdotal and statistical, supporting the existence of the Werther effect in news and entertainment media [19, 5, 31, 54]. These findings indicate that the effect varies in its persistence, peaking by about three days and leveling out by about two weeks [17]. The effect is also associated with the amount and prominence of media coverage, and it has consistently been observed to be prevalent in diverse cultures [43, 63, 16]. Hence literature has also critically examined the role of media as a risk factor of suicide [56, 54].

A complementary line of work also found that repetitive or high-profile suicide events led to imitative behaviors [61] — especially with media consumers with similar characteristics to the celebrity. Explicit depiction of particular methods has been known to lead to increases in completed suicides employing that method — this phenomenon is also known as "copycat suicides" [33].

Previous work on the Werther effect has measured actual suicides, which do not lend direct insights into the nature of suicidal ideation. Moreover, little has been investigated in terms of the role of online suicide discussion and support platforms, and their relationship to the manifestation of the Werther Effect. Relatedly, much of the psychology research into suicidality and suicidal ideation relies on surveys and self-report. These methods can be intrusive, expensive, vulnerable to participants' memory bias, vulnerable to experimental demand effects, and often lack temporal granularity. These are further complicated by impediments due to the stigma and sensitivity surrounding suicide. In contrast, social media, especially public online communities geared towards supporting suicidal individuals, can provide us with a rich, real-time source of information about the phenomena, without many of the drawbacks of more traditional approaches. Here, we measure suicide related interest and intent by looking at conversations on a prominent suicide forum on Reddit, called SuicideWatch. This focus on online communities allows us to look at content around suicide interest and intent, allowing complementary insight into the problem.

2.2 Psychology of Suicide

Several studies have examined linguistic and behavioral attributes associated with suicide. Due to the inherent challenge of obtaining information shared by suicidal individuals, most prior work focuses on poetry as the source of content, analyzing suicidal tendencies

of poets, or publicly available corpus of suicide notes [52]. [57] leveraged the popular and widely validated psycholinguistic lexicon LIWC to understand the various linguistic constructs manifested in poems written by suicidal poets. An important finding of this work was that the suicidal poets showed higher usage of first-person singular nouns in their writing when compared to a control group of poets, interpreted as lowered social integration or stronger inward focus. In general they found that suicidal thoughts can be associated with detachment from the social realm and higher preoccupation with the self. Along similar lines, others [26, 53, 42, 15, 28, 60] have independently found that suicidal poets showed ambivalence towards death in their writing, exhibited cognitive distortion and emotional inhibition, and over time their linguistic style shifted to a personal, expressive form and stronger inward focus. Authors in [44] found cognitive impairment to be a characteristic predictor of suicide ideation based on a standardized battery of questionnaires. Petrie and Brook found that repeated suicide attempts were associated with lowered coherence and self-esteem, and greater hopelessness [42].

Beyond suicide, literature in psychology has focused on attributes of mental illness and other behavioral health concerns [1]. Pennebaker and colleagues used LIWC in a number of different populations and scenarios to identify language related markers of anxiety, stress, neurotic tendencies and psychiatric disorders [41, 47].

Taken together, this suggests the potential of leveraging behavioral and linguistic cues for understanding vulnerability in individuals and populations. While this paper does not focus on inferring suicidality of individuals based on the content they share online, we do examine how such behavioral and linguistic cues may be mined from data gathered from social platforms, with particular focus on the Werther Effect.

2.3 Health, Well-being and Social Media

Social media research has indicated that psychological states, health, well-being, and social support status of individuals may be gleaned via analysis of language and conversational patterns. These include utilizing social media to understand conditions and symptoms related to diseases [37, 38], influenza propagation [49] and prediction [39], cyberbullying and teenage distress [14], substance abuse [29, 30], postpartum depression [10], mental health [12, 36, 22, 8, 9, 50], and insomnia [24].

Contrastively, research on suicide in social media is limited. Authors in [62] focused on South Korean blogs to predict nationwide suicide rate data. An interesting aspect of this work is that economic, meteorological, and celebrity suicide count variables were used as controls in the prediction model. Similarly, there is some evidence of announcements of suicidal thoughts on Facebook [48], and public health consequences of suicide related content on social media was examined in [27].

This paper builds on this emergent body of research. We utilize data shared on a social media platform, Reddit, to probe the psyche and social milieus of individuals contemplating suicide or seeking support to fight such tendencies.

3. DATA

3.1 Social Media Data

As mentioned earlier, we examine data from Reddit. We provide a description of the features of this social media platform, which are important to understand the context of our research problem. Reddit allows users to submit content in the form of links or text posts, organized by areas of interest or sub-communities called "subreddits" (e.g., politics, programming, science). Users can voice their

---

[3]http://www.cdc.gov/injury/wisqars/pdf/10lcid_all_deaths_by_age _group_2010-a.pdf
[4]http://www.pewinternet.org/fact-sheets/social-networking-fact-sheet/

It just feels like death is the only option but also so conflicted and wanting to live. I cannot think anymore.
I desperately need some help from this subreddit! I feel I am right on the edge.
It will be one more week, and I'll be done.
There's just no one I can talk to if my life is worth living. I fear they'd think it is a suicide threat and manipulation. Maybe I should just do it.
Just want to let you know, I'll be ending it this Weekend

Table 1: Example titles of postings in SW dataset, modified to protect the privacy of the authors.

opinion on the post via a voting mechanism which allows more popular submissions to be featured more prominently according to their score: the difference between the "upvotes" and "downvotes" cast on each post (also known as "score"). Users can also engage with each other via a comment thread attached to each post. In 2014, Reddit had 71 billion page views, over $8,000$ active communities, 55 million posts, and 535 million comments[5].

In this paper, we focus specifically on the subreddit called "SuicideWatch", a forum for users contemplating suicide and who seek help, advice, and support. It is a strong support community with (currently) about 35K subscribers. The community is highly moderated, with many of its moderators and active subscribers adopting prominent roles in providing support to individuals showing vulnerability. In this subreddit, votes on posts are used as a proxy for support and to increase or decrease a post's prominence, rather than as a statement of agreement/disagreement.

We used Reddit's official API[6] to collect posts, comments, and associated metadata from r/SuicideWatch (hereafter SW). Our analysis in this paper is based on all posts made to SW between October 16, 2013 and December 19, 2014 – 66,059 posts from 19,159 unique users. Example (paraphrased) titles of posts from r/SuicideWatch are given in Table 1. We collected the title of the post, the body or textual content, ID, timestamp, author ID, the number of upvotes and downvotes the post obtained, including the difference between upvotes and downvotes on the post (i.e. score.)

3.2 Wikipedia Data

Next we compiled a list of reported celebrity suicides which fell within the time range of our Reddit data. Defining who is a "celebrity" is nontrivial, so we refer to the Wikipedia page listing celebrity suicides,[7] as a way to measure who has sufficient celebrity status for inclusion. We obtained 10 reported celebrity suicides in the same period as our Reddit data; their names and reported suicides are shown in Table 2.

We measure the prominence of a celebrity's death by measuring the change in Wikipedia page views for the celebrity's Wikipedia page. Wikipedia provides daily page view statistics for each page.[8] We compare the number of page-views in the two weeks prior to their death with the two weeks following their death in terms of z-score (Figure 1). Here z-scores are computed by converting the page views to standard normal variable with 0-mean and standard deviation of 1. For 9/10 of the cases, we see a notable spike in number of views, showing that the suicides of these individuals were well-known enough to be viewable on such a macro scale and for examining the presence of Werther Effect in social media.

We note two aspects related to the above analysis, and which will be used through the rest of this paper. First, since we are focusing on different types of data sources—Wikipedia and Reddit, we use

[5] http://www.redditblog.com/2014/12/reddit-in-2014.html
[6] http://www.reddit.com/dev/api
[7] http://en.wikipedia.org/wiki/List_of_suicides
[8] http://en.wikipedia.org/wiki/Wikipedia:Pageview_statistics

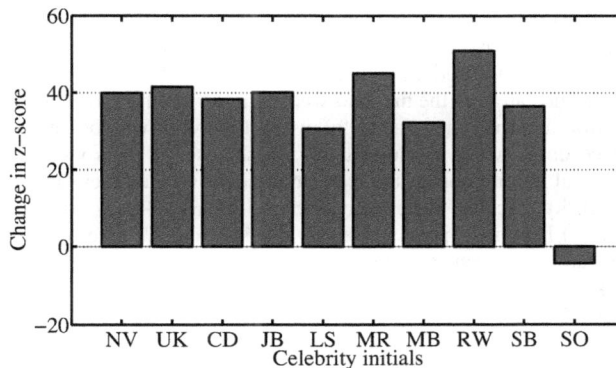

Figure 1: z-score change for Wikipedia celebrity page views succeeding a celebrity suicide.

Celebrity	Profession	Reported suicide
Ned Vizzini	Writer	12/19/2013
Uday Kiran	Actor	1/5/2014
Charlotte Dawson	Television personality	2/22/2014
Jurgen Brummer	Gymnast	2/25/2014
L'Wren Scott	Stylist/Model	3/17/2014
Michael Ruppert	Writer/Activist	4/13/2014
Malik Bendjelloul	Filmmaker/Journalist	5/13/2014
Robin Williams	Actor/Comedian	8/11/2014
Simone Battle	Actress/Singer	9/5/2014
Sean O'Haire	Wrestler	9/8/2014

Table 2: List of Wikipedia derived celebrity suicides.

z-score conversion as a normalization technique for the Wikipedia page views and Reddit's SW posting activity volume. Further, the above observation in Wikipedia data, and the analyses that ensue, focus on observing changes over a two week window preceding and succeeding a celebrity suicide; this choice is motivated by our initial analyses and from the literature on Werther Effect [17].

4. METHODS

Our goal is to measure the change in both the quantity and quality of posts to SW following a celebrity suicide. First, we will measure the volume of posts on SW preceding and succeeding a celebrity suicide to obtain a measure of increased interest in the topic of suicide. Next, we will use a series of content analysis techniques to examine the nature of these posts: how the topic of posts changed in the wake of the suicide.

4.1 Measuring Post Volume

4.1.1 Developing a Baseline

We begin by constructing a baseline as to the expected variability in posts by measuring pairs of subsequent two week periods. Deviations from these expected trends following a celebrity suicide

depression	mentalhealth	Anger
traumatoolbox	psychoticreddit	EatingDisorders
getting_over_it	survivorsofabuse	alcoholism
rapecounseling	bipolarreddit	addiction
hardshipmates	StopSelfHarm	socialanxiety
MakeMeFeelBetter		ptsd
depersonalization, derealization		feelgood
Borderline Personality Disorder		panicparty

Table 3: Control group mental health subreddits.

would provide evidence for the Werther effect. Our goal is therefore to identify, per celebrity, a set of k consecutive two-week time period pairs in the entire timeframe of our data. We refer to the first item of the pair (i.e., the first two-week window) as the "preceding" window, and the immediately following two-week window as the "succeeding" window. Collectively, these baseline pairs yield an empirical distribution of the expected variation when there is not a celebrity suicide. Specifically, each of the k two-week window pairs (1) have no reported celebrity suicide, and (2) take periods that start on the same as the day of week. This accounts for day-of-week related variations on SW. For the purposes of this paper, we choose k as 20.

4.1.2 Developing a Control

Next, we develop a control to establish that changes in volume of posts in SW succeeding a celebrity suicide compared to that preceding it is attributed to the topic of suicide in particular, and such changes are not part of a broader shift in interest in mental health topics. For this purpose, we identified a set of "control group" subreddits, which are on topics related to mental health, but are unlikely to be specifically about suicide or suicidal ideation. These mental health subreddits (henceforth referred to as MH subreddits) were compiled based on our prior work in [11]; refer to the paper for details on how these subreddits are identified and crawled. Table 3 lists the control subreddits, crawled in the same timeframe as SW. We obtained 32,509 posts from 23,807 unique users. Like SW, all of these subreddits are public.

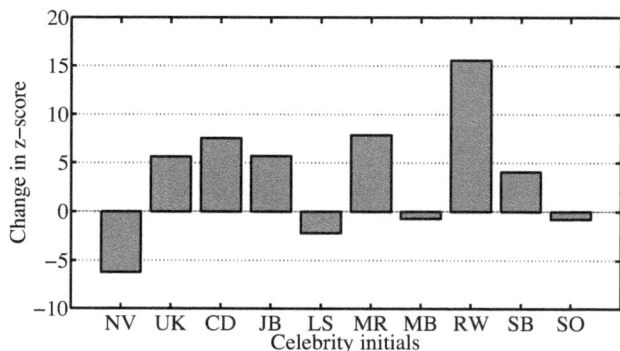

Figure 3: z-score changes in SW post volume succeeding and preceding a celebrity suicide.

4.2 Content Analysis

4.2.1 Linguistic Measures

We propose four categories of linguistic and non-linguistic attributes to examine preceding/succeeding celebrity suicides. These are: (1) **affective attributes**, (2) **cognitive attributes**, (3) **linguistic style attributes**, and (4) **social attributes**. Measures belonging to all of these attribute categories are largely based on the psy-

cholinguistic lexicon LIWC [40], and were motivated from prior literature that examine associations between the behavioral expression of individuals and their responses to traumatic context and crises, including vulnerability due to mental illness [7, 11]. Note that LIWC has been extensively validated to perform well on Internet language [7, 18].

(1) We consider two measures of affect derived from LIWC: positive affect (PA), and negative affect (NA), and four other measures of emotional expression: *anger*, *anxiety*, *sadness*, and *swear*.

(2) We use LIWC to define the cognitive measures as well: (a) cognition, comprising *cognitive mech*, *discrepancies*, *inhibition*, *negation*, *death*, *causation*, *certainty*, and *tentativeness*; and (b) perception, comprising set of words in LIWC around *see*, *hear*, *feel*, *percept*, *insight*, and *relative*.

(3) Next, we consider four measures of linguistic style: (a) **Lexical Density**: consisting of words that are *verbs*, *auxiliary verbs*, *nouns*, *adjectives* (identified using NLTK's [2] POS tagger), and *adverbs*. (b) **Temporal References**: consisting of *past*, *present*, and *future* tenses. (c) **Social/Personal Concerns**: words belonging to *family*, *friends*, *social*, *work*, *health*, *humans*, *religion*, *bio*, *body*, *money*, *achievement*, *home*, and *sexual*. (d) **Interpersonal Awareness and Focus**: words that are *1st person singular*, *1st person plural*, *2nd person*, and *3rd person* pronouns.

(4) For social attributes we utilized a variety of content sharing, social interaction, and social support indicators. These are: *post length*, *number of comments*, *vote difference* (difference between upvotes and downvotes, divided by total upvotes and downvotes), *comment arrival rate* (average time difference between any two subsequent comments in a post's comment thread), *time to first comment* (time elapsed between the first comment and the timestamp of the corresponding post), and *median comment length*[9].

We compute each of the above linguistic measures of behavior at the post level – the value of a measure is given by the ratio of the number of words in a post that match words belonging to the measure, to the total number of words in the post. For each measure we take the average across all celebrities, to ensure each suicide event is equally weighted, i.e., to avoid skew due to a single suicide. For statistical comparison, we used the Welch t-test; a negative t-statistic value means the measure increased after suicide.

4.2.2 n-gram Analysis

We also present an analysis of the usage of various n-grams in posts shared succeeding and preceding celebrity suicides. Specifically, we focus on uni-, bi-, and tri-grams — we refer to them as n-grams throughout the paper. For comparison of the post and pre-celebrity suicide periods, we compute log likelihood ratios of each n-gram given as the logarithm of the ratio of the probability of occurrence of the n-gram in the post-suicide period, to the probability of the same n-gram over the pre-suicide period. Thus, when a n-gram is equally frequent, its log likelihood ratio will be zero; it would be greater than 1 if it is more frequent post celebrity suicides, whereas less than 1 if the reverse.

4.2.3 Topic Model Analysis

Our final content analysis method used a topic model, which have been commonly employed to analyze health data [45, 37, 38]. We obtain topics by running Latent Dirichlet Allocation (LDA) [3]

---

[9]Although comments in Reddit can be nested, we do not consider the nesting structure, rather focus on all comments associated with a post ordered by their timestamps.

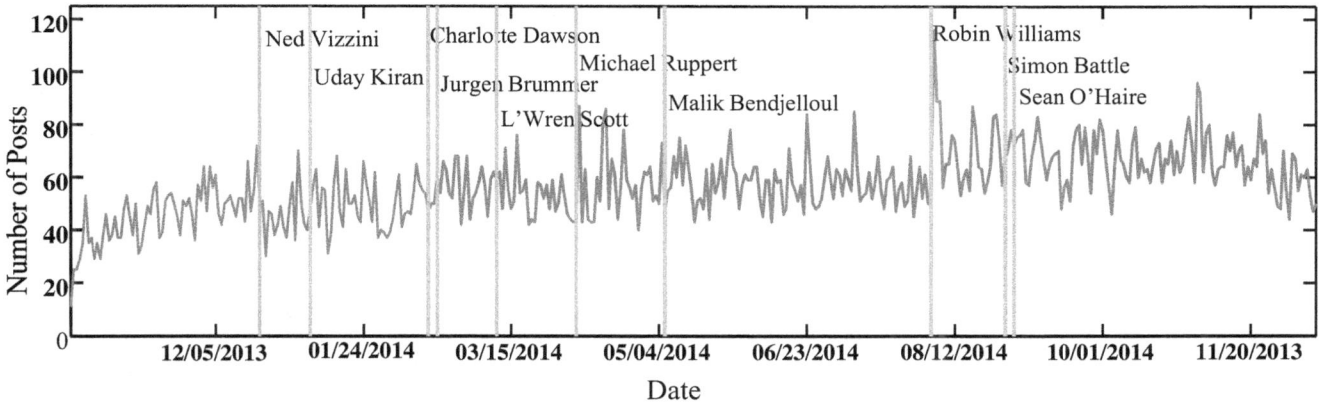

Figure 2: Number of posts on SW with markers of celebrity suicides.

Celebrity	Actual Change in z-score	Baseline Change in z-score	t-stat.	Std. Err.	p	Control Change in z-score	Std. dev.
Ned Vizzini	-6.2247	4.8708	-31.362	2.5018	$< p^{-10}$	0.7822	±2.50
Uday Kiran	5.6022	3.1108	3.7312	4.7215	$< .001$	2.5407	±4.72
Charlotte Dawson	7.5475	1.9654	8.8301	4.4706	$< p^{-10}$	-0.8699	±1.47
Jurgen Brummer	5.6801	0.8948	7.5050	4.5085	$< p^{-10}$	-1.2648	±2.50
L'Wren Scott	-2.1786	2.2798	-7.0382	4.4792	$< p^{-8}$	0.4181	±2.47
Michael Ruppert	7.8587	1.7304	8.4508	5.1277	$< p^{-10}$	-0.1192	±1.12
Malik Bendjelloul	-0.7002	1.7444	-3.5361	4.8887	$< .001$	-0.9398	±4.88
Robin Williams	15.561	0.6006	22.842	4.6314	$< p^{-10}$	1.6456	±3.63
Simone Battle	4.0460	1.3554	4.2296	4.4981	$< .001$	-0.4795	±2.49
Sean O'Haire	-0.7781	0.9866	-2.6803	4.6554	$< .01$	2.6393	±1.65
Mean	3.6414	1.9539				0.4353	

Table 4: *Left:* Actual change in z-scores of post volume over a two-week period following each celebrity suicide, compared to the same period before. *Center:* Paired t-tests comparing z-score changes after each celebrity suicide and that over 20 similar windows with no celebrity death (baseline). *Right:* changes compared to the 21 mental health subreddits (control).

over the combined set of posts shared in a two week period preceding and succeeding the celebrity suicide events. We use Gensim's [46] implementation of online LDA from [21]. We use the default hyper-parameter settings and 50 topics, which we found to work well in initial experiments. To measure topic increases in post-suicide posts we first compute the posterior probability of each topic separately for the pre-suicide and post-suicide posts. We then compute the rate of increase for each topic as the difference between the posterior probability post-suicide and pre-suicide, divided by the probability of topic pre-suicide.

5. RESULTS

5.1 Measuring Post Volume

Figure 2 shows trends in posting activity on SW (raw frequencies of posts), overlaid with the times of reported celebrity suicides. To quantify changes in the aftermath of the celebrity suicides, we use z-scores of the number of posts in the pre celebrity suicide and post celebrity suicide two week periods[10]; change per celebrity is given by the difference between post-suicide z-scored #posts and the pre-suicide z-scored #posts (Figure 3). Posting activity increased after most celebrity suicides; combining all suicides, we find a strong increase of SW posts (Table 4).

---
[10]Use of z-scores for the daily volume of posts helps us account for an observed gradual increase in the number of posts over time.

Compared to the observed changes in the empirical background distribution (§4.1.1) we find that the actual change combined across all 10 celebrities is 3.64 (mean difference between post-celebrity suicide z-score of posts and pre-suicide z-score across all celebrities), whereas, although positive, the same change is nearly half the mean baseline change (1.95) (Table 4). Further, paired t-tests indicate that the change associated with each celebrity suicide event is significantly different from the corresponding baselines ($p < .001$). Thus the observed increase in SW posts is unlikely due to a random fluctuation in posting volume.

Finally, comparing the z-score posting change of SW (3.64) to the MH subreddits control group (0.43) we find that these increases are specific to SW (Table 4). These three findings support the manifestation of the Werther Effect in the forum.

5.2 Content Analysis

5.2.1 Linguistic Measures

Table 5 summarizes the linguistic measures of behavior derived from SW content, comparing the two week period following celebrity suicides to a period of same length before.

(1) Affective Attributes: *Post-suicide content is more negative, angry, sad, and anxious.* Prior literature indicates increased negative affect to be associated with increased emotional vulnerability such as mental instability, helplessness, loneliness, and restlessness [59].

(2) Cognitive Attributes: *Post-suicide content shows greater cog-*

Category	Pre-	Post-	t-stat.	p
Affective				
negative emotion	0.0317	0.0587	-5.821	**
anger	0.0121	0.0656	-7.431	**
anxiety	0.0082	0.0348	-8.628	**
sad	0.0122	0.0219	-3.276	*
Cognitive				
negation	0.0311	0.0573	-4.234	*
certainty	0.0409	0.0170	3.094	*
inhibition	0.0533	0.0042	7.388	**
death	0.0173	0.0925	-7.942	**
feel	0.0013	0.0092	-5.845	**
Linguistic Style				
Lexical Density				
nouns	0.2032	0.1145	6.934	**
adjectives	0.1263	0.0668	5.437	**
adverbs	0.0362	0.0121	1.696	*
Temporal Ref.				
past tense	0.0937	0.1733	-6.374	**
future tense	0.2478	0.1035	9.852	**
Social/Personal Concerns				
social	0.1841	0.0686	5.268	**
work	0.0782	0.0440	2.364	*
humans	0.0191	0.0176	1.257	*
Interpersonal Awareness				
1st pp singular	0.1184	0.3615	-11.548	***
2nd pp	0.0445	0.0122	8.270	**
3rd pp	0.0729	0.0083	8.482	**
Social				
post length	107.37	324.02	-14.521	***
#comments	6.3914	10.757	-7.431	**
vote difference	5.1800	1.7526	3.864	*
comm. arrival rate	12.423	6.699	8.548	***
med. comment len.	37.236	86.935	-10.448	***

Table 5: Welch t-test between content preceding and succeeding celebrity suicides; negative values mean the measure increased after suicide. We report results for α=.05(*), .01(**), .001(***). p values are adjusted after adopting the Bonferroni correction (number of measures m=49).

nitive biases. Posts are less certain, show increased negation, and use more perception centric words, such as words in the category 'feel'. The psychology literature indicates such cognitive biases to be associated with lower emotional stability and increased self-consciousness [44, 25, 12]. Additionally, *post-suicide content has more death related conversation and shows lowered inhibition.* These are known to be associated with greater health concerns as well as suicidal thoughts [58, 7]. Lowered inhibition also indicates an increased tendency for self-disclosure [42, 57] – suicidal ideation or suicide interest, lowered self-esteem and display of self-derogatory thoughts are extreme forms of self-disclosure and inhibition.

(3) Linguistic Style Attributes: *Post-suicide content has lower lexical density.* Greater mental health challenges and suicidal tendency is known to show this characteristic – such content is mostly about the self, hence people attribute less to things, happenings or people around them [60, 11]. The literature also associates lower lexical density to high drive states, which are typical in suicidal individuals [35]. *Post-suicide content is less concerning about the future and more fixated on the past* – likely due to the manifestation of suicidal tendencies [55]. Lowered future orientation is a known attribute of negative attitude towards one's own life and actions. Additionally, *post-suicide content shows little social and personal concerns.* It is known that suicidal thoughts are accompanied by thoughts about the self and self-occupation, hence they are less likely to talk about words relating to social, work, and humans [7].

(4) Social Attributes: *Post-suicide content shows more use of first person singular pronouns and fewer second and third person pronouns.* This suggests that posters are less socially concerned or bothered. Suicidal ideation is associated with *greater self-attentional focus* [57, 60, 12]. In fact, together with the fact that they also exhibit fewer social and personal concerns, it is likely that the post-suicide cohort in SW share more personal stories and in general, high self-preoccupation [4]. *Post-suicide content is longer* – literature on self-disclosure on stigmatized topics, such as suicide interest, shows that greater self-disclosure is associated with longer and more verbose content [20, 23, 11]. Further, the SW community seems to provide more support through a greater number of and longer comments, likely because of their high degrees of expressed vulnerability. However, they get fewer upvotes – suicide interest or ideation related content are unlikely to garner positive approval. People also tend to comment faster – we presume due to the increased sensitive content, the community volunteers to provide help and advice quickly.

5.2.2 *n-gram Comparison*

Going beyond the linguistic measures, we now investigate whether and how usage of n-grams change following celebrity suicides. Per section 4.2.2, we obtained frequencies and log likelihood ratios of all uni-, bi-, and tri-grams from the SW posts in the two weeks following the suicides and also that in the same period before.

An analysis of the n-grams that exhibit the greatest changes pre- and post- celebrity suicide demonstrate a similar trend (Section 4.2.2). We also measured the adjusted mutual information between the frequencies of occurrence of the n-grams (frequencies > 50) after celebrity suicides and that before: yielding a score of 0.21. This indicates that there is little correlation in terms of frequencies of these n-grams before and after celebrity suicide reports. Further, a Welch t-test informs that this difference to be statistically significant – the t-statistic is found to be 3.7 ($p < .001, df = 6892$).

Table 6 gives a list of 75 n-grams and their associated log likelihoods — we present them in three categories, 25 n-grams each with highest and lowest log likelihoods, and most frequent 25 n-grams with log likelihood zero. The first column indicates those n-grams more frequent in the post celebrity suicide period versus before, the second indicates the reverse, and the third column is a set of n-grams which equally co-occur in both categories.

Our findings align with those from the previous subsection — qualitative inspection of the n-grams in the first column suggest SW content shifts to a more vulnerable tone following the celebrity suicides (first column) compared to before (second column). We organize the inspected themes into various broad categories in line with literature on analysis of content in suicide notes [35, 51, 57].

In the aftermath of the celebrity suicides, we find evidence of expression of anxiety and depression, sense of guilt and regret ("i hate it", "piece of shit", "hate myself so", "give a shit", "without me. i"), hopelessness ("i gave up", "i ended"), sorrow ("alone i", "leave me"), and explicit desire to end their life ("to hang myself", "wanting to kill", "of suicide", "tired of living"). During this period we also observe heightened conflicting thoughts ("but right now", "i'm probably"), and a sense of urgency and help seeking ("really just want", "to let me", "help me").

On the other hand, n-grams that are more frequent in the period before the celebrity suicides tend to be less sensitive or vulnerable. In many cases use of n-grams like "be happy. i", "a good person", "be happy", "hope" indicate a tendency for individuals to strive towards maintaining a positive spirit. We also observe greater intent to seek help from the SW community — "if anyone has", "feel free to", "want people to", "tell my parents". Mentions of close friends

n-gram (post>pre)	LLR	n-gram (pre>post)	LLR	n-gram (pre=post)	LLR
few weeks ago	0.717	i feel ,	-0.780	thinking of	0
leave me	0.712	be happy. i	-0.675	they would n't	0
days i	0.693	hope	-0.571	a therapist ,	0
of suicide ,	0.693	my life with	-0.511	phone	0
without me. i	0.673	a cry for	-0.375	badly	0
anxiety and depression	0.634	even worse	-0.375	that point	0
hate myself so	0.631	a good person	-0.346	any kind of	0
tired of living	0.623	i feel bad	-0.288	we 're all	0
really just want	0.623	tired of the	-0.288	i 've just	0
i ended up	0.620	if anyone has	-0.323	i 've struggled	0
alone , i	0.619	thought it would	-0.465	i 'll have	0
i 'm extremely	0.619	friends , no	-0.464	cope with	0
i 'm probably	0.609	tell my parents	-0.452	call me	0
to let me	0.609	family , i	-0.448	i believe i	0
i gave up	0.606	she says she	-0.442	at times	0
to hang myself	0.598	my father is	-0.421	miss me ,	0
i 've lived	0.598	people , but	-0.419	i feel really	0
give a shit	0.575	a friend of	-0.386	reason to live.	0
wanting to kill	0.574	my dad and	-0.533	dont even know	0
help me ,	0.573	no one would	-0.357	feel bad for	0
i ended	0.569	be happy.	-0.357	unhappy	0
but right now	0.566	to her. i	-0.357	put up	0
piece of shit.	0.565	want people to	-0.343	helped me	0
year and a	0.563	feel free to	-0.343	love me and	0
i hate it	0.556	so hard for	-0.323	going through with	0

Table 6: Log likelihood ratios (LLR) of n-grams more frequent in posts after celebrity suicides (left); those of n-grams more frequent in posts before celebrity suicides (center); and those equally frequent in both sets (right).

and family are also widely common ("friends, no", "family, i", "she says she", "my father is", "people, but", "my dad and", "to her. i"). To contrast with the n-gram usage following the suicides, it thus seems that individuals are typically keen to derive help and support from the SW community, however this reduces significantly in the short time period following the celebrity suicides.

Compared to the above two categories of n-grams, we observe that certain types of content are prevalent in SW posts irrespective of the time of reports of celebrity suicides. These include reflection ("thinking of", "don't even know", "they wouldn't", "we're all", "reason to live"), illustration of one's experiences of coping with distress ("i've struggled", "cope with", "going through with", "a therapist ,"), and negative tone ("badly", "unhappy", "feel bad for"). We also observe some n-grams suggesting call for help ("call me", "helped me", "phone"). This indicates the manner in which the broader SW community might be catering to some of the prime needs of this population in a consistent fashion irrespective of external agents or events.

5.2.3 Topic Model Analysis

Finally, we provide a topic analysis to determine how topics discussed in SW prior to celebrity suicides differ from those following the suicides. For the purpose, we use the method described in section 4.2.3. From Figure 4, we observe that the mean (absolute) change across all topics is 2.34% ($\pm$9.16%) in the two-week period succeeding the suicides compared to that before. Specifically, we observe that topics #4, 50, 30, 8, 17 (five topics with highest absolute change) show notable changes in use in the post-celebrity suicide period, compared to that preceding the suicides. Now we analyze change in the content of these topics, like with n-grams, based on prior literature on analysis of suicide notes [35, 51, 57]. We present top changing five topics along with a set of their representative words that capture the essence of the topics.

(1) *lost, useless, done, poisoning, alone, fucking, angry, shitty, hate, suffocate, damn*: This topic (#4) describes self-derogatory and self-critical thoughts relating to self destruction (increase: 13%).

(2) *suicidal, sorry, lifeless, kill, death, withdraw, horrible, anxiety, rough, afraid, hotline, flashes, numb, scars, harsh, scared*: This topic (#50) manifests confessions and regrets of individuals and their desire to commit suicide, particularly via distress expression (increase: 7%).

(3) *maybe, though, probably, except, however, if, but, admit, reason, finally, support, wanted, hurt, bad, sure, nothing, pain, best*: This topic (#30) illustrates the struggling and conflicting feelings that are often known to ensue suicidal ideation [51] — cognitive functioning under competing motives, e.g., self-criticism vs. self-protection, aggression vs. affection towards others (increase: 6%).

(4) *talk, help, ask, emergency, advice, happy, sober, smile, trying, comforted, believe, promise, hopeful, love, sure, friend, family, relationship, parents, school, domestic, guy, undergrad*: This topic (#8) mixes requests for help, including constructs related to demand, command, and request. It expresses needs of the individual and requires some behavior on the part of the listener for their satisfaction [20]. We conjecture such requests are a prime reason why individuals join the SW community. We also notice manifestation of positive and compassionate cognitive thoughts, as well as content around societal, practical and familial concerns. Alarmingly, this topic decreases after celebrity suicide (decrease: 6%).

(5) *really, anything, want, always, never, everything, unable, still, every, unwilling*: This topic (#17) reflects information under high drive or emotion and tend to be more extreme, polarized or ambivalent in their assertions [34]. This is indicated by use of terms that permit no exception (increase: 5%).

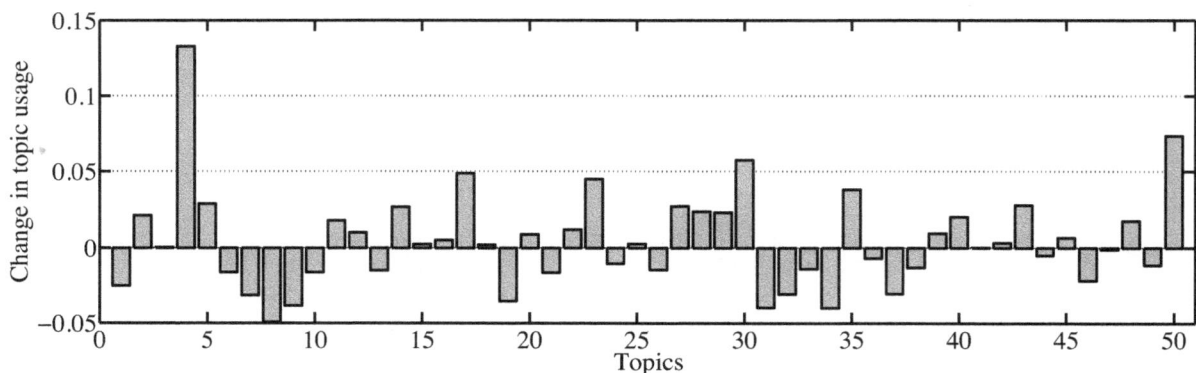

Figure 4: Changes in use of topics over two weeks succeeding a celebrity suicide compared to that over two weeks before. Positive change indicates value increased in post-suicide period.

6. DISCUSSION

Our empirical findings suggest that social media (Reddit in this work) contain subtle yet significant changes in language and activity around suicide content following celebrity suicide events. To the best of our knowledge, this is one of first studies examining the prevalence of the Werther effect centered around suicidal ideation manifested online.

However, we urge caution in deriving causal implications from our findings. While SW is a great resource for suicide related support, it is a platform wherein individuals discuss *why* they desire to end their lives, instead of a channel for communicating or sharing suicide notes. We cannot assess how increased activity on SW compares with increased attempted or completed suicides. In fact, participation in such online support groups may decrease suicide attempts. Nevertheless, our study provides insight into a previously difficult facet of suicide to explore — discussion and ideation.

Next, one presumed explanation of the observed SW post changes might be that the users are, in fact, discussing the celebrity suicides themselves. To examine the validity of this conjecture, we calculated the number of times each celebrity was mentioned — 8/10 celebrities were never mentioned, L'Wren Scott was mentioned once, and Robin Williams was mentioned 52 times. This suggests that the ensuing linguistic changes of post content are not attributable to discussion of the suicide events of the celebrities themselves.

Additionally, we note that one celebrity suicide is perhaps qualitatively different than the rest (as is evidenced in the preceding paragraph) – that of Robin Williams. To ensure that our observed effects were not driven by this singular event, we repeated our empirical investigation excluding his suicide; our findings remain true. For instance, even after disregarding this suicide, the changes in the period succeeding suicides compared to that before was significantly higher than the baselines and the control group (MH subreddits), although it decreased to some extent (32% decrease for the former, and 8% for the latter). The different LIWC categories continued to show significance, while the difference between the posterior probabilities of the pre-celebrity suicide and post-celebrity suicide topics was also distinct.

We also comment on the generalizability of our findings. We acknowledge that the results presented in this paper are limited to those individuals who participate in the SuicideWatch support forum on Reddit. It is possible there is a self-selection bias in this population. For instance, it is likely it is a set of individuals who are seeking help on this sensitive issue. Second, it is also a group who are choosing an *online* platform for seeking help, instead of, or in addition to other (offline) modalities of suicide support. Caution

is advised given the known bias of Reddit user base as well—the average redditor is a 20-something male[11], and perhaps more "tech-savvy" than the general set of individuals contemplating suicide. Finally, even though some of the linguistic and content cues that we mined are Reddit-specific (language characteristic of the platform's culture), our methods could be extended to other social media platforms as well—especially to those online platforms which possess similar attributes implicitly or explicitly, and which allow sharing of textual content.

Implications of Findings. There are many practical implications of this work. Community moderators may develop strategies for the aftermath of celebrity suicides, allowing them and other interested/committed volunteers to be more proactive with the help they offer, as well as provide some unstated context relevant to support during the period immediately following a celebrity suicide report. Awareness of this phenomenon on SW will also allow moderators and volunteers to pay specific attention to redditors who show increased signs of suffering exacerbated by the suicide event. Additionally, individuals whose content contain phrases and other linguistic constructs of high suicidality may be connected to community members who have volunteered to provide help and support— social support and higher levels of social capital can help individuals fight such vulnerable tendencies. Thus, adequately deployed interventions following celebrity suicides can actually motivate potentially suicidal individuals to steer away from their final decision, and encourage them to continue living.

Ethics. Finally, we identify the ethical challenges of this line of research. The interventions outlined above need to honor the privacy of the individuals and those who volunteer to provide help and support. Further, beyond the design suggestions outlined above, *how* to actually intervene, deploy, and offer support to individuals of high likelihood of suicide is a research and ethical question of its own. Especially given the (semi)-anonymous ecosystem that Reddit's SW forum provides to this sensitive population, we need to inculcate utmost care in the manner in which help and support are catered to them following the evidence of existence of the Werther Effect. Unthoughtful interventions may actually lead to counter-helpful outcomes—for instance, chilling effects in participation in the community, or suicide ideation related expression moving on to other alternative or peripheral platforms online where such populations might be difficult to discover and therefore extend help to. Broadly, the ethical dimensions of interventions and their deploy-

---

[11] http://www.pewinternet.org/files/old-media/Files/Reports/2013/PIP_reddit_usage_2013.pdf

ment need to ensure that communities like the SW can continue to be safe and powerful platforms for seeking help, advice, and support around suicidal tendencies, and for online psychotherapy.

7. CONCLUSION

We have presented preliminary findings on the manifestation of the Werther effect in the prominent Reddit suicide support forum r/SuicideWatch. We found significant changes manifested following reports of several celebrity suicides – impacting the frequency of posting activity as well as the nature of content shared. Our findings are among the first to demonstrate the Werther effect on suicidal ideation and have implications for building suicide prevention interventions following high-profile suicides.

There are several interesting directions to future work. Examination of other suicide support forums and social media, observations over longer periods of time and more celebrities and across varied cultural contexts will help us generalize our findings on presence of Werther Effect online. We also intend to investigate to what extent Werther Effect in social media relates to actual changes in completed (government-reported) suicide numbers in regions where the Reddit platform is widely adopted. Causal relationships between the change observed following celebrity suicides and the reporting of these suicide events can be better inferred through a predictive setting, which also constitutes a promising future research direction. Finally, given our observation that more prominent suicidal thoughts are expressed in posts succeeding the celebrity suicides, automated or semi-automated suicide ideation detectors may be developed using machine learning approaches, that can be used to bring timely help and support to these vulnerable communities.

ACKNOWLEDGEMENTS

We thank Shawndra Hill for suggesting the idea of investigating the Werther Effect in social media. De Choudhury was partly supported by a National Institutes of Health grant #1R01GM11269701.

8. REFERENCES

[1] A. G. Billings and R. H. Moos. Coping, stress, and social resources among adults with unipolar depression. *Journal of personality and social psychology*, 46(4):877, 1984.

[2] S. Bird. NLTK: the natural language toolkit. In *COLING/ACL Interactive presentation sessions*, 2006.

[3] D. M. Blei, A. Y. Ng, and M. I. Jordan. Latent dirichlet allocation. *Journal of Machine Learning Research (JMLR)*, 3:993–1022, 2003.

[4] A. Boals and K. Klein. Word use in emotional narratives about failed romantic relationships and subsequent mental health. *Journal of Language and Social Psychology*, 24(3):252–268, 2005.

[5] A. T. Cheng, K. Hawton, T. H. Chen, A. M. Yen, C.-Y. Chen, L.-C. Chen, and P.-R. Teng. The influence of media coverage of a celebrity suicide on subsequent suicide attempts. *Journal of Clinical Psychiatry*, 68(6):862–866, 2007.

[6] A. Chester and A. O'Hara. Image, identity and pseudonymity in online discussions. *International Journal of Learning*, 13(12), 2007.

[7] C. Chung and J. W. Pennebaker. The psychological functions of function words. *Social Comm.*, pages 343–359, 2007.

[8] G. Coppersmith, M. Dredze, and C. Harman. Quantifying mental health signals in twitter. In *ACL Workshop on Computational Linguistics and Clinical Psychology*, 2014.

[9] G. Coppersmith, C. Harman, and M. Dredze. Measuring post traumatic stress disorder in twitter. In *International Conference on Weblogs and Social Media (ICWSM)*, 2014.

[10] M. De Choudhury, S. Counts, E. Horvitz, and A. Hoff. Characterizing and predicting postpartum depression from facebook data. In *Computer-Supported Cooperative Work and Social Computing (CSCW)*, 2014.

[11] M. De Choudhury and S. De. Mental health discourse on reddit: Self-disclosure, social support, and anonymity. In *International Conference on Weblogs and Social Media (ICWSM)*, 2014.

[12] M. De Choudhury, M. Gamon, S. Counts, and E. Horvitz. Predicting depression via social media. In *International Conference on Weblogs and Social Media (ICWSM)*, 2013.

[13] M. De Choudhury, M. R. Morris, and R. W. White. Seeking and sharing health information online: Comparing search engines and social media. In *Human factors in computing systems (CHI)*, 2014.

[14] K. Dinakar, B. Jones, H. Lieberman, R. Picard, C. Rose, and M. T. R. Reichart. You too?! mixed initiative lda story-matching to help teens in distress. In *International Conference on Weblogs and Social Media (ICWSM)*, 2012.

[15] R. M. Fernquist and P. Cutright. Societal integration and age-standardized suicide rates in 21 developed countries, 1955–1989. *Social Science Research*, 27(2):109–127, 1998.

[16] K.-w. Fu and C. Chan. A study of the impact of thirteen celebrity suicides on subsequent suicide rates in south korea from 2005 to 2009. *PloS one*, 8(1):e53870, 2013.

[17] K.-w. Fu and P. S. Yip. Long-term impact of celebrity suicide on suicidal ideation: Results from a population-based study. *Journal of Epidemiology and Community Health*, 61(6):540–546, 2007.

[18] S. A. Golder and M. W. Macy. Diurnal and seasonal mood vary with work, sleep, and daylength across diverse cultures. *Science*, 333(6051):1878–1881, 2011.

[19] M. S. Gould. Suicide and the media. *Annals of the New York Academy of Sciences*, 932(1):200–224, 2001.

[20] S. H. Hemenover. The good, the bad, and the healthy: Impacts of emotional disclosure of trauma on resilient self-concept and psychological distress. *Personality and Social Psychology Bulletin*, 29(10):1236–1244, 2003.

[21] M. Hoffman, F. R. Bach, and D. M. Blei. Online learning for latent dirichlet allocation. In *Neural Information Processing Systems (NIPS)*, 2010.

[22] C. M. Homan, N. Lu, X. Tu, M. C. Lytle, and V. Silenzio. Social structure and depression in trevorspace. In *Computer-Supported Cooperative Work and Social Computing (CSCW)*, 2014.

[23] D. J. Houghton and A. N. Joinson. Linguistic markers of secrets and sensitive self-disclosure in twitter. In *Hawaii International Conference on System Science (HICSS)*, 2012.

[24] S. Jamison-Powell, C. Linehan, L. Daley, A. Garbett, and S. Lawson. I can't get no sleep: discussing# insomnia on twitter. In *Human factors in computing systems (CHI)*, 2012.

[25] N. Lapidot-Lefler and A. Barak. Effects of anonymity, invisibility, lack of eye-contact on toxic online disinhibition. *Comp in human behavior*, 28(2):434–443, 2012.

[26] M. A. Long. As if day had rearranged into night: suicidal tendencies in the poetry of anne sexton. *Lit Psychol*, 39:26–41, 1993.

[27] D. D. Luxton, J. D. June, and J. M. Fairall. Social media and suicide: A public health perspective. *American Journal of Public Health*, 102(S2):S195–S200, 2012.

[28] T. R. Lynch, J. Cheavens, J. Q. Morse, and M. Rosenthal. A model predicting suicidal ideation and hopelessness in depressed older adults: The impact of emotion inhibition and affect intensity. *Aging & Mental Health*, 8(6):486–497, 2004.

[29] M. A. Moreno, D. A. Christakis, K. G. Egan, L. N. Brockman, and T. Becker. Associations between displayed alcohol references on facebook and problem drinking among college students. *Archives of Pediatrics & Adolescent Medicine*, 166(2):157–163, 2011.

[30] E. L. Murnane and S. Counts. Unraveling abstinence and relapse: smoking cessation reflected in social media. In *Human factors in computing systems (CHI)*, 2014.

[31] T. Niederkrotenthaler, K.-w. Fu, P. S. Yip, D. Y. Fong, S. Stack, Q. Cheng, and J. Pirkis. Changes in suicide rates following media reports on celebrity suicide: a meta-analysis. *Journal of epidemiology and community health*, 66(11):1037–1042, 2012.

[32] T. Niederkrotenthaler, A. Herberth, and G. Sonneck. The "werther-effect": legend or reality? *Neuropsychiatrie: Klinik, Diagnostik, Therapie und Rehabilitation: Organ der Gesellschaft Osterreichischer Nervenarzte und Psychiater*, 21(4):284–290, 2006.

[33] T. Niederkrotenthaler, B. Till, N. D. Kapusta, M. Voracek, K. Dervic, and G. Sonneck. Copycat effects after media reports on suicide: A population-based ecologic study. *Social science & medicine*, 69(7):1085–1090, 2009.

[34] I. O'Donnell, R. Farmer, and J. Catalan. Suicide notes. *The British Journal of Psychiatry*, 163(1):45–48, 1993.

[35] C. E. Osgood and E. G. Walker. Motivation and language behavior: A content analysis of suicide notes. *The Journal of Abnormal and Social Psychology*, 59(1):58, 1959.

[36] M. Park, D. W. McDonald, and M. Cha. Perception differences between the depressed and non-depressed users in twitter. In *International Conference on Weblogs and Social Media (ICWSM)*, 2013.

[37] M. J. Paul and M. Dredze. You are what you tweet: Analyzing twitter for public health. In *International Conference on Weblogs and Social Media (ICWSM)*, 2011.

[38] M. J. Paul and M. Dredze. Discovering health topics in social media using topic models. *PLoS ONE*, 9(8), 2014.

[39] M. J. Paul, M. Dredze, and D. Broniatowski. Twitter improves influenza forecasting. *PLOS Currents Outbreaks*, 2014.

[40] J. W. Pennebaker, M. E. Francis, and R. J. Booth. Linguistic inquiry and word count: Liwc 2001. *Mahway: Lawrence Erlbaum Associates*, 71:2001, 2001.

[41] J. W. Pennebaker, T. J. Mayne, and M. E. Francis. Linguistic predictors of adaptive bereavement. *Journal of personality and social psychology*, 72(4):863, 1997.

[42] K. Petrie and R. Brook. Sense of coherence, self-esteem, depression and hopelessness as correlates of reattempting suicide. *British Journal of Clinical Psychology*, 31(3):293–300, 1992.

[43] J. E. Pirkis, P. M. Burgess, C. Francis, R. W. Blood, and D. J. Jolley. The relationship between media reporting of suicide and actual suicide in australia. *Social science & medicine*, 62(11):2874–2886, 2006.

[44] D. W. Prezant and R. A. Neimeyer. Cognitive predictors of depression and suicide ideation. *Suicide and Life-Threatening Behavior*, 18(3):259–264, 1988.

[45] K. W. Prier, M. S. Smith, C. Giraud-Carrier, and C. L. Hanson. Identifying health-related topics on twitter. In *Social computing, behavioral-cultural modeling and prediction*, pages 18–25. Springer, 2011.

[46] R. Řehůřek and P. Sojka. Software Framework for Topic Modelling with Large Corpora. In *LREC Workshop on New Challenges for NLP Frameworks*, 2010.

[47] S. Rude, E.-M. Gortner, and J. Pennebaker. Language use of depressed and depression-vulnerable college students. *Cognition & Emotion*, 18(8):1121–1133, 2004.

[48] T. D. Ruder, G. M. Hatch, G. Ampanozi, M. J. Thali, and N. Fischer. Suicide announcement on facebook. *Crisis: The Journal of Crisis Intervention and Suicide Prevention*, 32(5):280–282, 2011.

[49] A. Sadilek, H. A. Kautz, and V. Silenzio. Modeling spread of disease from social interactions. In *International Conference on Weblogs and Social Media (ICWSM)*, 2012.

[50] H. A. Schwartz, J. Eichstaedt, M. L. Kern, G. Park, M. Sap, D. Stillwell, M. Kosinski, and L. Ungar. Towards assessing changes in degree of depression through facebook. In *Association for Computational Linguistics (ACL)*, 2014.

[51] E. S. Shneidman. Suicide notes reconsidered. *Psychiatry*, 36(4):379–394, 1973.

[52] E. S. Shneidman and N. L. Farberow. Clues to suicide. *Public Health Reports*, 71(2):109, 1956.

[53] M. A. Silverman and N. P. Will. Sylvia plath and the failure of emotional self-repair through poetry. *The Psychoanalytic Quarterly*, 1986.

[54] M. Sisask and A. Värnik. Media roles in suicide prevention: a systematic review. *International journal of environmental research and public health*, 9(1):123–138, 2012.

[55] J. M. Smyth. Written emotional expression: effect sizes, outcome types, and moderating variables. *Journal of consulting and clinical psychology*, 66(1):174, 1998.

[56] S. Stack. Media coverage as a risk factor in suicide. *Journal of epidemiology and community health*, 57(4):238–240, 2003.

[57] S. W. Stirman and J. W. Pennebaker. Word use in the poetry of suicidal and nonsuicidal poets. *Psychosomatic Medicine*, 63(4):517–522, 2001.

[58] J. Suler. The online disinhibition effect. *Cyberpsychology & behavior*, 7(3):321–326, 2004.

[59] Y. R. Tausczik and J. W. Pennebaker. The psychological meaning of words: Liwc and computerized text analysis methods. *Journal of Language and Social Psychology*, 29(1):24–54, 2010.

[60] K. M. Thomas and M. Duke. Depressed writing: Cognitive distortions in the works of depressed and nondepressed poets and writers. *Psychology of Aesthetics, Creativity, and the Arts*, 1(4):204, 2007.

[61] I. M. Wasserman. Imitation and suicide: A reexamination of the werther effect. *American sociological review*, pages 427–436, 1984.

[62] H.-H. Won, W. Myung, G.-Y. Song, W.-H. Lee, J.-W. Kim, B. J. Carroll, and D. K. Kim. Predicting national suicide numbers with social media data. *PloS one*, 8(4):e61809, 2013.

[63] P. S. Yip, K.-W. Fu, K. C. Yang, B. Y. Ip, C. L. Chan, E. Y. Chen, D. T. Lee, F. Y. Law, and K. Hawton. The effects of a celebrity suicide on suicide rates in hong kong. *Journal of affective disorders*, 93(1):245–252, 2006.

A Human-annotated Dataset for Evaluating Tweet Ranking Algorithms

Dominic Rout
The University of Sheffield
d.rout@sheffield.ac.uk

Kalina Bontcheva
The University of Sheffield
k.bontcheva@sheffield.ac.uk

ABSTRACT

Social media monitoring is now an essential part of brand management, political science, and news production. Automatic tweet ranking and content recommendation methods are required, in order to support human analysts in deriving useful insights from large-scale social media data. To facilitate the development and comparative evaluation of tweet ranking methods, a task for which re-tweets do not form a reliable gold standard, a new, openly available Twitter corpus has been created. A number of results for several popular recommendation algorithms are presented for this corpus.

Categories and Subject Descriptors

[**Information systems**]: [World Wide Web, Web applications, Social networks]

General Terms

Human Factors

1. INTRODUCTION

The unprecedented volume and velocity of social media has resulted in users only "seeing a tiny subset of what was going on" [5]. In the context of Internet use, research on information overload has already demonstrated that people are ineffective at processing high volumes of incoming information [1]. Automatic tweet ranking methods (e.g. [19, 18]) have been proposed as a way of addressing problems within organisations that carry out high-volume, time-critical social media monitoring (e.g. brand and reputation management, political analysis, news outlets).

Tweet ranking methods are typically evaluated using retweet counts as the gold standard indicator for relevance [19, 18], i.e. it is assumed that universal tweet popularity translates into user- and task-specific relevance. As shown in Section 2, however, in a professional social media monitoring context

only 36.36% of relevant tweets were re-tweeted. This empirical finding demonstrates that a new, human-curated gold standard corpus is needed, in order to reliably compare the performance of tweet ranking algorithms aimed at professional Twitter users. Targeting professional Twitter users, in particular, is motivated by recent findings [2] that 38% of twitterers use the platform in both professional and personal capacity, and 24% exclusively use it professionally. Such users tend to carry out exploratory search and analysis tasks, which present challenges to traditional full text search and relevance ranking methods [13].

This paper first discusses the interactive, user-directed annotation methodology used for the creation of this new gold standard tweet dataset for political social media monitoring. Next this new, openly available expert-curated tweet relevance dataset is presented, followed by a comparative evaluation of several tweet ranking approaches, targeting social media monitoring applications.

The key contributions of this work are as follows:

- Creation of an openly available dataset, manually created by professional analysts.

- Comparative evaluation of tweet ranking methods on this new dataset, also including common baselines.

2. GOLD STANDARD CREATION

Political analysts were recruited to manually annotate a new gold standard corpus for tweet relevance, in a professional use context. The dataset is available online [1].

It is comprised of a stream of tweets followed by an Austrian social research institute (SORA), which monitors social media during election campaigns, key political debates, and for evidence based policy. The tweets are authored primarily by Austrian political and journalist figures. Therefore it is not representative of trending tweets and topics on Twitter as a whole, but is instead curated to meet specific professional needs.

There are 1,799,924 tweets in the timeline, collected over a period of one year starting from the 1st of September 2012. A smaller subset of these tweets were annotated for topics and interestingness. The tweets were authored by nearly 2000 Twitter users and are mostly in German, with a few in English. The value of tweets varied over time and covered numerous topics. Most importantly, only 36.6% of the tweets marked relevant had ever been re-tweeted, which confirms our motivation for creating a human annotated tweet relevance dataset.

---

[1] https://gate.ac.uk/projects/trendminer/relevance_data.html

Figure 1: The interactive cloud interface

2.1 The Interactive Annotation Methodology

The political analysts from SORA were consulted on their media monitoring practices and Twitter tools used. Based on their requirements to go beyond simple keyword, hashtag, and user mention tweet searches, a temporally-aware interactive annotation approach was designed, allowing annotators to specify which tweets were relevant to their professional information seeking needs.

The political analysts annotated tweets for relevance in the following manner:

1. The analyst first chooses a temporally bounded window of tweets (typically hourly) from a set of available time periods.

2. Based on this selection, topics and named entities are extracted automatically and visualised in an interactive word cloud.

3. The analyst then chooses one or more topics and entities of interest, and thus narrows down the set of tweets to be read and annotated.

4. The annotator selects the top 8 most relevant tweets.

In more detail, the interactive annotation process was carried out in the following four stages.

Temporal Bounding: Incoming tweets were collected continuously and made available to the analysts in a web interface. Temporal windows were formed, where each window contained the most recent tweets returned by a single Twitter API request, with cut-offs to prevent overlaps with tweets in previous time periods. The analysts then selected the time window of interest via a calendar interface.

Selecting topics: In previous work, topics used to restrict the relevant tweets were chosen *a priori* by the researchers themselves [7, 17, 6]. Our interactive, user-driven approach instead allows the analysts to explore all available topics, shown as an interactive cloud, to better accommodate their information exploration and seeking behaviour. The interactive cloud is populated automatically with terms and named entities discovered by the LODIE named entity disambiguation system [3].

The interactive clouds are animated in a moving 3D sphere, to assist in browsing large numbers of terms and entities.

When a term/entity is selected, the analyst sees live feedback on how many tweets from the chosen temporal window contain the chosen term/entity. The annotators can then continue to select other related terms and/or entities of interest, which in turn would widen further the set of matching tweets. They were instructed to continue selecting terms/entities until at least 50 matching tweets were returned, ensuring a sufficient number of tweets for analysis in the gold standard.

Tweet Selection: The analysts were asked to select the most relevant 8 tweets amongst the subset of fifty or more they selected through the terms and entities in the interactive cloud. Post-annotation interviews with the political analysts established that these relevance selections were based on novelty, diversity, and interestingness.

The relevance selection interface was designed to closely resemble the Twitter web based interface, where tweets were shown in a random order to prevent annotation bias [16]. The author's photo, tweet text, clickable links, and time stamp were also included. Users selected relevant tweets and could easily revise their decisions, as they browsed through the list of matching tweets. We showed exactly 50 tweets in response to the query, selecting at random where there were more. We did not choose a higher number to prevent annotator fatigue.

Retweets are ubiquitous in micro-blog streams and lead to duplicates; a preliminary annotation experiment showed that users would mark as relevant at most one instance of the same post. Therefore, a post-processing step was introduced, which groups together and marks all retweets of a relevant tweet also as being relevant.

2.2 The Annotated Dataset

Over the period of April 2013 to October 2013, SORA analysts annotated a total of 62 sets of tweets using the interactive relevance annotation interface. As discussed above, each set contains 50 tweets, of which 8 were marked as relevant. It is possible that fewer or greater than 8 tweets in a set may be relevant, however the understanding of 'interesting' can differ, creating large variances which hinder meaningful comparison between algorithms. We chose to restrict annotators to mark 8 in 50 most interesting tweets, as this was established as the mean number of relevant posts in earlier work [16], though this does introduce some negativity to the task - most tweets are considered uninteresting, but some are more relatively interesting.

In total, the annotated dataset consists of 3100 German language tweets, with 496 positive and 2604 negative examples. The queries used to create these 62 manually annotated subsets included combinations of names of politicians, parties and/or places, involved in events of interest to the analysts which occurred during the chosen time window (e.g. ZIB, Grosse Koalition, Wien, Donau). Of the relevant tweets, only 36.36% had been retweeted at least once.

2.3 Validation

The relevance annotations in the corpus were produced by SORA analysts, with the self-declared aim of guiding and informing political analysis. In order to determine the repeatability of these annotations, we requested that the task be repeated one year later by the original organisation, on a random selection of 15 tweet sets from the originally annotated dataset (the 62 sets described above). Given the

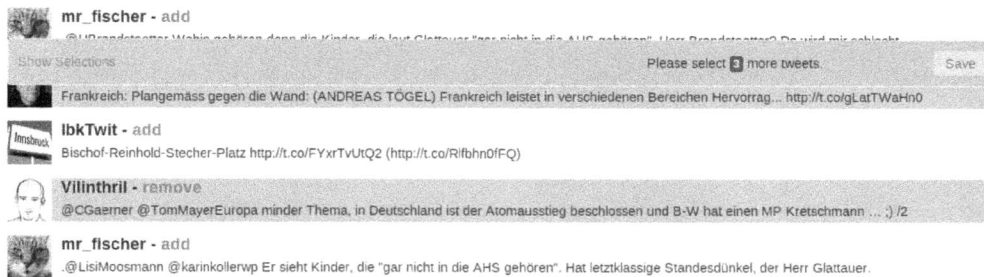

Figure 2: Selecting the most interesting tweets in a collection

difference in time, and our decision to hide both the query and the date of the original set, the observed agreement between the new annotations and the original gold standard was 0.0743 (Fleiss' Kappa), indicating some agreement.

3. EVALUATION EXPERIMENTS

This section focuses on using the new manually curated dataset for the evaluation of several tweet ranking approaches, including the social baselines of retweets and favourites, the former of which has been used in previous work as a source of gold standard judgements [18, 19].

As discussed in Section 2, the gold standard contains binary judgements indicating which tweets are interesting and which ones are not. Tweet rankers, however, produce a ranked list or a series of scores. Thus a better ranking should ideally place the interesting posts towards the top of the list, followed by the uninteresting ones.

To compare binary judgements in the gold standard against continuous relevance scores from the ranking algorithms, Mean Average Precision (MAP) [11] is used. Results for the ROUGE-1 metric [9] are also reported, since it has been used in related work [10, 6]. ROUGE-1 also captures content overlap, not just tweet identity, making the evaluation scores more robust in cases where there are several very similar or identical tweets. For ROUGE, the top 8 relevant tweets are used to form the model summary. German stop words [14] are removed prior to evaluation.

3.1 Results

3.1.1 Baselines

Table 1 shows the performance of several social baselines, namely ranking tweets based on the number of retweets or favourites they have. The results show that the number of times a tweet has been favourited by users is the best performing social baseline. On the other hand, retweets are significantly weaker.

The reverse chronological baseline, wherein tweets are ordered according to posting time stamp, performed similarly to ordering randomly. In other words, the current ordering used in the Twitter web interface is sub-optimal for professional users, who need tweets ordered by relevance.

Several text-only baselines were also evaluated (see Table 2). The cosine score is the similarity between the query terms, which are derived from the tag cloud as described in Section 2, and the candidate tweet, and it outperforms retweets and reverse chronological ordering. The IDF weighted scores are lower, since the queries were unlikely to contain

Feature	MAP	ROUGE-1		
		P	R	F
Number of Retweets	23.44%	28.01%	31.79%	29.53%
Number of Favourites	**27.58%**	**36.88%**	**36.29%**	**36.28%**
Reverse Chronological	21.32%	27.12%	28.16%	27.37%

Table 1: Performance of social and temporal baselines

uninformative parts, as the user selects only entities of interest from the interactive cloud. Hybrid TF.IDF [8] outperforms cosine-based ranking on ROUGE-1 precision and F-score. A threshold of 0.85 was used for Hybrid TF.IDF on this dataset, which was derived using grid search.

The score for random ordering under ROUGE-1 is higher than the corresponding MAP score, since the fifty tweets are already pre-filtered through the interactive cloud, which lowers the overall topical diversity.

Feature	MAP	ROUGE-1		
		P	R	F
Random ranking	22.75%	28.40%	27.55%	27.69%
Cosine	**30.20%**	35.38%	**32.45%**	33.59%
Cosine with IDF	25.99%	31.01%	26.68%	28.42%
Hybrid TF.IDF	28.65%	**39.94%**	30.92%	**34.50%**

Table 2: Performance of the Textual Baselines

3.1.2 Centroid and TextRank

We also investigated methods which aim to prioritise the most relevant, or central, tweets in each tweet set of fifty. The intuition behind centrality-based ranking is that the representative tweets capture the key messages and thus alleviate the need to read the entire tweet set.

The Centroid algorithm [15] selects tweets with the most vocabulary shared with the rest of the collection. The TextRank [12] algorithm tries to identify tweets which are typical of salient themes in the collection.

We used a number of textual n-gram features, when evaluating these two algorithms (see Table 3). IDF weights were created from the complete timeline of curated tweets, with hourly sections used as documents. Unless otherwise stated, all words were lower cased and stop words were removed.

Even though the ROUGE-1 results for TextRank are higher than those for Centroid, the scores do not differ significantly (p=0.33 for unweighted unigrams). Experiments using unigrams with IDF appeared more effective than those using unweighted terms, although there is also no statistically significant difference in ROUGE-F (p=0.72 for Centroid unigram, p=0.06 for TextRank unigram). Likewise, no significant differences were found when bigrams were included alongside weighted unigrams (p=0.8 for Centroid, p=0.25 for TextRank).

Even though some of the approaches appear to outperform the social baselines described in Section 3.1.1, the best performing, TextRank with unigrams and bigrams, is not significantly better than the favourites baseline (p=0.58).

3.1.3 Dimensionality Reduction

The final set of experiments investigate whether dimensionality reduction helps with tweet ranking, when compared to n-gram based features alone. This is motivated by the fact that tweet vocabulary often contains several lexical variants of the same concept (abbreviations, hashtags, misspellings, typos). Latent Semantic Indexes (LSI) [4] are used to map the higher dimensional n-gram feature space onto a lower dimensional space of topics. Then Centroid is applied to rank the tweets, as before. LSI was not incorporated as a pre-processing stage for TextRank, as the resulting graphs are generally very dense, whereas TextRank performs well on sparser text graphs.

The LSI models are trained on the entire 1.8 million tweet dataset, where each hour of tweets is considered a separate document, based on the intuition that there may be lower topical variance within each hour.

As shown in Table 4, using topic models in this way significantly outperforms using Centroid ranking with IDF alone (p=0.008, LSI 200 topics), as well as the favourites baseline (p=0.017, LSI 200 topics). The reported figures in Table 4 are for unigrams with IDF.

Topics	MAP	ROUGE		
		P	R	F
10	33.50%	36.90%	38.49%	37.41%
50	33.83%	38.43%	38.36%	38.17%
100	39.68%	44.14%	43.43%	43.59%
200	**41.44%**	**46.67%**	**44.54%**	**45.36%**
400	40.49%	45.40%	43.40%	44.14%
600	39.51%	45.44%	43.14%	44.01%
800	38.37%	44.13%	41.70%	42.62%
1000	38.34%	44.86%	42.34%	43.30%

Table 4: Performance with Dimensionality Reduction

3.2 Discussion

The majority of tweet ranking methods evaluated here outperformed the reverse-chronological baseline. This demonstrates that current Twitter monitoring tools need to cater better for information seeking and exploratory analysis tasks, as frequently carried out by professional Twitter users. The results also demonstrate that more sophisticated tweet ranking algorithms do outperform ranking based on retweets and favourites alone. They also show that the use of these general popularity-based indicators, in lieu of human-curated evaluation datasets is not appropriate as a ground truth for this type of social media monitoring in a professional context, nor are such indicators useful for ranking tweets for political analysis.

4. RELATED WORK

Tweet recommendation research has used both automatic and manual evaluation methods on different datasets. The most readily available source of gold standard data is retweets [18, 19]. Our new gold-standard dataset, however, demonstrated that only 36.36% of the tweets considered useful by professional Twitter users had been retweeted by anyone. To our knowledge, there have been no attempts to directly use favourite counts as a source of gold standard data.

Therefore, there is a clear need for human curated datasets of tweets, ranked by interestingness. Some researchers [8] asked volunteers to summarise tweets belonging to topically coherent clusters which they had themselves produced or which were created by the experimenters based on predetermined topics [7, 17, 6]. The topics were not chosen by the users themselves, however, a limitation addressed in our interactive, user-driven annotation methodology.

The dataset in this paper is, to our knowledge, the first to be curated and annotated entirely by professional social media analysts. Moreover, the interactive, user-directed annotation methodology enables analysts to select specific topics of professional relevance, instead of ranking tweets on generic trending topics or news.

5. CONCLUSION

This paper presented a new gold standard for training and/or evaluating tweet ranking algorithms for political social media monitoring. To enable professional Twitter users to better express their information needs and identify sets of relevant tweets amongst the 1.8 million tweets collected from their Twitter feed, an interactive social media annotation tool was implemented. This supports exploratory tweet search via entity and term clouds, through which analysts dynamically narrow down the set of relevant tweets, prior to ranking them for interestingness. The interactive clouds support knowledge discovery by exposing terms and named entities from within a chosen time period and enabling analysts to find connections between groups of actors and other entities or events.

A number of social baselines and tweet ranking algorithms were evaluated on the new dataset for professional social media monitoring. Experiments showed that Centroid-based tweet ranking with dimensionality reduction outperforms both the Twitter status quo (reverse chronological ordering) and the most widely used social baselines (i.e., retweet counts, tweet favourites counts). In future work we will create a similar dataset for general personal Twitter timelines, and develop machine learning-based tweet ranking, integrating dimensionality reduction.

6. ACKNOWLEDGEMENTS

This work was supported by funding from the Engineering and Physical Sciences Research Council (grant EP/I004327/1) and the Trendminer project, EU FP7-ICT Programme, grant agreement no.287863.

Algorithm	Features	MAP	ROUGE-P	ROUGE-R	ROUGE-F
Centroid	Unigram	26.61%	31.30%	33.73%	32.26%
	Unigram (case preserved)	25.93%	30.14%	32.82%	31.22%
	Unigram with IDF	33.04%	35.66%	36.36%	35.76%
	Unigram with IDF (case preserved)	32.00%	34.45%	35.42%	34.67%
	Bigram only	30.67%	33.47%	34.16%	33.44%
	Unigram with IDF & bigram	33.27%	**35.97%**	36.49%	**35.98%**
	Trigram	29.57%	31.25%	35.45%	32.98%
	Unigram with IDF, bigram & trigram	**33.30%**	35.49%	**36.59%**	35.82%
TextRank	Unigram	27.45%	32.89%	33.89%	33.17%
	Unigram (case preserved)	26.70%	31.63%	33.14%	32.16%
	Unigram with IDF	32.15%	40.01%	35.69%	37.43%
	Unigram with IDF (case preserved)	30.86%	38.62%	34.79%	36.36%
	Bigram only	27.30%	34.47%	30.54%	32.01%
	Unigram with IDF & bigram	33.60%	**40.51%**	**35.92%**	**37.76%**
	Trigram	27.64%	33.78%	32.12%	32.72%
	Unigram with IDF, bigram & trigram	**33.78%**	40.18%	35.83%	37.58%

Table 3: Performance of Centroid and TextRank

7. REFERENCES

[1] C. Beaudoin. Explaining the relationship between internet use and interpersonal trust: Taking into account motivation and information overload. *Journal of Computer Mediated Communication*, 13:550—568, 2008.

[2] K. Bontcheva, G. Gorrell, and B. Wessels. Social media and information overload: Survey results. Technical Report 1306.0813 [cs.SI], arXiv, 2013. http://arxiv.org/abs/1306.0813.

[3] D. Damljanovic and K. Bontcheva. Named Entity Disambiguation using Linked Data. In *Proceedings of the 9th Extended Semantic Web Conference*, 2012.

[4] S. Deerwester, S. Dumais, G. Furnas, T. Landauer, and R. Harshman. Indexing by latent semantic analysis. *Journal of the American Society for Information Science*, 41:391–407, 1990.

[5] F. Douglis. Thanks for the fish - but i'm drowning! *IEEE Internet Computing*, 14:4–6, 2010.

[6] Y. Duan, L. Jiang, T. Qin, M. Zhou, and H.-Y. Shum. An empirical study on learning to rank of tweets. In *COLING*, pages 295–303, 2010.

[7] S. Harabagiu and A. Hickl. Relevance Modeling for Microblog Summarization. In *Proceedings of the Fifth International Conference on Weblogs and Social Media (ICWSM)*, 2011.

[8] D. Inouye and J. K. Kalita. Comparing Twitter summarization algorithms for multiple post summaries. In *SocialCom/PASSAT*, pages 298–306, 2011.

[9] C.-Y. Lin. Rouge: A package for automatic evaluation of summaries. In *Text Summarization Branches Out: Proceedings of the ACL-04 Workshop*, pages 74–81, Barcelona, Spain, July 2004. Association for Computational Linguistics.

[10] S. Mackie, R. McCreadie, C. Macdonald, and I. Ounis. Comparing algorithms for microblog summarisation. In E. Kanoulas, M. Lupu, P. Clough, M. Sanderson, M. Hall, A. Hanbury, and E. Toms, editors, *Information Access Evaluation. Multilinguality, Multimodality, and Interaction*, volume 8685 of

Lecture Notes in Computer Science, pages 153–159. Springer International Publishing, 2014.

[11] C. D. Manning, P. Raghavan, and H. Schütze. *Introduction to information retrieval*. Cambridge University Press, New York, NY, 2008.

[12] R. Mihalcea and P. Tarau. TextRank: Bringing order into text. In *Proceedings of the Conference on Empirical Methods in Natural Language Processing (EMNLP)*, pages 404–411, 2004.

[13] P. Pirolli. Powers of 10: Modeling complex information-seeking systems at multiple scales. *IEEE Computer*, 42(3):33–40, 2009.

[14] M. Porter. Snowball: A language for stemming algorithms, 2001.

[15] D. R. Radev, H. Jing, M. Styś, and D. Tam. Centroid-based summarization of multiple documents. *Information Processing and Management*, 40(6):919–938, Nov. 2004.

[16] D. Rout, K. Bontcheva, and M. Hepple. Reliably evaluating summaries of twitter timelines. In *Proceedings of the AAAI Symposium on Analyzing Microtext*, 2013.

[17] B. Sharifi, M. A. Hutton, and J. Kalita. Summarizing Microblogs Automatically. In *Human Language Technologies: The 2010 Annual Conference of the North American Chapter of the Association for Computational Linguistics*, pages 685–688, Los Angeles, California, June 2010.

[18] I. Uysal and W. B. Croft. User oriented tweet ranking: a filtering approach to microblogs. In *Proceedings of the 20th ACM Conference on Information and Knowledge Management, CIKM 2011, Glasgow, United Kingdom, October 24-28, 2011*, pages 2261–2264, 2011.

[19] R. Yan, M. Lapata, and X. Li. Tweet recommendation with graph co-ranking. In *Proceedings of the 50th Annual Meeting of the Association for Computational Linguistics*, pages 516–525, Jeju Island, Korea, 2012.

From Small Sensors to Big Data

Barry Smyth
Insight Centre for Data Analytics
School of Computer Science
University College Dublin
Dublin, Ireland
barry.smyth@insight-centre.org

ABSTRACT

In our increasingly digitized world almost everything we do creates a record that is stored somewhere, whether we are purchasing a book, calling a friend, ordering a meal, or renting a movie. And in today's world of sensors and internet-enabled devices, smartphones and wearables, this is no longer just limited to our online activities. Exercising in the park, shopping for groceries, falling asleep, or even taking a shower, are just some of the everyday real-world activities that are likely to generate data. This is the big data world of the so-called Sensor Web. It is enabled by the widescale availability of high-performance computing, always-on communications, and mobile computing devices that come equipped with a variety of powerful sensors. This provides for a powerful computing and sensing ecosystem with important applications across all aspects of how we live, work, and play.

The primary challenge for us now is to understand how we can (and whether we should) use this information. On the one hand, the promise of big data analytics is better decisions: better decisions about where we might live or where to send our kids to school; better decisions about the food we eat and the exercise we should take; and better decisions about some of the biggest choices facing modern societies when it comes to health, education, energy, and climate. On the other hand, this potential has a darker side, in the form of a gradual erosion of personal privacy as businesses and even governments seek to exploit our personal data for their own purposes, often without our informed consent.

What is certain is that the combination of mobile computation, cheap but powerful sensors, and big data analytics points to new ways of thinking about some of society's toughest challenges. But to take advantage of these benefits we must reconcile the promise of big data with the pitfalls of privacy. Only then can these technologies can have a meaningful impact on how we can all benefit from the big data revolution as part of a healthier, safer, fairer world.

Categories and Subject Descriptors

H.4 [**Information Systems Applications**]: Miscellaneous

General Terms

Human Factors

Keywords

Big Datal Sensor Web; Data Analytics; Mobile Computing

Acknowledgement

This work is supported by Science Foundation Ireland through through the Insight Centre for Data Analytics under grant number SFI/12/RC/2289.

Examining Personalization in Academic Web Search

Sara Salehi
WebTech and Security Lab
Mawson Lakes Campus
University of South Australia
sara.salehi@mymail.unisa.edu.au

Jia Tina Du
Strategic Information
Management Lab
Mawson Lakes Campus
University of South Australia
Tina.Du@unisa.edu.au

Helen Ashman
WebTech and Security Lab
Mawson Lakes Campus
University of South Australia
Helen.Ashman@unisa.edu.au

ABSTRACT

Personalization promises to improve the accuracy of Web search and has been drawing much research attention recently. Some evidence indicates that for educational purposes, the disadvantages of personalized search are not justified by its benefits. The potential issues with search personalization, especially in an educational context, include loss of serendipity and capability, commercialization of education and the 'Filter Bubble' effect where users are denied information if search engine algorithms decide it is irrelevant to them. The majority of students in higher education make use of general-purpose search engines to find academic information, however we have little knowledge about the effects of personalization on learners' experience and achievements. This observation motivates the research in this paper. First, we surveyed 120 university students to investigate which research sources, including search engines they predominately use and how much they depend on each for educational purposes. We learned that the majority of students prefer Google to other search engines; indeed sometimes it is their primary or only information-seeking tool. Additionally, about 80% of them use search engines for educational purposes on daily basis. Second, we measured the difference between personalized and non-personalized search results for 120 academic search queries divided equally into four categories: Education, IT, Health sciences and Business. Our results showed that on average only 53% of links appear, not necessarily in the same order, in both personalized and non-personalized search results. Interestingly, we observed only slight differences in the extent of personalization based on academic topics.

Categories and Subject Descriptors

H.3.3 [Information Storage and Retrieval]: Information Search and Retrieval – Search process, Selection process.
H.5.4 [Information Storage and Retrieval]: Hypertext/ Hyper-media – User issues

Keywords

Personalized search; University Students; Academic Web search; Measurement; Google

1. INTRODUCTION

In 2005, Google began the era of personalized search by modifying the search results for each user based on the knowledge about her/his current needs, preferences and behavior [20]. As the world's most popular search engine, Google holds 67% of search engine market share in the USA and over 90% in Europe [26]. Since 2009 Google has been providing personalized search results for all users, even those without a Google account [13]. Personalized search promises to improve users' Web experience by giving them the right information at the right time and it benefits users in apparent ways such as better understanding the real meaning of their ambiguous queries or retrieving locally-relevant results [12].

Although details of Google personalization process are unclear, in general personalization of search results takes place based on a user's browser cookies, geographical location, language, Web history and Google+ social connections [12, 24]. According to Google official blog, the aim of personalizing search results is to make a connection with users and provide them with the best possible results. For this purpose Google attempts to understand who users are and what they like, provides them with the results that are assumed to fit their purpose best and finally observes user's reaction and adjusts the fit [19]. However, Pariser [19] argues that although the system's perception of 'who users are' and 'what they like' depends on the sophistication of search algorithms and user models, yet humans are very complicated and no specific set of data can define who they are.

Personalization of search is seemingly a free personal service. However there are potentially a number of negative effects arising from personalization such as loss of serendipity and capability [2, 19]. Since, the Internet is the gateway through which users view and gather information about the world, personalization of search does not only influence advertising and users' shopping behavior, but also affects people's perception of important matters and defines how information flows. Users have a strong faith in what the search engines think is best and that affects their choice of search results. Users tend to choose positive information over negative and prefer search results higher in position even if the abstracts are less relevant to what they need [17, 28].

White's study [28] shows that these biases ultimately change the search results based on what a user prefers, as search engines tend to please the searchers by keeping them within their comfort zone and providing them with familiar concepts in their domain of interest while leaving out potentially important but less agreeable information. This is known as the *filter bubble effect* [19]. Pariser [19] argues that personalization of the search results could limit users' serendipity and negatively affect creativity and innovation.

Search engines are part of our everyday routine to find information for different purposes including completing academic tasks. Despite all the advances in eLearning systems, students continue to depend heavily on general-purpose search engines such as Google to find information and conduct research [16, 21]. Analyzing Internet usage logs from student-driven learning sessions showed that undergraduate medical students spent, on average, 69.8% of each session using Google to find and access biomedical context [14]. A study of PhD students has shown that 82% of the participants considered Google and Google Scholar as their first choice for seeking information [5].

Considering university students and future researchers' strong dependency on Google for academic purposes and rising concerns over the filter bubble effect and Web search biases [12, 28], to date, there has been little scientific examination of personalization of academic search results and how much of a difference it makes to students' learning and educational outcomes. This key observation underlies and motivates the research in this paper.

1.1 Objectives

First, learning the scope in which university students depend on Google for research and other educational purposes: we ask 120 participants from different groups of undergraduate, research and taught postgraduate students from a variety of subjects and attendance statuses to complete a survey about their academic information-seeking behavior and preferences. The aim is to learn what proportion of university students use search engines as their primary or even only source of information, how important they find search engines as an academic information source and finally which search engine they predominantly use.

Second, measuring the difference between personalized and non-personalized search results for academic search queries and analyzing the difference: we use a methodology to measure the difference between personalized and non-personalized search for four sets of academic search queries. Each set of queries belongs to a specific field of study e.g. Business. Search queries are designed using the key words of the most popular/cited papers of each field. The personalized search results of each query are compared to non-personalized search results for the same query and non-personalized searches are executed at the same time and machine as the personalized version. For conducting personalized search we create four Google accounts and assign a unique search history and set of search queries to each of them.

1.2 Terminology

Terms that are often used in this paper when referring to Google search are explained in this section. A typical search *query* is made of one to three words [22] e.g. "credit crunch". The Google search engine returns a *page* of *results* for each query. Each page contains approximately 10 result *links*. We were interested in the *organic links* that point to third party websites and appear in the search results due to their relevance and not for advertisement or redirecting users to other Google

services such as Google news. Examples of organic links that were used for our experiment are highlighted with red arrows in Figure 1.

Figure 1. Example of Google search result page

2. RELATED WORKS

Research on Web search is a multidisciplinary study; it investigates search engines from different perspectives, ranging from information retrieval to social sciences [31]. However, prior studies mainly focused on technical aspects of personalization such as identifying factors that power personalization, personalization measurement and improvement techniques [6, 12, 30].

Hannak et al. [12] developed a methodology for measuring personalization of Web search results and identifying the factors causing Google search personalization e.g. user's location or gender. They indicated that measurable personalization happens when users are searching with their logged in Google accounts and also based on their IP addresses. Their experiments also showed that only 11.7% of the differences in the search results were caused by personalization. Since these experiments took place with a different objective, methodology and under different circumstances we cannot compare our findings with theirs.

Regarding the scope of personalized search and its social and behavioral impacts, we looked into previous studies on university students [2, 5, 11, 14]. Haglund et.al [11] performed a multiple case study at three universities in Sweden and observed that regardless of their information needs; university users preferred direct and easy access to online resources and were more likely to avoid complex information resources. The majority of students used Google search engine for all their information needs, since Google was considered an easy information source compared to other resources such as libraries. Judd et.al [14] came to a similar conclusion after evaluating undergraduate medical students' online information seeking skills. They monitored how students use five popular websites to access biomedical information. Despite students rating Google and Wikipedia as the least reliable sources among the five examined website, these two were the most frequently used websites for accessing academic information. Moreover, less that 40% of the webpages located by students during this study were reliable and of high quality. Another study by Du et.al [5] on 42 postgraduate students pointed to Google search forms as the most popular choices for seeking academic information. This study indicated that as much as 82% of students start their information retrieval process by using Google and Google Scholar.

The study by Ashman et.al [2] focused on the ethical and social effects of personalization technologies in education. They draw attention to the pitfalls of using personalized information in learning such as loss of privacy, serendipity and capability. They discussed that despite obvious benefits of personalization for students such as improving their involvement with the system, personalization should not limit students' search space by denying them access to the same information viewed by others.

3. METHODOLOGY

Our experimental methodology consists of two parts. In part I, we explain the design of our survey, its scope, participants, validity and margin of error. In part II we describe the experiment design that measures the difference between personalized and non-personalized search results for academic queries. We will also talk about noise-cancelling techniques and the reason behind employing or ignoring them during the experiment. Then, we describe the implementation of the experiment and introduce the test queries.

3.1 Part I: Survey

A short survey was designed to observe information-seeking attitudes of university students and the role general-purpose search engines play in them. The survey was made of nine questions. First six questions were about participants' demographic information including age, gender, field of study and level of education. In the last three questions participants were given a set of options and were asked to consider them as information resources for the purpose of completing their academic tasks such as their assignments, reports or research. Participants then ranked each option based on:

- How important they find each of the information resources.
- How often they use each of the information resources.
- How often they use each of the information resources as their first point of enquiry

Ranking was done based on a Likert scale of 1, meaning the lowest, to 5, meaning the highest.

General-purpose search engines were given to the participants among other options as we did not want the participants to know the exact purpose of the survey in case it led to biased answers. The options included library resources, online database and journal subscriptions, Wikipedia or other online encyclopedias or dictionaries, textbooks, lecture notes and discipline-specific online sources such as Medline.

3.1.1 Scope and Participants

A total of 120 students from the University of South Australia, Adelaide, Australia were recruited to take part in the survey. Participants included undergraduate (58%), research postgraduate and taught postgraduate (42%) students from a variety of subjects and attendance statuses. Involving students from a cross-section of the university makes it possible to find if there are discipline-specific differences in search engine usage.

Although this survey covered other aspects of participants' information seeking behavior, this paper only focuses on their attitude towards search engines.

3.1.2 Validity Discussion

We chose a confidence level of 95% for this survey. The confidence level determines how confident we are that the margin of error captures the true population value. At a 95% confidence level, the maximum margin of error (MoE) is calculated as follow where n is the sample size:

$$\text{MoE} \approx \pm\, 0.98/\sqrt{n}$$

Considering that our sample size of 120 students is a random sample of a large population, in this case University of South Australia student population of 37000 students that fit our demographic, the margin of error for the survey is $\approx \pm\, 0.09$. This means if for example 70% of participants gave a particular answer to a question we are 95% sure that (70±9)% of the general population would give the same answer. In other words, we are 95% confident that our survey results are applicable to the general population with a margin error of ±9%.

3.2 Part II: Experiment

This experiment seeks to answer a broad question:
Using the Google search engine for academic queries, what are the differences between personalized and non-personalized search in terms of actual search results?

3.2.1 Experiment Design

Since the result of our survey (see section 4) and also previous research has shown that Google search is the most popular search engine among users and students in particular [26, 29], we run our experiment only on the Google search engine.

This experiment design is based on previous experiments measuring personalization of search for general queries while we are specifically focusing on academic queries.

They showed that measurable Google search personalization accrues based on users' geographical locations and while they are searching with their logged in accounts, assuming these accounts normally store third party cookies [12]. For this reason, to gather personalized search results we created four different Google accounts (test accounts) and a control account identical to one of the test accounts.

These accounts were assumed to belong to four students studying in different areas: Education, IT, Business and Health Sciences.

In order to access non-personalized search results for comparison, we used the *Startpage* search engine on a *Tor* browser. Startpage grabs the best Google search results without revealing or storing any of user's personal information such as IP address (location), identifying cookies or search histories [25]. Startpage has been awarded European Privacy Seal, a certification that confirms users' privacy is taken very seriously by the firm [7]. We ran Startpage private searches on the Tor browser that consists of a modified Mozilla Firefox ESR Web browser with proxy applications and extensions that hides user's location and online activities by redirecting internet traffic through an international network of over five thousand transmits. Third party cookies and Web history are not stored in this browser [27]. Using Startpage on Tor browser prevents the search results from being localized based on Tor exit nodes.

Hannak et al. [12] considered a series of possible noises that might alter the search results and used noise-cancelling techniques to limit their effect, as their aim was to measure the personalization of Web search and discover the factors that influence Google search personalization algorithms. Although, we too are measuring the difference between personalized and non-personalized search results, here this measurement is done to understand what search results a typical student would receive in every-day scenarios if he/she did not use personalized search and how different these search results compare to what students normally receive from Google personalized search. Therefore, we take into account some of the noise-canceling techniques and overlook others:

User's Location and Demographics: Since we were comparing personalized to non-personalized search results for each query and not to the results from other test accounts, all the test accounts had the same IP address. Moreover, we assigned the same demographic information to all the test accounts and used the same operating system and Web browser for all of them, since differences in user's demographics, operating system and browser do not result in measurable personalization [12].

The non-personalized searches were obviously conducted without a Google account and minus all the above information including user's location or IP address.

Google Index Updates: as Google frequently updates its search index, search results for the same query might change over time. Therefore, we ran both personalized and non-personalized searches for each query at the same time and from the same machine.

Google Randomized Testing: to improve user search experience, Google occasionally alters the search results and observes how users respond to them [18].
In order to measure the level of noise caused by these tests, we created a control account identical to one of the test accounts and ran one set of search queries once more while logged in with the control account. As control and test accounts were identical and both executed the queries at the same time and under the same conditions, any difference in their search results must be due to the noise.

Sequential Queries: as it is shown in previous studies, sequentially submitting search queries from a user can refine search results [23]. Hannak et al. [12] called this occurrence the *carry-over effect* where search results of a subsequent query are affected by the preceding query. However their experiment indicated that the carry-over effect disappears after 10 minutes. For this reason and also because we were trying to simulate a real-world scenario, we did not run the queries immediately after one another and allowed at least an 11-minute gap between subsequent queries.

3.2.2 Implementation

All Google accounts that were used to collect personalized search results were created manually with the same profile information: male, 25 years old and living in Australia. Each account had a profile picture and a unique name. Accounts were created two weeks prior to the start of the experiment and during this time we formed a search and browser history for each account containing a variety of academic search queries and visited webpages in students' respective fields (see section

3.2.3) and several general topics pulled from Google Zeitgeist 2013 [9]. There was not any overlap between these queries and the experimental queries. During the experiment we clicked on up to 3 search result links in the first page of the results for each query. We selected these results according to their relevance and reliability. Considering that there is no standard in place for this purpose we made these selection based on our own judgment and expertise. For instance, we favored government and educational URLs (.gov and .edu) over commercial or personal webpages, and read all the abstracts in the first page of the search results regardless of where the link was positioned within the page, in order to choose the most relevant link.

Account cookies and search and browser history were stored normally as set by default settings prior and throughout the experiment. We opened the welcome emails, checked pending notifications, and Google+ announcements for all the accounts to ensure all of the accounts are working in usual order.

Since we set up each account to belong to a student in a specific field of study, we assigned 30 academic search queries in the relevant field to each respective account. Personalized and non-personalized searches for each query were conducted at the same time and on the same machine using the Mac operating system and Mozilla Firefox browser (version 32.0.3). Personalized searches were conducted on Google search main page while users were logged into their Google account and non-personalized searches were carried on at the same time on https://startpage.com. After performing every non-personalized search, the Tor browser session was terminated which automatically cleared all privacy-sensitive data.

We waited at least 11 minutes between submitting consecutive queries and for each account all the search queries were executed within a 48-hour window.
This experiment was conducted in September 2014 at the University of South Australia.

3.2.3 Search Queries

In this experiment we designed 120 *informational* search queries, divided equally into four categories: Education, IT, Business and Health Sciences. Informational queries aim to find the information that is expected to be available on one or more webpages [3], as opposed to *navigational* or *transactional* queries that look for site location and online purchases.

We tried to cover a wide range of academic topics by selecting our categories based on the four main divisions at the University of South Australia. Each of our four Google accounts, putatively belonging to a university student, searched for a particular set of queries consisting of 30 queries on a specific topic in the student's field of study. Table 1 shows the categories, topics and examples of the queries used in the experiment.

Table 1. Categories of search queries

Category	Topic	Query Examples
Education	Effect of Educational Computer Games on Learning	Cooperative learning, Educational beliefs
Health Sciences	Diabetes Type 2 and Life Style	Pre-diabetic state, Oxidative stress
IT	Computer Vision and Pattern Recognition	Object tracking, Motion analysis
Business	Recovery from Financial Crises	Mortgage, Fiscal policy

Since it is impossible to test all potential queries, it was important to at least ensure our queries covered a representative range of popular topics and impact a large number of real students in different fields. We used Google Scholar metrics on top publications [8] and targeted the most cited papers in each of our categories. We then ran through the papers that cited the key paper in each category and made a list of their keywords. Search queries consisted of one to three words from the most frequent keywords in the lists.

4. SURVEY RESULTS

The survey aimed to discover the degree in which university students, from different disciplines and education levels, rely on all-purpose search engines as an information source for academic purposes.

4.1 Results

From 83% of the survey participants who answered the question regarding the general search engine they predominantly use, 99% of them selected Google. Figure 2 shows which search engines participants mainly use. The fact that our survey result identified Google as the most prevalent search engine among university students is consistent with previous studies on information seeking behavior of students [5, 16, 21].

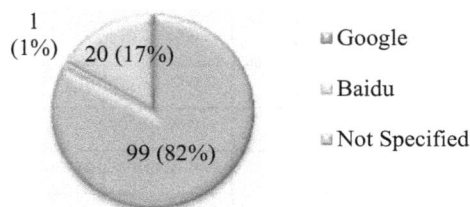

Figure 2. Participants' search engine usage

Next we asked participants to consider general-purpose search engines as educational tools and specify how important they are, how often they are used and finally in what regularity they start researching a topic by referring to a search engine. Participants chose their answers on a 5-point Likert scale from 1, the lowest meaning to 5 the highest meaning. The average point for each question was calculated as follow, where n is the number of participants choosing a specific point and N is the number of participants answering the question:

Average point= $(n \times 5) + (n \times 4) + (n \times 3) + (n \times 2) + (n \times 1) / N$

$1 \leq$ Average point ≤ 5

Table 2 shows a summary of survey findings with average Likert points indicating to what degree university students depend on all-purpose search engines for their education. Since, we did not observe any significant differences in average points for different groups of students; the table only shows the average points for students in different education levels.

Table 2. Average Likert points for students in different education levels

Participants	Importance	Frequency	First point of enquiry
Undergrad (N=70)	4.5	4.7	4.4
Postgrad (N=50):	3.9	4.6	4.0
PhD (N=30)	4.1	4.6	4.1
Masters & GradDip (N=20)	3.8	4.5	4.0
Total (N=120)	4.2	4.7	4.2

According to our findings, not only do higher education students prefer Google to other search engines, they also depend on it as a reliable source of information for conducting assignments and research. More than 83 % of participants found search engines an *important* or *very important* source of academic information. Participants ranked the importance of search engines for the purpose of completing their academic tasks on a 5-point Likert scale: 1 meaning not important at all to 5 meaning very important. The average importance of the search engine for all the participants was 4.2. We did not observe any significant differences in the average points for students from different education levels, field of study, gender or age groups (all ≈ 4).

Despite recommendations that students mainly depend on their library resources including academic journals for educational purposes instead of all-purpose search engines and Wikipedia, the result of our survey and previous studies show that university students frequently use online resources such as Google search engine for learning and research [16]. We asked the participants to indicate how often they use search engines in general and also as their first/starting point of enquiry for seeking information on the topic of their assignments or research. For instance, if they use Google to search for a subject and choose a link from the search results, the first point of enquiry is Google not the webpage they were directed to by the search results.

Their responses were ranked based on a 5-point Likert scale: 1 meaning *never* to 5 meaning *daily*. The average point for how frequently all participants use search engines for educational purposes was 4.7. This number indicates that the majority of our participants, a sample size of 120 higher education students, use general-purpose search engines on daily basis as an educational tool. Although, we expected PhD students to depend less on search engines as a learning resource compared to undergraduate students, the survey results did not show a meaningful dissimilarity between students from different education levels, fields of study, gender or age groups with all different groups' average points being approximately 4.5. This suggests that information-seeking habits are entrenched amongst students by their undergraduate years and are not changed as their education progresses.

The results also indicated an average point of 4.2 for the frequency in which participants use all-purpose search engines as their first/starting point of enquiry for seeking academic information. This means that at least once a week our participants start their self-directed learning sessions by using a search engine. Once more, we did not identify any significant differences between different groups of participants.

4.2 Reflections

Results of this survey were, to some extent, predictable. Although, we predicted that in general students would rely heavily on Google for educational purposes, we did not expect the degree of this dependency to be relatively the same for all groups of students. It was expected of postgraduate students, especially at doctoral level, not to consider all-purpose search engines as one of their primary research resources, especially given that the general-purpose search engines are not tailored to the provision of quality research results.

Students are more likely to choose an information source for research that is convenient, accessible and of high quality [15] and the Google search engine seems to offer all these features. It provides all its users even those without a Google account with personalized search results [13]. The humanizing effect of personalization, efficiency of search results and its convenience and novelty could be a major factor in students' positive attitude towards the Google search engine. Providing students with a personal touch makes them feel that they really matter and it seems to increase their motivation to use the search engine [1].

Students' reliance on Google and its effect on their learning process are very important, as distance and traditional education are becoming more self-driven. There is the possibility of this phenomenon creating new opportunities to improve learning or causing unexpected pedagogical problems, such as providing different search results based on academically-inappropriate personalization factors such as location. This motivated us to look at Google personalized search as a widespread educational tool and conduct the next experiment to find out the extent in which Google personalizes academic search results.

5. EXPERIMENT RESULTS

This experiment was designed to identify the difference between personalized and non-personalized Google search results for academic search queries. For this purpose, we collected the first 10 result links on the first page of the search results for 120 queries, where queries were divided equally into four categories with different topics: Business, IT, Education and Health Science.

Each query was run twice, once anonymously and once personalized to a user studying the topic of query's respective category. Personalized and non-personalized search results of each query were compared to each other to measure their difference. We observed that not only on average 47% of non-personalized search result links are different from the personalized ones, but also the majority of common links appear in different positions in two lists. We also noticed some dissimilarity in level of personalization based on academic topics where the search results of IT queries were less personalized compare to search results in Education category. The next two sections discuss these observations in detail.

5.1 Measuring the Differences

For comparing personalized and non-personalized search results, we used percentage of the overlap between the two sets of results and the *Hamming distance* to measure the difference in order of the links.

The Hamming distance is applicable to two lists with equal lengths and measures how many substitutions are needed to turn one list into another one. In other words, it represents the number of positions in the search results where the corresponding links are different. For instance, the Hamming distance for the following two lists is 3, meaning it takes three substitutions to convert list B into list A:

$$A= 0123456789$$
$$B= 1123556779$$

When these metrics are considered together for two sets of search results we can realize how similar the results are. For instance, as shown in Table 3, there is 50% overlap between personalized and non-personalized results for "Diabetes Risk factor" query. The Hamming distance for this query is 9, meaning we need to substitute 9 links in a list to make it identical to the other. In other words, although 5 out of 10 search result links were common between two lists only one link appeared in the same position in both lists. Table 3 highlights the matching links with the same color.

Table 3. Comparing search results for "Diabetes Risk factor" query

Personalized Results	Non-personalized Results
www.aihw.gov.au/...	www.webmd.com/...
www.mayoclinic.org/...	www.mayoclinic.org/...
www.diabetesqld.org.au/...	www.diabetes.org.uk/...
diabetesaustralia.com.au/...	www.ndep.nih.gov/...
diabetesaustralia.com.au/...	www.idf.org/...
diabetesaustralia.com.au/...	www.aihw.gov.au/...
www.webmd.com/...	www.heart.org/ ...
www.idf.org/...	professional.diabetes.org/...
www.health.gov.au/...	www.diabetes.org/...
diabetes.about.com/...	www.diabetesqld.org.au/...

Our findings show that the difference between personalized and non-personalized search results for typical students, regardless of their study subject, is quite significant. Almost half the links in the first page of the search results are completely different and common links between two lists mainly appear in different orders. Considering that most users do not scroll down to results *below the fold* [4, 10], the order in which a link appears in the result page is very important.

Considering the importance of the first position link in the first search result page and the fact that almost half of the users click on this link [10], for each query we observed if the first links in personalized and non-personalized lists were similar.
For each topic and for all the queries in total, Table 4 shows the average overlap, Hamming distance and the number of times similar links appeared in the first position for both lists.

The significance of results ranking is specifically noticeable for the first result link and more than 30% dissimilarity between links in the top position could indicate that personalized and non-personalized search results can lead students to different or even contrary information about the same topic.

Table 4. Experiment results for total of 120 search queries

Topic	Overlap	Hamming Distance	Matching First Link
Education	47%	8	70%
Health Sciences	50%	8	57%
IT	60%	7	77%
Business	54%	8	70%
Total	53%	8	68%

On one hand, a user's search experience could be immensely improved when search engines use their knowledge about a user in order to generate more relevant results for nonspecific queries. On the other hand, it could be frustrating if the search engine inaccurately guesses user's intention or even misleading if the search engine correctly understands user's intent but hides useful links because they are not in user's anticipated domain of interest. Table 5 shows the most and least personalized queries in our experiment.

Table 5. Most/Least personalized queries

Most Personalized (Overlap ≤ 10%)	Least personalized (Overlap ≥ 90%)
Secondary education	Educational computer games
Recovery services	Family history of diabetes
Public policy	Dietary fatty acids
Gender studies	Oxidative stress
Learning	Diabetes and urbanization
Public health	3D position
Obesity	
Weight management	
Regulations	
Housing market	
Mortgage	

Although, similar to previous studies [12, 23], our general observation of the search results showed that user's geographical location causes notable personalization, we did not expect this factor to affect academic queries as much as general queries. We did not specifically measure the difference between personalized and non-personalized search results based on user's location, as our aim was not to discover the role of different features in search personalization. This observation was attained by revising search results of most personalized queries with average overlap percentage of equal or less that 20% between personalized and non-personalized search results. Personalized search results mainly include links from Australian institutions whereas non-personalized search results seem to be all-inclusive. This pattern was obvious in majority of our most personalized search results. Such a focus on 'local' research institutions may not always be academically beneficial and may skew a student's understanding of their chosen field.

5.2 Noise Level

Comparing search results of the control account to its test account duplicate (the health science account) determined the level of noise in this experiment, for instance noise caused by Google randomized testing. One set of queries were executed three times at the same time and under the exact same conditions for the control account, its identical test account and once more anonymously to obtained non-personalized search results. The search results from both control and test accounts were compared to the non-personalized search results where Hamming distance and the overlap between the two lists were calculated. To determine the baseline of noise, we then compared these metrics from the control account against the test account.

As shown in Figure 3, these comparisons did not demonstrate any significant dissimilarity between the test and the control search results. There is on average 50% overlap between personalized and non-personalized search results in both cases. The average Hamming distance for control account was 9 whereas for the test account the average was 8. This means that compared to the test search result list, on average, we need only 1 more substitution in the control list to make it identical to non-personalized results. These measurements indicate that the difference between personalized and non-personalized search results in our experiment seems to be mainly due to personalization rather than noise.

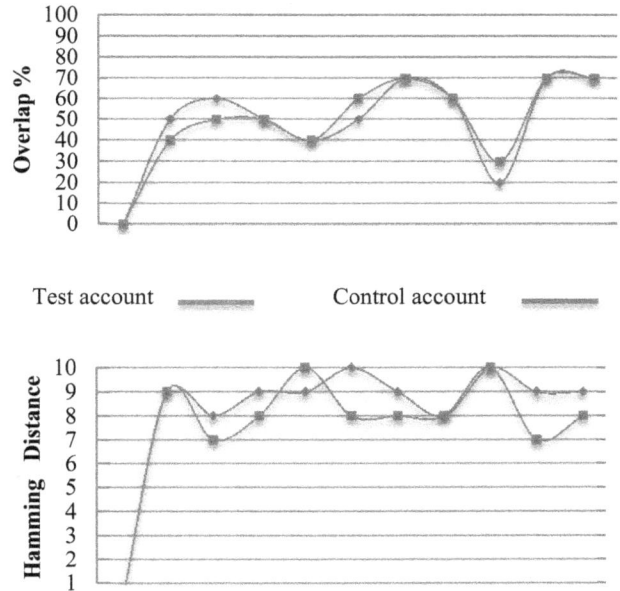

Figure 3. Comparing personalized control and test results to non-personalized results

6. DISCUSSION

Students' reliance on Google and its effect on their learning process are very important, as distance and traditional education are becoming more self-driven. The possibility of this phenomenon creating new opportunities to improve learning or causing unexpected pedagogical problems motivated us to look at Google personalized search as a widespread educational tool.

It seems that Google is providing personalized learning experiences for students and therefore has the power to significantly influence society by shaping the mindset of future researchers and professionals. The majority of students depend greatly, sometimes exclusively, on Google for their educational information needs even when they think of Google as a less reliable source compared to other academic information sources such as university libraries and journal databases. Moreover, Google search results are personalized for all the users even those without a Google account. Considering these facts, there is potential for concern here, given that the personalization and indeed the search engine itself is not intended as an educational or research tool, as it aims to service domestic and recreational requests as well. While, Google personalization has been measured in past studies to understand the difference personalization makes in the search results, these studies mainly focused on the general public and personalization of popular everyday search queries. There is little understanding about the educational and social effects of this personalization and of search engines' ranking methods, applied in the educational context.

In this study, first we questioned a group of students from different disciplines, levels of education, age groups and genders about their educational information-seeking attitudes. We were specifically interested in their approach towards commercial search engines and whether they view them as a reliable source for research and other educational purposes. Our results indicated Google is the most popular search engine among students. We also learned that not only the majority of undergraduate students, but also postgraduate research students depend on Google as their primary or even only source of academic information. More than 83% of participants found search engines an *important* or *very important* learning resource. The majority of students stated that not only do they use search engines for educational purposes on daily bases, but also they refer to search engines as their first point of enquiry at least once a week. The degree in which the participants relied on search engines for their education was relatively the same for all groups of students.

Second, we focused on higher education students and quantified the difference personalization makes in the Google search results of academic queries for a typical student. We compared personalized and non-personalized top 10 search results for 120 informational search queries, divided equally into four categories: Education, IT, Business and Health Sciences. We discovered that on average only 53% of the links were shared between personalized and non-personalized search results; these shared links mostly appeared in different orders. There was not any significant difference in the level of personalization based on topic of the search queries. Moreover, comparing the results of the control account to the search results of the test account indicated that the difference between personalized and non-personalized search results in our experiment seems to be mainly due to personalization rather than noise.

We observed that results of most queries were unnecessarily personalized based on user's geographical location. One of the main objectives of personalized search is altering the search results to fit each user as oppose to the 'one size fits all' approach where every user receives the same results for the same query despite of their characteristics and information needs. However, at times, the discrimination between users is not helpful and the current approach to personalization itself is a 'one size fits all' process in that it applies personalization regardless of the context or the genuine need for it. In this case,

it seems that Google search algorithms fail to distinguish between queries that need to be personalized based on user's location and academic queries for which user's location is irrelevant. Although, it is practical to give users locally-relevant results when they are looking for restaurants or attractions the same does not apply to most academic informational queries. One can argue that when users submit search queries to Google to find academic information they expect to receive the most relevant and reliable links on that topic regardless of where they live or what their IP address is. In the academic domain it can be counterproductive to deny users information simply because that information comes from an organization located in a different country.

As the result of our methodology, we realized the scope in which university students use Google search engine as an educational tool, and the level of Google search personalization for academic search queries. Considering the significant difference personalization makes in search results coupled with students' substantial dependency on Google search and the limitations of this study, we discussed some of the potential benefits and disadvantages of using personalized search as an academic resource which gives us direction for future research in this area.

We aim to continue this work by semantically comparing personalized and non-personalized search results. For instance, after determining that link A is different from link B, we study whether they contain different information or one is more reliable than the other. We determine the quality of search results by asking academic experts in different fields to rank Google personalized and non-personalized search results for several queries in their respective fields in terms of usefulness, reliability and relevance.

Furthermore, we will investigate the effects of personalized search on students' learning process. Through self-directed study sessions, we will study the effects of personalized search on students' satisfaction and outcomes including originality of research and quality of assignment.

7. REFERENCES

[1] Ashman, H. Brailsford, T and Brusilovsky, P. 2009. Personal Services: Debating the Wisdom of Personalisation. In *Proceedings of the 8th International Conference on Advances in Web Based Learning* (Aachen, Germany, August 19-21, 2009). Springer-Verlag Berlin, Heidelberg, 1-11.

[2] Ashman, H. Brailsford, T. Cristea, A.I. Sheng, Q.Z. Stewart, C. Toms, E.G. and Wade, V. 2014. The Ethical and Social Implications of Personalization Technologies for e-learning. *Inf. Manage.* 51 (Sep. 2014), 819-832.

[3] Broder, A. 2002. A Taxonomy of Web Search. *ACM SIGIR Forum.* 36 (Fall 2002), 3-10.

[4] Cutrell, E and Guan, Z.2007. What Are You Looking for? An Eye-tracking Study of Information Usage in Web Search. In *Proceedings of the SIGCHI Conference on Human Factors in Computing Systems* (San Jose, California, USA, 28 April – 3 May, 2007). ACM, New York, NY, 407-416.

[5] Du, JT and Evans, N. 2011. Academic Users' Information Searching on Research Topics: Characteristics of Research Tasks and Search Strategies. *The Journal of Academic Librarianship.* 37 (July. 2011), 299-306.

[6] Dou, Z. Ruihua Song and R. Wen, J. 2007. A Large-scale Evaluation and Analysis of Personalized Search Strategies. In *Proceedings of the 16th international conference on World Wide Web* (Banff, Alberta, Canada, May 18-12, 2007). ACM, New York, NY, USA, 581-590.

[7] European Privacy Seal for Ixquick and Startpage. http://bit.ly/1OH4P5k.

[8] Google Scholar Top Publications. http://bit.ly/1zcwBmp.

[9] Google Zeitgeist. http://www.googlezeitgeist.com.

[10] Guan, Z and Cutrell, E.2007. An Eye Tracking Study of the Effect of Target Rank on Web Search. *In Proceedings of the SIGCHI Conference on Human Factors in Computing Systems* (San Jose, California, USA, 28 April - 3 May, 2007). ACM, New York, NY, 407-416.

[11] Haglund, L. & Olsson, P. 2008. The Impact on University Libraries of Changes in Information Behavior Among Academic Researchers: A Multiple Case Study. *The Journal of Academic Librarianship*, 34 (Jan. 2008), 52-59.

[12] Hannak, A. Sapiezynski, P. Kakhki, A.M. Krishnamurthy, B. Lazer, D. Mislove, A. and Wilson, C. 2013. Measuring Personalization of Web Search. In *Proceedings of the 22nd international conference on World Wide Web* (Rio de Janeiro, Brazil, May 13-17, 2013), International World Wide Web Conferences Steering Committee Republic and Canton of Geneva, Switzerland, 527-538.

[13] Horling, B and Kulick, M. Personalized Search for Everyone. *Google Official Blog*, 2009. http://bit.ly/71RcmJ.

[14] Judd, T and Kennedy, G. 2011. Expediency-based Practice? Medical Students' Reliance on Google and Wikipedia for Biomedical Inquiries. *BJET*. 42 (Mar. 2011), 351–360.

[15] Kim, K. Sin, S.J.2007. Perception and Selection of Information Sources by Undergraduate Students: Effects of Avoidant Style, Confidence, and Personal Control in Problem-Solving. *The Journal of Academic Librarianship*. 33 (Dec. 2011), 655–665.

[16] McClure, R and Clink, K. 2009. How Do You Know That? An Investigation of Student Research Practices in the Digital Age, *Portal: Libraries and the Academy*. 9 (Jan. 2009), 115-132.

[17] Pan, B. Hembrooke, H. Joachims, T. Lorigo, L. Gay, G. and Granka, L. 2007. In Google We Trust: Users' Decisions on Rank, Position, and Relevance. *CMC*. 12 (June 2007), 801-823.

[18] Pansari, A and Mayer, M. This is a Test. This is Only a Test. *Google Official Blog*, 2006. http://bit.ly/Ldbb0.

[19] Pariser, E. 2011. *The Filter Bubble: What The Internet Is Hiding From You*. Penguin Press, New York, NY.

[20] Personalized Search Graduates from Google Labs. *News from Google Blog*, 2005. http://bit.ly/Tndpgf.

[21] Purdy, JP. 2012. Why First-year College Students Select Online Research Resources as Their Favorite. *First Monday*. 17 (Sep. 2012).

[22] Senthil Kumar, N and Saravanakumar, K. 2013. Web Query Expansion and Refinement Using Query-level Clustering. *IJET*. 5 (Apr. 2013). 705-712.

[23] Shen, Y. Yan, J. Yan, S. Ji, L. Liu, N and Chen, Z. 2011. Sparse Hidden-Dynamics Conditional Random Fields for User Intent Understanding. In *Proceedings of the 20th international conference on World Wide Web* (Lyon, France, April 26-20, 2012). ACM, New York, NY, USA, 7-16.

[24] Singhal, A. Some Thoughts on Personalization. *The Official Google Search Blog, 2011.* http://bit.ly/tJS4xT

[25] StartPage Privacy Policy. http://bit.ly/1qxOC9x.

[26] Sterling, G. Google Market Share: 67 Percent On PC, 83 Percent In Mobile, *Search Engine Land*, 2014, http://selnd.com/1uBLegh

[27] Tor: Overview. http://bit.ly/1dZ2zvZ

[28] White, R.W. 2013. Beliefs and Biases in Web Search. In *Proceedings of the 36th international ACM SIGIR conference on Research and development in information retrieval* (Dublin, Ireland, July 28 - August 01, 2013), ACM, New York, NY, 3-12.

[29] Yadav, D. Sharma, A.K and Gupta, J.P. 2010. Users Search Trends on WWW and Their Analysis. *In Proceedings of the First International Conference on Intelligent Interactive Technologies and Multimedia* (Allahabad, India, December 28 - 30, 2010). ACM, New York, NY, 59-66.

[30] Zhu, Yun. Xiong, L. Verdery, C. 2010. Anonymizing User Profiles for Personalized Web Search. In *Proceedings of the 19th international conference on World Wide Web* (Raleigh, NC, USA, April 26-30, 2010). ACM, New York, NY, USA, 1225-1226.

[31] Zimmer, M. 2010. *Web Search Studies: Multidisciplinary Perspectives on Web Search Engines.* Springer Netherlands, Dordrecht.

An Interactive Method for Inferring Demographic Attributes in Twitter

Valentina Beretta
University of Milano-Bicocca
DISCo
Viale Sarca 336
Milano, Italy
v.beretta3@campus.unimib.it

Daniele Maccagnola
University of Milano-Bicocca
DISCo
Viale Sarca 336
Milano, Italy
daniele.maccagnola@disco.unimib.it

Timothy Cribbin
Brunel University
Department of Computer Science
Kingston Lane
Uxbridge, United Kingdom
timothy.cribbin@brunel.ac.uk

Enza Messina
University of Milano-Bicocca
DISCo
Viale Sarca 336
Milano, Italy
messina@disco.unimib.it

ABSTRACT

Twitter data offers an unprecedented opportunity to study demographic differences in public opinion across a virtually unlimited range of subjects. Whilst demographic attributes are often implied within user data, they are not always easily identified using computational methods. In this paper, we present a semi-automatic solution that combines automatic classification methods with a user interface designed to enable rapid resolution of ambiguous cases. TweetClass employs a two-step, interactive process to support the determination of gender and age attributes. At each step, the user is presented with feedback on the confidence levels of the automated analysis and can choose to refine ambiguous cases by examining key profile and content data. We describe how a user-centered design approach was used to optimise the interface and present the results of an evaluation which suggests that TweetClass can be used to rapidly boost demographic sample sizes in situations where high accuracy is required.

1. INTRODUCTION

Social scientists, policy makers and marketers are keen to find ways to mine social media (SM) data in order to gain insights into public attitudes and opinion. Traditional survey research methods (questionnaires, interviews etc.) are becoming less attractive, due to falling response rates and increasing costs [9]. At the same time, members of potential target populations are increasingly sharing their views, for free, on SM platforms such as Twitter and Facebook. For this reason, mining SM is seen by many as a key part of the next generation in survey research methods [23]. There are several features that make SM based research attractive. that are particularly attractive. First large datasets can be collected rela-

tively cheaply and are already digitally encoded. Second, SM users tend to comment in a responsive, ad hoc manner, allowing a more timely polling of opinion on current events, in comparison to 'designed' research. Third, despite being public forums, the perceived anonymity of SM platforms means that views expressed online may often be more honest and expressive than those collected using designed instruments [21].

A key barrier to the use of SM data is the absence of explicit and/or reliable demographic attribute data. Such metadata is essential in survey research to make comparisons between population groups. Without ready demographic data, researchers tend to resort to making subjective judgments by explaining the qualitative characteristics of user's posted content and virtual profile.

However, this method is very time consuming. On the other hand, automatic techniques can be used for deriving the demographic attributes, but in some cases (for instance in age identification task) their results are not always reliable [22, 26].

Given this problem, we propose a semi-automatic framework to facilitate and accelerate the human judgment process. The framework relies as much as possible on automatic techniques, essential for handling the huge amount of data that originates from SM, only requiring human intervention for cases that cannot be classified with high confidence by the algorithms. We incorporate this approach into a proof-of-concept tool, called TweetClass, designed to support researchers in the identification of demographic attributes of a Twitter user sample. In order to evaluate the capabilities of our tool, our experiments include an extensive analysis of the interface design. Moreover, even if our focus is not on the classification method, we investigated the best approach among few popular techniques for facilitating the refinement process for the end-user.

The rest of the paper is structured as follows. In Section 2 we present previous work related to demographic attribute inference and semi-automatic approaches to classification. In Section 3 we explain the rationale behind combining automatic and interactive methods and how we combine them. Section 4 describes how we collected our dataset, followed by Section 5 which describes the experiments carried out to find the best approach for automatically identifying age and gender class. Finally, in Section 6, we focus our attention on an essential part of the work, the interface design and the method employed for evaluating it. In particular, here the description of the first prototype is followed by the description of

HT '15, September 1–4, 2015, Guzelyurt, Northern Cyprus.
© 2015 ACM. ISBN 978-1-4503-3395-5/15/09 ...$15.00.
DOI: http://dx.doi.org/10.1145/2700171.2791031.

his evaluation that highlighted several problem addressed with the development of a second prototype interface.

2. RELATED WORKS

Previous research has explored the problem of automatically inferring key demographic variables such as gender, age, ethnicity, political orientation, occupation and regional origin [20, 10, 18]. Here, we focus our attention on gender and age, since they are fundamental attributes required in social research. Existing approaches have exploited different feature types that can be used for deriving age and gender. The three main approaches can be distinguished as: profile-based, content-based and hybrid.

Profile-based approaches use metadata associated with the user's account or profile. In Twitter, such features include real name, description, location, followers and friends. For instance, the simplest profile-based method assigns gender class based on a dictionary look-up of the user's first-name, see [13, 22]. An alternative approach is to infer a user's gender based on profile colour preference [1]. When it comes to age inference, profile-based features tend not to be used alone, but combined with content-based features.

Content-based methods exploit the language expressed in the text of users' posts. One of the earliest content-based approaches focused on gender and age class inference is [20]. Their method processes unigrams and bigram features using a Support Vector Machine (SVM) algorithm. Similarly, in [17], n-grams are used with a combination of Chi-square based feature selection and SVM. Other work has also used n-gram features in combination with logistic and linear regression models [14, 15].

In addition to n-grams, stylistic features have also been studied. For instance, several approaches describe methods to derive gender and/or age based on the usage of smileys, abbreviations, punctuation, possessive bigrams, repeated letters, pronouns, hashtags and other grammatical features[20, 6, 4].

In contrast, hybrid approaches leverage profile data for enhancing the accuracy of results obtained using content-based features. Notable examples of the hybrid approach include [26, 10, 11, 5, 3].

Comparing the efficacy of these and other methods is not straightforward because of the tendency to use different datasets for training and testing. Moreover, different studies tend to vary in the intervals used for age classes. Despite these problems, it is possible to draw some key conclusions:

- Regarding gender classification studies, it is evident that profile-based classification methods are faster than content-based ones, but the former achieve lower accuracy than the latter.

- Age inference tends to be the more challenging task, particularly with respect to older age groups, see [14]. This seems to be due to the fact that the way a person speaks is influenced by many factors, beside age: for instance, whilst adults tend to be more conservative in their language, factors such as their profession and culture can also impact on their content and style of expression.

- Generally, in studies where several machine learning techniques are compared, SVM performs better than other classification methods.

- Content-based methods have an high computational complexity due to the number of features generated from the text. This is particularly true for n-gram approaches.

- Gender and age classification are treated as independent tasks, although gender has been used as an additional binary feature of the age feature set ([16, 17]).

We hypothesised that features characterising age and gender might be co-dependent. Argamon et al. used factor analysis for identifying 20 coherent factors of words linking gender and age [2]. They show that male components of language increase with age, while female ones decrease. Therefore we decided to introduce a hierarchical approach, whereby the first step derives user's gender and in the second one derives user's age class conditioned to his gender class.

The results obtained with automatic methods, as described, tend to fall in the ranges of 70%-92% of accuracy for gender inference and 71%-88% for age class (levels of accuracy in excess 80% are only possible if the age classes are divided by a gap of several years). To become a credible alternative to designed survey research, it must be feasible and practicable to sample demographic groups to a much higher level of accuracy.To this end, we developed a semi-automatic approach in which a user interface presents the results of automatic classification and enables the user make refinements on the basis of additional profile and content information. This kind of method has been adopted successfully in other domains (e.g. [24, 27]).

3. APPROACH

TweetClass combines automatic classification with human interaction. The use of automatic methods is essential to manage the huge amount of data that originates from SM, however a reliable and accurate automatic classification may not be possible for all cases and human intervention may be required. Indeed in some cases determining a user's gender or age might be a simple task for a human, based on examination of a photograph or profile description, yet the same task is very difficult to reliably achieve using automatic methods. Moreover, for a given a Twitter user, humans are able to explore additional information. For instance, they can explore the user's digital footprint on the Web. If the name is not meaningful, they can see profile images from other platforms, explore SM relationships and so on. Just reading extracts from a user's timeline, can be sufficient to discover nuanced clues that might not be found by automatic methods amongst a much larger corpus of data.

Gender and age class inference is achieved through a process that is summarized in Figure 1. At each major step, the end-user is provided with the option to scrutinize and refine the results of automatic classification algorithms. The most critical part of the pro-

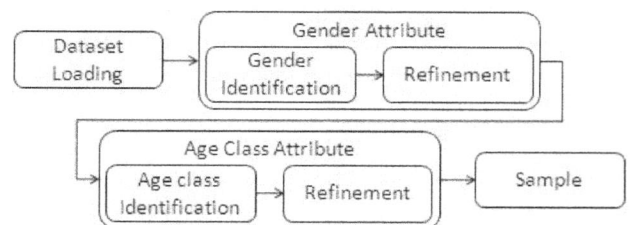

Figure 1: TweetClass process.

cess regards the identification of age class demographic attribute. Our experimental data show that gender does influence the age class identification. As such, a two phase hierarchical procedure was used to build the classification model. Hence, gender is derived as first attribute to increase the classification accuracy of the user's age class.

The gender of each Twitter user is determined using the user's first-name that appears in the profile. Identifying a person's gender from their name is not always straightforward. For instance, users may use pseudonyms or transpose their surname and first-name. The latter case becomes more problematic if the user's surname is equivalent to a common first-name (e.g. Michael Stewart).

In our work, we decided to use a dictionary based approach, primarily because of its efficiency in terms of computational time. In particular, we used the 40N database [22] that contains a list a more than 44000 first names and related gender from 54 different states covering the vast majority of first names in all European Countries. Therefore, given a string u containing user's name, we have that $u \in \{F, mF, M, mM, U\}$, where F is female, mF is unisex but mostly female, M is male, mM is unisex but mostly male, and U is either unisex (with no prevalence of female or male) or not found. To increase the accuracy of this classification a refinement classification phase follows the automatic one in order to manually inspect the ambiguous classification $u \in \{mF, mM, U\}$.

Once the gender class is assigned, the process continues to the age inference step. During age inference phase the Twitter users are classified into two major demographic sets: users below 30 (younger) and users above 30 (older).

While this binary categorization may seem too simple, we must consider that age is a difficult attribute to learn. Not only does it change constantly, age-sensitive communication behavior differs based on numerous socioeconomic variables, and there is no well known indicator for age on Twitter [20].

We model the tweet contents, for each gender class, using a feature vector approach. Unigram features are selected after a preprocessing phase. Chi-Square feature selection is used to reduce the number of attributes and to take into account only the most predictive words. We derived the remaining stylistic features additionally using a POS-tagging procedure and partially using regular expressions, for instance the presence of stretched word (hellooo, SUNNY). Since an user can write more than one tweet, user's age class is identified taking into account a sample of their recent posts. Single tweets are then classified independently by using classification models such SVM or Naive Bayes. From this classification phase we obtain the label probability distribution and we assign to the tweet the label with the maximum likelihood. Once each single tweet of the user is classified the results are aggregated in order to obtain an overall age classification probability for each user. The probabilities for a user to belong to younger and older class are computed using the following formulas:

$$p\{u \in younger\} = \alpha \sum_{i=0}^{N} p\{tweet_i \in younger\}$$

$$p\{u \in older\} = \alpha \sum_{i=0}^{N} p\{tweet_i \in older\}$$

(1)

where α is a normalization factor and N is the number of tweets that belong to him/her. For each user u_j we define a confidence value $Conf_j$ given by the following formula:

$$Conf_j = max(p\{u_j \in younger\}, p\{u_j \in older\}). \quad (2)$$

The confidence level can be interpreted as the probability of how sure end-user can be regarding a certain classification. All user instances classified with a confidence level lower than a certain threshold are displayed to end-user.

4. DATASET

There is a lack of both gender and age labeled datasets in the public domain. Given this, we collected a new dataset using Twitter API. The absence of suitable datasets is a result of two key factors. First, to gather private information such as gender and age of a user is a resource intensive task. Second, issues relating to privacy and Twitter data user terms limit data diffusion. Indeed, datasets of Twitter Content or an API that returns Twitter Content can be downloaded only if they contain or return IDs (tweet IDs or user IDs).

To obtain our data collection we adopted a similar idea used in [26]. In order to identify age labeled users, they collected all tweets in which an individual announced his or her own birthday (e.g., "Happy ##th/st/nd/rd birthday to me").

As reported in Figure 2, we developed a crawler, based on the Streaming Search API provided by the Twitter site, able to filter only particular tweets from the stream.

Figure 2: Dataset collection process.

We filtered all the tweets containing the word "birthday" and identifying the owner's birthday. At this point, we derived the age of each user using the regular expressions. We filtered all tweets including two consecutively digits that were not part of fractions, urls, usernames, hours, dates and three or more-digit numbers. In fact, with high probability, the remaining two digit numbers represent the age. We eliminated all users with follower number greater than 5000 because these users were likely to be celebrities or big companies that would not be representative of behaviour Twitter population.

In order to validate the dataset, a manual inspection was necessary and during this phase the gender labels were added.

Using this method we were able to collect a dataset of 386 users. It is composed of 62 younger male, 88 older male, 152 younger female and 84 older female. For each of these users we retrieved between 20 and 200 tweets from their timeline. In this way, we obtained a tweet dataset where 8368 tweets belong to younger male, 12868 to older male, 21288 to younger female and 12002 to older female authors. To create a balanced dataset for both gender and age class attributes, we randomly sampled the dataset retrieving for each gender-age class a number of tweets equal to 8368 (minimum number of tweet in gender-age class combination). Using the collected dataset we conducted the following experiments.

5. EXPERIMENTS

5.1 Gender identification

Since social scientists are interested in maximizing the accuracy of the assigned demographic attributes, the automatic gender classification should ideally either assign the correct gender if possible or leave the classification to the refinement phase. For this reason we decided to reduce from 5 to 3 the number of classes presented to the end-user, namely (female, male and unknown). During the experiments we used two configurations to identify these three classes:

1. $u^* \in \{F, M, U^*\}$ where $U^* = \{mF \cup mM \cup U\}$;

2. $u^+ \in \{F^+, M^+, U\}$ where $F^+ = \{F \cup mF\}$ and $M^+ = \{M \cup mM\}$;

Social scientists need a sample of users with specific demographic attribute values and it is very important that these values match the real ones. So, the first configuration seems to be more desirable than the second one. Indeed, in configuration 1 the users with names that are considered mostly male or mostly female are classified as "unknown". In this way, social scientists can be assured that if a user is classified as "male" or "female", he/she belongs to this class with high reliability. Nonetheless, we decided to analyse both the situations to obtain a much deeper investigation.

Moreover, we analysed performance changes considering either all words contained in the user name field or just the first word that appeared in it. Therefore we conducted experiments with the following resulting configurations:

- *method G1*, we derived gender of u^* using all user's name field;

- *method G2*, we derived gender of u^* using first word in user's name field;

- *method G3*, we derived gender of u^+ using first word in user's name field;

Note that, in all the experiments, we used the C library written by Micheal et al.[12] for exploiting the 40N database. The library is able to check first-names and determine their gender automatically.

Results

The results of these experiments are reported in Table 1. Note that we were interested in computing only the evaluation measures over the instances classified as "male" or "female". In fact, due to the huge amount of Twitter users, social scientists are likely to be less worried about loss of some users, if this results in a significant improvement in classification accuracy. So, the instances considered "unknown" were just discarded and we focused our attention only on male and female classified instances. We observed

	Class	Precision	Recall	F1	Acc
G1	F	97.7%	90.7%	94.07%	93%
	M	86.7%	96.6%	91.38%	
G2	F	98.4%	96.1%	97.2%	97%
	M	93.7%	97.4%	95.51%	
G3	F	97.4%	94.94%	96.15%	95%
	M	92.23%	95.96%	94.06%	

Table 1: Gender classification results

that the *method G2* achieves the best result. In this case, the error rate is only 3%. Instead, the worse performances were obtained with *method G1*. The difference between this method and the other ones was the part of user name field used to derive gender. As already explained, in *method G1* all name field was considered, while in *method G2* and in *method G3* only the first word of name field was used. Since typically Twitter users fill their name field writing first name followed by surname, taking into account the entire name field could be a problem. Indeed, several surnames are also first names. In *method G1*, this affects the gender classification task increasing the number of gender misclassified instances. For example, a possible name field could be "Rylee Ross" (first name + surname). In this situation, considering all the name field (*method G1*), user would be misclassified as male. Indeed, while "Rylee" is a mostly female name," Ross" can be also used as first name, and, in particular as a male name leading to an overall classification as male user.

Usually, in all the experiments, the number of incorrectly female classified instances was higher than the male one. Inspecting these misclassified instances we found that in several cases female users do not write their name, but acclaim related to some male celebrity, such as "I love you Ashton". After all these observations, since we want to assure to social scientist the best reliability, we decided to use the *method G2* to infer gender attribute of each user in Tweet-Class tool.

5.2 Age class identification

The feature set that represents each tweet was composed of 108 attributes where 80 are term-based and 28 are stylistic-based features. For the preprocessing phase we employed the StringToWord-Vector filter, present in Weka's libraries, to obtain the unigram features. This filter is able to transform a input char set into a output token set where each token has specific value. This value is also called weight and it is derived from frequency of the token. During the tokenization phase we applied the stopword list, but not the stemming. Then, we applied the Chi-square feature selection techniques for reducing the number of unigrams to 80. Then we used regular expressions and the "Twitter NLP and Part of Speech Tagging" for identifying the stylistic features, as detailed in [8].

During the experiments we investigated the best method to identify the age class, among a set of popular classification methods: SVM, Naive Bayes, Multinomial Naive Bayes and K Nearest Neighbours. Moreover, we were interested in understanding if gender attribute value influenced age classification. For this reason, we performed several experiments using different dataset compositions:

- *dataset A*, composed of all instances belonging to the dataset;

- *dataset B*, composed of only male instances of *dataset A*;

- *dataset C*, composed of only female instances of *dataset A*.

For each aspect that we explored, we conducted experiments using 10-fold cross validation technique.

Results

A set of experiments was conducted using several machine learning techniques, aimed at inferring the age class of each single tweet, over the three dataset. The SVM obtained the best results among the considered approaches as shown in Table 2. Furthermore, other

	Dataset A	Dataset B	Dataset C
SVM	64%	65%	66%
NB	59%	59%	60%
NBMultinomial	62%	62%	62%
kNN (k=7)	60%	60%	61%

Table 2: Tweet-level accuracy obtained using different machine learning techniques over the different dataset.

experiment outcomes reported in Table 3 show the different performances achieved, over *dataset A*, *dataset B* and *dataset C*, using SVM with different feature set: only unigram features, only stylistic features and both. Note that, in all the experiments, the highest performances were obtained considering all features, while the lowest were obtained considering only unigram features.

Once we discovered the best configuration to obtain the age class of each single tweet, we decided to study the performances from the user point of view. The experimental campaign was conducted using all the datasets (*dataset A*, *dataset B* and *dataset C*). Table 4 shows the outcomes. So, in order to obtain the best outcomes, we

Dataset	Features	Accuracy
Dataset A	Unigrams	61.88%
	Stylistic	63.12%
	All	64.45%
Dataset B	Unigrams	62.69%
	Stylistic	63.09%
	All	65.17%
Dataset C	Unigrams	62 .53%
	Stylistic	63.67%
	All	65.76%

Table 3: Accuracy performances using SVMs.

decided to learn two different model to infer age: one for male and one for female instances. Both the model are trained using SVM, using the entire feature set (unigrams + stylistic features).

Dataset	Accuracy
Dataset A	71.28%
Dataset B	72.82%
Dataset C	75.43%

Table 4: User-level accuracy performances achieved using SVM in combination with the entire feature set.

The effect of size variation in the tweet set available for each author to infer his/her age class was also analyzed. In particular, the experiments shown that the variation of accuracy for each Twitter user was reduced as the number of tweets available decreased (see Figure 3). To judge age class from just one tweet is a complex task. Therefore, to address this difficulty it is useful to increase the number of tweets examined for each Twitter user. In order to balance effectiveness and efficacy of age classification, in the tool a set of 55 tweets was considered for each user.

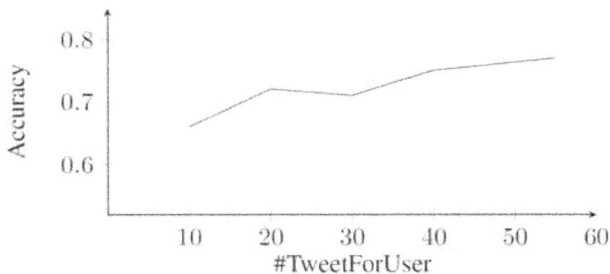

Figure 3: User-level accuracy variation respect to tweet test-set dimension variation.

6. INTERFACE DESIGN

The aim of the interface design is to support the users with all instances that are difficult to classify automatically. Any instance classified as "unknown" can be processed manually by the end-users through the refinement step. The interface is composed of two main areas: the process timeline viewer *(a)* and the data viewer *(b)* on the left and on the right part of Figure 4, respectively.

The process timeline viewer shows all the steps of the procedure, and highlights the one currently performed. The content of the data viewer varies, depending on the relevant information for the current process phase. For instance, during this refinement phase, additional information related to the Twitter profile of each user is

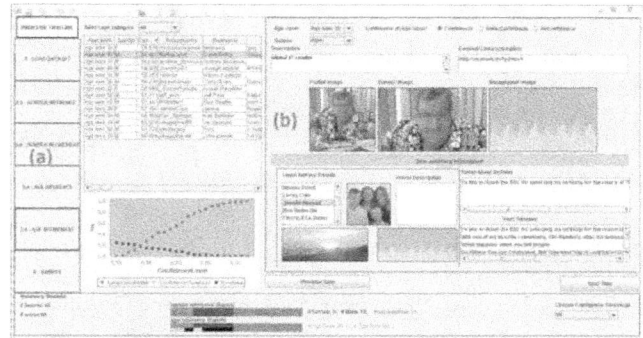

Figure 4: Tool interface, there are the process timeline bar (a) on the left and the data viewer (b) on the right.

shown to the end-user. For the gender inspection, screen name, description, profile image, banner image and background profile image are shown. All this information can be used to infer a user's gender. Indeed, frequently, the images could show a self-portrait and the description could give indications about their gender. In the same way, the age class identification step is followed by a user refinement step. Here, since during the automatic classification stage a confidence level (see Formula 2) is associated to each classified instance, all instances whose age class is identified with a low confidence level are refined by the end-user. Once again, during this phase, the end-user can process the data by using additional information. Beside all the information already described for the gender refinement step, the end-user can also see external links, a list of least famous friends, the user's timeline and the user's tweets about "birthday". All this kind of additional information is useful for different reasons. For instance, external links could be able to connect the unclassified users with their other web-pages. Here, suggestions about a user's age class could be found. In a user's timeline the end-user could read about a specific topic highly related to a particular age class. In user's tweets about birthday a user could celebrate his/her birthday indicating his/her age. Moreover, as reported in [26], an indicator of user's age class is the set of least famous friends. They are friends of user who have the fewest followers, which are more likely to be friends in real life (versus celebrities or organizations) and therefore belong to the same age group. For each friend of this kind, information like description, profile image, background image and banner image, is displayed. After the age class refinement phase, the final aim of the tool is reached: a set of users with their gender and age class is obtained.

6.1 Cognitive Walkthrough

To understand if the interface that we designed is intuitive and easy to use for typical end-users, we decided to conduct a formal evaluation using a method called cognitive walkthrough. The cognitive walkthrough entails an usability analyst stepping through the cognitive tasks that a user must carry out in interacting with technology. The aim of a walkthrough is to evaluate the design of a user interface, with special attention to how well the interface supports "exploratory learning", i.e., first-time use without formal training. In brief, users start with a goal and some sort of plan(task sequence) as how to achieve the goal. Users then look for apparently relevant actions, activate the most probable option, consider the system response (system feedback) and decide whether the right effect has been achieved.

For each individual step, performed by the end-users, in the interaction the analyst asks the following questions:

- Will the user try to achieve the right effect?

- Will the user notice that the correct action is available?

- Will the user associate the correct action with the effect to be achieved?

- If the correct action is performed, will the user see that progress is being made towards solution of the task? [25]

These questions permit to understand in which tool part end-user has difficult to do tasks. For instances the case in which a button produces unexpected effect, the order of displayed information is wrong, the end-user is not able to proceed in the process, etc. In all these cases improvements of the tool interface are required in order to maximize the easiness of it. In fact, the final aim of the cognitive walkthrough is to realize an interface that not required it explanation to end-users before it usage.

Procedure

For our cognitive walkthrough we recruited 2 domain experts (both male with age between 30 and 35). both are social scientists who work in a major market research organization in the UK that conducts surveys for a wide range of major clients, including commercial and government organisations. They are comfortable with computers and very familiar with Twitter Social Media.

Before beginning the cognitive walkthrough, the participants received a 10 minute of presentation about the tool, which presented the aim and all basic conceptual steps required to obtain it. The presentation described some background to the work and explained the limitations of automatic methods, but no reference to the interface was made at this stage. In this way the participants were not influenced in how to achieve the requested goals. We asked participants to attempt to reach the following two goals:

1. to obtain a sample composed of older users, only using automatic method procedure (no refinement phase for either gender and age class inference);

2. to obtain a sample composed of older users, using both automatic method procedure and refinement phase for just few users for either gender and age class inference. After that, to load another dataset.

The sequences of tasks needed for both first and second goal are reported in Table 5 and 6, respectively.

Step	Task
1	Load new tweet dataset
2	Start gender inference process
3	Do not do gender refinement phase
4	Start age class inference phase
5	Do not do age class refinement phase
6	Save author sample (save only older authors)

Table 5: Task sequence to achieve goal 1.

During the procedure we recorded our observations on paper data sheets. We used the "thinking aloud" methods, whereby participants were asked to verbalize their thoughts while performing the tasks. Comments made by the participants are often valuable complements to observed behaviors in the test, and "thinking aloud" can help participants communicate what they are feeling about a tool and problems they may encounter while using it.

The post-study survey was used to gather the test participants' opinions about the tool, after the test. The participants were asked

Step	Task
1	Load new tweet dataset
2	Start gender inference process
3	Do gender refinement phase and set the gender for some authors
4	Start age class inference phase
5	Do age class refinement for some authors
6	Save author sample (save all authors)
7	Save author sample (save only older authors)
8	Load new dataset

Table 6: Task sequence to achieve goal 2.

to answer questions that cover all the different aspects of usability. For instance, the questions regard effectiveness, efficiency, information understanding, and easiness of use of the tool. All these aspects are very important to create a usable interface. Indeed, our aim was to create a tool that was usable by a non-technical user, therefore the easiness for learning and using it is essential. Also the easiness of information understanding is important: the end-user has to use the additional information to judge demographic attributes of Twitter users.

Results

The cognitive walkthrough highlighted several problems:

1. Both participants suggested that a continuous update about the age and gender composition of the current set of Twitter users should be available. In this way the end-users can decide with more confidence about the number of instances to refine.

2. Both complained about the absence of options for selecting the confidence threshold that split the entire set of Twitter users into instances to refine or not.

3. During the two refinement phases, we noticed that the attention of the experts was captured by the images, while the textual information was mainly ignored.

4. The pop-up messages that appeared between two phases was not clear. The participants suggested to simplify the messages in order to make more simple and fast end-user choice.

5. In the gender refinement screen, the experts clicked on the "Next" button for selecting other users to refine. Actually, they obtained an unexpected effect: the age class identification started. Moreover, for the same screen, one of the cognitive walkthrough participant complained about the absence of label indicating which kind of images were shown in the user panel.

6. In the age refinement screen they suggested we simplify the top part of the screen designed to set the new age class or gender of a Twitter user, but they appreciated the facility to modify gender class at this stage. Moreover, they suggested to explain more clearly the meaning of word "confidence". In this screen they also found another problem related to going back in the process using buttons.

On the basis of this feedback, a second interface prototype was designed. A key feature in the new interface is an additional visualization component: the summary panel (see Figure 5). It is the main improvement made on the previous version and displays a breakdown of labelled and unlabelled user cases. A new combo box was

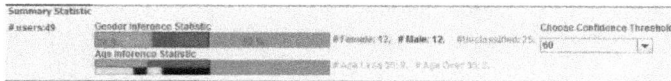

Figure 5: Summary panel.

added which allows the end-user to set the confidence threshold for user refinement. Having chosen the threshold, the tool presents all instances that require examination (all instances with a confidence level lower than threshold level).

The graph presented in Figure 6 is particularly useful for the user to establish an optimal trade-off between accuracy and sample size. It can be used by the end-user for understanding which is the best confidence level threshold to choose based on his/her needs (a social scientist could prefer a highest level of error and refine a lowest number of instances or viceversa). For supporting the end user in the choice of the confidence level threshold, during the age class refinement step, we incorporated the graph reported in Figure 6 in the tool interface. This graph has been obtained over the dataset where 55 tweets are used for identifying the age class of each user. It shows the variation of the number of instances that required a refinement (classified with lower confidence level than a certain threshold) and the variation of the error rate with respect to the variation of confidence level. Using this graph the end-user can follow two possible strategies for choosing the best threshold: one based on error rate requirements and one based on the size of the user sample required.

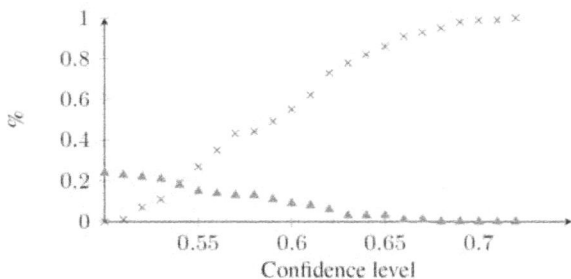

Figure 6: Percentage of instances to refine (x marks) and error rate (triangle marks) with respect to confidence level variation.

In the summary panel is also possible to see the sample composition in each step of the process. The information displayed is: number of initial users, number of female, male and unknown classified users during the gender inference phase, number of younger and older users classified with a certain confidence level. It is also possible to see the proportion of age classified users respect to gender. The rectangle below "Gender inference statistic" label represents percentage of Twitter users, belonging to the initial dataset, that are gender classified as female (fuchsia bar), male (blue bar) and unknown (gray bar). While the rectangle below "Age inference statistic" label represents also the proportion of females and males that are age classified with a confidence level higher than the threshold (green bar) and with a confidence level lower than the threshold (black bar).

The new gender refinement screen is presented in Figure 7. Here, for the gender inspection, screen name *(a)*, description *(b)*, profile image *(c)*, banner image *(e)* and background profile image *(d)* are shown. Essentially, we changed the order of information and we highlighted all the text boxes in order to attract user attention towards text areas.

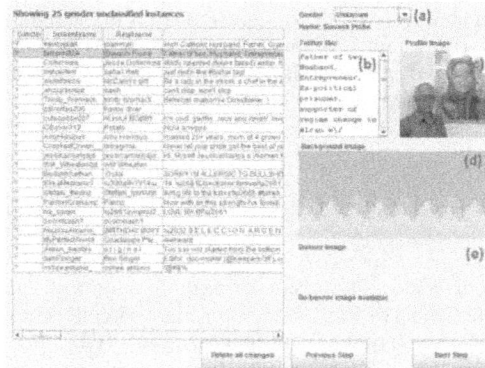

Figure 7: Gender refinement screen.

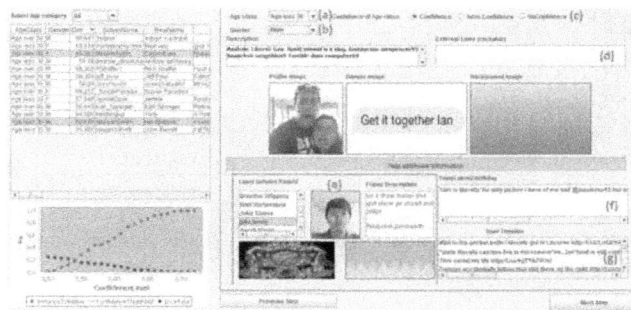

Figure 8: Age refinement screen.

The second age refinement screen is shown in Figure 8. Here, the user can see all the information already described for the gender refinement step, as well as external links *(d)*, list of least famous friends *(e)*, user's timeline *(f)* and user's tweets about "birthday" *(g)*. Another improvement on the age refinement screen was to move the text boxes above the images and highlight their texts. Moreover, we introduced combo boxes *(a)* and *(b)* for simplify how to set the new age/gender class. Both in age class and gender combo box the actual class value of an instance is shown. When the user selects another class, this class is automatically assign to the selected user. In this way, the process of setting age or gender class becomes more fast and simple. The user can specify their confidence level about refined instances, using a three radio buttons *(c)* that replace the earlier slider control. Now, the user only needs to specify if he/she is confident, semi-confident or completely unconfident about their classification.

6.2 Summative Evaluation

We also conduced a summative evaluation of the second interface prototype. This evaluation was quantitative and about testing if the objective of enabling users to make quick and confident judgments was met.

Through a traditional "time and errors" usability test, three dependent variables were collected for both gender and age class refinement tasks: completion time, inter-rater agreement and success rate. Task completion time was measured by recording the time when users clicked on a row related to a user until they made a final decision by selecting one of the possible classes. Inter-rater agreement is the degree of agreement among two or more evaluators. It describes how frequently they assign the exact same rating (if all give the same rating, they are in agreement) and it gives a score of how much homogeneity, or consensus, there is in the ratings given by judges. It is useful in refining the tools given to human judges, for example by determining if a particular scale is appropriate for measuring a particular variable. Success rate is the percentage of users' correct classification decision.

Procedure

We recruited 22 participants (15 males and 7 females), of which 12 PhD students, 7 researchers and 3 master students in the Department of Computer Science both of Brunel University and Milano-Bicocca University. All of them were comfortable with computers and familiar with Twitter. A dataset for trial was collected using an experimental version of Chorus Tweetcatcher (TCD)[1] that is able to collect a table of Twitter users where each of them has all the attributes listed in Table 7.

UserId	ScreenName	RealName
Description	URL	Language
Location	GeoEnabled	TimeZone
UTCOffset	Followers	Friends
StatusCount	Favourites	CreatedAt
Verified	Protected	ProfileImage
BannerImage	BackImage	TweetSample
BirthdayTweets		

Table 7: Meta-data available for each user in the table obtained using Chorus TCD.

The dataset obtained through Chorus TCD was composed of 50 Twitter users. The test participants had to inspect 25 gender unclassified users and 21 age unclassified users belonging to this dataset.

Before beginning the study, participants received 10 minute training on final interface. The training session consisted of a brief explanation of the tool's purpose and basic concepts, and a short demonstration of the interface and detailed instruction on the usage of the interface. The tutorial was administered by the same person following a basic script (explanations and demonstrations). In addition to demonstrating the features of the interfaces, the administrator explained basic strategies to complete the tasks (for example, comparing the additional information of the considered user to assign gender class).

Tasks did not have a time limit. Once the participants completed the refinement of gender, they repeated the same procedure for assigning age to those user falling beneath the specified threshold.

After the participants finished all the tasks, they were asked to complete post-study questionnaire about the interface. Subjective measures including satisfaction, usability, and learnability were collected along with participants' comments and suggestions during the post-study survey session.

Results

Regards the summative evaluation the results that we collected show that the gender refinement phase required less time than the age one. The assignment of a gender to an instances takes around 8.3 sec, while the assignment of an age class takes around 16 sec. This confirms the idea that age classification is also more difficult for human judges than the gender one. A deep investigation of the decision time shows that the users do not tend to slow down in their judgment task as the trials proceeded, with decision time depending on how clear the additional information is for them. Figure 9 shows bar charts that represent, respectively, average task completion time to refine user gender and age class.

---

[1]This software is available at http://chorusanalytics.co.uk

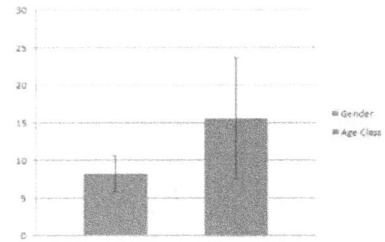

Figure 9: Average time in sec for gender and age refinement.

Furthermore, we find that in age refinement phase more time is required to load all the information (4 sec) than in gender refinement phase (0.5 sec). Indeed, least famous friend information, for user's age class inspection, was collected real-time, while all the other information required for gender refinement was already present as attributes of the user table. Indeed, this data was part of the input-data collected, a priori, using Chorus TCD.

Then, we studied the inter-agreement rate between participants for both gender and age refinements. We used an adaptation of Cohens' Kappa test for multiple raters proposed by Fleiss [7]. Fleiss' kappa is a variant of Cohen's kappa, a statistical measure of inter-rater reliability. Whereas Cohen's kappa works for only two raters, Fleiss' kappa works for any constant number of raters giving categorical ratings, to a fixed number of items. It is a measure of the degree of agreement that can be expected above chance. The Fleiss' Kappa statistic for gender was equal to 77.34%, and for age was equal to 70.45%. We find again that age inference seems to be more difficult than gender. Although 70.45% is a good level of agreement is less than the one obtained in gender refinement.

We also attempted to understand the accuracy level obtained by participants. We performed a 3-fold cross-validation separating the evaluation given by participants into two groups. Each time with the evaluation of 66% of the raters we created a gold standard and with the evaluation of other 33% of the raters, we created the test set from which we computed their accuracy. We found that for gender refinement the level of accuracy reached is equal to 92%, while for age refinement the level of performances achieved is 91%. Also from this point of view, we obtained worse results in the age identification, the most difficult task, than in gender derivation.

Moreover, we studied how effective is the confidence value in finding the users misclassified by the automatic method, and whether the manual labeling had improved the results. We analyzed the agreement between the participants and the automatic method, and we found that the 80% of the misclassifications happen when the confidence value is in the range 50-60%.

In the post-study survey, the participants were asked to answer questions about easiness of use, easiness of learning, easiness of navigation and easiness of information understanding. Their overall satisfaction and confidence toward the interface was high. The main qualitative feedback was to increase the size of tweet windows in order to facilitate their reading.

As the summative evaluation showed, the visualization of additional information helped users make decisions faster. Users who have participated in our trials have been very positive about the interactive approach supported by the TweetClass tool.

7. CONCLUSION AND FUTURE WORKS

In this paper, we presented a semi-automatic approach to boost the accuracy of demographic attribution of users contributing to a Twitter corpus. We presented TweetClass, as a proof-of-concept tool, that supports social scientist researchers in the identification of demographic attributes of a Twitter users sample by combining both automatic and interactive class inference methods. This is a difficult problem because these attributes (e.g. age class, gender) are not directly obtainable from tweets or user account meta-data. As first step we built the hierarchical model to automatically identify demographic attributes, then we developed an interface that enables the user to intervene in the classification process. The interface is necessary for inspecting and refining the Twitter users of the initial set for which an automatic classification of their gender or age class is very hard. In this way, the end-users can increase the quality or/and the dimension of Twitter user samples.

Future work of this study will concern how to exploit the knowledge provided by the end-users' refinement. For instance, we could use the inspected Twitter users as new instances in the training set obtaining an active learning model able to improve itself each time that new Twitter users are refined by TweetClass end-users. Moreover, another future work could relate to incorporate in the tool other automatic techniques able to increase the performance of the existing demographic attribute classification or new automatic techniques to identify other demographic attribute such as profession, marital status and so on. Since, after the end of the study, a new dataset, with both gender and age label, became available [19], we want to expand our experiments over this large dataset for a better evaluation of our approach.

8. REFERENCES

[1] J. S. Alowibdi, U. A. Buy, and P. Yu. Language independent gender classification on twitter. In *Proceedings of the 2013 IEEE/ACM International Conference on Advances in Social Networks Analysis and Mining*, pages 739–743. ACM, 2013.

[2] S. Argamon, M. Koppel, J. W. Pennebaker, and J. Schler. Mining the blogosphere: Age, gender and the varieties of self-expression. *First Monday*, 12(9), 2007.

[3] J. D. Burger, J. Henderson, G. Kim, and G. Zarrella. Discriminating gender on twitter. In *Proceedings of the Conference on Empirical Methods in Natural Language Processing*, pages 1301–1309. Association for Computational Linguistics, 2011.

[4] N. Cheng, R. Chandramouli, and K. Subbalakshmi. Author gender identification from text. *Digital Investigation*, 8(1):78–88, 2011.

[5] M. Ciot, M. Sonderegger, and D. Ruths. Gender inference of twitter users in non-english contexts. In *EMNLP*, pages 1136–1145, 2013.

[6] C. Fink, J. Kopecky, and M. Morawski. Inferring gender from the content of tweets: A region specific example. In *ICWSM*, 2012.

[7] J. L. Fleiss, B. Levin, and M. C. Paik. The measurement of interrater agreement. *Statistical methods for rates and proportions*, 2:212–236, 1981.

[8] K. Gimpel, N. Schneider, B. O'Connor, D. Das, D. Mills, J. Eisenstein, M. Heilman, D. Yogatama, J. Flanigan, and N. A. Smith. Part-of-speech tagging for twitter: Annotation, features, and experiments. In *Proceedings of the 49th Annual Meeting of the Association for Computational Linguistics: Human Language Technologies: Short Papers - Volume 2*, HLT '11, pages 42–47, Stroudsburg, PA, USA, 2011. Association for Computational Linguistics.

[9] R. M. Groves. Three eras of survey research. *Public Opinion Quarterly*, 75(5):861–871, 2011.

[10] J. Ito, T. Hoshide, H. Toda, T. Uchiyama, and K. Nishida. What is he/she like?: Estimating twitter user attributes from contents and social neighbors. In *Proceedings of the 2013 IEEE/ACM International Conference on Advances in Social Networks Analysis and Mining*, ASONAM '13, pages 1448–1450, New York, NY, USA, 2013. ACM.

[11] W. Liu and D. Ruths. What's in a name? using first names as features for gender inference in twitter. In *Analyzing Microtext: 2013 AAAI Spring Symposium*, 2013.

[12] J. Michael. 40000 namen, anredebestimmung anhand des vornamens, 2007.

[13] A. Mislove, S. Lehmann, Y.-Y. Ahn, J.-P. Onnela, and J. N. Rosenquist. Understanding the demographics of twitter users. *ICWSM*, 11:5th, 2011.

[14] D. Nguyen, R. Gravel, D. Trieschnigg, and T. Meder. "how old do you think i am?" a study of language and age in twitter. In *ICWSM*, 2013.

[15] D. Nguyen, R. Gravel, D. Trieschnigg, and T. Meder. Tweetgenie: automatic age prediction from tweets. *ACM SIGWEB Newsletter*, 4(Autumn):4, 2013.

[16] D. Nguyen, N. A. Smith, and C. P. Rosé. Author age prediction from text using linear regression. In *Proceedings of the 5th ACL-HLT Workshop on Language Technology for Cultural Heritage, Social Sciences, and Humanities*, pages 115–123. Association for Computational Linguistics, 2011.

[17] C. Peersman, W. Daelemans, and L. Van Vaerenbergh. Predicting age and gender in online social networks. In *Proceedings of the 3rd international workshop on Search and mining user-generated contents*, pages 37–44. ACM, 2011.

[18] M. Pennacchiotti and A.-M. Popescu. Democrats, republicans and starbucks afficionados: User classification in twitter. In *Proceedings of the 17th ACM SIGKDD International Conference on Knowledge Discovery and Data Mining*, KDD '11, pages 430–438, New York, NY, USA, 2011. ACM.

[19] F. Rangel, P. Rosso, M. Koppel, E. Stamatatos, and G. Inches. Overview of the author profiling task at pan 2013. *Notebook Papers of CLEF*, pages 23–26, 2013.

[20] D. Rao, D. Yarowsky, A. Shreevats, and M. Gupta. Classifying latent user attributes in twitter. In *Proceedings of the 2nd international workshop on Search and mining user-generated contents*, pages 37–44. ACM, 2010.

[21] C. Seale, S. Ziebland, and J. Charteris-Black. Gender, cancer experience and internet use: a comparative keyword analysis of interviews and online cancer support groups. *Social science & medicine*, 62(10):2577–2590, 2006.

[22] L. Sloan, J. Morgan, W. Housley, M. Williams, A. Edwards, P. Burnap, and O. Rana. Knowing the tweeters: Deriving sociologically relevant demographics from twitter. *Sociological Research Online*, 18(3):7, 2013.

[23] T. W. Smith. Survey-research paradigms old and new. *International Journal of Public Opinion Research*, page eds040, 2012.

[24] R. O. Tachibana, N. Oosugi, and K. Okanoya. Semi-automatic classification of birdsong elements using a linear support vector machine. *PloS one*, 9(3):e92584, 2014.

[25] C. Wharton, J. Rieman, C. Lewis, and P. Polson. Usability inspection methods. chapter The Cognitive Walkthrough Method: A Practitioner's Guide, pages 105–140. John Wiley & Sons, Inc., New York, NY, USA, 1994.

[26] F. A. Zamal, W. Liu, and D. Ruths. Homophily and latent attribute inference: Inferring latent attributes of twitter users from neighbors. In *ICWSM*, 2012.

[27] Y. Zhang, D. Wang, and T. Li. idvs: an interactive multi-document visual summarization system. In *Machine Learning and Knowledge Discovery in Databases*, pages 569–584. Springer, 2011.

Text, Topics, and Turkers: A Consensus Measure for Statistical Topics

Fred Morstatter
Arizona State University
699 S. Mill Ave.
Tempe, AZ, 85281
fred.morstatter@asu.edu

Jürgen Pfeffer
Carnegie Mellon University
5000 Forbes Ave.
Pittsburgh, PA, 15213
jpfeffer@cs.cmu.edu

Katja Mayer
University of Vienna
Universitätsring 1
1010 Vienna, Austria
katja.mayer@univie.ac.at

Huan Liu
Arizona State University
699 S. Mill Ave.
Tempe, AZ 85281
huanliu@asu.edu

ABSTRACT

Topic modeling is an important tool in social media analysis, allowing researchers to quickly understand large text corpora by investigating the topics underlying them. One of the fundamental problems of topic models lies in how to assess the quality of the topics from the perspective of human interpretability. How well can humans understand the meaning of topics generated by statistical topic modeling algorithms? In this work we advance the study of this question by introducing *Topic Consensus*: a new measure that calculates the quality of a topic through investigating its consensus with some known topics underlying the data. We view the quality of the topics from three perspectives: 1) topic interpretability, 2) how documents relate to the underlying topics, and 3) how interpretable the topics are when the corpus has an underlying categorization. We provide insights into how well the results of Mechanical Turk match automated methods for calculating topic quality. The probability distribution of the words in the topic best fit the Topic Coherence measure, in terms of both correlation as well as finding the best topics.

Categories and Subject Descriptors

I.5.4 [**Applications**]: Text Processing; I.2.7 [**Natural Language Processing**]: Language Generation

Keywords

Topic Analysis; Topic Modeling; Text Analysis; Text Mining

HT '15, September 1–4, 2015, Guzelyurt, Northern Cyprus.
ACM 978-1-4503-3395-5/15/09.
http://dx.doi.org/10.1145/2700171.2791028 .

INTRODUCTION

Text analysis has proven to be one of the cornerstones of social media analysis. Researchers can usually rely on text to give them signal for their specific problem. Text has been used to greatly aid problems such as opinion mining [27], and user home location detection [15], and to find users in crisis situations [19]. Topic modeling is one of the fundamental text analysis techniques in social media. Topic modeling takes a corpus of text and finds the underlying topics in it. This process is akin to organizing newspaper articles by the "section" in which they appear, and simultaneously ranking words for that section. Topic modeling algorithms have been widely used for many tasks in social media research, such as using text to find important topics of discussion in crisis scenarios [12], event detection and analysis [9], and finding a Twitter user's home location [5].

Latent Dirichlet Allocation [2], commonly known as LDA, is the dominating topic modeling algorithm. The key advance with LDA is that it models a document as a distribution over topics, and a topic as a distribution over the vocabulary in the corpus. The topic distributions are manually inspected in many studies to show that some underlying pattern exists in the corpus. The meaning behind these topics is often interpreted by the author, and topics are often given a title or name to reflect the author's understanding of the underlying meaning of the topics. One existing concern with topic modeling algorithms lies with how well human beings can actually understand the topics produced by these algorithms. It may be true that when presented with a group of words a human will always be able to assign some meaning. Measuring the consensus of this meaning against the known underlying properties of the data is the major thrust of this work. We focus on three measures that can be used to calculate the interpretability of topics. First, we reproduce two measures previously introduced in Chang et. al [4]. We find that while these two measures can help to measure the interpretability, they do not show how well the statistical topics illuminate the underlying themes in the data. We continue to introduce Topic Consensus, which measures topic quality based on how well the humans are able to understand the consensus between the topics and the underlying themes. We show that Topic Consensus approximates a different aspect of the LDA topics, helping researchers to better understand the topics generated from their data.

Consensus and interpretability measures for topics rely on crowdsourcing, having human participants answer questions regarding the topics. While this is an important analytical step, these methods can be expensive and time consuming to reproduce, making this analysis out of reach to many researchers. To overcome this problem, we propose a method that uses automatic, computational measures to assess the quality of topics without the need for "Turkers": the human workers who carry out the tasks for our experiments. We compare the performance of several automated measures introduced previously as well as in this work against those that rely on crowdsourcing to give researchers insight into which measures can be used to assess the quality of their topics. In this way we allow for scalable and cheap methods to assess the topics generated by any topic modeling algorithm.

The main contributions of this work are as follows:

- We propose a new consensus measure, Topic Consensus, that can estimate how well an individual topic represents an underlying topic in the corpus.

- By employing automated measures on the topics, we show that the process of measuring the quality of the topics both from the interpretability and consensus perspectives can be automated. This will allow future researchers to incorporate this topic evaluation framework at scale.

RELATED WORK

Chang et. al conducted the first interpretability study on topic models [4]. In their paper, the authors focus on two main validation schemes for topic models: "Word Intrusion" which studies the top words within a topic by discovering how well participants can identify a word that does not belong. They also introduce "Topic Intrusion", which studies how well the topic probabilities for a document match with a human's understanding of this document by showing three highly-probably *topics*, and one improbably topic, and asking the worker to select the "intruder". These experiments focus on the humans' understanding of the dataset. Lau et. al [13] furthers this study by building heuristics to guess the actions of the workers. Other investigations into measuring topic quality include Roder et. al [22], who automatically explore the space of topic quality measures and aggregation functions to find the measure that best approximates model precision. Moreover, Wallach et. al [28] proposes Topic Size and Topic Coherence which we include in this work. Newman et al. [21] proposes a measure for topic coherence based on Pointwise Mutual Information. Furthermore, Aletras and Stevenson [1] measure the quality topics by inspecting the vector similarity. We use these measures by including them in our suite of automated measures that we use to test the crowdsourced measures later in the paper. We assess which of these measures can help us to predict which topics will perform well without the help of the Turkers.

LDA has been used in a wide array of domains. LDA was verified on scientific corpora to show that the topics that were produced by the model made sense [2, 6]. Recently, LDA has been used to study the trends in scientific topics (for example, "Information Retrieval", and "HIV") over time, to see how scientific interest has changed over time. LDA has been used in even more varying domains. For example,

Schmidt [23] uses LDA to cluster 1820's ship voyages. By treating trips as documents and nightly latitude/longitude checkins as words, the authors are able to find trading and whaling topics, amongst others.

Topic analysis can also be used to understand the content of tweets. In the context of disaster-related tweets, Kireyev et. al [12] tries to find disaster-related tweets, finding two types of topics: informational and emotional. Joseph et. al [10] studies the relation between users' posts and their geolocation. Other works [29, 8] focus on identifying topics in geographical Twitter datasets, looking for topics that pertain to things such as local concerts and periods of mass unrest. In Morstatter et. al [20], the authors use LDA to find evidence of bias in Twitter's Streaming API.

OVERVIEW OF LATENT DIRICHLET ALLOCATION

LDA discovers "topics" from a large corpus of text. LDA's definition of a topic is a probability distribution over the corpus vocabulary such that each word in the corpus has some probability of occurring within that topic. LDA will find K topics in the text, where K is a positive integer that indicates the number of topics in the text. K is set by the LDA user, and the process for setting this parameter is largely unknown. LDA will also find the probability of each document to belong to each topic.

LDA takes two inputs: A bag-of-words corpus containing d documents and a vocabulary of size v, and a scalar value K, which indicates the number of topics that the algorithm will learn. LDA then outputs a model, m, which consists of a vector $\mathbf{z}^m$ containing each token's topic assignment. The output of LDA is twofold:

1. A *Topic* × *Vocabulary* matrix, $\mathbf{T}^m \in \mathbb{R}^{K \times v}$, with entry $\mathbf{T}^m_{i,j}$ representing the probability of that word j belongs to topic i.

2. A *Document* × *Topic* matrix, $\mathbf{D}^m \in \mathbb{R}^{d \times K}$, with entry $\mathbf{D}^m_{i,j}$ representing the probability that document i is generated by topic j.

TOPIC INTERPRETABILITY

The key questions evaluated in this work are: 1) are topics produced by LDA interpretable?, and 2) can we automate the process used to evaluate the topics' interpretability to reduce the dependence on Amazon Mechanical Turk?

To measure the interpretability of topics, we extend upon the framework proposed in Chang et. al [4]. We reproduce the two experiments proposed in their paper: *Word Intrusion*, and *Topic Intrusion*, and continue on to introduce our own measure, *Topic Consensus*. This new measure builds upon the existing crowdsourced methods to tie the topics to a score that measures them based upon their ground truth assignment.

All of the measures used to answer the first question rely on crowdsourcing to verify results. This can be a cumbersome task for researchers, taking ample amounts of both time and money to perform the experiments. In the subsequent section we introduce automatic measures that gauge the quality of topics. We continue to show that not only do these measures approximate the performance of the crowdsourced experiments, but we provide recommendations on

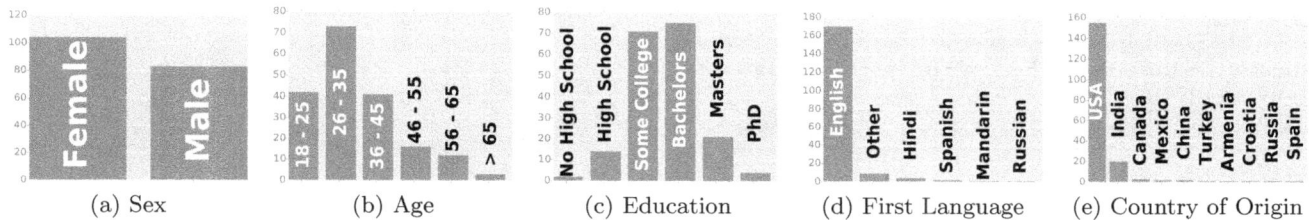

| (a) Sex | (b) Age | (c) Education | (d) First Language | (e) Country of Origin |

Figure 1: Demographic breakdown of the 188 Turkers who participated in this study.

how to use these automated measures to build better LDA topics for future experiments.

Data

The text corpus focused upon in this study consists of 4,351 abstracts of accepted research proposals to the European Research Council[1]. In the first 7 years of its existence, the European Research Council (ERC) has funded approximately 4,500 projects, 4,351 of which are used in this study. Abstracts are limited to 2,000 characters, and when a researcher submits an abstract, they are required to select one of the three scientific domains their research fits into: Life Sciences (LS), Physical Sciences (PE), or Social Sciences and Humanities (SH). These labels will be used in the crowdsourced measure we propose.

Mapping scientific research areas has become of growing interest to scientists, policymakers, funding agencies and industry. Traditional bibliometric data analysis such as co-citation analysis supply us with basic tools to map research fields. However, Social Sciences and Humanities (SH) are proven to be especially difficult to map and to survey, since the fields and disciplines are embedded in diverse and often diverging epistemic cultures. Some are specifically bound to local contexts, languages and terminologies, and the SH domain is lacking coherent referencing bodies or citation indices, and dictionaries [16]. Furthermore, SH terminology is often hard to identify as it resembles everyday speech. Innovative semantic technologies such as topic modeling promise alternative approaches to mapping SH, but the basic question here is: how interpretable are they and how can their results be evaluated in a systematic way. This raises further questions into the interpretability of the LDA topics we study in this paper.

The abstracts used in this research were accepted between 2007 - 2013, written in English, and classified by the authors into one of the three main ERC domains. Table 1 shows some statistics of the corpus. The aim of each abstract is to provide a clear understanding of the objectives and methods to achieve them. Abstracts are also used to find reviewers or match authors to panels.

In addition to the ERC data that lies at the heart of this work, we also created a corpus consisting of the top stories from the New York Times. We do this in the first experiments to act as a control for the specialized topics that may arise from the ERC corpus. These topics are presented to give the reader a point of reference for the ERC topics. The New York Times data was collected using LexisNexis[2].

Table 1: Properties of the European Research Council accepted abstracts and top stories in the New York Times (NYT).

Property	ERC Data	NYT Data
Total Documents	4,351	156
Life Sciences	1,573	—
Physical Sciences	1,964	—
Social Sciences	814	—
Tokens	649,651	9,188
Types	10,016	772

Extracting Topics from Text

We apply LDA to extract topics from the text. We run LDA on the ERC dataset four times, with $K = 10, 25, 50, 100$, yielding a total of 185 ERC topics. Furthermore, we also ran LDA on the New York Times dataset with $K = 25$. All LDA runs were carried out using the Mallet toolkit [17] using the default hyperparameter values of $\alpha = 5.0$ and $\beta = 0.01$.

In addition to the LDA runs, we extract two additional topic groups from the corpus. The first is a set of *random topics*. To generate these topics, we weight the words by their frequency in the corpus and randomly draw words from this distribution. Our topics have a roughly equal mixture of the three ERC domains.

To complement our random topics, we also create a set of *social sciences topics*. To generate these topics, we calculate each word's probability of occurring in a SH, LS, or PE document. We then select words that occur most in the SH category and least in the other two. These topics lie in contrast to the random topics in that they are strongly skewed to represent a single group.

In both the case of the random and social sciences topics, these topics are different from traditional LDA topics, containing only a *set* of 20 words. For both processes, we generate 25 such topics. We use both of these auxiliary topic sets for validation of the results obtained using the LDA topics. Table 2 shows an overview of all of the topic sets generated for this study.

Amazon Mechanical Turk

The crowdsourced experiments carried out in this work were performed using Amazon's Mechanical Turk[3] platform. Mechanical Turk is a crowdsourcing platform that allows requesters to coordinate Human Intelligence Tasks (HITs) to be solved by Turkers. The formulation of each HIT will be described in the corresponding section for each experiment.

---

[1] http://erc.europa.eu/projects-and-results/erc-funded-projects
[2] http://www.lexisnexis.com/hottopics/lnacademic/

[3] http://www.mturk.com

Table 2: The topic sets used in this study. These indicate the different values of "m" used throughout the experiments.

Name	Dataset	Algorithm	No. Topics
ERC-010	ERC	LDA	10
ERC-025	ERC	LDA	25
ERC-050	ERC	LDA	50
ERC-100	ERC	LDA	100
NYT-025	NYT	LDA	25
RAND-025	ERC	Random	25
SH-011	ERC	Manual	11

In all cases, each HIT was solved 8 times to overcome issues that arise from using non-expert annotators [24].

Prior to solving any HITs, we require the Turker to fill out a demographic survey. The demographic survey consists of five questions about the Turker's background: their sex, age, first language, country of origin, and highest level of education achieved. In order to understand the demographic makeup of our Turkers, we plot the distribution for each answer in Figure 1. In Figures 1(d) and 1(e), we see a strong skew towards American Turkers who speak English as their first language. This could be partly attributed to a recent change in the Mechanical Turk terms of service that requires Turkers to provide their Social Security Number[4] in order to solve HITs on the site. This allows us to go forward knowing that the participants are largely English speakers, and we cannot attribute poor performance in our analysis to poor language understanding.

Experiment 1: Word Intrusion

Word Intrusion, introduced by [4], measures the "coherence" of an individual topic. For each topic, we show the Turker the top 5 most probable words from the topic's probability distribution along with one of the *least* probable words in the distribution (the "intruded" word). We then ask the Turker to select the word that they think is the intruded word. We define model precision as the number of times a Turker was able to guess the intruded word divided by the number of times the HIT was solved, formally:

$$MP_k^m = \frac{1}{|\mathbf{s_k^m}|} \sum_{i=1}^{|\mathbf{s_k^m}|} \mathbb{1}(g_k^m = \mathbf{s}_{k,i}^m), \qquad (1)$$

where MP_k^m indicates the model precision k-th topic from model m, g_k^m is the ground-truth intruded word for topic k, and $\mathbf{s}_k^m$ is the vector of choices made by Turkers on topic k.

Results

The results of the experiments are shown in Figure 2. We see that the median model precision goes down as a function of K. In [4], we see that the authors attain an average model precision of approximately 90% with both $K = 50$ and 100 on their topics derived from New York Times and Wikipedia data. To compare, our topics achieve median scores of 75% at $K = 50$, and 65% at $K = 100$. These results reflect the difference in Model Precision results that can occur when this methodology is applied to different data.

[4]https://www.mturk.com/mturk/help?helpPage=worker#tax_no_have_tin

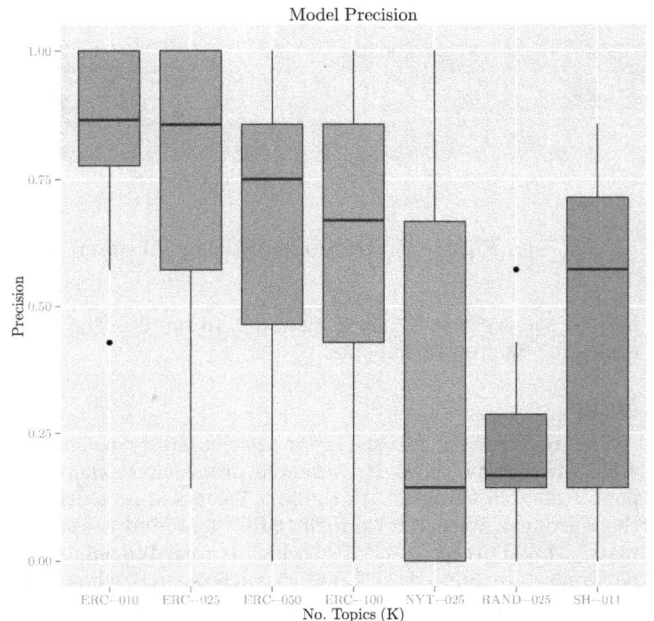

Figure 2: Model Precision aggregated by LDA model. Higher is better. We see a trend of decreasing performance with increasing K, and the New York Times corpus performs, on average, worse than the random topics.

Furthermore, see that our reference topics do not perform as expected. While the randomly-generated topics achieve the consistent poor performance that we would expect, the New York Times topics get an even worse score, indicating that humans are worse at detecting an intruded word in our New York Times dataset than they are at random. Furthermore, while the SH topics perform the best of our control topic sets, they still perform worse than any ERC corpus.

Experiment 2: Topic Intrusion

Topic intrusion, introduced by Chang et. al [4], measures how well the *Document × Topic* matrix, $\mathbf{D}^m$, produced by the LDA model can be deciphered by humans. This matrix is a reflection of how well each document is described by each topic produced by the model. Each row of this matrix $\mathbf{D}_d^m$ is a probability distribution over all of the topics with entry $\mathbf{D}_{d,i}^m$ being the probability that document d is made up of topic i.

In this task, a document is shown to the Turker, along with three highly-probable topics and one improbable topic. The highly-probable topics are selected as the three highest values in $\mathbf{D}_d^m$, and the improbable topic is randomly select from the bottom three non-zero values of $\mathbf{D}_d^m$. The Turker is told to identify the improbable, or intruded, topic. To calculate the error, we adopt the Topic Log Odds (TLO) calculation, defined as follows:

$$TLO_d^m = \frac{1}{|\mathbf{s_d^m}|} \sum_{i=1}^{|\mathbf{s_d^m}|} \left(log(\mathbf{D}_{d,s^*}^m) - log(\mathbf{D}_{d,\mathbf{s}_{,i}^m}^m) \right), \qquad (2)$$

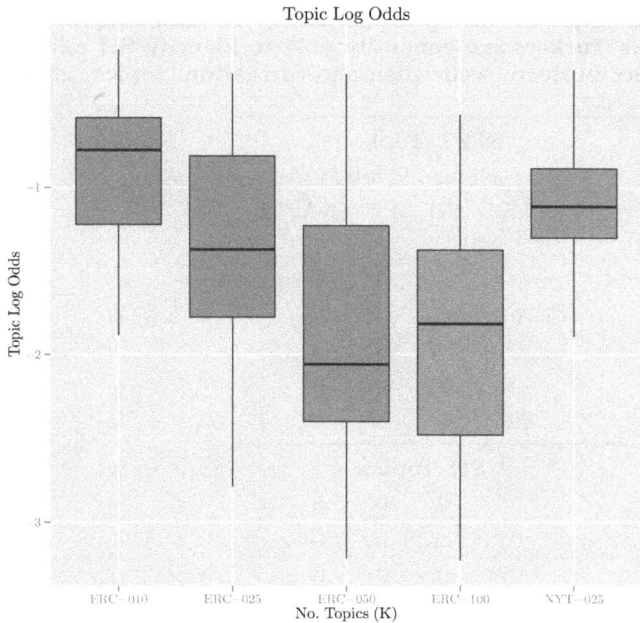

Figure 3: Topic Log Odds on the ERC and New York Times data. Higher is better.

where $\mathbf{s}_d^m$ is the vector of Turker answers for document d on model m, s^* is the index of the true intruded topic, and $\mathbf{s}_{d,i}^m$ is the index of the i-th Turker's answer.

Results

The results of the experiments are shown in Figure 3. Due to the way the SH and Random topics were generated, we were unable to perform this analysis on these datasets. In Chang et. al [4], the Turkers get median scores of -1.5, and -1.6 for $K = 50$, and $K = 100$, respectively. To compare we get results of -2.1, and -1.8 for these groups. Again, we compare with [4] to show how a different dataset can influence the results of these measures.

Experiment 3: Topic Consensus

The previous experiments test the intrinsic coherence of individual topics using Word Intrusion, and the fit of the topics to the documents using Topic Intrusion. We have not yet measured the ability of the topics to conform to the natural topics underlying the text. Explicit topics are often present in many corpora, such as newspaper articles, due to their manual categorization by "sections", and our ERC abstracts which explicitly label each abstract with an ERC domain. We measure this conformity to the underlying topic distribution by leveraging the ground-truth topic labels that comes from the ERC domains when the abstract is submitted.

To understand how well the statistical topics mimic the underlying topics, we show the Turker the top 25 words of a statistical topic and ask him to choose which of the three ERC domains the topic describes: "Life Sciences", "Physical Sciences", or "Social Sciences". We provide a fourth option, "No Topic Matched", in case the topic does not make sense to the Turker.

To compute the topic's ability to represent the underlying topics in the dataset, we compare the distribution of the Turkers' responses for that topic with the distribution of the topic over the ERC domains. To perform this analysis, we construct an LDA Topic × ERC domain matrix $\mathbf{R}$, where $\mathbf{R}_{i,c}$ indicates topic i's probability of occurring in ERC domain c. By defining $\mathbf{R}$ in this way, we are able to obtain values for topics that were not generated through LDA. The structure of each row of $\mathbf{R}$ is dependent on the type of topic group it comes from. We construct the rows as follows for each topic group:

- **ERC-*** — The $\mathbf{R}_i$ row vector for an ERC topic is created by taking the sum of the columns of the $\mathbf{D}$ matrix. This sum is taken for each row (document) of $\mathbf{D}$ labeled with the corresponding ERC domain. This is defined as:

$$\mathbf{R}_{i,c} = \frac{\sum_{j \in M_c} \mathbf{D}_{j,i}}{\sum \mathbf{D}_{*,i}}, \qquad (3)$$

where M_c is the set of documents containing the label corresponding to the column of $\mathbf{R}$, i.e. "SH", "LS", or "PE". This gives us an understanding of the ERC domain makeup for each LDA topic.

- **SH-011** — The $\mathbf{R}_i$ row vector for an SH topic contains a 1 for the SH category and a 0 for the other two. This is because due to the way the SH topics are generated, they contain purely SH words.

- **NYT-025** and **RAND-025** — Both Random and NYT topics have an evenly split row vector of 1/3 for each category as they do not belong to any category. The aggregate of the Turkers' responses should be confused over all of the ERC categories. We will measure this disparity in subsequent sections.

Using the responses from the Turkers, we build a separate *Topic × Domain* matrix, $\mathbf{R}^{\mathbf{AMT}}$ where $\mathbf{R}^{\mathbf{AMT}}_{i,j}$ represents the Turkers' probability of choosing domain j when presented with topic i. In this way, $\mathbf{R}^{\mathbf{AMT}}$ is the representation of $\mathbf{R}$ obtained from the Turkers' responses. A row in $\mathbf{R}^{\mathbf{AMT}}$ indicates the distribution over ERC domains for a given LDA topic from the Turker's responses.

To compute the topic consensus of the topics, we compute the Jensen-Shannon divergence [14] between the two distributions $JS(\mathbf{R}^{\mathbf{AMT}}_d || \mathbf{R}_d)$, defined as:

$$JS(\mathbf{R}^{\mathbf{AMT}}_d || \mathbf{R}_d) = \frac{K(\mathbf{R}^{\mathbf{AMT}}_d || M) + K(\mathbf{R}_d || M)}{2}, \quad (4)$$

where K is Kullback-Leibler divergence [11], and $M = \frac{1}{2}(\mathbf{R}^{\mathbf{AMT}}_d + \mathbf{R}_d)$. Jensen-Shannon is a natural choice as the rows of $\mathbf{R}$ and $\mathbf{R}^{\mathbf{AMT}}$ are probability distributions over the 3 ERC topics and Jensen-Shannon is a measure of the similarity of two distributions.

Results

The results of the topic consensus experiment are shown in Figure 4, and a confusion matrix comparing the Turkers' responses with the ground truth is shown in Table 3. In Figure 4, we see that the SH topics perform the best, showing that Turkers are able to match these handpicked words with the topic they come from. The New York Times topics perform worst of all. This is partly explained by Table 3,

Table 3: Confusion matrix of ground truth ERC domain assignments of topics against the domain assignments made by the Turkers. In the ERC topics, we see that the Turkers are generally able to identify SH and LS topics, but overall fail to identify PE topics. The Turkers perform well when shown random topics, giving most of these topics a "not applicable" label.

	ERC Topics				NYT Topics			
	Ground Truth				Ground Truth			
	LS	SH	PE	NA	LS	SH	PE	NA
AMT Classification								
LS	45	0	2	0	0	0	0	1
SH	3	10	8	0	0	0	0	22
PE	1	0	60	0	0	0	0	0
NA	4	0	52	0	0	0	0	2
Accuracy	62%				8%			
	Random Topics				SH Topics			
LS	0	0	0	1	0	0	0	0
SH	0	0	0	5	0	11	0	0
PE	0	0	0	0	0	0	0	0
NA	0	0	0	19	0	0	0	0
Accuracy	76%				100%			

where we see that many NYT topics are classified as SH by the Turker, indicating that the Turkers may have an over-interpretation of what constitutes an SH topic. This could also help to explain their poor performance in the Word Intrusion task.

The Difference between Topic Measures

We have executed three measures on our data thus far: Word Intrusion, Topic Intrusion, and Topic Consensus. At this point we should step back and discuss the differences observed between these three measures. First, in Word Intrusion, we measured the Turker's ability to identify a word randomly inserted into the top words in a topic. This measure approximates a topic's intelligibility to the reader. Next, we studied Topic Intrusion, in which we saw how well the user could understand the Document by Topic matrix **D** generated by LDA. Both of these measures were proposed in Chang et. al [4].

After reproducing these two measures, we continued to propose our own Topic Consensus measure to assess the quality of the topics. The main difference between this measure is that it refers to properties of the corpus from which the topics were generated in order to compare the quality of the topics. Simultaneously, it helps us to identify topics whose makeup of real, corpus-level groups are discernible to the reader. This measure can be useful for statistical topics generated on any corpus with corpus-level groups, such as newspaper articles or even Wikipedia entries.

In our crowdsourced experiments, we see that the Turkers perform admirably. We also see that the Turkers performance differs from that obtained in [4]. This is likely due to the nature of the data used in our study. Clearly, there is a need for automated measures that can supplement the knowledge of the Turkers. In the next section we test a suite of possible measures for measuring topic quality.

MEASURING TOPIC QUALITY AUTOMATICALLY

In the previous sections we reproduced and introduced a variety of approaches to measure the coherence and consensus of topics. All of these measures rely on crowdsourcing to get the results, which can cause for a bottleneck in the research process. Automating the task of the Turkers can make for more accessible empirical comparison, saving researchers both the time and cost of performing crowdsourced experiments. In this section we compare measures that can be used to automatically discover topics that are of high quality according to the measures above.

Automatic Topic Quality Measures

Here, we discuss several methods for automatically assessing the quality of topics. Each measure is defined as follows:

1. **Topic Size (TS):** This is a count of the number of tokens in the input corpus that are assigned to the topic. This was used in Mimno et. al [18] as a possible measure for topic quality. The hypothesis behind this measure is that a larger topic (with more tokens) will represent more of the corpus, and thus convey a larger understanding.

2. **Topic Coherence (TC):** Also introduced by Mimno et. al [18], this measures the probability of top words co-occuring within documents in the corpus:

$$TC(\mathbf{w}) = \sum_{j=2}^{|\mathbf{w}|} \sum_{k=1}^{j-1} log \frac{D(\mathbf{w}_j, \mathbf{w}_k) + 1}{D(\mathbf{w}_k)}, \qquad (5)$$

where **w** is a vector of the top words in the topic sorted in descending order, and D is the number of documents containing all of the words provided as arguments. This measure is computed on the top 20 words of the topic.

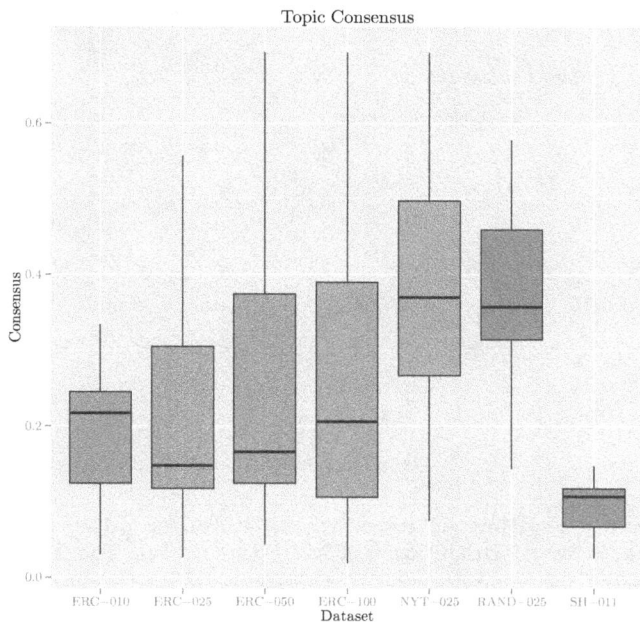

Figure 4: Topic consensus scores across all models. Lower scores are better. On the left we see the form that is shown to the workers. On the right we see that the random topics perform worse than any of the ERC topics, and the SH topics perform the best.

3. **Topic Coherence Significance (TCS):** We adapt the measure above to understand the significance of the top words in the topic when compared to a random set of words. To calculate this measure we select 100 groups of words at random, following the topic's word distribution. We then recompute the Topic Coherence measure for each of the random topics, obtaining a vector, $\mathbf{d}$, of topic coherence scores. We calculate the mean, $\bar{\mathbf{d}}$, and standard deviation, $std(\mathbf{d})$. Significance is defined as:

$$TCS(\mathbf{w}) = \frac{TC(\mathbf{w}) - \bar{\mathbf{d}}}{std(\mathbf{d})}. \qquad (6)$$

4. **Normalized Pointwise Mutual Information (NPMI):** Introduced by Bouma [3], this metric measures the probability that two random variables coincide. This measure was used to estimate the performance of Model Precision in Lau et. al [13], where the authors adapted it to measure the coincidence of the top $|\mathbf{w}|$ words. In this paper, two variables "coinciding" is the probability that they will co-occur in a document. The authors named this version OC-Auto-NPMI, formally:

$$\text{OC-Auto-NPMI}(\mathbf{w}) = \sum_{j=2}^{|\mathbf{w}|} \sum_{k=1}^{j-1} \frac{log \frac{P_D(\mathbf{w}_j, \mathbf{w}_k)}{P_D(\mathbf{w}_j) P_D(\mathbf{w}_k)}}{-log(P_D(\mathbf{w}_j, \mathbf{w}_k))}, \qquad (7)$$

where $P_D(\cdot) = D(\cdot)/|N|$, where $|N|$ is the number of documents in the corpus. P_D measures the probability that a document in the corpus contains the words given to $D(\cdot)$. We will refer to this measure as NPMI.

5. **ERC-Distribution HHI (ERC-HHI):** The Herfindahl-Hirschman Index [7], or HHI, is a measure proposed to find the amount of competition in a market. This is calculated by measuring the market share of each firm in the market, formally:

$$HHI = \frac{(H - 1/N)}{(1 - 1/N)}, \qquad (8)$$

Where $H = \sum_i s_i^2$, N is the number of firms in the market, and s_i is the market share of firm i, as a percentage. HHI ranges from 0 to 1, with 1 being a perfect monopoly (no competition), and 0 being an evenly split market. In this way we measure how focused the market is on a particular firm.

By treating ERC categories as firms, and the market share distribution as $\mathbf{R}_i$, we can calculate how focused each topic is around a particular ERC domain.

6. **Topic-Probability HHI (TP-HHI):** Using the same formulation as ERC-HHI, this time we treat every *word* in the vocabulary as a firm, and $\mathbf{T}_i^m$ as the probability distribution. In other words, the topic's probability distribution is the market, and TP-HHI measures the market's focus any word, or group of words. This measures whether the focus of a topic is around a handful of words, or whether it is evenly spread across the entire vocabulary used to train the model.

Correlation with Crowdsourced Measures

To see how well these automatic topic measures compare with the crowdsourced topic measures from the "Topic Interpretability" section, we calculate the Spearman's ρ [25] rank correlation coefficient between the crowdsourced measure and the automatic measure. We omit the "topic log odds" score as it is not a true topic measure, but instead a measure of the documents over topics. The correlations between each pair of crowdsourced and automatic measure are shown in Table 4. In this table, we present the Spearman's ρ, as well an indication of the significance for the following hypothesis test:

H_0 : The two sets of data are uncorrelated.

Instances where the hypothesis is rejected at the $\alpha = 0.05$ significance level are shown in the table.

In Table 4, we see that the measure most correlated with Model Precision is NPMI, meaning that documents whose words co-occur more are apt to achieve higher Model Precision values. We see that higher (better) values of model precision are accompanied by lower NPMI values.

On the other hand, we see that the measure most correlated with Topic Consensus is TP-HHI. Once again, these lists exhibit negative correlation, indicating that the more peaked a distribution is, the lower (better) the Topic Consensus will be. This is a hopeful result for researchers, as the measure does not rely on the topic's domain distribution information, meaning that an approximate ranking of the topics could be obtained *without* ground truth.

Precision with Crowdsourced Measures

In the previous section correlation was used to determine the dependence between the automated measures and the crowdsourced measures. To accompany this analysis, we also want to see the automated measures' *precision* in predicting the best topics from the LDA model. To measure this, we

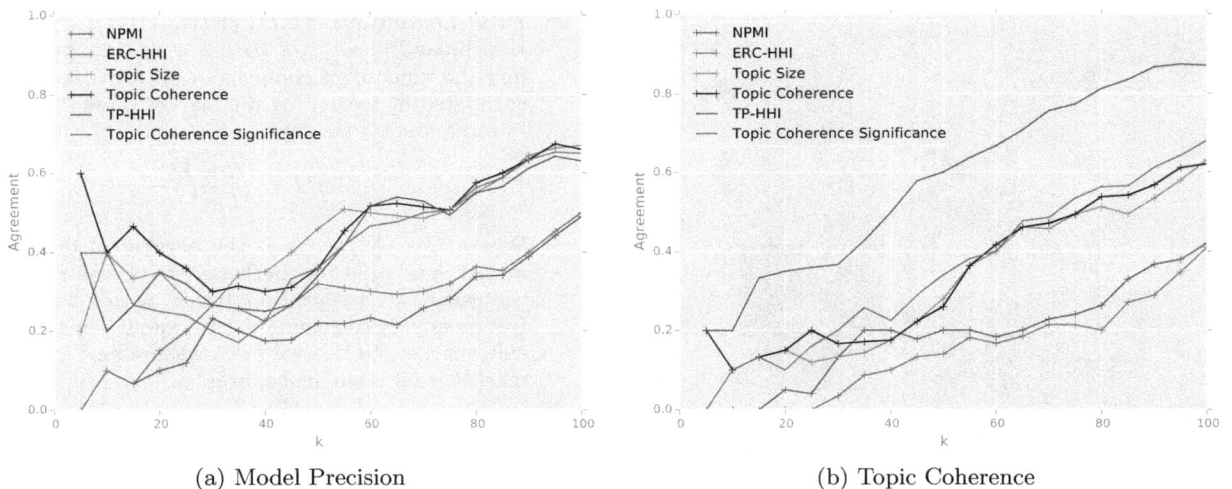

(a) Model Precision   (b) Topic Coherence

Figure 5: Agreement between the automated measures and crowdsourced measures for different values of k. In the case of Topic Coherence, TP-HHI yields the best agreement. In the case of Model Precision, the Topic Coherence does best at the shorter lists, however is matched by other measures at longer lists.

Table 4: Spearman's ρ between measures requiring Mechanical Turk and automated measures. Instances where we reject the null hypothesis at the $\alpha = 0.05$ significance level are denoted with *, and instances where we reject the null hypothesis at the $\alpha = 10^{-6}$ significance level are denoted with **.

	Model Precision	Topic Consensus
TS	0.152*	-0.532**
TC	0.359**	-0.584**
TCS	-0.074	-0.788**
ERC-HHI	0.103	-0.478**
TP-HHI	-0.471**	**-0.885****
NPMI	**-0.562****	-0.774**

calculate the agreement between the top k topics determined by ranking the crowdsourced measures as well as the top k topics determined by ranking the automated measures. The results of this experiment are shown in Figure 5. Here we see that **TP-HHI** is the best at finding the best topics at lists of any size with respect to Topic Coherence. In the case of model precision the best measure is less clear: **Topic Coherence** is best for shorter lists while **TP-HHI**, and **Topic Size** compete for the best performance of some of the mid-length lists.

Predicting the True Crowdsourced Values

So far we have evaluated the quality of our automated measures by seeing how well the value of the automated measures changes as compared to the crowdsourced measures. While correlation can be used to find the quality of the measure, and precision to find the best topics, there is value in being able to predict the *actual* value of the topics' crowdsourced measures.

Using linear regression, we train a model to predict the true value of the crowdsourced measures using the automated measures. We build two models: one where the dependent variable is "Model Precision", and another where the dependent variable is "Topic Coherence". In both cases, the independent variables are all of the automated measures introduced previously. We use 10-fold cross validation and report both the mean and standard deviation of the performance of the models across all 10 runs. In this experiment we achieved a root-mean-square error of 0.12 ± 0.02 for Topic Coherence and 0.27 ± 0.05 for Model Precision.

CONCLUSION AND FUTURE WORK

We investigate how well topics can be interpreted by humans. To do this we generated topics from a collection of scientific abstracts, consisting of abstracts of proposals accepted by the European Research Council. Using this data we ask how well crowdsourced techniques can be used to evaluate topic models. Further, we investigate how well automatic measures can approximate the crowdsourced measures, making way for scalable and reproducible research.

We reproduced existing topic measures on a corpus consisting of scientific abstracts. We received inferior results compared to the original results which were performed on Wikipedia and New York Times data. This could be due to the nature of the Amazon Mechanical Turk workers changing, but is likely due to the nature of the dataset.

We propose a new crowdsourced topic measure, "topic consensus", that includes ground truth information about the label of the topic. This method allows researchers to see how well the topics generated from their dataset can be understood in relation to the underlying topics in the corpus. Furthermore, by inspecting the Turker's results on the NYT topics we were able to see how the Turker's understanding of the topics influences their answers.

We investigate how to estimate these crowdsourced topic measures without the need of crowdsourcing tools such as Mechanical Turk. We find some automated measures that are very highly correlated with crowdsourced measures, allowing future researchers to reproduce these topic quality measures at scale. Additionally, we find that the measures that best estimate the ground truth topics do not require ground truth information themselves, allowing for researchers to perform topic consensus analysis when ground truth information about the underlying ground truth topics in their dataset is not known.

One direction for future work is to catalogue the performance of all crowdsourced measures across different datasets to provide a benchmark for different types of data. Future work also includes seeing how these measures perform when K is taken out of the equation, using nonparametric topic modeling algorithms such as Hierarchical Dirichlet Processes [26]. Other areas of interest include the role that both "interpretability", and "coherence" contribute to the measures proposed in this work.

ACKNOWLEDGEMENTS

This work is sponsored, in part, by Office of Naval Research grant N000141410095 as well as LexisNexis and HPCC Systems.

REFERENCES

[1] N. Aletras and M. Stevenson. Evaluating Topic Coherence using Distributional Semantics. In *IWCS*, pages 13–22, 2013.

[2] D. M. Blei, A. Y. Ng, and M. I. Jordan. Latent Dirichlet Allocation. *The Journal of Machine Learning Research*, 3:993–1022, 2003.

[3] G. Bouma. Normalized (Pointwise) Mutual Information in Collocation Extraction. *Proceedings of GSCL*, pages 31–40, 2009.

[4] J. Chang, J. L. Boyd-Graber, S. Gerrish, C. Wang, and D. M. Blei. Reading Tea Leaves: How Humans Interpret Topic Models. In *NIPS*, volume 22, pages 288–296, 2009.

[5] J. Eisenstein, B. O'Connor, N. A. Smith, and E. P. Xing. A Latent Variable Model for Geographic Lexical Variation. In *EMNLP*, pages 1277–1287, 2010.

[6] T. L. Griffiths and M. Steyvers. Finding Scientific Topics. *PNAS*, 101(Suppl 1):5228–5235, 2004.

[7] A. O. Hirschman. *National Power and the Structure of Foreign Trade*. University of California Press, Berkeley, CA, 1945.

[8] L. Hong, A. Ahmed, S. Gurumurthy, A. J. Smola, and K. Tsioutsiouliklis. Discovering Geographical Topics in the Twitter Stream. In *WWW*, pages 769–778, 2012.

[9] Y. Hu, A. John, F. Wang, and S. Kambhampati. ET-LDA: Joint Topic Modeling for Aligning Events and their Twitter Feedback. In *AAAI*, volume 12, pages 59–65, 2012.

[10] K. Joseph, C. H. Tan, and K. M. Carley. Beyond "Local", "Categories" and "Friends": Clustering foursquare Users with Latent "Topics". In *UbiComp*, pages 919–926, 2012.

[11] J. M. Joyce. Kullback-Leibler Divergence. In *International Encyclopedia of Statistical Science*, pages 720–722. Springer, 2011.

[12] K. Kireyev, L. Palen, and K. Anderson. Applications of Topics Models to Analysis of Disaster-Related Twitter Data. In *NIPS Workshop on Applications for Topic Models: Text and Beyond*, volume 1, 2009.

[13] J. H. Lau, D. Newman, and T. Baldwin. Machine Reading Tea Leaves: Automatically Evaluating Topic Coherence and Topic Model Quality. In *Proceedings of the European Chapter of the Association for Computational Linguistics*, pages 530–539, 2014.

[14] J. Lin. Divergence Measures Based on the Shannon Entropy. *Information Theory, IEEE Transactions on*, 37(1):145–151, Jan 1991.

[15] J. Mahmud, J. Nichols, and C. Drews. Where Is This Tweet From? Inferring Home Locations of Twitter Users. In *ICWSM*, pages 511–514, 2012.

[16] K. Mayer and J. Pfeffer. Mapping Social Sciences and Humanities. *Horizons for Social Sciences and Humanities*, 09 2014.

[17] A. K. McCallum. MALLET: A Machine Learning for Language Toolkit. http://mallet.cs.umass.edu, 2002.

[18] D. Mimno, H. M. Wallach, E. Talley, M. Leenders, and A. McCallum. Optimizing Semantic Coherence in Topic Models. In *EMNLP*, pages 262–272, 2011.

[19] F. Morstatter, N. Lubold, H. Pon-Barry, J. Pfeffer, and H. Liu. Finding Eyewitness Tweets During Crises. In *ACL 2014 Workshop on Language Technologies and Computational Social Science*, 2014.

[20] F. Morstatter, J. Pfeffer, H. Liu, and K. M. Carley. Is the Sample Good Enough? Comparing Data from Twitter's Streaming API with Twitter's Firehose. In *Proceedings of ICWSM*, pages 400–408, 2013.

[21] D. Newman, J. H. Lau, K. Grieser, and T. Baldwin. Automatic Evaluation of Topic Coherence. In *NAACL*, pages 100–108, 2010.

[22] M. Röder, A. Both, and A. Hinneburg. Exploring the Space of Topic Coherence Measures. In *WSDM*, pages 399–408, 2015.

[23] B. M. Schmidt. Words Alone: Dismantling Topic Models in the Humanities. *Journal of Digital Humanities*, 2(1):49–65, 2012.

[24] R. Snow, B. O'Connor, D. Jurafsky, and A. Y. Ng. Cheap and Fast—But is it Good? Evaluating Non-Expert Annotations for Natural Language Tasks. In *EMNLP*, pages 254–263. Association for Computational Linguistics, 2008.

[25] C. Spearman. The Proof and Measurement of Association between Two Things. *The American Journal of Psychology*, 15(1):72–101, 1904.

[26] Y. W. Teh, M. I. Jordan, M. J. Beal, and D. M. Blei. Hierarchical Dirichlet Processes. *Journal of the American Statistical Association*, 101(476), 2006.

[27] A. Tumasjan, T. O. Sprenger, P. G. Sandner, and I. M. Welpe. Predicting Elections with Twitter: What 140 Characters Reveal about Political Sentiment. In *ICWSM*, pages 178–185, 2010.

[28] H. M. Wallach, I. Murray, R. Salakhutdinov, and D. Mimno. Evaluation Methods for Topic Models. In *ICML*, pages 1105–1112, 2009.

[29] Z. Yin, L. Cao, J. Han, C. Zhai, and T. Huang. Geographical Topic Discovery and Comparison. In *WWW*, pages 247–256, 2011.

Media Bias in German Online Newspapers

Alexander Dallmann
Data Mining and Information
Retrieval Group
University of Würzburg
dallmann@informatik.uni-
wuerzburg.de

Florian Lemmerich
Computational Social
Science Group
GESIS - Leibniz Institute for
the Social Sciences
florian.lemmerich@gesis.org

Daniel Zoller
Data Mining and Information
Retrieval Group
University of Würzburg
zoller@informatik.uni-
wuerzburg.de

Andreas Hotho
Data Mining and Information
Retrieval Group
University of Würzburg & L3S
Research Center
hotho@informatik.uni-
wuerzburg.de

ABSTRACT

Online newspapers have been established as a crucial information source, at least partially replacing traditional media like television or print media. As all other media, online newspapers are potentially affected by media bias. This describes non-neutral reporting of journalists and other news producers, e.g., with respect to specific opinions or political parties. Analysis of media bias has a long tradition in political science. However, traditional techniques rely heavily on manual annotation and are thus often limited to the analysis of small sets of articles. In this paper, we investigate a dataset that covers all political and economical news from four leading German online newspapers over a timespan of four years. In order to analyze this large document set and compare the political orientation of different newspapers, we propose a variety of automatically computable measures that can indicate media bias. As a result, statistically significant differences in the reporting about specific parties can be detected between the analyzed online newspapers.

Categories and Subject Descriptors

H.4 [**Information Systems Applications**]: Miscellaneous

General Terms

media analysis, computational social science

1. INTRODUCTION

Online newspapers have been established as a crucial information source in modern societies, at least partially replacing traditional media like television or print media. As all other

media, online newspapers are potentially affected by media bias. This describes non-neutral reporting of journalists and other news producers, e.g., with respect to specific opinions or political parties. Identifying and recognizing biases in media is crucial for an open society due to the large influence of the news media as the *fourth estate*. Additionally, making biases transparent can also have practical implications: it allows journalists and publishers to assess their own work objectively, and readers to interpret statements of that source in the correct context or choose an online newspaper according to their own political preference. Analysis of media bias has a long tradition in political science. However, many traditional techniques require access to a wide range of newspapers and rely heavily on manual annotation and are therefore often limited to the analysis of small sets of articles and thus focus on small time spans, e.g., election campaigns. This paper investigates how online newspapers that are freely available on the web can be analyzed automatically with respect to potential bias towards political parties.

In this paper, we are not interested in the overall political orientation of online news media as a whole, but focus on a comparative analysis in order to identify relative biases between online newspapers. In that direction, we focus on the German online newspaper landscape. We collected a large dataset composed of all articles published in politics and economics sections of four leading online newspaper in Germany, that is, *faz.net*, *spiegel.de*, *taz.de*, and *zeit.de*, in a four-year period.

Thus, the contribution of this paper is twofold: First, we discuss several measures that allow us to identify potential bias towards a political party in online newspapers in an automatic manner. This not only enables the analysis of large document sets with reasonable costs, but also grants results that are not influenced by the subjectivity of human annotations. Second, we show for our exemplary dataset what biases four leading German online newspapers exposed in the analyzed time frame in comparison to each other. In that regard, we can identify statistically significant differences in the coverage of different parties among the analyzed online newspapers.

The rest of the paper is structured as follows: Section 2 reviews related work. Then, Section 3 introduces a variety of metrics that indicate potential bias towards political parties in online newspapers. Next, Section 4 presents the utilized datasets. Section 5 reports on experimental results. Afterwards, Section 6 discusses limitations of the proposed approach. Finally, Section 7 concludes the paper with a summary and an outlook on future research directions.

2. RELATED WORK

The analysis of media bias is a well developed and active research field in political sciences, but traditionally relies heavily on manual annotation of articles. This not only makes analytical studies very costly, but also introduces another form of bias through the annotators. Therefore, "text as data", i.e., the automated analysis of large text corpora, has been recognized as an useful tool in political science in the last years, cf. [3]. In that direction, large sets of parliamentary speeches [11], the political orientation of parties [8, 12, 9], party classification of speeches [17] and the distribution of topics in congressional bills [5] have been investigated. In contrast to these approaches, this paper focuses on the large-scale analysis of online newspapers.

Literature on media bias analysis distinguishes between three types of media bias, that is, *gatekeeping bias, coverage bias* and *statement bias* [1]. Gatekeeping bias describes the selection of stories out of the potential stories and is generally hard to quantify. Coverage bias expresses how much space political positions (or in our case, parties) receive in media. For traditional newspapers, this has been measured by column inches of paper covered [14], see also [1]. As an alternative, also counting occurrences in the headlines has been performed for this task [13]. While counting occurrences is a tedious task to do manually for full texts of articles, it is easy to perform in an automatic approach as advocated in this paper. Statement bias denotes how an author's own opinion is woven within a text. Traditionally, this is often handled by manual annotation of whether a text is "favorable" to a party or not. As one of many examples, Ho and Quinn investigated the political position of media in the US party system by labeling and analyzing the agreement of editorials with Supreme Court decisions. For their study they employed a team of 14 law students and manually labeled 1500 editorials [7]. These efforts clearly illustrate the advantages of automatic approaches as proposed in this paper. Regarding automatic analysis, Groseclose and Milyo measure bias in newspaper media by first computing a score for think tanks based on the citations of Democrat or Republican party members. Using these scores, newspapers are then evaluated indirectly by investigating which think tanks are referenced [4]. Such a method could be additionally implemented to augment the analysis in our setting. However, results could be expected to be less significant for the German political landscape since think tanks are mostly publicly funded and obligated to political neutrality. Gentzkow and Shapiro investigate overall bias of US newspapers by determining the number of occurrences of typical phrases (as identified by a quantitative analysis of congressional records) for Democratic and Republican congressman in newspapers [2]. While this is related to our method for measuring vocabulary similarity to party manifestos, unlike our work their approach is tailored to the US two-party system. Additionally, this paper uses a variety of different measures for a more comprehensive picture and is focused on online newspapers.

3. ANALYSIS

Measuring bias in printed media is a long-term research topic in political science. However, established methods often involve manual inspection of documents, and are difficult to apply automatically on a large corpus. In addition, existing methods are often tailored to the two-party system as it is established in the United States, but are less suited to a multi-party system as it exists, e.g., in Germany. Therefore, we present in the following a set of metrics that indicate possible bias of newspapers towards certain political parties in our corpus of German online newspapers. We start by introducing some notations.

3.1 Notation

The corpus for each online newspaper $N = \{d_{N,1}, \ldots, d_{N,k}\}$ consists of a set of documents (articles). For each document, the title $T(d)$, the full text $F(d)$, and a set of keywords $K(d)$ from the HTML header of the online article are available. If a title $T(d)$ contains a subsequence s of one or more words, then this is denoted in this paper as $s \sqsubseteq T(d)$ (or $s \sqsubseteq F(d)$, $s \sqsubseteq K(d)$ analogously). Furthermore, the length of the respective article in number of words is denoted by $|F(d)|$.

We focus our analysis on a set of political parties $\mathcal{P} = \{P_1, P_2, \ldots, P_p\}$. Since parties are commonly referenced by their acronym in Germany (e.g., "FDP" is the prevalent notion for the party "Freie Demokratische Partei"), we only consider those acronyms. In this paper, we write the acronym of a party P as $acr(P)$. Furthermore, we consider for each party a set of prominent party members $M(P) = \{m_{P,1}, \ldots, m_{P,l}\}$. We use the notation $m_{P,i} \sqsubseteq T(d)$ if the full name (first, middle and last name) of a party member is contained in the title of an article ($m_{P,i} \sqsubseteq F(d), m_{P,i} \sqsubseteq K(d)$ for full texts and keywords respectively).

3.2 Coverage Bias Metrics

The first group of metrics is concerned with the coverage political parties receive. These measures should be interpreted in comparison to the values for other political parties. Therefore we apply standard normalization procedures. Given any raw measure $\overline{M_x}(P, N)$, the normalized measure $\widehat{M_x}(P, N)$ is computed as $\widehat{M_x}(P, N) = \frac{1}{Z} \cdot \overline{M_x}(P, N)$, with the normalization constant $Z = \sum_{P' \in \mathcal{P}} \overline{M_x}(P', N)$. Additionally, differences between newspaper are easier to spot when only the deviation for this newspaper in comparison to the average values for the complete set of newspapers $\mathbb{N}$ are displayed: $M_x(P, N) = \widehat{M_x}(P, N) - \frac{\sum_{N \in \mathbb{N}} \widehat{M_x}(P,N)}{|\mathbb{N}|}$. Please note that our measures do not consider multiple occurrences of acronyms or names and count every article only once.

3.2.1 Party as Main Article Topic

A first group of measures indicates how often a party appears as the main topic of an article. In that direction, $M_{Title}(P, N)$ describes how often political parties appear in the titles of a newspaper's articles:

$$\overline{M}_{title}(P, N) = |\{d \in N : acr(P) \sqsubseteq T(d)\}|.$$

Since we are analyzing a corpus of online news, each article is associated by its publisher with certain keywords in the *HTML* header section. These keywords can also be used to identify articles, which are directly concerned with a political party. The respective measure $M_{keywords}$ is computed as:

$$\overline{M}_{keywords}(P, N) = |\{d \in N : acr(P) \sqsubseteq K(d)\}|.$$

3.2.2 Party and Party Member Mentions

Further measures are concerned with the overall coverage political parties receive within the full text of the articles. In that direction, we count the number of distinct articles that contain a reference to a political party.

$$\overline{M}_{Full}(P, N) = |\{d \in N : acr(P) \sqsubseteq F(d)\}|.$$

As an extension, we do not consider references to the party itself, but to prominent party members, i.e., all parliament members of the respective party. Then, we count the proportion of articles in each newspaper that contain the exact name (first, middle and family name) of a prominent member. Using the exact name ensures that members are detected with high precision.

$$\overline{M}_{Full\_mem}(P, N) =$$
$$|\{d \in N : (\exists m_{P,i} \in M(P) : m_{P,i} \sqsubseteq F(d))\}|.$$

3.3 Statement Bias Metrics

The second group of metrics is designed to indicate statement bias, i.e., (un-)favorable reporting about specific political positions.

3.3.1 Sentiment Analysis

We use state-of-the art sentiment analysis for German language and identify for a neighborhood, i.e., four words before and four words after a mentioning of a party P, the mood $S(N, P)$. All party mentions are classified by *SentiStrength* [15] for a scaled sentiment strength using the full text $F(d)$ of an article. We configure SentiStrength for the syntax of the German language (negation words can occur after the sentiment). An overall sentiment towards a political party in a newspaper can then be computed as the sum of the individual mood ratings.

3.3.2 Vocabulary Similarity

Although party manifestos show in general a strong overlap in the used vocabulary, each party lays a distinct emphasis on specific ideological terms such as *freedom*, *solidarity*, *environment*, etc., cf. [10]. Common usage of the same terms in an online newspaper and a political party can indicate a related ideology. To capture such similarities, we first determine a list of keywords that specifically point at certain political orientations. For each party, the number of keyword occurrences in recent party manifestos is counted and stored in a vector. Analogously, another vector then provides the number of keyword occurrences in each online newspaper. A formal measure for the vocabulary similarity between an online newspaper and a party is then given by the *cosine similarity* of the corresponding vectors.

4. DATASET

For our analysis, we utilized a large dataset consisting of articles published on four of the leading online news sites in Germany, that is, *faz.net*, *spiegel.de*, *taz.de*, and *zeit.de*. We restrict our analysis to the time between 27th October 2009 and 22th October 2013 covering the 17th legislative session of the German federal parliament. Six main political parties sent members to the parliament in this time frame: the conservative sister parties *CDU* and *CSU*, the liberal party *FDP*, the greens (*Grüne*), the social-democratic *SPD* and the left-wing party *Linke*. The government in this time span

Table 1: Dataset overview: The number of articles ($|N|$), their average length (l, measured in words), the share of articles that mention at least one party (s_P) or party member (s_M) or either party or member (s_C) in the full text, and the percentage of articles that mention a party acronym in the title (s_T) or in the keywords (s_K)

N	$|N|$	l	s_P	s_M	s_C	s_T	s_K
faz.net	40,209	513.5	30.5%	24.5%	35.1%	4.1%	20.1%
spiegel.de	51,560	472.1	31.7%	30.6%	37.5%	6.0%	10.0%
taz.de	23,610	477.5	35.9%	27.6%	40.0%	2.5%	2.9%
zeit.de	17,926	445.5	36.6%	35.7%	43.2%	6.8%	32.3%
Average	33,326	477.2	33.7 %	29.6 %	39.0 %	4.9 %	16.3 %

was formed by a conservative-liberal coalition of the parties *CDU*, *CSU* and *FDP*, led by chancellor Angela Merkel.

For the analyzed time frame we retrieved all articles that have been published in the respective *politics* and *economics* sections. We parsed the article pages and extracted the *date*, the article *title*, the *full text*, and the *keywords* added by the publisher as meta-information. For each part of the article, we identified mentions of the parties and party members that are also members of the parliament, see also Section 3.

Table 1 shows dataset characteristics including the share of articles that contain references to parties or party members as defined in section 3. Overall, our dataset features more than 130,000 newspaper articles containing more than 62,000,000 words. For each of the four online newspapers more than 370 articles are available on a monthly average. However, not all these articles can be easily associated with party politics as the dataset also includes other articles on e.g., economic topics or foreign politics. On average, only 39% of articles mention a party either directly or indirectly, i.e., by mentioning a prominent party member. From the analyzed news sites, *zeit.de* published the smallest amount of articles in the analyzed time frame, but it has the highest percentage of articles that mention a party.

taz.de started adding *keywords* only after February 2012. As a result only 2.9% of taz.de articles contain a party acronym in the *keyword* meta-information. Also care must be taken when judging results for keywords since we found that some articles are missing important *keywords*.

For vocabulary analysis, we relied on additional data from previous research in political science: Pappi, Seher and Kurella provide a short list of key vocabulary (such as *freedom*, *solidarity*, etc.) including the number of mentions in the respective election programs[1] aggregated from 1990 until 2009 [10].

5. RESULTS

This section presents experimental results of the described measures on the German online newspaper dataset.

5.1 Coverage Bias

In the following, we present results for the measures that indicate coverage bias, cf. Section 3.2. For these measures, the overall values for each party and online newspaper over the complete time interval are reported. In order to additionally test the statistical significance of our findings, we calculate

---

[1] Manifestos for the CSU have been excluded, since they have been identical to those of the CDU for most elections.

Table 2: Differences in coverage: acronyms in titles.

(a) Articles with party acronyms in title ($\overline{M}_{title}$).

N	CDU	CSU	FDP	Grüne	Linke	SPD
faz.net	315	167	481	213	57	543
spiegel.de	605	296	848	355	266	1,007
taz.de	104	28	120	127	99	146
zeit.de	224	118	381	147	90	369

(b) Normalization over every online newspaper ($\widehat{M}_{title}$).

N	CDU	CSU	FDP	Grüne	Linke	SPD
faz.net	17.7%	9.4%	27.1%	12.0%	3.2%	30.6%
spiegel.de	17.9%	8.8%	25.1%	10.5%	7.9%	29.8%
taz.de	16.7%	4.5%	19.2%	20.4%	15.9%	23.4%
zeit.de	16.9%	8.9%	28.7%	11.1%	6.8%	27.8%
Average	17.3%	7.9%	25.0%	13.5%	8.5%	27.9%

(c) Differences in coverage using titles (M_{title}).

N	CDU	CSU	FDP	Grüne	Linke	SPD
faz.net	+0.4%	+1.5%	+2.1%	−1.5%	**−5.2%**	+2.7%
spiegel.de	+0.6%	+0.9%	+0.1%	**−3.0%**	−0.6%	+1.9%
taz.de	−0.6%	**−3.4%**	**−5.8%**	**+6.9%**	**+7.4%**	−4.5%
zeit.de	−0.4%	+1.0%	+3.6%	−2.4%	−1.7%	−0.1%

Table 3: Differences in coverage: acronyms in keywords ($M_{keywords}$).

N	CDU	CSU	FDP	Grüne	Linke	SPD
faz.net	**+6.1%**	+1.1%	**+5.5%**	**−10.7%**	−2.3%	+0.3%
spiegel.de	−0.5%	+1.3%	−0.8%	−0.3%	+1.3%	−1.0%
taz.de	−7.5%	**−2.7%**	−6.2%	**+10.8%**	+1.8%	+3.8%
zeit.de	+1.9%	+0.3%	+1.6%	**+0.2%**	−0.8%	**−3.1%**

Table 4: Differences in coverage: acronyms in full text (M_{Full}).

N	CDU	CSU	FDP	Grüne	Linke	SPD
faz.net	+1.4%	**+0.5%**	+0.3%	+0.0%	−2.5%	+0.3%
spiegel.de	−0.1%	**+1.0%**	+0.7%	−1.0%	−0.2%	−0.3%
taz.de	−1.9%	**−2.0%**	**−2.5%**	**+2.4%**	**+3.1%**	**+0.8%**
zeit.de	+0.7%	+0.5%	**+1.5%**	**−1.5%**	−0.4%	−0.8%

Table 5: Differences in coverage: party members in full text (M_{Full_mem}).

N	CDU	CSU	FDP	Grüne	Linke	SPD
faz.net	**+3.7%**	+0.2%	−0.8%	−1.4%	**−1.6%**	−0.0%
spiegel.de	+1.8%	+0.4%	+1.0%	−1.1%	**−1.8%**	−0.4%
taz.de	**−6.5%**	−0.6%	−2.3%	**+4.2%**	**+4.3%**	+0.9%
zeit.de	+1.0%	+0.0%	**+2.1%**	**−1.6%**	−0.9%	−0.5%

5.1.2 Articles that Mention Parties

Table 4 is obtained by counting articles that contain the party acronym in the full text. Again, faz.net favors conservative parties over the Linke in terms of overall coverage. In contrast, taz.de favors the Linke and Grüne over the conservative and liberal parties. zeit.de and spiegel.de display slight bias towards the liberal FDP and against the Grüne.

Table 5 shows results for counting articles that contain a reference to a prominent party member in the full text (see Section 3.2.2). The obtained values support the observations for Table 4. However, the deviations on party member level seem to be even more significant in comparison to the deviations for party acronyms.

5.2 Statement Bias

Regarding statement bias, we first investigate results for sentiment analysis. Table 6 shows the average scaled sentiment strength (see Section 3.3.1) of all parties in each online newspaper. As we can observe from the table, the average party scores do not deviate significantly from zero. Based on these scores, there is a slight tendency for all newspapers to present the CDU in a slightly positive and the FDP in a slightly negative way. This could be inferred from the fact that the party got entangled in several affairs in the considered time interval. faz.net reports overall slightly more positive about parties, in particular the conservative ones CDU and CSU. However, in summary results for the sentiment analysis are inconclusive. In [16] Atteveldt et al. report similar findings for Dutch newspapers. That is possibly due to the fact that party bias is not expressed bluntly in newspapers, but in a more indirect way, indicating the need for more sophisticated specialized techniques for sentiment analysis.

Finally, results for the similarity of key vocabulary in articles and party manifestos are shown in Table 7. It can be seen that the usage of key terms for the faz.net is more similar to governing coalition parties CDU and FDP than it is for other newspapers, especially compared to spiegel.de and taz.de. By contrast, party manifestos of Grüne and Linke are more

all metrics on a monthly basis in the considered time span. With the computed values, we conduct a *Student's t-test* for a single sample for each party and online newspaper and test if the mean value is significantly different from zero. We mark the *Bonferroni* corrected ($m = 24$) significant values at a level of 0.05 bold in the result tables.

5.1.1 Articles about Parties

Table 2 shows results of analyzing party occurrences in article titles (M_{title}). Using this measure, we also demonstrate the normalization procedures. First, the overall count of occurrences $\overline{M}_{title}$ is displayed in Table 2(a). Then, this table is normalized to obtain the share of counts $\widehat{M}_{title}$ for each party, see Table 2(b). Finally, the average value for each party over all online newspapers is subtracted from the individual newspaper values. Thus, the displayed values show how much more or less coverage compared to the average a party got in each newspaper. Due to constraint space, results for other measures are only reported after normalization.

Table 2(c) shows the differences of party mentions in article titles. The newspaper faz.net tends to slightly favor the governing parties CDU, CSU and FDP to the leftist Linke and Grüne. Results for taz.de indicate an opposite ideology. For the newspapers zeit.de and spiegel.de, the picture is less clear since there are few significant findings. This indicates that these newspapers are ideologically in the center of the analyzed spectrum of online newspapers. These findings are in line with the public perception of these newspapers.

Party mentions in HTML keywords, see Table 3, show overall similar results, but with unusual outliers, i.e., mentions of the party Grüne.

Table 6: Average sentiment scale for every online newspaper and party.

N	CDU	CSU	FDP	Grüne	Linke	SPD
faz.net	0.002	0.067	−0.013	0.002	0.005	0.014
spiegel.de	−0.026	0.028	−0.057	0.015	−0.065	0.021
taz.de	−0.018	0.041	−0.034	−0.020	−0.014	0.002
zeit.de	−0.023	0.066	−0.061	−0.014	−0.048	0.011

Table 7: Similarity of the distribution of key vocabulary between online newspaper articles and party manifestos (possible range 0 to 1).

N	CDU	FDP	Grüne	Linke	SPD
faz.net	0.863	0.853	0.731	0.794	0.838
spiegel.de	0.808	0.802	0.756	0.831	0.833
taz.de	0.756	0.774	0.759	0.835	0.802
zeit.de	0.846	0.842	0.787	0.845	0.864

dissimilar. Also for other newspapers interesting results can be observed: for taz.de, large distances to CDU and FDP vocabularies are evident. Results for zeit.de show higher similarities to the left parties SPD, Grüne, and Linke than other newspapers. Vocabulary used in party manifestos of Grüne is most dissimilar to articles in the analyzed online newspapers. Overall, the results point in a similar direction about the political orientation of online newspapers as findings with coverage bias measures.

6. DISCUSSION

It is important to notice that the proposed measures for coverage bias detection analyze a set of online newspapers comparatively, that is, the obtained results should only be interpreted in relation to the other analyzed online newspapers. As such, our method is highly dependent on the selection of online newspapers, e.g., a moderate paper would appear to be leftist when compared only to conservative ones.

Counting mentions of party acronyms and member names is subject to some issues: parties in government tend to generate more news and are differently framed depending on the party status [6]. Additionally, acronyms and names might be ambiguous. However, these factors influence all online newspapers in the same way and consequently don't distort the comparative analysis significantly.

For the proposed measures, different variations could additionally be considered. For example, the measures count each party only once for each article. Instead, each occurrence could also be counted individually. Since these variations lead to very similar results in our initial experiments, we do not report them in this paper. Several metrics proposed in this paper expose similar tendencies, cf. Section 5. Thus, not every measure is crucial on its own. However, by considering a broad spectrum of different measures, a more stable picture of the overall political orientation emerges.

7. CONCLUSIONS

This paper was concerned with the large-scale analysis of online newspapers. In that direction, we discussed several automatically computable metrics that indicate potential bias towards a political party. These considered the mentions of parties and party members in the title, the keyword and the full text of articles, the sentiment in the direct neighborhood of article mentions, and the vocabulary used in online newspapers in comparison to party manifestos. Using these metrics, we investigated a large dataset containing all articles from the politics and economics sections from four of the leading German online news sites, that is, *faz.net*, *spiegel.de*, *taz.de*, and *zeit.de* over a four-year period. As a result, we were able to detect statistically significant reporting differences across the analyzed online newspapers.

In the future we want to extend our work in different directions. First, we will enlarge our dataset by adding more news sites and by considering longer time intervals. Furthermore, we aim at developing more sophisticated measures by integrating more data sources such as political speeches. Additionally, while this paper focused on bias towards political parties, similar techniques could be used to study other types of biases, for example, gender bias or bias against racial minorities. Finally, a comparative analysis of newspaper sites with social media sources such as Twitter is an interesting topic of future work.

8. REFERENCES

[1] D. D'Alessio and M. Allen. Media bias in presidential elections: a meta-analysis. *Journal of communication*, 50(4):133–156, 2000.

[2] M. Gentzkow and J. M. Shapiro. What drives media slant? Evidence from US daily newspapers. *Econometrica*, 78(1):35–71, 2010.

[3] J. Grimmer and B. M. Stewart. Text as data: The promise and pitfalls of automatic content analysis methods for political texts. *Political Analysis*, 2013.

[4] T. Groseclose and J. Milyo. A measure of media bias. *The Quarterly Journal of Economics*, pages 1191–1237, 2005.

[5] D. Hillard, S. Purpura, and J. Wilkerson. Computer-assisted topic classification for mixed-methods social science research. *Journal of Information Tech. & Politics*, 4(4):31–46, 2008.

[6] G. Hirst, Y. Riabinin, J. Graham, and M. Boizot-Roche. Text to ideology or text to party status? *From Text to Political Positions: Text analysis across disciplines*, 55:93, 2014.

[7] D. E. Ho, K. M. Quinn, et al. Measuring explicit political positions of media. *Quarterly Journal of Political Science*, 3(4):353–377, 2008.

[8] M. Laver and K. Beniot. Estimating Irish party position using computer wordscoring: the 2002 elections. *Irish Political Studies*, 17(2):97–107, 2003.

[9] W. Lowe, K. Benoitt, S. Mikhaylov, and M. Laver. Scaling policy preferences from coded political texts. *Legislative Studies Quarterly*, 36(1):123–155, 2011.

[10] F. U. Pappi, N. M. Seher, and A.-S. Kurella. Das Politikangebot deutscher Parteien bei den Bundestagswahlen seit 1976 im dimensionsweisen Vergleich, 2011.

[11] K. M. Quinn, B. L. Monroe, M. Colaresi, M. H. Crespin, and D. R. Radev. How to analyze political attention with minimal assumptions and costs. *American Journal of Political Science*, 54(1):209–228, 2010.

[12] J. B. Slapin and S.-O. Proksch. A scaling model for estimating time-series party positions from texts. *American Journal of Political Science*, 52(3):705–722, 2008.

[13] G. H. Stempel. The prestige press in two presidential elections. *Journalism & Mass Communication Quarterly*, 42(1):15–21, 1965.

[14] G. H. Stempel and J. W. Windhauser. Coverage by the prestige press of the 1988 presidential campaign. *Journalism & Mass Communication Quarterly*, 66(4):894–919, 1989.

[15] M. Thelwall, K. Buckley, G. Paltoglou, D. Cai, and A. Kappas. Sentiment strength detection in short informal text. *Journal of the American Society for Information Science and Technology*, 61(12):2544–2558, 2010.

[16] W. Van Atteveldt, J. Kleinnijenhuis, N. Ruigrok, and S. Schlobach. Good news or bad news? conducting sentiment analysis on dutch text to distinguish between positive and negative relations. *Journal of Information Technology & Politics*, 5(1):73–94, 2008.

[17] B. Yu, S. Kaufmann, and D. Diermeier. Classifying party affiliation from political speech. *Journal of Information Technology & Politics*, 5(1):33–48, 2008.

Characterizing Smoking and Drinking Abstinence from Social Media

Acar Tamersoy, Munmun De Choudhury, Duen Horng Chau
College of Computing
Georgia Institute of Technology
{tamersoy, munmund, polo}@gatech.edu

ABSTRACT

Social media has been established to bear signals relating to health and well-being states. In this paper, we investigate the potential of social media in characterizing and understanding abstinence from tobacco or alcohol use. While the link between behavior and addiction has been explored in psychology literature, the lack of longitudinal self-reported data on long-term abstinence has challenged addiction research. We leverage the activity spanning almost eight years on two prominent communities on Reddit: StopSmoking and StopDrinking. We use the self-reported "badge" information of nearly a thousand users as gold standard information on their abstinence status to characterize long-term abstinence. We build supervised learning based statistical models that use the linguistic features of the content shared by the users as well as the network structure of their social interactions. Our findings indicate that long-term abstinence from smoking or drinking (~one year) can be distinguished from short-term abstinence (~40 days) with 85% accuracy. We further show that language and interaction on social media offer powerful cues towards characterizing these addiction-related health outcomes. We discuss the implications of our findings in social media and health research, and in the role of social media as a platform for positive behavior change and therapy.

Categories and Subject Descriptors

H.4 [**Information Systems Applications**]: Miscellaneous

Keywords

addiction; social media; smoking; drinking; abstinence; health; well-being; Reddit

1. INTRODUCTION

Health and well-being challenges such as smoking, alcoholism, and impulsive eating are known to be influenced by individuals' social environment [13], which are moving online, as social media sites become more popular. Indeed, the use of social media for health-related discourse have increased sharply in recent years [12].

Permission to make digital or hard copies of all or part of this work for personal or classroom use is granted without fee provided that copies are not made or distributed for profit or commercial advantage and that copies bear this notice and the full citation on the first page. Copyrights for components of this work owned by others than ACM must be honored. Abstracting with credit is permitted. To copy otherwise, or republish, to post on servers or to redistribute to lists, requires prior specific permission and/or a fee. Request permissions from Permissions@acm.org.
HT '15, September 1–4, 2015, Guzelyurt, Northern Cyprus.
© 2015 ACM. ISBN 978-1-4503-3395-5/15/09 ...$15.00.
DOI: http://dx.doi.org/10.1145/2700171.2791247.

Figure 1: Examples of the users' abstinence badges on the StopSmoking and StopDrinking subreddits. The abstinence stage is displayed inside the badge icon (e.g., smiley face for "under one week") and the actual number of days of abstinence is reported next to it (e.g., 4 days).

Such use acts as a constantly available and conducive source of information, advice, and support, as well as known to foster positive behavior change [20]. Meanwhile, this new social interaction paradigm has begun to provide us with an opportunity to observe individuals' psychological states and social milieu, often in a real-time, longitudinal fashion.

This paper focuses on the health challenge of addiction, specifically addiction to tobacco or alcohol. Alcohol and tobacco are among the top causes of preventable deaths in the United States [25]. In addition to contributing to traumatic death and injury, alcohol is associated with chronic liver disease, cancers, acute alcohol poisoning, and fetal alcohol syndrome. Similarly, smoking is associated with lung disease, cancers, and cardiovascular disease [17]. Achieving long-term abstinence of tobacco or alcohol is difficult [36]—most abstainers are known to relapse within one to three months of cessation. In fact, many individuals who want to quit have been observed to go through short phases of relapse and cessation [14]. While there is a rich body of research on identifying factors associated with such short-term relapse or cessation [35, 37, 28], limited research examines the cues associated with long-term abstinence. This is largely due to the difficulty in compiling high quality self-reported data on abstinence from suitable populations, spanning over long periods of time.

In this paper, we examine how social media language and interactions may be leveraged to *characterize long-term abstinence from tobacco or alcohol*. As of May 2013, 72% of online adults use social networking sites; the number is more than 80% for individuals under the age of 50.[1] Based on reports from the Centers for Disease Control and Prevention (CDC), this demographic aligns well with the age group in which heavy smoking and/or drinking are prevalent [34]. This suggests that social media may be a viable platform for mining cues associated with abstinence.

To this end, we focus on two prominent smoking and drinking abstinence communities on the social media site Reddit: StopSmoking[2] and StopDrinking[3]. These two communities together consist of more than 65,000 subscribed Reddit users as of April 2015, and as described on their public pages, serve as "a place for Reddit users to motivate each other to control or stop smoking/drinking". A participating user may request to have a "badge" (see Figure 1) that indicates self-reported information about the duration of their smoking/alcohol abstinence. The badges are dynamically updated in the system on a daily basis, unless the users request a change to their badges. The main contributions of this paper include:

- We collect and study a novel dataset from Reddit that describes 1,153 users' self-reported information on their duration of smoking or drinking abstinence via the badges. We use the badge information to identify short-term and long-term abstainers.

- We formulate and identify the key linguistic and interaction characteristics of short-term and long-term abstainers based on activity spanning eight years, from 2006 to 2014.

- We build a supervised learning framework based on the characteristics above to distinguish long-term abstinence from short-term abstinence with over 85% accuracy, 88% precision, and 82% recall.

- Our findings present a number of significant discoveries that may help researchers better understand the role of social media language and interactions in assessing and determining tobacco or alcohol use. We find that:

  - the nature of affect manifested in Reddit posts and comments as well as the tenure of participation in Reddit communities are indicative of short-term or long-term abstinence;

  - the network properties of the users (e.g., indegree) based on their interaction patterns also bear significant explanatory power towards characterizing these addiction-related health outcomes.

We note here that our goal in this work is not to predict future success or failure in abstaining from tobacco or alcohol use. That is, we do not attempt to predict which individual will transition from being a short-term abstainer to long-term abstainer or will relapse while being a short-term or long-term abstainer. Rather, we study a set of successful abstainers and attempt to characterize the attributes of long-term smoking or drinking abstinence from social media. Through such characterization, we evoke the potential use of social media towards addressing public health challenges, in particular addiction to tobacco or alcohol.

2. BACKGROUND AND PRIOR WORK

2.1 Behavioral Science and Addiction

Clinical research on addiction shows that decreased psychosocial stress is associated with transitions from smoking to abstinence [30]. Smokers who fail to quit or relapse after a short period

[1] http://www.pewinternet.org/data-trend/social-media/social-media-use-all-users/
[2] http://www.reddit.com/r/StopSmoking
[3] http://www.reddit.com/r/StopDrinking

report high levels of stress prior to initial abstinence or at one, three, and six months after cessation [36]. Additionally, recent work analyzing the size and structure of individuals' social networks has found that their connections and interactions therein are related to health-related behaviors and goals [5]. Availability of a strong, trusting network of friends can provide practical and emotional support, which can reduce their smoking or drinking urges [22, 6].

The findings of this extensive body of research provide evidence on the relationship between behavior and addiction. However, they rely heavily on small, often homogeneous samples of individuals, not necessarily representative of the larger population. Furthermore, these studies are typically based on surveys, relying on retrospective self-reports about mood and observations regarding addiction episodes. This method limits temporal granularity as it involves recollection of historical facts. Some of these limitations are circumvented through the use of wearable sensors and other electronic equipment that capture behavioral and affective data in real time without explicit intervention [35]. However, these methods are often expensive and intrusive because they need participants to use the equipment over a period of time.

As such, most behavioral science research on substance abuse has focused on relapse [31, 24, 37]. In fact, few population-based cohort studies have examined long-term abstinence (a year or more) among former smokers or alcoholics. It is important to quantify the relationship between the duration of abstinence and the likelihood of continued abstinence for the evaluation of ongoing public health interventions and the design of smoking or drinking cessation programs. Additionally, understanding factors associated with long-term abstinence is critical due to the high rate of relapse—most individuals attempting to quit tobacco or alcohol abuse go through multiple short-term phases of abstinence and relapse [13].

Our research specifically tries to address this problem. We develop computational approaches that can characterize the attributes of long-term smoking or drinking abstinence from social media. We derive a promising non-intrusive way to examine psychosocial attributes associated with long-term health outcomes by analyzing longitudinal and fine-grained activity in online communities.

2.2 Social Media, Health, and Addiction

Social media research has indicated that individuals' psychological states and social support status relating to health and well-being may be gleaned via analysis of language and conversational patterns. These include utilizing social media, largely Twitter, to understand conditions and symptoms related to diseases [33], cyberbullying and teenage distress [10], postpartum depression [8], mental health [9, 32, 19, 7], obesity and public health [1], exercise and mental health [11]. Broadly, this body of work investigated the role of linguistic attributes in describing or predicting health challenges.

We extend this body of research by examining the role of both language and social interactions gleaned from social media. Specifically, we build statistical language models that go beyond dictionary approaches. Additionally, we explore how network measures (e.g., indegree, neighborhood density, centrality, etc.) derived out of social interactions may bear explanatory power in the context of tobacco or alcohol addiction. Furthermore, we focus on Reddit, which remains underexplored in comparison to other social media platforms like Twitter.

There has been some research examining addiction behavior manifested on social media, however this body of work is limited. Relationship between displayed alcohol use on Facebook and self-reported information on alcohol abuse was examined in [26, 3, 27]. The authors in [4] explored sentiment manifested by individuals in Twitter by following a pro-marijuana profile. The structure of social circles of prescription drug abusers was investigated in [16]. Using Twitter, the authors in [29] examined perceptions of tobacco products. Another work conducted a study examining characteristics of individuals who express a desire to quit smoking on Twitter [28]. More recently, researchers have studied the prescription drug abuse recovery community Forum77 [23]. In a method similar to [28], they identified dictionary-based linguistic attributes of individuals in various phases of recovery, and were able to characterize recovery trajectory of these individuals.

With the exception of [27] and [23], none of the above pieces of research focuses on predicting health challenges related to addiction. Furthermore, it is important to note that, the ground truth labels on recovery in [28] and [23] were obtained via crowdsourcing. Simply looking at social media posts may not always allow third-party judges to reliably capture abstinence status. Additionally, reasons such as idiosyncratic or personal usage patterns of social media as well as differential social norms and stigma may motivate or preclude some individuals from explicitly reporting abstinence information in social media content. Hence, self-reported abstinence information is extremely valuable. In this paper, we leverage self-reported abstinence information on smoking and drinking.

3. DATA

We begin with a short overview of Reddit. Reddit is a highly popular social media platform, where the users are often referred to as "redditors". They can submit content in the form of link posts or text posts. Posts are organized by areas of interest or subcommunities called "subreddits". For instance, some popular subreddits are r/Politics, r/programming, and r/science.[4] Redditors can engage on a post via "upvotes" or "downvotes"; the post's *score* is the difference between these two quantities. They can also post comments on a post and respond in a comment thread. Over time, redditors accrue reputation in two forms: *link karma* and *comment karma*. Link karma is proportional to the difference between the upvotes and downvotes in all the link posts users made. Comment karma refers to the same difference for all their comments. In 2014, Reddit had 71 billion page views, over 8,000 active communities, 55 million posts, and 535 million comments.[5]

In this paper, we focus on the following two self-improvement subreddits: StopSmoking and StopDrinking. We refer to them as SS and SD, respectively. Both subreddits host *public* content that can be viewed without a Reddit account. At the time of the writing of this paper, SS had 33,690 subscribed users, while SD had 25,542 subscribed users.

As we described before, both subreddits allow users to acquire "badges" to help track their abstinence progress (see Figure 1). Such badges are subreddit-specific, and are displayed next to the username whenever the user posts or comments on the subreddit (ref. Figure 1). Both SS and SD identify different stages of abstinence inside the badge icon (e.g., smiley face for "under one week"), although the actual number of days of abstinence is reported next to it as well.

Typically, a user makes a badge request to the moderators of the subreddit they are interested in, through the subreddit's interface or by privately messaging the moderators. Badges are then awarded by the subreddit moderators either manually (SD) or automatically through an application known as "badgebot" (SS). Both subreddits are heavily moderated and follow a set of guidelines. For instance,

---

[4]Subreddits are typically referred to with the prefix "r/". We omit the prefix when no ambiguity arises.
[5]http://www.redditblog.com/2014/12/reddit-in-2014.html

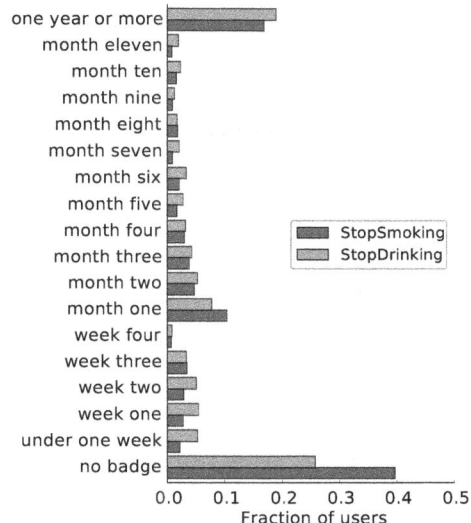

Figure 2: Distributions of the users in StopSmoking (SS) and StopDrinking (SD) across the various smoking and drinking abstinence stages, displayed in the subreddit-specific badges.

SD cautions against providing medical advice on the forum, conducting surveys, or advertising links to recovery centers.

3.1 Data Collection

We used Reddit's official API[6] to collect posts, comments, and associated metadata from the subreddits. Our data collection proceeded in three phases.

Phase 1. We collected a sample of users in SS and SD. The Reddit API limits crawling historical posts on a subreddit to the past 1,000 posts, so we obtained the most recent 1,000 posts from each of the two subreddits. The crawl took place in November 2014. For each post, we collected the title of the post, body or textual content, ID, timestamp, author ID, author's comment and link karmas, and score of the post. We collected the same information for each comment on the post as well. We then used the API to obtain the badge value of the post author and each of the comment authors, if available.

Phase 2. We extracted the list of unique authors of the posts and comments who had a badge. This gave us 1,859 users for SS and 1,383 for SD (ref. Table 1). The distributions of the SS and SD users across the various abstinence stages displayed in the badges are shown in Figure 2. The badge values of these users were eventually used to construct ground truth data on smoking and drinking abstinence, which we will discuss below. We purposefully excluded the users for whom the API did not return any badge value. No badge information meant that we did not know about their smoking or drinking abstinence status at the time of the crawl.

Phase 3. For users with badges, we collected their posts, comments, and associated metadata, this time across Reddit. Note that these posts and comments could have been shared on any subreddit, outside of SS/SD. Like before, for every user, the Reddit API limits crawling to the most recent 1,000 posts or comments shared by the user. Using this method, we obtained 86,835 posts and 766,574 comments for the 1,859 SS users, and 59,201 posts and 492,573 comments for the 1,383 SD users.

---

[6]http://www.reddit.com/dev/api

	StopSmoking (SS)		StopDrinking (SD)	
	All data	Ground truth data	All data	Ground truth data
Users	1,859	635	1,383	533
Total posts from users	86,835	36,713	59,201	30,178
Total comments from users	766,574	306,560	492,573	229,656
Date of earliest post	Dec. 09, 2006	Dec. 09, 2006	Feb. 18, 2006	Feb. 18, 2006
Date of earliest comment	Aug. 29, 2006	Aug. 29, 2006	Aug. 02, 2007	Aug. 02, 2007
Date of latest post	Nov. 23, 2014	Nov. 23, 2014	Nov. 23, 2014	Nov. 23, 2014
Date of latest comment	Nov. 23, 2014	Nov. 23, 2014	Nov. 23, 2014	Nov. 23, 2014
Mean / Median comment karma	4,390.2 / 846	5,065.4 / 1,391	3,808.6 / 406	4,610.2 / 745
Mean / Median link karma	1,312.7 / 88	1,626.2 / 201	1,184.7 / 7	1,794.9 / 38
Mean / Median comments per post	6.8 / 5	7.1 / 5	12.6 / 9	13.2 / 9
Mean / Median post score	37.5 / 4	36.9 / 4	34.3 / 5	34.1 / 5
Mean / Median comment score	5.5 / 1	5.5 / 2	5.2 / 2	5.0 / 2
Mean / Median post length in words	55.2 / 15	55.3 / 14	67.5 / 17	62.7 / 15
Mean / Median comment length in words	31.9 / 16	32.6 / 17	36.7 / 18	39.2 / 19

Table 1: Summary statistics of the crawled dataset.

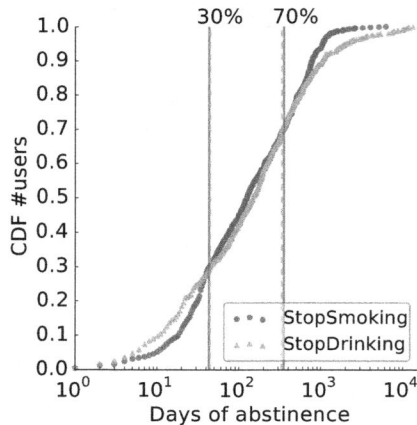

Figure 3: Cumulative distribution functions (CDFs) of the number of users over the abstinence duration (in days) in StopSmoking (SS) and StopDrinking (SD).

We report the summary statistics of the crawled data in the "All data" columns for SS and SD in Table 1. Also important to note here that, per our crawl, each user in the dataset had a recent post or comment in SS/SD, therefore our dataset is likely to be free of any users who stopped being active in SS/SD and do not pay attention to their badges therein.

3.2 Ground Truth Creation

We constructed ground truth information on smoking and alcoholism abstinence from the crawled badges of the users. Since the badge information is self-reported, we consider it as a reliable, high-quality signal of a user's abstinence status. While characterizing the different abstinence statuses would be insightful, the skewness in the number of users among the different abstinence stages and the sparsity of users per stage (see Figure 2) debarred us from pursuing this direction. Instead, we examined whether we could utilize Reddit activity and interaction of users towards a binary classification task—determining whether a user is likely to belong to the short-term abstinence category or to the long-term abstinence category, given his or her historical data.

To identify the suitable durations to qualify for short-term or long-term abstinence, we leverage the cumulative distribution functions (CDFs) of abstinence duration obtained from the badges in SS and SD (Figure 3). The CDFs show stable patterns before the 30 percentile and after the 70 percentile. The 30 percentile mark for SS is 43 days while it is 44 days for SD; the 70 percentile mark is

Explanatory variables
Language variables:
counts for the 300 uni/bi/trigrams
mean, median PA, NA SS/SD
Addiction variables:
addiction words count
mean, median PA, NA OSR
Interaction variables:
#posts, #comments SS/SD
#posts, #comments OSR
mean, median Δ between contents SS/SD
mean, median Δ between contents OSR
mean, median content scores SS/SD
mean, median content scores OSR
mean, median content lengths SS/SD
mean, median content lengths OSR
link, comment karma
tenure, recency SS/SD
tenure, recency OSR
#contents in each of the 15 related subreddits
indegree, outdegree, degree
reciprocity, #triangles, clustering coefficient
betweenness, closeness, eigenvector centralities
SCC size, WCC size

Table 2: List of the explanatory variables used in the statistical models for StopSmoking (SS) and StopDrinking (SD).

350 days and 333 days for SS and SD, respectively. Prior research in addiction [36] indicates frequent relapse to happen at 1-2 months after quitting, which aligns with our 30 percentile mark. Furthermore, individuals who successfully abstain from smoking/alcohol for a year or more have been found to be less likely to relapse in the future [37]. Therefore, we consider the users within the 30 percentile mark to be the short-time abstainers and those beyond the 70 percentile mark to be the long-term abstainers.

This categorization gave us 635 users in SS (318 users/50.07% long-term abstainers) and 533 users in SD (268 users/50.28% long-term abstainers). In the rest of this paper, we use this user set for the task of characterizing long-term abstinence from tobacco or alcohol. Summary statistics on these users can be found in the "Ground truth data" columns for SS and SD in Table 1.

4. STATISTICAL METHOD

We now present the statistical method we employ to characterize long-term abstinence from tobacco or alcohol. For this goal, we introduce the variables outlined below and summarized in Table 2.

Response variable. Our binary response variable represents if a user is a *short-term* or a *long-term* abstainer of smoking/drinking.

Explanatory variables (Language). Our first set of explanatory variables focuses on extracting linguistic attributes from a user's posts and comments in SS/SD. Here, we converted the textual content of all the posts and comments in SS/SD to lowercase and extracted the top-100 most frequent unigrams, bigrams, and trigrams (three sets of 100 items each) following the conventional bag-of-words model.[7] These 300 n-grams do not include any phrase that is solely comprised of stopwords. We introduce a count variable for each n-gram, representing the total number of times that the corresponding n-gram appears in the user's posts or comments.

As another dimension of language, we also consider the sentiment of the posts and comments with VADER [21]. VADER is a lexicon and rule-based sentiment analysis tool that is tailored to specifically detect sentiment expressed in social media. Using VADER, we introduce four variables that correspond to the mean and median of the positive sentiment (PA) and negative sentiment (NA) scores of a user's posts and comments in SS/SD. Together, this set of explanatory variables contains 304 variables and we refer to them as the *language variables*.

Explanatory variables (Addiction). Our second set of explanatory variables focuses on the content (posts or comments) shared by a user in subreddits other than SS/SD (we henceforth refer to this set of subreddits as OSR).[8] To examine if smoking or drinking related content in OSR could potentially help characterize long-term abstinence, we complied two addiction-related lexicons for smoking and drinking based on words in Urban Dictionary[9]. Urban Dictionary is a suitable choice due to the informal nature of online language. Specifically, we utilized a snowball approach in which we seeded the dictionary searches with "smok*" and "alcohol*". We followed the "related words" returned by the dictionary results on these two seed words. We recursively adopted this approach over three more iterations. The final two lexicons are shown in Table 3. Since a user is unlikely to use every word in the lexicon, we consider a single count variable that represents the total number of times that any of the words in the lexicon appears in the user's posts or comments. We also introduce four variables that correspond to the mean and median of the PA and NA scores of the users' posts and comments in OSR—we again use VADER for this purpose. This set of explanatory variables contains 5 variables and we refer to them as the *addiction variables*.

Explanatory variables (Interaction). Our third set of explanatory variables focuses on the various aspects of interaction.

(1) *Activity measures.* We introduce variables for the number of posts and comments in SS/SD and OSR, the mean and median differences in hours (Δ) between consecutive contents in SS/SD and OSR, the mean and median content scores in SS/SD and OSR, the mean and median content lengths (in characters) in SS/SD and OSR, and the user's link and comment karmas. Also, we include variables that represent the number of days since the earliest and latest contents (tenure and recency, respectively) in SS/SD and OSR.

(2) *Participation in related subreddits.* Since abstainers might seek support from or contribute to other subreddits as well, we also extracted the list of the 100 most widely used subreddits, other than

SS and SD themselves, based on the posts and comments of the users. Two researchers familiar with Reddit thereafter individually scanned the list to rate their relevance to our task. Researchers referred to prior addiction literature during this task to identify behavioral attributes associated with smoking/alcohol addiction [6]. Subreddits with the following characteristics were deemed relevant—emotional discourse subreddits (e.g., r/depression), religious discourse subreddits (e.g, r/Buddhism and r/atheist), fitness subreddits (e.g., r/Fitness), and subreddits on other types of addiction and recovery (e.g., r/cripplingalcoholism). Abstainers are known to engage to greater emotional expression, including personal and subjective topics like religion [30]. Fitness and exercise are also known to be a helpful characteristic of abstinence [6].

The final set of related subreddits considered here are shown in Table 4. For each of these subreddits, we introduce a count variable that represents the total number of posts and comments that the user made in the corresponding subreddit.

(3) *Graph measures.* To further quantify the interaction between the users in SS/SD, we construct a network based on the users' posting and commenting patterns in SS/SD. Specifically, if user A comments on user B's post or comment, we establish a directed edge with a weight of 1 from user A to user B in the network. The total weight of an edge denotes the number of "directed" interactions between the corresponding users. We introduce several graph-centric variables, representing a user's local and global relations with other users in SS/SD: the indegree, outdegree, and degree; reciprocity, the number of triangles to which the user participates (#triangles), and clustering coefficient; the betweenness, closeness and eigenvector centralities; and the number of users in the strongly (SCC) and weakly connected components (WCC) to which the user belongs. Note that for #triangles, clustering coefficient and the centrality measures, we consider an undirected network in which an edge exists only if it appears in both directions in the original network. We refer the reader to [2] for the details of these measures. This set of explanatory variables contains 48 variables and we refer to them as the *interaction variables*.

Statistical models. We employ Ridge regression [18] to classify our binary response variable (short-term or long-term smoking/drinking abstinence). Most of our explanatory variables correspond to English phrases, which posit the collinearity (i.e., excessive correlation between phrases) and sparsity (i.e., some phrases occurring infrequently) properties. Ridge regression guards against problems related to collinearity and sparsity by shifting the weights of the correlated and sparse variables to the more explanatory ones. We use 10-fold cross-validation to determine the best tuning constant that controls the strength of the ridge penalty and also to prevent overfitting to the dataset.

To understand the explanatory powers of our independent variables, we consider three statistical models: (i) the Language model, (ii) the Language + Addiction model, and (iii) the Language + Addiction + Interaction model, which consist of (i) the language, (ii) the language and addiction, and (iii) the language, addiction, and interaction variables, respectively. The first two models are motivated from prior work [28, 23], and through the third, we examine the additional role of interaction in characterizing abstinence. In these models, we represent each user as feature vectors that are standardized to zero mean and unit variance.

5. RESULTS

In this section, we present the results of our two tasks: characterizing long-term abstinence from tobacco and from alcohol.

---

[7] Our statistical models suffered from high dimensionality when we considered more than 300 n-grams.

[8] SD (SS) becomes an OSR when we focus on smoking (drinking).

[9] www.urbandictionary.com

Smoking:	acid, alcohol, baked, blaze, blazed, blunt, blunts, bong, bongs, bowl, bowling, bowls, bud, cannabis, chew, chronic, cig, cigar, cigarette, cigarettes, cocaine, coke, crack, dank, dip, doobie, dope, drug, drugs, drunk, ecstasy, fag, ganja, grass, grizzly, herb, heroin, high, hit, hookah, joint, joints, lsd, marijuana, meth, nicotine, party, piece, pills, pipe, pipes, pot, reefer, ripped, roach, school, sex, shit, skoal, smoke, smokes, smoking, snuff, spliff, stone, stoned, stoner, stones, tobacco, toilet, toke, toking, wasted, weed, fucked up, mary jane
Drinking:	acid, alcohol, alcoholic, alcoholism, awesome, bar, beer, beers, beverage, booze, boozing, brew, cocaine, cocktail, coke, college, crack, crazy, crunk, dance, dope, drink, drinking, drinks, drug, drugs, drunk, ecstasy, friends, fucked, fun, girls, hammered, hangover, heroin, high, intoxicated, liquor, lsd, marijuana, meth, parties, party, partying, pills, pissed, pong, pot, rave, rum, sex, shitfaced, shot, shots, smashed, smoke, sober, stoned, trashed, up, vodka, wasted, weed, whiskey, wine

Table 3: Addiction-related lexicons for smoking and drinking.

Smoking:	StopDrinking, electronic_cigarette, BabyBumps, Fitness, relationships, Christianity, personalfinance, atheism, IAmA, MakeupAddiction, SkincareAddiction, loseit, Frugal, Showerthoughts, Buddhism
Drinking:	REDDITORSINRECOVERY, alcoholism, StopSmoking, relationships, cripplingalcoholism, depression, Christianity, Drugs, CasualConversation, IAmA, atheism, Fitness, MakeupAddiction, electronic_cigarette, DebateReligion

Table 4: Related subreddits—subreddits other than StopSmoking (SS) and StopDrinking(SD) where users post/comment.

5.1 Deviance Results

To evaluate the goodness of fits of our three models, namely Language, Language + Addiction, and Language + Addiction + Interaction, we use *deviance*. Briefly put, deviance is a measure of the lack of fit to data, hence lower values are better. It is calculated by comparing a model with the saturated model—a model with a theoretically perfect fit, which we consider to be the intercept-only model and refer to as *Null*. Table 5 provides a summary of the different model fits. Due to the randomness introduced by cross-validation, we ran our models 10 times and here we report the results corresponding to the lowest deviances that we obtained in any of the runs.

Compared to the Null models, we observe that all three of our models provide considerable explanatory power with significant improvements in deviances in both SS and SD. The difference between the deviance of a Null model and the deviances of the other models approximately follows a χ^2 distribution, with degrees of freedom equal to the number of additional variables in the more comprehensive model. As an example, comparing the deviance of Language with that of Null in SS, we see that the information provided by the language variables has significant explanatory power: $\chi^2(304, N = 635) = 880.3 - 438.9 = 441.4, p < 10^{-6}$. This comparison with the Null model is statistically significant after Bonferroni correction for multiple testing ($\alpha = \frac{0.01}{3}$ since we consider three models). We observe similar deviance results for the Language + Addiction and Language + Addiction + Interaction models in both SS and SD, with the latter models possessing the best fits and highest explanatory powers.

From the fits of the Language + Addiction + Interaction models, Table 6 presents the top-30 positive and top-30 negative β values for the variables corresponding to the n-grams and the top-7 positive and top-7 negative β values for the other variables. The variables with negative and positive β values classify a user as short-term and long-term abstainer, respectively. Note that we standardize the feature vectors before regression, hence the β values correspond to standardized features. We do not report the statistical significance of the β values in the form of p-values because they are hard to interpret for strongly biased estimates such as those arise from Ridge regression [15].

The contribution of the different explanatory variables in the two characterization tasks is notable. In both, phrases are notable variables that distinguish short-term and long-term abstinence. In fact, the variables that have the highest explanatory power for short-term abstinence in SS/SD are the phrases *"i started"* and *"in the past"*, respectively. We conjecture that the short-term abstainers use these

phrases to indicate new intentions: *"i started an attempt on monday..."* and *"it feels great to be sober and have my dark drinking days in the past"*, respectively. Furthermore, the phrases associated with short-term abstinence are related to current sensation, urge, or confession (*"i need to"*, *"i feel"*), and appreciation and acknowledgement of support, perhaps because they are newcomers in the community (*"thanks for the"*, *"thank you"*). E.g., notice the post excerpt below:

i need to find more friends that don't drink so much

In contrast, the phrases associated with long-term abstinence are mostly about encouragement and boosting morale (*"keep it up"*, *"hang in there"*) and advisory (*"worked for me'*, *"was able to"*):

for those of you behind me, keep it up! i believe in you!

Examining some of the non-phrase variables with negative β values, we observe that indegree is a strong indicator of short-term abstinence. This is likely because the short-term abstainers' contents are typically support-seeking in nature, which attract responses from a variety of users in the SS/SD communities. The negative sentiment of contents is also a significant indicator of short-term abstinence. We conjecture that this is likely due to the tendency of the short-term abstainers' disclosures about recent failures, challenges, and struggles related to quitting. Addiction literature also indicates that increased negative affect and stress are associated with early abstainers of smoking/drinking [35]:

i [...] struggle with depression and used alcohol to escape from my often difficult reality

Focusing on some of the non-phrase variables with positive β values, we observe that tenure in SS/SD and OSR are strong indicators of long-term abstinence. Prior work has indicated that long-term social engagement has a positive impact on the psychological states of individuals [8]. Hence, we conjecture that longer tenure on Reddit helps keep individuals intending to abstain from smoking/drinking more motivated and focused towards their respective self-improvement goals. Furthermore, users' comment karma characterizes long-term abstinence in SS, suggesting that social endorsement obtained from the greater Reddit community in the form of upvotes possibly motivated individuals to succeed in their abstinence goals.

We also see that the mean content score in SS and the mean positive sentiment of contents in SD are strong indicators of long-term abstinence from smoking and drinking, respectively, which are likely related to the supportive tone expressed in such content. Addiction literature indicates social support to act as a mediator of stress during smoking/drinking urges [35]. E.g., the following excerpt expresses positive sentiment:

Model	StopSmoking (SS)				StopDrinking (SD)			
	Deviance	df	χ^2	p-value	Deviance	df	χ^2	p-value
Null	880.3	0			738.9	0		
Language	438.9	304	441.4	$< 10^{-6}$	353.5	304	385.4	10^{-3}
Language + Addiction	418.5	309	461.8	$< 10^{-7}$	340.8	309	398.1	$< 10^{-3}$
Language + Addiction + Interaction	326.9	357	553.4	$< 10^{-9}$	273.2	357	465.7	$< 10^{-4}$

Table 5: Summary of different model fits. Null is the intercept-only model. Deviance measures the goodness of fit. All comparisons with the Null models are statistically significant after Bonferroni correction for multiple testing ($\alpha = \frac{0.01}{3}$).

every time when i remember i quit smoking it makes me happy and a little proud

5.2 Classification Results

To evaluate how well our three statistical models distinguish the long-term and short-term abstinence categories, we randomly split the dataset into 90% training and 10% testing partitions. We trained our models only on the training partitions and measured their classification performance on the testing partitions. Due to the randomness introduced by cross-validation, we performed the aforementioned procedure 10 times to obtain accurate performance estimates. Assuming that long-term abstinence is our positive class, Table 7 presents the classification results with respect to the F1 score, accuracy, precision, recall, and specificity metrics. We report for each metric the mean and standard deviation of the 10 values that we obtained from the 10 iterations on the testing sets.

In general, we observe that the best performing model in both SS and SD is Language + Addiction + Interaction, which achieves the mean F1 scores of 0.86 and 0.85 in SS and SD, respectively. Considering the minimum of the values for SS and SD, this model also achieves a mean accuracy of 0.85, a mean precision of 0.88, a mean recall of 0.82, and a mean specificity of 0.88. This model is followed by Language + Addiction and then Language in terms of performance. Not only the mean values of the performance metrics for Language + Addiction + Interaction are higher than those for the other two models, the ranges of the values are also narrower in Language + Addiction + Interaction (lower standard deviations).

The good performance of Language + Addiction + Interaction is also evident from the receiver operator characteristic (ROC) curves in Figure 4. To obtain the ROC curves, we first sorted the probabilities that the users are long-term abstainers as output by the models in ascending order. We then generated 250 threshold points equidistant in the range [0, 1] and applied them on the probabilities of the users in the testing partitions; for each threshold value, all users with probabilities above that value are labeled as long-term abstainers, or short-term abstainers otherwise. This process generated 250 pairs of true positive (TP) rate and false positive (FP) rate values for each testing partition, plotting the average of the 10 TP rate and FP rate values computed using the same threshold value across the 10 experiments on the testing partitions gave us the ROC curves in Figure 4. We observe from the figure that the performance of Language + Addiction + Interaction is superior to the other two models in both SS and SD in the whole spectrum of the average TP rate and FP rate values.

6. DISCUSSION

6.1 Clinical Relevance

Our findings indicate that linguistic and interaction cues gleaned from activity in SS and SD forums may be used to understand short-term or long-term abstinence tendencies among users. Such ability to proactively identify one's abstinence status may be used to create early warning systems or interventions that are integrated in social

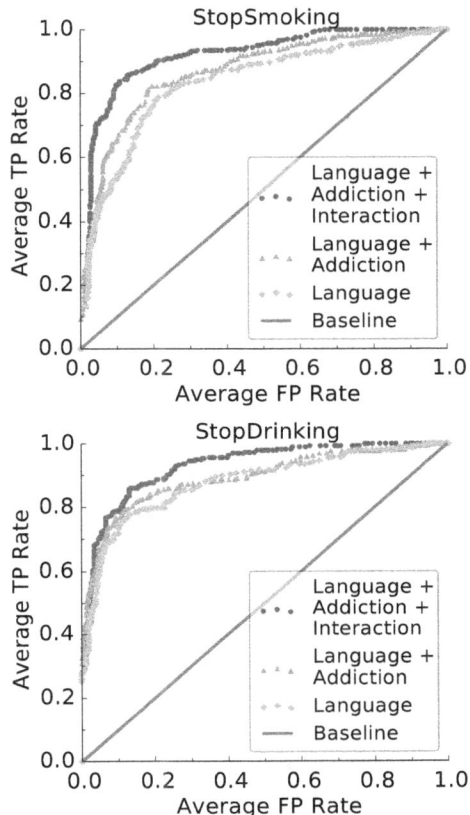

Figure 4: Receiver operating characteristic (ROC) curves corresponding to the three statistical models for StopSmoking (SS) and StopDrinking (SD). Long-term abstinence is the positive class.

platforms. These early warning systems could analyze one's activity on the platform and engage appropriately if the probability of long-term abstinence drops below a certain level. Certainly, such systems could raise ethical and privacy concerns, and must therefore be carefully designed and developed. However, if successful, these systems may be used in clinically meaningful ways that provide great benefits. For instance, an individual may more easily keep track of his or her activities and interactions on a social media platform and share them with a therapist, which may subsequently lead to more effective treatment.

Broadly, tracking the patterns of changes in the explanatory variables we identified could help clinicians, medical professionals, and policy makers better understand people's experiences around long-term abstinence from tobacco or alcohol, and the strategies that may have worked for them. Since, traditionally, it has been challenging to understand and identify factors associated with long-term smoking or drinking abstinence [36], our research can also help identify previously underexplored variables that may contribute towards the success or failure of abstinence.

StopSmoking (SS)				StopDrinking (SD)			
feature	β	feature	β	feature	β	feature	β
indegree	-0.28	tenure SS	0.75	indegree	-0.26	tenure SD	0.83
median content length SS	-0.24	#comments OSR	0.35	closeness centrality	-0.20	#comments OSR	0.25
degree	-0.23	tenure OSR	0.24	median NA SD	-0.16	r/REDDITORSIN RECOVERY	0.24
r/Buddhism	-0.18	mean content score SS	0.20	mean NA OSR	-0.16	mean PA SD	0.18
recency SS	-0.17	comment karma	0.18	r/Fitness	-0.15	tenure OSR	0.16
median NA SS	-0.16	addiction words count	0.18	link karma	-0.15	#posts OSR	0.14
outdegree	-0.16	r/electronic_cigarette	0.14	SCC size	-0.15	r/relationships	0.13
feature (n-gram)	β	feature (n-gram)	β	feature (n-gram)	β	feature (n-gram)	β
i started	-0.31	year	0.32	in the past	-0.33	year	0.33
i need to	-0.26	keep it up	0.27	i'm going to	-0.31	i got sober	0.27
this time	-0.23	think about it	0.21	week	-0.24	months	0.25
i'm going to	-0.23	pack a day	0.20	i know i	-0.18	i quit drinking	0.23
i want to	-0.22	i still	0.19	i need to	-0.17	i don't drink	0.23
as much as	-0.19	keep it	0.18	day	-0.17	a drink	0.19
trying to quit	-0.19	never	0.18	i need	-0.17	meetings	0.19
thanks for the	-0.19	since i quit	0.18	i feel	-0.16	find	0.19
if you don't	-0.18	if you want	0.18	i don't know	-0.14	was able to	0.17
in the morning	-0.18	a year	0.17	to quit	-0.14	years	0.16
feel like	-0.17	worked for me	0.16	and i don't	-0.14	as much as	0.16
i don't want	-0.16	you want	0.16	last	-0.13	keep up the	0.15
started	-0.16	going to be	0.16	want to be	-0.13	stay	0.14
the last	-0.13	i would	0.15	the first time	-0.12	stay sober	0.14
try to	-0.13	i smoked	0.15	have a problem	-0.12	in the first	0.13
feeling	-0.13	hang in there	0.15	so much	-0.12	sobriety	0.13
last	-0.13	a non smoker	0.14	back to	-0.12	at a time	0.13
i want	-0.13	you'll	0.14	don't know	-0.11	still	0.13
thanks for	-0.13	get a	0.14	i'm	-0.11	part of	0.13
you don't have	-0.13	you're	0.14	i can't	-0.11	one day at	0.13
i've	-0.13	so much	0.13	i think i	-0.11	people	0.12
right now	-0.12	keep	0.12	i'm not	-0.11	a time	0.12
2	-0.12	you don't need	0.12	i know that	-0.11	i was drinking	0.12
in the past	-0.12	helped me	0.12	i don't want	-0.11	congrats on	0.12
in my life	-0.11	you quit	0.12	not drinking	-0.11	i really	0.12
to quit smoking	-0.11	it gets	0.12	drinking i	-0.10	i got	0.12
i quit smoking	-0.11	like a	0.12	i've been	-0.09	aa	0.12
able to	-0.11	years	0.12	thank you	-0.09	life	0.12
i got	-0.11	you want to	0.12	i feel like	-0.09	if you don't	0.12
as well	-0.10	a pack a	0.12	i want to	-0.09	you don't want	0.11

Table 6: β values corresponding to the 74 features with the highest explanatory power for StopSmoking (SS) and StopDrinking (SD). "OSR" stands for subreddits other than SS/SD. The prefix "r/" indicates a related subreddit. "aa" stands for Alcoholics Anonymous.

Finally, and importantly, through our statistical models that identify short-term and long-term abstainers, we can begin to determine the abstinence status of those individuals for whom badge or other self-reported information on abstinence is not available. This can be particularly valuable in bringing in-time help and support to individuals who intend to quit smoking or drinking and use a social media platform, however have not adopted the practices of accruing badges, imbibed in the two online communities we study.

6.2 Implications for Social Media Research

Design Considerations. We believe our findings have strong design-related implications for social media research. Below, we describe several design ideas inspired by our research, which may help tailor social media platforms to cater to individuals aiming to abstain from smoking or drinking. Literature indicates that individuals desirous of quitting smoking or drinking often go through repetitive phases of cessation and relapse [14]. Hence, new users joining these abstinence communities, or those who have been short-term abstainers may benefit from content on the forum that discusses the challenges and struggles in this early phase. Mechanisms could be created to engage in a conversation with other long-term members on what to expect during this phase, how to combat desires of smoking or drinking urges, or for general positive reinforcement of their abstinence goal.

Post excerpts containing phrases and other linguistic constructs associated with long-term abstinence may also be promoted to users intending to quit smoking or drinking. They may also be directed to connect with other users in the community who have had success in tobacco or alcohol abstinence over a period of time—social support and higher levels of social capital have been known to help individuals fight addiction urges [13]. Moderators of these recovery communities may also direct requests for advice or help to appropriate users in the community who are actively engaged and have had experiences of long-term abstinence. Since we also found that posting activity or commentary in certain other subreddits were associated with long-term abstinence, users may also be recommended to participate in those other communities or forums where they might additionally obtain support for beating addiction urges or gather general positive reinforcement of their desire to abstain from smoking or drinking.

In addition, our work showed that network features derived out of the social interaction offered considerable explanatory power. That is, the presence of a strong support network on the forum is likely to play an important role in encouraging long-term abstinence. As a design idea, newcomers' posts could be promoted to

Measure	Language		Language + Addiction		Language + Addiction + Interaction	
	StopSmoking	StopDrinking	StopSmoking	StopDrinking	StopSmoking	StopDrinking
F1 score	0.70 ± 0.06	0.78 ± 0.04	0.78 ± 0.05	0.80 ± 0.05	0.86 ± 0.03	0.85 ± 0.05
Accuracy	0.74 ± 0.05	0.81 ± 0.04	0.80 ± 0.04	0.81 ± 0.04	0.86 ± 0.03	0.85 ± 0.05
Precision	0.81 ± 0.06	0.91 ± 0.07	0.83 ± 0.05	0.91 ± 0.06	0.90 ± 0.04	0.88 ± 0.06
Recall	0.62 ± 0.09	0.69 ± 0.06	0.74 ± 0.06	0.71 ± 0.07	0.82 ± 0.04	0.83 ± 0.06
Specificity	0.86 ± 0.04	0.93 ± 0.04	0.86 ± 0.05	0.93 ± 0.05	0.91 ± 0.04	0.88 ± 0.05

Table 7: Performance metrics corresponding to the three statistical models for StopSmoking (SS) and StopDrinking (SD).

prominent positions in the forums' timelines to attract more attention, increasing their likelihood of receiving responses. In turn, this would broaden engagement of the whole community, decrease user churn, and thereby increase member retention. This could lead to a self-reinforcing positive cycle that attracts and helps increasingly more people.

Furthermore, in these Reddit communities, reputation is associated with "badges" that indicate the duration of abstinence of a user from smoking/drinking. In a way, making such badge information accessible to visitors and users of the forum not only is likely to boost self-esteem because of improved reputation in the community, but also in general, is likely to induce positive feelings towards abstinence, and encourage and inspire others to do so as well.

Uniqueness of Reddit. We also discuss the effectiveness of addiction recovery communities like SS or SD in general. Although many online communities exist to help individuals in addiction recovery, SS and SD are unique because they encourage long-term abstinence. This is indicated by the fact that almost 50% of the users in our dataset were abstainers for three or more months. We thus believe that participation in these Reddit forums are likely to help individuals adopt a positive attitude and approach towards addiction recovery. Moreover, the ability to be anonymous or pseudonymous can be an additional facilitating element of abstinence—Reddit accounts do not need any personally identifiable information. Users can thus engage in candid and honest discourse, without worrying about the social stigma that often comes with being a victim of addiction. In fact, a considerable fraction (10%) of users in our dataset explicitly only posted on these two subreddits, perhaps indicating that either they are on Reddit simply to participate in these abstinence forums, or have alternate account(s) on Reddit for non-addiction recovery related discourse. Also, even though some of the explanatory variables that we consider in our statistical models are Reddit-specific, our statistical models can be generalized to other social media platforms, especially to those that possess similar attributes implicitly or explicitly (e.g., link karma on Reddit vs. number of retweets on Twitter as a manifestation of a user's reputation on the online platform).

6.3 Limitations and Future Directions

Our work is of course not free from limitations. We acknowledge that generalizations of our work might not be easily applied across large populations or on arbitrary addiction contexts. As we pointed out, SS and SD are specialized self-improvement communities; most likely, individuals who choose to join them are already motivated to quit addiction. Moreover, since these are largely communities of abstainers, it is possible that individuals new to quitting may feel uncomfortable joining the communities or can feel uncomfortable to be participating. Further biases inherent to Reddit exist as well—the average redditor is a 20-something male[10], perhaps more "tech-savvy", and therefore more likely to resort to online platforms to obtain abstinence support compared to the gen-

eral population. Additionally, since we did not have information on whether the long-term abstainers sought support through offline means, we are limited in the way we evaluate the effectiveness of the particular forums for addiction recovery. We also note that we focused on smoking and drinking addiction recovery, obviously extending our findings to other kinds of addiction (e.g., prescription or recreational drugs) would need additional investigation.

As we also pointed out earlier, an important point to note about this work is that we do not *predict* abstinence of individuals in SS/SD. That is, based on our findings, we are not able to make (causal) claims as to whether someone will continue to abstain smoking or drinking in the future, or will relapse. This requires tracking an individual's activity and their abstinence reports, i.e., the badge values, over time, which construes an important future research direction we intend to pursue. In fact, in prior literature on clinical studies of addiction behavior, use of survival analysis methods have been found to be particularly helpful in forecasting the likelihood of experiencing a relapse. We intend to leverage these statistical approaches in the future to predict smoking or drinking relapse based on social media activities.

We also note that a known concern with many recovery communities is member retention—failure to recover often demotivates individuals and leads them to leave the platform. While it is challenging to measure the overall retention rate for SS and SD based on our data, the focus on both self-reported abstinence information through badges and the users who had a recent post or comment in SS/SD ensures that we consider a population of individuals who are attempting to abstain from smoking/drinking and continuing to use Reddit. Also, as mentioned earlier, in our ground truth dataset, we had nearly 50% users who are short-term abstainers. However, per our current data, we cannot be sure of the nature of such short-term abstinence—i.e., whether individuals were attempting to quit smoking/drinking for the first time, or it followed a recent relapse experience. This is because Reddit's API allows our program to access only the *current* badge of a user. Hence, we were not able to determine the nature of short-term abstinence of users in our dataset. For instance, we do not know if they had relapsed shortly before, or if they are attempting to quit for the first time. Finally, as Reddit also imposes that only the most recent thousand posts and comments of every user may be retrieved, we were limited in how far back we could go to examine redditors' historical activity.

7. CONCLUSION

We presented a computational framework to understand smoking and drinking abstinence of individuals from social media. We compiled and studied a previously unexplored source of data—activity on the Reddit communities StopSmoking and StopDrinking. We leveraged the badge feature in these forums to construct self-reported ground truth information on the abstinence status of users to characterize long-term abstinence. Our statistical models incorporated a variety of language and interaction attributes to distinguish long-term abstinence from smoking or drinking from short-term abstinence with 85% accuracy. We found that linguis-

---

[10]http://www.pewinternet.org/files/old-media/Files/Reports/2013/PIP_reddit_usage_2013.pdf

tic cues like affect, activity cues like tenure, and network features like indegree to be indicative of short-term or long-term abstinence. Through our findings, we provided insights into how social media may be leveraged to tackle addiction-related health challenges.

8. REFERENCES

[1] S. Abbar, Y. Mejova, and I. Weber. You tweet what you eat: Studying food consumption through twitter. In *Proc. CHI*, 2015.

[2] C. C. Aggarwal. *Social Network Data Analytics*. Springer, 1st edition, 2011.

[3] K. Beullens and A. Schepers. Display of alcohol use on facebook: a content analysis. *Cyberpsychology, Behavior, and Social Networking*, 16(7):497–503, 2013.

[4] P. Cavazos-Rehg, M. Krauss, R. Grucza, and L. Bierut. Characterizing the followers and tweets of a marijuana-focused twitter handle. *Journal of Medical Internet Research*, 16(6):e157, 2014.

[5] N. A. Christakis and J. H. Fowler. The collective dynamics of smoking in a large social network. *New England Journal of Medicine*, 358(21):2249–2258, 2008.

[6] S. H. Cook, J. A. Bauermeister, D. Gordon-Messer, and M. A. Zimmerman. Online network influences on emerging adults' alcohol and drug use. *Journal of Youth and Adolescence*, 42(11):1674–1686, 2013.

[7] G. Coppersmith, C. Harman, and M. Dredze. Measuring post traumatic stress disorder in twitter. In *Proc. ICWSM*, 2014.

[8] M. De Choudhury, S. Counts, E. Horvitz, and A. Hoff. Characterizing and predicting postpartum depression from facebook data. In *Proc. CSCW*, 2014.

[9] M. De Choudhury, M. Gamon, S. Counts, and E. Horvitz. Predicting depression via social media. In *Proc. ICWSM*, 2013.

[10] K. Dinakar, B. Jones, H. Lieberman, R. W. Picard, C. P. Rosé, M. Thoman, and R. Reichart. You too?! mixed initiative lda story-matching to help teens in distress. In *Proc. ICWSM*, 2012.

[11] V. L. Dos Reis and A. Culotta. Using matched samples to estimate the effects of exercise on mental health from twitter. In *Proc. AAAI*, 2015.

[12] S. Fox and S. Jones. The social life of health information. *Pew Internet & American Life Project*, 2009.

[13] S. Galea, A. Nandi, and D. Vlahov. The social epidemiology of substance use. *Epidemiologic Reviews*, 26(1):36–52, 2004.

[14] E. A. Gilpin, J. P. Pierce, and A. J. Farkas. Duration of smoking abstinence and success in quitting. *Journal of the National Cancer Institute*, 89(8):572–576, 1997.

[15] J. J. Goeman. L1 penalized estimation in the cox proportional hazards model. *Biometrical Journal*, 52(1):70–84, 2010.

[16] C. L. Hanson, B. Cannon, S. Burton, and C. Giraud-Carrier. An exploration of social circles and prescription drug abuse through twitter. *Journal of Medical Internet Research*, 15(9):e189, 2013.

[17] H. J. Harwood. Updating estimates of the economic costs of alcohol abuse in the United States: Estimates, update methods, and data. *NIH Publication No. 98-4327*, 2000.

[18] A. E. Hoerl and R. W. Kennard. Ridge regression: Biased estimation for nonorthogonal problems. *Technometrics*, 12(1):55–67, 1970.

[19] C. M. Homan, N. Lu, X. Tu, M. C. Lytle, and V. Silenzio. Social structure and depression in trevorspace. In *Proc. CSCW*, 2014.

[20] J. Huh and M. S. Ackerman. Collaborative help in chronic disease management: Supporting individualized problems. In *Proc. CSCW*, 2012.

[21] C. J. Hutto and E. Gilbert. Vader: A parsimonious rule-based model for sentiment analysis of social media text. In *Proc. ICWSM*, 2014.

[22] L. A. Kaskutas, J. Bond, and K. Humphreys. Social networks as mediators of the effect of alcoholics anonymous. *Addiction*, 97(7):891–900, 2002.

[23] D. MacLean, S. Gupta, A. Lembke, C. Manning, and J. Heer. Forum77: An analysis of an online health forum dedicated to addiction recovery. In *Proc. CSCW*, 2015.

[24] G. Marlatt and D. Donovan. *Relapse prevention: Maintenance strategies in treatment of addictive behaviors*. Guilford Publications, 2nd edition, 2005.

[25] A. H. Mokdad, J. S. Marks, D. F. Stroup, and J. L. Gerberding. Actual causes of death in the United States, 2000. *Journal of the American Medical Association*, 291(10):1238–1245, 2004.

[26] M. A. Moreno, D. A. Christakis, K. G. Egan, L. N. Brockman, and T. Becker. Associations between displayed alcohol references on facebook and problem drinking among college students. *Archives of Pediatrics & Adolescent Medicine*, 166(2):157–163, 2012.

[27] M. A. Moreno, J. D'Angelo, L. E. Kacvinsky, B. Kerr, C. Zhang, and J. Eickhoff. Emergence and predictors of alcohol reference displays on facebook during the first year of college. *Computers in Human Behavior*, 30:87–94, 2014.

[28] E. L. Murnane and S. Counts. Unraveling abstinence and relapse: Smoking cessation reflected in social media. In *Proc. CHI*, 2014.

[29] M. Myslín, S.-H. Zhu, W. Chapman, and M. Conway. Using twitter to examine smoking behavior and perceptions of emerging tobacco products. *Journal of Medical Internet Research*, 15(8):e174, 2013.

[30] R. S. Niaura, D. J. Rohsenow, J. A. Binkoff, P. M. Monti, M. Pedraza, and D. B. Abrams. Relevance of cue reactivity to understanding alcohol and smoking relapse. *Journal of Abnormal Psychology*, 97(2):133–152, 1988.

[31] M. E. Pagano, K. B. Friend, J. S. Tonigan, and R. L. Stout. Helping other alcoholics in alcoholics anonymous and drinking outcomes: Findings from project match. *Journal of Studies on Alcohol*, 65(6):766–773, 2004.

[32] M. Park, D. W. McDonald, and M. Cha. Perception differences between the depressed and non-depressed users in twitter. In *Proc. ICWSM*, 2013.

[33] M. J. Paul and M. Dredze. You are what you tweet: Analyzing twitter for public health. In *Proc. ICWSM*, 2011.

[34] C. Schoenborn, P. Adams, and J. Peregoy. Health behaviors of adults: United States, 2008-2010. *Vital and Health Statistics*, 10(257), 2013.

[35] S. Shiffman. Relapse following smoking cessation: A situational analysis. *Journal of Consulting and Clinical Psychology*, 50(1):71–86, 1982.

[36] A. B. Whitworth, F. Fischer, O. M. Lesch, A. Nimmerrichter, H. Oberbauer, T. Platz, A. Potgieter, H. Walter, and W. W. Fleischhacker. Comparison of acamprosate and placebo in long-term treatment of alcohol dependence. *Lancet*, 347(9013):1438–1442, 1996.

[37] X. Zhou, J. Nonnemaker, B. Sherrill, A. W. Gilsenan, F. Coste, and R. West. Attempts to quit smoking and relapse: Factors associated with success or failure from the attempt cohort study. *Addictive Behaviors*, 34(4):365–373, 2009.

Twitter-based Election Prediction in the Developing World

Nugroho Dwi Prasetyo
Web Information Systems
Delft University of Technology
NugrohoDwiPrasetyo@student.tudelft.nl

Claudia Hauff
Web Information Systems
Delft University of Technology
c.hauff@tudelft.nl

ABSTRACT

Elections are the main instrument of democracy. Citizens decide which entity or entities (a political party or a particular politician) should represent them. Traditionally, pre-election polls have been used to learn about trends and likely election outcomes. Predicting an election outcome based on user activity on Twitter has been shown to be a cheap alternative. While past research has focused on election prediction in the *developed* world (where its use is debatable), in this paper we provide a comprehensive argument for the use of Twitter-based election forecasting in the *developing* world. For our use case of Indonesia's presidential elections 2014, the most basic Twitter-predictor outperforms the majority of traditional polls, while the best performing predictor outperforms all traditional polls on the national level.

Keywords: election forecasting, microblogs, Twitter

1. INTRODUCTION

Elections are the main instrument of democracy. Citizens decide which entity or entities (a political party or a particular politician) should represent them. One important aspect of elections are pre-election polls which provide citizens and political entities the opportunity to adjust the vote or campaign strategy if necessary.

Opinion polls have existed since the early 19th century [22], and have over time been improved with statistical models which allow (in general) to reliably forecast elections [25]. While in developed countries election polling failures are relatively rare [16], they are still a regular occurrence in developing countries such as Indonesia — the country we consider in our work. Several aspects play a role in poll prediction failure, including the "house effect" [1] (polling organizations themselves are often leaning towards one political camp) which can be caused by non-random sampling, sampling over a very short period of time or post-stratification strategies (the adjustment of raw polling data). Over time, the comparatively high costs of traditional opinion polling (which

requires person-to-person contact) has led to a range of alternatives including telephone polls, SMS polls and Web-based polls. These cheaper alternatives can suffer from a range of issues including a strong sample bias and a low response rate [14].

With the increased usage of the social Web as a platform for individuals to share details about their daily lives [29] (including their political leanings), researchers began to consider social Web portals as potential sources for opinion poll mining. Here, instead of explicitly requiring users to answer a set of fixed questions (about their voting preferences), their opinions are *inferred* from the content and/or the connections they have created over time. This in turn allows researchers to gather information about a much larger sample of users. Twitter in particular has become a widely investigated source for election forecasting [2, 3, 4, 5, 8, 10, 9, 12, 17, 24, 26, 27, 31, 33, 35], due to data availability as well as the widespread use of Twitter all across the world.

Existing work in Twitter-based election forecasting has several shortcomings as most prominently discussed by Gayo-Avello [20, 19]. Data selection (including which political parties to investigate [24]) and data pre-processing have a considerable influence on the prediction accuracy. Experiments are always conducted post-hoc, i.e. after the election result is known (the election result constitutes the *the ground truth* to predict), and often only consider one or two different elections. These issues limit the generalizability of the results. Moreover, the nature of the social Web itself (its bias, issues of trust, credibility, etc.) requires the attention of researchers when relying on it for election forecasting.

The ultimate objective of Twitter-based election polling[1] is to be a *cheap* (close to zero cost) alternative to traditional "offline" polling while achieving the same level of *prediction accuracy* and *reliability*. Past works have shown that predictions based on Twitter data often lack behind traditional polls in accuracy (cf. Table 1). The vast majority of works have investigated elections in the developed world, where traditional polls tend to be highly accurate and occur frequently throughout election campaigns. In these instances the added value of Twitter-based polls is at least questionable. In the developing world, however, traditional polls are less likely to be reliable and often result in a high forecasting error. In the specific case of the Indonesian presidential elections (2 candidates) in 2014 for instance, the *Mean Absolute prediction Error* (MAE) of the twenty

---

[1]In this work we focus on Twitter as social media source, but consider the points raised as generalizable across a range of social media platforms.

most well-known polling institutions was 4.2%[2], while even the simplest Twitter-based predictor achieved an MAE of 3.3%, thus providing a better forecast than the majority of polling institutions (cf. Table 6). We believe that this observation does not only hold for Indonesia but that more generally, Twitter-based election polling can yield opinion polls that are more accurate than traditional polls across many parts of the developing world. One aspect which requires special attention in this scenario is the *de-biasing* of the gathered data [10]. The demographic bias of Twitter users (young, male and living in urban areas) is considerably higher in developing countries compared to the developed world. During our crawling efforts for instance, we collected more than 50,000 tweets from users residing in the capital Jakarta (9.6 million inhabitants), while we were only able to gather 26 tweets from users residing in the Kalimantan Tengah province (more than 2.2 million inhabitants).

The work we present in this paper has 2 goals:

1. To conduct Twitter-based election forecasting a five-step pipeline is required. While past works have investigated the impact of a particular factor or a small set of factors (e.g. using spam detection in the filtering step or using sentiment analysis in the prediction step) on Twitter-based election prediction, we aim to gain a *comprehensive understanding* of the influence of *all* factors introduced in the past.

2. Using the specific case of the 2014 Indonesian presidential election, we aim to provide a detailed & in-depth analysis, comparing the Twitter-based prediction accuracy to 20 polls conducted by the most well-known polling institutes in Indonesia during the election campaign.

2. PREVIOUS WORK

First, in order to provide the reader with an intuition of past work, we sketch a basic Twitter election prediction approach that may be employed (and actually has been employed in the past). Lets assume we want to predict the winner of the 2016 US Presidential elections with the two candidates being Hillary Clinton and Jeb Bush. We decide to collect all tweets published through Twitter's public streaming API[3] in the run-up to the election. All tweets $T_{clinton}$ containing one of the terms {*hillary, clinton, democrat*} are considered as a "vote" for Clinton, while all tweets T_{bush} containing one of the terms {*bush, jebbush, republican*} constitute a "vote" for Bush.
The predicted percentage of votes for Hillary Clinton is then calculated as $|T_{clinton}|/(|T_{clinton}| + |T_{bush}|)$ (and similarly for Jeb Bush). Lastly, the accuracy of the forecast is evaluated by computing the difference of the forecast to the actual election outcome.

This basic setup can be broken down into five different components (thus expanding the three components introduced in [19]) of the *Twitter election forecasting pipeline*, namely: (i) **data collection** (e.g. should the streaming API be used?), (ii) **data filtering** (should some tweets or users be removed from the dataset?), (iii) **de-biasing** of the data (should some "votes" count more than others?), (iv) the

prediction (can tweets represent votes?) itself, and finally (v) the **evaluation** of the prediction. We have categorized a representative selection of past work along these dimensions in Table 1 and will now provide a more in-depth overview of each of these components. Note that we focus solely on Twitter, as it is by far the most popular social Web platform to gather election prediction data from.

2.1 Data collection

The data collection process involves four different aspects: (i) election type, (ii) data access (searching vs. streaming), (iii) the duration of monitoring, and, most importantly, (iv) which keywords or phrases to use in order to extract tweets pertaining to the election. As evident in Table 1 there are no standard settings for any of these factors.

Election Type: The most commonly investigated election type is the presidential election which selects one winner from several candidates. The second most common type is the general election where political parties (usually 5-10) compete against each other. The most noticeable difference is the number of candidates; intuitively the larger the pool of candidates the more difficult the prediction becomes [28]. Besides the number of candidates, the election type also affects the keyword selection.

Data Access: Collecting Twitter data is possible in two ways: we can either retrieve all tweets that match a small set of election-related manually defined keywords (the *search* setup), or we can *stream* all tweets that Twitter makes accessible through the streaming API (roughly 1% of all tweets) and search within them in a post-processing step. While the former method is very storage efficient, it is also restrictive in the sense that once the keywords are fixed it is not possible to look back beyond a small timeframe and collect additional data. As Table 1 shows, both approaches are equally popular with researchers.

Duration: The duration of the data collection is another aspect which has been shown to influence the prediction accuracy. There is no agreement on the timespan to consider, e.g. [37, 17, 27] started collecting tweets more than 6 months prior to the election, while Jensen & Anstead [23] collected data only within the last 2 days of the election. Bermingham & Smeaton [3] empirically showed that relying on the 24 hour time window before the election produces the best prediction accuracy when compared to time windows covering several days.

Keyword Selection: Arguably the most important aspect of data collection are the selected keywords as they determine what tweets will appear in the final dataset[4]. Most research relies on candidate/party names and abbreviations as keywords. Using more fine-grained keywords such as candidate addresses, election related hashtags, and campaign hashtags has also been investigated. The assumption is that using more keywords related to the election leads to a larger dataset and thus a higher predictive power.

2.2 Data Filtering

The goal in the data filtering step is to reduce the noise in the dataset. Few works have considered this step in the

---

[2] A lower MAE value indicates a better prediction.
[3] These tweets constitute roughly 1% of all tweets and are considered a random sample of all tweets.

[4] In the Twitter streaming data access setup, once streaming ends, these keywords will be used to extract the election related tweets from the streamed data. In the Twitter search setup, all tweets containing at least one of these keywords is collected.

	Country	Type	#Ca.	Methods	MAE	Stream / Search	Duration	Keywords	Filtering	De-bias
[35]	Germany	Federal	6	Count tweets/hashtags	1.7%	N/A	5 weeks	party names	N/A	-
[10]	Singapore	Presidential	4	Count tweets & sentiment	6.1%	Search	1 week	Candidate names	English tweets only	computer literacy & social media support and age group from previous election
[18]	USA	Presidential	2	Count tweets & sentiment	11.63%	Search	6 months	Candidate names	N/A	location and age based on previous election
[3]	Ireland	General	5	Count tweets & sentiment	3.7-5.9%	N/A	3 weeks	party names and election hashtag	delete tweets about poll result	-
[33]	NL	Senate	12	Count tweets	1.3%	Stream	1 month	Dutch words	N/A	user
[9]	USA	Presidential	2	Count tweets	1.7%	N/A	6 weeks	N/A	non english tweets	internet penetration per-state & social media supporters from previous election
[24]	Germany	Federal	6	Count hashtags & sentiment	N/A	N/A	4 months	party name and election hashtags	N/A	-
[31]	USA, France	Presidential	2	sentiment	N/A	N/A	2 months	candidate names and election hashtags	delete retweet	-
[27]	USA	Republican nomination	7	Count tweets & sentiment	N/A	Search	1 year	candidate names	N/A	-
[17]	Venezuela, Paraguay, Ecuador	Presidential	2(V) 3(P) 2(E)	Count tweets & user	0.1-19%	N/A	7 months	candidate names and aliases	filter tweets based on predefined keywords	-
[37]	USA	Presidential	2	Count (re)tweets & sentiment	N/A	Stream	8 months	selected keywords	N/A	-
[2]	USA	Presidential	2	sentiment	N/A	N/A	2 months	Daily top words	N/A	-
[23]	USA	Republican nomination	4	Count tweets	3.1%	Stream	2 days	candidate names and Account name	N/A	-
[15]	Nigeria	Presidential	4	Count tweets & sentiment	11.0%	Search	1 year	candidate names and Popular names	N/A	-
[26]	Canada	General	4	Count interactions, followers & followees	N/A		1 month	N/A	Delete spammer	N/A	-
[8]	Italy, France	Presidential	7(I) 2(F)	Count tweets & sentiment	2.4-5.7 %	N/A	1 month	candidate names	N/A	-
[7]	USA, Italy	Presidential	2(U) 5(I)	Count tweets & sentiment	0.4%-9.7%	N/A	6 weeks	N/A	N/A	-

Table 1: Overview of previous research in Twitter-based election forecasting. The references are ordered from oldest (top) to most recent (bottom). For each work, we list, among others, the country (or countries) under investigation, the number of candidates (#Ca.), the prediction error with respect to the election outcome (in MAE if available) as well as data collection and processing details.

past. Makazhanov et al. [26] used a spam classifier to determine spam users. Overall, they did not find this to be a significant issue with less than 0.5% of users (with election pertaining tweets) being classified as spam users. A more significant fraction of users were so-called non-personal users (1.8%), i.e. Twitter accounts that represent organizations, businesses, etc. instead of individual users. In contrast, Cook et al. [13] found the rise of Twitter bots [11], which we can consider spam in the election context, to be a significant issue in the 2013 Australian federal elections where many of a candidate's followers were actually bots.

Gaurav et al. [17] filtered tweets not pertaining to the election by modifying their approach to only consider tweets that contain the candidate names as well as specific keywords such as "eleccion" or "election".

Finally, filtering Twitter users based on their geo-location may also be desirable [18], especially for elections that are of global interest with many users from all around the globe weighing in. To reduce the convolution between the voting (users who live in the election country) and non-voting users, geo-location filtering can be employed: users whose tweets originate from the election country are included in the prediction model, the remainder are ignored.

2.3 Reducing Bias

Addressing the data bias has attracted little attention among the research community. A country's social Web users are not necessarily representative of the overall population, especially in developing countries. In [18] (US presidential election) it was attempted to de-bias the data according to user age by crossing the full names and county of residence with online public records, though the success was minimal. Similarly, Choy et al. [10] (Singapore presidential election) also considered external data sources to enhance the Twitter-based prediction by taking into account the percentage of population and social media users in each age group, and the vote share of each candidate at the previous general election, thereby adjusting the prediction. Again, the prediction only improved marginally.

We hypothesize that the lack of success is partially due to the elections investigated in countries with a high Internet penetration rate (87% and 80% respectively in the US and Singapore vs. 17% in Indonesia[5]).

---

[5]Estimates based on http://www.internetlivestats.com/internet-users/

2.4 Predicting the Election Outcome

Different data characteristics have been employed to predict the election outcome. The essence is the counting of items and the implied correlation between counts and votes. What exactly to count differs across past works.

One of the earliest works [35] assumed that vote proportions in an election correspond to the number of tweets mentioning a candidate or party's name. Later it was argued that one vote per user (instead of one vote per tweet) is a more realistic approach [33]. Counting only a selected number of tweets (namely those containing an interaction with a candidate's or party's Twitter account) was evaluated in [26]. These counts are directly translated into predicted voting shares.

A common criticism of this approach is the fact that the mentioning of a candidate's name or party is not sufficient to detect whether or not the user (or tweet) is in favour of the candidate. Sentiment analysis (based on lexica [34], machine learning [32] and crowdsourcing [6]) have been employed in past works to determine whether or not a tweet's or user's vote should count towards a particular candidate's vote share.

2.5 Evaluating the Forecast

Finally, the evaluation component determines the quality of the prediction. Two questions need to be answered: (i) what is the prediction compared against, and, (ii) how is the difference between the prediction and ground truth measured. Prior work has considered two types of ground truth for comparison: the election outcome itself as well as polls released by traditional polling institutions. The common goal is to determine whether the Twitter-based prediction can have a similar or even higher accuracy than traditional polls. In order to quantify the difference between the prediction and ground truth, the vast majority of works rely on the *Mean Absolute Error* defined as:

$$MAE = \frac{1}{n}\sum_{i=1}^{n}|P_i - R_i| \qquad (1)$$

where n is the number of candidates, P is the predicted vote percentage and R is the true election result percentage. Alternatives such as the root mean squared error [17] have not gained traction.

3. ELECTION USE CASE

We determined the 2014 Indonesian Presidential Election to be a good use case for our work and research questions as Indonesia is a highly populated country of the developing world with a relatively large Twitter user base which is highly skewed towards urban centers, which we hypothesize will require substantial de-biasing of the data.

The election took place on July 9, 2014 with two candidates in the running (the incumbent was not standing for re-election): **Joko Widodo** with running mate Jusuf Kalla and **Prabowo Subianto** with running mate Hatta Rajasa. Both candidates officially announced their candidacy on May 20, 2014.

Election Outcome: Widodo won the election with 53.15% of the votes (Subianto received 46.85%). Of Indonesia's 33 provinces, Widodo won in 23 while Subianto won in 10. Most provinces were highly contested with less than 10% difference between vote shares. Interestingly, Widodo was

supported by a coalition of parties that received only 36% of the votes in the legislative election earlier in 2014, while Subianto was supported by a group of parties that had gathered 53% of votes in that election.

Polling Institutes: We collected the poll results published by the 20 most well-known polling institutes in Indonesia. These institutes conduct traditional (offline) polls. We compiled their poll results as well as the self-reported margin of error in Table 2. All institutes randomly select samples in several randomly drawn provinces (akin to multistage random sampling).

The final column in Table 2 contains the error (MAE) of each poll with respect to the actual election outcome. The result vary greatly between institutes, even for polls conducted within the same time frame.

4. METHODOLOGY

Having outlined the different pipeline components and their various instantiations, we now turn to our own experiments. We aim to provide a **comprehensive overview** of all the different influences the various components have on the prediction, based on the eight research hypotheses outlined in this section.

4.1 Data Collection

We employed the Twitter *search* approach and collected all tweets (starting April 15 and ending July 8, 2014) containing at least one term from a *manually curated* list of terms (keyword selection). This setup allows us to investigate the following hypothesis:

Hypothesis 1. *Using several days of data (which implies a larger data sample) in the run-up to the election leads to a more accurate election forecast.*

The final keyword list can be found in Table 4. Since over time the discussion around an election may change, we started our keyword list with the popular names of the candidates (and their running mates) as well as their Twitter usernames. We dynamically updated the keyword list by monitoring daily the Twitter Trending Topics localized for Indonesia. We added those hashtags (identifying the trending topic) to our list that were related to the upcoming election. We can thus investigate to what extent the keyword list plays a role in the accuracy of election prediction.

Hypothesis 2. *Using more election-related keywords yields more relevant data and thus improves the accuracy of the Twitter-based election forecast.*

In an additional pre-processing step, to select mainly tweets from potential voters, we only include tweets that originate from Indonesia. This geo-restriction was enforced via a parameter setting within the Twitter search API. Twitter itself estimates the location from geo-tagged messages and from the location stated in the users' profile.

We also consider the following two hypotheses about users:

Hypothesis 3. *The number of users in the Twitter-based dataset positively correlates with the accuracy of the election forecast.*

Hypothesis 4. *Using users instead of tweets as indicators of "votes" enhances the accuracy of the prediction.*

Institute	%Widodo	%Subianto	%Undecided	Poll date	Sample Size	Error Margin	MAE
ARC	38.8	29.0	32.2	May 18-28	1,440	2.64%	4.08%
Cyrus Network	53.6	41.1	5.3	May 25-31	1,500	2.60%	3.45%
IDM	34.4	48.7	16.9	June 22-30	3,324	1.80%	11.75%
Indobarometer	49.1	36.5	14.4	May 28-Jun 4	1,200	3.00%	4.21%
INES	37.6	54.3	8.1	June 25-Jul 2	7,000	1.31%	12.24%
IRC	43.0	47.5	9.5	June 14-20	1,200	2.80%	5.64%
ISI	46.9	53.1	0.0	July 2-6	999	3.00%	6.25%
Kompas	42.3	35.3	22.4	June 1-15	1,950	2.20%	1.36%
LIPI	43.0	34.0	23.0	June 5-24	790	3.51%	2.69%
LSI Network	47.8	44.2	8.0	July 2-5	2,400	2.00%	1.19%
LSN	39.9	46.6	13.5	June 23-26	1,070	3.00%	7.02%
Median	44.3	46.2	9.5	June 15-20	2,200	2.10%	4.20%
PDB	32.3	40.6	27.1	June 23-July 1	2,688	5.00%	8.84%
Pol Tracking	48.5	41.1	10.4	May 26-June 3	2,010	2.19%	0.98%
PolcoMM	45.3	46.8	7.9	June 23-27	1,200	3.10%	3.96%
Populi Center	47.5	36.9	15.6	May 24-29	1,500	2.53%	3.13%
Puskaptis	42.79	44.69	12.52	June 16-21	2,400	2.00%	4.24%
Roy Morgan	52.0	48.0	0.0	June 15	3,117	1.80%	1.15%
SSSG	51.0	43.4	5.6	June 21-July 5	1,250	2.78%	0.87%
Vox Populi	37.7	52.8	9.5	June 3-15	4,898	1.80%	11.49%

Table 2: **Results of traditional polls conducted before the election. Columns 2-4 contain the predicted voting shares for both candidates and swing voters (if available in the poll). The MAE of the last column is calculated with respect to the election outcome (swing voters are ignored).**

Crawling period	April 15 - July 8, 2015
Number of electoral tweets	7,020,228
Max. tweets in a day	375,064
Number of users	490,270
Max. active users in a day	148,135
Percentage of retweets	29.24%

Table 3: **Overview of POLLDATA statistics.**

An overview of our collected data (referred to as POLLDATA dataset) is provided in Table 3; more than 7 million tweets were collected from $\sim$ 490,000 different users. In this setup, only tweets containing at least one term of our keyword list are included. To gather more in-depth information about the users, within the period of July 25-30, 2014 (i.e. after the election) we attempted to collect the most recent 100 tweets of all users appearing in POLLDATA. This was possible for 84.9% of the users, resulting in an additional 42 million tweets. We refer to this dataset as USERDATA. Note that we did not rely on the tweets appearing in USERDATA for prediction purposes, but to gain qualitative insights into factor such as age, gender and person vs. non-personal users as outlined next.

4.2 Data Filtering

4.2.1 Qualitative Insights

To determine the influence of spam and non-personal users in our dataset, we randomly selected 600 users from USER-DATA and *manually* labelled these users as either spam (or bot), non-personal (e.g. an account from a poltical organizaton) or "slacktivist" (a social media user that is only active during an election campaign [36, 13]). We based the labelling on the content of the user profiles as well as the content of the most recent 100 tweets.

We found that:

- 7.4% of users can be classified as spam (or bot); most of these can be distinguished based on their re-tweet frequency, their peculiar use of hashtags, etc.;

- 3.8% of users are non-personal users;

- 2.1% of users can be classified as slacktivists through their specific activities prior to the election (newly created account, all tweets relate to the election, no match between user profile and tweeted content, etc.).

Taken together, more than 10% of Twitter accounts in this sample do not belong to a human user. We believe that filtering out those accounts before conducting the election forecast will yield a more accurate prediction.

Hypothesis 5. *Removing spam users, non-personal users and slacktivists from our dataset improves the accuracy of the election forecast.*

4.2.2 Rule-based classification

To detect bots we follow the methodology outlined in [11] (based on time intervals, the regularity of URLs, etc.). To detect non-personal users, spam and slacktivists we built up a set of hand-curated rules during the just described manual annotation phase (e.g. a user with at least 10% of his tweets containing one of the terms {*twitter, 10rb, follower, 1k*} is considered a spammer; a user tweeting every day about the election with a recently created account is a slacktivist). We used these rules to classify all users appearing in POLLDATA as either a personal user or not (collapsing all non-personal types into one type). In total, in this manner we found 4,323 users whose tweets are discarded from POLLDATA when running data filtering experiments.

	Keywords Widodo	Keywords Subianto
Popular names	*Jokowi, Kalla, jokowi-jk*	*Prabowo, PrabowoHatta, hatta*
Twitter user-name	*@Pak_JK, @jokowi_do2*	*@Prabowo08, @hattarajasa*
Trending topics	*IndonesiaHebat, revolusimental, salamDUAjari, JKW4P, JK-WJK*	*DukungPrabowoHatta, SelamatkanIndonesia, indonesiabangkit, SalamSAT-Ujari, Salam1jari, prabowoforpresident*

Table 4: List of keywords employed during data collection. Since in Indonesia people rarely refer to each other by their last names the candidates' family names do not appear as keywords.

4.3 Reducing Bias

We consider two hypotheses in relation to the data bias that was already outlined anecdotally in Section 1.

Hypothesis 6. *Weighting the contribution of tweets/users to votes depending on their geographical location improves the election forecast.*

Hypothesis 7. *Weighting the contribution of tweets/users to votes depending on the users' demographic information improves the election forecast.*

Although other sources of bias exist, e.g. education or income, we restricted ourselves to those two as they can be automatically inferred with high precision and leave other factors to future work.

To recognize and subsequently reduce bias, we rely on demographic information made available by the Indonesian Statistics Institution[6]. For each of the 33 administrative districts (provinces) in Indonesia and the country as a whole we gather the number of citizens, the gender distribution as well as the age distribution in three age ranges: $\{0-19, 20-49, 50+\}$.

4.3.1 Qualitative Insights

In Table 5 we compare the population's age and gender distribution to our dataset by *manually* annotating the previously randomly selected 600 users (minus those deemed spam/non-personal) according to their age range and gender. We based the labelling on user profile information (including users' names, school or university names and the profile images) and tweet content. We find that in terms of age, the 20-49 year olds are overrepresented in our Twitter dataset, while female users are underrepresented.

In terms of location bias, we rely on the latitude/longitude information provided by Twitter and convert these coordinates into the corresponding province via Google's reverse geo-coding service[7].

Shown in Figure 1 is the province-level percentage of the population that is active on Twitter. To this end, we related the number of users identified from each province (found in POLLDATA) to the provinces' population data. As expected, Jakarta has a very active Twitter user base (approx. 0.6% of

[6]http://www.bps.go.id/
[7]https://developers.google.com/maps/documentation/geocoding/#ReverseGeocoding

	Twitter	Population
Age Distribution		
0-19	33.8%	37.7%
20-49	64.7%	46.3%
50+	1.5%	16.0%
Gender Distribution		
Female	42.0%	50.3%
Male	58.0%	49.7%

Table 5: Comparison of gender and age distribution between Indonesia's population as a whole and our labelled sample of Twitter users.

Jakarta's population is active on Twitter), while provinces such as Maluku or Kalimantran Tenagh have close to zero coverage.

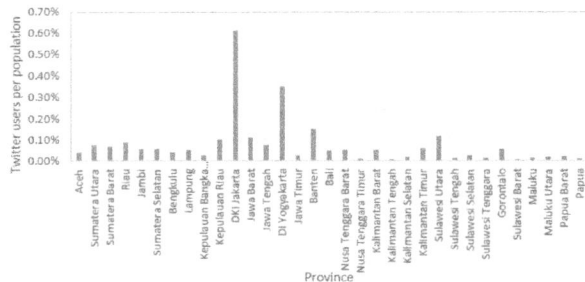

Figure 1: Percentage of Twitter users in each of Indonesia's 33 provinces.

4.3.2 Gender Classification

While the identification of a user's province is relatively straight-forward due to available reverse geo-coding services, classifying each user in POLLDATA according to gender is more difficult.

We investigated the use of a name list to distinguish the users' gender. We collected roughly 6500 popular Indonesian male and female names[8] and compare a users's name (as listed on Twitter) against this list. In this manner we are able to identify the gender of about 140,000 users from POLLDATA. To verify the accuracy of this method, we manually labelled 2,500 randomly selected users; the accuracy of this approach is 96.01%. Although highly accurate, this approach did not allow us to label 71.4% of our users in POLLDATA. In subsequent de-biasing experiments based on gender, we only use those users from POLLDATA for which the gender assignment was possible.

Finally, we note that we also investigated the use of age classifiers based on Twitter content as proposed in [30]. However, we found the classification accuracy of this approach to be too low (61% correctly classified instances based on 10-fold cross-validation and our 600 sampled users) to be useful in practice. We hypothesize that the discrepancy between our findings and [30] is due to the difference in language

[8]Note that in Indonesia many people go by a single name (instead of using the first-name family-name convention).

(Dutch vs. Indonesian) as well as the lack of sufficient annotated training data.

4.4 Predicting the Election Outcome

To determine the vote share of a candidate C, each tweet mentioning any of the candidate's associated keywords is considered a vote for C. If a tweet contains keywords related to several candidates, it counts as a vote towards the candidate with the majority of mentioned keywords (in a tie situation, the user is categorized as "undecided" and not further considered). On a per-user bases, a user is considered to vote for C if the user mentions C more often than any other candidate in the collected dataset[9]. Although we collected tweets for nearly three months, we usually want to restrict the dataset to the final d days before the election (i.e. $d = -1$ indicates all data within the last day before the election, $d = \{-1, .., -7\}$ encompasses the entire week before the election, etc.). Similarly, we may want to consider only tweets containing the popular names of either candidate, instead of all keywords, indicated with *keywords=popularNames* vs *keywords=all*. In either setup, we only consider those tweets that fall within these restrictions as a basis for the prediction.

4.4.1 Sentiment Analysis

Past studies that have relied on sentiment analysis for Twitter-based election forecasting have shown that it can reduce the error of the prediction.

Hypothesis 8. *Taking the expressed sentiment into account when tallying the Twitter-based votes improves the prediction accuracy.*

We aim to classify each tweet according to its sentiment into positive, negative or neutral. We use an established methodology to create training data from tweets in POLL-DATA: we rely on tweets containing positive emoticons, e.g. :), as positive training data (12,287 tweets) and tweets containing negative emoticons, e.g. =(, as negative training data (7,290 tweets). We pre-process the tweets by removing *@mentions*, URLs, electoral keywords (Table 4), emoticons and single characters. The tweets are turned into word vectors and a standard Naïve Bayes classifier setup is employed for classification.

Following the guidelines in [21], we use a class prediction probability threshold of 0.8 to filter out low confidence prediction results, i.e. tweets that cannot be classified as positive or negative with a high confidence are classified as neutral instead.

Employing 10-fold cross-validation (using the training data as input) yields a precision of 0.799. We deem this to be a sufficiently well performing approach for our purposes and classified all tweets in POLLDATA with our generated model. Overall, 27.97% of tweets are identified as positive, 10.88% as negative and 60.62% as neutral.

5. RESULTS

The main results are summarized in Table 6, both on the national level and broken down to the province levels. We report the MAE with respect to the election outcome on the

[9]Note, that for both the tweet-count and user-count setup, we only rely on the POLLDATA dataset (no tweets from the USERDATA dataset is employed).

national level as well as the number of polls that performed better and worse than our prediction (20 polls in total). At the province level we report for how many (out of 33) provinces the winner was correctly predicted as well as the spread in MAE we observed indicated through the minimum and maximum MAE in a province.

From Tweets to Users: Hypothesis 4 is based on the assumption that each citizen has at most one vote in a democratic election and it should be beneficial to count users instead of tweets, thereby naturally down-weighting the undue influence of highly active Twitter users. Past work has indicated that this hypothesis holds [17, 33]. Table 6 rows (1) & (2) compare the two setups (with parameter settings $d = -1$, *keywords=all*). Indeed, on the national level we observe the same result as prior work - the MAE decreases from 3.3% to 1.3% when switching from tweet to user counts. If we break the results down to the province level though, we hardly observe any changes (for one additional province the winner is correctly predicted and the maximum MAE observed in a province decreases slightly from 26% to 25%). This discrepancy can be explained by the fact that the user-based MAE significantly decreased in the two provinces DKI Jakarta and Jawa Barat where more than 50% of our Twitter users live.

We thus accept Hypothesis 4, but point out that in practice it only plays an important role in areas (provinces) with a large fraction of Twitter users.

Keyword Selection: To investigate the influence keyword selection has on the prediction accuracy (Hypothesis 2) we employ three different tweet counting strategies: (i) we only use a single keyword per candidate (the candidates' respective popular names), (ii) we use all keywords as listed in Table 4, and, (iii) we randomly select 5 keywords from that list for each candidate. Comparing rows (1), (3) and (4) in Table 6 (the results for the user-count based approach are not shown but similar) shows that keyword selection has a limited effect. Our carefully manually curated keyword list performs best with an MAE of 3.3%; surprisingly though using a single keyword (each candidate's popular name) performs slightly better than using five keywords per candidates. For each strategy the prediction accuracy (tweet-count based with $d = -1$) in all provinces can be seen in Figure 2 — although using *all* keywords does not always lead to the best prediction, it is never far away from the best one. Since those 5 keywords per candidate are randomly drawn from all identified keywords in Table 4, we can conclude that a careful selection of keywords is needed. Simply using more keywords does not always lead to better results, thus we cannot unconditionally accept Hypothesis 2.

Duration of Data Collection: The usual paradigm of "the more data, the better" does not necessarily hold in the election prediction context. Instead of fixing the collection time frame to d days before the election we vary d and investigate its effect on the prediction accuracy. In order to derive a prediction based on several day's of data, we evaluate two possibilities: (i) the *Moving Average* (for each day the predicted vote share is computed separately and then averaged), and, (ii) the *Aggregate* (we simply aggregate all data across the considered days). For selected values of d, the results are shown in Table 7, both for the tweet-count and user-count based approach. We observe that d has a significant influence on the MAE — while for the tweet-count based approach $d = -1$ is the best setting, the best user-count results

Approach	Predicted Votes % Widodo	Subianto	MAE	Polls +	Polls -	At Province Level #Correct	min. MAE	max. MAE
(1) *TweetCount* $d=-1, keywords=all$	56.45	43.55	3.3	7	13	23/33	0.27	26.09
(2) *UserCount* $d=-1, keywords=all$	54.45	45.55	1.3	4	16	24/33	0.05	25.01
(3) *TweetCount-Keywords* $d=-1, keywords=1$	57.2	42.8	4.05	9	11	23/33	0.12	26.82
(4) *TweetCount-Keywords* $d=-1, keywords=5$	57.27	42.73	4.12	10	10	23/33	0.19	26.82
(5) *TweetCount-FILTER* $d=-1, keywords=all$	56.66	43.34	3.51	8	12	22/33	0.01	25.33
(6) *UserCount-FILTER* $d=-1, keywords=all$	54.59	45.41	1.44	5	15	24/33	0.38	27.36
(7) *TweetCount-LOCATION* $d=-1, keywords=all$	55.14	44.86	1.99	5	15	N/A	N/A	N/A
(8) *UserCount-LOCATION* $d=-1, keywords=all$	54.26	45.74	1.11	2	18	N/A	N/A	N/A
(9) *TweetCount-GENDER* $d=-1, keywords=all$	56.36	43.64	3.21	7	13	21/33	0.33	28.05
(10) *UserCount-GENDER* $d=-1, keywords=all$	54.89	45.11	1.74	5	15	23/33	0.1	26.72
(11) *TweetCount-SENTI-POS* $d=-1, keywords=all$	53.98	46.02	0.83	0	20	14/33	0.01	54.90
(12) *UserCount-SENTI-POS* $d=-1, keywords=all$	54.02	45.98	0.87	0	20	19/33	0.26	26.51
(13) *TweetCount-SENTI-POS-NEG* $d=-1, keywords=all$	50.67	49.33	2.48	5	15	14/33	0.01	49.79
(14) *UserCount-SENTI-POS-NEG* $d=-1, keywords=all$	53.77	46.23	0.62	0	20	19/33	0.01	26.40

Table 6: Overview of the main results on the national and per-province level. For each approach, we report the predicted vote shares for each candidate, the MAE (with respect to the election outcome) and the number of offline polls with a smaller MAE (+ indicates "better") and larger MAE (- indicates worse). The rightmost three columns break the prediction outcome down on a per-province level: #Correct indicates for how many out of 33 provinces the winner was correctly predicted; minimum and maximum MAE indicate the spread in prediction accuracy across the provinces. Note that the location de-biasing (rows (7) & (8)) only affects the national prediction.

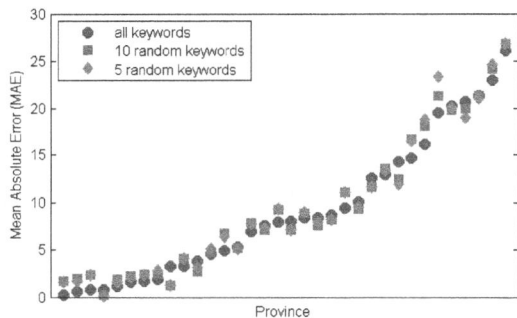

Figure 2: Influence of keyword selection on the prediction accuracy province-by-province (provinces are ordered according to their MAE).

	1 day	7 days	14 days	21 days	30 days
Tweet Count					
Average	3.30	5.37	8.50	7.28	6.11
Aggregate	3.30	5.34	8.40	6.42	5.34
User Count					
Average	1.30	0.06	3.71	2.20	1.17
Aggregate	1.30	1.42	3.62	0.57	0.02

Table 7: Overview of the MAE when varying the data collection duration, where *n days* indicate the timespan of the final *n* days before the election.

are achieved for $d = \{-1, .., -7\}$ and $d = \{-1, .., -30\}$. For the user-count approach the manner in which the prediction is derived across several days also plays an important role. To get more insights into the development of the prediction across the 2 months prior to the election, we plotted the daily prediction of the tweet-count approach in Figure 3, treating each day as if it were the final day before the election (i.e. using $d = -1$). The plot shows the predicted vote share for both *keywords=all* and *keywords=1*. Notable is the dynamic nature of the prediction, it varies in the extremes between a 72/28 split in early June and a 52/48 split in early July. At all times though, the same candidate (the actual winner) is predicted to receive the majority of the votes.

Data Filtering: Overall, we filter 4.12 % of users in POLLDATA and subsequently 15.99% of tweets. The data filtering hypothesis (Hypothesis 5) suggests that the removal of selected users from the dataset will improve the prediction. The results in Table 6, rows (5) and (6) show that this hypothesis does not hold for the overall election result and has to be rejected. The MAE increases slightly from 1.3% to 1.44% (user-count) and from 3.3% to 3.51% (tweet-count) respectively. On a province level, the prediction actually slightly improves for 20 out of 33 provinces (i.e. the MAE decreases). This though is not sufficient to raise the overall prediction accuracy, as the provinces with the largest number of users do not benefit from this filtering step.

Reducing bias: Hypothesis 6 suggests that de-biasing the Twitter-based prediction with population data (i.e. decreasing the influence of tweets from locations overrepresented in the dataset and increasing the influence of tweets

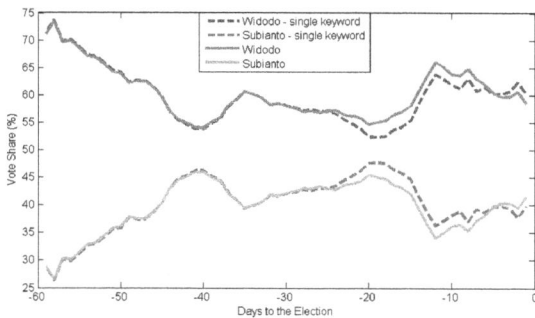

Figure 3: Daily prediction results based on tweet-counts computed individually (i.e. separately for each 24 hours) for the 60 days leading up to the election.

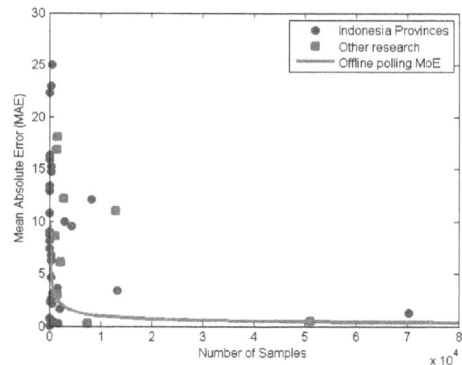

Figure 4: Margin of Error: comparison between Twitter-based predictions and offline polls.

from locations that are underrepresented) improves the prediction accuracy. The results are shown in Table 6, rows (7) & (8). Indeed, location-based de-biasing is beneficial, the MAE is reduced for both tweet-count and user-count approaches, though more significantly for the former than the latter (from 3.3% MAE to 1.99% MAE). In contrast to this result we do not find gender de-biasing (Hypothesis 7) to yield improvements. In Table 6, rows (9) and (10), we observe generally a degradation of the prediction both on the national as well as the province level. Recall though, that the gender-based results are based on a small set of users in POLLDATA (28.6% of all users due to the labeling restrictions), which is likely to affect the prediction considerably. Based on the empirical evidence found though, we cannot accept Hypothesis 7.

Sentiment Analysis: Hypothesis 8 is based on the assumption that sentiment information should be a guiding factor when determining whether or not to count a tweet (or user) as a vote towards a candidate. Having classified all tweets according to their sentiment, we investigate two approaches: (i) only positive tweets towards a candidate C are used as votes for C (SENTI-POS, Table 6 rows (11) & (12)), and, (ii) not only positive tweets towards C count, but also tweets negatively directed at the opposing candidate [18] (SENTI-POS-NEG, Table 6 rows (13) & (14)). In the user-based count approach, we determine which candidate the user has the majority of positive associations with. On the national level, sentiment analysis aids the prediction, as also found in past work, e.g. [8]. We observe though, that the impact of negative tweets in the prediction is ambiguous: the tweet-count based prediction degrades (compared to SENTI-POS), while the user-count based prediction improves. Notable is the fact that on the national level both tweet-count and user-count approaches predict better than *all* traditional polls. On the province level, we observe a highly negative impact of sentiment analysis on the prediction accuracy. In particular, while in our tweet-count baseline (row (1)), 23 provinces have their winner predicted correctly, this degrades to 14 provinces after the employment of sentiment analysis. The degradation for the user-based approach is evident, though not as stark: in the baseline (row (2)) 24 provinces are correctly predicted, after sentiment analysis this result degrades to 19 provinces. Interestingly, the maximum MAE in a province rises sharply for the tweet-count approach (up to 54.9%), while it remains rela-

tively constant compared to the baseline for the user-count approach.

Initial investigations make us believe that the diversity of languages spoken in Indonesia is behind this surprising result. The national language, Indonesian, is only used on a daily basis in large urban areas. Within Indonesia more than 700 languages are spoken, while our POLLDATA is dominated by tweets in Indonesian (we found 88% of tweets to be in this language). Thus, the MAE improvement on the national level is due to the benefit of sentiment analysis in the large (urban) provinces, where most of the Twitter users live.

Sample Size Influence: When reporting the results of a survey or poll, the estimated margin of error is dependent on the confidence interval and the number of samples employed. Based on hypothesis 3 we investigate the correlation between the number of users and the margin of error. We combine our user-count based approach ($d = -1, keywords=all$) on a province-by-province level with the results in [15, 17] and present them in Figure 4. Shown in red is the standard margin of error, computed as $MoE = z \times \sqrt{\frac{p(1-p)}{n}}$, where p is the sample proportion, n is the sample size, and z is the appropriate critical value for the desired level of confidence. In Figure 4 we use $p = 0.5$, $z = 1.96$ (95% confidence level) and vary n. The error decreases with a greater number of users (samples). Twitter-based prediction errors are considerably larger than those reported for offline polls, and in particular at sample sizes that are sufficient for well-performing traditional polls large errors are still evident in Twitter-based prediction.

6. CONCLUSIONS

We have investigated the effect of different factors on Twitter-based election prediction with a specific focus on the developing world.

For the use case of Indonesia, we found the most basic Twitter-based predictor to lead to more accurate predictions than the majority of offline polls. Interestingly, the best performing predictors outperformed *all* available offline polls on the national level. We can thus conclude that Twitter-based election prediction, in a developing country such as Indonesia, offers competitive prediction accuracy.

We conducted a thorough analysis of various factors (gender, location, sentiment, keyword selection, spam removal, data collection duration) that may influence the accuracy of the prediction. We find most factors useful to some degree. At the same time, we also acknowledge the prediction challenges on the province level, where the diversity of the languages and the lack of technology penetration impedes a thorough use of more involved prediction pipelines.

As in all prior works, we have conducted the experiments post-hoc, i.e. after the election outcome was known. This is a limitation. We have implemented an election forecasting framework that allows us to make predictions for elections at the time of the election campaign in a real-time fashion. We used the insights gained in this paper to implement the five main components & are currently investigating its generalizability across a range of elections.

7. REFERENCES

[1] K. Arzheimer and J. Evans. A new multinomial accuracy measure for polling bias. *Political Analysis*, 22(1):31–44, 2014.

[2] N. Beauchamp. Predicting and interpolating state-level polling using Twitter textual data. In *New Directions in Analyzing Text as Data Workshop*, 2013.

[3] A. Bermingham and A. F. Smeaton. On using Twitter to monitor political sentiment and predict election results. In *SAAI '11*, 2011.

[4] A. Boutet, H. Kim, E. Yoneki, et al. What's in Your Tweets? I Know Who You Supported in the UK 2010 General Election. In *ICWSM '12*, pages 411–414, 2012.

[5] A. Bruns, J. Burgess, et al. # ausvotes: How Twitter covered the 2010 Australian federal election. *Communication, Politics & Culture*, 44(2):37–56, 2011.

[6] J. D. Burger, J. Henderson, G. Kim, and G. Zarrella. Discriminating gender on Twitter. In *EMNLP '11*, pages 1301–1309, 2011.

[7] A. Ceron, L. Curini, and S. M. Iacus. Using Sentiment Analysis to Monitor Electoral Campaigns Method Matters: Evidence From the United States and Italy. *Social Science Computer Review*, 33(1):3–20, 2015.

[8] A. Ceron, L. Curini, S. M. Iacus, and G. Porro. Every tweet counts? How sentiment analysis of social media can improve our knowledge of citizens' political preferences with an application to Italy and France. *New Media & Society*, 16(2):340–358, 2014.

[9] M. Choy, M. Cheong, M. N. Laik, and K. P. Shung. US presidential election 2012 prediction using a census corrected Twitter model. *arXiv preprint arXiv:1211.0938*, 2012.

[10] M. Choy, M. L. Cheong, M. N. Laik, and K. P. Shung. A sentiment analysis of Singapore Presidential Election 2011 using Twitter data with census correction. *arXiv preprint arXiv:1108.5520*, 2011.

[11] Z. Chu, S. Gianvecchio, H. Wang, and S. Jajodia. Who is tweeting on Twitter: human, bot, or cyborg? In *ACSAC '10*, pages 21–30, 2010.

[12] J. E. Chung and E. Mustafaraj. Can collective sentiment expressed on Twitter predict political elections? In *AAAI '11*, pages 1770–1771, 2011.

[13] D. M. Cook, B. Waugh, M. Abdipanah, O. Hashemi, and S. Abdul Rahman. Twitter Deception and Influence: Issues of Identity, Slacktivism, and Puppetry. *Journal of Information Warfare*, 13(1):58–71, 2014.

[14] J. Down and S. Duke. Sms polling. a methodological review. In *ASC*, pages 277–286, 2003.

[15] C. Fink, N. Bos, A. Perrone, E. Liu, and J. Kopecky. Twitter, Public Opinion, and the 2011 Nigerian Presidential Election. In *SocialCom '13*, pages 311–320, 2013.

[16] L. Fumagalli and E. Sala. The total survey error paradigm and pre-election polls: The case of the 2006 Italian general elections. Technical report, Iser Working paper Series (No. 2011-29), 2011.

[17] M. Gaurav, A. Srivastava, A. Kumar, and S. Miller. Leveraging candidate popularity on Twitter to predict election outcome. In *SNA-KDD Workshop*, 2013.

[18] D. Gayo-Avello. Don't turn social media into another 'Literary Digest' poll. *Communications of the ACM*, 54(10):121–128, 2011.

[19] D. Gayo-Avello. A meta-analysis of state-of-the-art electoral prediction from Twitter data. *Social Science Computer Review*, 31(6):649–679, 2013.

[20] D. Gayo-Avello, P. Metaxas, and E. Mustafaraj. Limits of electoral predictions using social media data. In *ICWSM '11*, pages 490–493, 2011.

[21] Y. He and D. Zhou. Self-training from labeled features for sentiment analysis. *Information Processing & Management*, 47(4):606–616, 2011.

[22] D. S. Hillygus. The evolution of election polling in the United States. *Public opinion quarterly*, 75(5):962–981, 2011.

[23] M. J. Jensen and N. Anstead. Psephological investigations: Tweets, votes, and unknown unknowns in the republican nomination process. *Policy & Internet*, 5(2):161–182, 2013.

[24] A. Jungherr, P. Jürgens, and H. Schoen. Why the pirate party won the German election of 2009 or the trouble with predictions: A response to … *Social Science Computer Review*, 30(2):229–234, 2012.

[25] M. S. Lewis-Beck. Election forecasting: principles and practice. *The British Journal of Politics & International Relations*, 7(2):145–164, 2005.

[26] A. Makazhanov, D. Rafiei, and M. Waqar. Predicting political preference of Twitter users. *Social Network Analysis and Mining*, 4(1):1–15, 2014.

[27] Y. Mejova, P. Srinivasan, and B. Boynton. GOP primary season on Twitter: popular political sentiment in social media. In *WSDM '13*, pages 517–526, 2013.

[28] P. T. Metaxas, E. Mustafaraj, and D. Gayo-Avello. How (not) to predict elections. In *SocialCom*, pages 165–171. IEEE, 2011.

[29] M. Naaman, J. Boase, and C.-H. Lai. Is it really about me?: Message content in social awareness streams. In *CSCW '10*, pages 189–192, 2010.

[30] D. Nguyen, R. Gravel, D. Trieschnigg, and T. Meder. "How Old Do You Think I Am?"; A Study of Language and Age in Twitter. In *ICWSM '13*, pages 439–448, 2013.

[31] F. Nooralahzadeh, V. Arunachalam, and C. Chiru. 2012 Presidential Elections on Twitter–An Analysis of How the US and French Election were Reflected in Tweets. In *CSCS '13*, pages 240–246, 2013.

[32] B. Pang, L. Lee, and S. Vaithyanathan. Thumbs up?: Sentiment classification using machine learning techniques. In *EMNLP '02*, pages 79–86, 2002.

[33] E. T. K. Sang and J. Bos. Predicting the 2011 Dutch Senate Election Results with Twitter. In *Workshop on Semantic Analysis in Social Media*, pages 53–60, 2012.

[34] M. Taboada, J. Brooke, M. Tofiloski, K. Voll, and M. Stede. Lexicon-based methods for sentiment analysis. *Computational linguistics*, 37(2):267–307, 2011.

[35] A. Tumasjan, T. O. Sprenger, P. G. Sandner, and I. M. Welpe. Predicting Elections with Twitter: What 140 Characters Reveal about Political Sentiment. In *ICWSM '10*, pages 178–185, 2010.

[36] B. Waugh, M. Abdipanah, O. Hashemi, S. A. Rahman, and D. M. Cook. The Influence and Deception of Twitter: the authenticity of the narrative and slacktivism in the Australian electoral process. In *14th Australian Information Warfare Conference*, pages 28–38, 2013.

[37] F. M. F. Wong, C. W. Tan, S. Sen, and M. Chiang. Quantifying Political Leaning from Tweets and Retweets. In *ICWSM '13*, pages 640–649, 2013.

Language, Twitter and Academic Conferences

Ruth García[1]   Diego Gómez[2]   Denis Parra[2]
Christoph Trattner[3]   Andreas Kaltenbrunner[1]   Eduardo Graells-Garrido[4]

[1]Eurecat. Barcelona, Spain
[2]Pontificia Universidad Católica de Chile. Santiago, Chile
[3]NTNU. Trondheim, Norway
[4]Telefónica I+D. Santiago, Chile

ABSTRACT

Using Twitter during academic conferences is a way of engaging and connecting an audience inherently multicultural by the nature of scientific collaboration. English is expected to be the *lingua franca* bridging the communication and integration between native speakers of different mother tongues. However, little research has been done to support this assumption. In this paper we analyzed how integrated language communities are by analyzing the scholars' tweets used in 26 Computer Science conferences over a time span of five years. We found that although English is the most popular language used to tweet during conferences, a significant proportion of people also tweet in other languages. In addition, people who tweet solely in English interact mostly within the same group (English monolinguals), while people who speak other languages interact more with different *lingua groups*. Finally, we also found higher interaction between people tweeting in different languages.These results suggest a relation between the number of languages a user speaks and their interaction dynamics in online communities.

Categories and Subject Descriptors

J.4 [**Social and Behavioral Sciences**]: Sociology

Keywords

Twitter; culture; language, academic conferences

1. INTRODUCTION

In the past few years, Twitter has been used as a conference backchannel platform in academic events targeting the expansion of the community's communication and participation [1, 10]. Attendees using Twitter are generally involved in note taking, sharing resources and reporting individual real-time reactions to events, covering both conference presentations and conference social activities. This supports scholars' activities such as disseminating their work and engaging general public and newcomer scientists into the research communities [8]. It is a common practice in research conferences to use hashtags in the tweets to identify that particular event (e.g. #hypertext2015).

HT '15, September 1–4, 2015, Guzelyurt, Northern Cyprus.
©2015 ACM. ISBN 978-1-4503-3395-5/15/09$15.00
DOI: http://dx.doi.org/10.1145/2700171.2791059.

International academic conferences have a diverse community, with different cultural backgrounds and languages. Thus, it is interesting to analyze how language affects the generation of content and interaction among attendees. Such study would allow to observe how integrated a research community is and will shed light for future research.

This can be of special interest to conference organizers not only to evaluate communication but also to have an overview of their audiences. Despite the research published in the past [6, 7, 13, 12] on academic conferences, little has been done on language communities and the communication established among them. To bridge this gap, we explore the language of 7M tweets posted by 18K users during 26 Computer Science conferences over five years (one week before and after for each conference).

We group users by the language(s) they use to tweet in order to explore how different language communities interact. Although English is expected to be the lingua franca of many international events, we wonder to what extent people use other languages on Twitter during academic conferences.

Research Questions. Overall, our study was driven by the following research questions:

- **RQ1. Conference attendees' languages**: To what extent do people tweet in other languages beyond English in conferences?
- **RQ2. Interactions between lingua groups**: How do lingua groups interact with each other?
- **RQ3. Effect of language**: Is there an effect of language or lingua group over online user interaction?

Main results. We find that most people tweet only in English (61%) in conferences but most of the tweets are posted by multilingual users and their participation varies significantly across conferences. Additionally, we observe that *English monolinguals* receive most of the attention and interact more within their lingua group while the opposite is observed for most of the members from other language communities.

Finally, we show that people who do not interact with other attendees are mostly monolinguals, while people who interact with others tweet in different languages (bilingual or trilingual).

2. DATASET

We selected a representative set of conferences in Computer and Information Science from the CORE Conference Ranking list[1]; 26 conferences active in Twitter every year between 2009 and 2013. Furthermore, we manually checked that the selected conferences did not overlap with other events. To retrieve the tweets from these events in previous years, we used the Topsy API and crawled

---

[1]http://www.core.edu.au/index.php/conference-rankings

Table 1: Percentage of monolinguals, bilinguals and multilinguals tweeting in each conference between 2009-2013 (col 2-4). Diversity percentage for interactions (reciprocated or not) (col 5-8) for tweets (TW) and retweets (RT).

| Conference | Lingua groups | | | Diversity percentage | | | |
| | 1-ling | 2-ling | ≥ 3-ling | General | | Reciprocated | |
				TW	RT	TW	RT
AAAI	81%	8%	11%	34%	29%	16%	20%
ACMMM	52%	38%	11%	53%	53%	48%	41%
CHI	76%	17%	7%	49%	48%	40%	30%
CIKM	66%	24%	10%	54%	54%	44%	40%
ECIR	58%	27%	15%	55%	57%	43%	31%
ECIS	57%	31%	12%	46%	44%	24%	0%
HT	64%	26%	10%	52%	53%	37%	29%
ICIS	67%	26%	7%	44%	41%	19%	16%
ICML	75%	17%	8%	52%	55%	20%	21%
ICMT	51%	30%	19%	70%	62%	31%	20%
ICSE	58%	32%	10%	47%	46%	40%	47%
ISMAR	64%	28%	8%	39%	37%	19%	21%
IUI	62%	21%	17%	59%	58%	45%	44%
KDD	73%	18%	9%	53%	50%	38%	37%
MobileHCI	66%	23%	11%	50%	47%	48%	39%
NIPS	74%	19%	7%	46%	48%	25%	20%
SIGGRAPH	77%	16%	7%	38%	32%	24%	19%
SIGIR	68%	21%	11%	56%	58%	36%	39%
SIGMOD	72%	23%	5%	58%	53%	19%	12%
SLE	59%	32%	9%	58%	58%	40%	40%
UBICOMP	71%	21%	8%	59%	57%	55%	44%
UIST	71%	24%	5%	60%	58%	35%	32%
VLDB	67%	26%	7%	56%	53%	29%	21%
WSDM	65%	22%	13%	61%	60%	48%	39%
WWW	52%	32%	16%	52%	51%	43%	40%
XP	58%	35%	7%	53%	52%	51%	54%

tweets containing the corresponding official hashtag (e.g., #chi12, #www2009) within a two-week time window around the dates each conference took place (from seven days before and until seven days after the conference ended). We found that these tweets were posted by 22,021 participants in total. We acknowledge that these participants also interact with others without the conference hashtag and because of this we also crawled their timeline tweets during the same period. In total, we obtained *6,993,693* tweets.

Language Identification. To identify the language of the tweets, we removed all URLs, mentions and hashtags. Then we set a minimum threshold of *4* remaining words in the tweets to identify their language. The language detection task was performed with a professional language tool provided by Yahoo! Labs that is able to identify over 40+ languages as in [9]. Following this process we were left with *6,184,775* tweets (88% from initial sample) with an identified language (see Table 5 in the Appendix). The tweets without a language are generally those containing symbols or links only. Finally, we proceeded to model each user by the three most frequent languages they used to tweet (setting a minimum threshold of *5* tweets per language). Consequently, we found *266* lingua groups with *18,347* users using at least three different languages in their tweets[2].

3. RESULTS

RQ1. To what extent do people tweet in other languages beyond English across conferences?

As expected, we found that the majority of tweets are written in English (76%). Nevertheless, due to the multicultural nature of conferences, there is a non-negligible 24% of tweets in languages different than English (en), such as French (fr), Spanish (es), German

---

[2]"The venue of the conference (city, country) might have had an impact on the languages used, but we leave that detailed analysis for future work.

Table 2: Statistics of top lingua groups (more than 90 users). We show the percentage of users belonging to each *lingua* (Users), the percentage of tweets (Tweets), the engagement (tweets/user), and the interquartile range of tweets per users (IQR).

Lingua	Users	Tweets	(tweets/user)	IQR
en	61.31%	31.56%	167.18	142.00
en-fr	6.46%	3.85%	193.88	164.75
en-es	3.79%	2.52%	216.14	191.00
de-en	2.18%	1.75%	260.68	249.25
en-nl	2.15%	1.58%	238.65	222.5
fr	2.00%	0.27%	43.61	43.00
en-ja	1.92%	1.16%	196.3	166.00
en-es-pt	1.62%	4.05%	809.84	611.50
en-pt	1.44%	0.37%	83.52	63.75
en-it	1.36%	1.68%	402.87	193.50
nl	1.36%	0.16%	37.46	31.00
ja	1.09%	0.16%	47.94	42.75
en-es-fr	0.93%	9.23%	3,224.06	1,771.00
ca-en-es	0.79%	2.18%	891.29	799.50
en-ko	0.57%	0.53%	301.94	300.00
es	0.52%	0.06%	35.24	40.00
Others	10.52%	38.88%	1,200.51	864.00

Table 3: *Most popular linguas*: lingua groups ordered by the attention they receive across all conferences. The *out-link* column represents the percentage of interactions going to other lingua groups.

| General | | | | | |
| Mentions (148,184) | | | Retweets (91,523) | | |
Ling.	Att.	out-links	Ling.	Att.	out-links
en	67%	37%	en	66%	37%
en-fr	7%	56%	en-fr	7%	54%
de-en	3%	74%	de-en	3%	78%
en-es	3%	79%	en-es	3%	80%
en-ja	2%	35%	en-ja	2%	42%
Reciprocated					
Mentions (25,956)			Retweets (6,496)		
Ling.	Att.	out-links	Ling.	Att.	out-links
en	57%	48%	en	51%	52%
en-fr	8%	52%	en-fr	8%	44%
de-en	4%	72%	en-es	5%	61%
en-es	4%	71%	de-en	4%	74%
en-nl	3%	71%	en-nl	3%	70%

(de) and Japanese (jp). Furthermore, we found in our dataset that many people post tweets in more than a single language.

We quantify this observation in Table 1 that shows the percentage of users who tweet in a single language (1-lingua), in two languages (2-lingua) or three or more (≥ 3-lingua) in each conference. We observe that the percentage of people who tweet in two or more languages goes from close to 20% (AAAI, SIGGRAPH) up to around 50% (ACMMM, ICMT, WWW) showing important differences among conferences in the distribution of users who tweet in one or more languages. Based on these results, rather than analyzing languages as isolated groups, we studied the lingua groups as communities of people who speak either one or more languages. Table 2 describes the top language communities by number of users. The table shows that the majority of users are classified as *English monolinguals* (61%) but interestingly only produce (29%) of all tweets with a moderate engagement (only 179.5 tweets per user). In contrast, we see that users of multilingual groups are the most engaged (3609.9 tweets/user for en-es-fr, 1016.7 for ca-en-es, and 944.93 for en-es-pt).

These results lead us to further analyze specific lingua groups to unveil the interaction between language communities and their online behaviour.

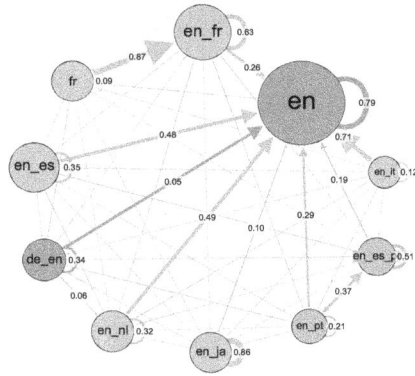

(a) Mentions between lingua groups. An edge from lingua x pointing to lingua y shows proportions of mentions that people in lingua x directed to people in lingua y. For readability, we only show probabilities ≥ 0.05.

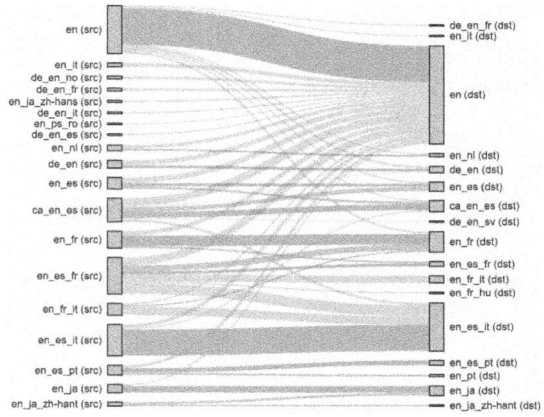

(b) Retweet interactions between top 50 most active lingua groups.

Figure 1: *(a)* Nodes representing the top 10 lingua groups based on mentions. *(b)* Interactions between lingua groups based on source language (src) retweeting posts in a target language (dst).

RQ2. How do lingua groups interact with each other?

To answer this question, we first define two types of interactions: (1) general interactions and (2) reciprocated interactions. We refer to *general interactions* to all (re)tweets containing mentions in the original text of the tweet, while *reciprocated interactions* correspond to the (re)tweets that were reciprocated by the users mentioned in the text.

Secondly, we measure diversity using the Gini-Simpson index, as in [3, 5] also called *diversity index*. This index ranges from 0 to 1 and it measures the probability that two lingua groups taken at random from a set of interactions are different. Participants of a conference with diversity index close to 0 will have the tendency to interact with people of the same lingua group. Conversely, values close to 1 show a uniform distribution of interactions with other lingua groups. We define diversity D of a lingua group as:

$$D(c, i) = 1 - \sum_{j \in S} \left(\frac{I_{i,j}^c}{N_i} \right)^2 \qquad (1)$$

with $N_i = \sum_{k \in S} I_{i,k}^c$ and where $I_{i,j}^c$ is the total number of interactions between people of lingua i and j. N_i is the total number of interactions of people of lingua i in conference c. To know the diversity of a conference, we average $D(c, i)$ over all the linguas in conference c.

We see in Table 1 the diversity percentage for each conference. We find some interesting patterns showing that a lower percentage of monolinguals is linked to higher diversity. For example, ICMT is the most diverse conference for the general type of interactions and the percentage of monolinguals is the lowest of all (51%). Conversely, AAAI shows high percentage of monolinguals (82%) and the lowest diversity for the general interactions. On the other hand, reciprocal interactions do not show to be related to the percentage of monolinguals. For example, UBICOMP presents a high percentage of monolinguals and the highest diversity for the reciprocal interactions.

Furthermore, we look at the attention *received* by members of each lingua by calculating the number of mentions and retweets received from different users. Table 3 shows the top 5 most popular lingua groups: English monolinguals are the most mentioned and retweeted in the general and reciprocated interactions. Albeit the fact that English monolinguals do not produce most of the tweets, they still receive most of the attention. This is mostly explained by the column *out-links*, which shows the percentage of mentions and retweets about *different* lingua group. For example, we see that only

37% of the mentions and retweets generated by English monolinguals refer to other groups. Interestingly, Japanese bilinguals also prefer to interact mostly within their group. Conversely, groups like *en-fr, de-en, en-es* interact more with users of *different* lingua groups.

The unequal activity between lingua groups is also seen in Figure 1, which considers only the top 10 lingua groups and shows (a) the mentions network (general type) and (b) the retweet network (general type) across lingua groups. Figure 1a shows that 79% of all mentions from the *en* group also belong to the same group. Moreover, 35% of mentions from the *en-es* lingua group refer to users from the same group, and 48% to the *en* group.

In Figure 1b, the Sankey plot represents the network of retweets. Again, here we see that for most of the cases the English group retweets members from the same group. At the same time, the English group receives most of the attention from other language communities. Interestingly, in similar proportion, lingua groups en-es-it, en-fr, en-es-pt and en-ja show a similar pattern, preferably retweeting users on their same lingua groups.

RQ3. Is there any effect of language or lingua group over online user interaction?

We addressed this question by studying how the number of languages a Twitter user speaks affects her online behavior. As already explained, if a user has posted tweets in only one language we consider her in the 1-lingua group (monolingual), while another user tweeting in two languages will be in the 2-lingua group, and so on. We found two results that show at general and at individual level the effect of the amount of languages on user interaction. At the general level, we found that among the users who posted tweets but who had not interacted with other people (by mentioning them), the percentage on monolinguals is considerably larger (80.6%) than multilinguals. A different picture is seen among users who interacted at least once during the conference (by mentioning someone in a tweet), since only 62.9% of those users are monolinguals and the rest are multilinguals. We conducted a chi-square test of proportions comparing the distribution of monolinguals, bilinguals and trilinguals between people who interacted (using mention or retweet) and people who did not. We found a statistically significant difference with $\chi^2 = 416.6$, $df = 2$, $p < .001$. This relation can be better observed in Figure 2, where the group who interacted (right-side plot) had a more balanced distribution and hence a higher entropy (a measure of diversity [11]) of $H(s) = 0.89$ compared to a smaller diversity on lingua groups among people who did not interact with

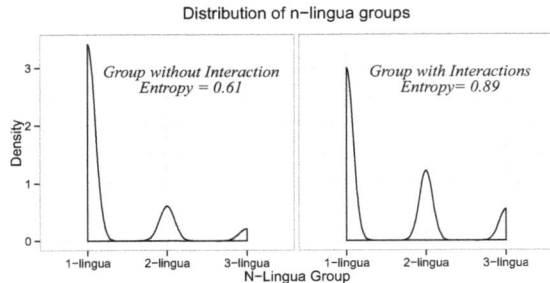

Figure 2: Distribution of users per n-lingua groups: users who interacted (right) and did not interacted (left) with others.

an entropy $H(s) = 0.61$. Moreover, at the individual level we found that the more the languages a user speaks, the larger the likelihood to interact with others. Table 4 shows the results of a logistic regression where the dependent variable measures whether the user *interacted* with other people or not. The factors in the regression are the *year* of the conference and the number of languages the user has used to tweet (*n_languages*). We observe that the number of languages has a significant β coefficient of 0.666 ($p < .001$), which can be interpreted by saying that, keeping all the other factors fixed, for each additional language the user speaks the odds ratio of interacting in the network increases by 95% (since $e^{0.666} = 1.95$).

4. RELATED WORK

The role of Twitter in academic conferences was also studied by Letierce *et al.* [6, 7]. They showed that Twitter is frequently used to spread information using the official conference hashtags. Wen *et al.* [13, 12] found that newcomer students receive little attention from senior members of the research community and identified factors that contribute to the continuing participation of users to the online Twitter conference activity. We have continued this line of research by exploring the influence of language during conferences. The role of language in Twitter has also been studied. Hong *et al.* [4] studied differences in usage patterns between language communities in Twitter, while Kim et al. [5] performed a sociolinguistic study on the role of mono- and bilinguals in Twitter across multilingual societies such as Qatar, Quebec and Switzerland. Inspired by them, we adopted similar methods to build language communities but we targeted different lingua groups interacting at conferences.

A broader but certainly related topic of study is the impact of *culture* in online communication. Garcia *et al.* [2] found that language and cultural dimensions are discriminative features influencing international active conversation and attention in Twitter. We find that focusing on language(s) we capture the multicultural nature of most researchers that attend international conferences.

5. CONCLUSIONS & FUTURE WORK

In this paper we show that most of the English tweets posted in Computer and Information Science conferences come from lingua communities different than English monolinguals. We also observe that English monolinguals still prefer to interact more with themselves. The same happens for other important communities such as English-Japanese bilinguals, while this behavior is not commonly replicated in other communities, who tend to interact more equally with members of other linguas.

We also find that there is more language diversity among people who interact with others on Twitter during conferences, compared to people who do not. This result suggests an important implication, which is that although English is the standard for scientific communication, the diversity in language use is a catalyst for interactions in a community.

Table 4: Results of L.R. where the D.V. is whether user interacted on Twitter (mentions) and the I.V.s are conference *year* and number of languages spoken.

Variable	β coeff.	S.E.
year(=2009)	2.049***	(0.390)
year(=2010)	2.458***	(0.385)
year(=2011)	2.453***	(0.385)
year(=2012)	2.294***	(0.383)
year(=2013)	2.423***	(0.383)
n_languages	0.666***	(0.035)
Constant	-1.371***	(0.385)
Observations	26,281	
Note:	*p<0.1; **p<0.05; ***p<0.01	

There are still several questions to address in future work. For example, does the attention received by the English monolingual group depend on popular users and/or venues? Furthermore, we will validate the result of RQ3 using a "test set" of tweets in the future.

Acknowledgments: This work was carried out during the tenure of an ERCIM "Alain Bensoussan" fellowship program by C.T.

6. REFERENCES

[1] M. Ebner. Introducing live microblogging: How single presentations can be enhanced by the mass. *Journal of research in innovative teaching*, 2009.

[2] R. García-Gavilanes, Y. Mejova, and D. Quercia. Twitter Ain'T Without Frontiers: Economic, Social, and Cultural Boundaries in International Communication. In *Proc. CSCW'14*, 2014.

[3] R. Guimera and L. A. N. Amaral. Functional cartography of complex metabolic networks. *Nature*, (7028), feb 2005.

[4] L. Hong, G. Convertino, and E. H. Chi. Language matters in twitter: A large scale study. In *Proc. ICWSM'11*, 2011.

[5] S. Kim, I. Weber, L. Wei, and A. Oh. Sociolinguistic analysis of twitter in multilingual societies. In *Proc. HT'14*, 2014.

[6] J. Letierce, A. Passant, J. Breslin, and S. Decker. Understanding how twitter is used to widely spread scientific messages. In *Proc. WebSci'10*, 2010.

[7] J. Letierce, A. Passant, J. G. Breslin, and S. Decker. Using twitter during an academic conference: The #iswc2009 use-case. In *Proc. ICWSM'10*, 2010.

[8] E. Mitchell and S. B. Watstein. The places where students and scholars work, collaborate, share and plan: endless possibilities for us! *Reference services review*, 35(4), 2007.

[9] B. Poblete, R. García-Gavilanes, M. Mendoza, and A. Jaimes. Do All Birds Tweet the Same? Characterizing Twitter Around the World. In *Proc. CIKM'11*, 2011.

[10] C. Ross, M. Terras, C. Warwick, and A. Welsh. Enabled backchannel: conference twitter use by digital humanists. *Journal of Documentation*, 67(2), 2011.

[11] C. E. Shannon. A mathematical theory of communication. *ACM SIGMOBILE Mobile Computing and Communications Review*, 5(1):3–55, 2001.

[12] X. Wen, Y. Lin, C. Trattner, and D. Parra. Twitter in academic conferences: Usage, networking and participation over time. In *Proc. HT'14*, 2014.

[13] X. Wen, D. Parra, and C. Trattner. How groups of people interact with each other on twitter during academic conferences. In *Proc. CSCW'14*, 2014.

APPENDIX

The following tables show detailed data used in our analyses.

Table 5:

	en	es	fr	pt	ja	ar	nl	ko	it	de	total tweets	number of users
AAAI	93%	1%	1%	0%	0%	0%	1%	0%	0%	0%	39,988	144
ACMMM	70%	4%	3%	1%	4%	0%	2%	1%	3%	4%	36,550	330
CHI	84%	3%	2%	1%	2%	0%	1%	1%	1%	1%	1,352,685	3,836
CIKM	80%	4%	1%	0%	2%	0%	1%	1%	0%	6%	239,461	1,064
ECIR	76%	8%	0%	1%	1%	0%	1%	0%	1%	1%	41,747	294
ECIS	75%	9%	1%	0%	0%	0%	7%	0%	0%	4%	27,466	173
HT	59%	3%	0%	3%	0%	0%	24%	0%	0%	2%	12,6873	631
ICIS	71%	0%	1%	0%	5%	11%	2%	0%	4%	2%	29,654	199
ICML	90%	3%	1%	0%	1%	0%	0%	1%	0%	1%	50,081	275
ICMT	92%	5%	1%	0%	0%	0%	0%	0%	1%	0%	27,445	71
ICSE	78%	6%	6%	3%	2%	0%	1%	0%	1%	1%	227,072	738
ISMAR	80%	1%	1%	0%	7%	0%	2%	3%	0%	2%	61,103	213
IUI	81%	4%	1%	0%	0%	0%	7%	1%	0%	4%	36,028	173
KDD	88%	3%	1%	1%	1%	1%	1%	0%	1%	0%	157,607	703
MobileHCI	76%	5%	1%	0%	0%	0%	2%	2%	1%	3%	25,572	204
NIPS	81%	2%	5%	0%	5%	0%	0%	2%	0%	1%	161,394	810
SIGGRAPH	84%	6%	2%	1%	1%	1%	0%	0%	1%	0%	1,096,484	3,303
SIGIR	86%	2%	0%	1%	1%	2%	0%	1%	0%	1%	138,094	702
SIGMOD	79%	1%	1%	2%	4%	1%	0%	5%	0%	1%	38,759	280
SLE	73%	2%	5%	1%	1%	0%	14%	0%	0%	2%	39,885	172
UBICOMP	79%	4%	1%	0%	6%	0%	1%	2%	1%	4%	75,100	349
UIST	77%	1%	1%	0%	17%	0%	0%	0%	0%	0%	51,563	362
VLDB	86%	2%	0%	0%	3%	1%	0%	0%	2%	1%	47,701	315
WSDM	85%	4%	1%	0%	1%	0%	0%	0%	1%	1%	53,951	368
WWW	64%	5%	18%	6%	0%	0%	1%	0%	1%	1%	1,785,006	5,081
XP	79%	9%	1%	2%	0%	0%	1%	0%	1%	3%	231,959	1,231

Table 5: The number of tweets per conference and the percentage of tweets in each language.

Table 6:

		AAAI	ACMMM	CHI	CIKM	ECIR	ECIS	HT	ICIS	ICML	ICMT	ICSE	ISMAR	IUI	KDD	MobileHCI	NIPS	SIGGRAPH	SIGIR	SIGMOD	SLE	UBICOMP	UIST	VLDB	WSDM	WWW	XP
2009	tweets	0	22	38932	122	40	2666	2559	87	12	3330	306	11746	176	619	543	1279	7932	27176	2	1719	241	1359	679	0	77243	2111
	retweets	0	1	459	14	11	30	169	8	0	3	14	327	2	355	32	44	213	745	1	151	46	107	139	1	770	263
	mentions	0	2	3932	74	34	64	719	27	4	19	76	881	41	498	81	293	954	2040	3	549	192	540	412	16	3753	1701
	urls	0	4	24102	33	26	2132	1111	35	1	1275	54	8003	21	330	100	724	2329	16639	0	1109	105	637	241	0	42538	364
2010	tweets	324	6822	152637	2753	4552	91	13837	700	91	343	15641	2054	4271	6586	747	18196	7916	3360	2448	4931	4912	2306	1120	5450	196200	25610
	retweets	93	935	9613	567	540	9	578	53	8	128	441	100	746	255	256	1056	239	506	415	371	983	358	201	543	10203	3142
	mentions	223	1798	35212	1119	1379	51	1036	139	18	289	1016	259	1590	582	489	1877	633	1321	896	693	1929	994	564	1532	22306	9670
	urls	72	3117	96384	826	3540	30	11039	276	8	113	11152	1040	3172	2330	363	9276	2505	961	910	2442	2658	1325	597	3157	124629	6737
2011	tweets	14514	2449	204498	9091	5440	1297	15815	2634	3628	4364	19659	7013	4436	16312	3263	11182	46757	4577	3298	847	10205	2586	5447	5668	117833	44334
	retweets	243	488	13411	2401	924	109	917	53	557	564	2403	223	911	1423	271	1376	1782	1240	616	2	1162	724	744	1308	6478	6971
	mentions	533	982	33244	4845	187a0	280	2343	195	1154	1261	4683	438	1709	2942	967	2690	3674	2822	1116	41	2856	1773	1960	2068	12703	22277
	urls	3744	1155	103827	4459	2190	599	4335	645	1291	962	8217	5856	1718	8702	1106	6408	20819	1879	1615	181	5604	950	2177	3087	71491	13372
2012	tweets	1182	5229	102553	14859	4607	4921	13425	1953	5836	781	18219	7639	4084	11632	5199	15283	178229	17235	7987	4459	3738	8186	6729	11780	351146	18580
	retweets	120	941	6580	2628	1085	106	1855	125	1183	149	2881	530	570	1173	750	1552	5714	2345	967	689	458	611	947	3569	19521	3604
	mentions	350	1884	18383	5342	2098	209	3647	228	2801	410	5922	1070	1134	1727	1538	3668	12588	4477	2092	1739	1060	1431	1916	3569	46939	11195
	urls	530	2511	46343	6953	2437	2880	5567	945	2529	205	7280	6700	1693	7904	2544	8755	102146	7400	3282	1691	1880	6125	3303	5338	153339	5875
2013	tweets	3297	5385	183168	96779	5679	3712	13961	9197	14584	4376	57411	2560	3681	44026	2512	39327	306407	18409	5580	5048	20140	9867	9501	4939	144870	22022
	retweets	203	1790	8436	5613	1078	206	994	527	1489	337	3566	268	732	3851	233	3409	10726	2798	754	730	913	1146	738	1265	9339	2972
	mentions	499	3648	23925	13310	2707	364	2953	871	3791	1135	7714	629	1863	7457	713	8125	23287	6126	1533	1935	2176	2234	1666	2416	21264	9962
	urls	1027	2972	84575	44217	3166	2504	6030	5807	914	22559	1359	1739	22637	1391	20743	178613	8990	2461	1557	14087	6012	5585	2430	66205	7484	

Table 6: Metrics of tweets, retweets, mentions and tweets with URLs per conference and year.

Table 7:

		AAAI	ACMMM	CHI	CIKM	ECIR	ECIS	HT	ICIS	ICML	ICMT	ICSE	ISMAR	IUI	KDD	MobileHCI	NIPS	SIGGRAPH	SIGIR	SIGMOD	SLE	UBICOMP	UIST	VLDB	WSDM	WWW	XP
2009		en 4	en 335	en 8	en 5	en 8	en 43	en 10	en 1	en 3	en 3	en 66	en 2		en 14	en 10	en 8	en 66	en 97	en 1	en 32	en 21	en 41	en 21	en 1	en 313	en 36
		fr 2	it 35	de 2	es 1	de 4	it 10	de 1		ar 1	fr 1	es 12		de 4	de 2	it 1	de 15	es 12		de 8	ja 4	ja 6	fr 5	es		es 112	no 9
		nl 1	ps 25	ja 1	hu 1	es 3	pt 10	fi 1		de 1	hi 1	de 10		it 2	it 2	es 1	it 15	it 9		no 5	fr 2	de 3	it 3	fr		it 77	sv 6
		ro 1	de 22	no 1	it 1	fi	de 6	ko 1		et 1		nl 9		el	ps 2	it 2	ps 7	pt 8		pt 3	cs	es 1	ro 2	ps		de 58	es 4
2010	en	en 20	en 100	en 802	en 54	en 58	en 35	en 4	en 20	en 87	en 39	en 48	en 49	en 17	en 132	en 71	en 91	en 37	en 41	en 87	en 53	en 19	en 77	en 1140	en 470		
	es	it 4	it 30	fr 88	it 6	fr 9	de 2	de 13	de 3	de 1	es 6	de 14	ko 12	de 10	es 8	ca 4	fr 19	it 12	es 13	de 3	de 12	it 15	ja 14	it 3	es 17	es 263	no 143
	ca	it 2	es 14	it 83	fr 4	de 7	no 2	es 8	no 3		nl 3	es 12	es 8	fr 6	es 3	de 14	it 11	ca 7	fr 3	es 7	de 8	nl 5	es 2	it 7	fr 172	de 53	
	de	nl 2	nl 11	es 81	ca 3	fr 4			sv 2	no 7	ar 7	ca 2	fr	ja 16	ja 16	de 159	no 17	fr 10	it 9	fr 5	es 10	fr 4					
2011	en	en 64	en 75	en 1280	en 157	en 98	en 44	en 141	en 30	en 52	en 30	en 270	en 44	en 62	en 189	en 77	en 185	en 293	en 88	en 63	fr 6	en 80	en 69	en 103	en 86	en 630	en 538
	it	es 16	fr 201	es 25	es 22	de 10	nl 93	de 6	es 8	es 10	es 12	de 16	es 30	sv 14	es 24	fr 61	es 17	el 10	en 4	ja 21	es 9	ja 15	es 17	es 165	es 189		
	tr	it 9	es 9	es 180	de 17	de 12	nl 8	es 39	no 6	it 6	fr 10	it 54	de 8	es 8	it 28	de 11	fr 23	it 55	it 16	de 6	de 4	de 15	fr 8	de 14	de 10	it 147	it 104
	es	it 8	ja 7	ps 132	ca 12	no 8	it 5	no 33	it 3	ro 5	da 5	ro 35	es 7	nl 7	fr 19	it 8	de 17	no 38	ja 8	es 4	ca 3	fr	fa 4	es 4	zh-hans 7	de 111	no 85
2012	en	en 37	en 101	en 1218	en 207	en 96	en 58	en 145	en 46	en 109	en 13	en 277	en 46	en 41	en 82	en 230	en 1216	en 283	en 119	en 71	en 90	en 86	en 117	en 190	en 2616	en 216	
	es	en 7	ja 23	es 151	es 37	es 25	es 22	es 29	de 8	de 11	es 4	es 47	ja 30	de 9	zh-hans 19	es 12	es 27	es 243	es 36	it 18	nl 34	it 11	ja 11	es 15	es 23	fr 1625	no 41
	pt	it 3	it 16	it 113	de 22	it 14	ca 11	de 23	nl 6	fr 8	fr 3	pt 44	zh-hans 6	it 7	zh-hant 9	it 11	it 18	fr 182	de 23	de 11	it 11	de	de 7	tr 11	de 17	it 821	sv 40
	ro	de 11	de 107	fr 22	de 9	it 11	de 7	ja 11	de 5	ru 7		fr 42	fr	ca 6	fr 9	ja 10	ja 16	de 159	no 17	fr 10	it 9	fr	es	es 5	fr	ca 627	es 39
2013	en	en 48	en 159	en 1605	en 799	en 124	en 89	nl 278	en 135	en 149	en 25	en 425	en 55	en 71	en 472	en 70	en 518	en 2281	en 378	en 111	en 66	en 158	en 222	en 115	en 96	en 1158	en 284
	de	de 6	fr 29	es 232	it 110	bg 18	de 19	no 61	nl 19	ja 14	fr 6	it 67	no 6	de 9	it 52	es 11	fr 54	it 372	es 39	ro 11	de 11	es 15	it 16	es 16	it 18	pt 368	it 59
	it	it 6	ca 19	it 190	fr 109	uk 18	fr 18	fr 60	it 16	fr 13	it 5	de 55	ja 4	it 7	de 38	ca 5	es 50	de 247	no 26	es 8	nl 10	nl 14	es 15	no 11	de 8	fr 237	sv 33
	ps	de 6	de 15	de 162	de 107	sr 17	sv 17	es 28	sv 15	fr 13																	

Table 7: Top three languages at every conference each year based on the number of users tweeting in each language.

163

First Women, Second Sex: Gender Bias in Wikipedia

Eduardo Graells-Garrido[*,1,2]   Mounia Lalmas[3]   Filippo Menczer[4,5]

| [1]Web Research Group Universitat Pompeu Fabra Barcelona, Spain | [2]Telefónica I+D Santiago, Chile | [3]Yahoo Labs London, UK | [4]Yahoo Labs Sunnyvale, USA | [5]Indiana University Bloomington, USA |

ABSTRACT

Contributing to the writing of history has never been as easy as it is today. Anyone with access to the Web is able to play a part on Wikipedia, an open and free encyclopedia, and arguably one of the primary sources of knowledge on the Web. In this paper, we study *gender bias* in Wikipedia in terms of how women and men are characterized in their biographies. To do so, we analyze biographical content in three aspects: meta-data, language, and network structure. Our results show that, indeed, there are differences in characterization and structure. Some of these differences are reflected from the off-line world documented by Wikipedia, but other differences can be attributed to gender bias in Wikipedia content. We contextualize these differences in social theory and discuss their implications for Wikipedia policy.

Categories and Subject Descriptors

H.3.4 [**Information Storage and Retrieval**]: Systems and Software—*Information networks*

Keywords

Wikipedia; Gender; Gender Bias; Computational Linguistics.

1. INTRODUCTION

Today's Web creates opportunities for global and democratic media, where everyone has a voice. One of the most visible examples is Wikipedia, an open encyclopedia where anyone can contribute content. In contrast to traditional encyclopedias, where a staff of experts in specific areas takes care of writing, editing and validating content, in Wikipedia these tasks are performed by a community of volunteers. Whether or not this *open source* approach provides reliable and accurate content [23, 47], Wikipedia has gained unprecedented reach. An extensive body of research covers Wikipedia [39], with topics like participation, structured data, and analysis of historical figures, among others.

In her book *The Second Sex*, Simone de Beauvoir widely discusses different aspects of women oppression and their historical

---

*Corresponding author: eduardo.graells@telefonica.com.

HT '15, September 1–4, 2015, Guzelyurt, Northern Cyprus.
Copyright is held by the owner/author(s). Publication rights licensed to ACM.
ACM 978-1-4503-3395-5/15/09 ...$15.00.
DOI: http://dx.doi.org/10.1145/2700171.2791036.

significance. She wrote in 1949 (in French, originally): "*it is not women's inferiority that has determined their historical insignificance: it is their historical insignificance that has doomed them to inferiority*" [16]. More than 60 years later, almost anyone with access to the Web can contribute to the writing of history, thanks to Wikipedia. In theory, by following its guidelines about verifiability, notability, and neutral point of view, Wikipedia should be an unbiased source of knowledge. In practice, the community of Wikipedians is not diverse in terms of gender, as women represent only 16% of editors [25]. This disparity has been called the *gender gap* in Wikipedia, and has been studied from several perspectives to understand why more women do not join Wikipedia, and what can be done about it. It is a problem because reportedly women are not being treated as equals to men in the community [30], and potentially, in content. For instance, Filipacchi [18] described a controversy where women novelists started to be excluded from the category *"American Novelists"* to be included in the specific category *"American Women Novelists."*

Instead of focusing on the participatory *gender gap*, we focus on how women are characterized in Wikipedia articles, to assess whether gender bias from the off-line world extends to Wikipedia content. The scale of Wikipedia, as well as its openness, allows us to perform a quantitative analysis of how women are characterized in Wikipedia in comparison to men. Encyclopedias characterize men and women in many ways, *e. g.*, in terms of their lives and the events in which they participated or were relevant. We concentrate on *biographies* because they are a good source to study gender bias, given that each article is about a specific person. In this paper, we understand gender bias as the *systematic asymmetry* [8] in the way that three dimensions of analysis favor one gender over the other: *meta-data*, *language*, and *network structure*. Then, the research questions that drive our work are:

> *Is there a gender bias in biographies of men and women in Wikipedia? If so, how to identify and quantify it? Can it be contextualized based on social theory?*

We present the following three major findings:

1. Differences in meta-data are coherent with results in previous work, where women biographies were found to contain more content related to marriage than men's.
2. Sex-related content is more frequent in women biographies than men's, while cognition-related content is more highlighted in men biographies than women's.
3. A strong bias in the linking patterns results in a network structure in which articles about men are disproportionately more central than articles about women.

These findings represent a quantification of gender bias in user generated content in Wikipedia. The main contributions of this paper are the aforementioned quantification of gender bias, a first contextualization of differences found in terms of social theory, and a discussion of the implications of our findings for policy design in Wikipedia. Furthermore, even though we focus on the English Wikipedia, our methods are generalizable to other languages.

2. BACKGROUND

Research on the community structure and evolution of Wikipedia has been prominent. In its first steps, the focus was on growth [2] and dynamics [45], without attention toward gender. Later, it was found that there is a gender gap, as Wikipedia has fewer contributions from women, and women stop contributing earlier than men [30]. Moreover, men and women communicate differently through the inner communication channels of Wikipedia [31]: they focus on different topics [30] and the level of content revision differs by gender but also by amount of activity [4]. In addition, Lam et al. [30] found that women are more *reverted* than men (*i.e.*, their contributions are discarded), and reportedly women contribute less because of aggressive behavior toward them [15, 52]. Efforts have been made to build a more welcoming community and to encourage participation [36, 14] with initiatives like *WikiWomen's Collaborative*.[1]

Content-wise, the study of biographies in Wikipedia enables the identification of cultural differences in content [42] and coverage [10], as well as the construction of social networks of historical (and current) figures [6]. Lam et al. [30] found that, in terms of interest of contributors, coverage of "female topics" (*i. e.*, topics of interest for women) was inferior to "male topics " when classifying topics as "male" or "female" according to the people who contributed to them. Reagle and Rhue [46] found that in characterization of women, in comparison to commercial encyclopedias like *Britannica*, Wikipedia has better coverage of notable profiles, although this coverage is quite low and is still biased toward men. Bamman and Smith [7] found that women biographies are more likely to include language related to marriage or divorce events. At large-scale, Hecht and Gergle [24] measured *self-focus bias* [24], which studies the relation of the language of a specific Wikipedia and its related cultures.

Addressing the gender gap from a content perspective may help to improve the quality and value of the content. Researchers have focused on predicting article quality in Wikipedia [3, 20]. However, focusing on quality without considering readers does not give the whole picture, as Wikipedia readers are not necessarily interested in the same topics as contributors [33] and might have a different concept of quality. Moreover, in our context, Flekova, Ferschke, and Gurevych [20] found that the quality of biographies is assessed differently depending on the gender of the portrayed person. Is it because the raters were biased? Or is it because biographies were written differently? Our hypothesis is that biographies are written differently, an idea inspired by seminal work by Lakoff [29] about how women are characterized by language.

Word frequency is commonly used to study differences in text. Word frequency follows Zipf's law [57, 49], an empirical distribution found in many languages [43]. An interesting property of Zipf distributions in language is that small sets of words that are semantically or categorically related also follow a Zipf distribution [43]. This property implies that, given two subsets of words that are related semantically or categorically, their frequency distributions can be compared. Thus, we compare frequency distributions according to gender for several semantic categories derived from the *Linguistic Inquiry and Word Count* (LIWC) dictionary. LIWC studies *"emotional, cognitive, structural, and process components present in individuals' verbal and written speech samples"* [40]. It

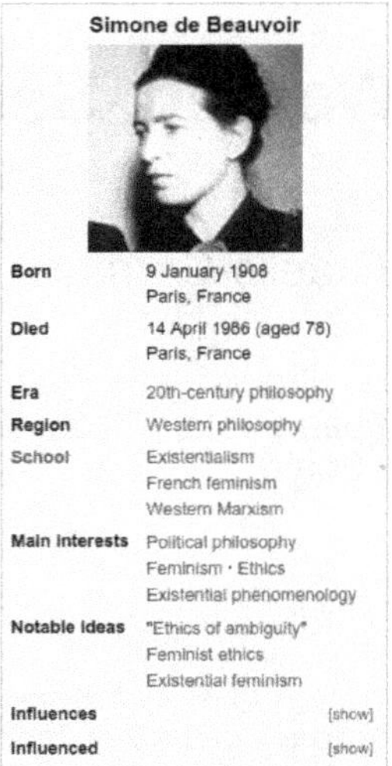

Figure 1: *Infobox* from the biography article of Simone de Beauvoir.

has been used to analyze interactions between Wikipedia contributors [26] and article content with respect to emotions [17]. In a context similar to ours, Schmader, Whitehead, and Wysocki [48] used LIWC to quantify differences in characterization of women and men in recommendation letters.

In our work, we quantify gender bias in Wikipedia's characterization of men and women through their biographies. To do so we approach three different dimensions of biographies, which we analyze in different sections on this paper: *meta-data*, provided by the structured version of Wikipedia, DBpedia [34]; *language*, considering how frequent are words and concepts [49]; and *network structure*. In terms of network structure, we build a biography network [6] in which we estimate PageRank, a measure of node centrality based on network connectivity [9, 21]. In similar contexts, PageRank has been used to provide an approximation of historical importance [6, 50] and to study the bias leading to the gender gap [50]. We measure bias in link formation by comparing the importance given by PageRank in the biography network with those of null models, *i. e.*, graphs that are unbiased by construction but that maintain certain properties of the source biography network.

3. DATA SOURCES

To study gender bias in Wikipedia, we consider three freely available data sources:

1. The DBpedia 2014 dataset [34].[2]
2. The Wikipedia English Dump of October 2014.[3]
3. Inferred gender for Wikipedia biographies by Bamman and Smith [7].[4]

In addition, we use the *Linguistic Inquiry and Word Count* dictionary of semantic categories to find if different genders have different characterizations according to those semantic categories.

DBpedia. DBpedia [34] is a structured version of Wikipedia that provides meta-data for articles, normalized article URIs (*Uniform Resource Identifiers*), normalized links between articles (taking care of redirections), and a categorization into a shallow ontology, which includes a *Person* category. To provide the structured meta-data,

---

[1] http://meta.wikimedia.org/wiki/WikiWomen's_Collaborative

[2] http://wiki.dbpedia.org/Downloads2014
[3] https://dumps.wikimedia.org/enwiki/20141008/
[4] http://www.ark.cs.cmu.edu/bio/

Table 1: Considered semantic categories from LIWC, and their two most frequent words found in biographies from each gender.

Category	Words (Men)	Words (Women)
Social Processes	team, son	daughter, received
– Family	son, father	daughter, family
– Friends	fellow, friend	fellow, partner
– Humans	people, man	female, women
Cognitive Processes	became, known	known, became
– Insight	became, known	known, became
– Causation	made, based	made, based
– Discrepancy	outstanding, wanted	outstanding, wanted
– Tentative	appeared, mainly	appeared, appearing
– Certainty	law, total	law, ever
– Inhibition	held, conservative	held, hold
– Inclusive	addition, open	addition, open
– Exclusive	except, whether	except, whether
Biological Processes	life, head	life, love
– Body	head, body	head, body
– Health	life, living	life, living
– Sexual	love, passion	love, sex
– Ingestion	water, food	food, water
Work Concerns	career, team	career, worked
Achievement Concerns	won, team	won, worked

Table 2: Number of biographies in the dataset for the *Person* class and its most common child classes (in terms of biographies with gender). *OutD* means Out Degree and *Len* means Length. In this and the following tables, we use this legend for *p*-values: ***: $p < 0.001$, **: $p < 0.01$, *: $p < 0.05$.

Ontology	With gender	% Women	OutD. t	Len. t
Person	893,380	15.53	20.77***	-2.65**
Athlete	187,828	8.94	10.64***	-2.83**
Artist	79,690	25.14	12.95***	-0.33
OfficeHolder	38,111	13.04	10.97***	3.77***
Politician	32,398	8.75	1.29	-4.02***
MilitaryPerson	22,769	1.67	4***	1.03
Scientist	15,853	8.79	4.91***	-0.01
SportsManager	11,255	0.62	0.79	-2.79**
Cleric	8,949	6.34	3.23**	0.02
Royalty	7,054	35.24	0.55	1.75
Coach	5,720	2.40	0.27	-2.65**
FictionalCharacter	4,023	26.08	3.03**	0.39
Noble	3,696	23.16	3.16**	2.05*
Criminal	1,976	12.45	1.08	-1.69
Judge	1,949	14.88	3.93***	2.97**

DBpedia processes content from the infoboxes in Wikipedia articles. Infoboxes are template-based specifications for certain kinds of articles. When DBpedia detects an infobox with a template that matches those of a person, it assigns the article to the *Person* class from the ontology, and to a specific subclass if applicable (*e. g.*, *Artist*). Thus, we consider an article to be a biography if it belongs to the *Person* class. For instance, Figure 1 displays the infobox of Simone de Beauvoir. The infobox contains specific meta-data attributes pertinent to a biography, such as date and place of birth, but it does not include gender (except in certain cases, see "Inferred Gender" next). DBpedia maps infobox properties to specific fields in a person's meta-data.

Wikipedia Biography Text. We consider two versions of the biographies: the overview and the full text. We analyze both in different contexts: in the overview we analyze the full vocabulary employed, while in the full text we analyze only the words pertaining to the LIWC dictionaries. The overview is described by Wikipedia as *"an introduction to the article and a summary of its most important aspects. It should be able to stand alone as a concise overview."* Since those aspects are subjective, the overview content is a good proxy for any potential biases expressed by Wikipedia contributors. At the same time we avoid potential noise included in the full biography text from elements like quotations and the filmography of a given actor/actress. In both cases (overview and full content), template markup is removed from analysis.

Inferred Gender. To obtain gender meta-data for biographies, we match article URIs with the dataset by Bamman and Smith [7], which contains inferred gender for biographies based on the number of grammatically gendered words (*i. e.*, *he*, *she*, *him*, *her*, etc.) present in the article text. Bamman and Smith [7] tested their method in a random set of 500 biographies, providing 100% precision and 97.6% recall. This method has also been used before by Reagle and Rhue [46] and DBpedia itself [34], making DBpedia to include gender meta-data in some cases. Note that the genders considered in these datasets (and thus, in this work) are only *male* and *female*.

Semantic Categories. The LIWC dictionary [40] includes, for each category (and its corresponding subcategories), a list of words and prefixes that match relevant words. We consider the categories (and their subcategories, if applicable): *Social Processes, Cognitive*

Processes, Biological Processes, Work Concerns, and *Achievement Concerns*. We believe these categories should be used in the same way when characterizing women and men. Other categories have been left out of analysis, such as *Positivity, Negativity, Relativity, Religion,* and *Death*, as they can be used in different ways in biographies (*e. g.*, it is expected that religious men have completely different characterizations from religious women). To generate the final dictionaries for analysis from the vocabulary, we matched the vocabulary found in biographies with the prefixes in our corpus. Then we performed manual cleaning of noisy keywords, such as places (*e. g.*, *Virginia* matches *virgin** from the *Sexual* category), names (*Victoria* matches *victor** from the *Achievement Concerns* category), and words with unrelated meanings. In total, our cleaned dictionary contained 2,877 words. Table 1 shows the two most frequent words found per gender for each considered category.

4. META-DATA PROPERTIES

In our first analysis we estimate the proportion of women in Wikipedia. We analyze meta-data by comparing how men and women proportionally have several attributes in the data from DBpedia.

Presence and Proportion According to Class. DBpedia estimates the length (in characters) of each article and provides the network of links between articles. Of the set of 1,445,021 biographies (articles in the DBpedia *Person* class), 893,380 (61.82%) have gender meta-data. Of those, only 15.5% are about women.

The mean article length is 5,955 characters for men and 6,013 characters for women (a significant difference according to a t-test for independent samples: $p < 0.01$, Cohen's $d = 0.01$). The mean out-degrees (number of links) of 42.1 for men and 39.4 for women also differ significantly ($p < 0.001$, Cohen's $d = 0.06$). Table 2 displays the number of biographies in the *Person* class, as well as its most common subclasses. From the table, in comparison to the global proportion of women, the following categories over-represent women: *Artist, Royalty, FictionalCharacter, Noble, BeautyQueen,* and *Model*. The others over-represent men. The differences in length and degree do not hold for all classes, hinting that a study according to semantic categories of people is needed. However, in this paper we focus on the global differences in *Person*.

Date of Birth. Figure 2 displays the distribution of biographies according to their corresponding *birthYear* property, considering

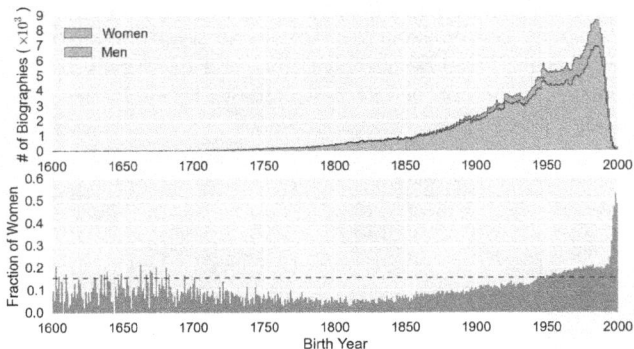

Figure 2: Distribution of biographies according to birth year.

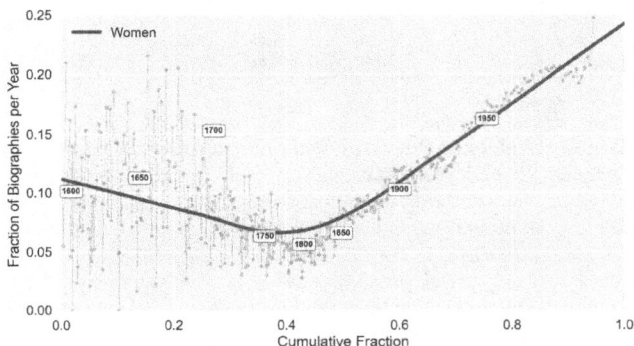

Figure 3: Relation between the cumulative fraction of women in time and the fraction of women per year (dots). The y-axis was truncated to 0.25 for clarity.

Table 3: Proportion of men and women who have the specified attributes in their infoboxes. Proportions were tested with a chi-square test, with effect size estimated using Cohen's w.

	% Men	% Women	χ^2	w
birthName	4.01	11.46	4.84*	0.81
careerStation	8.95	1.13	6.84**	0.94
deathDate	32.82	19.35	5.53*	0.64
deathYear	44.68	25.45	8.28**	0.66
formerTeam	4.40	0.24	3.94*	0.97
numberOfMatches	8.60	1.06	6.61*	0.94
occupation	12.52	23.28	4.97*	0.68
position	13.62	1.68	10.46**	0.94
spouse	1.56	6.86	4.10*	0.88
team	14.06	1.97	10.39**	0.93
title	9.17	19.65	5.59*	0.73
years	8.95	1.12	6.84**	0.94

only those biographies between years 1600 and 2000 (inclusive). This accounts for 65.48% of biographies with gender (note that 34.07% do not have date of birth in meta-data). The distribution per gender (top chart) shows that most of the biographies of both genders are about people from modern times. The distribution of the fraction of women per year (bottom chart) shows that since the year 1943 the fraction of women is consistently above the global fraction of 0.155. Note that, of the biographies that have date of birth in their meta-data, 53% are from 1943 until 2000. To explore the evolution of growth of women presence, in Figure 3 we display the relationship between the cumulative fraction of biographies in time and the yearly fraction of biographies of women. The chart includes a *LOWESS* (LOcally Weighted Scatterplot Smoothing) fit of the data, to be able to see the tendency of changes in representation. This tendency became positive in the period 1750–1800. These results are discussed in terms of historical significance in Section 7.

Infobox Attributes. Given that there are different classes of infoboxes, there are many different meta-data attributes that can be included in biographies. In total, we identified 340 attributes. For each one of them, we counted the number of biographies that contained it, and then compared the relative proportions between genders with a chi-square test. Only 3.53% presented statistically significant differences. Those attributes are displayed in Table 3. All of them have large effect sizes (Cohen's $w > 0.5$). Inspection allows us to make several observations:

- Attributes *careerStation*, *formerTeam*, *numberOfMatches*, *position*, *team*, and *years* are more frequent in men. All these attributes are related to sports, and thus, these differences can be explained by the prominence of men in sports-related classes (*e. g.*, *Athlete*, *SportsManager* and *Coach* in Table 2).
- Attributes *deathDate*, *deathYear* are more frequent in men. According to Figure 2, most women are from recent times, and thus they are presumably still alive.
- Attribute *birthName* is more frequent in women. Its values refer mostly to the original name of artists, and women have considerable presence in this class (see Table 2). In addition, even though it depends on the cultural context, another possible explanation is that married women usually change their surnames to those of their husbands.
- Attributes *occupation* and *title* are more frequent in women, and seem to serve the same purpose but through different mechanisms. On one hand, *title* is a text description of a person's occupation (the most common values found are *Actor* and *Actress*). On the other hand, *occupation* is a DBpedia resource URI (*e.g.*, http://dbpedia.org/resource/Actress). These attributes are present in the infoboxes of art-related biographies. On the contrary, the infoboxes of sport-related biographies do not contain these attributes because their templates are different and contain other attributes (such as the aforementioned *careerStation* and *formerTeam*) which already indicate their occupations. Thus, athletes (which are mostly men) do not contain such attributes.
- The *spouse* attribute is more frequent in women. This attribute indicates whether the portrayed person was married or not, and with whom. In some cases, it contains the resource URI of the spouse, while in other cases, it contains the name (*i. e.*, when the spouse does not have a Wikipedia article), or the resource URI of the article of *"divorced status."* Our manual inspection did not offer a direct explanation for the tendency to include this attribute in women's biographies more than in men's. For instance, the most common class with the spouse attribute is *Person* (without a more specific subclass), with 45% of the instances of the attribute.

5. LANGUAGE PROPERTIES

In this section we explore the characterization of women and men from a lexical perspective. First, we analyzed the vocabulary used in the overview of each biography through word frequency, and we use the estimated frequencies to find which words are associated with each gender. To estimate relative frequencies, words were considered once per biography, and we estimated bi-gram word collocations to identify composite concepts (*e. g.*, *New York*). We obtained a vocabulary of size $V_m = 1,013,305$ for men, $V_w = 376,737$ for women, with $V = 272,006$ common words.

Figure 5: Words most associated with women (left) and men (right), estimated with *Pointwise Mutual Information*. Font size is inversely proportional to PMI rank. Color encodes frequency (the darker, the more frequent).

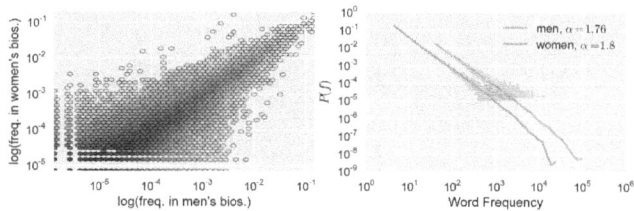

Figure 4: A density hexbin plot of word frequencies in men/women's biographies (left), and the PDF of word frequency distribution according to gender (right).

Figure 4 displays a density plot of word frequency, and the Probability Density Functions (PDFs) for both genders. The frequency distributions are similar across genders. Word frequencies in the common vocabulary for both genders follow a Zipf distribution $P(f) \sim f^{-\alpha}$ with similar exponents $\alpha \approx 1.8$, consistent with the value found by Serrano, Flammini, and Menczer [49]. In addition, frequency with respect to gender presents a high rank-correlation $\rho = 0.65$ (p < 0.001). For reference, consider that the inter-language rank correlation of words with the same meaning across languages is 0.54 [11]. This implies that words share meanings when referring to men and women.

Associativity of Words with Gender. To explore which words are more strongly associated with each gender, we measure *Pointwise Mutual Information* [13] over the common vocabulary V for both genders. PMI is defined as:

$$\text{PMI}(c, w) = \log \frac{p(c, w)}{p(c)p(w)}$$

where c is a class (*men* or *women*), and w is a word. The value of $p(c)$ can be estimated from the proportions of biographies about men and women, and the other probabilities can be estimated from the corresponding proportions of words and bi-grams. Since PMI overweights words with very small frequencies, we consider only words that appear in at least 1% of men or women biographies.

Associativity results are displayed as word clouds in Figure 5. The top-15 words associated to each gender are (relative frequency in parentheses):

- Women: *actress* (15.9%), *women's* (8.8%), *female* (5.6%), *her husband* (4.1%), *women* (5.3%), *first woman* (1.9%), *film actress* (1.6%), *her mother* (1.8%), *woman* (4.4%), *nee* (3.6%), *feminist* (1%), *miss* (1.9%), *model* (3.3%), *girls* (1.5%) and *singer* (6.5%).

- Men: *played* (14.2%), *footballer who* (3%), *football* (4.5%), *league* (5.9%), *john* (7.9%), *major league* (1.8%), *football league* (1.6%), *college football* (1.5%), *son* (7%), *football player* (2.2%), *footballer* (2%), *served* (11.7%), *william* (4.6%), *national football* (2%) and *professional footballer* (1%).

There is an evident difference in the kind of words most associated to each gender. The words most associated with men are related to sports, football in particular, which refers to both popular sports of soccer and American football (recall from Table 2 that *Athlete* is the largest subclass of *Person*). For women, the most associated words are related to arts (recall from Table 2 that *Artist* is the second largest subclass of *Person*), gender (*women's, female, first woman, feminist*), and family roles (*her husband, her mother*, and *nee* (adjective used when giving a former name of a woman in some cultures). This is consistent with the results from the meta-data analysis, where women are more likely to have a *spouse* attribute in their infoboxes (see Table 3), and with the results of Bamman and Smith [7].

Gender Differences in Semantic Categories of Words. To compare the distributions of words in the semantic categories, we employed two metrics: relative frequency in overviews, as previously done with PMI, and burstiness in the full text. Word frequencies identify how language is used differently to characterize men and women in terms of semantic categories. However, word frequency alone does not give insights on how those semantic categories portray a given biography, or in other words, the importance that editors give to those categories. Burstiness is a measure of word importance in a single document according to the number of times it appears within the document, under the assumption that important words appear more than once (they appear in *bursts*) when they are relevant in a given document. We use the definition of burstiness from Church and Gale [12]:

$$B(w) = \frac{E_w(f)}{P_w(f \geq 1)}$$

where $E_w(f)$ is the mean number of occurrences of a given word w per document, and $P_w(f \geq 1)$ is the probability that w appears at least once in a document. The differences in frequency and burstiness are tested using the Mann-Whitney U test, which indicates if one population tends to have larger values than another. It is non-parametric, *i. e.*, it does not assume normality. For all categories under consideration, we report the test value. A positive value indicates that the distribution is biased towards men, and a negative value indicates bias towards women. If the test is significant, we calculate the *common language effect size* (ES) as the percentage of words that had a greater relative frequency for the dominant gender.

Table 4: Word frequency in biography overviews. For each LIWC category we report vocabulary size, median frequencies, and the result of a Mann-Whitney U test. M and W mean men and women, respectively.

category	V	Median (M)	Median (W)	U
Social Processes	498	0.04%	0.05%	-1.12
– Family	43	0.03%	0.09%	-0.85
– Friends	33	0.05%	0.05%	-0.58
– Humans	59	0.13%	0.17%	-1.34
Cognitive Processes	1043	0.02%	0.02%	2.05*
– Insight	354	0.02%	0.02%	0.73
– Causation	181	0.02%	0.02%	1.32
– Discrepancy	57	0.02%	0.02%	0.06
– Tentative	150	0.01%	0.01%	0.85
– Certainty	110	0.03%	0.02%	0.92
– Inhibition	229	0.01%	0.01%	1.75
– Inclusive	7	0.25%	0.29%	-0.06
– Exclusive	6	0.11%	0.07%	0.48
Biological Processes	638	0.01%	0.01%	-1.63
– Body	193	0.01%	0.01%	-0.60
– Health	274	0.01%	0.01%	-0.40
– Sexual	105	0.00%	0.01%	-3.02**
– Ingestion	122	0.01%	0.01%	-0.51
Work Concerns	570	0.04%	0.03%	1.12
Achievement Concerns	364	0.05%	0.04%	1.06

Table 4 shows the result of the test applied to word frequency in biography overviews. Note that, although the medians are very similar for each category, the U test compares differences in the distribution instead of differences in means or medians. Of the 20 categories under consideration, two of them (one top-level) showed significant differences between genders: *Cognitive Processes* ($U = 2.04$, ES = 63%) is dominated by men, while *Sexual* (subcategory of *Biological Processes*, $U = -3.02$, ES = 85%) is dominated by women. Burstiness distributions in full biographies per semantic category are displayed in Table 5. There are three (two top-level) categories with significant differences, both dominated by men: *Cognitive Processes* ($U = 2.85$, ES = 60%), its subcategory *Causation* ($U = 2.17$, ES = 71%), and *Work Concerns* ($U = 2.62$, ES = 64%).

In this section, we have analyzed generic semantic categories with words that should be used in the same way to describe women and men. Although the results found imply more similarities than differences, in the discussion section we elaborate over the importance of such differences and the implications of these findings.

6. NETWORK PROPERTIES

To study structural properties of biographies, we first built a directed network of biographies from the links between articles in the *Person* DBpedia class. This empirical network was compared with several null graphs that, by construction, preserve different known properties of the original network. This allows us to attribute observed structural differences between genders either to empirical fluctuations in such properties, such as the heterogeneous importance of historical figures, or to gender bias. To do so, we consider PageRank, a measure of node centrality based on network connectivity [9, 21].

Empirical Network and Null Models. We study the properties of the directed network constructed from the links between 893,380 biographical articles in the *Person* class. After removing 192,674 singleton nodes, the resulting graph has 700,706 nodes and 4,153,978 edges. We use this graph to construct the following null models:

Table 5: Word burstiness in full biographies for LIWC categories. Columns are analog to Table 4.

category	V	Median (M)	Median (W)	U
Social Processes	498	1.21	1.22	0.21
– Family	43	1.31	1.35	-1.12
– Friends	33	1.23	1.26	-1.06
– Humans	59	1.35	1.44	-1.00
Cognitive Processes	1043	1.12	1.11	2.82**
– Insight	354	1.13	1.12	1.75
– Causation	181	1.15	1.13	2.17*
– Discrepancy	57	1.10	1.14	-1.05
– Tentative	150	1.12	1.10	1.80
– Certainty	110	1.11	1.10	1.62
– Inhibition	229	1.10	1.10	1.09
– Inclusive	7	1.27	1.29	-0.45
– Exclusive	6	1.27	1.20	0.48
Biological Processes	638	1.26	1.25	1.87
– Body	193	1.27	1.26	1.24
– Health	274	1.24	1.24	1.33
– Sexual	105	1.27	1.31	-0.51
– Ingestion	122	1.29	1.24	1.30
Work Concerns	570	1.23	1.20	2.62**
Achievement Concerns	364	1.15	1.15	0.54

- *Random.* We shuffle the edges in the original network. For each edge (u,v), we select two random nodes (i,j) and replace (u,v) by (i,j). The resulting network is a random graph with neither the heterogeneous degree distribution nor the clustered structure that the Wikipedia graph is known to have [58].
- *In-Degree Sequence.* We generate a graph that preserves the in-degree sequence (and therefore the heterogeneous in-degree distribution) of the original network by shuffling the sources of the edges. For each edge (u,v), we select a random node (i) and rewire (u,v) to (i,v). Each node has the same in-degree, or popularity, as the corresponding biography.
- *Out-Degree Sequence.* We generate a graph that preserves the out-degree sequence (and therefore the out-degree distribution) of the original network by shuffling the targets of the edges. For each edge (u,v) select a random node (j) and rewire (u,v) to (u,j).
- *Full Degree Sequence.* We generate a graph that preserves both in-degree and out-degree sequences (and therefore both distributions) by shuffling the structure in the original network. For a random pair of edges ((u,v), (i,j)) rewire to ((u,j), (i,v)). We repeat this shuffling as many times as there are edges. Note that although the in- and out-degree of each node is unchanged, the degree correlations and the clustering are lost.
- *Small World.* We generate a undirected small world graph using the model by Watts and Strogatz [55]. This model interpolates a random graph and a lattice in a way that preserves two properties of small world networks: average path length and clustering coefficient.

All null models have the same number of nodes $n = 700,706$ and approximately the same mean degree $k \approx 4$ as the empirical network.

Gender, Link Proportions and Self-Focus Ratio. For each graph, we estimated the proportion of links from gender to gender, and we tested those proportions against the expected proportions of men and women present in the dataset using a chi-square test. Table 6 shows the results. None of the null models show any bias in link proportions. The observed graph, on the other hand, shows a significant difference in the proportion of links from women biographies. In particular, articles about women tend to link to other women

Table 6: Comparison of the empirical biography network and the null models. *M* and *W* mean men and women, respectively.

	Nodes	Edges	Clust. Coeff.	Edges (M to M)	Edges (M to W)	χ^2 (M to W)	Edges (W to M)	Edges (W to W)	χ^2 (W to W)	SFR
Observed	693,843	4,106,916	0.16	90.05%	9.95%	2.38	62.19%	37.81%	37.83***	6.55
Small World	693,843	2,775,372	0.16	84.45%	15.55%	0.00	84.15%	15.85%	0.01	5.41
Random	693,843	4,106,916	0.00	84.41%	15.59%	0.00	84.39%	15.61%	0.00	5.41
In Deg. Seq.	693,843	4,106,916	0.00	85.36%	14.64%	0.06	85.27%	14.73%	0.05	5.75
Out Deg. Seq.	693,843	4,106,916	0.00	84.43%	15.57%	0.00	84.37%	15.63%	0.00	5.42
Full Deg. Seq.	693,843	4,106,916	0.00	85.34%	14.66%	0.06	85.39%	14.61%	0.06	5.74

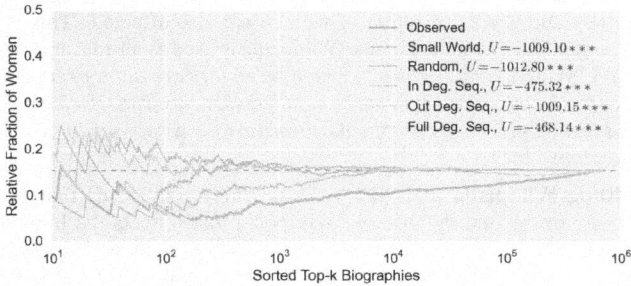

Figure 6: Women fraction in top biographies sorted by PageRank.

biographies more than expected ($\chi^2 = 40.54, p < 0.001$, Cohen's $w = 0.76$). Men biographies show a greater proportion of links to men and a lesser proportion to women than expected, but the difference is not statistically significant, although it has an impact on the estimated *Self-Focus Ratio* [24]. In our context, this ratio is defined as the relation between the sum of PageRank for men and the sum of PageRank for women. A SFR above 1 confirms the presence of self-focus, which, given the proportions of men and women in the dataset, is expected. In fact, given those proportions, the expected SFR is 5.41. Note that the null models have similar SFRs to the expected value, in contrast with the observed model with SFR of 6.55.

Biography Centrality. As an approximation for importance in our biography network we considered the ranking of biographies based on their PageRank values. To compare the observed distribution of PageRank by gender to those of the null models, we analyzed the fraction of women biographies among the top-r articles by PageRank, having $r \geq 10$. In the absence of any kinds of bias, whether endogenous to Wikipedia or exogenous, one would expect the fraction of women to be around 15% (the overall proportion of women biographies) irrespective of r. In the presence of correlations between popularity or historical importance and gender, we expect the ratio to fluctuate. But such fluctuations would also be observed in the null models.

The results are shown in Figure 6. While the null models stabilize around the expected value by $r \leq 10^4$, the proportion of women in the observed network reaches 15% only when the entire dataset is considered. This systematic under-representation of women among central biographies is not mirrored in the null models. We tested the differences between observed and null models using a Mann-Whitney U test, and found that the observed model is significantly different with all null models (U values shown in Figure 6, p < 0.001 for all pairwise comparisons with the observed model, Holm-Sidak corrected). This implies an asymmetry that cannot be explained by any of the heterogeneities in the structure of the network preserved by the null models. For instance, even if men biographies tended to have more incoming links (as they do),

or to be more densely clustered, those factors would not explain the lower centrality observed in women biographies.

7. DISCUSSION

Even though we found more similarities than differences in characterization, in this section we contextualize those differences in social theory and history. We do this to understand why such differences exist, and whether they can be attributed to bias in the English Wikipedia or to a reflection of the society documented in it.

Meta-data. We found that there are statistically significant differences in biographies of men and women. Most of them can be explained because of the different areas to which men and women belong (mostly *sports* and *arts*, respectively), as well as the recency of women profiles available on Wikipedia. Other differences, like article length and article out-degree, although significant, have very small effect sizes, and depend on the person class being analyzed.

The greater frequency of the *spouse* attribute in women can be interpreted as specific gender roles attributed to women. Regarding this *Implicit Association*, Nosek, Banaji, and Greenwald [37] found that Internet visitors tended to associate women and language related to family and arts. Arguably, an alternative explanation is that people in the arts could be more likely to marry a notable spouse than people in sports. Yet, we found that the most common specific class was the generic one, not assigned any of its sub-classes.

In terms of time, we found that the year 1943 marked a hit on the growth of women presence. According to Strauss and Howe [53], the post-war *Baby Boomers* generation started in 1943. The following generations are *Generation X* (1961–1981) and *Millenials* (1982–2004). The social and cultural changes embraced by people from those generations, plus the increased availability of secondary sources, might explain this growth. We also observed that the cumulative growth of women presence started in dates nearby the French Revolution (1789–1799), where women had an important role, although they were oppressed after it [1]. During these years seminal works about feminist philosophy and women's rights were published, like the works of *Mary Wollstonecraft* (1792) and *Olympe de Gouges* (1791). It is reasonable to assume that these historical events paved the way for women to become more notable.

The imbalance found in the *Artist* (women) and *Athlete* (men) classes is not a sign of bias from Wikipedians. Instead, it could be a reflection of physical world phenomena under study by the social sciences. For instance, according to Lauter [32], in the 20th century women became *mythmakers* through arts, an hypothesis that is supported by our results.

Language. We found that the words most associated with men are mostly about sports, while the words most associated with women are about arts, gender and family. Of particular interest are two concepts strongly associated with women: *her husband* and *first woman*. These results are arguably indicative of systemic bias: the usage of *her husband* was found in concordance with our meta-data results and previous work by Bamman and Smith [7], and the aforementioned work on *Implicit Association* [37]. These results can be contextualized in terms of *stereotyping theory* [44], as they categorize women, either as norm breaking (being the first is an exception to the norm) or as with predefined roles (being wives). As Fiske and Neuberg [19] indicate in their *continuum model of impression formation*, such categorization makes individuals more prone to stereotyping than those who are not categorized. The usage of *first woman* might indicate notability, but it also has been seen as an indicator of gender bias, as indicated by the Bechdel-inspired *Finkbeiner-test*[5] about scientific women, where it is explicitly mentioned that an article about a woman does not pass the test if it mentions *"How she's the 'first woman to ...' "* Despite being informal, the Finkbeiner-test raises awareness on how gender becomes more important than the actual achievements of a person.

According to Nussbaum [38], one possible indicator of *objectification* is the *"denial of subjectivity: the objectifier treats the object as something whose experience and feelings (if any) need not be taken into account."* This idea is supported as, in the overviews, men are more frequently described with words related to their *Cognitive Processes*, while women are more frequently described with words related to *sexuality*. In the full biography text, the *Cognitive Processes* and *Work Concerns* categories are more bursty in men biographies, meaning that those aspects of men's lives are more important than others at the individual level.

It could be thought that, instead of gender bias, such use of language could be a consequence of the imbalance in *Person* sub-classes like *Artist* and *Athlete* (recall Table 2). However, the semantic word categories under study are neutral in that aspect, as each word should be used equally (in terms of meaning) when portraying a person, regardless of her/his gender. Recall that we omitted categories that could be prone to be different for each gender (*e. g.*, *Religion*). We acknowledge that the study of specific sub-classes should be approached in future work, specially from a social science point of view. For instance, the *Athlete* class can be analyzed from a *sociology of sports* framework [35].

Presence and Centrality of Women. Women biographies tend to link more to other women than to men, a disproportion that might be related with women editing women biographies in Wikipedia, one of the reported interests of women editors [52]. Since we are considering notable people, it is known that men and women's networks evolve differently through their careers [27], not to mention the set of life-events that influence those changes like child-bearing and marriage (see an in-depth discussion by Smith-Lovin and McPherson [51]). Thus, link proportion between women cannot be attributed to bias in Wikipedia, as it seems to be more a reflection of what happens in the physical world.

We found that network structure is biased in a way that gives more importance to men than expected, by comparing the distribution of PageRank across genders. The articles with highest centrality, or historical importance [6], tend to be predominantly about men, beyond what one could expect from the structure of the network. As shown in Figure 6, there are women biographies with high centrality, but their presence is not a sign of an unbiased network: *"the successes of some few privileged women neither compensate for nor excuse the systematic degrading of the collective level; and the very fact that these successes are so rare and limited is proof of their unfavorable circumstances"* [16].

7.1 Implications

At this point, considering the *gender gap* that affects Wikipedia [25], it is pertinent to recall the concept of *feminine mystique* by

Friedan [22], developed from the analysis of women's magazines from the 50s in the United States, which were edited by men only. Fortunately, as discussed earlier, we have found women in different fields, mostly *arts*, in contrast to the *"Occupation: Housewife"* identified by Friedan [22], as well as more similarities in characterization than differences. Moreover, the presence of women is increasing steadily and most of the differences found are not from an inherent bias in Wikipedia. Nevertheless, the identified language differences objectify women and the network structure diminishes their findability and centrality. Hence, the gender bias in Wikipedia is not just a matter of women participation in the community, because content and characterization of women are also affected. This is important, for example, because Wikipedia is used as an educational tool [28], and *"children learn which behaviors are appropriate to each sex by observing differences in the frequencies with which male and female models as groups perform various responses in given situations"* [41].

Editing Wikipedia and NPOV. Critics may rightly say that by relying on secondary sources, Wikipedia just reflects the biases found in them. However, editors are expected to write in their own words, *"while substantially retaining the meaning of the source material,"*[6] and thus, the differences found in terms of language that objectify women are caused explicitly by them. In this aspect, Wikipedia should provide tools that help editors reduce sexism in language, for instance, by considering already existing manuals like [5]. Furthermore, their neutral point of view guidelines should be updated to explicitly include gender bias, because biased language is a clear violation of their guidelines.

Affirmative Action for Women in Notability Guidelines. The current notability guidelines for biographies in Wikipedia state: *"1. The person has received a well-known and significant award or honor, or has been nominated for one several times. 2. The person has made a widely recognized contribution that is part of the enduring historical record in his or her specific field."*[7] However, the boundary between not being notable according to sources and exclusion from history is blurred when evaluating the notability of women. For instance, consider a discussion about women in philosophy: *"Feminist historians of philosophy have argued that the historical record is incomplete because it omits women philosophers, and it is biased because it devalues any women philosophers it forgot to omit. In addition, feminist philosophers have argued that the philosophical tradition is conceptually flawed because of the way that its fundamental norms like reason and objectivity are gendered male"* [56]. Women, specially in historical contexts before 1943, should be targeted by affirmative actions that would allow them to appear in the content if they are not there, and be linked from other articles. We acknowledge that this is not easy, because relaxing notability guidelines can open the door to original research, which is not allowed. However, a correctly defined affirmative strategy would allow to grow the proportion of women in Wikipedia, make women easier to find, both through search (as it increases relevance) and exploratory browsing.

8. CONCLUSIONS

We studied gender bias in Wikipedia biographies. Our results indicate significant differences in meta-data, language, and network structure that can be attributed not only to the mirroring of the offline world, but also to gender bias endogenous to content generation in

---

[5]http://www.doublexscience.org/the-finkbeiner-test/

[6]https://en.wikipedia.org/wiki/Wikipedia:No_original_research
[7]https://en.wikipedia.org/wiki/Wikipedia:Notability_(people)#Any_biography

Wikipedia. Our contribution is a quantification of *systematic asymmetries* [8], which we define as gender bias with respect to content and structure, as well as a contextualization of the differences found in terms of social theory. In concluding remarks, we proposed that Wikipedia may wish to consider revising its guidelines, both to account for the non-findability of women and to encourage a less biased use of language, as such a bias is a violation of the neutral point of view guideline.

Limitations. Our study has two main limitations. First, our focus is on the English Wikipedia, which is biased towards western cultures [24]. However, a parallel work to ours by Wagner et al. [54] focused on hyperlingual quantitative analysis, and obtained similar results for other languages. Our methods can be applied in other contexts given the appropriate dictionaries with semantic categories. The second limitation is a binary gendered view, but we believe this is a first step towards analyzing the gender dimension in content from a wider perspective, given the social theory discussion we have made.

Future Work. At least three areas are ripe for further work. The first is the construction of editing tools for Wikipedia that would help editors detect bias in content, and suggest appropriate actions. The second is a study of individual differences among contributors, as our work analyzed user generated content without considering *who* published and edited it. This aspect can be explored by analyzing how contributors discuss and edit content based on their gender and other individual factors. The last area is a further exploration of bias considering more fine-grained ontology classes and metadata attributes. For instance, it may be possible that gender bias is stronger or weaker for different ontology classes (e.g., *Scientist* vs. *Artist*) or in biographies of people from different regions and religions. Finally it would be helpful to study whether gender bias depends on the quality of an article: does bias decrease with increasing number of edits or other measures of article maturity?

Acknowledgments. We thank Daniela Alarcón Sánchez for fruitful discussion and Luca Chiarandini for tool code, as well as the anonymous reviewers for their advice to improve the paper. This work was partially funded by Grant TIN2012-38741 (Understanding Social Media: An Integrated Data Mining Approach) of the Ministry of Economy and Competitiveness of Spain.

References

[1] Jane Abray. "Feminism in the French Revolution". In: *The American Historical Review* (1975), pp. 43–62.

[2] Rodrigo Almeida, Barzan Mozafari, and Junghoo Cho. "On the Evolution of Wikipedia." In: *International Conference on Weblogs and Social Media*. 2007.

[3] Maik Anderka, Benno Stein, and Nedim Lipka. "Predicting quality flaws in user-generated content: the case of Wikipedia". In: *Proceedings of the 35th international ACM SIGIR conference on Research and development in information retrieval*. ACM. 2012, pp. 981–990.

[4] Judd Antin et al. "Gender differences in Wikipedia editing". In: *Proceedings of the 7th International Symposium on Wikis and Open Collaboration*. ACM. 2011, pp. 11–14.

[5] APA. "Publication Manual of the American Psychological Association". In: Sixth. American Psychological Association, 2000. Chap. General Guidelines for Reducing Bias.

[6] Pablo Aragón et al. "Biographical social networks on Wikipedia: a cross-cultural study of links that made history". In: *Proceedings of the Eighth Annual International Symposium on Wikis and Open Collaboration*. ACM. 2012, p. 19.

[7] David Bamman and Noah A Smith. "Unsupervised Discovery of Biographical Structure from Text". In: *Transactions of the Association for Computational Linguistics* 2 (2014), pp. 363–376.

[8] CJ Beukeboom. "Mechanisms of linguistic bias: How words reflect and maintain stereotypic expectancies". In: *Social Cognition and Communication* (2014), pp. 313–330.

[9] Sergey Brin and Lawrence Page. "The anatomy of a large-scale hypertextual Web search engine". In: *Computer networks and ISDN systems* 30.1 (1998), pp. 107–117.

[10] Ewa S Callahan and Susan C Herring. "Cultural bias in Wikipedia content on famous persons". In: *Journal of the American society for information science and technology* 62.10 (2011), pp. 1899–1915.

[11] Andreea S Calude and Mark Pagel. "How do we use language? Shared patterns in the frequency of word use across 17 world languages". In: *Philosophical Transactions of the Royal Society of London B: Biological Sciences* 366.1567 (2011), pp. 1101–1107.

[12] Kenneth W Church and William A Gale. "Poisson mixtures". In: *Natural Language Engineering* 1.02 (1995), pp. 163–190.

[13] Kenneth W Church and Patrick Hanks. "Word association norms, mutual information, and lexicography". In: *Computational linguistics* 16.1 (1990), pp. 22–29.

[14] Giovanni Luca Ciampaglia and Dario Taraborelli. "MoodBar: Increasing new user retention in Wikipedia through lightweight socialization". In: *Proceedings of the 18th ACM Conference on Computer Supported Cooperative Work & Social Computing*. ACM. 2015, pp. 734–742.

[15] Benjamin Collier and Julia Bear. "Conflict, criticism, or confidence: an empirical examination of the gender gap in Wikipedia contributions". In: *Proceedings of the ACM 2012 conference on Computer Supported Cooperative Work*. ACM. 2012, pp. 383–392.

[16] Simone De Beauvoir. *The second sex*. Random House LLC, 2012.

[17] Michela Ferron and Paolo Massa. "Psychological processes underlying Wikipedia representations of natural and man-made disasters". In: *Proceedings of the Eighth Annual International Symposium on Wikis and Open Collaboration*. ACM. 2012, p. 2.

[18] Amanda Filipacchi. "Wikipedia's sexism toward female novelists". In: *The New York Times, April 28th, 2013* (2013).

[19] Susan T Fiske and Steven L Neuberg. "A continuum of impression formation, from category-based to individuating processes: Influences of information and motivation on attention and interpretation". In: *Advances in experimental social psychology* 23 (1990), pp. 1–74.

[20] Lucie Flekova, Oliver Ferschke, and Iryna Gurevych. "What makes a good biography?: multidimensional quality analysis based on Wikipedia article feedback data". In: *Proceedings of the 23rd international conference on World wide web*. International World Wide Web Conferences Steering Committee. 2014, pp. 855–866.

[21] S. Fortunato et al. "On local estimations of PageRank: A mean field approach". In: *Internet Mathematics* 4.2–3 (2007), pp. 245–266.

[22] Betty Friedan. *The feminine mystique*. WW Norton & Company, 2010.

[23] Jim Giles. "Internet encyclopaedias go head to head". In: *Nature* 438.7070 (2005), pp. 900–901.

[24] Brent Hecht and Darren Gergle. "Measuring self-focus bias in community-maintained knowledge repositories". In: *Proceedings of the fourth international conference on Communities and technologies*. ACM. 2009, pp. 11–20.

[25] Benjamin Mako Hill and Aaron Shaw. "The Wikipedia Gender Gap Revisited: Characterizing Survey Response Bias with Propensity Score Estimation". In: *PloS ONE* 8.6 (2013), e65782.

[26] Daniela Iosub et al. "Emotions under discussion: Gender, status and communication in online collaboration". In: *PloS ONE* 9.8 (2014), e104880.

[27] Jerry A Jacobs. *Revolving doors: Sex segregation and women's careers*. Stanford University Press, 1989.

[28] Piotr Konieczny. "Teaching with Wikipedia and other Wikimedia foundation wikis". In: *Proceedings of the 6th International Symposium on Wikis and Open Collaboration*. ACM. 2010, p. 29.

[29] Robin Tolmach Lakoff. "Language and woman's place". In: *Language in Society* 2, No. 1, Apr. (1973), pp. 45–80.

[30] Shyong Tony K Lam et al. "WP: clubhouse?: an exploration of Wikipedia's gender imbalance". In: *Proceedings of the 7th International Symposium on Wikis and Open Collaboration*. ACM. 2011, pp. 1–10.

[31] David Laniado et al. "Emotions and dialogue in a peer-production community: the case of Wikipedia". In: *Proceedings of the Eighth Annual International Symposium on Wikis and Open Collaboration*. ACM. 2012, p. 9.

[32] Estella Lauter. *Women as mythmakers: poetry and visual art by twentieth-century women*. Indiana University Press, 1984.

[33] Janette Lehmann et al. "Reader preferences and behavior on Wikipedia". In: *Proceedings of the 25th ACM conference on Hypertext and Social Media*. ACM. 2014, pp. 88–97.

[34] Jens Lehmann et al. "DBpedia - A Large-scale, Multilingual Knowledge Base Extracted from Wikipedia". In: *Semantic Web Journal* (2014).

[35] Michael A Messner. "Sports and male domination: The female athlete as contested ideological terrain". In: *Sociology of sport journal* 5.3 (1988), pp. 197–211.

[36] Jonathan T Morgan et al. "Tea and sympathy: crafting positive new user experiences on Wikipedia". In: *Proceedings of the 2013 conference on Computer supported cooperative work*. ACM. 2013, pp. 839–848.

[37] Brian A Nosek, Mahzarin Banaji, and Anthony G Greenwald. "Harvesting implicit group attitudes and beliefs from a demonstration web site." In: *Group Dynamics: Theory, Research, and Practice* 6.1 (2002), p. 101.

[38] Martha C Nussbaum. "Objectification". In: *Philosophy & Public Affairs* 24.4 (1995), pp. 249–291.

[39] Chitu Okoli et al. "Wikipedia in the eyes of its beholders: A systematic review of scholarly research on Wikipedia readers and readership". In: *Journal of the American Society for Information Science and Technology* (2014).

[40] James W Pennebaker, Martha E Francis, and Roger J Booth. "Linguistic inquiry and word count: LIWC 2001". In: *Mahway: Lawrence Erlbaum Associates* 71 (2001), p. 2001.

[41] David G Perry and Kay Bussey. "The social learning theory of sex differences: Imitation is alive and well." In: *Journal of Personality and Social Psychology* 37.10 (1979), p. 1699.

[42] Ulrike Pfeil, Panayiotis Zaphiris, and Chee Siang Ang. "Cultural differences in collaborative authoring of Wikipedia". In: *Journal of Computer-Mediated Communication* 12.1 (2006), pp. 88–113.

[43] Steven T Piantadosi. "Zipf's word frequency law in natural language: A critical review and future directions". In: *Psychonomic bulletin & review* (2014), pp. 1–19.

[44] Felicia Pratto, Peter J Hegarty, and Josephine D Korchmaros. "How communication practices and category norms lead people to stereotype particular people and groups". In: *Stereotype dynamics: Language based approaches to the formation, maintenance, and transformation of stereotypes* (), pp. 293–313.

[45] Jacob Ratkiewicz et al. "Characterizing and modeling the dynamics of online popularity". In: *Physical review letters* 105.15 (2010), p. 158701.

[46] Joseph Reagle and Lauren Rhue. "Gender bias in Wikipedia and Britannica". In: *International Journal of Communication* 5 (2011), p. 21.

[47] Roy Rosenzweig. "Can history be open source? Wikipedia and the future of the past". In: *The Journal of American History* 93.1 (2006), pp. 117–146.

[48] Toni Schmader, Jessica Whitehead, and Vicki H Wysocki. "A linguistic comparison of letters of recommendation for male and female chemistry and biochemistry job applicants". In: *Sex Roles* 57.7-8 (2007), pp. 509–514.

[49] M Ángeles Serrano, Alessandro Flammini, and Filippo Menczer. "Modeling statistical properties of written text". In: *PloS ONE* 4.4 (2009), e5372.

[50] Steven S. Skiena and Charles B. Ward. *Who's Bigger?: Where Historical Figures Really Rank*. Cambridge Univ. Press, 2014.

[51] Lynn Smith-Lovin and J Miller McPherson. "You are who you know: A network approach to gender". In: *Theory on gender/feminism on theory* (1993), pp. 223–51.

[52] Sarah Stierch. *Women and Wikimedia Survey 2011*. https://meta.wikimedia.org/wiki/Women_and_Wikimedia_Survey_2011. [Online; accessed April 2015]. 2013.

[53] William Strauss and Neil Howe. *Generations: The history of America's future, 1584 to 2069*. Morrow New York, NY: 1991.

[54] Claudia Wagner et al. "It's a Man's Wikipedia? Assessing Gender Inequality in an Online Encyclopedia". In: *Ninth International AAAI Conference on Web and Social Media* (2015).

[55] Duncan J Watts and Steven H Strogatz. "Collective dynamics of 'small-world' networks". In: *Nature* 393.6684 (1998), pp. 440–442.

[56] Charlotte Witt and Lisa Shapiro. "Feminist History of Philosophy". In: *The Stanford Encyclopedia of Philosophy*. Ed. by Edward N. Zalta. Winter 2014. 2014.

[57] George Kingsley Zipf. *Human behavior and the principle of least effort*. Addison-Wesley Press, 1949.

[58] Vinko Zlatić et al. "Wikipedias: Collaborative web-based encyclopedias as complex networks". In: *Physical Review E* 74.1 (2006), p. 016115.

Cultures in Community Question Answering

Imrul Kayes
University of South Florida
Tampa FL, USA
imrul@mail.usf.edu

Nicolas Kourtellis
Telefonica Research
Barcelona, Spain
nicolas.kourtellis@telefonica.com

Daniele Quercia
University of Cambridge
Cambridge, United Kingdom
dquercia@acm.org

Adriana Iamnitchi
University of South Florida
Tampa FL, USA
anda@cse.usf.edu

Francesco Bonchi
Yahoo Labs
Barcelona, Spain
bonchi@yahoo-inc.com

ABSTRACT

CQA services are collaborative platforms where users ask and answer questions. We investigate the influence of national culture on people's online questioning and answering behavior. For this, we analyzed a sample of 200 thousand users in Yahoo Answers from 67 countries. We measure empirically a set of cultural metrics defined in Geert Hofstede's *cultural dimensions* and Robert Levine's *Pace of Life* and show that behavioral cultural differences exist in community question answering platforms. We find that national cultures differ in Yahoo Answers along a number of dimensions such as temporal predictability of activities, contribution-related behavioral patterns, privacy concerns, and power inequality.

Categories and Subject Descriptors

K.4.0 [**Computers and Society**]: General; J.4 [**Social and Behavioural Sciences**]: Sociology

Keywords

Community question answering; cultures; crowdsourcing

1. INTRODUCTION

Cultural differences exist in almost all aspects of social interactions. For example, in some cultures in Asia it may be considered disrespectful for people to express their opinions or ask questions to authority figures (e.g., teachers, elders). In other cultures (such as USA or Canada) asking questions is expected or even encouraged.

Cross-country cultural variations have been studied in the real world via small-scale experiments and opinion surveys. Geert Hofstede [13] administered opinion surveys to a large number of IBM employees from different countries in the 1960s and 1970s. He discovered five cultural dimensions (individualism, power distance, uncertainty avoidance, masculinity, and long term orientation), that can be attributed to the existence of cultural variations. Three of these dimensions, individualism, power distance, and uncertainty avoidance, have been used to assess cultural differences in online contexts such as Twitter communication [8], emoticon usage [27] and online scheduling [30]. In brief, individualism reflects the extent to which an individual is integrated into a group (e.g., individualistic cultures like USA emphasizes mostly on their individual goals, as opposed to collectivist cultures like China that emphasizes on group harmony and loyalty). Power distance is the extent to which the less powerful members of an organization or society expect and accept that power is distributed unequally (e.g., in high power distance countries subordinates simply comply with their leaders). Uncertainty avoidance defines the extent to which society members feel uncomfortable with uncertainty and ambiguity (e.g., the stereotypical Swiss plans everything ahead supposedly to avoid uncertainty).

Psychologist Robert V. Levine [21] proposed the *Pace of Life* metric based on the walking speed of city people over a distance of 60 feet, the service time for standard requests for stamps, and the clock accuracy of city banks. During the 1990s, Levine employed 19 experimenters in large cities from 31 countries and computed country-specific Pace of Life ranks. He found significant differences in Pace of Life across cultures and ranked the cultures based on that.

Such cross-cultural variations that sociologists and psychologists already found in the offline world lead to our main research question: Does national culture determine how we participate in online Community Question Answering (CQA) platforms? CQAs such as Yahoo Answers (*YA*), Quora and Stack Overflow have been popular in the last decade. These platforms are rich and mature repositories of user-contributed questions and answers. For example, *YA*, launched in December 2005, has more than one billion posted answers,[1] and Quora, one of the fastest growing CQA sites has seen three times growth in 2013.[2]

National cross-cultural variations have been studied in a number of online contexts, including social networks (e.g., Twitter [10], Facebook [29]), location search and discovery (e.g., Foursquare [34]) and online scheduling (e.g., Doodle [30]). While CQA platforms have been intensively studied [32, 6, 28, 16], to the best of our knowledge, there has

---

[1] http://www.yanswersbloguk.com/b4/2010/05/04/1-billion-answers-served/
[2] http://www.goo.gl/MfK83y

been no study focusing on users' cultural differences and how they shape asking, answering, or reporting abuses in CQA platforms. If cultural variations exist in CQA platforms, they could be used for more informed system design, including question recommendation, follow recommendation, and targeted ads.

To fill this gap, we analyzed about 200 thousand sampled *YA* users from 67 countries who were active between 2012 and 2013. We tested a number of hypotheses associated with Hofstede's cultural dimensions and Levine's Pace of Life. Our results show that *YA* is not a homogeneous subcultural community: considerable behavioral differences exist between the users from different countries. We find that users from individualistic countries provide more answers, have higher contribution than take away, and are more concerned about their privacy than those from collective cultures. Users from individualistic countries are also less likely to provide an answer that violates community norms. We also find that higher power distance countries show more indegree imbalance in following relationships compared to lower power distance countries. Finally, we find that users from higher Pace of Life and lower uncertainty avoidance countries have more temporally predictable activities.

The rest of the paper is structured as follows. Section 2 discusses previous analysis of CQA platforms and the existing body of work on online cultural variations. Section 3 presents the *YA* functionalities relevant to this study and the dataset used. We introduce the hypotheses and present the results relating to Levine's Pace of Life and Hofstede's cultural dimensions in *YA* in Section 4 and Section 5, respectively. We discuss the impact of these results in Section 6.

2. RELATED WORK

Golder and Macy [10] studied collective mood in Twitter across countries from 509 million Twitter posts by 2.4 million users over a 2-year period. Despite having different cultures, geographies, and religions, all countries (USA, Canada, UK, Australia, India, and English-speaking Africa) in their study showed similar mood rhythms—people tended to be more positive on weekends and early in the morning. Park et al. [27] examined the variation of Twitter users' emoticon usage patterns in cross cultures. They used Hofstede's national culture scores of 78 countries and found that collectivist cultures favor vertical and eye-oriented emoticons, where people within individualistic cultures favor horizontal and mouth-oriented emoticons. Hofstede's cultural dimensions have also been used to study whether culture of a country is associated with the way people use Twitter [9]. In another study on cross-country Twitter communication, Garcia et al. showed that cultural variables such as Hofstede's indices, language and intolerance have an impact on Twitter communication volume [8].

Silva et al. [34] used food and drink check-ins in Foursquare to identify cultural boundaries and similarities across populations. They showed that online footprints of foods and drinks are good indicators of cultural similarities between users, e.g., lunch time is the perfect time for Brazilians to go for slow food places more often, whereas Americans and English people go for slow foods more at dinner time. Extracted features like these allow them to apply simple clustering algorithms such as K-means to draw cultural boundaries across the countries.

Quercia [29] used *Satisfaction With Life* tests and measured happiness of 32,787 Facebook users from 12 countries (Australia, Canada, France, Germany, Ireland, Italy, New Zealand, Norway, Singapore, Sweden, UK, USA). He found that despite comparative economic status, country-level happiness significantly varies across the countries and that it strongly correlates with official well-being scores.

Reinecke et al. [30] used about 1.5 million Doodle polls from 211 countries and territories and studied the influence of national culture on people's scheduling behavior. Using Hofstede's cultural dimensions, they found that Doodle poll participants from collectivist countries find more consensus than those from predominantly individualist societies.

CQA platforms have also attracted much research interest focusing on content, user behavior and applications. Research on CQA content has analyzed textual aspects of questions and answers. Researchers have proposed algorithmic solutions to automatically determine the quality of questions [23] and answers [32]. Research on CQA user behavior has been mostly about understanding why users contribute content: that is, why users ask questions (askers are failed searchers, in that, they use CQA sites when web search fails [24]); and why they don't answer questions (e.g., they refrain from answering sensitive questions to avoid being reported for abuse and potentially lose access to the community [6]). As for applications, researchers have proposed effective ways of recommending questions to the most appropriate answerers [28], automatically answering questions based on past answers [33], and retrieving factual answers [1] or factual bits within an answer [39]. Our previous work [16] used user-provided rule violation reports and user social network features to detect the content abusers in *YA*.

However, there has been no empirical cross-cultural analysis of CQA platforms. This paper is a first step in this direction and it verifies whether cultural differences are manifested in one such platform, *YA*.

3. YAHOO ANSWERS

After 9 years of activity, *YA* has 56M monthly visitors (U.S. only).[3] The functionalities of the *YA* platform and the dataset used in this analysis are presented next.

3.1 The Platform

YA is a CQA platform in which community members ask and answer questions on various topics. Users ask questions and assign them to categories selected from a predefined taxonomy, e.g., *Business & Finance*, *Health*, and *Politics & Government*. YA has about 1300 categories. Users can find questions by searching or browsing through this hierarchy of categories. A question has a title (typically, a short summary of the question), and a body with additional details.

A user can answer any question but can post only one answer per question. Questions remain open for four days for others to answer. However, the asker can select a best answer before the end of this 4-day period, which automatically *resolves* the question and archives it as a *reference* question. The best answer can also be rated between one to five, known as *answer rating*. If the asker does not choose a best answer, the community selects one through voting. The asker can extend the answering duration for an extra four days. The questions left unanswered after the allowed

---

[3]http://www.listofsearchengines.org/qa-search-engines

duration are deleted from the site. In addition to questions and answers, users can contribute comments to questions already answered and archived.

YA has a system of points and levels to encourage and reward participation.[4] A user is penalized five points for posting a question, but if she chooses a best answer for her question, three points are given back. A user who posts an answer receives two points; a best answer is worth 10 points.

A leaderboard, updated daily, ranks users based on the total number of points they collected. Users are split into seven levels based on their acquired points (e.g., 1-249 points: level 1, 250-999 points: level 2, ..., 25000+ points: level 7). These levels are used to limit user actions, such as posting questions, answers, comments, follows, and votes: e.g., first level users can ask 5 questions and provide 20 answers in a day.

YA requires its users to follow the Community Guidelines that forbid users to post spam, insults, or rants, and the Yahoo Terms of Service that limit harm to minors, harassment, privacy invasion, impersonation and misrepresentation, fraud and phishing. Users can flag content (questions, answers or comments) that violates the Community Guidelines and Terms of Service using the "Report Abuse" functionality. Users click on a flag sign embedded with the content and choose a reason between violation of the community guidelines and violation of the terms of service. Reported content is then verified by human inspectors before it is deleted from the platform.

Users in *YA* can choose to follow other users, thus creating a follower-followee relationship used for information dissemination. The followee's actions (e.g., questions, answers, ratings, votes, best answer, awards) are automatically posted on the follower's newsfeed. In addition, users can follow questions, in which case all responses are sent to the followers of that question.

3.2 Dataset

We studied a random sample of about 200k users from *YA* who were active between 2012 and 2013. These users posted about 9 million questions (about 45 questions/user), 43 million answers (about 215 answers/user), and 4.5 million abuse reports (about 23 reports/user). They are connected via 490k follower-followee relationships in a social network. The indegree and outdegree distributions of the social network follow power-law distributions, with an exponential fitting parameter α of 1.83 and 1.85, respectively.

In our dataset, we have users from 67 countries. Figure 1 shows the number of users in our dataset as a function of the number of Internet users taken from the World Bank.[5] We find a linear relationship between the number of users per country in our *YA* dataset and the number of Internet users in the World Bank dataset for each country. It means that the *YA* users from our dataset are not skewed by country. Instead, they represent a sample of global Internet users.

To investigate how sensitive this correlation is to the number of users per country, we computed the Pearson correlation between the number of *YA* users in x countries and their respective internet population. The x countries were ranked based on the number of *YA* users found in the dataset, and x was varied from top 20 to all 67 countries. Figure 2 shows that there are several peaks in the correlation, but the values are high and between 0.5 and 0.7. We select as a threshold

---

[4]https://answers.yahoo.com/info/scoring_system
[5]http://www.data.worldbank.org/indicator/IT.NET.USER.P2

the second highest correlation peak and thus included in the study 41 countries which have at least 150 users per country.

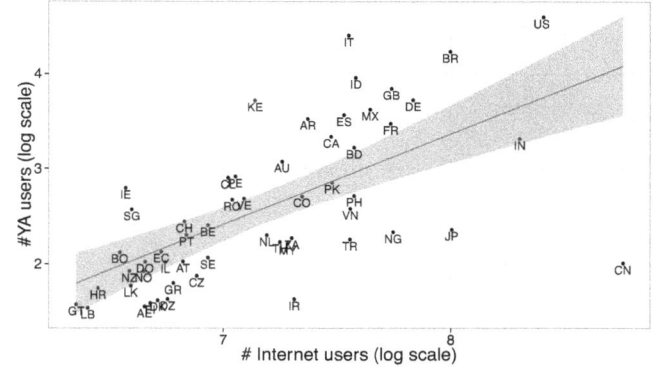

Figure 1: The number of Internet users and YA users for 67 countries. The regression line and 95% confidence interval area are also shown. The countries are represented by a 2-letter country code based on ISO 3166.

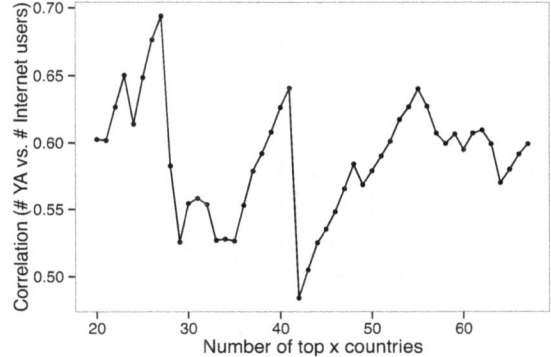

Figure 2: Number of top countries based on the number of YA users and correlation with their number of Internet users. All correlations are statistically significant with p-value<0.05.

4. LEVINE'S PACE OF LIFE

In this section, we analyze Levine's Pace of Life cultural dimension in the context of *YA* and show how it relates to user activities such as questioning, answering and reporting. In his book [20], psychologist Robert Levine defines Pace of Life as "the flow or movement of time that people experience". With the help of 19 experimenters, he collected and compared three indicators of the Pace of Life in 36 large cities from 31 countries around the world during a warm summer month between 1992 and 1995 [21]. The indicators are:

- **Walking speed:** They measured walking speed of 35 men and 35 women over a distance of 60 feet in main downtown areas in each city. Measurements were done during prime business hours after controlling a number of variables such as sidewalks, crowd, effects of socialization. They found significant differences in pedestrians walking speed—for example, pedestrians in Rio de Janeiro, Brazil walked only two-thirds as fast as pedestrians in Zurich, Switzerland.

- **Postal speed:** In each city, they measured the time it took postal workers to serve a standard request for stamps and considered this time as a proxy for work speed. They handed each clerk money and a note written in the local language requesting a common stamp. For example, in the United States, the clerk was handed a 5 dollar bill with a request for one 32-cent stamp. They found that overall Western Europe was the fastest to serve a standard request.

- **Clock accuracy:** To quantitatively measure time concerns, the researchers checked the clock accuracy of randomly selected 15 downtown banks in each city. The reported times were then compared to those reported by the telephone company, which was considered accurate.

Levine combined these three scores into a country-specific Pace of Life score and concluded that "the Pace of Life was fastest in Japan and the countries of Western Europe and was slowest in economically undeveloped countries. The pace was significantly faster in colder climates, economically productive countries, and in individualistic cultures" [21].

Intuitively, to cope with the rigid perception of time, people from the higher Pace of Life countries have to be planned and organized in their daily activities. On the other hand, people from lower Pace of Life countries might allow some unstructured activities, as in those countries the expectation of following the 'right' time is more relaxed.

Applying these findings to online communities such as CQA platforms, we expect that people from higher Pace of Life countries, such as the USA, will be less likely to ask or answer questions during busy hours of the day, e.g., office hours. From these ideas, we hypothesize the following in *YA*:

[H1] *Users from countries with a higher Pace of Life score show more temporally predictable activities.*

To test this hypothesis, we calculate how probable a country's users are in asking, answering and reporting at different times of day and correlate that with that country's Pace of Life rank. For example, if a user only asks or answers questions in the evening, he is temporally more predictable than a user who asks or answers in the morning, afternoon and night. In a Twitter study [10], Golder and Macy also find diurnal mood rhythms in different cultures.

In order to calculate temporal predictability, we only consider working days, as weekends are less predictable. More specifically, similar to [9], we divide the working day in five time intervals: morning (6:00 - 8:59), office time (9:00-17:59), evening (18:00-20:59), late night (21:00- 23:59), sleeping time (00:00 - 05:59). All the reported times are users' local time. We use *information entropy* [3], a measure of disorder, to calculate the temporal predictability.

For a given activity (asking, answering, or reporting) and C intervals, we can compute $p(c)$, the probability of an activity belonging to interval c. We measure the normalized entropy for user u for all activities as:

$$Entropy_u = \frac{-\sum_{c \in C} p(c) log(p(c))}{|log C|} \quad (1)$$

We calculate users' normalized entropies for all their questions, answers and abuse reports and refer to them as *question*, *answer* and *report entropy*, respectively. In our dataset, each country has on average 134k questions, 642k answers and 67k abuse reports. Normalized entropy ranges from 0 to 1. A normalized question entropy close to 0 indicates that most of the questions the user asked are within one time interval of the day, whereas the closer to 1, the more likely is that the user asked questions during all intervals. Finally, the question/answer/report entropy for a country c, $Entropy_{q/a/r,c}$, is defined as the geometric mean of all $Entropy_{q/a/r,u}$ computed for the users of that country:

$$Entropy_{q/a/r,c} = \left(\prod_{u \in U_c} Entropy_{q/a/r,u} \right)^{\frac{1}{|U_c|}} \quad (2)$$

where U_c is the set of users in country c. We use geometric mean to account for the skewed distribution of the entropy scores, something that the regular arithmetic mean cannot handle.

Table 1 shows Pearson correlations between question, answer, report entropy and Pace of Life ranks, where lower ranks mean higher Pace of Life. For both questions and answers, the overall Pace of Life ranks have positive correlations with question and answer entropy with $r = 0.67$ and $r = 0.37$, respectively. These positive relationships are seen in the Figures 3 and 4. We find positive correlations between walking speed rank, post office service time rank, and clock accuracy time rank with question entropy with $r = 0.48$, $r = 0.60$ and $r = 0.48$, respectively. For answers, we find positive correlations between post office service time rank, and clock accuracy time rank with entropy with $r = 0.38$ and $r = 0.29$, respectively. However, we do not find any statistically significant relationships between report entropy and Pace of Life ranks.

These results confirm that users from countries with a higher Pace of Life score show more temporally predictable asking and answering behavior in *YA*.

Pace of Life	Entropy		
	Question	**Answer**	**Report**
Overall	0.67***	0.37*	0.18
Walking speed	0.48**	0.18	0.06
Post office	0.60**	0.38*	0.19
Clock accuracy	0.48**	0.29*	0.21

Table 1: Pearson correlations between question, answer, report entropy and Pace of Life rank. Lower ranks mean higher Pace of Life. *p*-values are indicated as: $p<0.005$(***), $p<0.05$ (**), $p<0.1$ (*).

5. HOFSTEDE'S CULTURAL DIMENSIONS

In this section, we analyze a number of cultural dimensions in *YA* proposed by Geert Hofstede. We show how three cultural dimensions defined by Hofstede—individualism, power distance and uncertainty avoidance are manifested in the ecosystem of *YA*.

Hofstede's cultural dimensions theory is a framework for analyzing cultural variability. In his original model [12],

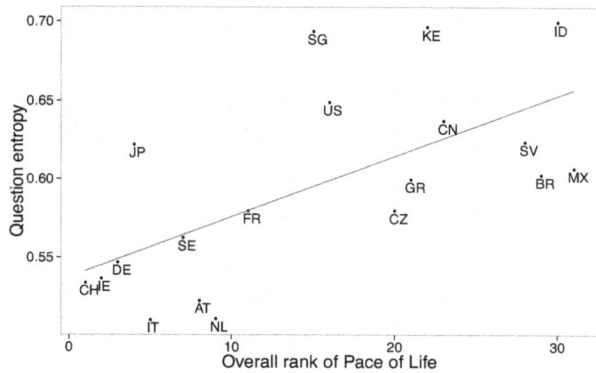

Figure 3: Pace of Life overall rank vs. average question entropy per country. Countries shown are the ones in our dataset for which a Pace of Life rank has been published. Countries are ranked in decreasing order of their Pace of Life value. A regression line is also shown.

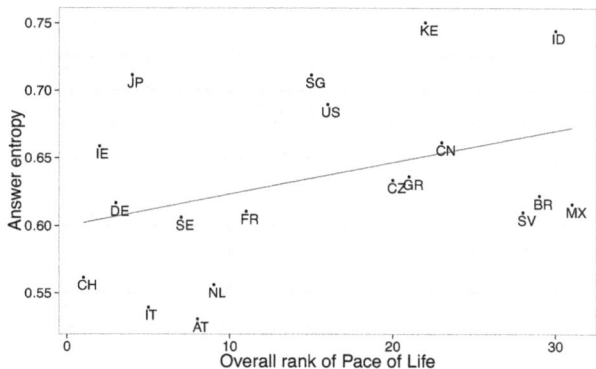

Figure 4: Pace of Life overall rank vs. average answer entropy per country. Countries shown are the ones in our dataset for which a Pace of Life rank has been published. Countries are ranked in decreasing order of their Pace of Life value. A regression line is also shown.

Hofstede proposed four primary dimensions by surveying in the 1960s and 1970s a large number of IBM employees from 40 countries: power distance (PDI), individualism (IDV), uncertainty avoidance (UAI) and masculinity (MAS). Later [13], he added two more dimensions: long-term orientation (LTO) and indulgence versus restraint (IVR). Three of the dimensions, individualism, power distance, and uncertainty avoidance, have been used in a number of recent studies of online behavior [8, 27, 30]. We also use these three Hofstede's cultural dimensions and relate them to a number of hypotheses in the context of YA.

5.1 Individualism (IDV)

Individualism is the extent to which an individual is integrated into a group. In individualistic societies (high IDV) such as the USA and England, personal achievements and individual rights are emphasized; an individual is expected to take care of only himself and his immediate family. In collectivist countries such as those of India, China, and Japan,

individuals are expected to place the family and group goals above those of self. In this work, we investigate how individualism is related to users' contribution, (un)ethical behavior and privacy settings in YA.

Individualism and contribution. The usage of the Internet takes time from a number of daily activities including face-to-face socialization. In collectivist countries, people are expected to give a fair amount of time on sociability, hence traditionally they seem to spend less time on the Internet compared to the people from the individualistic cultures [5]. In YA we expect that users from individualistic countries spend more time online, hence they can provide more answers and eventually they can contribute more to the community than their direct benefits from the community. We hypothesize the following:

[H2] *Users from countries with higher individualism index provide more answers.*
[H3] *Users from countries with higher individualism index contribute more to the community than what they take away from the community.*

We correlate the geometric mean of the number of answers posted by the users from a country with that country's individualism index (a higher score means higher individuality). We use geometric mean as an average because of the skewed distributions of the number of answers. In the calculation of the geometric mean, we exclude the users who have not provided any answers. We observe a positive correlation, shown in Figure 5, with $r = 0.46, p < 0.005$. This means that, on average, users from individualistic countries provide more answers.

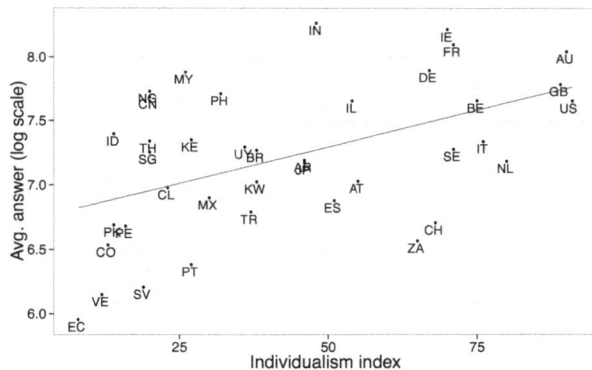

Figure 5: Individualism index vs. the average number of answers posted by users per country. A regression line is also shown.

To quantify users' contribution compared to their take away, we compute *yielding scores* of the users. The *yielding score* of a user is simply a difference between his contribution and his take away. For yielding scores, we consider YA's point system, which awards two points for an answer, ten points for a best answer, and penalizes five points for a question:

$$\text{Yielding}_u = f(contribution) - f(takeaway)$$
$$= 2.0 * A_u + 10.0 * BA_u - 5.0 * Q_u \quad (3)$$

179

where Q_u is the number of questions posted by user u, A_u is the number of answers posted by u, and BA_u is the number of best answers posted by u.

Finally, a country's yielding score $Yielding_c$ is defined as the geometric mean of all $Yielding_u$ computed for the users of each country c:

$$Yielding_c = \Big(\prod_{u \in U_c} Yielding_u \Big)^{\frac{1}{|U_c|}} \qquad (4)$$

where U_c is the set of users in country c and we take only those users having yielding scores more than zero. We correlate a country's geometric mean of the yielding score with the country's individualism index and we obtain a positive correlation (Figure 6) with $r = 0.37, p < 0.05$. This result suggests that the more individualistic a country is, the more its users contribute to YA than what they take away from the community.

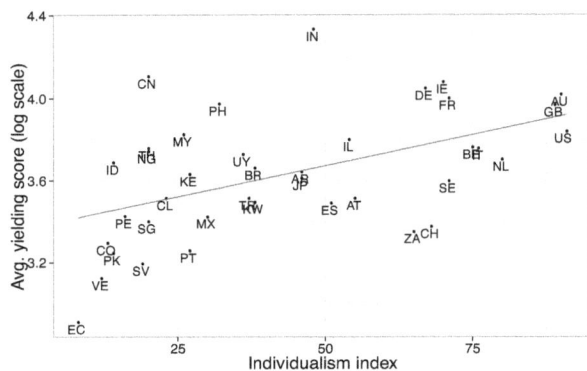

Figure 6: Individualism index vs. yielding score per country. A regression line is also shown.

There might be multiple explanations about why users from individualistic countries contribute more to the community as reflected by hypotheses H2 and H3. One explanation is that individualistic cultures have a more favorable collaborative environment [35], so individuals feel the urge to contribute to the community. Another explanation could be that users from individualistic cultures simply want more points than collectivist cultures. As points are awarded for contribution (e.g., an answer earns two points) and participation (e.g., each login earns one point), users might be tempted to contribute more. In fact, we obtain a positive and significant correlation ($r = 0.42, p < 0.01$) between a country's points (calculated as geometric mean of the country's user points) and its individualism index. Finally, there might be other confounding factors (e.g., internet penetration) that affect the contribution of a country's users on the platform. Thus, it is difficult to confirm whether the users' behavioral differences on contribution are due to their cultural differences.

Individualism and (un)ethical behavior. The degree to which a culture is collectivist or individualistic has an implication on its users' online (un)ethical behavior. For example, the more individualistic (less collectivistic) a culture, the lower the rate of software piracy [14] and online music piracy [19]. Personal rights are paramount in individualistic cultures, where people do not feel obligated to engage

in group cooperation that involves conspiracy. Group cooperation and conspiracy are two key elements for the real world unethical behaviors such as corruption [26]. Triandis et al. [37] used Hofstede's individualism index and found that the countries with higher collectivist scores show the most corruption.

Based on this online and offline user unethical behavior that is influenced by culture, our intuition is that we could observe a similar trend in YA. In CQA platforms, the expectation is that users would provide helpful answers to posted questions. As such, users are required to follow the Community Guidelines and the Yahoo Terms of Service while answering. When users post bad answers, community members flag them. Later, human moderators check whether these flags are applied correctly or not. We expect that the more collective a culture is, the more probable the answers from its users will be flagged as abusive. Formally, we hypothesize that:

[H4] *Users from more collective (less individualistic) cultures have higher probability to violate CQA norms.*

To this end, for each user u, we first calculate p_u, the probability that his answers violate community norms (and thus are correctly flagged by other users):

$$p_u = \frac{\text{\# correctly flagged answers from u}}{\text{\# total answers from u}} \qquad (5)$$

Finally, P_c, the geometric average of all p_u probabilities computed for each country c:

$$P_c = \Big(\prod_{u \in U_c} p_u \Big)^{\frac{1}{|U_c|}} \qquad (6)$$

where U_c is the set of users in country c.

The Pearson correlation $r = -0.48, p < 0.05$ shows that the probability of abuses in answers provided by the users from a particular country is negatively correlated with that country's individualism index. Figure 7 indeed shows that the probability decreases with an increasing individualism index, meaning that if an answer comes from an individualistic country, it is less probable to violate community rules.

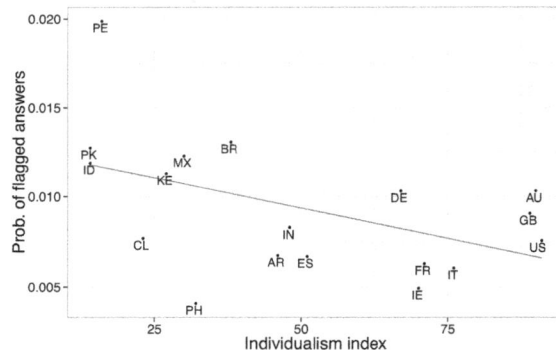

Figure 7: Individualism index vs. the probability that an answer from a country is correctly flagged. A regression line is also shown.

Individualism and privacy concerns. Although online privacy concerns are global, the extent to which people perceive these concerns as real varies across cultures. For example, in the United States, privacy is a basic human right, endorsed by the American Bill of Rights, while Asian countries show little or no recognition on privacy in their legal systems [5]. A survey of 1261 Internet users from five big cities—Bangalore, Seoul, Singapore, Sydney and New York—shows that Internet users from individualistic cultures are more concerned about privacy than those in collective cultures [2]. We expect that a similar trend also exists in CQA platforms. We hypothesize that:

[H5] *Users from higher individualism index countries exhibit higher level of concern about their privacy.*

We use the modifications of the privacy settings on users' *YA* accounts as a proxy of privacy concern. In *YA*, privacy settings are typically available for users to personalize for content (questions or answers) and follower-followee network. Intuitively, privacy-concerned users would take the opportunity to change the default privacy settings. So, we consider the fraction of public privacy profiles in a country to draw a conclusion on how concerned its users are about their privacy. However, the default privacy in YA is public. It might be possible that many of the users in the public group are dormant: users who signed up, asked and answered some questions, and disappeared quickly. These users might skew the results of our study, thus, we only consider active users from our dataset— users who have asked and answered more than 10 questions during our observation interval. These active users are about 79% of our dataset. We note that our conclusions remain the same if we consider more active users by filtering users who have asked and answered more than 20 questions.

Based on Hofstede's Individualism index, the Hofstede Centre[6] has tagged countries as individualistic or collectivist. In our study, we use this classification. Figure 8 shows the percentage of user profiles with public privacy settings in a country, as function of the country's ranking in the collectivist and individualistic class. The figure shows that, on average, collectivist countries have a higher percentage of public profiles: collectivist countries such as Spain, Peru, Argentina, and Mexico have higher percentage of public profiles than individualistic countries such as United Kingdom, United States, Australia or Italy.

5.2 Power Distance Index (PDI)

PDI is the extent to which the less powerful members of an organization or society expect and accept that power is distributed unequally. This dimension sheds light on how a society handles inequalities among its members. In countries with high PDI, such as countries from Latin, Asian, African and Arab world, everybody has a place in the social hierarchy and people accept the situation without questioning it. However, in Anglo and Germanic countries, which are low power distance countries, people seek distribution of power and ask for justifications of power inequality.

PDI essentially measures the distribution of wealth and power between people in a country or culture. In *YA*, we can use the indegree (number of followers) as a proxy of wealth and power. For example, the larger the number of followers users have, the larger an audience they have for direct communication. Higher indegree users are also found to

[6]http://geert-hofstede.com/countries.html

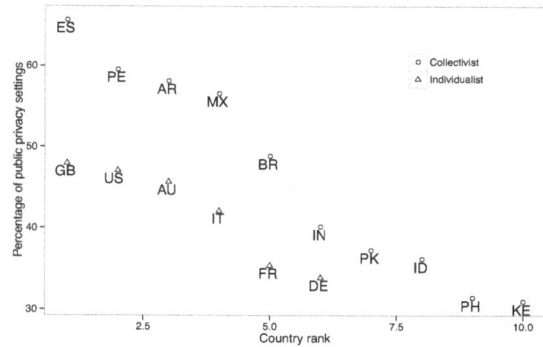

Figure 8: Percentage of public privacy settings vs. rank of collectivist and individualistic countries, respectively. Country ranks are based on the percentage of public privacy settings and they are separately done for collectivist and individualistic countries.

be more central (thus more retained [18]) across a number of network centrality metrics [17]. Moreover, these users' questions are forwarded to more users, hence more likely to be getting an answer. A study [16] on *YA* shows that users receive more answers from close neighborhoods. Given the high number of questions that remain unanswered (42% in *YA* reported by a study [31]) in CQA platforms, bringing answers not only shows a user's potential capability, but also makes the platform mature and informative. Taking ideas from the unequal distribution of wealth and power in higher power distance countries, we expect that in *YA*, users from those countries also have inequality in their indegrees. Garcia et al. [8] have found similar indegree inequality in Twitter. We hypothesize the following in *YA*:

[H6] *Users from higher power distance countries show a larger indegree imbalance in follow relationships.*

We correlate countries power distance index (higher index means power distance is high) with their users' indegree imbalance. A user's indegree imbalance is calculated as the difference between her friends' average indegree and her indegree. Finally, a country's indegree imbalance is the geometric mean of the indegree imbalance of its users.

For all countries, except Panama and Philippines, we obtained a positive indegree imbalance, meaning that for those countries, on average, a user's contacts have more contacts than the user. This supports a well-known hypothesis *friendship paradox* in sociology. The friendship paradox states that your friends have on average more friends than you have, however, most people think that they have more friends than their friends have [7]. It has been shown that the paradox holds for both Twitter [11] and Facebook [38]. Now we also show it for *YA*.

Figure 9 shows the relation between PDI and indegree imbalance (excluding Panama and Philippines). The figure indeed shows a positive correlation. We obtained a positive correlation $r = 0.65, p < 0.005$ between indegree imbalance and PDI for all countries (including Panama and Philippines). This supports the hypothesis that users from countries with higher PDI are more comfortable with indegree imbalance.

181

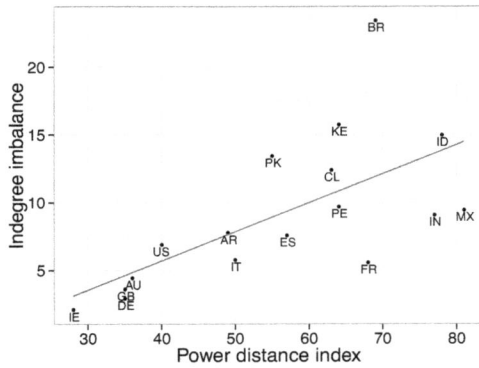

Figure 9: Power distance index vs. indegree imbalance. A regression line is also shown.

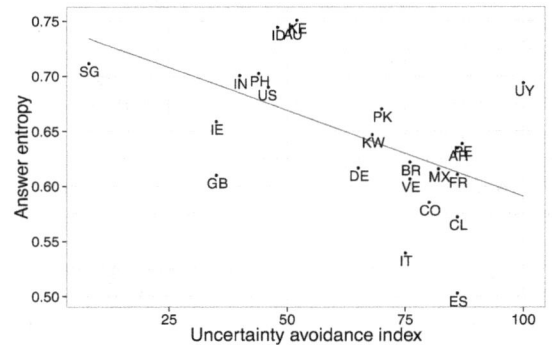

Figure 10: Question entropy vs. uncertainty avoidance index. Only countries having more than 300 users are plotted. A regression line is also shown.

5.3 Uncertainty Avoidance Index (UAI)

UAI is the extent to which people feel uncomfortable with uncertainty and ambiguity. Individuals from countries exhibiting strong UAI tend to minimize uncertainty and ambiguity by careful planning, and enforcing rules and regulations. On the other hand, low uncertainty avoidance cultures maintain a more relaxed attitude in unstructured situations.

For example, Switzerland has a reasonably high uncertainty avoidance index (58) compared to countries such as Singapore (8) and Sweden (29). In fact, an online scheduling behavior study [30] on Doodle (http://doodle.com/) shows that Switzerland and Germany have a high advance planning time of 28 days. In YA, our related hypothesis is:

[H7] *Users from countries with higher uncertainty avoidance index exhibit more temporally predictable activities.*

Figures 10, 11, 12 show the relationship between question, answer and abuse report entropy vs. uncertainty avoidance index, respectively. Note that a higher UAI means lower uncertainty and ambiguity. The negative relations in the figures indicate that users from countries with higher uncertainty avoidance index tend to have lower question, answer and abuse report entropies, thus they are more temporarily predictable. All the entropies have negative relation to uncertainty avoidance index: $r = -0.43$ for questions, $r = -0.55$ for answers, and $r = -0.51$ for abuse reports. All correlation values are statistically significant with $p < 0.05$.

6. SUMMARY AND DISCUSSION

Observing the global spread of information and communication technologies, researchers sometimes predicted that the online world would be converging into a "one-world culture" [22]. With the advent of the large-scale online behavioral datasets in the past decade from online platforms like Twitter, Facebook and Foursquare, researchers showed that the Internet does not have a homogeneous culture. Instead, country-specific cultural variations do exist. We showed the same non-homogeneity, but in a very different online context—community question answering.

In this work, we analyzed about 200 thousand sampled Yahoo Answers users from 67 countries. We studied users' behavioral patterns such as temporal predictability of activ-

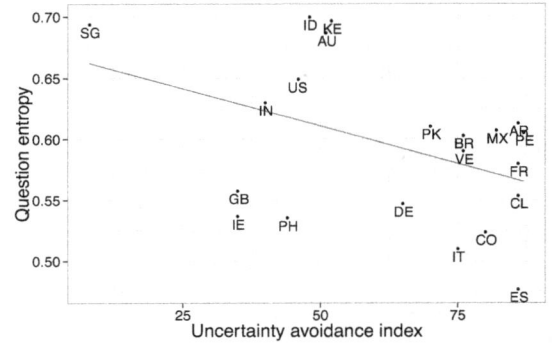

Figure 11: Answer entropy vs. uncertainty avoidance index. Only countries having more than 300 users are plotted. A regression line is also shown.

ities, engagement, (un)ethical behavior, privacy concerns, and power inequality and how they compare with a number of cultural dimensions (Pace of Life, Individualism, Uncertainty Avoidance and Power Distance). We find that behavioral differences exist across cultures in YA. Table 2 shows a summary of all the hypotheses involving cultural indices and the results found.

We acknowledge that our study is observational and lacks controlled experimental ground truth data. Therefore, we cannot draw causal conclusions whether cultures shape the ecosystem of YA. However, our results hint at the importance of culture-aware CQA moderation. Note that CQA platforms like YA employ human moderators to evaluate reported abuses and determine the appropriate responses, from removing content to suspending user accounts. We find that collective cultures are more probable to provide bad answers. At a minimum, more attention of moderators are expected in these cultures to keep the environment clean.

We find that individualistic cultures are more engaged in YA, e.g., by providing more answers and contributing more than their take away. These results confirm the generalization that individualistic cultures are highly attracted to the Internet. Researchers often attribute the egalitarian, democratic nature of the Internet to this engagement [4].

The evidence of different engagement patterns and difference in pace of life across cultures in CQA platforms imply that some core functionalities such as *question recommenda-*

Pace of Life	Correlation
Users from countries with a higher Pace of Life score show more temporally predictable activities (asking, answering and reporting)	$r_q = 0.67^{***}$ $r_a = 0.37^{**}$ $r_r = 0.18$
Individualism	**Correlation**
Users from higher individualism index countries provide more answers	$r = 0.46^{***}$
Users from countries with higher individualism index contribute more to the community than what they take away from the community	$r = 0.37^{**}$
Users from more collective (less individualistic) cultures have higher probability to violate CQA norms	$r = -0.48^{**}$
Users from higher individualism index countries exhibit higher level of concern about their privacy	NA
Power distance	**Correlation**
Users from higher power distance countries show larger indegree imbalance in follow relationships	$r = 0.65^{***}$
Uncertainty Avoidance	**Correlation**
Users from countries with higher uncertainty avoidance index exhibit more temporally predictable activities (asking, answering and reporting)	$r_q = -0.43^{**}$ $r_a = -0.55^{**}$ $r_r = -0.51^{**}$

Table 2: **Pearson correlation coefficients in hypotheses related to pace of life, individualism, uncertainty avoidance and power distance.** p-values are indicated as: $p<0.005(***)$, $p<0.05$ (**), $p<0.1$ (*).

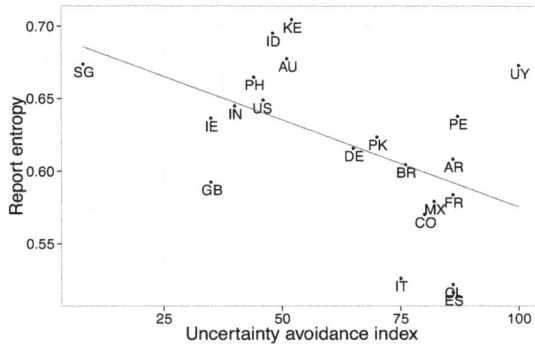

Figure 12: **Report entropy vs. uncertainty avoidance index. Only countries having more than 300 users are plotted. A regression line is also shown.**

tion and *follow recommendation* could benefit from exploiting cultural factors. In *question recommendation*, questions are routed to the most appropriate answerers. To find out such answerers, factors such as followers, interests, question diversity and freshness [36] are considered. Our study suggests that including cultural variables such as individualism can be useful. For example, as users from collective cultures are less probable to answer, questions from those communities should be routed to a larger number of potential answerers.

Another variable, Pace of Life, could also be a factor in *question recommendation*. Our results show that users from countries with a higher pace of life are temporally more predictable. In those cultures, if questions are forwarded to answerers during the busy hours of the day (e.g., during office hours), the questions are less likely to get an answer. Solutions could include routing questions to a larger number of potential answerers, diversifying the set of answerers to include users from countries with a lower Pace of Life, or delaying routing for after work hours.

In the *follow recommendation*, CQA platforms recommend which other users one can follow based on shared interests, common contacts, and other related factors. We find that in YA, lower power distance countries show less indegree imbalance in follow relationships. For follow recommendation in

those countries, users to be followed may be recommended to a user with the same level of indegree as them.

CQA platforms could also exploit cultural differentiations to improve targeted ads. Okazaki and Alonso [25] analyzed online advertising appeals such as "soft sell" appeal (that works by creating emotions and atmosphere via visuals and symbols) and "hard sell" appeal (that provides focus product features, explicit information, and competitive persuasion) across a number of cultures. They found individualistic cultures like the USA are more attracted to "hard sell" appeal, where collective cultures like Japan are attracted to "soft sell" appeal. Ju-Pak's study [15] also confirms that fact-based appeal is dominant in the USA, but text-limited, visual layouts are popular in collective cultures like South Korea. Linguistic aspects in the ads might also be important. For example, focusing on 'I', 'me' in individualistic cultures and 'us' and 'we' in collective cultures. Finally, CQA sites could leverage cultural variations in their platforms by, for example, placing textual, informative feature ads to users from individualistic cultures and visual and symbolic ads to users from collective cultures.

7. ACKNOWLEDGMENTS

The work was funded by the National Science Foundation under the grant CNS 0952420, and by the Yahoo's Faculty Research and Engagement Program.

8. REFERENCES

[1] J. Bian, Y. Liu, E. Agichtein, and H. Zha. Finding the right facts in the crowd: Factoid question answering over social media. In *Proceedings of the 17th International Conference on World Wide Web*, pages 467–476, 2008.

[2] H. Cho, M. Rivera-Sánchez, and S. S. Lim. A multinational study on online privacy: global concerns and local responses. *New media & society*, 11(3):395–416, 2009.

[3] T. M. Cover and J. A. Thomas. Elements of information theory 2nd edition. *Willey-Interscience: NJ*, 2006.

[4] M. De Mooij. The future is predictable for international marketers: converging incomes lead to diverging consumer behaviour. *International Marketing Review*, 17(2):103–113, 2000.

[5] M. De Mooij. *Global marketing and advertising: Understanding cultural paradoxes*. Sage Publications, 2013.

[6] D. Dearman and K. N. Truong. Why users of yahoo!: Answers do not answer questions. In *Proceedings of the*

SIGCHI Conference on Human Factors in Computing Systems, pages 329–332, 2010.

[7] S. L. Feld. Why your friends have more friends than you do. *American Journal of Sociology*, pages 1464–1477, 1991.

[8] R. Garcia-Gavilanes, Y. Mejova, and D. Quercia. Twitter ain't without frontiers: Economic, social, and cultural boundaries in international communication. In *Proceedings of the 17th ACM conference on Computer supported cooperative work & social computing*, pages 1511–1522, 2014.

[9] R. Garcia-Gavilanes, D. Quercia, and A. Jaimes. Cultural dimensions in twitter: Time, individualism and power. *Proceedings of the 7th International AAAI Conference on Weblogs and Social Media*, 13, 2013.

[10] S. A. Golder and M. W. Macy. Diurnal and seasonal mood vary with work, sleep, and day length across diverse cultures. *Science*, 333(6051):1878–1881, 2011.

[11] N. O. Hodas, F. Kooti, and K. Lerman. Friendship paradox redux: Your friends are more interesting than you. In *Proceedings of the 7th International AAAI Conference on Weblogs and Social Media*, 2013.

[12] G. Hofstede. National cultures in four dimensions: A research-based theory of cultural differences among nations. *International Studies of Management & Organization*, pages 46–74, 1983.

[13] G. Hoftede, G. J. Hofstede, and M. Minkov. *Cultures and organizations: software of the mind: intercultural cooperation and its importance for survival*. McGraw-Hill, 2010.

[14] B. W. Husted. The impact of national culture on software piracy. *Journal of Business Ethics*, 26(3):197–211, 2000.

[15] K.-H. Ju-Pak. Content dimensions of web advertising: a cross-national comparison. *International Journal of Advertising*, 18(2):207–231, 1999.

[16] I. Kayes, N. Kourtellis, D. Quercia, A. Iamnitchi, and F. Bonchi. The social world of content abusers in community question answering. In *Proceedings of the 24th International World Wide Web Conference*, pages 570–580, 2015.

[17] I. Kayes, X. Qian, J. Skvoretz, and A. Iamnitchi. How influential are you: Detecting influential bloggers in a blogging community. In *Proceedings of the 4th international conference on Social Informatics*, pages 29–42, 2012.

[18] I. Kayes, X. Zuo, D. Wang, and C. Jacob. To blog or not to blog: Characterizing and predicting retention in community blogs. In *Proceedings of the 7th ACM/ASE International Conference on Social Computing (SocialCom'14)*, 2014.

[19] E.-J. Ki, B.-H. Chang, and H. Khang. Exploring influential factors on music piracy across countries. *Journal of Communication*, 56(2):406–426, 2006.

[20] R. Levine. *A Geography of Time: The Temporal Misadventures of a Social Psychologist or How Every Culture Keeps Time Just a Little Bit Differently*. University Press, 2006.

[21] R. V. Levine and A. Norenzayan. The pace of life in 31 countries. *Journal of cross-cultural psychology*, 30(2):178–205, 1999.

[22] T. Levitt. The globalization of markets. *International Business: Strategic management of multinationals*, 3:18, 2002.

[23] B. Li, T. Jin, M. R. Lyu, I. King, and B. Mak. Analyzing and predicting question quality in community question answering services. In *Proceedings of the 21st International Conference Companion on World Wide Web*, pages 775–782, 2012.

[24] Q. Liu, E. Agichtein, G. Dror, Y. Maarek, and I. Szpektor. When web search fails, searchers become askers: Understanding the transition. In *Proceedings of the 35th International ACM SIGIR Conference on Research and Development in Information Retrieval*, pages 801–810, 2012.

[25] S. Okazaki and J. Alonso. Right messages for the right site: on-line creative strategies by japanese multinational corporations. *Journal of Marketing Communications*, 9(4):221–239, 2003.

[26] H. Park. Determinants of corruption: A cross-national analysis. *Multinational Business Review*, 11(2):29–48, 2003.

[27] J. Park, Y. M. Baek, and M. Cha. Cross-cultural comparison of nonverbal cues in emoticons on twitter: Evidence from big data analysis. *Journal of Communication*, 64(2):333–354, 2014.

[28] M. Qu, G. Qiu, X. He, C. Zhang, H. Wu, J. Bu, and C. Chen. Probabilistic question recommendation for question answering communities. In *Proceedings of the 18th International Conference on World Wide Web*, pages 1229–1230, 2009.

[29] D. Quercia. Don't worry, be happy: The geography of happiness on facebook. In *Proceedings of the 5th Annual ACM Web Science Conference*, pages 316–325, 2013.

[30] K. Reinecke, M. K. Nguyen, A. Bernstein, M. Näf, and K. Z. Gajos. Doodle around the world: Online scheduling behavior reflects cultural differences in time perception and group decision-making. In *Proceedings of the conference on Computer supported cooperative work*, pages 45–54, 2013.

[31] M. Richardson and R. W. White. Supporting synchronous social q&a throughout the question lifecycle. In *Proceedings of the 20th international conference on World wide web*, pages 755–764, 2011.

[32] C. Shah and J. Pomerantz. Evaluating and predicting answer quality in community qa. In *Proceedings of the 33rd International ACM SIGIR Conference on Research and Development in Information Retrieval*, pages 411–418, 2010.

[33] A. Shtok, G. Dror, Y. Maarek, and I. Szpektor. Learning from the past: Answering new questions with past answers. In *Proceedings of the 21st International Conference on World Wide Web*, pages 759–768, 2012.

[34] T. H. Silva, P. O. Vaz de Melo, J. M. Almeida, M. Musolesi, and A. A. Loureiro. You are what you eat (and drink): Identifying cultural boundaries by analyzing food and drink habits in foursquare. In *Proceedings of the 8th International AAAI Conference on Weblogs and Social Media*, 2014.

[35] J. J. Sosik and D. I. Jung. Work-group characteristics and performance in collectivistic and individualistic cultures. *The Journal of social psychology*, 142(1):5–23, 2002.

[36] I. Szpektor, Y. Maarek, and D. Pelleg. When relevance is not enough: Promoting diversity and freshness in personalized question recommendation. In *Proceedings of the 22Nd International Conference on World Wide Web*, pages 1249–1260, 2013.

[37] H. C. Triandis, P. Carnevale, M. Gelfand, C. Robert, A. Wasti, T. Probst, E. Kashima, T. Dragonas, D. Chan, X. Chen, et al. Culture, personality and deception: A multilevel approach. *International Journal of Cross-Cultural Management*, 1:73–90, 2001.

[38] J. Ugander, B. Karrer, L. Backstrom, and C. Marlow. The anatomy of the facebook social graph. *arXiv preprint arXiv:1111.4503*, 2011.

[39] I. Weber, A. Ukkonen, and A. Gionis. Answers, not links: Extracting tips from yahoo! answers to address how-to web queries. In *Proceedings of the 5th ACM International Conference on Web Search and Data Mining*, pages 613–622, 2012.

Mining Affective Context in Short Films for Emotion-Aware Recommendation

Claudia Orellana-Rodriguez
Insight Centre for Data Analytics
University College Dublin
Dublin, Ireland
claudia.orellana@insight-centre.org

Ernesto Diaz-Aviles
IBM Research
Dublin, Ireland
e.diaz-aviles@ie.ibm.com

Wolfgang Nejdl
L3S Research Center
University of Hannover
Hannover, Germany
nejdl@L3S.de

ABSTRACT

Emotion is fundamental to human experience and impacts our daily activities and decision-making processes where, e.g., the affective state of a user influences whether or not she decides to consume a recommended item – movie, book, product or service. However, information retrieval and recommendation tasks have largely ignored emotion as a source of user context, in part because emotion is difficult to measure and easy to misunderstand. In this paper we explore the role of emotions in short films and propose an approach that automatically extracts affective context from user comments associated to short films available in YouTube, as an alternative to explicit human annotations. We go beyond the traditional polarity detection (i.e., positive/negative), and extract for each film four opposing pairs of primary emotions: joy–sadness, anger–fear, trust–disgust, and anticipation–surprise. Finally, in our empirical evaluation, we show how the affective context extracted automatically can be leveraged for emotion-aware film recommendation.

Categories and Subject Descriptors

H3.3 [**Information Search and Retrieval**]: Information filtering; K.4 [**Computer and Society**]

General Terms

Human Factors, Experimentation, Measurement

Keywords

Computational Social Science; Sentiment Analysis; Social Media Analytics; YouTube.

1. INTRODUCTION

Amateur and professional filmmakers can reach large communities of viewers worldwide thanks to YouTube, which has drastically changed the way people access and critique films since its creation in 2005. This video-sharing platform provides its users with mechanisms – e.g., like/dislike buttons, comments – to publicly express their opinions about the uploaded movies, short films, or documentaries, thus shifting the role of users from being mere spectators to becoming active critics of the social media creations.

These user interactions, ratings and comments available in YouTube constitute a valuable source of data, which can be exploited to detect opinions, trends, or for ranking and recommendation tasks; however, the rapid pace at which users generate this content increases the difficulty of its analysis. Manually extracting useful information from different media is too slow, expensive, and requires considerable human effort, particularly if one needs to better understand users' emotions evoked by the videos.

In this paper, we explore two approaches for short film-emotion association. On the one hand, we obtain emotional annotations by crowdsourcing on Amazon Mechanical Turk and conduct an extensive study to better understand the affective content extracted by human intelligence from different short films and the role of emotions therein. On the other hand, we automatically extract affective context from the user-generated comments available in YouTube and empirically evaluate its usefulness by addressing an emotion-aware recommendation task. We do not limit our analysis to polarity extraction (positive-negative) but rather exploit Plutchik's four opposing emotion pairs (joy–sadness, anger–fear, trust–disgust, and anticipation–surprise) to better describe people's emotional context [32].

We focus on short films since they are motion pictures with all the components of a feature film but with less running time. As such, in only a few minutes, they express and elicit a whole gamut of emotions oriented to impact the audience and communicate a story, becoming an ideal test bed for our study of emotion association. We use a collection of short films that participated in two major festivals which leverage YouTube as their dissemination platform, namely *Tropfest* [5] and *Your Film Festival* [6].

In particular, our goal in this work is to address the following research questions:

RQ1. What is the role of emotions in short films?

RQ2. How can we leverage the wisdom of the crowd to detect emotions evoked by short films?

RQ3. How similar is the emotional context automatically associated to a short film compared to the one explicitly annotated by humans? and

RQ4. Are the automatically extracted emotions useful for personalized recommendations?

The association of emotions to films has several practical applications, for instance, to provide a personalized ranking of movies considering the emotions a person prefers to experience – e.g., by recommending *happy* short films to an audience who looks forward to experiencing *joy* – or for filmmakers to understand their audience and thus, provide more content with a higher degree of certain emotions to improve user experience. In summary, the main contributions of this paper are:

- We present an analysis on the responses elicited via crowdsourcing and on how the presence or absence of certain emotions may affect users decisions on what to watch.

- We propose a method for automatically detecting and extracting the different emotions and polarity evoked by short films.

- We show the usefulness of the extracted emotions in a context-aware film recommendation scenario.

2. RELATED WORK

We build upon the promising results of our previous work [31]. This paper differs from [31] by providing a more detailed and general overview: (i) We explore more extensively the crowdsourced association between short films and emotions, and share useful insights from this study in Section 3. (ii) We formally introduce our automatic approach for emotion extraction (AEX), offering clear details to ease its implementation and adoption for practitioners (Section 4). (iii) We also empirically compare the human emotion annotations against the automatically extracted affective context from user comments, using a context-aware recommender system as benchmark evaluation (Section 5).

The research we present in this work is mainly related to the areas of sentiment analysis, content ranking and recommendation exploiting user-generated posts, and context-aware recommendation.

Sentiment Analysis in the Social Web. Online Social Networks, with their growing popularity and availability, provide a constant stream of real users posts whose analysis sheds light on understanding human behavior, preferences, and diverse societal issues. Xu et al. [35] propose a fast training procedure to automatically recognize common emotions in bullying. The model is applied to Twitter posts and the findings reveal that the most common emotion in bullying traces is *fear*, followed by *sadness, anger*, and *relief*.

The detection of sentiments in short informal texts is described in [22] and in [27]. In [22] the authors present a system for sentiment detection based on a supervised statistical text classification approach and derive the sentiment features from tweet-specific sentiment lexicons. The work in [27] shows emotion-word hashtags as good labels for emotions in tweets and proposes the use of emotion-labeled tweets as a method to generate a word-emotion association lexicon.

In [17] the authors introduce a method for automatic emotion extraction from tweets and blog posts in Spanish – collected by tracking mentions of personal names of 18 Latin

American presidents – in order to measure the emotional effect of each president over the public opinion.

In this paper we focus on exploiting social media comments to extract emotions related to short films accessible in YouTube. Our work goes one step beyond the aforementioned approaches as we present how the automatically extracted emotions can be useful for the task of personalized short film recommendation.

User-Generated Content for Ranking and Recommendation. The role of user-generated content for ranking and recommendation tasks is studied in diverse research scenarios. Zhang et al. [37] examine brands by incorporating users posts and information about users interactions. Their experiments on Facebook data show that negative comments generate greater awareness of a brand than positive comments. The usefulness of check-ins and text-based tips in improving location recommendation is explored in [36].

Lipczack et al. [24] study Flickr user actions and tags across network relations to gain understanding on ways to enhance similarity-based recommendation applications and in social network analysis. The authors in [20] analyze YouTube, Flickr, and Last.fm comments to predict the popularity of Web 2.0 items.

Our work explores YouTube comments to detect emotions evoked by short films. In contrast to recent works, we analyze the impact these emotions have in various contexts and leverage our findings for the task of emotion-aware recommendation.

Context-aware Recommendation. Context-aware recommender systems (CARS) [9, 10] improve recommendation quality by incorporating contextual information to the recommendation process – e.g., time [18], location [26], social ties [16], or mood [34] – which enables them to adapt to the specific user's situation. In this work we are particularly interested in emotional context and its impact in CARS.

Gonzalez et al. [19] introduce a system that embeds users' emotional information, which is captured incrementally via small surveys, to enrich recommendations. More recently, Odic et al. [29, 30] demonstrate that emotions can be influential contextual variables in making recommendations. The role of emotions in CARS is explored by Zheng and co-authors in [38] where they study the influence of emotional context for rating prediction.

Similar to these studies, which rely on surveys to extract the emotional context with respect to the items of interest (e.g., movies), we ask humans to associate emotional vectors to short films. However, we go further and also explore how the emotional context can be automatically extracted from social feedback (YouTube comments) and then use a CARS setting as benchmark to assess its usefulness.

3. ROLE OF EMOTIONS IN SHORT FILMS

Our goal is to create a collection of short film-emotion associations to better understand the role of affective context in short films (RQ1). In addition, the emotional context extracted by humans will provide a gold-standard[1] to evaluate our automatic approach for emotion extraction, which we introduce in Section 4. To this end, we use Amazon Mechanical Turk (AMT) [3], a crowdsourcing marketplace where businesses and individuals (known as *requesters*) have access to an on-demand, scalable workforce (*workers*). The

---

[1]Our dataset is available upon request to the first author.

requesters post jobs, known as Human Intelligence Tasks (*HITs*), and the workers complete them in exchange for a monetary reward.

We design a HIT per short film. The HITs are designed following the structure used in [28] but slightly modified in order to adjust them to the films. Each HIT involves watching one single short film and answering sixteen questions. Eight of these questions ask the user to rate the degree of association of the short film to each emotion presented in Plutchik's psychoevolutionary theory [32]. This theory considers that there are eight primary emotions forming four opposing pairs, joy–sadness, anger–fear, trust–disgust, and anticipation–surprise. The next two questions ask for the sentiment polarity that the user would associate to the film (i.e., positive or negative). Five questions aim to get additional context relevant data for the user-short film pair such as time, audience, companion, emoticon, and genre. Finally, one question asks the user to label the film with a *like* or a *dislike* according to her/his personal preference. Appendix A shows an example of a HIT.

Short film collection. A short film is a motion picture with running time of 40 minutes or less [2]. As such, it contains all the elements of a feature film with the difference that the entire plot is much more condensed: there are only a few minutes to tell the story, transmit emotions, and impact the audience.

As a video-sharing website, YouTube hosts content ranging from a funny episode in a family trip to full length movies and documentaries, and unless private, each one of the videos can receive views, ratings and comments from audiences worldwide. Due to its popularity, accessibility and reach, short films festivals such as *Tropfest* [5] and *Your Film Festival* [6] use YouTube to host the films submitted to the competitions.

Tropfest is the world's largest short film festival, it started in Australia twenty two years ago and has expanded to regions including South East Asia and North America [1]. The finalists and winner films of *Tropfest* are uploaded to the festival's YouTube channel which has more than 68K subscribers and 35M views. *Your Film Festival*, sponsored directly by YouTube, took place in 2012 and it offered a $500K grant as the prize. Over 15K films were uploaded to YouTube to enter the competition and the 10 finalists were selected by YouTube users.

Focusing on the two aforementioned festivals, we used YouTube's Data API [7] to collect a set of the participant short films. For each of them, we collected its metadata – i.e., number of views, likes, dislikes – and corresponding comments. The final collection consists of 235 short films and a total of 21,043 comments. The minimum and maximum number of comments per short film is 3 and 996, respectively. The average is 91 and the median is 27 comments per video.

Participants. Each user decided which HIT to annotate or skip. In total we had 107 different participants of which 27 were discarded after a quality control screening. The annotations of the remaining 80 participants constitute the input of this study. The users annotated 7 HITs on average and each HIT was completed by approximately 3 users. In total we captured 631 user-item interactions for the 235 short films.

Emotional vectors from the crowdsourced annotations. To extract emotional vectors from the crowd-

Response	Value
This short film is not associated with the emotion e	0
This short film is weakly associated with the emotion e	1
This short film is moderately associated with the emotion e	2
This short film is strongly associated with the emotion e	3

Table 1: **Mapping responses to numerical values. In each question, e denotes the corresponding emotion.**

sourced annotations we considered the questions related to the emotions and polarity and associated a numerical value to each response. Table 1 shows the possible responses and the associated numerical values. Using the numerical scores, we normalized the responses to obtain probability vectors, i.e., whose values add up to 1.

For example, an emotional vector for a short film over dimensions [joy, sadness, anger, fear, trust, disgust, anticipation, surprise], can correspond to: [0.22, 0.15, 0.07, 0.08, 0.10, 0.06, 0.17, 0.15]. The components of the vector add up to 1 and each of them is a positive number between 0 and 1. Similarly, a polarity tuple (positive, negative) can correspond to: (0.6, 0.4).

3.1 Emotions and Contexts

Contextual information is important if one wants to better understand the users' needs and provide them with higher quality ranking or recommendations. On each HIT, besides the emotions and polarity questions, we asked the user to label the film according to: (i) the audience(s) she perceived as being the most appropriate for the film, (ii) the companion(s) she would choose to watch the film with, (iii) the time when she would watch the film, (iv) the emoticon(s) that would be more representative of her experience while watching the film, and (v) the genre(s) she thinks the film belongs to. We also asked the user to indicate if she liked or disliked the film. Note that we did not ask the users to associate emotions to these different contexts.

The purpose of these questions is to explore if and how emotions, implicitly, affect the decision on what to watch.

In what follows we analyze the emotions present in the videos associated by the users to each context.

Likes and Dislikes

We obtained 631 crowdsourced responses (e.g., user-item interactions). In 72.9% (460) of these cases the users indicated they liked the short film while in 27.1% (171) they disliked it.

Since each user also indicated what emotions and polarity she associates to the video, we explore how these emotions are distributed for both the *liked* and *disliked* films. For example, for all the *liked* videos we calculate the overall joy score by adding all the scores given for the emotion joy and dividing it by the number of videos (average joy). We follow the same procedure for all the emotions.

Figure 1 shows the average distribution of emotions and polarity in *liked* and *disliked* videos. As we can see in Figure 1(a), the most prominent emotion in the *liked* videos is joy, followed by anticipation, surprise and sadness. In the *disliked* videos the distribution of emotions is slightly different, sadness is the most prominent, followed by joy, anticipation and surprise (Figure 1(b)). It is also worth noting that the emotions disgust and anger increase when compared with those in the *liked* videos.

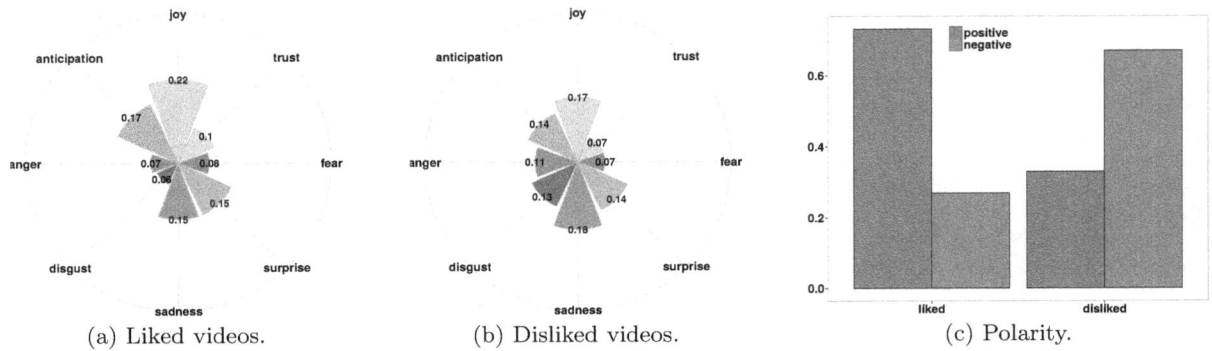

(a) Liked videos. (b) Disliked videos. (c) Polarity.

Figure 1: **Emotions and polarity in *liked* and *disliked* videos.**

Besides our questions related to Plutchik's eight basic emotions, we also asked users to indicate how positive or negative a film was. The possible responses were similar to those shown in Table 1.

In all cases where users labeled the video with a *like* we find an average score of 0.73 (the max. possible score is 1) for positive polarity and a score of 0.27 for negative polarity, while in the videos labeled with a *dislike*, there is an average score of 0.33 and 0.67 for positive and negative polarity, respectively. Figure 1(c) shows the distribution of polarity in the *liked* and *disliked* videos.

As shown in Figure 1, *Liked* videos are more associated with joy, anticipation, surprise, sadness, trust, and positive polarity, while *disliked* videos are more associated with sadness, joy, anticipation, surprise, a higher degree of disgust and anger, and negative polarity.

Audience

On each HIT, we asked the user to select the audience she/he thought as being the most adequate for the given short film. The question had six possible answers: *children, teenagers, young adults, adults, seniors*, and *all audiences*.

One reason behind this question is to better understand if there are certain emotions which a user considers more appropriate for a given demographic. Another reason is to explore how users preferences would change according to the context, for example, parents may forbid their child to watch a film if it is known to contain a high degree of anger.

As in this question the users were allowed to select more than one answer, for the analysis we considered each film as many times as audiences were thought as appropriate. 5% of the films (56 films) were marked as appropriate for *children*, 16% (184) for *teenagers*, 28% (322) for *young adults*, 29% (337) for *adults*, 10% (112) for *seniors*, and 12% (135) for *all audiences*.

Figure 2 shows the average distribution of the emotions associated to the films that the users selected as adequate for each audience. It is interesting to note that for the audiences *children, teenagers* and *all audiences* the emotion with higher average is joy; however, as the audience's age increases (*young adults, adults, seniors*) the appropriate films contain less joy and a higher presence of sadness, disgust and fear, according to the respondents.

Children (Figure 2(a)) and *seniors* (Figure 2(e)) are the audiences for which the users selected the lowest number of videos when compared to the rest of the groups. The films

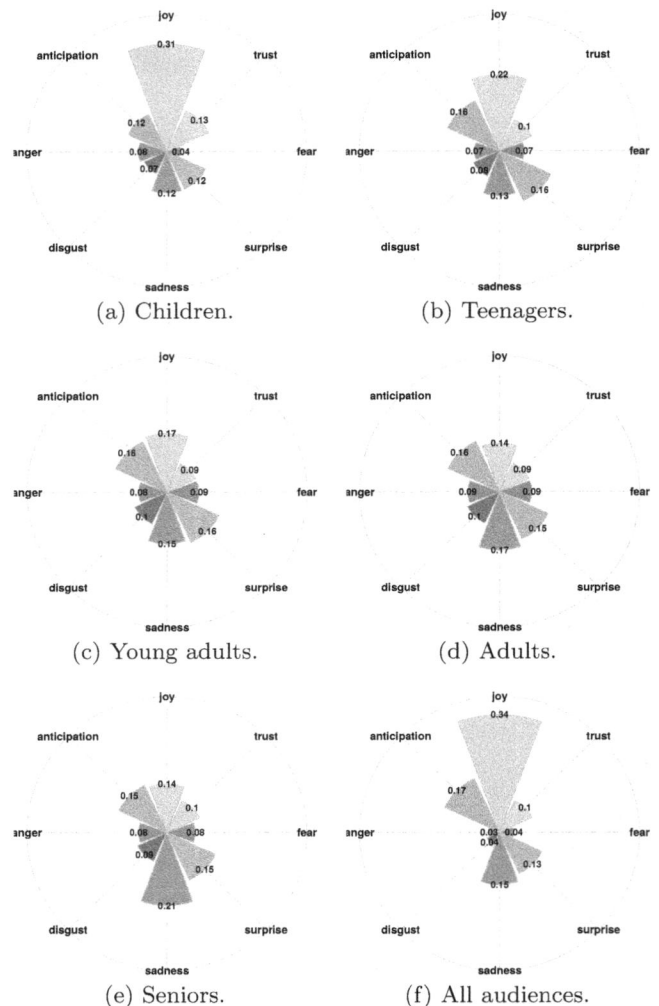

(a) Children. (b) Teenagers.

(c) Young adults. (d) Adults.

(e) Seniors. (f) All audiences.

Figure 2: **Emotions per audience.**

for *children* have a high score for joy (0.31) and a low score for fear (0.04), disgust (0.07) and anger (0.08), while the films for *seniors* have the highest sadness score (0.21) and the lowest joy score (0.14) among all the audiences.

The short films marked as appropriate for *all audiences* (Figure 2(f)) are those associated with joy (0.34), anticipation (0.17), sadness (0.15), surprise (0.13), and trust (0.10). The low scores for disgust (0.04), fear (0.04) and anger (0.03) could indicate the influence of these particular emotions on the selection of an adequate audience.

The highest number of associated videos are for the audiences *young adults* (Figure 2(c)) and *adults* (Figure 2(d)). Contrary to other audiences, the videos in these groups show a more balanced distribution of emotions (scores ranging from 0.08 to 0.17), and while disgust, anger and fear are not dominant, there is an increase with respect to the other groups.

Time

Time is one of the most studied contexts when trying to determine meaningful items for users. Users preferences vary according to the time of the day, day of the week, or weekday and weekend.

We asked users to indicate when they would prefer watching the given film. The question had four possible answers: *to relax after work*, *during a break at work*, *for entertainment during weekends or on vacation*, and *at anytime*. More than one answer was permitted.

Rather than specifying a time of the day (i.e., morning, afternoon) we consider a combination of activity and time.

For *relaxing after work* 13% (89) of the films would be watched, 17% (115) during a *break at work*, 28% (195) *for entertainment during weekends or on vacation*, and 42% (292) at *anytime*. Figure 3 shows the average distribution of emotions for each time.

Joy, surprise, and anticipation are the strongest emotions in the videos selected for *relaxing after work*, with anger, fear and disgust being the least present (Figure 3(a)). *During a*

break at work (Figure 3(b)) and *for entertainment on weekends or vacations* (Figure 3(c)) the films show an increase in anger, disgust, sadness, and fear. For the videos that would be watched at *anytime* (Figure 3(d)) the dominant emotions are joy, anticipation, sadness, and surprise.

Companion

One of the factors that influences users' decisions on what to watch is their companion at that specific moment. For example, a teenager might not watch a war film if she is with family, but would be keen on watching it when she is with friends or alone, or a person would not dare to watch a horror movie while alone, but would watch it when surrounded by friends.

We asked the users to indicate the companion with whom they would watch the short film presented in the HIT. The possible answers were: *friends, family, partner, alone,* and *anybody*. More than one answer was permitted.

Figure 4 shows the average distribution of emotions per companion. 7% (59) and 12% (94) of the films would be watched with *family* and *partner* (e.g., boyfriend/girlfriend,

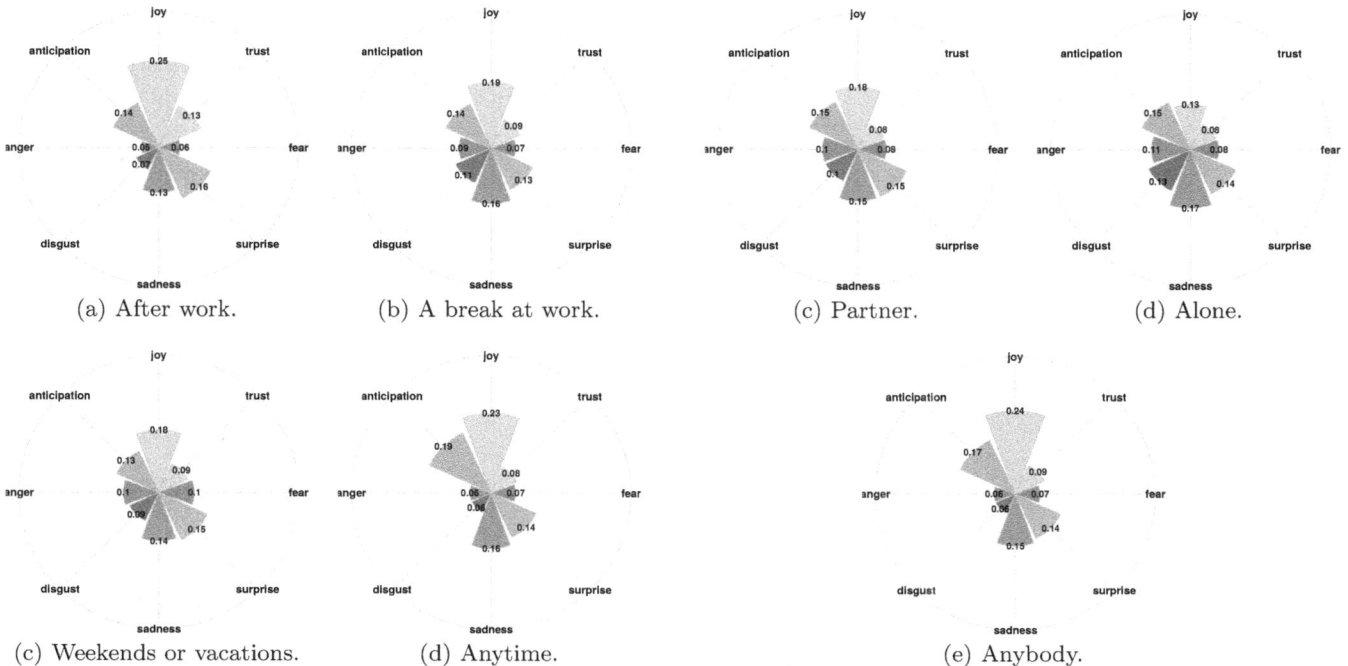

(a) Friends. (b) Family.

(c) Partner. (d) Alone.

(e) Anybody.

Figure 4: **Emotions per companion.**

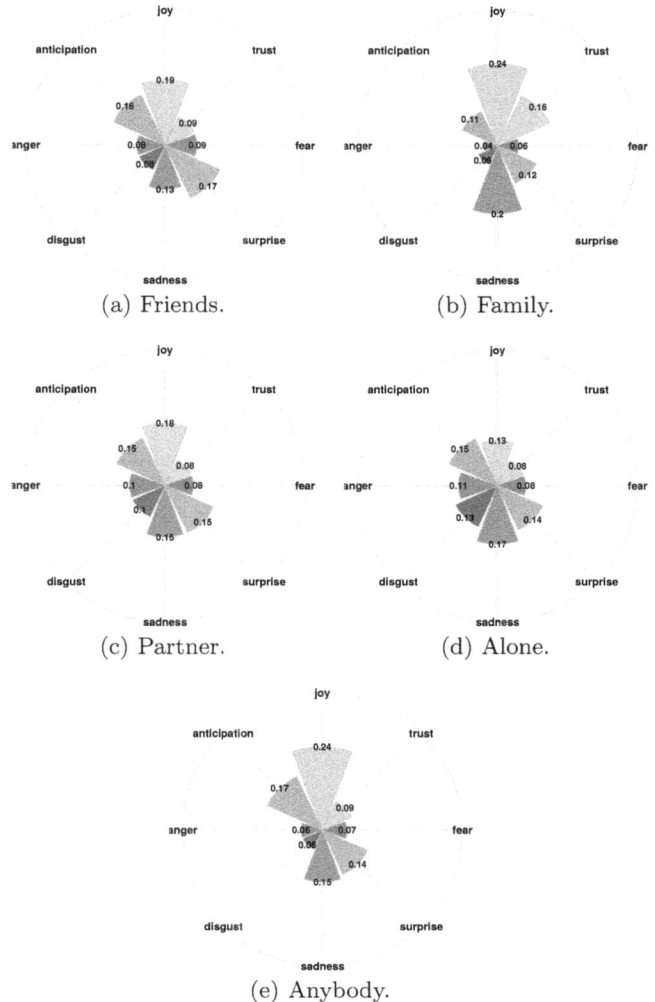

(a) After work. (b) A break at work.

(c) Weekends or vacations. (d) Anytime.

Figure 3: **Emotions per time.**

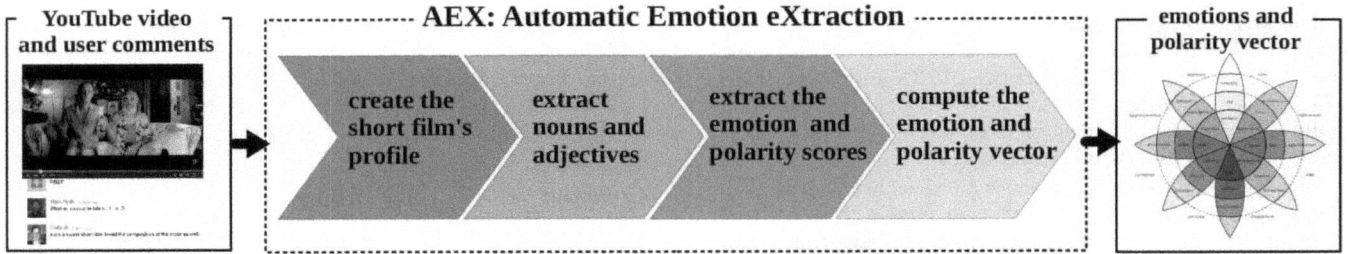

Figure 5: Extraction of emotions and polarity vectors from YouTube Comments. (1) Aggregate the short film's comments to form the film's profile. (2) Tag the profile with part-of-speech and extract the identified nouns and adjectives. (3) Search a match in EmoLex for each noun and adjective. When there is a match, add and process the related scores to form the emotions and polarity vector.

husband/wife), respectively, 20% (155) with *friends*, 23% (187) *alone*, and 38% (303) with anybody.

The films that the users would watch with *friends* (Figure 4(a)) have a high association with the emotions joy, surprise, anticipation, and sadness, and the highest presence of fear among all the companions. With *family* (Figure 4(b)), joy, sadness and trust are the dominant emotions, and fear has a lower score than in any other group of companions. For the option *alone* (Figure 4(d)), users selected those films with the lowest average of joy but with the highest average of disgust and anger.

With *partner* (Figure 4(c)), the average distribution of emotions is similar to that shown in (Figure 4(d)) with the main differences being joy, sadness, and disgust scores. The films to watch with *anybody* have joy as their dominant emotion, followed by anticipation and sadness. Anger, fear, and disgust have the lowest average scores among the emotions in this category.

In summary, under the settings of this study:

- Emotions impact the decisions on what to watch given different contexts.

- The most popular emotions (in terms of average score) found across the different contexts are joy, sadness, surprise, and anticipation. The least popular emotions and possibly the most discriminative – a strong presence of one or more of these emotions may help users distinguish in which contexts to watch the film – were anger, disgust, trust, and fear.

- Contexts involving children, seniors, or family resulted in a more unbalanced (very different average scores) distribution of emotions in the videos considered as appropriate, while for audiences such as adults, the selected videos had a more balanced (more similar average scores) presence of emotions.

4. AUTOMATIC EMOTION EXTRACTION

The explicit associations between short films and emotions via crowdsourcing provide very useful insights as detailed in Section 3. However, such effort can be costly and time consuming, particularly if done at large scale. In addition to that and given the accelerated pace of film production, an automatic approach for emotion detection represents a more desirable alternative.

In this section we address RQ2 and present our Automatic Emotion eXtraction approach (*AEX*) that exploits the large

amount of YouTube comments associated to a short film – as an important source of opinions and discussions about the video – in order to track the emotions it evokes.

AEX is comprised of the steps outlined in Procedure 1 and illustrated in Figure 5. Our approach is motivated by promising results reported in recent studies for emotion detection from short and sparse text [17, 31, 22].

Procedure 1 AEX: Automatic Emotion eXtraction

Input: User comments associated to a short film p.
Output: Emotional vector e_p and polarity tuple τ_p for the short film.
1: Create a *profile* for short film p by aggregating its user comments.
2: Extract the terms from the profile – i.e., nouns and adjectives.
3: Automatically associate each extracted term to a set of *emotions* and *polarity*.
4: Compute the *emotion vector* e_p and *polarity tuple* τ_p for the short film p.
5: **return** $[e_p, \tau_p]$

First we build a *profile* for each of the short films. The profile consists of all the user comments collected for the corresponding short film.

After building the profiles we perform part-of-speech tagging on each of them, using LingPipe [8] and MorphAdorner [4], in order to extract the *nouns* and *adjectives*, which have been shown to be good predictors for this task [17]. Part-of-speech tagging is necessary because the same word can act as a different part-of-speech depending on the context of the sentence.

Then, using a term-based matching technique, we associate each term with emotion and polarity values. To this end, we use in our study the NRC Emotion Lexicon (EmoLex) [28], a large set of human-provided word-emotion association ratings annotated according to Plutchik's psychoevolutionary theory [32]. Besides including annotations for each primary emotion, namely joy–sadness, anger–fear, trust–disgust, and anticipation–surprise, EmoLex also includes positive and negative sentiments associated to the words.

For instance, the word *friend* is associated to the emotion *joy* and to *positive* polarity, whereas the word *violent* is associated to the emotions of *anger, disgust, fear, surprise*, and *trust*, and a *negative* polarity.

We use EmoLex in order to be consistent with the affective context associated by humans in Section 3 and we also use the same data set – 235 short films and a total of 21,043 comments. The minimum and maximum number of comments per short film is 3 and 996, respectively. The average is 91 and the median is 27 comments per video.

AEX's goal is to automatically obtain an emotional vector and polarity tuple with the same structure as the ones elicited via crowdsourcing (see Section 3). To this end, we define the emotional vector, e_p, for short film p as follows. Let T_p be the set of terms extracted from the short film's profile p, and T_m the set of all terms in EmoLex annotated with emotion m, where $m \in M$; $M := \{joy, sadness, anger, fear, trust, disgust, anticipation, surprise\}$, i.e., Plutchik's eight basic emotions. Then, the mth dimension of emotional vector $e_p \in \mathbb{R}^{|M|}$ is given by:

$$e_p[m] := \sum_{t \in T_p} \mathcal{I}_m(t) * \text{tf-idf}(t)$$

where $\mathcal{I}_m(t)$ is an indicator function that outputs 1 if the term $t \in T_p$ is associated to emotion m, and 0 otherwise. tf-idf(t) denotes the tf-idf score of the term t, which weights the importance of the term contribution to the emotional vector.

Finally, we normalize vector e_p to produce a stochastic vector $\hat{e}_p = \frac{e_p}{Z_e}$, where $Z_e = ||e_p||_1$ is a normalization constant.

Similarly as in the case of emotions, we compute the polarity tuple $\tau_p = (positive, negative)$ of short film p as follows:

$$\tau_p = \frac{1}{Z_{polarity}} \left(\sum_{t \in T_p} \mathcal{I}_+(t) * \text{tf-idf(t)}, \sum_{t \in T_p} \mathcal{I}_-(t) * \text{tf-idf(t)} \right)$$

where the indicator functions and normalization constant are defined analogously as in the case of the emotions.

AEX offers the possibility to associate emotions to videos based on the social comments and discussion about it. Note that while this work focuses on short films, AEX is applicable to other scenarios using other types of textual resources, such as tweets, blog posts or users product reviews. In the next section we quantify to what extent the emotions extracted automatically compare to the ones associated by humans using a recommendation task as a benchmark.

5. EMPIRICAL EVALUATION

In this section we address RQ3 and measure to what extent the emotional context extracted using AEX compares to the one explicitly assigned by humans. We also assess the usefulness of the extracted context for a recommendation task, which tackles RQ4.

5.1 User Self-Similarity

AEX should capture the same, or a very similar, emotional context as the one extracted from the explicit human annotations. We take a user-centric perspective in order to measure the similarity among both strategies for emotion extraction.

We represent each observed user-item pair interaction – e.g., user watches a short film – using two emotional vectors corresponding to the manual and automatic strategy, respectively. Then, we compute the Cosine Similarity (CS) and Pearson Correlation Coefficient (PCC) between these two vectors and average the corresponding scores user-wise

in order to measure the self-similarity of the user across the approaches.

The average CS and PCC over all users is $CS = 0.6893$ ($\sigma = 0.166$) and $PCC = 0.4992$ ($p < 0.001$) respectively, which indicates a positive correlation between the strategies.

5.2 Emotion-aware Recommendation

Our goal in this part of the evaluation is to answer RQ4, i.e., we want to assess how useful is the emotional context extracted by AEX for a recommendation task.

Emotions and CARS. A natural way to include emotional information into a recommender system is by following a context-aware approach. Context-aware recommender systems (CARS) [10] generate more relevant recommendations by (i) incorporating contextual information in the recommendation process and by (ii) adapting the recommendations to the specific contextual situation of the user. In this evaluation we are concerned with the former and leave the latter for future work, e.g., leveraging the different dimensions explored in Section 3 for adaptation.

We incorporate the emotional context into the recommender system by following a Collaborative Ranking (CR) approach [12, 16] – other state-of-the-art alternatives for CARS include Factorization Machines [33] and N-dimensional Tensor Factorization [21]. The main idea behind this approach is to cast the recommendation problem into a (personalized) learning-to-rank task [25].

The emotion-aware recommendation problem can be placed into the learning-to-rank framework [25] by noting that the users correspond to queries and short films to documents. For each user-item pair the observed binary rating (like/dislike) indicates the relevance of the corresponding item (short film) with respect to that user and can be used to optimize the parameters of a ranking function that will be used for recommendation. As in the case of the self-similarity computation, we represent each observed user-item pair interaction by the corresponding emotional vectors given by the manual and automatic strategy (AEX). Figure 6 shows an example of a standard CARS-CR data representation.

```
------------------------------------------------------------
 1 qid:1 1:0.05 2:0.17 3:0.04 4:0.06 5:0.27 6:0.06 7:0.11 8:0.22
-1 qid:1 1:0.12 2:0.12 3:0.16 4:0.06 5:0.16 6:0.06 7:0.16 8:0.12
-1 qid:1 1:0.00 2:0.20 3:0.03 4:0.06 5:0.23 6:0.00 7:0.07 8:0.38
 1 qid:2 1:0.11 2:0.12 3:0.12 4:0.10 5:0.15 6:0.09 7:0.07 8:0.20
-1 qid:2 1:0.04 2:0.23 3:0.03 4:0.02 5:0.22 6:0.01 7:0.14 8:0.26
------------------------------------------------------------
```

Figure 6: **Collaborative Ranking data representation for CARS. In each row the first column represents the label, the second represents the user id (qid), and the rest of the columns are the emotional features of the user-item pair interactions, which correspond to the 8-dimension emotional vector (the 2 dimensions representing the polarity tuple are omitted in this example).**

CARS-CR learning-to-rank method. We use LambdaMART as the learning-to-rank method [13] for our emotion-aware recommendation task. We choose this method due to its ability to directly optimize Information Retrieval (IR) metrics and for the good performance exhibited in recent ranking competitions [14, 15].

LambdaMART is a learning-to-rank (ensemble) method that uses Multiple Additive Regression Trees or MART as base learners. One of the main features of LambdaMART is that it can optimize arbitrary IR metrics by guiding the learning process using so-called λ-gradients, which reflect small changes in the IR metric while iterating over the training set. We omit a detailed description of the model, since it is out of the scope of this report, and refer the reader to [13] and [14] for a comprehensive analysis of LambdaMART.

Protocol. The dataset is split user-wise into training, validation, and test set. First, 20% of the users – with their respective items – are randomly assigned to the test set. Then, we randomly sample 10% of the remaining users to form a validation set, which will help us to select the hyperparameters of our model. Finally, the rest of the user-item interactions are used for training.

After the selection of the best hyperparameters through grid-search, we retrain our models on the union of the training and validation sets, i.e., using 80% of the users. To account for variability, the results reported are the average of 100 rounds of experiments considering 95% confidence intervals.

Metrics. In order to measure the recommendation quality and to reflect our goal of recommending a short list of items to a user, we look to *precision* and *mean reciprocal rank* at cut-off level 5 – i.e., $P@5$ and $MRR@5$ [11]. The metrics are computed for each user in the test set and then averaged.

Parameters settings. Using the validation set we found that for LambdaMART a number of 64 base trees, with 5 leaves each, and a learning rate (or shrinkage) equal to 0.1 led to good results. We use RankLib's implementation of LambdaMART to learn the ranking function [23].

Results. Figure 7 shows the recommendation performance for the CARS-CR model trained using the emotional vectors derived from human intelligence (HI) and the one trained using the affective context automatically extracted with AEX. The $P@5$ for the CARS-CR models using HI and AEX are 75.95% and 69.50%, respectively, which corresponds to a difference of 6.45 percentage points.

CARS-CR using HI achieves a $MRR@5 = 83.43\%$ which ties with the AEX-based approach ($MRR@5 = 81.83\%$) since the difference is not statistically significant.

5.3 Discussion

After our experimental evaluation, we can answer our research questions RQ3 and RQ4.

The emotional context automatically associated to a short film is similar and positively correlated to the one explicitly annotated by humans ($CS = 68.93\%$ and $PCC = 49.92\%$). This level of user self-similarity between the emotional contexts is important for recommender systems, for example, user- or item-based collaborative filtering (CF), which use a k-nearest-neighbor approach to deliver recommendations, could use the AEX emotional vectors – instead of the human annotated ones – to compute the user or item neighborhoods required to produce a short list of personalized recommendations. This answers RQ3.

For RQ4, the results illustrated in Figure 7 show that the recommender system based on AEX is very competitive, specially in terms of $MRR@5$. This indicates that the automatic approach is capable of inferring an affective context useful in learning an emotion-aware personalized ranking model. Given the inherently human nature of emotions, the fact that the HI-based approach achieves a slightly better performance is somewhat expected; however, the promising results of the AEX-based model open the doors to compute

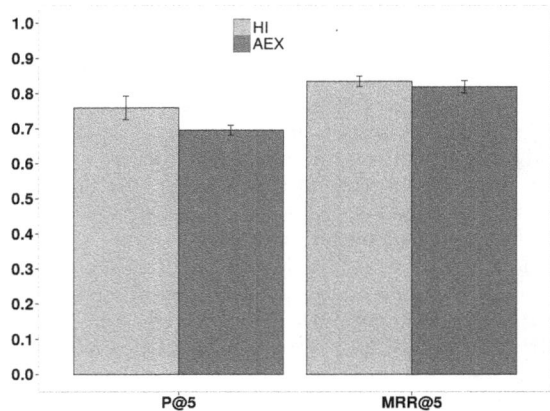

Figure 7: **Recommendation performance for the CARS-CR model using human intelligence (HI) and automatically extracted affective context (AEX).**

emotional context at scale and then leverage it to improve recommender systems.

6. CONCLUSION

In this paper we tackled the issue of extracting emotions associated to short films. We approached the task from two different fronts: (i) using crowdsourcing to obtain emotional labels and (ii) automatically extracting affective context based on the users criticism expressed in YouTube comments. Furthermore, we explored the usefulness of the extracted emotions for the task of context-aware recommendation.

We crowdsourced emotional labels by asking people on Amazon Mechanical Turk to complete HITs of sixteen questions, which aimed at identifying the emotions and polarity they associated with the short film and other relevant information on the different contexts (i.e., time, audience) at the moment of making the decision on whether to watch a film or not. The results obtained reveal that the emotions and polarity associated to short films have an impact on users liking/disliking the films and on the circumstances they would consider appropriate for watching a film or not.

We proposed AEX, an automatic emotion extraction approach, which makes use of YouTube comments to identify emotions associated to short films. Our findings reveal that users' comments indeed provide the information required to automatically extract emotions associated to short films.

Lastly, we measured the similarity of the emotional context automatically associated to a short film to that explicitly annotated by humans. In addition, we assessed the usefulness of the emotional context extracted by AEX for a recommendation task. Our results reveal that the emotional contexts extracted by the two different approaches are similar, and that the automatic approach is capable of inferring a useful affective context for emotion-aware personalized ranking.

The dataset used in this work was collected from two popular short film festivals available in YouTube. One of the reasons being reducing the inclusion of spam and ensuring a better quality of the selected films. We are aware, however, that the size of our final dataset is one limitation of this work. In the future, we plan to enlarge and diversify our dataset and to address tasks of short films ranking and recommendation considering, along with emotions and polarity, other contextual information such as time, companion, or target audience.

Acknowledgements. This work was supported in part by Science Foundation Ireland - Grant Number: 12/RC/2289.

7. REFERENCES

[1] About Tropfest. http://tropfest.com/about/. Accessed: 2015-04.

[2] Academy of Motion Picture Arts (AMPAS). http://www.oscars.org/oscars/rules-eligibility. Accessed: 2015-03.

[3] Amazon Mechanical Turk. https://www.mturk.com/mturk/welcome. Accessed: 2015-04.

[4] MorphAdorner. http://morphadorner.northwestern.edu. Accessed: 2015-03.

[5] Tropfest YouTube Channel. https://www.youtube.com/user/tropfest. Accessed: 2015-03.

[6] Your Film Festival. https://www.youtube.com/user/yourfilmfestival. Accessed: 2015-03.

[7] YouTube API. http://developers.google.com/youtube/v3/. Accessed: 2015-04.

[8] Alias-i. LingPipe 4.1.0. http://alias-i.com/lingpipe, 2008. Accessed: 2015-03.

[9] G. Adomavicius, B. Mobasher, F. Ricci, and A. Tuzhilin. Context-aware recommender systems. *AI Magazine*, 32(3), 2011.

[10] G. Adomavicius and A. Tuzhilin. Context-aware recommender systems. In F. Ricci, L. Rokach, B. Shapira, and P. B. Kantor, editors, *Recommender Systems Handbook*, pages 217–253. Springer US, 2011.

[11] R. A. Baeza-Yates and B. A. Ribeiro-Neto. *Modern Information Retrieval - the concepts and technology behind search, Second edition*. Pearson Education Ltd., Harlow, England, 2011.

[12] S. Balakrishnan and S. Chopra. Collaborative ranking. In *Proceedings of the Fifth ACM International Conference on Web Search and Data Mining*, WSDM '12, pages 143–152, New York, NY, USA, 2012. ACM.

[13] C. J. Burges. From ranknet to lambdarank to lambdamart: An overview. Technical Report MSR-TR-2010-82, Microsoft Research, June 2010.

[14] C. J. C. Burges, K. M. Svore, P. N. Bennett, A. Pastusiak, and Q. Wu. Learning to rank using an ensemble of lambda-gradient models. In *Yahoo! Learning to Rank Challenge*, pages 25–35, 2011.

[15] O. Chapelle and Y. Chang. Yahoo! learning to rank challenge overview. In *Yahoo! Learning to Rank Challenge*, pages 1–24, 2011.

[16] E. Diaz-Aviles, H. T. Lam, F. Pinelli, S. Braghin, Y. Gkoufas, M. Berlingerio, and F. Calabrese. Predicting user engagement in twitter with collaborative ranking. In *Proceedings of the 2014 Recommender Systems Challenge*, RecSysChallenge'14, 2014.

[17] E. Diaz-Aviles, C. Orellana-Rodriguez, and W. Nejdl. Taking the pulse of political emotions in latin america based on social web streams. *Web Congress, Latin American*, 2012.

[18] Z. Gantner, S. Rendle, and L. Schmidt-Thieme. Factorization models for context-/time-aware movie recommendations. In *Proceedings of the Workshop on Context-Aware Movie Recommendation*, CAMRa '10, 2010.

[19] G. Gonzalez, J. de la Rosa, M. Montaner, and S. Delfin. Embedding emotional context in recommender systems. In *Data Engineering Workshop, 2007 IEEE 23rd International Conference on*, 2007.

[20] X. He, M. Gao, M.-Y. Kan, Y. Liu, and K. Sugiyama. Predicting the popularity of web 2.0 items based on user comments. In *Proceedings of the 37th International ACM SIGIR Conference on Research and Development in Information Retrieval*, SIGIR '14, pages 233–242, New York, NY, USA, 2014. ACM.

[21] A. Karatzoglou, X. Amatriain, L. Baltrunas, and N. Oliver. Multiverse recommendation: N-dimensional tensor factorization for context-aware collaborative filtering. In *Proceedings of the Fourth ACM Conference on Recommender Systems*, RecSys '10, pages 79–86, New York, NY, USA, 2010. ACM.

[22] S. Kiritchenko, X. Zhu, and S. M. Mohammad. Sentiment analysis of short informal texts. *Journal of Artificial Intelligence Research (JAIR)*, 2014.

[23] Lemur Project. Ranklib. http://www.lemurproject.org/, 2015. Accessed: 2015-03.

[24] M. Lipczak, B. Sigurbjornsson, and A. Jaimes. Understanding and leveraging tag-based relations in on-line social networks. In *Proceedings of the 23rd ACM Conference on Hypertext and Social Media*, HT '12, 2012.

[25] T.-Y. Liu. *Learning to Rank for Information Retrieval*. Springer, 2011.

[26] C. Mettouris and G. A. Papadopoulos. Ubiquitous recommender systems. *Computing*, 96(3):223–257, 2014.

[27] S. M. Mohammad and S. Kiritchenko. Using hashtags to capture fine emotion categories from tweets. *Computational Intelligence*, 2014.

[28] S. M. Mohammad and P. D. Turney. Crowdsourcing a word-emotion association lexicon. *Computational Intelligence*, 2011.

[29] A. Odić, M. Tkalčič, A. Košir, and J. F. Tasič. Relevant context in a movie recommender system: Users' opinion vs. statistical detection. In *Proceedings of the 4th Workshop on Context-Aware Recommender Systems*, 2012.

[30] A. Odić, M. Tkalčič, J. F. Tasič, and A. Košir. Predicting and detecting the relevant contextual information in a movie-recommender system. *Interacting with Computers*, 25(1), 2013.

[31] C. Orellana-Rodriguez, E. Diaz-Aviles, and W. Nejdl. Mining emotions in short films: User comments or crowdsourcing? In *Proceedings of the 22nd*

International Conference on World Wide Web Companion (Posters), WWW '13, 2013.

[32] R. Plutchik. *A General Psychoevolutionary Theory of Emotion*. Academic press, New York, 1980.

[33] S. Rendle, Z. Gantner, C. Freudenthaler, and L. Schmidt-Thieme. Fast context-aware recommendations with factorization machines. In *Proceedings of the 34th International ACM SIGIR Conference on Research and Development in Information Retrieval*, SIGIR '11. ACM, 2011.

[34] Y. Shi, M. Larson, and A. Hanjalic. Mining mood-specific movie similarity with matrix factorization for context-aware recommendation. In *Proceedings of the Workshop on Context-Aware Movie Recommendation*, CAMRa '10, 2010.

[35] J.-M. Xu, X. Zhu, and A. Bellmore. Fast learning for sentiment analysis on bullying. In *Proceedings of the First International Workshop on Issues of Sentiment Discovery and Opinion Mining*, WISDOM '12, 2012.

[36] D. Yang, D. Zhang, Z. Yu, and Z. Wang. A sentiment-enhanced personalized location recommendation system. In *Proceedings of the 24th ACM Conference on Hypertext and Social Media*, HT '13, 2013.

[37] K. Zhang, S. Bhattacharyya, and S. Ram. Empirical analysis of implicit brand networks on social media. In *Proceedings of the 25th ACM Conference on Hypertext and Social Media*, HT '14, 2014.

[38] Y. Zheng, R. Burke, and B. Mobasher. The role of emotions in context-aware recommendation. In *ACM RecSys' 13, Proceedings of the 3rd International Workshop on Human Decision Making in Recommender Systems*, 2013.

APPENDIX

A. EXAMPLE OF A HIT

Title: Emotions in Short Films
Keywords: Emotions, Sentiment Analysis, Video
Reward : $:0.15
Description: You will be shown a short film and asked to indicate the different emotions you associate to the film

Q1. Did you like this short film?
  • yes
  • no

Q2. How positive (good, praising) is this short film?
  • this short film is not positive
  • this short film is weakly positive
  • this short film is moderately positive
  • this short film is strongly positive

Q3. How negative (bad, criticizing) is this short film?
  • similar choices as in Q2

Q4. How much would you associate this short film with the emotion joy? (for example, *happy* and *funny* scenes are strongly associated with joy)
  • this short film is not associated with joy
  • this short film is weakly associated with joy
  • this short film is moderately associated with joy
  • this short film is strongly associated with joy

Q5. How much would you associate this short film with the emotion sadness? (for example, *gloomy* and *hearthbreaking* scenes are strongly associated with sadness)
  • up to Q11 the answers are similar to those in Q4

Q6. How much would you associate this short film with the emotion fear? (for example, *horror* and *scary* scenes are strongly associated with fear)

Q7. How much would you associate this short film with the emotion anger? (for example, *rage* and *shouting* scenes are strongly associated with anger)

Q8. How much would you associate this short film with the emotion trust? (for example, *loyalty* and *integrity* scenes are strongly associated with trust)

Q9. How much would you associate this short film with the emotion disgust? (for example, *gross* and *cruelty* scenes are strongly associated with disgust)

Q10. How much would you associate this short film with the emotion surprise? (for example, *astonishing* and *sudden* scenes are strongly associated with surprise)

Q11. How much would you associate this short film with the emotion anticipation? (for example, scenes that keep you *interested* and *expecting* something are strongly associated with anticipation)

Q12. Who would you watch this short film with?
  • friends
  • family
  • boyfriend/girlfriend (husband/wife)
  • alone
  • with anybody

Q13. When would you watch this short film?
  • for relaxing after a working day
  • during a break at work
  • for entertainment on weekends or on vacation
  • at anytime

Q14. Who do you think would be the most appropriate audience(s) of this short film?
  • children (0-12 years)
  • teenagers (13-17 years)
  • young adults (18-24 years)
  • adults (25-64 years)
  • seniors (> 65 years)
  • all audiences

Q15. Please select the emoticons (one or more) representing the emotions you experienced while watching this short film
  :)   :(:D   :o   :&   :@
  |-) ;(:| (whew) :S   :^)

Q16. What would you say is the genre (or genres) of this short film?

action	adventure	biography	animation
comedy	crime	documentary	drama
family	fantasy	film-noir	game-show
history	horror	music	musical
mystery	news	reality-tv	romance
sci-fi	sport	talk-show	thriller
war	western		

194

An Investigation into the Use of Logical and Rhetorical Tactics within Eristic Argumentation on the Social Web

Tom Blount
Web and Internet Science
ECS
University of Southampton
tb12g09@ecs.soton.ac.uk

David E. Millard
Web and Internet Science
ECS
University of Southampton
dem@ecs.soton.ac.uk

Mark J. Weal
Web and Internet Science
ECS
University of Southampton
mjw@ecs.soton.ac.uk

ABSTRACT

Argumentation is a key aspect of communications and can broadly be broken down into problem solving (dialectic) and quarrelling (eristic). Techniques used within argumentation can likewise be classified as fact-based (logical), or emotion/audience-based (rhetorical). Modelling arguments on the social web is a challenge for those studying computational argumentation as formal models of argumentation tend to assume a logical argument, whereas argumentation on the social web is often largely rhetorical. To investigate the application of logical versus rhetorical techniques on the social web, we bring together two ontologies used for modelling argumentation and online communities respectively, the Argument Interchange Format and the Semantic Interlinked Online Communities project. We augment these with our own ontology for modelling rhetorical argument, the Argumentation on the Social Web Ontology, and trial our additions by examining three case studies following argumentation on different categories of social media. Finally, we present examples of how rhetorical argumentation is used in the context of the social web and show that there are clear markers present that can allow for a rudimentary estimate for the classification of a social media post with regards to its contribution to a discussion.

Categories and Subject Descriptors

H.4.3 [**Information Systems Applications**]: Communications Applications—*Social media*

Keywords

argumentation; dialectic; eristic; logic; rhetoric; social web

1. INTRODUCTION

Argumentation is fundamental to human communication – it is how people share new information and new ideas, and propose courses of action that see them carried out [5, 12] and can be (broadly) separated into two categories based on the intended outcome: dialectic, in which the participants are engaged in rational discourse with the aim of either discovering the particular truth behind a matter, or formulating a solution to a problem [14], and eristic, in which

HT '15, September 1–4, 2015, Guzelyurt, Northern Cyprus.
ⓒ2015 ACM. ISBN 978-1-4503-3395-5/15/09...$15.00.
DOI: http://dx.doi.org/10.1145/2700171.2791052

the participants are quarrelling with the aim of being seen to win [7]. Orthogonally to this, there are the notions of logic and rhetoric. While often used in modern parlance as a pejorative term, rhetoric is the art of discourse and convincing an audience based on one's knowledge of the topic at hand and of the audience themselves. Logical argumentation uses the facts of a case to draw conclusions but, it is important to note that the "facts" do not necessarily need to be correct: they may be warped to fit a particular purpose, or even outright fabricated. The key element is that the argument relies on these facts and the reasoning between them, even if fallacious. In contrast, rhetorical argument focuses on swaying an audience to one's cause by other means, such as appealing to camaraderie or making threats. There is a tendency to view argumentation tactics in relatively stark terms: that dialectic/logical arguments are good and eristic/rhetorical arguments are bad, which leads to eristic and rhetorical argumentation being discounted from formal models. However, this should be resisted: logical argument can also be used in a hostile manner and, by contrast, eristic or rhetorical arguments are often used recreationally, for humour or catharsis [18].

As the social web grows, the potential for using it to investigate how truly massive communities interact, communicate and argue increases dramatically. However, the social web presents a number of challenges for extracting and analysing arguments, particularly due to use of informal language [17], and by the number of distinct ecosystems on the social web with their own constraints and cultures [8]. There are also challenges when considering maintaining the social web as an inclusive platform for diverse and vibrant discussion. Because of the tendency for users to interact with others who are similar in terms of traits and beliefs, sites can become "echo-chambers" in which well-known views and opinions are repeated, little original content is produced and there is virtually no dissent or debate [4, 19]. Such spaces can quickly become stale or, at worst, incredibly hostile to those with opposing views, culminating at is most extreme in anti-social behaviour including vulgar abuse, threats of sexual violence, and death threats [6]. Disregarding these interactions from argumentation models is a mistake; indeed, accurately modelling them is the first step towards understanding how social media is used, and creating tools and environments that discourage these types of abuse to facilitate more social argumentation. As a result, current models must be combined and adapted to be fit for purpose when examining the social web.

2. BACKGROUND
2.1 Argument Interchange Format

The Argument Interchange Format (AIF) is a framework for representing argumentation as a directed graph [3]. Created as part of the Argument Web project [15], the AIF is primarily a description, with specifications in a number of languages including RDF and SQL. Data, claims and conclusions are modelled by Information nodes (I-nodes). I-nodes are linked by intermediary Scheme nodes (S-nodes). These S-nodes are subdivided into three applications: Rule of Inference Applications (RA-nodes), Conflict Applications (CA-nodes) and Preference Applications (PA-nodes). RA-nodes and CA-nodes denote an inference or conflict between one or more pieces of information, whereas PA-nodes denote a preference of one piece of information over another. In their work on an extension to the AIF, dubbed AIF+, Reed et al. build on the work of O'Keefe to differentiate between two separate notions of argumentation [13, 16]: the first, which they term $argument_1$, is a logically constructed set of claims and evidence used to back these claims (or attack other claims). The second, termed $argument_2$, refers to a dialogue – the exchange of ideas and opinions between two or more people. A result of this work was to introduce three new node types. Locutions (L-nodes) model locutionary acts in an $argument_2$; that is, they record precisely what was said. Transition Applications (TA-nodes) represent transitions between L-nodes, with associated forms such as a challenge or response. Illocutionary Applications (YA-nodes) represent the "illocutionary force" and serve to link each $argument_1$ to the overall $argument_2$.

2.2 Semantically Interlinked Online Communities

The Semantically Interlinked Online Communities project (SIOC), a semantic-web vocabulary for representation social media, aims to enable the cross-platform, cross-service representation of data from the social web [2]. This allows for semantic representations of Sites, which hold Forums, which contain Posts, authored by a UserAccount (explicitly *not* a person, as a person can own and manage more than one UserAccount). While an extension to SIOC for the purposes of capturing and representing argumentation does exist [10], it is based on the Issue Based Information System (IBIS) model, a highly dialectic approach [9]. IBIS struggles to model eristic arguments due to the focus on the notion of issues and solutions, rather than quarrelling for its own sake.

3. ARGUMENTATION ON THE SOCIAL WEB ONTOLOGY

In our previous work, we examined the capability of existing frameworks used to capture and model both argumentation and social communities [1]. It became apparent that the AIF, while a powerful tool for modelling dialectic argument, lacked the ability to capture certain aspects of social argumentation. While some logical fallacies, such as the *ad hominem attack* can be suitably modelled within the AIF, the rhetorical force of simple abuse is difficult to capture. However, that does not mean it is not valuable to model such outbursts. A heckler in a debate, for example, may resort to throwing vulgarities, but by simply disrupting the proceedings they are voicing their dissent at the positions offered which can act to catalyse further argumentation on the subject between the main participants. While the AIF can model the locution, the rhetorical force behind it goes uncaptured. In addition, there are other socio-rhetorical tactics that are often employed, such as spamming to drown out other posters, deliberate deviation from the topic at hand, bringing up non-sequiturs in an attempt to derail the argument and "meta-argumentation" – criticising the way in which an opponent argues, but not the argument itself. There are also social features to consider: for example, the number of "Likes" or "Favourites" a post has can demonstrate audience support.

Key elements of the AIF and SIOC ontologies have been combined as parts of the Argumentation on the Social Web Ontology (ASWO), to explicitly capture the social component of argumentation on the social web. This is achieved by linking the concept of a Post with that of a Locution. We consider each post as an atomic unit of the dialogue, or $argument_2$. In the majority of cases, a single locution will translate to a single self-contained $argument_1$. In this paper we focus on extending ASWO to include rhetorical support and attack. While this is only one aspect of rhetorical argument they feature heavily in eristic dialogue and showcase both the positive and negative aspects of rhetorical argument. Rhetorical support is often relatively benign and can be used to show solidarity with other members of the dialogue or to encourage more dialectic debate. Consider the extract *"I commend you for admitting that debt & deficits are important...If only more [people] felt the way you do"*, which disagrees with the overall stance presented by their opponent, but commends them for conceding some common ground. Conversely, rhetorical attacks are often extremely hostile. They differ from logical attacks by attacking the person behind the argument rather than the argument itself (not to be confused with *ad hominem*, which attacks a person's argument by calling their character into question – these are logical, even though they are fallacious). We model the notion of rhetorical support and attack by introducing three new types of nodes to the ontology. Firstly, the Persona node represents a user's character and (purported) authority on a given subject, and is bound to a UserAccount. Introducing the notion of personas allows each UserAccount to present a different view of themselves (that can be supported or attacked accordingly) when engaging in multiple discussions or topics. PersonalConflict (PC-nodes) nodes link from a YA-node to a Persona node to denote this type of personal support and, likewise, PersonalSupport (PS-nodes) nodes follow the same structure to denote support of a person's intentions and character.

4. INVESTIGATIONS

To investigate the application of logical versus rhetorical techniques in eristic dialogue on the social web, and trial our augmentations made to the AIF and SIOC ontologies within the ASWO, we performed three case studies on $arguments_2$ taking place on different areas of the social web. A sample of two hundred and seventy posts from within three different threads were manually annotated using our modified framework, allowing us to analyse the relation between logical and rhetorical $arguments_1$ used, and compare the features of the annotation structure with the content of each post.

4.1 Methodology

A single topic of argumentation was chosen to be examined for three case studies. To ensure the stimulation of debate, the selected topic needed to be controversial, have a large number of respondents and have been active for a long enough period of time to generate a rich and complete content. The Oct. 2013 United States government shutdown caused by Congress's failure to agree on a budget, and the following condemnation this received from the presidency, was a suitable match for these requirements. This topic was then tracked across three of Kaplan's social media categories: Twitter, a microblogging service; Facebook, a social network; and Reddit, a social news and networking site. The source of the posts themselves again needed to be both publicly available and have a large number of followers to ensure a maximally stimulated debate. As an authoritative public figure at the heart of the crisis, content from or relating to Barack Obama's social media profiles was chosen, and three posts dated 15 October 2013 were selected for study.

Table 1: Metrics of discussions sampled from Twitter, Facebook and Reddit

Metric	Twitter	Facebook	Reddit	Total
Posts	90	90	90	270
Direct replies	77	0	67	144
Number of users	26	85	43	154
Average posts per user	3.5	1.1	2.1	1.8
Average words per post	15.83	41.36	42.34	33.18
Average characters per post	96.51	265.27	243.31	201.70
Time between first and last posts	0d 6h 53m 40s	3d 4h 51m 27s	3d 0h 50m 12s	n/a
Average time between posts	04m 39s	51m 49s	49m 06s	35m 11s

Table 2: Summary of AIF and ASWO nodes in each sample

Metric	Twitter	Facebook	Reddit	Total
L-nodes	90	90	90	270
TA-nodes	52	9	15	76
YA-nodes	58	74	70	202
I-nodes	56	98	86	240
RA-nodes	13	20	24	57
CA-nodes	18	1	34	53
PA-nodes	4	4	2	10
PS-nodes	2	2	3	7
PC-nodes	26	6	12	44

Because of the volume of the data produced over the course of the tracked event and the time-intensive nature of manually annotating the data, it was necessary to sample the data to a more manageable size before annotation could take place. To ensure that the sampled graph maintained properties similar to those of the original graph, forest-fire sampling [11] was utilised to preserve the overall structure of the data. Table 1 shows an overview of the sample structures and some key characteristics of each thread. Manual annotation was required to derive the premises and conclusions (and subsequent relations) from each post. Each post is considered to contain zero or more separate $argument_1$. A YA-node is created for each $argument_1$ made, and links the L-node to each I-node in the $argument_1$. Information that met one (or more) of the following criteria was not considered relevant: off-topic posts that do not relate to the topic being discussed (Example: *"Ataturk did revolution ! building moderate muslim network is oxymoron which has been destroy secular , democratic, rule of law in Turkey."*); conversational posts (Example: *"I thank you, have a good night!"*) and meta-argumentation (Example: *"Down voting = disagree Upvoting = agree" "The rules say explicitly not to do that..."*). Repeated information does not create a new I-node; instead the YA-node links to the I-node already present. A TA-node is created to link two Locutions whenever a transition is present in the $argument_2$ – a step that contributes to the overall structure without providing any information, most often in the form of an interrogative. Support and attack between different I-nodes is denoted through the use of RA- and CA-nodes and preference with PA-nodes, while rhetorical support and attack utilises the new PS- and PC-nodes. Some nodes in the graph may not be complete as a result of the nature of sampling the graph. For example, it may be possible to detect that a user attacks another user's persona, but not exactly which user they are attacking. Table 2 shows an overview of the number of AIF and ASWO nodes added during the annotation process.

4.2 Results and Analysis

Firstly, we present how the argumentation structure changes and grows over time, in both a logical and rhetorical capacity, by graphing how the number of logical support and attack nodes (i.e. RA- and CA-nodes) and rhetorical support and attack nodes (i.e. PS- and PC-nodes) changes with each post contributed to the $argument_2$. Figures 1b and 1c show that in the cases of Facebook and Reddit use of rhetorical tactics rises slowly compared to the use of logical tactics. However, Figure 1a shows that in the case of Twitter, the rhetorical contributions rise in parallel to the logical contributions. In both samples from Twitter and Reddit, the distribution of logical supports and attacks also remain approximately equal. In all three examples, rhetorical conflict far outweighs rhetorical support. Overall, it appears that there is no sudden shift in tactics from arguing logically to adopting a rhetorical approach – rhetorical argument forms an underlying and consistent strategy throughout the $argument_2$.

In addition, we examined the proportion of logical versus rhetorical contributions made by each user. Figures 2a and 2c show that users in the Twitter and Reddit cases made more individual contributions to the argumentation structure than those in the Facebook sample, shown in Figure 2b. This suggests that there is more engagement in these cases than in the Facebook sample. All samples also display a tendency for rhetorical contributions to be distributed across the scale, with grouping towards either end. This has two connotations; firstly, users that contribute most to a discussion are also most likely to use rhetorical techniques, and secondly, users that contribute no logical contributions at all are most likely to provide a rhetorical contribution.

Correlations were drawn between the structure of the annotated argument graph, including elements such as the number of logical or rhetorical supports or conflicts and replies to and from each post, and features of the post content and structure, such as post length, number of expletives, percentage of spelling errors and again, replies to and from the post. Due to the largely discrete (and often binary) nature of the features and values studied the correlations seen are relatively weak. However, there are some stronger correlations which show potential early indicators of the structure and value of an argument. For example, as might be expected, longer posts are more likely to contain more I-nodes. Posts that use a large number of expletives are likewise more likely to contain a rhetorical attack. When examining all three case studies together, posts made in reply correlated with posts that were replied to, implying that when one or more users engage in a discussion, they are more likely to be engaged with in return.

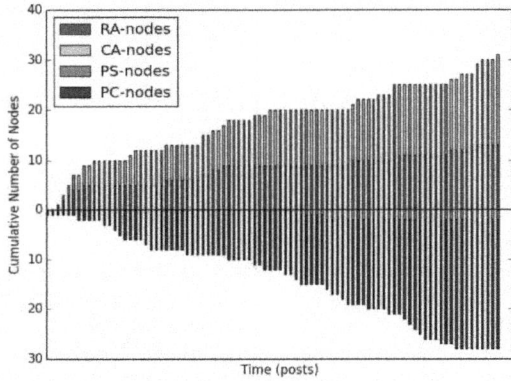

(a) Logical and rhetoric tactics over time on Twitter

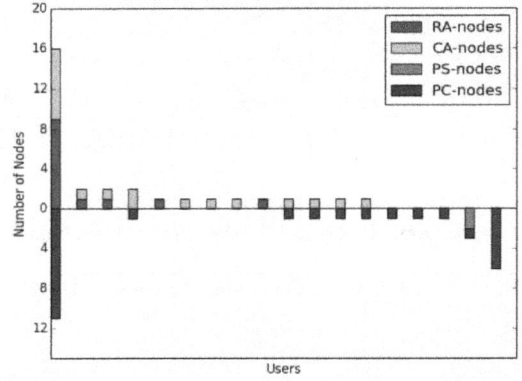

(a) Logical and rhetorical contributions by Twitter users

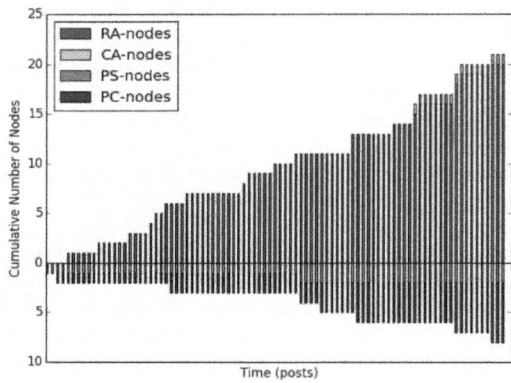

(b) Logical and rhetoric tactics over time on Facebook

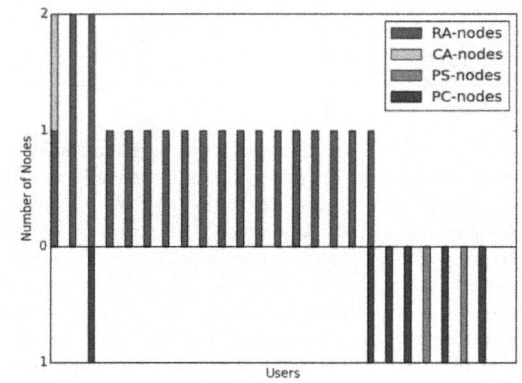

(b) Logical and rhetorical contributions by Facebook users

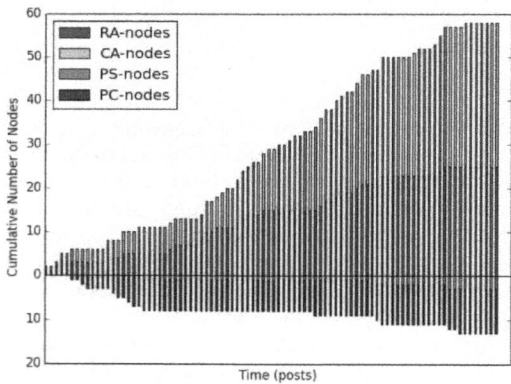

(c) Logical and rhetoric tactics over time on Reddit

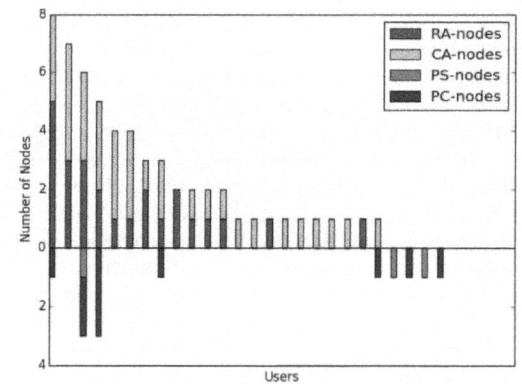

(c) Logical and rhetorical contributions by Reddit users

Figure 1: Cumulative use of logical and rhetorical tactics over time

Figure 2: Logical and rhetorical contributions per sampled user

5. CONCLUSIONS AND FUTURE WORK

Argumentation, like the social web itself, is a diverse construct that is challenging to model but has huge potential if correctly harnessed. To do this, both the logical and rhetorical features must be taken into account, particularly when modelling eristic arguments. The work presented in this paper provides a novel framework for modelling a subset of rhetorical argumentation, ideal for use in modelling social argumentation, then demonstrates some of the structures this allows us to observe when applied to three case studies. From these case studies, we draw three major conclusions. Firstly, and most importantly, rhetorical tactics are shown to be present throughout the argumentation in the case studies, even when only accounting for a small subset of rhetorical argumentation. Clearly, failure to accurately model these social argumentation strategies is detrimental to the goal of studying how discussions evolve on the social web. Secondly, in our three case studies, rhetorical tactics are most often used by either those contributing the most to the discussion overall, or by those who do not contribute logically at all. Finally, while the features of the argumentation structure above are challenging to detect automatically and expensive to manually annotate, the markers present in the social media sphere are relatively trivial to detect. When given enough data, it is possible to draw correlations between these argumentation and social features to give an estimation of the likelihood that a contribution is logical, positively rhetorical or negatively rhetorical. Given enough data, it may also be possible to estimate the weight or impact a given post will have on the overall argumentation structure. However, it must be noted that without further augmentations to the model, the structure of the annotated graph itself gives no indication to the quality of argument present.

There are a number of avenues that can be taken to further this research. Firstly more data can be collected and annotated from the social web to refine the estimates presented here. This can be approached with respect to breadth, by examining additional sites not covered here, such as virtual worlds; or depth, examining multiple additional sites for each of Kaplan's categories, to determine whether the correlations described hold true for each category, or are site-dependant. Secondly, additional annotations can be made with respect to the given case studies. This can also be approached from the perspective of breadth or depth; either categorisation of additional logical and rhetorical strategies or by sub-categorisation of those areas that are currently annotated. Thirdly, a node structure could be applied to the notion of audience perception, to directly reflect the social attributes of the argument$_2$ as a part of the argumentation structure itself. The computational modelling of social media argumentation has the potential to be a powerful tool in both our understanding of social media use and the development of new tools to encourage more sophisticated argument and counter antisocial behaviour. Current formal models of argument do not well suit the eristic arguments found on the social web, or cope well with the rhetorical tactics used. Our hope is that our work shows both how formal models can be extended to describe these features, and that those descriptions are necessary to create a complete picture of online argumentation.

6. REFERENCES

[1] T. Blount, D. E. Millard, and M. J. Weal. Towards Modelling Dialectic and Eristic Argumentation on the Social Web. In *14th workshop on Computational Models of Natural Argument*, 2014.

[2] J. G. Breslin, S. Decker, A. Harth, and U. Bojars. SIOC: an approach to connect web-based communities. *International Journal of Web Based Communities*, 2(2):133–142, 2006.

[3] C. Chesñevar, J. McGinnis, S. Modgil, I. Rahwan, C. Reed, G. Simari, M. South, G. Vreeswijk, and S. Willmott. Towards an argument interchange format. *Knowledge Engineering Review*, 21(4):293–316, 2006.

[4] E. Gilbert, T. Bergstrom, and K. Karahalios. Blogs are echo chambers: Blogs are echo chambers. In *42nd Hawaii International Conference on System Sciences, HICSS'09*, pages 1–10. IEEE, 2009.

[5] U. Hahn, M. Oaksford, and A. Corner. Circular arguments, begging the question and the formalization of argument strength. In *Proceedings of AMKLC'05, International Symposium on Adaptive Models of Knowledge, Language and Cognition*, pages 34–40, 2005.

[6] E. A. Jane. "Your a Ugly, Whorish, Slut" Understanding E-bile. *Feminist Media Studies*, 14(4):531–546, 2014.

[7] C. Jørgensen. Public Debate – An Act of Hostility? *Argumentation*, 12(4):431–443, 1998.

[8] A. M. Kaplan and M. Haenlein. Users of the world, unite! The challenges and opportunities of Social Media. *Business horizons*, 53(1):59–68, 2010.

[9] W. Kunz and H. W. Rittel. *Issues as elements of information systems*, volume 131. Institute of Urban and Regional Development, University of California Berkeley, California, 1970.

[10] C. Lange, U. Bojars, T. Groza, J. G. Breslin, and S. Handschuh. Expressing Argumentative Discussions in Social Media Sites. In *Proceedings of the Workshop on Social Data on the Web*, Karlsruhe, Germany, 2008.

[11] J. Leskovec and C. Faloutsos. Sampling from large graphs. In *Proceedings of the 12th ACM SIGKDD international conference on Knowledge discovery and data mining*, pages 631–636. ACM, 2006.

[12] A. d. Moor and M. Aakhus. Argumentation support: From technologies to tools. *Communications of the ACM*, 49(3):93–98, Mar. 2006.

[13] D. J. O'Keefe. *Readings in argumentation*, volume 11, chapter 5, pages 79–91. Walter de Gruyter, 1992.

[14] Plato. *Book V. The Republic*. Basic Books, 380BC. (Bloom, A.D. Trans. 1991).

[15] I. Rahwan, F. Zablith, and C. Reed. Laying the foundations for a world wide argument web. *Artificial intelligence*, 171(10):897–921, 2007.

[16] C. Reed, S. Wells, J. Devereux, and G. Rowe. AIF+: Dialogue in the Argument Interchange Format. *FRONTIERS IN ARTIFICIAL INTELLIGENCE AND APPLICATIONS*, 172:311, 2008.

[17] J. Schneider, B. Davis, and A. Wyner. Dimensions of argumentation in social media. *Lecture Notes in Computer Science*, 7603:21–25, 2012.

[18] J. Schneider, S. Villata, and E. Cabrio. Why did they post that argument? Communicative Intentions of Web 2.0 Arguments. In *Arguing on the Web 2.0*, Amsterdam, 2014. SINTELNET, European Network for Social Intelligence.

[19] W. Sherchan, S. Nepal, and C. Paris. A survey of trust in social networks. *ACM Computing Surveys (CSUR)*, 45(4):47, 2013.

Predicting Answering Behaviour in Online Question Answering Communities

Grégoire Burel
Knowledge Media institute
Open University, UK
gregoire.burel@open.ac.uk

Paul Mulholland
Knowledge Media institute
Open University, UK
paul.mulholland@open.ac.uk

Yulan He
School of Engineering &
Applied Science
Aston University, UK
y.he@cantab.net

Harith Alani
Knowledge Media institute
Open University, UK
h.alani@open.ac.uk

ABSTRACT

The value of Question Answering (Q&A) communities is dependent on members of the community finding the questions they are most willing and able to answer. This can be difficult in communities with a high volume of questions. Much previous has work attempted to address this problem by recommending questions similar to those already answered. However, this approach disregards the question selection behaviour of the answers and how it is affected by factors such as question recency and reputation. In this paper, we identify the parameters that correlate with such a behaviour by analysing the users' answering patterns in a Q&A community. We then generate a model to predict which question a user is most likely to answer next. We train Learning to Rank (LTR) models to predict question selections using various *user*, *question* and *thread* feature sets. We show that answering behaviour can be predicted with a high level of success, and highlight the particular features that influence users' question selections.

Categories and Subject Descriptors

H.4 [**Information Systems Applications**]: Miscellaneous

Keywords

social Q&A platforms; online communities; user behaviour; social media

1. INTRODUCTION

Online Question Answering (Q&A) communities such as

HT '15, September 1–4, 2015, Guzelyurt, Northern Cyprus.
©2015 ACM ISBN 978-1-4503-3395-5/15/09 ...$15.00.
DOI: http://dx.doi.org/10.1145/2700171.2791041

Stack Exchange,[1] Yahoo! Answers,[2] and Quora,[3] have witnessed a rapid increase in popularity in recent years as more and more people are going online to seek answers to their questions.

In Q&A communities, such as Stack Exchange, more than $3,700$ new questions are posted every day.[4] As a result, users need effective methods to help them find the questions they are interested in, or capable of, answering. In this context, much research has focused on question routing [23, 10, 11, 9, 5]; the automatic identification of relevant potential answerers for a given question. Another approach is user-centric question recommendation [12], where the focus is on identifying the most suitable question to a given potential answerer.

All such techniques aim at more efficiently connecting questions and potential answerers to boost community reactivity. Such techniques are largely based on matching the user's topic affinity and expertise with available questions, often overlooking the possible influence of users' behavioural patterns and preferences on their question selections. In this paper, we extract such behavioural patterns and use them to predict the questions that each answerer will select in the Stack Exchange *Cooking* community (CO);[5] which is a food oriented Q&A website. The main contributions of this paper are:

1. Demonstrate a method for extracting patterns of question-selection behaviour of individual users in a Q&A community.

2. Study the influence of 62 *user*, *question*, and *thread* features on answering behaviour and show how combining these features increases the quality of behaviour predictions.

3. Investigate the use of Learning to Rank models (LTR) for identifying the most relevant question for a user at any given time.

---

[1] http://stackexchange.com/.

[2] http://answers.yahoo.com/.

[3] lhttps://www.quora.com/.

[4] lhttps://api.stackexchange.com/docs/info#filter= default&site=stackoverflow&run=true

[5] http://cooking.stackexchange.com.

4. Construct multiple models to predict question-selections, and compare against multiple baselines (question recency, topic affinity, and random), achieving high precision gains (+93%).

In the following section we discuss existing works in question recommendation, question routing and answering behaviour. In Section 3 we introduce our approach for extracting and representing answering behaviour and discuss the set of features used for building our question-selection prediction model. In Section 4, we present our experiment and results. Discussions and conclusions are provided in Sections 5 and 6 respectively.

2. RELATED WORK

Question routing and recommendation can be seen as a sub-branch of content recommendation, the task of recommending items based on item description and user interests [14]. Since the goal of recommendation systems is to identify what content is likely to interest users, it shares many similarities with behaviour modelling. In the context of Q&A, question routing is generally contrasted from question recommendation as the task of identifying potential answerers for a given question whereas question recommendation is typically restricted to the recommendation of questions given a query or question (e.g. retrieval of similar questions). A slightly different task is answerer-centric question recommendation, the task of recommending questions to potential answerers.

Although question routing [22, 15, 23, 10, 12, 11, 6, 17, 9, 5, 20] and question recommendation [3, 7] research aim at different problems, both approaches have similar methodologies. Question recommendation approaches can be easily used for question routing and vice versa.

Most research has focused on the computation of language or topic similarity between questions and users in order to decide how relevant is a user given a question. Many works rely on topic models or similar approaches [22, 23, 15, 10, 17, 5, 20, 21] as part of the features used for classifying user as relevant for a question.

In general, the majority of works have relied on supervised binary classifiers trained on different features that can classify questions as relevant and irrelevant. Although providing good recommendation results, such methods do not necessary take into account relations between recommended items due to the type of algorithms used. Moreover, previous techniques are normally insensitive to the constant change in the community, available questions, and the status of those questions. For example, a question may receive a new answer from the community and render it less attractive to other potential answerers, or a new relevant question posed by a reputable user could divert the attention of potential answerers. Capturing such dynamic behaviour patterns impose the need for more complex approaches. In order to account for the relations between the content to be recommended and provide better recommendations, [12] and [19] used LTR models as part of their classifier. Although better than binary models, such approaches still considered non-dynamic features and do not consider the evolution of communities.

Besides routing the questions that fit user needs or topics and other standard text features, works like [10] and [5] integrated some behaviour factors in the recommendation process, such as user performance and availability in order to maximise the chances of getting good answers. To some extent, these works can be related with best answer identification within a thread such as [2] and [21]. Nevertheless, these methods also mostly focused on non dynamic features or where not trying to directly model answerer behaviour.

Few works in this domain have also looked at graph based techniques. However, rather than focusing on user decisions, such models focused on user reputation graphs [9] or topic hierarchies [3].

Our approach differs from all the above for three main reasons:

1. We use a mixture of dynamically-calculated *question*, *thread* and *user* (potential answerer) features.

2. We consider *all available questions* at each contribution time rather than only recently posed questions.

3. We identify which features correlate the most with user behaviour.

3. MODELLING QUESTION SELECTION BEHAVIOUR IN Q&A COMMUNITIES

Identifying the questions that a user will answer requires the definition of the choices and activities that the user is presented with at any given point in time. Once these choices and user behaviours are modelled, we can then construct a method to automatically predict question-selections based on available choices (i.e. predicting the correct user action given a set of possible outcomes).

3.1 Answerer Behaviour in Q&A Websites

In this section we describe some typical answering dynamics in Q&A websites, which naturally influence and guide answerers' behaviour. Q&A websites tend to have similar designs and contribution mechanisms. Such systems apply various ranking algorithms to present users with a list of questions that need answering. For example, Stack Exchange uses the number of community votes by default to rank questions, whereas Yahoo! Answers tends to rank questions based on their recency. Most Q&A websites enable users to flag best answers, and use this information to halt promoting those questions further. Users are usually encouraged to update their answers rather than posting new ones to the same questions. In the community we analyse in this paper, we found no cases where a user replied more than once to the same question.

On a typical Q&A website, a user is presented with a list of available and open questions to browse and select one question at a time to answer. Once an answer is provided, the question is dropped from the list of available questions, which will be given back to that user to select further questions to answer. In summary, the answering behaviour of users can be broadly divided into a two-step iterative process:

1. Obtain the list of available questions.

2. Select a question and answer it.

Next we try to model these steps, along with the features that could influence them.

3.2 Representing Answerer Behaviour

In order to introduce the method used for learning the behaviour of answerers, we need to formally represent the different actions and choices a user can make at interaction time, as well as the different factors that a user may take into account when deciding which question to select.

A question $q \in Q$ is characterised by two statuses that change over time, from opened or available ($\mathcal{O}$) to closed or solved ($\mathcal{C}$). We denote the status of a question q at time $t \in T$ as $S : T \times Q \to \{\mathcal{O}, \mathcal{C}\}$ ($S(q,t)$). We also define the status of question in relation to a particular user $u \in U$ at time t as $S_U : T \times Q \times U \to \{\mathcal{O}, \mathcal{C}\}$ ($S_U(q,t,u)$) in order to account for the potential previous answer of a user to a question. When a user answers a question, its status will be closed even if the question is not yet marked as solved by the community.

Using the previous notation, the set of available questions $Q_{t_u} = \{q_1, q_2, \dots, q_n\}$ at t for user u can be defined as function $A : T \times U \to Q'$ where Q' ($A(t,u)$) is a set of non overlapping elements of Q. For a set of available questions Q_{t_u} at time t for user u, a user selects one question to answer within Q_{t_u}. Such a selection can be defined as $C : Q' \times U \to q \in Q'$ ($C(Q', u)$). The decision to pick a particular question over a set of available questions can be represented as a vector of decision labels over questions. By combining all such vectors we obtain a time indexed matrix for each user containing all the questions $q \in Q$ and the selection and status of each question. At a particular activity time $t \in T$ for a particular user $u \in U$, an answering choice can be represented as a Boolean where only one question is labelled as selected.

By using such a matrix, a model of a particular user behaviour can be constructed (Figure 1a). For each matrix column (i.e. activity time), a decision graph representing the decision relations between the selected question and the unselected available ones can be constructed (Figure 1b). By using such a representation, we obtain a partially ordered set. Such a graph can then be used for training learning algorithms to automatically determine the answering behaviour of Q&A community members (Section 3.4).

3.3 Features for Predicting Question Selections

Many different types of features can influence users' selection of questions to answer. We divide such features into question (F_Q), thread (F_T) and user (F_O) categories. Question features are intrinsic to the content of the question itself, whereas Thread features represent all the answers given to a particular question. User features capture the status of the answerer at answering time, and measure affinity between a user and a considered question. It is important to note that all these features evolve during the lifetime of a question as new answers are posted from different users.

For a given user $u \in U$, time $t \in T$ and question $q \in Q$, the features that represent a question are defined by $F : Q \times T \times U \to F_Q \times F_T \times F_O$ ($F(q,t,u)$). Using the notation used in the previous section, a decision function $D : Q' \times F \to Q'$ ($D(Q', F)$) can be used for deciding which question to select for every answering activity. As a consequence, understanding how users select questions to answer could be achieved by modelling $D(Q', F)$ and learning the parameters that identify selected questions.

Below we describe 62 features used in this paper, which are strictly generated from the information available at the time when a user selected a question to answer (i.e. future information are not taken into account when calculating those features).

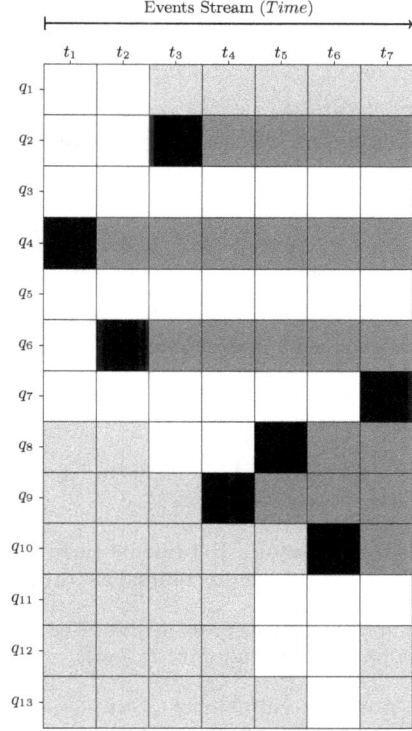

(a) Matrix-like representation of question statuses and answering behaviour for a user.

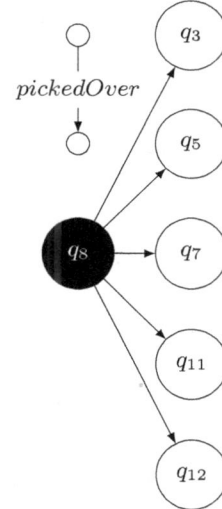

(b) Decision graph for a
user at answering time t_5.

Figure 1: (a) is matrix-like representation of the behaviour of a user $u \in U$ with 7 answering activities out of a total of up to 13 questions $Q = \{q_1, q_2, q_3, \cdots, q_{13}\}$. (b) is a decision graph representing which question is favoured at time t_5 by u. Grey areas are unavailable questions (i.e. not opened yet, already selected, or solved). Black areas represent users selections. White areas are open questions.

Although many features can be potentially selected for predicting users' selection of questions to answer, we decide to use features similar to the ones we have explored previously while investigating the issue of best answer identification [2] and the measurement question complexity [1]

3.3.1 User Features

Features of users who are considering answering a question.

- *Number of Answers*: The number of answers posted by the user so far.

- *Reputation*: Aggregation of user's contribution ratings.

- *Answering Success*: Number of user's previous answers that were flagged as best answers.

- *Number of Posts*: Number of questions and answers previously posted by the user.

- *Number of Questions*: Total number of questions posted by the user until now.

- *Question Reputation*: Represents how liked are the user's questions based on community ratings.

- *Answer Reputation*: Represents how liked are the user's answers based on community ratings.

- *Asking Success*: Number of previous user questions that were identified as solved.

- *Topic Reputation*: Measures user's reputation for a given question. It is derived from the topics or tags[6] T_q associated with a question q. Given a user u, and a question q with a set of topics T_q, the reputation associated with a given question q for user u is given by summing up the score values of user u's previous answer A_u about a particular topic $t \in T_q$:

$$E_P(q, u) = \sum_{t \in T_q} \sum_{a \in A_u} S(a^t) \qquad (1)$$

- *Topic Affinity*: Represents the likelihood of a user to answer a question with similar topics. It is calculated from the intersection $t \in T_u \cap T_q$ between the topics or tags T_u of a user u and the topics or tags T_q associated with a potential question q and the probability of u to contribute to each of those topics $P(t|u)$. Given a user u, the user topic affinity associated with a question q is given by:

$$A_u(T_q) = \prod_{t \in T_u \cap T_q} P(t|u) \qquad (2)$$

We also include the following features which we derive from the list above: *average answer reputation, average question reputation, ratio of successfully answered questions, ratio of successfully solved questions, average observer reputation, ratio of reputation for a potential question,* and *average topic reputation.* Total number of User Features is therefore 17.

---

[6]For the dataset used in this paper (CO), we use the community assigned tags attached to each questions.

3.3.2 Question Features

- *Question Age*: No. of days since question creation.

- *Number of Words*: Number of words in the question.

- *Referral Count*: Number of hyperlinks in the question.

- *Readability with Gunning Fog Index*: Measures question readability using the Gunning index of a question q which is calculated using the average sentence length asl_q and the percentage of complex words pcw_q:

$$G_q(asl_q, pcw_q) = 0.4 \, (asl_q + pcw_q) \qquad (3)$$

- *Readability with LIX*: Measures readability using the LIX metric of a question q which is calculated using the number of words contained in the question w_q, the number of periods, colon or capital first letters c_q and the number of words with more than six letters $w_q^{>6}$:

$$LIX_q(w_q, c_q, w_q^{>6}) = \frac{w_q}{c_q} \times \frac{w_q^{>6}}{w_q} \times 100 \qquad (4)$$

- *Cumulative Term Entropy (Complexity)*: Represents the distribution of words in a question using cumulative entropy. Given question q, its vocabulary V_q, and the frequency of each word $f_w, w \in \{1, 2, ..., |V_q|\}$, cumulative term entropy $C_d(q)$ can be defined as:

$$C_d(q) = \sum_{w=1}^{|V_q|} \frac{f_w \times (\log |V_q| - \log f_w)}{|V_q|} \qquad (5)$$

- *Question Polarity*: Measures the average polarity of a question using SentiWordNet[7]. It is calculated from each unique word w contained in a given question q, $w \in \{1, 2, ..., |V_q|\}$, and the positive $pos(w)$ and negative $neg(w)$ weights of word w:

$$QP_q = \frac{1}{|V_q|} \times \sum_{w=1}^{|V_q|} pos(w) - neg(w) \qquad (6)$$

Additionally, we include **asker features**, which are the user's features but applied to the asker of the each question. The aim is to take into account the possible influence of the user who posed a question, on the probability of that question being selected by others for answering. Therefore each question has also all the 17 user features, calculated for each question asker, thus totalling 23 Question Features.

3.3.3 Thread Features

This feature set aggregates the features of all the answers already posted to a question by the time a user is selecting a question to answer.

Each thread feature (F_T) is calculated using the same question features above, apart from *question age*, and normalised (i.e. averaged) across all the questions posted at any given time. Total number of Thread Features is 22.

---

[7]SentiWordNet, http://sentiwordnet.isti.cnr.it/.

3.4 Learning Behaviour using LTR Models

The question-selection function can be seen as a Learning to Rank problem where a learning algorithm tries to generate a list of ranked items based on derived relevance labels. In our case, the goal is to find the question that is most likely to be answered by a particular user. In other words, for each selection time, we try to label one question from the list as relevant, and label all the others as irrelevant. Such a decision representation can be built from the decision graphs discussed in Section 3.2.

One simple approach is to use a *pointwise* LTR method [13], which applies standard classifiers to rank questions directly by only considering them individually and then ordering them. For a binary relevance label, one approach is to use regression models and then rank the results by the predicted scores. More standard classifiers can also be used by ranking the results using the probability of a question belonging to a given class. For example, in our case, we can train a Logistic model or any other binary classifier $\mathcal{L}(f)$ and then label the question with the highest likelihood of being selected from a given list of available questions:

$$D(Q', F) = \underset{q \in Q', f \in F}{\mathrm{argmax}} \ P(q | \mathcal{L}(f)) \qquad (7)$$

Besides the pointwise approach, LTR algorithms can also use *pairwise* and *listwise* algorithms [13]. On the one hand, the pairwise method uses binary classifiers for comparing question pairs within a list in order to decide the most relevant one. Such an approach has the advantage of taking into account the relation between the questions that need to be ranked. On the other hand, the listwise approach uses machine learning methods that try to optimise a general evaluation measure such as the Mean Reciprocal Rank (MRR). The advantage of such a method is that it can be optimised on a particular evaluation metric. In our case, such a metric can be Precision at one ($P@1$) since we want to identify the one question selected by answerers at a time. Such question should be ranked on top for accurately predicting questions selections.

In this paper we evaluate *Random Forests* as a pointwise method. LambdaRank [16] as a pairwise approach, and, ListNet [4] for a listwise method. These algorithms are implemented on top of the RankLib[8] and Weka[9] frameworks.

4. DATASET

Our work and experiment are performed on the Stack Exchange *Cooking* (CO) Q&A community, which supports a range of Q&A features such as *voting*, *reputation* and *best answer labelling*. Our data is extracted from the April 2011 Stack Exchange public dataset [10] and consists of $3,065$ questions, $9,820$ answers and $4,941$ users. In our experiment we randomly selected 100 users out of the 283 users that have answered at least five questions. Users with less activity are currently deemed too underrepresented for our prediction task.

In our dataset, on average the number of questions available for each user to select and answer at every observed selection time is 328 questions. There were 1757 question-selections made by our 100 users, which translates to over

575K question-selection possibilities to consider, and many millions of feature calculations.

Note that in some Q&A platforms, such as the one we experiment with, users are allowed to answer questions multiple times or answer questions that have already been marked as resolved. In our datasets, we did not find cases of multiple answers by the same user for the same question. However, we found that in many cases, users were answering after a question was marked as solved (71%). The reason for this behaviour might be due to two reasons:

1. User may feel that they can provide an answer that is better than the existing best answer, or;

2. Although the best answer has already been posted, the question may not yet be marked as resolved.

To resolve this issue, we include all recently resolved questions (i.e. less than three weeks old) to the list of available questions if a user has not already selected them. Such an approach enables us to reduce the number of questions affected by the previous issue to only 5%. We discard these remaining questions from our dataset in order to focus on user activities that highlight a more common behaviour (i.e. users that do not reply to questions that have been resolved a long time ago).

5. EXPERIMENT & EVALUATION

In this section we apply LTR models for identifying questions that users are most likely to answer, using the dataset described in the previous section. In order to validate our answering behaviour model, we try to predict which questions a user is going to select and answer.

We train a model for each user, using a 80%/20% chronologically ordered training/testing split based on the number of answers posted by each user. Then, for each user, we generate their historical question-selection lists and attach the *user*, *question* and *thread* features. Then, in each list we label selected questions as 1 and unselected questions as 0. We merge the training/testing lists and train LTR models, excluding any information on user selections from the testing set.

Three different types of LTR models are trained in this experiment (Section 3.4):

1. A pointwise algorithm based on *Random Forests*.

2. A pairwise *LambdaRank* model.

3. *ListNet*, a listwise algorithm.

For baselines, in addition to these algorithms, we also use *question age* (selecting most recent question, as in [12]) and *topic affinity* (selecting the question that is most similar to user topics, using Formula 2 in Section 3.3), as well as a *random* algorithm that selects a question randomly.

We evaluate each model using the Mean Reciprocal Rank (MRR) and the Mean Average Precision at n ($MAP@n$) metrics. For the $MAP@n$ metric we compare the results at different levels using $n = \{1, 2, 4, 8, 16, 32\}$. MRR represents the average rank of the relevant question in each list, and $MAP@n$ can be seen as the average position of the relevant question within the top n items of each list.

We run two experiments:

---

[8]http://sourceforge.net/p/lemur/wiki/RankLib.
[9]http://www.cs.waikato.ac.nz/ml/weka.
[10]www.clearbits.net/get/1698-apr-2011.torrent

1. First experiment compares the performance of our models for identifying selected questions for 100 users, using *user*, *question* and *thread* features separately, then all features combined. We also evaluate the models using the baseline features described above.

2. The second experiment focuses on evaluating the influence of each feature on question selection behaviour in order to better understand how users select the questions to answer. Using those results, we re-evaluate the previous models with a restricted number of features to look for any improvements in the results.

5.1 Results: Model Comparison

For our first experiment, we train our models on different feature subsets and compare the results using the previous metrics in order to better understand the importance of each features groups (Table 1). As expected, the *Random* approach performs very poorly with $MRR = 0.007$. As for *topic affinity*, it also proved incapable of making any accurate predictions of answerer behaviour. The *question age* model performs better, with $MRR = 0.094$ and the highest $P@1$ of 0.036. Hence a ranking solely based on the age of questions can enable users to find the question they are willing to answer within the first 10 questions. Much higher $P@1$ can be expected in communities where the default is to organise questions by recency, such as Yahoo! Answers, where a $P@1$ of 0.2445 was reported in [12]. We also observe that *user features* when used alone perform the worst overall, whereas *question features* provide a better average ($MMR = 0.182$) across all models.

Although *ListNet* performs better than the other approaches and baselines with $MMR = 0.139$, user features alone did not provide a good prediction of selected questions. This could be because most *user* features are only useful when linked with *question* and *thread* features. For example, the *reputation* of a user may be only used while coordinated with the average reputation of a thread.

In our prediction models, except for *ListNet*, *Question features* shows more value than *user features* with an average ($MMR = 0.182$) across all models. The best performing model is *Random Forests* with $MRR = 0.397$ which is much higher than both *LambdaRank* (+88.92%) and *ListNet* (+73.30%). *Thread features* seem less useful than *question features* with an average $MRR = 0.135$

When combining all features, *Random Forests* provides the best results with $MMR = 0.446$ meaning that selected questions are found on average in the 2nd or 3rd position. We also get $P@1 = 0.307$, a gain of +88.27% over our best baseline. Combining all features enables the ranking method to better consider the relations and influences between users, threads and questions, which seem to improve our predictions.

In general we observe that *Random Forests*, a pointwise algorithm, performs much better than the other models. Although in theory listwise methods are expected to perform better [13], in our case the simplest form of LTR models generated the best results. Such results may be explained by the fact that contrary to both *LambdaRank* and *ListNet*, the pointwise *Random Forests* method was optimised specifically for identifying question selection behaviour (i.e. there is only one relevant document per list).

5.2 Results: Feature Assessment

In this section, we aim to identify the features that are most useful for predicting question selection behaviour. We use standard Correlation Feature Selection (CFS) and Information Gain Ratio (IGR) by converting our problem into a classical binary classification task since such methods are not designed for LTR tasks. For each method we use 10-fold cross validation on the training dataset.

We also propose to rank features by dropping each individual feature one by one based on the full *Random Forests* LTR model and accounting for the drop in MRR (ablation method). Such a method has the advantage of including the LTR structure of our approach even though it does not take into account correlations between each behaviour feature. We apply the feature drop approach on the training split and evaluate it on the testing set defined earlier in Section 5. Finally, we merge the different ranks obtained from previous methods by calculating the average rank of each feature using CFS, IGR and feature-drop ranks.

The top rankings obtained by each individual method are listed in Table 2. The top fifteen features obtained from each feature selection method contain measures from each of the groups discussed in Section 3.3. Most of the top features are *question* features (40%) followed by the *thread* (31%) and *user* (29%) groups. Such results seem to indicate that all predictor types are equally important in determining the behaviour of answerers. This result is not really surprising as the best model obtained so far is generated when all the features are used.

Although IGR and CFS share similar top fifteen features (73%), it appears that the feature drop methodology produce quite different results by sharing only 20% of the features with IGR and 27% with CFS. Such a result is very likely due to the difference in methodology used by each feature selection method. Both IGR and CFS are applied on a simplification of our LTR tasks (i.e. binary classification task) while feature drop method is applied on the full *Random Forest* LTR model.

Table 3 compares the average ranks of each of our features. Most of the top fifteen features are *question* features. The top two *question* features are the number of hyperlinks contained in questions (*referral count*) and the reputation of the previous asker's questions (*questions reputation*). Other important features are *question age* and the total *number of answers* received by the question asker. Other *question* features show that users' choices of questions to answer are largely affected by the popularity of the previous questions of a given asker (*number of answers* and *questions reputation*). Looking in more detail into the first two features (Figure 2) we observe that users are more likely to select questions with a low referral count ($p = 1.53 \times 10^{-31}$)[11] and questions from users that have a high *question reputation* ($p = 1.20 \times 10^{-37}$). Such results suggest that users prefer to answer questions from popular askers and questions that do not require reading additional (hyperlinked) material.

By inspecting the distribution of the LIX metric we see that questions with simpler answers draw more selections

---

[11]We consider that the null hypothesis (H_0) is given when *there is no impact of referral count on question selection behaviour* and perform a two tailed t-test for understanding if *high or low referral count is associated with question selections* (H_1). We calculate the other p-values of other features similarly.

Table 1: Mean Reciprocal Rank (MRR) and Mean Average Precision ($MAP@n$) for identifying the most likely question-selection for 100 users randomly selected from those with more than 5 question answers for *Cooking*.

Model	Feature	MRR	Mean Average Precision ($MAP@n$)					
			$MAP@1$	$MAP@2$	$MAP@4$	$MAP@8$	$MAP@16$	$MAP@32$
Baseline	Random	0.007	0.007	0.007	0.007	0.007	0.007	0.006
	Question Age	0.094	0.036	0.053	0.069	0.082	0.089	0.090
	Topic Affinity	0.018	0.000	0.004	0.007	0.008	0.009	0.011
Random Forests	Observer	0.048	0.023	0.031	0.036	0.039	0.041	0.042
	Question	0.397	0.279	0.350	0.384	0.391	0.393	0.394
	Thread	0.246	0.212	0.222	0.224	0.225	0.234	0.239
	All	0.446	0.307	0.380	0.428	0.440	0.444	0.444
LambdaRank	Observer	0.045	0.018	0.018	0.023	0.028	0.033	0.038
	Question	0.044	0.028	0.032	0.034	0.036	0.037	0.039
	Thread	0.046	0.000	0.000	0.001	0.001	0.029	0.043
	All	0.234	0.222	0.222	0.223	0.226	0.227	0.228
ListNet	Observer	0.139	0.059	0.089	0.110	0.121	0.126	0.133
	Question	0.106	0.041	0.053	0.074	0.085	0.095	0.099
	Thread	0.112	0.039	0.056	0.076	0.094	0.098	0.104
	All	0.114	0.036	0.066	0.081	0.093	0.101	0.107

($p < 2.2 \times 10^{-16}$). Similarly, answerers seem to prefer questions that have not attracted skilled answerers yet ($p < 2.2 \times 10^{-16}$). Finally, the top *user* features are all related to user ability to answer and ask questions. Such features are probably highly ranked as they can be used for differentiating knowledgeable users from less skilled answerers. Therefore, a ranking model can use *user* information to adapt the ranking depending on the type of potential answerer.

5.2.1 Feature Reduction

We trained the *Random Forests* model for each set of features selected by the CFS, IGR, features drop, and average ranking methods. In order to select the minimal and most effective number of features, we gradually add in features according to their discriminative power and determine the best number of features based on the MRR score (Figure 3).

As shown in Figure 3, for each ranking approach, the optimum number of features are: 1) IGR: 60 ($MRR = 0.458$); 2) CFS: 58 ($MRR = 0.451$); 3) Feature drop (ablation method): 58 ($MRR = 0.491$), and 4) Average rank: 52 ($MRR = 0.463$). This implies that almost all our features are required for training the *Random Forests* LTR model. Nevertheless, we observe that by using the feature drop subset, we can outperform the best previous result by more than 9% MRR (Table 4). Although it appears that feature selection does not reduce significantly the number of features required for getting quality behaviour predictions, we can observe that by using only the top 15 features from average ranking, we get a result similar to our best previous result. As a consequence, it is possible to reduce the computational complexity of the behaviour model without sacrificing much prediction ability.

6. DISCUSSION

Modelling the behaviour of answerers is a complex task and it is generally difficult to obtain high precision for such a problem [12]. In this paper, we showed that by using dynamic features and LTR algorithms, we obtained a good precision ($MAP@1 = 0.5168$). For the CO community, we found that

Table 3: Top fifteen features ranked using their average rank computed by merging the Information Gain Ratio, Correlation Feature Selection and Features Drop results for *Cooking*. Type of feature is indicated by U/Q/T for User/Question/Thread.

	Merged Rank (IGR+CFS+Drop)	
R.	AR.	Feature
1	1.66	Referral Count (Q)
2	6.66	Question Reputation (Q)
3	9.33	Number of Answers (Q)
4	10.33	Average Readability LIX (T)
5	10.33	Average Answer Success (T)
6	11.66	Answer Success Ratio (U)
7	14.66	Question Age (Q)
8	17.33	Number of Questions (U)
9	18.33	Questions Success (U)
10	18.33	Reputation (Q)
11	18.66	Average Answer Success Ratio (T)
12	18.66	Polarity (Q)
13	21	Question Success (U)
14	21.33	Number of Answers (U)
15	21.33	Average Readability Fog (T)

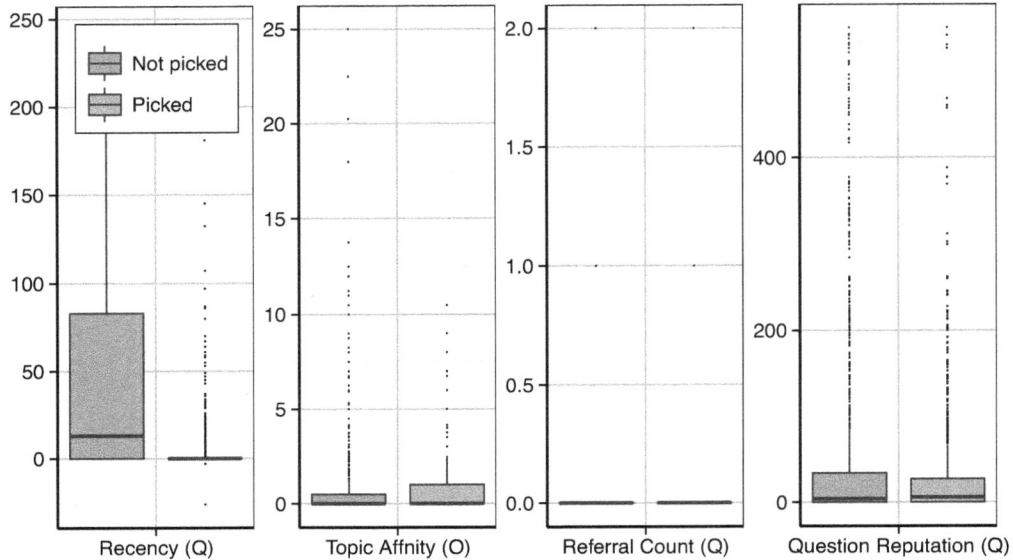

Figure 2: Box plots representing the distribution of different features and question selection for *Cooking*.

answering behaviour is mostly affected by three different features: the ability of askers to obtain good answers, the recency of questions and the syntactical complexity of existing answers. Questions asked by users that had difficulties to obtain good answers were more likely to get selected ($p = 9.723e - 05$). Naturally, recent questions had a higher chance of being selected by answerers ($p < 2.2e - 16$) and questions that had less complex answers were also more likely to be selected by answerers ($p < 2.2e - 16$)

Our approach generated high MRR and $P@1$ ($MAP@1$) indicating that on average, the questions a user will select to answer are positioned within the first two list elements returned by our LTR model. Although our dataset consisted of a randomly selected 100 users only, our analyses considered all open and available questions as possible candidates for users to select to answer, which was 328 questions per user per time t. In [12] only the latest 20 questions were considered. To further optimise our approach, we plan to study whether the influence of our prediction features change when the size of the question list is smaller or bigger. Our analyses showed that using a smaller subset of features can produce high prediction accuracies, which facilitates applying our approach to much larger community datasets.

In order to better understand how answerers select their questions, we applied different automatic methods for ranking features according to their ability to model answering behaviour. Although such methods were originally designed for standard classification tasks (e.g. binary classification) and are theoretically suboptimal for LTR problems, we managed to maintain the quality of our results by cutting the number of required features considerably. As a consequence, we observed that for the CO community, it is not necessary to have many different predictors in order to identify the questions selected by users. Although it is necessary to validate this finding on bigger and more diverse communities, it is possible to apply it to the CO community in order to

reduce the amount of computation required for creating behaviour models. In particular, by reducing the number of required features, it becomes possible to go beyond the 100 user sample that we used for our study of CO.

In this paper, we also removed 5% of the questions that were answered even if they were solved and older than three weeks. Although we argue that such a percentage of questions is unlikely to affect our results, future work could investigate the identification of these type of questions and study a method for predicting behaviour with those particular items.

Users' question selection time was known when predicting our answering behaviour. One extension is to also predict those selection times, as partially studied in [21] and [16]. This would enable us to predict when a user answers a question, as well as which question the user selected for answering.

Another point worth highlighting is that we experimented with a single Q&A community, on Cooking. It would be worth applying our approach to other communities on cooking, as well as to other communities on different topics, to see if similar behaviour patterns are exhibited. Such an extension is necessary to determine the portability of our findings across different communities and topics [18].

Finally, we limited our number of features to 62 *user*, *question* and *thread* features. Although there is potentially an infinite number of features that could be evaluated for the task presented in this paper, we found that question features were the most associated with question selection behaviour. Future work could investigate additional features in this particular area such as different readability metrics [8] or question complexity measures [1].

7. CONCLUSIONS

This paper proposed an approach for identifying the questions that users are most likely to answer in a Q/A website.

Table 2: Top fifteen features ranked using their average rank computed using Information Gain Ratio, Correlation Feature Selection and Features Drop for the *Cooking* dataset and the corresponding *MRR* performance. Type of feature is indicated by O/Q/T for Observer/Question/Thread.

	Info. Gain Ratio			CFS			Feature Drop.		
R.	AR.	IGR	Feature	AR	AC	Feature	R.	MRR	Feature
1	4	0.011	Answer Succ. Ratio (O)	1.8	0.022	Answer Succ. Ratio (O)	1	0.414	Referral Count (Q)
2	4.2	0.011	Referral Count (Q)	2.2	0.021	Referral Count (Q)	2	0.418	Nb. of Answers (Q)
3	6.8	0.010	Question Reputation (Q)	4.4	0.022	Question Age (Q)	3	0.418	Avg. Nb. of Questions (T)
4	7.7	0.010	Avg. Readability LIX (T)	5.7	0.022	Question Reputation (Q)	4	0.422	Asker Reputation (Q)
5	8.1	0.010	Question Age (Q)	6.4	0.023	Avg. Readability Fog (T)	5	0.423	Avg. Question Reputation (T)
6	9.1	0.013	Avg. Reputation (O)	7.5	0.022	Nb. of Answers (Q)	6	0.425	Avg. Question Reputation (O)
7	11.4	0.010	Answers Succ. Ratio (Q)	9.2	0.022	Avg. Readability LIX (T)	7	0.427	Topic Reputation (O)
8	11.8	0.010	Topic Affinity (Q)	9.5	0.022	Avg. Referral Count (T)	8	0.427	Topic Affinity (O)
9	11.9	0.010	Avg. Referral Count (T)	13.9	0.022	Topic Affinity (Q)	9	0.430	Readability LIX (Q)
10	12	0.346	Avg. Quest. Reputation (Q)	14	0.022	Avg. Quest. Succ. Ratio (T)	10	0.431	Polarity (Q)
11	12.6	0.010	Avg. Quest. Succ. Ratio (T)	15.1	0.021	Avg. Reputation (O)	11	0.432	Length (Q)
12	14	0.010	Avg. Polarity (T)	15.2	0.022	Avg. Answer Succ. (T)	12	0.432	Avg. Reputation (T)
13	14.2	0.010	Avg. Answers Succ. Ratio (T)	15.6	0.022	Questions Succ. (O)	13	0.434	Question Reputation (Q)
14	14.4	0.010	Avg. Answer Succ. (T)	16.3	0.022	Nb. of Posts (O)	14	0.434	Avg. Reputation (O)
15	15.4	0.009	Questions Succ. (O)	17.2	0.022	Nb. of Answers (O)	15	0.434	Nb. of Questions (O)

Table 4: Mean Reciprocal Rank (*MRR*) and Mean Average Precision (*MAP@n*) for identifying the most likely question-selection for 100 users randomly selected from those with more than 5 answers for *Cooking* using different feature selections approaches.

Model	Feature	*MRR*	Mean Average Precision (*MAP@n*)					
			MAP@1	*MAP@2*	*MAP@4*	*MAP@8*	*MAP@16*	*MAP@32*
	All	0.446	0.307	0.380	0.428	0.440	0.444	0.444
	IGR	0.329	0.326	0.399	0.438	0.453	0.456	0.456
	CFS	0.451	0.326	0.394	0.433	0.447	0.449	0.449
	Drop	0.491	0.364	0.439	0.478	0.485	0.488	0.489
	IGR+CFS+Drop	0.463	0.326	0.398	0.449	0.459	0.461	0.462
LambdaRank	All	0.234	0.222	0.222	0.223	0.226	0.227	0.228
	IGR	0.227	0.209	0.213	0.215	0.219	0.220	0.220
	CFS	0.226	0.212	0.213	0.215	0.219	0.220	0.220
	Drop	0.245	0.233	0.233	0.233	0.235	0.236	0.239
	IGR+CFS+Drop	0.228	0.212	0.216	0.217	0.220	0.221	0.221
ListNet	All	0.114	0.036	0.066	0.081	0.093	0.101	0.107
	IGR	0.105	0.039	0.062	0.073	0.083	0.091	0.098
	CFS	0.086	0.026	0.037	0.054	0.064	0.074	0.079
	Drop	0.111	0.041	0.053	0.070	0.088	0.097	0.106
	IGR+CFS+Drop	0.091	0.034	0.047	0.066	0.072	0.079	0.085

We introduced different LTR models for learning user behaviours, and showed that a *Random Forests* ranking model can identify question selections efficiently with a *MRR* of 0.491 with 52 features and an *MRR* of 0.441 with 15 features. We found that question selections are highly influenced by question features such as whether they contain hyperlinks, have already received some answers, or have been asked by a reputable user. We also found that users tend to answer more recent questions and that the readability of existing answers affect users' selections.

8. ACKNOWLEDGEMENT

This work is partly funded by the EC-FP7 project DecarboNet (grant number 265454).

9. REFERENCES

[1] G. Burel and Y. He. A question of complexity: Measuring the maturity of online enquiry communities. In *Proceedings of the 24th ACM Conference on Hypertext and Social Media*, HT '13, pages 1–10, New York, NY, USA, 2013. ACM.

[2] G. Burel, Y. He, and H. Alani. Automatic identification of best answers in online enquiry communities. *The Semantic Web: Research and Applications*, 2012.

[3] Y. Cao, H. Duan, C.-Y. Lin, Y. Yu, and H.-W. Hon. Recommending questions using the mdl-based tree cut model. In *Proceedings of the 17th international conference on World Wide Web*. ACM, 2008.

[4] Z. Cao, T. Qin, T.-Y. Liu, M.-F. Tsai, and H. Li. Learning to rank: From pairwise approach to listwise approach. In *Proceedings of the 24th International Conference on Machine Learning*, ICML '07, New York, NY, USA, 2007. ACM.

[5] S. Chang and A. Pal. Routing questions for collaborative answering in community question answering. In *Proceedings of the 2013 IEEE/ACM International Conference on Advances in Social Networks Analysis and Mining*. ACM, 2013.

[6] G. Dror, Y. Koren, Y. Maarek, and I. Szpektor. I want to answer; who has a question?: Yahoo! answers recommender system. In *Proceedings of the 17th ACM*

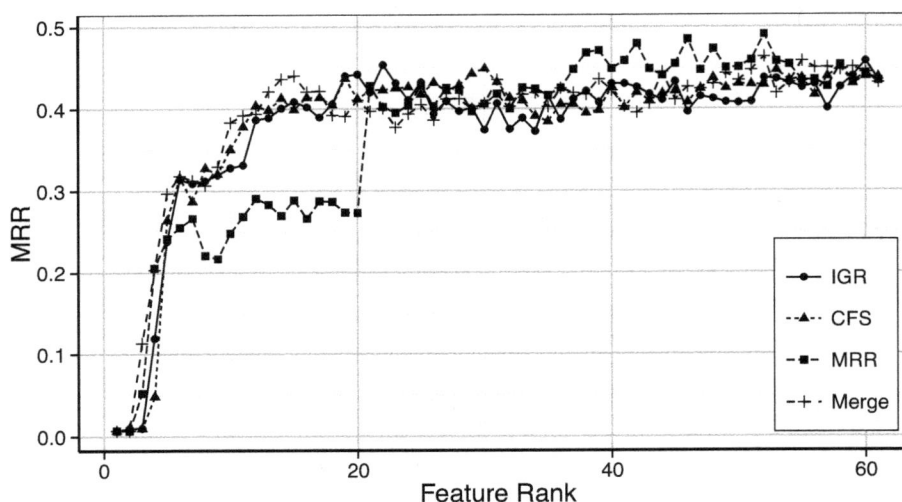

Figure 3: *MRR* vs. feature rank for the Information Gain Ratio, Correlation Feature Selection, Features Drop feature selection and Merged Ranking methods for *Cooking*.

SIGKDD international conference on Knowledge discovery and data mining. ACM, 2011.

[7] H. Duan, Y. Cao, C.-Y. Lin, and Y. Yu. Searching questions by identifying question topic and question focus. In *ACL*, 2008.

[8] L. Feng, M. Jansche, M. Huenerfauth, and N. Elhadad. A comparison of features for automatic readability assessment. In *Proceedings of the 23rd International Conference on Computational Linguistics: Posters*, COLING '10, pages 276–284, Stroudsburg, PA, USA, 2010. Association for Computational Linguistics.

[9] L.-C. Lai and H.-Y. Kao. Question routing by modeling user expertise and activity in cQA services. In *The 26th Annual Conference of the Japanese Society for Artificial Intelligence*, 2012.

[10] B. Li and I. King. Routing questions to appropriate answerers in community question answering services. In *Proceedings of the 19th ACM international conference on Information and knowledge management.* ACM, 2010.

[11] B. Li, I. King, and M. R. Lyu. Question routing in community question answering: putting category in its place. In *Proceedings of the 20th ACM international conference on Information and knowledge management.* ACM, 2011.

[12] Q. Liu and E. Agichtein. Modeling answerer behavior in collaborative question answering systems. In *Advances in Information Retrieval.* Springer, 2011.

[13] T.-Y. Liu. Learning to rank for information retrieval. *Found. Trends Inf. Retr.*, 3(3), Mar. 2009.

[14] M. J. Pazzani and D. Billsus. Content-based recommendation systems. In *The adaptive web.* Springer, 2007.

[15] M. Qu, G. Qiu, X. He, C. Zhang, H. Wu, J. Bu, and C. Chen. Probabilistic question recommendation for question answering communities. In *Proceedings of the 18th international conference on World wide web.* ACM, 2009.

[16] C. Quoc and V. Le. Learning to rank with nonsmooth cost functions. *NIPS'07*, 2007.

[17] F. Riahi, Z. Zolaktaf, M. Shafiei, and E. Milios. Finding expert users in community question answering. In *Proceedings of the 21st international conference companion on World Wide Web.* ACM, 2012.

[18] M. Rowe and H. Alani. Mining and comparing engagement dynamics across multiple social media platforms. In *ACM 2014 Web Science Conference*, Bloomington, Indiana, USA, 2014.

[19] M. Surdeanu, M. Ciaramita, and H. Zaragoza. Learning to rank answers to non-factoid questions from web collections. *Computational Linguistics*, 37(2), 2011.

[20] I. Szpektor, Y. Maarek, and D. Pelleg. When relevance is not enough: promoting diversity and freshnessin personalized question recommendation. In *Proceedings of the 22nd international conference on World Wide Web.* International World Wide Web Conferences Steering Committee, 2013.

[21] Y. Tian, P. S. Kochhar, E.-P. Lim, F. Zhu, and D. Lo. Predicting best answerers for new questions: An approach leveraging topic modeling and collaborative voting. In *Social Informatics.* Springer, 2014.

[22] H. Wu, Y. Wang, and X. Cheng. Incremental probabilistic latent semantic analysis for automatic question recommendation. In *Proceedings of the 2008 ACM conference on Recommender systems.* ACM, 2008.

[23] Y. Zhou, G. Cong, B. Cui, C. S. Jensen, and J. Yao. Routing questions to the right users in online communities. In *Data Engineering, 2009. ICDE'09. IEEE 25th International Conference on.* IEEE, 2009.

A Long-Term Study of a Crowdfunding Platform: Predicting Project Success and Fundraising Amount

Jinwook Chung and Kyumin Lee
Department of Computer Science
Utah State University
Logan, Utah 84322
{jinwook.chung@aggiemail.usu.edu, kyumin.lee@usu.edu}

ABSTRACT

Crowdfunding platforms have become important sites where people can create projects to seek funds toward turning their ideas into products, and back someone else's projects. As news media have reported successfully funded projects (e.g., Pebble Time, Coolest Cooler), more people have joined crowdfunding platforms and launched projects. But in spite of rapid growth of the number of users and projects, a project success rate at large has been decreasing because of launching projects without enough preparation and experience. To solve the problem, in this paper we (i) collect the largest datasets from Kickstarter, consisting of all project profiles, corresponding user profiles, projects' temporal data and users' social media information; (ii) analyze characteristics of successful projects, behaviors of users and understand dynamics of the crowdfunding platform; (iii) propose novel statistical approaches to predict whether a project will be successful and a range of expected pledged money of the project; and (iv) develop predictive models and evaluate performance of the models. Our experimental results show that the predictive models can effectively predict project success and a range of expected pledged money.

Categories and Subject Descriptors: H.3.5 [Online Information Services]: Web-based services

Keywords: crowdfunding; kickstarter; twitter; project success; fundraising amount

1. INTRODUCTION

Crowdfunding platforms have successfully connected millions of individual crowdfunding backers to a variety of new ventures and projects, and these backers have spent over a billion dollars on these ventures and projects [8]. From reward-based crowdfunding platforms like Kickstarter, Indiegogo, and RocketHub, to donation-based crowdfunding platforms like GoFundMe and GiveForwad, to equity-based crowdfunding platforms like CrowdCube, EarlyShares and Seedrs - these platforms have shown the effectiveness of

HT '15, September 1–4, 2015, Guzelyurt, Northern Cyprus.
© 2015 ACM. ISBN 978-1-4503-3395-5/15/09 ...$15.00.
DOI: http://dx.doi.org/10.1145/2700171.2791045.

funding projects from millions of individual users. The US Congress has encouraged crowdfunding as a source of capital for new ventures via the JOBS Act [2].

An example of successfully funded projects is E-paper watch project. The E-paper watch project for smartphones on a crowdfunding platform was created by Pebble Technology corporation on April 2012 in Kickstarter, expecting $100,000 investment. Surprisingly, in 2 hours right after launching the project, pledged money was already exceeding $100,000. In the end of the project period (about 5 weeks), the company was able to get investment over 10 million dollars [25]. This example shows the power of collective investment and a crowdfunding platform, and a new way to raise funding from the crowds.

Even though the number of projects and amount of pledged funds on crowdfunding platforms has dramatically grown in the past few years, success rate of projects at large has been decreasing. Besides, little is known about dynamics of crowdfunding platforms and strategies to make a project successful. To fill the gap, in this paper we are interested to (i) analyze Kickstarter, the most popular crowdfunding platform and the 373rd most popular site as of March 2015 [4]; and (ii) propose statistical approaches to predict not only whether a project will be successful, but also how much a project will get invested. Kickstarter has an All-or-Nothing policy. If a project reaches pledged money lower than its goal, its creator will receive nothing. Predicting a range of expected pledged money is an important research problem.

Specifically, we analyze behaviors of users on Kickstarter by answering following research questions: Are users only interested in creating and launching their own projects? or Do they support other projects? Has the number of newly joined users been increased over time? Have experienced users achieved a higher project success rate? Then, we analyze characteristics of projects by answering following research questions: How many projects have been created over time? What percent of project has been successfully funded? Can we observe distinguishing characteristics between successful projects and failed projects? Based on the analysis and study, we answer following research questions: Can we build predictive models which can predict not only whether a project will be successful, but also a range of expected pledged money of the project? By adding a project's temporal data (e.g., daily pledged money and daily increased number of backers) and a project creator's social media information, can we even improve performance of the predicative models further?

Kickstarter projects	151,608
Kickstarter users	142,890
Kickstarter projects with temporal data	74,053
Kickstarter projects with Twitter user profiles	21,028

Table 1: Datasets.

Toward answering these questions, we make the following contributions in this paper:

- We collected the largest datasets, consisting of all Kickstarter project pages, user pages, each project's temporal data and each user's Twitter account information, and then conducted comprehensive analysis to understand behaviors of Kickstarter users and characteristics of projects.

- Based on the analysis, we proposed and extracted four types of features toward developing project success predictors and pledged money range predictors. To our knowledge, this is the first work to study how to predict a range of expected pledged money of a project.

- Finally, we developed predictive models and thoroughly evaluated performance of these models. Our experimental results show that these models can effectively predict whether a project will be successful and a range of expected pledged money.

2. DATASETS

To analyze projects and users on crowdfunding platforms, and understand whether adding social media information would improve project success prediction and pledged money prediction rates, first we collected data from Kickstarter, the most popular crowdfunding platform, and Twitter, one of the most popular social media sites. The following subsections present our data collection strategy and datasets.

2.1 Kickstarter Dataset

Kickstarter is a popular crowdfunding platform where users create and back projects. As of March 2015, it is the 373rd most visited site in the world according to Alexa [4].

Static Data. Our Kickstarter data collection goal was to collect all Kickstarter pages and corresponding user pages, but Kickstarter site only shows currently active projects and some of the most funded projects. Fortunately, Kicktraq site[1] has archived all project page URLs of Kickstarter. Given a Kicktraq project URL[2], by replacing Kicktraq hostname (i.e, www.kicktraq.com) of the project URL with Kickstarter hostname (i.e., www.kickstarter.com), we were able to obtain the Kickstarter project page URL[3].

Specifically, our data collection approach was to collect all project pages on Kicktraq, extract each project URL, and replace its hostname with Kickstarter hostname. Then we collected each Kickstarter project page and corresponding user page. Note that even though Kickstarter do not reveal an old project page (i.e., a project's campaign duration was ended), if we know the project URL, we can still access the project page on Kickstarter.

[1] http://www.kicktraq.com/archive/
[2] http://www.kicktraq.com/projects/fpa/launch-the-first-person-arts-podcast/
[3] https://www.kickstarter.com/projects/fpa/launch-the-first-person-arts-podcast/

Finally, we collected 168,851 project pages which were created between 2009 and September 2014. Note that Kickstarter site was launched in 2009. A project page consists of a project duration, funding goal, project description, rewards description and so on. We also collected corresponding 146,721 distinct user pages each of which consists of bio, account longevity, location information, the number of backed projects, the number of created projects, and so on. Among 168,851 project pages, we filtered 17,243 projects which have been either canceled or suspended, or in which the project creator's account has been canceled or suspended. Among 146,721 user pages, we filtered corresponding 8,679 user pages. Finally, 151,608 project pages and 142,890 user pages presented in Table 1, have been used in the rest of this paper.

Temporal Data. To analyze and understand how much each project has been pledged/invested daily and how many backers each project has attracted daily, whether incorporating these temporal data (i.e., daily pledged money and daily increased number of backers during a project duration) can improve project success prediction and expected pledged money prediction rates, we collected temporal data of 74,053 projects which were created between March 2013 and August 2014 and were ended by September 2014.

2.2 Twitter Dataset

What if we add social media information of a project creator to build predictive models? Can a project creator's social media information improve project success and expected pledged money prediction rates? Can we link a project creator's account on Kickstarter to Twitter? To answer these questions, we checked project creators' Kickstarter profiles. Interestingly 19,138 users (13.4% of all users in our dataset), who created 22,408 projects, linked their Twitter user profile pages (i.e., URLs) to their Kickstarter user profile pages. To use these users' Twitter account information in experiments, we collected their Twitter account information. Specifically, we extracted a Twitter user profile URL from each Kickstarter user profile, and then collected the user's Twitter profile information consisting of the basic profile information (e.g., a number of tweets, a number of following and a number of followers) and tweets posted during a project period. In a step of the Twitter user profile collection, we noticed that some of Twitter accounts had been either suspended or deleted. By filtering these accounts, finally, we collected 17,908 Twitter user profiles and tweets, and then combined these Twitter information with 21,028 Kickstarter project pages created by the 17,908 users.

3. ANALYZING KICKSTARTER USERS AND PROJECTS

In the previous section, we presented our data collection strategy and datasets. Now we turn to analyze Kickstarter users and projects.

3.1 Analysis of Users

Given 142,890 user profiles, we are interested in answering following research questions: Are users only interested in creating and launching their own projects? or Do they support other projects? Has the number of new users joined Kickstarter been increased over time? Do experienced users have a higher probability to make a project successful?

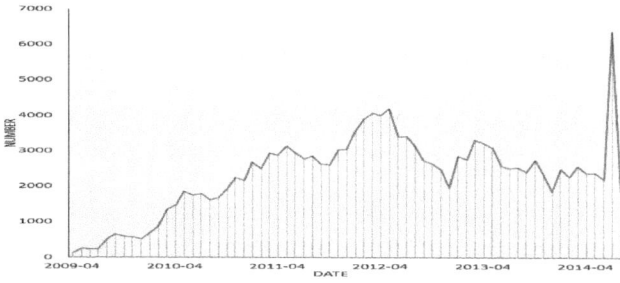

Figure 1: Number of newly joined Kickstarter users in each month.

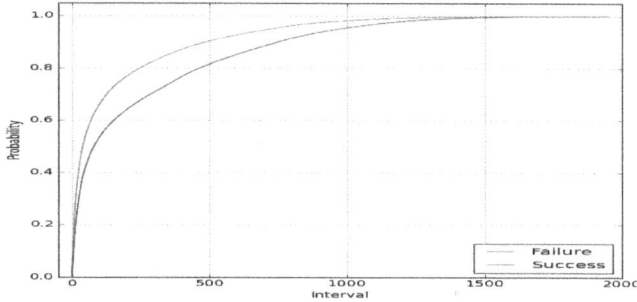

Figure 2: CDFs of intervals between user joined date and project creation date (Days).

First of all, we present general statistics of users in Table 2. The user statistics show that average number of backed projects and created projects are 3.48 and 1.19, respectively. It means that users backed larger number of projects and created less number of their own projects. Each user linked 1.75 websites on average into her profile so that she can get trust from potential investors. Examples of websites are company sites and user profile pages in social networking sites such as Twitter and YouTube. 13.4% Kickstarter users linked their Twitter pages, and 6.89% Kickstarter users linked their Youtube pages.

Next, we categorized Kickstarter users based on their project backing and creating activities. We found two groups of users: (i) all-time creator (AT creator), who only created projects and did not back other projects; and (ii) active user, who not only created her own projects but also backed other projects. As shown in Table 3, there are 66,262 (46.4%) all-time creators and 76,628 (53.6%) active users. Each all-time creator created 1.12 projects on average. These creators were only interested in creating their own projects and sought funds. Interestingly, the average number of created projects per all-time creator reveals that these creators created just one or two projects. However, each of 76,628 active users created 1.25 projects and backed 6.49 projects on av-

	Total
Total number of users	142,890
Number of backed projects per user	3.48
Number of created projects per user	1.19
Number of websites per user	1.75
Twitter connected	13.4% users
YouTube connected	6.89% users

Table 2: Statistics of Kickstarter users.

	Number	Avg. backed	Avg. created
AT creators	66,262	N/A	1.12
Active users	76,628	6.49	1.25

Table 3: Two groups of users: all-time (AT) creators and active users.

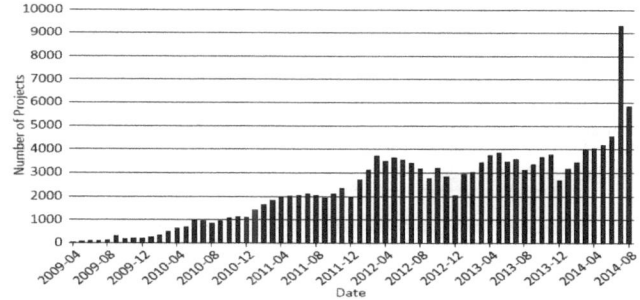

Figure 3: Number of created projects per month has been increased over time with some fluctuation.

erage. These active users created a little more projects than all-time creators, and backed many other projects.

Next, we analyze how many new users joined Kickstarter over time. Figure 1 shows the number of newly joined Kickstarter users per month. Overall, the number of newly joined users per month has been linearly increased until May 2012, and then has been decreased until June 2014 with some fluctuation. In July 2014, there was a huge spike. Note that we tried to understand why there was a huge spike in July 2014 by checking news articles, but we were not able to find a concrete reason. Interesting observation is that the number of newly joined users was the lowest during winter season, especially, December in each year. We conjecture that since November and December contains several holidays, people may delay to join Kickstarter.

A follow-up question is "Do experienced users achieve a higher project success rate?". We measured experience of a user based on when they create a project after joining Kickstarter. Figure 2 shows cumulative distribution functions (CDFs) of intervals between user joined date and project creation date in successful projects and failed projects. As we expected, successful projects had longer intervals. We conjecture that since users with longer intervals become more experienced and familiar with Kickstarter platform, their projects have become successful with a higher probability.

3.2 Analysis of Projects

So far we have analyzed user profiles. We now analyze Kickstarter projects. Interesting research questions are: How many projects have been created over time? What percent of projects has been successfully funded? Can we observe clearly different properties between successfully funded projects and failed projects? To answer these questions, we analyzed Kickstarter project dataset presented in Table 1.

Number of projects and project success rate over time. Figure 3 shows how the number of projects has been changed over time. Overall, the number of created projects per month has been increased over time with some fluctuation. Interestingly, lower number of projects in December of each year (e.g., 2011, 2012 and 2013) has been created. Another interesting observation was that the largest number of projects (9,316 projects) were created in July 2014. The

	Success	Failure	Total
Percentage (%)	46	54	100
Classified project count	69,448	82,160	151,608
Duration (days)	33.21	36.2	34.83
Project Goal (USD)	8,364.34	35,201.89	22,891.15
Final money pledged (USD)	16,027.96	1,454.18	8,139.37
Number of images	4.63	3.37	3.95
Number of videos	1.18	0.93	1.04
Number of FAQs	0.84	0.39	0.6
Number of rewards	9.69	7.49	8.5
Number of updates	9.59	1.59	5.26
Number of project comments	77.52	2.45	36.89
Facebook connected (%)	61.00	59.00	60.00
Number of FB friends	583.48	395.15	481.54
Number of backers	211.16	19.34	107.33

Table 4: Statistics of Kickstarter projects.

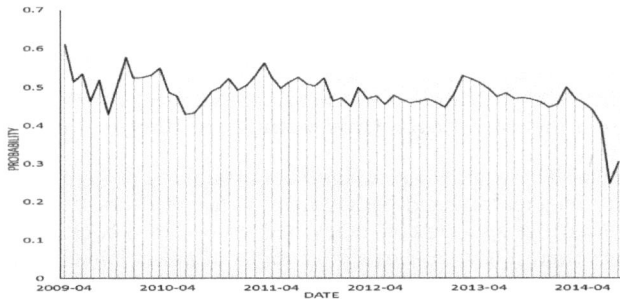

Figure 4: Project success rate in each month.

phenomena would be related to the number of newly joined users per month shown in Figure 1 in which less number of users joined Kickstarter during Winter season, especially in December in each year, and many users joined in July 2014.

Next, we are interested in analyzing how project success rate has been changed over time. We grouped projects by their launched year and month. Interestingly, the success rate has been fluctuated and overall project success rate in each month has been decreased over time as shown in Figure 4. In July 2014, the success rate was dramatically decreased. We conjecture that since many users joined Kickstarter in July 2014, these first-time project creators caused the sharp decrease of success rate.

Statistics of successful projects and failed projects.
Next, we analyze statistics of successful projects and failed projects. Table 4 presents the statistics of Kickstarter projects. Overall, percentage of the successful projects in our dataset is about 46%. In other words, 54% of all projects was failed. We can clearly observe that the successful projects had shorter project duration, lower funding goal, more active engagements and larger number of social network friends than failed projects.

Figure 5 shows more detailed information about how project success rate was changed when a project duration was increased. This figure clearly shows that project success rate was higher when a projet duration was shorter. Intuitively, people may think that longer project duration would be helpful to get more fund, but this analysis reveals the opposite result. To show how many projects have what duration, we plotted Figure 6. 39.7% (60,191 projects) of all projects had 30 day duration and then 6.5% (9,784 projects) of all projects had 60 day duration. We conjecture that since 30 day duration is the default duration on Kickstarter, many users just chose 30 day duration for their projects.

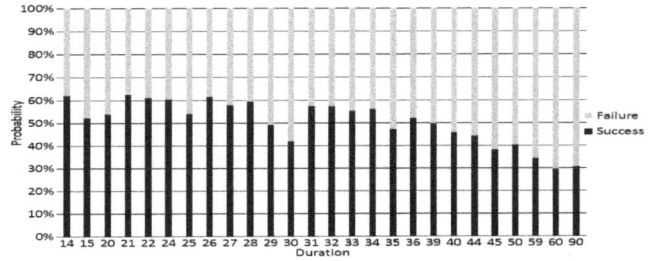

Figure 5: Project success and failure rates according to a duration that more than 1,000 projects has.

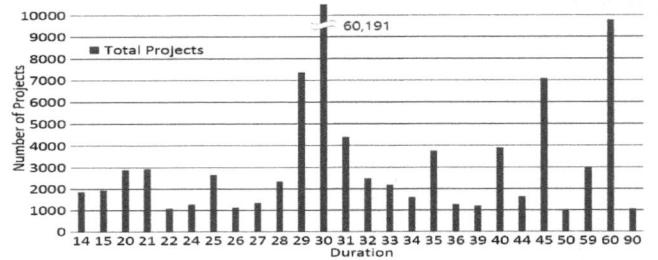

Figure 6: Number of Projects according to a duration that more than 1,000 projects has.

While the average project goal of successful projects was 3 times less than failed projects, the average pledged money of successful projects was 10 times more than failed projects. Project creators of successful projects spent more time to make better project description by adding a larger number of images, videos, FAQ and reward types. The creators also frequently updated their projects. Interestingly, project creators of the successful projects had a larger number of Facebook friends. It means that the creators' Facebook friends might help for their project success by backing the projects or spreading information of the projects to other people [19].

When a user creates a project on Kickstarter, she can choose a category of the project. Does a category of a project affect a project success rate? To answer this question, we analyzed project success rate according to each category. As you can see in Figure 7, projects in Dance, Music, Theater, Comics and Art categories achieved between 50% and 72% success rate which is greater than the average success rate of all projects (again, 46% success rate).

Location. A user can add location information when she creates a project. We checked our dataset to see how many

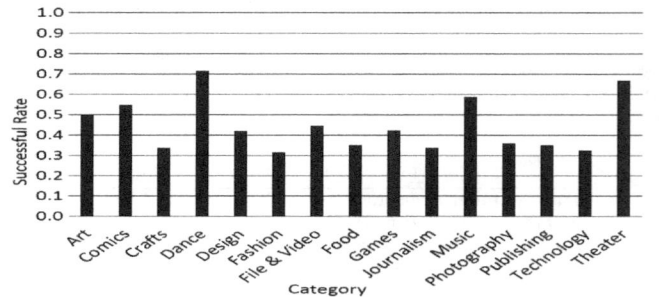

Figure 7: Project success rate under each of 15 categories.

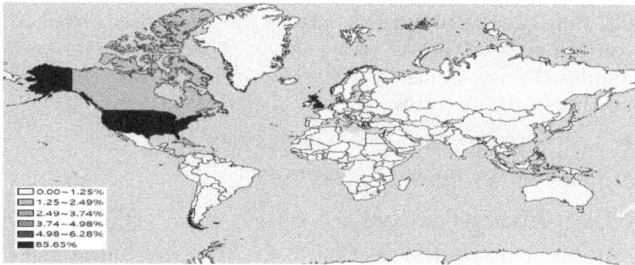

Figure 8: Distribution of projects in the world.

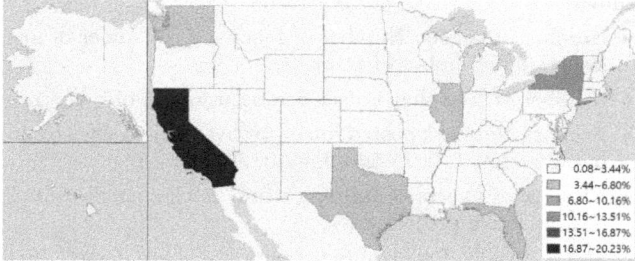

Figure 9: Distribution of projects in US.

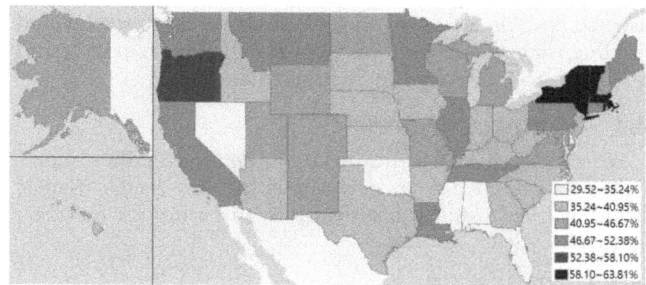

Figure 10: Project success rate across states in US.

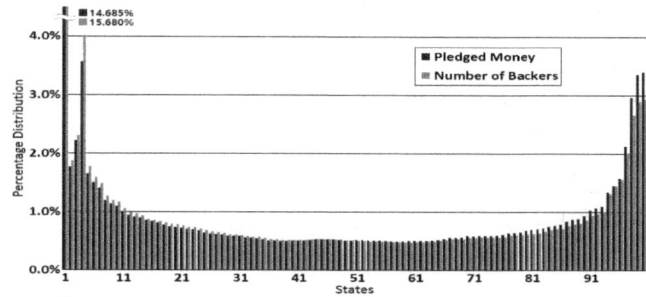

Figure 11: Percentage distribution of pledged money and number of backers per state.

projects contain location information. Surprisingly, 99% project pages contained location information. After extracting the location information from the projects, we plotted distribution of projects on the world map in Figure 8. 85.65% projects were created in US. The next largest number of projects were created in the United Kingdom (6.23%), Canada (2.20%), Australia (1%)and Germany (0.92%). Overall, the majority of projects were created in the western countries. The project distribution across countries makes sense because initially only US based projects on Kickstarter were created, and then the company allowed users in other countries to launch projects since October 2012. Since over 85% projects were created in US, we plotted distribution of the projects on US map in Figure 9. Top 5 states are California (20.23%), New York (12.93%), Texas (5.45%), Florida (4.57%) and Illinois (4.03%). This distribution mostly follows population of each state.

A follow-up question is how project distribution across states in US is related to projects success rate. To answer this question, we plotted project success rate of each state in Figure 10. Top 5 states with the highest success rate are Vermont (63.81%), Massachusetts (58.49%), New York (58.46%), Rhode Island (58.33%) and Oregon (53.56%). Except New York state, small number of projects were created in the four states. To make a concrete conclusion, we measured Pearson correlation between distribution of projects and project success rate. The correlation value was 0.25 which indicates that they are not significantly correlated.

Analysis of Kickstarter Temporal Data. As we presented in Table 1, we collected temporal data of 74,053 projects (e.g., daily pledged money and daily increased number of backers). Using these temporal data, we analyzed what percent of total pledged money and what percent of backers each project got over time after launching a project. Since each project has different duration (e.g., 30 days or 60 days), first, we converted each project duration to 100 states (time slots). Then, in each state, we measured percent of pledged money and number of backers.

Figure 11 shows the percentage distribution of pledged money and number of backers per state over time. One of the most interesting observations is that the largest amount of money was pledged in the beginning and end of a project. For example, 14.69% money was pledged and 15.68% backers were obtained in the first state. Other researchers also observed the same phenomena in smaller datasets [13, 15].

Another interesting observation is that there is another spike after the first spike in the beginning of project durations. We conjecture that the first spike was caused by a project creator's family and friends who backed the project [6], and the second spike was caused by other users who noticed the project and heard of a trend of the project.

The other interesting observation is that after 60th state, the number of backers and the number of pledged money have been exponentially increased. Especially, people rushed investing a project, as a project was heading to the end of the project duration. The phenomenon is called the Deadline effect [21, 24]. Even amount of invested money has been increased more quickly than the number of backers. This may indicate that people tend to purchase more expensive reward item. They may want to make sure a project become successful, achieving higher amount of pledged money than a project goal[4]. In another case, they knew that other people already supported the project with a large amount of money which motivated them to back the project with high trust.

4. FEATURES AND EXPERIMENTAL SETTINGS

In the previous section, we analyzed behaviors of Kickstarter users and characteristics of projects. Based on the analysis, in this section we propose features which will be

---

[4]Kickstarter has an All-or-Nothing policy. If a project reaches at or over its goal, its creator will receive pledged fund. Otherwise, the project creator will receive nothing.

used to develop a project success predictor and an expected funding range predictor. We also describe our experimental settings which are used in Sections 5 and 6.

4.1 Features

We extracted 49 features from our collected datasets presented in Table 1. Then, we grouped the features to 4 types: (i) project features; (ii) user features; (iii) temporal features; and (iv) Twitter features.

4.1.1 Project Features

From a project page, we generated 11 features as follows:

- Project category, duration, project goal, number of images, number of videos, number of FAQs, and number of rewards.
- SMOG grade of reward description: To estimate the readability of the all rewards text.
- SMOG grade of main page description: To estimate the readability of the main page description of a project.
- Number of sentences in reward description.
- Number of sentences in the main description of a project.

The SMOG grade estimates the years of education needed to understand a piece of writing [17]. The higher SMOG grade indicates that project and reward descriptions were written well. To measure SMOG grade, we used the following formula:

$$1.043\sqrt{|polysyllables| \times \frac{30}{|sentences|}} + 3.1291$$

, where the number of Polysyllables is the count of the words of 3 or more syllables.

4.1.2 User Features

From a user profile page and the user's previous experience, we generated 28 features as follows:

- Distribution of the backed projects under the 15 main categories (15 features): what percent of projects belongs to each main category.
- Number of backed projects, number of created projects in the past, number of comments that a user made in the past, number of websites linked in a user profile, and number of Facebook friends that a user has.
- Is each of Facebook, YouTube and Twitter user pages connected? (3 features)
- SMOG grade of bio description, and Number of sentences in a bio description.
- Interval (days) between a user's Kickstarter joined date and a project's launched date.
- Success rate of the backed projects by a user.
- Success rate of the projects created by a user in the past.

4.1.3 Temporal Features

As we mentioned in Section 2, we collected 74,053 projects' temporal data consisting of daily pledged money and number of daily increased backers. First, we converted these temporal data points (i.e., daily value) to cumulated data points. For example, if a project's daily pledged money for 5 days project duration are 100, 200, 200, 100 and 200, cumulated data point in each day will be 100, 300, 500, 600 and

800. Since each project has various duration, we converted a duration to 100 states (time slots). Then, we normalized cumulated data points by 100 states. Finally, we generated two time-series features:

- Cumulated pledged money over time.
- Cumulated number of backers over time.

4.1.4 Twitter Features

As we mentioned in Section 2, 17,908 users linked their Twitter home pages to their Kickstarter user pages. From our collected Twitter dataset, we generated 8 features as follows:

- Number of tweets, Number of followings, Number of followers and Number of favorites.
- Number of lists that a user has been joined in.
- Number of tweets posted during active project days (e.g., between Jan 1, 2014 and Jan 30, 2014).
- Number of tweets containing word "Kickstarter" posted during active project days.
- SMOG grade of aggregated tweets which are posted during active project days.

The first five features were used for any project created by a user. The rest three features were generated for each project since each project was active in different time period.

Finally, we generated 49 features from a project and a user who created the project.

4.2 Experimental Settings

We describe our experimental settings which are used in the following sections for predicting project success and expected pledged money range.

Datasets	|Projects|	|Features|
KS Static	151,608	39
KS Static + Twitter	21,028	47
KS Static + Temporal + Twitter	11,675	49

Table 5: Three datasets which were used in experiments.

Datasets. In the following sections, we used three datasets presented in Table 5. Each dataset consists of a different number of projects and corresponding user profiles as we described in Section 2. Two datasets (KS Static + Twitter, and KS Static + Temporal + Twitter) contained Twitter user profiles as well.

We extracted 39 features from KS Static dataset (i.e., project features and user features), 47 features from KS Static + Twitter dataset (i.e., project features, user features and Twitter features), and 49 features from KS Static + Temporal + Twitter (i.e., all four feature groups). Note that in this subsection we presented the total number of our proposed features before applying feature selection.

Predictive Models. Since each classification algorithm might perform differently in our dataset, we selected 3 well-known classification algorithms: Naive Bayes, Random Forest, AdaboostM1 (with Random Forest as the base learner). We used Weka implementation of these algorithms [11].

Feature Selection. To check whether the proposed features were positively contributing to build a good predictor, we measured χ^2 value [23] for each of the features. The larger the χ^2 value is, the higher discriminative power the corresponding feature has. The feature selection results are described in following sections.

Evaluation. We used Accuracy as the primary evaluation metrics and Area under the ROC Curve (AUC) as the secondary metrics, and then built and evaluated each predictive model (classifier) by using 5-fold cross-validation.

5. PREDICTING PROJECT SUCCESS

Based on the features and experimental settings, we now develop and evaluate project success predictors.

5.1 Feature Selection

First of all, we conducted χ^2 feature selection to check whether the proposed features were all significant features. Since we had three datasets, we applied feature selection for each dataset. All features in KS Static dataset had positive distinguishing power to determine whether a project will be successful or not. But, in both of KS Static + Twitter dataset and KS Static + Temporal + Twitter, "Is each of Facebook, YouTube and Twitter user pages connected" features were not positively contributing, so we excluded them. Overall, some of project features (e.g., category, goal and number of rewards), some of user features (e.g., number of backed projects, success rate of backed projects, number of comments), some of Twitter features (e.g. number of lists, number of followers and number of favorites), and all temporal features were the most significant features.

5.2 Experiments

Our experimental goal is to develop and evaluate project success predictors. We build project success predictors by using each of the three datasets and evaluate performance of the predictors.

Classifier	Accuracy	AUC
Naive Bayes	67.3%	0.750
Random Forest	75.2%	0.827
AdaboostM1	**76.4%**	**0.838**

Table 6: Experimental results of three project success predictors based on Kickstarter static features.

Using KS Static dataset. The first task was to test whether only using Kickstarter static features (i.e., project and user features) would achieve good prediction results. To conduct this task, we converted Kickstarter static dataset consisting of 151,608 project profiles and user profiles to feature values. Then, We developed project success predictors based on each of 3 classification algorithms – Naive Bayes, Random Forest and AdaboostM1. Finally, we evaluated each predictor by using 5-fold cross-validation. Table 6 shows experimental results of three project success predictors based on Kickstarter static features. AdaboostM1 outperformed the other predictors, achieving 76.4% accuracy and 0.838 AUC. This result was better than 54% accuracy of a baseline which was measured by a percent of the majority class instances in Kickstarter static dataset (54% projects were unsuccessful). This result was also better than the previous work in which 68% accuracy was achieved [10].

Using KS Static + Twitter dataset. What if we add Twitter features to Kickstarter static features? Can we even improve performance of project success predictors? To an-

Classifier	Accuracy	AUC
Kickstarter		
Naive Bayes	60.3%	0.722
Random Forest	72.8%	0.790
AdaboostM1	**73.9%**	**0.798**
Kickstarter + Twitter		
Naive Bayes	56.5%	0.724
Random Forest	73.4%	0.800
AdaboostM1	**75.7%**	**0.826**

Table 7: Project success predictors based on Kickstarter static features vs. based on Kickstarter static features and Twitter features.

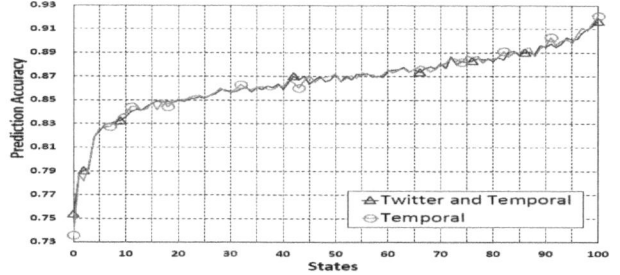

Figure 12: Project success prediction rate of predictors based on Kickstarter static and temporal features with/without Twitter features.

swer these questions, we compared performance of predictors without Twitter features with performance of predictors with Twitter features. In this experiment, we extracted Kickstarter static features from 21,028 projects and corresponding user profiles, and Twitter features from corresponding Twitter user profiles. As you can see in Table 7, AdaboostM1 classifier with Twitter features achieved 75.7% accuracy and 0.826 AUC, increasing accuracy and AUC of AdaboostM1 classifier without Twitter features by 2.5% ($= \frac{75.7}{73.9} - 1$) and 3.5% ($= \frac{0.826}{0.798} - 1$), respectively.

Using KS Static + Temporal + Twitter dataset. What if we replace Twitter features with Kickstarter temporal features? Or what if we use all features including Kickstarter static, temporal and Twitter features? Would using all features give us the best result? To answer these questions, we used KS Static + Temporal + Twitter dataset consisting of 11,675 project profiles, corresponding user profiles, Twitter profiles and project temporal data. Since each project has a different project duration, we converted each project duration to 100 states (time slots). Then we calculated temporal feature values in each state. Finally, we developed 100 predictors based on KS Static + Temporal features and 100 predictors based on KS Static + Temporal + Twitter features (each predictor was developed in each state). Note that in the previous experiments AdaboostM1 consistently outperformed the other classification algorithms, so used AdaboostM1 for this experiment. Figure 12 shows two project success predictors' accuracy in each state. In the beginning, KS Static + Temporal + Twitter features based predictors were slightly better than KS Static + Temporal features based predictors, but both of approaches performed similarly after 3rd state because temporal features became more significant. Overall, accuracy of predictors has been sharply increased until 11th state and then consistently increased until the end of a project duration. In 10th state (i.e., in the first 10% duration), the predictors achieved 83.6% accuracy which was increased by 11% ($= \frac{83.6}{75.3} - 1$) compared with 75.3% accuracy when a state was 0 (i.e., without temporal features). The more a state value increased, the higher accuracy a predictor achieved.

In summary, we developed project success predictors with various feature combinations. A project success predictor based on Kickstarter static features achieved 76.4% accuracy. Adding social media features increased the prediction accuracy by 2.5%. Adding temporal features consistently increased the accuracy. The experimental results confirmed that it is possible to predict a project's success when a user creates a project, and we can increase a prediction accuracy further with early observation after launching the project.

6. PREDICTING AN EXPECTED PLEDGED MONEY RANGE OF A PROJECT

So far we have studied predicting whether a project will be successful or not. But a project's success depends on a project goal and pledged money. If pledged money is equal to or greater than a project goal, the project will be successful. On the other hand, even though a project received a lot of pledged money (e.g., $99,999) , if a project goal (e.g., $100,000) is slightly larger than the pledged money, the project will be failed. Remember the All-or-Nothing policy. If we predict how much a project will get invested in advance, we can set up a realistic project goal and make the project successful. A fundamental research problem is "Can we predict expected pledged money? or Can we predict a range of expected pledged money of a project?". To our knowledge, no one has studied this research problem yet. In this section, we propose an approach to predict a range of expected pledged money of a project.

6.1 Approach and Feature Selection

In this section, our research goal is to develop predictive models which can predict a range of pledged money of a project. We defined the number of classes (categories) in two scenarios: (i) 2 classes; and (ii) 3 classes. In a scenario of 2 classes, we used a threshold, $5,000. The first class is $\leq$ $5,000, and the second class is $>$ $5,000. In other words, if pledged money of a project is less than or equal to $5,000, the project will belong to the first class. Likewise, in a scenario of 3 classes, we used two thresholds, $100 and $10,000. The first class is $\leq$ $100, the second class is $100 < project \leq$ $10,000$ and the third class is $>$ $10,000. Now we have the ground truth in each scenario.

Next, we applied feature selection to our datasets. In 2 classes, "Is Youtube connected" feature was not a significant feature in KS Static and KS Static + Temporal + Twitter datasets. "Is Twitter connected" feature was not a significant feature in KS Static + Twitter and KS Static + Temporal + Twitter datasets. In 3 classes, "Is Twitter connected" feature was not a significant feature in KS Static + Twitter and KS Static + Temporal + Twitter datasets.

6.2 Experiments

We conducted experiments in two scenarios – prediction in (i) 2 classes and (ii) 3 classes.

Using KS Static dataset. The first experiment was to predict a project's pledged money range by using KS Static dataset (i.e., generating the static features – project features and user features). A use case is that when a user creates

Classifier	Accuracy	AUC
Naive Bayes	75.9%	0.780
Random Forest	85.6%	**0.906**
AdaboostM1	**86.5%**	0.901

Table 8: Experimental results of pledged money range predictors based on Kickstarter static features under 2 classes.

a project, this predictor helps the user to set up an appropriate goal. We conducted 5 fold cross-validation in each of the two scenarios. Table 8 shows experimental results in 2 classes. AdaboostM1 outperformed Naive Bayes and Random Forest, achieving 86.5% accuracy and 0.901 AUC. When we compared our predictor's performance with the baseline – 74.8% accuracy (percent of the majority class, assuming selecting the majority class as a prediction result) –, our approach increased 11.5% ($= \frac{86.5}{74.8} - 1$).

Classifier	Accuracy	AUC
Naive Bayes	49.4%	0.713
Random Forest	73.3%	**0.817**
AdaboostM1	**74.2%**	0.811

Table 9: Experimental results of pledged money range predictors based on Kickstarter static features under 3 classes.

We also ran another experiment in 3 classes. Table 9 shows experimental results. Again, AdaboostM1 outperformed the other classification algorithms, achieving 74.2% accuracy and 0.811 AUC. When we compared its performance with the baseline – 63.1% –, it increased 17.6% ($= \frac{74.2}{63.1} - 1$). Regardless of the number of classes, our proposed approach consistently outperformed than the baseline. The experimental results showed that it is possible to predict an expected pledged money range in advance.

Classifier	Accuracy	AUC
Kickstarter		
Naive Bayes	70.6%	0.759
Random Forest	81.4%	0.889
AdaboostM1	**82.5%**	**0.896**
Kickstarter + Twitter		
Naive Bayes	70.7%	0.763
Random Forest	83.1%	0.904
AdaboostM1	**84.2%**	**0.910**

Table 10: Experimental results of pledged money range predictors based on Kickstarter static features and Twitter features under 2 classes.

Using KS Static + Twitter dataset. What if we add Twitter features? Will these improve a prediction accuracy? To answer this research question, we used KS Static + Twitter dataset in each of 2 classes and 3 classes. Experimental results under 2 classes and 3 classes are shown in Tables 10 and 11, respectively. In case of 2 classes, AdaboostM1 with Twitter features increased 2.1% ($= \frac{84.2}{82.5} - 1$) compared with a predictor without Twitter features, achieving 84.2% accuracy and 0.91 AUC. In case of 3 classes, AdaboostM1 with Twitter features also increased 1.8% ($= \frac{77.2}{75.8} - 1$) compared with a predictor without Twitter features, achieving 77.2% accuracy and 0.843 AUC. The experimental results confirmed that adding Twitter features improved prediction performance.

Using KS Static + Temporal + Twitter dataset. What if we add temporal features? Can we find a sweet spot

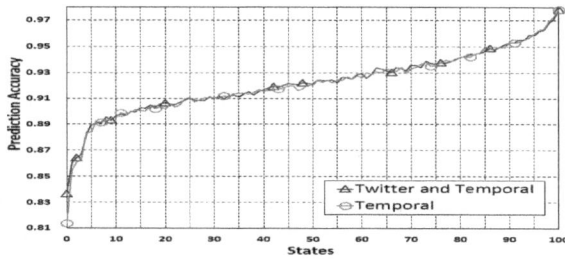

(a) Under 2 classes   (b) Under 3 classes

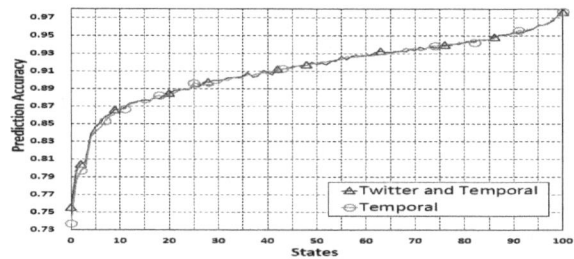

Figure 13: Pledged money range prediction rate of predictors based on Kickstarter static and temporal features with/without Twitter features under 2 and 3 classes.

Classifier	Accuracy	AUC
Kickstarter		
Naive Bayes	48.6%	0.677
Random Forest	74.2%	0.829
AdaboostM1	**75.8%**	**0.830**
Kickstarter + Twitter		
Naive Bayes	48.8%	0.668
Random Forest	75.4%	0.841
AdaboostM1	**77.2%**	**0.843**

Table 11: Experimental results of pledged money range predictors based on Kickstarter static features and Twitter features under 3 classes.

where we can reach to a high accuracy in a short period? To answer these questions, we used KS Static + Temporal + Twitter dataset. Again, each project duration was converted to 100 states (time slots). Figure 13 shows how accuracy of predictors has been changed over time under 2 classes and 3 classes. Prediction accuracy of AdaboostM1 classifiers with all features (project features + user features + temporal features + Twitter features) has been sharply increased until 5th state in 2 classes and 10th state in 3 classes. The classifiers reached to 90% accuracy in 15th state under 2 classes, and in 31st state under 3 classes.

What if we do not use Twitter features? In both 2 and 3 classes, adding Twitter features slightly increased prediction accuracy until 3rd state in 2 classes, and 9th state in 3 classes compared with predictors without Twitter features.

In summary, our proposed predictive models predicted a project's expected pledged money range with a high accuracy in 2 classes and 3 classes. Adding Twitter and Kickstarter temporal features increased a prediction accuracy even higher than only using Kickstarter static features. Our experimental results confirmed that predicting a project's expected pledged money in advance is possible.

7. DISCUSSION

In previous section, we described our proposed approaches with a list of feature, and showed experimental results. In this section, we discuss other features that we tried to use but finally excluded because of degrading performance of our predictive models.

7.1 N-gram Features

In the literature, researcher have generated and used n-gram features from texts such as web pages, blogs and short text messages toward building models in various domains like text categorization [1], machine translation [16] and social spam detection [14].

We extracted unigram, bigram and trigram features from Kickstarter project descriptions after lowercasing the project descriptions, and removing stop words. Then, we conducted χ^2 feature selection so that we could only keep n-gram features which have positive power distinguishing between successful projects and failed projects. Finally, we added 22,422 n-gram features to our original feature set (i.e., project features, user features, temporal features and Twitter features) described in Section 4. Then, we built and tested project success predictors. Unfortunately, adding n-gram features deteriorated performance of project success predictors compared with only using the original feature set described in Section 4. The experimental results were the opposite of our expectation because other researchers [18] reported that using n-gram features improved their prediction rate in their own Kickstarter dataset. We conjecture that the researchers used smaller dataset which might give them some improvements. But, given the larger dataset containing all Kickstarter projects, using n-gram features decreased a prediction rate.

7.2 LIWC Features

We were also interested in using the Linguistic Inquiry and Word Count (LIWC) dictionary, which is a standard approach for mapping text to psychologically-meaningful categories [20], to generate linguistic features from a Kickstarter project main description, reward description and project creator's bio description. LIWC-2001 defines 68 different categories, each of which contains several dozens to hundreds of words. Given a project's descriptions, we measured linguistic characteristics in the 68 categories by computing a score of each category based on LIWC dictionary. First we counted the total number of words in the project description (N). Next we counted the number of words in the description overlapped with the words in each category i on LIWC dictionary (C_i). Then, we computed a score of a category i as C_i/N. Finally, we added 68 features to the original features described in Section 4. Then we built project success predictors and evaluated their performance. Unfortunately, the predictors based on 68 linguistic features and the original features were worse than predictors based on only the original features.

8. RELATED WORK

In this section we summarize crowdfunding research work in three categories: (i) analysis of crowdfunding platforms; (ii) analysis of crowdfunding activities and backers on social media sites; and (iii) project success prediction.

Researchers have analyzed crowdfunding platforms [5, 8, 9, 12]. For example, Kuppuswamy and Bayus [13] examined the backer dynamics over the project funding cycle. Mollick [19] studied the dynamics of crowdfunding, and found that personal networks and underlying project quality were associated with the success of crowdfunding efforts. Xu et al. [22] analyzed the content and usage patterns of a large corpus of project updates on Kickstarter.

In another research direction, researchers have studied social media activities during running project campaigns on crowdfunding platforms. Lu et al. [15] studied how fundraising activities and promotional activities on social media simultaneously evolve over time, and how the promotion campaigns influence the final outcomes. Rakesh et al. [3] used a promoter network on Twitter to show the success of projects depended on the connectivity between the promoters. They developed backer recommender which recommends a set of backers to Kickstarter projects.

Predicting the success of a project is one of important research problems, so researchers have studied how to predict whether a project will be successful or not. Greenberg et al. [10] collected 13,000 project pages on Kickstarter and extracted 13 features from each project page. They developed classifiers to predict project success. Their approach achieved 68% accuracy. Etter et al. [7] extracted pledged money based time series features, and project and backer graph features from 16,000 Kickstarter projects. Then, they measured how prediction rate has been changed over time. Mitra et al. [18] focused on text features of project pages. They extracted phrases and some meta features from 45,810 project pages, and then showed that using phrases features reduced prediction error rates.

Compared with the previous research work, we collected the largest datasets consisting of all Kickstarter project pages, corresponding user pages, each project's temporal data and each user's social media profiles, and conducted comprehensive analysis of users and projects. Then, we proposed and extracted comprehensive feature sets (e.g., project features, user features, temporal features and Twitter features) toward building project success predictors and pledged money range predictors. To our knowledge, we are the first to study how to predict a range of expected pledged money of a project. Since the success of a project depends on a project goal and the amount of actually pledged money, studying the prediction is very important. This research will complement the existing research work.

9. CONCLUSION

In this paper we have presented comprehensive analysis of users and projects in Kickstarter. We found that 46.4% users were all-time creators and 53.6% users were active users who not only created their own projects but also backed other projects. We also found that project success rate in each month has been decreasing as new users jointed Kickstarter and launched projects without enough preparation and experience. When we analyzed temporal data of our collected projects, we noticed that there were two peaks in the beginning of a project duration and there was the deadline effect, rushing to invest the project as the project was heading to the end of its duration. Then, we proposed 4 types of features toward building predictive models to predict whether a project will be successful and a range of pledged money. We developed the predictive models based on various feature

sets. Our experimental results have showed that project success predictors based on only static features achieved 76.4% accuracy and 0.838 AUC, by adding Twitter features, increased accuracy and AUC by 2.5% and 3.5%, respectively. Adding temporal features consistently increased the accuracy. Our pledged money range predictors based on the static features have achieved up to 86.5% accuracy and 0.901 AUC. Adding Twitter and temporal features increased performance of the predictors further.

10. REFERENCES

[1] N-Gram-Based Text Categorization, 1994.
[2] Jumpstart our business startups act. http://www.gpo.gov/fdsys/pkg/BILLS-112hr3606enr/pdf/BILLS-112hr3606enr.pdf, 2012.
[3] What Motivates People to Invest in Crowdfunding Projects? Recommendation using Heterogeneous Traits in Kickstarter, 2015.
[4] Alexa. kickstarter.com site overview - alexa. http://www.alexa.com/siteinfo/kickstarter.com, March 2015.
[5] P. Belleflamme, T. Lambert, and A. Schwienbacher. Crowdfunding: Tapping the Right Crowd. SSRN Electronic Journal, 2012.
[6] Economist. The new thundering herd. http://www.economist.com/node/21556973, 2012.
[7] V. Etter, M. Grossglauser, and P. Thiran. Launch hard or go home!: Predicting the success of kickstarter campaigns. In COSN, 2013.
[8] E. M. Gerber and J. Hui. Crowdfunding: Motivations and deterrents for participation. ACM Trans. Comput.-Hum. Interact., 20(6), Dec. 2013.
[9] E. M. Gerber, J. S. Hui, and P.-Y. Kuo. Crowdfunding: Why people are motivated to post and fund projects on crowdfunding platforms. In CSCW, 2012.
[10] M. D. Greenberg, B. Pardo, K. Hariharan, and E. Gerber. Crowdfunding support tools: Predicting success & failure. In CHI Extended Abstracts, 2013.
[11] M. Hall, E. Frank, G. Holmes, B. Pfahringer, P. Reutemann, and I. H. Witten. The weka data mining software: An update. SIGKDD Explor. Newsl., 11(1):10–18, Nov. 2009.
[12] J. S. Hui, M. D. Greenberg, and E. M. Gerber. Understanding the role of community in crowdfunding work. In CSCW, 2014.
[13] V. Kuppuswamy and B. L. Bayus. Crowdfunding Creative Ideas: The Dynamics of Project Backers in Kickstarter. Social Science Research Network Working Paper Series, Mar. 2013.
[14] K. Lee, J. Caverlee, and S. Webb. Uncovering social spammers: Social honeypots + machine learning. In SIGIR, 2010.
[15] C.-T. Lu, S. Xie, X. Kong, and P. S. Yu. Inferring the impacts of social media on crowdfunding. In WSDM, 2014.
[16] J. B. Mariòo, R. E. Banchs, J. M. Crego, A. de Gispert, P. Lambert, J. A. R. Fonollosa, and M. R. Costa-jussà. N-gram-based machine translation. Comput. Linguist., 32(4):527–549, Dec. 2006.
[17] H. G. McLaughlin. SMOG grading - a new readability formula. Journal of Reading, pages 639–646, May 1969.
[18] T. Mitra and E. Gilbert. The language that gets people to give: Phrases that predict success on kickstarter. In CSCW, 2014.
[19] E. Mollick. The dynamics of crowdfunding: An exploratory study. Journal of Business Venturing, 29(1):1–16, 2014.
[20] J. Pennebaker, M. Francis, and R. Booth. Linguistic Inquiry and Word Count. Erlbaum Publishers, 2001.
[21] A. E. Roth, J. K. Murnighan, and F. Schoumaker. The deadline effect in bargaining: Some experimental evidence. The American Economic Review, pages 806–823, 1988.
[22] A. Xu, X. Yang, H. Rao, W.-T. Fu, S.-W. Huang, and B. P. Bailey. Show me the money!: An analysis of project updates during crowdfunding campaigns. In CHI, pages 591–600. ACM, 2014.
[23] Y. Yang and J. O. Pedersen. A comparative study on feature selection in text categorization. In ICML, 1997.
[24] M. Yildiz. Optimism, deadline effect, and stochastic deadlines. 2004.
[25] N. Zipkin. The 10 most funded kickstarter campaigns ever. http://www.entrepreneur.com/article/235313, March 2015.

Analyzing Book-Related Features to Recommend Books for Emergent Readers

Maria Soledad Pera
Department of Computer Science
Boise State University
Boise, Idaho, U.S.A.
solepera@boisestate.edu

Yiu-Kai Ng
Computer Science Department
Brigham Young University
Provo, Utah, U.S.A.
ng@compsci.byu.edu

ABSTRACT

We recognize that emergent literacy forms a foundation upon which children will gage their future reading.[1] It is imperative to motivate young readers to read by offering them appealing books to read so that they can enjoy reading and gradually establish a reading habit during their formative years that can aid in promoting their good reading habits. However, with the huge volume of existing and newly-published books, it is a challenge for parents/educators (young readers, respectively) to find the right ones that match children's interests and their readability levels. In response to the needs, we have developed K3Rec, a recommender which applies a multi-dimensional approach to suggest books that simultaneously match the *interests/preferences* and *reading abilities* of emergent (i.e., K-3) readers. K3Rec considers the grade levels, contents, illustrations, and topics, besides using special properties, such as length and writing style, to distinguish K-3 books from other books targeting more mature readers. K3Rec is novel, since it adopts an unsupervised strategy to suggest books for K-3 readers which does not rely on the existence of personal social media data, such as personal tags and ratings, that are seldom, if ever, created by emergent readers. Furthermore, unlike existing book recommenders, K3Rec explicitly analyzes book illustrations, which is of special significance for emergent readers, since illustrations assist these readers in understanding the contents of books. K3Rec focuses on a niche group of readers that has not been explicitly targeted by existing book recommenders. Empirical studies conducted using data from BiblioNasium.com and Amazon's Mechanical Turk have verified the effectiveness of K3Rec in making book recommendations for emergent readers.

Categories and Subject Descriptors

H.3.3 [**Information Search and Retrieval**]: Information filtering

---

[1]http://www.deafed.net/publisheddocs/sub/9807kle.htm

Keywords

Book recommendations; emergent readers; K-3

1. INTRODUCTION

Reading is an activity performed on a daily basis: from reading news articles and books to cereal boxes and street signs. According to the National Institute of Child Health and Human Development, "reading is the single most important skill necessary for a happy, productive, and successful life",[2] which is the reason why focusing on *emergent* (or early) *reading* that refers to the knowledge, skills, and dispositions acquired in reading (and writing) in primary school grades prior to and up till the 3rd grade [23], is particularly significant. As stated in [27], learning to read is a key milestone for children living in a literate society, specially given that reading provides the foundation for children's academic success. A recent study [4] highlights the fact that children who "do not read proficiently by the end of third grade are four times more likely to leave school without a diploma than proficient readers." The results of the study correlate with earlier statistics [11] which confirm that 88% of children who are poor readers by the end of the first grade remain so by the end of the fourth grade. Moreover, young readers who successfully learn to read in the early primary years of school will more likely be prepared to read for pleasure and learning in the future [18]. The aforementioned findings constitute the essence of encouraging good reading habits early on. Identifying books appealing to emergent readers (i.e., readers up till the 3rd grade), however, can be challenging, given the amount of books made available on a regular basis that address a diversity of topics and target readers at different reading levels. It is essential to provide emergent readers with reading materials matching their preferences/interests and reading abilities, since exposing young readers to materials that are either too easy/difficult to understand or involving unappealing topics could diminish their interest in reading [1].

In the quest for locating print materials (especially books) which can help develop/improve the reading skills of K-3 readers, parents, educators, and young readers can turn to online book recommendation systems which suggest books of potential interest. Unfortunately, existing book recommenders [10, 25] require user-defined information, such as tags, ratings, connections, and accessing patterns, to make suggestions for the respective individuals. Personal information of K-3 users, however, may not exist owing to the lack

---

[2]http://www.ksl.com/?sid=15431484

of online social networking sites targeting K-3 users or may not be publicly accessible due to the ethical obligation of everyone to respect the online privacy of children. Moreover, majority of these recommenders fail to explicitly consider (i) the reading ability of a reader, which is necessary in making recommendations for readers with diverse reading skills [26], and/or (ii) unique characteristics that distinguish books targeting emergent, as opposite to advanced, readers [22].

To solve the problems in suggesting books for emergent readers, we have developed *K3Rec*, an unsupervised books recommender, which facilitates one of the tasks undertaken by parents/educators/young readers on a daily basis: to identify books that help improve their reading abilities of K-3 readers. K3Rec applies a multi-dimensional analysis on a book known to be of interest to a reader R and identifies other relevant books from existing book repositories, such as OpenLibrary.org, that match (to a degree) the preferences and reading ability of R. While the criteria that dictate an appropriate K-3 book are determined using a number of pre-defined features that commonly apply to "good" books targeting emergent readers [22], its correlation with the preferences and reading ability of R is analyzed by conducting an in-depth examination on a brief description of its content, pictorial perspectives, reading level, and topics as defined based on Library of Congress Subject Headings.

K3Rec is a novel recommender that exclusively targets emergent readers, an audience who has not been catered by existing recommendation systems. K3Rec is a self-reliant recommender which, unlike others, does not rely on the availability of *personal information* about its users to make book suggestions. Instead, K3Rec takes advantage of book metadata, which are either readily and freely available from reputable online sources, such as the Library of Congress (catalog.loc.gov), or inferred from user-defined metadata, such as book reviews and book ratings, that are publicly accessible online from popular book-related websites, e.g., Google Books (http://books.google.com/) and Amazon.com. K3Rec is unique, since it explicitly considers one of the most distinguishable aspects of books for emergent readers [9, 22]—their illustrations—by employing OpenCV (opencv.org) an open source computer vision/machine learning software.

K3Rec is designed for solving the *information overload* problem while minimizing the *time* and *efforts* imposed on parents/educators/young readers in discovering unknown, but suitable, books for pleasure reading or knowledge acquisition. The current implementation of K3Rec is tailored towards recommending books written in English and classified based on the K-12[3] grade level system. K3Rec, however, can be easily adopted to make suggestions based on diverse grade-level scales and in languages other than English.

The remaining of this paper is organized as follows. In Section 2, we discuss existing recommenders that have been used for identifying books for individual readers, including young readers. In Sections 3, we introduce K3Rec and its overall design methodology. In Section 4, we present the results of the empirical studies on K3Rec conducted to assess its performance. In Section 5, we give a concluding remark and present directions for future work on K3Rec.

---

[3]K-12, which is a term used in the educational system in the United States and Canada (among other countries), refers to the primary and secondary/high school years of public/private school grades prior to college. These grades are kindergarten (K) through 12th grades.

2. RELATED WORK

To the best of our knowledge, there is no existing book recommendation system developed specifically for emergent readers. At present, parents/educators/young readers often rely on existing book websites, including, but not limited to, ARbookfind.com, Kidsread.com, Scholastic.com, and World-Cat.org, which offer different tools to search for books in various domains. These sites, however, either (i) supply (read-alike) non-personalized booklists [8], (ii) require a particular topic/subject area of interest to be selected from a pre-defined list,[4] which limits the themes of books that can be obtained from the sites, (iii) offer reading choices grouped by age/grade ranges,[5] which is undesirable, since readers in the same grade or age group might not reach the same reading level, or (iv) allow users to create keyword queries to specify their information needs, which often yield an overwhelming volume of items to choose from and impose an additional burden on users to sort though. Unlike the aforementioned websites, K3Rec eliminates their constraints imposed in locating books, which enhances the process in finding books relevant to the information needs of emergent readers and at a reading level appropriate for the readers.

Even though there are no book recommenders for emergent readers, a number of book recommendation systems that have been designed for general audience are available. The recommendation module offered by Amazon.com suggests books based on the purchase patterns of its users [14], whereas Yang et al. [28] analyze users' access logs to infer the users' preferences and apply the traditional collaborative-filtering (CF) strategy to make book recommendations. The authors in [10] combine CF and social tags to capture the content of books for making recommendations. Sieg et al. [25], on the other hand, rely on the standard user-based CF framework and incorporate semantic knowledge in the form of a domain ontology to capture the topics of interest to a user. BReK12 [19], which is based on content and readability analysis, relies heavily on the availability of bookmarking information offered by social bookmarking sites to suggest K-12 books. Unlike K3Rec, these recommenders require (i) historical data on the users in the form of ratings and bookmarking information, which may not always be accessible, or (ii) an ontology, which can be labor-intensive and time-consuming to construct. In addition, none of these recommenders (with the exception of BReK12) considers the readability level of their users as part of their recommendation strategies.

It is worth mentioning that even though K3Rec is not a recommender for direct learning, its design goal is to enhance reading selections for emergent readers by locating suitable books among the overwhelming number of choices available these days. (For an in-depth description of existing recommenders in the educational domain, see [16].)

3. OUR PROPOSED RECOMMENDER

In making book suggestions for a K-3 reader R, K3Rec first analyzes a given book B known to have been read by R and identifies books that are compatible with the readability level of R (detailed in Section 3.1). These books are treated as *candidate books* to be considered for recommendation. Candidate books are selected among the books

---

[4]http://www.readingrockets.org/books/booksbytheme
[5]http://goo.gl/78X7i6

available at one of the (online) book repositories, which include, but are not limited to, (i) *reputable websites*, such as OpenLibrary.org or WorldCat.org, which are two of the largest online library catalogs, (ii) *school/public libraries*, and (iii) book-related *bookmarking sites*, such as Biblionasium.com, which is a website that encourages reading among children/teenagers. K3Rec computes a ranking score (in Section 3.3) for each candidate book CB, which captures not only the degree of *context closeness* of CB and B, but also the *desired properties* of books for emergent readers that apply to CB for R based on the analysis of multiple book-related features (presented in Section 3.2).

3.1 Identifying Candidate Recommendations

One of the design goals of K3Rec is to suggest books that its readers can comprehend. It is imperative for K3Rec to locate books with grade levels suitable for a reader R, since "reading for understanding cannot take place unless the words in the text are accurately and efficiently decoded" [17]. K3Rec determines the readability level of R based on the grade level of a given book B, which is computed using TRoLL [20], a regression-based readability prediction tool. Unlike existing popular readability-level prediction formulas/tools, such as Flesch-Kincaid, Lexile Framework, and ATOS (discussed in details in [2]), TRoLL computes the grade level of a book using metadata on books publicly accessible from reputable online sources, even in the absence of book excerpts. Hence, TRoLL is not constrained by the availability of sample text of a book, which is not always freely accessible due to copyright laws. Experimental results [20] show that TRoLL is highly accurate in predicting the grade levels of K-12 books and outperforms other existing readability formulas/tools, such as Flesch-Kincaid and Accelerated Reader (AR), which rely on books excerpts.

Based on the readability level of a reader R through B, K3Rec applies Equation 1 to determine the set of candidate books considered for recommendation to R.

$$SCB(B) = \{CB \mid CB \in Rep \land RL(CB) \in [RL(B) \pm 0.25]\} \quad (1)$$

where CB is a candidate book available at a book repository Rep and $RL(CB)$ ($RL(B)$, respectively) is the grade level of CB (B, respectively) determined by TRoLL. By selecting books within *half a grade*[6] of the grade level of B, K3Rec considers books for recommendation within an appropriate level of (text) complexity for R based on the grade level of B that R is interested in the past.

EXAMPLE 1. Consider a reader R_A, who has read the books "If you give a pig a party" by Laura Numeroff and "Fancy Nancy" Nancy O'Connor. Using TRoLL, K3Rec determines that the readability levels of these books are 1.10 and 1.40, respectively. Based on this information, K3Rec establishes 1.25 ($= \frac{1.10+1.40}{2}$) as the readability level of R_A. Using Equation 1, K3Rec generates a set of candidate books which includes books from the BiblioNasium dataset (introduced in Section 4.1) with readability levels between 1.0 and 1.5. Consequently, books such as "The paperboy" by Dav Pilkey, "If you give a mouse a cookie" by Laura Numeroff,

and "Cat and dog" by Else Holmelund with readability levels 1.15, 1.3, and 1.45, determined by TRoLL, respectively, are considered as candidate books to be considered for recommendations for R_A, since they can be read and comprehended by R_A. Furthermore, books such as "Harry, the Poisonous Centipede" by Lynne Reid Banks and "Football Genius" by Tim Green with readability levels 0.25 and 2.2, computed by TRoLL, respectively, are excluded from the candidate set, since they are too easy and too challenging for R_A, respectively. □

3.2 Book-Related Feature Analysis

K3Rec suggests relevant books not only readers are interested in, but also they can comprehend. This is accomplished by examining candidate books (determined using Equation 1) using diverse publicly accessible book metadata to analyze (i) *book contents* appealing to R (in Section 3.2.1), (ii) the *type of illustrations* of interest to R (in Section 3.2.2), and (iii) the general *traits* applied to CB that are significant factors to be considered for books targeting emergent readers (in Sections 3.2.3 - 3.2.6).

3.2.1 Content Analysis

K3Rec analyzes the content description of CB, which can be extracted from reputable book-related websites, such as Amazon.com and the Library of Congress, to determine the degree to which CB addresses subject matters that are appealing to R based on the overview of B. As shown in Equation 2, K3Rec computes the *content similarity* score between CB and B, denoted $CSim(CB, B)$, based on the "bag-of-words"[7] representation of the description of CB and B. $CSim(CB, B)$ considers the word-correlation factor (wcf) [13] of each word in the description of B with respect to each word in the description of CB, and prioritizes candidate books based on their degree of shared content with B. Word-correlation factors in the pre-computed word-correlation matrix reflect the degree of similarity between any two words according to their (i) frequencies of co-occurrence and (ii) relative distances in a collection of Wikipedia(.com) documents. K3Rec relies on word-correlation factors, instead of similarity measures [3] based on WordNet(.pricenton.edu), since it has been empirically verified that the former correlates with human assessments on word similarity more accurately than the latter [19].

$$CSim(CB, B) = \frac{\sum_{i=1}^{n} Min\{\sum_{j=1}^{m} wcf(B_i, CB_j), 1\}}{n} \quad (2)$$

where n (m, respectively) is the number of distinct words in the description of B (CB, respectively), B_i (CB_j, respectively) is a word in the description of B (CB, respectively), and $wcf(B_i, CB_j)$ is the correlation factor, i.e., degree of similarity, of B_i and CB_j in the word-correlation matrix.

The Min function in Equation 2 imposes a constraint on summing up the correlation factors of words in the description of CB and B. Even if a word in the description of B (i) matches exactly one of the words in CB and (ii) is similar to some of the remaining words in CB, which yields a value greater than 1.0, K3Rec limits the sum of their similarity measure to 1.0, which is the word-correlation factor of an *exact* match. This constraint ensures that if B contains a

---

[6] We have empirically verified that by selecting 0.25 as a threshold in Equation 1, the overall processing time of K3Rec is shortened, without significantly affecting its accuracy.

[7] From now on, unless stated otherwise, "word" refers to non-stop, stemmed word.

dominant word w in its description which is highly similar to a few words in CB, w alone cannot dictate the content resemblance value of B with respect to CB. Words in the brief overview of CB that are similar to most of the words in B should yield a greater $CSim$ value than the $CSim$ value of words in the description of CB that are similar to only one dominant word in B.

3.2.2 Illustration-Based Analysis

One of the features commonly associated with a book for emergent readers is its illustrations. Since illustrations play an important role in "directly encouraging children's emergent literacy development" [12], it is imperative for K3Rec to consider book illustrations as part of its recommendation process. Similar to the textual content of a book, its illustrations are not always freely accessible due to copyright laws. However, there are a number of websites that offer API access to book covers, such as LibraryThing.com and Google Books. K3Rec takes advantage of such resources and calculates $Isim(CB, B)$, a score that reflects the degree of resemblance between the illustrations as shown on the book covers of CB and B. K3Rec prioritizes candidate books partially based on the illustrations as shown in their covers with similar images to the book known to be appealing to R.

It is not an easy task, however, to compute $Isim(CB, B)$, given that the similarity between images is based on accurately identifying the same (or similar) object(s) or scene(s) even if they are presented under different imaging conditions, such as viewpoint changes, image blur, and illumination changes [15]. To facilitate the task of determining the degree of similarity between any two book covers, K3Rec applies the Open Source Computer Vision (OpenCV) library. Given any two images, i.e., the book covers of CB and B, OpenCV models them as matrices of multiple image features. These matrices are then compared to determine $Isim(CB, B)$ that quantify the degree of resemblance between the two images.

EXAMPLE 2. Consider the book covers as shown in Figure 1, which correspond to "Don't let the pigeon drive the bus" by Mo Willems ($Book_A$), " The pigeon finds a hot dog" by Mo Willems ($Book_B$), and "Pat the bunny" by Dorothy Kunhardt ($Book_C$). Using OpenCV, K3Rec determines that $Isim(Book_A, Book_B)$ is higher than $Isim(Book_A, Book_C)$. This is anticipated, since although the covers of $Book_A$ and $Book_C$ share very similar background colors, the covers of $Book_A$ and $Book_B$ share similar images, i.e., the pigeons and dialogue bubbles. Based on the computed $Isim$ scores, K3Rec prioritizes $Book_B$ over $Book_C$ in making suggestions for a reader given his/her interest in $Book_A$. □

3.2.3 Topical Analysis

Besides considering the relatedness of CB and B based on their content representations and illustrations, K3Rec examines topical information of CB to determine its suitability for R. This analysis is based on Library of Congress Subject Headings (LCSH) assigned to CB by professional cataloguers. LCSH, which is a de facto universal controlled vocabulary, constitutes the largest general indexing vocabulary in the English language [29]. LCSH, which are terms or phrases that denote concepts, events, or names, are used by librarians to categorize and index books according to their themes. Examples of LCSH include "Fairy tales" and "Fear of the dark–Fiction".

Figure 1: Sample book covers

Features derived from the LCSH of CB, which are publicly accessible from the Library of Congress, include their (i) total count and (ii) associated grade levels.

Total Count of LCSH. K3Rec considers the *count* of LCSH assigned to CB, since books that are *more difficult* to comprehend are often assigned *more* LCSH[8]. The degree of difficulty in comprehending CB (based on its subjects), denoted $Diff(CB)$, is computed by K3Rec using Equation 3, which penalizes candidate books that have been assigned more LCSH than other books in the set of candidate books considered for recommendation, since the *lower* the number of LCSH assigned to CB, the *more likely* the audience targeted by CB are emergent readers.

$$Diff(CB) = \frac{1}{|LCSH_{CB}|} \quad (3)$$

where $LCSH_{CB}$ is the set of LCSH assigned to CB and $|LCSH_{CB}|$ denotes the size of $LCSH_{CB}$.

LCSH and Grade Levels. Besides using the *count* of LCSH, K3Rec also considers the grade levels associated with LCSH assigned to a (candidate) book. Using Equation 4, K3Rec determines the proportion of LCSH of CB that are associated with grade levels similar to the grade (i.e., readability) level of R (through book B). K3Rec favors candidate books that address subjects suitable to the reading level of R, which is one of the major goals of K3Rec, i.e., suggesting books tailored to the reading abilities of individual readers.

$$LC(CB, B) = \frac{\sum_{j=1}^{|LCSH_{CB}|} isSuitable(CB_j, RL(B))}{|LCSH_{CB}|} \quad (4)$$

where $LCSH_{CB}$ and $|LCSH_{CB}|$ are defined in Equation 3, CB_j is the jth LCSH in $LCSH_{CB}$, and $isSuitable(CB_j, RL(B))$ is a function that returns "1" if the grade level of CB_j is within a quarter of $RL(B)$ (as defined in Equation 1), and is "0" otherwise. Note that the grade level associated with a given LCSH is determined based on the mapping between grade levels and LCSH defined in [20]. (See Table 1 for sample mappings between LCSH and their grade levels, where "1.5" indicates that the corresponding LCSH, i.e., "Babar fictitious character," is often assigned to books between the first and second grade.)

---

[8] The authors in [20] have empirically verified the correlation between the number of LCSH assigned to K-12 books and their corresponding grade levels. The analysis in [20] has shown that the lower the number of LCSH assigned to a books is, the lower is the grade level defined for the book.

Table 1: Sample mapping between LCSH and grade levels

LCSH	Grade Level
Babar fictitious character	1.5
Bedtime fiction	1.8
Bedtime prayer	0.2
Dora the explorer fictitious character	0.8
Scary stories	2.8
Zoo-children-fiction	0.4

Table 2: Sample appeal terms associated with each of the appeal factors considered by ABET

Appeal Factors	Appeal Terms
Characterization	Believable, distant, dramatic
Frame	Bittersweet, contemporary, descriptive
Language and Writing Style	Candid, complex, conversational, extravagant, poetic, prosaic
Pacing	Easy, fast, slow
Special Topics	Addiction, bullying, violence
Storyline	Action-oriented, character-centered
Tone	Dark, happy, surreal

3.2.4 Book-Length Analysis

Another desired property of books for emergent readers is the *length*, i.e., the number of pages, of the books. As stated in [21], books for emergent readers are on an average of 32 pages in length. Relatively *short* books are preferred, since they can be read in one (or few) sittings, which offers their readers a sense of accomplishment in finishing a book.[9] K3Rec applies Equation 5 to measure the degree to which the length of CB is within the expected length of a book targeting emergent readers.

$$Len(CB) = \begin{cases} 1 & \text{if } Pages(CB) \leq 32 \\ \frac{1}{Pages(CB)-32} & \text{otherwise} \end{cases} \quad (5)$$

where $Pages(CB)$ is the number of pages of CB, which can be obtained by accessing the publicly available catalog record for CB from the Library of Congress.

As shown in Equation 5, K3Rec imposes a penalization on books longer than 32 pages. This penalization is scaled to the number of pages of CB such that the *more* pages that exceed the average number of pages expected for a K-3 book, the *lower* the chance CB targets K-3 readers.

3.2.5 Writing Style-Based Analysis

Another characteristic often applied to books for emergent readers is the *simplicity* and *directness* of their texts [21]. Identifying the writing style of books, however, is non-trivial, given the lack of access (due to copyright laws) to sample text on books required to perform semantic/syntactic analysis. An alternative to gather this information is to turn to book metadata available at online sources, such as NoveList, which provide a description of the literary elements of a book. Literary elements are "elements of a book—whether definable or just understood—that make readers enjoy the book" [24]. These elements, which include characterization, frame, pacing, storyline, language and writing style, and tone, capture general traits of a book [5]. Access to these resources, however, requires a paid subscription. K3Rec relies on ABET [20] instead to obtain a description of the writing style of each candidate book CB.

ABET is a newly-developed, unsupervised tool that automatically generates a description of the literary elements of CB by analyzing (up to) 500 distinct reviews on CB, which can be retrieved from well-known book-related websites, such as Amazon.com and Powell.com. By analyzing reviews, ABET determines diverse readers' opinions on a book based on terms (also known as appeal terms) that describe the corresponding literary elements (i.e., appeal factors) of the book. A sample of the appeal terms and appeal factors considered by ABET are included in Table 2.

ABET, which performs *linguistic* and *semantic* analysis on sentences in reviews using Stanford Part-of-Speech Tagger and Dependency Parser (nlp.stanford.edu/software/lex-parser.shtml), employs a number of *extraction rules* on word pairs in sentences included in reviews that capture the semantic link between literary elements and terms used to describe them, which are based on typed dependency relations. It is natural for ABET to turn to typed dependencies, since they capture the *semantic connection*, i.e., association, between words in sentences. For this reason, the rules defined for ABET simply look for words in sentences that (directly or indirectly) describe the literary elements of a book, which are often the subjects or objects of sentences[10].

The rules introduced in [20] to extract a writing-style description for a book based on its corresponding reviews are defined in Table 3. These rules, which are used to generate descriptions of appeal factors, including writing style, are based on common writing patterns identified in book reviews and capture the semantic link between appeal factors and their corresponding terms that describe them. Consider the sentence S_A, "The words in the book are simple", and sentence S_B, "The author creates unmistakable, classic characters". In S_A the *subject* of the sentence, i.e., "words," is characterized as being "simple", whereas in S_B its *object*, i.e., "characters", is described as "classic". In these examples, it is clear that if the subject/object of a sentence is an appeal factor, then a word in the sentence that semantically describes, i.e., is directly linked to, the mentioned object/subject is often its descriptive keyword, i.e., appeal term. ABET captures these connection patterns using Rules 1 and 2 as defined in Table 3.

An appeal term can also be indirectly connected with an appeal factor in a sentence. Consider sentence S_C, "The characters portrayed are funny." "Funny" is *indirectly* related to the subject of S_C, i.e., "characters", through the word "portrayed". Using Rule 3, ABET examines pairs of grammatical relations that involve indirect connections among words. Next, consider S_D, "The writing is not direct". Based on Rule 1, ABET would mistakenly describe the appeal factor "Writing Style" using the keyword "direct." This exam-

---

[9]http://www.rif.org/documents/us/choosing_books.pdf

[10]Despite being comprehensive, the taxonomy defined for ABET that enumerates appeal factors and appeal terms cannot account for every variation of appeal factors/terms that can be specified in readers' reviews. For example, a reviewer may refer to the "Storyline" of a book as "story" or "narrative", and (s)he may also use either "easy" or "simple" as the keyword that describes the "Writing Style" of a book. To handle these variations during the extraction process, ABET uses (stemmed) synonyms of each appeal factor/term, which can be identified using WordNet.

Table 3: Rules considered by ABET to extract writing-style descriptions in book reviews

Notations
$rel(A, B)$ is a *grammatical relation* between a *dominant*, i.e., *governor* or *head*, word (A) and a *subordinate*, i.e., *dependent* or *modifier*, word (B)
L_F, L_T, EL_F, and EL_T are the list of appeal factors, list of appeal terms, extended list of appeal factors, and extended list of appeal terms, respectively.
w_f is an appeal factor in L_F, and w_t is an appeal term in L_T
$w \rightsquigarrow w_f$ ($w \rightsquigarrow w_t$, respectively) denotes that w is a synonym of w_f (w_t, respectively)
$POS(w)$ is the part-of-speech tag of w which is a verb (adverb, respectively) if $POS(w) = $ "VB" ("RB", respectively)
Abbreviation: adv(erbial)mod(ifier), a(djectival)mod(ifier), c(lausal)comp(lement), d(irect)obj(ect), neg(ation modifier), nn (noun compound modifier), n(ominal)subj(ect), nsubjpass (passive nominal subject), prep(_*) (Prepositional modifier)
ABET only extracts a pair $< w_f, w_t >$ if w_t is in the corresponding vocabulary defined for w_f

Rule	Objective	Conditions	Identified Factors/Terms
1	To capture the written patterns based on a keyword, i.e., appeal term, that immediately precedes/ follows the subject or object of a sentence S, i.e., appeal factor	$A \in EL_T, B \in EL_F, rel \in \{$nn, nsubj$\}$ $A \rightsquigarrow w_t$	$B \rightsquigarrow w_f$
2		$A \in EL_F, B \in EL_T, rel \in \{$advmod, amod, prep_in, prep_about$\}$	$A \rightsquigarrow w_f$ $B \rightsquigarrow w_t$
3	To identify an appeal term that qualifies its indirectly related appeal factor in S	$rel \in \{$nn, nsubj$\}$, $B \in EL_F$, and $\exists rel_2(C, D) \in \{$amod, dep, ccomp$\}$, $A = C, D \in EL_T$	$B \rightsquigarrow w_f$ $D \rightsquigarrow w_t$
4	To explicitly consider *negated* appeal terms in S	$B \in EL_F, rel \in \{$nn, nsubj$\}$, $\exists neg(C, D)$, $A (= C)$ is an antonym of $\bar{A} \in EL_T$, D is a negation term	$B \rightsquigarrow w_f$ $\bar{A} \rightsquigarrow w_t$

ple shows the necessity of examining pairs of grammatical relations in the presence of negated terms. ABET applies Rule 4, which identifies a negated term as a modifier of a keyword k and then extracts as the keyword description for the corresponding feature the antonym of k (if it is included in the vocabulary defined in ABET's taxonomy for the feature). Together, Rules 1 to 4 account for the most common written patterns for appeal factors/terms observed in reviews. These rules look for words in sentences that (directly or indirectly) describe the qualitative features of a book, which are often the subjects or objects of sentences. Rules 3 and 4 take precedence over Rules 1 and 2, since once a dependency in a sentence is used by either of the former rules, it cannot be considered by the latter ones.

It is important to note that the description of the writing style of CB determined by ABET involves not only the terms extracted from reviews on CB that describe the language and writing style of CB, but also their *frequency of occurrence*. The latter captures the relative *degree of significance* of a term in describing the writing style of CB based on reviewers' varied opinions expressed in their reviews.

Using the ABET-generated writing style description of CB, K3Rec applies Equation 6 to compute $WTS(CB)$, which quantifies the degree of *directness* and *simplicity* of (the textual content of) CB. The *higher* $WTS(CB)$ is, the *larger* the number of reviewers who describe the writing style of CB as simple/direct, which reflects the *more likely* that CB includes text expressed in a simple/direct manner, a criteria of books suitable for emergent readers.

$$WTS(CB) = \frac{\sum_{i=1}^{|WSDsc|} isDirect(WSDsc_i)}{\sum_{i=1}^{|WSDsc|} |WSDsc_i|} \quad (6)$$

where $WSDsc$ is the set of distinct terms in the ABET-generated writing style description of CB, $|WSDsc|$ is the size of $WSDsc$, $WSDsc_i$ is the ith term in $WSDsc$,

- **Jayne Eyre** by Charlotte Brontë

Complex (8), passionate (6), simple (1), unusual (9), classic (6)

- **The Pigeon Finds a Hot Dog!** by Mo Willems

Simple (9), dramatic (1), direct (5), classic (1)

Figure 2: Example of ABET-generated writing style descriptions, where the number (in parentheses) indicates the *frequency* in which a term was used to describe the corresponding writing style of books in reviews

$|WSDsc_i|$ denotes the *frequency* in which $WSDsc_i$ appears in the ABET-generated writing style description of CB, and $isDirect(WSDsc_i)$ denotes the *frequency* of $WSDsc_i$ if the term is "simple" or "direct," and is "0" otherwise.

EXAMPLE 3. Consider the ABET-generated descriptions of the writing style of the books "Jane Eyre" by Charlotte Bronte and "The pigeon finds a hot dog!" by Mo Willems as shown in Figure 2. WTS("Jane Eyre") = $\frac{1}{30}$ = 0.03, whereas WTS("The pigeon finds a hot dog!") = $\frac{14}{16}$ = 0.88. Based on the WTS scores, K3Rec favors the latter for recommendation, which is anticipated, since the latter is indeed a book for emergent readers. □

3.2.6 Rating Assessment

Another feature considered by K3Rec in estimating the degree of appealing of CB is its *rating*. As product ratings capture an independent measure of the quality of a product based on the opinions of a number of appraisers who are familiar with the product [7], it is natural for K3Rec to prioritize books that have been assigned a *high* rating. The rating score of CB, denoted $Rate(CB)$, is extracted from

Google Books' API[11] which is the *average* of the ratings given to CB by Google Book users.

Note that even though K3Rec turns to the "wisdom of crowds" for another appeal measure, i.e., rating, on candidate books, it is completely different from the strategies employed by existing book recommenders [28]. The latter rely on the availability of *personal ratings* assigned to books by an individual user (to reflect the degree to which a book matches his interests/preferences), which are seldom, if ever, made by K-3 readers, and which K3Rec does not rely on.

3.3 Ranking Candidate Books

Having determined the appropriate readability level of each candidate book CB (defined by using Equation 1) and quantified the properties of CB applicable to emergent readers, K3Rec computes a single, overall *ranking score* of CB by using $CombMNZ$ [6] (as defined in Equation 7). CombMNZ, which is a popular linear combination strategy, is applied to the aforementioned scores to determine the degree to which CB (i) matches the content and illustration preferences of a reader and (ii) shows evidence of addressing book properties desirable for K-3 readers.

$$Rank(CB) = \sum_{c=1}^{7} score^c \times |score^c > 0| \qquad (7)$$

where $score^c$ is the (normalized) value of one of the scores computed in Section 3.2 and $|score^c > 0|$ is the number of non-zero scores of CB.

CombMNZ combines multiple existing lists of rankings on an item into a joint ranking, a task known as *rank aggregation* or *data fusion*. The aggregation strategy adopted by K3Rec accounts for the fact that not all candidate books are assigned a non-zero score for each of the measures computed in Section 3.2, i.e., $Csim(CB, B)$, $Isim(CB, B)$, $Diff(CB)$, $LC(CB, B)$, $Len(CB)$, $WTS(CB)$, and $Rate(CB)$. The joint ranking considers the *strength* of each evidence regardless whether any evidence yields a zero value, as opposed to simply positioning higher in the ranking candidate books with non-zero scores for all the measures. After the joint ranking score has been computed for each candidate book, the top-3 highest-ranked books are suggested to R.

EXAMPLE 4. Consider a reader R who has read and enjoyed "Too Princessy!" by Jean Reidy, i.e., $Book_R$ as shown in Figure 3. By performing a multi-dimensional analysis on $Book_R$ using books in the BiblioNasium dataset, K3Rec suggests "Too Purpley!" by Jean Reidy ($Book_1$), "Birdie Plays Dress-Up" by Sujean.Rim ($Book_2$), and "Wacky Wednesday" by Dr. Seuss ($Book_3$) in the dataset in the respective order. We have manually verified that the suggestions are relevant recommendations for R, not only because their grade levels correlate with the reading ability of R, which is at the 1.4 grade level, but also because they share similar content, have similar illustrations, and are highly-regarded and relatively-short books (in terms of their ratings and page counts, respectively) that include simple and direct narratives and address topics (i.e., LCSH such as "Stories in rhyme", "Play", and "Pictorial books") suitable for K-3 readers. □

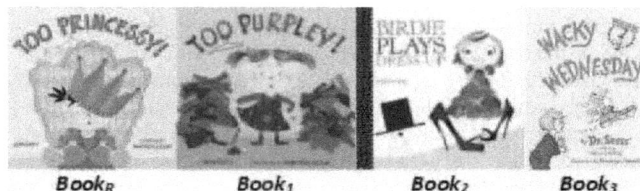

Figure 3: Top-3 recommendations generated by K3Rec based on the interest of the reader R on the book "Too Princessy" by Jean Reidy

4. EXPERIMENTAL RESULTS

In this section, we first introduce our evaluation framework (in Section 4.1). Hereafter, we present the results of the empirical studies conducted to assess the performance of K3Rec (in Sections 4.2 and 4.3).

4.1 Evaluation Framework

Although the BookCrossing dataset[12] has been employed to evaluate book recommenders tailored to a general audience, it is not specifically designed for assessing the performance of book recommenders for emergent readers. We conducted a number of empirical studies, presented in Sections 4.2 and 4.3, on their respective dataset to validate the effectiveness of K3Rec.

The first empirical study relies on data from BiblioNasium.com, a bookmarking site set up exclusively to encourage children and teenagers to read. The BiblioNasium dataset consists of 1,705 K-3 users and their bookmarks, i.e., books assigned to the respective "bookshelves" by each of the users. The second empirical study depends on data collected using Amazon's Mechanical Turk (https://www.mturk.com/mturk/welcome), which is a "marketplace for work that requires human intelligence", which allows individuals or businesses to programmatically access thousands of diverse, on-demand workers and has been and is being used to collect user feedback on various information retrieval designs.

Regardless of the study, the current implementation of K3Rec uses close to 20,000 books available at BiblioNasium.com as its book repository. Note, however, that besides BiblioNasium, any other book repository, such as OpenLibrary.org, can also be employed by K3Rec to make recommendations. Furthermore, as the design methodology of K3Rec relies on *topical*, *brief content*, and *writing style* descriptions, in addition to *covers*, predicted *grade levels*, *page counts*, and *ratings* of books, we retrieved the brief book descriptions, LCSH, and page count from the Library of Congress, their ratings and covers from Google Books, their writing style descriptions from book reviews (available at reputable book-related websites) using ABET, and their readability levels using TRoLL.

It is worth mentioning that the *statistical significance* of the results presented in the following sections were determined using the Wilcoxon signed-ranked test.

4.2 Evaluation of K3Rec Versus BReK12

Using the BiblioNasium dataset, we conducted an evaluation on the performance of K3Rec, which we compared with

---

[11]Popular book-related sites, such as Amazon.com, GoodReads.com, or Kidsread.com, also archive ratings on books.

[12]Informatik.unifreiburg.de/~cziegler/BX

the performance of BReK12 (as introduced in Section 2). We compared K3Rec with BReK12, since to the best of our knowledge BReK12 is the only existing recommender that explicitly considers the readability level of its users in making personalized book recommendations. Furthermore, we excluded other state-of-the-art approaches for (book) recommendations for comparison purpose, since (as stated in Section 2) they require *personal ratings* on books provided by individual users which are neither available for K-3 readers nor are included in the BiblioNasium dataset.

We assessed the performance of K3Rec and BReK12 using two metrics: *Mean Reciprocal Rank* (MRR) and *Normalized Discounted Cumulative Gain* (nDCG). While MRR computes the *average ranking position* of the *first* relevant book suggested by a recommender, nDCG determines the *overall* (ranking) performance of the recommender and penalizes relevant books positioned lower in the recommendation list. The penalization is based on a reduction, which is logarithmically applied to the position of each relevant book in a ranked list. To compute the aforementioned metrics, given a reader R in the BiblioNasium dataset, we treated one of his/her bookmarked books B as a book "of interest" to R. Hereafter, a book suggested to R by a recommender is treated as *relevant* to R if it is one of the remaining bookmarks of R, and is *non-relevant* otherwise, which is a commonly-employed evaluation protocol. (This evaluation is repeated for each of R's bookmarks.) Since only books that have been bookmarked by a user are considered *relevant*, it is not possible to account for potentially relevant books a user has not bookmarked, which is a well-known limitation of this evaluation protocol. As the limitation applies to both BReK12 and K3Rec, the results of the empirical studies are consistent for the comparison purpose.

As shown in Figure 4, K3Rec achieves a significant improvement ($p < 0.001$) over BReK12 in terms of nDCG, which are 0.79 and 0.65, respectively. Moreover, according to the computed MRR scores, users of K3Rec are expected to browse, on the average, *one* ($= \frac{1}{0.77} = 1.2$) book suggestion before locating a relevant one, as opposed to BReK12 users who are required to browse through *two* ($= \frac{1}{0.62} = 1.6$) before a relevant book is located. The difference in MRR between the recommenders is statistically significant ($p < 0.001$). The experimental results verify not only the effectiveness of K3Rec in applying its the multi-dimensional recommendation strategy, but also the choice of using book meta-data, instead of bookmarks on books used by BReK12. Unlike bookmark data created by more mature readers, bookmarks are rarely created by K-3 readers.

4.3 Mechanical Turk Appraisers

To further assess the performance of K3Rec, we conducted a survey using Mechanical Turk appraisers[13] who identified, among a provided set of three books (generated using K3Rec), the ones that relate to a given book B. The purpose of this survey is to emulate the behavior of K3Rec when presented with B, and quantify the degree of relevance of the generated suggestions based on the opinion of independent appraisers. This survey quantifies the degree of

---

[13] We are aware that crowdsourcing assessments can be affected by spam. To address this issue, we included in each of our surveys a book that did not align with the task in the survey. Appraisers that selected said book were treated as spammers and their assessment discarded.

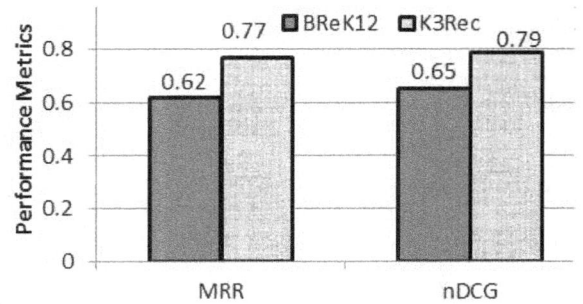

Figure 4: Performance evaluation of BReK12 and K3Rec using the BiblioNasium dataset

relevant suggestions made by K3Rec based on the opinions of independent appraisers.

We created ten HITs (Human Intelligent Task) on Mechanical Turk, each with a different book and its corresponding set of suggestions made by K3Rec. (A sample HIT is shown in Figure 5.) We collected responses to the HITs from 400 independent appraisers during the month of April 2014. The responses provided by each appraiser are treated as the "gold standard", i.e., the chosen books are treated as *relevant* to the given book in the corresponding HIT.

The accuracy ratios computed using the collected responses, which reflect the proportion of books treated as relevant by independent appraisers among the top-3 books included in each HIT, are shown in Figure 6. Among the appraisers who provided their occupation, 63% were teachers, parents of young readers, or librarians. Given that (i) parents/teachers/ librarians are the ones who often select books for K-3 readers and (ii) the impossibility of directly interacting with K-3 readers using Mechanical Turk, it is appropriate to quantify the performance of K3Rec reflected by the opinions of librarians, parents of young readers, and teachers separately from other appraisers with diverse occupations/professions. As shown in Figure 6, the accuracy ratios calculated according to parents/teachers/librarians responses yield a statistically significant improvement ($p < 0.001$) over the one based on all the collected responses. The results compiled using the opinion of "experts," i.e., parents/teachers/librarians, in books targeting emergent readers are of special importance in assessing the performance of K3Rec, given the lack of benchmark datasets to evaluate recommendation tools for K-3 readers. Moreover, the fact that appraisers who are "experts" appreciate the recommendations made by K3Rec more than general appraisers provides further evidence of the usefulness of K3Rec in suggesting books for K-3 readers in locating suitable reading materials. Based on the feedback collected through Mechanical Turk, we have observed that consistently, almost 2 out of the 3 generated book recommendations were treated as relevant by Mechanical turk appraisers, which demonstrates the effectiveness of K3Rec in locating books suitable for emergent readers.

To evaluate the degree to which books recommended by K3Rec are preferred over those suggested by recommendation modules at well-known book-related websites, we created another set of 10 HITS using Mechanical Turk. We have selected several well-known recommenders that adopt diverse strategies in making book suggestions: (i) Ama-

Give us your opinion about books you have read and
the corresponding "read-alikes"

- If you have read (or are familiar with) **Too Princessy!** by Jean Reidy,
  select, among the ones shown below, the book(s) that are (to a degree)
  related to Too Princessy! and that you would also like to read (provided
  that you are familiar with the following books as well):

☐ **Too Purpley!** by   ☐ **Birdie Plays Dress**   ☐ **Wacky Wednesday** by
Jean Reidy   **Up** by Sujean Rim   Theo LeSieg

- What is your occupation?

☐ Teacher   ☐ School Staff   ☐ Other
☐ Librarian   ☐ Parent of young readers

Figure 5: A sample survey conducted on Mechanical Turk to determine the relevance of K3Rec-generated recommendations

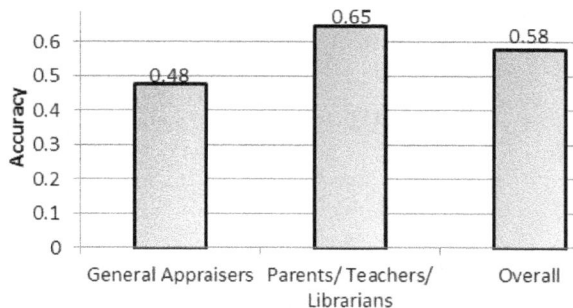

Figure 6: Performance evaluation of K3Rec-generated recommendations based on the opinions of parents/teachers/librarians and other appraisers

Give us your opinion about books you have read and
the corresponding "read-alikes"

If you have read **To Be Like the Sun** by **Susan Marie Swanson**, choose the
top **two** most related books that you would also like to read, among the ones
given below (provided that you are familiar with the following books as well):

☐ **City Dog, Country   **How a Seed   **Love You
Frog** by Mo Williems   Grows** by Helene J.   ☐ Forever** by Robert
                         Jordan   Munsch

☐ **Planting a   **That's Not a
Rainbow** by Lois   ☐ Daffodil!** by Elizabeth ☐ **Weslandia** by Paul
Ehlert   Honey   Fleischman

Figure 7: A Mechanical Turk HIT on the book "To Be Like the Sun"

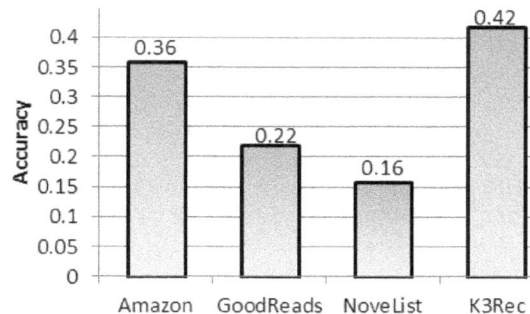

Figure 8: Accuracy achieved by Amazon, GoodReads, NoveList, and K3Rec based on the opinions of Mechanical Turk appraisers

zon, which considers purchasing patterns of its users [14], GoodReads, [14] which "combines multiple proprietary algorithms that analyze 20 billion data points to better predict which books people want to read next", and (iii) NoveList,[15] which examines a number of book-related information, such as title and publication date, for recommending books.

Each HIT (see Figure 7 for a sample) included the top-2 recommendations (in which some of them are identical) made by NoveList, GoodReads, Amazon, and K3Rec for a given sample book B, respectively. Appraisers were asked to select the top-two books most closely related to B, which were treated as the *gold standard* for B.

Based on the 400 responses collected during the month of April 2014, we computed the accuracy of the top-2 recommendations made by K3Rec and each of the recommenders considered for comparison purpose. As shown in Figure 8, recommendations made by K3Rec and Amazon are preferred over the suggestions made by GoodReads and NoveList. Furthermore, the improvement, in terms of accuracy ratios, achieved by K3Rec over GoodReads and NoveList is statistically significant ($p < 0.001$).

In terms of the overall accuracy, K3Rec outperforms Amazon ($p < 0.05$). While K3Rec considers books provided directly by K-3 readers (or their parents/teachers) to generate personalized suggestions, recommendations made by Amazon that target children are the results of extensive analysis of the purchasing patterns of adults, which might not accurately reflect the direct interests/preferences of emer-

gent readers in books. More importantly, K3Rec can treat a book K as a candidate suggestion immediately after K is published, unlike Amazon which requires a number of purchasing transactions involving K to recommend it.

5. CONCLUSIONS AND FUTURE WORK

We have presented K3Rec, an unsupervised book recommender developed for K-3 readers who are not currently targeted by existing recommenders. K-3 readers are an essential audience, given that individuals' reading habits are developed early in life. Unlike current state-of-the art recommenders, K3Rec does not rely on personal social media data, such as personal ratings or bookmarks, which are rarely created by emergent readers, to make recommendations. Instead, K3Rec takes advantage of publicly-available (meta)data on books and (i) examines properties of books that target young audiences, such as their short length and simple and direct writing style, (ii) considers the suitability of topics addressed in books, (iii) analyzes books' contents, and (iv) compares book illustrations, which offer children joy in reading while at the same time help them develop visual thinking skills. The design goal of K3Rec is to assist K-3 readers, their parents, and teachers in their quest for books, either for pleasure reading or knowledge acquisition. K3Rec enriches its readers' choices on books and encourages them to read so that they could become lifelong readers. We have conducted empirical studies using data from BiblioNasium to validate the effectiveness of K3Rec and its superiority over existing recommenders that explicitly consider the reading ability of its users. Conducted experiments using a crowdsourcing platform have further verified the relevance

---

[14] http://goo.gl/AZ8xvv

[15] support.epnet.com/knowledge_base/detail.php?id=4772

of books suggested by K3Rec, which outperforms the recommenders at Amazon, GoodReads, and NoveList.

For future work, we would like to extend the performance evaluation on K3Rec to determine the impact K3Rec has on the reading and learning habits of emergent readers. Furthermore, we would like to enhance the functionality of K3Rec by examining existing image-matching models and, if necessary, develop one that would allow us to perform a more in-depth examination of book illustrations to distinguish, for example, *a little girl from a doll*. In doing so, we anticipate that more relevant book suggestions could be generated, which will improve the effectiveness of our proposed recommender.

6. REFERENCES

[1] R. Allington and E. Gabriel. Every Child, Every Day. *Reading: The Core Skill*, 69(6):10–15, 2012.

[2] R. Benjamin. Reconstructing Readability: Recent Developments and Recommendations in the Analysis of Text Difficulty. *Educational Psychology*, 24:63–88, 2012.

[3] A. Budanitsky and G. Hirst. Evaluating WordNet-based Measures of Lexical Semantic Relatedness. *Computational Linguistics*, 32(1):13–47, 2006.

[4] The Annie E. Casey Foundation. Early Warning Confirmed: A Research Update on Third-Grade Reading. Available at http://goo.gl/HQrPOA, 2013.

[5] C. Coulter and M. Smith. The Construction Zone: Literary Elements in Narrative Research. *Educational Researcher*, 38(8):577–590, 2009.

[6] W. Croft, D. Metzler, and T. Strohman. *Search Engines: Information Retrieval in Practice*. Addison Wesley, 2010.

[7] R. Dong, M. O'Mahony, M. Schaal, K. McCarthy, and B. Smith. Sentimental Product Recommendation. In *Proceedings of ACM conference on Recommender systems (RecSys)*, pages 411–414, 2013.

[8] I. Fountas and G. Pinnell. *Matching Books to Readers: Using Leveled Books in Guided Reading, K-3.* Heinemann, 1999.

[9] L. Girard, L. Girolametto, E. Weitzman, and J. Greenber. Educators' Literacy Practices in Two Emergent Literacy Contexts. *Journal of Research in Childhood Education*, 27(1):46–60, 2013.

[10] S. Givon and V. Lavrenko. Predicting Social-Tags for Cold Start Book Recommendations. In *Proceedings of ACM conference on Recommender systems (RecSys)*, pages 333–336, 2009.

[11] C. Juel. Learning to Read and Write: A Longitudinal Study of Fifty-Four Children from First Through Fourth Grade. *Journal of Educational Psychology*, 80:437–447, 1988.

[12] L. Justic and J. Kaderavek. Using Shared Storybook Reading to Promote Emergent Literacy. *Teaching Exceptional Children*, 34(4):8–13, 2002.

[13] J. Koberstein and Y.-K. Ng. Using Word Clusters to Detect Similar Web Documents. In *Proceedings of Second International Conference on Knowledge Science, Engineering, and Management (KSEM 2007)*, pages 215–228, 2006.

[14] G. Linden, B. Smith, and J. York. Amazon.com Recommendations: Item-to-item Collaborative Filtering. *IEEE Internet Computing*, 7(1):76–80, 2003.

[15] H. Mai and M. Kim. Utilizing Similarity Relationships Among Existing Data for High Accuracy Processing of Content-Based Image Retrieval. *Multimedia Tools and Applications*, January:1–30, 2013.

[16] N. Manouselis, H. Drachsler, K. Verbert, and E. Duval. *Recommender Systems for Learning*. Springer Briefs in Electrical and Computer Engineering, 2013.

[17] J. Oakhill and K. Cain. The Precursors of Reading Ability in Young Readers: Evidence from a Four-Year Longitudinal Study. *Scientific Studies of Reading*, 16(2):91–121, 2012.

[18] Ministry of Education of Ontario. A Guide to Effective Instruction in Reading, Kindergarten to Grade 3. Available at http://goo.gl/UCo5e3, 2005.

[19] M. Pera and Y.-K. Ng. What to Read Next?: Making Personalized Book Recommendations for K-12 Users. In *Proceedings of ACM conference on Recommender systems (RecSys)*, pages 113–120, 2013.

[20] M. Pera. *Using Online Data Sources to Make Recommendations on Reading Materials for K-12 and Advanced Readers*. PhD Dissertation, Brigham Young University, April 2014.

[21] M. Renck. *Young Children and Picture Books (2nd Ed.)*. National Association for the Education of Young Children, 2004.

[22] C. Robinson, J. Larsen, J. Haupt, and J. Mohlman. Picture Book Selection Behaviors of Emergent Readers: Influence of Genre, Familiarity, and Book Attributes. *Reading Research and Instruction*, 36(4):287–304, 1997.

[23] K. Roskos, J. Christie, and D. Richgels. The Essentials of Early Literacy Instruction. *Young Children*, 58(2):52–60, 2003.

[24] J. Saricks. *Readers' Advisory Service in the Public Library, 3rd Ed*. ALA Store, 2005.

[25] A. Sieg, B. Mobasher, and R. Burke. Improving the Effectiveness of Collaborative Recommendation with Ontology-based User Profiles. In *Proceedings of International Workshop on Information Heterogeneity and Fusion in Recommender Systems (HetRec 2010)*, pages 39–46, 2010.

[26] S. Vanneman. Keep Them Reading. *School Library Monthly*, 27(3):21–22, 2010.

[27] G. Whitehurst and C. Lonigan. *Handbook of Early Literacy Research, Volume 1*, chapter Emergent Literacy: Development from Prereaders to Readers. The Guilford Press, 2003.

[28] C. Yang, B. Wei, J. Wu, Y. Zhang, and L. Zhang. CARES: A Ranking-oriented CADAL Recommender System. In *Proceedings of ACM/IEEE Joint Conference on Digital Libraries (JCDL)*, pages 203–212, 2009.

[29] K. Yi and L. Chan. Revisiting the Syntactical and Structural Analysis of Library of Congress Subject Headings for the Digital Environment. *Journal of the Association for Information Science and Technology (JASIST)*, 61(4):677–687, 2010.

Pairwise Preferences Elicitation and Exploitation for Conversational Collaborative Filtering

Laura Blédaitė[*]
Faculty of Computer Science
Free University of Bozen - Bolzano
Piazza Domenicani 3, I - 39100, Bolzano
laura.bledaite@gmail.com

Francesco Ricci
Faculty of Computer Science
Free University of Bozen - Bolzano
Piazza Domenicani 3, I - 39100, Bolzano
fricci@unibz.it

ABSTRACT

The research and development of recommender systems is dominated by models of user's preferences learned from ratings for items. However, ratings have several disadvantages, which we discuss, and in order to address these issues we analyse another way to articulate preferences, i.e., as pairwise comparisons: item A is preferred to item B. We have developed a recommendation technology that, combining ratings and pairwise preferences, can generate better recommendations than a state of the art solution uniquely based on ratings.

Categories and Subject Descriptors

H.3.3 [**Information Storage and Retrieval**]: Information Search and Retrieval—*Information Filtering*

Keywords

Pairwise preferences; collaborative filtering; recommender systems

1. INTRODUCTION

Recommender systems (RSs) are popular Web applications that generate personalised recommendations for items that are estimated to be relevant and useful for their target users [20]. The research and application of RSs is dominated by the usage of ratings, which indicate absolute preferences for items. In its core computational step, e.g., by using collaborative filtering [3], a RS builds a prediction model that, analysing the available ratings, estimates unknown ones.

However, ratings have several disadvantages. First of all, they must be expressed in a predefined scale, which has its own characteristics, and measures taken according to a scale cannot be easily converted to another one [6]. Hence, choosing the right scale is always an issue. Moreover, since ratings represent evaluations measured against an absolute benchmark, it could be difficult for the user to consistently rate items. For instance, if a user rates an item

with the highest value and succesively finds another item which she likes more, then there is no way to express such a preference.

Considering these issues, we have analysed another way to express preferences, i.e., as pairwise comparisons of alternative options, such as, A is preferred to B. However, whether entering pairwise preferences is easier than ratings is debatable. In [9] the authors claim that it is easier to decide which item is preferred among two, rather than rating them in some predefined scale. Conversely, in [17] comparing alternative interfaces for rating and ranking the authors conclude that "rating is the more familiar and less cognitively demanding form of judgement", and found that a rating interface, with the additional support of showing one example item for each star level, was preferred to an interface supporting pairwise comparisons of items. Moreover, while pairwise preferences have been studied in the learning to rank literature [5, 19, 8], they have been rarely used for building RSs (in combination with ratings).

Working on the proposition that pairwise preferences might provide a viable complement to ratings in RSs, we have developed a recommendation technology that combines ratings and pairwise preferences to model user preferences and to generate recommendations. We have compared that solution with a state of the art rating-based approach (based on matrix factorization [11]), and validated the following hypotheses:

1. Pairwise preferences can be as easy to enter as ratings (provided that an effective interface is built);

2. Pairwise preferences can help users more than ratings to understand their preferences;

3. The proposed pairwise-based recommendation technology has a better accuracy and ranking quality;

The rest of this article is organised in the following way. In Section 2 we illustrate the implemented preference acquisition interaction and we describe the implemented ranking and recommendation technique. In Section 3, the evaluation strategy is described and in Section 4 the results are presented. Finally, we discuss some related work and draw the conclusions of our research.

2. PAIRWISE-BASED RECOMMENDER

In order to validate our research hypotheses, we have implemented two movie recommender systems: RAO (RAtings Only) which is based on ratings and Matrix Factorization (MF) (SVD method [11]), and PPR (Pairwise Preferences and Ratings) which analyses user preferences in the form of pairwise preferences (pairscores) and makes recommendations using them together with a possibly pre-existent ratings data set. In this section we illustrate the important features of these systems.

---

[*]Current affiliation: Twitter Inc.

HT '15, September 1–4, 2015, Guzelyurt, Northern Cyprus.
© 2015 ACM. ISBN 978-1-4503-3395-5/15/09 ...$15.00.
DOI: http://dx.doi.org/10.1145/2645710.2645757.

2.1 Preference Acquisition

Preference elicitation requires a suitable GUI. We have implemented a standard five-stars rating interface for the RAO system. Figure 1 instead shows the GUIs that we designed for the PPR system. It enables the users to compare pairs of items and to enter to what extent an item is preferred to another (pair-score). We decided to use a slider: the closer the slider pointer is dragged to an item the more this item is preferred to the other.

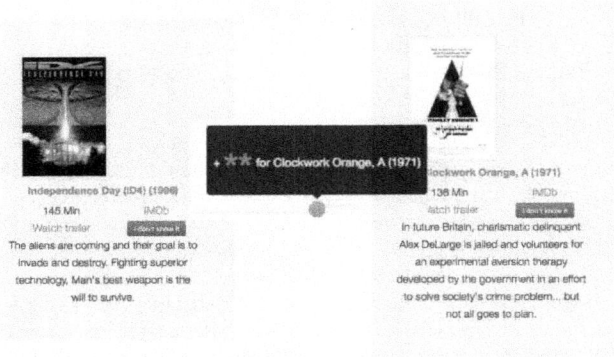

Figure 1: Items' comparison interface producing pair-scores

The main problem that arises in system controlled preference acquisition is the choice of the items, movies in our recommender system, to be shown to the user to rate (rating scenario), or the choice of the movie pairs to compare (pairwise preferences scenario). This is an active learning problem that has received already some attention in the RS community [21, 4]. "Active learning" means that the system actively decides what (preference) data to acquire before starting the learning phase, which in RSs is the rating prediction model building.

For ratings' acquisition in RAO, we adopted a variation of a popular active learning strategy, namely: $log(pop)entropy$ [18]. But, we replaced entropy with variance, because variance is a diversity measure for ordinal data, hence, it is more suitable for measuring the rating diversity. The chosen scoring measure for ranking the items to present to the user to rate - $LpopVar$ - is given in Equation 1. It scores and ranks higher the most popular movies (log factor) with the most diverse ratings ($variance$ factor). The higher the score for item i, the higher i is ranked in the list of items presented to the user to rate. We denote with $u \in U$ a user, with $i \in I$ an item, and with r_{ui} the rating that u gave to i. U_i is the set of users that rated item i, and $\bar{r}_i$ is the average of the ratings of item i.

$$LpopVar(i) = log(|U_i|) \left(\frac{1}{|U_i|} \sum_{u \in U_i} (r_{ui} - \bar{r}_i)^2 \right) \quad (1)$$

While the literature offers several options for the selection of the item to ask the user to rate, acquiring pairwise preferences in recommender systems has not been considered so far. This is challenging since the number of potential pairs of items that the user could compare is quadratic in the number of items and without some well designed system support, in the form of a selection or ranking of item pairs, the task would be hard to complete. Hence, we have introduced a scoring function, which is analogous to $LpopVar$ and it is shown in Equation 2. It is used in the PPR system for ranking the item pairs to be presented to the user to compare.

$$log(|U_i|) \, log(|U_j|) \, (1 - \rho_{ij}) \quad (2)$$

Here, ρ_{ij} denotes the Pearson correlation between the ratings of the items i and j expressed by the users in $U_{ij} = U_i \cap U_j$, i.e., the users that rated both i and j. Items' popularity is considered as in the rating scenario, but we also incorporate a measure of the de-correlation of the ratings of the items in the pair $(1 - correlation)$. The formula implements the heuristics that the more de-correlated the ratings of the two items are, the more the user preference for one of the two will help the system to understand the user tastes. Using this ranking approach the same item may be shown several times in different pairwise comparisons.

2.2 Pairwise-based Recommendations

With a collection of ratings or/and pairwise preferences the PPR system uses a recommendations' ranking technique described in this section. We first illustrate a "non personalised" ranking method based on the pairwise comparison of items in the form of pair-scores [12]. Then, we describe our original modification aimed at obtaining a personalised ranking.

If a set of ratings is available, a skew-symmetric $n \times n$ matrix K is defined, where $n = |I|$, and with entry k_{ij} as in Equation 3.

$$k_{ij} = \frac{1}{m_{ij}} \sum_{u \in U_{ij}} r_{uij} \quad (3)$$

$$r_{uij} = r_{ui} - r_{uj} \quad (4)$$

where $U_{ij} = U_i \cap U_j$ is the set of users that rated both i and j, and $m_{ij} = |U_{ij}|$. In [12] (chapter 9) the following "scoring" vector $\nu = (\nu_1, \ldots, \nu_n)$ is computed:

$$\nu_i = \frac{\sum_{j=1}^{n} k_{ij}}{n} \quad (5)$$

The entries of ν are obtained by simply averaging the rows of the matrix K. It is shown that these entries determine a ranking of the items with the property that $\nu_i - \nu_j$ gives the best approximation of k_{ij}, i.e., the difference of the ν scores of two items tells us how much on average an item receives more star ratings than the other. It is worth noting that such a ranking can be obtained even if in the K matrix there are conflicting preferences such as: $k_{ij} > 0$, $k_{jl} > 0$ and $k_{li} > 0$, i.e., item i is preferred to j, j is preferred to l, but also l is preferred to i.

Our personalised version of this ranking technique, which is illustrated below, incorporates user-to-user similarity weights in the computation of K, hence computing a $K(u)$ matrix for each user u and then producing a personalised ranking of the items using again the formula 5. Namely, k_{uij}, the entries of $K(u)$, are the system predictions of how much the user u will prefer i over j. Hence, while in ratings based systems one predicts ratings, in pairwise preferences approaches [5] one first estimates how much a user likes an item more that another and then aggregates these predictions in the final ranking function, as in Equation 5.

We note that the user ratings for two items can be easily converted into a pair score, as it is shown in equation 4. But also, with the help of the slider-based GUI shown in Figure 1, we are able to directly collect pair-scores. When the user u moves the slider towards item i, this means that u prefers i to j ($i \succ_u j$) and he can also select how much i is preferred to j, hence we can assign a positive value to r_{uij}. While, if user u moves the slider towards j a negative value is assigned to r_{uij} ($i \prec_u j$) (see Equation 6).

We decided to collect pair scores in the range $[-4, +4]$ to be able to exploit a collection of pre-existent ratings in the $[1, 5]$ scale. But the method described here can be used without any modification, even when the pair scores are in the range $\{-1, 0, 1\}$, that is, when the user simply states that she prefers an item to another or says that the two are equally preferred.

$$
r_{uij} = \begin{cases} \in \{4, 3, 2, 1\} & i \succ_u j \\ 0 & \text{no preference} \\ \in \{-1, -2, -3, -4\} & i \prec_u j \end{cases} \quad (6)
$$

Hence, in order to generate personalised recommendations using a collection of ratings and pair-scores the system converts all the available ratings (if there are any) in pair-scores, adds the available pair-scores, and then for the target user u, the personalised values of the $K(u)$ matrix are calculated as follows:

$$
k_{uij} = \frac{1}{\sum_{v \in U_{ij}} w'_{u,v}} \sum_{v \in U_{ij}} w'_{uv} \, r_{vij} \quad (7)
$$

where the user-to-user similarity w'_{uv}, as defined in Equation 8, is a generalisation to pair scored of the original Pearson correlation defined on ratings [3]. Actually, it is the Pearson correlation computed among the users' pair-scores, multiplied by a significance score:

$$
w'_{uv} = \frac{min\,(|\mathcal{I}_{uv}|, \gamma)}{\gamma} \, w_{uv} \quad (8)
$$

$$
w_{uv} = \frac{\sum_{(i,j) \in \mathcal{I}_{uv}} (r_{uij} - \bar{r}_u)(r_{vij} - \bar{r}_v)}{\sqrt{\sum_{(i,j) \in \mathcal{I}_{uv}} (r_{uij} - \bar{r}_u)^2 \sum_{(i,j) \in \mathcal{I}_{uv}} (r_{vij} - \bar{r}_v)^2}} \quad (9)
$$

Here $\bar{r}_v$ is the user's u average of all pairwise preferences, and $\mathcal{I}_{uv}$ is the set of all pairs (i, j) of items that both user u and user v rated (or compared), and such that $i < j$. The significance score $\frac{min(|\mathcal{I}_{uv}|, \gamma)}{\gamma}$ decreases the similarity w_{uv} when $|\mathcal{I}_{uv}|$ is smaller that γ, i.e., when users u and v compared few common pairs of items. γ is a parameter that must be cross-validated. In our experiments we obtained the best performance for $\gamma = 7$.

3. EXPERIMENTAL STRATEGY

We recall that we have implemented two fully operational recommender systems that interact with the users, acquire preferences (ratings or pairwise comparisons), and rank items in order to select the top-n recommendations for the users: RAO - which is based on RAtings Only and uses Matrix Factorization; PPR - which is based on a mixture of Pairwise Preferences acquired during the interaction with the users and possibly pre-existent Ratings. By using the two mentioned systems we have validated our research hypotheses by performing a live user study, as an A/B test (between group).

The initial data set of ratings is common for both systems and contains those for the top 100 movies scored by the $LpopVar$ criterion (Equation 1) that are present in the MovieLens 100K data set (http://grouplens.org/datasets/movielens/).

The evaluation strategy of the systems, included the following stages and steps:

- Stage 1: Initial preference elicitation
  - User preference elicitation (ratings or pairwise preferences);
  - User evaluation of the preference elicitation procedure (questionnaire).
- Stage 2: Recommendation and preference revision

  - Recommendation presentation and user assessment of a first set of recommendations I;
  - User input of additional preferences;
  - Recommendation presentation and user assessment of a second set of recommendations II;
  - User evaluation of the recommendations quality (questionnaire).

The above listed steps are further described in the following. The users were recruited for the experiment mostly by using social media channels and e-mail address lists. Many of them are aged between 25 to 35. A high percentage of them are either undergraduate, graduate, PhD students, recent graduates or university staff. We think that the sample is quite representative of the real users of such a movie recommender system, and more in general for such type of systems.

There were 97 users registered to the experiment. However, not all the users finished the whole experiment (precise numbers are given later). During the initial "preference elicitation" stage of the experiment, user preferences were gathered in the form of either ratings or pairwise preferences, depending on the system to which the users were assigned. Items to rate or item pairs to compare where ranked and presented using the active learning technology that is described in Section 2.1. In case a user was assigned to the RAO system, she was asked to provide ratings for the items. In case she was assigned to the PPR system, she was asked to provide pairwise preferences (Figure 1). We did not ask users to provide a precise number of ratings or pairwise preferences, we simply let the user add as many preferences as she liked. In fact, we were interested in measuring the effort that users freely decide to devote to preference elicitation, estimated as the number of inserted preferences. Preference elicitation is typically seen by the users as a burden, hence we wanted to understand which preference elicitation method may be better accepted and used by the users.

In the second step of the first stage, users were asked to evaluate the preference elicitation process. 89 users completed the first stage (RAO 44 and PPR 45) and answered to the following questionnaire on the preference elicitation process:

1. I have fun using the system;
2. Using the system is a pleasant experience;
3. The system makes me more aware of my choice options;
4. I feel bored when I am using the system.

We took these questions from a survey designed for measuring the perceived system effectiveness and fun that was elaborated by Knijnenburg et al. [10].

The second stage of the experiment (recommendation and preference revision) was run after 15 days, when all the 89 users that accessed the system in the first stage did complete the preference elicitation process. The 15 days interruption between the two stages is not deemed as problematic. It is a common practice to enter ratings in a session (stage 1 of the experiment) and to request recommendations subsequently (the user task in the second stage of the experiment).

In the first step of the second stage of the experiment, the users were given top 5 recommendations displayed in a list (Figure 2). Ranking of the recommendations were computed using SVD matrix factorization for RAO [11] and using the proposed technique for PPR, and were based on the preferences that all the users provided during the first stage (plus the ratings for the selected 100 items that were already present in MovieLens). While browsing the recommendations the users could watch a trailer of the recommended movie or access the corresponding IMDb page. Moreover, users were asked to mark the items that they considered "good recommendations" and the ones they "have seen". This information enabled us to compare the accuracy of the two recommendation processes in terms of precision, which is calculated as the proportion of the relevant items (good recommendations) among the 5 recommended items. Moreover, in order to assess the quality of

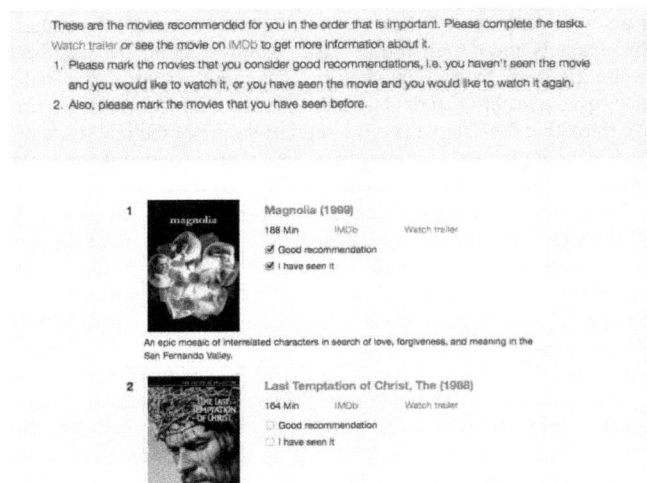

Figure 2: List of Recommendations

the systems' generated rankings we used normalized Discounted Cumulative Gain ($nDCG$) [15, 3], which is a popular and well accepted measure of ranking quality.

In the second step of the second stage the users were asked to provide additional preferences (ratings or pairwise preferences depending on the system they were assigned to) about the items that they marked as seen in the previous step (recommendation I), by using again the same preference elicitation interface that they used in the first step of the first stage. Note that our ranking approach can handle preferences that are possibly conflicting with those already expressed (see Section 2.2). The goal of this step was to involve the user by interacting with the system in order to offer her better and better recommendations.

Next, the users were given an improved set of recommendations based on all the entered preferences (both in the first and second stage) (again as in Figure 2). They marked again the good and the seen recommendations. This approach enabled us to test the improvement of the accuracy of the two recommendation processes after additional preferences, using both approaches, were acquired. We measured again precision and $nDCG$ for both system.

We conjectured that the subsequent recommendation list, which is computed by using also the additional preferences collected on items belonging to the first recommendation list, could be more accurate than the first list, and the usage of pairwise preference could improve more the recommendation accuracy (precision and nDCG).

Finally, the users were asked to provide an overall feedback to the recommendations quality in general. The feedback was collected using a questionnaire (answers in a Likert scale). This questionnaire was already used in similar experiments [10]:

1. I liked the items recommended by the system;

2. The recommended items fitted my preference;

3. The recommended items were well-chosen;

4. The recommended items were relevant;

5. The system recommended too many bad items;

6. I didn't like any of the recommended items;

7. The items I selected were "the best among the worst".

69 (34 from RAO and 35 from PPR) users finished both stages of the experiment. Thus, 69 users filled in the questionnaire at the end of the second stage of the experiment. We use this data to compare their perceived recommendation quality. We note that among these 69 users only 30 provided additional ratings or preferences (16 using system RAO and 14 using system PPR), i.e., 39 skipped this phase. Thus we have used only this data when comparing recommendation prediction accuracy and ranking quality before/after additional preferences were entered.

4. RESULTS

Analysing the replies of the users to the first questionnaire on the satisfaction for the preference elicitation process we found a larger overall score of 66.66 for PPR as compared to 62.78 for RAO (this validates the fist research hypothesis listed in the Introduction). This score is computed by taking each reply to the four given statements and converting them into a score in the range 0-4. For sentences where larger agreement means a higher perceived satisfaction, i.e., the first three, the score contribution is the scale position minus 1. For sentences where larger agreement means a lower perceived satisfaction (the fourth) the contribution is 5 minus the scale position. The resulting score was then scaled to [0, 100].

We also discovered that the system that elicits pairwise preferences makes users more aware of their choice options, i.e., users replied to question 3 with a much larger agreement. We conducted Mann-Whitney and Kruskal-Wallis tests and both of them proved significant difference in favour of PPR (both p-values ≈ 0.0001). This proves the second research hypothesis that we made.

When analysing the scores for separate questions of the questionnaire about the perceived recommendation quality, which the user gave at the end of the complete recommendation process, i.e., end of stage 2, we observed a clear tendency of PPR to outperform RAO. The pooled score, which was computed similarly to the score of the first questionnaire on the user satisfaction of the preference elicitation process, for RAO is 61.34 and for PPR is 63.27. However, because of a small sample size, a significant difference was not observed.

Discussing now the recommendation accuracy of the two systems, Table 1 shows $nDCG$ and precision of RAO and PPR before and after additional preferences were entered in stage two and p-values of the tests for significance of $nDCG$ and precision differences: a) between systems before and after the additional preferences; and b) within each system before versus after additional preferences. We note that we could compute these evaluation metrics because the users were asked to mark the recommendations that they considered as good. Hence, we stress that the results shown here are not offline estimations of precision and nDCG, but the effective performance of the system recommendations as evaluated by the users.

As it can be seen from Table 1, before the additional preferences are entered, i.e., when comparing the initial recommendation lists, PPR performs significantly better than the RAO in terms of $nDCG$ (p-value = 0.024). PPR has also a better precision than RAO, but in this case the difference is not significant. After the additional

Table 1: Recommendation accuracy and its improvement after additional preferences were entered

	nDCG			precision		
	before	after	p-value	before	after	p-value
RAO	0.54	0.66	0.180	0.45	0.49	0.346
PPR	0.79	0.84	0.295	0.51	0.64	0.035 *
p-value	0.024 *	0.046 *		0.35	0.044 *	

preferences are entered by the users, i.e., when comparing the improved recommendation lists presented by the two systems, PPR performs significantly better than RAO in terms of both $nDCG$ (p-value = 0.046) and precision (p-value = 0.044).

Table 1 also shows, as expected, that there is always an improvement in precision and $nDCG$ for both systems after the user has provided additional preferences. But, there is a significant improvement of recommendation accuracy, in terms of precision, only after additional preferences were entered in PPR (p-value = 0.035). These results prove the third hypothesis that we made, i.e., the usage of pairwise preferences, compared to the exploitation of ratings, improves more the recommendation accuracy and ranking quality.

We also looked at the number of preferences entered in the systems in the two stages. In the first stage of the experiment, $1,415$ ratings and $2,262$ pairwise preferences were collected. In the second stage, on average per user, 2.06 additional ratings and 1.93 additional pairwise preferences were provided by the users using RAO and PPR, respectively. Hence, there was a difference in terms of the number of preferences entered by the users using the two systems; it is noteworthy that more pairwise preferences than ratings were acquired in the first stage. We can conclude that overall these results confirm our main research hypothesis, that is, pairwise preferences are a viable approach to preference elicitation and the generated recommendations are even superior to those produced by Matrix Factorization.

5. RELATED WORK

In [2] the authors discuss issues related to rating inconsistency and the user difficulty in mapping preferences to ratings, while [16] addresses these problems by introducing improved user interfaces to support the preference to rating mapping process. The suggested methods include personalised tags and exemplars to relate rating decisions to prior ones. It has been concluded that, notwithstanding the usefulness of their proposed solutions, it remains hard for the user to enter ratings.

The authors of [9] have already guessed that pairwise preferences are easier to formulate and to reason about than ratings. Namely, it is easier to decide which item (and how much more) is preferred to another, rather than to rate both items in some arbitrary scale, e.g., the common 5-star scale.

Besides, in [17] the authors compare alternative interfaces for rating and ranking by measuring the user perceived: speed, accuracy, mental demand, suitability for organization, fun to use, and overall preference. In that study the user task was to rank 20 movies. It is worth noting that in their scenario they derive results that are very different from ours. For instance, they found that a rating interface, with the additional support of showing one example item for each star level, was preferred to an interface supporting pairwise comparisons of items. This diversity stresses the importance to evaluate preference elicitation interfaces in the context of their usage, since one cannot derive absolute measures of a goodness of an approach without embedding it in a fully operational system.

In the RS literature some formal ranking models based on pairwise preferences exist [23, 7, 22, 19]. However, none of them has been developed, together with an appropriate GUI, for supporting the full interaction of the user with the system: preference elicitation, preference revision, and recommendation browsing.

A notable example of a recommender system based on pairwise preferences is described in [13]. However, there are several differences between this approach and that one presented in this paper. For instance, in our system the user is entering preferences by comparing pairs of movies while in [13] the user is asked to compare sets of movies. Moreover, the number of comparisons in our case is essentially not limited by any condition and we have developed a novel active learning strategy for helping the user to compare items. In [13] the number of comparisons is equal to the number of factors of the used matrix factorization model, which is necessary in order to bootstrap the approach. For that reason, the factor model must be rather simple, since for each factor the system generates a preference elicitation comparison of two sets of movies. It is unlikely that a user can go through many of these questions, while an accurate factor model can require a very large number of factors (hundreds, thousands and even more).

6. CONCLUSION AND FUTURE WORK

By conducting an online A/B test, we have shown that it is possible to build recommender systems that incorporate pairwise preferences and perform better than state of the art rating-only based solutions (in terms of recommendation accuracy measured by $nDCG$ and precision). We have also shown that such type of systems can improve more the recommendation accuracy after the user provides additional preferences. Additionally, we have shown that asking a user to compare movies makes her more aware of her choice options, and by doing that the system is able to collect more preferences (pairwise comparisons vs. ratings). We have therefore validated the research hypotheses that we stated in the Introduction of this paper.

We want here to mention some limitations of the presented work and suggest some branches of further research. First of all, a deeper analysis of the pairwise preference request generation is required. In that respect, further work is needed in the development of effective user interfaces that make use of active learning strategies for the PPR model and may elicit mixed preference data, i.e., both ratings and pairwise preferences. This is especially important when there are no pre-existent ratings (cold-start), as we have assumed in our experiments, and it is therefore important to acquire users' preference information efficiently. Another important research line is the better usage of session data in PPR. In fact, preference elicitation is strongly influenced by the interaction context which varies at each single session [14, 1].

Finally we must explicitly note that the proposed ranking method illustrated in Section 2.2 is just one possible solution for the considered ranking problem. We imagine that other label ranking techniques could be applied to recommender systems and we believe that in the future more research works could be dedicated to this interesting topic.

7. REFERENCES

[1] G. Adomavicius, B. Mobasher, F. Ricci, and A. Tuzhilin. Context-aware recommender systems. *AI Magazine*, 32(3):67–80, 2011.

[2] A. Bellogín, A. Said, and A. P. de Vries. The magic barrier of recommender systems - no magic, just ratings. In *User Modeling, Adaptation, and Personalization - 22nd International Conference, UMAP 2014, Aalborg, Denmark, July 7-11, 2014. Proceedings*, pages 25–36, 2014.

[3] C. Desrosiers and G. Karypis. A comprehensive survey of neighborhood-based recommendation methods. In F. Ricci, L. Rokach, B. Shapira, and P. B. Kantor, editors, *Recommender Systems Handbook*, pages 107–144. Springer, 2011.

[4] M. Elahi, F. Ricci, and N. Rubens. Active learning in collaborative filtering recommender systems. In *E-Commerce and Web Technologies - 15th International Conference, EC-Web 2014, Munich, Germany, September 1-4, 2014. Proceedings*, pages 113–124, 2014.

[5] J. Fürnkranz and E. Hüllermeier. Preference learning and ranking by pairwise comparison. In J. Fürnkranz and E. Hüllermeier, editors, *Preference Learning*, pages 65–82. Springer Berlin Heidelberg, 2011.

[6] C. Gena, R. Brogi, F. Cena, and F. Vernero. The impact of rating scales on user's rating behavior. In *User Modeling, Adaption and Personalization - 19th International Conference, UMAP 2011, Girona, Spain, July 11-15, 2011. Proceedings*, pages 123–134, 2011.

[7] D. F. Gleich and L.-H. Lim. Rank aggregation via nuclear norm minimization. In *Proceedings of the 17th ACM SIGKDD International Conference on Knowledge Discovery and Data Mining, San Diego, CA, USA, August 21-24, 2011*, pages 60–68, 2011.

[8] E. Hüllermeier, J. Fürnkranz, W. Cheng, and K. Brinker. Label ranking by learning pairwise preferences. *Artificial Intelligence*, 172(16-17):1897–1916, Nov. 2008.

[9] N. Jones, A. Brun, A. Boyer, and A. Hamad. An exploratory work in using comparisons instead of ratings. In *E-Commerce and Web Technologies - 12th International Conference, EC-Web 2011, Toulouse, France, August 30 - September 1, 2011. Proceedings*, pages 184–195, 2011.

[10] B. P. Knijnenburg, M. C. Willemsen, Z. Gantner, H. Soncu, and C. Newell. Explaining the user experience of recommender systems. *User Modeling and User-Adapted Interaction*, 22:441–504, 2012.

[11] Y. Koren and R. Bell. Advances in collaborative filtering. In F. Ricci, L. Rokach, B. Shapira, and P. B. Kantor, editors, *Recommender Systems Handbook*, pages 145–186. Springer Science and Business Media, 2011.

[12] A. N. Langville and C. D. Meyer. *Who's #1?: The Science of Rating and Ranking*. Princeton University Press, 2012.

[13] B. Loepp, T. Hussein, and J. Ziegler. Choice-based preference elicitation for collaborative filtering recommender systems. In *Proceedings of the SIGCHI Conference on Human Factors in Computing Systems*, CHI '14, pages 3085–3094, New York, NY, USA, 2014. ACM.

[14] T. Mahmood and F. Ricci. Improving recommender systems with adaptive conversational strategies. In *HYPERTEXT 2009, Proceedings of the 20th ACM Conference on Hypertext and Hypermedia, Torino, Italy, June 29 - July 1, 2009*, pages 73–82, 2009.

[15] C. D. Manning, P. Raghavan, and H. Schütze. *Introduction to Information Retrieval*. Cambridge University Press, 2008.

[16] T. T. Nguyen, D. Kluver, T.-Y. Wang, P.-M. Hui, M. D. Ekstrand, M. C. Willemsen, and J. Riedl. Rating support interfaces to improve user experience and recommender accuracy. In *Proc. RecSys 2013*, pages 149–156. ACM, 2013.

[17] S. Nobarany, L. Oram, V. K. Rajendran, C.-H. Chen, J. McGrenere, and T. Munzner. The design space of opinion measurement interfaces: Exploring recall support for rating and ranking. In *Proceedings of the SIGCHI Conference on Human Factors in Computing Systems*, CHI '12, pages 2035–2044, New York, NY, USA, 2012. ACM.

[18] A. Rashid, I. Alberta, D. Cosley, S. Lam, S. McNee, J. Konstan, and J. Riedl. Getting to know you: Learning new user preferences in recommender systems. In *in Proc. of the International Conference on Intelligent User Interfaces*, pages 127–134, 2002.

[19] S. Rendle, C. Freudenthaler, Z. Gantner, and L. Schmidt-Thieme. Bpr: Bayesian personalized ranking from implicit feedback. In *Proceedings of the Twenty-Fifth Conference on Uncertainty in Artificial Intelligence*, UAI '09, pages 452–461, Arlington, Virginia, United States, 2009. AUAI Press.

[20] F. Ricci. Recommender systems: Models and techniques. In R. Alhajj and J. G. Rokne, editors, *Encyclopedia of Social Network Analysis and Mining*, pages 1511–1522. Springer, 2014.

[21] N. Rubens, D. Kaplan, and M. Sugiyama. Active learning in recommender systems. In F. Ricci, L. Rokach, B. Shapira, and P. Kantor, editors, *Recommender Systems Handbook*, pages 735–767. Springer Verlag, 2011.

[22] Y. Shi, A. Karatzoglou, L. Baltrunas, M. Larson, N. Oliver, and A. Hanjalic. Climf: Learning to maximize reciprocal rank with collaborative less-is-more filtering. In *Proceedings of the Sixth ACM Conference on Recommender Systems*, RecSys '12, pages 139–146, New York, NY, USA, 2012. ACM.

[23] S. Wang, J. Sun, B. J. Gao, and J. Ma. Adapting vector space model to ranking-based collaborative filtering. In *21st ACM International Conference on Information and Knowledge Management (CIKM '12)*, 2012.

Surpassing the Limit: Keyword Clustering to Improve Twitter Sample Coverage

Justin Sampson, Fred Morstatter, Ross Maciejewski, Huan Liu
School of Computing, Informatics, and Decision Systems Engineering
Arizona State University
{justin.sampson, fred.morstatter, ross.maciejewski, huan.liu}@asu.edu

ABSTRACT

Social media services have become a prominent source of research data for both academia and corporate applications. Data from social media services is easy to obtain, highly structured, and comprises opinions from a large number of extremely diverse groups. The microblogging site, Twitter, has garnered a particularly large following from researchers by offering a high volume of data streamed in real time. Unfortunately, the methods in which Twitter selects data to disseminate through the stream are either vague or unpublished. Since Twitter maintains sole control of the sampling process, it leaves us with no knowledge of how the data that we collect for research is selected. Additionally, past research has shown that there are sources of bias present in Twitters dissemination process. Such bias introduces noise into the data that can reduce the accuracy of learning models and lead to bad inferences. In this work, we take an initial look at the efficiency of Twitter limit track as a sample population estimator. After that, we provide methods to mitigate bias by improving sample population coverage using clustering techniques.

Categories and Subject Descriptors

H.3.3 [**Information Search and Retrieval**]: Clustering; Retrieval models

Keywords

Clustering; Text Processing; Social Media

1. INTRODUCTION

The use of social media as a data source has allowed for an extremely wide-reaching range of topics and phenomena to be studied on a large scale. Highly prominent among sources for data gathering is the microblogging site Twitter. The popularity of Twitter as a source can be attributed to the type of data that is produced by its users, tweets must

HT '15, September 1–4, 2015, Guzelyurt, Northern Cyprus.
© 2015 ACM. ISBN 978-1-4503-3395-5/15/09 ...$15.00.
DOI: http://dx.doi.org/10.1145/2700171.2791030.

be concise due to the 140 character limit imposed by the service, and the data gathering limits are relaxed compared to most other similar services. The combination of these favorable traits, found almost uniquely in Twitter, have allowed it to become organically selected as the "'model-organism' for research with social media data" [21]. The Twitter streaming API allows users to gather up to 1% of all tweets that pass through the service at any time. According to Twitter, around 500 million tweets are posted every day meaning that a single user can gather up to 5 million tweets in this period of time.[1] While this generous data rate allows for large samples to be gathered over time, rate limiting still poses significant challenges for any research which requires as close to a complete data set as possible.

Recent works have shown that there is significant bias in the sampling method used by Twitter's filtered streaming API. However, this sampling method remains unpublished, making it difficult for end users to detect and correct for the resulting bias in their data sets. Attempting to create generalized models or make any form of measurement based on a data set with ingrained bias is dangerous and can result in large margins of error that may not be acceptable. Additionally, the inverse is also true. When the total population size for a data set is known bias can be minimized making it possible to make good predictions based on principled statistical and machine learning techniques. In the absence of the ability to measure and correct for sources of bias, the only available recourse is to ensure that the coverage of the gathered sample is as close as possible to the total sample population during the gathering process. However, in order to measure the difference between a sample and the complete set, a useful population measure is required.

The Twitter streaming API uses a mechanism called "limit track" which informs the user of the number of tweets that were not delivered to them due to exceeding the 1% rate limit. The limit track data is provided periodically along with tweets delivered in a particular stream. Unfortunately, if the limit track value provided by Twitter is not a reliable measurement, then it becomes significantly more difficult to determine the overall sample population, and, as a result, the level of bias in the sample remains unknown. In addition, the usefulness of the limit track value is further reduced as it does not allow for any method to retroactively obtain the lost data. Unfortunately, since the method used for sampling tweets, as well as how the limit track value is obtained, is not yes published, it is imperative to know (1) whether Twitter's

---

[1]https://about.twitter.com/company

limit track is accurate and, if it is not, we (2) must find another way to decide if information is being lost.

With these limitations in mind, this work will attempt to answer the following questions:

- Is the Twitter limit track an accurate measure of the amount of data missing from a sample?
- How can we structure our search to reduce the volume of missed data?

While data sets created using completely random sampling methods are known to preserve important statistical properties that allow a smaller sample size to generalize well to the entire set [7, 19], the introduction of deterministic processes into sample creation introduces bias that can cause erroneous and dangerous conclusions to be drawn from the data. Unfortunately, the incredible size and rigidity inherent to the infrastructure of these services, such as Twitter, do not necessarily lend themselves well to producing the type of random sampling necessary. This shifts the burden of responsibility for creating and using unbiased data from the service to the user. However, producing unbiased samples from inherently biased data sources is nontrivial. Regardless of biases in the sampling method, increasing the ratio of coverage between the sampled data and the complete dataset will reduce sample error and improve results. While gathering the complete set of data would be optimal, most services impose strict sampling rate limitations. In other cases, where the complete data samples are available, exorbitant pricing can be a roadblock. This work proposes several methods to overcome these limitations by increasing sample coverage, thereby minimizing bias in incomplete samples. Though the proposed methods were implemented and tested on Twitter, the results should generalize well to any keyword-based data gathering services.

2. RELATED WORK

The predictive power of social media services, such as Twitter, has been used to effectively track and predict the spread of disease [1, 6, 8]. Other efforts have also shown promising results by using social media to discover a wide range of collective knowledge such as real-time political polling [4, 22] and the potential success of movies at box-office [2, 14]. However, there are very few standards governing how data from social media is gathered and how research and predictions should be approached [16]. A number of studies have shown that the method used for sampling can introduce various forms of bias which introduce error into results and remain largely unnoticed [9, 19]. Very little research has gone into methods for correcting for bias. Morstatter et al. proposed using bootstrapping [5] and secondary data sources to obtain a confidence interval for the occurrence rate of a hashtag between the two sources. Such a statistical difference could be used as a red flag for the presence of bias in the stream [18].

Several relevant works have attempted to uncover the underlying mechanisms with which Twitter disseminates tweets through its various streaming APIs. In 2013, Morstatter et al. tested the differences between the public Twitter streaming API, which is commonly used by researchers but will only return up to 1% of all available data, and the prohibitively priced "firehose" stream, which offers all of the available data to those willing to pay for it [19]. This work uncovered a number of anomalies such as varying top hashtags, differing topic distributions, and varying network mea-

sures when using the same searches on both the paid and free services. They explain that according to the "law of large numbers" if the sample is truely random then it should relate well with the results from the population, in this case the "firehose" results [19]. These differences indicate that the streaming API introduces some form of bias when determining how to limit the results sent to a stream [18].

The possible causes of this sampling bias have been a continuing source of inquiry. Joseph et al. used five independent streaming sources the differences between multiple streaming results taken at similar but varying time windows [10]. They used a set of keywords and usernames including stop words such as "the" and "i" and words that they specifically invented for the experiment. In order to determine if starting time had an impact on the results they staggered each start by a fraction of a second. After running these tests multiple times, they showed that, when using the same keywords across each stream, 96% of unique tweets were captured by all streams [10]. Since the experiment used stop words that undoubtedly make up a significant portion of English tweets, a random distribution method would have given results that varied wildly across the separate streaming connections. This is strong proof that the sampling method used by Twitter is highly deterministic.

Kerg et al. found further evidence of non-random sampling. In earlier forms of the Twitter streaming API, the three data streaming levels which provided 1%, 10%, and 100% of Twitter data were named "Spritzer", "Gardenhose", and "Firehose" respectively. These streams, unlike the filter-based stream, provide data from the entire body of current tweets. Through analysis of the unique tweet IDs provided by Twitter, the authors discovered that the unique IDs included data, such as the timestamp when the tweet was created, the data center that created it, and other information related to the underlying technical infrastructure of the Twitter data centers. Analysis of the timestamp in particular showed that, in the limited streams, the timestamps only fell over a specific interval of milliseconds directly related to the percentage of sample coverage specified by the service level [11]. Though no similar timestamp-based sampling method appears to be used in the filtered search stream, the non-random nature of the filtered data, in addition to the use of simple deterministic methods in past dissemination schemes, indicates that there are underlying artifacts in the filtered stream infrastructure as well that may be adding bias to gathered samples.

The 1% boundary has proven to be a significant hindrance for applications and research that require as close to a complete set of data as possible. These include mission critical response situations, such as those necessary for emergency response and monitoring applications [12, 17, 23], as well as any form of research that is highly affected by sample bias. As a direct result of the high cost of the "firehose" service, many users have attempted to develop novel solutions for gathering data to improve either the size and coverage of the dataset [13] or the overall quality of results for a smaller sample [7]. Li et al. proposed a system that uses "automatic keyword selection" to determine the best search terms to use for a given search through a keyword cost-based system. Using this method improved topic coverage from 49% of targeted tweets obtained through human-selected keywords to 90% in the automatic system [13]. Ghosh et al. took an alternate approach and attempted to improve the quality of their sample by gathering topic-based twitter data from experts and comparing the "diversity, timeliness, and trust-worthiness" to a larger sample of community tweets of the same topic. While the expert-based search did show an improvement in all of these areas, they cautioned that crowd-based data could not be entirely discounted as it captured other significant properties such as the flow of conversation in the topic that is otherwise ignored by experts [7].

3. KEYWORD SPLITTING APPROACH

The Twitter Streaming API allows anyone to gather real-time data from Twitter by specifying a set of parameters that include search terms, user names, or location boxes. In the case that the search terms specified for a stream surpass the 1% limit, the API informs the user of the total number of tweets missed since the streaming connection began. Ideally, this would give the user a quantitative measure of the overall sample size for their search. The total size of the dataset would then be the sum of the number of unique tweets gathered added to the limit track value provided by Twitter. Knowing the exact quantity of missing data is of paramount importance when it is necessary to adjust the data gathering method to account for gaps in the sample.

The Twitter limit track is designed to give a measurement of lost data for a single stream. However, our proposed methods revolve around using multiple streams to increase the effective sample size. In order to determine if the limit track is a useful measure for the overall sample, when viewed from the context of multiple streams, we ran a number of trials simultaneously. At the first level, all keywords used in the search were tracked using a single stream. For each level beyond the first, the keywords were separated as evenly as possible among the streams. In the example shown in Figure 1, all keywords are split between crawlers based on the number of crawlers required at each level. For example, split level two separates all 400 keywords between two crawlers. All split levels are run simultaneously up to a maximum split level of five which required a total of fifteen streaming clients. After a set period of time, all crawlers terminate and any duplicate tweet IDs are discarded from the set for each split level. Since no keywords were added or duplicated between the streams, the total number of possible tweets should be equivalent to the unsplit streams number of caught tweets as well at the reported limit value. However, in nearly every experiment, there was always a number of splits that would result in a larger number of unique tweet IDs than should be possible according to limit track. As shown in Figure 1, we accumulated 107.3% of the tweets that were indicated by the limit track, meaning that we received more tweets than were estimated by Twitter. Furthermore, using a four-split approach, we collected 137.2% of the tweets indicated by the limit track In order for the limit track to be an accurate measurement of the sample population it should not be possible to gather unique tweets much beyond 100%. This data can also be seen in Table 1 where N/A is used for the missing data and the totals columns when splitting was used because each stream is only capable of indicating the number of missed tweets and not which tweet IDS were missed. Since multiple crawlers may have overlap in the tweets that they do not receive, it is not possible to determine the number of unique tweet IDs missed across each crawler. Additionally, if limit track is an accurate metric, then the number of missed tweets for a single stream with

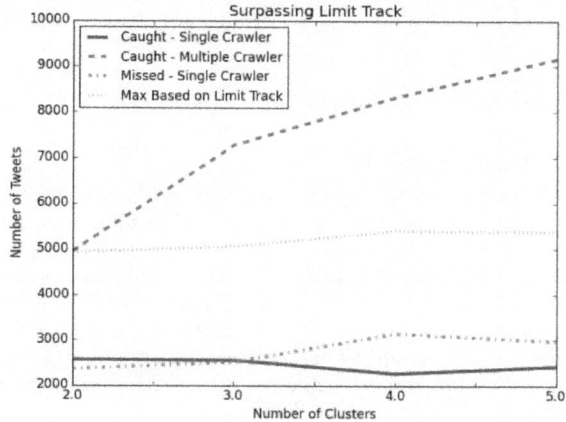

Figure 1: Using a single crawler it is possible to gather tweets from at most 400 keywords. As can be seen, the rate of tweets caught remains stable for a single crawler. Splitting the same keywords across multiple crawlers results in immediate improvement in the number of unique tweets caught as well as allowing the sampled population to go beyond the population size indicated by Twitter.

Table 1: Impact of Additional Crawlers on Sample Coverage. Since multiple crawlers may have overlap in the tweets that they do not receive, it is not possible to determine the number of unique tweet IDs missed across each crawler - we use N/A when this is the case.

	Caught	Missed	Total	Coverage
Unsplit	3632	4488	8120	44.7%
2-split	5060	N/A	N/A	62.3%
3-split	8714	N/A	N/A	107.3%
4-split	11143	N/A	N/A	137.2%

all possible keywords should indicate the total population. These figures provide strong evidence that the limit track reports supplied by Twitter are either inaccurate or they are an estimation.

In order to get the most tweets in a time period, we run multiple crawlers. Given a list of keywords, the Twitter streaming API will return every new tweet that contains any of the words specified. Therefore, by splitting the keyword list among multiple crawlers it becomes possible to gather tweets beyond the 1% limitation. Under perfect conditions, each additional stream increases the effective limit rate by 1%. Unfortunately, when partitioning keywords, it is important to keep in mind the possibility of overlap between the streams. For example, a tweet that contains keywords that were split between a number of crawlers will be duplicated in each stream. Tweet duplication in this manner reduces the overall efficiency of each stream. The stream splitting methods must be able to account for, and attempt to minimize, the potential for overlap between keywords.

In order to gather samples closer to the population size, we propose and evaluate three different splitting algorithms

- each with varying characteristics for the initial rate of growth and growth stability as additional crawlers are added:
- Round Robin
- Spectral Clustering
- K-Means Round Robin

4. EXPERIMENTS

Each of the following experiments is designed to test the efficiency of the given splitting method in obtaining a sample closer to the total sample population than is possible with the standard single stream method. The key factors that we will focus on include: speed of initial growth with a small number of crawlers, how stable the splitting method is for increasing growth as additional crawlers are added, and how many crawlers are required before we pass the population size estimation established by Twitter.

In each of the experiments, we drew from a pool of twenty-one streams. This allows us to use a single stream with all possible keywords as a baseline measure for standard gathering rate and population estimation with the limit track. The remaining twenty streams are then used for performing keyword splitting up to twenty ways. Each of these streams was able to track up to 400 keywords, the maximum number of keywords allowed by Twitter in any given stream. While twenty streams could easily track more than 400 keywords, we limit our search to all 400 keywords from a single stream split across up to twenty streams to allow for direct comparison with the performance of a single crawler. The keywords used were chosen by taking the most frequently occurring keywords from the Twitter sample stream in a ten minute period of time. These keywords contained a broad spectrum of topical words as well as multiple source languages. Keywords were chosen in this manner to ensure a high data rate from Twitter and represent a worst possible scenario for keyword splitting since a single keyword represents an atomic element that can not be further split. The set of keywords discovered in this fashion were used throughout.

For the purpose of these experiments, it was not necessary to track specific users or geographic coordinates simply because the volume of data obtained from these sources is minuscule in comparison to the top words used on Twitter. In cases where segmenting geoboxes is necessary, it is possible to segment it into any number of geographic regions while introducing no overlap between regions. In addition, the proposed solutions can be applied to the tracking of Twitter user names since they act as tokens in a similar manner to keywords. Limiting the number of keywords split between crawlers to the maximum capability of a single stream enables comparison by examining the change in sample population between each method while keeping the set of keywords constant. For example, using a single stream we know the number of tweets obtained, n, as well at the number of tweets left undelivered, m. Therefore, we should know the total sample size, N, such that $N = n + m$. Considering that the number of undelivered tweets is reported without any indication as to which data was lost, this total sample size is the only quantitative measurement given by Twitter as to the overall volume of the data. Furthermore, in cases where we want to employ multiple streaming accounts in a search strategy, the number of tweets missed, reported on a per-stream basis, becomes an unreliable measure due to the potential of separate streams to count a single missed tweet multiple times.

Each streaming agent captures text data from each tweet in order to create a word-to-word co-occurrence network. This data takes the form of word tuples followed by the number of times that the word pairs were observed across each tweet. The co-occurrence can then be used to create a network graph where each word is a graph node and the number of observations become undirected weighted edges. The resulting network graph G takes the standard form $G = (V, E, W)$ where each $v \in V$ is a word and each $e \in E$ is a co-occurrence observation with weight, W indicating the number of times a (v, v) pair was observed.

4.1 Experiment 1 - Round Robin

In order to reduce the initial overlap between crawlers, an additional "priming" step was added before each crawling experiment. Priming a search requires running an initial single level crawler for up to 10 minutes before creating any additional streams. During this stage the priming crawler observes all word pairs. Since words with a large number of pair observations are more likely to occur together, reducing the overlap between words will reduce the number of duplicated tweets. Though this priming step is a requirement for each splitting technique described here, it is possible to perform a very short initial priming search and subsequently update the clusters later as the word-to-word graph improves in quality. The priming step is not used in the results and is instead a method to obtain a word co-occurrence graph to be used in performing the initial splits.

The round robin method of stream keyword splitting is an effective baseline for other splitting methods as it is a straightforward method that requires very little additional processing power. Sampling the amount of tweets gathered and missed at each split level requires running one baseline stream that contains all selected keywords as well as k additional streams that contain the keywords split between each stream. While it is possible to sample all split levels simultaneously, the number of required accounts for a test of this type is $x_k = \frac{k(k+1)}{2}$ where k is the number of split levels and x is the number of accounts. Sampling all splits up to a split level of 7 would require 28 separate account which is unfeasible for our purposes. Additionally, the processing power required to maintain the set of unique tweet IDs for each stream becomes problematic very quickly. Alternatively, using a single baseline stream that contains all keywords and comparing the results to each split level independently requires a much lower number of accounts, $x_k = k+1$. It is this latter method that we use for each stream splitting analysis. At the completion of the priming stage, the word pairs, from the most frequently occurring to the least frequently occurring, are assigned to streams in a round robin fashion. Each split level runs for 30 minutes before resetting all streams, including the baseline stream, and beginning the next split level. Resetting the baseline stream is key to analyzing each stream level in this method as it allows a comparison of the difference between a single stream and multiple split streams over a given window of time and thereby making it unnecessary to maintain all data for every level of split at once.

The graph shown in Figure 2 show that we were able to eclipse the limit track maximum by 12 splits at which point we were able to gather six times as many unique tweets containing proper keywords than was possible with a single stream. Reaching 20 split levels nearly doubled the number of unique tweets gathered over the maximum indicated by

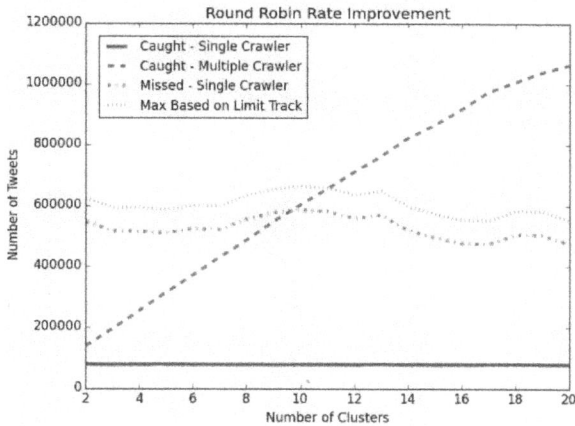

Figure 2: **Round robin splitting based on word co-occurrence tends to show a steady rate of gain as additional crawlers are added.**

Twitter. Constructing round robin splits can be found in Algorithm 1.

Algorithm 1: Round Robin Splits Construction
---
input : graph G, num_clusters k
output: array of lists
for *node v in G(V, E)* **do**
  | keywordList += v
end
sortedList := Sort(keywordList by occurrence rate);
for *word, index in sortedList* **do**
  | listNum := index % k;
  | assign word to split list k
end

4.2 Experiment 2 - Spectral Clustering

Spectral clustering, an extension of K-Means clustering which performs "low-dimension embedding" [20], directly leverages the word occurrence graph. Unlike K-Means, spectral clustering requires an affinity matrix in order to create accurate clusters based on how the items relate to one another. This clustering method allows us to define a number of clusters, k, and the spectral clustering algorithm will incorporate the nuances of the similarity between the items in order to improve cluster results. Like most clustering algorithms, spectral clustering does not make any guarantee on the size of each cluster. As a result, cluster size can vary to a large degree which has implications for the usefulness of this method.

The combined effect of these properties of spectral clustering manifest themselves as a number of interesting properties. First, as the number of requested clusters increased, keywords in each sub cluster also became increasingly biased towards individual languages. This is a favorable trait for reducing overlap since two or more streams gathering keywords of differing language should have a low rate of word overlap except in the case of multi lingually authored tweets. Secondly, despite the ability to specify the number of clusters, if the underlying similarity does not lend itself well to a high number of partitions a few of the resulting

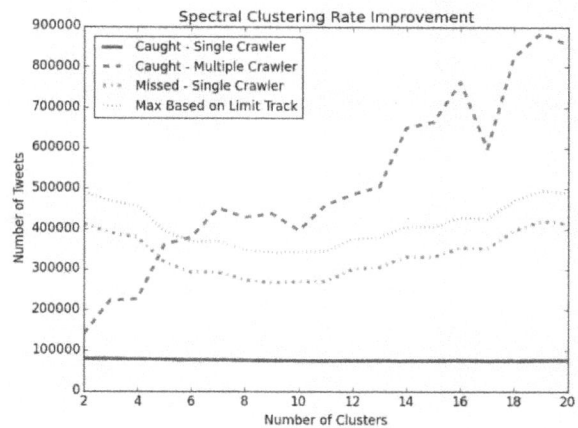

Figure 3: **The results of Spectral Clustering do show an increase of sample coverage overall. However, the clustering creates unbalanced splits where one stream, while still a good cluster, may contain significantly more words than others. The lack of balance manifests through instability in the rate of gain from each additional crawler.**

clusters will be very large while many will be small. Though this behavior is preferable for most applications that employ clustering, a significant difference in the size of clusters causes some streams to significantly over perform the 1% limit and subsequently become severely rate limited while streams based on smaller clusters fail to reach a limiting rate at all. This effect can be seen in Figure 3. Clustering based on word occurrence quickly passes the Twitter limit with only 6 streams active but shortly thereafter struggles to gain much ground. Wild fluctuation can be observed between each split level and while there is overall growth it is possible to gather a smaller sample with a larger split level. Such inconsistencies were not observed in Figure 2 further indicating how detrimental sensitivity to cluster size is when considering methods for gathering tweet samples. Spectral clustering based splits can be found in Algorithm 2.

4.3 Experiment 3 - K-Means Round Robin

The K-Means Round Robin (KMRR) approach looks to incorporate the strengths of both previous splitting methods. It borrows the near equivalently sized groups found in the round robin method which enable stable growth across split levels and the use of intelligent clustering from the spectral clustering method to reduce tweet duplication, or overlap. Rather than using spectral clustering, however, we use K-Means clustering [15]. In order to accomplish this type of non-standard clustering with K-Means we first need to convert the network graph into a dissimilarity matrix. This can be done by constructing the standard network graphs weighted adjacency matrix and normalizing by the highest occurring word pair. Next, we use the dissimilarity matrix in a process called Multidimensional Scaling, or MDS [3]. Multidimensional Scaling uses the computed dissimilarity values to transform data into another graph space - in this case two dimensions. MDS leverages the dissimilarity between each point as a measurement distance and seeks to find an embedding in the new dimensional space that maintains these

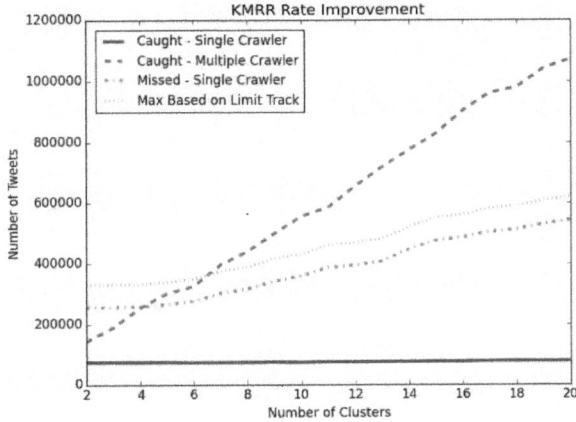

Figure 4: **KMRR splitting displays quick initial gains with a low number of crawlers while eventually settling into a steady growth rate as additional crawlers are added.**

Algorithm 2: Spectral Clustering Splits Construction

---

input : graph G, num_clusters k
output: array of lists
matrix A := [][];
for *node v in G(V, E, W)* **do**
 | wordIDs[v] := unique ID
end
/* create affinity matrix for spectral
 clustering   */
for *word pair (v1,v2) in G(V, E, W)* **do**
 | Construct symmetric matrix A for all words such
 | that v1,v2 := E.weight;
end
labels := the result of Spectral Clustering with k
clusters and the matrix A;
for *label, cluster in labels* **do**
 | splitLists[cluster].append(label)
end

---

distances as closely as possible. With our network newly transformed into a two dimensional graph, K-Means is run on the data to find centroid locations. It is important to note that we do not use the learned K-Means labels as this would not satisfy the requirement for relatively balanced keyword splits. Instead, keywords are assigned to clusters in a round robin fashion based on euclidean distance from the centroid. The combination of MDS transformation with round robin k-means centroid assignments is shown in Figure 5.

It is obvious to see that assigning words to centroids in a round robin style introduces intruding words into clusters. Accounting for word intrusion is accomplished through a convergence step. The convergence process examines the items assigned to each centroid and swaps the centroid assignment for any pair of items where doing so would reduce the average distance to each centroid following the inequality, $\frac{b_{c1}+a_{c2}}{2} < \frac{b_{c2}+a_{c1}}{2}$, where $c1$ and $c2$ are cluster centroids and the remaining variables follow the notation that a_{c1} is the distance to centroid 1 from item a. This process is repeated until no improvement can be found between

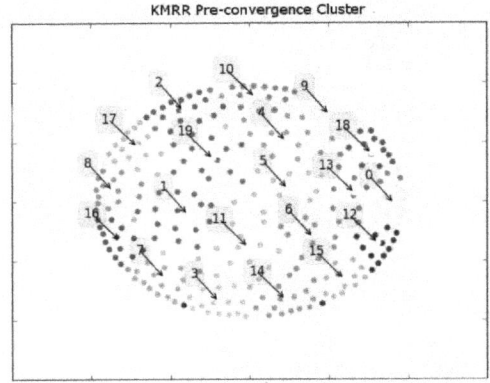

Figure 5: **After performing Multidimensional Scaling on the data set, the words are clustered according to K-means. The discovered cluster centroids are then used to create balanced groupings by assigning a centroid to the closest unassigned word in a round robin manner. However, this process introduces intruding words as the number of remaining assignments decreases.**

any pair of nodes. The convergence process is depicted in Figure 6. While performing the convergence step would normally be time consuming, the number of items clustered is never larger than 400 items. Figure 7 shows the final cluster assignments after the completion of the convergence step. These clustering assignments are completely absent of intrusion. Using this method the rate at which multiple crawlers exceed the limit track becomes comparable to spectral clustering at 7 splits as can be seen in Figure 4. Additionally, K-Means Round Robin does not suffer from the problem of inconsistency between split levels showing consistency similar to that found in the round robin experiment. KMRR-based splits can be found in Algorithm 3.

A comparison of each splitting method can be seen in Figure 9. These results, shown also in 2, are the average coverage rates related to the total sample size estimated from the limit track over 20 trials. Though the Twitter limit track is not a perfect indicator of the total population of data available from a complete set, it is used in this comparison as a relative measure as opposed to an absolute. Given additional crawlers, it is very likely that the limit track would again be eclipsed. Each splitting method was able to produce a sample significantly closer to the total population as estimated by Twitter and sometimes many times larger than a single stream.

5. CLUSTER REALIGNMENT

The next step is determining if there is a difference between results when the clusters are computed at some time variable above the reconnection limit imposed by Twitter. To accomplish this, we use one stream that runs indefinitely and constantly updates the observed weight for each word occurrence pair. This stream does not maintain a tweet set in order to keep the memory footprint from growing too large. Every 1000 seconds the cumulative network is clustered and new splits are designated for every stream.

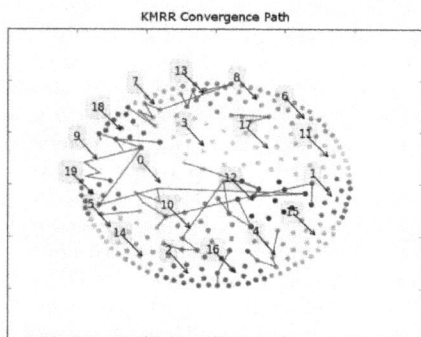

KMRR Convergence Path

Figure 6: The convergence step maintains group size by operating on pairs of nodes with differing centroid assignments. On each pass, if a pair of nodes is discovered for whom swapping them will reduce the average distance between centroids then it is considered a good swap and immediately performed. The lines between each node indicate the swap path as a pair of cluster assignments gradually improve.

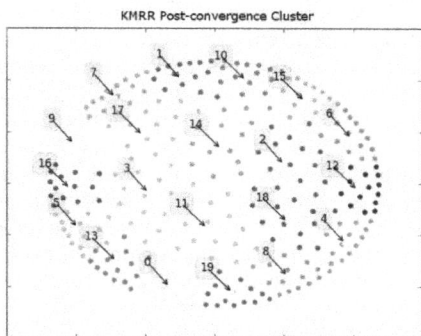

KMRR Post-convergence Cluster

Figure 7: At the completion of the KMRR convergence step, the resulting clusters can be seen to have no intruding assignments while maintaining the balanced group size between clusters.

This time step was chosen in order to avoid connection rate limiting from Twitter which will block connections from a stream if it attempts to reconnect more frequently than every 15 minutes. Unfortunately, Twitter does not supply any method for changing the search parameters of a stream without performing a reconnection so any method of cluster realignment will be unable to perform these steps more frequently than the 15 minute interval.

Cluster realignment seeks to improve the performance of the spectral clustering method as well as KMRR. Since one stream is dedicated solely to maintaining and updating the word-occurrence network, performing either of the cluster-based splitting methods at a later period of time should improve the resulting clusters. Using cluster realignment, it becomes possible to run a very short priming step or even eliminate the priming step altogether. This allows the streams to begin gathering data immediately while also reducing the overlap between each stream over time. The effect of cluster realignment can be seen in Figure 8. While the initial data

---

Algorithm 3: K-Means Round Robin Splits Construction

input : graph G, num_clusters k
output: array of lists
matrix dissimilarity := [][];
counter := 0;
for *node v in G(V, E, W)* **do**
  | wordIDs[v] := unique ID
end
max := compute highest rate of occurrence for normalization;
/* **create dissimilarity C matrix for MDS** */
for *word pair (v1,v2) in G(V, E, W)* **do**
  | Construct symmetric dissimilarity matrix for all words such that v1,v2 := | $E.weight - max$ | ;
end
wordGraph is the result of Multidimensional Scaling of the dissimilarity matrix to 2 dimensions;
labels := KMeans(num_clusters = k, data = wordGraph)
for *i := 0 to number_of_keywords* **do**
  | assign keyword i to the closest cluster centroid
end
/* **enter convergence step** */
while *any improvement can be found* **do**
  | **for** *i := 0 to number_of_clusters* **do**
  | | **for** *j := i to number_of_clusters* **do**
  | | | **if** *swapping a point in each cluster would reduce the average distance to each centroid* **then**
  | | | | swap cluster assignments
  | | | **end**
  | | **end**
  | **end**
end
for *label, cluster in labels* **do**
  | splitLists[cluster].append(label)
end

gathering rate using this method can be somewhat unstable, over a period of time the number of tweets gathered per second does become stable and shows an overall increase. Over larger periods of time, the word occurrence network becomes increasingly stable, and, as a result, the overall increase of performing realignment becomes less efficient. This is especially true when considering that performing clustering, disconnection, and reconnection can take some time and introduce small gaps into the dataset. Twitter streams also do not return immediately to their highest potential data rate which introduces a dip in the number of tweets obtained for a small period of time. Overall, cluster realignment improves the possible data rate but these factors should be considered when implementing a realignment scheme.

6. LANGUAGE CLUSTERING

In spectral clustering based on word co-occurrence, about 72% of the largest clusters were one language with a mix of words from other languages. When k = 20, many of the smaller clusters were completely biased towards their language to the point that they were always very close to, if not completely from, a single language. The high rate of

243

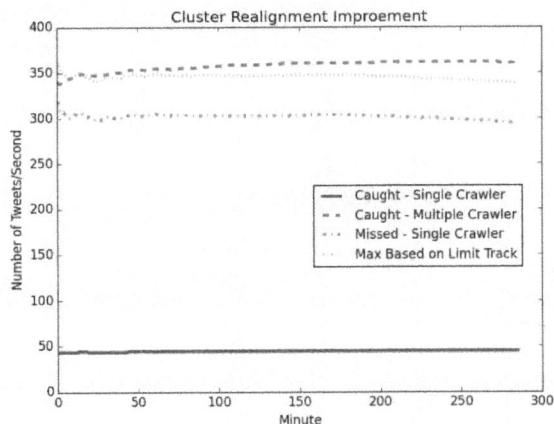

Figure 8: Performing cluster realignment by maintaining and updating the word co-occurrence graph over a long period of time can improve the number of tweets gathered per second without the need to introduce additional crawlers. Initially, the lack of a significant sample for the co-occurrence graph causes fluctuations in the gathering rate but as the sample size increases the volume of data per second becomes stable and is still able to maintain a constant rate of growth even as the amount of data in the population (limit maximum) reduces.

strong language clusters is a good indicator of correct cluster assignments. In all methods, a high rate of language clustering should result in searches with less overlap. Future methods for search improvement should seek a balance between language clusters, word co-occurrence overlap reduction, and maximum per-crawler stream utilization.

KMRR also displayed this property by produced heavily language-biased clusters but, as is likely the result of the round robin process, few of the clusters were completely from a single language. There is a potential for optimization within the KMRR clustering process where by producing slightly less balanced clusters in exchange for improved language clustering may produce better results. On the far end of the spectrum, the round robin method seemed to produce a completely mixed set of language keywords as is expected. Further experiments would need to be run with attention paid particularly to the language bias from these clustering methods in order to obtain a better understanding of the effect of language clusters on streamed search results.

7. CONCLUSION

We ask whether the volume of data missed, as reported by the Twitter limit track system, is an accurate and useful measurement for determining sample size. Furthermore, we ask whether standard methods used for gathering streamed data from the Twittersphere can be improved to increase coverage for a gathered dataset. To answer these questions, we used a battery of twenty streams as well as a single comprehensive baseline stream to gather tweets for a large number of high volume keywords. We provide a methodology for comparing relative improvement in sample size in the absence of reliable reporting as well as a series of algorithms capable of a multiplicative increase in sample coverage.

We started our analysis by inspecting the performance of the Twitter limit track process in single and multi-stream situations. It has been assumed that the Twitter limit track provides an accurate metric for the overall size of a dataset with a given set of keywords. When using a single stream, the limit values returned, in addition to the number of tweets gathered, should be the size of the complete data set if it were possible to obtain all 100%. However, the simple addition of extra streams operating on subsections of the same keywords were able to quickly overtake the hypothetical maximum volume of unique tweets. Such ease in producing beyond the maximum limit as calculated by Twitter cast serious doubts on the validity of the limit track system. In the absence of a well-defined baseline we employed a relative method to measure improvement obtained through alternative streaming methods.

Next, we proposed a series of methods for separating keywords in order to obtain the best possible sample coverage. The simplest proposed method, Round Robin splitting, displayed stable sample growth with the addition of each stream and was able to overtake the Twitter-calculated complete set. The stability of growth indicated the importance of balancing keywords across streams - a property that would later be employed in K-Means Round Robin.

The second method, Spectral Cluster splitting, again employed a word co-occurrence graph to build a similarity matrix. The clusters obtained in this manner tended to vary significantly in size but showed interesting properties, such as a tendency for languages to cluster together. Spectral Cluster-based streams showed the sharpest rate of initial growth with a smaller number of streams. However, when the number of streams grew large the volume of increase with each stream became unstable as a result of small clusters failing to fully populate the stream bandwidth.

Using the lessons learned from Round Robin splitting and Spectral Cluster splitting, we proposed a balanced solution in K-Means Round Robin. KMRR uses K-Means clustering before following a convergence process to produce balanced cluster sizes while maintaining as much of the original clustering properties as possible. KMRR showed the rapid initial growth displayed by Spectral Clustering as well as the stability obtained from Round Robin splitting. While clusters still displayed a tendency to group by language, each cluster had a higher rate of out-of-language word intrusion than was seen in the Spectral Clustering results. Each of these methods allow for cluster re-computation on the fly, and improvements to the rate of tweets obtained per second were seen when periodically realigning from an improved word co-occurrence graph.

There are many interesting possible extensions to this work. Since it can be shown that the Twitter limit track is not a true indication of the overall population for a given search, further inquiry into the methods used for calculating the limit may reveal interesting features of the Twitter tweet dissemination process and provide insight to the source of bias observed in Twitter streams. While our experiments focused on a single feature of each keyword, the co-occurrence rate, the language clustering side effect indicates that there are potentially other features that may introduce sources of overlap. An example of this would be the semantic meaning between each keyword where there may be potential for further reduction of overlap by seperating keywords with similar meaning. Identification of other such features could

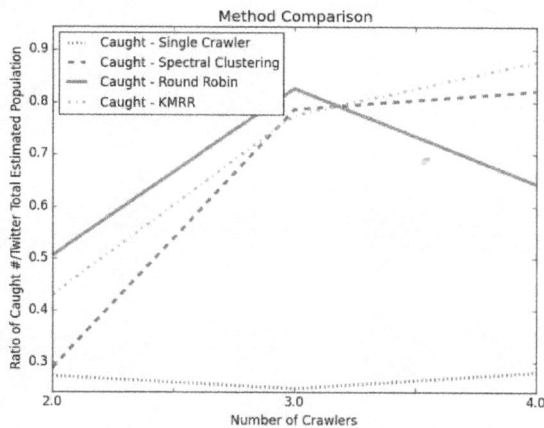

Figure 9: This graph shows the average sample coverage for a given set of search keywords across 20 trials. Each of our sampling methods significantly outperform the single stream with some variation in characteristics between each method.

Table 2: Sample Coverage of Total Population

	Unsplit	2-split	3-split	4-split
Round Robin	19.02%	50.54%	82.58%	64.34%
Spectral Clustering	19.02%	28.95%	78.63%	82.08%
KMRR	19.02%	42.93%	77.45%	87.63%

further strengthen the gathering process and lead to better and less biased samples.

8. ACKNOWLEDGEMENTS

This work is sponsored, in part, by Office of Naval Research grant N000141410095.

9. REFERENCES

[1] H. Achrekar, A. Gandhe, R. Lazarus, S.-H. Yu, and B. Liu. Predicting Flu Trends using Twitter Data. In *INFOCOM*, pages 702–707. IEEE, 2011.

[2] S. Asur and B. A. Huberman. Predicting the Future with Social Media. In *WI-IAT*, volume 1, pages 492–499. IEEE, 2010.

[3] I. Borg and P. J. Groenen. *Modern Multidimensional Scaling: Theory and Applications*. Springer Science & Business Media, 2005.

[4] A. Ceron, L. Curini, S. M. Iacus, and G. Porro. Every Tweet Counts? How Sentiment Analysis of Social Media can Improve our Knowledge of Citizens' Political Preferences with an Application to Italy and France. *New Media & Society*, 16(2):340–358, 2014.

[5] B. Efron and R. J. Tibshirani. *An Introduction to the Bootstrap*. CRC press, 1994.

[6] M. Garcia-Herranz, E. Moro, M. Cebrian, N. A. Christakis, and J. H. Fowler. Using friends as sensors to detect global-scale contagious outbreaks. *PLoS ONE*, 9(4):e92413, 04 2014.

[7] S. Ghosh, M. B. Zafar, P. Bhattacharya, N. Sharma, N. Ganguly, and K. Gummadi. On Sampling the

Wisdom of Crowds: Random vs. Expert Sampling of the Twitter Stream. In *CIKM*, pages 1739–1744. ACM, 2013.

[8] J. Gomide, A. Veloso, W. Meira Jr, V. Almeida, F. Benevenuto, F. Ferraz, and M. Teixeira. Dengue Surveillance Based on a Computational Model of Spatio-temporal Locality of Twitter. In *WebSci*, pages 1–8. ACM, 2011.

[9] S. González-Bailón, N. Wang, A. Rivero, J. Borge-Holthoefer, and Y. Moreno. Assessing the Bias in Samples of Large Online Networks. *Social Networks*, 38:16–27, 2014.

[10] K. Joseph, P. M. Landwehr, and K. M. Carley. Two 1%s Don't Make a Whole: Comparing Simultaneous Samples from Twitter's Streaming API. In *Social Computing, Behavioral-Cultural Modeling and Prediction*, pages 75–83. Springer, 2014.

[11] D. Kerg, R. Roedler, and S. Seeber. On the Endogenesis of Twitter's Spritzer and Gardenhose Sample Streams. In *ASONAM*, pages 357–364, 2014.

[12] S. Kumar, G. Barbier, M. A. Abbasi, and H. Liu. TweetTracker: An Analysis Tool for Humanitarian and Disaster Relief. In *ICWSM*, pages 661–662, 2011.

[13] R. Li, S. Wang, and K. C.-C. Chang. Towards Social Data Platform: Automatic Topic-focused Monitor for Twitter Stream. *VLDB*, 6(14):1966–1977, 2013.

[14] Y. Lu, F. Wang, and R. Maciejewski. Business Intelligence from Social Media: A Study from the VAST Box Office Challenge. *Computer Graphics and Applications, IEEE*, 34(5):58–69, Sept 2014.

[15] J. MacQueen et al. Some Methods for Classification and Analysis of Multivariate Observations. In *BSMSP*, volume 1, pages 281–297. Oakland, CA, USA., 1967.

[16] L. Madlberger and A. Almansour. Predictions Based on Twitter-A Critical View on the Research Process. In *ICODSE*, pages 1–6. IEEE, 2014.

[17] F. Morstatter, N. Lubold, H. Pon-Barry, J. Pfeffer, and H. Liu. Finding Eyewitness Tweets During Crises. *ACL*, pages 23–27, 2014.

[18] F. Morstatter, J. Pfeffer, and H. Liu. When is it Biased?: Assessing the Representativeness of Twitter's Streaming API. In *WWW*, pages 555–556, 2014.

[19] F. Morstatter, J. Pfeffer, H. Liu, and K. M. Carley. Is the Sample Good Enough? Comparing Data from Twitter's Streaming API with Twitter's Firehose. In *ICWSM*, pages 400–408, 2013.

[20] A. Y. Ng, M. I. Jordan, and Y. Weiss. On Spectral Clustering: Analysis and an Algorithm. In *NIPS*, pages 849–856. MIT Press, 2001.

[21] Z. Tufekci. Big Questions for Social Media Big Data: Representativeness, Validity and Other Methodological Pitfalls. In *ICWSM*, pages 505–514, 2014.

[22] A. Tumasjan, T. O. Sprenger, P. G. Sandner, and I. M. Welpe. Predicting Elections with Twitter: What 140 Characters Reveal about Political Sentiment. *ICWSM*, 10:178–185, 2010.

[23] S. Vieweg, A. L. Hughes, K. Starbird, and L. Palen. Microblogging During Two Natural Hazards Events: What Twitter May Contribute to Situational Awareness. In *CHI*, pages 1079–1088. ACM, 2010.

Other Times, Other Values:
Leveraging Attribute History to Link User Profiles across Online Social Networks

Paridhi Jain
Indraprastha Institute of
Information Technology (IIIT-D),
India
paridhij@iiitd.ac.in

Ponnurangam Kumaraguru
Indraprastha Institute of
Information Technology (IIIT-D),
India
pk@iiitd.ac.in

Anupam Joshi
University of Maryland, Baltimore
County (UMBC),
USA
joshi@cs.umbc.edu

ABSTRACT

Profile linking is the ability to connect profiles of a user on different social networks. Linked profiles can help companies like Disney to build psychographics of potential customers and segment them for targeted marketing in a cost-effective way. Existing methods link profiles by observing high similarity between most recent (current) values of the attributes like name and username. However, for a section of users observed to evolve their attributes over time and choose dissimilar values across their profiles, these current values have low similarity. Existing methods then falsely conclude that profiles refer to different users. To reduce such false conclusions, we suggest to gather rich history of values assigned to an attribute over time and compare attribute histories to link user profiles across networks. We believe that attribute history highlights user preferences for creating attribute values on a social network. Co-existence of these preferences across profiles on different social networks result in alike attribute histories that suggests profiles potentially refer to a single user. Through a focused study on *username*, we quantify the importance of username history for profile linking on a dataset of real-world users with profiles on Twitter, Facebook, Instagram and Tumblr. We show that username history correctly links 44% more profile pairs with non-matching current values that are incorrectly unlinked by existing methods. We further explore if factors such as longevity and availability of username history on either profiles affect linking performance. To the best of our knowledge, this is the first study that explores viability of using an attribute history to link profiles on social networks.

1. INTRODUCTION

Today, Online Social Networks (OSNs) offer innovative services that ease the access to news, campaigns, art, talent, business opportunities and personal connections. For instance, Twitter's retweet feature enables quick access to news, campaigns, and crisis information while pin boards of Pinterest facilitate reach to the work of artists, photographers, and fashion designers. In order to enjoy these services simultaneously, a user innocuously registers herself on multiple OSNs. During registration, she shares personal infor-

mation, lists her friends and later creates content to share with her friends. The quality, quantity and veracity of the information created and shared by her vary with the OSN, thereby resulting in dissimilar profiles of the same user, scattered on the world wide web, with no explicit links directing to one another. These disparate profiles liberate her from any privacy concerns that could emerge if the profiles were implicitly collated. However, linking these disparate unlinked profiles can benefit various stakeholders.

Companies like Disney and PepsiCo carry out psychographic segmentation based upon customers' activities, interests, opinions and lifestyles to adapt marketing strategies on their needs [2]. It is the most effective segmentation citing a rise of 24% in business performance [27]; however includes high cost in both time and money [8]. The cost of constructing psychographics of each customer can be brought down with the use of her linked social profiles [4]. Social media marketers often run a campaign on multiple online social platforms like blogs and OSNs and offline platforms like TV to maximize reach to their customers. Often, they need to estimate audience size to measure the success of the campaign. An arithmetic sum of users from each platform is inflated as users can engage in the same campaign via their multiple OSN profiles. Therefore, it is important to de-duplicate users across platforms by linking their profiles in order to estimate campaign ratings and invest accordingly [1, 5].

Profile linking methods compare attributes like username and name to find connection between a pair of profiles. However, challenges like dissonant social platforms with partially overlapping list of supported attributes and heterogenous attributes holding veracious values impede effective profile linking. Literature suggests various methodologies equipped with tools that compare overlapping attributes of examined user profiles and match attributes on different metrics. Similarity between text attributes like name is estimated using Jaro similarity while media attributes like profile-picture are compared using face detection algorithms and histogram matching [13, 14, 17, 20, 26]. These methodologies consider most recent (current) values of the attributes and assume high similarity to infer a link between respective profiles. However, the low similarity between these values need *not* imply different users for reasons such as attribute evolution over time [16, 18]. Consider the following scenario – A user registers on Twitter and Facebook with the same username value, she favors Twitter and updates her Twitter profile more frequently than her Facebook profile. After a few weeks, she chooses a new username on Twitter but makes no such changes on Facebook. Due to evolution of username over time on a favored social network, she now owns dissimilar usernames on her profiles. On observing dissimilarity, existing methods that match

HT '15, September 1–4, 2015, Guzelyurt, Northern Cyprus.
© 2015 ACM. ISBN 978-1-4503-3395-5/15/09$15.00
DOI: http://dx.doi.org/10.1145/2700171.2791040.

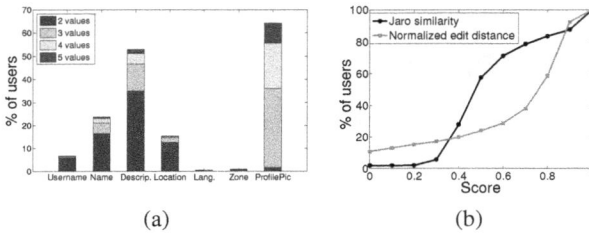

Figure 1: Attribute evolution on Twitter. (a) Around 73.21% users tend to change their attributes on Twitter. (b) Users who evolve their username have low similarity between usernames across their profiles. For these users, attribute history can be leveraged for profile linking.

only username falsely conclude that Twitter and Facebook profiles refer to different users.

To examine if a significant section of users change attributes, we deploy an automated system to track 8.7 million Twitter users every fortnight and record changes to their attributes. Figure 1(a) shows the distribution of users that evolve over time and hold distinct values for their attributes. On a two month period, we observe that 73.21% users change their attributes and assign distinct values. Thereby, we gather that attribute evolution is an evident phenomenon. Further, we test if evolution causes dissimilar current values across profiles of users and hence, filter users who evolve their usernames. We compute Jaro similarity and Edit distance between usernames across their profiles and plot the user distribution (see Figure 1(b)). Observe that 78% users have usernames with Jaro similarity < 0.7 and 62% users with Edit distance > 0.7 implying dissimilar values for a majority section of users. Thus, due to username evolution, current usernames have low similarity which is falsely manipulated by existing methods as different users.

For the section of users who evolve and select dissimilar attribute values across profiles, we propose to collect rich information created due to their tendency towards evolution i.e. past values. These past values created by a user, termed as *attribute history*, reveal her preferences and behavior while creating them like the choice of length or characters of username. Co-existence of user preferences across her profiles on different OSNs for a prolonged period of time create alike attribute histories, thus suggesting a potential link to a single user. We, therefore, present the first study that quantifies importance of attribute history to link profiles that are missed by existing methods on observing dissimilar current values. For the aforementioned scenario, due to user's initial choice to select same username across her profiles, past username on Twitter is an exact match to current username on Facebook, and hence an inspection of username history correctly links the profiles. We also cater to the likelihood of different user profiles with similar attribute values.

Scope: A user profile is composed of multiple attributes; each signifies a unique characteristic of the user. Among the attributes, literature suggests username to be an important and discriminating attribute for profile linking [19, 22, 28]. Though a small section of users change username on Twitter (<10%), it is the most common publicly available attribute across OSNs that can uniquely identify users within an OSN. In addition to availability and uniqueness, usernames can only contain alphanumeric and special characters irrespective of the preferred language of the user profile, thereby allowing clean string comparisons. We, therefore, choose to track changes to *username*, collect a set of values, and use the value set for profile linking. History of other attributes like name, description and profile-picture can further help in identifying user profiles of the same user; however lack of their universal support and

availability across social platforms direct us to limit our scope to only username. For this study, we ask following research question: *Given two user profiles and respective username histories on a pair of OSNs, can we predict that profiles belong to the same user?*

Contributions: On a labelled dataset of 128,251 pairs of username histories accessed from users with profiles on four popular social networks – Twitter, Instagram, Facebook and Tumblr, we examine the viability of using username history for profile linking and impact of various factors that govern its effectiveness. We show that:

- Out of 89% profile pairs that current values fail to link, a comparison of username histories correctly link 44% profile pairs while keeping a false positive rate of 1.65%. Therefore, attribute history helps profile linking.

- Out of 45% profile pairs that username history fails to link, 90.88% results from Twitter-Tumblr profile comparisons, while 5.50% results from Twitter-Instagram profile comparisons. Therefore, effectiveness of attribute history varies with the choice of OSNs user profiles belong to.

- Availability of username history only on one profile increases false linkings by 12% as compared to its availability on both.

- Importance of username history for profile linking is directly proportional to its longevity.

To the best of our knowledge, this is the first study that provides insights about estimating the use of attribute history for profile linking. We believe that attribute history can also help other applications that are build on derived behavioral characteristics of users.

2. PROBLEM STATEMENT

We now formally define the research question using following definitions and notations. User profiles under examination belong to a pair of social networks, SN_A and SN_B, termed as *source profile S* and *candidate profile C*, respectively. An evolved *username* set U is a set of pairs, where each pair contains new value and time of evolution of the attribute, ordered on time of evolution i.e. $U = \{(u_1, t_1), (u_2, t_2), \cdots, (u_L, t_L)\}$, where $t_i < t_{i+1}$. Here, L denotes the length of the username set, t_1 denotes the time when first username change is recorded and t_L denotes the time last username change is recorded; u_L represents the most recent (current) value. Username sets on source and candidate profiles are denoted by U_S and U_C, respectively. If past usernames of the candidate profile are *not* available, set U_C is replaced by the current username u_c. We define our problem as –

Given a source profile S on SN_A, a candidate profile C on SN_B and their respective username sets U_S and U_C, each composed of pairs of usernames and their receptive evolution timestamps, find if U_S and U_C refer to the same user $\mathcal{I}$.

A collection of methods can solve the problem. Heuristic approaches like rule based methods, collaborative approaches like crowd sourcing and manual tagging, and algorithmic approaches like machine learning can look for similarities between username sets and infer the potential link between them.

We model profile linking as a classification problem with three phases – feature extraction, labelled dataset collection and supervised machine learning algorithm usage for correct profile identification (see Figure 2). Features extract similarities between usernames across username sets by capturing unique behavioral charac-

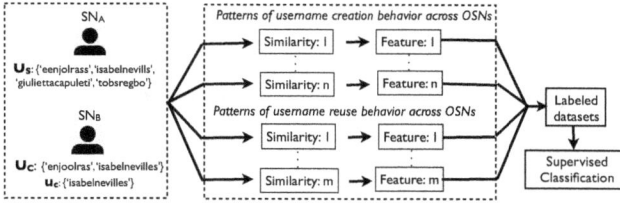

Figure 2: Proposed methodology to compare username sets and capture similarities based on unique behavioral patterns while creating and reusing usernames over time.

teristics and consistent preferences that a user exhibits while choosing usernames across her profiles over time (Section 3); Labelled datasets collect users who evolve their usernames on popular social networks (Section 5) followed by supervised classification by a single and an ensemble of classifiers organized in a framework (Section 6). Section 7 describes relevance of our study to related literature. Finally, Section 8 presents discussion and Section 9 concludes this research with directions for future work.

3. FEATURES

Users often exhibit consistent behavior while creating their attribute values across their profiles on different social networks. Cross-OSN analysis of users on OSNs shows that 85% users have more then 50% matching attribute values across different OSNs [7]. These attributes, however, evolve over time, leading to matching histories than current values. Further, a recent study shows that users exhibit similar choices while selecting usernames across OSNs [28]. We believe that such choices may co-exist and repeat over time.

User preferences while creating usernames on her profiles are affected by self-bias and limited memory. Biased choices push users to create similar usernames across her profiles resulting in username creation behavioral patterns. Limited memory constrains users to reuse a username either used in the past within or across OSN profiles, thus producing username reuse behavioral patterns. We discuss these patterns and quantify them into features.

3.1 Username creation

On a social network, users converse by tagging another user's username with '@' tag. Tagged user specifies username properties that aid these interactions. For instance, a user chooses short usernames on OSNs that restrict message length to help her friends post more content when tagging her [3]. Choice of username properties that remain static over time as well as repeat across OSNs constitute *static behavioral patterns*. For instance, a static choice of a user to create short username across OSNs is a static behavioral pattern.

With time, changing expectations from an OSN can push her to change a few username properties but reflect the same changes across her other OSN profiles. Similar transitions in username properties constitute *temporal behavioral patterns*. For instance, the user later realizes that short usernames confuse her followers, therefore now creates long personalized usernames. Such a transition in user behavior, if evident across all her OSN profiles, results in a temporal behavioral pattern. We now explore methods to quantify these patterns.

3.1.1 Static behavioral patterns

Username creation behavior can be captured by observing three string properties of usernames – length, choice of characters, and the arrangement of characters. It is likely for a user to create usernames of similar length with a limited set of characters compiled in

similar fashion. For both source and candidate username sets, we calculate these properties and compare using different methods.

Length of a username l_{u_i} is calculated by counting alphanumeric characters in the username. Length distribution of usernames in source $\mathcal{L}_S$ is compared with that of usernames in candidate username set $\mathcal{L}_C$ using JS divergence. The low divergence hints use of similar username lengths across OSNs.

To compare choice of characters, we compare character distribution of usernames in source $\mathcal{C}_S$ with that of usernames in candidate username set $\mathcal{C}_C$ using Jaccard similarity index J and cosine similarity cos. The best value at '1' for both metrics implies same choice of characters on username sets, made by the same user.

To compare the arrangement of characters, we compute string similarity between usernames of different sets. We calculate normalized Longest Common Subsequence (LCS) similarity score between u_i and u_j such that u_i, u_j belong to different sets and estimate mean, median and standard deviation of score distribution $\mathcal{A}$. The low standard deviation of the distribution hints similar arrangement of characters likely to be made by the same user while high mean and median values denote the high similarity among usernames in the two sets. In a nutshell, static features are:

$$F_{static} : (JS(\mathcal{L}_S || \mathcal{L}_C), J(\mathcal{C}_S, \mathcal{C}_C), cos(\mathcal{C}_S, \mathcal{C}_C), \mathbb{E}(\mathcal{A}),$$
$$med(\mathcal{A}), \ \sigma(\mathcal{A}))$$

3.1.2 Temporal behavioral patterns

With changing requirements on an OSN over time like privacy concerns, a user can consider to change a few properties of new usernames she creates within an OSN. For instance, user can start using initials over full name in her username, thereby anonymizing and shortening its length. It is likely that her new preferences influence usernames created on other OSNs as well. Similar transitions in selected properties of username with time across OSNs result in similar evolutionary patterns of properties. We capture such patterns by comparing evolution sequence of the username properties computed for each username set.

Consecutive usernames of each username set are compared on length, character distribution and arrangement of characters, resulting in three comparison vectors for each set – length, character, and arrangement vector. Length vector $\mathbb{L}$ is a sequence of lengths l_{u_i}, character vector $\mathbb{C}$ is a sequence of Jaccard index and cosine similarity scores between character distribution while arrangement vector $\mathbb{A}$ is a sequence of string similarity scores between consecutive usernames of a username set. For the arrangement vector, we use four string similarity metrics – Edit distance, Jaro similarity, LCS similarity and Longest Common Substring similarity (LCSub). Multiple similarity metrics ensures different penalties for character insertion and deletions. Normalized versions of string similarity scores are used in the arrangement vectors.

Length, character and arrangement vectors for two username sets are compared to find any correlation between the two sets. We use normalized cross-correlation (NCC) to compute the correlation, whose values ranges from -1 to 1. This metric is used to find correlation between two time series data lists as a function of lag τ at which the time series best align each other, also used for temporal analysis on Twitter in [24]. A positive correlation implies similar pattern of evolution of the username property on both username sets, from which we may link username sets to the same user. In a nutshell,

$$F_{temporal} : (NCC(\mathbb{L}_S, \mathbb{L}_C), NCC(\mathbb{C}_S, \mathbb{C}_C), NCC(\mathbb{A}_S, \mathbb{A}_C))$$

3.2 Username reuse

With an increasing number of OSNs and evolving preferences, a user struggles to remember her latest usernames on all OSNs in order to sign in or use the usernames for interactions. However, a naive reuse of a username borrowed from her other OSN profiles can ease her cognitive load [28]. Reused username can either be a latest username or an old username from any of her OSN profiles. Frequent tendency to reuse a username from other profiles results in a set of common usernames appearing in the same order at the same time across user profiles indicating user synchronous behavior across her profiles.

3.2.1 Occasional reuse

User's choice of reusing a username from her other profiles at least once results in observing that username on different profiles at different times. To find the common username, we intersect username lists extracted from each username set. If the intersection results in an empty set, there is a possibility that the username she wants to use is already taken by a different user within the OSN. In that case, user can make minor modifications to the selected username to create an available version and use the available version on the OSN. With minor modifications, selected username and its available version have a high string similarity score. We, therefore, perform pairwise comparisons between usernames from different sets to find best matching username pair,

$$\max_{(u_i,t_i)\in U_S,(u_j,t_j)\in U_C} Sim(u_i,u_j)$$

We compute the similarity based on four string based metrics – edit distance, jaro similarity, LCSub similarity and LCS similarity. We acknowledge that the existence of a common username or a pair of similar usernames between two username sets can be co-incidental. It is likely that different users pick the same username at some point in their past. This can happen to usernames derived from celebrity, brand or popular names. Therefore, we calculate second best similarity score between usernames from different sets. A low second best similarity indicates that the best similarity can be an outlier, implying that username sets refer to different persons.

3.2.2 Frequent reuse

Repeated use of borrowed usernames results in a set of common usernames between profiles of a user. We examine if there exists a set of common usernames and compute a boolean feature. We estimate the ratio of common usernames to the size of smaller username set which denotes if all (or few) usernames are copied from other OSN profiles. A sequential and simultaneous use of common usernames across OSNs lends support to the belief that username sets refer to the same user. It is highly unlikely for different users to choose same usernames in the same order at the same time across multiple OSNs. Further, similar sequential ordering of common usernames in both sets is an indicator of a single user consistently choosing same usernames over time across her profiles. Earlier research suggests Smith-Waterman algorithm as an effective algorithm to measure sequential ordering [13], originally proposed to perform sequence alignment in protein sequences [25]. We use Smith-Waterman similarity to estimate sequential ordering between common usernames in the username sets. To capture temporal synchrony, we use timestamps of evolution to find if same usernames are used on both sets at the same time.

As described earlier, users may make minor modifications to a selected username, in order to create an available version to use on the OSN. We incorporate such minor modifications while calculating set of common usernames. We consider two usernames as

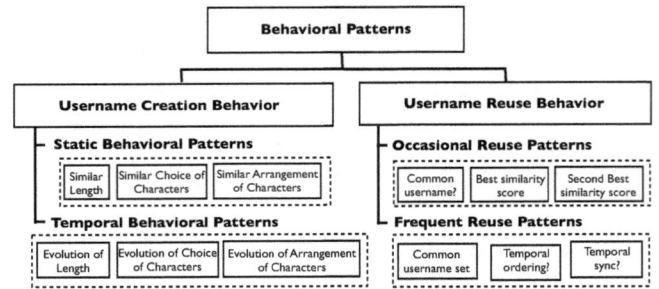

Figure 3: Various username creation and reuse behavioral patterns of users.

variations of the same username, if LCS string similarity is above a threshold. We adjust the threshold from 0.8 to 1 and compute set of common usernames and other features accordingly.

To summarize, we list possible similarities between username sets resulting from synchronous user behavior when selecting usernames within and across OSNs over time. Discussed methods quantify these similarities into a set of twenty-six normalized features. We extract these features from a labeled dataset of username sets, learn a supervised classifier and use it to predict connection between test username sets. In scenarios where past usernames are accessible only on one user profile, we compute static behavioral patterns of username creation and occasional reuse between the source username set on source profile and candidate current username.

4. FRAMEWORK

We experiment with two plausible supervised frameworks – Independent framework and Cascaded framework.

4.1 Independent framework

Most profile linking approaches use a feature set, labelled dataset and a single classifier to predict link between test profiles [17, 19, 22, 28]. Classifier decision is not revised further either manually or computationally. We experiment with such a framework by learning a supervised classifier on proposed features extracted from username sets in the labelled datasets (see Figure 4(a)). However, we suspect the dominance of a subset of features that extract similarities between histories than current values. Hence, trained classifier can be biased towards finding similar histories and can falsely label username sets with dissimilar past but similar current values as negative. To avoid this, we suggest cascaded framework.

4.2 Cascaded framework

Cascaded framework is an ensemble of two classifiers trained on different features to uncover link between two profiles and is extensively used in machine learning domain [12]. **Classifier I** extracts current username features and uses an existing method to classify username sets while **Classifier II** extracts proposed username set features and uses a supervised classifier to re-classify username sets labelled as negative by **Classifier I** (see Figure 4(b)). We further experiment with two existing profile linking methods as **Classifier I** and different supervised classification techniques as **Classifier II** of the framework. These existing methods act as baselines, also used in [19, 28] to evaluate performance of the suggested features:

- **Exact matching (b1):** Two username sets are linked if current usernames are an exact match.

- **Substring matching (b2):** Two username sets are linked if substring similarity score between respective current usernames is beyond a threshold. We use Jaro similarity score to

(a) Independent framework

(b) Cascaded framework

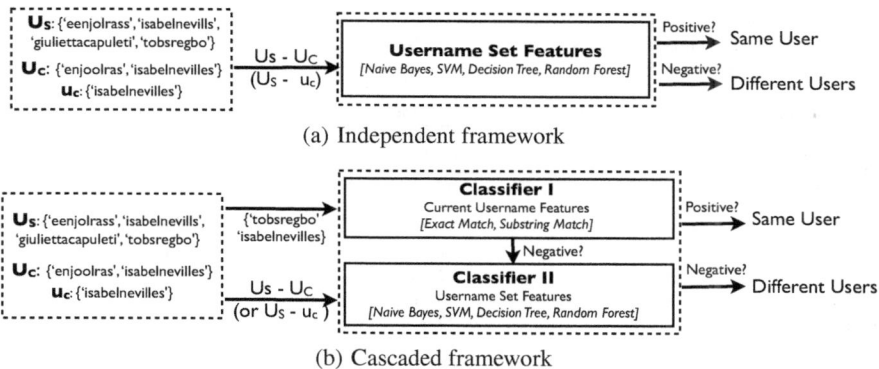

Figure 4: Independent v/s cascaded framework. Independent framework uses proposed features to classify username sets while cascaded framework uses proposed features to re-classify username sets predicted as negative by another classifier.

compute substring similarity, and vary the threshold to report best achieved accuracy.

5. DATA COLLECTION

For a positive dataset, we need to know accounts of a user on multiple OSNs. We start with Twitter, choose a random set of users and find their profiles on three popular social networks that contain quality information about a user[1] – Facebook, Instagram, and Tumblr. All networks, except Facebook, allow multiple changes to username. Facebook allows username change only once.

Ground Truth: One way to identify other OSN profiles of selected Twitter users is by manually search for the profiles, which is cumbersome and time-consuming. Another way is to exploit the tendency of users to broadcast hyperlinks to other OSN profiles via URL attribute of their Twitter profiles [15]. Such users *self-identify* themselves on other OSNs. For instance, a user posts *www.facebook.com/username* on her URL attribute, thereby informing other Twitter users about her Facebook profile. Similar methods are used in literature to create positive datasets either from social aggregation sites, forums or social networks where users *self-list* their OSN accounts [28].

Username History: Once user profiles are identified across OSNs, we collect past usernames owned by the user profiles. We build an independent tracking system for Twitter to monitor any changes to 8.7 million randomly chosen Twitter profiles as on October 2013. Tracking system repeatedly query Twitter Search API with *user_id* of the user profile after every fortnight and store responses mentioning username, name, URL and similar details, user owns at the time of the query. The system then compare consecutive API-responses to take a note of any changes to usernames, names, URLs, etc. Unique usernames chosen by the queried user profile over the tracking period of October 1, 2013 to November 26, 2013, constitute past username set on Twitter. Note that, the system collects only publicly available data on social networks and does not engage in any user authorization asking for private data.

To gather past usernames used on other OSN profiles of the user, one can deploy a similar independent tracking system to track each OSN profile. However, configuring and deploying a tracking system for each OSN requires extensive infrastructure.[2] To reduce infrastructure costs, we use an alternate way to record user-

name changes on other OSNs. We record URL attribute of the Twitter user profile to mark any changes to her username on other OSN. For instance, a Twitter user puts her URL attribute from *www.instagram.com/happygu!* to *www.instagram.com/gulben!* to notify Twitter followers (or others) about her new username on Instagram. We exploit this method to record username changes on users' Facebook, Instagram or Tumblr profiles. We also time username changes on the social networks. Other methods to collect past usernames are discussed in Section 8.

Pre-processing: Recorded usernames on Twitter, Facebook, Instagram and Tumblr profiles are processed prior comparison. Usernames on most social networks are case-insensitive, therefore, usernames are converted to lower case. Further, different OSNs allow a different set of special characters in the usernames. Twitter allows underscore '_', Tumblr allows the hyphen '-', Instagram and Facebook allow dot '.'. A user's wish to reuse a past username on other OSN in its exact form can be restricted by the use of special characters. She needs to replace the special characters with those allowed on the other OSN. To avoid low similarities or miss exact username matches between two username sets, we remove special characters from the usernames. Since no feature captures choice of special characters, their removal will not affect our results.

Dataset: Without the loss of generalizability, we use Twitter profile as a source profile and the corresponding username set as a source username set U_S for our experiments. We use other OSN profile (Tumblr, Facebook or Instagram) as a candidate profile and the respective username set as a candidate username set U_C. If candidate usernames set is not accessible, current username of the candidate profile is used as u_c. Post processing, we collect 18,959 $U_S - U_C$ username set pairs and 109,292 $U_S - u_c$ pairs, totaling 128,251 instances whose username sets are known to belong to a single user and hence are positive instances (see Table 1). We create an equal number of negative instances, by randomly pairing a username set of a positive instance with a username (set) of a different positive instance, which are known to belong to different users. We extract features from positive and negative instances and use features in an engineered framework that effectively classifies username sets as same or different users.

Table 1: Datasets capture username changes of 128,251 users within two months on source and candidate networks.

	Tumblr	Facebook	Instagram	Total
$U_S - U_C$	14,301	1,166	3,492	18,959
$U_S - u_c$	58,285	31,076	19,931	109,292

---

[1] http://mashable.com/2013/04/12/social-media-demographic-breakdown/

[2] Tumblr API does not share a unique *user_id* of a user to keep track of changes to her Tumblr profile, hence development of an automated tracking system is challenging.

Table 2: Accuracy, FNR and FPR of supervised frameworks, baselines learned using current username features and their integration with another classifier learned on proposed feature set using different supervised classification techniques.

Framework Config.	$U_S - U_C$ Accuracy	FNR	FPR	$U_S - u_c$ Accuracy	FNR	FPR
Independent [Naive Bayes]	72.19%	55.86%	0.13%	73.58%	48.15%	4.7%
Cascaded [b1→Naive Bayes]	72.48 %	55.27%	0.14%	73.59%	47.12%	5.7%
Exact Match (b1)	55.38%	89.34%	0.00%	59.26%	84.61%	0.00%
Substring Match (b2)	60.99%	78.46%	0.00%	58.25%	83.53%	0.00%
b1 → Naive Bayes	72.48%	55.27%	0.14%	73.59%	47.12%	5.7%
b1 → SVM [Linear]	**76.74%**	**45.16%**	1.65%	74.75%	47.9%	2.6%
b1 → SVM [RBF]	76.02%	47.33%	0.94%	74.52%	49.18%	1.8%
b1 → Decision Tree	67.95%	30.31%	33.76%	66.92%	31.79%	34.35%
b1 → Random Forest	72.09%	32.47%	23.4%	70.13%	33.4%	26.33%
b2 → Naive Bayes	72.51%	54.97%	0.17%	73.44%	46.2%	6.77%
b2 → SVM [Linear]	**76.84%**	**45.16%**	1.25%	74.88%	47.89%	2.21%
b2 → SVM [RBF]	75.92%	47.33%	0.94%	74.42%	49.18%	1.84%
b2 → Decision Tree	67.74%	30.89%	33.4%	66.86%	31.87%	34.19%
b2 → Random Forest	72.46%	32.06%	22.86%	70.17%	33.24%	26.22%
b1 w/o Tumblr	66.17%	67.51%	0.00%	57.56%	85.35%	0.00%
b2 w/o Tumblr	70.95%	57.9%	0.00%	61.8%	76.69%	0.00%
(b1 → SVM [Linear]) w/o Tumblr	**91.20%**	**16.6%**	0.96%	83.7%	30.56%	2.1%
(b2 → SVM [Linear]) w/o Tumblr	91.04%	16.6%	0.96%	83.56%	30.56%	2.18%

6. EVALUATION

We evaluate listed frameworks on two genre of instances: $U_S - U_C$ instances (18,959 positive; 18,959 negative) and $U_S - u_c$ instances (109,292 positive; 109,292 negative) and on three metrics – *accuracy, false negative rate* (FNR) and *false positive rate* (FPR). Accuracy shows number of username sets correctly classified. False negative rate shows number of username sets falsely classified as unlinked while false positive rate shows the number of username sets falsely classified as linked. We use Naive Bayes classifier for both independent or cascaded framework with **b1** as the **Classifier I** (see Table 2). We observe that cascaded framework gives a slight better accuracy and false negative rate than independent framework while maintaining a low false positive rate.

Performance of Cascaded Framework: We now experiment with different baselines used as **Classifier I** and different supervised machine learning algorithms as **Classifier II** in the cascaded framework. Table 2 details 10-fold cross validated accuracy, FNR and FPR of the framework. Classifying $U_S - U_C$ instances with only **b1** results in false negative rate of 89.34% and an accuracy of 55.38%. The high false negative rate alerts that most users have non-matching current usernames across their OSN profiles. **Classifier II** learned using Naive Bayes technique exploits username set features of **b1** negative predictions and reclassifies them. Reclassification reduces false negative rate to 55.27% thereby boosting accuracy to 72.48%. A significant reduction in false negative rate by 34% is due to the comparison of username history. We experiment with other supervised methods to learn the classifier, and achieve best accuracy with SVM (reduction by 44.18%) while maintaining a low FPR. With baseline **b2** as **Classifier I**, the framework achieves best accuracy of 76.84% and reduction in false negative rate by 33.30% with SVM classifier learned on username set features as **Classifier II**. ROC curves in Figure 5 shows that in order to gain higher TPR with **Classifier II**, which directly contributes to the reduction in FNR of the framework, we need to compromise on FPR of the framework.

Significant reduction in FNR of the framework implies that the username history helps in linking user profiles and is an important feature for profile linking methods. An example where baselines fail to link with current usernames but cascaded framework compares the username sets and finds the link is two chronologically ordered sets – { U_S: ['*eenjolrass*', '*isabelnevills*', '*giuliettacapuleti*',

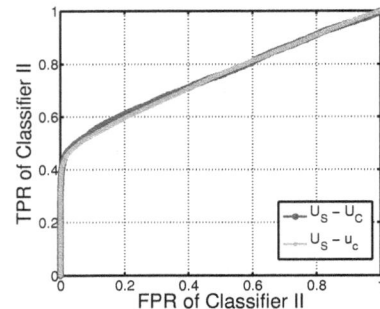

Figure 5: ROC curve when SVM with RBF kernel is used as **Classifier II**. 40% TPR at low FPR implies that FNR of the framework reduces by 40%.

'*tobsregbo*'], U_C: ['*enjoolras*', '*isabelnevilles*'] }. We see that current usernames do not match, however two of the past usernames are similar.

Classification of $U_S - u_c$ instances shows similar trends. On comparing classification accuracies of $U_S - U_C$ and $U_S - u_c$ instances, we observe that without access to candidate's past usernames, framework achieves a little less but similar accuracies. Lower linking accuracies for $U_S - u_c$ can be attributed to a slight increase in FPR. We, therefore, investigate if history availability on both profiles is beneficial for profile linking. Using $U_S - U_C$ instances, we create another dataset where we access only the current username of the candidate profile. With **b1** and SVM classifier (linear), we achieve an accuracy of 70.43% (FNR: 45.25%, FPR: 13.77%). Observe that due to increased FPR, profile linking accuracy fall from 76.74%, when username history on both profiles is available, to 70.43%, when username history is available only on source profile. Therefore, a comparison of a single username with a set may lead to higher FPR than a comparison of two username sets.

Impact of choice of OSNs: Though cascaded framework significantly reduces false negative rates, we are curious why false negative rates are still high (~45%). To answer the question, we plot a distribution of false negative instances among the three candidate social networks (see Figure 6(a) and 6(b)). We find that an enormous 90.88% of false negatives results from Twitter-Tumblr username set comparisons. A high false negative rate on Tumblr can be attributed to the lowest Jaro similarity between most sim-

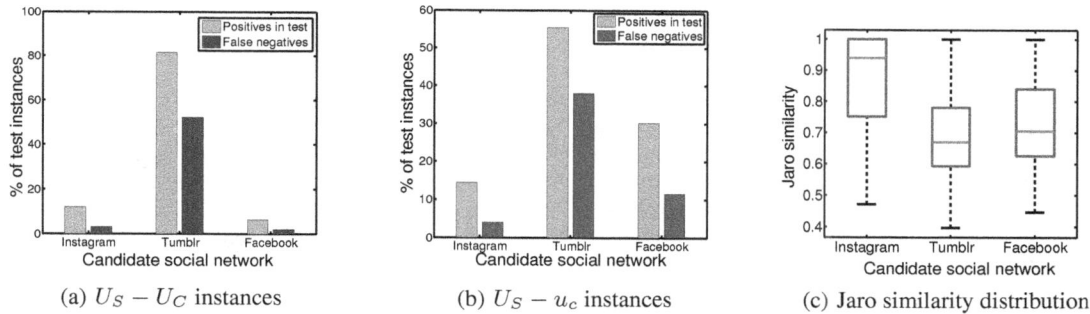

(a) $U_S - U_C$ instances   (b) $U_S - u_c$ instances   (c) Jaro similarity distribution

Figure 6: False negatives distribution among three candidate networks; Tumblr results in most false negatives. On further analysis, we observe that among the three candidate networks, Tumblr usernames have least Jaro similarity with corresponding Twitter usernames.

ilar usernames from Tumblr and Twitter username sets (see Figure 6(c)). For instance, a user's usernames on Twitter – [*'articulatedan'*, *'radicaliguori'*, *'satanichowell'*] do not hold any similarity with her usernames on Tumblr – [*'ptvkitty'*, *'piercethecait'*, *'ptvcait'*]. Best Jaro similarity score for the username sets is 0.56. For instances like this, we need support of other attributes like name, location to find link between the two profiles. We thus evaluate cascaded framework only on instances with candidate profile on either Facebook or Instagram. We achieve an accuracy of 91.20% on 4,658 $U_S - U_C$ instances (FNR: 16.6%, FPR: 0.96%) and 83.70% on 51,007 $U_S - u_c$ instances (FNR: 30.56%, FPR: 2.1%). On removal of candidate network Tumblr, a significant improvement in the accuracy shows that proposed cascaded framework can accurately find links between two user profiles given the username sets resemble and are created with similar behavioral characteristics.

To summarize, the key observations are – i) Cascaded framework performs better than an independent framework, ii) A comparison of username history reduces false predictions by 44% which are caused by the only comparison of current usernames, iii) Cascaded framework returns lower FPR with availability of past usernames on both profiles than on only one, iv) Success of the framework relies on the platforms to which examined profiles belong to; Twitter-Tumblr username set comparisons lead to 90.88% false negatives while Twitter-Instagram leads to 5.50% for U_S - U_C instances (FNR on U_S - u_c for Twitter-Tumblr: 70.81%; Twitter-Instagram: 7.82%). Our experiments on fairly large datasets give a detailed proof of concept on the importance of using username history for profile linking. Applicability and dependencies of the framework are discussed in Section 8.

6.1 Feature importance

We now detail features that help the most during classification of usernames sets. We examine feature weights to estimate their importances for the most accurate framework configuration – Exact matching (**b1**) followed by temporal matching using SVM and compute them by squaring coefficients of features returned by **Classifier II** as suggested in [11]. Top-10 features, calculated between source and candidate username sets, are –

1. Maximum normalized LCSub similarity.

2. Second best normalized LCS similarity.

3. Minimum normalized edit distance.

4. Maximum normalized jaro similarity.

5. Median of LCS similarity between source and candidate username pairs.

6. Standard deviation of LCS similarity between source and candidate username pairs.

7. Mean Jaccard similarity between alphabet distribution of source and candidate username pairs.

8. Second best normalized edit distance.

9. Maximum normalized LCS similarity.

10. Second best normalized LCSub similarity.

Note that, top-10 features capture username creation behavior of a user. Username creation behavior play an important role for classification, but username evolutionary features and reuse behavior have relatively weaker roles. We analyze if evolutionary and frequent reuse patterns can contribute better given a longer history to find connections between the user profiles in Section 8.

7. RELATED WORK

Profile linking is a well studied problem in literature. Existing literature addresses the problem of connecting user profiles across social networks by comparing current values of the attributes of user profiles. The suggested methods explore combination of attributes to compare and techniques to measure the similarity. Profile attributes such as username and name are compared using string similarity measures [13, 17, 22, 28], content attributes such as posts and message length are compared using language models [10, 13, 17], and network attributes such as number of friends and nature of ties with friends are compared using graph algorithms [6, 17, 21]. Few studies suggest crowd-sourced mechanisms to match user profiles across OSNs [23]. Others have examined the effectiveness of using only usernames to connect user profiles across OSNs [22, 28]. The state-of-the-art method MOBIUS compares a candidate username with a set of usernames owned by a user profile on other OSNs. MOBIUS assumes that user's unique behavior often leads to redundancies / similarities among the usernames across OSNs, which can be captured into features. Supervised classification techniques then predict if a candidate username and usernames on other OSNs are linked [28].

Most profile linking methods compare user profiles based on current values of the attributes observed at the time of executing the method. Existing methods are successful when users do not evolve their attribute values over time. However, recent studies show that users frequently change their attributes to suit their changing preferences on different OSNs [18, 29], similar to our observations in the study. In these scenarios, current values of the attributes on multiple profiles of a user may not match, thereby leading existing methods to falsely infer that user profiles as different users.

To address the limitations of existing methods and complement MOBIUS, we suggest considering attribute history to find links between user profiles. We propose to compare a candidate username with a set of past usernames of multiple user profiles across networks, not just with current values. We re-implement MOBIUS and build a framework with **Classifier I** extracting top-10 features by comparing candidate username with a set of current usernames on other OSNs, as proposed by the authors and **Classifier II** extracting username set features by comparing candidate username history with other profiles' username histories as proposed in this work. On a dataset of 8,997 users who have profiles on more than two social networks as well past history on all the social networks, 42.67% instances are false negatives i.e. **Classifier I** miss the link among profiles. **Classifier II** identifies links among 30.72% more instances, reducing false negatives to 11.95%. Therefore, we see that attribute history complements state-of-the-art method and extends support to existing profile linking methods.

8. DISCUSSION

On a dataset of real-world users, we show that username history holds its significance by extending performance to existing methods for profile linking. However, its effectiveness varies with the choice of OSNs. We observe that majority users create different usernames on Tumblr as compared to their profiles on Twitter, Facebook or Instagram. Differences between the username sets hints disparate user needs and choices across OSNs. We think that profile linking strategies need to tune according to the nature and genre of the OSN with a prior knowledge of popular user behavior on that OSN. Now, we discuss applicability of attribute history along with other dependencies of the framework that uses attribute history for linking.

8.1 Applicability

Apart from observing users over time on OSNs, one can get user history archived by external services like DataSift[3] or Gnip[4]. We further suggest other two methods to collect past usernames – via timeline and via public datasets.

8.1.1 Via timeline

On social networks like Twitter and Instagram, users converse by tagging another user's username with '@' tag. When a user changes her username, old tweets and replies where others tagged her with her old username stay on her timeline. By listing old posts with replies and extracting mentions from the tweets, one may list her past usernames. We believe that a recent history of past usernames can be captured by this method.

8.1.2 Via public datasets

Multiple researchers collect private and public posts related to a topic, event or a campaign ranging over a period of time. They often store information about authors who created these posts. One may query these databases with the *user_id* of a user and find posts created by her at different times. If the author details are recorded with each post, one may list unique usernames used by the user in the past. With this methodology, we find past usernames of 4% of 128,251 Twitter users, via datasets shared by an event monitoring tool, MultiOSN [9].

With the listed methods, applicability of the proposed profile linking framework can be extended to random users who are not tracked continuously over time.

[3]http://datasift.com/platform/historics/
[4]https://gnip.com/products/historical/

8.2 Dependency

We test the proposed framework for dependency on the grounds of understanding how much history is required for efficient profile linking. In other words, does a longer history on source username set impact framework accuracy? To answer the question, we create a dataset of $U_S - u_c$ username sets with 502 users from the dataset of 109,292 users who had changed their Twitter username maximum number of times (5 times) within tracking period of two months. We further partitioned 502 $U_S - u_c$ sets into 4 datasets $(d_i)_{i=2}^5$, where dataset d_i contains instances with first i past usernames from their respective U_C sets. For instance, d_2 contains 502 $U_S - u_c$ instances, where each U_C contains only first two usernames of the five usernames in the username set. FNR by cascaded framework with respect to the baseline **b1** on the derived datasets with varying set sizes is shown in Figure 7.

Observe that as past username set size increases, difference between FNR of the framework and FNR of the baseline increases, thereby indicating that longer the username history of a Twitter user, better the matching with a candidate username or set.

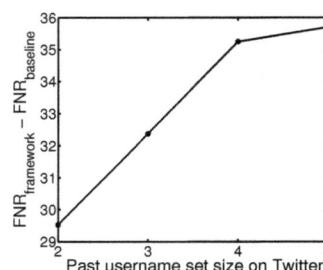

Figure 7: Higher FNR reduction with increasing source username set size.

8.3 Importance of temporal creation and reuse behavior

Section 6.1 suggests that username creation behavior helps better than other behavioral patterns to suggest if username sets refer to a single user. We suspect that a user's evolutionary behavior or her tendency to reuse usernames across social networks over time are of little help to the classification process due to fewer instances with these features. We, therefore, repeat feature importance analysis for another dataset with longer username history. We randomly sample a set of 10,000 users from 128,251 users on Twitter and record their attributes every fifteen minutes for 12 months (November 26, 2013 - November 28, 2014). Out of 10,000 users, 47% users change their username at least once during the tracking period. To create ground truth dataset, we filter users who self-identify themselves on at least one of the candidate social networks – Instagram, Tumblr or Facebook. For 682 users, we retrieve their current username on either of the candidate networks while for 155 users we retrieve their past usernames on both Twitter and one of the candidate networks. SVM classifier with linear kernel, used as **Classifier II**, ranked 'username reuse' features above 'username creation' features deemed important earlier – ratio of common usernames to candidate set size, and number of common usernames found between source and candidate username sets are ranked above than mean Jaccard similarity between two sets. Therefore, we gather that relative importance of behavioral patterns to reveal a potential link between two user profiles varies with the longevity of the attribute history on either profiles. Username reuse behavior can be only observed over a prolonged track of history, however has proven useful feature for profile linking.

9. CONCLUSION AND FUTURE WORK

In this work, we emphasize that attribute values evolve over time on one or multiple profiles of a user. This causes non-matching current attribute values on the profiles. Existing methods do not consider attribute evolution and falsely predict non-matching user profiles as different users. To avoid such mistakes, we propose to compare attribute's past values, not just current values, to revise the prediction. Focusing on username, we find similarities between username sets, comprised of past and current username of a user profile. We assume that user behavior of username creation and its reuse across her profiles is unique; these user behavioral patterns can remain static or vary over time and are captured into a set of features. Novel cascaded framework of classifiers uses proposed features to rectify erroneous classifications based only on current values. We show that our framework outperforms existing profile linking methods by reducing false negative errors by 44%. In conclusion, comparing username history along with current values help in effective profile linking.

In future, we plan to extend our work on two fronts. First, further reduce the false negative rate with the help of other features such as name, description and profile picture, and second, evaluate the proposed framework on a random set of users rather than users who self-identify themselves. We believe that an accumulation and knowledge of a user's past profiles can also help in other research domains other than profile linking. Our work can be extended to profile search frameworks, which is an important part of profile resolution process [15], however is not the focus of this study.

10. REFERENCES

[1] The Five Biggest Mistakes in Measuring Social Media. www.clickz.com/clickz/column/1716119/the-five-biggest-mistakes-measuring\\social-media, 2009.

[2] Segmenting Target Markets. thewaltdisneyco.blogspot.in/2011/11/chapter\-8\-segmenting\-targeting\-markets.html, 2011.

[3] 4 Reasons Why You Need to Change Your Username on Twitter. www.adweek.com/socialtimes/twitter-username-tips/453851?red=at, 2012.

[4] How Social Media Influences Market Segmentation. http://www.marketingtechnews.net/news/2012/mar/16/how-social-media-influencing-\\marketing-segmentation/, 2012.

[5] Deduplicate Audiences With Cross-Media Planning. http://www.beet.tv/2015/01/br15nielsenhohnan.html, 2015.

[6] Sergey Bartunov, Anton Korshunov, S Park, Wonho Ryu, and Hyungdong Lee. Joint Link-Attribute User Identity Resolution in Online Social Networks. In SNAKDD, 2012.

[7] Terence Chen, Mohamed Ali Kaafar, Arik Friedman, and Roksana Boreli. Is More always Merrier?: A Deep Dive into Online Social Footprints. In WOSN, 2012.

[8] G. Cockerell. Making Marketing Meaningful. Kendall Hunt Publishing Company, 2010.

[9] Prateek Dewan, Mayank Gupta, Kanika Goyal, and Ponnurangam Kumaraguru. Multiosn: Realtime monitoring of real world events on multiple online social media. In I-CARE, 2013.

[10] Oana Goga, Howard Lei, Sree Hari Krishnan Parthasarathi, Gerald Friedland, Robin Sommer, and Renata Teixeira. Exploiting Innocuous Activity for Correlating Users across Sites. In WWW, 2013.

[11] Isabelle Guyon, Jason Weston, Stephen Barnhill, and Vladimir Vapnik. Gene Selection for Cancer Classification using Support Vector Machines. Machine learning, 2002.

[12] Geremy Heitz, Stephen Gould, Ashutosh Saxena, and Daphne Koller. Cascaded Classification Models: Combining Models for Holistic Scene Understanding. In NIPS, 2009.

[13] Tereza Iofciu, Peter Fankhauser, Fabian Abel, and Kerstin Bischoff. Identifying Users Across Social Tagging Systems. In ICWSM, 2011.

[14] Danesh Irani, Steve Webb, Kang Li, and Calton Pu. Large Online Social Footprints–An Emerging Threat. In CSE, 2009.

[15] Paridhi Jain, Ponnurangam Kumaraguru, and Anupam Joshi. @ I seek 'fb. me': Identifying Users across Multiple Online Social Networks. In WWW Companion, 2013.

[16] Pei Li, Xin Luna Dong, Andrea Maurino, and Divesh Srivastava. Linking Temporal Records. VLDB, 2011.

[17] Siyuan Liu, Shuhui Wang, Feida Zhu, Jinbo Zhang, and Ramayya Krishnan. HYDRA: Large-scale Social Identity Linkage via Heterogeneous Behavior Modeling. In SIGMOD, 2014.

[18] Yabing Liu, Chloe Kliman-Silver, and Alan Mislove. The Tweets They are a-Changin': Evolution of Twitter Users and Behavior. In ICWSM, 2014.

[19] Anshu Malhotra, Luam Totti, Wagner Meira, Ponnurangam Kumaraguru, and Virgilio Almeida. Studying User Footprints in Different Online Social Networks. In ASONAM, 2012.

[20] Marti Motoyama and George Varghese. I seek You: Searching and Matching Individuals in Social Networks. In WIDM, 2009.

[21] Arvind Narayanan and Vitaly Shmatikov. De-anonymizing Social Networks. In SP, 2009.

[22] Daniele Perito, Claude Castelluccia, Mohamed Ali Kâafar, and Pere Manils. How Unique and Traceable Are Usernames? In PETS, 2011.

[23] Mohamed Shehab, Moo Nam Ko, and Hakim Touati. Social Networks Profile Mapping using Games. In USENIX, 2012.

[24] Xiaolin Shi, Ramesh Nallapati, Jure Leskovec, Dan McFarland, and Dan Jurafsky. Who Leads Whom: Topical Lead-lag Analysis across Corpora. In NIPS Workshop, 2010.

[25] Temple F Smith and Michael S Waterman. Identification of Common Molecular Subsequences. Journal of molecular biology, 1981.

[26] Martin Szomszor, Ivan Cantador, Escuela Politecnica Superior, and Harith Alani. Correlating User Profiles from Multiple Folksonomies. In HT, 2008.

[27] A. Weinstein. Handbook of Market Segmentation: Strategic Targeting for Business and Technology firms. Haworth Press, 2004.

[28] Reza Zafarani and Huan Liu. Connecting Users across Social Media Sites: A Behavioral-modeling Approach. In KDD, 2013.

[29] Jun Zhang, Chaokun Wang, and Jianmin Wang. Learning Temporal Dynamics of Behavior Propagation in Social Networks. In ICWSM, 2014.

Only One Out of Five Archived Web Pages Existed as Presented

Scott G. Ainsworth
Old Dominion University
Norfolk, VA, USA
sainswor@cs.odu.edu

Michael L. Nelson
Old Dominion University
Norfolk, VA, USA
mln@cs.odu.edu

Herbert Van de Sompel
Los Alamos National Laboratory
Los Alamos, NM, USA
herbertv@lanl.gov

ABSTRACT

When a user retrieves a page from a web archive, the page is marked with the acquisition datetime of the root resource, which effectively asserts "this is how the page looked at a that datetime." However, embedded resources, such as images, are often archived at different datetimes than the main page. The presentation appears temporally coherent, but is composed from resources acquired over a wide range of datetimes. We examine the completeness and temporal coherence of composite archived resources (composite mementos) under two selection heuristics. The completeness and temporal coherence achieved using a single archive was compared to the results achieved using multiple archives. We found that at most 38.7% of composite mementos are both temporally coherent and that at most only 17.9% (roughly 1 in 5) are temporally coherent and 100% complete. Using multiple archives increases mean completeness by 3.1–4.1% but also reduces temporal coherence.

Categories and Subject Descriptors

H.3.7 [**Information Storage and Retrieval**]: Digital Libraries

General Terms

Design, Experimentation, Standardization

Keywords

Digital Preservation, Temporal Coherence, Web Architecture, Web Archiving, Resource Versioning, HTTP, Memento, RFC 7089

1. INTRODUCTION

When a user retrieves an archived page from a web archive such as the Internet Archive [28], the page is marked with a Memento-Datetime (the datetime the archived resource was acquired) of the root resource, which effectively asserts "this page appeared in this state at the datetime indicated." The page is recomposed from archived resources in an attempt to provide an appearance as similar as possible to that which the user would have experienced had the original page been visited on the indicated Memento-Datetime.

The presentation appears as real as those from the live web. However, appearances can be deceiving.

Figure 1 shows a presentation for *wunderground.com* on Thursday 2004-12-09 19:09:26 (all times GMT). The large radar image near the page center shows the weather in Varina, Iowa, USA was clear and sunny. A closer look tells a different story. The daily image for Thursday shows cloudy with a chance of rain and the rest of the daily images are partly cloudy. These discrepancies indicate temporal incoherence between the archived root and the embedded archived resources.

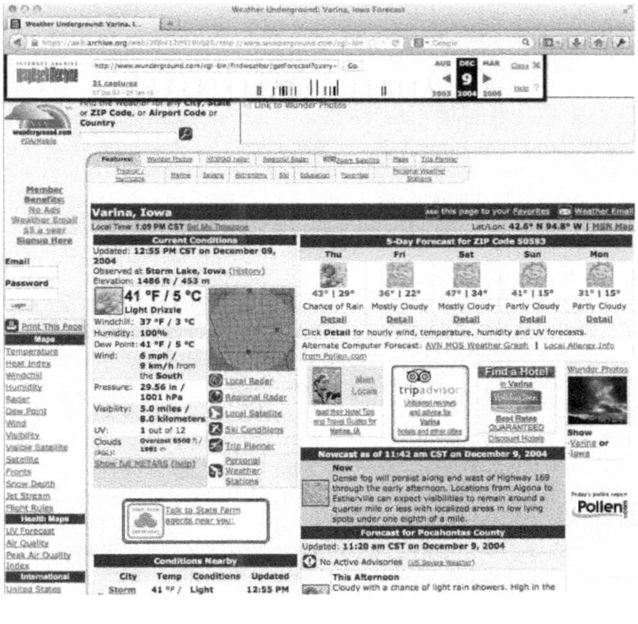

Figure 1: Wunderground Composite Memento, Memento-Datetime 2004-12-09 19:09:26

An archived web page is a composite resource, generally a composition of a root HTML page, images, Javascripts, stylesheets, and other resources. As shown in Figure 2, although the *wunderground.com* root page itself was acquired on 2004-12-09, the embedded resources were acquired from −20 days before to +9 months after the root. Many archived resources are missing embedded resources. Some of these are apparent (as indicated at the top of Figure 2), but many are not. Web archive user interfaces attempt to create a smooth simulation of browsing the past web. Thus, the temporal incoherence shown in Figure 2 and hidden incompleteness are mostly ignored by these interfaces.

Figure 2: Wunderground Composite Memento, Memento-Datetime 2004-12-09 19:09:26

Public web archives now hold hundreds of billions of archived web pages. Indeed, as of May 25, 2015, the Internet Archive claims 479 billion pages [21]. These web archives have become trusted sources. For example, after the shoot down of Malaysian Flight 17, Arthur Bright, writing for the Christian Science Monitor, cited the Internet Archive when arguing that the flight had been shot down by pro-Russian rebels [10]. Knowing what a web site previously contained is also important in litigation and other legal proceedings. Howell [19] addresses these uses with an emphasis on the meeting for rules of evidence and admissibility requirements.

In the data we studied, it is common for the temporal spread between the oldest and newest captures to be weeks, months, and sometimes a year or more. Unexpected though were spreads exceeding five years; a few even exceed ten years. The difference between expectations and the data, along with our work on Memento [34], motivates us to explore archive completeness and temporal coherence of archived web pages. Our previous studies of existing web archive content examined the coverage on a broad scale [1] and the temporal drift that occurs as web archives are browsed [3]. This paper examines the completeness and temporal coherence of archived composite resources with a focus on these questions:

- How prevalent is temporal incoherence?

- Current web archive user interfaces enable access to a single archive's resources. If multiple archives are used, is temporal coherence improved?

- The *best* memento for an embedded resource can be selected using many different heuristics. Currently, most web archives use the Minimum Distance heuristic (see 4.2.1). How do other heuristics compare?

2. RELATED WORK

Large-scale web archiving requires resolution of issues and approaches on several axes. Although somewhat dated, Masanès [25]

is an excellent introduction and covers a broad range of web archiving topics. Of significance to this research are the technical aspects of acquisition, quality, and completeness. An area not addressed by Masanès is standardized access to archived resources, which Van de Sompel et al. [35] addressed with IETF RFC 7089 [34].

2.1 Acquisition

Acquisition is the technical means of bringing content into a web archive. *Client-side* archiving works by emulating web users following links; Heritrix [27] is a widely-used tool. Most client-side archiving suffers from two major limitations: first, only linked resources are captured; second, root and embedded resources are commonly acquired at different times. (Some archives, such as WebCite [17], attempt to prevent the second.) *Transactional* archiving [16, 18], such as *SiteStory* [12], is specifically designed to overcome client-side limitations by inserting the acquisition process between users and the data source. Unique request-response pairs are archived, including requests for resources that are not linked and might not be discovered by client-side archiving. *Server-side* archiving makes a direct copy of the content from the server, bypassing HTTP altogether. This is a common approach for content management systems and wikis. Although conceptually simple, access to the resulting server-side archive can be difficult, requiring different URIs and navigational structures than the original. This can be mitigated by implementing the Memento Protocol, as Jones, et al. [20] did for MediaWiki.

2.2 Access

Until recently, there were neither standard methods nor a standard protocol for access to archived resources. Each archive provided (and still provides) a unique user interface (UI), such as the Wayback Machine [33] shown in Figures 1 and 2, for access to the archive's resources. In general, UI access to archives starts with a user-selected URI and datetime, after which the archive allows the user to simply click links to browse the collection.

Van de Sompel et al. addressed the lack of standards with Memento [35, 34]. Memento is an HTTP-based protocol that bridges web archives with current resources. Each original resource has zero or more archived resources (mementos) which encapsulate its state at various acquisition times. Memento provides a standard protocol for identifying and dereferencing mementos through datetime negotiation. Similar to the way clients use HTTP content negotiation, clients use datetime negotiation to request mementos for original resources by datetime.

2.3 Quality and Completeness

In general, quality is defined as fitting a particular use; objectively, it is defined as meeting measurable characteristics. Our examination of web archive content is concerned with the latter. For web archives, quality issues stem from difficulties inherent in acquiring content over HTTP [25]: content can be temporarily unavailable, leaving coverage gaps; web content changes more frequently than archival crawls can occur, creating temporal gaps; embedded resources may change after root resource acquisition but before the embedded resources themselves have been acquired, leading to temporal incoherence.

2.3.1 Completeness (Coverage)

When crawling to acquire content, the tradeoffs required and conditions encountered routinely lead to incomplete coverage. For example, the archive may not have the resources required to acquire and store all desired content; thus, only high priority content is crawled and stored. Desired content may not be available at crawl time due to server downtime or network disruption. The combination of compromises and resource unavailability create undesired, undocumented gaps in the archive.

Although much has been written on the technical, social, legal, and political issues of web archiving, little detailed research has been conducted on the coverage, completeness, and coherence of existing holdings. Day [14] surveyed web archives while investigating the methods and issues associated with web archiving, but did not address coverage. Thelwall touched on coverage when he addressed international bias in the Internet Archive [32], but did not directly address how much of the Web is covered. McCown and Nelson addressed coverage [26], but their research was limited to search engine caches. Ben Saad et al. [8, 7] addressed qualitative completeness through change detection to identify and archive important changes. Leveraging the Memento Protocol and pilot infrastructure, Ainsworth et al. [1] showed that 35–90% of publicly-accessible URIs have at least one publicly-accessible archived copy, 17–49% have two to five copies, 1–8% have six to ten copies, and 8–63% at least ten copies. The number of URI copies varies as a function of time, but only 14.6–31.3% of URIs are archived more than once per month.

The ad-hoc nature of web archiving causes many composite mementos to be incomplete. Brunelle et al. [11] studied the value of missing embedded resources on user perception of the damage caused. In this study, 19.7%–23.9% of composite mementos were found to be incomplete.

2.3.2 *Temporal Coherence*

Spaniol et al. define temporal coherence as meaning that a web archive's contents appear to be "as of" timepoint x or within interval $[x; y]$ [31]. The same constraints and conditions that negatively impact completeness also affect temporal coherence. Spaniol et al. [30] note that crawls may span hours or days, increasing the risk of temporal incoherence especially for large sites. Thus, the simple "as of" timepoint x or within interval $[x; y]$ requirement is *impossible to achieve* in a crawler-based paradigm. (It is not impossible in a transactional archiving or on-demand approach.) Also introduced is a model for identifying coherent sections of archives, which provides a measure of quality, and a crawling strategy which helps minimize temporal incoherence in web site captures. Spaniol et al. [31] also develop crawl and site coherence visualizations. Spaniol et al.'s work, while presenting a measure of quality, addresses the quality of new acquisition crawls; the quality of existing holdings is not addressed.

Denev et al. also address the quality of new acquisition crawls with the SHARC framework [15], which introduced a stochastic notion of *sharpness* (a quality measure). Site changes are modeled as Poisson processes with page-specific change rates, which allows reasoning on the expected sharpness of an acquisition crawl. The authors propose crawl-time quality assessments and page revisits to improve the quality of future crawls.

Ben Saad et al. [9] show that different methods and measures are required *a priori* and *a posterior*, that is during acquisition and post-acquisition respectively. Like Denev et al. [15], the *a priori* solution is designed to optimize the crawling process for archival quality. The *a posteriori* solution uses metadata collected by the *a priori* process to direct the user to the most coherent archived versions. Combining *a priori* and *a posterior* measures and methods into a single solution is shown to produce the most coherent result.

The above research shares a common thread: evaluation and control of completeness and temporal coherence during acquisition with the goal of improving future archive holdings. Our research focuses on the temporal quality of *existing* holdings.

One temporal quality issue we have documented is temporal drift as users navigate from page to page using web archives. The drift is subtle, but can be observed by examining Memento-Datetime. We examined temporal drift under two target datetime policies [3]. The sliding policy emulated web archive user interfaces by allowing the target datetime to shift; the sticky policy held the target datetime to the user's originally selected value. Although some drift is inevitable due to the sparse nature of web archive collections, we found that the sticky policy reduced median drift by 30 days compared to the sliding policy.

Continuing our temporal coherence focus, the present research addresses temporal coherence of composite resources under two heuristics and when embedded mementos are selected from the same archive as a web page or from multiple archives.

3. COMPOSITE MEMENTOS

3.1 Original Resources and Mementos

As mentioned in Subsection 2.2, Memento [34] extends HTTP to provide standard protocol for recognizing and accessing archived resources using datetime negotiation. Each original resource (URI-R) has zero or more mementos (URI-M_i), that encapsulate the URI-R's state at times t_i. A timemap (URI-T) provides a list of mementos for a URI-R. Each archived URI-R will have a timemap for each archive holding mementos for the URI-R.

Memento has become the de facto standard for web archive interoperability. Some web archives support Memento natively (Memento support was added to version 1.6 of the Wayback Machine in 2011), and for others the Los Alamos National Laboratory Research Library Prototype Team and Old Dominion University Computer Science Web Science and Digital Libraries Group have developed Memento proxies. The proxies allow the Memento aggregator to simultaneously access native and proxied Memento archives [6]. This study did not use the aggregator. All timemaps and mementos were collected directly from archives that support the Memento Protocol natively or by proxy.

3.2 Composite Mementos

Given a *root URI-R* (rURI-R), which contains *embedded URI-Rs* (eURI-Rs), which may contain eURI-Rs, etc., a Composite Memento comprises mementos for the rURI-R (rURI-M) and for all eURI-Rs (eURI-Ms); that is, all the URI-Ms needed to recompose the the original representation. Figure 3 shows a tree representation of a composite memento[1]. For HTML, a composite memento

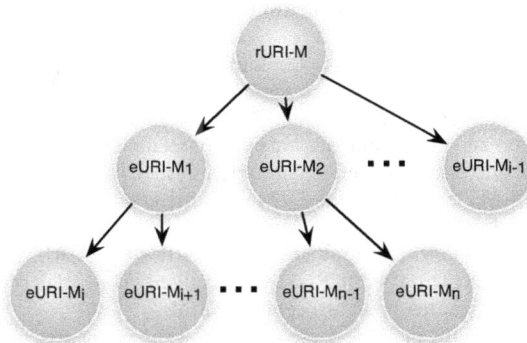

Figure 3: Composite Memento Tree

---

[1] Composite mementos are actually directed graphs, but in this context can be treated as trees without loss of generality.

URI-R	Last-Modified	Memento-Datetime	Delta	Root?	Bracket?	Coherence	Color
`http://www.rpgdreamers.com/`	N/A	2006-11-10 04:37:51	–	Y	–	C	Black
`.../aslmain.js`	2006-04-25 14:03:39	2006-11-10 23:44:02	–	N	Y	C	Green
`.../home_exp_leader_728x90_468x60.js`	2006-11-11 00:30:18	2006-11-11 01:02:19	19.9h	N	N	V	Red
`http://www.rpgdreamers.com/`	N/A	2006-12-06 08:04:42	–	Y	–	C	Black
`.../aslmain.js`	2006-04-25 14:03:39	2006-12-07 01:07:32	–	N	Y	C	Green
`.../home_exp_leader_728x90_468x60.js`	2006-12-05 17:54:31	2006-12-05 18:30:00	13.6h	N	N	PC	Blue
`.../show_ads.js`	N/A	2006-12-06 12:00:00	3.9h	N	N	PV	Yellow
`http://www.rpgdreamers.com/`	N/A	2007-01-01 21:31:16	–	Y	–	C	Black
`.../aslmain.js`	2006-04-25 14:03:39	2007-01-02 16:23:01	–	N	Y	C	Green
`.../home_exp_leader_728x90_468x60.js`	2006-12-09 14:41:27	2006-12-09 15:04:45	23.3d	N	N	PC	Blue
`.../show_ads.js`	N/A	2007-01-05 12:00:00	86.5d	N	N	PV	Yellow

generally includes an archived web page and archived embedded resources (e.g., images and stylesheets).

Recomposing a composite memento follows a process analogous to a web browser rendering a web page. The process starts with a rURI-R and target datetime, which are use to select a rURI-M. The rURI-M is dereferenced to retrieve its representation from the web archive. Recomposition continues recursively for each eURI-R until eURI-Ms have been retrieved for every rURI-R. It is likely that not every eURI-R will have been archived; these are considered missing.

3.3 Temporal Coherence

We define an eURI-M as temporally coherent with respect to an rURI-M when it can be shown that the eURI-M's representation existed at the rURI-M's Memento-Datetime [4]. However, temporal coherence is more nuanced than simply coherent or not. Determining the coherence state of an eURI-M requires examining the relationship between rURI-M using Memento-Datetime, Last-Modified datetime, and possibly content equality and similarity. Relationships between eURI-Ms and rURI-Ms form patterns. An example pattern, which we call [4] the *Two-Memento Bracket Pattern (2B)* is shown in Figure 4. Here, $\mathcal{L}$ represents a Last-Modified

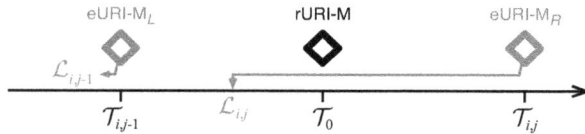

Figure 4: Two-Memento Bracket Pattern (2B)

datetime and $\mathcal{T}$ is a Memento-Datetime. The horizontal axis represents time and the URI-Ms are represented as diamonds plotted at the URI-M's Memento-Datetime. The black diamond is the rURI-M; the left and right diamonds are two consecutive eURI-Ms (subscripts L and R indicate left and right respectively). Note that the eURI-M$_R$ Last-Modified, $\mathcal{L}_{i,j}$, and its Memento-Datetime, $\mathcal{T}_{i,j}$, time *Bracket* the rURI-M's Memento-Datetime, $\mathcal{T}_0$, as shown by the thin green line. This time bracket shows that the eURI-M$_R$ representation existed when rURI-M was acquired. Thus, eURI-M$_R$ is temporally Coherent with respect to rURI-M.

The mementos in Table 1 are a subset of the mementos needed to recompose three `http://www.rpgdreamers.com/` composite mementos. Figure 5 is a scatter plot of these mementos. Each Composite Memento is a single row with diamonds representing individual rURI-Ms and eURI-Ms. The vertical axis is time. The horizontal axis is the delta between the rURI-M Memento-Datetime

and the eURI-M Memento-Datetime, with the scale in days (d). For datetimes outside the two-day range, the delta is shown in the plot area. Composite Mementos are positioned vertically based on their rURI-M Memento-Datetime. Black diamonds are rURI-Ms. eURI-Ms are represented by colored diamonds with the color indicating there coherence state as defined by Ainsworth et al. [4]:

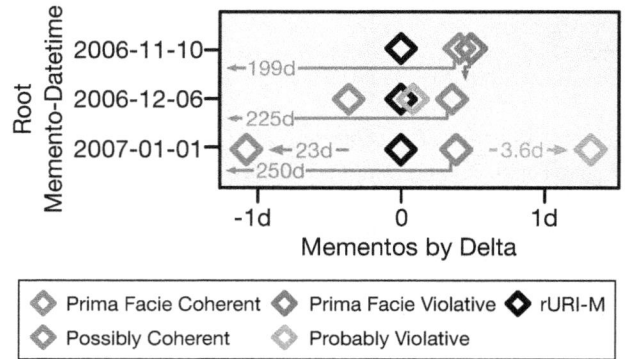

Figure 5: Scatter Plot Sample

Prima Facie Coherent (green). The eURI-M was acquired after the rURI-M Memento-Datetime and its Last-Modified datetime is on or before the rURI-M Memento-Datetime, bracketing rURI-M Memento-Datetime. Therefore, the eURI-M's representation existed at the time the rURI-M was acquired.

Prima Facie Violative (red). The eURI-M was acquired after the rURI-M and its Last-Modified datetime is after the rURI-M Memento-Datetime. Therefore, the eURI-M's representation did not exist at the time the rURI-M was acquired.

Possibly Coherent (blue). The eURI-M was acquired before the rURI-M. Therefore, its representation could have existed at the time the rURI-M was acquired.

Probably Violative (yellow). The eURI-M was acquired after the rURI-M Memento-Datetime and lacks a Last-Modified datetime. Without Last-Modified, the eURI-M cannot be considered Prima Facie Violative or Prima Facie Coherent. Finally, unlike Possibly Coherent, there is no evidence that the eURI-M's representation existed at rURI-M Memento-Datetime.

Table 2 contains temporal coherence statistics for the three sample composite mementos discussed above. The composite mementos have 37 or 39 eURI-Rs each, 72.5%–78.9% of which are Prima

Table 2: Sample Composite Memento Statistics

Description	'06-11-10	'06-12-06	'07-01-01	Mean
eURI-Ms	37	39	39	38.3
Coherent	78.9%	72.5%	72.5%	74.6%
Possibly Coherent	2.6%	12.5%	12.5%	9.3%
Probably Violative	0.0%	2.5%	2.5%	1.7%
Violative	7.9%	0.0%	0.0%	2.5%
Missing	10.5%	12.5%	12.5%	11.9%

Table 3: Archival Rates

Sample	This study	Jan'13 [1]	Jan'11 [3]
DMOZ	97.0%	95.2%	79%
Search Engine	55.2%	26.4%	19%
Bitly	28.3%	23.5%	16%
Delicious	95.0%	91.9%	68%
Aggregate	68.9%	59.4%	46%

Facie Coherent. Another 2.6–12.5% are Possibly Coherent. Prima Facie Violative (0–7.9%), Probably Violative (0–2.5%), and missing mementos (10.5–12.5%) account for the remainder. These are individual statistics for three mementos. (Subsection 3.3 and Table 9 present statistics for the entire sample set.)

The full scatter plot shown in Figure 6 reveals interesting patterns. Many embedded resources are archived infrequently; these create right-to-left diagonals. Also, some resources are archived much later than the root resources, which results in unexpectedly large deltas. For example, the 2005-03-10 03:21:27 composite memento (indicated by the dashed green line) includes several embedded resources that were archived well after the root. Of particular note is media.gif[2], which had only a single URI-M with Memento-Datetime 2011-06-06 20:10:22 and was acquired nearly seven years after the rURI-M. Full details for all sample URIs can-

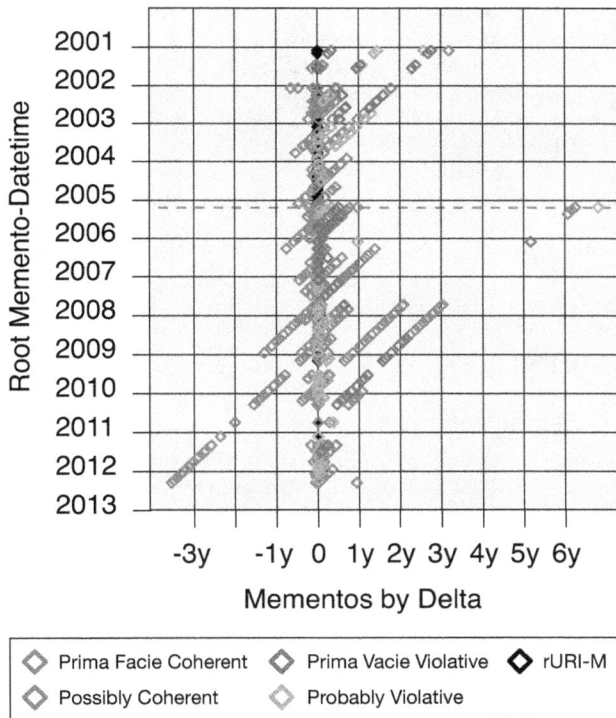

Figure 6: Full Scatter Plot

not be made available within this paper. We will provide the scatter plots and statistics for the entire sample set online at http://coherence.cs.odu.edu.

---

[2] http://www.rpgdreamers.com/rpgworld/logo/media.gif

4. EXPERIMENT

4.1 Sample URIs

Building on previous work, we used the same four URI sample sets (from DMOZ, search engine, Bitly, and Delicious) as in [1]. Each sample contains 1,000 randomly-selected URI-Rs for 4,000 URI-Rs total. Random selection details can be found in [2].

The percentage of sample URI-Rs found to be archived at the time of the experiment is shown in Table 3. There are several significant differences from our 2011 results [1, 36] and January 2013 results [3]. The 2013 results noted increased holdings availability provided by the Internet Archive [22], which helped increase archival rates. This experiment again found that archival rates increased. Most significant difference from [1] and [3] is the use of additional archives, including seven with primary languages other than English.

4.2 Parameters

The experiment recomposed four variants of each sample composite memento. Each variant used one of two memento selection heuristics and either a single archive or multiple archives.

4.2.1 Heuristics

Public web archives currently use a single heuristic to select mementos. We call this heuristic *Minimum Distance*. As explained in subsection 3.3, less than 50% of the embedded mementos selected by this heuristic are Prima Facie Coherent. Anticipating that a more sophisticated heuristic would improve coherence, this experiment also included a second heuristic we call *Last-Modified Datetime/Memento-Datetime Bracket*, or *Bracket* for short. Both heuristics are defined below:

Minimum Distance (Mindist) Select the URI-M with Memento-Datetime closest to the root's (it can be before or after). The heuristic cost is absolute value of the difference between the two Memento-Datetimes.

Last-Modified/Memento-Datetime Bracket (Bracket) Establish URI-M lifetime using the range starting from Last-Modified datetime and ending with Memento-Datetime. This range is the time frame when the URI-M's representation is known to have existed in its archived state. When an eURI-M's lifetime overlaps an rURI-M Memento-Datetime, it is Prima Facie Coherent with cost 0. When the lifetime does not overlap, this heuristic falls back to a modified form of Mindist, which computes cost for both Memento-Datetime and Last-Modified, selecting the least as heuristic cost.

4.2.2 Source Constraint

Composite mementos are recomposed using a single or multiple archives. Using a single archive mimics the behavior of existing web archive user interfaces; all eURI-Ms are chosen from the same archive as the rURI-M. Using multiple archives enables eURI-Ms to be selected from multiple archives, possibly filling completeness and datetime gaps. The archives used are listed in Appendix A.

Table 4: rURI-R Timemap Statistics

Desc.	DMOZ	S.Eng.	Bitly	Deli	Total
URI-Rs	1,000	1,000	1,000	1,000	4,000
URI-Rs Archived	971	552	282	951	2,756
in Multiple Archives	14.5%	11.1%	23.0%	57.5%	29.5%
Timemaps	1,154	682	404	2,167	4,252
per URI-R	1.19	1.14	1.43	2.28	1.58
Mementos	120,765	11,508	36,816	174,214	343,303
per URI-R	124.37	20.85	130.55	183.19	124.57

Table 5: rURI-M Statuses

Status	DMOZ	S.Eng.	Bitly	Deli.	Total	Percent
200	46,242	4,461	2,876	28,846	82,425	93.6%
503	2,989	254	155	1,046	4,444	5.0%
404	324	42	26	191	583	0.7%
403	161	6	28	193	388	0.4%
400	41	10	10	42	103	0.1%
Other	34	17	7	53	111	0.1%
Total	49,791	4,790	3,102	30,371	88,054	100.0%

4.3 Procedure

The examination of temporal spread was accomplished using the procedure described below. Timemaps and mementos were collected in May 2013. The proxies described in Subsection 3.1 were used to obtain timemaps for all archives except the Internet Archive, which was the only native Memento Protocol archive for the duration of preparation and data collection. Data collection was accomplished in two phases:

- Selection of rURI-Ms, and
- Recomposition of composite mementos.

Phase I. Selection of rURI-Ms

Phase I selected rURI-Ms by retrieving timemaps for all sample URI-Rs and choosing a subset of URI-Ms from the timemaps.

Process. We attempted to retrieve timemaps for all 4,000 sample rURI-Rs from 15 archives. Table 4 shows that 2,756 sample rURI-Rs had at least one timemap available; these are considered archived. Of the archived rURI-Rs, 29.5% are held in multiple archives and had multiple timemaps available, with an average of 1.58 timemaps each. The timemaps listed 343,303 rURI-Ms, averaging 124.57 per archived rURI-R. Of these 343,303 rURI-Ms, 88,054 (25.6%) were sampled for retrieval and evaluation. Specifically, we selected the rURI-M that was acquired closest to midnight on the 12th of each month during which the the rURI-R was archived.

Phase II. Recomposition of composite mementos

This phase recomposed composite mementos for each rURI-M selected in Phase I. It was executed four times, once for each combination of heuristic and source constraint. For each selected root URI-M, the following steps were performed.

Step 1. Download rURI-M. The rURI-M was retrieved using *curl*. A failure at this step stopped recomposition.

Of the 88,054 rURI-Ms, 93.6% were available and returned a 200 HTTP status. As shown in Table 5, the most common failure status was HTTP 503, which generally means the URI-M is not currently available (perhaps its data store is offline). Status 503 is generally considered temporary, so each 503 was retried twice over the course of a week before considering the 503 final for this study. The next most common failures were 403 and 404, access restricted and the memento does not exist, respectively.

Step 2. Extract eURI-Rs. The BeautifulSoup Python package (version 4.1.3) was used to extract eURI-Rs from HTML documents. Additionally, eURI-Rs were extracted from CSS files using regular expressions. If the memento did not contain eURI-Rs (or could not; e.g., images), processing finished.

Note: Steps 3–6 were repeated for each eURI-R found in step 2.

Step 3. Retrieve the eURI-R timemap. The eURI-R timemaps were retrieved using *curl*. Status 503 Failures were retried twice. If timemaps could not be retrieved, processing finished.

Step 4. Select eURI-M for eURI-R . A heuristic was used to select the best eURI-M, which is the eURI-M with lowest score according to the heuristic in use. For the Mindist heuristic, the closest eURI-M was selected directly from the eURI-R's timemaps. For the Bracket heuristic, two candidate eURI-Ms were selected: one acquired before and one acquired after the root's Memento-Datetime (final selection is part of step 5). If no closest memento was available, processing finished.

Step 5. Download embedded memento. The representation for the selected eURI-M was retrieved using *curl*. Status 503 Failures were retried twice. For the Bracket heuristic, the "on or after" eURI-M was retrieved first. If it bracketed the root, it was considered best. If it did not bracket the root, the Bracket heuristic fell back to Minimum Distance (which may have caused the "before" eURI-M to be selected and retrieved).

Step 6. Recursion. Steps 2–5 were repeated for HTML frames and other resources containing eURI-Rs.

As Table 6 shows, 1,619,805–1,623,354 eURI-Rs were found varying by source constraint and heuristic. Timemaps and mementos were found for 1,250,641–1,332,993 (73.1%–78.1%) of URI-Rs. rURI-Ms average 21.2–21.2 eURI-Rs each, of which only 14.2–15.1 had available eURI-Ms. The primary reason for not finding mementos was that 19.3%–24.4% of eURI-Rs were not archived, as shown by the *No timemaps* reason. The next most common cause was 404 status (2.5%-2.9% of URI-Ms), which indicates the archive was not able to acquire a copy of the eURI-R. Other reasons account for about 1% of eURI-Rs.

5. RESULTS

5.1 Completeness

Completeness is the ratio of available mementos to required mementos. A rURI-M with no eURI-Ms (for example a plain HTML page with no CSS or JavaScript) is inherently 100% complete. That same web page with a single embedded image is 50% complete if no mementos for the image can be found (i.e., were never archived or not retrievable). Completeness is affected by both source constraint and heuristic.

Source Constraint and Completeness

As shown in the first line of Table 7, using multiple archives improves completeness by 4.1% for both heuristics. This is less than we expected. We hypothesize that the primary cause is minimal URI-R and Memento-Datetime overlap across the archives studied.

Heuristic and Completeness

Changing heuristic had a negligible impact on completeness, differing by just 0.01% for both single- and multi-archive recompositions. This is as we anticipated because the Bracket heuristic is an enhancement of the Minimum Distance heuristic. What is a little

Table 6: eURI-M Retrieval Statistics

Description	Mindist Single	Mindist Multi	Bracket Single	Bracket Multi
Memento Counts				
eURI-Rs	1,620,597	1,623,354	1,619,805	1,623,127
per rURI-M	19.7	19.7	19.7	19.7
eURI-Ms available	1,250,641	1,330,858	1,252,125	1,332,993
per rURI-M	14.2	15.1	14.2	15.1
eURI-Ms not found	369,956	292,494	367,680	290,134
Not-Found Reasons				
No timemaps	395,545	312,843	395,065	312,641
404	41,588	46,330	40,428	44,852
403	6,186	6,194	6,105	6,116
503	6,092	5,806	5,697	5,442
Other	2,970	3,746	2,810	3,508

Table 7: Completeness and Temporal Coherence

Description	Mindist Single	Mindist Multi	Bracket Single	Bracket Multi
Completeness				
Mean complete	76.1%	80.2%	76.2%	80.3%
Mean missing	23.9%	19.8%	23.8%	19.7%
Temporal Coherence				
Mean Prima Facie Coherent	41.0%	40.9%	54.7%	54.6%
Mean Possibly Coherent	27.3%	28.7%	12.8%	14.2%
Mean Probably Violative	2.5%	5.3%	2.5%	5.3%
Mean Prima Facie Violative	5.3%	5.3%	6.2%	6.2%

surprising is that there is any difference at all—both heuristics will either find or not find an eURI-M for the same URI-R and target datetime. The difference has two causes. First, the heuristics can select different eURI-Ms for the same URI-R and target datetime; one may be available and the other not. Second, even when both are available, they may have different eURI-Rs.

5.2 Temporal Coherence

Mean temporal coherence values for eURI-Ms are in the lower section of Table 7. These means represent the percentage of all required URI-Ms in the specified coherence state. Most of the available URI-Ms were Prima Facie Coherent, ranging from a mean of 41.0% for Mindist/Single to 54.7% for Bracket/Single. Adding Possibly Coherent increases the means to 63.8%–69.6%. On the other hand, 7.8%–11.5% of required mementos were violative, with 5.3%–6.2% Prima Facie Violative.

Source Constraint and Temporal Coherence

Unlike completeness, multiple archives have little effect on temporal coherence, just 0.1%. However, using multiple archives appears to reduce Prima Facie Coherence. This is a side effect of the fact that during this study only the Internet Archive returned original Last-Modified headers[3]. Thus, only the Internet Archive's URI-Ms could be Prima Facie Coherent. When using multiple archives, Internet Archive rURI-Ms can be paired with eURI-Ms from other archives. Since Last-Modified is not available from other archives, those eURI-Ms cannot be Prima Facie Coherent. If paired with an Internet Archive rURI-M, the eURI-Ms may have been Prima Facie Coherent. Using multiple archives improves the Possibly Coherent mean. More available eURI-M increases the likelihood that the

---

[3] Several other web archives now also return original Last-Modified headers.

Table 8: eURI-M Temporal Coherence Counts

Description	Mindist Single	Mindist Multi	Bracket Single	Bracket Multi
Prima Facie Coherent	622,565	621,447	864,736	859,625
Possibly coherent	497,405	466,046	244,104	215,585
Probably violative	104,376	53,734	104,339	53,694
Prima Facie Violative	100,760	103,662	114,062	117,469
Total	1,325,106	1,244,889	1,327,241	1,246,373

eURI-M selected will match a Possibly Coherent pattern. Multiple archives also increase Probably Violative counts. The primary reason is the increase in eURI-M without Last-Modified datetimes. Multiple archives also increase completeness by 4.1%, but 2.8% is an increase in Probably Violative URI-Ms. The violative eURI-Ms ratio stays the same with multiple archives.

Heuristic and Temporal Coherence

Compared to Mindist, the Bracket heuristic increased Prima Facie Coherent eURI-Ms by 13.7%. However, Possibly Coherent eURI-Ms decreased by 14.5% and Prima Facie Violatives eURI-Ms by 0.9%. This appears to be reduction in coherence—quite unexpected. Indeed, we expected to see the coherence values increase and the violatives decrease. The Bracket heuristic makes two changes when Last-Modified is available. First, when selecting the best eURI-M and the rURI-M Memento-Datetime is bracketed by an eURI-M lifetime (see 4.2.1), then the eURI-M is Prima Facie Coherent. Compared to Mindist's Memento-Datetime-only calculation, Bracket is much more likely to select a Prima Facie Coherent eURI-M over a Possibly Coherent eURI-M, increasing Prima Facie Coherent eURI-Ms and decreasing Possibly Coherent eURI-Ms as shown in Table 8. Second, when the root is not bracketed, Last-Modified is used in the fall-back Mindist calculation, which increases the selection of eURI-Ms captured after the root. All these are Prima Facie Violative by definition (see 3.3). However, because Bracket uses eURI-M lifetime instead of just a point in time whenever possible, even with the increase in violatives, Bracket still provides a more accurate representation of the composite memento.

Composite Memento Coherence

Figure 7 and Table 9 provide two other, more compelling, views of the same data. (The figure shows only the Bracket heuristic and Single Archive source constraint due to space limitations.) Each row on the plots represents one sample URI-R. The horizontal axis represents the rURI-M Memento-Datetime. Only 2,756 of the the rows contain data; the other 1,244 sample URI-Rs had no timemaps (see Table 4) or were not publicly available (i.e., 403 status). For the available URI-Rs, 88,054 rURI-Ms were selected (see 4.3). Of these, 93.6% could be retrieved and were recomposed as shown under *Bracket Single* column in the *All Coherence States* row. Excluding composite mementos containing Prima Facie or Probably Violative eURI-Ms, leaves 54.8%–65.1% (*Possibly Coherent & Prima Facie Coherent* row). And, as the last row of Table 9 shows, only 12.4%–17.9% are both 100% Prima Facie Coherent and 100% complete. Figure 7 provides a visual depiction: 7(a) includes all composite mementos, 7(b) excludes composite mementos with Prima Facie or Probably Violatives, and 7(c) includes only composite mementos that are both 100% complete and composed only from Prima Facie Coherent eURI-Ms. These results are striking and could have significant implications for non-casual uses such as litigation [19] and historical research. Still, public web

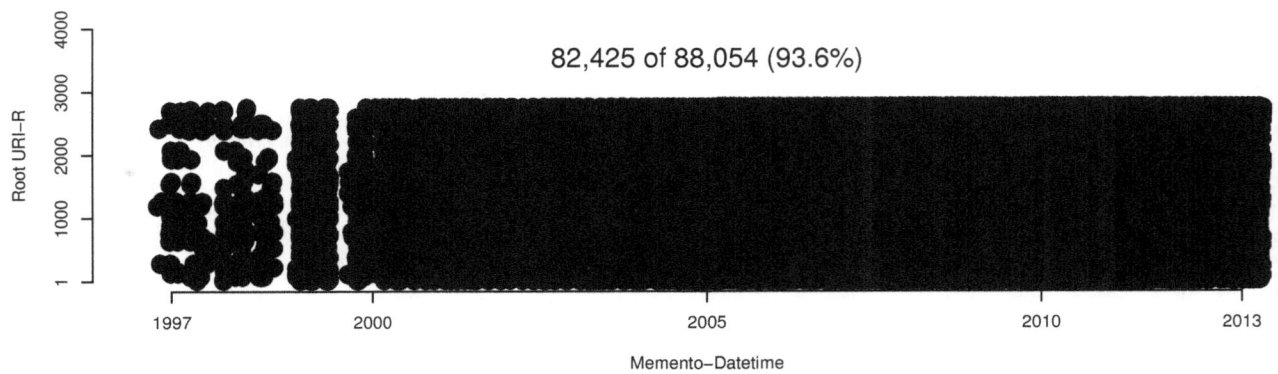

82,425 of 88,054 (93.6%)

Memento–Datetime

(a) All Composite Mementos

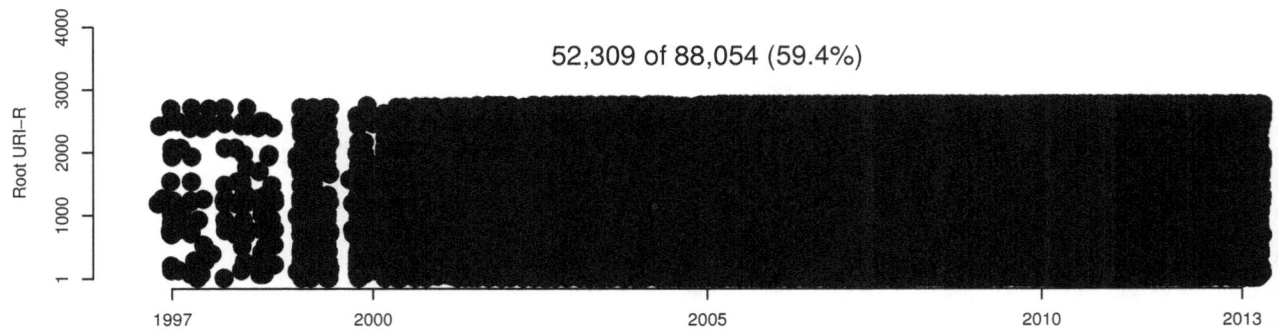

52,309 of 88,054 (59.4%)

(b) No Prima Facie or Probably Violatives

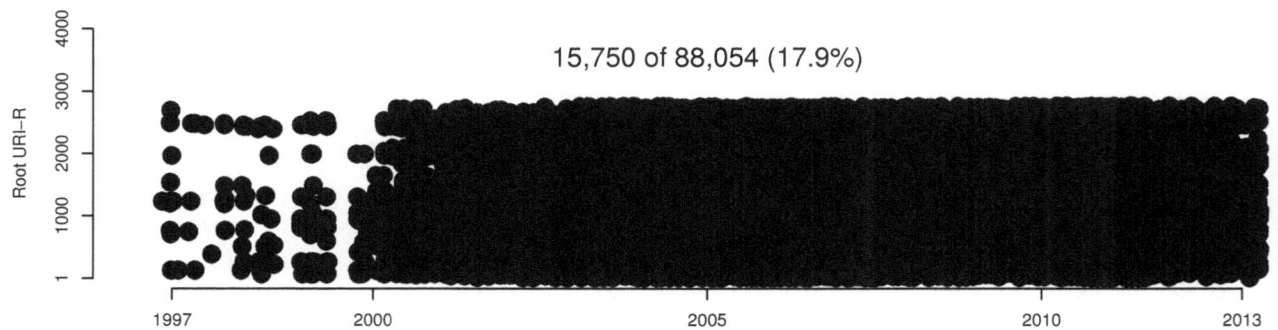

15,750 of 88,054 (17.9%)

(c) Complete and Prima Facie Coherent

Figure 7: Composite Memento Coherence

Table 9: Composite Memento Coherence

Description	Mindist Single		Mindist Multi		Bracket Single		Bracket Multi	
	Quantity	Percent	Quantity	Percent	Quantity	Percent	Quantity	Percent
All Root Mementos in Timemaps	88,054	100.0%	88,054	100.0%	88,054	100.0%	88,054	100.0%
All Composite Mementos (complete and incomplete)								
All Coherence States	82,425	93.6%	82,425	93.6%	82,425	93.6%	82,425	93.6%
Probably Violative through Prima Facie Coherent	62,749	71.3%	62,603	71.1%	60,525	68.7%	60,525	68.7%
Possibly Coherent & Prima Facie Coherent	54,120	61.5%	48,289	54.8%	52,309	59.4%	52,309	59.4%
Prima Facie Coherent only	23,147	26.3%	20,262	23.0%	34,074	38.7%	34,074	38.7%
Complete Composite Mementos Only								
All Coherence States	26,969	30.6%	29,200	33.2%	27,077	30.8%	27,077	30.8%
Probably Violative through Prima Facie Coherent	23,284	26.4%	25,180	28.6%	22,678	25.8%	22,678	25.8%
Possibly Coherent & Prima Facie Coherent	21,576	24.5%	21,976	25.0%	21,010	23.9%	21,010	23.9%
Prima Facie Coherent only	10,944	12.4%	10,901	12.4%	15,750	17.9%	15,750	17.9%

archive interfaces give no indication that on average only 17.9% of holdings are both 100% complete and 100% Prima Facie Coherent.

6. FUTURE WORK

6.1 Redirection and Missing Mementos

The research conducted so far has accepted the lists of URI-Ms in timemaps as ground truth; however, timemaps only tell part of the story. For example, a URI-M listed in a timemap may redirect to another with a different Memento-Datetime [5]. Redirections are likely to impact temporal coherence, which could change the coherence state of some eURI-Ms. Redirection could also be an indication of duplication; however, timemaps and archives provide no indication of cause for redirections, so we cannot be sure. Timemaps also list URI-Ms that do not exist or are not accessible, which this study simply considers missing. A heuristic that searches the timemap to locate reasonable substitutes for missing URI-Ms could be developed.

6.2 Duplicates and Similarity

This study calculated deltas as the simple difference between rURI-M and eURI-M Memento-Datetimes (as is common practice for web archives). We have observed that web archives frequently return identical representations for multiple Memento-Datetimes. Consider an rURI-M with a Memento-Datetime of July 5 and two eURI-Ms with Memento-Datetimes of July 1 and July 10. It appears that the best delta is four days (July 5 – July 1). However, if the eURI-Ms have identical representations (e.g., a logo that has not changed), then the July 1 eURI-M should be considered Prima Facie Coherent instead of Possibly Coherent. For file types such as images, duplicates are easily identified using message digest algorithms (e.g., SHA-256). However, text (and especially HTML), is commonly modified for branding and user interface purposes by every web archive we have studied. This is evident in Figure 1, which shows the banner added by the Internet Archive's Wayback Machine. The changes are inconsequential to human users but prevent simple machine duplicate detection. Lexical Signatures [29, 23] and the *SimHash* [13, 24] algorithm may be able to help determine if modified files similar enough to be considered semantically equivalent and thus Prima Facie or Possibly Coherent. Ainsworth et al. [4] define equality and similarity patterns that can be used once appropriate similarity methods and measures are identified.

6.3 Communicating Status

One significant issue with existing web archive user interfaces is that temporal coherence is not communicated to the user. An icon or symbol that quickly communicates the temporal coherence of composite mementos would be very useful.

7. CONCLUSIONS

This study addressed temporal coherence of composite mementos recomposed from existing web archive holdings, comparing the use of Single and Multiple Archives and two eURI-M selection heuristics: Bracket and Minimum Distance. Using a sample of 4,000 original URIs with 343,303 corresponding URI-Ms, 88,054 (25.6%) URI-Ms were selected for recomposition. Of these, 82,425 (93.6%) were available and recomposed. We found that using multiple archives improves completeness by 4.1% but has no significant impact on temporal coherence. We also found that the Bracket heuristic improved temporal coherence, in particular increasing the number of Prima Facie Coherent mementos by 13.7%, compared with the Minimum Distance heuristic typically employed by web

archives. To maximize completeness, multiple archives provide the best results; changing heuristic provided no significant benefit. To maximize coherence, the Bracket heuristic with a single archive provides the best results (privided that the archive has significant holdings for the URI-R). Truly significant is the finding that at most 17.9% of composite mementos held by web archives are both complete and Prima Facie Coherent.

As of this study, only the Internet Archive returns the original Last-Modified header, which significantly improves both eURI-M selection and temporal coherence evaluation. We recommend that all web archives capture and return all original headers.

Acknowledgments

Memento is a joint project between the Los Alamos National Laboratory Research Library and Old Dominion University. We are grateful to the Internet Archive for their continued support of Memento access to their archive.

8. REFERENCES

[1] S. G. Ainsworth, A. AlSum, H. SalahEldeen, M. C. Weigle, and M. L. Nelson. How much of the Web is archived? In *Proceedings of JCDL'11*, pages 133–136, June 2011.

[2] S. G. Ainsworth, A. AlSum, H. SalahEldeen, M. C. Weigle, and M. L. Nelson. How much of the Web is archived? Technical Report arXiv:1212.6177, Old Dominion University, December 2012.

[3] S. G. Ainsworth and M. L. Nelson. Evaluating sliding and sticky target policies by measuring temporal drift in acyclic walks through a web archive. In *Proceedings of JCDL'13*, July 2013.

[4] S. G. Ainsworth, M. L. Nelson, and H. Van de Sompel. A framework for evaluation of composite memento temporal coherence. Technical Report arXiv:1402.0928, Old Dominion University, February 2014.

[5] A. AlSum, M. L. Nelson, R. Sanderson, and H. Van de Sompel. Archival HTTP redirection retrieval policies. In *Proceedings of WWW'13 Companion*, pages 1051–1058, Republic and Canton of Geneva, Switzerland, 2013.

[6] A. AlSum, M. C. Weigle, M. L. Nelson, and H. Van de Sompel. Profiling web archive coverage for top-level domain and content language. *International Journal on Digital Libraries*, 14(3):149–166, 2014.

[7] M. Ben Saad and S. Gançarski. Archiving the Web using page changes patterns: a case study. In *Proceedings of JCDL'11*, pages 113–122, 2011.

[8] M. Ben Saad and S. Gançarski. Improving the quality of web archives through the importance of changes. In *Proceedings of DEXA'11*, pages 394–409, 2011.

[9] M. Ben Saad, Z. Pehlivan, and S. Gançarski. Coherence-oriented crawling and navigation using patterns for web archives. In *Proceedings of TPDL'11*, pages 421–433, 2011.

[10] A. Bright. Web evidence points to pro-Russia rebels in downing of MH17. *Christian Science Monitor*, 2014.

[11] J. F. Brunelle, M. Kelly, H. SalahEldeen, M. C. Weigle, and M. L. Nelson. Not all mementos are created equal: Measuring the impact of missing resources. In *Proceedings of JCDL'14*, pages 321–330, September 2014.

[12] J. F. Brunelle, M. L. Nelson, L. Balakireva, R. Sanderson, and H. Van de Sompel. Evaluating the SiteStory transactional web archive with the ApacheBench tool. In *Proceedings of TPDL'13*, pages 204–215, 2012.

[13] M. S. Charikar. Similarity estimation techniques from rounding algorithms. In *Proceedings of STOC'02*, pages 380–388, New York, NY, USA, 2002.

[14] M. Day. Preserving the fabric of our lives: A survey of web preservation initiatives. In *Proceedings of ECDL'05*, pages 461–472, 2003.

[15] D. Denev, A. Mazeika, M. Spaniol, and G. Weikum. SHARC: Framework for quality-conscious web archiving. *Proceedings of the VLDB Endowment*, 2(1):586–597, August 2009.

[16] C. E. Dyreson, H. ling Lin, and Y. Wang. Managing versions of web documents in a transaction-time web server. In *Proceedings of WWW'04*, 2004.

[17] G. Eysenbach and M. Trudel. Going, going, still there: Using the WebCite service to permanently archive cited web pages. *Journal of Medical Internet Research*, 7(5), 2005.

[18] K. Fitch. Web site archiving: an approach to recording every materially different response produced by a website. In *9th Australasian World Wide Web Conference, Sanctuary Cove, Queensland, Australia,*, pages 5–9, 2003.

[19] B. A. Howell. Proving web history: How to use the Internet Archive. *Journal of Internet Law*, 9(8):3–9, 2006.

[20] S. M. Jones, M. L. Nelson, H. Shankar, and H. V. de Sompel. Bringing web time travel to MediaWiki: An assessment of the Memento MediaWiki Extension. Technical Report arXiv:1406.3876, Old Dominion University and Los Alamos National Laboratory, June 2014.

[21] B. Kahle. Wayback Machine just grew today to 479,160,477,000 pages. Go @internetarchive ! https://archive.org/web [Twitter post]. Retrieved from `https://twitter.com/brewster_kahle/status/603611567276589056`.

[22] B. Kahle. Wayback machine: Now with 240,000,000,000 URLs. `http://blog.archive.org/2013/01/09/updated-wayback/`, January 2013.

[23] M. Klein and M. L. Nelson. Revisiting lexical signatures to (re-)discover web pages. In B. Christensen-Dalsgaard, D. Castelli, B. Ammitzbøll Jurik, and J. Lippincott, editors, *Research and Advanced Technology for Digital Libraries*, volume 5173 of *Lecture Notes in Computer Science*, pages 371–382. Springer Berlin Heidelberg, 2008.

[24] G. S. Manku, A. Jain, and A. Das Sarma. Detecting near-duplicates for web crawling. In *Proceedings of WWW'07*, pages 141–150, New York, NY, USA, 2007.

[25] J. Masanès. *Web Archiving*. Springer, Heidelberg, 2006.

[26] F. McCown and M. L. Nelson. Characterization of search engine caches. In *Proceedings of IS&T Archiving 2007*, pages 48–52, May 2007. (Also available as arXiv:cs/0703083v2).

[27] G. Mohr, M. Stack, I. Rnitovic, D. Avery, and M. Kimpton. Introduction to Heritrix, an archival quality web crawler. In *Proceedings of IWAW'04*, September 2004.

[28] K. C. Negulescu. Web archiving @ the Internet Archive. `http://www.digitalpreservation.gov/news/events/ndiipp_meetings/ndiipp10/docs/July21/session09/NDIIPP072110FinalIA.ppt`, 2010.

[29] S.-T. Park, D. M. Pennock, C. L. Giles, and R. Krovetz. Analysis of lexical signatures for finding lost or related documents. In *Proceedings of the 25th annual international ACM SIGIR conference on Research and development in information retrieval*, pages 11–18, New York, NY, USA, 2002.

[30] M. Spaniol, D. Denev, A. Mazeika, G. Weikum, and P. Senellart. Data quality in web archiving. In *Proceedings of WICOW'09*, pages 19–26, 2009.

[31] M. Spaniol, A. Mazeika, D. Denev, and G. Weikum. "Catch me if you can": Visual analysis of coherence defects in web archiving. In *Proceedings of IWAW'09*, pages 27–37, 2009.

[32] M. Thelwall and L. Vaughan. A fair history of the Web? examining country balance in the Internet Archive. *Library & Information Science Research*, 26(2):162–176, 2004.

[33] B. Tofel. 'Wayback' for accessing web archives. In *Proceedings of IWAW'07)*, 2007.

[34] H. Van de Sompel, M. Nelson, and R. Sanderson. HTTP framework for time-based access to resource states—Memento (IETF RFC 7089), December 2013. `http://tools.ietf.org/html/rfc7089`.

[35] H. Van de Sompel, M. L. Nelson, R. Sanderson, L. L. Balakireva, S. Ainsworth, and H. Shankar. Memento: Time travel for the Web. Technical Report arXiv:0911.1112, 2009.

[36] M. C. Weigle. How much of the Web is archived? `http://ws-dl.blogspot.com/2011/06/2011-06-23-how-much-of-web-is-archived.html`, June 2011.

APPENDIX

A. WEB ARCHIVES

Table 10 lists the web archives used for this study.

Table 10: Web Archives Used in This Study

Archive	Home Page
Archiv Českého Webu	wayback.webarchiv.cz
Archive-It!	wayback.archive-it.org
Archief Web EU	www.archiefweb.eu
Archuivo de la Portuguesa	arquivo.pt
L'Arxiu Web de Catalunya	www.padi.cat
Library and Archives Canada	www.collectionscanada.gc.ca
Hrvatski arhiv weba	haw.nsk.hr
Internet Archive	www.archive.org
Icelandic Web Archive	wayback.vefsafn.is
Library of Congress Web Archives	webarchive.loc.gov
The National Archives (UK)	webarchive.nationalarchives.gov.uk
NTU Web Archive	webarchive.lib.ntu.edu.tw
UK Web Archive (British Library)	www.webarchive.org.uk
Wikia	wikia.com
Wikipedia	www.wikipedia.org

Opportunistic Layered Hypernarrative

Harold T. Goranson
Sirius-Beta, Inc.
1976 Munden Point Rd
Virginia Beach, Virginia, US
tedg@@sirius-beta.com

ABSTRACT

We are designing a system to model narrative structures as expressed in lightly formalized text-centric chunks. The system is novel in shifting much of the organizational complexity to a categoric reasoning system in a two sorted logic. We optimize for two goals. One goal is to grow a pool of stored insights concerning complex narrative constructions, learned by aggregating crowd-sourced insights. These emphasize qualities that escape capture by existing methods, and include deliberate ambiguities, poetic allusions, irony, self reference, dynamic reinterpretation and cinematic devices. A second goal, described here, is to present suggested, machine generated narrative paths for an unskilled user, generated on the fly and informed by developing insights of multiple narrative situations. The narrative paths may follow the target video's narrative, annotative machine constructed essays or some synthesis of these.

Categories and Subject Descriptors

H.5.4 [**Hypertext/Hypermedia**]: Theory

General Terms

Human Factors

Keywords

Narrative structure, Two-sorted logic, Ontology graphs.

1. INTRODUCTION

In information environments such as data-fed websites and expert systems, users have access to many narrative elements. These can take the form of: small chunks of locally structured information (often internally structured using natural language), finer grained data elements (usually structured in databases and/or graphs) and agents (currently presented as contacts in social graphs, but sometimes as services). These environments are growing in scale and potential utility faster than we can usefully assemble and navigate them. Each has robust engineering communities and associated scientific disciplines.

The general problem that we address here is one often posed: how to identify appropriate candidate elements from large pools and structure them opportunistically to provide value, itself dynamically defined. (A more specific application is described later.) Current approaches, which appear inadequate to serve this need, [16, 34] can be categorized as:

1) *locally hardwired*, where users make point-to-point connections that can be serially followed by other users or services to build useful insights. 'Connections' in this context are usually hyperlinks, social affiliations and data/ ontological relations. A key limit in this case is that the local connections are blind to the user's intended purpose and constrained to only a few options for global structure. In the case of the Web, these connections are go-to navigational links; a user has to visit a candidate to evaluate its utility.

2) *local options*. Where the previous case consists of fine-grained connections that the user has to assemble, this case has the same fine-grained elements, but in curated contexts whose coherent topic may be closely related to the desired information structure, for example, a real or virtual essay. Curated link farms served this purpose in early years of the Web, whereas search engines (covering the Web or data pools) are popular today. Social trust is growing as a strategy, relying on the circular assumption that likeminded people will have similar interests (and report promising paths).

3) *global curation*. These are sources that have information already coherently structured in larger assemblies that can be digested for a generic purpose.

The Web as it exists today is an example of the first. Xanadu [32] and Memex [10] are examples of the second. (Memex assumed an automatic text recognition driven facility to create the hard links.) Subscriptions from social networks, RSS feeds, email lists and so on often present curated links of the second kind. Wikipedia is an example of the third, but special purpose blogs are proliferating, indicating a strong user pull.

In practice, an ordinary user starts with one of these three strategies and, following hunches, explores possibilities enabled by the others. All of these strategies are expected to

HT '15, September 1–4, 2015, Guzelyurt, Northern Cyprus.

improve in the ability to help a user assemble the information he/she wants, whether for insight or amusement. But we believe that a more radical rethinking is required; suppose you had a system that understood how to structure information, had the ability to learn the types of structures you found useful and was able to 'look ahead' at possibilities to guide you.

This system will construct candidate narratives and suggests them as links, as whole essays or instead conduct a conversation with you to query and guide. The system we call *redframer* would help you follow a path that had coherence with your goal, whether the goal was to assemble an essay-like insight or simply be entertainingly engaged.

The focus domain is long form film (and television) stories. The approach depends on narrative in several ways, both as the subject of analysis and in order to understand how humans structure chunked information. The products of *redframer* are essays, conversations or entertaining explorations about films and the general film experience.

The presented possible navigation paths are based on an understanding of three primary narrative layers: the narrative of the film (or other narratively based source), the narrative of known successful types of the opportunistic hypertext 'narratives' being created and the inferred narrative of what the user is up to with the endeavor.

We opportunistically link chunks in structures to create these experiences. For us, 'links' are of three types: semantic relations of the ontological kind (regulated by a combination of a management system for local ontologies, the user and situated narrative reasoner); narrative influences that model the current and possible influences in the possible narratives, and navigation links that are associated with the former. (All these are described in more detail below.)

We rely on a few esoteric tools, recently become practical: emerging work in cognitive science that leverages a broad notion of narrative; situation theory as the formal framework on the human side; and categoric, scalable functional reactive programming on the machine(s) side.

The focus of this paper is on underlying structure, with the user interface accommodation (discovery, registration and presentation) reported elsewhere [26, 20, 23, 21]. Parts of the initial study were performed for the US intelligence community [18].

The project fits squarely in the hypertext domain. We operate at the boundary of machine and human reader; we are text-centric and we link text (and other media) chunks by relations, some of which are serially navigable by a user. Our intent is to build a machine reasoning system that understands stories well enough to create them and stories about stories as well as a human. We use some techniques new to the machine reasoning domain, yet based on solid, individually proven component technologies.

A simple, broadly used application is described here. The machine observes feature films, initially understood by an automated interpreter [19]. More pertinent is the 'learning'

about films by aggregating insights from human annotators. The learning infrastructure is wholly novel; it works with narrative structures and metanarratives, but employs mathematics outside logic. An implicit assumption is that logic is inadequate in approaching narrative [15].

Companion papers describe these novel operations [24, 25]. This paper provides a high level view in the hypertext/hypermedia context. *redframer* has machine-generated links that are dynamically generated on the fly, peculiar to the instant situation, user and history, and that generate only narratively coherent path suggestions. They are linked via text but refer to cinematic features. Interacting with *redframer* improves the machine's understanding.

redframer supports annotation of video media to create closely allied metadata, as do many examples. In addition, the system described here automatically structures the metadata as narratives, using the narrative structure of the source (with others) as a reference. The project as currently scoped is not intended to support interactivity with the media directly. A user instead will navigate a specially designed presentation of the media object as described in [22].

2. NARRATIVE AS INFORMATION COHERENCE

We leverage several areas of research in concert to enable the system; central is the notion that narrative captures causal transformation/coherence. This work has been influenced by Paul Thagard's theories of cognitive coherence [36] in that coherence can occur indirectly and across an entire system. It also draws from Thagard and Kuhn's work on conceptual transformation [35, 28], where the achievement of such coherence might involve the integration of incompatible elements, and require a fundamental change in the structure of the system in order to do so.

The influence of these theories is philosophical only; we do not use Thagard's model of beliefs, goals and actions, and instead draw from narrative processes to develop a system based on narrative causal agency [12], where causal agency is determined by the distinguishing of an anomalous agent from a particular field or context [17]. Our agents drive the assembly of narratives, so they are compelling and coherent at many levels.

The approach relies on the way humans structure information chunks in narrative. We opportunistically link chunks into models to create narrative experiences. Links in part provide layered navigation paths, based on an understanding of three main layers: the narrative of the film (or other narratively based source), the narrative of successful cases of types of the opportunistic hypertext being created and the inferred narrative of what drives the user's activities.

The original research motivation was to support a community of intelligence analysts with diverse skills and goals, in order to discover: what is happening in certain places, or did; what is going on in the minds (the worlds) of key participants; how are other actors (including nonhumans) changing this; and what new or enhanced activity would change that and how? All these are narratives.

The current focus is easier because it is more limited: what is going on in a film and films in general; why do they engage (including cinematic effects); what can be said as metanarrative that is itself engaging?

But the new focus is also more challenging in terms of ontology management. The intelligence case had manageable notions of truth and causality. In film, we allow fictional worlds, magical causality and we don't particularly care if the metanarrative is 'true.' While we prefer useful, portable insights in some resulting narrative, sheer entertainment value is sufficient for others in our *redframer* project.

3. METANARRATIVES IN AND ABOUT FILM

Our work is expressly interested in the kind of rich narratives representative in literature and long form films. This domain has traditionally challenged AI and formally constructed hypertext both of which require (at least temporally) single threads of meaning and have trouble with ambiguity and poetic resonance. Also, existing methods poorly handle retroactive reinterpretation; this quality is common but explicit in mysteries and con stories.

The approach outlined below captures these engaging qualities. Since starting the project over a decade ago, we have been surprised by the many levels a typical narrative contains. Typically these employ irony, self-awareness and self-reference in creative combination. Moreover, the techniques in modern film are getting more novel over time and many cases leverage knowledge of prior cases.

To understand these, we initiated a simple, broad study named *filmsfolded* to observe the forms of these internal metalevels and relationships in long form film. Thousands of films were viewed over a dozen years, with thousands of participants commenting on the piecewise published observations [5, 2]. Useful dynamics were extracted [3].

Independently, a co-researcher, Cardier, developed a formalism for capturing multilayered, dynamic causality in narrative [12]. We employ it for modeling soft dynamics and retroactive interpretation in the situated reasoner described below. *redframer*'s goal is to allow user-created metanarratives to be layered onto existing film narratives and metanarrative structures with as much richness as the internal layers, using the same folding vocabulary where effective.

4. SITUATION THEORY AS A FORMAL FOUNDATION

The basic challenge is that formal logic of any kind is not amenable to narrative — this is a well understood problem in the logic community [27]. A workable, formal, philosophical framework for this type of problem was developed in the 1980s as situation theory [9]. It suggests a second reasoning system over situations that control the interpretive semantics of logical statements.

Later, a type system for the theory was refined for the logical components [13], allowing some reasoning over the (typically open set of) facts that constitute salient situations and that move in and out of influence. The result is practical for use, supporting a two sorted logic. One system (that of serialized facts) can be supported in a computer, the other in that system is supported in human brains albeit guided by the formalism of the theory [14].

Recent advances in mathematical metamodeling [8] concern modeling quantum effects in physics, using a two sort, with the second sort abstracting logical structures (but not semantics) and 'reasoning' about structural dynamics using category theory. This is a dynamically developing area of mathematics with maturing methods, suitable for coding in a computer.

Developments in yet another field, that of functional programming, provide a maturing family of functional reactive programming techniques that can support just these kinds of second sorts: categoric, massively scaled and dynamic [31]. This style of programming is developing quickly and even in the last five years competing mainstream frameworks have appeared for mission critical work [4, 1].

Together, these developments allow situations and their transformation to be coded. Our work explores how far such a development can probe, capture and perhaps even embellish on long-form narratives.

Note that use of these categoric reasoning systems to model and create narrative structures does not unduly constrain the first logic. You can still use modal logics, Bayesian systems and graph reasoning. The requirement for a first sort logic to work in our system is lightweight: only that it can be linearized. In our experience this is nearly automatable so long as the connectives fit the 'and-then' and 'while' vocabulary [29, 30] natural to both narrative expressions and the representations [13] of modern situation theory.

5. LOCAL ONTOLOGICAL REGISTRATION

A well understood barrier in formal systems that build structure is the burden on the user to work within the formalism [33]. In our work, the way the situated reasoner (the second sort) suggests and learns narrative constructions requires little of the user. It should be fluid, pleasant and often delightful. Everything we have done is designed to increase the reward to the user while lowering the cost of registering an item in the system.

The problem is in what we call the first sort, where a user enters a statement in natural language and registers it in the system. Only with proper registration in the system can any assisted structuring method work, but in order for the system to be at all attractive at scale and with users of ordinary skill, this task has to be light-weight.

By introducing a semantic-free second sort, and focusing only on narrative structure, the burden to register content is lowered. Current natural language processing systems are inadequate for this; there is already a discernible shift from lexical to compositional semantics [11]. Conceptually, we are just further extending the scope to larger compositions, and reducing the need for lexical registration.

Figure 1: Each phrase is clarified in a lightweight assisted NLP system. In this case, the writer is creating a Joker-friendly essay about a Batman movie, humorously referencing the original comics. 'Swat' is highlighted because it is a synonym. The action has different resonance in three worlds. The next chunks in the essay are dynamically suggested by *redframer*. The user can move distance, make/move connections and enter new nodes. In this example, he has previously entered 'bizarro world' but not connected it here.

Our ontological requirements differ from those of a conventional system: all interpretation is within a construction of situations, some governing others. The effective notion of an ontology changes as the narrative progresses and different situations (as managed by categoric functions of the second sort) come to bear. This means that each narrative fragment (a 'chunk') needs only be registered in the local situations the originator intends. In other words, the heavy lifting is done by reasoning over situations in the second sort, not by structure captured from the user. All the user has to do is help the system understand the initial, local meaning of a small chunk of semantically bounded information.

While technology in the rest of the system has been piece-meal validated, we are still refining this process. Our current approach is to present a small directed graph of ontological nature, with no more than a dozen labeled nodes. It represents the system's best guess at what the user meant, being primarily a lexical mapping of the chunk's text into our baseline common knowledge reference ontology as situationally transformed at that instant by the second sort.

For example, if the focus is the movie 'The Dark Knight' and the observed context is the creation of an essay about iconography, then an appearance of the word 'bat' in the chunk is a large semantic distance from the verb and sport interpretations in the global semantic graph, and these will not be displayed. The user will instead see nodes clarifying the semantic distance to flying mammals, and certain cartoon behavior, asking for refinements. Perhaps this user will note that he is more concerned with qualities of a character found in an external knowledge of comic books.

The elements of the graph that are displayed are computed by both sorts. The first sort's match is a simple lexical one: the term 'bat' for instance will match that term in a global knowledgebase we maintain, for example ConceptNet [7]. The second sort, knowing the relative (narrative) contexts, filters the lexical matches. A user can extend the range of the displayed graph to clarify, and the second sort may adjust what is displayed if an unusual structure is noticed. For example, the essay the user is creating may use a hitting metaphor in the essay on Batman.

It will take some larger user testing with this UI to find the right balance of precision, prediction and ease. But we have enough experience to know that the user has to have an immediate reward: instant feedback on how his information bends the semantic space at large (in the situation/narrative he is creating) by display of his information rippling through a larger section of the graph and a second graphical display as the narrative lattice (not shown here) that the system has assembled.

This can switch among relevant narratives, including the focus narrative, which in this case is the movie. Another required narrative is the construction the user is currently creating. Other narratives may be interesting to this user, for example how her new information changes the default, constructed essay that gives a noir interpretation of the film (perhaps from the perspective of the Joker.)

We present three options for hypertext views. One has been mentioned: the essay. This is a linear presentation with outline structure. It may be constructed by the system after the current chunk. All content, including externally referenced content (perhaps a segment of a video interview with Heath Ledger) is displayed in-line by default.

Figure 1 shows this view on the left with outliner controls. Figure 2 below shows another location in the same essay, also on the left, but in text flow.

Another option gives the user more control over the next displayed chunks. In this search-like view, everything that has gone before is considered a query of the *redframer* system and options are presented to the right. These are all next steps in different coherent narratives. The system still presents what it thinks is the best suggested narrative in the remaining outline, but has these more radical, opportunistic paths offered. As usual, a user can choose to initiate a wholly new and (to the system) surprising turn.

A tag (the left facing arrow) at each chunk preserves past branches in this session, by this user, by other users who may have visited a saved session, or by what the system believes other users of interest might have created.

A conversational mode is being explored as well, where the 'narrative' is a conversation that emulates and possibly integrates with existing social networks and involves known friends, others optionally accepted with similar interests and of course the *redframer* system. We consider this a way to better introduce branches from outside. We have not yet designed a good way to toggle governing editorship, namely how much influence a single participant can have over the group narrative. An advisory group [6] is guiding this.

6. A CATEGORIC, TWO-SORTED REASONING SYSTEM

The unique component is the reasoning system. So far as the user is concerned, the *redframer* system knows a lot about movies in general, including the one the user is considering. She also knows how classes of people and social groups interact with film. All of this is from large numbers of crowd-sourced chunks, both contributed and observed, strung together in intersecting narratives. Moreover, the system may

← Think I am kidding about Batman being the bad guy in this movie? Consider this scene where Joker's back is turned, and he is walking away, and yet his Moriarty throws a shuriken. The Joker bats away the threat and walks away without seeking a fight!

It is only later that he gets mean, after being provoked. ▶

← Heath Ledger mentions this reversal in an interview days before his death. He saw the Joker as the hero. ▼

▶ But most reporters present at the interview thought he was kidding… ▶

▶ In *Batman's Skinny Girlfriend* DC#4966, it is revealed that Bethany is Joker's cloned sister; killing Joker frees her from… ▶

▶ Ledger has a history of introducing conflicting subplots in his character's backstory. In *Brokeback Mountain,* tire salesmen… ▶

▶ A survey of movie and TV Joker characters… Cesar Romero's notion reflected his childhood abuse and loss of a sister… ▶

▶ Rollover image for suggestion…

Figure 2: The left side of the image has the essay as created or explored to that point by the user. In this case, the next chunk about the interview is suggested by the system and lightly displayed with the inline video expanded. The right side shows some alternative branch points suggested by the system. Hovering over them indicates suggested further paths and characteristics of the chunk like system-level modification and whether content is external.

know a lot about this user and what engages him, and so can opportunistically present new narrative paths for him to explore.

Superficially, the reasoner utilizes two pools of structure. One consists of the relatively small chunks of information that exist in the large graph structure. This has every (lexically-based) concept ever encountered by the combined users and every conceptual link ever made.

This pool also contains the registration of chunks against this session's fabric. New links and nodes may have been created. (The user may have noted that an upside down bat symbol on the Joker's underpants is a unique kind of joke.) The influence of some links will have been increased and some decreased. Though the first sort uses these adjusted graphs collectively as 'story ontologies,' the second sort uses them as a source for structure abstracted from semantics.

The process is one of extracting topology from logical structures. Because our logic statements are story fragments, it is easy to limit the connectives to an 'and-then' and 'while' vocabulary. With other constraints (a fact syntax and type system), this presents an easily abstractable structure that can target many possibilities for categories. Details have been described in a biomedical research context [24, 25].

Most of the work in so-called categoric quantum two-sorted logic targets monoids, but we have had success with a simpler abstraction chain. Narrative connections among chunks are represented as lattices. (Note, these are not navigational connections.) This allows for simple visualization of the nar-

rative influences, and use of mature tools from the conceptual graph and formal concept analysis communities.

The extracted categories can be skeletal in the form of half-duals. These have some intuitive utility in the interface. The second sort has a rough equivalent of an ontology that captures narrative dynamics, created (by experts) and discovered (by observation of *redframer* users) analogous to ontologies. These are implemented as reactive functors so any change in the semantic fabric in the first sort can have worldwide effect as the second sort changes the semantic distances.

7. CONCLUSION

Key components of the system have been piecewise demonstrated. We have confidence in the ability to present opportunistically derived narratives and narrative possibilities based on familiar story expression, have some initial insights to seed the second sort dynamics, and presume they constitute a critical mass.

Many elements of the first sort are straightforward engineering challenges, including management of the large chunk graphs. Functional reactive frameworks are now mainstream and could readily support more sophisticated category typed second sorts if required.

We are refining a strategy to mitigate problems in user requirements for semantic registration, natural language recognition, scalability and user interaction. Still to be proved is whether all the pieces can be put together in a non-research, mainstream context for useful work and fun.

8. REFERENCES

[1] Clojure web page. Clojure Site: https://clojure.org. Accessed: 2015-03.

[2] Filmsfolded database, 2000-2015. Filmsfolded Annotation Database: http://tedgoranson.filmsfolded.com.2015. Accessed: 2015-03.

[3] Filmsfolded essays, 2000-2015. Filmsfolded Annotation Database: http://filmsfolded.tedgoranson.com.2015. Accessed: 2015-03.

[4] Swift web page. Apple Developer Site: https://developer.apple.com/swift/. Accessed: 2015-03.

[5] Tedg comments, 2000-2015. The Internet Movie Database: http://www.imdb.com/user/ur0643062/comments. Accessed: 2015-03.

[6] redframer advisors. redframer Site: http://redframer.com/Forum. Accessed: 2015-03.

[7] Various. ConceptNet5 Web Site: http://conceptnet5.media.mit.edu. Accessed: 2014.

[8] S. Abramsky and B. Coecke. A categorical semantics of quantum protocols. In Proc. of the 19th Annual IEEE Symp. on Logic in Computer Sc., pages 415–425, 2001.

[9] J. Barwise and J. Perry. Situations and Attitudes. MIT Press, Cambridge, MA, 1983.

[10] V. Bush. As we may think. The Atlantic Monthly, 176(1), 1945.

[11] E. Cambria and B. White. Jumping NLP curves: A review of natural language processing research. IEEE Comp. Intelligence Mag., 9(2):48–57, 2014.

[12] B. Cardier. Unputdownable. PhD thesis, University of Melbourne, Melbourne, Australia, 2013.

[13] K. Devlin. Logic and Information. Cambridge University Press, Cambridge, UK, 1995.

[14] K. Devlin. Language at work. Technical report, Center for the Study of Logic and Information, Stanford University, Palo Alto, CA, 1996.

[15] K. Devlin. Goodbye, Descartes: The End of Logic and the Search for a New Cosmology of the Mind. Wiley, 1998.

[16] K. Devlin. Modeling Real Reasoning, pages 234–252. Springer-Verlag, Berlin, 2009.

[17] H. Einhorn and R. Hogarth. Judging probable cause. Psychological Bulletin, (99):3–19, 1986.

[18] H. T. Goranson. The Agile Virtual Enterprise: Cases, Metrics, Tools. Praeger, Westport, CT, 1999.

[19] H. T. Goranson. System and method for scalable semantic stream processing. Technical report, Sirius-Beta Corp., Virginia Beach, VA, 2011.

[20] H. T. Goranson. System and method for situated reasoning. USPTO 13/919,751, 2013.

[21] H. T. Goranson. System and method for space-time annotation-capable media scrubbing. USPTO 61/973,841, 2014.

[22] H. T. Goranson. System and method for space-time, annotation capable media scrubbing. Technical report, Sirius-Beta Corp., Virginia Beach, VA, 2014.

[23] H. T. Goranson and B. Cardier. System and method for ontology derivation. USPTO 14/093,229, 2013.

[24] H. T. Goranson and B. Cardier. A two-sorted logic for structurally modeling systems. Progress in Biophysics and Microbiology, 113(1):141–178, 2013.

[25] H. T. Goranson and B. Cardier. Pragmatic phenomenological types. To appear in Progress in Biophysics and Molecular Biology, 2015.

[26] H. T. Goranson and T. Schachman. Digital system for organizing diverse information. USPTO 8,751,918, 2007.

[27] R. Heuer. Psychology of intelligence analysis. Technical report, Center for the Study of Intelligence, Central Intelligence Agency, Washington, DC, 2001.

[28] T. S. Kuhn. The Structure of Scientific Revolutions. University of Chicago Press, Chicago, IL, 1973.

[29] D. Lehmann. A presentation of quantum logic based on an and then connective. J. of Logic and Computation, 18(1), 2008.

[30] D. Lehmann. Concrete foundations for categorical quantum physics. Technical Report TR- 2010-40, Leibniz Center, School of Engineering, Hebrew University, 2010.

[31] S. Lindley, P. Wadler, and J. Yallop. The arrow calculus. Jour. of Functional Prog., 20(1):51–69, 2010.

[32] T. H. Nelson. A file structure for the complex, the changing and the indeterminate. In ACM '65 Proceedings of the 1965 20th National Conference, pages 84–100, 1965.

[33] F. Shipman and C. Marshall. Formality considered harmful: Experiences, emerging themes, and directions on the use of formal representations in interactive systems. Computer-Supported Cooperative Work, (4):333–352, 1999.

[34] J. Sowa. The Role of Logic and Ontology in Language and Reasoning, pages 231–263. Springer, Berlin, 2010.

[35] P. Thagard. Conceptual Revolutions. Princeton University Press, Princeton, NJ, 1992.

[36] P. Thagard. Coherence in Thought and Action. MIT Press, Cambridge, MA, 2002.

No Reciprocity in "Liking" Photos: Analyzing *Like* Activities in Instagram

Jin Yea Jang   Kyungsik Han   Dongwon Lee

College of Information Sciences and Technology
The Pennsylvania State University, USA

{jzj157|kuh178|dlee}@ist.psu.edu

ABSTRACT

In social media, people often press a "Like" button to indicate their shared interest in a particular content or to acknowledge the user who posted the content. Such activities form relationships and networks among people, raising interesting questions about their unique characteristics and implications. However, little research has investigated such Likes as a main study focus. To address this lack of understanding, based on a theoretical framework, we present an analysis of the *structural*, *influential*, and *contextual* aspects of Like activities from the test datasets of 20 million users and their 2 billion Like activities in Instagram. Our study results first highlight that Like activities and networks increase exponentially, and are formed and developed by one's friends and many random users. Second, we observe that five other essential Instagram elements influence the number of Likes to different extents, but following others will not necessarily increase the number of Likes that one receives. Third, we explore the relationship between LDA-based topics and Likes, characterize two user groups—specialists and generalists—and show that specialists tend to receive more Likes and promote themselves more than generalists. We finally discuss theoretical and practical implications and future research directions.

Categories and Subject Descriptors

J.m [Computer Applications]: Miscellaneous

General Terms

Measurement, Experimentation

Keywords

Like activity; Like network; Social media analysis; Instagram

1. INTRODUCTION

The recent dramatic increase in the usage and prevalence of social media has led to the creation and sharing of a significant amount of information in various formats such as texts, photos, or videos [7][26]. It has become commonplace for people to actively access or appreciate shared content as well as to interact with the content by adding tags, comments, or Likes. A recent report by Public

Broadcasting Service (PBS)[1] shows this trend in which teens and young adults are actively adding Likes and trying to receive more Likes and attention from others through Likes.

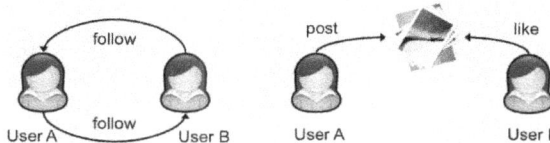

Figure 1. Two networks formed by a follow activity (left) and a Like activity (right).

In particular, Like-based interactions imply a personal preference or interest in the content shared by other users. Unlike followship-based relationships illustrated in Figure 1 (left), Liking does not necessarily require a pre-existing relationship. Instead, anyone can access and show interest by pressing a Like button on the media (Figure 1, right). Such expressions of preference from users for content in social media can take many diverse forms: for example, "LIKE" in Facebook, "+1" in Google+, "favorite" in Flickr, "re-pin" in Pinterest, and "heart" in WeChat. These micro-expressions are examples of a "content-based" relationship, and in this paper, we refer to this as *Like activities*.

Like activities imply many opportunities that can be understood in different contexts. For example, research has started to study Like activities with respect to social phenomena, because they can be interpreted as indications of one's shared interest in the content or the user who posted that content [8]. Like activities also imply business opportunities [26], where many companies take strategic approaches; for example, creating vivid and interactive posts or having more positive comments on the posts, to increase Liking on and people's interest in their brand posts [11].

Despite those research values and business implications of Like activities, however, most prior research studies have utilized them as a means to answer their other questions or hypotheses, such as a degree of popularity. Relatively, there is a lack of understanding on the intrinsic and extrinsic characteristics of Like activities, including their network structures, their relationships with other elements, and contextual aspects, which will provide unique and additional insights in the study of social media. Therefore, in this paper, we present an in-depth and comprehensive analysis on Likes and Like activities based on several test datasets drawn from the base dataset of 20 million users and their 2 billion Like activities in Instagram. We chose Instagram as a media platform, because it is currently one of the most popular social media sites with many users and ample Like activities therein. For example, a

---

[1] http://www.pbs.org/wgbh/pages/frontline/generation-like/

recent Pew research report indicates that Instagram is one of the most popular social media platforms for digital photo sharing and users with ages between 18 and 29 account for 43% of Instagram users [13].

To theoretically guide our research, we employed some research insights that have been applied in previous social media studies. The followings are our three research questions:

RQ1 (Structure): What are the structural characteristics of Like activities? How is the network formed by Like activities different from the one by Followships?

RQ2 (Influence): To what extent do user's other activities (photos, tags, comments, followers, and follows) influence Like activities?

RQ3 (Context): What are the contextual characteristics of Like activities that have been less studied?

In the balance of this paper, we first describe the theoretical framework for understanding Like activities and present previous studies on Like activities in social media. Next, we describe the process of data collection and details of the data used in the analysis. We then present our findings that show some insights on answering our research questions. Lastly, we conclude the paper with a discussion of the implications, limitations, and future work of our study and, more broadly, Likes in social media.

2. RELATED WORK
2.1 Theoretical motivations and guidelines
First, much research has presented various structural aspects of one's online social network, ranging from its component and formation to its comparison to other network types. For example, [17] showed that, in social media, people form interlinked personal communities based on their follow and following connections as well as the norms, languages, and techniques used by them within the network. Somewhat differently, [9] argued that not all members are fully connected with each other and many relationships are missing in online social networks. They presented a new structure-based approach that leverages social communications (i.e., posts and replies) among users to identify different communities in which they engage. [23] found that a followship link between any two people in social media was not positively related to a network of people whom they actually interact with. They emphasized the importance of eliciting a hidden social network that goes beyond simple follow-based relationships. By taking a similar approach, we show how a Like network (to be defined in Definition 1; Section 4.1) formed from Like activities is structured and developed as well as how it is different from a follow-based network, which has not been studied in social media research.

Second, when it comes to the influence of online social media, we are in particular interested in the extent to which different elements that exist in a social media platform influence one particular element in the same platform. There are a number of studies that detail those relationships. For example, [29] explored the different levels of influence of profile elements on the number of friends on Facebook. They found that the number of friends was positively associated with several common referents, such as

high school, hometown, same major, and same school, even after controlling for gender, time on the system, and the updated time. Similarly, in the study on Pinterest, [15] posited that being female, having fewer followers, and using four specific verbs (i.e., use, look, want, and need) will lead to having more re-pins. In Twitter, studies have found that having tags and URLs show the strongest effects on having more retweets [39]. Similar to these studies, we also aimed at exploring the relationship between the number of Likes and other elements that specifically pertains to "Instagram design interfaces," including the number of photos, comments, tags, followers, and followings. These are the direct indicators of one's engagement and activities in Instagram.

Lastly, much research has investigated the contextual aspect of social media. For instance, it has been found that social media creates a communication space for presidential elections [40], workspaces [10], and major incidents or disasters [41][42]. Studies have also indicated that social media reengineers the way of interactions between doctors and patients [20], provides richer local information to residents and facilitates local interactions [38], and helps teachers maintain professional ties with different educational communities as well as share resources and make connections with students [33]. Based on these studies, we found that, in most cases, the contextual information was obtained from the text-based content. However, Instagram is different, because it is a photo-based social media platform. [22] presented content categories from Instagram photos; however, the small sample size (200 photos from 50 users) used in the analysis limits their findings. In our study, to infer its content, we decided to leverage tags, because users tend to add tags that meaningfully describe the photo content [21]. With this rationale, we have applied a probabilistic topic model-based tag analysis and measured the relationship between photo topics and Like activities.

Extracting photo information also allowed us to study an additional contextual aspect. One study method utilized in many social media studies is to articulate different use cases by different groups. For example, [35] analyzed gender roles and behaviors in Pinterest, and found that females tend to have more diverse interests but males tend to be more interested in specific topics. [18] studied self-presentation in social media, and found that females are more likely to use online social networking sites for comparing themselves with others, while males tend to use them to find friends. Since Instagram does not officially provide gender or age information, based on the topics identified through tags, we decided to characterize users through an entropy measurement and analyzed Like activities for two user groups, namely specialists and generalists.

2.2 Studies on Likes in social media
Like activities (or a similar type of content-based activities) do not necessarily need a pre-existing interpersonal relationship. Rather, it mostly asks for a similar or even the same interest in and reflection on content [24]. In this regard, the number of contents that users added Likes to could be an indication of the degree of connections. For example, when a user A added a total of 20 Likes and a user B added a total of 2 Likes to the photos posted by a user C (suppose C posted more than 20 photos), A may have more interests or stronger feelings toward C's photos (or perhaps to C) compared to B.

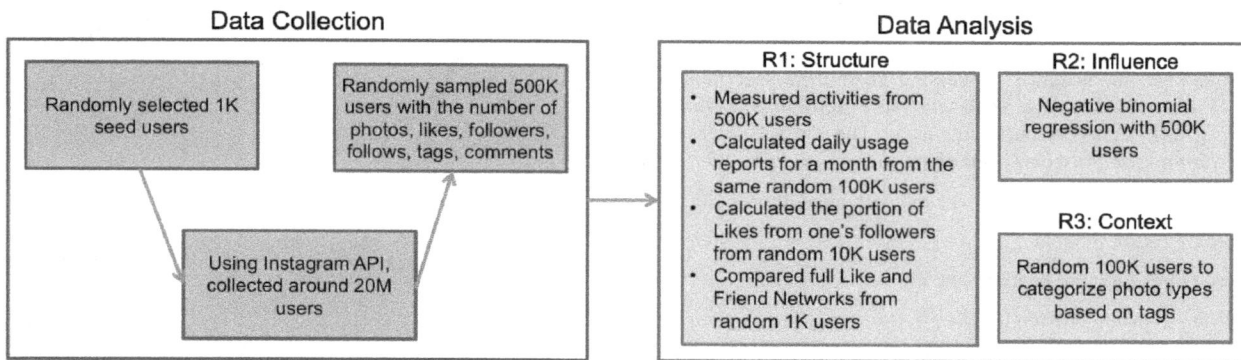

Figure 2. Workflow of data collection and analysis.

There have been research efforts on discovering the characteristics of a content-based relationship in social media. For example, [6] suggested that people tend to think that recommendations, which were derived from profile similarities and rating overlaps, are more useful and meaningful than those from one's familiarity with the recommender. [5] reported that having similar music interests can create interpersonal bonds between people. [3] studied the concept of homophily from two online social networks (BlogCatalog and Last.fm) and found that there was no significant difference among the sub-communities that were clustered based on the personal network ties for each network. This suggests that the level of one's interest is not always consistent with that of one's familiarity, and a content-based network can have more interesting items that attract people than a person-based network.

In Twitter, as retweeting has been perceived as a way of expressing one's agreement with the content, studies have shown the factors of retweeting and found that some features such as URLs and hashtags (i.e., content features), the number of followers and follows, and the age of the account (i.e., contextual features) are closely correlated to re-tweetability [8][39]. More recently, exploring the characteristics and possible applications of Like activities to predict other latent features of users in social media has appeared in [28]. They reported that Likes in Facebook could be utilized to predict user's personal traits such as gender, ethnicity, religion, etc. However, other key aspects of Likes and Like activities, such as the network structure and their relationship with other key elements in each social media site, have not been studied and investigated yet.

As its growing popularity, Instagram has gained attention from research communities, and there have been a few research studies on Like activities. Such examples include studying tag-based Like networks formed by Instagram users who have the same tags [19], studying differences in online social behaviors and engagement presented by teen and adult users in Instagram [25], exploring the relationship between the content of photos and the types of users [2], studying the relationship between online popularity of users and tag-based topical interests of their photos [14]. In every case, however, we found that Likes were primarily used as a method of measuring popularity of photos or users, where having more Likes means being more popular.

In summary, although there have been many research studies on Like activities in social media, we found that relatively little has investigated the diverse characteristics of Like activities as the main study focus. To better understand the characteristics and

implications of Like activities and interactions in social media, we present our analysis from the empirical usage datasets drawn from Instagram. In particular, our rationale was to leverage existing directions used in prior studies as a theoretical guideline. We found that the application of systematic approaches toward Like activities is relatively new in social media literature; therefore, we believe that our study will provide novel insights and additional methods in the research of social media that later social media studies can leverage.

3. DATA COLLECTION

Among many social network sites, we chose Instagram for the following reasons: (1) Instagram is one of the most popular social network sites in the U.S., as reported by the Pew report [13], with a sufficient user base; (2) Compared to other social network sites such as Facebook and Twitter, Instagram has been less studied and understood; (3) With an easy interface to post photos and like others' photos, there is abundance of Like activities in Instagram; and (4) Instagram provides a well-designed and easy-to-access programming API that facilitates our data collection process.

Starting from 1,000 random seed individuals in Instagram, from March to May in 2014, we crawled to obtain the base dataset of about 20 million related users and their 2 billion Likes. To capture relatively complete Like activities across users in a chain, we exploited users' Like relationships. In other words, the dataset include those users who "liked" the photos posted by other users. In this sense, the unique aspect of our dataset is that they are all centered on users' Like activities. To collect complete Like activities, we checked each photo that a user has posted and obtained the number of Likes associated with the photo.

From user's account in Instagram, we obtained user information (e.g., user ID, name, homepage, etc.), photo information (e.g., Likes, comments, tags, etc.), and social relationship information (e.g., followers and follows). As a result, our base dataset consisted of around 20 million users and 2 billion Likes. To reduce biases from the data collection and speed up subsequent data analysis, then, we randomly generated several subsets of users of different sizes (e.g., 1K, 10K, 100K, and 500K users) from 20M users and used them for different analyses (see Figure 2). For instance, to answer RQ1 (structure), we used 500K users to understand overall Like activities, but used 100K users to closely monitor their daily usage over a month. In addition, we used 10K users to calculate the portion of Likes from one's followers and 1K users to generate and compare Like and Follow Networks at a more fine-grained level. For RQ3 (contexts), we used 100K random users.

By using different sizes of datasets for different measurements, we were able to handle different data formats required for a particular study and speed up the processing time for analyzing data. Otherwise, for instance, processing 20 million users and 2 billion Likes in the base dataset was prohibitively time-consuming and highly resource-intensive. The datasets that we collected from Instagram consisted of seven types as follows:

Posters: (Instagram) users who posted/uploaded photos

Photos: Posters' photos

Likes: Likes added to posters' photos

Tags: Tags added to posters' photos

Comments: Comments added to posters' photos

Followers: Users who follow posters

Follows: Users whom posters follow

Note that Photos, Tags, Followers, and Follows pertain to posters, whereas Likes and Comments are added from other users who access posters' photos.[2]

4. RESULTS

4.1 RQ1: Structure of Like Network

We first explored the basic structural characteristics of Like activities, namely a Like Network (LN), and their difference with the followship-based relationship, namely a Follow Network (FN). We formally define a LN as follows.

Definition 1 (Like Network): A Like Network (LN) is a directed graph $G=(V, E)$, where V is a set of users in a social network, and E is a set of directed relationships among users. An edge $e_i: u_j \rightarrow u_k$ indicates that a user u_j "Likes" a photo posted by a user u_k (u_j is not equal to u_k).

Variable	Median	Mean	Max	S.D.
# Photos	166	309	57,925	487
# Likes	1,984	11,122	61,606,804	224,292
# Tags	21	228	97,249	1,034
# Comments	58	320	1,112,862	3,861
# Followers	623	2,404	2,751,722	16,488
# Follows	292	734	5,291,779	19,026

Table 1. Descriptive statistics of the dataset (N=500K).

4.1.1 Likes and other Instagram elements

Table 1 shows the basic statistics of six variables from 500K posters. In general, there is a wide spectrum of variances in all variables, indicated by their high standard deviations. In particular, the variance for the number of Likes is higher. While there are many users whose photos have received no Likes at all, for instance, there is a user whose photos have garnered as many as 61 million Likes. In general, the number of Likes that a user or a photo has received shows a typical long-tail distribution with only a small fraction of dominating users or photos. As empirical evidences, four graphs in Figure 3 illustrate different functional relationships between the number of Likes and: (1) the number of

[2] Dataset is available at https://goo.gl/lyDB52

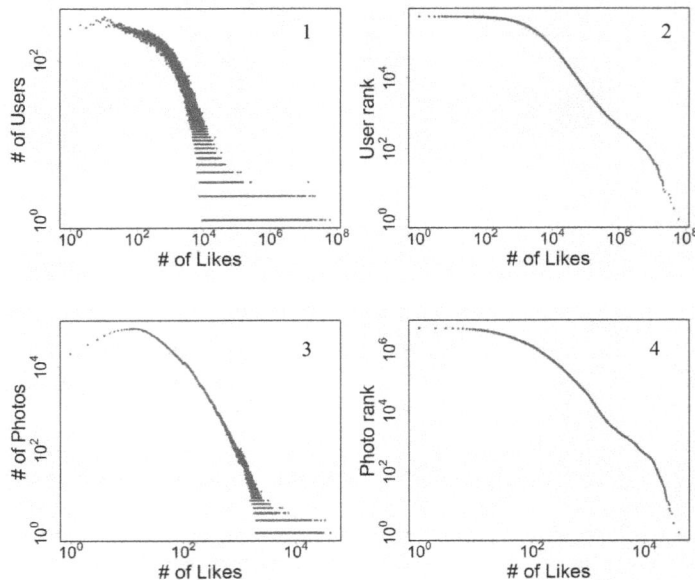

Figure 3. Distributions of # of Likes with respect to: (1) # of user, (2) user rank, (3) # of photos, and (4) photo rank. (1) and (2) are based on 500K users, and (3) and (4) are based on around 5M photos posted by randomly selected 100K users. All graphs in log-log plot.

users, (2) user rank, (3) the number of photos, and (4) photo rank. Note that (1) and (2) are based on all 500K users, and (3) and (4) are based on around 5M photos posted by randomly selected 100K users. While not identical, all four graphs exhibit similar characteristics—i.e., power-law distributions hold approximately only over a limited range (as the number of Likes increases on x-axis), and only a small number of dominating users or photos receive a disproportionally large number of Likes.

4.1.2 Trends of Liking and following

We measured the trend of a LN formed over time compared to a FN. A challenge was that the Instagram API does not provide information about "when" users received Likes or started following others. To obtain this information, therefore, for the same 100K posters reported in Figure 3, we collected the total number of photos, Likes, tags, comments, followers, and follows once a day over a month period, and monitored the evolution of Like activities.

Figure 4 presents three time series graphs over a month where each data point in x-axis represents the difference (i.e., delta) of Likes, followers, and follows between two consecutive days. One finding is that all three elements increased over time in general. However, there are two differences between Likes and followers/follows. First, the average increase in Likes was much higher than the other two. For example, the number of Likes increased by 2 millions everyday on average, while the average increase in followers and follows was 93K and 15K, respectively. Second, while there was a steady increase in Likes, the variance for followers and follows somewhat fluctuated, and there was even a decrease in some days as indicated by red circles in Figure 4. This might be influenced by the way of following others in Instagram. Unlike Facebook, people do not need to be approved by others to be a friend in Instagram. Because of this, it is very common for people to follow or un-follow others as they wish, resulting in an occasional drop in a time series.

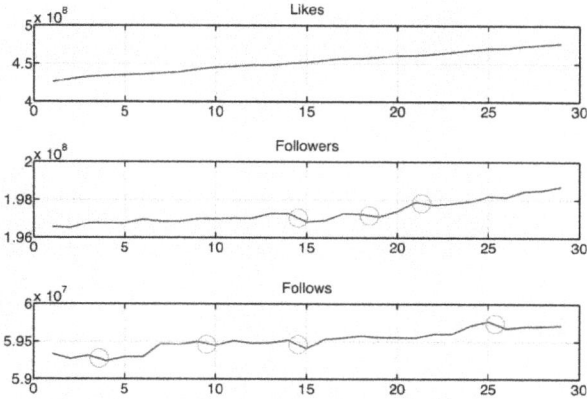

Figure 4. The difference (delta) of Likes, Followers, and Follows between two days over a month (the same 100K posters as Figure 3; x-axis is day and y-axis is daily frequency). Red circles indicate a noticeable decrease.

This occasional drop also occurs in Like activities, because "un-Liking" is also simply a one-click action that is the same as Liking. However, given that people tend to add Likes everyday whenever they like the content, but usually do not track their Like activities, they are less likely to "un-like" photos that they already "liked." In comparison, most social media sites provide an interface that allows users to manage their friends, making it easier for them to "un-follow" others. In this sense, it might be more reasonable to see a steady increase (instead of an occasional drop) in the number of Likes over time.

4.1.3 Likes from followers

Next, we investigated a LN based on the number of Likes that a poster receives from other users. From randomly chosen 10K posters, we calculated the ratio of Likes added by each poster's followers. With the IDs of users who added Likes and those of followers, we were able to check the percentage of Likes received by one's followers. As a result, interestingly, we found that almost a half of Likes were from random users with no follow-relationship (Table 2). This in part indicates that Instagram users not only check photos from people they follow, but they also navigate random photos and simply add Likes if they like those photos. This randomness of adding or receiving Likes implies another reason for a significant increase in a LN.

	Mean	Median
# Photos per user	47	29
# Likes per user	1,333	1,009
# Likes from one's followers per user	742 (55.6%)	476 (47.1%)

Table 2. Total number of Likes from all users and the ratio of Likes from one's followers (N=10K).

Figure 5 shows the examples of the LN from two random posters, p_1 and p_2, visualized by Gephi [1], where p_1 and p_2 received a total of 10,889 and 62,821 Likes, respectively. In each figure, nodes represent other users (p_1 and p_2 not shown; located in the middle), and their sizes are proportional to the number of Likes that each node provided to the poster, p_1 or p_2. The right graph for p_2 has more users who gave many Likes to p_2, while the left graph

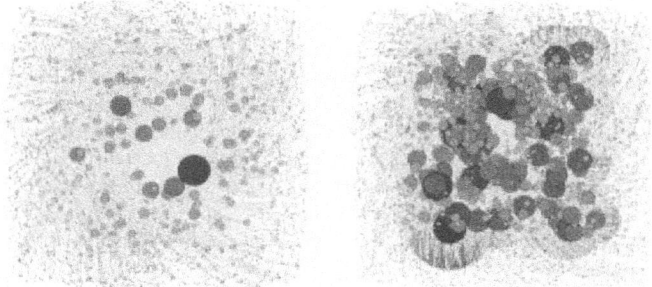

Figure 5. Example LNs of two posters, p_1 (left) and p_2 (right). p_1 and p_2 received 10,889 and 62,821 Likes, respectively. A significant number of Likes were from users who gave only a single Like (i.e., the smallest nodes) to either p_1 or p_2.

exhibits only a few users who gave many Likes to p_1. Similar to what we have shown in Table 2, these two examples show that there are many users who only gave a "single" Like. We found that both p_1 and p_2 have received 66% and 44% of their Likes from people who added a Like only once.

Having a single Like could be explained by a unique characteristic of Instagram. Instagram users can easily access many random photos shared by random users. For example, Instagram provides photo pages that display hot photos (e.g., photos of this month), or photos by specific hashtags (e.g., #halloween, #christmas), making it easy for any user to add Likes to random photos or receive Likes from random users.

4.1.4 Like and follow networks

Lastly, we compared a LN with a FN. Starting from the same 1K users, we measured the links among users up to two depths to create a FN and a LN. With these data, we again ran the network analysis using Gephi. In particular, we measured the degree of each network to show the number of links that each node has and indicate a level of network size and future growth.

	FN	LN
Avg. # Nodes	97,092	169,974
Avg. # Edges	116,444	536,599
Avg. Degree (total)	2.34	6.18
Avg. In-Degree (follower for FN; receive for LN)	1.24	3.15
Avg. Out-Degree (follow for FN; give for LN)	1.10	3.03

Table 3. Degree comparison between a FN and a LN derived from the same 1K users. All degrees were weighted.

Table 3 summarizes the degree centrality of two networks. Regarding the number of nodes and edges from the same 1K users, the LN has many more nodes and edges than the FN. There are differences in terms of degree as well. On the one hand, in-degree indicates how many followers that users have for the FN and how many Likes users received for the LN. On the other hand, out-degree indicates how many others users are following back for the FN and how many Likes that users gave back to others for the LN. As a result, both in-degree and out-degree were found to be higher in the LN than the FN, indicating that the LN tends to contain more interactions and expand more rapidly from the same number of users.

4.2 RQ2: Influences on Like Activities

Our second question examines factors that influence the number of Likes. Our assumption was that a poster might receive "more" Likes due to: (1) the posting of many interesting photos, (2) having many followers or follows, (3) the addition of many tags to photos (which are used in the "search" feature), or (4) the people's tendency to add Likes while adding comments to photos. Articulating the relationships among these factors may provide another perspective of Like activities. For this analysis, we used a negative binomial regression model, which is a statistical method to model Like activities by considering other variables as the predictors. This model has been previously used to understand the relationship among variables in other social networking sites [2][15]. The fact that the dependent variable, which is the number of Likes, is a count and conditional variance of each variable that exceeds its conditional mean suggests that using the negative binomial regression model is appropriate. We used STATA software for the analysis.

Variable	β	IRR	Std. err.	z	p
Followers	0.079	1.082	0.0004	173.0	< 0.0001
Photos	0.046	1.047	0.0004	102.3	< 0.0001
Comments	0.032	1.033	0.0002	114.5	< 0.0001
Tags	0.028	1.028	0.0002	120.7	< 0.0001
Follows	-0.005	0.994	0.0005	-9.7	< 0.0001

Note: Alpha (estimate of the dispersion parameter): 1.40, Likelihood-ratio test of chi-square: 2.3e+0.9, p < 0.0001

Table 4. The result of the negative binomial regression. The dependent variable is # of Likes, which is also countable (N: 500K; IRR: Incident Rate Ratio).

Table 4 presents the result of the negative binomial regression where p-value indicates that the model is statistically significant (p < 0.0001) and the number of Likes is the dependent variable. The alpha value of the model refers to the estimate of the dispersion parameter, and the fact that alpha is greater than zero (1.40) indicates that the data are over dispersed and better estimated using a negative binomial model than a Poisson model. The model also shows the large test statistic of the likelihood-ratio chi-square test, again indicating that using the negative binomial model is appropriate.

The IRR (Incident Rate Ratio) result refers to the change in the dependent variable in terms of a percentage increase or decrease, which measures the effects of the independent variable on the dependent variable. More specifically, the IRR for followers (1.082) means that for each one-unit increase in followers, the expected number of Likes increases by 8.2% (p < 0.0001), while holding the other variables in the model constant. This in part indicates that people are likely to add Likes to the photos posted by those whom they are following, and having more followers is likely to lead to having more Likes.

Likewise, the expected number of Likes increases by 4.7%, 3.3%, and 2.8% with every one-unit increase in photos, comments, and tags, respectively (p < 0.0001), while holding the other variables in the model constant. For photos, although we had expected to see a higher percentage of its influence on the number of Likes (i.e., more photos, more chances to get Likes), the results still show a relatively significant effect. Commenting is another (could be more explicit) way of expressing one's thought, and people might add Likes while adding comments. In addition, the result for tags seems to be supported by an interesting culture in Instagram where the tags can

be used as a way of promoting oneself or one's photos, similar to the way hashtag (#) is used in Twitter. Lastly, regarding follows, it shows a negative effect (-0.5%) on the Like count. This result can be partly explained by the fact that many popular and active posters that have many followers (i.e., they also tend to receive many Likes) do not always follow back with a similar number of others. This also implies that following more people does not always guarantee receiving more Likes back from those people.

In summary, the results show that all independent variables, except follows, are positively related to the number of Likes to different extents. Especially, we found that having more followers and adding more photos seem to be more influential with respect to having more Likes.

ID	Topic	Tag examples
1	Nature	sky, nature, flowers, ocean, beach
2	Fashion/beauty	makeup, jewelry, model, fashion, beauty
3	Location/place/area	nyc, boston, spain, italy, brazil, home
4	Art/photos/design	photo, interior, architect, design, art
5	Holiday/vacation	party, holiday, vacation, friday, rest
6	Mood/emotion	love, cute, happy, smile, great, good
7	Social/people/family	family, girlfriend, boyfriend, gay, folks
8	Sports/activity	skateboarding, hiking, soccer, basketball
9	Entertainment	music, movie, pop, rock, song, play, star
10	Follow/shoutout/like	tagsforlike, followme, likes, shoutout
11	Food/drink	food, coffee, yummy, delicious, eat
12	Health/fitness	fitness, cleaneating, fit, yoga, workout
13	Animal	cat, kitty, instacat, pet, puppy, animal
14	Car/airplane	ford, Toyota, dodge, hotcars, bmw, truck
15	Travel	mytravelgram, trip, instatravel, traveling
16	Religion/belief	blessed, god, faith, truth, jesus, mind
17	Funny/quotes	lol, funny, jokes, quotes, saying, lmfao
18	Technology	samsung, galaxy, iphone, ipad, computer
19	Smoking	weedstagram, high, weed, dope, smoker
20	Apps/games/comics	instahub, webstagram, comics, gamer

Table 5. LDA-discovered topics in Instagram (N=100K).

4.3 RQ3: Contexts and Like Activities

Our third question explores the contextual aspects of Like activities. In particular, we extract contextual information from photos by means of the tags in photos.

4.3.1 Topics and Likes

Topic models are often useful for analyzing a large collection of unlabeled texts. It is reasonable to assume that each poster may have a few selected topics of interest, and there is a higher probability that they will post photos on such topics. However, Instagram does not provide a set of pre-defined topics or genres for photos. By viewing all tags added to photos by a poster, as a bag of words, therefore, we tried to identify latent topics of the poster. To do this, we first randomly selected 100K posters. We then applied a Latent Dirichlet Allocation (LDA) model [4], using Mallet [32], an open-source machine learning toolkit, to identify a list of latent topics per poster.

As Mallet generated different topics for each execution, we ran Mallet 50 times to extract 100 well-presented topics. Mallet generates two types of outputs—a list of keywords for each topic and the ratio of each topic per poster. Because we found that there were some overlaps among the 100 topics, we categorized them by taking a bottom-up approach. First, to obtain ground-truth tag categories, we investigated a number of third-party websites that present a list of popular or hot tags in different time frames (i.e., daily, weekly, monthly) and finally chose two websites (i.e., tagsforlikes.com, tagstagram.com). Based on those categories, three human judges then inductively coded the types of topics and continued this process until all judges agreed. At the end, through this process, we were able to identify 20 mutual Instagram topics. Each poster had 20 topics with a different ratio depending on the tags added to the photos. Table 5 shows a list of final 20 topics with some tag examples. Lastly, to obtain the number of Likes per topic, we multiplied the ratio of each topic with the total number of Likes. We believe this was a reasonable method to find the relationship between Likes and topics, because we found that the number of Likes tends to be evenly distributed over one's photos.

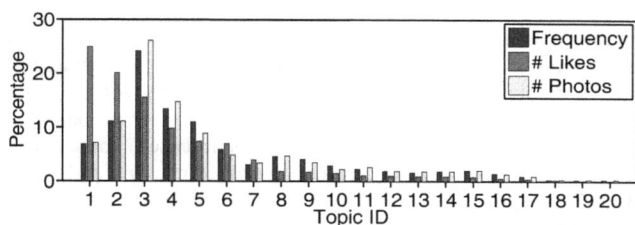

Figure 6. Ratio of frequency, # of Likes, and # of photos for the topics in Instagram (N=100K).

Figure 6 shows the ratio of frequency, the number of Likes, and the number of photos for each topic. First, regarding frequency, "Location/place/area" (3rd topic in Table 5) was the most frequent topic to be found in Instagram, followed by "Art/photos/design" (4th), "Fashion/beauty" (2nd), and "Holiday/vacation" (5th). We found that the tags in "Follow/shoutout/like" (10th) especially represented a unique and interesting culture in Instagram, as we can assume that posters with those tags in "Follow/shoutout/like" tend to desire to have their photos more widely searched and accessed by other users. Second, the most frequent topic is not necessarily the one receiving the most number of Likes. For example, the frequency in "Nature" (1st) was only 6%, but its number of Likes (24%) was the highest. "Location/place/area" (3rd) had the highest frequency (24%), but was not the highest regarding the number of Likes (15%). Lastly, unlike the Like results, the number of photos broadly showed a similar pattern to their frequency, which further implies that in general tags were quite well distributed across one's photos.

As to the number of Likes and photos, most topics showed a small difference except for the first four topics. "Nature" (1st) received more Likes than photos, whereas "Location/place/area" (3rd) had more photos than Likes. Regarding the "Nature" (1st) topic, we speculate that there might be many high-quality photos showing the beauty of the nature that affect user behavior. That is, users who posted those photos might prioritize the quality of photos, but not necessarily their quantity, which might attract more users and make them to add Likes. "Location/place/area" (3rd) showed the highest number of photos, because the tags in this topic seem to describe a wide range of photos that are used together with many other topics. This perspective can be partly supported by a high frequency of their usage.

Overall, based on our dataset, it appears that the first five topics (IDs between 1 and 5) represent the main contents posted and shared by users in Instagram with respect to their frequency of usage, and the number of Likes and photos. This may not be generalized to the whole set of activities in Instagram. However, we believe that this result shows the connection between photo topics and Like activities in an online photo-sharing community.

4.3.2 Poster groups and Likes

We further investigated the characteristics of posters based on the topics. Once we represented each poster as a 20-dimensional topic vector via LDA, we calculated the entropy values for all 100K posters. The entropy of a poster p is a measure of the uncertainty in a random variable, defined as follows:

$$Entropy\ (p) = -\sum_{i=1}^{20} P(x_i) \log P(x_i)$$

where $P(x_i)$ is the probability of the topic x_i in this study. When applied to our data, a higher entropy value means that a poster p tends to post photos with diverse topics, while a lower entropy value means that p tends to post photos with a specific topic. As a result, we found that the range of entropy values is between 0 and 3.5 (see Figure 7)—that is, at minimum one topic ($2^0 = 1$) and maximally twelve topics ($2^{3.5} \approx 12$). We then defined those posters who had an entropy value smaller than 1 (i.e., less than $2^1 = 2$ topics) as specialists (those who tend to post photos with a specific theme) and those who had an entropy value higher than 3 (i.e., more than $2^3 = 8$ topics) as generalists (those who tend to post photos with diverse topics).

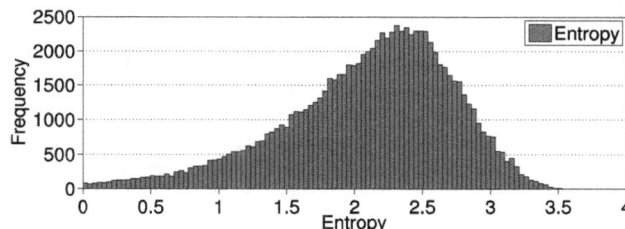

Figure 7. Distribution of entropy scores of posters (N=100K).

Table 6 shows a summary of Likes for specialists and generalists. Although the variance was high for both groups, the median results show that specialists received five times more Likes (10,893) than generalists had (2,375). In addition, the ratio of the number of Likes and the number of photos for each group indicates that on average specialists' photos appear to be more Like-inducing (e.g., high-quality landscape and architectural photos) than generalists' photos. We transformed the values to a logarithmic scale, where the t-test result showed a significant difference between two groups (i.e., $t(8823) = 133.4$, $p < 0.0001$).

Type	# Likes			# Likes / # Photos (Median)
	Mean	Median	S.D.	
Specialists (5,594)	101,666	10,893	1,358,885	35.3
Generalists (3,230)	15,989	2,375	367,911	12.5

Table 6. Summary of specialists and generalists.

Further, to verify how accurate it is to use entropy results to distinguish specialists and generalists, we randomly picked around 10% of specialists (500) and manually checked their photos based on three criteria (i.e., whether there was a specific theme in the photos; whether they have an external personal site; whether they specify a promotion site) as shown in Table 7. From the specialist group, we found that 404 posters (80.8%) have high-quality photos. However, we identified that 49 posters (9.8%; false positive) should have been considered as generalists, because we were not able to identify a specific theme from their photos. Interestingly, we found that 83 posters (16.6%) have a commercial website to advertise their photos or products (e.g., fashion items), and 129 posters (25.8%) provide a link to their personal webpage (e.g., Twitter, Facebook, Tumblr, etc.) to reach out to more people.

Question	Count (%)
How many **specialists** have a specific theme?	404 (80.8%)
How many **specialists** have a personal site?	129 (25.8%)
How many **specialists** have a promotion site?	83 (16.6%)
How many **generalists** have a specific theme?	49 (16.3%)
How many **generalists** have a personal site?	30 (10.0%)
How many **generalists** have a promotion site?	5 (1.6%)

Table 7. Differences between randomly selected specialists (N=500) and generalists (N=300) with respect to having a theme in their photos and an additional personal website.

This result implies some meaningful insights on why specialists have more Likes. It seems that a number of posters in the specialist group want to have more people visit their homepage and see their photos. Because of this, they might try to take and share high-quality photos, making their photos more distinctive, unique, and professional than others. Moreover, it seems that they tend to add tags that best describe their photos and use many tags in "Follow/shout-out/like" to get more attention (e.g., becoming a friend will expose their photos more) as well as showing their personal webpages for self-promotion or sale.

We also randomly picked around 10% of generalists (300) and checked their photos. As a result, 251 posters (83.6%) are likely to post photos that mostly describe individual stories, experiences, or thoughts. Topics in this group are diverse and more individual- and social-oriented. Such topics include "Mood/Emotion," "Social/People/Family," "Holiday/Vacation," "Sports/Activity," and "Travel." In addition, we found that photos posted by 49 posters (16.3%; false positive) have a specific theme, and thus should have been considered as specialists. There were only 5 generalists that had promotion sites (1.6%) and 30 generalists that had personal websites (10.0%). This implies that generalists tend to use Instagram to share their personal stories and experiences with others.

5. DISCUSSION

We have studied Likes and Like activities in Instagram. These small actions of adding Likes to published content (or other similar micro-activities in social media) have become a salient part of interactions in social media. As social media has become one of the primary communication channels, it has also become more natural for people to engage in "Liking." However, based on our literature review, we found that little research has studied Like activities as a main focus nor articulated their intrinsic and extrinsic aspects. In this regard, based on the research approaches applied in many social media studies, we specifically explored

and studied Like activities through the lenses of their structural, influential, and contextual characteristics.

5.1 RQ1: Structure

Using large-scale Like activities in Instagram, our statistical results indicated that a LN (Like Network) expanded rapidly with respect to both the size of users and other variables (i.e., photos, comments, tags, followers, and follows). Compared to a FN (Followship Network), a LN had more nodes and links and showed a higher degree of centrality. In addition, we found that the number of Likes steadily increased over time, whereas that of followers and follows fluctuated and sometimes decreased. We also identified that a great number of Likes were from random users who only gave a "single" Like, which also accounts for the typical characteristics of a LN. We speculate that the design of Instagram (e.g., its functionality and UI; users can access not only photos by others whom they follow, but a set of random or popular photos by tags or through search) or many photo-sharing events hosted by the official Instagram blog (blog.instagram.com) might influence the size and randomness of a LN.

Another interesting implication from the randomness of Likes is that certain information can be spread very quickly and widely to a great number of people. However, most existing social media research has studied the possibility of spreading or propagating information based on one's social (followship-based) connections or networks, profile characteristics, text-based content, and so on [30][37]. In this sense, we believe that our study results open up a possibility of studying the speed and effectiveness of leveraging Like activities in spreading information to wider audience.

In addition, the structural findings that we observed here may not be repeated among other Like activities in other platforms such as Flickr, whose user demographics may be different from those of Instagram (e.g., Flickr users are generally older than Instagram users, and many professional photographers in Flickr, etc.). We leave the investigation on Like activities in other platforms for future work.

5.2 RQ2: Influence

We investigated the extent to which other Instagram factors influence Like activities. The statistical results indicated that the number of Likes was positively related to that of photos, comments, tags, and followers to different extents. In particular, followers showed the highest influence on having Likes, followed by photos, comments, and tags. Gaining attention from others was one of the motivations for using and engaging in social media [27][31]. As Public Broadcasting Service (PBS) recently noted the popularity of adding Likes among teens and young adults, and given that those populations are the main users of Instagram, our results raise an interesting question about how users tend to be involved in Like activities (e.g., the patterns of the activities; they might try to have more followers and add Likes to others' photos, etc.) compared to other older populations in social media.

Conversely, having more follows (i.e., number of users that I follow) did not show a positive influence on receiving Likes. Note that this may not be applied to every single user. However in general and when we consider a large number of users together, we can see that, even if a user decides to "follow" other users more, that action does not necessarily guarantee that the user would receive a more number of Likes from others. Perhaps this is also influenced by the fact that some very popular users have many followers and receive numerous Likes everyday, but had only few or no follows. More follow-up research is needed to find out the reasons behind the relationship between the number of Likes and the number of follows that one has

Prior studies on Twitter showed that tags and URLs exhibited the highest influence on having retweets followed by the number of followers and followings [39], which is somewhat different from our results. However, given that retweeting has many implications (e.g., Like, conversations, self-promotion, bookmark, and thanks) [16] and Liking pertains mostly to one's simple appreciations to or interests in photos, having more followers and more photos, which will increase the visibility of photos, might show a stronger effect on having more Likes.

5.3 RQ3: Context

Using topic models, based on the tags annotated to their photos, we semi-manually identified 20 prevalent topics in Instagram and found that the frequency and the number of Likes and photo for each topic were positively correlated. Based on their relationships, topics such as "Nature," "Art/photos/design," "Fashion/beauty," "Location/places/area," and "Holiday/vacation" were found to be the main ones posted, shared, and appreciated by users, which compliment the topic results from previous studies [22].

We identified two user groups, specialists and generalists, based on entropy scores for the topics. By and large, we found that specialists tend to receive more Likes in total and per photo than generalists. From the manual inspection of the samples, we found that more specialists have a personal webpage visible to others for self-promotion or sale than generalists.

Regarding topic relevance through our manual verification, our results showed around 80-85% accuracy for each group. This highlights a reasonable method of utilizing tags as a way of topic identification. It also suggests an additional feedback mechanism to Instagram users to encourage them be more engaged in online social activities. For example, Instagram can recommend a user who posts similar photos and shows similar Like activities and patterns, and users might find Like-based recommendations useful and meaningful. This design idea could further lead to creating and fostering social relationships by accessing new photo updates that are based on one's interests and adding Likes or comments.

5.4 Limitations and future work

Despite the presented interesting findings, we acknowledge a few limitations in our study. First, our results may not represent overall Like activities in Instagram or other online social media that have the Like function or a similar interface. In addition, despite the large 20 million Instagram users in the base dataset that we collected, there may exist a possibility of biases induced by the random sampling-based data collection procedure of this paper. Furthermore, by expanding our study on Like activities to other related photo-sharing social media platforms (e.g., Flickr, Pinterest, Snapchat, etc.), we want to repeat and validate if our findings are consistent across platforms. Research has also found that people show different usage patterns in social media based on the number of social media sites that they use [36], and this idea can be also applied to our study. We leave this as future work.

Second, the quantitative and statistical analysis that we have conducted cannot reveal users' motivations to add Likes and expectations to receive Likes from others, which is also a critical perspective to better understand a LN. Prior research in an online photo-sharing community [34] shows that people participate in photo-sharing activities because of intrinsic and extrinsic

motivations. As our analysis already showed a relatively high correlation between comments and Likes, perhaps the texts used in comments could provide some insights on motivations for adding Likes. We are also interested in applying a qualitative approach to this idea.

Lastly, we are also interested in a co-likeness relationship, which is formed when two users liked the same photo or a user liked two photos concurrently. A similar research idea has been explored in document term co-occurrence analysis or bibliometric co-author analysis. This problem is also closely related to the collaborative filtering techniques in recommender systems. As the practical implications of such co-liked items in social media are especially high, we plan to conduct a comprehensive co-likeness analysis based on Like activities.

6. CONCLUSION

This paper contributed to an exploration and articulation of one of the most popular activities in social media—"Liking"—according to three research perspectives—structure, influence, and context. Using several datasets of different sizes that were randomly drawn from a base of 20 million users and 2 billion Likes in Instagram, we found that a Like network (LN) is a fast-expanding network, formed and developed by both one's friends and random users. We found that five other Instagram elements influence the number of Likes received to different extents. In addition, using an LDA-based tag analysis, we identified 20 latent topics, prevalent among tags added to photos, and presented top 5 topics in Instagram. Furthermore, we distinguished among posters with special topics (specialists) and those with diverse topics (generalists) and found that specialists tend to receive more Likes and provide additional channels for self-promotion, whereas generalists showed opposite characteristics.

7. ACKNOWLEDGEMENT

This research was in part supported by NSF CNS-1422215 award.

8. REFERENCES

[1] Bastian, M., Heymann, S., & Jacomy, M. (2009). Gephi: an open source software for exploring and manipulating networks. *ICWSM*, 361-362.

[2] Bakhshi, S., Shamma, D. A., & Gilbert, E. (2014). Faces engage us: Photos with faces attract more likes and comments on instagram. *CHI*, 965-974.

[3] Bisgin, H., Agarwal, N., & Xu, X. (2010). Investigating homophily in online social networks. *Web Intelligence and Intelligent Agent Technology*, 533-536.

[4] Blei, D.M, Ng, A.Y., & Jordan, M.I. (2003). Latent dirichlet allocation. *J. of Machine Learning Research*, 3, 993-1022.

[5] Boer, D., Fischer, R., Strack, M., Bond, M., Lo, E., & Lam, J. (2011). How Shared Preferences in Music Create Bonds Between People: Values as the Missing Link. *Personality and Social Psychology Bulletin*, 1-13.

[6] Bonhard, P., Harries, C., McCarthy. J., & Sasse, A. (2006). Accounting for Taste: Using Profile Similarity to Improve Recommender Systems. *CHI*, 1057-1066.

[7] boyd, d. & Ellison, N. (2007). Social Network Sites: Definition, History, and Scholarship. *J. of Computer-Mediated Communication*, 13(1), 210-230.

[8] boyd, d., Golder, S., & Lotan, G. (2010). Tweet, Tweet, Retweet: Conversational Aspects of Retweeting on Twitter. *HICSS*, 1-10.

[9] Chen Y., Chuang, C., & Chiu, Y. (2014). Community detection based on social interactions in a social network. *JASIST*, 65(3), 539-550.

[10] Davison, R.M., Ou, C., Martinsons, M. G., Zhao, A. Y., & Du, R. (2014). The Communicative Ecology of Web 2.0 at Work: Social Networking in the Workspace. *JASIST*, 65(10), 2035-2047.

[11] De Vries, L., Gensler, S., & Leeflang, P. S. (2012). Popularity of brand posts on brand fan pages: an investigation of the effects of social media marketing. *J. of Interactive Marketing*, 26(2), 83-91.

[12] Duggan, M. & Brenner, J. (2012). The Demographics of Social Media Users - 2012. *Pew Research Center's Internet & American Life Project*.

[13] Duggan, M. (2013). Photo and Video Sharing Grow Online. *Pew Research Center's Internet & American Life Project*.

[14] Ferrara, E., Interdonato, R., & Tagarelli, A. (2014). Online popularity and topical interests through the lens of instagram. *HT*, 24-34.

[15] Gilbert, E., Bakhshi, S., Chang, S., & Terveen, L. (2013). "I Need to Try This!": A Statistical Overview of Pinterest. *CHI*, 2427-2436.

[16] Gorrell, G. & Bontcheva, K. (2015). Classifying Twitter favorites: Like, bookmark, or Thanks?. *JASIST*.

[17] Gruzd, A., Wellman, B., & Takhteyev, Y. (2011). Imagining Twitter as an Imagined Community. *J. of American Behavioral Scientist*, 55(10), 1294-1318.

[18] Haferkamp, N., Eimler S.C., Papadakis, A.M., & Kruck, J.V. (2012). Men are from Mars, women are from Venus? Examining gender differences in self-presentation on social networking sites. *Cyberpsychology behavior and social networking*, 15(2), 91-98.

[19] Han, K., Jang, J., & Lee, D. (2015). Exploring Tag-based Like Networks. *CHI*, 1941-1946.

[20] Hawn, C. (2009). Take Two Aspirin And Tweet Me In the Morning: How Twitter, Facebook, And Other Social Media Are Reshaping Health Care. *Health Affairs*, 28(2), 361-368.

[21] Hollenstein, L. & Purves, R.S. (2010). Exploring place through user-generated content: Using Flickr tags to describe city cores. *J. of Spatial Information Science*, 1(1), 21-48.

[22] Hu, Y., Manikonda, L., & Kambhampati, S. (2014). What we instagram: A first analysis of instagram photo content and user types. *ICWSM*.

[23] Huberman, B.A., Romero, D.M., & Wu, F. (2009). Social networks that matter: Twitter under the microscope. *First Monday, Peer-Reviewed J. on the Internet*, 14(5).

[24] Jacovi, M. et al. (2011). Digital Traces of Interest: Deriving Interest Relationships from Social Media Interactions. *ECSCW*, 21-40.

[25] Jang, J., Han, K., Shih, P. C., & Lee, D. (2015). Generation Like: Comparative Characteristics in Instagram. *CHI*, 4039-4042.

[26] Kaplan, A.M. & Haenlein, M. (2009). Users of the world, unite! The challenges and opportunities of Social Media. *J. of Business Horizons*, 53(1), 59-68.

[27] Kietzmann, J., Hermkens, K., McCarthy, I., & Silvestre, B. (2011) Social media? Get serious! Understanding the functional building blocks of social media. *J. Business Horizons*, 54, 241-251.

[28] Kosinski, M., Stillwell, D., & Graepel, T. (2013). Private traits and attributes are predictable from digital records of human behavior. *PNAS*, 110(15), 5733-5734.

[29] Lampe, C., Ellison, N., & Steinfield, C. (2007). A Familiar Face(book): Profile Elements as Signals in an Online Social Network. *CHI*, 435-444.

[30] Lee, K., Mahmud, J., Chen, J., Zhou, M., & Nichols, J. (2014). Who Will Retweet This? Automatically Identifying and Engaging Strangers on Twitter to Spread Information. *IUI*, 247-256.

[31] Leung, L. (2009). User-generated content on the internet: an examination of gratifications, civic engagement and psychological empowerment. *New Media & Society*, 11(8), 1327-1347.

[32] McCallum, A. K. (2002). "MALLET: A Machine Learning for Language Toolkit." http://mallet.cs.umass.edu/

[33] Moran, M., Seaman, J., & Kane, H.T. (2011). Teaching, Learning, and Sharing: How Today's Higher Education Faculty Use Social Media for Work and for Play. *Pearson Learning Solutions*.

[34] Nov, O., Naanam, M., & Ye, C. (2009). Analysis of Participation in an Online Photo-Sharing Community: A Multidimensional Perspective. *JASIST*, 61(3), 555-566.

[35] Ottoni, R., Pesce, J., Casas, D., Franciscani, G., Meira, W., Kumaraguru, P., & Almeida, V. (2013). Ladies First: Analyzing Gender Roles and Behaviors in Pinterst. *ICWSM*.

[36] Petrocchi, N., Asnaani, A., Martinez, A., Nadikarni, A., & Hofmann, S. (2015). Differences between People who Use Only Facebook and Those who Use Facebook Plus Twitter. *J. of Human-Computer Interaction*, 31(2), 157-165.

[37] Pfitzner, R., Garas, A., & Schweitzer, F. (2012). Emotional Divergence Influences Information Spreading in Twitter. *ICWSM*.

[38] Schroeter, R. (2012). Engaging New Digital Locals with Interactive Urban Screens to Collaboratively Improve the City. *CSCW*, 227-236.

[39] Suh, B., Hong, L., Pirolli, P., & Chi, E. (2010). Want to be Retweeted? Large Scale Analytics on Factors Impacting Retweet in Twitter Network. *SocialCom*, 177-184.

[40] Tumasjan, A., Sprenger, T.O., Sandner, P.G., & Welpe, I.M. (2010). Predicting Elections with Twitter: What 140 Characters Reveal about Political Sentiment. *ICWSM*.

[41] Vieweg, S., Hughes, A.L., Starbird, K., & Palen, L. (2010). Microblogging During Two Natural Hazard Events: What Twitter May Contribute to Situational Awareness. *CHI*, 1079-1088.

[42] Yardi, S. & boyd, D. (2010). Tweeting from the Town Square: Measuring Geographic Local Networks. *ICWSM*.

Build Emotion Lexicon from Microblogs by Combining Effects of Seed Words and Emoticons in a Heterogeneous Graph

Kaisong Song[1], Shi Feng[1,2], Wei Gao[3], Daling Wang[1,2], Ling Chen[4], Chengqi Zhang[4]
[1]School of Information Science and Engineering, Northeastern University, Shenyang, China
[2]Key Laboratory of Medical Image Computing (Northeastern University), Ministry of Education, China
[3]Qatar Computing Research Institute, Hamad Bin Khalifa University, Doha, Qatar
[4]Centre for Quantum Computation and Intelligent Systems, University of Technology, Sydney, Australia
kaisongsong@gmail.com, {fengshi, wangdaling}@ise.neu.edu.cn
wgao@qf.org.qa, {ling.chen, chengqi.zhang}@uts.edu.au

ABSTRACT

As an indispensable resource for emotion analysis, emotion lexicons have attracted increasing attention in recent years. Most existing methods focus on capturing the single emotional effect of words rather than the emotion distributions which are helpful to model multiple complex emotions in a subjective text. Meanwhile, automatic lexicon building methods are overly dependent on seed words but neglect the effect of *emoticons* which are natural graphical labels of fine-grained emotion. In this paper, we propose a novel emotion lexicon building framework that leverages both seed words and emoticons simultaneously to capture emotion distributions of candidate words more accurately. Our method overcomes the weakness of existing methods by combining the effects of both seed words and emoticons in a unified three-layer heterogeneous graph, in which a multi-label random walk (MLRW) algorithm is performed to strengthen the emotion distribution estimation. Experimental results on real-world data reveal that our constructed emotion lexicon achieves promising results for emotion classification compared to the state-of-the-art lexicons.

Categories and Subject Descriptors

H.3.1 [**Information Storage and Retrieval**]: Content Analysis and Indexing—*Dictionaries, Thesauruses*; H.3.4 [**Information Storage and Retrieval**]: Systems and Software—*Web 2.0*; I.2.7 [**Artificial Intelligence**]: Natural Language Processing—*Text analysis*

Keywords

emotion lexicon; heterogeneous graph; microblogs; emoticon; seed word

HT '15, September 1–4, 2015, Guzelyurt, Northern Cyprus.
© 2015 ACM. ISBN 978-1-4503-3395-5/15/09 ...$15.00.
DOI: http://dx.doi.org/10.1145/2700171.2791035.

1. INTRODUCTION

Nowadays, more and more people are willing to express their attitudes and feelings in social media such as Twitter[1] and Weibo[2] rather than just passively browse and receive information. With the prolific rise of user-generated content in social media, how to effectively analyze users' sentiments has received much attention in the past decade. Emotion lexicons, which annotate words with their expressed emotions, are crucial to the success of sentiment analysis. Therefore, building high-quality emotion lexicons becomes essential for many different kinds of sentiment analysis applications [12, 13, 22, 10, 11, 7, 24].

A lot of works have been done for building emotion lexicons [4, 6, 8, 18], where each word is given a positive or negative label automatically. However, the binary representation of emotion may be oversimplified. For example, rather than simply assigning a negative emotion label to the word "self-abasement", it is more accurate to annotate the expressed emotion as sadness and disgust. Therefore, studies on constructing emotion lexicons that assign the entry words into fine-grained categories of emotions, such as *happiness, like, disgust, sadness,* and *anger*, have emerged recently [29, 30, 34]. In addition, for many sentiment analysis applications, it is beneficial to know not only the binary or multiple emotion classes of a word, but also the emotion intensity. For example, how favorably or unfavorably do people feel about a new product, movie or a TV show. As a result, several recent lexicons [3, 5, 25, 30] associate words with both emotion classes and corresponding valence scores to represent emotion intensity. In this paper, we propose a more generalized solution that derives the emotion distributions of entry words. That is, for each entry word, we estimate its probabilities belonging to various emotion classes.

Traditional lexicon construction overly depends on the seed emotion words selected from large set of words [28, 32], but ignores the emotion of the entire post which accommodates the entry words. We observe that many microblog posts are accompanied by abundant *emoticons* that naturally convey the overall sentiment of the post. It is thus expected that emoticons play complementary roles with seed words in building fine-grained emotion lexicon. For instance,

---

[1]http://www.twitter.com/
[2]http://www.weibo.com/

let us consider the following two example microblogs[3]:

(1) I must **accuse** myself. So *sad*, her injury was my fault...

(2) He must be **accused**. Her injury was his fault! 😖

where *sad* is a seed word and **accuse** is the candidate emotion word. To annotate the emotion of **accuse**, if we consider its co-occurrence with seed word only, we may infer from the first post that **accuse** is associated with the emotion class *sadness*. However, considering its occurrence in the second post, which conveys an overall emotion of *anger* represented by the emoticon 😖, we may also assign **accuse** to the emotion class *anger*. Hence, considering either seed words or emoticons may produce incomplete and inaccurate representation of sentiment. Our idea is to combine the effects of both seed words and emoticons using a unified method, which captures the emotion of candidate words from different perspectives.

Intuitively, the more frequently a candidate emotion word co-occurs with seed words and emoticons bearing specific emotions, the more likely the candidate word converges to the real emotion distribution. In this paper, we propose a novel and extensible emotion lexicon building method by formulating the lexicon building as a multi-label random walk (MLRW) problem for estimating the emotion distributions of candidate words. The candidate words with probabilities of some main emotion classes greater than a specified threshold are selected into lexicon. Our contributions are three-fold:

- We propose a unified framework that combines the effects of seed words and emoticons co-occurring with candidate words in microblogs, which captures the fine-grained emotion of candidate words more accurately.

- We develop an effective multi-label random walk algorithm for emotion distribution estimation based on a three-layer heterogeneous graph, where vertices at different layers represent emoticons, seed words and candidate words jointly and the edges represent their corresponding co-occurrence relationships.

- We conduct sentence-level emotion classification experiments on a real-world microblog dataset using our constructed emotion lexicon, which shows promising performance in single-label and multi-label classification compared to emotion lexicons built by state-of-the-art approaches. We make our learned lexicon public accessible.

The remainder of this paper is organized as follows: In Section 2, we introduce related work on building emotion lexicons and their applications to sentiment analysis; we describe general inference method for finding the emotion distributions of emoticons in Section 3 and seed words selection method in Section 4; in Section 5, we present our effective multi-label random walk algorithm for emotion distribution estimation based on a three-layer heterogeneous graph; Section 6 provides the detailed results of evaluation; we conclude our work and give future directions in Section 7.

2. RELATED WORK

It is important to build high-quality emotion lexicons for sentiment analysis tasks. Most of the existing methods focus on building coarse-grained emotion lexicons where each entry is assigned with a positive or negative sentiment label [4, 6, 8, 14, 18]. In contrast to such lexicons, methods of building fine-grained emotion lexicon have also been proposed [20, 23, 30]. Our work fits in the latter category for building a fine-grained emotion lexicon. In addition, an emotion word conveying multiple emotions may associate different intensity with each emotion. Similar to Staiano et al. [25], we represent emotion words in our lexicon as emotion distributions such that for a given emotion word, the score in each emotion dimension represents the emotion strength.

Existing methods build emotion lexicons largely from a set of selected seed emotion words. Strapparava and Valitutti [26] created WordNet-Affect, an affective extension of WordNet, by leveraging seed words to make all WordNet synonyms have the same emotion. Xu et al. [30] used pointwise mutual information (PMI) to measure the correlation strength between seed words and candidate words. Xu et al. [28] adopted a graph-based algorithm which allows candidate words to learn emotion from connected seed words. Yang et al. [32] proposed an emotion-aware LDA model to build a domain-specific emotion lexicon using a minimal set of domain-independent seed words. All these approaches stem from the basic intuition that the emotion of a candidate word is determined by its frequently co-occurring seed words. However, they heavily rely on the subjective selection of seeds, rendering the low coverage of the constructed lexicons. Moreover, they ignore the overall emotion of the entire post which cannot be fully reflected by the selected seed words.

Graphical emoticons naturally reflect the emotion of a user and the post as a whole. Some studies [23, 34] even leveraged people's affective tags for online news articles as annotations. Zhao et al. [35] proposed a microblog emotion classifier trained on posts using emoticons as the ground truth. Yang et al. [31] adopted a variation of PMI to measure the similarity between emoticons and candidate words. Further, Feng et al. [6] integrated emoticons and candidate words into a graph model to mutually reinforce the ranking of candidate words. Unlike seed words, emoticon may convey multiple complex emotions, which is inherently versatile. Nevertheless, emoticons are generally noisy and the embedded complex emotions sometimes are hard to differentiate. In this paper, we model the sentiment as an emotion distribution and aim to strengthen the estimation of emotion distribution of candidate words by combining the effects of seed words and emoticons in a unified framework. A multi-label random walk algorithm is proposed to capture the emotion distribution accurately.

Emotion lexicons have been used by all kinds of sentiment analysis and other related applications [12, 13, 22, 10, 11, 7, 24]. While we focus on building a high-quality fine-grained emotion lexicon, we resort to a basic voting-based sentiment classification method to assess the quality of lexicon generated by our proposed method.

3. EMOTION DISTRIBUTION OF EMOTICONS

Emoticons are commonly contained in microblog posts which are of rich quantity and can reflect users' overall emotion in the post explicitly [1, 31, 35]. Unlike emoticons, seed emotion words are selected in a subjective manner

---

[3]The example microblogs are translated from Sina Weibo (http://weibo.com) posts.

Table 1: Polarity vs. fine-grained emotion

Sentiment Polarity	Emotion Category
Positive	happiness, like, surprise
Negative	disgust, sadness, anger, fear

and usually convey the most intensive emotion rather than overall emotion. Further, as opposed to the binary emotion polarity, an emoticon can express complex emotions which in nature can be modeled as a distribution of different e-motions. To capture such fine-grained emotion types, we first introduce an inference method for finding the emotion distribution for emoticons in this section, and then the inferred distribution is leveraged to guide building the emotion lexicon by incorporating seed emotion words for further distinguishing similar emotions.

3.1 Building Emoticon Dataset

We make use of a publicly available microblog dataset named NLPCC2014 corpus[4] (see Section 6.1 for details) to train an emotion classifier for inferring the emotion distribution of emoticons. In this corpus, human annotators identify the emotion-bearing sentences in the microblogs and annotate each identified sentence with one or two emotion labels that reflect the major (for the one-label case) or the major and secondary emotions (for the two-label case) of the sentence. To build our training data, we extract a subset with 3,232 sentences that all contain emoticons by discarding the pure text sentences in the corpus. Each sentence sen in this subset is preprocessed into the following form:

$$sen = [\{emc_1, emc_2, ..., emc_N\}^*, emo]$$

where $\{emc_1, emc_2, ..., emc_N\}$ is the full set of N emoticons in our system, $\{...\}^*$ is a subset of it meaning the specific emoticons contained in the sentence and emo is the emotion label. Note that if a sentence has two emotion labels, we split it into two instances each containing a unique emotion label. As a result, we build a training set with 3,600 sentences.

3.2 Inferring Emotion Distribution

Here we aim to estimate the emotion distribution for each emoticon. Let C denote the possible label for emo and A denote the possible emoticon in the full set of emoticons. Given an emoticon, we can obtain the probability of its classified emotion based on Baysian rule:

$$P(C = c_j | A = a_i) = \frac{P(C = c_j)P(A = a_i | C = c_j)}{\sum_j P(C = c_j)P(A = a_i | C = c_j)}$$

where a_i denotes the i-th emoticon emc_i of A (i.e., $i = 1...N$) and c_j is the j-th emotion of C. Based this formula, we represent each emoticon as a f-dimensional vector of emotion distribution $v = < P_1, ..., P_f >$ (so $j = 1...f$). Specifically, we adopt the popular seven-level categorization of fine-grained emotion following [27, 30], which are described in Table 1 (therefore $f = 7$).

Based on the results of inference, we demonstrate 32 most frequently used emoticons and their emotion distributions in Figure 1. We can observe that some emoticons convey only a single prominent emotion like 🙂, but many of them

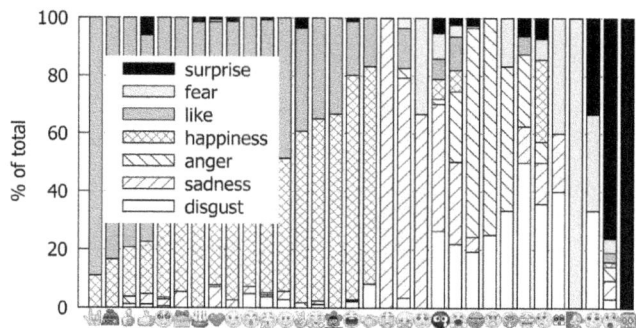

Figure 1: Emotion distribution of emoticons

suggest multiple complex emotions like 😵, and some others such as 😠 have a major emotion *anger* and a secondary emotion *disgust*. We expect that the emotions of such different granularity from emoticons can be used to help capture the emotion distribution of candidate words.

4. SEED EMOTION WORDS

Although emoticons are natural and versatile, there is at times subtle difference among emoticons, such as those containing emotions of anger and sadness (see Figure 1). In addition, emoticons are noisy sentiment labels [9]. Therefore, only using emoticons for selecting candidate words would be suboptimal in the sense that their effect on distinguishing similar emotions of candidate words in fine-grained level is problematic. As mentioned earlier, the seed emotion words typically bear some salient emotion, which can provide benefit to distinguish the subtle difference among the emotions of candidate words resulting from the co-occurring emoticons.

In this paper, we adopt a semi-automatic approach to choose seed words and ensure that the selected seed words can have straightforward impact on the co-occurring candidate words. Specifically, we rank all the words in the microblog dataset (see Section 6.1) according to their occurrence frequency; For those high-frequency words, we cross-reference the entries of a state-of-the-art manually created emotion lexicon from DUTIR group[5] called EWN (i.e., Emotion Words Noumenon) [27, 30], which provides seven possible emotions (i.e., happiness, like, surprise, disgust, sadness, anger, fear), five level of emotion intensity (i.e., 1, 3, 5, 7, 9) and no more than two emotion labels for each entry word. For each emotion, we manually select five high-frequency words with strong intensity as seed words. To represent the selected seed words, we adopt the same vector representation as that of emoticons. The only difference is that the probability value of the element is replaced by the ratio of the corresponding emotion's intensity with respect to all possible emotions' intensity.

5. BUILDING EMOTION LEXICON

We aim to overcome the weakness of relying on either seed words or emoticons alone: although seed words have strong indicative and discriminative capacity, seeds selection is subjective, which cannot induce to fully cover fine-grained emotions of candidate words; emoticons are finer grained, but

---

[4] http://tcci.ccf.org.cn/conference/2014/index.html

[5] http://ir.dlut.edu.cn/

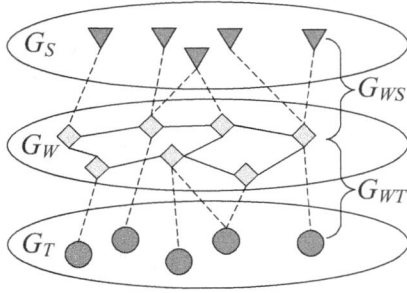

Figure 2: Our heterogeneous graph, where circles denote emoticons, diamonds denote candidate words, triangles denote seed words, solid lines and dotted lines correspond to different types of edges

are prone to noise and less discriminative. In this section, we try to combine their effects to infer the emotion distribution of candidate words more accurately. Specifically, we build a unified framework based on a three-layer heterogeneous graph, where nodes at each layer corresponds to seed words, emoticons and candidate words. Then we propose a multi-label random walk (MLRW) algorithm to strengthen the emotion distribution of candidate words resulting from complementary effect of seed words and emoticons. Finally, we output candidate words with the resulted emotion distribution as a lexicon.

5.1 Symbols and Notations

We first introduce some notations which are frequently used later. Let $W = \{w_1, w_2, ..., w_{|W|}\}$ be a candidate word set, $S = \{s_1, s_2, ..., s_{|S|}\}$ be a seed word set, and $T = \{t_1, t_2, ..., t_{|T|}\}$ be an emoticon set. For any element in W, T and S, we represent it as a vertex v in the graph. So we have three vertex sets V_W, V_T and V_S, and the entire vertex set $V = V_W \cup V_T \cup V_S$. Each $v \in V$ is a f-dimensional vector of emotion distribution $v = < P_1, ..., P_f >$ and $\sum_{i=1}^{f} P_i = 1$. If a vertex v_i often co-occurs with v_j, then there will be an edge e_{ij} between them. Let $E_{WW} = \{e_{ij}|i, j \in W, i \neq j\}$ denote the edges between candidate words, $E_{WT} = \{e_{ij}|i \in W, j \in T\}$ as edges between candidate words and emoticons, and $E_{WS} = \{e_{ij}|i \in W, j \in S\}$ as edges between candidate words and seed words. So edge set $E = E_{WW} \cup E_{WT} \cup E_{WS}$. As a result, the dataset is formulated as a heterogeneous graph $G = (V, E)$, as illustrated in Figure 2. Emoticons and seed words are priori knowledge, so V_S and V_T are fixed. Our goal is to estimate the vector of emotion distribution for V_W.

5.2 Building Heterogeneous Graph

We assign the edge weights for E_{WW}, E_{WS} and E_{WT} on the graph. Let $\mathbf{WW}$, $\mathbf{WS}$ and $\mathbf{WT}$ be the adjacent matrices of subgraphs $G_W = (V_W, E_{WW})$, $G_{WS} = (V_W \cup V_S, E_{WS})$ and $G_{WT} = (V_W \cup V_T, E_{WT})$, respectively. We resort to a variant of pointwise mutual information (PMI) [19] for measuring the correlation between nodes. The weight of edge e_{ij} in G_W is defined as follow:

$$\mathbf{WW}_{ij} = \begin{cases} c(w_i, w_j) * \delta\left(\frac{P(w_i, w_j)}{P(w_i)P(w_j)}\right) & \text{if } i \neq j \\ 0 & \text{otherwise} \end{cases}$$

where $\delta(x) = \frac{1}{1+e^{-x}}$ is a logistic function instead of logarithm function in PMI (logistic function ensures all the elements in the vector of emotion distribution are positive), $P(w) = \frac{|M_w|}{|M|}$ is the probability of candidate word w occurring in the entire microblog set M (M_w is the microblogs contain w), $c(w_i, w_j) = |M_{w_i} \cap M_{w_j}|$ is co-occurrence count of w_i and w_j (M_{w_i} and M_{w_j} are the microblogs containing words w_i and w_j, respectively), and $P(w_i, w_j) = \frac{c(w_i, w_j)}{|M|}$ is the probability that w_i and w_j co-occur. Similarly, we can also define adjacent matrix $\mathbf{WS}$ and $\mathbf{WT}$ as follow:

$$\mathbf{WS}_{ij} = c(w_i, s_j) * \delta\left(\frac{P(w_i, s_j)}{P(w_i)P(s_j)}\right)$$

$$\mathbf{WT}_{ij} = c(w_i, t_j) * \delta\left(\frac{P(w_i, t_j)}{P(w_i)P(t_j)}\right)$$

where $P(s) = \frac{|M_s|}{|M|}$ is the probability of seed word s occurring in M, $P(t) = \frac{|M_t|}{|M|}$ is the probability that emoticon t occurs, $P(w_i, s_j) = \frac{c(w_i, s_j)}{|M|}$ is the probability that w_i and s_j co-occur, and $P(w_i, t_j) = \frac{c(w_i, t_j)}{|M|}$ is the probability that w_i and t_j co-occur. Note that our variant of PMI is aimed for generating positive edge weights. This is necessary to ensure the probabilities in the generated emotion distribution to be non-negative (see Section 5.3).

5.3 Multi-label Random Walk (MLRW)

We propose the MLRW algorithm over the above undirected heterogeneous graph. Previous variants of PageRank-based methods [6, 36] for building emotion lexicon are aimed for ranking graph nodes all with single values, and the ranking scores of nodes could become negative during iterations. This is not directly applicable to our case. We intend to generate (and update) the emotion probability distribution for each node based on the distributions of other nodes and the edge weights, rather than just ranking candidate words. Meanwhile, we need normalization in adjacent matrices to ensure the probabilistic distribution for candidate words in each iteration. We adopt the form of power iteration formula [17] for updating the distribution in each round:

$$\mathbf{P}_W^{(k+1)} = (1-\alpha)\mathbf{e} + \alpha\mathbf{X}_W^{(k)}, \quad and$$

$$\mathbf{X}_W^{(k)} = \beta_1 \widetilde{\mathbf{WW}}\mathbf{P}_W^{(k)} + \beta_2 \widetilde{\mathbf{WT}}\mathbf{P}_T^{(k)} + (1-\beta_1-\beta_2)\widetilde{\mathbf{WS}}\mathbf{P}_S^{(k)}$$

where $\mathbf{P}_W : |W| \times f$, $\mathbf{P}_T : |T| \times f$ and $\mathbf{P}_S : |S| \times f$ are output matrices of candidate words, emoticons and seed words, respectively, $\mathbf{e}$ is an identity vector and α is damping factor [2], β_1 and β_2 are adjustable relative weights, $\widetilde{\mathbf{WW}}$, $\widetilde{\mathbf{WT}}$ and $\widetilde{\mathbf{WS}}$ are the corresponding stochastic matrices after normalizing $\mathbf{WW}$, $\mathbf{WT}$ and $\mathbf{WS}$.

Normalization: As $\mathbf{P}_T$ and $\mathbf{P}_S$ are known and fixed, we transform the w-th row vector $\mathbf{P}_{w.}^{(k+1)}$ ($w \in W$) to emotion distribution $\widetilde{\mathbf{P}}_{w.}^{(k+1)}$ by column-wise and row-wise min-max normalization in each round as follow:

$$\widetilde{\mathbf{P}}_{w.}^{(k+1)} = < \frac{\mathbf{P}_{w,1}^{(k+1)} - min_1}{(max_1 - min_1) \times Z}, ..., \frac{\mathbf{P}_{w,f}^{(k+1)} - min_f}{(max_f - min_f) \times Z} >$$

where notations $min_i = \min\{\mathbf{P}_{w,i}^{(k+1)}|w \in W\}$, $max_i = \max\{\mathbf{P}_{w,i}^{(k+1)}|w \in W\}$ and $Z = \sum_{i=1}^{f} \frac{\mathbf{P}_{w,i}^{(k+1)} - min_i}{(max_i - min_i)}$. This ensures that the values in the i-th column vector $\widetilde{\mathbf{P}}_{.i}^{(k+1)}$ ($1 \leq$

Algorithm 1: Multi-Label Random Walk Algorithm

Input : word-word matrix $\widetilde{\mathbf{WW}}$; word-emoticon matrix $\widetilde{\mathbf{WT}}$; word-seed word matrix $\widetilde{\mathbf{WS}}$; word output matrix $\mathbf{P}_W$; emoticon output matrix $\mathbf{P}_T$; seed word output matrix $\mathbf{P}_S$; relative weight $\beta = \{\beta_1, \beta_2\}$; damping factor α; threshold ε.

Output: word output matrix $\mathbf{P}_W$

1 **foreach** *emotion word w of word set W* **do**
2 $\quad \mathbf{P}_w$ is initialized with a uniform distribution
3 **foreach** *emoticon t of emoticon set T* **do**
4 $\quad \mathbf{P}_t$ is initialized with v_t
5 **foreach** *word s of seed emotion word set S* **do**
6 $\quad \mathbf{P}_s$ is initialized with v_s
7 $k = 1$
8 **repeat**
9 $\quad \mathbf{P}_W^{(k+1)} = (1 - \alpha)\mathbf{e} + \alpha \mathbf{X}_W$
10 $\quad$ **foreach** *candidate word w of word set W* **do**
11 $\quad\quad \mathbf{P}_w^{(k+1)}$ is normalized to emotion vector $\widetilde{\mathbf{P}}_{w\cdot}^{(k+1)}$.
12 $\quad \mathbf{P}_W^{(k+1)} = \widetilde{\mathbf{P}}_W^{(k+1)}$
13 $\quad k = k + 1$
14 **until** $\| P_W^{(k+1)} - P_W^{(k)} \| < \varepsilon$
15 **return** $P_W = P_W^{(k+1)}$

$i \leq f$) are within $[0, 1]$ and comparable among different columns, and Z makes the sum of all elements in the vector equal to 1. The detail of MLRW algorithm is described in Algorithm 1.

We obtain the vectors of emotion distribution for all candidate words in W based on Algorithm 1. We reserve the candidate words whose probability of the main emotion in the resulted distribution $\max\{P_i | 1 \leq i \leq f\}$ larger than assigned threshold τ are selected into final emotion lexicon. We show some example entries of our generated emotion lexicon based on Chinese Sina Weibo in Table 2.

In Table 2, we show some example entries of our generated lexicon, which include typical emotion words or popular buzzwords in social networks. The scores in lexicon represents the strength of a given word with respect to the corresponding dimensions we consider. For example, 作呕 (feel like vomiting) has a predominant weight in *disgust* (0.35), 笑哈哈 (laughter) has a predominant weight in *happiness* (0.44), while 孬种 (coward) has predominant weights in *disgust* and *anger* (0.30 and 0.30 respectively). Therefore, the weights can reflect multiple complex emotion of the word. In addition, we also display some network buzzwords with superscript $\star$. Network buzzword conveys strong personal emotion. For example, 屌丝 (loser), 尼玛 (damn), 抽风 (puzzling behavior), 童鞋 (classmate) and 给力 (brilliant/awesome). As we can see, the lexicon captures emotion distribution of network buzzwords in real-world scenarios well. The lexicon generated contains $17k$ entries in total.

6. EXPERIMENTAL EVALUATION

We conduct experiments based on real-world Chinese microblogs from Sina Weibo[6] (a popular Twitter-like online so-

---
[6]http://www.weibo.com/

cial network in China) since Chinese emotion lexicons, especially with fine-grained emotion categories, are not common. However, our method can be generalized to other languages easily.

6.1 Data Resources

We crawled 3.5 million public Chinese microblogs with emoticons, via Weibo API[7], to construct our lexicon. The microblog posts are crawled randomly so that they are not limited to particular topics. By covering any possible topics, the dataset is expected to produce a more general emotion lexicon. We preprocess the dataset to obtain a cleaner corpus. The microblogs without typical emoticons (See Section 3.2) or selected seed words (See Table 7) are discarded; the ones containing negation words (e.g., 不 (not)) or adversative conjunctions(e.g., 但是 (but) and 然而 (however)) are filtered because they will complicate the inference of emotion orientation. Finally, we obtain a large enough corpus with 1.5 million microblogs.

Different from English, there is no separator between adjacent Chinese words. Therefore, we utilize NLPIR[8], a state-of-the-art Chinese word segmenter, to segment microblogs into words and assign them Part-of-Speech (POS). In order to guide the word segmenter to identify emotional network buzzwords more accurately, we introduce a self-built network buzzword lexicon named NetLex with these network buzzwords[9]. In addition, we use existing lexicons (i.e., sentiment lexicons HowNet[10], NTUSD [15] and emotion lexicon EWN) to filter unemotional words. Note that, we resort to these lexicons only to identify candidate words but neglect their original emotion labels in lexicons. Basically, we adopt the following two rules to select candidate words from the corpus: (1) Meaningless stop words and infrequent words appearing less than 10 times are discarded; (2) Words existing in aforementioned lexicons and POS tagged words (adjective, verb, noun and adverb)[11] are reserved. Finally, we consider all the remaining words as candidate words and construct our fine-grained emotion lexicon based on these words. Our constructed emotion lexicon has been made publicly available[12].

Recall that we quantitatively evaluate the constructed lexicon through an emotion classification task. For this task, we use an annotated Chinese microblog dataset named EACWT (i.e., Emotion Analysis in Chinese Weibo Texts) to build the training set for inferring the emotion distribution of emoticons and the test set for evaluating lexicon-based emotion classification. EACWT dataset is the standard corpus used in NLPCC2014 emotion analysis shared task[13]. Each sentence in EACWT is annotated with one or two emotion labels that represent the major or the major and the secondary emotions, respectively. The task, namely Emotion Sentence Identification and Classification, aims to identify the emotion-bearing sentences and determine the emotion category for each sentence. We extract all sentences

---
[7]http://open.weibo.com/
[8]http://ictclas.nlpir.org/newsdownloads?DocId=389
[9]http://wangci.net/
[10]http://www.keenage.com/html/e_index.html
[11]Only part of most relevant subtypes of POS are considered.
[12]https://github.com/songkaisong/EmotionLexicon
[13]http://tcci.ccf.org.cn/conference/2014/dldoc/ evsam1.rar (Sample data is only available on the website, but complete data is provided with our lexicon together.)

Table 2: Examples of entries in our emotion lexicon, where superscript ⋆ denotes the network buzzwords

Entries	disgust	sadness	anger	happiness	like	fear	surprise
作呕 (feel like vomiting)	**0.35**	0.15	0.22	0.04	0.04	0.01	0.09
孬种 (coward)	**0.30**	0.10	**0.30**	0.03	0.06	0.16	0.05
嚎啕大哭 (burst into tears)	0.19	**0.33**	0.07	0.11	0.13	0.12	0.05
于心有愧 (have a guilty)	0.17	**0.40**	0.06	0.08	0.11	0.14	0.04
不共戴天(absolutely irreconcilable hatred)	0.34	0.09	**0.43**	0.01	0.00	0.08	0.05
怒火冲天 (towering rage)	0.32	0.09	**0.43**	0.00	0.01	0.08	0.07
笑哈哈 (laughter)	0.16	0.05	0.05	**0.44**	0.17	0.08	0.05
好笑 (funny)	0.22	0.06	0.07	**0.33**	0.14	0.09	0.09
好人 (good person)	0.07	0.05	0.04	0.17	**0.42**	0.22	0.03
甜美 (sweet)	0.16	0.06	0.03	0.20	**0.41**	0.08	0.06
鬼魔 (ghost)	0.09	0.04	0.04	0.15	0.22	**0.43**	0.03
地狱 (hell)	0.05	0.03	0.04	0.12	0.30	**0.44**	0.02
叹为观止 (amazing)	0.15	0.07	0.06	0.10	0.18	0.09	**0.35**
吃惊 (surprise)	0.16	0.11	0.09	0.15	0.11	0.12	**0.27**
童鞋 (classmate)⋆	0.17	0.07	0.06	0.26	**0.30**	0.07	0.07
屌丝 (loser)⋆	0.22	0.10	0.08	**0.26**	0.16	0.10	0.10
给力 (brilliant/awesome)⋆	0.15	0.04	0.04	**0.32**	0.30	0.07	0.08
抽风 (puzzling behavior)⋆	**0.24**	0.11	0.18	0.11	0.12	0.13	0.11
尼玛 (damn)⋆	**0.34**	0.12	0.30	0.04	0.04	0.10	0.06

with emotion labels, preprocess the sentences and then divide them into two parts: 3,600 sentences with emoticons are used for inferring emotion distribution of emoticons (see Section 3.1) and the remaining 6,799 labeled sentences are used for evaluating our learned lexicon.

Our method is implemented using the Java programming language based on a linear algebra package JAMA[14] for its efficiency. We run the program on a commodity PC with Intel Core i7-3537U CPU, 4G RAM and Windows-8 64-bit operating system.

6.2 Experiments and Results

We compare our lexicon with others built by the state-of-the-art methods. Rather than directly comparing the lexicons that may have different emotion types, which is difficult, we compare these automatically built emotion lexicons with respect to a manually created emotion lexicon called EWN [30]. EWN is regarded as the de facto standard because it has large size and the systems based on it has achieved state-of-the-art performance in sentiment classification evaluation [27]. We configure all methods compared in our experiments to produce word entries with the same seven possible emotions as EWN. We conduct two sets of experiments to examine (1) the quality of the lexicons generated by different methods; (2) the performance of sentence-level emotion classification based on these different lexicons.

6.2.1 Quality of Generated Lexicons

Evaluation Metrics: We use Precision, Recall and F-measure to assess the quality of the lexicons generated by different methods with respect to the manual lexicon EWN. We assess lexicon quality based on the major emotion because most of the EWN entry words are not provided with secondary emotion. We define the three metrics as follows:

$$P = \frac{\sum_{e \in E} |W_{EWN}(e) \cap W_{LEX}(e)|}{\sum_{e \in E} |W_{LEX}(e)|}$$

---
[14] http://math.nist.gov/javanumerics/jama/

$$R = \frac{\sum_{e \in E} |W_{EWN}(e) \cap W_{LEX}(e)|}{\sum_{e \in E} |W_{EWN}(e)|}$$

where E is the set of all seven possible emotions, $W_{EWN}(e)$ is the word set with emotion label of e in EWN, $W_{LEX}(e)$ is the word set with emotion label e in the produced lexicon. And we further define F-measure as $F = \frac{2 \cdot P \cdot R}{P+R}$. High precision P indicates the generated lexicons performs well in capturing major emotion, and high recall R indicates a high coverage with respect to EWN.

In addition, we use an auxiliary metric KL-divergence [16] to assess whether generated lexicons have good word distribution over emotion classes. Similarly, we also define this metric based on the major emotion as follow:

$$D_{KL} = \sum_{e \in E} \log \left(\frac{P_{LEX}(e)}{Q_{EWN}(e)} \right) P_{LEX}(e)$$

where $P_{LEX}(e) = \frac{|W_{LEX}(e)|}{\sum_{e \in E} |W_{LEX}(e)|}$ is the proportion of words with emotion label e in EWN, $Q_{EWN}(e) = \frac{|W_{EWN}(e)|}{\sum_{e \in E} |W_{EWN}(e)|}$ is the proportion of words with emotion label of e in the produced lexicon. A better lexicon will have a smaller difference with EWN.

Baseline Methods: We compare our method with the following emotion lexicon generation approaches:

- **PMI_e:** Yang et al. [31] use a variant of PMI to get the correlation strength $co(w, t)$ between word w and emoticon t. Emoticons (see Figure 1) are classified into seven emotion sets, so emoticons in emotion set T_l are associated with the same emotion label l (i.e., $l \in \{1, 2, 3, 4, 5, 6, 7\}$). For each word w, its score under emotion class l is represented by maximum correlation strength based on emoticons in emotion set T_l. Then, w's emotion vector can be represented as $< \max_{t \in T_1} \{co(w, t)\}, ..., \max_{t \in T_7} \{co(w, t)\} >$.

- **PMI_s:** Xu et al. [30] use standard PMI to get the correlation strength $co(w, s)$ between word w and seed word s. Seed words and their emotion partition will

Table 3: Quality of lexicon on all emotion

	DM	PMLs	PMLe	Lex_s	Lex_e	Lex_c
P	0.202	0.282	0.361	0.403	0.484	**0.541**
R	0.060	0.083	0.106	0.118	0.143	**0.159**
F	0.092	0.128	0.164	0.183	0.221	**0.246**

Table 4: Statistics of idioms and non-idioms in EWN and Lex_c lexicons

	# of non-idioms	# of idioms
EWN	12,480	14,986
Lex_c	15,328	1,682

Table 5: Capacity of different lexicons

Lexicon	Emotion type	# of entries
HowNet	positive, negative	8,936
NTUSD	positive, negative	11,086
NetLex	no classification	675
Lex_c	seven emotions	17,010
EWN/Idiom	seven emotions	12,480
EWN	seven emotions	27,466

be introduced later (see Table 7). Similar to PMLe, word w's score under emotion class l is represented by maximum correlation strength based on seed words in emotion set S_l. Then, the emotion of w can be represented as
$$< \max_{s \in S_1}\{co(w,s)\}, ..., \max_{s \in S_7}\{co(w,s)\} >.$$

- **DM**: Depeche Mood (DM) is an emotion lexicon proposed by Staiano and Guerini [25]. It first constructs the document-by-emotion matrix and the word-by-document matrix based on tf*idf, then applies matrix multiplication to represent each word as an emotion vector.

- **Lex_e**: This lexicon is generated using the special case of our model which only involves emoticons and candidate words in the graph. This essentially reduces to the model in [6] using the multiple emotion representation.

- **Lex_s**: This lexicon is generated as a special case of our model using only seed emotion words to produce emotion distributions of candidate words.

- **Lex_c**: This lexicon is built based on the full configuration of our proposed method that combines seed words and emoticons.

Results: As shown in Table 3, we find that the constructed lexicons Lex_c, Lex_e and Lex_s have obvious advantages over DM, PMLe and PMLs methods. Especially, the Lex_c combining the effects of seed words and emoticons performs the best, which manifests that our method can produce a high-quality and high-coverage emotion lexicon.

The following example illustrates such effect:
(1) My kitty **smirks** and sticks tongue out! 😀
(2) The star's **smirk** let me feel *disgusting*.
In (1), the candidate word 'smirk' co-occurring with the emoticon 😀 is assigned an emotion vector <0.16, 0.07, 0.04, **0.26**, 0.21, 0.23, 0.03> by Lex_e; In (2), 'smirk' co-occurring with the seed word 'disgusting' has an emotion vector <**0.40**, 0.15, 0.11, 0.04, 0.08, 0.12, 0.10> by Lex_s. We can see that in the respective lexicon, 'smirk' mainly conveys either 'happiness' or 'disgust', which is not complete. By considering both seed words and emoticons, Lex_c assigned 'smirk' the emotion vector <**0.24**, 0.09, 0.06, **0.24**, 0.13, 0.10, 0.14>, where the emotions *disgust* and *happiness* receive balanced weights, which is closer to its real emotion distribution.

We observe that the overlap with the manual lexicon EWN in Table 3 is notably low. This is because EWN contains too many idioms which are not commonly used in the microblog. We show statistical results of idioms and non-idioms in Lex_c and EWN in Table 4, respectively. From Table 4, we find that idioms and non-idioms in EWN show almost the same proportions, but Lex_c has a much larger percentage of the non-idioms. Therefore, too many idioms in EWN which are rarely used in microblog posts leads to a low recall in

Table 3. But our Lex_c lexicon built from the corpus has much more non-idioms and can be extended automatically with the increase of corpus size.

We further compare the capacity of Lex_c with existing binary emotion lexicons HowNet and NTUSD, fine-grained emotion lexicon EWN and its simplified version exclusive of idioms EWN/Idiom, and network buzzword lexicon NetLex in Table 5. Although these available lexicons with different emotion types are based on different construction methods, we still compare them together for indicating that our generated lexicon is large enough to be used. From Table 5, we can easily find that Lex_c is much larger than most available Chinese lexicons HowNet, NTUSD, NetLex and EWN/Idiom in size, which indicates that Lex_c is more universal compared to most existing lexicons.

As most candidate words are supposed to be emotional based on specific context, we reserve as many words as possible. As a consequence, the lexicons built automatically by our method and other comparable methods are similar in size. However, the distributions of these words in each lexicon under each emotion class are remarkably different and displayed based on the major emotion in Table 6. It is difficult to tell whether Lex_c has a good word distribution from Table 6. Therefore, we again resort to auxiliary metric KL-divergence to measure the difference between each generated lexicon with respect to the manual lexicon EWN. The results are plotted in Figure 3. We can easily find that our Lex_c performs the best by achieving the smallest KL-divergence between Lex_c and EWN. In contrast, DM performs the worst in identifying words under emotion *like*, and PMLe behaves poor since it identifies few words under emotion *disgust* and *fear*.

We follow the semi-automatic approach (see Section 4) and select 5 representative seed words respectively from each

Table 6: Word distributions of different lexicons, where di, sa, an, ha, li, fe, su denote the seven emotions *disgust, sadness, anger, happiness, like, fear* and *surprise*, respectively

	PMLs	PMLe	DM	Lex_s	Lex_e	Lex_c	EWN
di	7,805	394	4,105	6,909	4,921	5,822	10,282
sa	1,627	3,384	1,568	1,224	22	401	2,314
an	1,307	2,433	2,986	1,063	63	642	388
ha	1,862	2,909	2,297	1,930	3,367	3,034	1,967
li	2,049	7,495	848	2,944	6,273	6,205	11,108
fe	1,389	16	2,102	1,111	2,716	670	1,179
su	1,382	825	3,173	840	34	236	228

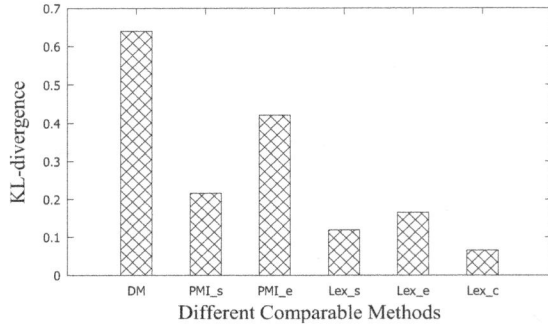

Figure 3: Word distribution under each emotion

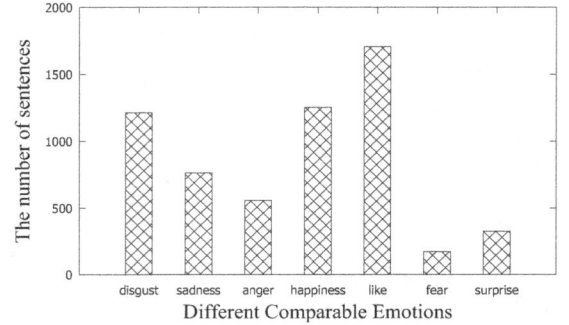

Figure 4: The number of testing sentences under each emotion category

Table 7: Seed Emotional Words

Emotion	Seed Words
disgust	讨厌 (disgusting), 多心 (suspicious) 厌烦 (boredom), 嫉妒 (jealousy), 可耻 (shame)
sadness	忧伤 (distressed), 伤心 (heart-broken) 绝望 (despair), 内疚 (compunction), 悲伤 (sad)
anger	恼火 (annoyed), 生气 (angry), 气愤 (furious) 悲愤 (grief and indignation), 火气 (anger)
happiness	高兴 (happy), 喜悦 (delightful), 欢喜 (joyful) 安心 (relieved), 踏实 (sureness)
like	尊敬 (respect), 赞扬 (praise), 相信 (believe) 喜爱 (inlove), 祝愿 (wish)
fear	害怕 (afraid), 恐惧 (dread), 吓人 (scary) 可怕 (horrible), 畏惧 (fear)
surprise	惊呆 (stunned), 震惊 (shock), 惊讶 (amazed) 惊奇 (surprise), 惊人 (astonishing)

emotion class. The 35 seed words from seven emotions we considered are shown in Table 7.

6.2.2 Sentence-level Emotion Classification

We also quantitatively evaluated the learned emotion lexicons through a sentence-level emotion classification task. The objective of the task is to assign the major emotion and secondary emotion to each sentence in test dataset from the NLPCC2014 corpus. We used a simple voting-based algorithm to assign class labels to a given sentence as follows. Let an entry word w in the lexicon represented by emotion distribution $< P_1^w, ..., P_7^w >$. For each emotion, we add up the values of all the emotion words contained in the sentence by looking up the lexicon:

$$sen \rightarrow < \sum_{i=1}^{n} P_1^{w_i}, ..., \sum_{i=1}^{n} P_7^{w_i} >$$

where n is the number of emotion words in sentence sen. Note that, this paper is not about improving the sentiment classification; we rather use emotion classification task as the standard task for measuring and comparing different lexicon generation methods. Therefore, we do not compare with emotion classification methods which are not based on lexicons.

Evaluation Metrics: We use popular Macro Metric [34] and Average Precision [33] to measure the effectiveness of single-label and multi-label emotion classification, respectively, based on the produced lexicons.

- **Macro Metric:** Macro Precision (MaP), Macro Recall (MaR) and Macro F-measure (MaF):

$$MaP = \frac{1}{7} \sum_i \frac{\#correct(emo_i)}{\#label(emo_i)}, MaR = \frac{1}{7} \sum_i \frac{\#correct(emo_i)}{\#gold(emo_i)}$$

where emo_i is any type of emotion, $\#correct(emo_i)$ is the number of microblogs with emo_i recognized correctly by algorithm, $\#label(emo_i)$ is the number of microblogs with emo_i recognized by algorithm and $\#gold(emo_i)$ is the number of microblogs labeled with emo_i. $MaF = \frac{2 \cdot MaP \cdot MaR}{MaP + MaR}$.

- **Average Precision:** For the top-2 emotion classification, we use Average Precision (AP) in multi-label classification as metric:

$$AP = \frac{1}{|n|} \sum_{j=1}^{n} \frac{1}{|Y_j|} \sum_{k=1}^{|Y_j|} \frac{|(emo \in Y_j | r(x_j, emo) \leq r(x_j, emo_k))|}{r(x_j, emo_k)}$$

where n is the number of sentences in test set, Y_j is the set of standard emotion labels for sentence x_j, emo is the system predicted emotion label, emo_k is one of the ground-truth emotions of x_j, and $r(x_j, y)$ is the ranked position of emotion y in x_j. Note that major emotion is always put ahead of secondary emotion, which gives an order of emotion labels in both ground-truth and prediction. AP indicates the average fraction of relevant labels ranked higher than the true label.

Parameter Setting: There are three adjustable parameters in our method, including the damping factor α, and the relative weights β_1 and β_2. According to the suggested setting to PageRank-like algorithm [2, 21], we set $\alpha = 0.85$. For tuning β_1 and β_2, we randomly choose 799 sentences into a development set, and the remaining 6,000 sentences are used for test. We display the number of testing sentences under each emotion category in Figure 4, which also reflects the fact that *like*, *happiness* and *disgust* play major roles in emotion expression. We use the parameter setting that gives the optimal F-measure value. For Lex_c, the optimal settings is $\beta_1 = 0.5$ and $\beta_2 = 0.4$; Lex_e and Lex_s just have a single β. We set it as 0.4 and 0.45, respectively. We set the convergence threshold $\varepsilon = 1e - 5$ and major emotion threshold $\tau = 0.20$ empirically.

Results: The results for single-label classification are shown in Table 8. We notice that the Lex_c model outperforms all the other automatic lexicon building methods. Its F-measure is just slightly lower than that of the manual lexicon EWN by 6.47%. This again confirms that our method

Table 8: Single-label emotion classification

Methods	MaP	MaR	MaF
PMLs	0.258	0.283	0.270
PMLe	0.390	0.313	0.347
DM	0.348	0.368	0.357
Lex_s	0.318	0.293	0.305
Lex_e	0.418	0.273	0.330
Lex_c	**0.579**	0.328	0.419
EWN	0.494	**0.411**	**0.448**

Table 9: Comparison of average occurrence number of seed words and emoticons in corpus

	Average occurrence number
Seed word	1,155
Emoticon	55,637

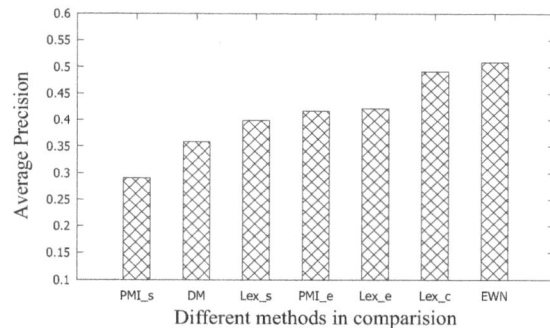

Figure 5: Multi-label emotion classification

combining emoticons and seed words is more effective in capturing major emotion of emotional words. We also find that the Lex_s and PMLs models do not perform as well as the DM, PMLe and Lex_e methods in terms of F-measure. This is mainly because seed words appear much fewer times than emoticons in the corpus. We further calculate the average occurrence number of seed words and emoticons, respectively, in corpus by formulas $\frac{\#emoticons}{\#microblogs}$ and $\frac{\#seedwords}{\#microblogs}$, and display results in Table 9 which explains the reasons for lower performance of Lex_s and PMLs models intuitively. The performance of Lex_e is close to PMLe and DM since all these methods are based on emoticons.

Then, we further study the multi-label emotion classification performance. The results are provided in Figure 5. We observe that PMLs performs much worse than the other models by failing to capture the secondary emotion. This is because PMLs does not leverage emoticons, which is especially a disadvantage for this multi-label task due to its potential incomplete emotion representation. Lex_c performs nearly as well as the manually built lexicon EWN, but Lex_e and Lex_s performs much worse, which implies that both emoticons and seed words contribute to estimating emotion distribution of words more accurately.

7. CONCLUSION AND FUTURE WORK

In this paper, we focus on building a high-quality emotion lexicon automatically from massive collection of microblogs. Our idea is to capture the emotion distributions of candidate words that convey multiple complex emotions by combining the effect of seed words and emoticons that co-occur with the candidate words. We resort to a three-layer heterogeneous graph to represent emoticons, seed words and candidate words and the correlations among them, on which a multi-label random walk algorithm is performed to strengthen the estimation of emotion distributions of candidate words. Experimental results based on real-world microblogs demonstrate that the performance of our lexicon in capturing words' emotion is nearly as well as a high-quality emotion lexicon created manually. Meanwhile, it outperforms other lexicons created by the state-of-the-art automatic methods in emotion classification.

In the future, we will introduce the syntax unit composed of word and Part-of-Speech into emotion lexicon building and study the emotion distribution of emotional words un-

der each POS. In addition, we will further improve the quality and capacity of our Chinese emotion lexicon Lex_c, and publish lexicons in other languages.

8. ACKNOWLEDGMENTS

This work is supported by the National Basic Research 973 Program of China under Grant No. 2011CB302200-G, the National Natural Science Foundation of China under Grant Nos. 61370074, 61402091 and the Fundamental Research Funds for the Central Universities of China under Grant Nos. N130604002, N140404012. This work is also partly supported by the Australian Research Council (ARC) Discovery Project under Grant No. DP140100545 and a national scholarship from China Scholarship Council (CSC) for building high level universities.

9. REFERENCES

[1] P. P. Alexander Pak. Twitter as a corpus for sentiment analysis and opinion mining. In *Proceedings of the International Conference on Language Resources and Evaluation*, pages 1320–1326, 2010.

[2] S. Brin and L. Page. The anatomy of a large-scale hypertextual web search engine. *Computer Networks*, 30(1-7):101–117, 1998.

[3] E. Cambria, R. Speer, C. Havasi, and A. Hussain. enticnet: A publicly available semantic resource for opinion mining. In *Proceedings of AAAI Fall Symposium on Commonsense Knowledge*, pages 417–422, 2010.

[4] Y. Chen and S. Skiena. Building sentiment lexicons for all major languages. In *Proceedings of the 52nd Annual Meeting of the Association for Computational Linguistics*, pages 383–389, 2014.

[5] A. Esuli and F. Sebastiani. Sentiwordnet: A publicly available lexical resource for opinion mining. In *Proceedings of the International Conference on Language Resources and Evaluation*, pages 417–422, 2006.

[6] S. Feng, K. Song, D. Wang, and G. Yu. A word-emoticon mutual reinforcement ranking model for building sentiment lexicon from massive collection of microblogs. *World Wide Web*, 18(4):949–967, 2015.

[7] S. Feng, D. Wang, G. Yu, W. Gao, and K.-F. Wong. Extracting common emotions from blogs based on fine-grained sentiment clustering. *Knowledge and Information Systems*, 27(2):281–302, 2011.

[8] D. Gao, F. Wei, W. Li, X. Liu, and M. Zhou. Co-training based bilingual sentiment lexicon learning. In *Proceedings of AAAI Workshops on Late-Breaking Developments in the Field of Artificial Intelligence*, 2013.

[9] A. Go, R. Bhayani, and L. Huang. Twitter sentiment classification using distant supervision. In *Technical report, Stanford*, 2009.

[10] Y. He, C. Lin, W. Gao, and K.-F. Wong. Tracking sentiment and topic dynamics from social media. In *Proceedings of the 6th International AAAI Conference on Weblogs and Social Media*, pages 483–486, 2012.

[11] Y. He, C. Lin, W. Gao, and K.-F. Wong. Dynamic joint sentiment-topic model. *ACM Transactions on Intelligent Systems and Technology*, 5(1):6:1–6:21, 2013.

[12] C. J. Hutto and E. Gilbert. Vader: A parsimonious rule-based model for sentiment analysis of social media text. In *Proceedings of the 8th International Conference on Weblogs and Social Media*, 2014.

[13] N. Kaji and M. Kitsuregawa. Building lexicon for sentiment analysis from massive collection of html documents. In *Proceedings of EMNLP-CoNLL*, pages 1075–1083, 2007.

[14] R. Krestel and S. Siersdorfer. Generating contextualized sentiment lexica based on latent topics and user ratings. In *Proceedings of the 24th ACM Conference on Hypertext and Social Media*, pages 129–138, 2013.

[15] L.-W. Ku and H.-H. Chen. Mining opinions from the web: Beyond relevance retrieval. *Journal of American Society for Information Science and Technology*, 58(12):1838–1850, 2007.

[16] S. Kullback and R. Leibler. On information and sufficiency. *Annals of MathematicalStatistics*, 22:79–87, 1951.

[17] B. Liu. *Web Data Mining: Exploring Hyperlinks, Contents, and Usage Data (Data-Centric Systems and Applications)*. Springer-Verlag New York, Inc., Secaucus, NJ, USA, 2006.

[18] Y. Lu, M. Castellanos, U. Daya, and C. Zha. Automatic construction of a context-aware sentiment lexicon: An optimization approach. In *Proceedings of the 20th International Conference on World Wide Web*, pages 347–356, 2011.

[19] C. D. Manning and H. Schütze. *Foundations of Statistical Natural Language Processing*. MIT Press, Cambridge, MA, USA, 1999.

[20] S. Mohammad and P. D. Turney. Crowdsourcing a word-emotion association lexicon. *Computational Intelligence*, 29(3):436–465, 2013.

[21] L. Page, S. Brin, R. Motwami, and T. Winograd. The pagerank citation ranking: Bringing order to the web. In *Technical Report 1999-0120, Computer Science Department, Standford University*, 1999.

[22] F. Peleja, J. Santos, and J. Magalhaes. Reputation analysis with a ranked sentiment-lexicon. In *Proceedings of the 37th International ACM SIGIR Conference on Research and Development in Information Retrieval*, pages 1207–1210, 2014.

[23] Y. Rao, J. Lei, W. Liu, Q. Li, and M. Chen. Building emotional dictionary for sentiment analysis of online news. *World Wide Web*, 17(4):732–742, 2014.

[24] K. Song, S. Feng, W. Gao, D. Wang, G. Yu, and K.-F. Wong. Personalized sentiment classification based on latent individuality of microblog users. In *Proceedings of the 24th International Joint Conference on Artificial Intelligence*, 2015.

[25] J. Staiano and M. Guerini. Depeche mood: a lexicon for emotion analysis from crowd annotated news. In *Proceedings of the 52nd Annual Meeting of the Association for Computational Linguistics*, pages 427–433, 2014.

[26] C. Strapparava and A. Valitutti. Wordnet-affect: an affective extension of wordnet. In *Proceedings of the 4th International Conference on Language Resources and Evaluation*, 2004.

[27] S. Wen and X. Wan. Emotion classification in microblog texts using class sequential rules. In *Proceedings of the Twenty-Eighth AAAI Conference on Artificial Intelligence*, pages 187–193, 2014.

[28] G. Xu, X. Meng, and H. Wang. Build chinese emotion lexicons using a graph-based algorithm and multiple resources. In *Proceedings of the 23rd International Conference on Computational Linguistics*, pages 1209–1231, 2010.

[29] J. Xu, R. Xu, Y. Zheng, Q. Lu, K.-F. Wong, and X. Wang. Chinese emotion lexicon developing via multi-lingual lexical resources integration. In *Proceedings of the 14th International Conference on Computational Linguistics and Intelligent Text Processing - Volume 2*, pages 174–182, 2013.

[30] L. Xu, H. Lin, Y. Pan, H. Ren, and J. Chen. Constructing the afective lexicon ontology. *Journal of The China Society For Scientific and Technical Information*, 27(2):180–185, 2008.

[31] C. Yang, K. H.-Y. Lin, and H.-H. Chen. Building emotion lexicon from weblog corpora. In *Proceedings of the 52nd Annual Meeting of the Association for Computational Linguistics*, pages 133–136, 2007.

[32] M. Yang, D. Zhu, and K.-P. Chow. A topic model for building fine-grained domain-specific emotion lexicon. In *Proceedings of the 52nd Annual Meeting of the Association for Computational Linguistics*, pages 421–426, 2014.

[33] M.-L. Zhang and Z.-H. Zhou. A review on multi-label learning algorithms. *IEEE Transactions on Knowledge and Data Engineering*, 26(8):1819–1837, 2014.

[34] Z. Zhang and M. P. Singh. Renew: A semi-supervised framework for generating domain-specific lexicons and sentiment analysis. In *Proceedings of the 52nd Annual Meeting of the Association for Computational Linguistics*, pages 542–551, 2014.

[35] J. Zhao, L. Dong, J. Wu, and K. Xu. Moodlens: An emoticon-based sentiment analysis system for chinese tweets in weibo. In *Proceedings of the 18th ACM SIGKDD International Conference on Knowledge Discovery and Data Mining*, pages 1528–1531, 2012.

[36] W. Zheng, C. Wang, Z. Liu, and J. Wang. A multi-label classification algorithm based on random walk model. *Chinese Journal of Computers*, 33(8):1418–1426, 2010.

Random Voting Effects in Social-Digital Spaces: A Case Study of Reddit Post Submissions

Tim Weninger[†]   Thomas J. Johnston[‡]   Maria Glenski[†]

[†]University of Notre Dame
[‡]University of Illinois Urbana-Champaign
tweninge@nd.edu, johnst26@illinois.edu, mglenski@nd.edu

ABSTRACT

At a time when information seekers first turn to digital sources for news and opinion, it is critical that we understand the role that social media plays in human behavior. This is especially true when information consumers also act as information producers and editors by their online activity. In order to better understand the effects that editorial ratings have on online human behavior, we report the results of a large-scale *in-vivo* experiment in social media. We find that small, random rating manipulations on social media submissions created significant changes in downstream ratings resulting in significantly different final outcomes. Positive treatment resulted in a positive effect that increased the final rating by 11.02% on average. Compared to the control group, positive treatment also increased the probability of reaching a high rating (≥ 2000) by 24.6%. Contrary to the results of related work we also find that negative treatment resulted in a negative effect that decreased the final rating by 5.15% on average.

Categories and Subject Descriptors

H.1.2 [**Models and Principles**]: User/Machine Systems— *Human information processing*; H.5.3 [**Information Interfaces and Presentation**]: Group and Organization Interfaces—*Web-based interaction*

General Terms

Human Factors, Experimentation

Keywords

social media; voting; herding effects

1. INTRODUCTION

What is becoming known as **collective intelligence** bares the potential to enhance human potential and accomplish

what is impossible individually. Indeed, the collective judgements of social groups have been shown to be remarkably accurate when their averaged judgements are compared with the judgements of an individual. For example, more than a century ago the experiments of Francis Galton determined that the median estimate of a group can be more accurate than estimates of experts[3]. Surowiecki's book *The Wisdom of the Crowds* finds similar examples in stock markets, political elections, quiz shows and a variety of other fields where large groups of people behave intelligently and perform better than an elite few[14]. However, other experiments have shown that when individuals' perceptions of quality and value follow the behavior of a group, the resulting **herd mentality** can be suboptimal for both the individual and the group [6, 8].

In modern, digital society, people frequently rely on the anonymous, aggregate ratings of others to make important decisions. The sheer volume of new information being produced and consumed only increases the reliance that individuals place on anonymous others to curate and sort massive amounts of information. But by relying on the judgements of others, we may be susceptible to malicious ratings with some ulterior motive.

With this vulnerability in mind, recent studies have attempted to determine if and how past ratings affect future ratings and the general opinion of the public. Unfortunately, causal determinations are difficult to assess. In a closely related experiment, Wu and Huberman measured rating behavior in two different online platforms. The first allowed users to see prior ratings before they voted and the other platform hid the prior ratings until after the user voted. They found that when no information about previous ratings or page views are available, the ratings and user-opinions expressed tend to follow regular patterns. However, in cases where the previous ratings were made known, the user-opinions tended to be either neutral or form a polarized consensus. In the latter case, new opinions tend to reinforce previous opinions and thus become more extreme [17].

In a separate line of work, Sorenson used mistaken omissions of books from the *NY Times* bestsellers list to identify the boost in sales that accompany the perceived popularity of a book's appearance on the list[13]. Similarly, when the download counters for different software labels were randomly increased, Hanson and Putler found that users are significantly more likely to download software that had the largest counter increase[5]. Salganik and Watts performed a study to determine the extent to which perception of quality becomes a "self-fulfilling prophecy." In their experiment they inverted the true popularity of songs in an online music marketplace, and found that the perceived-but-false-popularity became real over time[12].

The recent popularity of social networks has led to the study of socio-digital influence and popularity cascades where models can be developed based on the adoption rate of friends (*e.g.*, share, retweet). Bakshy *et al.*, find that the friendship plays a significant role in the sharing of content[2]. Similarly, Leskovec *et al.* were able to formulate a generative model that predicts the size and shape of information cascades in online social networks [7].

Like social networks, online *social news* platforms allow individuals to contribute to the wisdom of the crowd in new ways. These platforms are typically Web sites that contain very simple mechanics. In general, there are 4 operations that are shared among social news sites:

1. individuals generate content or submit links to content,

2. submissions are rated and ranked according to their rating scores,

3. individuals can comment on the submitted content,

4. comments are rated and ranked according to their rating scores.

Simply put, social news platforms allow individuals to submit content and vote on the content they like or dislike.

The voting mechanism found in socio-digital platforms provides a type of Web-democracy that is open to all comers. Given the widespread use and perceived value of these voting systems[4], it is important to consider whether they can successfully harness the wisdom of the crowd to accurately aggregate individual information.

In our study, we determine what effect, if any, post ranking and vote score has on rating behavior. This is accomplished via an *in vivo* experiment on the social media Web site, Reddit, by inserting random votes into the live rating system.

Reddit is a social news Web site where registered users can submit content, such as direct posts or links. Registered users can then up-vote submissions or down-vote submissions to organize the posts and determine the post's position on the site; posts with a high vote score (*i.e.*, up-votes – down-votes) are ranked more highly than posts with a low vote score. Reddit is organized into many thousands of "subreddits," according to topic or area of interest, *e.g.*, news, science, compsci, datamining, and theoryofreddit. Posts must be submitted to a subreddit. A user that subscribes to a particular subreddit will see highly ranked posts from that subreddit on their frontpage, which Reddit describes as 'the front page of the Internet.'

It is important to note that, unlike other online social spaces, Reddit is not a social *network*. the notion of friendship and friend-links, like on Facebook, is mostly absent on Reddit. Although usernames are associated with posts and comments, the true identity of registered users is generally unknown and in many cases fiercely guarded.

In fact, we attempted to find friendship by looking at user-pairs that frequently reply to each other in comments; unfortunately, more than 99.9% of the comments were in reply to a user that they had never previously replied to. Thus, we typically refer to Reddit a social non-network, and the vast amount of previous social *network* literature does not apply.

Although this is the first in-vivo Reddit experiment, our work is motivated and informed by multiple overlapping streams of literature and build on substantial prior work from multiple fields such as: herding behavior from theoretical and empirical viewpoints [11, 16]; social influence [2]; collective intelligence [6, 1]; and online rating systems [9].

A recent study by Muchnik *et al* on a small social news Web site, similar to Reddit, found that a single up-vote/like on an online comment significantly increased the final vote count of the treated comment; interestingly, the same experiment also found that a single negative rating had little effect on the final vote count[10].

We report the results of a large ($N = 93,019$) in-vivo experiment on Reddit that up-voted or down-voted posts at random. Based on these experimental treatments we observe the effects that votes have on the final score of a post as a proxy for observing herding effects in social news. Unlike the experimental study performed by Muchnik *et al.*, and other behavioral studies our experiment: 1) manipulates votes of posts rather than comments, 2) leverages Reddit's dynamic, score-based ranking system rather than a time-only ranking system, 3) does not involve friendship or the use of social networks, and 4) randomly delays the vote treatment rather than always performing the treatment immediately upon creation.

2. METHODS

During the 6 months between September 1, 2013 and January 31, 2014 a computer program was executed every 2 minutes that collected post data from Reddit through an automated two-step process. First, the most recent post on Reddit was identified and assigned to one of three treatment groups: up-treated, down-treated, or control. Up-treated posts were artificially given an up-vote (a +1 rating) and down-treated posts were given a down-vote (a -1 rating). Up-treatment, down-treatment and the control have an equal likelihood of being selected. Vote treated posts are assigned a random delay ranging from no delay up to an hour delay in intervals of 0, .5, 1, 5, 10, 30 and 60 minutes. Second, each post was re-sampled 4 days later and final vote totals were recorded.

These treatments created a small, random manipulation signalling positive or negative judgement that is perceived by other voters as having the same expected quality as all other votes thereby enabling estimates of the effects of a single vote while holding all other factors constant. This data collection resulted in 93,019 sampled posts, of which 30,998 were up-treated and 30,796 were down-treated; each treatment type was randomly assigned a delay interval with equal likelihood. Treatments were removed from the vote scores before data analysis was performed, *i.e.*, up-treated post-scores were decremented by 1 and down-treated post-scores were incremented by 1.

During the experimental time period, Reddit reported that their up-vote and down-vote totals were "fuzzed" as an anti-spam measure; fortunately, they certified that a post's score (*i.e.*, up-votes minus down-votes) was always accurate. In July of 2014, after the data gathering phase of this experiment had ended, Reddit removed the vote totals from their Web site and replaced it with a semi-accurate points system.

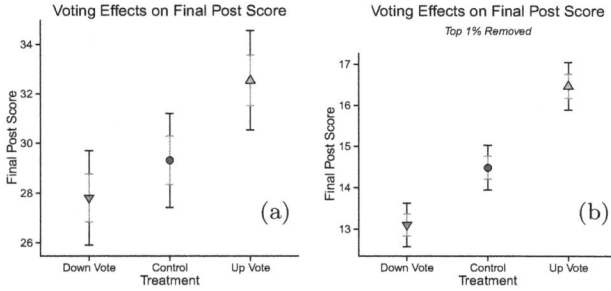

Figure 1: Final scores for artificially, randomly up-treated posts, down-treated posts, and scores for untreated posts in the control group are shown. Red inner error bars show the standard error of the mean; black outer error bars show the 95% confidence interval. Fig. (a) shows the scores in the heavily skewed full distribution. When the highest 1% of scores are removed as in Fig. (b), the score distribution becomes much less skewed resulting in tighter error bounds, which further result in significant increases for up-treated posts and significant decreases for down-treated posts when compared to the control group.

3. RESULTS

We first compared the final vote totals of posts in each treatment group. These findings measure the overall effect that up-treatments and down-treatments have on the overall life of a post.

Figure 1(a) shows the distribution of the final post scores for each treatment group. Black outer error bars show the 95% confidence interval and red inner error bars show the standard error of the mean. The distribution of scores is extremely positively skewed with a skewness of 11.2 and a kurtosis of 149.8. If we remove the top 1% highest scoring posts from the data set the skewness and kurtosis values drop to 6.5 and 54.9 respectively giving a better, although still skewed, view of the treatment effects. Figure 1(B) shows the distribution of the final post scores with the top 1% of posts removed. In this case, the up-treated posts have a significantly higher final score, and the down-treated posts have a significantly lower final score.

Kolmogorov-Smirnov (K-S) tests showed that the final score distribution of all up-treated posts were more positively skewed than posts in the control group (K-S test statistic: 0.08; $p < 2.2 \times 10^{-16}$), which were more positively skewed than down-treated posts (K-S test statistic: 0.11; $p < 2.2 \times 10^{-16}$). Student's T-Test on log-scores also showed that the up-treated posts were significantly higher than the control group ($p = 1.69 \times 10^{-20}$), and that the down down-treated posts were significantly lower than the control group ($p = 1.69 \times 10^{-09}$) although scores less than or equal to 0 were removed to calculate the log of the final scores.

Up vote and down vote treatments were performed after a 0, 0.5, 1, 5, 10, 30 or 60 minute delay chosen at random, and Figure 1 does not distinguish between the effects of vote-treatments performed after the various delay peri-

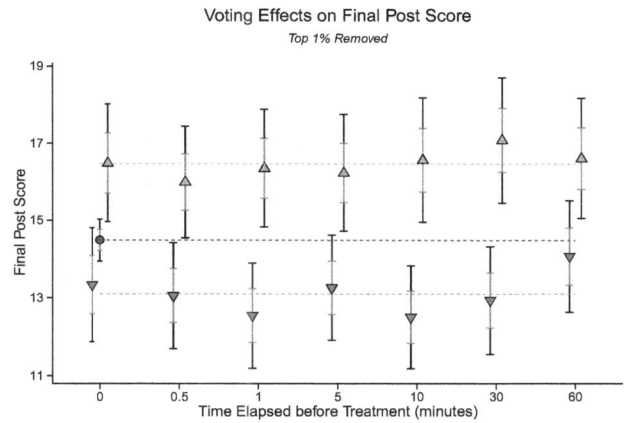

Figure 2: Final scores for artificially, randomly up-treated posts, down-treated posts, and scores for untreated posts in the control group separated into their respective treatment delay intervals. Horizontal lines show the overall mean of each treatment group. The top 1% of scores were removed to un-skew the score distribution. These results show that treatment delay had little effect on the mean final score.

ods. Figure 2 separates the results from Figure 1 into their respective treatment delay groups. We expected that immediate votes would have a larger effect than votes performed after a long delay. However, these results show, surprisingly, that a delay in treatment generally had little effect on the mean outcome. Unfortunately, displayed error bounds have little meaning when the data is so highly skewed; K-S tests again showed that all up-treated posts were more positively skewed than posts in the control group and that the effects generally diminished as the delay interval increased: (K-S test statistic: 0.087(0 min), 0.087(.5 min), 0.087(1 min), 0.083(5 min), 0.082(10 min), 0.087(30 min), 0.078(60 min); $p < 2.2 \times 10^{-16}$).-Similarly, the control group was more positively skewed than the down-treated posts, but the effects were mixed as the delay interval increased: (K-S test statistic: 0.119(0 min), 0.110(.5 min), 0.110(1 min), 0.112(5 min), 0.119(10 min), 0.097(30 min), 0.099(60 min); $p < 2.2 \times 10^{-16}$).

Unlike the results presented by Muchnik *et al.* [10] on a similar experiment, we find that the positive and negative treatments show mostly symmetric results, *i.e.*, the up-treatments and down-treatments result in similar, yet opposite, departures from the control group. The reason for the differences is unclear and worthy of further investigation.

We are careful to note that reports of mean-averages and standard error are often misleading on such highly skewed data. With this in mind, Figure 3 shows the inner-deciles of the results as a function of their treatment delay. Taken together these results show graphically what the KS tests imply: that up-treated posts tend to be skewed more highly than the control group, and that down-treated posts tend not to be as highly skewed as the control group. The decile plots also show that the majority of posts (deciles $\leq 50\%$) receive at most a final score of 2. A single up-treatment actually does not change the median (50% decile) final score, but a down-treatment does lower the median score from 2 to 1.

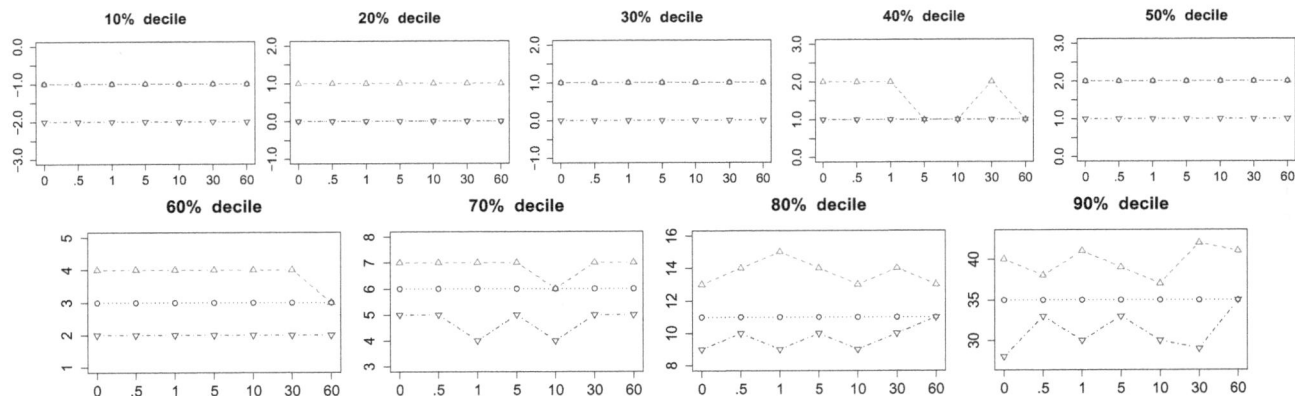

Figure 3: The middle 9 deciles of up-treated, down-treated and control group posts are shown according to their interval times. These results show that most posts receive a median score of 2 or less, and that the treatment has the most effect in the higher deciles of the score distribution.

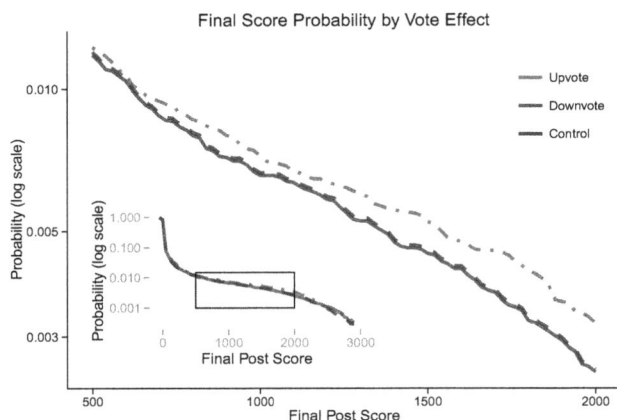

Figure 4: The probability of a post receiving a corresponding score by treatment type. The inset graph shows the complete probability distribution function. The outer graph shows the probability of a post receiving scores between 500 and 2000 – an approximation for *trending* or *frontpage* posts. Up-treated posts are 24% more likely to reach 2000 votes than the control group.

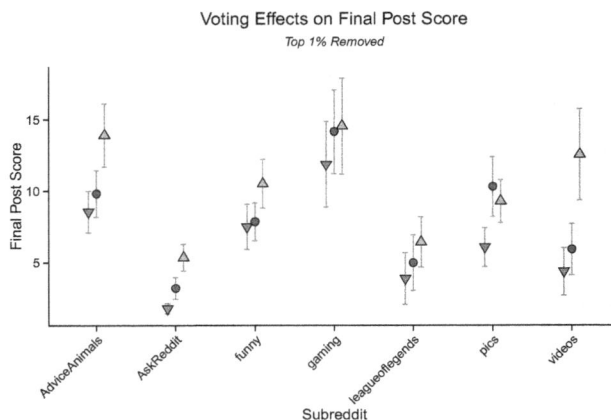

Figure 5: Mean scores of down-treated, control group and up-treated posts shown with 95% confidence intervals on the top 8 most active subreddits.

Overall, the results suggest that an up-treatment increases the probability that a post will result in a high score relative to the control group, and that down-treatments decrease that probability relative to the control group. However, on Reddit and other social news sites only a handful of posts become extremely popular. On Twitter and Facebook this is generally referred to as a *trending* topic, but on Reddit the most popular posts are the ones that reach the front page. Unfortunately, reaching the front page is a difficult thing to discern because each user's homepage is different, based on the topical subreddits to which the user has subscribed. Nevertheless, we crudely define a post as having become popular, *i.e.*, is trending, on the frontpage, etc., if it has a score of more than 500. Using this definition Figure 4 shows the probability of a post reaching a given final score under the two treatment conditions. This probability distribution

function is monotonically decreasing, positively skewed, and shows that up-treatments result in a large departure from the control group. However, despite our earlier claims of up-treatment and down-treatment symmetry, these results show that, in the upper limits of the distribution, down-treatments do not effect the final score results. These results mean that, compared to the control group, an up-treated post is 7.9% more likely to have a final score of at least 1000, and an up-treated post is 24.6% more likely to have a final score of at least 2000.

We finally investigated treatment effects in the top 10 most frequent subreddits. These do not necessarily correspond to the top 10 most popular subreddits, but are rather the subreddits to which posts are most frequently submitted. From the top 10, we removed **politic** and **friendsafari** because posts in **politic** are automatically submitted by a computer program, and because posts in **friendsafari** cannot be down-treated according to the subreddit rules. Results show significant positive effects in **AdviceAnimals**, **AskReddit** and **videos**, and significant negative effects in **AskReddit** and pics. Within the top 500 subreddits, we found that 22% had significant up-treatment effects, 21.6% had significant down-treatments, and 5.4% of subreddits had significant differences in both the up-treatment and down-treatment results as compared to the control group. Also in the top 500 there was no correlation between up-treatment significance and number of submissions the subreddit received ($r^2 = 0.014$; p-value $= 0.007$), nor down-treatment significance and number of submissions the subreddit received ($r^2 = 0.010$; p-value $= 0.026$)

4. DISCUSSION

We find that the positive treatment of a single, random "upvote" on a Reddit post has a corresponding positive herding effect that increases post scores on average and in the top limits of the heavily skewed score distribution. We further found that the negative treatment of a single, random "downvote" on a post has a corresponding negative herding effect that significantly decreased the post scores on average, in contrast to the asymmetric findings of Muchnik *et al.* [10], who found no significant effects of a negative treatment. However, our results begin to resemble asymmetry in the top limits of the score distribution meaning that a negative treatment does not decrease the probability that a post will receive a high score.

When treatments were separated according to their delay intervals we found that immediate treatments have a slightly larger positive effect than those with longer delays, but the negative delay results did not follow a clear trend. The time of day a vote is placed did not change the overall effect.

The nature of the manner in which social platforms rank items for viewing typically utilizes the ratings, in this case the post scores, of the items being ranked. The results of our experiment show that random vote perturbations through vote treatments impact the post scores of postings on Reddit. These results underscore the need for counter measures against vote chaining and social engineering strategies as multiple artificial votes are likely to increase the herding effect.

Finally, we re-draw attention to what Eric Gilbert calls, the 'widespread underprovision of votes' in social media like Reddit [4]. Although our data does not draw these figures explicitly, we estimate that only .25% of the of the daily visitors to Reddit actually vote on the items they view. This seems to be an even further skewed anecdote of the 1-9-90 rule of social networking [15], and may be the an underestimated reason behind the results presented in this paper.

Similar work on post comment threads has been collected and will be presented in future reports.

5. ACKNOWLEDGMENTS

We thank Michael Creehan for his help and discussion. This research is sponsored by the Air Force Office of Scientific Research FA9550-15-1-0003. The research was approved by University of Notre Dame institution review board and the Air Force Surgeon General's Research Compliance Office. Raw data files, and statistical analysis scripts are available on the corresponding authors Web site at http://www3.nd.edu/~tweninge/data/reddit_report.html. Reddit Inc was not involved in the experimental design, implementation or data analysis.

6. REFERENCES

[1] A. Anderson, D. Huttenlocher, J. Kleinberg, and J. Leskovec. Discovering value from community activity on focused question answering sites. In *SIGKDD*, page 850, New York, New York, USA, 2012. ACM Press.

[2] E. Bakshy, B. Karrer, and L. A. Adamic. Social influence and the diffusion of user-created content. In *EC*, page 325, New York, New York, USA, July. ACM Press.

[3] F. Galton. The Ballot Box. *Nature*, 75:509–510, 1907.

[4] E. Gilbert. Widespread underprovision on Reddit. In *CSCW*, page 803, New York, New York, USA, Feb. ACM Press.

[5] W. A. Hanson and D. S. Putler. Hits and misses: Herd behavior and online product popularity. *Marketing Letters*, (4):297–305, Oct.

[6] D. A. Hirshleifer. The Blind Leading the Blind: Social Influence, Fads and Informational Cascades. In K. Ierulli and M. Tommasi, editors, *The New Economics of Human Behaviour*, chapter 12, pages 188–215. Cambridge University Press.

[7] J. Leskovec, A. Singh, and J. Kleinberg. Patterns of influence in a recommendation network. *Advances in Knowledge Discovery and Data Mining*, pages 380–389, Apr.

[8] J. Lorenz, H. Rauhut, F. Schweitzer, and D. Helbing. How social influence can undermine the wisdom of crowd effect. *Proceedings of the National Academy of Sciences*, (22):9020–5, May.

[9] Y. Lu and C. Zhai. Opinion integration through semi-supervised topic modeling. In *WWW*, page 121, New York, New York, USA, Apr. 2008. ACM Press.

[10] L. Muchnik, S. Aral, and S. J. Taylor. Social Influence Bias: A Randomized Experiment. *Science*, (6146):647–651, Aug.

[11] M. J. Salganik, P. S. Dodds, and D. J. Watts. Experimental Study of Inequality and Unpredictability in an Artificial Cultural Market. *Science*, 311(5762):854–856, Feb. 2006.

[12] M. J. Salganik and D. J. Watts. Leading the Herd Astray: An Experimental Study of Self-Fulfilling Prophecies in an Artificial Cultural Market. *Social psychology quarterly*, (4):338, Jan.

[13] A. T. Sorensen. Bestseller Lists and Product Variety. *The Journal of Industrial Economics*, (4):715–738.

[14] J. Surowiecki. *The Wisdom of Crowds*. Anchor.

[15] T. van Mierlo. The 1% rule in four digital health social networks: An observational study. *J Med Internet Res*, 16(2):e33, Feb 2014.

[16] T. Weninger, X. A. Zhu, and J. Han. An Exploration of Discussion Threads in Social News Sites: A Case Study of the Reddit Community. In *ASONAM*, Niagra Falls, Canada, 2013.

[17] F. Wu and B. A. Huberman. How Public Opinion Forms. In C. Papadimitriou and S. Zhang, editors, *Internet and Network Economics*, Lecture Notes in Computer Science. Springer Berlin Heidelberg, Berlin, Heidelberg.

Tag Me Maybe:
Perceptions of Public Targeted Sharing on Facebook

Saiph Savage   Andrés Monroy-Hernández   Kasturi Bhattacharjee   Tobias Höllerer
University of California Santa Barbara
Universidad Nacional Autónoma de México
Microsoft Research
{saiph, kbhattacharjee, holl }@cs.ucsb.edu saiph@unam.mx amh@microsoft.com

ABSTRACT

Social network sites allow users to publicly tag people in their posts. These tagged posts allow users to share to both the general public and a targeted audience, dynamically assembled via notifications that alert the people mentioned. We investigate people's perceptions of this mixed sharing mode through a qualitative study with 120 participants. We found that individuals like this sharing modality as they believe it strengthens their relationships. Individuals also report using tags to have more control of Facebook's ranking algorithm, and to expose one another to novel information and people. This work helps us understand people's complex relationships with the algorithms that mediate their interactions with each another. We conclude by discussing the design implications of these findings.

Author Keywords Social media; access controls; social networks; narrowcast; broadcasting; algorithmic filtering

ACM Classification Keywords H.5.3 Group and Organization Interfaces

1. INTRODUCTION

On social networking sites (SNS), people have contacts from different facets of their lives, e.g., college or work. This can lead to unintentionally sharing sensitive content with subsets of friends [7]. People engage in a spectrum of sharing modes to overcome this problem, from targeted sharing, where messages are shared with specific individuals, e.g., in an email [1], to public broadcasts where people share messages that are appropriate for all [7].

There has been growing interest in understanding people's perceptions of these sharing modalities. Bernstein et al. [1] studied targeted sharing in private messages and found that people saw this modality as a way to share personally relevant content. Kairam et al. [10] used Google+ to study selective sharing, i.e., the sharing of content with specific predefined groups such as "family" or "work." Their results indicate that people use selective sharing to evangelize, ask questions, or start conversations. Hogan [7], in studies of public broadcasting in social media, found that in this sharing

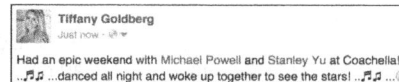

Figure 1: Example of public targeted sharing on Facebook.

mode, people often speak to the "lowest common denominator" to allow everyone to understand the message.

Few studies have fully addressed the public targeted sharing modality of SNS. Figure 1 presents an example of a Facebook post with this sharing mode. Public targeted sharing combines elements of targeted sharing and broadcasting. When a person tags others, the tagged individuals receive a direct notice of the post. However, the post's public nature also reaches a wider audience similar to a broadcast (e.g., the entire social graph of the content producer). This hybrid sharing mode also represents a public display of social connections, as the public posts carry the names of certain friends and links to their personal Facebook profiles [2]. Previous research has studied particular aspects of this interaction, such as the identity concerns it triggers [11] or the types of conversations that such posts elicit [9, 8]. Little is known, however, regarding people's different views and uses of this sharing modality.

The aim of this investigation is to organize and understand the variety of perceptions of this hybrid sharing mode on Facebook. Although Facebook has a particular design for public targeted sharing, the concepts involved are not unique. Sites such as Twitter or Soundcloud also provide hyperlinks to the profiles of the people tagged in content. Google+ links tags to people's profiles and allows people to broadcast to the social circles of those tagged. Gold users of reddit receive notifications when others tag them.

Our interview-based study of 120 individuals discovers that individuals feel public targeted sharing strengthens friendships. They also believe it can be used to overcome the algorithmic filtering powers in play, bringing each other greater exposure to more surprising content and people.

2. METHODS

To examine the perceptions of public targeted sharing, we employ a methodology similar to that used in a study about people's perceptions of Facebook disclosures [11]. Similar to Lampinen et al. [11], instead of pursuing a longitudinal study, our goal is to shed light on the variety of interpretations that individuals have regarding this sharing modality. We conducted interviews to understand the perceptions.

2.1 Data Collection

We recruited participants both offline and online to avoid having only highly active Facebook users. To recruit online, we posted invitations to our study in different Facebook groups and to pages randomly selected from public listings. To recruit offline, we approached people in public spaces such as bus stops and parks and invited them to take part in our study. We labeled participants recruited directly from Facebook as F# and those recruited from public spaces as P#. Our recruitment material avoided the term "tagging" to not exclude people who rarely tag.

Of the 120 individuals participated in our study, 32 were recruited from Facebook, and 88 from public spaces. Participants used Facebook to varying degrees. The individuals recruited from Facebook were 18-52 years old; 44% were female, 56% were male. The participants from public spaces were 18-68 years old; 52% were female, and 48% were male. The interviews had a median duration of 11 minutes, with the longest lasting 40 minutes, and the shortest 8 minutes. The interviews covered participants' interpretations of this sharing modality from the perspectives of the different social roles involved, such as content producers (individuals who tag friends in content they share on Facebook), taggees (individuals tagged in the content), and viewers (individuals who view the tagged content). We counterbalanced the order in which we asked participants about each role. Participants voiced which roles they had taken and only responded for those that they had personally assumed. All participants had been viewers at least once, 87% had been taggees at least once, and 83% had been content producers at least once.

Our study began by asking each participant to write down examples of public targeted sharing. On average, each participant provided two examples (for instance, two Facebook posts where friends were tagged). For each role, we used the examples to start a discussion. For instance, we asked: "What are your thoughts when someone tags you in this type of post?" We encouraged the participants to lead the discussion. Our goal was mainly to get them to elaborate and exemplify. Participants mostly reported on their perceptions of public targeted sharing in posts (Facebook status updates or wall posts). Some also referred to tagging in comments, photos, or videos. However, participants did not highlight any difference among content types. The interviews also covered participants' background in SNS use (sites and devices used, type of content they or their friends share, number of Facebook friends, etc.) We did not witness any difference in interview responses across age groups or SNS usage.

2.2 Categorization Perspectives

We used qualitative coding to analyze interview responses. This allowed us to establish a categorization of perceptions of public targeted sharing. Our overarching goal was to identify patterns in these perceptions. We transcribed all audio recordings and separated each interview into sections based on the social role that the interviewee was reporting on. Two researchers then jointly read each interview transcript for each social role to identify key concepts and ideas. These initial concepts were then discussed with a third researcher. We decided that a category would cover a general type of perception and that, when possible, it would include perspectives specific to each social role. Concepts were then aggregated and similar ones renamed.

We also quantified the number of participants who viewed the tagging of Facebook users in posts as a mechanism that involved two mixed audiences. We considered this would help to further contextualize our results. Two researchers, unfamiliar with the work, read each interview and classified whether the person saw

tagging as involving two audiences. The researchers found that all interviewees referred to tagging as a mixed sharing mode. Additionally, 71% of the interviewees specifically used the term "share" to describe tagging on Facebook.

3. RESULTS

The following five main categories cover participants' perceptions of public targeted sharing. One person can be associated with more than one category, as a person can have more than one perception associated with the sharing modality. We did not identify differences between participants' Facebook usage and their perceptions on sharing.

Stronger Relationships. A majority of our interviewees (79%) perceived public targeted sharing as a way to build stronger relationships. From our interviews, it appears that tagging builds stronger friendships because the targeted audience feels that someone is making time for them:

> "I think the best thing about being tagged is that there is somebody who is considering and thinking about you. I always comment on the things people tag me because they took the time to think about me." 28, male F2.

This result matches theory on disclosure, which states that the more an interaction makes people feel singled out, the more value they attribute to it [2]. Being publicly tagged has become a social signal that helps individuals feel unique and noteworthy. Content producers appear to be aware of this dynamic. Interviewees stated that, via public targeted sharing, they secured higher-quality responses from their network:

> "[Tagging] ensures that you are working with only loyal people that you know will help and promote your cause, not sabotage it." 30, male, F1.

Individuals appear to use targeted sharing to jump start discussions with sympathetic crowds. Interviewees also believed that, via tagging, Facebook's ranking algorithm was more likely to share their content with others. Therefore some people use public targeted sharing to revive relationships:

> "...I basically hope that friends I haven't seen in a while will see this [a tagged post], and they will comment, and we can reconnect [...] Basically I have had other people in mind when I have tagged – sort of thinking about the fact that they are also watching." 21, male, F55.

Surprising Content. Interviewees (61%) perceived this sharing mode as a way to expose audiences to information outside of what they normally viewed on Facebook. Interviewees believe that friends have similar tastes. Facebook's recommendation algorithm thus tends to show more of one type of content to the members of a particular social circle. Tagging broke this by enabling content producers to reach multiple social graphs and share surprising information, outside the social graph's norms:

> "I like to tag people that I know are interested in something and whose audience will also care. But my interest is in creating a crossover. So I involve audiences that follow people in dance, but I share with them something totally different, such as poetry..." 25, female, F10.

This is similar to the finding of Huang et al. [9] of how people tagged on Twitter to direct content to certain social graphs. However, perhaps due to Facebook's recommendation algorithms, we observed here an emphasis on using tagging to diversify a social graph's information.

Participants also had folk theories about how tags influenced Facebook's ranking algorithm:

> "If I tag someone and then he comments, the post becomes "active" and it'll appear at the top of the News Feed. So I'll sometimes tag someone directly in the post, or in the comments. In either case, if it makes him comment, the post will be pushed to the top." 25, female, F10.

Participants also believed that this sharing mode facilitates the introduction of audiences to new and surprising people:

> "Being a group of friends, I want them to meet other people who they might find interesting. The whole idea of social media is that we can share. So they might see a face, but they don't know who they are; with the tag, they can find more information about them" 26, male, P3.

Public Image. Interviewees (60%) believed that public targeted sharing can help refine one's public image:

> "I tag friends to represent something I want to project. So let's say that I want to project that I am a super hipster, well then I will tag friends in support of a cause, I will casually mention that my friends and I are out writing in our Moleskine journals..." 29, female F5.

Interviewees also reported that they tagged to link their content to the reputation or image of their friends and increase the value of the content. Participants cherry-picked who they tagged. They analyzed how influential or relevant the image of a person whom they planned on tagging was in reference to the content they wanted to share. Similarly, participants also believed that Facebook's ranking algorithm would give more visibility to posts linked to high-profile users. Individuals thus tagged users with influential public images in an attempt to garner more visibility for the posts they wanted to broadcast:

> "Facebook will always rank higher content tied to verified, well known accounts. You're losing a lot of visibility if you don't link your content. You have to select well who you tag." 41, male, P83.

In contrast to selective sharing [10], public targeted sharing is also a public display of social connections [2]. This might cause individuals to relate it to public image construction, as everyone (people and algorithms included) can view how one interacts with others.

Participants saw public targeted sharing as an opportunity to tailor not only their own public image but also that of their friends. They tagged as a way to collectively help friends find content that favored them. Interviewees also expressed that, in general, they felt honored to be tagged and be a part of their friends' posts. However, some also voiced identity concerns because others selected the content linked to them and the content might not match what they wanted to portray:

> "[Tagging] is a very public thing. It allows anyone to broadcast something about you, something that might mislead the idea of who you are. Through tags your identity can be created for you. Your identity becomes what other people broadcast about you, their idea of you." 26, male, O3.

Content producers were aware that others are self-conscious about the type of content that is posted about them. We found that most empathized with their friends and usually alerted them offline that they were going to tag them:

> "A lot of people don't want to be tagged at a party. People are self-conscious of what they want or what they don't want about them online. [...] I always ask people if they want to be tagged. I am in the car and I say: Hey guys I am making a Facebook status and I am going to tag all you guys!" 19, male O7.

This echoes the findings of Lampinen et al. [11] regarding people negotiating self-disclosures before conflicts emerge. However, we found that, despite the negotiations taking place, individuals occasionally had to untag themselves. This occurred when individuals were excessively tagged in their friends' content. Individuals wanted to show their involvement in their friends' lives (as it helped strengthen friendships). Yet, showing too much of that involvement, e.g., being tagged in too many posts, obscured who they were:

> "In every wedding photo they posted, they included my name regardless of whether I was in the photo or not [...] Because I don't have any other posts on my profile, that one wedding event began dominating my page and it began characterizing me because it was the only thing that people saw on my profile. When people went into my page, they thought I was really into weddings [...] My identity was made up by someone's wedding. I felt that was too emphasized. I thought about untagging myself from the photos but decided to leave them. I felt it was sad to disassociate myself from my friend's wedding." 29, male, O8.

The nature of this mixed sharing modality generates struggles, as individuals want to show support for friends, while also portraying their desired public image.

Unwanted Content. Interviewees (38%) perceived this sharing modality as annoying, because it brought them undesired data. Individuals thought that the content should have been shared privately with the targeted audience. Some taggees also found this sharing modality annoying because they received excessive Facebook notifications. Some untagged themselves as a result. Taggees and viewers alike felt annoyed with tagged posts generated by companies, especially if they were advertisements. Individuals appeared tolerant of targeted ads created by friends. They considered that at least their friends thought about them to tag them and that the posts were a chance to be updated about their friends' lives:

> "It's usually interesting to see what my friends are selling. One girl was tagging so we could see her ceramics creations [...] it's really interesting to see what they're up to..." 25, female, P52.

Content producers are aware that this sharing modality can be annoying. They are thus careful about how often they publicly target others and in what content they target others. Interestingly, some see this annoyance as a chance to play with friends:

> "One friend of mine was an Obama supporter [...] I was tagging them in some anti-Obama stuff

to mess with them [...] I succeeded in being annoying...hehe..." 24, male, F15.

Despite this, taggees and viewers felt that unwanted content could also bring them serendipitous discoveries, as it could expose them to interesting strangers:

> *"...I have personally met several people through this "spam", like people with whom I've had an interest to collaborate, and people with whom I've shared interests on this and other topics. It isn't common that you get to meet people in spam. They are rare exceptions. Marvelous exceptions that bring you marvelous opportunities." 20, male, F3.*

Recollection. Interviewees (33%) perceived public targeted sharing as a type of virtual diary that helped to document who played a part in their lives. Participants reported that they enjoyed returning later to these posts to reminisce. Interviewees thought it helped them to reminisce not only individually but also collectively. Individuals surfaced posts from the past to encourage their audiences to relive memories:

> *"...For me, they [tagged posts] are more like a path for sharing memories. They are really about making your friends relive these experiences again..." 28, female, P60.*

Content producers also have the perception that by including a person's name in a post, they can implicitly remind the taggees of events that they will conduct together. In this case, content producers admitted to mentioning certain persons so that their posts would be favored by Facebook's ranking algorithm and people would be reminded of their event:

> *"...tagging helps to build the fan base of your event, and people will be constantly reminded of the event. Their friends are also more likely to see it [i.e., the content] if you tag. That's one of the things which Facebook loves and favors: tagging!" 21, male, F202.*

4. DISCUSSION

We used Facebook as a medium to investigate perceptions on an increasingly popular sharing modality: public targeted sharing. In general, individuals feel that this modality helps to reinforce relationships, as content producers publicly show that they are taking the time to consider a particular targeted audience. Tagged posts generated automatically by companies are likely to not be perceived as positively, because individuals do not see any real person making time for them. This is similar to what was observed in the Scratch online community, where people valued credit granted automatically less than credit given by humans [12]. SNS and UI designers could contemplate how to help companies better engage with their online clients, perhaps by encouraging more humanized sharing. This result is important especially given the recent lawsuit over people's name appearing in tagged advertising.

Individuals appeared to use public targeted sharing to build collaborative spaces, such as a space to reminisce collectively about the past, or a type of backstage to collectively help friends craft a desired public image. Individuals seem to have adopted public targeted sharing as a building block to create the flexible online social spaces they desire. We believe that it is important to design digital structures that allow people to collectively experiment with building on the technology. It is not about just user-testing all elements of an interface but, rather, testing whether people can make use of those elements to construct jointly the dynamic spaces they want.

Our study revealed that individuals view public targeted sharing as a way to expose each other to surprising content or to other people beyond those recommended by Facebook's algorithms. Recommendation algorithms in general have sought to filter out opinions, people, and items that are different from us, potentially limiting the diffusion of information. Individuals appear to use this sharing modality as a means to free audiences from these "algorithmic biases" and distribute information that they consider fresh and interesting.

Individuals also perceive public targeted sharing as a way to reach audiences outside their immediate social circles. Facebook does not officially present tagging as a way to reach foreign social graphs but rather as a way simply to let people know when they are involved in the posts that are shared. Our findings thus raise the question of whether social media would benefit from more official digital structures tailored for targeting and assessing novel audiences [13, 4, 3, 14]. Audiences could be bombarded with more unwanted content in this setting, however, it might also enable more serendipitous discoveries. Future work could further explore this trade-off.

Across categories, we uncovered how individuals feel they can use this sharing modality to try to manipulate or "game" Facebook's ranking algorithm and obtain the viewership they want. This result is consistent with the recent work of Gillespie [5], which points out, "Teens have been known to tag their status updates with unrelated brand names, in the hopes that Facebook will privilege those updates in their friends' feeds." Editors were traditionally the gatekeepers of information. Today, it is filtering algorithms that determine what is relevant [15] and even how we interact with content, products and prices [6]. Our results raise the question of what the role of human-centered SNS should be regarding the algorithmic powers in play. Again, there is a trade-off: allowing manipulations could expose audiences to more unwanted content, yet it might also help disseminate more diverse, unpredictable, noteworthy content.

Finally, similar to [11], we call for caution in generalizing our results. Although we took care to recruit a diverse set of participants, the pool of interviewees recruited outdoors belonged to particular cultural settings. We tried to counter this issue by triangulating their responses with those participants recruited online. However, future work could focus on a quantitative analysis with a more varied population.

Acknowledgements Special thanks to all our participants, as well as Leif Singer, Angus Forbes, Airi Lampinen for the immense feedback and iterations on this work. This work was partially supported by the U.S. Army Research Laboratory under Cooperative Agreement No. W911NF-09-2-0053 and by NSF grant IIS-0747520.

5. REFERENCES

[1] Bernstein, M. S., Marcus, A., Karger, D. R., and Miller, R. C. Enhancing directed content sharing on the web. In *Proc. of the SIGCHI Conf. on Human Factors in Computing Systems*, CHI '10, ACM (2010), 971–980.

[2] Donath, J., and Boyd, D. Public displays of connection. *BT Technology Journal 22*, 4 (Oct. 2004), 71–82.

[3] Forbes, A. G., Hollerer, T., and Legrady, G. behaviorism: A framework for dynamic data visualization. *Visualization and Computer Graphics, IEEE Transactions on 16*, 6 (2010), 1164–1171.

[4] Forbes, A. G., Savage, S., and Höllerer, T. Visualizing and verifying directed social queries. In *IEEE Workshop on Interactive Visual Text Analytics. Seattle, WA*, Citeseer (2012).

[5] Gillespie, T. The relevance of algorithms. *Media Technologies* (2013).

[6] Hannak, A., Soeller, G., Lazer, D., Mislove, A., and Wilson, C. Measuring price discrimination and steering on e-commerce web sites. In *Proceedings of the 2014 Conference on Internet Measurement Conference*, ACM (2014), 305–318.

[7] Hogan, B. The presentation of self in the age of social media. *Bulletin of Science, Technology & Society* (2010).

[8] Honeycutt, C., and Herring, S. C. Beyond microblogging: Conversation and collaboration via twitter. *2013 46th Hawaii International Conference on System Sciences 0* (2009), 1–10.

[9] Huang, J., Thornton, K. M., and Efthimiadis, E. N. Conversational tagging in twitter. In *Proceedings of the 21st ACM conference on Hypertext and hypermedia*, ACM (2010), 173–178.

[10] Kairam, S., Brzozowski, M., Huffaker, D., and Chi, E. Talking in circles: selective sharing in google+. In *Proc. of the SIGCHI Conf. on Human Factors in Computing Systems*, CHI '12, ACM (2012), 1065–1074.

[11] Lampinen, A., Lehtinen, V., Lehmuskallio, A., and Tamminen, S. We're in it together: interpersonal management of disclosure in social network services. In *Proceedings of the SIGCHI Conference on Human Factors in Computing Systems*, CHI '11 (2011).

[12] Monroy-Hernández, A., Hill, B. M., Gonzalez-Rivero, J., and boyd, d. Computers can't give credit: How automatic attribution falls short in an online remixing community. In *Proc. of the SIGCHI Conf. on Human Factors in Computing SystemsI* (2011).

[13] Savage, S., Forbes, A., Toxtli, C., McKenzie, G., Desai, S., and Hollerer, T. Visualizing targeted audiences. In *Proceedings of the International Conference on the Design of Cooperative Systems*, COOP'15 (2015).

[14] Singer, L., Filho, F. M. F., Cleary, B., Treude, C., Storey, M.-A. D., and Schneider, K. Mutual assessment in the social programmer ecosystem: an empirical investigation of developer profile aggregators. In *Proc. of the 2013 Conf. on Computer-Supported Cooperative Work* (2013), 103–116.

[15] Tufekci, Z. Algorithms in our midst: Information, power and choice when software is everywhere. In *Proceedings Conference on Computer Supported Cooperative Work & Social Computing*, CSCW '15 (2015).

Hypertext 2015 Doctorial Consortium Chairs' Message

The Hypertext 2015 Doctorial Consortium session is held the first day of the 26th ACM Conference on Hypertext and Social Media. It offers Ph.D. students an opportunity to present their ongoing research towards obtaining a Ph.D. degree in the disciplines related to the conference, mostly in Computer and Information Sciences but not limited to them. The themes of the submissions are strongly connected to the research tracks of this year's conference: Digital Connectivity, Data Connectivity and Digital Humanities. The Digital Connectivity track targets developing insights into the mechanisms of information generation and dissemination, characterization of evolutionary processes on online social networks, and studies of models and systems that support these processes. The second track, Data Connectivity, deals with the methods, techniques and technologies that can be used to make data available on the Web, with a special focus on how heterogeneous data sources can be connected to each other. Finally, the track of Digital Humanities seeks to attract work from an interdisciplinary perspective, on the intersection between computer science on one hand, and the humanities and social sciences on the other.

During the DC session, students receive constructive feedback from their peers and from a panel of mentors to support them in envisioning added-value contributions to the state-of-the-art research in Hypertext and Social Media. The consortium session is open to all doctorial students by application. Each submission was reviewed by three senior researchers in the topics the students made their submissions. The DC session is aimed in particular at students who have defined a dissertation topic but are still more than one year from graduating at the time of application in order to obtain benefits from feedback.

This year, the committee has accepted three contributions to be presented during the Doctorial Consortium session:

- *Automated Methods for Identity Resolution in Heterogeneous Social Platforms* by Paridhi Jahin. In this work, connected to the digital and data connectivity tracks of the conference, the author proposes novel methods to search and link user identities scattered across heterogeneous social networks. The methods consider carefully users' privacy, so they are designed to access only public and historic data. The evaluation is proposed on large datasets over multiple platforms to prove their significance in identity resolution of an online user.

- *Language Innovation and Change in On-line Social Networks* by Daniel Kershaw. As a fundamental aspect for human communication, this research focuses on forecasting online language change through the use of predictive and descriptive methodologies. This work is framed within structuration theory which helps the researcher in structuring the analysis of the dynamics of language (re)production - i.e. by the agent (user), the social structure and their interplay.

- *A Framework to Provide Customized Reuse of Open Corpus Content for Adaptive Systems* by Mostafa Bayomi. This work deals with issues of reusability of contents on adaptive systems. Adaptive systems tailor content specific to user's needs, but they face two big problems: (a) they use a closed corpus content that has been prepared for them a priori, and (b) the content is tightly coupled with other parts of the system, which hinders its reusability. This work presents a proposal that leverages the semantic web by extending an existing content provision system, Slice-pedia.

We acknowledge ACM SIGWEB for providing traveling grants to support students whose work was accepted to be presented in the Hypertext 2015 Doctorial Consortium session.

Denis Parra
Pontificia Univesidad Católica de Chile
Santiago, Chile
dparras@uc.cl

Christoph Trattner
NTNU & Know-Center
Trondheim, Norway & Graz, Austria
ctrattner@know-center.at

Automated Methods for Identity Resolution across Heterogeneous Social Platforms

Paridhi Jain*
Indraprastha Institute of Information Technology (IIIT-D), India
paridhij@iiitd.ac.in

ABSTRACT

Users create identities on multiple social platforms for various purposes but often do not link them. Unlinked identities raise concerns for enterprises and security practitioners. To address the concerns, we propose novel methods to search and link user identities scattered across heterogenous social networks. Our methods are automated and access only public current and historic data of a user. Evaluation on fairly large datasets from multiple platforms prove our methods' efficiency in identity resolution of an online user.

1. INTRODUCTION

Today, Online Social Networks (OSNs) offer innovative services that ease the access to news, campaigns, art, talent, business opportunities and personal connections. For instance, Twitter's retweet feature enables quick access to news, campaigns, and crisis information while pin boards of Pinterest facilitate reach to the work of artists, photographers, and fashion designers. In order to enjoy these services simultaneously, a user innocuously registers herself on multiple OSNs. During registration, she shares personal information, lists her friends and later creates content to share with her friends. The quality, quantity and veracity of the information created and shared by her vary with the OSN, thereby resulting in dissimilar identities of the same user, scattered across Internet, with no explicit links directing to one another. These disparate identities liberate her from any privacy concerns that could emerge if the identities were implicitly collated. However, disparate unlinked identities is a concern for various stakeholders.

Enterprises like multinationals and news companies, non-profit organisations, and political parties spend resources to seek user sentiment towards their organisation, events or products via social media. They create accounts on multiple OSNs and ask users to 'like' or 'follow' their accounts and promote users to share their feedback on these accounts. Often, there is a need to estimate the volume of appreciators i.e. social audience. With multiple accounts attracting users on each OSN, it is difficult to estimate correct size of the audience as a single user can participate in the same activity via her multiple OSN accounts. An arithmetic sum of 'followers' or 'view-

*Research presented here has been jointly done with my Ph.D. Thesis Advisor, Prof. Ponnurangam Kumaraguru.

HT '15, September 1–4, 2015, Guzelyurt, Northern Cyprus.
ⓒ 2015 ACM. ISBN 978-1-4503-3395-5/15/09$15.00
DOI: http://dx.doi.org/10.1145/2700171.2791040.

ers' from each organisation's OSN account can then inflate the real correct audience size [1, 7]. Therefore, it is necessary to deduplicate users by linking their multiple OSN identities. Security practitioners often need to verify individual's credentials for security reasons. Recently, New York Times reports that 'Skout', a mobile social networking app, found that three adults masqueraded as 13 to 17-year olds. They contacted kids and sexually harassed them, according to a police report [2]. In such scenarios, security practitioners as well as platforms need to verify portrayed identity of a user. Within the limits of a social network, the task is non-trivial, which raises concerns in the community. However, attribute verification is plausible with identity resolution. One can draw links between user's multiple identities and aggregate information to effectively highlight attribute value discrepancies, thereby contributing to identity verification.

Formally, an identity of a user on an OSN refers to a collective set of her attributes namely, profile, content and network. Profile attributes describe her persona like username, name, age, location. Content attributes describe the content she creates or is shared with her such as text, time of post. Network attributes refer to the connections of the user like number of friends, number of followers. The task of finding and linking disconnected identities of a user across multiple social platforms is known as *Identity resolution.* Formally, given an identity I_A of user I on social network SN_A, find her correct identity I_B on social network SN_B. Challenges like dissonant social platforms with partially overlapping list of supported attributes, heterogenous attributes holding veracious values and missing attribute information to safeguard one's privacy impede effective identity resolution.

Contribution: In purview of these challenges, we devise novel algorithms that surface current identity of a user on different OSNs with the only use of public attributes of the user. Further, we ideate and evaluate methods that accurately link correct identities of a user based on comparisons between past and current versions of important attributes of respective identities. These methods are given absolute access to *public* data of the user only to avoid any ethical, legal or privacy concerns. Evaluations on large datasets shows effectiveness and efficiency of our algorithms on four popular social networks – Twitter, Facebook, Instagram, Tumblr.

2. MAJOR TASKS AND LITERATURE

Identity resolution on OSNs can be divided into two tasks – *identity search* and *identity linking*. Identity search lists a set of candidate identities on SN_B, which are similar to given identity I_A and possibly belong to user I. Identity linking then calculates the similarity score between I_A and every candidate identity returned by identity search on certain metrics. Candidate identities are then ranked on similarity score; highest ranked candidate identity is returned as I_B. We briefly define and describe each task now:

- **Identity Search**: *For a user I, given her identity I_A on social network SN_A and a search parameter S, find a set of identities I_{Bj} on social network SN_B s.t. $S(I_A) \simeq S(I_{Bj})$.* Identity I_{Bj} is termed as *candidate identity* and the set as *candidate set.* The size of the candidate set is denoted by N. For an identity search algorithm, source can be a given identity I_A and search parameters can be I_A's attributes like profile, content or network.

- **Identity Linking**: *Given an identity I_A of user I on social network SN_A, a set of candidate identities $Q = \{I_{B1}, \ldots, I_{Bj}, \ldots, I_{BN}\}$ on social network SN_B and a match function M, locate an identity pair (I_A, I_{Bj}) s.t. $M(I_A, I_{Bj}) = \max\{M(I_A, I_{B1}), \ldots, M(I_A, I_{BN})\}$. I_{Bj} with highest match score is I_B.* For an identity linking method, match function can compare attributes that are likely to repeat across a user's identities like name and profile image.

To the best of our knowledge, researchers have exploited *only* profile attributes (private and public) to search for candidate identities of a user on social network SN_B, given her identity on social network SN_A [11, 16, 17, 21]. However, search algorithms based on profile attributes have limitations. Firstly, search by profile attributes is restrictive and dependent on the availability of same profile attributes across networks. For example, 'gender' profile attribute is available only on Facebook. Therefore, a search algorithm may have access to limited profile attributes to use as search parameters. Secondly, search by limited profile attributes results in many candidate identities with similar profile attributes e.g. same name, or location; linking large number of candidate identities becomes computationally expensive and time consuming. Thirdly, search by profile attributes may miss identities for users who use different profile attributes across OSNs, either purposely or unintentionally. For such users, candidate set never contains the correct identity of the user. This lowers the accuracy of the identity resolution. Fourthly, URL attribute of a profile has been discussed in literature but has not been exploited in any of the profile based identity search methods. We think that URLs mentioned as a profile attribute on one social network may help in locating a user's identity on other social networks. Therefore, we infer that search by limited profile attributes may not give satisfying results and there is a need to explore other public identity search methods.

Researchers have suggested various identity linking methods – Syntactic linking [10, 11, 17, 19, 22], Semantic linking [6, 8, 20], Crowd-sourced linking [21], Graph linking [5, 18], and behavioural linking [3, 4, 23] to match and rank candidate set and infer the most similar candidate identity as I_B. Image linking algorithms calculate similarity between profile (background) images used by two identities. Graph linking methods calculate the friend network structure similarity of two identities. Crowd-sourced linking methods generate human intelligence tasks to assign a match score to each candidate identity, on the basis of their background knowledge and apprehension. These existing identity linking algorithms access only latest versions of the examined user identities. They assume high similarity among the current values of the attributes for respective users. However, current values may remain dissimilar for a user's accounts for reasons such as attribute evolution over time or a user's choice of dissimilar values to avoid de-anonymization. In both scenarios, current values falsely direct existing identity linking algorithms to infer accounts of a single user as different users. Therefore, there is a need to consider history of values along with current values to examine a potential link between two user identities.

3. IDENTITY SEARCH

The objective here is to search for identities across social networks, termed as candidate identities, that are similar to a given identity on one social network. At this phase, we devise novel identity search algorithms and use state-of-the-art identity linking methods to evaluate effectiveness of search algorithms.

3.1 Methodology

We propose to leverage complete set of public attributes namely, profile, content, network and introduce novel identity search methods as follows:

3.1.1 Profile Search

A user on an OSN list profile attributes that give basic information about her such as username, name, location, description, etc. If the user does not demonstrate any active obfuscation or maintains anonymity on an OSN, it is likely that she re-uses certain profile attributes' value on the social networks she joins. If the user demonstrates such behavior, profile attributes can be used as a search parameter S to find her identity on other social networks. We consider only those profile attributes which are publicly available on atleast one OSN – username, name, profile image and URL. The algorithm searches with the listed profile attributes to retrieve a candidate set of profiles on other OSNs.

3.1.2 Content Search

A user creates content to share her activities, interests and knowledge with others. Owing to the popularity of social aggregation sites and ways to link multiple networks together, a user is facilitated with a choice to push the same content on multiple networks. For example, Twitter provides a functionality to connect Twitter and Facebook identity to post user's tweets on her Facebook timeline. Because of such services, it is likely that a user generates same content on multiple OSNs. Content Search method uses content as a search parameter S. We filter out candidate identities with zero cosine similarity between the post created by them and the queried post of the given user and constitute a non-ranked set of candidates.

3.1.3 Self-mention Search

This method exploits a user's tendency to cross-pollinate information across OSNs [13]. The method explores content attributes of I_A and assumes that if I_A has accounts on two or more networks, she can cross refer to her other account in few of her tweets. For example, I_A can post a tweet with a URL referring to an album on Flickr, indirectly revealing her Flickr identity. We term this behavior of posting URLs indirectly but consciously directing to user's other OSN identity as "*Self-mention*". This method exploits self-mention behavior to search for a user identities across networks.

3.1.4 Network Search

Connections of a user on a social network constitute her network. A user needs other users to define her connection attributes. If any user in the connection network leaks her identity on any other social network, it is likely that identities of users associated with her may also get leaked. Network Search algorithm explores the possibility of a user's identity leak via her network attribute.

Candidate identities of each search method are collated together and ranked using standard approaches for identity linking. We use username syntactic linking and profile image linking for matching. We then rank the candidate set on the basis of the match-score associate with each candidate set. The aim of ranking is to retrieve the correct identity of the queried user within top results. The ranked candidate set is then presented to a human manual verifier to locate the correct identity among the candidate identities. We assume that the human verifier is 100% accurate, in making the inferences. In this work, authors are the human verifiers.

3.2 Evaluation

We evaluate the identity resolution framework build with novel identity search and state-of-the-art identity linking methods on two popular social networks – Twitter and Facebook. We assume access to a Twitter profile, use it as a source identity of the user and look for candidate identity on Facebook, in order to retrieve her correct identity. We borrow the ground truth dataset from [16] collected from Social Graph API. The dataset consists of 543 users who self-identify themselves on both Twitter and Facebook. We query the framework with 543 users, denoted by U_{total}, and record the number of users for whom the framework retrieves correct Facebook identity in the candidate set, denoted by $U_{correct}$. Therefore, *accuracy* of the framework is the ratio of $U_{correct}$ to U_{total}.

Search Algorithm	$U_{correct}$	Accuracy
Profile Search (P)	205	37.7%
Content Search (C)	3	0.5%
Self-mention Search (SM)	31	5.7%
Network Search (N)	1	0.2%
Identity Search (P+C+SM+N)	212	**39.0%**
P (without URL)	149	27.4%
P (with URL) + (C+SM) + N	149+71	27.4% **+11.6%**

Table 1: Listing accuracy of each search algorithm. Note a contribution of 11.6% to the accuracy with proposed identity search methods.

We observe that for 212 Twitter users (39.0%), the system retrieves their correct Facebook identities. Table 1 lists the contributions of each search algorithm. We further compare our identity search with the traditional profile search used in literature, assuming access to only public profile attributes. Traditional profile search method finds candidate identities on the basis of search parameters – username, name and location. To the best of our knowledge, no profile search method exploited an important profile attribute, URL attribute of an identity, to understand if a user herself has directly or indirectly self-identity themselves. We include the URL attribute and improvise profile search method. Table 1 shows a comparison of using traditional profile search methods with improvised and proposed identity search methods, to search for a user's Facebook identity. We observe that an additional 11.6% users are identified by the combination of improvised profile and proposed identity search methods.

4. IDENTITY LINKING

We improvise methods to link two user identities i.e. source and a candidate identity and suggest to incorporate historical values of the respective attributes, along with their current values.

4.1 Methodology

Our assumption is that though users can evolve and change their attributes over time, their choice or preference for attribute creation remain consistent across OSNs. Therefore, if current values of the attributes do not match, it is likely that the histories can. Limiting our focus to only *username* i.e. a publicly available attribute across most OSNs, an investigation of past usernames of user profiles [1] reveal consistent creation and reuse behavior across OSNs, captured via a set of twenty six features (see Figure 1). Features are then evaluated using a cascaded machine learning framework to avoid missing potential links between user profiles owing to dissimilar current values. We briefly describe these patterns as follows:

---
[1] Since we leverage only profile attributes for this work, we interchangeably use profile for identity.

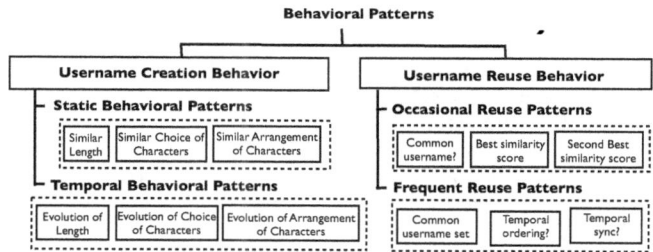

Figure 1: Various username creation and reuse behavioral patterns of users.

4.1.1 Username Creation

On an OSN, users define the following properties of a username – length, characters and arrangement of characters. They often tune these properties to their requirements. For instance, a user can choose short usernames that restrict message length to help her friends post more content when tagging her. Choice of username properties that remain static over time and repeat across OSNs constitute *static behavioral patterns*. However, with time, changing expectations on an OSN can push her to change username properties but reflect the same changes across her other OSN profiles. Similar transitions in username properties constitute *temporal behavioral patterns*. For instance, if user later realizes that short usernames confuse her followers, she can now create long personalized usernames. Such a transition in user behavior if evident across all her OSN profiles results in a temporal behavioral pattern.

4.1.2 Username Reuse

With an increasing number of OSNs and evolving preferences, a user struggles to remember her latest usernames on all OSNs in order to sign in or use the usernames for interactions. However, a naive reuse of a username borrowed from her other OSN profiles can ease her cognitive load [23]. Reused username can either be a latest username or an old username from any of her OSN profiles. Frequent tendency to reuse a username from other profiles results in a set of common usernames appearing in the same order at the same time across user profiles indicating user synchronous behavior across her profiles.

4.2 Evaluation

We evaluate our features for profile linking using a novel cascaded framework. Unlike earlier profile linking frameworks where all features are used together and the classifier's prediction is never revised, either manually or computationally [15], cascaded framework revises classification predictions to avoid missing potential links between examined user profiles.

Framework: Cascaded framework is an ensemble of two classifiers trained on different features to uncover link between two profiles and is extensively used in machine learning domain [9]. **Classifier I** extracts current username features and use an existing method to classify username sets while **Classifier II** extracts proposed username set features and use a supervised classifier to re-classify username sets labelled as negative by **Classifier I** (see Figure 2). We further experiment with two existing profile linking methods as **Classifier I** and different supervised classification techniques as **Classifier II** of the framework. These existing methods – Exact Matching and Substring Matching between usernames, act as baselines and are used to evaluate performance of the suggested features on users who register on four popular social networks – Twitter, Facebook, Instagram and Tumblr. We start with Twitter, choose a random set of users and find their profiles on the other three networks.

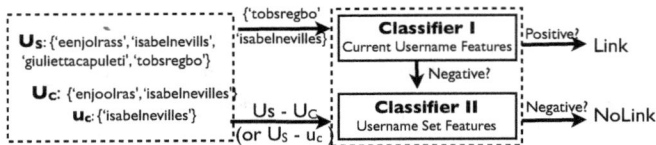

Figure 2: Cascaded framework uses proposed features to re-classify username sets, falsely predicted as 'unlinked' by an earlier classifier on observing dissimilar current usernames.

Ground Truth: We gather positive dataset by exploiting the user tendency to broadcast hyperlinks to their other OSN profiles via URL attribute of their Twitter profiles [12]. Such users *self-identify* themselves on other OSNs. For instance, a user puts her URL as *www.facebook.com/username*, thus informing others about her Facebook profile. Once user profiles are identified across OSNs, we collect past usernames owned by these profiles. We build a tracking system for Twitter to monitor any changes to 8.7 million randomly chosen Twitter profiles as on October 2013. Tracking system repeatedly query Twitter Search API with *user_id* of the user profile after every fortnight and store responses mentioning their username at the time of the query. The system then compare consecutive API-responses to take a note of any changes to usernames. Unique usernames chosen by the queried user profile over the tracking period of two months, constitute past username set on Twitter. To gather past usernames on user's Facebook, Instagram or Tumblr profiles, we record changes to their Twitter profile's URL attribute and time the changes to her username on the other OSN.

Dataset: For experimental purposes, we use Twitter profile as a source profile and the corresponding username set as a source username set U_S. We use other OSN profile (Tumblr, Facebook or Instagram) as a candidate profile and the respective username set as a candidate username set U_C. If candidate usernames set is not accessible, current username of the candidate profile is used as u_c. Post processing, we collect 18,959 $U_S - U_C$ username set pairs and 109,292 $U_S - u_c$ pairs, totalling 128,251 instances whose username sets are known to belong to a single user and hence are positive instances. We create an equal number of negative instances, by randomly pairing username sets of different positive instances, known to belong to different users. We extract features from positive and negative instances and use features in an engineered framework that effectively classifies username sets as same or different users.

Performance of Cascaded Framework: We experiment with two baselines used as **Classifier I** and different supervised learning algorithms as **Classifier II** in the cascaded framework. Classifying $U_S - U_C$ instances with only **b1** results in false negative rate of 89.34% and an accuracy of 55.38%. The high false negative rate alerts that most users have non-matching current usernames across their OSN profiles. **Classifier II** learned using Naive Bayes technique exploits username set features of **b1** negative predictions and reclassifies them. Reclassification reduces false negative rate to 55.27% thereby boosting accuracy to 72.48%. A significant reduction in false negative rate by 34% is due to the comparison of username history. We experiment with other supervised methods to learn the classifier, and achieve best accuracy with SVM (reduction by 44.18%) while maintaining a low FPR. With baseline **b2** as **Classifier I**, the framework achieves best accuracy of 76.84% and reduction in false negative rate by 33.30% with SVM classifier as **Classifier II**. We obtain similar results for $U_S - u_c$ comparisons. Our experiments on fairly large datasets show that comparison of username history reduces false predictions by 44% which are caused by the only comparison of current usernames.

5. FUTURE PLAN

For future, our plan is to experiment with various authorship styles to link user profiles. Authorship analysis is widely used on forensic evidences, such as SMS text messages and tweets to link texts to authors based on the assumption that writing styles of distinct users differ, clearly attributing the questioned text to the right author. We also plan to look for other identifiable attributes such as phone numbers to link user profiles as our earlier work shows that users often post their phone numbers publicly on OSNs [14].

6. ACKNOWLEDGEMENT

Thanks to TCS Research Labs and my friends at CERC@IIIT-D for their continuous feedback and support on the research.

7. REFERENCES

[1] The Five Biggest Mistakes in Measuring Social Media. http://bit.ly/1dbuhXa, 2009.

[2] Cross-media Interactivity Metrics, 2012. http://nyti.ms/1AasvKU.

[3] Fabian Abel, Samur Araújo, Qi Gao, and Geert-Jan Houben. Analyzing cross-system user modeling on the social web. In *Web Engineering*. 2011.

[4] Fabian Abel, Nicola Henze, Eelco Herder, and Daniel Krause. Interweaving public user profiles on the web. In *UMAP*, 2010.

[5] Sergey Bartunov, Anton Korshunov, S Park, Wonho Ryu, and Hyungdong Lee. Joint Link-Attribute User Identity Resolution in Online Social Networks. In *SNAKDD*, 2012.

[6] AnHai Doan and Alon Y. Halevy. Semantic-integration research in the database community. *AI Magazine.*, 2005.

[7] J.G. FitzGerald. Cross-media Interactivity Metrics, 2009.

[8] Jennifer Golbeck and Matthew Rothstein. Linking social networks on the web with FOAF: a semantic web case study. In *AAAI*, 2008.

[9] Geremy Heitz, Stephen Gould, Ashutosh Saxena, and Daphne Koller. Cascaded Classification Models: Combining Models for Holistic Scene Understanding. In *NIPS*, 2009.

[10] Tereza Iofciu, Peter Fankhauser, Fabian Abel, and Kerstin Bischoff. Identifying Users Across Social Tagging Systems. In *ICWSM*, 2011.

[11] Danesh Irani, Steve Webb, Kang Li, and Calton Pu. Large Online Social Footprints–An Emerging Threat. In *CSE*, 2009.

[12] Paridhi Jain, Ponnurangam Kumaraguru, and Anupam Joshi. @ I seek 'fb. me': Identifying Users across Multiple Online Social Networks. In *WWW Companion*, 2013.

[13] Paridhi Jain, Tiago Rodrigues, Gabriel Magno, Ponnurangam Kumaraguru, and Virgílio Almeida. Cross-pollination of information in online social media: A case study on popular social networks. In *SocialCom*, 2011.

[14] Prachi Jain, Paridhi Jain, and Ponnurangam Kumaraguru. Call Me Maybe: Understanding Nature and Risks of Sharing Mobile Numbers on Online Social Networks. In *COSN*, 2013.

[15] Siyuan Liu, Shuhui Wang, Feida Zhu, Jinbo Zhang, and Ramayya Krishnan. HYDRA: Large-scale Social Identity Linkage via Heterogeneous Behavior Modeling. In *SIGMOD*, 2014.

[16] Anshu Malhotra, Luam Totti, Wagner Meira, Ponnurangam Kumaraguru, and Virgilio Almeida. Studying User Footprints in Different Online Social Networks. In *ASONAM*, 2012.

[17] Marti Motoyama and George Varghese. I seek You: Searching and Matching Individuals in Social Networks. In *WIDM*, 2009.

[18] Arvind Narayanan and Vitaly Shmatikov. De-anonymizing Social Networks. In *SP*, 2009.

[19] Daniele Perito, Claude Castelluccia, Mohamed Ali Kâafar, and Pere Manils. How Unique and Traceable Are Usernames? In *PETS*, 2011.

[20] E. Raad, R. Chbeir, and A. Dipanda. User Profile Matching in Social Networks. In *NBiS*, 2010.

[21] Mohamed Shehab, Moo Nam Ko, and Hakim Touati. Social networks Profile Mapping using Games. In *WebApps*, 2012.

[22] Martin Szomszor, Ivan Cantador, Escuela Politecnica Superior, and Harith Alani. Correlating User Profiles from Multiple Folksonomies. In *HT*, 2008.

[23] Reza Zafarani and Huan Liu. Connecting Users across Social Media Sites: A Behavioral-modeling Approach. In *KDD*, 2013.

Language Innovation and Change in On-line Social Networks

Daniel Kershaw
Highwire CDT
Lancaster University
d.kershaw1@lancaster.ac.uk

Matthew Rowe
School of Computing and
Communication
Lancaster University
m.rowe@lancaster.ac.uk

Patrick Stacey
Management Science
Lancaster University
p.stacey@lancaster.ac.uk

ABSTRACT

Language is fundamental to human communication - throughout the course of history language has constantly evolved. This can currently be seen in the changing forms of colloquial language in various on-line social networks (OSN's). These innovations in language are even appearing in every day life with the recent induction of 'lol' and 'rofl' into modern dictionaries. Changes and varying forms of language pose challenges to both academics and people in business when attempting to assess and communicate with different communities.

In this Ph.D, we aim to forecast online language change through the use of predictive and descriptive methodologies. Through using data sets mined from a number of OSNs, we aim to develop generalizable models and theories for assessing and predicting such language changes. We philosophically frame this work by drawing on structuration theory [11] which helps us structure our analysis of the dynamics of language (re)production - i.e. by the agent (user), the social structure and their interplay. We draw on state-of-the-art work and methods, including the development of neural nets to analyse language usage, along with network and community classification too uncover social structures within language. Preliminary results have identified statistically significant innovations usage across communities across a number of OSN's, this was done by operationalizing known linguistic models of innovation acceptance.

Categories and Subject Descriptors

H.3.1 [**Information Storage and Retrieval**]: Content Analysis and Indexing—*Linguistic processing*
; H.3.3 [**Information Storage and Retrieval**]: Information Search and Retrieval—*Clustering, Information filtering*

Keywords

OSN; Language; Evolution; Innovation; Change

1. INTRODUCTION

Language is a faculty of human life that people take for granted; it allows for the communication of ideas, thoughts and emotions from one person to another or a group of people. Language is necessary yet fragile in that it is in constant flux through numerous pressures and constraints in usage [9]. The aim of this Ph.D is to answer the following question 'How can one forecast language change in on-line social media, and if so what are the factors that it depends on'. By using the on-line social networks (OSN's) as the medium allows for an in-depth analysis into the patterns of communication between people.

The study of variation in language has been the endeavor of linguistics; famous studies from Lobov showed variation in pronunciations of English across classes in New York [15]. However these studies were time consuming requiring interviews, transcriptions and hand analysis of data; through the use of computers the cost of performing this work has decreased, though there has been a limited investigation into a continuous time series analysis of language change.

This work ultimately looks into language change/evolution; this is a term that not only draws attention to the difference in the states of a language at two points in time, but also gives an in-depth look at which components within the language have altered and the reasons for these alterations. By separating the language change into structural (e.g. grammar and word formation) and non-structural components (e.g. content that the language is used in, user latent variables) the term allows for the explanation of linguistic variation that cannot be solely explained by the structure of the language itself [4].

The impact of this work though is not limited to the academic fields. Social sensemaking in on-line social media is an ever growing field, though one of the limiting factors is the ever-changing nature of language used by different communities on-line, thus by understanding how and when language changes should allow for a greater success rate within the field. Marketers draw on the understanding of the consumers who they are trying to target; successful campaigns in recent times have lead to brand terms being embedded into every day language; Google, Facebook and iPhone. The importance of understanding OSN's for marketers has been seen in the implementation and development of a large body of work in understanding and predicting influential users within the network that can aid the dissemination of a message during a campaign.

2. PROBLEM

Ultimately this research is aiming to answer one over-arching research question: "How can one forecast language change in on-line social media, and if so what are the factors that it depends on?". To break this work into three core questions we look too Giddens [11]. According to this theory of structuration theory social structure is produced and reproduced through the actions of agents; thus structure and agency are inextricably linked. In terms of language and communications, the actions of the agents can be both verbal and written. The social structures that actions draw on are not physically constrained, but rather exist as memory traces within each agent, thus the structure is self reflexive. As with action per se, language is formed by the individual and the social structure the individual sits within, for this reason the over-arching question can be looked at by analysing three components:

- The agent
- The social structure
- The interplay between social structure and the agent

Question 1 How can we detect language change in on-line social networks? This question can be seen as focusing on agency - it will be used to explore the individual user's language innovations in on-line communication. This work will initially draw upon theoretical frameworks for the forms of language innovations that were developed by [1], as well as more recent work for the computational detection of these innovations [7].

Question 2 How does community influence language change? In contrast to the first question, this focuses on the social structure in the system. However the methods developed for the first question will be equally useful for this question. Initially it will look into the diffusion of language innovation though varying forms of community structure, social ties and reinforcement; pulling on work such as [20, 21].

Question 3 What is the role of social constructs in language innovation and use within on-line social networks? Social structure and the agent are brought together within this final question. It is aiming to model and understand the dynamics of language innovation in the relationship of the individual and social structure, drawing on Gidden's assertion that: "[a]lthough language only exists in those instances where we speak or write it, people react strongly against others who disregard its rules and conventions [12]"

The question will be used to explore issues of power and solidarity within language and language innovation. It will also be used to identify key influencers and users that gain greater power in comparison to others, in much the same way as marketers attempt to identify key users in a network to maximize message diffusion. Ultimately it will look at how people change and adapt their language in situations, and how this can be utilized to detect events within the network.

3. STATE OF THE ART

There has been growing interest in studying language change and evolution through the use of computational means. Computational models have shown that traditional language diffusion models (gravity and wave) can be applied to on-line social media data, identifying new terms diffusing over the geographical landscape of the USA [10]. This work also identifies correlations between demographic data, geography and language styles; though the pre-filtering to identify candidate innovations was performed over the whole data set, thus innovations specialized to smaller communities would have been push out in favour of innovations from the larger community.

Social factors including age and gender have been shown to have a strong influence on communication styles in on-line discourse [19]; a users position within OSNs can be predicted though the use of language models such as variation in topics and emoticon usage. Gender of Twitter users was predicted again though the use of emoticons and variations in punctuation [19]. Though again there was limited acknowledgement of the communities of practice, and generalisation of the population as a whole.

It has been shown that through assessing the morphological characteristics of word blends introduced in OSNs means that the source words of the blends can be determined [7]. However it is also the change of meaning that heavily influence language change, large scale semantic changes have been shown in the Google N-gram corpus and social media data sets [14]. Again both these studies generalized to a whole population, without identifying that the meaning of words is dependent on the community that is using them.

As mentioned it is not only the individual that changes language, but the interactions and roles within a community that influence the change. Social roles of users within OSNs have been studied in earnest (though not looking at language). Through assessing and automatically classifying interaction patterns within Reddit [5], models were able to predict 'answer' roles within Reddit; and showed that the users roles transcended multiple communities within the network, meaning users' maintain the same interaction patterns within different communities and potentially different networks. Though this was limited to highly specialist communities that had highly dynamic interactions on a specific topics. Again through the use of topic specific networks, opinion leaders where identified and assessed for there reach within the network [23] and ignored the dynamics of user roles over time.

As inferred throughout this work language change and evolution is dependent on the dynamics of the social network. The dynamics of social network has been shown [22] to highly influence the diffusion and propagation of news and memes thought on-line and offline social networks, with the rate of diffusion being a factor of; time, network structure, randomness and numerous other factors. Through time series and feature based classification one is able to identify and predict the success or failure of meme diffusion through a social network, this was done by identifying communities, and thus the audience size, network structure, and speed of growth. However this only has the ability to detect static meme diffusion, through the use of NLP systems and fuzzy matching the evolution of news reports and options is able to be seen to propagate through social network, showing that blog propagation of news events peaks 2hrs after that of main stream news [16]. Though this was not on a word level, and needed the whole article to identify similar content.

4. PROPOSED APPROACH

The main focus of this work is to forecast language change in OSNs (Twitter, Reddit); this though brings a number of challenges, this section will address the approach that will be taken in performing this research. Each research question will require different approaches, for this reason we list each question and the approach we propose to take.

Question 1: The initial question will be looking at the agent and their usage of innovations. First innovation will need to be identified; by using the BNC (British National Corpus) as a gold standard of the English Language one can infer that if a word is an innovation if it falls outside of the BNC and is composed of all alphanumeric characters. To classify if an innovation is a morphological change a number of methods are proposed for identifying innovations. Methods can come from text normalization for abbreviation detection [18]. Semantic is more complicated, this will be assessed in a number of ways; with basic semantic changes can be assessed though word correlation and distribution metrics [14].

Question 2: The second question will look at communities' acceptance and rejection of innovations; this will use the latent features mentioned above; patterns of innovations will be inferred through the usage of temporal topic models per community, along with morphological features such as character-grams. Through then modeling survival and diffusion of innovation we aim to show innovations dependency on community and what allows for an innovation to pass though communities.

Question 3: The final question will investigate identifying the dynamics of the agent and the community, this will ultimately aim to predict the diffusion of new innovations though a network by looking at the agents that are using the innovations. This will be investigated though computing a number of features, including; diffusion paths of innovation in conjunction with the identification of influential users, with the aim of predicting the speed and range of the diffusion of an innovation.

Finally the data that is being currently mined is large (400Gb+ currently) and to process the data there is going to be a number of different stages and tools needed. For this reason large data analytics distributed systems are going to be used. Open source code will be developed in scalable manner, utilizing know frameworks such as Hadoop and Spark to name a few. Ultimately this will lead to the development of a scalable framework to aid in future research, including tools for network analysis, time series analysis, and NLP at scale.

5. METHODOLOGY

The following section will discuss the methodology that will be used during the process of research as discussed in this work. The methodology applied is that of deductive mixed methods, yet is epistemologically post-positivist; this will be used to apply theories, build hypothesis, and test the operationalization through the approach mentioned above on the selected data sets.

Within this work the theories of language change and social networks will be drawn upon. These theories will come from the fields of linguistics for the process and pressures of language change and evaluations [8], but also from management science for grounded theory in the formation of social systems though structuation theory [11], and explaining the dynamics of OSNs through the use of social reinforcement [6] and homophiliy [2]. We hypothesise that the grounded theories can be applied to the detection of language innovations in on-line social networks, and the forecast of these innovations. Verification will mainly happen though offline validation, this will be done though applying the same models across social networks and comparing different results. On-line validation could be done on deltas of dictionaries as they are updated, though this could be infrequent and not a reliable method.

6. RESULTS

Results so far attempting to answer questions one and two. By applying two widely cited models of language acceptance (VFRGT [3] and FUDGE [17]) we have made progress in classifying innovations and accepted innovations. By identifying innovations as words not in the BNC, and detecting statistical significant changes in frequency over time (Figure 1) has shown variations in innovation patterns across two social networks (Reddit and Twitter). However when looking at communities within these networks one can see variations in innovation patterns based on different network structure (geographical based and interest based). This variation in language and geography was seen in previous published work [13] which showed variation in language around the consumption of alcohol on Twitter.

7. CONCLUSIONS AND FUTURE WORK

In summary we aim to model and forecast language change and innovations within OSNs. Initial analysis and framing of the problem has been done so in a heavily grounded framework, that frames the problem in such as way that allows for a structured analysis of the three components of social interactions; the agent, the network and the interplay of the two. By critiquing state-of-the-art work in relation to the three components, has allow for this work to be position in a gap that is novel and relevant within the fields of research. The proposed approach identifies the need large scale preprocessing to identify innovations, along with performing time-series based assessments of the dynamics of user and network. A deductive methodology with on-line and off-line validation is also applied, allowing for conformation of results from though the use of a rigorous method of inquiry.

Future work will be focused around modeling the dynamics of OSNs and how the networks themselves affect the probability of acceptance or rejection of the innovations. This will use time series and interaction analysis, identifying which factors of a network that affect the possibility of that community accepting or rejecting the innovation.

8. ACKNOWLEDGEMENTS

This work is funded by the Digital Economy program (RCUK Grant EP/G037582/1), which supports the High-Wire Centre for Doctoral Training (http://highwire.lancaster.ac.uk).

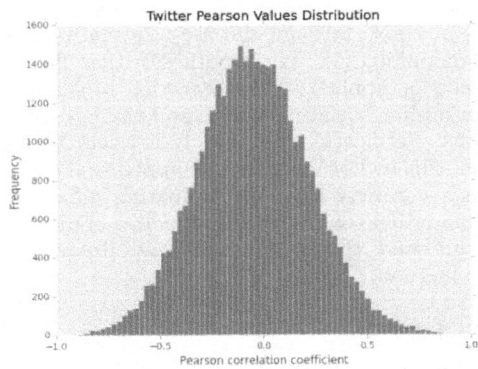

(a) Pearson Value Distribution

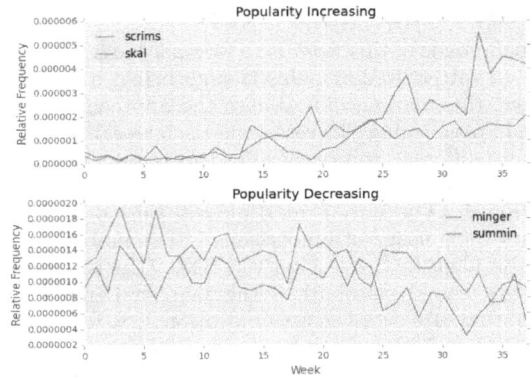

(b) Sample of words from the 95% confidence interval

Figure 1: Distribution of Pearson values for OOV innovations increasing or decreasing in popularity on Twitter

9. REFERENCES

[1] J. Algeo. Where Do All the New Words Come from? 55(4):264–277, Dec. 1980.

[2] J. Alstott, S. Madnick, and C. Velu. Homophily and the Speed of Social Mobilization: The Effect of Acquired and Ascribed Traits. *arXiv.org*, Apr. 2014.

[3] D. K. Barnhart. A Calculus for New Words. 28(1):132–138, 2007.

[4] R. K. Blot. *Language and Social Identity*. Greenwood Publishing Group, Jan. 2003.

[5] C. Buntain and J. Golbeck. Identifying social roles in reddit using network structure. In *WWW Companion '14: Proceedings of the companion publication of the 23rd international conference on World wide web companion*. International World Wide Web Conferences Steering Committee, Apr. 2014.

[6] D. Centola. The Spread of Behavior in an Online Social Network Experiment. 329(5):1194, Sept. 2010.

[7] C. P. Cook. Exploiting Linguistic Knowledge to Infer Properties of Neologisms, 2010.

[8] W. Croft. *Explaining Language Change*. An Evolutionary Approach. Pearson Education, Jan. 2000.

[9] W. Croft. Mixed languages and acts of identity: An evolutionary approach William Croft. *The mixed language debate: Theoretical and empirical . . .* , 2003.

[10] J. Eisenstein, N. A. Smith, and E. P. Xing. Discovering sociolinguistic associations with structured sparsity. In *HLT '11: Proceedings of the 49th Annual Meeting of the Association for Computational Linguistics: Human Language Technologies*. Association for Computational Linguistics, June 2011.

[11] A. Giddens. *The Giddens Reader*. Stanford University Press, Jan. 1993.

[12] A. Giddens and C. Pierson. Conversations with Anthony Giddens: Making sense of modernity, 1998.

[13] D. Kershaw, M. Rowe, and P. Stacey. Towards tracking and analysing regional alcohol consumption patterns in the UK through the use of social media. *WebSci*, pages 220–228, 2014.

[14] V. Kulkarni, R. Al-Rfou, B. Perozzi, and S. Skiena. Statistically Significant Detection of Linguistic Change. *arXiv.org*, page 3315, Nov. 2014.

[15] W. Labov. *The social stratification of English in New York city*. Cambridge University Press, 2006.

[16] J. Leskovec, L. Backstrom, and J. Kleinberg. Meme-tracking and the dynamics of the news cycle. In *KDD '09: Proceedings of the 15th ACM SIGKDD international conference on Knowledge discovery and data mining*, pages 497–506, New York, New York, USA, June 2009. ACM Request Permissions.

[17] A. A. Metcalf. *Predicting New Words*. The Secrets of Their Success. Houghton Mifflin Harcourt, 2004.

[18] D. Pennell and Y. Liu. Toward text message normalization: Modeling abbreviation generation. In *Acoustics, Speech and Signal Processing (ICASSP), 2011 IEEE International Conference on*, pages 5364–5367. IEEE, 2011.

[19] D. Rao, D. Yarowsky, A. Shreevats, and M. Gupta. Classifying latent user attributes in twitter. In *SMUC '10: Proceedings of the 2nd international workshop on Search and mining user-generated contents*. ACM Request Permissions, Oct. 2010.

[20] I. Sahin. Detailed Review of Rogers' Diffusion of Innovations Theory and Educational Technology-Related Studies Based on Rogers' Theory. *Online Submission*, 5(2), Mar. 2006.

[21] H. Tajifel. *Differentiation Between Social Groups*. Academic Press, Inc, Jan. 1979.

[22] L. Weng and Y.-Y. Ahn. Predicting Successful Memes using Network and Community Structure. *arXiv.org*, page 6199, Mar. 2014.

[23] Y. Zhao, G. Wang, P. S. Yu, S. Liu, and S. Zhang. Inferring social roles and statuses in social networks. In *KDD '13: Proceedings of the 19th ACM SIGKDD international conference on Knowledge discovery and data mining*, page 695, New York, New York, USA, Aug. 2013. ACM Request Permissions.

A Framework to Provide Customized Reuse of Open Corpus Content for Adaptive Systems

Mostafa Bayomi
CNGL Centre for Global Intelligent Content, Knowledge and Data Engineering Group
School of Computer Science and Statistics, Trinity College Dublin, Ireland
bayomim@scss.tcd.ie

ABSTRACT

One of the main services that Adaptive Systems offer to their users is the provision of content that is tailored to individual user's needs. Some Adaptive Systems use a closed corpus content that has been prepared for them *a priori*, hence, they accept only a narrow field of content. Furthermore, the content is tightly coupled with other parts of the system, which also hinders its re-usability. To address these limitations, recent systems started to make use of open Web content to provide a wider variety of content. Previous approaches have attempted to harness the information available on the web by providing adaptive systems with customizable information objects. Since adaptive systems are evolving towards the Semantic Web and the use of ontologies, existing systems are limited by their ability to service these documents solely through keyword-based queries. In this research we propose a novel framework that extends existing content provision system, Slicepedia. Our framework uses the conceptual representation of content to segment it in a semantic manner. The framework removes unnecessary content from web pages, such as navigation bars, and then semantically reveals the structural representation of text to build a tree-like hierarchy. This tree can be traversed to obtain different levels of content granularity that facilitate content discoverability and adaptivity.

Categories and Subject Descriptors

H3.3 [**Information Search and Retrieval**]: Information Filtering; Retrieval Models; Selection Process;
H.5.4 [**Hypertext/Hypermedia**]: Architectures; User Issues;

Keywords

Open Corpus Content; Semantic Web; Content Semantic Slicing;

1. INTRODUCTION AND MOTIVATION

The amount of content on the World Wide Web is continuously growing. Several research fields have emerged that particularly focus on the challenges associated with this growing body of global content. These challenges include: how to identify, handle and retrieve content from different sources; how to search for information in multiple languages; and how to deliver this content in a personalized form that is most suitable for the user.

Various systems [6,9,16] have tried to address the challenge of producing adaptive compositions from open information sources in order to deliver content in a form that is most suitable to an individual user. Adaptive systems focus on providing such compositions based on a variety of user dimensions, such as user interests, prior knowledge, preferences or context. At the heart of these systems is the adaptive engine which deals with multiple loosely coupled models that are integrated as desired. Content, however, is still very tightly coupled to these engines and as a result strongly impedes the re-usability of this content.

Consider an E-Learning portal as an adaptive system that provides users with learning materials about specific subject. The portal has a user model that is responsible for personalizing content according to different dimensions, such as the user's interests, prior knowledge, preferences or preferred style of content (concise or detailed content). Since the dimensions are not the same for all users, the portal should: i) have various content resources, ii) be able to provide different levels of content granularity, iii) provide content at low production costs iv) and provide content that is amenable to be reused.

Early proposed adaptive systems have relied on closed document corpus with content specifically authored for their usage [7], hence they accept only a narrow field of content. As a result, Open corpus content is increasingly seen as providing a solution to these issues [3]. However, most systems incorporating open corpus content have mainly focused on linking such content with the internal content as a path for more content exploration [9]. Moreover, adaptive systems must strict to specific content structures to be able to make use of it which limits the amenability of content reuse.

The one-size-fits-all nature of Web content calls for automatic approaches that can tailor the content in a way that facilitates its reuse – whether in part or in full. This tailoring must be performed based upon various aspects, such as: granularity, content format and associated metadata [11]. Various systems have been proposed to address the challenge of producing adaptive content from open corpus content. These systems focused on separating the content from other models in the adaptive systems (such as domain and user models). Slicepedia [11], for example, was introduced as a service to process open corpus resources and extract content for reuse by right-fitting it to specific content requirements of individual adaptive system.

Since adaptive systems are moving towards the Semantic Web and the use of ontologies, Slicepedia and other systems are limited by the ability to service these documents solely through keyword-based queries. This means they only provide limited capabilities to capture the conceptualizations associated with adaptive system needs and content.

HT '15, September 1–4, 2015, Guzelyurt, Northern Cyprus.
© 2015 ACM. ISBN 978-1-4503-3395-5/15/09$15.00
DOI: http://dx.doi.org/10.1145/2700171.2804450

Hence, there is a need for a service that can provide adaptive content based on the conceptual needs of an adaptive system.

The research question of this study is: *To what extent can content be automatically adapted to intelligently meet the requirements of individual applications?*

Section 2 highlights the state of the art approaches and the key challenges. Section 3 presents the research proposal and the research objectives that are derived from the main research question. Section 4 presents the ongoing research work. Finally, section 5 gives the plan ahead of the research.

2. KEY CHALLENGES & RELATED WORK

As the vast quantity and diversity of content on the Web continues to grow, various systems [6,9,16] have tried to address the challenge of producing adaptive compositions from open information sources to deliver information in a form that is most suitable for an individual user. Adaptive systems attempt to perform such compositions using different methods: *manual* [9], *community-based* [2], *automatic linkage* [16] or *IR approaches* [14]. In manual methods, documents are manually incorporated within the adaptive system, however, these methods require a significant amount of time and effort due to the difficulty in identifying adequate content. Automatic linkage approaches attempt to improve this situation by providing guidance with respect to the relevant content that is available. However, these methods only provide an indication of the relative closeness of content and do not provide the details needed to support user guidance. The community-based approaches also tried to overcome the burden proposed by the manual approaches by analyzing the quantity of users stepping between various resources in order to derive this information. IR approaches provide a pluggable search service for the adaptive systems to support open corpus content identification and incorporation. The OCCS system [10] for example, uses focused crawling techniques to harvest large amounts of web resources and identify those most relevant to specific contexts of use, based on arbitrarily pre-selected topic boundaries. Various schemas such as LOM (Learning Object Metadata in e-learning) were developed to provide usage-agnostic solutions, however they require a lot of development effort thus prohibiting scalability [8].

All these approaches are limited in that they use harvested resources in their native form (web pages) as one-size-fits-all documents. As pointed out by Lawless [10], "*there is an inverse relationship between the potential reusability of content and its granularity*", i.e. the more granularity the content is, the more amenable it is to be reused.

As a result, various approaches have been proposed to utilize open corpus content to convert the wealth of information available on the web into customizable information objects. Slicepedia [11], for example, was introduced as a service to process open corpus resources and extract content for reuse by right-fitting it to the specific content requirements of individual adaptive system. Slicepedia converts original resources into information objects called *slices*. The concept of a *slice* is an abstract notion representing a stand-alone piece of information, originally part of an existing document, extracted and segmented to fulfil a specific information request. After slicing content, *slices* are stored in a repository to be provided and right-fitted to specific adaptive system requirements.

As adaptive systems are moving towards the Semantic Web and the use of ontologies [15], Slicepedia and other systems [13] are considered limited in that they are keyword-based content providing services, which means that they provide limited capabilities to capture the conceptualizations associated with adaptive system needs and content.

Hence, there is a need for a service that can provide adaptive content based on the conceptual needs of an adaptive system. By conceptual representation of content we mean the semantic metadata that describes it. Leveraging such semantic metadata is very important, but content published on the Web generally lacks the presence of such information [1].

Recent research looked at leveraging Semantic Web technologies in order to enrich content through annotation [4]. Such approaches use Named Entity Recognition to extract concepts (mostly people, locations and companies) from text. As a result, in our approach, instead of relying on the available semantic metadata for the open corpus content, we semantically annotate content to extract its conceptual structure and segment (slice) it based on the ontological relation between its constituents.

3. RESEARCH PROPOSAL

The research question posed in this study can be broken into three main objectives:

1- To investigate how existing content-provider systems, which are based on traditional keyword approaches, can be enhanced using semantic techniques.

2- To explore the effectiveness of semantic-based approaches in discovering and delivering content that best matches specific application requirements.

3- To explore the impact of the proposed approach in an industry case study, and measure the extent at which cost, time, and effort are saved when producing tailored content.

To achieve these objectives, we propose a service that: i) works as a pluggable content providing service; ii) separates the content model from other adaptive system models (such as domain and user models); iii) slices content based on its semantic (ontological) meaning to suit ontology based adaptive systems; iv) organizes content into tree-like structure. The benefits of the proposed service are a) improving content discoverability, b) facilitating its personalization, and c) maximizing its reusability.

4. Ongoing Work:

In order to investigate how existing systems can be enhanced using semantic techniques (objective 1) and to explore the effectiveness of the semantic approaches in discovering and delivering content (objective 2), we built a service that extends Slicepedia. The service is provided by an intelligent content provider framework which consists of the following modules (see Figure 1):

1) Harvester: Acquires open corpus resources, from the web, in their native form (HTML pages). Standard IR systems or focused crawling techniques [10] are used to gather relevant documents, which are then cached locally for further analysis. We will use the same harvester used by Slicepedia, the 80Legs[1] web crawler.

---

[1] http://www.80legs.com/

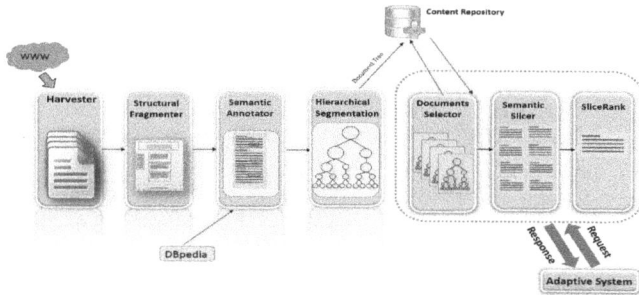

Figure 1. The Framework Structure

2) Structural Fragmenter: Once resources have been identified, the structural fragmenter starts to fragment the content into atomic pieces and the unnecessary fragments are removed. Plain fusion Densitometric Content Fragmentation (DCF) [9] is used by Slicepedia and also is selected as the structural fragmentation approach in our framework. The output of this module is a document that consists of plain text only.

3) Semantic Annotator: After removing the unneeded content from the web page, the remaining content is treated as one text document without barriers. The text is then semantically annotated using a named entity recognition algorithm, and text entities (names, places, organizations, etc.) are extracted. Each entity is then mapped to its class or classes in an ontology. For example, *Barack Obama*, as an entity, is mapped to DBpedia ontology classes: *["Person", "Agent", "Officeholder"]*. The text is then represented as a sentence-based vector-space where each sentence in the text is represented as a vector of entities, and each entity is represented by a set of classes that match the entity from the ontology. This vector space is then used as an input to the following phase. As our framework can work across different content domains, in this research we use *DBpedia*[2] ontology as the underlying knowledge- base as it is considered a cross-domain ontology. *DBpedia Spotlight*[3] is used as the named entity recognition system to extract entities from text.

4) Hierarchical Segmentation: After semantically annotate text and building sentence-based vector-space, text is segmented into hierarchically semantically coherent segments. Unlike traditional text segmentation approaches [5], our approach to text segmentation measures the similarity between text blocks based on the ontological similarity between them. A text block is considered the elementary unit of the segmentation algorithm, which could be one sentence or multiple sentences (paragraphs). To measure the ontological similarity between two text blocks, we measure the similarity between the classes of their entities using the **is-a** relation. In ontology structure, the **is-a** relations group the classes according to how they are conceptually related to each other. After measuring the similarity between text blocks, a Hierarchical Agglomerative Clustering (HAC) algorithm is applied. Conceptually, the process of agglomerating blocks into successively higher levels of clusters creates a cluster hierarchy (or dendrogram) for which the leaf nodes correspond to individual blocks, and the internal nodes correspond to the merged groups of clusters. When two groups are merged, a new node is created in

---

[2] http://dbpedia.org/

[3] https://github.com/dbpedia-spotlight/dbpedia-spotlight/wiki

this tree corresponding to this larger merged group. The output is a tree-like hierarchy of the text. This tree is then stored in a repository with its structure and with the entities that were extracted from the text. Figure 2 depicts a tree representation of a sample text of 10 sentences.

The benefit of this tree is that it represents different levels of granularity of the document, which means that the document can be sliced semantically at different levels of granularity. This is a powerful criterion in the hierarchical representation of text. In contrast to linear representation, in each level of the structure (tree), slicing with different levels of details could be obtained and can be usefully applied to different adaptive systems' needs.

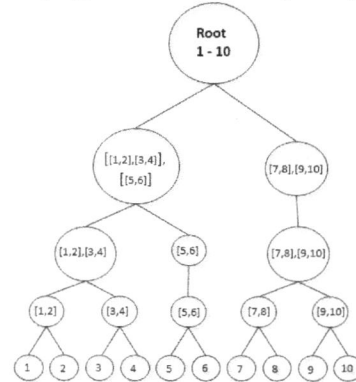

Figure 2. A tree representation for a text from 10 sentences

In the current state of the framework, we have built the text segmentation module that builds a structure of text based on the ontological similarity between text blocks. We conducted several experiments to evaluate this module on a well-known dataset [5] in the text segmentation field. The results show that text segmentation based on the ontological similarity is feasible with a low error rate. Table 1 reports the results of the best run of the experiments.

Table 1. Error rates for different subsets

Range of n	3-11	3-5	6-8	9-11
Error rate	0.15	0.19	0.15	0.11

5) Documents Selector: It is an ontology-based IR system that ontologically matches an adaptive system query with the documents in the repository. As the documents are hierarchically stored (as trees), this structural representation enhances the accuracy of the retrieval process. For example, suppose we have a query with two entities $E1$ and $E2$ and we have two documents $D1$ and $D2$. $E1$ and $E2$ are found in the same branch of $D1$'s tree (i.e. they are near to each other in the hierarchy) while in $D2$'s tree the two entities are in different branches (i.e. they are far from each other in the hierarchy). Intuitively, $D1$ is considered to be more relevant to the query as it contains the two entities in the same region of the document. The output is a set of documents that are ranked based on the relevancy between the entities in the query and the entities existence and location within the document tree structure.

6) Semantic Slicing: After retrieving and ranking the relevant documents based on how they match the request query, the slicing process starts. For each retrieved document, the semantic slicer starts to traverse its tree and based on the request, the slicer starts to slice the tree. For example, if the adaptive system requests a slice of six sentences that contains a specific entity in the request query. In a document tree like the one depicted in figure 2, suppose the entity is found in sentence number 4. In this circumstance, the algorithm needs to select five additional sentences that are related to sentence 4 in order to match the adaptive system request. From the document tree (Figure 2), it is clear that the most related sentences to sentence 4 are sentences from 1 to 6 as they are all clustered in one node based on the ontological relation between each other.

7) SliceRank: Bringing order into slices

The output from the previous step (the semantic slicer) is a set of slices that are extracted from different documents and match with the adaptive system request. At this point a question naturally arises. "Among slides created which one is the most appropriate slice to be retrieved to the adaptive system?" In a similar way in which a ranking mechanism can be used to rank documents, we apply what we call *SliceRank* to rank slices. Ranking slices is different than ranking documents in the sense that documents are ranked based on their relevance to the query, while slices are ranked based on the richness of information contained in them.

SliceRank is an unsupervised graph-based ranking model derived from TextRank [12] for text summarization. *SliceRank* ranks slices according to the ontological relation between their entities. Slices are represented as vertices in a graph; edges are created based on the ontological relation between entities within two slices. Edges are typically undirected and are weighted to reflect a degree of similarity between two slices. The idea behind *SliceRank* is that slices recommend each other based on the ontological similarity between their entities. A slice gets a high rank because it has entities that are ontologically similar to many entities found in the other slices. Which means that this slice has more information more than other slices even if it is extracted from a document that is not highly related with the request query.

In summary, the completed work so far involved identifying conceptually similar content fragments and structuring them into tree-like hierarchy which is the first step towards enhancing content discoverability and re-usability. In this step, the *Semantic annotator* and the *Hierarchical Segmenter* modules have been developed and evaluated. As for the ongoing work, it involves implementing the remaining modules of the framework.

5. Plan for Next Phase

Moving forward, future work will involve exploring the impact of the proposed approaches on industry and measuring the extent at which cost, time and effort are saved when employing our proposed service in producing tailored content (objective 3). The Documents Selector, Semantic Slicer, and SliceRank modules are yet to be evaluated. This will involve user studies and state of the art standard evaluation methodologies to measure the effectiveness of each module independently. Furthermore, a user study will also be carried out to evaluate the overall efficacy of the framework based on user evaluations within the context of adaptive systems and industry use cases.

Acknowledgements. This work is supported by Science Foundation Ireland (Grant 12/CE/I2267) as part of CNGL Centre for Global Intelligent Content (www.cngl.ie) at Trinity College Dublin. Special thanks to Prof. Séamus Lawless, Dr. Killian Levacher, and Dr. M. Rami Ghorab for their guidance, support, and fruitful advice.

6. REFERENCES

[1] Bizer, C., Eckert, K., Meusel, R., Mühleisen, H., Schuhmacher, M., and Völker, J.Deployment of RDFa, Microdata, and Microformats on the Web – A Quantitative Analysis. *The Semantic Web – ISWC, Springer Berlin Heidelberg*, 2013, pp. 17–32.

[2] Brusilovsky, P., Chavan, G., and Farzan, R.Social Adaptive Navigation Support for Open Corpus Electronic Textbooks. *Adaptive Hypermedia and Adaptive Web-Based Systems*, 2004, pp. 24–33.

[3] Brusilovsky, P. and Henze, N.Open Corpus Adaptive Educational Hypermedia. *The Adaptive Web SE - 22*. Springer Berlin Heidelberg, 2007, 671–696.

[4] Butuc, M.-G.Semantically enriching content using opencalais. *EDITIA 9*, 2009, 77–88.

[5] Choi, F.Y.Y.Advances in Domain Independent Linear Text Segmentation. *Proceedings of the 1st North American Chapter of the Association for Computational Linguistics Conference*, (2000), 26–33.

[6] Conlan, O., Staikopoulos, A., Hampson, C., Lawless, S. & O'Keeffe, I. *The Narrative Approach to Personalisation*. New Review of Hypermedia and Multimedia, 2013,132 - 157

[7] Dieberger, A. and Guzdial, M.CoWeb — Experiences with Collaborative Web Spaces. *From Usenet to CoWebs SE - 8*. Springer London, 2003, 155–166.

[8] Farrell, R.G., Liburd, S.D., and Thomas, J.C.Dynamic Assembly of Learning Objects. *Proceedings of the 13th International World Wide Web Conference on Alternate Track Papers &Amp; Posters, ACM* (2004), 162–169.

[9] Henze, N. and Nejdl, W.Adaptation in open corpus hypermedia. *International Journal of Artificial Intelligence in Education* 12, 4 (2001), 325–350.

[10] Lawless, S.Leveraging Content from Open Corpus Sources for Technology Enhanced Learning. *Doctoral Thesis*, 2009.

[11] Levacher, K., Lawless, S., and Wade, V.Slicepedia: Providing Customized Reuse of Open-web Resources for Adaptive Hypermedia. *Proceedings of the 23rd ACM Conference on Hypertext and Social Media, ACM* (2012).

[12] Mihalcea, R. and Tarau, P.TextRank: Bringing Order into Texts. *Proceedings of EMNLP 2004, Association for Computational Linguistics* (2004), 404–411.

[13] Savić, G., Segedinac, M., and Konjović, Z.Automatic generation of E-courses based on explicit representation of instructional design. *Computer Science and Information Systems* 9, 2 (2012), 839–869.

[14] Speretta, M. and Gauch, S.Personalized search based on user search histories. *Web Intelligence* (2005), 622–628.

[15] Sudhana, K.M., Raj, V.C., and Suresh, R.M.An ontology-based framework for context-aware adaptive e-learning system. *Computer Communication and Informatics*, (2013).

[16] Zhou, D., Goulding, J., Truran, M., and Brailsford, T.LLAMA: Automatic Hypertext Generation Utilizing Language Models. *Proceedings of the Eighteenth Conference on Hypertext and Hypermedia, ACM* (2007).

VizTrails: An Information Visualization Tool for Exploring Geographic Movement Trajectories

Martin Becker
University of Würzburg
becker@informatik.uni-wuerzburg.de

Philipp Singer
GESIS - Leibniz Institute for the Social Sciences
Cologne, Germany
philipp.singer@gesis.org

Florian Lemmerich
GESIS - Leibniz Institute for the Social Sciences
Cologne, Germany
florian.lemmerich@gesis.org

Andreas Hotho
University of Würzburg and L3S Research Center
hotho@informatik.uni-wuerzburg.de

Denis Helic
Graz University of Technology
dhelic@tugraz.at

Markus Strohmaier
GESIS - Leibniz Institute for the Social Sciences and University of Koblenz-Landau
markus.strohmaier@gesis.org

ABSTRACT

Understanding the way people move through urban areas represents an important problem that has implications for a range of societal challenges such as city planning, public transportation, or crime analysis. In this paper, we present an interactive visualization tool called VizTrails for exploring and understanding such human movement. It features visualizations that show aggregated statistics of trails for geographic areas that correspond to grid cells on a map, e.g., on the number of users passing through or on cells commonly visited next. Amongst other features, VizTrails allows to overlay the map with the results of SPARQL queries in order to relate the observed trajectory statistics with its geo-spatial context, e.g., considering a city's points of interest. The systems functionality is demonstrated using trajectory examples extracted from the social photo sharing platform Flickr. Overall, VizTrails facilitates deeper insights into geo-spatial trajectory data by enabling interactive exploration of aggregated statistics and providing geo-spatial context.

Categories and Subject Descriptors: H.5.3 **[Information Interfaces and Presentation]**: Group and Organization Interfaces—*Web-based interaction*

Keywords: Human Trails; Flickr; Hypotheses; HypTrails

1. INTRODUCTION

Understanding the way people move through urban areas represents an important problem that has implications for a range of societal challenges such as city planning, public transport or crime. Recent research has studied human movement trajectories in cities through a variety of data sources including mobile phone data, GPS and WiFi tracking, location-based social media platforms, online photo sharing sites, and others (cf. related work section of [1]).

Recently, we have extended this line of research by studying the underlying processes of a set of trails derived from human

HT '15, September 1–4, 2015, Guzelyurt, Northern Cyprus.
ACM 978-1-4503-3395-5/15/09.
http://dx.doi.org/10.1145/2700171.2791021

movement exemplified in urban photo trails [1]. In that direction, the HypTrails approach [2] allows to formulate and compare different hypotheses about the production of these trails. In order to better understand how the original photo trails materialize, and also to gain further insights on how our own hypotheses explain these trails, we have implemented a visualization tool called VizTrails[1]. In this article, we present VizTrails including an overview of its architecture (Section 2) and visualization aspects (Section 3).

VizTrails shows aggregated information for grid cells on a map featuring interactive visualization of statistics, such as the number of users passing through cells, the in- and out-degree from and to other cells or the cells commonly visited next. Amongst other tools, VizTrails enables overlaying the map with content from arbitrary SPARQL queries for relating the observed trajectory statistics with geo-spatial context. VizTrails is designed for minimizing the required pre-processing steps. Overall, VizTrails facilitates deeper insights into geo-spatial trajectory data by enabling interactive exploration of aggregated statistics and providing geo-spatial context.

2. ARCHITECTURE

VizTrails is a web application based visualization system. It consists of two independent layers: the REST-layer for serving data and the UI-layer for visualizing the provided data.

The REST-layer is connected to a database and provides endpoints for accessing data points, user trajectories, grid cells, cell transitions, and more. It is built to be modular, i.e., the underlying database is easily exchangeable. Thus, it can not only serve data from relational databases like MySQL or PostgreSQL, but can also directly access data from distributed NoSQL databases like HBase or Cassandra. This is especially useful when large amounts of trajectory data are processed via parallel computation frameworks like Hadoop or Spark which directly write to such distributed data storage systems.

The UI-layer is browser-based. It pulls the data from the endpoints provided by the REST-layer and visualizes it via HTML, JavaScript and corresponding frameworks like jQuery or OpenLayers. As a primary goal of VizTrails, the UI-layer enables data exploration in real-time. Since the listing of available grids and transitions is directly coupled with the REST-layer, new grid and transition types are immediately available in the user interface. This allows for a smooth workflow from generating and analyzing data towards visualizing it.

---

[1] http://dmir.org/viztrails

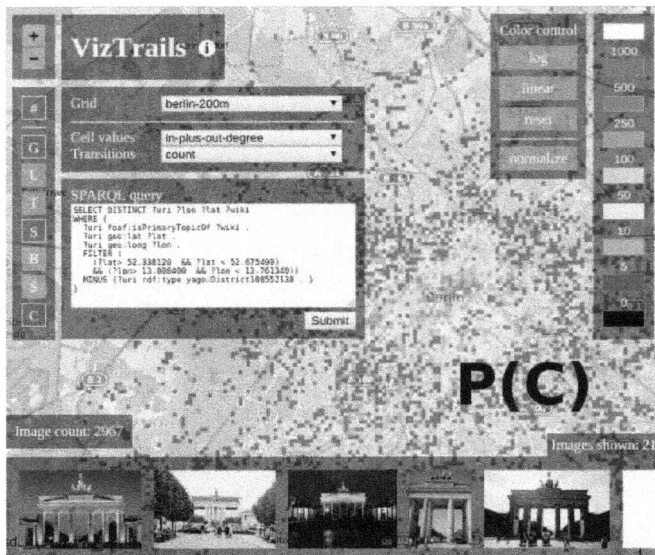

(a) Grid View

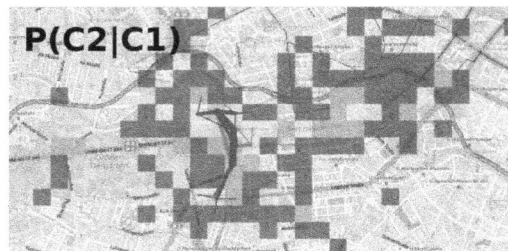

(b) Transitions

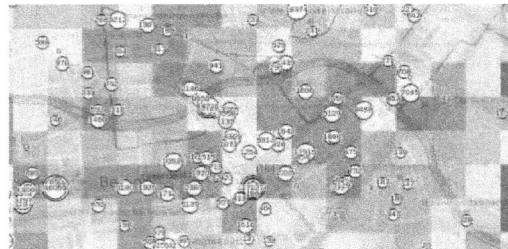

(c) POIs

Figure 1: *Visualization components (map tiles from OpenStreetMap).* In (a) we show the general grid view visualizing different values for individual grid cells providing a general overview of some global statistics. In this case, photo counts (e.g., $P(C)$) in Berlin are depicted. The second subfigure (b) demonstrates how transitions from or to a cell are visualized when clicking on that particular cell (e.g., $P(C2|C1)$). This allows to explore how people move from or to different places. Third, (c) shows how entities from DBPedia and their respective view counts on Wikipedia are visualized providing trajectories with spatio-semantic context. These different visualization modes aid in exploring data about human movement trajectories in an intuitive and explorative way.

3. VISUALIZATIONS

We visualize geo-spatial trajectory data by discretizing an area defined by a bounding box into grid cells as depicted in Figure 1a. Trajectories are then projected onto this grid. This allows us to visualize aggregated statistics on the set of all trails that contain a location within this grid cell. These include single cell statistics, cell transitions, and the respective geo-spatial context. In the following, we describe these visualizations in the same order.

Cell frequencies. For an overview of the general spatial distribution of the recorded datapoints, we color each grid cell according to the number of data points in that cell. The color as well as the value intervals associated with each color can be freely chosen. In addition to the number of data points in each cell, this visualization can be used to visualize any other scalar valued statistics depending on the values the grid provides (in our case we also provide in- and out-degree for each cell). A dialog allows to choose from a number of different grids and associated values and updates as new grids are available in the database. Upon choosing a grid the map automatically pans and zooms to the appropriate extent.

Markov chain transitions. Now, in order to explore trajectories, the UI allows to visualize first-order Markov chain transitions. When clicking on a cell, cell colors change from a coloring based on overall statistics, to colors associated with the count of transitions starting at a point within the clicked cell. We also show lines for the most probable trails from (red) or to (blue) that cell. Thus, for example in the Flickr case, it can easily be judged where people will go from the current cell in order to take their next picture. Figure 1b shows the transitions from the "Brandenburg Gate" in Berlin. Here people mostly move towards three destinations, namely the "Reichstag" building, the "Potsdamer Platz" and the "Museum Island" (marked in orange on the screenshot). Note, that this feature not only allows to visualize actual trajectories, but can also be used to contrast them with hypotheses about transitions as applied in [1, 2].

Spatio-semantic context. In previous work [1], we have found that the processes resulting in human trajectories are strongly connected with geo-spatial features such as points of interest and their corresponding popularity in the social and semantic web. In order to be able to directly correlate trajectories with such features, we provide the possibility to query and visualize geo-spatial entities from DB-Pedia via SPARQL. In addition, these entities can be weighted by the view counts of the respective Wikipedia articles[2] (if available), as shown in the example screenshot show in Figure 1c.

Flickr. Although VizTrails can visualize arbitrary geo-spatial trails, our demonstration example features urban *photo* trails from the Flickr platform. As an additional feature for this dataset, we can also search for particular photo ids or show public photos that have been taken within a bounding box drawn on the map, cf. Figure 1a.

4. CONCLUSION

In this paper, we have introduced an interactive visualization tool called VizTrails that allows exploring human movement and corresponding trails. To this end, we have used a grid-based approach to visualize a number of metrics as well as mutual transitions between cells. VizTrails also allows to set these trails into geo-spatial context using semantic web data via SPARQL queries. Thus, it enables interactive exploration and also facilitates deeper insights into spatial trajectory data.

Acknowledgements. This work was partially funded by the DFG in the research project "PoSTs II".

References

[1] M. Becker, P. Singer, F. Lemmerich, A. Hotho, D. Helic, and M. Strohmaier. Photowalking the city: Comparing hypotheses about urban photo trails on flickr. 2015. under review http://dmir.org/pub/2015/photowalking.pdf.

[2] P. Singer, D. Helic, A. Hotho, and M. Strohmaier. Hyptrails: A bayesian approach for comparing hypotheses about human trails on the web. In *International Conference on World Wide Web*, 2015.

---

[2]extracted from http://dumps.wikimedia.org/other

"I like ISIS, but I want to watch Chris Nolan's new movie": Exploring ISIS Supporters on Twitter

Walid Magdy, Kareem Darwish, and Ingmar Weber
Qatar Computing Research Institute, HBKU, Qatar Foundation
Doha, Qatar
{wmagdy,kdarwish,iweber}@qf.org.qa

ABSTRACT

The recent rise of the "Islamic State of Iraq and Syria" (ISIS) has sparked significant interest in the group. We explore the tweets of a large number of Twitter users who frequently comment on this subject by either showing support or opposition. ISIS supporters dedicate on average 20% of their tweets to ISIS related content, compared to 4.5% for those who oppose ISIS. Thus, the vast majority of tweets for both groups are on general topics, covering many aspects in life, including politics, religion, and even jokes and funny photos. Our demo allows users to search and explore 123 million tweets of 57 thousand Twitter users who have declared explicit positions towards ISIS. Given a query, our system displays a comparative report that shows the difference in views between supporters and opponents of ISIS on the search topic. The report includes a timeline of per day mentions of query terms in the tweets of each group, the top retweeted tweets, images, videos, and tagcloud of top terms in results for each group. Time navigation allows the exploration of content shared by both groups on specific dates, which can go back in time to the period before ISIS appeared.

Categories and Subject Descriptors

J.4 [**Computer Applications**]: Social and Behavioral Sciences

Keywords

ISIS; Twitter data analysis; Violent groups supporters

INTRODUCTION

There is a popular belief that supporters of violent organizations are poor, uneducated, isolated, and/or unstable. Many social psychology studies have shown the exact opposite: Such individuals are typically more educated, financially better off, generally more accomplished than average, more exposed to Western culture, and psychologically more resilient than most people [2, 3, 5]. A recent study on supporters of the "Islamic State in Iraq and Syria" (ISIS) suggests a common theme among supporters, namely support for the Arab spring and opposition to regional regimes, and they moved to supporting ISIS after the missteps of the Arab Spring [4].

HT '15, September 1–4, 2015, Guzelyurt, Northern Cyprus.
ACM 978-1-4503-3395-5/15/09.
DOI: http://dx.doi.org/10.1145/2700171.2794352.

Our demonstration is built over the data collection used for studying the antecedent of ISIS supporters. It includes 123 million tweets from the timelines of 57K Twitter users who showed interest in ISIS group [4]. We have studied the leaning of these users, and automatically classified them into supporters (pro-ISIS) and opposers (anti-ISIS) with 98% accuracy. We noticed that ISIS supporters dedicate on average 20% of their tweets to ISIS and the remaining on different topics. This percentage is only 4.5% for ISIS opponents. We found that the other topics discussed by both groups are not always political and include topics such as jokes, movies, religious content, and nature photos. For example, a tweet by one of the ISIS supporters was: "*I like ISIS, but I want to watch Chris Nolan's new movie*".

In this demonstration, we present a search and analysis system over the tweets collection of pro- and anti-ISIS Twitter users. The collection contains the tweet timelines of 11.3k and 45.6k accounts supporting and opposing ISIS respectively. Once a query is submitted to our system, the top shared content is displayed for each group individually showing the different views of each group on a given topic. Search results could be configured to include text tweets, tweets containing images or videos, or both. The trend of the query terms over time is plotted for both groups, and two tagclouds of popular terms in the search results are presented showing the difference in views between both groups on the search topic. Navigation through search results over time is enabled to allow users to see the top shared content on a given topic on specific dates for each group. Since our collection was collected for users mostly coming from the Arab World, we enable Google translate to allow search and display of results in English for non-Arabic speakers.

DATA COLLECTION

We collected our data through several steps. Initially, we collected Arabic tweets mentioning ISIS by any of its name forms between mid October and end December 2014 using Twitter's streaming API. The name variations were of two types, namely: those who used the full name of the group such as "الدولة الإسلامية" ("Islamic State"), and those who used the abbreviated version of the name such as "داعش" (Arabic acronym similar to ISIS in English). In all, we collected 3.1 million Arabic tweets authored by more than 180k users. For all users, we collected the last 3,200 tweets in their timeline.

To classify users into Pro- or Anti-ISIS, we got a hint from recent reports [6] that state that ISIS supporters usually use the full name of ISIS (or its variants), while the abbreviated form (or its variants) is preferred by those who oppose ISIS. To validate this claim, we manually labeled 1,000 random tweets containing the full name and another 1,000 containing the abbreviated form as either Pro-ISIS, Anti-ISIS, or neutral (news or spam). We found that for tweets that use the full name of group, 93% were pro-ISIS, while only 1.2% were anti-ISIS, and the rest were neutral. On the other hand, for tweets that use the abbreviated name, 77% were anti-ISIS, and 7.5% were pro-ISIS. From the set of 180k collected accounts, we retained those who had at least 10 ISIS-related tweets to ensure that they are engaged with the topic of ISIS. Based on our findings, we labeled users who used the full name of ISIS more than 70% of the time as pro-ISIS, and those who use the abbreviated name more than 70% of the time as anti-ISIS. We picked 70%, because 90% of users use the full or abbreviated name forms in 70% of the their tweets. Automatic labeling of Twitter accounts yielded 11,332 pro-ISIS accounts and 45,628 anti-ISIS, and the remaining accounts were discarded from our collection. A manual validation of 200 sample users showed that the automatic labeling is 98% accurate. Our final collection contained 123 million tweets authored by 56,960 users, who had an explicit leaning towards or against ISIS. More details about the data and its nature with full analysis can be found in [4].

SYSTEM ARCHITECTURE

The collection of tweets was indexed using Solr[1] with all the tweets' metadata. Metadata included: tweet ID, user name, user ID[2], links in tweets, if the tweet has a link to YouTube, if the tweet has an embedded image, and the number of retweets. In addition, we added our user classification indicating for each tweet whether it is authored by a pro- or anti-ISIS user. We also indicate whether the tweet was authored *before* or *after* explicitly declared positions towards ISIS. Since the majority of tweets are in Arabic, we have applied one of the available tools for Arabic social text normalization [1], which performs character normalization, word elongation resolution, and emotion detection. It was reported in [1] that these steps significantly improve retrieval effectiveness when searching Arabic social text.

Once a query is submitted to the system, the following steps are applied:

1. Text normalization of tweets text similar to the indexed text.
2. Top 1,000 resulting tweets of searching the index are retrieved for each user group and displayed in parallel. Results are sorted by the number of retweets.
3. An option is available to display only tweets with text, images, or videos.
4. Timeline plot of query terms popularity for both sides over time is displayed, see Figure 1(b). Specific date could be selected to display results for it only.
5. Tag cloud of top terms in results of each group is presented to summarize the view of each group toward the searched topic.

DEMONSTRATION

Figure 1(a) presents a snapshot of the preliminary design of our search system interface. A search box is provided for users to write their queries. A selection of results type is indicated by the users (tweets with images are selected in the shown example). Results are displayed for users sorted by the number of retweets on a split screen, where the left and right sides of the screen show the top shared content by the pro-ISIS and anti-ISIS users on the search topic, respectively. Google translate is enabled on our website to translate Arabic content into English.

Our demonstration enables users to issue a query about an entity or an event, for example "Free Syrian Army" and "Muslim

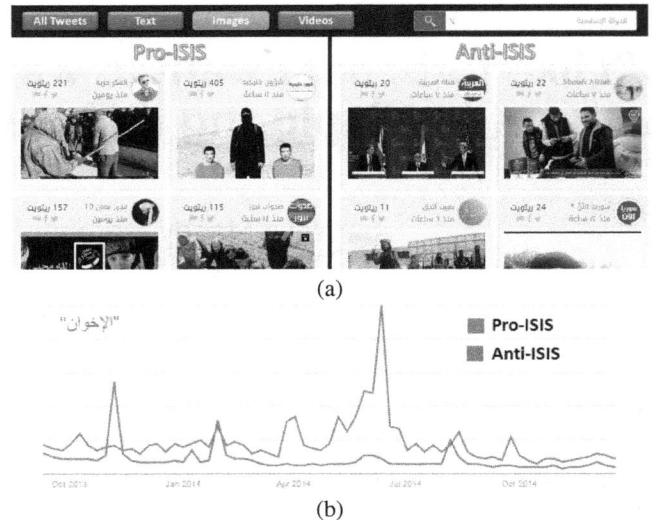

---

[1] http://lucene.apache.org/solr/
[2] In actual demo, we hide users' identifiable information

(a)

(b)

Figure 1: Example of displayed results and plotted timeline for a given search query

Brotherhood". Seeing tweets from both pro- and anti-ISIS camps before and after declarations of explicit stances may serve to shed light on how attitudes of people shift, contingent on their view on ISIS. For example, one user authored the following tweet in March 9, 2013 "*An important message from your brother in Syria #jihad #Alnusra_Front #Free_Syrian_Army (link)*". The same user wrote nearly a year later (on Feb. 19, 2014) the following tweets: "*Islamic State retakes Babila (Syrian town) after #Free_Syrian_Army betrayal*". The tweets signal a shift from supporting the Free Syrian Army to opposing it. The displayed tweet timeline (Figure 1(b)) allows user to see the development of the search topic for both sides over time, and can navigate to see search results on specific dates.

Users are allowed to search the collection for various topics, including immaterial ones such as jokes or pictures of kittens and flowers, which we noticed to exist in the accounts of ISIS supporters as well as opponents. Searching through a collection of 123 million tweets can bring a lot of insight about how ISIS supporters think about different topics, even before the appearance of ISIS itself.

REFERENCES

[1] K. Darwish, W. Magdy, and A. Mourad. Language processing for arabic microblog retrieval. In *CIKM*, 2012.

[2] J. Horgan. The search for the terrorist. *Terrorists, victims and society: Psychological perspectives on terrorism and its consequences*, 2003.

[3] W. Louis. If they're not crazy, then what? the implications of social psychological approaches to terrorism for conflict management. In *Terrorism and Torture: An Interdisciplinary Perspective*. Cambridge University Press.

[4] W. Magdy, K. Darwish, and I. Weber. #failedrevolutions: Using twitter to study the antecedents of isis support. *arXiv preprint arXiv:1503.02401*, 2015.

[5] L. Miller. The terrorist mind i. a psychological and political analysis. *International journal of offender therapy and comparative criminology*, 50(2), 2006.

[6] P. Ross. Isil, isis, islamic state, daesh: What's the difference?, Sept. 2014.

Sentiment Analysis with Incremental Human-in-the-Loop Learning and Lexical Resource Customization

Shubhanshu Mishra
The iSchool/ GSLIS
University of Illinois at
Urbana Champaign
Champaign, IL - 61820
(217) 721-8520
smishra8@illinois.edu

Jana Diesner
The iSchool/ GSLIS
University of Illinois at
Urbana Champaign
Champaign, IL - 61820
(217) 721-8520
jdiesner@illinois.edu

Jason Byrne
Anheuser Busch InBev
St. Louis, MO - 63118
(314) 765-4483
jason.byrne@anheuser-busch.com

Elizabeth Surbeck
Anheuser Busch InBev
St. Louis, MO - 63118
(314) 765-4991
elizabeth.surbeck@anheuser-busch.com

ABSTRACT

The adjustment of probabilistic models for sentiment analysis to changes in language use and the perception of products can be realized via incremental learning techniques. We provide a free, open and GUI-based sentiment analysis tool that allows for a) relabeling predictions and/or adding labeled instances to retrain the weights of a given model, and b) customizing lexical resources to account for false positives and false negatives in sentiment lexicons. Our results show that incrementally updating a model with information from new and labeled instances can substantially increase accuracy. The provided solution can be particularly helpful for gradually refining or enhancing models in an easily accessible fashion while avoiding a) the costs for training a new model from scratch and b) the deterioration of prediction accuracy over time.

Categories and Subject Descriptors

I.2.7 [Natural Language Processing]: Text analysis

General Terms

Algorithms, Design, Experimentation, Human Factors

Keywords

Sentiment Analysis; Incremental Learning; Lexical Resource Customization

1. INTRODUCTION

Sentiment Analysis aims to assign a single best fitting valence category to (terms or short phrases in) text data documents [17]. The commonly considered valence categories are "positive", "negative" and "neutral" [1; 16]. While other categories have been proposed, tested and implemented [20], these labels are particularly useful for assessing reviews of consumer products [15], and are therefore widely used for commercial applications.

Many sentiment analysis tools apply previously trained models with fixed features and weights to new and unseen data; hoping to obtain accuracy rates similar to those obtained when evaluating the models via k-fold cross-validation. However, trained models can be skewed towards the genre and domain of the training data.

Moreover, as language use and the perception of products might change over time, such static models might need to be updated by a) relabeling some prediction results and/or b) adding new labeled instances for learning, and considering either one modification for model updating. This step can be realized via incremental learning, which keeps computational costs low as it updates a model based on changed labels or added instances [2; 3].

Another issue with sentiment analysis is that several solutions rely on predefined lexicons for mapping tokens from the text data to sentiment categories, or as an additional feature for learning (some cutting edge solutions use bag-of-word approaches that consider more context [7; 11], or word vector-based deep learning [6; 10; 18] instead). Due to their intended general applicability, existing resources – though convenient to use – can lead to errors when general terms have different connotations in specific domains. Prior research has shown that sentiment prediction accuracy can be improved by adjusting these lexical resources to a new dataset and domain [5; 8]. This adjustment entails removing false positives from lexicons and adding in false negatives.

We have been addressing both of these issues by building a free and open tool (Sentiment Analysis and Incremental Learning, short SAIL, https://github.com/uiuc-ischool-scanr/SAIL) that allows for a) incremental learning and b) adjusting lexical resources (positive and negative filters) (overview shown in Figure 1). SAIL's baseline model is trained on SemEval data [12]. Users can also train a model from scratch using their own annotated data and even their own categories.

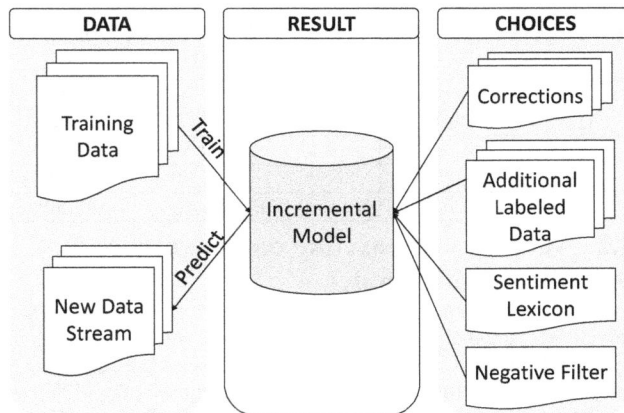

Figure 1. SAIL overview: Incremental learning and prediction with adjustable lexical resources and additional labeled data.

2. DATA

We provide illustrative results for a case study where a model was trained on public Twitter data that were hand-coded for sentiment (data collection and labeling done by Anheuser-Busch InBev, in the following AB). The annotation for the neutral class was ambiguous and hence the class was not considered for learning. After disambiguating and balancing the data, 14,298 instances of the positive and the negative class were used for training.

3. METHOD

3.1 Preprocessing and feature extraction

For each tweet, the content of hashtags, URLs, mentions, emoticons and double quotes was converted into binary mentions (_HASH, _URL, _MENTION, _EMO, _DQ). Each tweet was converted into a vector with the following features: a) **Meta:** Count of hashtags, emoticons, URLs, mentions, double quotes; b) **POS:** Count of parts of speech using the ark-tweet-nlp tool [13; 14]; c) **Word:** Presence of the top 10,000 unigram and bigram with at least three occurrences; d) **Sentiment lexicon:** Count of positive and negative words matching a widely used sentiment lexicon [19], which the user can edit; e) **Negative filter:** A user generated list of words, hashtags and usernames that may represent false positives with respect to the sentiment lexicon, and hence are omitted from consideration for feature d).

3.2 Incremental human-in-the-loop learning

Incremental learning leverages instance based learning techniques to minimize the loss for a given instance or batch of instances based on a prior model. A model was trained using stochastic gradient decent (SGD) [2] as implemented in Weka; using the log-loss function and epoch of 500. SGD has shown to be highly effective for online learning [3]. With appropriate usage of parameters and loss-functions, SGD has been found to perform on par or even better than static models (e.g. batch gradient descent or SVM). It has been argued that SGD can help alleviate key issues with large scale learning, e.g. faster convergence, convergence to global minima for convex functions, incremental learning, and lower computational costs for model retraining [4].

4. RESULTS

4.1 Static versus adjustable baseline model

The comparison shows that SVM (as implemented in Weka [9]) is only outperformed by SGD (by about 0.9%) when using a large amount of tokens for the word feature (Table 1).

Table 1 Prediction accuracy depending on training algorithm and feature sets

Features considered			Accuracy (F1)	
Meta	POS	Word	SVM	SGD
X	X		70.50%	70.40%
X	X	X (N=2K)	85.70%	85.60%
X	X	X (N=20K)	**86.60%**	**87.50%**

4.2 Accuracy of baseline model versus domain-specific model

Two individuals having no affiliation with AB hand-tagged two sets of new, unlabeled tweets from the same content domain as the first set (N=1,000 (dataset 1) and N=470 (dataset 2)); achieving an inter-coder reliability of ~78%. Next, the accuracy of applying the SGD-based model (from the same domain as the new, i.e. focused on selected consumer products) versus SAIL's baseline model was identified for these new data. SAIL's baseline model was trained on SemEval (2013, Task 2) data, which has ~5K tweets

labeled as positive or negative; achieving an accuracy rate of ~80%. On dataset 1+2, using the baseline model, the accuracy is ~50%, versus ~75% when using the domain-aligned model.

4.3 Human-in-the-loop incremental learning

We simulated the situation of considering additional labeled tweets for model adjustment. For both new datasets, prior models (starting from the SGD model) were retrained incrementally by adding 10% of each batch with every step (10 steps total). Our results show that using the prior model as is on datasets 1, 2 and 1 after 2 results in accuracy rates (F1) of 77.4%, 70.1% and 79.1%; while incremental learning increases these values to 78.5%, 73.4% and 82.7%, respectively, after ten steps (Figure 2).

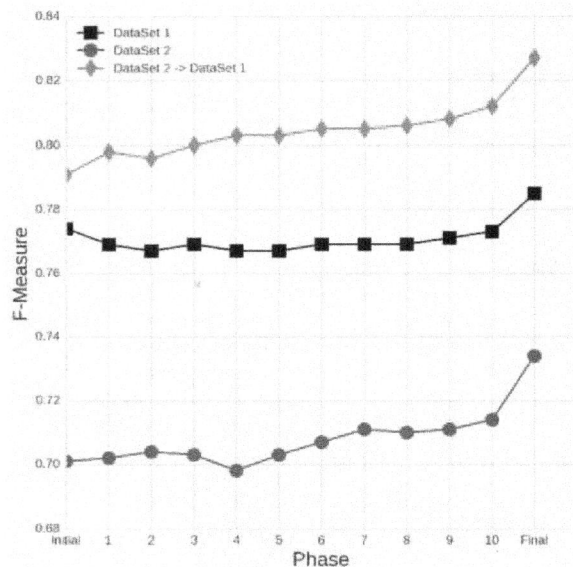

Figure 2. Accuracy gain from incremental learning with additional labeled data.

5. CONCLUSIONS

We provide a GUI-based technology that supports the prediction of standard sentiment classes and allows for a) relabeling predictions or adding labeled instances to retrain the weights of a given model, and b) customizing lexical resource to account for false positives and false negatives. The tool supports interactive result exploration and model adjustment. This might be particularly helpful for users from the computational social sciences and humanities, where distant reading techniques, e.g. sentiment analysis, are often combined with close reading techniques, i.e. zooming into selected relevant data points.

Our results show that updating given models with information from new, labeled instances increases accuracy. This approach allows users to account for changes in natural language use, such as the emergence of new terms and concepts, subtle changes in norms and vernacular, and cultural shifts; thereby reducing the risk of model accuracy deterioration over time.

6. ACKNOWLEDGEMENTS

This work is supported by Anheuser-Busch InBev. Marie Arends from AB InBev provided invaluable advice on this work. We thank the following people from UIUC: Liang Tao and Chieh-Li Chin for their help with technology development, and Jingxian Zhang and Aditi Khullar for their contributions to the technology.

7. REFERENCES

[1] Baccianella, S., Esuli, A., and Sebastiani, F., 2010. SentiWordNet 3.0: An Enhanced Lexical Resource for Sentiment Analysis and Opinion Mining. In *Proceedings of the Seventh International Conference on Language Resources and Evaluation (LREC)*, 2200-2204.

[2] Bottou, L., 1991. Stochastic gradient learning in neural networks. *Proceedings of Neuro-Nîmes*.

[3] Bottou, L., 1998. Online learning and stochastic approximations. *On-line learning in neural networks*, 1-34.

[4] Bottou, L., 2010. Large-Scale Machine Learning with Stochastic Gradient Descent. In *Proceedings of International Conference on Computational Statistics (COMPSTAT)*, Paris, France, 177-186.

[5] Diesner, J. and Evans, C., 2015. Little Bad Concerns: Using Sentiment Analysis to Assess Structural Balance in Communication Networks. In *Proceedings of the IEEE/ACM International Conference on Advances in Social Networks Analysis and Mining (ASONAM), Short paper* (Paris, France2015).

[6] Glorot, X., Bordes, A., and Bengio, Y., 2011. Domain Adaptation for Large-Scale Sentiment Classification: A Deep Learning Approach. *Proceedings of the 28th International Conference on Machine Learning*, 513-520.

[7] Go, A., Bhayani, R., and Huang, L., 2009. Twitter sentiment classification using distant supervision. *CS224N Project Report, Stanford*.

[8] Grimmer, J. and Stewart, B.M., 2013. Text as Data: The Promise and Pitfalls of Automatic Content Analysis Methods for Political Texts. *Political Analysis 21*, 3, 267-297.

[9] Hall, M., Frank, E., Holmes, G., Pfahringer, B., Reutemann, P., and Witten, I.H., 2009. The WEKA data mining software: an update. *ACM SIGKDD Explorations Newsletter 11*, 1, 10-18. DOI= http://dx.doi.org/10.1145/1656274.1656278.

[10] Maas, A.L., Daly, R.E., Pham, P.T., Huang, D., Ng, A.Y., and Potts, C., 2011. Learning word vectors for sentiment analysis. In *Proceedings of the 49th Annual Meeting of the Association for Computational Linguistics: Human Language Technologies (HTL)*, 142-150.

[11] Mohammad, S.M., Kiritchenko, S., and Zhu, X., 2013. NRC-Canada: Building the State-of-the-Art in Sentiment Analysis of Tweets. In *Proceedings of the seventh international workshop on Semantic Evaluation Exercises (SemEval-2013)* Association for Computational Linguistics, 321-327.

[12] Nakov, P., Rosenthal, S., Kozareva, Z., Stoyanov, V., Ritter, A., and Wilson, T., 2013. SemEval-2013 Task 2: Sentiment Analysis in Twitter. In *Proceedings of the 7th International Workshop on Semantic Evaluation* Association for Computational Linguistics, 312-320.

[13] Owoputi, O., O'Connor, B., Dyer, C., and Gimpel, K., 2013. Improved Part-of-Speech Tagging for Online Conversational Text with Word Clusters. In *Human Language Technologies: Conference of the North American Chapter of the Association of Computational Linguistics (HLT-NAACL)*, Atlanta, Georgia, USA, 380-390.

[14] Owoputi, O., O'Connor, B., Dyer, C., Gimpel, K., and Schneider, N., 2012. Part-of-Speech Tagging for Twitter: Word Clusters and Other Advances. *Cmu-Ml-12-107*.

[15] Pang, B. and Lee, L., 2008. *Opinion Mining and Sentiment Analysis*. Now Publishers Inc.

[16] Pang, B., Lee, L., and Vaithyanathan, S., 2002. Thumbs up? In *ACL Conference on Empirical Methods in Natural Language Processing (EMNLP)* Association for Computational Linguistics, Morristown, NJ, USA, 79-86. DOI= http://dx.doi.org/10.3115/1118693.1118704.

[17] Shanahan, J.G., Qu, Y., and Wiebe, J.M., 2006. *Computing attitude and affect in text: theory and applications*. Springer.

[18] Socher, R., Perelygin, A., and Wu, J., 2013. Recursive deep models for semantic compositionality over a sentiment treebank. In *Proceedings of the Conference on Empirical Methods in Natural Language Processing (EMNLP)*, 1631-1642.

[19] Wilson, T., Wiebe, J., and Hoffmann, P., 2005. Recognizing contextual polarity in phrase-level sentiment analysis. In *Proceedings of the Conference on Human Language Technology and Empirical Methods in Natural Language Processing (HLT)* Association for Computational Linguistics, 347-354.

[20] Zhao, J., Dong, L., Wu, J., and Xu, K., 2012. MoodLens: an emoticon-based sentiment analysis system for chinese tweets. In *Proceedings of the 18th ACM SIGKDD International Conference on Knowledge Discovery and Data Mining (KDD)*, New York, New York, USA, 2-5.

Everything is Filed under 'File' –
Conceptual Challenges in Applying Semantic Search to Network Shares for Collaborative Work

Dirk Ahlers   Mahsa Mehrpoor

NTNU – Norwegian University of Science and Technology
Trondheim, Norway
dirk.ahlers@idi.ntnu.no, mahsa.mehrpoor@ntnu.no

ABSTRACT

Lots of professional collaborative work relies on shared networked file systems for easy collaboration, documentation, and as a joint workspace. We have found that in an engineering setting with tens of thousands of files, usual desktop search does not work as well, especially if the project space is huge, contains a large number of non-textual files that are difficult to search for, and is partially unknown by the users due to information needs reaching into previous years or projects. We therefore propose an approach that joins content and metadata analysis, link derivation, grouping, and other measures to arrive at high-level features suitable for semantic similarity and retrieval to improve information access for this case of professional search.

Categories and Subject Descriptors

H.3.3 [**Information Systems**]: Information Storage and Retrieval—*Information Search and Retrieval*

General Terms

Design, Documentation

Keywords

Collaboration, File System, Network Shares

1. INTRODUCTION

The most common content management system or digital library is arguably a shared file system on a network share that is used as a collaborative workspace. It does not provide actual management functions, but is often the easiest way for users to collaborate on large amounts of files. The challenge is that it is not always a very well structured library. We find no content-focused metadata and apart from textual documents, there is a huge number of varied, non-textual, partly proprietary file types that are hard to index and that

HT '15, September 1–4, 2015, Guzelyurt, Northern Cyprus.
ACM 978-1-4503-3395-5/15/09
DOI: http://dx.doi.org/10.1145/2700171.2791046.

have no explicit relations between them. This is not new, but we want to explore what this means in a professional environment where access to information is vital, yet not always properly supported. We share thoughts on solutions to these issues informed by an ongoing project that aims to provide improved information access by deploying semantic recommendation and search solutions.

Our scenario is shared folders or network shares that are used as shared file systems by a group of engineers in a collaborative professional environment [1, 5]. The engineers form a multidisciplinary group with many different domains of expertise with respective documentation as well as specific file types. However, these issues are more general and may also occur in other types of storage systems, such as intranets, digital libraries, or online collaboration tools, as well as in other collaborative settings. Apart from retrieving known files within the shared project workspace, an issue is retrieving files from previous projects that might have solved similar problems, but have almost no personnel overlap with the current project team. This makes knowledge transfer much more difficult as finding files or even getting a good overview is time-consuming. This is different from the local desktop search scenario, which often deals with re-finding of information. In the professional search scenario, on the other hand, routine operations are getting an overview or finding something in a non-personal unfamiliar storage.

We aim to solve this with a solution that supports exploration, search, and recommendation tasks on the corpus. In the following, we discuss the background of the scenario, highlight interesting issues and discuss potential approaches to develop semantic search to collaborative file system workspaces.

2. SCENARIO

The approach includes common document indexing, inferring links and grouping from both textual and non-textual documents, similarity measure, and using recommendation approaches to generate item or workflow-based recommendations, supporting individual views of relevance within the file system.

Contrary to content management systems (CMS) or digital libraries, there is no or very limited user-provided metadata annotated to files. Directly available metadata is mostly related to the file system storage, not to the content, so there is no deeper semantics directly available. More specific, we have two types of sources available, similar to desktop search. First, on the filesystem-level, there are file and directory names as well as filesystem metadata, such as creation or modification date, size, owner etc. Second, there is the application-level that depends on the support of the file types and can include metadata as well as file content. For simple file types such as text, no metadata is available, the file is pure textual content. For application-specific formats, specific metadata can be available. Some is mandatory, such as the length of a video, other is optional, such as the title of a presentation. This depends on the support for the file format inside the operating system and the indexer of the search engine. Without application-specific adapters, the content can be undecipherable binary data. We will therefore extend available search tools.

In the engineering case we are looking at, we have additional issues that a lot of the 3D files are binary, but even if we have a parser, there is little textual information inside them that's available and useful for search. A simple keyword search is insufficient in easily bringing up relevant files in this scenario; therefore we aim to use a recommender systems approach. We aim to automatically build an index that contains additional derived metadata, grouping, links, and similarity information.

3. STRATEGIES/METHODOLOGY

There are several disadvantages of a file system compared to the Web, but also some unique features that can be used. In a way, it is similar to single domain site search. However, there are no links between documents, there is a different structure and organization than theInformation Architecture of a Web site and there is a huge amount of relevant yet non-textual files. Also, there is much less frequent interaction between users and documents that in a normal recommender system setting. For example, collaborative filtering could be less useful due to few users, with highly different requirements and roles and the added cold-start problem.

We propose to complement the usual full-text indexing and similarity with additional metadata and annotations, especially for non-textual or no-textual-content files, with features that can be derived from the organization of the file system and its use. A related approach aims to replace directory location with semantic tags [3] and others, such as the Nepomuk project aim for semantic desktops [4]. Another option is to infer a graph structure of semantic links in a file system. It was shown that simple features such as content overlap, file name overlap, and name reference (a filename mentioned in another file) can be used for ranking [2]. The file system can be thought of as providing important context for the files [6], an approach we want to follow up on. The general approach is to automatically generate high-level annotations from low-level features. Annotations and classifications can partially be derived automatically from content, metadata, and file and path names.

Files could be conceptually grouped (i.e. Excel calculation, Word documentation, CAD 3D model) without there being a direct content similarity. Yet, there exists the possibility to group by some other measure of similarity. Examples are the location in the file system, shared paths, similar file names, being in the same folder as other relevant documents, access by same user or group, or, if content is available, mention of entity/product/part names, or general content similarity. This measure can be weighted by the number and type of other files in that directory. For example, a folder that is deep in the hierarchy and has a rather specific name and contains only 3 files, we can assume that they all belong to the same concept. We may find additional features such as similar names, matching parts of names (example, drawing, sketch, 3d). Yet, in a folder filled with hundreds of pdfs, we cannot assume a relation of all of them to each other and need to weight name and content similarity higher. Additional contextual similarity can be based on derivations, such as backup files derived from a file or standard groupings from programming languages or compiler runs that produce a predictable set of files. Some files are only important in conjunction with others, or are superseded by others. In other cases, related documents are distributed over different places in the hierarchy, for example one general design document, a detailed file about the actual model, a separate folder for programming of electronic components, purchases in the finance folder, and related documents from the previous project that has a similar part. Initial work on these features looks promising.

From previous interviews with about ten stakeholders we understand that people mostly work in their individual domains. General documents that are used by more team members are often easier to find and it is clearer where they are. Thus, this will help to search the long tail of project and workspace files.

4. CONCLUSION

Shared file systems are easily mounted in a local system and are easy to use with all available tools and programs. Thus, file systems are used as a workspace as well as a documentation of finished results. In most cases, document management systems are used for finished work, while users are still doing their work locally. The lines get more blurred with online tools or systems such as SharePoint that allow office applications to direct open from and save to a web system or other tools such as Google Drive or Microsoft OneDrive. We expect to be able to use our approaches there as well, as they strongly depend on the file structure that users set up to organise their files as well as files' contents. Our future work concerns a deeper analysis of the contents and distributions of shared file systems, including analyses of the performance of the different parts of our approach on file sets drawn from professional workspaces.

5. REFERENCES

[1] D. Ahlers and M. Mehrpoor. Semantic social recommendations in knowledge-based engineering. In *Social Personalization Workshop 2014*. CEUR, 2014.
[2] D. Bhagwat and N. Polyzotis. Searching a File System Using Inferred Semantic Links. Hypertext '05, 2005.
[3] O. Eck and D. Schaefer. A semantic file system for integrated product data management. *Advanced Engineering Informatics*, 25(2), 2011.
[4] T. Groza, S. Handschuh, et al. The Nepomuk project - On the way to the social semantic desktop. In *I-Semantics' 07*. JUCS, 2007.
[5] M. Mehrpoor, J. A. Gulla, D. Ahlers, K. Kristensen, S. Ghodrat, and O. I. Sivertsen. Using process ontologies to contextualize recommender systems in engineering projects for knowledge access improvement. In *ECKM2015*, 2015.
[6] C. A. N. Soules and G. R. Ganger. Connections: Using context to enhance file search. SOSP '05. ACM, 2005.

On Recommending Newly Published Academic Papers

Jiwoon Ha
Dept. of Computer & Software
Hanyang University
Seoul, Korea
jiwoonha@hanyang.ac.kr

Soon-Hyoung Kwon
Dept. of Electronics &
Computer Engineering
Hanyang University
Seoul, Korea
rikar@agape.hanyang.ac.kr

Sang-Wook Kim[*]
Dept. of Computer & Software
Hanyang University
Seoul, Korea
wook@hanyang.ac.kr

ABSTRACT

To recommend newly-published papers that did not receive any citations yet, this paper proposes a novel method by using the authors' interest on the papers cited in the newly-published paper. Compared to citation-network based methods, the empirical validation shows a significant improvement with our method in accuracy of 11%–41% in precision and 8%–34% in recall.

Categories and Subject Descriptors: H.2.8 DATABASE MANAGEMENT: Database applications—*Data mining*

Keywords: Paper recommendation, data mining, singular value decomposition

1. INTRODUCTION

With the rapid development of technologies and disciplines, there have been a number of services and approaches created using academic papers. Among them, recommendation of academic papers to a researcher is recognized as one of the most interesting research issues [1, 2].

An experienced researcher who has published some papers in a research field already understands the overall research flow of the field very well, and is thus interested in tracking *recent research trends* in the field. For this type of researchers, it is crucial to recommend *newly-published* (rather than existing) papers under their interest. Moreover, in case s/he is in the stage of paper writing, the recommendation of newly-published papers becomes more important because missing those papers could make the completion of her/his current work useless.

Most existing methods exploit such researchers' actions as citations or bookmarks as their interest on a paper in recommendation [2]. These methods could be effective in recommending an *existing paper*. It is infeasible, however, to apply them to recommending a newly-published paper since it did not receive any actions yet.

In this paper, we propose a novel method for recommending newly-published papers that have not been cited by other papers. While writing a paper, researchers cite the papers that address the topics with which the paper deals. Thus, the papers cited by a newly-published paper can be regarded as highly related to the paper. If a researcher has high interest on the papers highly related to the newly-published paper, s/he is likely to have interest on the paper. To measure the target user's interest on a newly-published paper, we predict her/his interest on its citing papers.

2. THE PROPOSED METHOD

To recommend newly-published papers, we first predict the degree of the target researcher's interest on each newly-published paper and recommend the top-N papers of her/his highest interest. For predicting the target researcher's interest on a newly-published paper, (1) we predict the degree of her/his interest on its citing papers, and then (2) predict the degree of her/his interest on the newly-published paper by using it.

Before proceeding, we need to define 'the interest of a researcher on a paper' more clearly. We regard the papers written by the researcher herself/himself and also the papers cited by her/him as those of interest. *Initially*, the interest, given to a pair of a researcher and a paper, is represented by a binary value of 0 or 1.

A straightforward way to measure the target researcher's interest on a newly-published paper is to count its citing papers that are written or cited by her/him. However, a target researcher has a very small number of papers written or cited by her/him. So, this simple way is inappropriate since, for most newly-published papers, it would decide the target researcher not to have any interest on them.

In order to solve this problem, we need to predict the target researcher's interest on all the papers other than those written or cited by her/him. To the end, we employ the *singular value decomposition (SVD)*. The SVD is one of most widely used methods for matrix factorization. It is frequently employed in ratings prediction and top-N recommendation [3]. Equations (1) and (2) show how the target researcher's interest on papers is computed by using the SVD. Equation (1) is for matrix factorization and Equation (2) is for interest prediction.

$$R \approx U \cdot \Sigma \cdot Q^T \qquad (1)$$

$$\hat{r}_{ui} \approx r_u \cdot Q \cdot q_i^T \qquad (2)$$

In Equation (1), matrix R represents each researcher's *explicit* interest on each paper. The element of the matrix, r_{ui}, has 1 if researcher u cited or wrote paper i, and 0 otherwise. Matrices U, Σ, and Q represent the relationship between researchers and latent factors, the importance of latent fac-

[*]Corresponding author

HT '15, September 1–4, 2015, Guzelyurt, Northern Cyprus.
ACM 978-1-4503-3395-5/15/09.
DOI: http://dx.doi.org/10.1145/2700171.2791047.

tors, and the relationship between papers and latent factors, respectively. In Equation (2), $\hat{r}_{ui}$ indicates (predicted) researcher u's interest on paper i. r_u and q_i represent the u-th row of matrix R and the i-th row of matrix Q, respectively. As a result, $\hat{r}_{ui}$ is predicted as a real number between 0 and 1.

Once the prediction of the target researcher's interest on those papers cited by a newly-published target paper is completed, we predict her/his interest on the newly-published target paper by aggregation as in Equation (3).

$$I_{uk} = \frac{\sum_{i \in Ref_k} \hat{r}_{ui}}{|Ref_k|} \qquad (3)$$

where I_{uk}, Ref_k, and $\hat{r}_{ui}$ indicate researcher u's interest on a newly-published paper k, a set of papers cited by the paper k, and researcher u's interest on the paper i cite by the paper k, respectively. Note that, $\hat{r}_{ui}$ becomes 1 if researcher u cited or wrote paper i, and (predicted) researcher u's interest on paper i, otherwise. For recommendation to a target researcher, we select the top-N (newly-published) papers according to their degree of predicted interest.

3. EVALUATION
3.1 Experimental Setup

For empirical validation of our method, we used a real-life DBLP data set. We first identified 5,896 distinct researchers from 6,241 papers published from 1971 to 2003 in databases and data mining fields. We split the data from 1971 to 2000 as a training set and those in 2001 as a test set. The ground truth data set consists of the papers published in 2001 and cited by target researchers during 2002 and 2003. There are 650 target researchers in the ground truth data set. As evaluation metrics, we used the well-known precision@N and recall@N, where N in top-N recommendation ranged from 1 to 5.

3.2 Results and Analyses

In order to accurately predict the target researcher's interest on a newly-published paper, we should accurately predict the target researcher's interest on the papers cited by the newly-published paper. Thus, we first examine the accuracy of the interest prediction by our method for the papers cited by the newly-published paper. In this experiment, we selected the user-/item-based collaborative filtering methods [4] for comparisons with our SVD-based method. Then, based on the prediction results through these methods, we predicted the target researcher's interest on newly-published papers and compared the top-N (newly-published) paper recommendation results.

In user-/item-based collaborative filtering, we set the number of nearest neighbors, k, as 30 that produced the highest accuracy in our preliminary experiments, and in our SVD-based method, we set the rank for the SVD as 2,000. Figures 1(a) and 1(b) show the results. The x-axis indicates the number of recommended papers, N, and the y-axis does precision@N and recall@N.

The results show that the SVD-based method performs best in both precision@N and recall@N. This is because the SVD successfully identifies latent factors from the relationships between researchers and papers, leading to more accurate prediction of the target researcher's interest.

Next, we show the effectiveness of our proposed method for recommending newly-published papers in comparisons

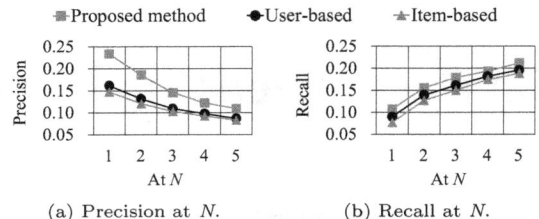

(a) Precision at N. (b) Recall at N.

Figure 1: Accuracies according to prediction methods for reference papers.

with citation-network based methods, i.e., PageRank based [1] and belief propagation based methods [5]. Figure 2 shows the results. The x- and y-axes are the same as in Figure 1. For the PageRank based method, we set the random jump probability as 0.6. For the belief propagation based method, we set the node prior as 0.8 when the target researcher cited or wrote the paper. Via preliminary experiments, we verified that these settings produce the best accuracy. The results reveal that the proposed method significantly outperforms both of the PageRank based method and the belief propagation based method.

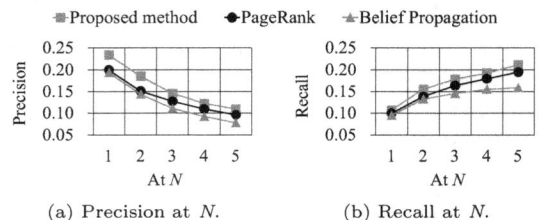

(a) Precision at N. (b) Recall at N.

Figure 2: Comparisons against citation-network based methods.

4. CONCLUSIONS

In this paper, we proposed a novel method that recommends newly-published papers. At first, we predicted a target researcher's interest on the reference papers of a newly-published paper. Then, we predicted his or her interest on the newly-published paper by referring to the interest on its reference papers. The experimental results reveal that the SVD performs best for prediction of the target researcher's interest on reference papers and that the proposed method provides accuracy higher than existing citation-network based methods.

5. ACKNOWLEDGMENTS

This work was supported by the National Research Foundation of Korea (NRF) grant funded by the Korea government (MSIP) (No. NRF-2014R1A2A1A10054151)

6. REFERENCES

[1] M. Gori and A. Pucci, Research paper recommender systems: a Random-Walk based approach, *IEEE/WIC/ACM WI*, pp.778-781, 2006.
[2] S. M. McNee et al., On the recommending of citations for research papers, *ACM CSCW*, pp.116-125, 2002.
[3] P. Cremonesi, Y. Koren and R. Turrin, Performance of recommender algorithms on top-N recommendation tasks, *ACM RecSys*, pp.39-46, 2010.
[4] G. Adomavicius and A. Tuzhilin, Toward the next generation of recommender systems: a survey of the state-of-the-art and possible extensions, *IEEE TKDE*, vol.17, no.6, pp.734-749, 2005.
[5] J. Ha et al., Top-N recommendation through belief propagation, *ACM CIKM*, pp.2343-2346, 2012.

On Recommending Job Openings

Yeon-Chang Lee
Hanyang University, Korea
lyc0324@hanyang.ac.kr

Jiwon Hong
Hanyang University, Korea
nowiz@hanyang.ac.kr

Sang-Wook Kim
Hanyang University, Korea
wook@hanyang.ac.kr

Sheng Gao
BUPT, China
gaosheng@bupt.edu.cn

Ji-Yong Hwang
AskStory, Korea
hwanghol@askstory.com

ABSTRACT

AskStory is a company providing an e-recruitment service where job seekers find a variety of job openings. This paper discusses an approach to recommending job openings attractive to job seekers.

Categories and Subject Descriptors

H.2.8 [**Database Applications**]: Data Mining

Keywords

e-recruitment services, job matching, job recommendation

1. INTRODUCTION

In e-recruitment services such as *AskStory* (askstory.com), *Indeed*, and *Reed*, there are a large number of job openings offered by many companies that would like to recruit employees. A number of job seekers search for job openings using these services. However, this is a very time-consuming and cumbersome task because of the vast number of job openings. In this situation, an automatic recommendation of job openings without much effort is crucial. In this paper, we address approaches to recommending job openings that are likely to be attractive to job seekers in *AskStory*.

AskStory has job openings and resumes posted by companies and job seekers, respectively. A job seeker has her/his resume, and a *resume* consists of a series of job records representing her/his career experiences. A *job record* consists of a *company*, a *job title*, and a working period. In this paper, we address how to model the *AskStory* data, and discuss how to recommend job openings to job seekers.

2. CHALLENGES

Suppose there are three persons A, B, and C that have similar career experiences. If B and C currently have a common job that A has not experienced and A is currently looking for a new job, it is highly likely that A may be interested in the current job of B and C. This situation agrees with that mainly targeted by collaborative filtering (CF), which recommends items for an *active user* by considering

the items liked by the users similar to her/him [1]. Thus, we try to solve this problem under the perspective of CF.

In *AskStory* data, there are two entities of *job seekers* and *job records* of <company, job title>. It can be simply modeled by a *bipartite graph* where a node represents a job seeker or a job record, and a link indicates that a job seeker had a job record in the past. Figure 1-(a) depicts a graph constructed with this model over a toy data. However, CF with this model could be confronted with the following problems.

- *New item problem*: If a newly offered job opening has a new <company, job title>, it is considered as a new item in CF. Such a new item can be never recommended to job seekers until the offer is closed. After that, the item becomes a *non-new item*, which is meaningless, however.

- *Data sparsity problem*: The number of job records owned by a person is very limited. For example, a person rates hundreds of movies but has only several job records. This makes the *AskStory* data much sparser than movie data such as *MovieLens* and *Netflix*.

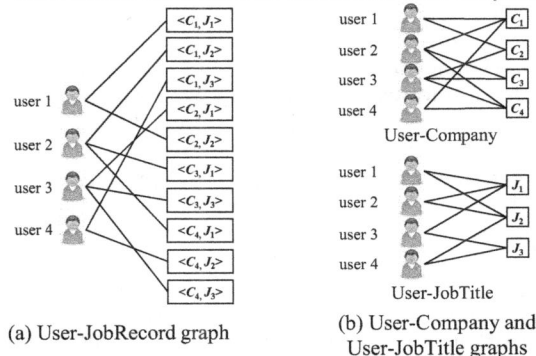

(a) User-JobRecord graph

(b) User-Company and User-JobTitle graphs

Figure 1: *AskStory* data with different modelings.

3. PROPOSED APPROACH

The basic model mentioned above regards (1) two job records of the same company but different job titles and (2) those of the same job title but different companies as four distinct items. As the number of distinct items increases, the new item and data sparsity problems get more serious. In order to solve the problems, we propose a new modeling that considers a company and a job title as distinct items instead of job records. The two problems can be successfully alleviated by this approach as follows.

- *New item problem*: Even when a job opening with a new <company, job title> is offered, this is not a new item any longer if both of a company and a job title are found in some (different) job records existing within the past data. This makes the new item problem considerably relieved.

- *Data sparsity problem*: Since a company and a job title are regarded as separate items, the job records with the same company but different job titles will be associated with the same company, and also those with the same job title but different companies will be associated with the same job title. Because the number of distinct items decreases in this way, the data sparsity problem could be significantly alleviated.

In order to model the data with our approach, we construct two bipartite graphs. Figure 1-(b) depicts two bipartite graphs built with our approach over the same data used in Figure 1-(a). The upper side and the lower side represent the relationships between job seekers and companies and the relationships between job seekers and job titles, respectively. In Figure 1-(a), the number of distinct items is 10 and the density is $0.25 (= 10/(4*10))$. In Figure 1-(b), however, the number of distinct items is reduced to $7 (= 4 + 3)$. In addition, the density is increased to $0.65 (= (10/(4*4) + 10/(4*3))/2)$ on average. Table 1 shows the statistics of the same data under different modelings.

Table 1: Statistics of the same data with (a) user-job record graph, and (b) user-company and user-job title graphs

	(a)	(b)
# users	46, 407	46, 407
# items	206, 693	company: 34, 683
		job title: 9, 463
Avg. # users/item	1.61	company: 6.53
		job title: 22.67
Density	0.004%	company: 0.015%
		job title: 0.050%

Using our approach, recommendation is performed as follows: Step 1 predicts the preferences of an active job seeker for each company and also for each job title; Step 2 predicts the preference for each job opening by combining the preferences for its company and job title; Step 3 finds the top-N job openings based on combined preferences.

There have been a lot of CF algorithms primarily based on user ratings over items. In our domain, however, there are no user ratings but only positive-or-not records over items; in Step 1, thus, predicting preferences on items can be considered as the *one-class collaborative filtering (OCCF)* problem [3]. We adopt three methods to solve the OCCF problem: OCCF, BP, and RWR methods. The OCCF method in [3] computes the active user's preference on an item by employing *weighted low rank approximation*; the BP method determines probabilistically the active user's preference on an item using the *belief propagation* [2]; the RWR method calculates a relevance score between the active user and an item based on the *random walk with restart* [1].

For combining the two preferences in Step 3, we simply multiply the preferences of a company and a job title, thereby obtaining the final score.

4. RESULTS AND ANALYSES

For evaluating the accuracy of our approach, we performed experiments with the *AskStory* data. We split the data into training and test sets. We regarded those users who have more than five job records as *test users*. We built the test set only with the latest job records of test users. We built

the training set with the rest of job records except for those in the test set.

To evaluate the accuracy, we computed how much proportion of recommended top-N $(= 3, 5, 10, 20, 30)$ companies, job titles, and job openings for each test user contains her/his latest job records (i.e., *recall*). We also performed extensive experiments with different parameter settings for OCCF, RWR, and BP methods, and took the best ones. For the OCCF method, we set # iterations as 50, and set the weighting scheme as the *user-oriented* one. For the BP method, we set # iterations and α of the propagation matrix in a user-company graph as 2 and 10^{-3}, and those in a user-job title graph to 3 and 10^{-5}, respectively. For the RWR method, we set the damping factor as 0.85.

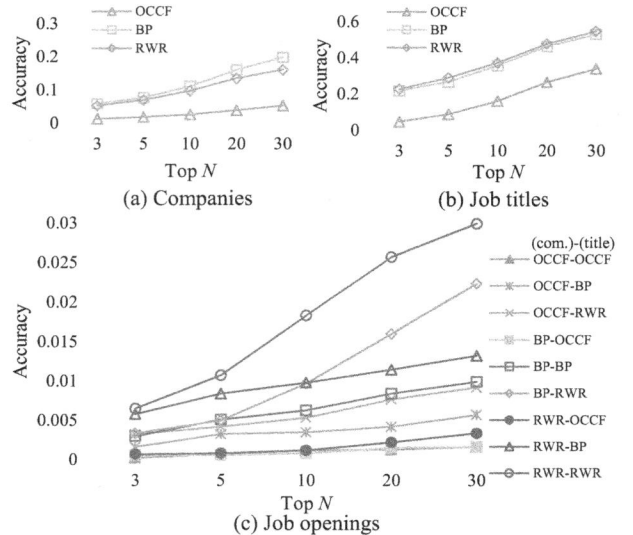

Figure 2: Accuracy of top-N recommendation.

Figure 2 shows the accuracy for companies, job titles, and job openings. It is surprising that the OCCF method shows the *worst* performance although we are solving the OCCF problem. We conjecture that the OCCF method has a weakness on the very sparse data like ours (as shown in Table 1). This phenomenon needs to be investigated later in more detail. For companies and job titles, the RWR and BP methods provide comparable performances (Figure 2-(a) and (b)). For recommendation of job openings, RWR-RWR shows the best performance in Figure 2-(c).

5. ACKNOWLEDGEMENTS

This research was supported by (1) Business (Grants No. C0191469) for Cooperative R&D between Industry, Academy, and Research Institute funded Korea Small and Medium Business Administration in 2014 and (2) the National Research Foundation of Korea (NRF) grant funded by the Korea government (MSIP) (NRF-2014R1A2A1A10054151).

6. REFERENCES

[1] F. Fouss et al. Random-walk computation of similarities between nodes of a graph with application to collaborative recommendation. *IEEE TKDE*, 19(3):355–369, 2007.

[2] J. Ha et al. Top-n recommendation through belief propagation. In *ACM CIKM*, pages 2343–2346, 2012.

[3] R. Pan et al. One-class collaborative filtering. In *IEEE ICDM*, pages 502–511, 2008.

Collaborative Learning in the Cloud– A Cross-Cultural Perspective of Collaboration

Kathrin Kirchner
Berlin School of Economics and Law
Alt-Friedrichsfelde 60
10315 Berlin, Germany
+49 30 30877 2411
kathrin.kirchner@hwr-berlin.de

Liana Razmerita
Copenhagen Business School
Dalgas Have 15
2000 Frederiksberg, Denmark
+45 38152182
lr.ibc@cbs.dk

ABSTRACT

This present study aims to investigate how students perceive collaboration and identifies associated technologies used to collaborate. In particular we aim to address the following research questions: What are the factors that impact satisfaction with collaboration? How do these factors differ in different collaborative settings? Based on data from 75 students from Denmark and Germany, the article identifies collaborative practices and factors that impact positively and negatively satisfaction with collaboration.

Categories and Subject Descriptors

K3.1 [Computers Uses in Education] Collaborative learning, H1.2 [User/Machine Systems]: Human factors, H4.3 [Communication Applications], H5.3 [Group and Organization Interfaces]: Collaborative computing, Computer-supported cooperative work

General Terms

Human Factors

Keywords

Collaboration; collaborative learning; cloud computing

1. INTRODUCTION

Collaborative learning is an important pedagogical tool used in modern higher education. "Collaborative learning describes a variety of educational practices in which interactions among peers constitute the most important factor in learning, although without excluding other factors such as the learning material and interactions with teachers." [1]

The "digital natives students" or "millennials" are multitasking, operating at "twitch speed" [2] in multiple modalities using mobile pervasive cloud technology and social media on regular basis. Social media is based on Internet and cloud computing technology that "allows users to easily create, edit, evaluate, and/or link to content or to other creators of content."[3].

HT '15, September 1–4, 2015, Guzelyurt, Northern Cyprus.
© 2015 ACM. ISBN 978-1-4503-3395-5/15/09…$15.00
DOI: http://dx.doi.org/10.1145/2700171.2804452

Collaboration may be organized through both traditional face to face group work or through online learning using e-collaboration via various cloud services. Cloud services have a big potential for expanding collaborative learning through both real time collaboration and social interaction [4, 5]. A new set of collaborative tools available in the cloud are supporting different collaborative/cooperative or learning processes:

- multi-user collaborative writing like Wikis (e.g., Wikipedia, Wikiversity, Wikimedia,), GoogleDocs or editing simultaneous notes, lists and ideas using Pads (e.g., TitanPad, SimplePad)
- communicating, sharing and social interaction using social networking (e.g., Twitter, Facebook, Podio) or instant messaging (e.g., WhatsApp)
- file sharing or document sharing (e.g., Dropbox or GoogleDrive)
- brainstorming and structuring of ideas like Mindmaps (e.g., Mindmeister, Freemind)
- sharing links and bookmarks using Social Bookmarking (e.g., Delicious, Digg)
- media sharing including video streaming or presentations using content communities (e.g., Slideshare, YouTube)
- computer-intensive e-learning services (e.g., Massive Open Online Courses (MOOCS), virtual worlds, simulations)

Collaborative services are the most potential applications for achieving collaborative learning that can be used to assist students in accomplishing a collaborative or cooperative learning task [5]. The aim of this study is to investigate collaborative learning and technologies associated with learning in the cloud adopted by student to support collaboration. In particular, the following research questions are addressed: What are the factors that impact satisfaction with collaboration? How do these factors differ in different collaborative settings?

2. RELATED WORK

A variety of approaches and interpretations to collaborative learning exist [1] (e.g., online collaboration [6], cross-cultural virtual teams [7], case-based learning [8]). Despite these different approaches, these studies agree on the benefits of peer interaction that stimulates knowledge production and cognitive gains [1, 9, 10]. However group work has many dependent variables and factors that influence group performance [11, 12] and satisfaction [13]. In particular the quality of learning is highly dependent of characteristics of the group [11, 14]. The literature related to motivation and collaborative learning shows that students' performance and learning depends not only to interest in the subject but also to the relation to peers, individual differences, personality traits, cultural backgrounds, gender differences, classroom as a learning environment [7, 11, 12, 14].

Based on an extensive literature review, the main benefits and affordances of cloud computing for education have been identified and discussed [15]. The main listed benefits are: availability of online applications, flexibility to create learning environments, support for mobile learning, computing intensive support, scalability and cost savings in hardware and software.

3. RESEARCH METHOD AND DATA

Our study employs a survey research design. Based on the literature review, a questionnaire was developed in previous study [12, 13], that was later revised and extended. The questions focused on students' perception of collaboration and e-collaboration. The last version of the questionnaire consists of 22 questions covering areas like general collaboration within the group, the support of knowledge processes, the challenges of group work, as well as the role of e-collaboration via cloud services (e.g. social media). Most of the questions used a 5-point Likert scale ranging from 1 (strongly agree) to 5 (strongly disagree). In order to get additional insights and enable student to comment regarding the group work, some open questions were included in the survey. The data was collected through an online survey, distributed at the end of the semester. Data was collected in two different courses, at bachelor level, one at Copenhagen Business School (CBS), one at Berlin School of Economics and Law (BSEL) in 2014 and 2015.

The course "Web Interaction Design and Communication: New Forms of Knowledge Sharing and Interaction" has run as an elective course at CBS in Spring and Fall 2014. The participating students were Danish bachelor students from different study programs as well as exchange students from all over the world. Students conducted research on a selected topic of interest, developed research ideas collaboratively and collected data in group. At the end of the course, student groups presented their results and received feedback on their work so far. The collaborative work was the starting point for their individual student projects.

Furthermore, data was collected from German Information Systems bachelor students at BSEL in Spring 2015. The students were enrolled into a cooperative study program - they work all in parallel for a company and gain practical experience in addition to their theoretical knowledge. These students attended a mandatory course in "Management of complex software systems". They worked together in groups on a case study over the semester. Although the case study tasks were assigned, some degrees of freedom allowed integrating their own ideas. Similarly to the previous case, the results of group work were presented at the end of semester.

4. DATA ANALYSIS AND FINDINGS

Altogether, we have collected answers from 35 students at CBS (out of 92 participants) and 40 students (out of 50 participants) from BSEL. In total, our sample includes 75 valid responses, among which we have 42 male students (56%) and 33 female (44%). The CBS student sample of respondents included 34% Danes and 66% non-Danes. During the group work, students could freely select what collaborative tools they use. In the course

at CBS, Podio, a social media-enhanced platform was used for providing course related materials, sharing information and interacting with the students. In the BSEL course, Moodle was used for similar purposes. Figure 1 shows the different usage of collaboration services. Facebook and Dropbox were the most preferred means of collaboration in both settings. Additionally to Skype, Prezi, GoogleDocs/Drive, a few students used WhatsApp and email.

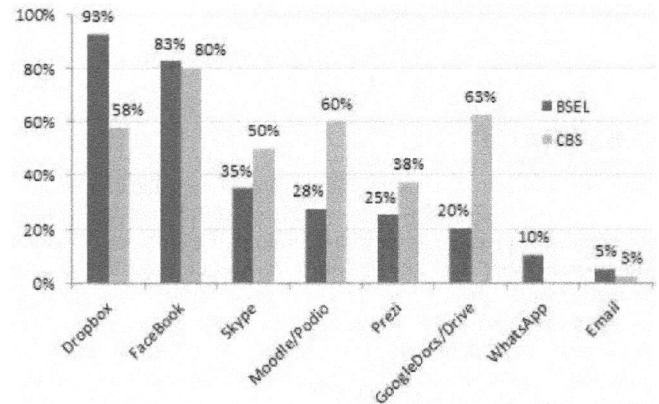

Figure 1. Usage of collaboration tools at BSEL and CBS

Furthermore, we have investigated the overall satisfaction of students in relation with their collaboration. As it can be seen in Figure 2, in the BSEL setting students were more satisfied (mean=1.68, SD=0.694) than in the CBS case (mean=2.31, SD=1.078). A T-Test showed a significant difference (sig. 0.003) between the two groups.

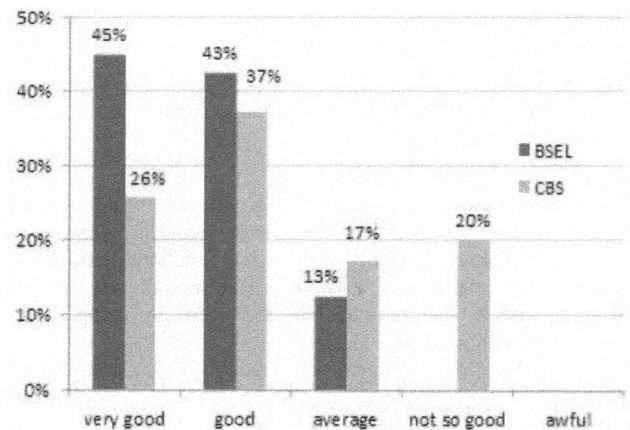

Figure 2. Overall satisfaction with collaboration

The "not so good" experience of some students at CBS may be explained due to the fact that some groups had experience conflict - "disagreements about approach to the subject" - and therefore some groups split-up or some members left the group before finalizing the group work. Group work is not a mandatory task at CBS as students' final grade depends only on their individual performance and therefore not all students engage voluntarily in group work.

Table 1. Overview of collaboration factors (Likert Scale, 1= strongly agree, 5=strongly disagree)

Survey	Item	Mean	SD
General Collaboration	Enjoy collaboration with peers	1.91	0.918
	Collaboration effect on learning and inspiration	2.49	1.143
	Equal contribution of team members	2.31	1.208
	Help to enhance project ideas	2.01	0.979
Support of knowledge processes	Creating Presentations	2.09	1.042
	Learning new perspectives	2.48	1.005
	Inspiring new ideas	2.51	0.991
	Enhancing social interaction	2.53	1.155
	Helping individual project work	2.56	1.068
	Helping in data collection	2.44	1.265
Collaboration challenges	Social Loafing	3.68	1.210
	Lack of coordination	3.27	1.212
	Lack of trust	4.20	1.053
	Conflict	4.19	0.968
	Different backgrounds of team members	3.92	1.112
	Cultural differences in the team	3.61	1.218
General e-collaboration	E-Collaboration important for group work	1.64	0.880
	Prefer social interaction	4.04	1.202
	Easy to use	1.81	0.940
	Fun	2.32	0.872
	Benefits	1.61	0.804
	Need	1.93	1.095
	e-collaboration important for work	1.64	0.880
E-collaboration use	For coordination and meeting	1.88	1.013
	For exchanging ideas	2.35	1.157
	For assigning tasks	2.49	1.155
	For brainstorming	3.27	1.223
	For knowledge sharing	2.29	1.136
	For creating drafts and editing	1.51	0.876
	For sharing articles and ideas	2.36	1.147
	For virtual social interaction	2.80	1.252
Social media advantages	Save time	1.87	0.905
	Enhance group work	1.73	0.890
	Facilitate knowledge sharing and quality of end result	1.76	0.803
	Useful for completing group work	1.83	0.991
	Integrating different ideas and group creativity	2.14	0.944

Table 1 presents an overview of the different factors influencing collaboration that have been considered in the survey. These factors have been clustered into six different groups, namely "general collaboration", "support of knowledge processes", "collaboration challenges", "general e-collaboration", "e-collaboration use" and "social media advantages". All factors were ordinal, measured on a Likert scale from 1 to 5.

Spearman's Rho was used to analyze the influence of the 37 factors from table 1. As can be seen in Fig. 3, for the CBS case, eight factors from the clusters "general collaboration", "support of knowledge processes" and "collaboration challenges" influenced

the overall satisfaction with collaboration. The factor with the highest impact in the CBS setting is "enjoy collaboration with peers" with Spearman Rho=0.968. Challenges like social loafing (Rho=-0.468) and lack of trust (Rho=-0.369) negatively influence the satisfaction with the group collaboration.

In the case of the BSEL setting, the factor "enjoy collaboration with peers" had also the highest impact on the overall satisfaction (Fig. 4). Nine factors from the clusters "general collaboration", "collaboration challenges" and "social media advantages" were significant factors. The challenge with the highest negative impact was the lack of trust.

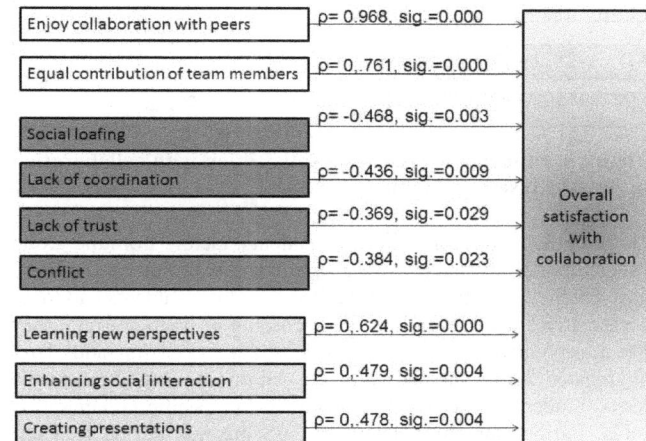

Figure 3. Influencing factors on satisfaction with collaboration in the CBS setting (n=35)

5. DISCUSSION

Even though collaboration settings are different in terms of backgrounds (students, tasks, type of group projects) most of the influencing factors are common in both settings.

In both cases, variables from the clusters "General collaboration" and "Collaboration Challenges" were significant influencing factors on the overall satisfaction with the group collaboration. In both settings, "enjoy collaboration with peers" had the highest impact, although at CBS, the Rho value was higher (0.986) than at BSEL (0.742). In the cluster "Collaboration challenges", four factors were the same in both settings, although at BSEL, "lack of trust" played a bigger role than at CBS (despite the fact that students know each other since 3 years). Interestingly, the factor "different backgrounds" played only a significant role for the BSEL group, but not for CBS students. This might seem intriguing, as BSEL students have known each other since three years and they are more homogeneous, as they are all Germans and belong to the same study program while CBS students are more heterogeneous - as they come from different study programs or countries. However, BSEL students had different practical knowledge and experience due to their practical work in different companies. Therefore, some of them had already some experiences with the topic covered in the case study for the group work.

For CBS students, factors from the cluster "support for knowledge processes" (including factors such as: learning new perspectives, enhancing social interaction, creating presentations) played a significant role, while it was not the case for BSEL students. That might be due to the fact that the project task for in the CBS setting was more open and students had the opportunity to be more creative.

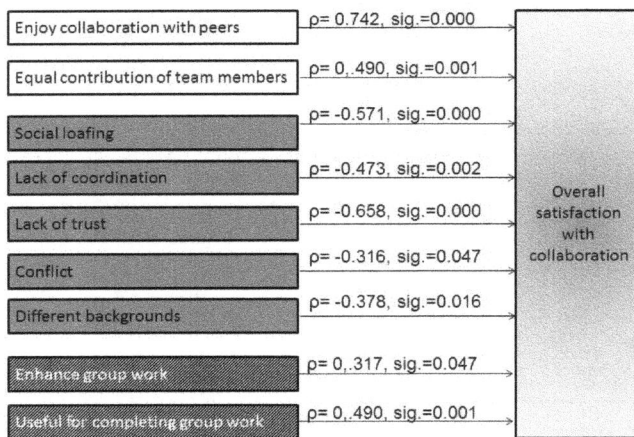

Enjoy collaboration with peers	ρ= 0.742, sig.=0.000
Equal contribution of team members	ρ= 0,.490, sig.=0.001
Social loafing	ρ= -0.571, sig.=0.000
Lack of coordination	ρ= -0.473, sig.=0.002
Lack of trust	ρ= -0.658, sig.=0.000
Conflict	ρ= -0.316, sig.=0.047
Different backgrounds	ρ= -0.378, sig.=0.016
Enhance group work	ρ= 0,.317, sig.=0.047
Useful for completing group work	ρ= 0,.490, sig.=0.001

Figure 4. Influencing factors on satisfaction with collaboration in the BSEL setting (n=40)

On the other hand, for the BSEL students, factors from the group "social media advantages" were significant, while this was not the case for the CBS students. In the BSEL setting, students had to do a case study with several tasks. According to their answers, they have separated the tasks among team members and later aggregated the results and defined a red threat using social media tools. Students were not prescribed to use specific collaboration tools. Furthermore the student at CBS are not graded for their group presentation and class participation and therefore some students are not that motivated to participate in the group work and presentations. BSEL students are graded based on their students' presentations and group report.

In a previous study [13] that examined the students' satisfaction with group collaboration, based only on data from CBS students from 2011-2012 - we found seven significant impact factors. The relationship to peers "enjoy collaboration" was found to be the most influential factor that impact satisfaction as well as "equal contribution of team members". Among the identified challenges were mostly the same as in this study: social loafing, lack of coordination and lack of trust. The present study identifies some additional factors (such as conflict as an additional challenge) and some context dependent factors which are influenced by specific collaboration settings and assignments.

6. SUMMARY AND OUTLOOK
Cloud computing has the potential to expand collaborative learning and teaching. The study sheds light on collaboration practices and perception of students' satisfaction with group work. In particular, the article has investigated the most important factors that impact collaboration satisfaction with group work in two different classroom settings with students working on different collaborative tasks, in two different countries. The study has identified critical factors that impact students' satisfaction with collaboration presented in two models. Thus, the study findings contribute to a better understanding of how to promote successful collaboration and of a better understanding of challenges that students encounter in their groupwork. Collaboration and group work skills are important for business school graduates as organizations demand employees to have strong interpersonal and group work skills. These skills are particularly important in an economic environment that is increasingly complex, rapidly changing and global. In the future we aim to collect and analyze more data from other courses, other countries and different collaborative settings in order to identify gender differences and validate context dependent factors that impact collaboration.

7. REFERENCES
[1] Dillenbourg, P., What do you mean by collaborative learning?, in *Collaborative-learning: Cognitive and Computational Approaches.* 1999, Oxford, Elsevier. p. 1-19.

[2] Prensky, M., *Digital natives, digital immigrants Part 1. On the Horizon,* 2001. 9(5): p. 1-6.

[3] Kaplan, A.M. and M. Haenlein, Users of the world, unite! The challenges and opportunities of Social Media. *Business Horizons,* 2010. 53(1): p. 59-68.

[4] Calvo, R.A., S.T. O'Rourke, J. Jones, K.Yacef and P. Reimann, Collaborative Writing Support Tools on the Cloud. *IEEE Transactions on Learning Technologies,* 2011. 4(1): p. 88-97.

[5] Huang, Y.-M., C.-S. Wamg, J.-Z. Guo, H.-Y. Shih and Y.-S. Chen, Advancing collaborative learning with cloud service, in *Information Technology Convergence.* 2013, Springer. p. 717-722.

[6] Xu, J., J. Du, and X. Fan, Students' Groupwork Management in Online Collaborative Learning Environments. *Journal of Educational Technology & Society,* 2015. 18(2): p. 195-205.

[7] Paul, S., P- Seetharaman and P. Mykytyn, Impact of Heterogeneity and collaborative conflict management style on the performance of synchronous global virtual teams. *Information and Management,* 2003. 41: p. 303-321.

[8] Mondahl, M. and L. Razmerita, Social Media, Collaboration and Social Learning-a study of Case-based Foreign Language Learning. *The Electronic Journal of e-Learning (EJEL),* 2014. 12(4): p. 339-352.

[9] Oliveira, I., L. Tinoca, and A. Pereira, Online group work patterns: How to promote a successful collaboration. *Computers & Education,* 2011. 57(1): p. 1348-1357.

[10] McConnell, D., *E-learning groups and communities.* 2006: McGraw-Hill International.

[11] Razmerita, L. and A. Brun, Collaborative Learning in Heterogeneous Classes: Towards a Group Formation Methodology. *Proceedings of 3rd International Conference on Computer Supported Education (CSEDU 2011),* 2011. 2: p. 189-194.

[12] Razmerita, L. and K. Kirchner. Collaboration and e-collaboration: A study of factors that influence perceived students' group performance. in *HICSS 2015 2015.* Kauai, USA: IEEE computer society.

[13] Razmerita, L. and K. Kirchner, Social media collaboration in the classroom: A study of group collaboration, in *Collaboration and Technology (CRIWG 2014),* G. Zurita, et al., Editors. 2014, Springer. p. 279-286.

[14] Ku, H.-Y., H.W. Tseng, and C. Akarasriworn, Collaboration factors, teamwork satisfaction, and student attitudes toward online collaborative learning. *Computers in Human Behavior,* 2013. 29(3): p. 922-929.

[15] González-Martínez, J.A., M.L. Bote-Lorenzo, E. Gomez-Sanchez and R. Cano-Rafael, Cloud computing and education: A state-of-the-art survey. *Computers & Education,* 2015. 80(0): p. 132-151.

Longitudinal analysis of low-level Web interaction through micro behaviours

Aitor Apaolaza, Simon Harper and Caroline Jay
University of Manchester
School of Computer Science
Kilburn Building, Oxford Road, MANCHESTER, M13 9PL, UK
[aitor.apaolaza|simon.harper|caroline.jay]@manchester.ac.uk

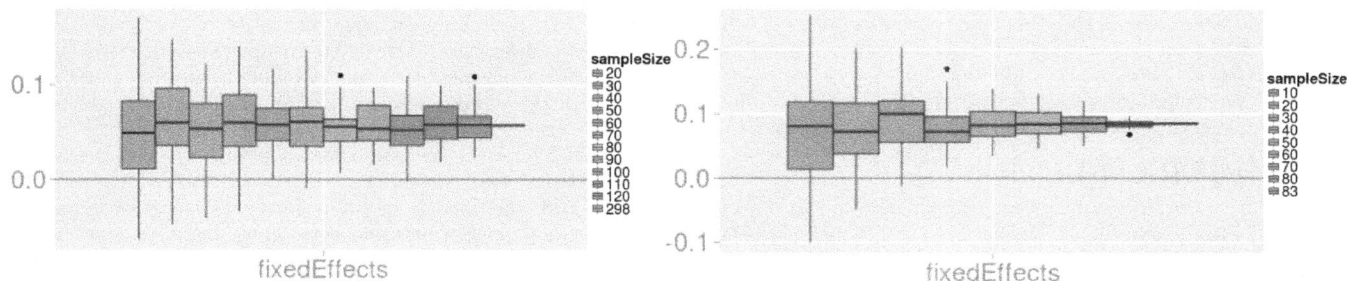

Figure 1: Evolution of the duration of users' episode over time in each phase.

ABSTRACT

To truly understand how people learn to navigate and use a Web site or application, we need to collect real usage data over extended periods of time. Detailed Web interaction data gathered in the wild (from URLs visited, to keystrokes and mouse movements) has the potential to provide an in-depth, ecologically valid view of interaction, and enable an understanding of how behaviour evolves over time. Interpreting such data is extremely challenging, however. We present a longitudinal data-driven analysis of fine-grained interaction data captured from 14,000 recurrent users over 12 months. At the core of our approach is the aggregation of low-level interaction data into *micro behaviours*. By analysing changes in these behaviours as a function of users' accumulated interaction time, we were able to demonstrate how users' interaction evolves as they become more familiar with a Web page. The results demonstrate that monitoring micro behaviours offers a simple and easily extensible *post hoc* means of understanding how Web-based behaviour evolves over time.

Keywords

Longitudinal; Web ergonomics; usability; behaviour; Web interaction

Categories and Subject Descriptors

H.5.2 [**User Interfaces**]: Evaluation/methodology, Ergonomics; H.5.4 [**Hypertext/Hypermedia**]: User issues

1. INTRODUCTION

Long-term studies are necessary to support the design of interfaces that accommodate interaction over long periods of time. Laboratory studies provide a constrained environment in which confounding variables can be controlled, but are not a feasible way of studying an individual user's interaction over days or weeks. Monitoring behaviour remotely provides a means of obtaining naturalistic, 'in the wild' observations, but analysing data collected in these circumstances is potentially challenging.

Existing approaches to the remote study of behaviour usually rely on prejudgements that help simplify the analysis step. Some investigations have either given participants predefined tasks or made assumptions about those that the user is likely to be performing, to enable the comparison of different interaction sequences [1, 11]. Predefining tasks means prejudging users' interaction goals, however, and making assumptions about the task being performed that may be inaccurate; in both cases, this risks the validity of the study.

We designed a remote capture solution and captured detailed Web interaction data continuously for over two years, and report here on how we are using this approach to understand long term, real world Web usage. Instead of employing a predefined longitudinal interaction metric [7] we were interested in discovering how users' interaction behaviour changes over time. At the heart of our approach is the transformation of low-level data (such as mouse movements) into manageable temporal units of interaction, while avoiding assumptions about users' tasks or goals. These units, which we term *micro behaviours*, describe small samples of user interaction. We describe a number of micro behaviours,

337

based on evidence from the literature and the application of a data-driven approach to analysis.

We hypothesised that the changes in these behaviours over time could be indicators of how users' interaction behaviour evolves as they get more familiar with the Web site or application. We compared our initial findings with an additional four months of captured interaction, supplemented with a survey that asks users about their familiarity with the site. The results support our hypothesis that the manifestation of certain micro behaviours are a valid proxy for users' familiarity with a website.

We present results discovering evolving aspects of different micro behaviours over time. When users scroll in a continuous way (such as scanning a page) the speed increases and the duration of this scroll action reduces as they get more familiar with the Web page. Users' interaction time with the mouse decreases as they become more familiar with the page, which may be caused by the lack of necessity to explore the page. Finally, we found that users' episode length within a Web page increases as they become more familiar, possibly indicating the reuse of a known page as reference.

2. CAPTURE SOLUTION

In order to obtain naturalistic observations, it was important that interaction data was captured unobtrusively. Our solution also needed to be scalable, as it would be required to manage large amounts of data captured over extended periods of time. The data reported here were obtained by monitoring the `cs.manchester.ac.uk` site. This site contains information about the School of Computer Science at the University of Manchester, covering news, events, teaching and research, and is used by a range of people (including current and prospective students and staff). As the site is frequently updated, the number of pages it contains varies; in this study we captured data from a total of 1411 different URLs.

We based our capture solution on the UsaProxy [3] tool, which supports the recording of low-level Web interaction events. The original tool was extensively modified, in particular, to allow deployment by adding Javascript code to the Web pages, rather than requiring users to set their browser to re-route all connections through a proxy server. Proxies have been successfully employed in short remote experiments in the past [5], but we discovered they are not suitable for longer term experiments. In particular, we found out that various bots and random internet requests made the server unstable and led to us closing the proxy connection altogether. More details about the capture tool can be found in [2][1].

Captured data.

Specific users are tracked via a unique, anonymised code stored in a cookie. Events captured include all mouse and keyboard interaction, as well as browser window events, changes to the state of the elements on the page, and other system information. The state of the DOM and its changes during interaction are also stored, allowing the context of interaction to be potentially recreated. All the data is stored in JSON format in a NoSQL database, which allows for extensibility and query scalability and means that further events can easily be included as required. The design also supports the modification or removal of existing events should they become deprecated.

---

[1]The source code for the capture tool is available in `iam-data.cs.manchester.ac.uk/data_files/12`.

Window events, indicating when the page is loaded, or when the page has lost focus, combined with user specific information, provide context for lower-level events. This information allows the grouping of events according to the specific environment in which they took place, such as the browser tab – identifiable via the page load timestamp – and URL. Logging the platform and browser version supports the control of event compatibility according to the system. The ever-changing nature of the Web and the possibility of enabling partially supported events makes this information useful for discerning problems with the way a given system handles interaction events.

3. ANALYSIS OF MICRO BEHAVIOURS

The focus of our analysis is to provide insight into how users' interaction changes over time. An important initial step when dealing with large amounts of freely instigated low-level interaction data is to group it appropriately from a temporal perspective. We decided to segment the data into 'episodes', which equate to a single, continuous session of Web use. We split data by applying an inactivity threshold of 40 minutes to user interaction [6, 8]. The threshold was determined by looking at the distribution of inactive periods, and calculating the point after which the variance between the length of inactive periods was small enough to be negligible. This helped ensure that the number of episodes containing a long interruption was minimal [12].

For each episode, we grouped low-level events (individual mouse movements, keystrokes etc.) into sequences that represent what we term *micro behaviours*. These behaviours represent a small sample of user interaction, such as clicking a link, typing in a text field, or scrolling down the page. Previous work has shown that it is possible to identify certain behaviours that are common across individuals through behavioural observation and interaction data analysis, and also that these behaviours are important indicators of both what the user is doing, and how successfully they are completing their task [9, 10]. For example, scrolling down quickly to the bottom of a page and then up again indicates that someone is struggling to find the information they are looking for [10].

We extracted several micro behaviours from the data, based on past research, and manual observation of individual user's interaction. As opposed to the aggregation of interaction data for each episode – e.g. total amount of scroll – extraction of micro behaviours allows us to group interactions into smaller units. Analysing finer grained groups of interactions provides a more detailed insight into users' behaviour, and supports comparisons that would not otherwise be possible. For example, if a user scrolls down fast for a short period of time, it would go unnoticed if data were aggregated for each episode. However, if the scroll actions are combined into micro behaviours, this interaction would stand out as a specific "fast scroll" micro behaviour.

We analysed the characteristics of these behaviours to find meaningful changes over time. In order to account for the uniqueness of each user, we employed linear mixed models, which allow the inclusion of random effects. If a linear mixed model is based on certain independent variables – in our case a time metric and a micro behaviour characteristic – the random effects represent the residual that cannot be accounted for by these variables. When random effects are added to the model, they explicitly model the inter-subject variability. In this case, adding users as random effects tells the model to consider their values as different subjects. The result is a more sensible interpretation of the data. The model

338

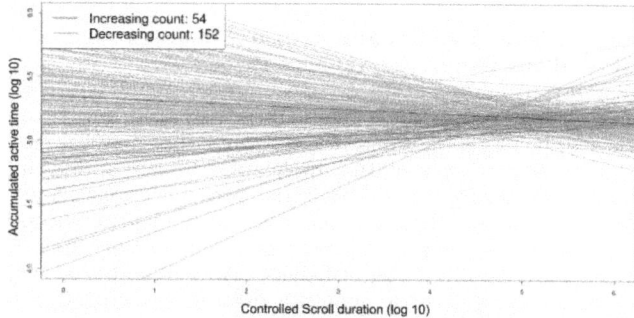

Figure 2: Mixed linear model showing the relation of users' aggregated active time against the duration of the "controlled scroll" behaviour in the cs.manchester.ac.uk page

is robust against unbalanced data [4] and calculates different intercepts and slopes for each user. It also takes into account how noisy the data from each user is and calculates a user specific intercept and slope taking into consideration data from other users.

In Figure 2 a plot of this model is shown, indicating the correlation of users' aggregated active time (aggregated amount of time the user was active on the page over the entire period of data capture) against the duration of the "controlled scroll" behaviour.

The black line represents the model prediction for the overall population, indicating that the value of this feature decreases over time. Despite this prediction, it can be seen that this same feature was found to be increasing over time for some users. Furthermore, these lines are the result of the prediction for those particular users taking into account the entire population's data into account, i.e. each line represents the model for that user "conditioned" by the rest of the available data.

Due to the linear mixed model's noise handling behaviour, the application of these models can be sensitive to certain users exhibiting particularly strong correlations. In this case, even if those correlations are not shared by other users, the model could still be biased towards them. To tackle this, we applied the model to different user sample sizes chosen at random from the population. We then observed the distribution of the model's fixed effect values – i.e. the value of the slope, indicating that particular feature's tendency to change over time. This approach results in a more conservative and reliable prediction of changes. In order to avoid disparity in the number of data points per user, we also enforce thresholds in the sampling of users. More precisely, we set a minimum amount of interaction for the user to be included in the analysis, as well as removing long-term interaction beyond which users became scarce, to prevent a small number of highly-recurrent users overpowering the model. The examples below include users who have interacted for at least 5 episodes, or have 4 minutes of aggregated active time, and exclude any data after 20 episodes, or 20 minutes of aggregated active time.

4. FINDING LONGITUDINAL FACTORS

We applied the technique introduced in Section 3 to look for characteristics that showed a correlation with the time the user spent in the Web site. Two different metrics were employed to measure time: episode count and users' aggregated active time. Aggregated active time is a precise measurement of the total amount of time the user spent active in the page. We aggregated the duration of all peri-

ods containing continuous interaction without an interruption longer than a stipulated threshold of 50 seconds. This threshold was obtained by applying the same technique described earlier, used to differentiate "episodes", changing the algorithm to use a scale of seconds.

Data was collected in two phases. "Phase 1" contains data captured over a year from 14,000 different recurring users. "Phase 2" occurred over the subsequent four months, and includes data from over 3,000 different recurrent users. Throughout phase 2, we concurrently carried out remote surveys of both first time users, and those who had visited more than once. More precisely, we compared self-reported levels of familiarity between first-time visitors and recurrent users. With 95 answers from first time visitors and 154 answers from recurrent visitors, a Wilcoxon test demonstrates that the familiarity level of recurrent users was significantly higher than first time visitors (p-value = 0.021). Therefore our hypothesis that users' familiarity increases over time was supported. We also limited the analysis to the most visited Web page in the site to remove any variance introduced by page dissimilarity. Lastly, data has been transformed using a logarithmic function to respect the necessary assumptions to apply Mixed Linear Models.

For each example, we present the results for each data set. The graphs shown in Figures 1, 3, 4 and 5, show the variance between different iterations of random sampling of users. We applied the analysis technique 50 times for each sample size and report the distribution of results. For each figure, sample sizes start at 10, and increase left to right by 10, until 120 or the maximum number of available users has been reached. In order to increase readability, the sample size legend has only been included in Figure 1. The most relevant aspect of these visualisations is the possibility of comparing if the result of applying the model to the entire population – last sample size, not showing any variance – differs drastically from using smaller samples.

We found that changes present in phase 1 were also found in phase 2. Some features were not found to have any temporal correlation, showing a normal distribution of results across the origin. For example, we found no change in the time from hovering over an element to clicking on it, while using the mouse.

Controlled scroll speed.

Figure 3 shows the occurrences of users scrolling down for a prolonged period of time at a controlled speed. As opposed to users scrolling down fast to the bottom of a Web page, this behaviour may occur when users are slowly scanning a Web page. We found that the speed of this scrolling action increased as users visited the page again.

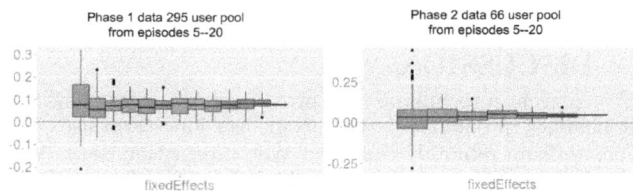

Figure 3: Evolution of the speed of controlled scroll over time in each phase.

Controlled scroll duration.

When examining the duration of the controlled scroll micro behaviour in Figure 4, we found that it was negatively correlated with users' active time. Taking into account the increasing speed of this micro behaviour (see Figure 3), users may scroll faster, and for less time, to find what they were looking for in the Web page.

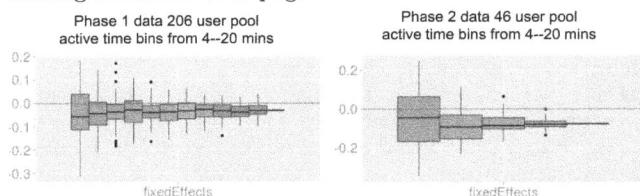

Figure 4: Evolution of the duration of controlled scroll over time in each phase.

Mouse inactive time.

For each episode, we extracted different micro behaviours concerning mouse interaction. In the example shown in Figure 5 we looked at the amount of time the user spent on a page without moving the mouse. In this case we analysed the median of all mouse inactive periods per episode. Our initial belief was that as they got more familiar with the Web page users would interact quicker, and take less time to decide what to do when presented with the page, resulting in shorter inactive times. Contrary to this initial belief, we found that users' mouse inactive time increased over time. This phenomenon could be the result of users not having to explore a page they are already familiar with – e.g. first-time users might want to hover over elements to determine what the interaction options are.

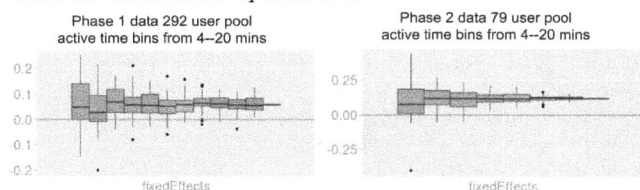

Figure 5: Evolution of the inactive time of mouse interaction over time in each phase.

Episode duration.

Figure 1 shows a positive correlation of episode duration with users' active time. This means that users' episodes get longer as they get more familiar with the page. Our initial belief was that users would need less time to navigate away from the page as their level of familiarity increases. One possible reason for this phenomenon is that users could be coming back to a page they already know to use it as reference. If the time between visits is smaller than the inactivity threshold set to separate episodes, both visits could be considered as part of the same episode. Therefore, rather than longer episodes, this tendency could be showing that the use of a reference page increases as the user becomes more familiar with it.

5. DISCUSSION

We present a technique that provides a means of identifying changes in behaviour that occur over long-term use of a Website from remotely captured Web interaction data. We tackle the problem of handling high levels of fine-grained data – such as mouse movement and scroll action – for extended periods of time, by grouping interaction data into *micro behaviours* representing particular aspects of user interaction. New micro behaviours can be included in the analysis, including data from different interfaces, or new interaction abstractions. Our contributions are threefold: we provide the means to achieve a **naturalistic observation of Web interaction**, remotely capturing data from

users' environments; we designed an **extensible longitudinal analysis technique**, enabling the addition of any new micro behaviour or feature *post hoc* in order to find new tendencies; and we present a **broadly applicable solution**, as it can be easily deployed in any Web site or application.

We present results of the application of our approach. Some of them supported our initial preconceptions about Web interaction, showing that the particular action of scrolling to scan the page becomes quicker over time. Other results challenged our initial beliefs. We found that users' interaction time with the mouse decreases as they become more familiar with the page. We also found that users' episode length within a Web page increases as they become more familiar – when using our interpretation of "episode".

6. ACKNOWLEDGEMENTS

This work was supported by the Engineering and Physical Sciences Research Council [EP/I028099/1].

7. REFERENCES

[1] D. Akers, M. Simpson, R. Jeffries, and T. Winograd. Undo and erase events as indicators of usability problems. In *Proceedings of the 27th international conference on Human factors in computing systems*, CHI '09, pages 659–668. ACM, 2009.

[2] A. Apaolaza, S. Harper, and C. Jay. Understanding users in the wild. In *Proceedings of the 10th International Cross-Disciplinary Conference on Web Accessibility*, W4A '13, pages 13:1–13:4. ACM, 2013.

[3] R. Atterer, M. Wnuk, and A. Schmidt. Knowing the user's every move: user activity tracking for website usability evaluation and implicit interaction. In *Proceedings of the 15th international conference on World Wide Web*, WWW '06, pages 203–212, New York, NY, USA, 2006. ACM.

[4] D. M. Bates. lme4: Mixed-effects modeling with r. 2010.

[5] J. P. Bigham, A. C. Cavender, J. T. Brudvik, J. O. Wobbrock, and R. E. Lander. WebinSitu: a comparative analysis of blind and sighted browsing behavior. In *Proceedings of the 9th international ACM SIGACCESS conference on Computers and accessibility*, Assets '07, pages 51–58. ACM, 2007.

[6] Google. How visits are calculated in analytics, 2014. [Online https://support.google.com/analytics/answer/2731565?hl=en-GB; accessed 8-April-2015].

[7] T. Grossman, G. Fitzmaurice, and R. Attar. A survey of software learnability: metrics, methodologies and guidelines. In *Proceedings of the 27th international conference on Human factors in computing systems*, CHI '09, pages 649–658. ACM. 00083.

[8] D. He and A. Göker. Detecting session boundaries from web user logs. In *Proceedings of the BCS-IRSG 22nd annual colloquium on information retrieval research*, pages 57–66, 2000.

[9] D. Lunn, S. Harper, and S. Bechhofer. Identifying behavioral strategies of visually impaired users to improve access to web content. *ACM Trans. Access. Comput.*, 3(4):13:1–13:35, 2011.

[10] M. Vigo and S. Harper. Considering people with disabilities as überusers for eliciting generalisable coping strategies on the web. In *Proceedings of the 5th Annual ACM Web Science Conference*, pages 441–444, 2013.

[11] J. Vlasenko. Exploring developer's tool path. In *Proceedings of the ACM international conference companion on Object oriented programming systems languages and applications companion*, SPLASH '11, pages 219–220. ACM, 2011.

[12] N. Zakay and D. G. Feitelson. On identifying user session boundaries in parallel workload logs. In W. Cirne, N. Desai, E. Frachtenberg, and U. Schwiegelshohn, editors, *Job Scheduling Strategies for Parallel Processing*, number 7698 in Lecture Notes in Computer Science, pages 216–234. Springer Berlin Heidelberg, 2013.

User-Adapted Web of Things for Accessibility

Ilaria Torre
Department of Computer Science, Bioengineering,
Robotics and Systems Engineering
University of Genoa,
Viale Causa, 13, Italy
Ilaria.torre@unige.it

Ilknur Celik
Computer Education and Instructional Technology,
Middle East Technical University
Northern Cyprus Campus,
Guzelyurt, Mersin 10 Turkey
cilknur@metu.edu.tr

ABSTRACT
This paper describes a new wave of the Web that is the user-adapted Web of Things. This is a new step in the evolution of the Web of Things and of adaptive web-based systems. The current proposals for the Web of Things focus on the augmentation of the physical objects in order to provide enhanced services. However, in our view, the Web of Things can also be a means to make physical objects accessible or more usable for people with special needs by exploiting adaptive and semantic techniques. The architecture presented in the paper describes the specific modules and components at the basis of this approach.

Keywords
Adaptive Web; Web of Things; Semantic Web; Linked Data; accessibility; adaptation techniques; user-adapted interaction; special needs.

1. INTRODUCTION
Back in a 2002 paper called "From Adaptive Hypermedia to the Adaptive Web" [1] Brusilovsky and Maybury explained a shift in paradigm at that time. Nowadays, there is a new shift, which is from Adaptive Web towards a User-adapted Web of Things.

The Web of Things (WoT) exposes Internet of Things (IoT) platforms and devices through the World Wide Web, making them accessible through their virtual representation [2], [3]. WoT exploits URIs to address things and Web technologies to access them, such as the HTTP protocol, the REST architecture and scripting APIs at the services layer. Moreover, the WoT Interest Group (www.w3.org/WoT) is working to define a *framework* for the development of standards and services based upon the Web technologies for a combination of the IoT with the Web of Data [4]. With respect to this, the semantics and data formats are the basis for interoperability; things are modeled as events, properties, and actions and query languages are used to retrieve metadata for things in a standard format, such as JavaScript Object Notation for Linked Data (JSON-LD).

The things in the WoT are virtual representations of objects. Thus, they can also include real-world objects (RWOs) that are not sensorized and connected the way devices are: people, objects, places, etc. [4]. Objects can be modelled at different levels of

abstraction and can have one or more virtual representations, and even multimodal representations. Therefore, the WoT enriches objects by linking them to their virtual counterpart, and, in this way, augmenting them.

The virtual representation may store additional information about the object, such as its history (for instance, an artwork can include data about its creator, past, and owners over the years), or may represent an object from points of view that are inaccessible with normal usage, e.g. inside view [5, 6]. Moreover, as well as adaptive techniques are deployed to provide personalized views of the web content and navigation assistance, similar techniques can be exploited to adapt the virtual representation of the physical objects in order to customize the interaction with them, so as to fit to various features of the users, including users' goals, background, preferences, special needs, devices, and environment.

The *research question* that we investigate in this paper is whether by combining adaptation techniques with WoT and semantic technologies, it is possible to make physical objects accessible and/or more usable for people with special needs.

The remainder of the paper presents our approach (Section 2), an example scenario (Section 3), the proposed architecture (Section 4) and a discussion of related works (Section 5).

2. THE APPROACH
In order to adapt the virtual side of a cyber-physical object [7] to make it accessible for people with special needs,

- the physical object has to be identified through a proper technology, depending on the design settings and on the type of the object (e.g. QR Code, RFID tag, GPS coordinates),

- a virtual representation of the physical object has to be built and linked to the RWO,

- the virtual representations of the object features have to include properties that can be matched against properties of real-world users, including needs, requirements, preferences and current environment,

- adaptive techniques have to be employed in order to adapt the web-based counterpart of the physical object to make it accessible. This step involves profiling the user's (accessibility) needs, preferences and context, and adapting the available data on the object according to reasoning rules, adaptation strategies and these data.

We propose the use of relevant ontologies and Linked Data (LD) as a paradigm to foster the integration of heterogeneous data, and enable connection and reuse of data about physical objects, user preferences and accessibility requirements.

3. EXAMPLE SCENARIO

In an example scenario regarding assisting people with special needs with the aid of Web technologies, one can imagine a person (user) with special needs shopping in a supermarket. This person may have hearing, visual or physical impairment, where each type of impairment has its levels. For instance, vision impairment could be low vision, color blindness or total blindness. Let us assume that the user in this scenario, *Ann*, has a degree of visual impairment that prevents her from reading and recognizing small objects. Similar problems could be experimented by a physically impaired user on a wheelchair who would not able to see objects on some shelves, or read their labels and prices.

The user, Ann, can use a device such as a smart phone with a specific application to navigate around the store and do her shopping (perhaps interacting with her pre-prepared shopping list as part of this application). To this aim, the specific application on the user's smart phone (developed in accordance with the proposed approach in this paper) will keep track of her shopping list, preferences, shopping history, special needs, context and location among other user features.

This application also allows the user to interact with the products in the store. That is, the products in the store may have either RFID tags or QR codes that will contain information about the product details, such as name, production date, expiry date, origin, brand, description, manufacturer, price, directions for use and so forth. Using the smart phone application, the user can read the QR code or the RFID tag with the inbuilt reader, and via a connection to the internet, access the corresponding web page via the URI. Following LD principles, this product could also be linked to similar products or to the details of product characteristics and specifications to enrich the available product information.

In our case, instead of overloading the user with all the available information, obtained from product tag or semantic enrichment, the smart application will filter some of this information according to the specific needs of this user. For instance, besides giving basic information about the product (such as name, price, usage instructions), if the user has any type of food allergies, the application will provide relevant allergy information, notify the user if this item is on the shopping list already, warn the user about expiry date, compare it to previous purchases or inform her about caloric intake. Moreover, based on this user's special needs and the preferences set in the user profile, the personalized information will be delivered as voice messages to the user (perhaps via headphones if this is a quite environment). The application can interact with the user via voice messages but the modality can be certainly changed. The user can ask for more specific information, and if she decides to purchase this item, the application will remove it from the current shopping list.

This scenario gives a simple abstract flow of how to provide intelligent guiding and support for people with special needs in a supermarket. The proposed approach can be utilized in different settings such as an electronics store, smart home, library, public buildings and so forth.

4. WOT ARCHITECTURE

Figure 1 displays the main components of the user-adapted WoT architecture. The bottom and central part of the figure represent the IoT sensing and networking layers, and the WoT above them, which are rather well-defined in the literature [8], [3]: RWOs can be physical objects with embedded sensors and processing capabilities, such as the smart shelves in Figure 1 or the powered wheelchair, but they can also be everyday artifacts (such as fruit crate, packaging box, aisle or panels in the picture[1] below) with attached tokens linked to a virtual counterpart on the Web. Users can access the virtual counterpart of these objects by scanning the attached token (e.g. QR code, RFID tag) and thus getting the object's URI [9]. Smart objects can also embed tiny Web servers, which make it possible both to communicate with such objects using the HTTP protocol or the REST paradigm, and to invoke services provided by these objects. CoAP is an HTTP-like application layer protocol that is intended for use in resource-constrained devices, such as Wireless Sensor Networks nodes.

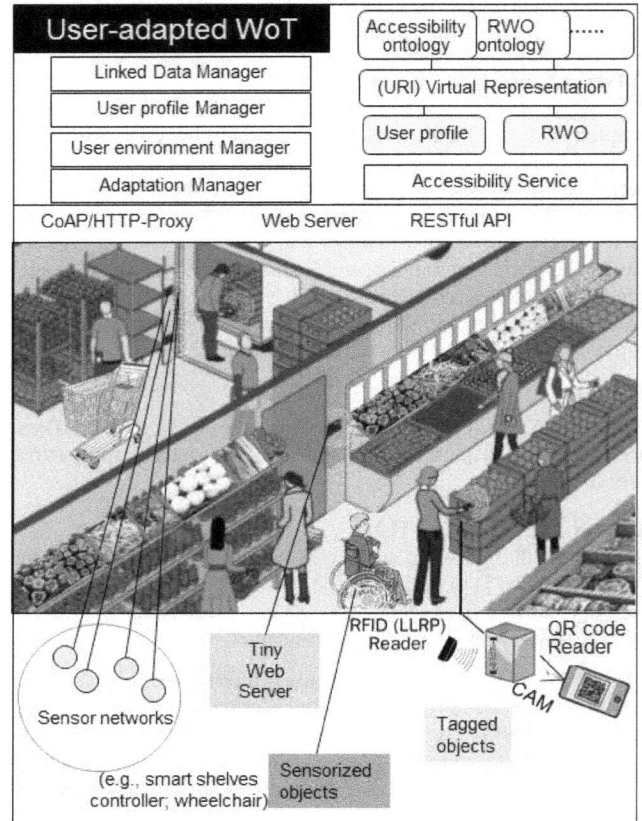

Figure 1. User-adapted WoT architecture.

The upper part of the figure represents the main modules and knowledge bases for the user-adapted WoT. The key module is the **Adaptation Manager** which is in charge of handling the interaction with the user and all the other modules of the architecture.

Literature on adaptive hypermedia systems is very vast and provides several approaches and models (as reported in "The Adaptive Web" collection by 10]). However these approaches and models are not specifically designed for the WoT. In the WoT, people interact with RWOs and exploit the Web as a way to:

(i) augment the physical objects (e.g. more information about a RWO, more views, usage instructions and simulation). This function follows the typical usage of WoT, namely providing enhanced services,

---

[1] The picture in Figure 1 is modified from RFID Arena, http://www.rfidarena.com/2013/4/11/grocery-industry-operations-are-facing-a-real-paradigm-shift.aspx.

(ii) augment their capabilities to interact with the RWO (through different modalities to access the object). In the architecture, the **Accessibility Service** is in charge of this task, coordinated by the **Adaptation Manager**. This function addresses specifically our initial research question, namely whether the WoT can be used to make physical objects accessible or more usable for people with special needs by exploiting adaptive and semantic techniques.

Hence, with respect to our example scenario and the research question, the adaptation may have to take into account several dimensions: the features of the RWO Ann is interacting with, her static and dynamic preferences and needs, the features of the device used by Ann to interact with the RWOs (its capabilities and equipment in terms of HCI modalities) and the features that relate Ann to the current environment.

These dimensions are handled by different modules, displayed in Figure 1.

- The user's *static* features such as general preferences and special needs are typically stored in the **user profile** (wrt the example scenario, they include the kind of impairment and its degree, or the type of food allergy). This information is usually supplied by the users. It is exploited by the **Adaptation Manager** and the **Accessibility Service**.

- The features of RWOs are described in the RWO **virtual representation**. Physical things are identified with a URI and such a URI can then be associated to other resources about the object. For example, in [11], RWOs are tagged with a QR code that contains the URI of their audio description on the Web. This simple cyber-physical object may be used to face accessibility problems of physical objects, but in this case it can handle just one type of disability. In a user-adapted WoT, the URI should identify the RWO and the **Accessibility Service** should redirect Ann to the audio track of the RWO virtual representation.

- The user's features that have to be monitored during the interaction (e.g. purchased products, favorite brands, and so on) are usually obtained through observation and reasoning of the user's interactions with the system based on assumptions. The information about each user can also be modified or updated by the **User Profile Manager** explicitly. For instance, our user Ann can edit or decide to delete her shopping history from last week, since she was shopping for a special occasion.

- The environmental features are monitored by the **User Environment Manager**, which keeps track of the user's context via the data from sensor networks, GPS and so on. The availability of a sensorized environment allows for exploiting several kinds of information, which augment the information that can be obtained by applications on the user's mobile device. This is useful to provide context-aware adaptation to the user, depending on whether the user is stationary, on the move, how fast, where, *etc.*, and is exploited by the **Adaptation Manager** and **Accessibility Service**. With the User Environment Manager, Ann can also edit her preferences of interaction. For instance, in our scenario, she can replace voice messages with bigger fonts for interaction with the device.

- The kind of device and applications exploited by the user to access the virtual representation (for instance, Ann uses an app on her smartphone) is a dimension that the **Accessibility Service** should take into account. The W3C Web Accessibility Initiative[2] (WAI) provides several guidelines to gain Web accessibility, such as: WCAG (Web Content Accessibility Guidelines), UAAG (User Agent Accessibility Guidelines) and WAI-ARIA (Accessible Rich Internet Applications). Managing user-adapted interfaces means that each adaptation has to follow the accessibility principles.

This last issue is specifically important since the adapted user interface has the objective to make a RWO accessible. With reference to the running example, the basic idea is that, even though food ingredients and usage instructions are not naturally accessible as RWOs, they can become accessible if the user interface is adapted to Ann's special needs. Moreover, the support to people with disabilities may require specific assistive equipment of their devices. The problem when dealing with assistive technologies is that impairments are heterogeneous and often a subject has more than one disability [12]. In this scenario, the possibility of dynamically identifying the kind of disability and adapting the virtual side of the physical object becomes a critical challenge.

The semantic representation of the features and properties described above enables reasoning mechanisms that improve the adaptation process [13]. For example, people with a certain disability may have different needs and preferences in different conditions which can be modeled by means of an ontology and rules running over it.

ACCESSIBLE[3] and AEGIS[4] are reference ontologies that represent an important effort toward the semantic representation of devices, platforms, characteristics of users with disabilities, functional limitations and impairments. ACCESSIBLE includes also verification rules for describing requirements and constraints. Due to space constraints, Figure 1 displays only an **accessibility ontology** and a generic **RWO ontology**, but other ontologies should be included, such as the User ontology, and so on. Indeed, people as well as artefacts, being real-world "objects", can have their own **virtual representation** and **URI** (see Figure 1). Such representation is particularly relevant to our approach, since it can store knowledge about the user features and needs concerning accessibility. Furthermore, this data can be used to adapt the interaction with the object. Of course, a vital requirement is the respect for the end-users' privacy when accessing this data. Privacy requirements depend on a variety of contextual socio-cultural factors and can be analyzed using privacy requirements distillation approach, such as [14].

A final consideration concerns the adoption of LD good practices to represent and link the information about a RWO and optionally about a person. The **Linked Data Manager** is in charge of this task. The adoption of LD best practices provides several advantages: *1)* LD practices are designed to foster the possibility of integrating heterogeneous data and reuse them in different ways [15], *2)* the LOD contains increasingly mass information that can complement and enrich the RWO semantic description and *3)* the object description can be freely enriched by the users, by creating new triple and thus adding new knowledge that subsequent user may find precious.

---
[2] http://www.w3.org/standards/webdesign/accessibility
[3] http://160.40.50.89/Accessible_Ontology/
[4] http://160.40.50.89/AEGIS_Ontology/

5. RELATED WORK AND CONCLUSION

In this paper we have sketched the main features of a User-Adapted Web of Things and how it can be exploited to support users with special needs so as to simplify the interaction with everyday objects.

Several FP7 European Projects have worked on providing frameworks and ontologies for accessibility – e.g. Open Accessibility Everywhere (www.aegis-project.eu), Accessibility Assessment Simulation Environment (www.accessible-eu.org), OASIS (oasis-project.eu). While the mentioned projects are most focused on providing augmented services, our approach is specifically focused on making current physical objects accessible. Additionally, our approach emphasizes the use of WoT and the use of LD to connect heterogeneous data about accessibility features.

Concerning IoT and accessibility, several application scenarios similar to our example scenario have been proposed before (as in [11], [8] and [16]). However they do not address the issue of adaptation, which, indeed, is accounted as a key challenge to assisting people with special needs in everyday life [8]. In our approach, we put forward the adaptation module of our proposed model in order to fill this gap and to provide customized support to those with special needs. In this respect, our approach is very close to GPII (http://gpii.net) and Cloud4all (cloud4all.info) projects since they propose the automatic personalization of user interfaces based on user preferences and context as a core feature of a global infrastructure for accessibility. These projects are aimed to make the Web, mobile technologies and devices accessible to everyone. Differently, we aim to make RWOs accessible to everyone, and we exploit the Web and mobile technologies to reach this goal. This represents a link between the projects and opens interesting possibilities of collaboration that would enhance the objective of accessibility, widening it from devices to things.

To sum up, our model *combines new approaches*, based on WoT, Semantic Web technologies and LD, *promotes the accessibility to physical objects* and *manages it as an integrated matter*, which requires: i) connecting and sharing data about accessibility requirements and real-world environment data, ii) annotating physical objects, making them available and linkable on the Web, iii) adapting the interaction with the virtual side of cyber-physical objects in order to make physical objects accessible.

The major contribution has been to propose an adaptive mechanism that manages and tunes the applications in order to make them fit the user needs and, in the meanwhile, avoiding the risk of users being overwhelmed by such applications. The basic idea is that through the virtualization of physical objects, even though such objects are not natively accessible and inclusive, they can become so if proper applications are developed to manage and adapt them.

6. ACKNOWLEDGMENTS
This research has been partially funded by the University of Genoa, within PRA 2013 projects, Prot. N. 9563.

7. REFERENCES

[1] Brusilovsky, P., and Maybury, M. T. 2002. *From adaptive hypermedia to the adaptive web. Communications of the ACM*, 45(5), 30-33.

[2] Guinard, D., Trifa, V., Mattern, F., and Wilde, E. 2011. From the internet of things to the web of things: Resource-oriented architecture and best practices. In *Architecting the Internet of Things*, Springer Berlin Heidelberg, 97-129, DOI: 10.1007/ 978-3-642-19157-2_5

[3] Atzori, L., Iera, A. and Morabito, G. 2010. The Internet of Things: A Survey. *Computer. Networks*. n 54(15), 2787–2805.

[4] Raggett, D., 2015. The Web of Things: Challenges and Opportunities, *Computer* , vol.48, no.5, 26-32. DOI: 10.1109/MC.2015.149

[5] Torre, I., 2013. Interaction with Linked Digital Memories. *Proc. of the Int. workshop on Personalized Access to Cultural Heritage within UMAP*, Rome, July 14, CEUR Proceedings, vol. 997, pp. 80-87, http://ceur-ws.org/Vol-997.

[6] Coccoli, M. and Torre I, 2014, Interacting with annotated objects in a Semantic Web of Things application, *Journal of Visual Languages & Computing* 25(6), 1012-1020. DOI:10.1016/j.jvlc.2014.09.008

[7] Fortino, G., Russo, W., Rovella, A., Savaglio, C. 2014, On the Classification of Cyberphysical Smart Objects in Internet of Things. *Proc. of the Int. Workshop on Networks of Cooperating Objects for Smart Cities 2014* (UBICITEC 2014). Vol. 1156, pp. 76-84.

[8] Domingo, M., C., 2012. An overview of the Internet of Things for people with disabilities, *Journal of Network and Computer Applications*, Vol. 35, pp. 584–596.

[9] Welbourne, E., Battle, L., Cole, G., Gould, K., Rector, K., Raymer, S., Balazinska, M. and Borriello, G, 2009. Building the Internet of Things Using RFID: The RFID Ecosystem Experience. *IEEE Internet Computing*, Vol. 13, No. 3, pp. 48-55.

[10] Brusilovsky, P., Kobsa, A., and Nejdl W. (eds.), 2007. *The adaptive web: methods and strategies of web personalization* Vol. 4321. Springer Science & Business Media.

[11] Al-Khalifa, Hend S., 2008. Utilizing QR code and mobile phones for blinds and visually impaired people. *LNCS* Vol. 5105, pp 1065-1069.

[12] Zhou, L., Parker, A. T., Smith, D. W., & Griffin-Shirley, N. 2011, Assistive technology for students with visual impairments: Challenges and needs in teachers' preparation programs and practice. *Journal of Visual Impairment & Blindness*, 105(4), 197-210.

[13] Torre, I., 2009. Adaptive systems in the era of the semantic and social web, a survey*, User Modeling and User-Adapted Interaction*, Vol. 19, pp 433–486, Springer Netherlands, DOI 10.1007/s11257-009-9067-3.

[14] Thomas, K., Bandara, A. K., Price, B. A., & Nuseibeh, B. 2014. Distilling privacy requirements for mobile applications. In *Proc. of the 36th International Conference on Software Engineering*. ACM, 871-882.

[15] Heath, T. and Bizer, C., 2011. *Linked Data: Evolving the Web into a Global Data Space*. Synthesis Lectures on the Semantic Web, Morgan & Claypool, 1-136.

[16] Stephanidis, C. and Antona, M. (eds), 2014, *Universal Access in Human-Computer Interaction*. LNCS, Vol. 8513.

Author Index

www.ingramcontent.com/pod-product-compliance
Lightning Source LLC
Chambersburg PA
CBHW080905220326

41598CB00034B/5478